Choose the Right Word

Choose the Right Word

A CONTEMPORARY GUIDE

TO SELECTING

THE PRECISE WORD

FOR EVERY SITUATION

S. I. HAYAKAWA

EUGENE EHRLICH,

REVISING EDITOR

HarperPerennial
A Division Of HarperCollinsPublishers

HarperCollins books may be purchased for educational, business, or sales promotional use. For information, please write: Special Markets Department, HarperCollins Publishers, Inc., 10 East 53rd Street, New York, NY 10022.

FIRST EDITION

Designed by C. Linda Dingler

Library of Congress Cataloging-in-Publication Data
 Choose the right word : a contemporary guide to selecting the precise word for every
 situation / [edited by] S. I. Hayakawa. — Rev. ed. / [edited by Eugene Ehrlich]
     p.   cm.
   Rev. ed. of: Cassell's modern guide to synonyms & related words.
   Includes index.
   ISBN 0-06-273131-9
   1. English language—Synonyms and antonyms. I. Hayakawa, S. I. (Samuel Ichiyé),
 1906- . II. Ehrlich, Eugene H.
PE1591.C445 1994   93-34206
423'.1—dc20

01 02 RRD-H 20 19 18 17 16 15 14 13

Contents

Introduction

by S. I. Hayakawa

English has the largest vocabulary and the greatest number of synonyms of any language in the world. This richness is due to the fact that the English language has grown over the centuries by constantly incorporating words from other languages. Even before the Norman Conquest, the Anglo-Saxon vocabulary included words borrowed from Latin (*street, mile,* the combining form *-chester* in the names of towns); Greek (*priest, bishop*); Celtic (*crag, bin*); and Scandinavian (*law, fellow, egg, thrall*). After the Norman Conquest, the English vocabulary was virtually doubled by the addition of French words, especially those reflecting a higher standard of living and a more complex social life: for example, words connected with food (*sugar, vinegar, boil, fry, roast*); clothing (*garment, robe, mantle, gown*); law (*plaintiff, perjury, legacy*); religion (*convent, hermitage, chaplain, cardinal*); and social rank and organization (*prince, duke, count, vassal, mayor, constable*).

While much of the new French vocabulary described new ideas and activities, a great deal of it duplicated existing Anglo-Saxon vocabulary, giving the writer or speaker a choice of synonyms: *cure* (French) or *heal* (Anglo-Saxon), *table* or *board, poignant* or *sharp, labor* or *work, mirror* or *glass, assemble* or *meet, power* or *might*. Sometimes, the duplication of vocabulary was used to make distinctions: *ox, swine, calf,* and *deer* were called—when killed and prepared for cooking—*beef, pork, veal,* and *venison; hitting, striking, stealing,* and *robbing* became, when viewed through the eyes of French law, *assault, battery, larceny,* and *burglary*.

With the enormous expansion of classical learning in the Renaissance, there was a great influx of words of Latin and Greek origin into the language, dictated by the demands of an enriched intellectual and cultural life. Also, the larger world discovered through travel (from the Crusades onward) and exploration (especially in the Elizabethan period) provided a great stimulus to culture and language. There also arose in the sixteenth century a fashion of ornamenting one's discourse with what were then called aureate or inkhorn terms drawn from Greek and Latin. Shakespeare's "multitudinous seas incarnadine" is a well-known example, and what happened to these particular words is typical of the fate of this new vocabulary: *multitudinous* stayed in the language as one of several synonyms for *many,* while *incarnadine* is not heard any more except in this context. In brief, many words of classical origin introduced into the language during the Renaissance became permanent additions, but most were soon forgotten or were relegated to special technical contexts, like *hebdomadary* (weekly) and *gressorial* (having to do with walking).

The adventures of English-speaking people as they traded and fought and traveled around the world in modern times—in Europe, North America, India, Australia, Africa—also expanded the vocabulary. Words were borrowed from Dutch (*tub, spool, deck*); Spanish (*sherry, armada, grenade*); American Indian (*squash, toboggan, hickory*); East Indian (*cashmere, punch, shampoo*); Afrikaans (*veldt, trek*); Italian (*soprano, casino, macaroni*); Mexican (*chocolate, tomato*); Australian (*kangaroo, billabong*); Japanese (*kimono, ricksha*); Malay (*amok, ketchup*); and many others.

Furthermore, the United States, as a separate nation with its own life and character and institutions, added vastly to the English vocabulary, beginning in Colonial times. With the rise of the United States to a position of world influence in politics, science, industry, trade, and the popular arts, American words and phrases have gained recognition and prestige everywhere. *Ice cream, jeep,* and *rock-and-roll* are internationally known terms, as are *containment* and *nuclear deterrence.* Moreover, American terminology for many things exists side by side with an English terminology, placing another whole group of closely related words at our service: *help* (American) and *servant* (British), *sidewalk* and *pavement, billboard* and *hoarding, movies* and *flicks, druggist* and *chemist, installment plan* and *hire-purchase system, water-heater* and *geyser, checkers* and *draughts, soft drink* and *mineral water,* and so on through an almost interminable list.

Near synonyms in English are therefore of many kinds. Some groups of similar words, like *foreword* (English), *preface* (French), *introduction* (Latin), and *prolegomenon* (Greek), seem to be an embarrassment of riches. Some, like *plain* (French), *steppe* (Russian), *pampas* (Spanish, from South American Indian), *prairie* (French voyageur), *savannah* (Spanish), and *tundra* (Russian, from Lappish), refer to geographical variants of the same kind of thing. Others, like *teach, educate, indoctrinate, instruct, school,* and *tutor,* differ from each other principally in degrees of abstraction: *teach* is certainly the most general word of this group, while the others are more specialized in application. Some words of quite similar meaning make distinctions at the concrete, descriptive level: *tip, cant, careen, heel, list, slant, slope,* and *tilt; screech, scream, clamor, yammer,* and *howl.* These are truly synonyms only if translated into more general form, the former group into *incline,* the latter into *outcry.*

It can be argued that there really are no exact synonyms—no exact equivalences of meaning. Such a position can be upheld if by meaning we refer to the total range of contexts in which a word may be used. Certainly, no two words are interchangeable in all the contexts in which either might appear. But within a given context, there is often exact synonymy: I *mislaid* my wallet; I *misplaced* my wallet. In a slightly different context, however, the two words are not interchangeable: it would not be idiomatic to say, I *mislaid* my suitcase—all of which may suggest that while *misplace* is applicable to both small objects and large, *mislay* applies only to small. Also, one may suffer disappointment because of *misplaced,* but never *mislaid,* trust. This example shows again that words synonymous in

one of their meanings may differ considerably in their other meanings.

Some groups of words describe the same actions, but imply different relationships among the parties concerned. We *accompany* our equals; we *attend* or *follow* those to whom we are subordinate; we *conduct* those who need guidance, *escort* those who need protection, and *chaperone* those who need supervision; merchant ships are *convoyed* in time of war.

Some differences in locution reveal differences in the degree of formality of the occasions described: a *luncheon* as distinguished from a *lunch.* Sometimes, different locutions reveal differences not in the situations described but in the formality of discourse about them: *He went to bed,* for instance, as compared to *He hit the sack.*

Semanticists and linguistic scholars continue to remind us that words change in meaning according to time and place and circumstance. Their warnings are certainly not to be ignored. The *democracy* of Sweden is not identical with that which bears the same name in England, Japan, or Germany; and the *democracy* of any of these nations may change from decade to decade, from year to year.

Yet, with all the changes that go on both in language and in the world described by language, there are remarkable elements of stability in a vocabulary with as rich a literary and cultural history as English. The distinctions between *bravery* and *foolhardiness,* between *weeping* and *whining,* between *fury* and *rage,* between *thought* and *deliberation,* between *desolate* and *disconsolate,* remain remarkably constant through Shakespeare to Swift to Jane Austen to Mark Twain to the present-day English or American (or Canadian or Australian) writer. It is gratifying to call the reader's attention to the many new words—even fad words—and new meanings discussed in the present volume. But I like to think that the reader will find equal pleasure—perhaps more—in the continuities and constancies in the meanings of English words that persist despite changes of time and changes of scene.

Nothing is so important to clear and accurate expression as the ability to distinguish between words of similar, but not identical, meaning. There are occasions in which we have to make choices between *transient* and *transitory, mutual* and *reciprocal, gaudy* and *garish, inherent* and *intrinsic, speculate* and *ruminate, pinnacle* and *summit,* because in a given context one is certain to be more appropriate than the other. To choose wrongly is to leave the hearer or reader with a fuzzy or mistaken impression. To choose well is to give both illumination and delight. The study of synonyms will help readers come closer to saying what they really want to say.

How to Use This Book

Using the Index

To find a word you want, turn first to the Index, beginning on p. 515. If the word is printed in small capital letters, as in the case of COURAGE, for example, that word appears as the headword of an entry. The page number on which that entry begins appears to the right of the word. You may then turn directly to the indicated page in the main section of the book. You will find COURAGE, for example, as the headword of an entry comparing *backbone, fortitude, grit, guts, nerve, pluck,* and *resolution* beginning on page 92. More often than not, the word you are interested in will not be a headword, but will appear in an entry listed under another word. In that event the Index will refer you to the headword, printed in small capital letters, under which the word you are seeking will appear. Suppose you want to find *indigent.* In the Index you will find: indigent PENNILESS 325. This means that *indigent* is discussed in an entry under the headword PENNILESS beginning on page 325.

Some words, like *good,* have so many important meanings that they must be included in several entries that discuss different aspects of meaning. In such cases the nature of the headword will suggest which meaning is discussed. For example:

good BENEFICIAL 33
good OBEDIENT 301

Headwords are always identified by part of speech when ambiguity would otherwise result. For example:

deluge FLOOD (v) 163
DEMAND (v) 107
retreat ESCAPE (v) 142

In a few cases the same word appears as the headword of more than one entry; the Index distinguishes between such entries by listing either the part of speech or, if both are the same part of speech, by the alphabetically first word discussed in each entry after the headword. For example:

PLAIN (n) 334
PLAIN (adj) 335
REQUEST (n) 377
REQUEST (v) 378
STOP (arrest) 437
STOP (cease) 438

A new feature of this edition of *Choose the Right Word* is usage notes dealing with words that are frequently confused. These notes are given in alphabetical order in the text as well as in the Index.

Finding the Word You Want

To aid you in locating the word you want, the headword of each entry is printed in large, boldface type at the beginning of where its entry begins. The other words discussed are printed in large, lightface type below their respective headwords.

Whenever there is insufficient room to list all the words on the first page of an entry, the headword is repeated on the following page with the word *continued* in parentheses with the remaining words treated in the entry listed below.

As a further aid in finding the word you want, the first occurrence of each word discussed within each entry appears in prominent boldface type, subsequent occurrences in italic type. Thus, if you are looking for a particular word, for example *perennial* in the entry PERMANENT, you need not read about *lasting, enduring, perpetual,* and *durable*—all discussed first—in order to get to it. Just scan the boldface words until you find what you are looking for. Of course, we hope you will more often want to read the entire entry, but we have made this guide to closely related words flexible enough to be useful for quick reference as well.

Cross-References

Cross-references at the end of entries, as in the Index, are always made to headwords which, as stated above, always appear in small capital letters. We have used cross-references liberally in the hope of stimulating the reader's interest to turn to other related entries and learn more about the fascinating relationships that exist between clusters of meaning in English. Cross-references, therefore, do not necessarily refer to a word of the same part of speech as the headword of the entry under which they appear. For instance, under SARCASTIC, an adjective, cross-references are made to CONTEMPTUOUS (an adjective), RIDICULE (a noun), SCOFF (a verb), and SOUR (an adjective). Cross-references are thus not intended to refer you to other synonyms or near-synonyms, but are used as a means of suggesting relationships that may interest you. Sometimes, these relationships are close enough to approximate synonymy, as in the cross-reference to CLEAN from SANITARY; at other times, the relationship is one of nuance or similarity of usual context and is far removed from synonymy, as in the cross-reference to MOUNTAIN and STEEP from ROUGH. In this way we hope to enlarge the reader's grasp of vocabulary and meaning, to lure him or her on, so to speak, into making more extensive inquiries than the reader perhaps originally intended, and thereby to discover how richly and subtly intertwined are the many elements of the English vocabulary.

Antonyms

Not every entry suggests a set of antonyms, and we have not attempted to force lists of antonyms into positions where they do not fit. Entries like CHARACTERISTIC, ROTATE, and SAMPLE can have no antonyms. Antonyms are listed at the end of those entries to which they apply following the word **Antonyms**. The antonym lists serve a different function from that of the cross-references, so the treatment accorded them is different. Antonym lists are commonly used by people searching for a word rather than a meaning. Antonym lists should therefore be of the same part of speech as that of the words discussed in the entry under which they appear. You will note that some antonyms are listed in lowercase letters in italic type, whereas others are listed in italicized small capital letters: for example, the antonyms of SAVORY are listed as *BLAND, insipid, tasteless.* Words listed in italicized small capital letters are headwords, and rather than repeat every word discussed in the entry designated, we refer the reader to the entry itself. The antonyms printed in lowercase letters in italic type are either not included in the work or are not included in a sense antonymic to that of the headword under which they appear. For example, *graceful* and *sure* are listed among the antonyms of CLUMSY, even though *graceful* is discussed under EXQUISITE and *sure* is a headword in its own right. But since all the words discussed at EXQUISITE and SURE are not antonyms of CLUMSY, we cannot fairly refer the reader to these entries. Thus, whenever an antonym appears in italicized small capital letters, you will find that each word discussed under that headword is also an antonym.

abjure. Do not confuse the verb *abjure* (renounce under oath) with the verb *adjure* (urge solemnly).

abrogate. Do not confuse the verb *abrogate* (cancel or repeal) with the verb *arrogate* (claim a power, privilege, etc., unduly).

absorb

assimilate
digest
imbibe
incorporate
ingest

These verbs, all relatively formal, indicate the taking in of one thing by another. **Absorb** is slightly more informal than the others and has, perhaps, the widest range of uses. In its most restricted sense it suggests the taking in or soaking up specifically of liquids: the liquid *absorbed* by the sponge. In more general uses *absorb* may imply the thoroughness of the action: not merely to read the chapter, but to *absorb* its meaning. Or it may stress the complete disappearance of the thing taken in within the encompassing medium: once-lovely countryside soon *absorbed* by urban sprawl. **Ingest** refers literally to the action of taking into the mouth, as food or drugs, for later absorption by the body. Figuratively, it designates any taking in and suggests the receptivity necessary for such a process: too tired to *ingest* even one more idea from the complicated philosophical essay she was reading. To **digest** is to alter food chemically in the digestive tract so that it can be *absorbed* into the bloodstream. In other uses, *digest* is like *absorb* in stressing thoroughness, but is even more emphatic. [You may completely *absorb* a stirring play in one evening, but you will be months *digesting* it.]

Assimilate is even more emphatic about the thoroughness of the taking in than either *absorb* or *digest*—in both its specific physiological and general uses. Physiologically, food is first *digested*, then *absorbed* by the bloodstream, and then *assimilated* bit by bit in each cell the blood passes. In more general uses, *assimilate*, unlike the previous verbs, often implies a third agent beside the absorber and the absorbed—an agent that directs this process: architects who *assimilate* their buildings to the environment. The process, furthermore, often implies the complete transformation of the absorbed into the absorbing medium. *Assimilate* also suggests a much slower process than *digest* and certainly than *absorb*, which can be nearly instantaneous: It would take the city generations to *assimilate* the newcomers into the patterns of a strange life.

Incorporate is the only verb here that does not have a specific use pertaining to the taking in of liquids or of food, meaning literally embody. It resembles the aspect of *assimilate* that stresses the loss of separate identity for the absorbed quantity: *incorporating* your proposals into a new system that will satisfy everyone. It is unlike *assimilate* in lacking that verb's suggestion of necessarily careful, time-consuming thoroughness.

Imbibe, while capable of uses comparable to those for *assimilate*, is mainly rooted still to its specific use for the taking in of liquids. Even this use, and certainly any others, now sound slightly archaic and excessively formal: Do you *imbibe* alcoholic beverages? See EAT.

Antonyms: *disgorge, disperse, dissipate, eject, emit, exude.*

abstain

forbear
refrain

The verb **abstain** means withhold oneself from an action or self-indulgence. [There were six votes in favor, two against, and two *abstaining*; She *abstained* from drinking.] **Refrain** has to do with withholding an action temporarily, or checking a momentary desire: He *refrained* from scolding his child until the company left. To **forbear**, in its intransitive sense, is to exercise self-control, often out of motives of patience or charity. [Though impatient, the customer *forbore* to upbraid the harried sales clerk; The teacher *forbore* to report Johnnie's misbehavior to his parents.] See FORGO, FORSWEAR.

Antonyms: *BEGIN, PERMIT.*

absurd

farcical
foolish
irrational
ludicrous
preposterous
ridiculous
senseless
silly
unreasonable

The adjective **absurd** means opposed to reason or truth, and may be applied to that which is grossly, and sometimes grotesquely, inconsistent with common sense or experience. **Preposterous** denotes a great contrariness to nature, reason, or common sense, and is used to describe that which is outrageously *absurd*. **Ridiculous** refers to that which is *absurd* in a way that invites ridicule or mockery. [It is *absurd* to predict that the sun will not rise tomorrow; It is *preposterous* that virtue should go unrewarded while vice goes unpunished; It is *ridiculous* to judge a foreign culture by the quality of its plumbing.]

Farcical and **ludicrous** are applied to that which is *absurd* in an amusing way. *Farcical* indicates a humorous distortion of fact, convention, or reason. *Ludicrous* implies playful absurdity, but may also be synonymous with *ridiculous* in describing something that is greeted with scorn or derision. [The *farcical* introduction of a talking horse gave the play its flavor; The *ludicrous* antics of the harlequins delighted the audience; The speaker made a series of *ludicrous* mistakes that were rewarded with hoots and catcalls.]

Foolish, **senseless**, and **silly** add a suggestion of folly or even of a trivial intellect to their synonymity with *absurd*. [To buy stocks in a company you have never heard of is a *foolish* investment; To beat a dead horse is *senseless*; To make unsupportable claims is *silly* affectation.]

Unreasonable and **irrational** mean contrary to reason, the difference between them being that *unreasonable* implies a bias or intent to go wrong and *irrational* suggests an uncontrollable lack of understanding. [It is *unreasonable* to maintain a geocentric theory of the universe; It is *irrational* to expect an adult reaction from a child.] See HUMOROUS.

Antonyms: *consistent, logical, rational, reasonable, sagacious,* SENSIBLE.

accomplice

abettor
accessory
confederate
conspirator
plotter

The nouns **accomplice** and **confederate** both denote a person who is associated with another in committing a crime, whether that association is limited to the planning stages or is extended to the entire execution of the wrongdoing. Thus, an *accomplice* or *confederate* may, but need not necessarily, be present at the scene of the crime. [The role of the murderer's *accomplice* was that of weapon procurer; Although Whitney planned the theft, it was one of his *confederates* who actually entered the house and stole the jewels.]

An **abettor** is an *accomplice* or *confederate* who is present and who participates in the execution of a crime. A lookout is an *abettor* in a bank robbery.

Accessory is the legal term for an *accomplice* who helps a felon without being present at the scene of the crime. If that person helps the felon's preparations, he or she is an *accessory* before the fact; if that person helps the felon to escape punishment once the crime has been committed, he or she is an *accessory* after the fact.

Conspirator and **plotter** refer to persons who are involved in a secret or underhanded agreement to perform some evil act. *Conspirators* are those who take part in a *conspiracy,* which is a legal term denoting an intention to violate the law; in general use, it is applied to major crimes and even more particularly to treason. *Plotters* are implicated in an activity that has a sinister purpose, but even though it is difficult to plan and execute, may be petty in scope. See ASSISTANT, ASSOCIATE, HELP.

Antonyms: OPPONENT.

accumulate

amass
collect
gather
hoard

The verbs **accumulate** and **amass** both mean to pile up by successive addition. To *accumulate* is to heap or pile up or bring together by degrees or by regular additions; to *amass* is to bring together a great quantity and usually suggests great value. A person may *accumulate* great piles of newspapers. A speculator may try to *amass* great wealth; an army may *amass* armaments for a final push. **Collect** and **gather** are interchangeable in the sense of bringing together into one place or into a group. *Collect,* however, suggests discriminating selection in a way that *gather* does not: to *collect* stamps as a hobby but with the idea of reselling them later at a profit; to *gather* a large bunch of wildflowers along a country road. **Hoard** means to *gather* and store for the sake of accumulation. It always connotes a selfish desire to keep permanently or for future use and suggests secrecy in the process. [Misers *hoard* their money; In wartime, individuals may *hoard* scarce items.] See PILE.

Antonyms: *disperse, dissipate, scatter, spend, squander, waste.*

accumulation
    aggregation
    collection
    conglomeration

All these nouns, as here considered, mean a mass of things that come or are brought together. They all imply that the things are neither merged with one another nor united organically in the resultant mass. **Accumulation** means that the things have come together by a series of additions rather than all at once. It often implies that the things are of the same kind, such as the *accumulation* of dust on surfaces, or of money in banks, and does not imply any coherence or organization in the mass gathered.

Collection and *accumulation* are often used interchangeably, but *collection* frequently implies a high degree of selection and organization in the mass collected: An *accumulation* of many specimens is needed when one is preparing a scientific *collection.*

Aggregation always denotes a mass brought together that forms, in some sense, a coherent whole, but one that has a lesser degree of organization than does a *collection:* An industrial empire is often an *aggregation* of unrelated enterprises.

Conglomeration implies that many different and sometimes even incongruous things are brought together from widely scattered sources or regions: The population of New York City is a *conglomeration* of many different kinds of people from various countries and cultures. See PILE.

accurate
    correct
    exact
    precise
    right
    true

The adjectives **accurate**, **exact**, **precise**, and **true**, as here considered, agree in implying close conformity to an objective standard. *Accurate* suggests that there are degrees of conformity to such a standard and stresses the painstaking care necessary for the attainment of fidelity to truth or fact: It took a week of investigation to get an even reasonably *accurate* account of the accident. *Exact* emphasizes extreme accuracy in measurable quantities and qualities: The *exact* wavelength assigned to a transmitting station must always be maintained. *Precise* stresses great accuracy in regard to minute details: The assembling of the parts of a watch must be *precise. True,* as here considered, implies absolute accuracy, particularly in reproductions of an original: a *true* copy of a birth certificate.

Correct suggests the absence of error or fault and a conformity to some standard. It is more general than the other adjectives in this group because it applies to such things as taste and fashion as well as to truth or fact: the *correct* dress for a formal dinner. **Right** is largely interchangeable with *correct,* but often adds a hint of moral approval: the *right* course of action. See DUPLICATE, GENUINE.

Antonyms: *erroneous, false, inaccurate, incorrect, inexact, wrong.*

accuse
    arraign
    charge
    impeach
    incriminate
    indict

These verbs all mean declare a person to be guilty of some offense or shortcoming. **Accuse** is the most general and may be used in formal or informal, official or personal, contexts. An investigating committee may *accuse* an officeholder of wrongdoing; a neighbor may *accuse* a man of playing his radio too loud.

Charge, in this context, means *accuse* formally, usually before a court; by extension, it means *accuse* informally of a violation of some accepted standard. [The police *charged* the driver with reckless driving; The candidate *charged* her opponent with evasion of the basic issues.]

Incriminate means *charge* a person with a crime directly, or involve that person in a crime by damaging testimony. In popular use, the latter is the more usual meaning: She was *incriminated* by an eyewitness who placed her at the scene of the crime.

Indict and **arraign** are legal terms. *Indict* is *charge* officially and make subject to an appearance before a jury or judge. In an extended sense, *indict* is *charge* unofficially but publicly: to *indict* a school of writing or painting as being obscurantist. To *arraign*, legally, is to call an *indicted* person before a court for trial; by extension, to *arraign* is to call publicly but unofficially a person or a movement to stand judgment before public opinion or some other standard.

Technically, **impeach** means *arraign* a public official before a competent tribunal on a charge of malfeasance in office. In the United States, the House of Representatives *impeaches* federal officeholders, and the Senate sits as the court. [In February 1868, President Andrew Johnson was *impeached* by the House; in May of that year he was acquitted by the Senate by a margin of one vote.] In extended use, to *impeach* is to discredit or call into question: to *impeach* a witness; to *impeach* a person's motives. See DISAPPROVAL, REBUKE.

Antonyms: *EXONERATE, PARDON.*

acknowledge
    admit
    concede
    confess

These verbs agree in meaning to accept openly, though with some reluctance, the truth or existence of a fact, condition, etc. One **acknowledges** something embarrassing or awkward, and usually not voluntarily; more often, the acknowledgment is extracted from one more or less unwillingly: The general *acknowledged* that the war had not been going as well as expected.

Admit is a bold acknowledgment of implication in something one has formerly tended to deny or to equivocate about: He *admitted* under questioning that he was in the service of a foreign power, but denied he was guilty of espionage. One **concedes**, usually because of overwhelming evidence, something he has been reluctant to *admit*. [She had no choice but to *concede* she had been guilty of bad judgment; In the face of the disastrous military battle, they *conceded* that victory was no longer attainable, and agreed to a negotiated surrender.] To **confess** is to *admit* guilt, as to a crime, or to *admit* to a shortcoming: *confessed* that he was an accomplice of the robber; The judge *confessed* he had never read the book that had been removed from the library. See ASSERT.

Antonyms: *CONTRADICT, FORSWEAR.*

acumen
    acuity
    insight
    perception

These nouns all refer to a highly developed mental ability to see or understand what is not obvious. **Acumen** has to do with keenness of intellect and implies an uncommon quickness and discrimination of mind. It requires *acumen* to solve an intricate problem in human relationships, or to emerge unscathed from a venture into penny stocks.

Insight and **perception** mean the power to recognize the hidden springs of behavior or the true nature or cause of a situation or condition: A psychiatrist's *insight* into human behavior may uncover the underlying cause of a child's delinquency; a doctor's *perception* may recognize a patient's complaints as symptoms of a personality disorder. *Perception* in its basic sense applies to anything recognized or understood by the senses, and in its extended sense to anything recognized or understood by the mind, thus suggesting a likeness between mind and the senses. *Perception* therefore suggests a view of the mind as a keenly receptive but nonetheless passive instrument, sensitive to very slight stimuli. *Insight*, on the other hand, is consistent with a view of the mind as an active agent, seeking and sifting ideas and probabilities as well as the evidence of sensations. In most contexts *insight* implies a more profound use of intellect and wisdom than does *perception; insight* suggests a knowledge of the inner character or essence of a thing, whereas *perception* relies primarily on the sharpness or **acuity** of one's senses.

Acuity means sharpness or keenness, and is applied exclusively to *perception:* visual *acuity;* The intelligence test was used as a basis for judging the applicant's mental *acuity.* See KEEN, SENSATION, VISION, WISDOM.

Antonyms: *bluntness, dullness, obtuseness, stupidity.*

adapt
    accommodate
    adjust
    conform
    fit
    reconcile

The verbs **adapt** and **adjust** mean to change someone or something to suit new circumstances or a different environment. *Adapt* involves considerable change to meet new requirements, while *adjust* implies a minor change, as in the alignment of parts: to *adapt* a novel for the stage; to *adjust* a motor; to *adjust* the differences between two parties in a dispute. *Adapt* emphasizes the purpose for which the change must be made: Shrewd politicians *adapt* their speeches to suit the interests of groups of voters. *Adjust* is also used to mean *adapt* oneself to a changed environment: Astronauts in flight must *adjust* to weightlessness.

Conform, as here considered, means correspond to a model or pattern: Any new building must *conform* to the building code. In a commonly used extended sense, *conform* means adhere or *adjust* to conventional behavior: When traveling in a foreign country, it is wise to *conform* to local customs. To **fit** something is to *adapt* it to a purpose or use: A prudent man *fits* his standard of living to his budget.

Accommodate and **reconcile** are similar to *adapt* in meaning change something or oneself in acknowledgment of an external condition. [American visitors to the Far East must *accommodate* themselves to habits of life that may seem very strange to them; A woman following a military career must *reconcile* herself to long absences from her family.] *Reconcile* implies an *accommodation* not without misgivings or resentment; one *reconciles* oneself to certain conditions because the alternatives are even less palatable. *Accommodate*, on the other hand, conveys no such connotation, but suggests that the adjustment will make one's own lot easier because it will gratify others. See CHANGE.

Antonyms: *derange, disarrange, discompose, disjoin, dislocate, displace, dissent, misfit, resist.*

Flexible and **elastic** have concrete applications to physical objects, in which case they suggest something with spring to it or something that will quickly resume its shape after being distorted. *Elastic* suggests stretching, as of a band or membrane; *flexible* suggests bending, as of a rod or tube. **Adjustable** is applied to objects that can be manually altered to suit different uses or purposes: An *adjustable* automobile seat slides backwards or forwards to accommodate the driver.

Used in the sense of *adaptable*, *elastic* suggests the ability to recover quickly in the face of a threat or upset: a leader who was amazingly *elastic* and imperturbable under pressure. *Elastic* can also refer to a projected set of requirements, rules, or figures when they are open to revision in the light of experience: an *elastic* budget that allows for unexpected outlays for new equipment; *elastic*, sensible rules drawn up by the students themselves. *Flexible*, in this context, is closer in meaning to *adaptable* than any other adjective here. It does not, however, necessarily suggest a permanent adjustment to change but rather temporary shifts of position to maintain balance: a society so *flexible* in the face of new influences as to lack unity or purpose. As in this example, *flexible* may suggest low standards or a chameleonic nature, whereas *adaptable* can suggest a slow, hard-won process of decisive movement in a new direction. See MALLEABLE, SUPPLE.

Antonyms: CLUMSY, *dilatory, fixed, inflexible, rigid, set, sluggish.*

adaptable

adjustable
elastic
flexible
yielding

These adjectives suggest the ease with which something will respond to an external force without breaking. **Adaptable** is the most general and the most abstract, suggesting the favorable quality of an ingenious or practical ability to alter habit as a response to changed circumstances: The ice ages exterminated many inadequately *adaptable* species. **Yielding** is nearly as abstract as *adaptable* but more readily suggests an unfavorable passivity or unassertiveness than a favorable ability to improvise responses to challenges: the damaging stereotype that makes all women out to be helpless and *yielding*.

add

affix
annex
append
attach

Add, the most general verb in this group, means join or unite so as to increase the importance, size, quantity, or scope of something: to *add* a new line of merchandise to one's goods; to *add* a new wing to a building; to *add* five new programmers to a department; to *add* a touch of levity to an otherwise solemn speech.

Attach, as here considered, means connect or join on as a part, and is close in some contexts to **append**: to *attach* a stipulation to a contract; to *append* a query to a manuscript. *Append* emphasizes that the addition is subordinate or minor in relation to the original work.

Both verbs are formal, but *attach* has a legalistic ring to it lacking in *append:* to *attach* a rider to a bill; to *append* a footnote. Note that *add* could be used in place of either of these verbs, but would make the tone less formal and therefore less impressive.

Affix means fix or attach to: to *affix* a seal to document. *Affix* is appropriate only in very formal contexts, as in the description of state affairs: The governor solemnly *affixed* her signature to the bill expanding educational opportunities.

Annex means add something supplemental. It implies not only that the addition is a subordinate part, but often that the addition remains distinct: to *annex* an adjoining territory; to *annex* a building to an older one. See ENLARGE.

Antonyms: *abstract, deduct,* LESSEN, REDUCE, *subtract.*

addition

> accessory
> adjunct
> appendage
> appendix
> appurtenance
> attachment
> supplement

These nouns all refer to parts of a whole, either integral or incidental. **Addition** and **supplement** share one sense in which the part and whole being joined are alike in kind, so that only an increase in quantity results. [The new members will be a welcome *addition* to the club; A vitamin *supplement* is said not to be necessary for the average diet.] Both nouns have uses, on the other hand, in which the part remains distinguishable from and subordinate to the whole. [What a charming *addition* the sunporch makes to your house; The paper-covered book of quizzes was a *supplement* to the assigned mathematics textbook.] A *supplement* can also be a standard or special section of a newspaper: the Sunday *supplement* on fall fashions. **Appendix**, like *supplement*, can refer to a part of a book, but is more often bound with the book itself. Neither of these is essential to the book's completeness, although both would offer additional details on given material.

Appendage refers to a more integral part of a whole than do any of the other terms. It is especially used in the life sciences to indicate the limbs or extremities of a plant or animal. No one except such a scientist, however, is likely—even in the most formal of contexts—to use *appendage* in preference to limb, branch, arm, leg, tail, or whatever. Biologists themselves, in fact, can be every bit as precise and certainly more succinct in speaking of a monkey's *tail* rather than its caudal *appendage*. In other uses of this noun, the subordination of the part to the whole is emphasized. Such uses may be rather stiff except when a note of mockery is conveyed. [It was apparent to everyone that the husband had become a mere *appendage* to his wealthy wife.]

Appurtenance and **adjunct** both refer to a part that becomes a valuable *addition* to a whole, though not essential to it. *Appurtenance* has a specific legal sense of an incidental property right that goes along with a major right, such as the right of way to a building. The sense of a gratuitous advantage pervades its other meanings as well: He was unusual in considering beauty as an *appurtenance* to a vigorous mind, and not vice versa. In *adjunct*, the separateness of the added part is stressed: Memorization is only an *adjunct* to real education, not its staple.

Attachment and **accessory** refer to parts that are neither essential to nor fused with the whole they complement. An *attachment* increases the usability of the original whole for which it is specifically designed, although its use is optional: If we had a flashbulb *attachment*, we could also take pictures at night. One meaning of *accessory* is identical to that of *attachment*, as in automobile *accessories*. Another sense of *accessory* points to its enhancing of the beauty, rather than the usefulness, of the whole to which it is added: the tastefully chosen *accessories* that dramatize the simplest dress or suit. See EXTRANEOUS.

Antonyms: *abstraction, deletion, omission, subtraction.*

adjure. Do not confuse the verb *adjure* (urge solemnly) with the verb *abjure* (renounce under oath).

administer. Do not confuse the verb *administer* (manage the business affairs of) with the verb *minister* (attend to people's needs).

adverse. Do not confuse the adjective *adverse* (unfavorable) with the adjective *averse* (disinclined).

afraid

aghast
alarmed
anxious
apprehensive
fearful
frightened
scared
terror-stricken

The adjective **afraid** means showing fear. When used by itself, no particular degree of fear is indicated. [He's *afraid* of dogs, even of puppies; We are *afraid* to walk in the park at night since the woman jogger was attacked there.] In most uses, being *afraid* is personal, and the fear has to do with bodily harm. *Afraid* is also used in polite discourse to indicate nothing more than mild concern: I'm *afraid* I'm a bit late for my appointment. Sometimes this use conceals great fear: If our present policy is continued, I am *afraid* that war is inevitable.

Frightened and **scared** often suggest fear of bodily harm, but both may be used to describe vague fears of unknown source. [When the lights went out I became *scared;* They are always *frightened* when their parents are not at home.] *Frightened* has a more genteel sound than *scared,* but both apply strictly to physically felt fear, even if the causes are emotional or imaginary.

Anxious means tense and worried. **Fearful** may mean full of terror or dread, but more often means merely **apprehensive**—that is, anticipating danger, failure, or trouble. In the latter sense, *fearful* shares with *anxious* the suggestion that the worry stems from inner concern without much relevance to external conditions, and is in this sense perhaps unreasonable. *Apprehensive* suggests awareness of impending danger caused by circumstances, and does not depend so much on one's personal nature or habitual state of mind. [They were *anxious* about their daughter's being out so late at night; The playwright was *fearful* that her first opening would be a failure; an investor who was *apprehensive* about his holdings during the recession; We are frankly *fearful* of another depression unless the economy improves radically in the next few months.]

Aghast, **alarmed**, and **terror-stricken** are applied to strong feelings of fear or fright. *Aghast* means *afraid* or *frightened* to the point of shock. A couple waking up in a burning house will be *aghast* at the thought that their children may be in grave danger. *Alarmed* means suddenly and sharply *afraid* or *frightened.* Parents will be *alarmed* by a sudden outbreak of tuberculosis in their community. *Terror-stricken* is the strongest adjective in this list and suggests fear so strong that normal reactions are suppressed. A *terror-stricken* person who is drowning may in panic resist the efforts of someone who is trying to save him. See EAGER, FEAR, FRIGHTEN, INTIMIDATE.

Antonyms: *audacious,* BRAVE, *calm, confident, unafraid.*

aggression

assault
attack
offensive

All these nouns refer to actions initiated against other persons or groups, especially in wars. **Aggression** means unprovoked belligerent action, as by one nation upon the territory of another. An **attack** is aimed at injuring or destroying others, often by catching them off guard and unprepared. An **assault** is a violent *attack,* so violent that it often implies personal abuse motivated by envy, malice, and the like. Both *attack* and *assault* can be applied to any violent conflict, verbal as well as physical: a personal *assault* on the character of the president; a vigorous *attack* on the trade policy of the new administration. [We will continue to resist *aggression* because tyranny must be resisted; The *attack* came just before dawn; The final *assaults* were designed to crush the last remnants of enemy resistance.] *Aggression,* as the first example illustrates, is now widely used among diplomats to describe a variety of actions contrary or hostile to the interests of their own countries; *aggression* has thus lost much of its meaning. *Assault* suggests perhaps more than *attack* the element of suddenness and surprise, as evidenced by the expression "surprise *attack*"; such emphasis is unnecessary with *assault.* In psychoanalytic usage *aggression* is a tendency toward hostile action. This sense has led to a number of analogous popular uses: He's just taking out his *aggressions* on me.

An **offensive** is a movement or position of offense or *attack.* In some contexts it is interchangeable with *attack,* but in others it applies to a large-scale coordinated military campaign of men and matériel: a major new *offensive* was launched in the western front. In recent diplomatic language, *offensive* is sometimes used synonymously with *initiative:* a peace *offensive* in the form of a 3-point offer to negotiate an end to the war. See ATTACK, FIGHT.

Antonyms: *defense, repulsion, retreat, surrender, withdrawal.*

alcoholic

boozer
drunk

alcoholic *(continued)*

drunkard
lush
sot

These nouns refer to a person who habitually drinks alcoholic beverages to excess. **Alcoholic** and **drunkard** are the most general of these, the first being the more formal and neutral of the two. *Drunkard* carries a tone of condemnation and can apply appropriately only to someone who frequently drinks past the point of sobriety: Anyone can see he's a common *drunkard* the way he staggers home night after night. *Alcoholic* was at one time simply a medical description for someone who could not moderate intake of alcohol after the first drink. It has since become so popular as a general term that it appears often in informal contexts as well. Even informally, *alcoholic* lacks the tone of disapproval implicit in *drunkard.* It should be noted, however, that an *alcoholic,* unlike a *drunkard,* may have abstained from alcohol completely for years: He used to be a *drunkard,* but now he refuses drinks at parties by saying, "Sorry, but I'm a recovering *alcoholic.*"

The rest of these nouns are either extremely informal or slang. A **boozer** might denote an acute *alcoholic,* one who alternates between periods of sobriety and intoxication in a pattern disruptive of normal life. On the other hand, *boozer* can be used almost admiringly to describe a person who drinks a great deal without losing control. [He was the most unbelievable *boozer* I ever saw; he could down six straight shots of bourbon and never bat an eye.]

Drunk is, of course, a shortening of *drunkard,* having greater informality than the latter and a tone of even greater contempt. A **sot** is one who is drunk most of the time. A **lush** may mean only a habitual drinker; sometimes it is used, however, for the drinker who enjoys the showy spending of money or who claims to drink strictly for the lift that liquor may provide.

Antonyms: *abstainer, nondrinker, teetotaler.*

allegiance

fealty
fidelity
loyalty

The noun **allegiance** refers to the obligation of faithfulness, that is, of **fidelity**, that citizens owe their country or sovereign in return for the benefits and privileges received by virtue of citizenship. *Allegiance* is now widely used to refer to any similar obligation a person feels, as to a principle or a political leader. [In the Declaration of Independence, the colonists renounced their *allegiance* to the British Crown; a lasting *allegiance* to the Democratic Party.] **Fealty** is used specifically of the feudal obligation a vassal owed his lord. The oath of *fealty* expressed both *allegiance* and *fidelity.*

Fidelity implies a strong and faithful dedication; His *fidelity* to the principles of justice never wavered. **Loyalty** is more often associated with personal relationships than is *fidelity.* Where *fidelity* suggests adherence, *loyalty* points to devotion. It emphasizes a profoundly personal commitment. [Her judgment was frequently faulty, but her *loyalty* to the nation could not be questioned; Company *loyalty* made him turn down many attractive job offers.] See TRUST.

Antonyms: *disaffection, disloyalty, rebellion, sedition, treachery, treason.*

allegory

fable
parable

These nouns all denote a story told about fictional persons and events to teach or illustrate a moral principle. In an **allegory** or **parable** the moral is not stated, but is left to the hearer or reader to discover. An *allegory* is usually long and elaborate, with many characters and incidents; a *parable* is brief and typically shows the application of a moral precept to a familiar situation. A **fable** usually states the moral at the end and is told in terms of animals that speak and reflect the nature of human beings. [Dante's *Divine Comedy* is an *allegory* based on the struggle between the city-states of what is now Italy; The *fable* of the tortoise and the hare drives home the moral that steady, persistent application is more rewarding in the end than arrogant, unstable brilliance; The *parables* of the New Testament make abstract moral principles concrete and vivid.] See NARRATIVE.

allude. Do not confuse the verb *allude* (direct attention to without mentioning) with the verb *refer* (direct attention to by mentioning). The distinction between these two verbs carries over into the nouns *allusion* and *reference.*

aloof

detached
reserved

These adjectives are comparable when applied to persons who are, or seem to be, emotionally distant from others. **Aloof** is applied to persons who are distant in manner or interest, as from a reluctance to associate with those whom they regard as intellectual or social inferiors, or because of habitual shyness or idiosyncrasy. [She now holds herself *aloof* from society, preferring to spend her days and nights dwelling on her memories; He always affected a grand, *aloof* manner with us poor middle-class people who work for a living.] **Detached** means free from emotional or intellectual involvement and often suggests the neutral attitude of the impartial observer: the surgeon's *detached* approach to pain. *Detached* may also mean inwardly distracted, emotionally untouchable. [He always seems so *detached* about everything: you just can't reach him at all.] **Reserved** implies reluctance to express one's feelings or thoughts.

Where *reserved* emphasizes manner, *detached* stresses attitude. Both *reserved* and *detached* can be associated with attractive qualities, whereas *aloof* is seldom so considered. [He was a diffident, scholarly fellow with a *reserved* but genial manner; She looked about her with a *detached* air and announced to no one in particular that she was about to be sick.] See DISTANT.

Antonyms: *communicative*, GREGARIOUS, *neighborly*, *sociable*, TALKATIVE.

amateur
dabbler
dilettante

These nouns are applied to a person who has some knowledge or proficiency in a certain area, but who is not an expert. **Amateur** usually means a person who pursues an interest, study, or skill as a hobby or avocation rather than as a profession. Thus, a physician who plays the violin in her spare time is an *amateur* in music, even if her playing is skillful. However, *amateur* is sometimes used disparagingly to stress that a person's skill, being nonprofessional, is not as good as it could be. If a man can't fix a leaky faucet, his children may chide him by saying, "Oh well, you're just an *amateur!*"

Dilettante means literally taking delight in and was originally applied to a person who was a lover of the arts. *Dilettante* has in recent years, however, come to be associated with frivolousness and shallowness. A *dilettante* is a person who, though showing interest in a field of knowledge or in an artistic skill, pursues it chiefly for enjoyment or ostentation, thus never attaining more than a superficial knowledge of it.

Dabbler is an even more disparaging term than *dilettante* and denotes a person who merely dips into something without serious intent or perseverance.

Antonyms: *connoisseur, expert, professional, specialist.*

ambassador
envoy
legate
minister
nuncio
plenipotentiary

These nouns all denote a diplomatic representative of a head of state or of a government. An **ambassador** is a diplomatic officer of the highest rank, appointed as the representative of one government to another. An *ambassador extraordinary* is one sent on a special mission, as distinguished from one, called an *ambassador ordinary*, who resides permanently in the country to which he or she is assigned.

A **minister** is a diplomatic representative of lower rank than an *ambassador*. A *minister* sent on a special mission is called an **envoy**. **Nuncio** and **legate** are diplomatic representatives of the Holy See, or Vatican State. A *nuncio* is an accredited ambassador of the Pope in a foreign country; a *legate* is a papal *envoy*, that is, a diplomatic representative of the Pope dispatched to a country on a special mission.

A **plenipotentiary** describes any person fully empowered to represent a government, whether as an *ambassador, minister,* or *envoy*. The term is most commonly applied to *ministers plenipotentiary*, who, though ranking below *ambassadors,* are nevertheless invested with full authority to conduct important matters of state in the name of their government.

ancestor
forebear
forefather
progenitor

The nouns in this list are very close in meaning, each being most strictly applied to a person from whom one is descended. **Ancestor, forebear**, and **forefather** are hardly ever applied to parents or grandparents, whereas **progenitor** is sometimes applied to them as well as to more remote *ancestors*. [Although Napoleon and his immediate *progenitors* were Corsicans, he is considered by most modern Frenchmen to have been as French as their own *ancestors*.]

Ancestor and *progenitor* are often applied to things other than people. [Eohippus was an *ancestor* of the horse; The *progenitors* of Italian lyric verse forms were those used by the troubadours of Provence.]

Progenitor, in this sense, points to an early form that created, caused, or led to the development of a newer one; *ancestor,* even in this extended sense, retains the idea of historical evolution, the course of which is determined by forces over which people have no control and little knowledge. [The impressionist movement was one of the *ancestors* of abstract art; Johnson's dictionary was the *progenitor* of many others that followed its style and treatment of the language.]

Forefather and *forebear* are usually used in the plural. *Forefathers* is most often used in a poetical context and frequently connotes strong family or racial feeling, or continuing habitation in one place, whereas *forebears* has such connotations to a much smaller degree. See DESCENT.

Antonyms: *descendant, offspring, progeny.*

ancient

    antique
    hoary
    immemorial
    old

The adjective **ancient** means existing or occurring in times long past: *ancient* rituals; *ancient* coins. As applied to history, *ancient* refers to the period beginning with the earliest times and ending about the time of the fall of the Roman Empire in A.D. 476. **Old,** a more general term, must be qualified to avoid ambiguity. It may mean *ancient:* cowrie shells and other *old* forms of currency; or aged: Oxford is an *old* university; or it can be used as a substitute in some contexts for any of the other adjectives in this group.

Antique is applied to that which has survived from the past, either from ancient times or from some less remote period. As used in describing furniture or other objects, *antique* may indicate an age of no more than several generations: an *antique* shop specializing in early nineteenth-century merchandise. **Immemorial** is applied to that which is so *ancient* that its origins are beyond all memory: *immemorial* customs. *Immemorial* is often used in the phrase *since time immemorial.* Otherwise its use tends to sound grand and affected. **Hoary,** which literally means white, gray, or having white or gray hair, is applied figuratively to things surviving from the distant past: *hoary* relics of *ancient* civilizations. See OLD.

Antonyms: *fresh,* MODERN, *new, novel, recent, up-to-date.*

anger

    fury
    indignation
    ire
    rage
    wrath

These nouns denote, in varying degrees, feelings of strong displeasure or antagonism directed against the causes of an assumed wrong or injury. **Anger,** the most general noun of this group, provides no clue as to the direction of this feeling or its means of expression. One may feel *anger* at an unfortunate turn of events, at oneself, or at another person. **Rage** often implies a loss of self-control, and **fury,** the strongest noun in the group, suggests a *rage* so violent that it may approach madness. [The surly insolence of the waiters drove her into a *rage,* and she flung her napkin to the floor and stalked out of the restaurant; The *fury* of a woman scorned, according to Congreve, is unmatched in hell; Mad with *fury,* he pounded his fists on the wall and beat his breast.]

Indignation denotes *anger* based on a moral condemnation of something felt to be disgraceful or ignoble: Abolitionists viewed the institution of slavery with *indignation.* **Wrath,** now limited in use to literature and figures of speech, suggests a strong *anger* directed at some specific person or thing. The source of *wrath* is always impressive, sometimes divine; hence, it traditionally inspires awe and fear: the *wrath* of the gods. **Ire,** meaning *anger* or *indignation,* is no longer encountered except in poetry and period literature: His *ire* was strongly provoked by the discourtesy of the host in failing to address him by his proper title. See RESENTMENT.

Antonyms: *amiability, calmness, clemency, docility, forbearance, gentleness, leniency, placidity, tranquility.*

animal

    beast
    brute
    creature

These nouns refer to living things other than plants. **Animal** may refer to all such beings, as in biological terminology, in which life is divided into two groups, plants and *animals.* In common use, however, *animal* is more specifically applied to all such beings with the exception of humans: people and the *animals* they live among. The contexts of some uses, furthermore, make it clear that birds, fish, and insects are also not included in the term. At its most restricted, *animal* can even refer strictly only to domestic quadrupeds: hogs, sheep, cattle, and other *animals.* When *animal* is applied to a human being in other than a scientific context, the emphasis is on depravity or amorality: a disgusting *animal* who cared for no one but himself. **Creature** does not have this range of possibility in meaning; it refers invariably to all living beings other than plants: all God's *creatures*. When a human being is referred to by this noun, however, pity or contempt is usually present: the poor little *creature;* what a vile *creature*.

Beast and **brute** both apply to *animals* other than people, but especially to the higher mammals: lions, tigers, and other *beasts* of the veldt; such *beasts* of burden as the donkey and the horse. While *beast*, thus, has a neutrally descriptive possibility, *brute* is charged with an emphasis on supposedly nonhuman qualities like wildness, viciousness, or stupidity: the jungle rule of *brute* versus *brute*. More commonly, *brute* is used to describe a strong, cruel, or stupid human being: a nasty *brute* of a man. *Beast* can also be applied to a human being, but unlike *brute,* it stresses mostly degradation and extreme inhumanity: the woman who was called the *Beast* of Belsen. In this use, *beast* is more pejorative than *brute,* but both are more negative than *animal* when it is used in this way.

answer
    rejoinder
    reply
    response
    retort
    riposte

These nouns apply primarily to something said or written to satisfy or acknowledge a question, call, request, charge, etc. **Answer** is the most general noun in this list, and though all the nouns here considered may be used figuratively of actions as well as words, *answer* is more variously used than any of them. When a question is asked, any words or actions in return may be called an *answer:* a prompt *answer* to a letter; His *answer* was an uppercut to the jaw. Indeed, any satisfactory conclusion may be styled an *answer:* She had hoped that divorce would be the *answer* to all her problems. An *answer* in the form of a statement appropriate to the question is a **reply**: General McAuliffe's famous *reply* to the German call to surrender in World War II was said to be "Nuts!"

A **response** is the reaction to a stimulus: Pavlov's experiments proved that a conditioned *response* to a given stimulus could be induced in rats by the learned association of the right *response* with satisfaction, and of the wrong *response* with pain. In more general use *response* refers to any *answer* to an urgent question or appeal, or to a set question: a *response* to a cry for help; the *responses* of a litany. A *reply* to a *reply* is a

rejoinder, often in the form of a second question or demand; *rejoinder* is particularly applicable to the give-and-take of a debate: a telling *rejoinder* that left her opponent momentarily speechless. **Riposte** first meant a return thrust in fencing. By extension, it came to be applied to a verbal duel, meaning a quick, clever, retaliatory *reply:* a brilliant, if somewhat savage, *riposte.* A **retort** is a sharp *answer,* as to an accusation or criticism: The libelous accusation provoked a bitter *retort.*

anxiety
    angst
    apprehension
    disquiet
    dread
    foreboding
    misgiving
    uneasiness
    worry

These nouns describe troubled states of mind in which a person feels frustrated and helpless concerning a present situation, or is beset by fear that some harmful event will occur in the future. **Anxiety**, the most general of these nouns, can relate on one hand to those terms here that describe a fearful state of mind concerning the future: *anxiety* about the outcome of the election. Unlike any of these other nouns, however, *anxiety* can refer to a fear of the future per se and not just of a single hazard. This meaning is particularly used by psychiatrists to refer to patients who are immobilized by such a feeling without being able to explain what it is they fear: The boy had been so mistreated that he faced each day with a vast, uncomprehending *anxiety.*

Anxiety also relates, on the other hand, to nouns of this group that are not necessarily tied to fear of the future. Existential philosophers developed this meaning to refer to the helpless, all-encompassing frustration of the human condition when confronted with the inexplicability of life. Today, this kind of *anxiety* is often referred to by the noun **angst**, from the Danish of the philosopher Søren Kierkegaard: In the Age of Anxiety, W. H. Auden claims that our fear of the future is really a fear of ourselves and our own irrepressible *angst.*

Dread, **apprehension**, and **foreboding** emphasize the fear of something that has yet to happen. *Dread* is the most intense of any of the nouns listed here, with overtones of helplessness in the face of something as inevitable as it is terrible. The thing *dreaded* may be a specific occurrence or a somewhat undefined evil that is nonetheless terrifying to consider.

[During the missile crises even diplomats were filled with the *dread* of nuclear war; She did not know what to expect on the dark road ahead, but every shadow filled her with *dread*.] *Dread* can, of course, be used hyperbolically for more trivial occasions: I *dread* rush-hour traffic so much that I often avoid it by getting to work late. *Apprehension* is more formal than either *dread* or *anxiety*, less intense in feeling, and applying to vaguer fears of a future happening. It is not so much a harmful inevitability that is foreseen as an uncertain outcome that keeps one in suspense: No matter how nearly perfect the weather, he never conquered the *apprehension* with which he saw his wife off at the airport. Like *anxiety*, *foreboding* is midway between *dread* and *apprehension* in its formality, its intensity, and its conviction of certain or possible harm. What sets *foreboding* aside is its aura of superstitiousness: Because it rained on her wedding day, she spent the rest of the week in gloomy *foreboding*. *Foreboding* can be used without this overtone, however, in which case it points to a more general nagging doubt about the future: He carried his report card home with a sharp *foreboding* of the nasty scene he would face that evening.

Worry is far less formal than the previous nouns and implies an obsessive concern for far more mundane matters. It frequently appears in the plural. [Forget your *worries* and relax.] It is often used as an abstraction for a habit of mind that compulsively frets about the future without real result: *Worry* never makes up for what hard work could have accomplished.

Misgiving is doubt about the outcome of an action, or a feeling of *apprehension* provoked by such doubt: They had some *misgivings* about investing in the stock, and the company's annual report soon justified their apprehension. **Uneasiness** and **disquiet**, unlike *misgiving*, do not necessarily apply to fear about the future. Both suggest that actual physical discomfort or restlessness accompanies the apprehensive or fearful state, *uneasiness* most strongly so. *Disquiet* refers to a more subtle *uneasiness* over an often ill-defined danger. [What had at first been merely a faint *disquiet* as the minutes passed became at last outright *uneasiness* that set him to pacing about the hospital waiting room.] See AFRAID, FEAR.

Antonyms: *assurance, calmness, composure,* CONFIDENCE, *ease, equability, equanimity, nonchalance, placidity, quietude, security.*

anxious. Do not confuse the adjective *anxious* (uneasy in mind) with the adjective *eager* (enthusiastic).

appearance
aspect
look
semblance

These nouns are all used to denote visual impressions of the way a person or thing is or seems. **Appearance**, in the sense here considered, is the most neutral of these terms, making only a flat assertion of what one perceives. [It had the *appearance* of an eighteenth-century church; He had the rugged *appearance* of an athlete.] *Appearance*, however, like the other nouns, can be used to accent the contrast between what seems to be so and what is the fact of the matter: a despot who assumes the *appearance* of a benefactor.

Look usually applies to facial expression or demeanor rather than to other forms of *appearance*, such as dress, although it may—implying an analogy with a person's face—be used to describe things as well: a Renaissance *look* to a building. Compare these two phrases: the *appearance* of a snob; the *look* of a snob. The former suggests dandyish clothes and an overly elegant manner; the latter suggests, along with other qualities, a supercilious expression.

Aspect is often interchangeable with *look*, but suggests more strongly the changing nature of *appearance* as it confronts the beholder: the pleasant *aspect* of a lake; an artist who had the *aspect* of a prizefighter. *Aspect* implies that the perception is a quality inherent in the thing perceived, a quality that is drawn out—into focus, as it were—by the eye of the beholder.

Semblance is almost invariably used to contrast *appearance* with reality: a doubtful assertion that has the *semblance* of truth; an enemy who cloaks threats with the *semblance* of civility. It may, however, be used to mean outward *appearance* without any suggestion of falseness: The faceless person in her dreams began to acquire the *semblance* of her dead brother.

applause
acclaim
acclamation

These nouns refer to simultaneous expressions of approval or praise by a number of persons. **Applause** may be given by voice or by clapping the hands. *Applause* does not suggest any particular degree of enthusiasm and depends on context or qualifying adjectives to indicate the intensity or sincerity of the approval. [At the end of the concert, the pianist was greeted with a smattering of *applause* and a few whistles; The crowd rose as one with a great roar of *applause*.] **Acclaim** and **acclamation** are more formal terms and refer specifically to vocal expressions of praise or approval. In parliamentary bodies, a measure adopted by *acclamation* is one adopted by shouts of approval and *applause* rather than by individual votes; *by acclamation* can therefore be taken to mean by enthusiastic endorsement of the assembly. *Acclaim* need not refer particularly to actual cries of approval, but is perhaps more commonly used nowadays to express figurative *applause:* Einstein's achievements earned him the *acclaim* of the entire scientific community.

Antonyms: *abuse, booing, censure, disapprobation, disapproval, execration, hissing, jeering, obloquy, reproof, vituperation.*

appoint
    assign
    designate
    name

The situation that unites these verbs is one in which a person is being chosen to fulfill a given function by someone else. Unlike other ways of matching people to tasks, these verbs imply an official situation—in an office, club, or government—in which the choice is made by means other than an elective process. **Appoint** indicates that the selection is made by someone officially charged with this duty, although the actual selection may itself be arbitrary or judicious: Some city officials are elected to their posts, while others are *appointed* by the mayor or the political leaders. Of this set, **name** is the most informal and tells least about the chooser or the method of choice adopted: Since no one has volunteered, I hereby *name* the following to serve on the credentials committee. Sometimes, therefore, *name* stresses outcome rather than process: a senator *named* to fill an unexpired term.

Designate is the most formal of all these terms, even to the point of stiffness. It can be useful, however, to distinguish from *appoint* a process of selection that is only quasi-official in nature: The candidate *designated* as her running mate the man who had been her main opponent in the primaries.

Assign differs from the other verbs here in that it most often refers, not to the picking of a person for a task, but to the delegation of a task to one or more members of a group. It sometimes has an overtone of arbitrariness. It is occasionally used of people rather than of the task; in this case, the person being *assigned* usually joins others already *designated* in a common task: Jones is *assigned* to KP, Smith is *assigned* to guard duty, and Anderson is *assigned* to the laundry detail. See NAME.

Antonyms: *discharge, fire, let go, suspend, withdraw.*

apprise. Do not confuse the verb *apprise* (inform) with the verb *appraise* (estimate).

approval
    approbation
    commendation
    sanction

These nouns are used for the formal assent given to a proposed undertaking or for the official honor given upon successful completion of a task. **Approval** is the most general and least formal of these. In the official context, it usually means the giving of permission to undertake a task. [We can't introduce our bill on the floor without first getting the committee's *approval;* Would you initial this requisition to signify your *approval?*] It can also simply mean concurrence in opinion: Your suggestion met with the president's highest *approval.*

Approbation, the most formal of these, refers to the giving of authoritative *approval,* especially in an ecclesiastical context. It carries overtones of warmth and congeniality in a more general context, but its use—even in many official situations—might be thought unnecessarily pretentious: Their controversial report gained the hearty *approbation* of other experts in the field.

Commendation and **sanction**, more formal than *approval,* are both limited almost exclusively to an official context. *Commendation* is further restricted, within this context, to formal recognition for a task well done: a *commendation* for your brilliant sales record. It can also refer to the written document of *commendation:* He framed his *commendation* for bravery and hung it on the wall. *Sanction* can mean either before-the-act *approval* or after-the-act *commendation.* [I'm sure you can get the committee's *sanction* to proceed with your project; Only after the crisis passed did he get the president's *sanction* for the way he had acted.] Caution must be observed in the use of *sanction,* however, for it can also mean official restrictive measures taken against a proposed act, a group of people, or a group's behavior: The civil rights group said it would seek *sanctions* against those businesses that still discriminated. See ENDORSE.

Antonyms: *censure, disapprobation,* DISAPPROVAL, *dissatisfaction.*

approximately

about
around
roughly

These adverbs all mean within some degree of exactness or closeness, as in distance, time, amount, etc. **Approximately** implies an accuracy so near to a standard that the difference is virtually negligible. [It was *approximately* 100° in the shade; π is *approximately* 3.14159.]

About is often used interchangeably with *approximately*, but it does not stress the closeness to accuracy that *approximately* does: a hat costing *about* twenty dollars; reaching home at *about* dinner time. **Around** sometimes appears in informal contexts in place of *approximately* or *about:* to go to bed *around* midnight; to invite *around* fifteen people to a picnic.

Roughly is often used in place of *approximately* or *about* when there is no real attempt to be exact. [The cost of the car repairs was estimated at *roughly* two hundred dollars; The population of Delaware is *roughly* 700,000.] *Roughly* also carries a suggestion of casualness or haste, which the other adverbs do not convey. [The books were shelved *roughly* in alphabetical order; *Roughly* speaking, I would guess that we are headed for a major recession.]

argue

debate
discuss
dispute
reason

All these verbs mean talk with others in order to reach an agreement, to persuade, or to settle a question of fact. **Argue**, the most general in the list, may refer to a reasoned presentation of views or to a heated exchange of opinion amounting to a quarrel. [The senator *argued* her position with such cogency and wit that even her adversaries were impressed; They *argued* vociferously over who should pay the bill.] **Debate** means argue formally, usually under the control of a referee and according to a set of regulations: The House of Representatives *debated* the proposal for three weeks. Any argument in which each person has strongly held opinions, however, can be styled a *debate. Debate* is also used less formally to mean to consider or think about alternatives: They *debated* about which train to take.

Discuss means talk over, usually in an informal, friendly way. It implies that the participants have less intensely held opinions than in a *debate,* and emphasizes their common desire to resolve the question sat-

isfactorily: a committee appointed to *discuss* and formulate recommendations on how to improve job opportunities for the underprivileged. *Discuss* points to the elucidation of an issue rather than to the narrow presentation of one's own view.

Reason means *argue* or *discuss* in a careful and painstaking manner in order to persuade or explore a subject in depth: Supreme Court justices *reason* with one another in interpreting the Constitution.

Dispute, in this context, means *argue* with more passion than logic, often from a factional point of view: Adherents of rival candidates at a convention frequently fall to *disputing* about subtle rules of procedure. See CONTROVERSY.

Antonyms: *CONSENT.*

arise

emanate
emerge
issue
originate
result
stem

These verbs refer to the development of one thing out of another. **Arise** suggests a chain of causality, possibly from simple to complex: new social organizations *arising* from the industrial revolution. **Emerge** suggests a gradual process that stresses simple change more than causality: a parliamentary system *emerging* slowly from the old order of absolute monarchy. **Originate** stresses the starting point for change: egalitarian sentiments that *originated* in contract theories of government. **Result**, by contrast, stresses the end product of change: contract theories of government that *resulted* in the growth of egalitarian sentiments.

Stem is closely related to *originate* in stressing the beginning of change, and is like *arise* in stressing direct causation. It usually appears with *from:* civil rights laws that *stemmed* from national indignation over the brutal suppression of the protest marchers. **Issue** is similar in force to *stem* but is considerably more formal in tone: a sense of freedom *issuing* from more than a decade of experimentation in the arts. **Emanate**, the most formal of these verbs so far, stresses the point of origin like *originate, stem,* and *issue,* but it might be thought too formal for many contexts. It can, however, suggest a less clearly defined pattern of causation to which many imponderable factors may have contributed: a new sense of security *emanating* from greater prosperity and cessation of the cold war. See BEGIN, BEGINNING.

Antonyms: *DECREASE, FINISH, STOP.*

arms

armament
arsenal
deterrent
matériel
munitions
ordnance
weapons

These nouns pertain to the guns and other military equipment used in fighting wars. **Arms** and **weapons** are general terms, nearly interchangeable, for the instruments of combat. A bow-and-arrow, sword, and rifle are all *arms* or *weapons*. Of the two terms, *arms* is more frequently restricted in use to those *weapons* that an individual soldier can employ, whereas *weapons* are anything used in the fight, from clubs to hydrogen bombs. In its most general sense, *arms* can also refer to the entire military capability of a country: Both nations bankrupted themselves in their race to manufacture *arms*.

Armament is similar in meaning to this last sense of *arms*, but it is much clearer in that it points without confusion both to the *weapons* and the military equipment used to wage war: The country's *armament* includes the most versatile planes, the fastest ships, and the most rugged tanks in the world. *Armament* may also be used to refer to the total weapons available to a military vehicle: The destroyer's *armament* comprises several small cannon, two torpedo bays, and a number of anti-aircraft guns. **Ordnance** may be used, like *armament*, for the total military effort of a country, but much more commonly refers specifically to heavy firearms, mounted cannon or mortars, and other heavy artillery.

Matériel and **munitions** both refer to equipment rather than to *weapons*. *Matériel* suggests all the supportive equipment and supplies necessary to combat, while *munitions* most commonly suggests ammunition only: Dry socks are as important an item of *matériel* as *munitions*.

Arsenal and **deterrent** have come into fairly recent use to refer to a country's nuclear *arms*. *Arsenal* previously meant simply a place where *weapons* are stored, but in this specific instance it indicates a stockpile of nuclear warheads. *Deterrent* is an almost euphemistic word for a nuclear *arsenal*: The atomic *arsenal* of either nation alone could lay waste to the entire planet, yet many countries clamor to build their own *deterrents* as well. See FLEET, TROOPS.

arrogate. Do not confuse the verb *arrogate* (claim a power, privilege, etc., unduly) with the verb *abrogate* (cancel).

artificial

ersatz
false
synthetic

The adjective **artificial** may be applied to anything made by human beings in imitation of something natural: *artificial* flowers; an *artificial* leg. **Synthetic** is synonymous with *artificial* in this sense, but there is a connotation in *synthetic* of production by chemical combinations or similar techniques: *synthetic* rubber. **False** and the formerly popular adjective **ersatz** both suggest a substitute made because of the costliness or lack of the original item: *false* teeth; the proliferation of *ersatz* goods during periods of war and inflation. *False* often implies the presenting of a misleading appearance when it refers to a function-masking decorative detail: *false* drawers that were actually a single door concealing stereo equipment. *Ersatz* commonly describes a cheap or inferior copy that can fool no one: bowls of wax fruit and a dusty collection of *ersatz* flowers in brass-plated planters. See MAKE, SHAM.

Antonyms: *GENUINE, natural.*

artisan

artificer
craftsman
creator
designer
executor
workman

These nouns all refer to makers or constructors of products at some level below that of artistic creation. An **artisan** falls midway between the full-scale artist who creates single inimitable works and the mere worker who turns out identical, anonymous products: Italian *artisans* were brought to New York expressly to carve the masonry on the brownstone buildings of the 1890's. *Artisan* was once much closer in meaning to artist, however, as witness the stained-glass windows of a medieval cathedral. These were created by anonymous *artisans*, but they are often great works of art nonetheless. **Artificer** still can suggest its earliest meaning of a worker who possesses mechanical facility: the *artificer* in an infantry company who cares for and repairs its weapons. In other uses *artificer* had begun to sound fusty until James Joyce reintroduced the word in *Portrait of the Artist as a Young Man* to stand for the artist as creator and controller of art and life. It has sometimes been used since in this highest sense.

Craftsman has risen somewhat in the scale to the artist end of the spectrum since the advent of machine-made objects in the nineteenth century: Replaced by factories, the furniture maker, the bookbinder, the dyer, and the weaver were all skilled *craftsmen* whose century-old secrets were lost during the Industrial Revolution. *Craftsman* is now a common term to describe a worker in the minor arts; a ceramist or a pottery maker would not feel insulted to be called a *craftsman*. In the other arts, *craftsman* is used of an artist unusually adept in the technical aspects of an art: The young poet was an extraordinary *craftsman* simply from the standpoint of the variety of poetic forms that he could command effectively. The terms *craftsperson* and *craftswoman* are now also in use with identical connotations.

Creator and **designer** in the minor arts are parallel terms and imply the existence of a subordinate **executor** who carries a plan or design into effect. The person named on the playbill as the *creator* of a play's costumes conceived and sketched them; someone else probably *executed* them. A fashion, book, or automobile *designer* plans the physical appearance of the completed product down to the smallest detail, but others are the *executors* of these designs.

Workman implies someone who has more craftsmanship than a worker would possess but far less than an artisan. [We called in an *artisan* to restore the broken pane in our Tiffany shade; At the same time, *workmen* arrived to repair our leaky roof.] See artist, laborer.

artist

craftsman
creator
painter
stylist
virtuoso

These nouns refer to people who produce works of art. **Artist**, in one of its uses, is the most general and all-inclusive of these, indicating a practitioner of any one of the fine or applied arts: *artists* who paint, compose music, or write novels. Its main usefulness lies in the fact that it can refer equally well as a group word to workers in diverse fields: a section of Paris where all kinds of *artists* lived. By extension, *artist* is often used of someone who shows unusual taste or discrimination in other tasks: a real *artist* when it came to planning and giving interesting parties. When *artist* is not clearly a group word, however, it can often be taken to apply more strictly to the visual arts, especially to painting: a gathering place for *artists* and writers. **Painter** thus specifically emphasizes one of the possible meanings of *artist*, to the exclusion of all others. In general, *artist* can be replaced to advantage by the more specific term whenever appropriate: gatherings of *painters*, sculptors, novelists, poets, and composers.

The remaining nouns all relate to *artist*, rather than *painter*, in grouping a variety of specific roles under one general heading. **Creator** emphasizes the origination of artistic ideas by a person working independently; it may or may not imply that others bring the idea to its realization: the *creator* of huge canvases teeming with scenes of Venetian life; a person credited as the *creator* of a film on which many had collaborated. *Creator* also may refer to an *artist* who works in a number of media: the *creator* of frescoes, architectural designs, and sonnets. It is also used in the applied arts, sometimes to lend aesthetic appeal to a business: the *creator* of a new line of fall fashions.

Craftsman, stylist, and **virtuoso** are general nouns that emphasize technical skill or flair when substituted for *artist*. In this context, *craftsman* suggests any *artist* who lavishes painstaking care on the construction of a work and is consciously concerned with fine details: a real *craftsman* showing ability to shape dialogue toward natural and inevitable climaxes. *Stylist* suggests an *artist* unusually gifted with a flair for working in one or a number of demanding modes: those rare, truly innovating *stylists* of the short story. *Stylist* can also be used of lesser or applied arts to suggest singularity or professionality: hair *stylist*; a unique song *stylist*. *Virtuoso* originally applied to a musical performer who was able to execute difficult passages with apparent ease and bravura. Now it may refer as well to any *artist* who shows unique mastery of technical difficulties or is especially given to displays of technical facility: a *virtuoso* in the sonnet form; a *virtuoso* who, for all his technique, remains a shallow and superficial *artist*. See CREATE.

artistic

aesthetic
artificial
arty
harmonious
mannered
precious
stylized
tasteful

These adjectives describe qualities in a work of art, its creator, or its appreciator. **Artistic** and **aesthetic** are closely related; most simply, the *artistic* instinct belongs to the creator, the *aesthetic* instinct to the beholder: *artistic* skill; *aesthetic* pleasure. In another sense, however, the *aesthetic* attitude might be taken as generic, the *artistic* attitude as a specific but by no means exhaustive example of the more general term. In this distinction, the *aesthetic* instinct expresses itself in all areas of life where taste, discrimination, style, and balance are desirable: an *aesthetic* flower arrangement; an *aesthetic* flair for matching the right wine to the right entrée. In yet another sense, *aesthetic* describes specifically those discriminations sorted out by aestheticians; one connotation here may be unnecessary refinement or passivity as opposed to the boldness and activity of the *artistic* attitude: too bogged down in *aesthetic* distinctions to have any *artistic* spontaneity. In describing a work of art rather than an attitude, *aesthetic* would be largely irrelevant, *artistic* inane or tautological. Both may be used to praise creations not commonly thought of as works of art: an *artistic* grouping of furniture.

Arty and **mannered** both refer to attitudes that tend toward parody of the *artistic* sensibility. *Arty,* the more strongly negative of the two, is also the most informal of any of these adjectives. It suggests the phoniness of the poseur or artist manqué, stressing particularly exaggerated and affected behavior that may be totally unrelated to the creation of works of art: the *arty* bohemian crowd who once flourished in Greenwich Village. *Mannered* is more formal and more restrained in its disapproval. It suggests behavior that is contrived and unnatural: the *mannered,* fey look of her costume. *Mannered* can also refer to the work of art itself, suggesting the same qualities of contrived artificiality.

Artificial most often refers only to the work, suggesting a lack of spontaneity and of naturalness. It is more negative in tone than *mannered.* The latter may suggest worthwhile content that has been harmed by unnecessary stylistic manipulation. *Artificial,* on the other hand, suggests a lack of content that a pretentious style is struggling to conceal. **Stylized** is like *mannered* and *artificial* in suggesting an emphasis on mode as opposed to content, but it contrasts with them in ranging from a neutral to an approving tone: the *stylized* patterns of the kabuki dances. It emphasizes the ordering of the artist's raw materials into significant, if unrealistic, designs.

Precious is the most negative in tone of any adjective here and is the most freewheeling in range, applying to the work, the artist, or to someone who is not artistic in any way. It points to a taste for the genteel and overelegant, especially when these qualities are as far removed as possible from reality or normality. It suggests a complaisant attempt to be different and striking, and typically results in over*stylized* affectation—cute, in the worst sense of the word: a *precious* writer of the Mauve Decade; a beauty queen who underlined her *precious* way of speaking with coy gestures and an exaggerated simper.

Tasteful and **harmonious** refer to *aesthetic* qualities that may be found in *artistic* works. *Tasteful* is extremely subjective in referring to what is in accordance with the canons of taste; what is *tasteful* to one person, such as a pink and purple Christmas tree, might be thought vulgar by another. *Harmonious* is more objective in pointing to a smooth, well-balanced relation of parts: a *harmonious* ordering of the room's spatial relationships. On the other hand, what one age thought chaotic or cacophonous, another finds simple, *tasteful,* and *harmonious.* All adjectives in this area, of course, are ultimately subjective. See FORMAL.

Antonyms: *displeasing, distasteful,* GAUDY, *inartistic, shoddy, tasteless, unaesthetic.*

assert

> affirm
> allege
> asseverate
> aver
> avouch
> avow
> maintain
> testify

These verbs all mean state positively, as though anticipating or countering argument or skepticism. Whereas **assert** means state with some force or conviction, **allege** means state without offering proof: It was *alleged* that he was present at the scene of the crime, but he *asserted* that he was in Europe at the time. Whatever one *asserts* would be defended in argument, but whether anyone believes something *alleged* is beside the point; the aim of *alleging* is to learn the truth by proving or disproving the claim made.

Affirm means declare or state positively that something is true; it indicates firm belief or unshakable conviction: to *affirm* one's faith in God. **Asseverate** is nearly synonymous with *assert* but even more positive and is uncommon even in formal writing. **Testify** means bear witness, as in a court of law, or declare solemnly to be true: to *testify* on behalf of the defendant; I can *testify* to this man's veracity and good character.

Maintain, as here considered, means *assert* something in the face of evidence or arguments to the contrary: In spite of circumstantial evidence pointing to her guilt, the woman on trial *maintained* that she was innocent. *Maintain* almost always involves controversy or disagreement; it presupposes a prior statement to which one is adhering, and in this sense is a reaffirming of one's position.

Aver means declare confidently as fact. **Avouch** means vouch for or affirm positively. **Avow** means declare openly: to *avow* one's guilt. These verbs are not common in contemporary writing; all occur only in formal writing, and *avouch* seldom even there. See DECLARE, UTTER.

Antonyms: CONTRADICT, *controvert, demur, dispute,* DOUBT, *refute.*

assistant

    adjutant
    aide
    helper
    subordinate

These nouns apply to a person who contributes to the accomplishment of a task. **Assistant** and **helper** are nearly identical except for the latter's greater informality. Because of this difference, *helper* may seem warmer in tone, implying affection, whereas *assistant* remains coolly objective. [She had to admit that her husband was a good *helper* around the house; It is not unusual now for a woman executive to have a man as her administrative *assistant*.] Furthermore, one might become someone else's *helper* out of generosity, whereas *assistant* usually implies a paid position. On the other hand, *helper* is frequently used in the area of manual labor, while *assistant* implies a position within a profession and is sometimes part of an official title: electrician's *helper; assistant* to the vice-president in charge of sales.

Subordinate emphasizes the inferiority of a *helper* or *assistant*, and its greater formality does not always mitigate an overtone of condescension, sometimes extending even to contempt. [The first sergeant treated the second lieutenants in the company as though they were merely her *subordinates*.] *Subordinate* can, however, be neutral in tone, merely describing an unequal relationship: a trusted *subordinate*. **Adjutant** and **aide** are drawn from military life to describe the administrative *assistant* or *subordinate* of a superior officer. *Aide*,

because of its brevity, has come to be used by journalists and especially headline writers to describe any government administrator. See ACCOMPLICE, ASSOCIATE.

associate

    affiliate
    ally
    coworker
    colleague
    fellow
    partner

The nouns in this set refer to professional, business, or work relationships between people. **Associate** is the least specific of these; its formality would suggest a business or professional context. While it implies close connection, the relationship might be the result of choice, chance, or necessity: a person's business *associates*. In a more specific use, *associate*, used attributively to modify a noun, is a component of some professional titles, denoting the second of three ranks: an *associate* editor; an *associate* professor. It is also used specifically to indicate less than full membership in a group: A member pays $200 annually in dues, but one can become an *associate* for $50. In this sense, the noun *associate* may refer either to a person or to a group within a larger group. **Affiliate** compares with this use of *associate* in being now mostly used of a group related to another group: the television *affiliate* of the town's only newspaper. It is frequently used to relate a small group to a national or international parent group: the local *affiliate* of the American Medical Association. *Affiliate* suggests that two *affiliates* are coequal in a loose relationship of autonomous groups, even when a smaller-to-larger hierarchy is involved. This contrasts with *associate* in its suggestion of subordinate membership in a group.

Ally and **partner** may apply either to individuals or to groups. *Ally* always suggests a relationship of choice. One's *allies* unite with one in a common cause and most often against a common enemy. *Allies* are not necessarily friends outside the cause that jointly concerns them: The two senators were enemies on questions of domestic affairs, but *allies* on foreign policy. *Ally* is chiefly used in reference to nations that are on the same side in an international war: England and Russia were our *allies* in World War II. *Partner*, like *ally*, may apply to one nation joined with another in a common cause: France and England were *partners* in an atomic power project. But *partner* often indicates a closer or a contractual relationship. It is the legal term for one of the co-owners of a business. She was made a *partner* in the law firm. And it may also refer to a much more personal association: marriage *partners*. Unlike the other nouns in this group, *partner* sometimes points to a one-to-one relationship involving a couple or a pair: his dance *partner;* to draw for *partners* in duplicate bridge.

The remaining nouns refer exclusively to person-to-person relationships, as does *associate* in its more general sense. **Coworker** is the least formal of these and applies as readily to manual labor as to more highly skilled occupations: his *coworkers* in the factory; her *coworker* on the space project. *Coworker* is distinctly neutral in tone, implying neither animosity nor the cordiality that may be suggested by *associate*. **Colleague** is restricted almost solely in use to professional association. It is formal in tone, but may range in feeling from neutrality to an expression of respect or approbation: my *colleagues* in the philosophy department. **Fellow**, as here considered, is now seldom used except as a title or component. In an academic context, it may mean a graduate student on a fellowship grant, but it may also be used of certain faculty positions: a Fulbright *fellow* at Padua; a *fellow* of All Souls College, Oxford. See ACCOMPLICE, ASSISTANT, FRIEND.
Antonyms: OPPONENT.

assure

guarantee
insure
promise

These verbs mean make or attempt to make something certain or secure by removing doubt. **Assure** can mean either make certain or cause to feel certain. [The doctor *assured* him that the child would recover from the illness; The fact that the hospital had a good reputation *assured* her that the child would be well taken care of.] **Insure**, or, as it is also spelled, *ensure*, means make certain as the consequence of some action or agent: To *insure* the child's quick recovery, the doctor gave him an antibiotic. *Insure* also means make safe, protect against harm: to *insure* freedom against tyranny.

Guarantee means assume responsibility for the quality of a product or for the performance of a service or obligation. One who *guarantees* a debt *assures* the creditor of full payment.

Promise, like *assure*, is often designed to make someone feel certain, but hardly *guarantees* that the outcome will measure up to expectations. *Promise* implies intention, not obligation, and every child knows that not all promises are kept: to *promise* some-

one a raise in pay; to *promise* to keep an appointment. In another sense, *promise* simply indicates grounds for favorable expectation. An invalid's renewed appetite may be deemed a *promising* sign. See PLEDGE.
Antonyms: *imperil, jeopardize, renege, warn.*

attack

assail
assault
besiege
bombard
charge
storm

These verbs all mean set upon violently or do battle with. **Attack**, the most general term of this group, may be applied to any offensive action, but more narrowly means begin hostilities: to *attack* an enemy stronghold; The watchdog *attacked* a would-be burglar and drove him off. *Attack*, like all these verbs, is also used figuratively: The senator *attacked* the views of a colleague.

Assail and **assault** have the same etymological origins but differ in meaning. *Assail* means *attack* violently and repeatedly, implying that victory depends not so much on the force or effectiveness of one's attack but on one's persistence and pertinacity. To be *assailed* is to be worn down, to have no respite: a person *assailed* by doubts. *Assault* typically suggests close physical contact and extreme violence, especially against one or a few people. *Assault* may be used as a euphemism for rape. [The two women were *assaulted* by a gang of hoodlums across the street from their home; The noise of car horns, jet planes, jackhammers, ambulance sirens, fire engines, subways, and helicopters *assaults* the ears of city dwellers.]

Charge and **storm** both suggest a forceful *assault* on a fixed position. To *charge* is to make a violent onslaught or attack upon an enemy: The tank brigade *charged* the hostile fort. But *charge* in this sense is most often used imperatively as a command. *Storm* means take or try to take by force, with all the rush and fury of a storm: Seasoned troops were picked to *storm* the difficult enemy position. *Storm* often conveys a feeling of desperation, an all-out effort to avert defeat and disaster.

Besiege means surround or beset with an armed force in order to capture: to *besiege* a fortified city. In its figurative uses it is close to *assail*, but retains some of its basic sense of being hemmed in or enclosed rather than punished repeatedly: *Besieged* with fears, he decided to seek the aid of a psychiatrist.

Bombard means *assail* with missiles or, in figurative senses, with abusive words. [The TV station was *bombarded* with complaints against a tasteless program; A prominent minister *assailed* the executives who had permitted it to be shown, and in the state legislature a senator *attacked* federal laxity in enforcing government regulations.] See AGGRESSION, FIGHT.

Antonyms: *aid,* PROTECT, UPHOLD.

attainment
    accomplishment
    acquirement
    acquisition

These nouns, as here considered, refer to a capability resulting, at least in part, from conscious effort. All are frequently used in the plural. **Attainment** is the loftiest term. It implies a fully developed talent that leads to eminence in the arts, in science, or in some comparable field of endeavor: Bertrand Russell was not only a distinguished philosopher but also a man of high literary *attainments*. **Accomplishment**, in this sense, refers to any ability or manner acquired from practice or experience; specifically, *accomplishments* are social graces meant to please or entertain. [In the nineteenth century, a young woman of many *accomplishments* might sing, play the piano, and paint; Skill in dancing and the ability to make small talk are *accomplishments* considered desirable by most American adolescents.]

An **acquirement** is a skill gained by study or practice rather than through natural talent. Where *accomplishments* may be showy and impressive, *acquirements* are substantial and useful: The ability to read Sanskrit is an *acquirement* rarely found among Western scholars. **Acquisition** usually refers to a newly obtained material possession, especially one of intrinsic value that is regarded as a sought-after prize: A library takes pride in its rare-book *acquisitions*. *Acquisition* may also apply to the *attainment* of a quality, skill, or body of knowledge that is valuable in itself: Self-discipline is an invaluable *acquisition*. See GENIUS, SKILL.

attraction
    affinity
    sympathy

The noun **attraction** refers to the power or quality that draws a person to another person, an idea, or a thing. An **affinity** is a natural or instinctive *attraction* or inclination: an *affinity* among children of the same age. *Attraction* means the power to attract. If a woman has an *attraction* for a man, he is attracted or has an *affinity* for her; nothing is implied about the woman's feelings toward the man. *Affinity* is also used to refer to any individual preference or liking that is presumed to be deep-seated or to stem from one's nature or background: an *affinity* for Italian movies; an *affinity* for mystery novels.

Sympathy, as here considered, refers to an agreement of affections, inclinations, or temperaments that makes people agreeable to one another. Two people are in *sympathy* if they have like *affinities*—for example, if they share similar tastes in art, recreation, or food. See LOVE.

Antonyms: *antagonism, antipathy, aversion, discord, estrangement, repugnance, repulsion.*

attribute
    ascribe
    credit
    impute

The verb **attribute** means consider one thing as belonging to or stemming from something else. [Some scientists *attribute* intelligence to ants; others say that the complex organizational life of ants should be *attributed* to instinct.]

Ascribe means assign or *attribute* a cause, quality, source, etc., to something as a property or as being characteristic of it: to *ascribe* good (or bad) motives to someone; to *ascribe* an unsigned painting to Picasso; to *ascribe* an artifact to the Paleolithic era.

Credit, as here considered, means *attribute* or *ascribe* in a favorable sense: to *credit* a scientist with a major discovery; to *credit* a seemingly trivial skirmish with being the turning point of a war.

Impute means attribute a fault, crime, etc., to a person: to *impute* nepotism to the senator because of her decision to give a lucrative government contract to her brother-in-law. *Impute*, however, is not invariably associated with derogatory contexts. It may also be used to mean simply to consider as the source or cause of: to *impute* one's happiness to modest ambitions. See PRESCRIBE.

Antonyms: *deny, dissociate, separate.*

authoritarian
    autocratic
    despotic
    dictatorial
    fascistic
    oligarchic

paternalistic
plutocratic
totalitarian
tyrannical

These adjectives refer to the wielding of power by a single person or a small group of people, usually without the consent of the governed. **Authoritarian**, the most general of these adjectives, is also the most objectively descriptive and least disapproving in tone, although any of them will have negative implications for the citizens of a democracy. *Authoritarian* may describe any form of rule—from a monarchy to a democracy—in which unquestioning obedience to those in power is expected or demanded: the military junta that instituted such *authoritarian* measures as censorship of the press; children whose upbringing was neither truly permissive nor *authoritarian*. **Paternalistic** refers to an *authoritarian* tendency that sees a populace as childlike and unable to govern itself *Paternalistic* may suggest either benevolent rule or a style of government determined to keep the governed helpless and dependent: the *paternalistic* stance of most banana republics; the *paternalistic* attitude of most postbellum whites toward the recently freed slave. **Oligarchic** refers to the rule of an elite, but does not suggest what grounds are used to determine who is a member of this ruling group: the *oligarchic* power of the English nobility before the rise of the monarchy. **Plutocratic** suggests an *oligarchic* rule based specifically on wealth: the first *plutocratic* industrial giants of the nineteenth century.

The remaining adjectives are all much harsher in tone than the foregoing. Of these, **autocratic** is the mildest, though stronger than *authoritarian*. It suggests the absolute rule of a single person, but such a rule may be as repressive or benevolent as the person chooses: *autocratic* rulers as different as Queen Elizabeth I and Louis XIV; the rare husband who still insists on *autocratic* control over his family.

Totalitarian is perhaps the least exact of these adjectives in its implications. It suggests concentration of power in the hands of the few; it also suggests the context of a modern collectivist state. A *totalitarian* government is certainly *authoritarian*, but may or may not be *oligarchic, plutocratic, paternalistic,* or *autocratic*. Such a state would certainly suppress civil liberties, but might still have a benevolent notion, however misguided, of its duties to the people. On the other hand, it might be based exclusively on the self-aggrandizement and greed of a ruling class: the Puritans of the New World who, in self-defense, constructed what amounted to a *totalitarian* state; a Stalinist regime that

was more *totalitarian* than those that preceded or followed it.

Dictatorial and **tyrannical** both may be simply descriptive of *autocratic* rule, but more often suggest strong disapproval for repressive tactics. *Dictatorial*, at its most neutral, specifically refers to leaders other than hereditary rulers such as kings. At its most negative, it suggests repressive harshness: Cromwell, who was less *dictatorial* than many kings; family life embittered by her *dictatorial* momism; corporations no longer *dictatorial* toward their employees. *Tyrannical* may once have been most appropriate to describe the power of a king, but now it applies more generally to any arbitrary, almost whimsical one-person rule: the *tyrannical* head of the congressional committee; his *tyrannical* outburst against the son's disobedience.

Fascistic and **despotic** are the most harshly negative of all these terms. *Fascistic* in its narrowest sense applies to a strongly nationalistic and militaristic right-wing regime that suppresses civil liberties and attacks selected minorities: the *fascistic* tendencies of many anti-Semites. *Fascistic*, however, is often used loosely as invective for any *authoritarian* stand: *fascistic* gangsters who took control of the neighborhood. *Despotic* could once be applied less negatively to any absolute, *autocratic* rule, but now it would be more often understood as indicating a fiercely cruel and savagely repressive ruler or government: the rapidly disappearing *despotic* family head; a government so *despotic* that citizens could be shot without a trial.

Antonyms: *compliant, constitutional, democratic, free, lenient, liberal, limited, permissive.*

auxiliary
ancillary
contributory
secondary
subsidiary

Auxiliary, like the rest of these adjectives, refers to something that gives additional help or support. The help given is usually similar to but less important than the main effort being made: The *auxiliary* police are called in only when the main force has been overtaxed. Sometimes, *auxiliary* can refer simply to additional or supplementary resources: an oil firm with *auxiliary* investments in shipbuilding and auto parts. And sometimes, *auxiliary* seems to be used almost euphemistically to avoid any suggestion of subordination or inferiority to the main item: My mother once headed the ladies' *auxiliary* club.

Like *auxiliary*, **ancillary** may refer to something

useful that may or may not be called into action. The *ancillary* item, however, may be dissimilar though closely related to what it supports: psychology as *ancillary* to the study of literature. In other instances, *ancillary*, more than any of the other adjectives, may suggest a dependence of the main thing on the *ancillary* thing, almost as if the latter were its prerequisite, or preceded it in time: Counterpoint and harmony are certainly *ancillary* to serious composition.

Contributory suggests a definite cause-and-effect relationship unique among these adjectives, indicating one of several factors that result in a particular effect. The *contributory* cause, however, only accompanies a major cause: Ever-escalating acts of sabotage were a *contributory* factor in the German retreat before the Allied onslaught. Unlike *ancillary* or *auxiliary* items, something that is *contributory* exists only if actually called into action; it cannot be held in abeyance and still be *contributory*. Also, a *contributory* factor may be part of a destructive as well as a constructive result: Cigarette smoking may be regarded as a *contributory* cause of cancer in his case.

Secondary and **subsidiary** both clearly state the subordination or inferiority of the added factor. *Secondary* relates to *contributory* in having a cause-and-effect meaning but, unlike *contributory*, can refer to both causes and effects. A *contributory* cause, for example, may result only in a *secondary* effect. *Secondary* may be applied in any context where comparison is made between primary values, goals, benefits, and less important or gratuitous ones. In this respect, *subsidiary* is more specific, meaning all the attached ramifications that may exist along with a primary situation: the author's *subsidiary* rights in the stage and film versions of her novel; a main store's *subsidiary* branches. *Subsidiary*, in this sense, is most like *auxiliary* in suggesting a similar but less important aspect of a larger whole. See ADDITION, ASSISTANT, SUBORDINATE.

averse. Do not confuse the adjective *averse* (disinclined) with the adjective *adverse* (unfavorable).

avoid
elude
escape
eschew
evade
shun

The verb **avoid** means keep away from or keep at a distance, either by design or as the automatic or accidental consequence of an action. [He drove home over the bridge to *avoid* the traffic congestion at the tunnel; By driving home over the bridge he unknowingly *avoided* the tunnel congestion.]

Escape in its basic sense refers similarly to a deliberate or accidental keeping clear of something. A criminal may adopt a ruse to *escape* detection, or he may *escape* apprehension by the death of the only witness. *Escape* is also used with the sense of manage to *avoid*, or remain untouched or uninfluenced by something evil or harmful: to *escape* from being injured by the falling debris.

To **elude** is to *avoid* or *escape* by the use of dexterity or artifice. A quarterback may *elude* tacklers by a feint; a fugitive may *elude* pursuers by planting false clues. **Evade** may sometimes be used in place of *elude*, but often carries the connotation of avoidance of duty or obligation by underhanded methods: a taxpayer who *evaded* taxes by falsifying accounts—a punishable offense—although she might legally have *avoided* a portion of the tax by taking advantage of allowable deductions; a soldier who *evades* hazardous duty by malingering.

Shun and **eschew** mean *avoid* with repugnance or distaste, or for reasons of morality or prudence. [A virtuous person will *shun* evil companions and practices; A person on a diet may *shun* or *eschew* rich foods.] *Eschew* is restricted to formal contexts and is narrower in application than *shun*. Whereas *eschew* points to abstention, *shun* may indicate either abstention or physical withdrawal; one can *shun* people as well as things. [During his illness he *shunned* all society, and in particular those who had been his dearest friends.]

Antonyms: *catch, encounter, face,* MEET, *seek, solicit.*

award
bounty
honor
premium
prize

These nouns involve the showing of favor either out of generosity or out of respect for achievement. **Award** and **prize** are now nearly identical in meaning, although *prize* is less formal in tone. Both refer to a tribute given for some outstanding accomplishment. Both may or may not imply the giving of a sum of money. [The Olympic winner was given only a gold medal as an *award;* An *award* of ten thousand dollars accompanied the *prize* for the best novel of the year.] *Prize* may also signify the objective or attainment of a struggle. [The platoon took the hill after an all-night battle, but it was a costly *prize;* Although he had not guessed it when he proposed, his wife turned out to be quite a *prize.*]

Honor is more general than the foregoing. Whereas *award* and *prize* may suggest an official ceremony of recognition, *honor* may share this implication or depart from it to indicate simply private, unofficial respect. [The visiting head of state was given the *honor* of a twenty-one gun salute; It is an *honor* to hear you speak so highly of me.]

Premium is most specific in meaning, referring to an additional value beyond an agreed-on sum, the *premium* being given when a further condition has been met: They gave her a *premium* for selling the most cars that month. More generally, *premium* may simply mean a high valuation, like *honor:* I put a high *premium* on the truth.

Bounty may mean generosity in general, or the gift given as a favor, a rather formal use: The land's *bounty* passed all expectation. *Bounty* is also used specifically to mean a sum of money given by a government for killing a predatory animal: the *bounty* offered for killing mountain lions. See APPROVAL.

Antonyms: *forfeit, penalty.*

aware

cognizant
conscious
mindful
on to

These adjectives mean having knowledge of the existence or fact of something. **Aware** is the broadest term and may mean having knowledge of something inside oneself or of some external fact or condition. Such knowledge may be based on the evidence of one's senses or on the intellect: to be *aware* of hunger pangs; *aware* of a sharp drop in temperature; *aware* of a new trend in public opinion.

Conscious at its most restricted is close to *aware* in indicating the mind's registering of a sensation, perception, or state of affairs: *conscious* of how dim the room had grown as the twilight deepened; *conscious* of what the other students thought of her. Even on this level, however, *conscious* may suggest the minimal registering of a perception, whereas *aware* more often implies a keener response or greater alertness that may encompass evaluation or rational judgment: People had been *conscious* of the problem before, but the new book made them *aware* of its magnitude. *Conscious,* furthermore, can apply as *aware* cannot to the waking state in general, as opposed to a sleeping or comatose state: a local anesthetic under which a person remains *conscious* throughout the operation. In a psychological context, *conscious* can apply to those contents of the psyche that are present or available to the ego: a *conscious* hatred of his mother; slowly becoming *conscious* of her long-buried feelings of inferiority. Less technically, it can refer to a deliberate or voluntary judgment: urged to make a *conscious* choice before events decided the question for them.

Cognizant implies knowledge of a more public character than the other adjectives here considered. To say that one is *cognizant* of a breeze would be absurdly pretentious, but one may without fear of ridicule claim to be *cognizant* of new methods in the teaching of foreign languages. [A congressman ought to be *cognizant* of the attitudes and opinions of voters.] *Cognizant* thus suggests a deliberate effort to know, and the things known are usually of some public importance. **Mindful**, like *cognizant* a rather formal word, emphasizes the giving of attention more than the acquisition of knowledge. [Because I am always *mindful* of my own mistakes, I am tolerant of the mistakes of others; *Mindful* of the strong opinions of voters, the congressman refused to support the bill.] **On to** is a colloquial expression meaning *aware of,* especially of something involving deception or skulduggery. It usually expresses a good deal of indignation, if not outright hostility. [I'm *on to* you and your fancy ideas about how I should spend my money; you're nothing but a crook!] See INFORM.

Antonyms: *blind,* HEEDLESS, *ignorant, insensible, unaware, unmindful.*

backcountry

backwoods
boondocks
inland
interior
midlands
sticks

These nouns refer to the inner portions of a country, to rural regions, or to those remote from cosmopolitan or urban centers. Many of these nouns also function attributively as adjectives. **Backcountry** is the most general of these and can apply to any of the three situations listed above. Its connotations imply a provincial, backward, and rude area that is sparsely settled or unimportant: tourists who stop over in the country's main port but seldom visit the *backcountry;* a *backcountry* doctor. **Backwoods** restricts the possibilities of *backcountry* to the notion of an out-of-the-way forested region: the *backwoods* of Maine. The note of provinciality is even clearer here: rednecks from the *backwoods.*

Interior and **inland** are restricted in reference to the inner portions of a country, rural or urban, both nouns having fewer connotations than the previous pair. *Inland* may suggest the greater remoteness of these two nouns: the *inland* of the continent; the *interior* of the island. *Interior* can, however, suggest greater inaccessibility: an *inland* lake; the first expeditions to the *interior* of Africa. **Midlands** can also function neutrally but is used mostly to refer to *inland* regions of England: the great industrial cities of the *midlands.* Neither remoteness nor inaccessibility is implied here, although provinciality may be indicated.

Boondocks, which comes from a Tagalog word for mountain, can refer to any stretch of rough country filled with dense brush or jungle: the *boondocks* of Luzon; headquarters personnel who are isolated from actual field conditions of troops in the *boondocks.* More recently, the term may refer informally to any rural or noncosmopolitan *backcountry*, especially with reference to its provincial isolation: a college town in the *boondocks.* **Sticks** is even more informal in concentrating exclusively on this last possibility of *boondocks,* pertaining to rural areas or provincial centers that are unsophisticated or backward. It is always somewhat derogatory or disparaging in tone: a hick from the *sticks;* like so many young men who left the *sticks* to seek their fortune in the big city. See PLAIN.

Antonyms: *CITY.*

bad

disagreeable
distasteful
objectionable
unpleasant

These adjectives describe qualities or situations that arouse feelings of displeasure or dislike, but usually not of strong aversion. **Bad**, the most general adjective of this group, may be a weak synonym for any of the other terms, indicating an unfavorable or undesirable quality. *Bad* government usually means corrupt government; a *bad* typist is an incompetent typist; a *bad* odor is often a disgusting or offensive odor; a *bad* child is a troublesome child; a *bad* situation may be either an unhappy or a dangerous situation.

Unpleasant is also a general adjective, but with a more limited application than *bad. Unpleasant* simply means not pleasant, failing to please: an *unpleasant* evening spent listening to a bore. However, *unpleasant* is often used as is *bad* to describe things that are displeasing or painful in various degrees of intensity. An *unpleasant* operation may be a polite description of a painful operation; an *unpleasant* day may be a tiring day or a stormy day; an *unpleasant* person may be a selfish, quarrelsome, or dirty person; an *unpleasant* taste may be a bitter or rancid taste.

Disagreeable and **distasteful** are stronger and more specific terms than *bad* and *unpleasant.* That which is *disagreeable* offends the senses, the feelings, or the opinions: the *disagreeable* taste of sour milk; to find the attentions of an unwanted suitor *disagreeable;* to find expressions of bigotry not only *disagreeable* to listen to, but almost impossible to eradicate. That which is *distasteful* is something one finds *disagreeable* or shuns, not because it is inherently *bad* or undesirable, but because it goes against one's tastes or nature. [Some people find hard work *distasteful;* Asking a favor from anyone was *distasteful* to my mother.] *Distasteful* is now only rarely applied to food or drink that is poorly prepared or has a *disagreeable* taste.

Objectionable carries strong overtones of disapproval and moral indignation: The censors declared the love scenes in the book to be *objectionable.* *Objectionable* may also apply to that which is counter to one's sense of what is proper, fitting, or aesthetically pleasing. [Sentimentality is *objectionable* to critical, informed lovers of art; The Japanese, with their love of simplicity and order, find cluttered interiors *objectionable*.] See FLAW, MISCHIEVOUS, PROFLIGATE, REPLUSIVE, SIN, WEAK.

Antonyms: *acceptable, desirable, good, pleasant,* PLEASING, *satisfactory, unobjectionable.*

banal
  fatuous
  inane
  insipid
  jejune
  vapid

These adjectives refer to what is offensive to good taste because of its want of sense, significance, or freshness. **Banal**, most strictly, refers to something that is so commonplace that it lacks freshness: *banal* jokes, hoary with age. But *banal* has gathered connotations that go beyond this strict meaning, referring to an odious or deplorable lack of taste: another season of *banal* television programs.

Both **insipid** and **vapid**, like the Latin words from which they come, can literally refer to foods that lack savor. In applying to what is tasteless or gauche, both adjectives also point to staleness, flatness, or want of spirit. They are often thought to be interchangeable, but subtle differences between them can be felt. *Insipid* is especially pertinent for describing instances of expression or behavior suggesting weakness or feebleness; this contrasts it with *banal,* which suggests outrageous bad taste: choosing between the *insipid* dullness of a drawing-room comedy and the *banal* brashness of a musical extravaganza. *Vapid,* on the other hand, might be thought more pertinent to describing a whole personality, one of limited mentality: a *vapid* celebrity who kept making *insipid* remarks about the weather. *Vapid,* when it describes behavior rather than character, often suggests patent insincerity: thanking him with a *vapid* smile.

Unlike the foregoing, **jejune** and **inane** are less concerned with something that has lost its freshness than with something that reveals a total lack of substance to begin with. *Jejune* derives from a Latin word meaning hungry and applies emphatically to what is worthless and uninteresting. [This play cannot be called *banal,* considering its novelty, nor *insipid,* considering its liveliness, nor *vapid,* considering its sensitivity; nevertheless, it is utterly unstimulating and *jejune* in every particular.]

Inane derives from a word meaning empty and refers to something that is regarded as worthless because it lacks sense to the point of becoming foolish or silly: attempts at flattery that would be laughable if they were not so *inane. Jejune* can also suggest an enduring state of mental exhaustion or emptiness: grimly resigning herself to the *jejune* patterns of suburban living. Because of confusion with *jeune,* the French word for *young, jejune* is also used disapprovingly to indicate immaturity or naiveté: *jejune* teen-age fads. **Fatuous** is an intensification of *inane* in that it adds a suggestion of self-contented smugness to the silliness suggested by *inane:* a *fatuous* grin that revealed how witty he imagined his *inane* remark to be. See MONOTONOUS, SENTIMENTAL, SUPERFICIAL, TRITE, TRUISM.

Antonyms: *meaningful,* SIGNIFICANT.

bare
  naked
  nude
  stripped

These adjectives mean devoid of clothing or of a usual covering. **Bare**, when applied to objects, means without covering or ornament: a *bare* outcropping of rock; a tree *bare* of leaves. When used of a person, *bare* usually applies to a part of the body rather than to the entire body: *bare* knees; *bare* arms and legs. By extension, it is also used to indicate the omission of fancy trappings or nonessential adjuncts: Just give us the *bare* facts, without embellishment.

Naked, when applied to a person, means completely devoid of clothing. *Naked* is often invested with moral or emotional connotations and may suggest sexual excitation or exhibitionism. [The hotel fire caught them both *naked;* She couldn't wear bikinis because they made her feel *naked.*] In other contexts, *naked* may suggest purity or innocence or simply be a neutral description: *naked* nymphs; *naked* children frolicking on the lawn; The body was *naked* when discovered. In the sense of *bare, naked* is also used about physical objects or forces, generally for poetic effect or for emphasis: *naked* boughs; *naked* power; the *naked* truth.

Nude applies only to persons and may be neutral in connotation by itself, but its context—sexual interest being what it is in modern society—often makes it highly charged with emotional feeling. The noun *nude* denotes an unclothed figure in painting or sculpture, and the association of the adjective with aesthetic appreciation often invests it with a kind of glamorous appeal lacking in *naked. Nude* has a more respectable tone than *naked;* thus, fashion writers can advertise some women's clothing as having a *nude* look, but dare not call it *naked.* For the same reason one speaks of sleeping in the *nude,* not *naked.*

Stripped literally means having been rendered *bare, naked,* or *nude* by some outside agency, but it is often used figuratively to mean deprived: *stripped* of his medals for disobeying a commanding officer; *stripped* of her rights pending appeal to a higher court. **Antonyms:** *clothed, covered, dressed.*

barter

    exchange
    swap
    trade

These verbs are alike in referring, most specifically, to a bargaining for goods or services that is conducted without the use of money.

Barter is the most formal and most specific of these. In the most primitive economic system, one gives the product he or she has made or grown in return for someone else's product—with no intermediary devices to assess abstract value. A farmer, in such a system, might *barter* several sacks of fodder for a pair of boots made by a shoemaker who happens to need feed for his horse. *Barter* in this strict definition does not involve middlemen; a person *barters* only for what he or she needs and intends to use. If the shoemaker, however, didn't need fodder at the exact time of the bargain, he might still take the fodder, planning to **trade** it with someone else for something he could use. In any but the most primitive societies, of course, *bartering* as such, except among children, is almost unknown, but many kinds of *trading* may exist. A person may *trade* merely for sustenance, as with *barter,* but more commonly in order to sell what he or she gets for a profit; *trading,* thus, can be an occupation or livelihood: a record number of shares *traded* at the stock exchange. In senses other than the economic, *barter* has fewer uses than *trade,* and would strike most ears as needlessly formal: diplomats who *bartered* for peace. *Trade,* more informal, also has a wider range of general application: *trade* compliments; *trade* glances in the crowded bar.

In *bartering* and *trading,* a person must **exchange** one item for another. *Exchange* is not limited to the economic sense, however, but applies to any reciprocal giving and receiving. In some uses, the things given and received may be equally valued: *exchange* partners at a dance. Or the value may not be an important aspect: *exchange* gifts at Christmas; *exchange* letters.

Perhaps more often, *exchange* implies the divesting of something unsuitable or unsatisfactory for something better: *exchanging* jobs; *exchanging* merchandise damaged in delivery.

Swap, most specifically, is like *barter,* except for its extreme informality. [The prospector *swapped* his gold dust for a jug of whiskey; I'll *swap* my slingshot for your caterpillar.] In some cases it may enter formal speech or writing when descriptive of a specific phenomenon: The sociologist did research on housewives who *swapped* husbands at Saturday night parties.

basic

    absolute
    categorical
    fundamental
    ultimate
    unlimited

These adjectives are concerned with concepts of totality and completeness or of necessity. **Basic** and **fundamental** suggest first principles that underlie more complex considerations. *Fundamental* is the more formal of the two and is more natural in a philosophical context when applied to the principles themselves: a *fundamental* truth. In an educational context, it strongly suggests something indispensable or prerequisite to more advanced development: reading as a *fundamental* skill. While *fundamental* often points to what is ideally necessary, *basic* may point to what is actually the case. [Lacking the *fundamental* ability to make distinctions, their *basic* vocabulary was greatly reduced.] *Basic* also has a wider range of application: the *basic* black of women's evening dress; a *basic* distrust of strangers. In these cases, *basic* may suggest not what is necessary but what is accepted or standard.

Absolute in one sense is used simply as an intensification of *basic:* an *absolute* dislike of women. *Absolute,* however, relates philosophically to **ultimate** and **categorical** in another sense. Here, it refers to totality of power. Where *fundamental* indicates an initial necessity, *absolute* suggests final and conclusive authority: The child's *fundamental* instinct toward cooperation was overruled by the *absolute* value the tribe placed upon competition. *Ultimate* also suggests the highest or final authority: the *ultimate* court of appeal. Unlike *absolute,* it carries an implication of something worked through in time: No one can say what our *ultimate* view of the universe will be. **Unlimited,** while suggesting totality, contrasts with *ultimate* in relating more often to quantity than to time: *unlimited* profits. It compares with *absolute* in suggesting less a highest authority than one to which no opposition exists. [The king's powers were *absolute* but hardly *unlimited,* considering the strictures of canon and common law.] *Categorical* in its philosophical sense refers to something, usually a principle, that is inescapable, undeniable, and universal. Like *fundamental,* it suggests an ideal necessity; like *absolute,* it suggests finality and totality. [The *categorical* imperative of Kant was a moral truth that the structure of the universe made inevitable.] See CENTER, KERNEL, SPECIFIC.

Antonyms: *circumscribed,* MARGINAL, *peripheral,* PROVISIONAL, *tangent,* TRIVIAL.

basis
    base
    foundation
    ground

These nouns all refer to something upon which something else rests or depends. **Basis** differs from **base** in being more often used in metaphorical senses: The *basis* of my argument is that the victory is unattainable without seriously jeopardizing our domestic programs. *Base,* on the other hand, normally refers to physical objects that form the lowest or supporting part of anything: the *base* of a statue. It can, however, be used metaphorically as well: the *base* of a theory. In this sense *basis* and *base* are practically synonymous; *base,* however, more often suggests the idea of an underlying **foundation**, whereas *basis* is broader in application and may suggest the idea of a central or fundamental part as well as that of an underlying principle. [Axioms are the *base* of geometry; the *basis* of our decision; On what *basis* do you propose to pay me?]

Foundation can mean the *base* on which something rests: the *foundation* of a building. *Foundation* suggests a more imposing, solid structure than *base,* which can apply to the bottom part of anything: the *base* of a lamp; the *foundation* of an ancient city. *Foundation* also means that on which anything is founded, and in this sense is close to *basis:* The *foundation* of democracy is the will of the people to preserve liberty. It should perhaps be noted that *foundation* is now used commercially to refer to a variety of feminine accouterments that supply an underlying *basis* or that give support, such as facial makeup applied beneath other makeup and certain undergarments that restrain vital parts of the body so that outergarments do not reveal their actual shape.

Ground, as here considered, means a *foundation* or *basis* for a decision, argument, or relationship. It is often used in the plural in this sense, and when plural, it may be construed as singular. [The *grounds* for his decision was never clearly stated; Absenteeism constitutes *grounds* for dismissal.] *Grounds* implies the underpinnings of reason: Leverrier's mathematical computations were the *grounds* for his theory that there was a planet beyond Uranus. See CENTER, KERNEL.

Antonyms: *superstructure, top.*

beat
    flagellate
    flog
    scourge
    spank
    thrash
    whip

These verbs refer to physical punishment meted out by means of blows administered primarily by hand or by some instrument held in the hand. **Beat** is the most general of these and the least specific. It perhaps most strongly suggests a pummeling with the fists; this may be the result of spur-of-the-moment anger between opponents: ruffians who *beat* the child up after school. But *beat* can also suggest a more deliberate inflicting of punishment on an inferior by a superior: a psychotic mother who *beat* her children unmercifully. In these latter cases, some sort of instrument may well be used: *beating* the dog with a rolled-up newspaper. **Thrash** is more likely to be restricted to the first situation, expressing spontaneous anger between opponents. Although fisticuffs might be the main element of the attack, *thrash* suggests a general sort of knocking about by any means whatsoever. *Thrash* may have a euphemistic flavor in that it seems to imply a less serious or cruel infliction of injury than *beat,* and may be an attempt to make light of the intent behind the act; but it can, despite this, indicate a more thorough or methodical act than *beat* and often suggests an act motivated by the wish to reprove someone for insolence or misbehavior: threatening to *thrash* the boy within an inch of his life unless he took back the insult.

Spank is more specific than either *beat* or *thrash* in its application. It refers unambiguously to the corrective or salutary punishment meted out by a parent on a child, with no intent to inflict actual harm. The action specifically involves hitting the child's buttocks with the open hand, often with the child laid facedown across the parent's knees. [G. B. Shaw wondered how parents could wait until their anger had cooled in order to *spank* their children in cold blood.] The remaining verbs all relate to punishment meted out by means of some instrument, usually one held in the hand.

The following verbs specifically stress the inflicting of physical injury to a degree that is not a necessary implication of the verbs discussed so far. **Whip** suggests the beating of someone usually by means of a flexible cord or series of cords expressly designed for this use, made of leather, metal, or rope and attached to a handle: *whipping* the horse into a quicker pace; ordering that the mutinous soldiers be put in irons and *whipped. Whip,* less specifically, can refer to any act of *beating* done by means of any sort of instrument, whether flexible or rigid, whether improvised or designed for the occasion: known to *whip* prisoners with a razor strop or a metal ruler; claiming that his interrogators had pistol-*whipped* him. **Scourge** is often used metaphorically for any calamity or harsh attack, but it refers most concretely to beating with a many-tongued or many-thonged whip. In this sense, however, it is less often used except in reference to the Biblical account of Christ's being *scourged.*

Flog may specifically suggest *whipping,* especially with a many-tongued lash, but it can also indicate *beating* with any sort of instrument, flexible or rigid: suspected informers who were *flogged* with chains before being killed. A historical context unique to *flog* is the nautical one in which this sort of punishment was inflicted upon sailors for certain infractions of orders. *Flog* might also apply in this way to military or penal situations. **Flagellate**, most strictly, has a religious or psychosexual context. In either case the infliction of pain is emphasized and is carried out by means of whip, lash, or other cord-like instrument, often many-tongued, knotted, barbed, or nettled, although this may be applied by oneself or by others, especially (as with *flog*) across the back. Religious zealots may engage in this activity to punish the flesh for its inherent sinfulness, and sado-masochistic neurotics may engage in flagellation for the sexual stimulation it affords them.

beautiful
    comely
    cute
    good-looking
    gorgeous
    handsome
    pretty
These adjectives refer to pleasing facial appearances. **Beautiful** indicates a strikingly desirable or attractive face, suggesting symmetry of features or perfection of proportion, although ultimately *beautiful* is

dependent on the subjective taste of the user. Because of this it is extremely unspecific in reference, although it would most often be used of a woman's face. **Good-looking** is equally as weak in specificity, but it can be used appropriately of both men and women: a *good-looking* couple.

Handsome and **pretty** are complementary terms in that *handsome* usually applies to men and *pretty* even more exclusively to women. *Pretty,* however, indicates a less elevated or more superficial appeal than *beautiful:* the rare woman who is truly *beautiful* as opposed to the many who are merely *pretty.* In this opposition, *pretty* might suggest vivacity and sweetness, while *beautiful* might suggest elegance and nobility. *Handsome,* used of men, is comparable to *beautiful,* used of women, suggesting regularity of features and a sturdy manliness. Sometimes *handsome* may be used of women as well, in which case it does not, strangely enough, suggest an epicene mannishness, but a radiant force of almost animal good health and vividness: insisting that Garbo was not merely *beautiful,* but breathtakingly *handsome. Handsome* in this sense would be used only of mature women, never of girls. *Pretty* would never be used of a man, except pejoratively to suggest effeminacy. *Beautiful* may rarely be used of a man without negative effect; in this case the face is usually regarded in an artistic light or as redolent of some special attribute: a man with *beautiful* features; a *beautiful* and expressive face that spoke both of strength and of suffering.

Because **comely** may now sound outdated, it is sometimes used to suggest earthy or rustic good looks in women: the *comely* milkmaid in a Constable painting. Once its particular emphasis, however, was on freedom from blemish, as in the Song of Solomon: "I am black, but *comely.*" **Cute** is an informal word for good looks in women that suggest cheerfulness and wholesomeness; *cute,* thus, gives less praise than *pretty* and far less than *beautiful. Cute* may also be used by women to describe men who may not be *handsome* but who are boyish or sweet-tempered. **Gorgeous** is sometimes used hyperbolically to refer to someone extremely *beautiful* or *handsome;* as with many hyperboles, extravagance has tended to strip it of meaning. See CHARMING, PLEASING.
Antonyms: UGLY, *uncomely.*

begin
    commence
    inaugurate

initiate
institute
launch
start

These verbs refer to the earliest period in a thing's existence. **Begin**, the broadest term of this group, means take the first step or do the first act or part of something: to *begin* a course of study leading to a doctorate; to *begin* to understand one's past mistakes. In many contexts **start** is interchangeable with *begin*: The engine *started* (or *began*) smoking. But *start* places more emphasis on the fact of making a beginning, the mere act of setting out, whereas *begin* often suggests the start of a process in fulfillment of a purpose. The relationship between *start* and *begin* is not unlike that between the nouns *speed* and *velocity*; the second verb, *start*, implies direction. [He was *beginning* to think of himself as an old man; She *started* (or *began*) skiing last winter; The train *started* with a lurch.]

Commence is a more formal term for *begin*. There are practically no contexts in which *begin* will not serve well in place of *commence*, but *commence*, and sometimes **institute**, is preferred in some contexts, especially legal, where *begin* is felt to be insufficiently formal, too much an everyday word, to dignify the proceedings. Thus, legal action is *instituted*, rarely *begun*, and judicial sessions *commence*, seldom *begin*. *Commence* is sometimes used vulgarly or humorously in other than solemn contexts: We *commenced* to drink our beer. *Institute* in other senses means *begin* with a view toward setting up or putting into operation: to *institute* needed reforms in Congress. *Institute* suggests a great deal of enterprise, and frequently foresight as well: to *institute* new management methods that save millions of dollars.

Initiate is close to *institute* in pointing to the motivating force or creator that starts something, but does not, like *institute*, convey the idea of carrying through what one has started to the point of seeing it in operation: to *initiate* legislation; The Arkansas governor *initiated* the reforms, but the state agency *instituted* them.

Inaugurate means *begin* formally or officially. Thus to *inaugurate* a new policy or legislation suggests some ceremony or traditional observance to commemorate it. [Once the president is *inaugurated*, he begins his term of office; The ball was *inaugurated* by the introduction to society of several young debutantes.] *Inaugurate* is also used for *begin* in historical contexts implying great scope or import: The Industrial Revolution *inaugurated* a new era.

Launch is a related word, but means to *begin* not so much with ceremony as with fanfare and publicity. [The Treasury is *launching* a new bond drive; The advertising agency will *launch* a campaign to introduce a new soap.] This sense doubtless derives from the fanfare once attached to the *launching* of large ocean-going vessels. See CREATE, ORIGIN.

Antonyms: *FINISH, STOP.*

beginner

apprentice
neophyte
novice
tyro

These nouns refer to someone who has not yet acquired the skills and experience required for qualifying in a given field. **Beginner** is the most informal of these nouns and is the least negative in tone, suggesting someone who has already begun to acquire the necessary abilities but has not worked long enough to master them; *beginner* may imply a young person, but this is not necessarily so: a ballet class for adult *beginners*; piano lessons for children and adult *beginners*. **Apprentice** most concretely refers to a young person taken on by a master to be taught the skills of a trade; this practice, more common in the past, is still reflected in the titles given by some trade unions in accordance with a person's amount of experience: the *apprentice* who becomes a journeyman and at last a master. In broader uses, *apprentice* refers to any *beginner*, often with an emphasis on the person's low or menial position or lack of polish: a writer whose first book reveals him or her to be an *apprentice* rather than a mature artist.

Both **novice** and **neophyte**, but especially the former, may refer to a newly introduced member of a religious order. In broader contexts, both are less factual and more uncomplimentary. *Novice* in this case may suggest clumsiness due to lack of training or even to an amateurish lack of discipline or application: measuring instruments made so that even the rankest *novice* can use them; a *novice* whose canvases show the lowest possible standards and the worst set of influences. *Neophyte* may be used somewhat less negatively than *novice*, especially since it implies an eagerness to learn and a humble respect for persons of superior knowledge: the *neophytes* who clustered around the established feminist writer in hopes of catching some pearl of wisdom she seemed always on the verge of dropping.

Tyro is perhaps the most negative of these nouns

in that it refers to an inexperienced and amateurish approach to a complicated field, suggesting a raw or young recruit who has yet to begin the task of mastering a craft: the *tyro* who has taken two survey courses in literature and proceeds to write profound reviews for the school paper. See AMATEUR.

Antonyms: *connoisseur, expert, old hand, old-timer, veteran, virtuoso.*

beginning
inchoate
incipient
primeval
rudimentary

These adjectives are used to refer to things that are in an initial or early stage of existence or to things that are unformed, undeveloped, or elementary in character. **Beginning**, the most general of the five, can mean either first or early. The *beginning* chapter of a book is its first chapter; the *beginning* section of the same book would embrace the first chapter but would also include several of the other early chapters. In another sense, *beginning* describes something that deals with elementary principles, skills, or routines: The *beginning* course in physics will not be offered this term.

Incipient shares with *beginning* the meaning of just coming into existence: the *incipient* stage of a urinary infection is often marked by high fever. **Inchoate**, like *beginning* and *incipient*, can describe a condition or activity that has just recently come into existence or operation. It more often suggests, however, the absence of order, form, or coherence: an *inchoate* plan, badly organized and full of contradictions. One of the general meanings of *inchoate*, that referring to a lack of completion or perfection, is part of the specialized terminology of the legal profession. An *inchoate* contract is one that has not been executed by all the parties involved.

Rudimentary, which means fundamental or elementary, is often used to express a limitation: The class had only a *rudimentary* knowledge of chemistry. It also can characterize something as primitive, undeveloped, or imperfectly developed. [Their dwelling was *rudimentary* in nature, rather more like a hut than a house; *Rudimentary* hind legs are part of the skeleton of the boa constrictor.]

Primeval refers to the earliest ages of the world, particularly to that time before the appearance of humans on earth: the *primeval* hills of Appalachia. It is applied by extension to things that are very old and

have existed since time immemorial: *primeval* forests. See BEGIN.

Antonyms: *closing, developed, ending, late,* MATURE.

behavior
conduct
demeanor
deportment
manners

These nouns refer to the characteristic ways that people reveal themselves in their actions. **Behavior** is the most general of these; at its most technical, it refers to all activity of people, singly or collectively, that might be studied by psychologists, sociologists, or anthropologists: paranoid *behavior;* peer-group *behavior* in preschool children; mating *behavior* in New Guinea. In everyday use, *behavior* more frequently refers to positive or negative social activity: promising to be on my best *behavior;* such incredibly rude *behavior*. **Conduct** can also refer to individual or group activity, but in a less technical sense than *behavior;* it also may be categorized positively or negatively. It does suggest a narrower range of activity than *behavior*, implying the breaking or following of prescribed rules: a bad-*conduct* discharge from the army; a prison sentence commuted for good *conduct*. *Conduct* is distinct from these other nouns in that it may suggest an ethical or moral basis for measuring *behavior: conduct* befitting an honest public official.

Manners refers not so much to adherence to ethical standards as to the arbitrary forms by which a social group has traditionally acted. Here a positive or negative evaluation may depend on subjective taste as much as anything else: the vulgar *manners* of the nouveau riche; the easy, natural *manners* that were second nature to her. *Manners* most often refers to individuals, but can sometimes apply collectively to a whole social group: the affected *manners* of our debased age.

Deportment is a more formal synonym for *conduct,* but the set of rules that measure *deportment* may be arbitrary choices to facilitate a goal or may be superimposed from above, instigated especially to instill a respect for authority. Its most common use is to describe the *behavior* of pupils in school: sending home remarks critical of her uncooperative *deportment;* measures to improve the *deportment* of the class. **Demeanor** is distinct from all these nouns in that it almost exclusively refers to the way a particular person acts at a particular time, and suggests an assessment of the person's dress, bearing, attitude, and expression: a habitually quiet man who had never shown such an agitated *demeanor;* a supervisor known for her invariably soft-spoken and relaxed *demeanor.* See ACT.

beleaguer

bait
heckle
hector
hound
ride

These verbs mean harass or torment another person so persistently as to disturb his or her peace of mind or undermine self-confidence. **Beleaguer**, from its literal meaning of surrounding and shutting in an enemy force with one's own army, carries the implication of a hemming in on all sides by a multitude, so that escape is virtually impossible: a landlord *beleaguered* by complaining tenants; a woman *beleaguered* by worries; a countryside *beleaguered* by a plague of locusts.

Hound strongly suggests the relentless and unflagging pursuit of a hunting dog on the scent: an escaped criminal *hounded* from state to state by the police. By extension, *hound* also implies repeated urging and nagging, especially to the point where the victim can do little except submit: to be *hounded* by bill collectors; teachers *hounded* from their jobs because of sexual orientation.

The literal meaning of **bait** is to set dogs for sport on a chained or penned animal, especially a bear or a bull. Figuratively, *bait* implies malicious pleasure in tormenting another by teasing and ridicule, especially when retaliation is difficult: *baited* by the other boys at school for his devotion to studies; to *bait* an old man whose ideas are not in agreement with yours. *Bait* may also mean to tease or twit in a more or less amiable way: She *baited* her husband for spending so much time talking on the telephone.

Ride, which is chiefly colloquial, evokes the action of urging a mount on to greater speed by the use of spurs or a whip. Therefore, *ride* may imply driving or goading someone to reach a goal (not necessarily an undesirable one), but often suggests mischievous or malicious intent. [Parents complain that the fifth-grade teacher *rides* his brighter pupils too hard; The boys at the office are always *riding* me because my wife calls me at five o'clock sharp every day to make sure I'm coming straight home; The old-timers *rode* the rookie shortstop unmercifully, calling him "Mama's boy."]

Heckle emphasizes the harassing of a speaker in public by means of taunts, questions, and other interruptions in order to confuse or intimidate the speaker or to ferret out weaknesses in argument: to *heckle* a candidate for political office; to *heckle* the leader of an anti-abortion demonstration.

Hector strongly suggests bullying and browbeating by scolding, nagging, or derision: an authoritarian father who *hectors* his children instead of trying to understand them; a warden who keeps order by *hectoring* his prisoners. See INTIMIDATE.

Antonyms: *ENCOURAGE, SPUR.*

believable

convincing
credible
plausible

These adjectives all mean capable of being believed or worthy of being accepted as real, true, or trustworthy. **Believable** is the most general term and describes anything that is possible, probable, or acceptable either because it is in accordance with one's everyday experience and observation or because it is not directly contrary to fact. [She gave us a frightening, but *believable*, account of her childhood in the slums; The boy's tale of meeting a pirate on the deserted beach is simply not *believable.*]

Credible is sometimes used interchangeably with *believable*: a *believable* excuse for lateness; a *credible* explanation for having failed to finish the assigned work. However, *credible* goes a step beyond *believable* in that something that is *credible* merits belief and is supported by known facts: a *credible* account of the causes of World War II. *Credible* is now rarely used of persons except in the expression *credible witness*—that is, a witness who is reliable and trustworthy in giving testimony.

Something that is **convincing** is *believable* because it overcomes any doubt, uncertainty, or hesitancy in accepting it. A *convincing* argument compels one's belief in its soundness because it satisfies the sense of logic or fitness.

The earlier meaning of **plausible** adhered closely to its etymology—worthy of applause—that is, commendable or capable of winning favorable acceptance by the mind. It now carries a strong implication of deception and speciousness. A *plausible* statement will very likely be one that appears to be *convincing* or *believable* on the surface, but which, upon closer examination, is not so. See ACCURATE, GENUINE, TRUTHFUL.

Antonyms: *DOUBTFUL, implausible, incredible, suspect, unbelievable, unreliable.*

belittle

deprecate
depreciate
detract
discredit
disparage
minimize

These verbs refer to criticism designed to diminish the worth of something. **Belittle** is the most general and informal of these; it may suggest a deliberately fault-finding attitude: *belittling* every practical suggestion she came up with. It may imply an attitude that simply cannot tolerate excellence or effort in others: *belittling* those who had continued to work on the project after most of us had given up. It may also suggest a cumulatively telling process of slight or trivial attempts to undermine another's position: constantly *belittling* everything we believed in.

Minimize is a more formal substitute for *belittle;* it refers specifically to the attempt to set a lower value on something than it commonly carries or deserves: *minimizing* the worth of labor laws previously in force. In contrast to *belittle,* any note of spiteful censoriousness may be absent from *minimize,* which by its formality may emphasize, instead, a judicious or reasoned reassessment: *minimizing* the effect of Augustine on later medieval thought. The sense of animus, by contrast, is definitely present in **detract**, even to a greater degree than in *belittle.* Where *belittle,* furthermore, may suggest a sniping at trivial failings, *detract* suggests an attempt at a more drastic lowering of esteem: a fiercely argued view that sought to *detract* from the usefulness of the earlier study.

Disparage and **deprecate** contrast with the foregoing verbs by suggesting a general effort to make something seem without worth or value. *Disparage* suggests the animus of *detract,* but may imply a seizing of any faults, small or large, to prove a judgment already formed: caustically *disparaging* each new production as further proof of the playwright's worthlessness. While *deprecate* may sometimes suggest only an attempt to devalue rather than to reject something utterly, its effect is strengthened by the amused, scornful, or sarcastic consideration it implies: *deprecating* the notion of racial integration with a weary laugh. Some purists assert that **depreciate** and not *deprecate* should be used in the sense of lowering or underestimating the value or worth of: the tendency of people who are not talented to *depreciate* those who are. Many excellent writers, however, use *depreciate* in this sense, and it can only be considered a well-established usage today

Discredit is the most severe of these verbs, exclusively suggesting criticism designed to demolish a position or accomplishment utterly, often by unfair means: attempting to *discredit* his opponent by glancing and suggestive references to her personal life. See DISAPPROVAL.

Antonyms: *credit,* ENCOURAGE, *enhance, exaggerate.*

beneficial

advantageous
good
healthful
profitable
salubrious
salutary
wholesome

These adjectives describe conditions that are positive in their effect on health or financial well-being. **Beneficial** is general and relatively formal. While it can refer to financial well-being, it more naturally applies to things conducive to mental or physical health: government programs *beneficial* to the poor; a sunny day's *beneficial* influence on my darkest moods; milk and vegetables *beneficial* to a growing child. In one sense, it suggests something that is an added help, but is not strictly necessary: a friendship *beneficial* to both of them. **Good** is, of course, the most general adjective here and the least formal; it has a multitude of uses in pointing to what promotes financial or physical strength: a *good* climate; *good* circulation; a *good* business proposal; a *good* stock. Its very generality invites the substitution of a more precise synonym.

Advantageous and **profitable** carry overtones of financial well-being. *Advantageous* can, of course, refer to anything chosen for its desirability or to improve one's situation: a more *advantageous* view of the sunset; resorts *advantageous* to wife-hunting. More often, an actual financial gain is present or implied: an *advantageous* position in the firm. *Profitable* is even clearer on this score: a *profitable* business in a *profitable* location; Good looks are a more *profitable* commodity in Hollywood than talent and hard work. In Victorian times, *profitable* was often used for something *beneficial* to the development of character: a *profitable* book to read for spiritual guidance. This use is less frequent today.

The rest of these adjectives relate more specifically to the promoting of health. **Healthful**, the most general, should be distinguished from healthy. The first refers to that which will give health, the second to the state of having it. The ill, rather than the healthy, are

33

most concerned with seeking out *healthful* climates. Both, however, may enjoy what is *healthful: healthful* exercise; *healthful* meals; the *healthful* sport of cross-country skiing. **Wholesome** suggests less the promoting of well-being than the inherently *good* or *healthful* situation in and for itself. It also carries a tone of moral uplift and is as often used of mental as of physical health: a *wholesome* movie for the entire family; *wholesome* food; *wholesome* good looks. Its Pollyanna overtones become clear when one considers that some *healthful* activities may not be considered *wholesome* in many situations.

Salutary suggests the correcting of a physical or mental lack: a *salutary* diet for hypertension; sea breezes *salutary* to insomniacs; an editorial *salutary* in its fierce honesty and forthright proposals. **Salubrious** is comparable to but more intense than *salutary*, suggesting a positive physical or mental enrichment, without suggesting any previous impoverishment. It also describes any invigorating or stimulating experience: the *salubrious* mineral waters of the spa; the *salubrious* effects of an ocean voyage; a *salubrious* shock to the complacent middle class. See FAVORABLE.

Antonyms: *bad, detrimental, disadvantageous, harmful, injurious, insalubrious, ruinous, unhealthful, unhelpful, unprofitable, unwholesome.*

benefit
advantage
favor
gain
profit

These nouns refer to some desirable good that can be given, acquired, or earned. **Benefit** is the most general of these, referring to any kind of good, however acquired, material or otherwise: lessons designed to be of *benefit* to growing minds; the *benefits* accorded to a person occupying a lofty position. **Advantage** is narrower in scope than *benefit*, since it can suggest more strictly either material *benefits* or things won in competition against an opponent: all the *advantages* of suburban living; a naturally fortified hill that would give them the *advantage* over the enemy. *Advantage*, of course, can function more abstractly and without any implication of depriving someone else of the same benefit: all equally free to take *advantage* of our tradition of free speech and respect for dissent. **Favor** may suggest being given the *advantage* in a competition: ruling in *favor* of the plaintiff; unequal odds that made the battle sure to come out in the

aggressor's *favor. Favor,* however, most often refers to *benefits* that result from securing the approval of others: a new product seeking *favor* in the marketplace; audiences that looked with *favor* on realistic plays. It can also be used to indicate narrow self-interest: acting only in his own *favor.*

Like *benefit,* **gain** can suggest an intangible good given or acquired at no one's expense: a law that resulted in a clear *gain* for civil liberties; a *gain* in technical competence over her previous work. More commonly, however, *gain* suggests material acquisition: capital *gains;* greedy for *gain.* **Profit** is even more restricted to material or monetary acquisition: realizing a ten percent *profit* on each sale; speculators eager for a quick *profit.* Sometimes, however, *profit* can refer to *gains* outside the context of moneymaking: a book anyone can read with *profit.* See HELP, IMPROVE.

Antonyms: *disadvantage, harm, loss.*

benevolence
altruism
generosity
goodwill
kindness
unselfishness

These nouns refer to a well-wishing friendliness or concern for the needs and desires of other people. **Benevolence** has the widest range of any of these nouns, suggesting an expansive and good-humored tolerance and sympathy for others: brimming over with a feeling of sunny *benevolence* toward everyone they encountered. Sometimes, *benevolence* implies the sympathy of a superior toward a subordinate, an implication strengthened by the term's formality: working conditions sought as a right, not as a *benevolence* of their employer. **Generosity** is more informal and focuses exclusively on the aspect of giving, referring to an unstintingly helpful act or habit: the *generosity* with which the child shared his toys. In contrast to *benevolence*, which may remain an unacted-upon feeling, *generosity* is measured by actual behavior: a plantation owner who looked on slaves with *benevolence* but could hardly be accused of treating them with *generosity.*

At a level of greater informality, **goodwill** and **kindness** are related somewhat like the previous pair, with *goodwill* referring primarily to feeling and *kindness* to action. *Goodwill* may refer to an open, charitable attitude, without reservation or bitterness: Christmas carolers full of merriment and *goodwill.*

Goodwill may also refer to a willingness to be fair-minded or impartial: both sides bargaining in *goodwill*. *Kindness* may suggest thoughtful or courteous consideration for the feelings of others: neighbors who were always the soul of *kindness*. Often, however, *kindness* specifically points to the help one person gives to someone less fortunate, less well, or less able: a nurse who treated the sick and wounded with almost reverent *kindness*. This noun, consequently, can sometimes have a patronizing flavor, like *benevolence*: insisting that he wanted only her *goodwill*, not her *kindness*.

Unselfishness and **altruism** both point to a *generosity* that is based on a lack of self-concern. Where *generosity* may emphasize the quantity given, possibly for ostentatious reasons, *unselfishness* stresses the effacing personal sacrifice required—even if a lesser amount is given: It was the tax deduction involved, rather than *unselfishness*, that prompted my *generosity* to the charity drive. While *unselfishness* is most often used to indicate a personal trait, the more formal *altruism* is usually reserved to indicate a moral or ethical principle. *Altruism* refers to the setting aside of special or personal interests in determining a course of action that will most benefit group welfare. This makes *altruism* a more specific and exact synonym for one possibility in *goodwill*: Peace Corps volunteers, searching for a way to put their youthful *altruism* into practice. See GENEROUS, HUMANE.

Antonyms: EGOISM, MALICE, *miserliness, stinginess*.

bequest

endowment
legacy

The noun **bequest** indicates something given or left to a person or an institution by the will of a benefactor. A **legacy** is something given or passed on by an ancestor, a predecessor, or an earlier era, and may be contained in a will or transmitted informally or automatically: to receive a *legacy* of a million dollars from the estate of a deceased aunt; to be heir to a *legacy* of goodwill through his father's reputation. [The United Nations was left a *legacy* of unsolved problems by the League of Nations.]

An **endowment** is something settled or bestowed on a person or institution, and is not necessarily a posthumous gift. Philanthropists may, during their lifetimes, establish *endowments* for scholarships at a university, or may bestow upon deserving students *endowments* for paying the great costs of higher education. See PRESENT.

between

amid
amidst
among
amongst
betwixt

The preposition **between**, as here considered, means flanked by two objects, one on either side. [Continental United States lies *between* Canada and Mexico; *between* a rock and a hard place.]

When *between* and **among** are used by extension to indicate a sharing, *between* is normally used when two objects are involved and *among* when more than two are involved: an inheritance divided *between* two heirs and one shared *among* three heirs. Occasionally, *between* is used to express such a relationship involving more than two objects, particularly if the relation involves each object individually or if it involves relationships between pairs of objects within the larger group: A political dispute involving six nations may be settled by an agreement *between* them.

Amid means surrounded by either separate objects or an undifferentiated mass or quantity. [A church stands *amid* skyscrapers; A reaper works *amid* the grain; A person may keep calm *amid* confusion.]

Among, as here considered, means surrounded by or included in a group of separate but similar objects. [Augustus Caesar was called *princeps*—chief *among* equals; A diary was *among* the effects left by the deceased.]

Amidst, **amongst**, and **betwixt** are variants of *amid, among*, and *between*. *Amongst* and *betwixt* are generally avoided as archaic, except when used poetically or rhetorically. *Amidst* is more common in Great Britain than in the United States.

biased

one-sided
partial
partisan
prejudiced
slanted
subjective

These adjectives refer to a lack of fairness in judging or reporting because of the favoritism given to one way of viewing a subject. **Biased** suggests that someone judging or reporting a controversy is already disposed for or against one of the contending sides: He insisted that the jury was already *biased* by improper remarks made by the prosecution; an education that gave her a *biased* view of cultures different from her own; a *biased* account referring to civil rights workers as carpetbaggers. **Prejudiced** in this context suggests a mind already disposed specifically against one view of something at issue; it also pertains more to judging something than to reporting it: a trial *prejudiced* by undue publicity; people who become *prejudiced,* however subtly, by the constant stereotyping of minority groups. **Subjective** refers to an inability to put personal interests aside in order to view a situation without preconceptions; it is a relative word in that even the most conscientious attempt at objectivity may not wholly overcome one's innately *subjective* perspective: a *subjective* account of the war, overstressing the importance of those things the author happened to see firsthand.

Slanted and one-sided pertain mostly to reports rather than to judgments. *Slanted* suggests deliberate suppression of some facts and expansion of others either to flatter the *biased* minds of readers or to convince them that the *biased* attitudes of the writer or publisher are correct: a news story *slanted* to make the incumbent candidate appear certain of reelection. *One-sided* suggests a far more extreme position than *slanted* in that only facts supporting a particular attitude are presented: a *one-sided* history of the conflict that made it appear to be a struggle between angels and monsters.

Partial and **partisan** suggest different degrees of alignment with a cause. *Partial* may suggest either an unconscious or conscious favoring of a particular stand: countries that claimed to be neutral but were actually *partial* to the West; frankly admitting that they were *partial* to the union's arguments. *Partisan* suggests wholehearted and unashamed commitment to and advocacy of a cause: to give equal time to *partisan* statements on the value of the proposed legislation. A *partisan* view of a matter is not necessarily unfair, provided the person is an advocate of that view and is not set up to judge between that view and another. One may even be *partisan* without being *one-sided,* if one is attentive to and considerate of other viewpoints. See BIGOTRY.

Antonyms: DISINTERESTED, open-minded, unbiased.

bigotry

bias
intolerance
narrow-mindedness
prejudice

These nouns refer to an unfair, irrational, or unexamined attitude toward issues or people based on blanket preconceptions. **Bigotry** now refers almost exclusively to an intense dislike or even violent hatred for a particular group, race, or religion. The comparable use of **prejudice** would indicate a similar but far less intense predisposition against such a group. *Bigotry* almost surely would be evidenced in unashamed public utterance or behavior, whereas *prejudice* might remain largely unexpressed—or even unknown to the person so afflicted: easier to cope with the outright *bigotry* of the Ku Klux Klan than the invisible walls of *prejudice* so commonly encountered. *Prejudice,* also, can apply to any preconception: an abhorrence for the maltreatment of animals that would make the judge unable to hear the case without *prejudice.*

Intolerance is now less commonly used in these senses than the previous pair, possibly because it sounds odd to pose these concerns in terms of whether or not one can tolerate—or put up with—a group of people; the question now is seen more often in terms of a genuine equalizing acceptance or lack of it. *Intolerance* is used widely outside the context of racial, religious, or ethnic *prejudice,* however, when it indicates an inability to give a fair hearing to ideas at variance with one's own: They looked with *intolerance* on the weird music preferred by their teenage children. **Bias** is unique among these nouns, since it can point to a predisposition either for or against something: He admitted that he had a sentimental *bias* for anything pertaining to Ireland; a strong *bias* in ghettos against police officers. Where *prejudice* can indicate a fixed, inflexible attitude, *bias* might suggest only a tendency to take a given view. Yet even such a mild predisposition could be disastrous where strict impartiality is required, as in a judge or juror: The lawyer argued that the judge's *bias* had affected the conduct of the case.

Narrow-mindedness points to a rigidity of preconceived attitudes, but specifically sees them as stemming from inexperience or a lack of exposure to a broader scale of values: the typical *narrow-mindedness* of people who stay in a rut without ever getting out of it to see how other people live. *Narrow-mindedness* often suggests habitual insularity, backwardness, provinciality, and lack of sophistication, but might be evidenced by an uneventful passivity or withdrawal rather than the hostile taking of stands suggested by the first pair: She was prevented from going to movies or dances by the *narrow-mindedness* of her parents. But *narrow-mindedness* can apply to any dogmatic rigidity of view: Permissive parents are often guilty of as much *narrow-mindedness* as those who are belabored for their authoritarian views on child-rearing. It frequently points specifically to a prudish or puritan attitude toward sex or pleasure: He accused her of *narrow-mindedness* for refusing to have dinner with him in his apartment. See BIASED.

Antonyms: *impartiality, objectivity, open-mindedness, tolerance.*

bisexual

androgynous
epicene
hermaphroditic
polymorphous perverse

These adjectives refer to the uniting of both sexes in one individual, either in a biological or psychological sense. **Bisexual** is the most general of these, having the widest range of possible meaning. In a biological sense, it can refer to any living organism in which both male and female organs are present. For many forms of life, this is normal: *bisexual* flowers; *bisexual* angleworms. Thus, as a generic term, *bisexual* can group together all normally double-sexed plants and animals. In its reference to people, however, *bisexual* would never refer to those rare individuals who are abnormally born with both male and female organs. On the contrary, it refers to those people who, physiologically male or female, are psychologically responsive to both sexes: that transitional phase when adolescents are *bisexual* in their sympathies and loyalties. This responsiveness may extend to erotic attraction or to sexual activity. Many psychologists view every individual as being normally *bisexual* in makeup, although only those men and women who have both homosexual and heterosexual relations can be called actively *bisexual.* The word is not likely to be used to describe someone whose appearance combines both male and female characteristics.

Hermaphroditic and **androgynous** are more clear-cut in their reference to biological description. *Hermaphroditic* refers most specifically as a zoological term to animals in which the organs of both sexes appear normally in each individual, whereas *androgynous* applies as a botanical term to such double-sexed plants: viewing the volvox either as a colony of cells or as a *hermaphroditic* organism; effecting the hybridizing of corn by the sexual polarization of a normally *androgynous* species. Among such sexually polarized species as man, of course, a *hermaphroditic* individual may rarely occur as a biological abnormality, but the word would be reserved for those cases in which both male and female sexual organs are anatomically present. Sometimes, *hermaphroditic* is used less technically to refer to general appearance that partakes of both sexes. In this case, *hermaphroditic* carries a tone of hyperbolic disapproval or amusement: The hair styles of many young people grow more and more *hermaphroditic. Androgynous* has a more formal ring even in its strict biological use, and can sound abstruse or curious when it applies more generally; here, it is not so likely to be confused with reference to biological structure: cultures in which sexual role-playing is relatively *androgynous* outside such biological functions as childbearing.

Epicene has no relevance whatever to biological classification, referring strictly to someone who in appearance or attitudes unites qualities of both sexes: a large, puffy face with soft features that were strikingly *epicene* in appearance. *Epicene* usually carries a disapproving or at least negative tone. Unlike *bisexual, epicene* may not refer to activity at all and may in fact suggest someone who appears sexless or is marked by no strong characteristics of either sex. In a culture that places a high value on manliness, *epicene* can often refer to effeminacy in men or even to neurasthenic male qualities: cultural stereotypes of the virile warrior and the *epicene* intellectual.

Polymorphous perverse is a fad phrase that oddly enough can carry an approving tone. It refers to sexual behavior that not only may be *bisexual* but guiltlessly pregenital in gaining satisfaction from other erogenous zones. The phrase, coined by Freud to describe the nonpolarized sexuality normal to the child, is now used loosely to describe a whole range of experimental adult sexual behavior: distinguishing between foreplay that is *polymorphous perverse* and a sole concentration on such acts.

bitterness

acerbity
acrimony
asperity
harshness
sourness

These nouns refer to a caustic, sharp, or rancorous temper or manner. **Bitterness** can indicate, most generally, a gloomy, dour, or cold disposition, but its special connotations suggest a deep-seated rage directed inward more than an anger directed at others, with disillusion or a conviction of injustice as its possible source and a smoldering cynicism as its possible result: life-long *bitterness* at losing the woman he loved. **Sourness** is less intense than *bitterness,* but suggests somewhat the same dour manner with an inward-directed disillusion as its source: What was *sourness* in Hamlet's view of the world has deepened to *bitterness* in Timon's. On the other hand, *sourness,* unlike *bitterness,* might suggest an external appearance only: a cheerful disposition that belied the *sourness* of her wrinkled face. **Harshness** relates more to manner than to disposition, suggesting not so much rancor as cruelty, either deliberate or unintentional: a teacher who met every infraction of the rules with *harshness.* *Harshness,* however, might merely be employed as a tactic: trying to soften his will first with wheedling, then with *harshness.*

The remaining nouns have a greater degree of formality than the foregoing. **Acerbity** relates most closely to *sourness,* suggesting an acidity of attitude that might, however, be expressed by a more directly sharp manner than with *sourness:* the abrupt *acerbity* with which he countered our every attempt at a casual conversation. **Asperity** relates most closely to *harshness,* with special emphasis on roughness or severity of treatment, implying even an arbitrary unevenness of disposition: the bewildering *asperity* of a parent who first ignored the child's questions and then punished her for asking them. **Acrimony** relates most closely to *bitterness,* but with a more outwardly directed rancor implied, even to the point of biting, irritating, and enraged actions: trying to make peace in a charged atmosphere clouded by *acrimony.* See SOUR, VINDICTIVE.

Antonyms: *blandness, mildness, sweetness.*

bizarre
fantastic
grotesque
outlandish
weird

These adjectives refer to anything that is thought extremely strange, eccentric, unusual, abnormal, ugly, or deformed. **Bizarre** points to the strange and unusual when they cause shock or surprise because of the unexpected, incongruous, or sensational forms they assume: skyscrapers that were as *bizarre* to them as their village of tiny houses would have been to us; the flamboyant Gothic style in which the stonework of the arches and windows took on *bizarre* convoluted designs. **Grotesque** suggests more readily the eccentric or deformed when seen as a comic or horrible caricature of some norm: Falstaff and the other *grotesque* cronies of the young prince; children with *grotesque,* cadaverous bodies, blighted by disease and malnutrition.

Fantastic is more general and less concrete than the previous adjectives. It can be used of anything that is fanciful or dreamlike or that appears to be a departure from common-sense reality: the *fantastic* nightmare world of Hieronymus Bosch; a *fantastic* tower made of concrete, bottles, hubcaps, and cans. *Fantastic* is overused as a hyperbole for anything pleasant, good, or out of the ordinary. **Weird** is similar to *fantastic* in suggesting a sharp break from ordinary reality: a *weird* feeling that time was standing still as the car hurtled down the cliff; *weird* forms of ocean life that flourish where sunlight never reaches them. *Weird,* too, is overused as a hyperbole for anything mildly unusual. **Outlandish** once suggested behavior typical of people on the periphery of a cultural center; now it more commonly suggests anything that is unusual to the point of shock or outrage: the *outlandish* look of the four backup singers.

Antonyms: NORMAL, *unexceptional.*

bland
dull
gentle
mild
moderate
soothing

These adjectives refer to taste, odors, and other sensations that are unassertive in character. **Bland** is the most specific of these, referring most appropriately to food that has not been heavily spiced: The doctor recommended a *bland,* salt-free diet for the patient. In other uses, *bland* may refer similarly to something of even disposition, without extremes, or lacking in tension: the *bland* domestic atmosphere in the house, free of argument and bickering; a *bland,* hazy spring day, neither too warm nor too cool. While these uses give a positive connotation, *bland* can become negative in tone when it suggests a lack of desirable excitement, flavor, or interest: the *bland,* anonymous cooking commonly attributed to the English; a *bland* novel that I began but couldn't finish; the *bland* attitudes of many college students during the 1980's.

Moderate is more neutral in tone than *bland,* being descriptive of a middle ground between extremes, without necessarily suggesting a positive or negative evaluation: a *moderate* winter and summer; a *moderate* conservative. Juxtaposed with a bad extreme, however, *moderate* can give an approving tone: a reign that was thought *moderate* and tolerant after the bloodbaths of the previous ruler. Both **gentle** and **mild** suggest an avoidance of extremes, but with a more forthrightly approving tone than *moderate* has. *Gentle* suggests a slight use of force to gain a result or a tender consideration for someone else: a *gentle* breeze off the patio; a *gentle* way of reprimanding her son. Unlike *gentle, mild* does not point to restrained power or considerate behavior so much as it indicates something thoroughly without harshness by its very nature: *mild* fall weather; *mild* suburban faces. Like *bland,* however, *mild* can suggest something so toned-down as to be uninteresting or unexciting: a comedy that offers only *mild* amusement; disclosures that were *mild* compared to those still forthcoming. The negative tone here is still far less intense or thoroughgoing than is true for *bland.*

Soothing is the most positive in tone of all these adjectives. Something may be *gentle* or *mild* and still not necessarily beneficial. By contrast, *soothing* suggests sensations that are positively comforting, helpful, or healing, either by the removal of irritation or by the application of something to overcome it: listening to the *soothing* silence; *soothing* music; a cloudless, sunny day that was *soothing* to the spirits; a *soothing* ointment to relieve serious sunburn. **Dull** compares strikingly with *soothing* in suggesting the complete absence of anything pleasurable. As such, it almost exclusively stresses, and with greater force, possibilities inherent in *bland* or *mild:* a *dull* evening playing cards with the neighbors; *dull* meals completely lacking in zest. *Dull* may of course apply more descriptively, like *moderate,* to low-key sensations: a *dull* gray sky; an artist who tended to use a palette of *dull,* subtly shaded colors. See MONOTONOUS, TRANQUIL.

Antonyms: *exciting, harsh,* KEEN, SOUR.

bleak
> barren
> desolate
> gaunt
> haggard

These adjectives refer to people or things that look wasted or inhospitable. **Bleak** is the most general of these and can apply equally well to people or things, especially landscapes or houses. It suggests a bare or unpleasant prospect: the *bleak,* ice-incrusted mountains of the Andes; the *bleak,* unpainted house that seemed almost uninhabitable. Used of people, it suggests a facial expression that is unhappy or unfriendly: She gave her husband a *bleak,* unsatisfied look. It can, of course, suggest anything unhopeful or unpromising: their one *bleak* hope for survival.

Gaunt and **haggard** are more closely tied to the physical appearance of people. *Gaunt* stresses leanness, but it may or may not suggest a wasted or

shrunken appearance: the sailor's *gaunt,* weather-beaten face. *Haggard,* however, insists on emaciation or at very least suggests a drawn expression resulting from strain or shock: the *haggard* faces of the prisoners in the concentration camp; a face *haggard* with grief. *Gaunt* can also apply to things or landscapes, in which case it suggests a harsh or bare scene: the *gaunt* moors of England. In this context, *bleak* is more intense than *gaunt:* grateful for even the *gaunt* prairies of the Midwest after the *bleak* deserts of Death Valley. *Haggard* would sound less natural in describing anything other than people, but used metaphorically, it might suggest a worn, run-down appearance: the rows of *haggard* houses that testified to poverty and neglect.

Desolate and **barren** refer to uninhabitable or unfeatured landscape. *Desolate* suggests an underpopulated starkness, *barren* a complete absence of life: only a few farmhouses strung out over the *desolate* countryside; *barren* rocks where the smallest shrub could find no foothold. *Desolate,* however, can also suggest solitariness or friendlessness: a *desolate* pine or two struggling for life above the timberline; a girl left *desolate* in the strange city. *Barren,* like *bleak,* can suggest an unpromising outlook: a plan *barren* of practical remedies. *Barren,* in the sense discussed here, could not be applied to people. See DISMAL, GLOOMY.

Antonyms: CHEERFUL, COMFORTABLE, HEALTHY, *luxurious.*

blithe
> convivial
> ebullient
> elated
> genial
> jovial
> lighthearted

These adjectives refer to a pleasant, warm, cheerful, or high-spirited disposition or manner. **Blithe** indicates an attitude that is cheerful, mirthful, joyous, or gay: *blithe* crowds enjoying the sunny weather in the park. *Blithe* can have a less favorable application to a manner that is casual, indifferent, or airy, particularly when directed toward something that should be taken seriously: listening to my grievance with a *blithe* lack of concern.

Genial points to a more low-key or long-term good-humored attitude that is exhibited in a kindly, pleasant, or warm manner; it suggests an unruffled or even temper and an ability to put people at ease: an always *genial* host. **Lighthearted** is closer in tone to *blithe,* since it suggests an absence of care or a positive state of buoyant delight: *lighthearted* youngsters singing as they hiked through the woods. A contrast with *genial* is apparent in that one may behave in a *genial* way regardless of how one feels, whereas the very essence of *lighthearted* is its suggestion of a spontaneous welling up of high spirits. *Genial,* furthermore, suggests friendly relationships with others; *lighthearted* may pertain to someone completely alone.

Convivial serves as an intensification of *genial,* suggesting jolly sociability and warm fellow-feeling; its Latin root pertains to a feast or banquet, and this is often reflected in the English use of the word: *convivial* merrymakers at Mardi Gras. **Jovial** may suggest sociability, but it is less specific in indicating any sort of good-natured amiability. *Jovial* is often used to describe a jolly but dignified fat person, so much so that it is sometimes taken to specify this situation. Similarly, *blithe* sometimes suggests a spry, elfin, or fey person, particularly a woman. Although neither of these associations is invariable, it would seem odd to speak of a *jovial* wisp of a girl or a *blithe* Santa Claus.

Elated and **ebullient** both refer, like *lighthearted,* to a welling up of high spirits. *Elated,* however, can often refer to a response to some external occurrence or news, whereas *ebullient* suggests the same spontaneity as *lighthearted. Ebullient* stems from the root of a Latin word meaning boil out, and the English word reflects this in pointing to a bubbling over with enthusiasm, excitement, or exuberance: fans who were *elated* when the team scored another touchdown; an *ebullient* personality that always seemed to overflow with vivacity and zest. See PLEASURE.

Antonyms: DISMAL, GLOOMY, *ill-humored, melancholic, morose,* SAD, *sullen,* TRANQUIL.

blockhead

boob
chump
dolt
dunce
fool
nincompoop
ninny

These nouns are all informal pejoratives for people who behave in stupid or foolish ways. **Blockhead, dolt,** and **dunce** suggest foolish behavior that results from a lack of intelligence. *Blockhead* suggests a dense, slow-witted person who predictably misunderstands information or is filled with exasperatingly obvious ideas or attitudes: a party at which she talked with one insufferable *blockhead* after another. *Dolt* specifi-

cally suggests a lack of flair, imagination, or perception that results from cloddish conventionality: *dolts* in the audience who liked his medley of show tunes better than his group of Schubert *lieder. Dunce* may suggest a momentary failure of intelligence rather than a permanent lack of it: He made a *dunce* of himself by forgetting the name of the guest of honor.

Fool and **chump** need not suggest a lack of intelligence at all. Both can suggest silly or ridiculous behavior that arises from any number of causes: letting the boys make a *fool* of him. *Chump,* besides being a much more informal substitute for *fool,* can indicate somebody who allows himself to become the butt of a joke or confidence game: looking for *chumps* who could be lured into buying Brooklyn Bridge. *Chump* can also be a severely contemptuous term for any sort of unsophisticated or ordinary person: *chumps* dumb enough to be taken in by tabloid journalism.

The remaining group of nouns relates to this last suggestion of *chump* in indicating contempt for ordinary or simple people. When it is not an informal substitute for *fool,* **boob** suggests a person crippled by middle-class values: H. L. Mencken used the term booboisie to refer to class rule of, by, and for *boobs.* **Nincompoop** has particular relevance in describing a foolish person, suggesting a weakling afflicted by timidity and passivity: situation comedies that stereotype husbands as bumbling *nincompoops.* **Ninny** can apply to either sex, but may be particularly useful in reference to foolish women, suggesting silly, precious, or prissy behavior: a *ninny* who still writes saccharine poems about butterflies and daffodils. See MORON.

Antonyms: *sage, savant, wise man.*

bloody

bloodthirsty
gory
sanguinary

These adjectives refer to the spilling of blood or to an attitude that delights in bloodshed. **Bloody** suggests freshly spilled blood or conflict that results in heavy casualties: the *bloody* hands of the suspect; the *bloody* four-day battle. It is also frequently used as an epithet for someone or something responsible for wanton slaughter: the *bloody* Stalinist purges; Hitler's *bloody* henchmen; *Bloody* Mary. In Britain, *bloody* can be used as a curse word for anything displeasing. This use was once taken as a blasphemous reference to Christ's blood, but overuse has weakened its force: He cursed the *bloody* tricycle he had tripped over in the dark. **Gory,** by contrast, suggests clotted or dried blood: television teams photographing the *gory* icepick. It may also refer to any production that revels in giving extremely detailed accounts of gruesome accidents or murders: a *gory* detective story. This use also appears in the cliché *the gory details*, which suggests the loving and minute description of anything unpleasant.

The remaining adjectives apply primarily to an eagerness to let blood, either literally or figuratively. **Bloodthirsty** is most specific here, suggesting a delight in inflicting harm on others, especially in armed combat: *bloodthirsty* generals who urged the king to declare war; *bloodthirsty* nightriders intent on terrorizing sharecroppers. *Bloodthirsty* can also be used figuratively to describe people who enjoy reading or seeing accounts of *bloody* happenings: *bloodthirsty* audiences that dote on *gory* television dramas.

Sanguinary is considerably more formal than these other words, giving a literary, almost euphemistic substitute for *bloody* or *bloodthirsty*: the *sanguinary* oppression of the conquered nation. It may also be used merely to refer to someone in a foul temper or ugly frame of mind: a *sanguinary* disposition. See GRUESOME.

Antonyms: *bloodless,* HUMANE, *merciful.*

boast

    brag
    crow
    gloat
    pride
    strut
    vaunt

These verbs refer to feelings of self-congratulation. **Boast** may suggest justifiable self-satisfaction: a college that *boasts* an unusually large number of distinguished alumni. More often, however, *boast* suggests a self-important and tasteless pointing out of one's own successes: He monopolized the conversation by *boasting* of his prowess at hunting and fishing; continually *boasting* and blowing his own horn. Occasionally, *boast* can refer to self-congratulation for a victory not yet won: He *boasted* that he would finish off the challenger in the first round. **Pride** is close to the justified self-satisfaction possible for *boast,* but it more often specifically suggests private self-regard rather than a public expression of it; it is usually reflexive: He secretly *prided* himself on a life of absolute honesty. *Pride* can suggest a stiff-necked self-righteousness, however, or a faulty estimate of one's own virtues: Though *priding* himself on tolerance, he nevertheless signed a restrictive housing clause.

Brag intensifies the note of tastelessness in *boast,* suggesting limitless conceit and, possibly, inaccuracy of the claims being made: *bragging* about his imaginary exploits in the last war; *bragging* about his son's success at college as a way of patting himself on the back. **Crow** suggests noisy or vociferous *bragging* of an extremely offensive kind: always *crowing* about the landslide defeat of his opponent. **Gloat** is an intensification of *crow,* although it need not be verbal and sometimes suggests taunting a person one has bested: rubbing his hands in secret and *gloating* over the way he had made the other applicants look foolish; *gloating* openly and lording it over the also-rans.

Strut suggests less animus than *gloat* but it is similar in not necessarily being verbal. It invariably suggests, however, an act done as a matter of public display: so puffed up and smug over his recent successes that he could not keep from *strutting* about and preening himself before his few remaining friends. **Vaunt** is considerably more formal than the other verbs here; it compares to the understandable self-satisfaction suggested by *boast,* but it is a shade more self-righteous, possibly suggesting a claim that cannot be substantiated. It differs from *pride* in usually implying a public expression of self-esteem: *vaunting* far and wide the cultural opportunities lying in wait for visitors to their small town. See CONCEITED, CONFIDENCE, EGOISM.

Antonyms: BELITTLE, *minimize, underrate.*

boil

    braise
    fry
    pan-broil
    poach
    sauté
    simmer
    steam
    stew

These verbs all refer to methods of cooking by direct heat or flame, especially on top of a range. **Boil** implies rapid cooking in more or less large quantities of water heated to the point (212° at sea level) where bubbles escape at the surface: to *boil* potatoes; to *boil* an egg.

Simmer means cook slowly in a hot liquid just below the boiling point, and usually for a long time.

To **steam** food is to cook it by direct exposure to steam or by using heat generated by steam, as in a double boiler. Direct *steaming* is usually accomplished by placing a metal rack above the level of the boiling water in a pot so that the food does not touch the water: to *steam* broccoli; to *steam* clams.

Poach implies a method of cooking a few foods, such as eggs without their shells, or pieces of chicken or fish, by dropping them into hot water, milk, or stock and *simmering* until done.

Stew is a close synonym of *simmer* in that both mean cook slowly in liquid over low heat: to *stew* prunes. However, to most people, *stew* strongly suggests the familiar dish that is cooked in this way—meat or fish combined with vegetables in a gravy or sauce. *Stewing* always involves *simmering,* but one may *simmer* (not *stew*) soups, vegetables, sauces, etc.

When cooks speak of *stewing* meat, they usually mean **braising** it. *Braise* implies the browning of meat (and often of accompanying vegetables) in a small amount of fat prior to adding a stock or other liquid and *simmering* in a covered pan.

Fry and **sauté** are closely related in that the food is cooked in hot fat. *Sautéing* is done very quickly with a minimum amount of fat and may or may not imply browning. Meat is usually *sautéed* before it is *braised. Frying* suggests cooking in greater amounts of fat than that used in *sautéing,* and may be done in a pan containing up to one or two inches of fat or in a pot designed for deep *frying,* in which large amounts of fat are used. Foods, especially potatoes, cooked in deep fat until crisp are often called French-*fried.*

The cooking of chops, small steaks, fish, etc., on the top of the stove in a dry pan with little or no fat is preferably referred to as **pan-broiling** rather than *frying.* See GRILL.

bold

    aggressive
    forward
    pushing

These adjectives share the connotation of self-assertive, confident, and energetic dispositions, with or without a disregard for the rights of others. **Bold** shares with **aggressive** the implication of a vigorous attack on a problem or prosecution of one's aims, and in this sense carries no derogatory connotation. An *aggressive* or *bold* entrepreneur will seek success farther afield and will risk more in this search than will a more timid competitor. *Bold* does, however, have a wider range of application than *aggressive.* In some contexts *bold* suggests impudence or sauciness, although this use is certainly less common now than it once was: The *bold* fellow simply put out his hand and asked for more money. In other contexts it suggests commendable enterprise: a *bold* new venture in space

science. *Aggressive* typically describes one who has a more lively sense of his or her own destiny than of other people's feelings.

Aggressive shares with **forward** and **pushing** a derogatory connotation of callousness in seeking one's ends. A *forward* or *pushing* social climber may resort to gossip, slander, and backbiting. *Pushing* may also be used in the less derogatory sense of *aggressive* to mean enterprising and energetic. See OPPORTUNISTIC, RECKLESS.

Antonyms: *AFRAID, COWARDLY, MODEST, TIMID.*

bombastic

    orotund
    purple
    turgid

These adjectives are used to describe styles of speaking or writing. **Bombastic** and **turgid** are alike in designating a lack of restraint and discipline that so inflates the language used in a piece of writing or in a speech that its style and content are thrown out of balance. *Bombastic* is derived from the noun *bombast,* which originally denoted the kind of cotton, wool, or other soft material used for padding and stuffing. The suggestion of padding is present in any reference to a *bombastic* style, which though not always connoting the complete absence of thought, certainly indicates an imbalance between the thought and the manner used to express it: For so trivial a topic, his speech was *bombastic* and cheaply theatrical. *Turgid* literally means swollen or distended, as by contained air or liquid: a healthy, *turgid* muscle; a leg *turgid* with infection. Like *bombastic, turgid* carries over a suggestion of its literal meaning into its figurative referral to style: a tiny idea that the author has blown up into this *turgid,* trying novel.

Orotund is used positively to describe a full, clear, round, and resonant tone of voice. The figurative sense of the adjective, however, is pejorative in its synonymity with *bombastic.* While *orotund* can apply to pompous, inflated speech or writing, because of its particular reference to sound, it is most often used to describe the spoken word: a speech so *orotund* as to cause yawns and whispers all over the auditorium. **Purple,** in the sense being compared here, means ornate or flowery. It is pejorative in its suggestion of too much color and showiness: a good playwright who ruined some of his most dramatic moments with passages of bad poetry and *purple* prose. It also has come to refer to the erotic, the lurid, the vulgar, or the profane: a TV emcee whose interviews led to such *purple* exchanges that a sponsor demanded her dismissal. See FORMAL.

Antonyms: *brief, precise, quiet, simple,* TERSE.

bony

> emaciated
> gaunt
> skeletal
> wasted

These adjectives refer to thinness so extreme that the underlying bones are evident. **Bony** is the most general term and is relatively free of connotations. It simply indicates a prominent bone structure, whether this is deemed a sign of attractiveness, asceticism, chronic undernourishment, or near-starvation: a crooner's *bony,* boyish face; a waiflike actress with *bony* shoulders and big eyes; a *bony* Indian fakir; a *bony,* sway-backed nag. *Bony* is frequently applied to a single part of the body: long, *bony* fingers; *bony* knees. And it may sometimes emphasize attributes of bone that are not seen but felt, such as hardness or sharpness: She jabbed me with her *bony* elbow.

Gaunt implies a paucity of flesh and prominence of bone. It comes from the Old Norse word for a tall, thin person, and it indicates an angular leanness: the tall, *gaunt* figure of Don Quixote. Specifically, *gaunt* often calls to mind the haggard look of the hungry, anguished, ill, or old. It suggests the weariness of long suffering or constant strain, describing one who seems to have been worn down to the bone: the *gaunt,* ascetic figure of a saint; a *gaunt* old man, hollow-eyed, with prominent cheekbones and attenuated limbs.

Wasted implies a loss of flesh, stressing the cause of *bony* thinness. A *wasted* body is one that has been gradually consumed—reduced to skin and bone by the ravages of time, grief, hunger, or disease: *wasted* away by AIDS-related disease; a pallid face and *wasted* frame. Hence, *wasted* implies physical weakness and frailty: the *wasted* form of a 100-year-old woman; a body *wasted* by disease.

Emaciated focuses on both the cause and the fact of abnormal leanness. It indicates a previous wasting away, implying the depletion of the body by grave illness, great suffering, or terrible privation. **Skeletal** is the most extreme of all these terms, pointing to the deathlike dominance of bone. Both *skeletal* and *emaciated* may suggest the leanness of living people who look like skeletons, their ribs and sharp bones showing through the skin: *emaciated* (or *skeletal*) survivors of a concentration camp. But *skeletal* has about it the fur-

ther suggestion of something lifeless or unreal, not fully human or alive: a painting of *skeletal* men and women in a barren future world; a novelist whose characters seem to be *skeletal* symbols, thoroughly analyzed but not fleshed out and never really brought to life. *Emaciated,* by contrast, is often expressive of human pity or horror at a *skeletal* appearance: the awful sight of *emaciated* children with distended bellies and glazed expressions. See LANKY, PALE, THIN, WEAKEN.

Antonyms: FAT, *nourished, well-fed.*

boss

> chief
> commander
> leader
> maestro
> master

These nouns all refer to persons who are in authority over others. **Boss** is a colloquial word that originated in the United States and in its strictest sense applies to an employer, foreman, or manager of a group of factory workers. By extension it has also become a popular term for any executive, supervisor, or immediate superior: the *boss* of the payroll department; my *boss,* the pharmacist; the *boss* of a large clothing store. *Boss* may also apply to any person who is in control of things, whether by prerogative or by tyrannical behavior. [A horse must understand who is *boss;* Many parents discover that a spoiled child has become *boss* of the household.] In another sense, a *boss* is a professional politician who controls a party organization: William M. Tweed was the *boss* of New York City politics right after the Civil War.

Chief, the most comprehensive of these nouns, can be applied to anyone who occupies the position of highest authority over a group, large or small: the editor in *chief* of a newspaper; the *chief* architect of the housing project. However, *chief* is more commonly used of the supervisor of some department of established government: a *chief* of staff; the *chief* of police; a fire *chief. Chief* and *boss* are sometimes used interchangeably: I need my *chief's* (or *boss's*) signature on these contracts. In its original sense, a *chief* is the ruler of a primitive or nomadic tribe.

A **leader** is one who is voluntarily followed because of an ability to guide and control others or because he or she has been selected by a group or party. One tends to think of a *leader's* having arrived at this position chiefly because of a talent for influencing others and for acting as a guiding force: the *leader* of the guerrilla band; a *leader* in the fashion world; the *leader* of a labor movement.

In its commonest sense a **master** is a person who has been given the authority to enforce obedience, but *master* does not suggest the innate ability of the *leader* to guide and influence others. A *master* may be one who employs servants, is a male teacher at a boy's private school, or owns an animal, such as a dog, that can be trained to obey him. *Master* is also the formal title for the captain of a merchant ship. A teacher or *leader* in philosophy, religion, etc., who has followers or disciples is often called a *master*, as is Jesus by many Christians. *Master* is also applied to people of exceptional skill or artistic ability: a *master* plumber; the old *masters* of Renaissance painting; a *master* of the keyboard.

Commander is narrower in its meaning than are the other nouns of this group. Originally, it meant one who commands, as a *leader, chief*, etc.; now it applies almost exclusively to highly placed personnel in the armed forces. In the Navy, a *commander* is an officer ranking next below a captain. The officer in charge of a military post is also called a *commander*, or *commanding* officer. The person holding supreme command of all the armed forces of a nation (as the President of the United States) is called a *commander* in chief, as is any high-ranking officer in charge of a fleet or a major force.

Maestro (from the Italian for *master*) is used of a person who is highly proficient in an artistic field, but it is now most often used of an eminent conductor, composer, or performer in music. *Maestro* sometimes carries overtones of affectionate veneration, as in its application to the late Arturo Toscanini.

Antonyms: ASSISTANT, *dependent, follower, servant, subordinate, underling.*

bother

disturb
harass
pester
plague
trouble
worry

These verbs imply one of two situations: either one in which a person is actively annoying another, or one in which a person is upset by something not necessarily the actions of someone else. Some of these verbs can carry either the active or passive implication; others are mainly restricted to one sense or the other.

Bother, **disturb**, and **plague** are often used in both active and passive senses. On the passive scale, *bother* usually indicates a minor complaint that may come and go: frequently *bothered* by a slight stiffness in his joints. *Disturb* is more intense, suggesting specifically, at its most extreme, mental derangement: the mentally *disturbed* patient. In milder uses, *disturb* points to a state of upset more thoroughgoing than that of *bother*: I was *bothered* by the lack of news at first, but now, after a month, I am really *disturbed*. *Plague*, in its passive sense, is perhaps the most intense of all these verbs, but suggests a specific kind of upset, one that repeatedly hammers inside the mind without letup. People who are *plagued*—by thoughts or by conditions around them—are by implication in control neither of the things that hound or harry them nor of their recurrence within their possibly unstable minds: *plagued* by constant recollections of his long-dead wife; *plagued* by the odor in the packing plant; *plagued* by a continuing lack of money.

These same three verbs—*bother, disturb*, and *plague*—give a somewhat different scale of effects in their active senses. In this case, *disturb* is the weakest in intensity. One person, for example, may *disturb* another unintentionally by actions not directed specifically to the latter: Did my whistling *disturb* you? *Bother*, here, is stronger than *disturb*, since an implication is present that the action may be done intentionally to *disturb*: Just pay the bill and I'll stop *bothering* you. *Plague* is even stronger in the active voice than in the passive, suggesting repeated, deliberate annoyances that may have an almost demoniacal insistence: The bill collector *plagued* us with unrelenting phone calls, letters, and threats.

Trouble and **worry** are largely confined to the passive implication of being upset about something. [I am *troubled* by the doctor's report; I'm *worried* that I'll fail the exam.] Both verbs are more forceful than the passive use of *bother* but less so than the same use of *disturb*. *Trouble* is slightly more formal than *worry* and suggests a definite cause for alarm; *worry* suggests less clear-cut reasons for uneasiness, specifically implying suspense over the outcome of something. *Trouble* is also more inclusive; one may be *troubled* without indulging in the helpless wasted motions of thought implied by *worry*.

In contrast, **pester** and **harass** are almost exclusively restricted to the active sense of someone annoying another person. [The platoon sergeant constantly *harassed* the recruits in ingeniously excruciating ways; Stop *pestering* me!] Both verbs are more forceful than the active use of *disturb* and even of *bother*. *Pester* is like the active use of *plague* in suggesting repeated and deliberate annoyances that interrupt someone else, but remains restricted mainly to trivial matters. *Harass* is considerably stronger, even carrying the possibility of physical punishment or worse: employers sexually *harassing* their female employees. *Harass* may even be stronger than *plague* in this case, since the latter stops short of any implication of physical violence. See ANGER, ENRAGE, UPSET.

Antonyms: *comfort, console, placate, solace.*

bounce
carom
deflect
ricochet

All these verbs describe ways in which the direction of a moving object can be radically changed. **Bounce**, the most general term, can be applied to virtually any missile that rebounds, such as a ball, stone, penny, or apple. [He didn't see me toss him the book; it *bounced* off his chest and fell to the floor.] But *bounce* commonly emphasizes resiliency. [The basketball *bounced* high in the air; My little girl loves to *bounce* up and down on her bed.]

Carom is a curious word, because the noun refers to a highly skillful and carefully controlled billiards shot, whereas the verb often implies lack of control and recklessness. In billiards, a *carom* is a shot in which the cue ball strikes against two other balls in succession. As a verb, *carom* means hit and rebound, often in a context that implies that the rebound is uncontrolled and damaging. [The car *caromed* off the telephone pole and hurtled into a parked mail truck.]

Deflect means turn aside or cause something to swerve from its course. **Ricochet** means glance from a surface in the fashion of a stone thrown over the surface of water, making a series of skips or bounds. Thus, *ricochet* in practice means to *bounce* away fast, with little loss of speed, whereas *deflect* stresses the change in direction of a moving object. Compare these two examples. [The bullet *ricocheted* off the sidewalk and shattered the window glass; The arrow, *deflected* by strong winds, missed its target completely.] In some contexts *ricochet* and *carom* are interchangeable, but *carom* emphasizes collision and the force of the rebound whereas *ricochet* emphasizes the speed of the deflection. *Bounce* can substitute in most contexts for *carom* and *ricochet*, but not for *deflect; deflect* differs essentially from the other verbs in not involving the actions of bounding away or collision. It means what

the others only imply: a change in the direction of movement of an object.

boundary
border
bounds
confines
frontier
limit

These nouns denote a line that marks the outermost part of an area, or a division between areas. **Boundary** is used chiefly of territory and suggests a definite demarcation, such as a line or mark that can be precisely located on a map. **Bounds** are less definite and may be used figuratively of behavior: His impudence exceeds all *bounds*. The colloquial expression *out of bounds*, derived from its use in various sports, is commonly used with the meaning of unfair, improper, or indecent: Holding hands was *out of bounds*, and as for kissing—that was unthinkable.

Whereas *boundary* points to an outermost limit, **border** emphasizes the division between two areas: the *border* between the Russia and Finland. [He crossed the *border* into Belgium; By international agreement the *boundary* of each nation fronting a body of water usually extends several miles from the coastline.] *Border* often suggests a territorial feature, such as a river or mountain range, and hence is not as precise as *boundary*. *Boundaries* may be changed by treaties, that is, on paper; *borders* may change by the changing course of a river or by military action.

Limit is the most general term of this group and can be applied to any outermost extent, range, demarcation, etc. As here considered, the term is usually plural: to pass beyond the city *limits*. In military usage *off limits* serves to notify military personnel not to enter the building or area so designated. **Frontier** may refer to the part of a nation's territory lying along the *border* of another country; it thus describes the *border* region of a country from an interior perspective. *Frontier* also means the part of a settled region lying along the *border* of an unsettled region. *Frontier* is often used in extended senses: beyond the *frontier* of knowledge; at the *frontier* of space exploration.

Confines, like *bounds*, define the extent of an area without reference to what lies beyond, but *confines* is less consistently restricted to the description of geographical *limits*: The political prisoner was not permitted to pass beyond the *confines* of his home. *Confines*, like *bounds*, is commonly used figuratively: Her genius soared beyond the narrow *confines* of her formal education; beyond all *bounds* of decency or common sense. See CIRCUMSCRIBE, EDGE, PERIMETER.

brand

> colophon
> logo
> logotype
> service mark
> trade name
> trademark

These nouns can all be used to describe commercial names, commodities, and services, and are in this sense related. They are not synonyms, however, and there are important distinctions to be made between them. **Brand** is generally understood to mean a definite, usually well-known and advertised type of commodity: the Savarin *brand* of coffee; a popular *brand* of soda water. By extension, *brand name* identifies a whole group of products made or sold by the same enterprise: General Electric is the *brand name* of a line of electrical appliances.

Trademark comes closest to having a definite legal status, especially when formally registered with the appropriate government agency. By federal law a *trademark* is "any word, symbol, or device or any combination thereof adopted and used by a manufacturer or merchant to identify his goods and distinguish them from those manufactured and sold by others." Of the thousands in active use most take the form of words, as *Kodak, Vaseline, Technicolor, Coca-Cola, Dacron,* etc. It will be noted that such words are spelled with an initial capital letter, a practice strongly recommended by their owners as a means of emphasizing exclusive rights to the goodwill and equity inherent in their commercial use.

Service mark extends this form of identification to enterprises engaged in providing a specified line of services under some slogan, monogram, title, etc.: Blue Cross is the *service mark* of the Associated Hospital Service of New York. **Trade name**, though used as a variant of *trademark,* is legally synonymous with the commercial name under which a firm, enterprise, corporation, association, etc., conducts its business. [*Dupont* is both the *trade name* and *service mark* of a manufacturer of chemical products, many of which carry *trademarks.*]

A **logotype** is any single piece of type containing several letters, a word, or words. In advertising, *logotype* applies specifically to a particular design or style used to represent the name of a company or a *trademark* so as to make it more readily identifiable and emphasize its protected status in the public mind. Thus, there are *logotypes*—or **logos**, as they are called for short—for many well-known *trademarks.*

A **colophon** was formerly an inscription placed at the end of a book, showing the title, the printer's name, date, and other information, such as the style and size of type used. Now *colophon* is more commonly used to refer to a design or emblem adopted by a publisher to represent a particular line of books or the publishing house as a whole; the *colophon* is now usually printed on the title page of books.

brandish

> flourish
> swing
> wield

These verbs are synonyms when they mean move something rapidly back and forth or in circles. **Brandish** means wave or shake a weapon, especially in public, so as to threaten or intimidate someone: The customer at the checkout counter suddenly *brandished* a gun, and everybody scrambled for cover. **Flourish** implies a display of self-confidence, triumph, or merely high spirits: The victorious army *flourished* a captured flag.

Swing, in this sense, means move rhythmically to and fro or backward and forward, like the pendulum of a clock or the clapper of a bell. It may imply a wide, sweeping motion, even rotation: to *swing* an ax; Huckleberry Finn recommended *swinging* a dead cat over one's head to cure warts. **Wield** emphasizes the command one has over the use of a weapon or instrument: to *wield* a hammer and chisel; to *wield* forceps with consummate skill. Sometimes, *wield* approaches *brandish* in meaning: He turned toward me and suddenly *wielded* a short, ugly knife.

Antonyms: *arrest, hang, suspend.*

brashness

> brass
> cheek
> chutzpah
> gall
> nerve
> sauciness

These nouns describe shameless, bold, or arrogantly brusque behavior. **Brashness** indicates a decisive, insistently aggressive, or come-what-may attitude. When *brashness* is approving, it expresses wonder or admiration for someone's audacity and zest; more commonly, it is used to criticize a rash lack of judgment or a lack of consideration for others: the *brashness* of such a small country in successfully defending itself against its enemies; a foolhardy *brashness* that often tempted him to tackle situations he knew nothing about; the *brashness* with which she pushed her way to the top of the heap, injuring the feelings of everyone else in the office. *Brashness* can also point to a garish vulgarity of taste: The *brashness* of his sports clothes almost made my eyeballs ache. **Sauciness** suggests, instead, an imperious, insouciant, and haughty manner, often exhibited in an inferior or in someone replying sharply or out of turn: the *sauciness* of that impertinent salesgirl; the indignant *sauciness* with which he refused to take his nap. Often, *sauciness* can be used humorously or affectionately to describe the spirited display of someone who is weak or powerless: the roguish *sauciness* of a small kitten; the boy's *sauciness* in grandly declining to play house with his older sister. **Chutzpah** is a U.S. slang word, derived from Yiddish, for brazen insolence or self-seeking: her *chutzpah* in demanding the best table in the restaurant. Like *brashness,* this noun can be approving for someone's audacity or disapproving for someone's effrontery: Give me someone who knows what he wants and has the *chutzpah* to go after it without shilly-shallying; a patient who had the *chutzpah* to charge into the doctor's office ahead of everyone else in the waiting room.

The remaining nouns are all informal words for the same idea expressed by *chutzpah*. Of these, however, only **nerve** can function with either positive or negative force. When approving *nerve* points to cool self-possession and courage in acting against odds: It took *nerve* for her to stand up for her rights in an atmosphere thick with recrimination and threats of reprisal. In disapproval, *nerve* suggests a shameless disregard for good taste or manners: Imagine the *nerve* of him inviting himself to stay the weekend! **Brass** and **cheek** both indicate an insistent and insolent self-assurance. *Brass* is the more disapproving of the two, suggesting a coarse or ingrained lack of sensitivity to the feelings of others: Not even the prosecutor had the *brass* to ignore the tears of the child on the witness stand. *Cheek* is milder in suggesting a smug or simpering self-regard that prompts uncritical, brazen, or tasteless behavior: the *cheek* to ask for a raise after only a week on the job. Like *sauciness, cheek* can be used humorously or affectionately for a cute forwardness in one's inferiors: the *cheek* of the boy in asking for another helping of dessert. **Gall** is the most severely disapproving of all these nouns, suggesting shameless acts of unwarranted discourtesy: the *gall* to

show up for dinner with three of his friends. But *gall* is very general, applying to any act one dislikes. See CONCEITED, EFFRONTERY, OVERBEARING.

Antonyms: *civility, meekness, politeness, self-effacement.*

brave
bold
courageous
dauntless
fearless
gallant
heroic
intrepid
plucky
undaunted
valiant
valorous

These adjectives indicate a readiness to face danger, difficulty, or even death when called upon by circumstance to do so. **Brave** is the most general term. It indicates the showing of one's mettle under stress, implying self-possession and resolution. **Courageous**, like *brave,* may focus on response to a situation, but it often implies firmness arising from strong moral convictions. Both adjectives imply a willingness to proceed with what is necessary in spite of external deterrents or internal misgivings. A *brave* or *courageous* soldier carries out a dangerous mission, not without fear, but without letting fear deter him from doing his duty.

Dauntless and **undaunted** indicate bravery under exceptionally trying circumstances. Both imply a refusal to be disheartened, intimidated, or otherwise discouraged from going on. [Scientists pursue their experiments with *dauntless* determination, despite repeated failures and disappointments; Stalemated negotiators must resume their talks each day with *undaunted* optimism.] **Fearless** and **intrepid** imply a resolute freedom from fear or a cool, unshakable determination. [A *fearless,* crusading newspaper exposes corruption in high places despite danger of reprisal; The *intrepid* pioneers traveled west in spite of hardships and the constant danger of armed attack.]

Valiant and **valorous** are applied to persons and actions that exhibit the kind of courage and fortitude associated with knighthood. *Valiant* may suggest bravery shown in a worthy cause, against impossible odds, or with commendable consequences. *Valorous* is usually applied to the spirit or deeds of the *valiant*. A *valiant* firefighter, showing *valorous* disregard of personal safety, may rescue persons trapped in a burning building. A dying person may put up a *valiant*, but hopeless, fight for life.

Heroic and **gallant** imply outstanding bravery coupled with nobility of motive or selfless dedication. *Heroic* stresses exceptional courage, fortitude, or enterprise, especially in time of war or danger. It implies a willingness to risk or sacrifice one's own life to save others. *Gallant* implies inner nobility that is manifested in chivalrous action. [The defense of the Alamo was a *heroic* action of *gallant* Texans.]

Plucky is somewhat informal and is usually applied to contenders who persist against unfavorable odds. A *plucky* prizefighter does his best to hold his own against a stronger, more skillful opponent. **Bold** indicates an actively *brave* nature or a confident audacity. The *bold* person is daring and is undeterred by fear of consequences: Washington's *bold* crossing of the Delaware caught the enemy by surprise and resulted in the fall of Trenton. See BOLD, DARING, RECKLESS.

Antonyms: AFRAID, COWARDLY, *daunted, intimidated,* TIMID.

break

interlude
intermission
letup
lull
pause
recess
respite

These nouns refer to intervals during which some activity stops or slackens. **Break** stresses the idea of interruption. It indicates a temporary time-out, as from work, for rest, refreshment, recreation, or other purpose: a coffee *break*. **Pause** is less abrupt and drastic, indicating a brief rest or a momentary suspension of action: the *pause* that refreshes. A scheduled interruption of a radio or TV program that is called a station *break* at the studio is referred to in milder terms on the air as a *pause* for station identification. *Pause* is also used to stress the temporary nature of a cease-fire: a *pause* in the bombing; Government sources said there would be no prolonged *pause* in the war. **Respite** is a much more formal synonym for *break*. A *respite* is an interval of relief, as from some source of strain: ceaseless toil that knows no *respite;* The holiday truce gave a welcome *respite* for the troops. One takes a *break* but is granted a *respite:* The construction workers took a *break*, and we enjoyed a brief *respite* from the noise.

A **recess** is an interval between the sessions of a school, court, legislature, or the like. It implies a formal adjournment for a limited time, with a temporary suspension of business: the university's spring *recess;* a legislative *recess* before elections. A *recess* may be as brief as a *break* or as long as a vacation, but it presupposes some sort of official authorization. [The cast decided to take a *break;* The judge declared a two-hour *recess.*] In grammar school, a *recess* is a free period between classroom sessions during which the children may play, relax, or get something to eat: boys and girls shooting marbles at *recess.*

An **interlude** is a period or episode that occurs in the course of a longer process and breaks its continuity: noise with *interludes* of quiet. By nature, an *interlude* contrasts with the activity it interrupts or the events it comes between—often occurring as an interval of calm, a time of content, or a touch of comic relief: *interludes* of lucidity in his delirium; a humorous *interlude* in a sober history; Their honeymoon was an idyllic *interlude*. An **intermission** is a scheduled *recess* between the acts of a play or the parts of a performance: to go out for fresh air during *intermission*. *Interlude*, on the other hand, may apply to an entertainment of a different kind that fills a *break* between the acts, as a brief, farcical comedy or a short, transitional passage of music: an orchestral *interlude*. In another sense, *intermission* may apply to any temporary cessation: The noise went on without *intermission*.

Letup is an informal word and is usually used negatively after *no* or *without*. It often indicates abatement rather than cessation, pointing to a lessening of force, a slackening of pace, or a reduction in number or intensity. [The rain came down without *letup;* We've worked two hours without *letup;* There has been no *letup* in the stream of complaints.] **Lull** designates an interval of stillness or calm that contrasts with prior and subsequent noise or confusion: a *lull* in a storm. *Lull* may also refer to a falling off of activity, implying a loss of momentum and suggesting the sluggishness of a slack period: a *lull* in business; a *lull* in the conversation.

break

burst
crack
crush
fracture
shatter
shiver
smash

These verbs refer to the forcible destruction, breaching, or injury of something. **Break** is the most general. It most often suggests the separation of a rigid body into pieces, implying either partial or total destruction of a whole: *breaking* the twigs in two for easier burning; *breaking* a vase by accident. *Break* may also indicate a temporary injury, as to a bone: *breaking* a leg in a fall. And it may involve getting free from some restraint or enclosure: to *break* out of jail; buds *breaking* open. **Burst** is close to *break* in this latter sense but involves much greater violence. It is a highly specific verb, suggesting a forceful *breaking* open that is due to internal pressure: squeezing a pimple until it *bursts* open; a dam so weakened by floods that it finally *burst;* blowing up a balloon until it *bursts.*

Crack usually means *break* without separation of parts. It suggests the *breaking* out across a surface of slitlike openings or hairline ruptures, either because of wear, age, or pressure: a window that he *cracked* by leaning against it; a *cracked* cup; linoleum that had faded and *cracked.* In other uses, however, *crack* may mean *break* apart or *break* into pieces: *cracking* open the walnut without *breaking* the meat. **Fracture** can suggest a deeper, more thorough, but also more localized *breaking* than *crack: fracturing* the bone in two places; boulders *fractured* by repeated freezing and thawing; old habit patterns *fractured* by changing technology.

Shatter and **shiver** most often suggest a total *breaking* up of a thin surface. *Shatter* is the more general of the two, implying the *breaking* of such a surface into sharp pieces or jagged fragments: heavy enough to *shatter* the melting ice; a well-aimed stone that *shattered* the already *cracked* window. *Shatter* can, however, refer to the *breaking* of any brittle object, in which case, it suggests reduction to many fairly small pieces: a marble statue that had been completely *shattered* in the earthquake *Shiver,* by contrast, is more closely restricted to glass or glasslike surfaces, suggesting a reduction into long, narrow shards or slivers: *shivering* the mirror. *Shiver* might now seem outdated except as a noun meaning fragment or splinter.

Crush and **smash** suggest forceful action taken to destroy or *break* something. *Crush* points to the effect of great external pressure; it suggests squeezing something out of shape: *crushing* the empty beer can in one hand; eggs that had been *crushed* by canned goods placed on top of them in the carton. *Smash* describes the kind of complete deformation resulting from a heavy, noisy blow. It suggests the *shattering* of something brittle either by throwing it or by throwing something against it: *smashing* the window with his bare fist; He *smashed* the bottle to smithereens against the rocks. See CRACK, DESTROY, EXPLODE.

Antonyms: CONNECT, REPAIR, *weld.*

bright

> beaming
> brilliant
> effulgent
> glowing
> incandescent
> radiant
> resplendent
> shining

All these adjectives refer most specifically to the intense, steady light emitted from a source, rather than to wavering or reflected light. **Bright** is the most general of these, stressing chiefly the intensity of the light: the *bright* stars. It is more useful than the other adjectives as a comparative: the *brighter* of the two bulbs. In its very generality, *bright* permits reference to wavering or reflected light, but only to emphasize intensity: a *bright,* cheerful fire; sun-*bright* ripples. **Brilliant** lends itself to the same uses as *bright,* but suggests even greater intensity: *brilliant* headlights. *Brilliant* can have a lyrical quality absent in the more matter-of-fact *bright,* and consequently it can imply excellence or beauty: the *brilliant,* cloudless day.

Incandescent suggests light created specifically by combustion, and it may or may not carry overtones of emitted warmth as well as light. *Incandescent* may simply refer technically to a white-hot light: an *incandescent* lamp. In other uses it suggests fierceness or intense whiteness rather than the excellence or beauty of *brilliant:* the *incandescent* glare of the streetlights.

Resplendent is in every way an intensification of *brilliant;* though more formal, it is even more lyrical, stressing vivid brightness and dazzling splendor: the *resplendent* sun; a sky *resplendent* with stars. *Resplendent* can refer to sources of reflected light as well, but with the same lyrical force and implication of luster: bedecked with diamonds and *resplendent* in her jeweled gown. **Effulgent** is like *resplendent* in lyricism and formality except that it is more precisely restricted to sources of light. Also, its extreme formality may make its use seem inflated or pretentious: *effulgent* rays streaming through the thunderhead.

While far less formal than *resplendent* or *effulgent,* **shining** as an adjective has been so overworked when used with lyrical intent that it may now strike one as a cliché in most contexts: a knight in *shining* armor. *Shining* may escape this liability when it is merely descriptive: the *shining* beacon far out at sea. Used in such a way, it contrasts with all the foregoing adjectives by describing light that need not be intense. **Glowing** and **radiant**, similarly, do not emphasize intensity. *Glowing* suggests a slow burning or the last stages of burning; it implies warmth as well, but faintness of both light and warmth may be the point of its use: the *glowing* remains of a fire. *Radiant* suggests the emission of light in all directions; it carries a unique connotation of mild, gentle warmth: a *radiant* June day, so unlike those of *incandescent* July. **Beaming** refers specifically to light sent out in long arms, either stationary or sweeping: the *beaming* searchlight.

All these adjectives can refer figuratively to qualities of personality, intelligence, or passion. Indeed, their metaphorical use has been extensive in describing all that is good or desirable in human nature—perhaps a comment on the high value people have continued to place on light. In brief, *bright* refers to intelligence, but more as potential than as accomplishment: a *bright* student. *Brilliant* goes beyond *bright* to indicate great intellect or talent. It may also refer to a highly admired accomplishment or illustrious achievement: a *brilliant* novel. *Resplendent* may suggest the blaze and brilliance of triumph or majesty: soldiers *resplendent* in victory. *Effulgent* may describe something that seems to radiate outward like light: her *effulgent* loveliness. *Glowing* suggests a being possessed by warm or passionate emotions; *radiant* suggests their satisfaction—or a being possessed by calmer, gentler feelings: eyes *glowing* with desire; a face *radiant* with tenderness. *Beaming* suggests pleasure or self-satisfaction, while *shining* in most of its figurative uses is decidedly trite. See LUMINOUS, SPARKLING.

Antonyms: *dim, dull,* GLOOMY, OBSCURE, *opaque.*

brusque

abrupt
bluff
blunt
curt
gruff
surly

All these adjectives point to a shortness or discourtesy of manner in a person's treatment of others. **Brusque** derives from an Italian word meaning rude. It is applied to a noticeably short, brisk, or terse manner that may or may not be rude, depending on intent and circumstance. [A no-nonsense woman, the gov-erness gave her employer a *brusque* handshake; Being in a hurry, he made an unintentionally *brusque* reply.] At worst, *brusque* may imply incivility, ungracious sharpness, or undue severity: a *brusque* dismissal. **Bluff**, by contrast, is not at all negative in tone but implies a hearty frankness—an openness that may lack finesse but does not intend discourtesy. *Bluff* is used almost exclusively to describe men. The *bluff* man talks and laughs loudly and freely, says and does whatever he pleases with fearless good nature, and with no thought of annoying or giving pain to others: A *bluff,* beefy man, he didn't mince his words, but there was a twinkle in his eye. **Blunt** is fairly close to *bluff* at one extreme, though it can imply only a well-meaning directness. Unlike *bluff*, however, *blunt* more often suggests a flat-footed forthrightness that verges on discourtesy. It may describe a manner of speech as well as a person. [Shall I lie politely to you, or shall I be *blunt?* Be as *blunt* as you like—I won't mind your rudeness if you tell me the truth.] At the other extreme, *blunt* may indicate a tactless frankness that is inconsiderate or needlessly cruel. *Blunt* people may say things they know to be disagreeable, either from a defiant indifference to the feelings of others or from the pleasure obtained in tormenting.

Abrupt and **curt** both suggest an uncooperative terseness, especially in reply to a question or appeal for help: His laconic answers to my repeated requests for directions were both unfriendly and *abrupt*. *Abrupt* may also imply a disconcerting directness: an *abrupt* refusal. *Curt* is stronger than *abrupt,* implying hardness or coldness of manner as well as a willful intent to be unpleasant: a *curt* rejoinder. [I can understand being a little *abrupt* if one is really busy, but she's always *curt* even when she's just passing time.]

Gruff and **surly** suggest bad-tempered or rude behavior, but they need not imply either straightforwardness, as in *bluff* and *blunt,* nor undue brevity of response, as in *abrupt* and *curt*. Of the two, *gruff* is more appropriately applied to a man and is most applicable to disposition. It describes one who is *brusque,* rough, and crusty in manner or hoarse and guttural in speech. [He'll grumble for minutes at a time when he's *gruff* and grouchy, but don't expect a straight answer from him then.] *Surly* suggests extreme discourtesy and may be applied to either sex. It implies not so much a sour frame of mind as an abiding attitude of hostility to people—a crabbed, churlish disposition evident in both speech and manner: a *surly,* insubordinate receptionist. [Give me the *gruffest* clerk in the world and I won't complain—just so long as I don't have to put up with that *surly* man in the credit department. I'll even take the *blunt* remarks about my figure from the woman in the dress department or the *curt* answers of the credit manager when I ask to pay by check. Believe me, a *surly* salesclerk is far worse.] See CANDID, TERSE.

Antonyms: *diplomatic, gracious, mannerly,* POLITE, *tactful, unctuous,* URBANE.

build

>construct
>erect
>fabricate

These verbs all indicate the assembling and fitting together of materials into a structure. **Build**, the most general and least formal, has the widest range of uses, from the most concrete and specific to the highly figurative and abstract. [Carpenters *build* houses, and birds *build* nests; Cave dwellers *built* fires at the mouths of their caves; The Wall Street broker hoped to *build* a business empire; Nations *built* their hopes for peace on the fear of nuclear war.] **Construct** has a much more limited range of application. It emphasizes the intricate or complex nature of a *building* process, where *build* may focus on the assembling of separate parts and the resulting connection: to *build* a bookcase; to *construct* an office building. The phrase *build a bridge* stresses the act of creation and the link created. The phrase *construct a bridge* emphasizes engineering problems and the workers and equipment involved. The same distinctions hold with reference to mental activities—*build* pointing to gradual, step-by-step creation through continued efforts. [Philosophers *construct* complicated systems for describing existence; Neurotics may be unable to *build* healthy relationships.] If substituted for *build* in the last example, *construct* would have an unfortunate overtone of artificiality.

Like *build*, **erect** may involve the assembling of parts. A child *builds* with blocks but may also play with an *Erector Set*. *Erect*, however, chiefly stresses height and vertical position, meaning put or set something up: to *erect* a skyscraper; to *erect* a monument; They finally *built* a road up the mountain to the tower that had been *erected* a century earlier. *Erect* also has figurative uses: to *erect* a tariff wall; to *erect* a trade barrier.

Fabricate has least the sense of building a structure on its intended location. In suggesting the assembly and fitting together of parts, it implies more the standardized manufacturing of smaller items in a factory: to *fabricate* parts for do-it-yourself furniture kits.

Recent techniques of house building have, of course, perfected the prefabrication of all units, which are then shipped and assembled on the spot. Unless this type of building or construction is meant, however, one would still not use *fabricate* of house or bridge building. In other uses, *fabricate* has taken on a strong negative overtone of artificiality or falsity: a friend who *fabricates* flimsy stories to conceal his irresponsibility. See CREATE, MAKE.

Antonyms: DESTROY, *devastate*.

burn

>brand
>cauterize
>char
>scald
>scorch
>sear
>singe

Burn, the general verb, means effect a change in an object through the action of heat or fire. The object may be changed only slightly, or it may be totally destroyed. [A cigarette *burned* the finish on the table; A fire *burned* the house down.] Although it usually connotes some degree of destruction, *burning* may accomplish a useful purpose. A householder *burns* fuel to heat the house. In autumn, gardeners formerly *burned* leaves to dispose of them. Not only heat but also extreme cold, corrosive chemicals, gases, electricity, radiation, friction, and the like may cause the kind of surface change or stinging sensation associated with a *burn*. Hence, acid is said to *burn* the skin, and a cutting wind may make the cheeks *burn*. *Burn* can also mean cause a feeling of heat in a part of the body: The hot spices *burned* her mouth and tongue.

To **scald** is to *burn* with a very hot liquid or steam. Thus, the careless chef may *scald* herself if she spills hot soup or boiling water.

Singe, **scorch**, and **char** are related in that they mean *burn* partially, slightly, or superficially. To *singe* is to *burn* the surface or ends of something: The fire *singed* his eyebrows. *Singeing* is sometimes done deliberately, as to remove bristles or to keep hair from splitting. A cook may *singe* a plucked chicken to remove pinfeathers by passing the fowl through an open flame. To *scorch* is to *burn* something to the point of discoloration, usually by hot metal: He *scorched* his shirt by setting the iron too high for the fabric. *Char* may imply a more advanced stage of combustion. It means reduce a substance to carbon, either completely, as in charcoal, or partially: Pieces of *charred* wood remained after the campfire had burned out; the *charred* remains of a burned-down house.

Sear, **brand**, and **cauterize** all connote deliberate *burning* to achieve a definite purpose. All are also used of flesh. Of the three, *sear* is the most general, as it can mean both *brand* and *cauterize*. *Searing* involves subjecting a surface to intense heat for a very short time. This may have the effect of hardening, sealing, drying up, destroying tissue, or leaving an ineradicable imprint. [Before stewing the beef, the cook *seared* it over high heat to seal the juices in.] To *brand* is to *sear* with a hot iron, burning a mark into the flesh, as to signify ownership. A rancher *brands* cattle so that they can be identified when they stray or are stolen. To *cauterize* is to *sear* tissue with a caustic agent or heated iron for curative purposes. A doctor may *cauterize* a wound to prevent infection. See COMBUSTIBLE, HOT, PASSIONATE, STIGMA.

busy

active
engaged
engrossed
occupied

These adjectives all refer to activity or involvement. **Busy** is the least formal. It may indicate nothing more than that a person is working on or doing something, or that a thing is in use. [Mr. Brown is *busy* right now; The line is *busy*.] Or it may imply constant, concentrated involvement in business, or intensive and varied activity of any kind: a *busy* woman; a *busy* day; a *busy* marketplace; a *busy* legislative session. The effort involved in being or staying *busy*, by implication, may be valuable or productive: Get *busy* and get something done. But in some cases, *busy* gives a special overtone of empty fuss and hollow results: *busy* work to keep pupils out of trouble; kept *busy* half the day by peddling neighborhood gossip. Another special use refers disapprovingly to a distracting elaborateness of design: such a *busy* pattern for a skirt.

Active stresses action, operation, or involvement as opposed to passivity or dormancy: an *active* senior citizen; an *active* life; an *active* listing. *Active* accounts are productive, and *active* investments yield interest. An *active* volcano is not extinct but may erupt, though it seldom does. Used of persons, *active* often points to actual work or participation as contrasted with mere approval or association: *active* on behalf of civil rights; *active* in community affairs; an *active* church member as opposed to a mere name on the rolls. A soldier on *active* duty is involved in military service full-time, but may not be *busy* all the time. *Active* may also mean brisk or lively, suggesting a heaviness of traffic or transactions: a day of *active* trading.

Occupied shares with *busy* and *active* a simple contrast with idle. When used of a person, it suggests involvement with a specific task: *occupied* with sweeping out the fireplace. When used of an object, it suggests its physical use at that moment. A telephone line can be *busy* but cannot be *occupied*. Conversely, a telephone booth can be *occupied* but cannot be *busy*. *Occupied*, when used of someone's mental state, means absorbed in thought, either purposive or idle: *occupied* in adding the columns of figures before her; He frequently *occupied* himself with trifles. In either case, it can suggest concentration to the point of distraction: so *occupied* in thought that the driver did not see the speeding car. **Engrossed** compares closely with this special use of *occupied*, implying even greater concentration, but with the added suggestion of pleasurable, willing, or fascinated involvement: *engrossed* in a good mystery story; *engrossed* in her research.

Engaged suggests involvement, like *busy*, but implies concentration on a specific task, like *occupied*. It also has a special sense of coming to grips with a situation: The *engaged* artist struggles to illuminate problems facing society. It has a military use for units involved in a hostile encounter: The *engaged* patrol was cut off from its own front line. It also refers to a man and woman in the formalized period of courtship just before marriage: an *engaged* couple. See ACTIVITY, DILIGENT, FIGHT, HIRE, OVERT, PREOCCUPIED.

Antonyms: *idle, inactive, inert, passive, relaxed, unoccupied.*

callous. Do not confuse the adjective *callous* (hardened) with the noun *callus* (an area of hardened skin).

candid

bluff
frank
ingenuous

These adjectives refer to the revealing or expressing of one's true thoughts or feelings. **Candid** can refer generally to a forthright manner or statement, but it has been heavily influenced by its related use to refer to impromptu or unposed photographs; a *candid* camera is one suitable for taking such pictures. Consequently, *candid* has acquired overtones pertaining to natural, informal, and unrehearsed statements as well: He agreed to give his *candid* opinion if his name weren't mentioned in the news story. **Frank** can also apply in a general way, but it is most often used to describe statements: a *frank* admission of guilt. In positive use, it can indicate an admirable openness and sincerity, but sometimes it can apply less favorably to someone who is unnecessarily blunt about things, despite other people's feelings: her *frank* disapproval of the way he treated their guests.

Bluff indicates a direct manner or blunt statements that may show little consciousness of or consideration for the vulnerabilities of other people, but that are usually without malicious intent: a *bluff* first sergeant who enjoyed ribbing soldiers about their inadequacies. *Bluff* can also convey, more favorably, a hearty candidness: a lovable, *bluff* old curmudgeon.

Ingenuous can refer descriptively to a lack of guile, but more often it can also suggest a person who is simple or unaware to the point of gullibility: She gave *ingenuous* answers to all of the stranger's questions. *Ingenuous* frequently applies more to manner or disposition than to individual statements. See BRUSQUE, OUTSPOKEN, SINCERE, TRUTHFUL.

Antonyms: *insincere,* MISLEADING, *sly, subtle, tricky, wily.*

capture

apprehend
arrest
bag
catch
nab
trap

These verbs all mean seize and take captive. **Capture** is the strongest. It implies the use of force or stratagem in overcoming active resistance: to *capture* an enemy fort; to *capture* an armed robber. **Catch** is the most general. It suggests seizure or detection of something fugitive or elusive—often implying active pursuit, clever entrapment, or taking by surprise: to *catch* a runaway horse; to *catch* a thief.

Arrest is applied only to persons and always carries the implication of a legal offense. It means take into custody by legal authority and may involve incarceration: An officer *caught* her fleeing the scene of the crime and *arrested* her as a suspect. **Apprehend** is a more formal word for *arrest,* involving the seizure of someone in the name of the law: He was *apprehended* five hours after his escape. *Apprehend* is the sort of term used in official documents and police reports; it seems stilted or pretentious in everyday contexts. **Nab** is an informal synonym for *catch* or *arrest.* It stresses the suddenness of the seizure, often implying rough grabbing: Police *nabbed* him as he ran out of the raided club.

In extended senses, *catch* and *capture* may mean seize something fleeting, grasp something hard to get hold of. *Capture* implies the greater difficulty and achievement: to *catch* a likeness in a sketch; an artist who *captures* a fleeting expression. Both *catch* and *capture* may also mean captivate or enthrall. [The song *caught* her fancy; The book *captured* his imagination.]

Four of these verbs are used of the seizure of animals in hunting. *Capture* is applied to wild animals brought back alive, as for exhibition in a zoo or training by an animal tamer: to *capture* lions and tigers. *Catch* is applied to small or harmless animals that are enticed by bait or fooled by camouflage: to *catch* fish; to *catch* a mouse in a trap; to *catch* a bird in a snare. **Trap** focuses on the use of a trap, snare, or pitfall to *catch* unsuspecting animals: to *trap* animals for their pelts. Persons may be *trapped* like animals by being *caught* in a cul-de-sac, cut off from all escape routes: *trapped* in a burning building; *trapped* in a dull job and a bad marriage. **Bag** is expressive of the hunter's satisfaction at having quarry literally in the bag: to *bag* an elk. In a figurative sense, *bag* stresses the triumph of the successful hunt, the bringing home of some sought-after prize: She *bagged* a prominent poet for her symposium. See GRASP, HUNT.

Antonyms: *free, let go, liberate, release.*

careful

conscientious
meticulous
punctilious
scrupulous

These adjectives are all used to describe people in reference to the care they exercise in their general behavior, in the performance of duties and in attention to detail. **Careful** is the most general term in the list. It can mean thorough or painstaking, and in this sense suggests avoidance of error by virtue of the care exercised: a *careful* writer who always checked her manuscripts repeatedly. It can mean concerned or mindful: *careful* about his manners at the party. It can mean cautious or watchful: Be *careful* when you drive on icy roads.

Conscientious and **scrupulous** agree in connoting a painstaking carefulness based on an ethical, logical, moral, or other standard. [A *conscientious* researcher, through a highly developed regard for the truth, is *careful* to avoid error or omission; A *scrupulous* juror is *careful* to weigh all the evidence and exclude all personal feelings.]

Meticulous and **punctilious** denote a strict, even excessive attention to details or standards. *Meticulous* suggests an almost finicky concern, often about trivial matters, based on a fear of making an error: A *meticulous* dresser is *careful* to avoid all violations of the canons of fashion. *Punctilious* implies an exaggerated regard for the fine points of the rules and forms prescribed by law or custom, as in etiquette: a *punctilious* social climber who was so *careful* about doing what others considered the right thing that he never developed any standards of his own. See CAUTIOUS.

Antonyms: HEEDLESS, *neglectful, negligent, remiss, sloppy.*

caress

cuddle
dandle
fondle
hug
neck
pet
smooch

These verbs refer to the pleasurable, desirous, or affectionate holding or stroking of something. **Caress** indicates a brief, gentle, or embracing motion expressive of love or desire: tenderly *caressing* her once more before boarding the train. **Fondle** may stress desire more than love, but carries the same connotations of gentleness as *caress*. Whereas *caress* might be done with the arms and body, however, *fondle* might more typically be done solely with the hands and so suggest a greater possible distance than *caress*: *fondling* the nape of her neck with his open palm. **Cuddle** is more informal than the foregoing; it specifically suggests body-to-body contact, but not necessarily to imply desire at all so much as affectionate pleasure: sleeping kittens *cuddled* next to their watchful mother. **Hug** emphasizes one possibility in *caress*, specifically suggesting an armclasp expressive of affection or desire. Being much more informal than *caress* or *fondle*, and even than *cuddle*, *hug* seems better suited to indicate earthier emotions, although it contrasts with all the foregoing by stressing intensity of feeling rather than gentleness: desperately *hugging* her injured child; turning to *hug* each other as soon as they were in a secluded part of the park. **Dandle** is perhaps the most specific of all these verbs, restricting itself most concretely to the bouncing or rocking of a child in one's lap or on one's knee: gently *dandling* the child as she sang a nursery rhyme.

Pet, in its oldest sense, is close to *fondle* in indicating the stroking of a body with one's hand: *petting* the purring cat. In a more recent sense, *pet* relates to *caress* and *fondle*, but more specifically suggests intense sexual play between lovers that stops short of intercourse: teenagers who find that *petting* in the back seats of automobiles only intensifies their frustrations. **Neck** is a slang term that exclusively pertains to this last sense of *pet*, but usually suggests kissing and may imply greater restraint than *pet*: couples who sat in the balcony of the theater and spent more time *necking* than watching the movie. **Smooch**, also a slang term, is similar in meaning to *neck*, but often suggests the loud, almost slobbery kind of kiss that has comic rather than serious or sexual overtones: the sometimes amusing, sometimes maddening spectacle of two teenagers *smooching* while munching popcorn. Unlike *pet* and *neck*, *smooch* has connotations of mutual affection; it is sometimes used in contexts meant to suggest physical displays of affection without any implication of sexual satisfaction: They've been married thirty-odd years and still love to *smooch*. See EMOTION, YEARN.

caricature

burlesque
mimicry

parody
takeoff
travesty

These nouns refer to an exaggerated rendering of the recognizable features of something in order to mock or poke fun at it. **Caricature**, most specifically, refers to a drawing or cartoon of someone in which salient features are distorted or overemphasized for comic effect. This may be done in good-humored fun or in an attempt at character assassination: a room filled with *caricatures* of Broadway stars; a *caricature* that represented the distinguished statesman as a masked gangster. *Caricature* can be used more widely of any production that deliberately distorts the recognizable features of something for whatever purpose: a novel that presents us with stereotyped *caricatures* rather than living human beings. **Takeoff** is the most informal and general of any of these nouns, referring to any exaggerated imitation designed to hold up its original to ridicule: a skit that was a *takeoff* on the absurdities of several reigning Broadway musicals; an imaginary transcript of a press conference that was a biting *takeoff* on the real thing.

Mimicry, most specifically, suggests the exaggerated acting out of another person's mannerisms and speech patterns; as with *caricature*, this may be done out of good humor or malice: his whining *mimicry* of the professor's voice; a series of impersonations in which her keen sense for *mimicry* is expertly displayed. *Mimicry* also is frequently used for a wider range of exaggerated imitations: his devastating *mimicry* of the most characteristic features of Hemingway's prose style. Sometimes, *mimicry* can be used for inept imitation of an admired figure or style: his pitiful *mimicry* of upper-class manners.

Burlesque suggests a rowdy or zany reduction to the absurd of the content or style of some production or work, especially when the original is afflicted with pomposity or excessive solemnity: a revue that was a *burlesque* of the typically woebegone naturalistic play. Sometimes, like *caricature* or *mimicry*, *burlesque* can indicate specifically the satirizing of the characteristics or mannerisms of a particular person: a figure in the novel that was clearly a *burlesque* of a well-known feminist of that day. **Parody** most specifically suggests the ridiculing of a literary work by an exaggerated imitation of its style: a howling *parody* of Longfellow's "Evangeline"; a virtuoso *parody* of the author's endlessly tortuous sentence structure. Where *burlesque* may imply broad, slashing strokes applied slapdash, *parody*, by contrast, more often suggests an extremely skillful and understated imitation that is all the more effective for so cleverly catching the style of its original. Sometimes *parodies* have been done so consummately as to be mistakenly admired as a serious effort; this could almost never happen with a *burlesque*.

Travesty was once and is still rarely used, like *burlesque* or *parody*, to suggest a broad or skillful mocking of someone else's style. It is now more often used to suggest an utterly inept or totally depraved debasement of something admirable; a shocking *travesty* of impartial judicial procedures. Sometimes, in its most hyperbolical uses, the standard to which something is compared is not even indicated: The whole concert was simply a *travesty*. See IMITATE, RIDICULE.

carry
bear
bring
convey
take
transport

These verbs are alike in referring to the moving of objects or people through space. **Carry** and **bear** both suggest the supporting of a load, but of the two only *carry* necessarily implies movement from place to place. A donkey can *bear* a heavy load simply by standing still, but *carrying* the load implies moving it somewhere: The bridge was designed to *bear* the heaviest load any train could *carry*. *Bear*, of course, can suggest movement as well, in which case a dignity of comportment and style is suggested: the royal carriage *bearing* the queen and her consort. *Carry*, on the other hand, need not emphasize the heaviness of the thing being moved: *carrying* only a small handbag and a pair of gloves. *Bear* has an additional connotation of suffering not implied by *carry*: He *bore* with him all his life the memory of her painful death.

Transport is more formal and technical than these and is normally restricted to the shipment of goods or people considered as freight: helicopters to *transport* troops to the battlefield. *Transport*, more than *carry*, emphasizes movement to a goal or destination. It contrasts with the style implied in *bear* by stressing the mere physical event of shipment as a problem in logistics.

Bring and **take** are the most informal of all these; *bring* refers to movement toward the speaker, *take* to movement away from the speaker. Both are often used imperatively: *Take* away this ghastly veal cutlet and *bring* me my dessert. In actual usage, the *to* or *from* distinction is not always observed; both may also imply an accompanied or guided movement rather than one in which one thing *carries* another. [*Take* me to the nearest hospital; The ski lift will *bring* you within a few feet of the mountaintop.]

Convey was in Shakespeare's time a simple synonym for *bring* or *take*. In this sense it is now extremely formal and is mainly used in referring to the transmitting of a message through an intermediary. [*Convey* my best wishes to the rest of your family; The ambassador personally *conveyed* the president's message to the prime minister.] *Convey* does not necessarily imply actual movement. [If my letter *conveyed* the impression that I was indifferent, please forgive me; His tone *conveyed* his real feelings more accurately than his words.] See MOVE, POSSESS.

Antonyms: LEAVE.

catastrophe

> calamity
> cataclysm
> debacle
> disaster

These nouns refer to misfortunes that result in grave loss or heavy casualties. **Catastrophe** is equally appropriate for a personal or public misfortune: taking along a team of medical personnel to cope with unexpected *catastrophes;* air pollution that has reached the proportions of a *catastrophe*. In personal application, *catastrophe* is often used hyperbolically of minor incidents: how to deal with the *catastrophe* of a stuck zipper. In reference to a general event, it may refer to the negative effect on a particular group rather than to the public as a whole: a land reform program that benefited the poor but was a *catastrophe* for rich landowners. **Cataclysm** is most sharply in contrast with these possibilities of *catastrophe* in allowing little use for personal misfortune and in restricting itself to severe mishaps that have negative results for everyone; it stresses, furthermore, a momentous disruption that results in severe damage and loss: a hairbreadth escape from nuclear *cataclysm*. More than these other nouns, *cataclysm* is especially suggestive of a natural upheaval: Eruption of the volcano would mean a *cataclysm* for the city.

Disaster is the most general of these nouns, referring both to personal and public misfortunes in a wide range of possibilities: household *disasters;* a country afflicted with the twin *disasters* of food shortages and an exploding population. Like *cataclysm, disaster* can refer to natural upheavals, but without the implications of total destruction present in *cataclysm:* a flood that was the worst *disaster* the city had ever faced. *Disaster* compares with *catastrophe* by stressing the actual harm done: They were glad they had survived the *catastrophe* and had met with no *disaster*. *Disaster*

can, of course, be used hyperbolically, like *catastrophe*, for minor misfortunes: a party that turned out to be a complete *disaster*.

Calamity is similar to *catastrophe*, but at a reduced level of intensity. It may also now sound more formal than these other nouns, or at least a shade outdated. It is more often used for a personal misfortune, seriously or hyperbolically, but it can also be used of public misfortunes on occasion, in which case it functions more abstractly or subjectively than *disaster:* a little *calamity* that happened on the way to school; a *calamity* that wiped out her savings; arguing that the bill's passage would result in a *calamity* for the whole country. **Debacle** once referred specifically to a serious disruption or natural upheaval, as of a flood, especially when severe damage or failure results: the savings-and-loan *debacle*; the Vietnam *debacle*. Now, *debacle* more often refers to an attempt that is ridiculously inept or that results in humiliating defeat: a high-level conference that was nothing short of a *debacle*. See DESTROY, FIRE.

Antonyms: BENEFIT, *blessing, boon, comfort, success*.

cautious

> circumspect
> discreet
> guarded
> prudent
> wary

These adjectives refer to thoughtful restraint in behavior. **Cautious** is the most general of these, suggesting a careful holding back from action until all possibilities have been considered: a *cautious* attitude toward buying into any company. *Cautious* can, as well, suggest careful action, in which case it suggests a slow, tentative, or even timid manner: their *cautious* crossing of the rickety bridge. **Wary** is an intensification of all the implications of *cautious*, stressing an extremely hesitant manner that sees every course of action fairly bristling with dangers: giving a *wary* reply to the enigmatic question of the stranger; asking campers to be particularly *wary* of starting a forest fire during the dry season.

Guarded also intensifies the implications of *cautious*, but puts special stress on a *wary* manner in social interchanges that is marked by a reluctance to reveal too much about oneself or give too much of oneself except to people with whom one is thoroughly familiar: a *guarded*, noncommittal answer to the interviewer's blunt questions. It may also suggest a deliberate suppression of one's feelings for fear of having them proved wrong: a *guarded* optimism about the outcome of the election. Whereas the former adjectives point to restrained behavior that might result from fear, unfamiliarity, or uneasiness, **prudent** suggests action that is the outcome of wisdom gained by experience. Such action need not be *cautious* or *wary* at all; these adjectives might, in fact, suggest the opposite of *prudent* when no real cause for fear exists: It was not *prudent* to be so *cautious* in climbing the slope, because it put her in constant danger of losing her balance.

Circumspect and **discreet** both refer primarily to social behavior. *Circumspect* indicates a strict adherence to social proprieties. [*Prudent* politicians must lead rigorously *circumspect* lives; if they cannot, they had best be *cautious* as to which temptations they allow themselves to surrender to.] *Discreet* refers to a different kind of social propriety than *circumspect*, indicating an ability to keep the confidences of other people and to be extremely *guarded* about entrusting personal details to others: wondering how *discreet* her friend could be about what he knew of her past life. In a less specific use, *discreet* approaches the meaning of *circumspect*, suggesting a *prudent* choice of inoffensive behavior or an ability to handle difficult matters with tact and delicacy. In this same sense, *prudent* nevertheless contrasts with *circumspect* in suggesting a more intuitive, less rigid approach to social behavior. See AFRAID, PRUDENCE.

Antonyms: BOLD, BRAVE, *confident*, DARING, *reckless*.

cave
burrow
cavern
grotto
tunnel

These nouns refer to a hollow or opening in the earth, either natural or artificial. **Cave** is least specific and can be applied to any hollowed-out area in the earth, usually one that occurs in the side of a mountain, cliff, or hill. The cliff dwellers found that natural *caves* gave them warmth and protection during the Ice Age. Bears, for similar reasons, hibernate in *caves* during the winter.

Cavern, when used in place of *cave*, tends to sound inflated in diction. It can be used accurately, however, to refer to a more extensive subterranean *cave* or set of *caves* indefinite in extent, especially when it suggests a natural chamber such as one formed in limestone by running water. In this case, the

sense of an opening into the slanted face of a hill is not necessarily maintained. One or more mouths of the *cavern* may open onto relatively level ground: The tourists clutched the guide rail and hurried along the shelf of the *cavern*, oppressed by its airlessness and lack of light. *Cavern* may also be used metaphorically for any obscure recess: the dark *caverns* of his mind.

Grotto is the most specific of these terms, though it can refer either to an artificial or natural hollow. When artificial, it is a cavelike, manmade structure built as a recreational retreat or shrine: The townspeople placed a Christmas tree within their quaintly decorated *grotto* and sang carols there throughout the holidays. When natural, a *grotto* is typically picturesque, often forming a recess in a *cavern*, one that may be filled with odd-shaped stalagmites and stalactites: Daylight must never touch the cave paintings in the *grotto* at Lascaux.

Burrow and **tunnel** are alike in suggesting an artificial opening in the earth and often implying a linear shape as contrasted with the roughly spherical hollow most typical of a *cave*. *Burrow* refers to the hollow dug by an animal, such as a gopher or a rabbit: The *burrow* of a gopher usually has two openings a considerable distance away from each other. *Tunnel* can refer to a hollow in the earth dug by an animal, but it is used most frequently to refer to one dug by people. If its purpose is to permit movement from one point to another, as in a subway system, a *tunnel* would be mainly horizontal over most of its course. If dug for purposes of mining, a *tunnel* would usually slant sharply downward into the depths of the earth: The miners were trapped in the *tunnel* by a cave-in along the passage just behind them. See HOLE.

celebration
ball
banquet
feast
festival
festivity
party

These nouns refer to joyful gatherings of people. **Celebration** and **party** are both general, suggesting any coming together of a number of people to rejoice over some happy event. *Celebrations* and *parties* can be large or small, public or private, formal or informal, but *celebration* usually connotes a large gathering and *party* a more intimate group, often of persons who are close friends or at least acquainted: a candidate's victory *celebration* that drew nearly a thousand people;

He felt fortunate to be a guest at one of her small, select dinner *parties*. **Ball** implies an official or stately occasion, and suggests a scrupulously selected guest list and formal attire: the debutante's coming out *ball;* the President's inaugural *ball.*

Festival suggests the *celebration* of an entire community either periodically at a significant time of the year or on some important occasion: the town's annual harvest *festival*. It is frequently applied to a planned series of cultural events: Lincoln Center's Mozart *festival;* such lures for summer tourists as the Salzburg and Spoleto *festivals*. It is also used to describe annual religious ceremonies: the *festival* of Trinity Sunday. **Feast**, like *festival*, has a religious connotation: the *feast* of Palm Sunday. But in wider applications, it suggests a single *celebration* at which a great deal of food is eaten: all the knights and ladies gathering for a sumptuous *feast*. Outside a religious or historical context, *feast* may sound outmoded now, except in metaphorical or hyperbolical uses: That dinner you gave was a real *feast*. **Banquet**, in fact, has almost replaced *feast* in the sense of a formal or official dinner; it suggests the honoring of a special event or guest or the observing of an important occasion: After the wedding *banquet*, there will be a formal *ball*.

Festivity is vaguer in reference than most of these related nouns. It now might sound like inflated diction when it replaces *festival* or, especially, *party:* promising to look in on the *festivities*. It is still viable, however, in suggesting a mood of convivial merry-making: the air of *festivity* that even the smallest town takes on during Christmas. See RITE.

censor. Do not confuse the verb *censor* (subject a book, film, etc., to examination or removal) with the verb *censure* (rebuke).

center

core
heart
hub
middle
midst

These nouns refer to a position equidistant from the extremities or periphery, or to the vital part of something. **Center**, most concretely, indicates such a point within the circumference of a circle or a sphere: the *center* of the earth. It can, of course, suggest an approximate location of this sort within any configura-

tion: at the *center* of the intersection. Used metaphorically, it suggests a place of extreme density or importance: a metropolitan *center;* at the very *center* of her philosophy. **Middle**, most typically, indicates a point equidistant from the two ends of something: folding the paper down the *middle*. It can be used more loosely, as an informal substitute for *center*, especially when an approximation is intended: right in the *middle* of the ocean. It is better used for a moment of time than *center:* in the *middle* of the day. It can also indicate a point or moment that occurs in the thick of things: in the *middle* of our other troubles. Here, it suggests passivity as compared with *center:* the man who was at the *center* of the controversy. **Midst** is now mostly used in this last sense of *middle* but without the implication of passivity; even here it might sound excessively formal except in some standard expressions: in the *midst* of battle.

Core specifically suggests the *center* of a solid figure: an apple *core;* the *core* of the Washington Monument. Metaphorically, it has a wide range of uses suggesting the irreducible minimum or quintessence of something that may in its fullness be extensive and manifold: The *core* of our appeal is freedom of speech; the *core* of his argument. **Heart**, at its most concrete, contrasts with all these other nouns in referring to a vital organ rather than to an exact or approximate *center*. In metaphorical uses, however, it may refer to the vital *center* of something: the very *heart* of the city. It may also, like *middle*, refer approximately to the point of greatest density: in the *heart* of the jungle. In more abstract uses, it relates most closely to *core* in suggesting the sine qua non of something, although in this case the irreducible *core* is also seen as animating principle. [The Bill of Rights is more than an addendum to the Constitution; it is the *heart* of our democracy.]

Hub, most concretely, refers to the *center* of a wheel; in metaphorical uses, it may refer to the psychological *center* of a city, even one laid out on a grid system: the *hub* of business activity in lower Manhattan. *Hub* seems more exactly used when a network with radiating arms is suggested: the *hub* of the White House party around whom the lesser known spread out in diminishing rank. See KERNEL.
Antonyms: BOUNDARY, EDGE, PERIMETER.

ceremonial. Do not confuse the adjective *ceremonial* (formal) with the adjective *ceremonious* (elaborately performed).

chance

accidental
adventitious
contingent
fortuitous
incidental

These adjectives refer to that which occurs either unexpectedly or without prearrangement or plan. **Chance** is the least formal of these. On one hand, it can indicate coincidence: a *chance* meeting in the street. On the other, it can suggest an occurrence that is governed by no known physical laws: the development of quantum theory to explain seemingly *chance* shifts in atomic particles. **Accidental** stresses the lack of intention or forethought, but is now strongly influenced by the noun accident, meaning mishap, to suggest an error that brings undesirable or even disastrous results: an *accidental* misreading of her bank balance; the specter of an *accidental* nuclear holocaust. **Fortuitous** can point to something that is apparently without cause or design, but it often suggests a good or desirable occurrence, an overtone that puts *fortuitous* in the strongest possible contrast with *accidental*: a *fortuitous* change of plan that kept them out of the city during the *accidental* blackout. Nevertheless, *fortuitous* is not to be used as a direct synonym of *fortunate*.

Contingent can refer, most simply, to what is unexpected or unforeseen: a *contingent* delay that inconvenienced travelers. More often, *contingent* points to something that is dependent on an uncertain event or condition; in this case *contingent* is used with *on* or *upon*: an increase in pay that is *contingent upon* increasing productivity.

Incidental points to something occurring without design or regularity: an *incidental* shrub or two beside the path. Thus, *incidental* can refer to something unplanned or unexpected, but usually of value, however slight, especially when this is a concomitant or side benefit gained in the pursuit of some other goal: an *incidental* knowledge of Nigerian folksongs gained during her stint in the Peace Corps. **Adventitious** can be a much more formal substitute for *incidental*, pointing to a *fortuitous* acquisition or coming together: *adventitious* circumstances that encouraged the rise of capitalism. Like *incidental*, *adventitious* can also indicate something that is not inherent, particularly something that is extrinsic to a primary consideration: *adventitious* flaws that did not detract from the power of the time-battered piece of sculpture. See MARGINAL, PROVISIONAL, RANDOM.

Antonyms: *CONCLUSIVE, INEVITABLE, INEXORABLE.*

change

alter,
convert
modify
transfigure
transform
transmogrify
transmute

These verbs all refer to the process of making something over or making it different. **Change**, the most general and least formal, can mean any process of differentiation, slight or great, in appearance or essence, in quality or quantity: *changing* the desert into farmland; *changing* his mind; *changing* the way they wore their hair.

Alter, **convert**, and **modify** suggest relatively slight revisions of something, generally in appearance or use. Each also has a use with somewhat different effect for a change in attitude or belief. As listed, these verbs move from the slightly to the highly formal, with perhaps a similar progression in implication, from lesser to greater change. *Alter*, most commonly, refers to *changing* the fit of clothes, either making them looser or tighter by letting out or taking in seams: the tailor who *altered* the hemline of the skirt. It also commonly refers to the redecoration of buildings: workmen *altering* the drugstore for the convenience of patrons. In both of these uses, *alter* implies that the basic structure is worked with and around rather than contravened, although no value judgment is present concerning the result. *Alter*, more than any of these verbs except *change*, has a wide range of application. [He *altered* his stand on abortion rights; The sales manager *altered* the price tag.] *Convert* suggests the adaptation of an object by a specially designed addition that will increase its usefulness; an attachment that *converts* a vacuum cleaner into a paint sprayer. When used of attitudes or beliefs, *convert* suggests a more drastic change than *alter*: the people who *converted* to Buddhism. *Modify*, when used of objects, suggests more basic changes than *alter* or *convert*, in which function, more importantly than appearance, is *changed*: car antennas *modified* by teenagers into lethal weapons. When applied to attitudes, however, *modify* implies less change than either *alter* or *convert*. It often has a special overtone of making less extreme. [She didn't *alter* her position so much as *modify* its severity; in any case, you could hardly say she was *converted* by the arguments of the opposition.]

The remaining verbs suggest more drastic changes than the preceding, changes so profound that an entirely new entity may appear to have taken the place of the old. **Transmute** emphasizes an elemental change in the inner structure of a material, often implying a shift from a lower to a higher state: coal *transmuted* to diamonds by eons of intense pressure; alchemists vainly trying to *transmute* lead into gold. Change of this magnitude, obviously, is not accomplished by revision, as in *alter*, or by addition, as in *convert*. **Transform** suggests change equally as profound, but in concentrating on outward form or appearance, it is perhaps slightly less intense than *transmute* and certainly more general. *Transform* may suggest change in a person or a definite entity, *transmute* in a less well defined quantity; *transmute* also tends to suggest a slow, analyzable or scientific process, *transform* a sudden or mystical change: the frog that was *transformed* into a prince; plans that were *transformed* overnight into reality. *Transform* also lends itself to hyperbole, perhaps overused: candles and a damask cloth that *transformed* the oak table into an elegant dining table.

Transfigure intensifies the mystical element in *transform,* adding a note of supernatural or religious rapture: the statue of St. Theresa *transfigured* by ecstasy. When used hyperbolically of more common circumstances, a positive or joyful change is indicated: her plain features *transfigured* with tenderness. **Transmogrify**, on the other hand, always stresses negative change, bizarre or ugly: the peasant lad *transmogrified* into a dragon. In more usual circumstances, the effect is comic: the graceful child *transmogrified* into a gangling adolescent. See ADDITION, BUILD, DEVISE.

Antonyms: *maintain, stabilize, sustain.*

characteristic

attribute
feature
mark
peculiarity
quality
trait

These nouns all refer to an aspect that is an identifiable part of a person, place, mood, or object. **Characteristic** may imply neutral description in referring to any aspect of something, without evaluating its relative importance to the whole: a psychological report that lists every possible *characteristic* of the person being studied. More often, however, the noun suggests an aspect of the whole that is regarded as typical: a town that had all the *characteristics* usual to any seaside resort; the preponderance of *characteristics* that supported the diagnosis of alcoholism. *Characteristic* has many scientific or technical uses in this sense, but may be overused in other contexts where a less formal word is available.

Attribute may escape the charge of inflated diction or imprecise jargon when used in place of *characteristic* for nontechnical situations. It also may be used to refer to something typical, but leans perhaps to greater neutrality in suggesting one of many possible aspects that make up a whole: eagerness to learn, an often overlooked *attribute* in small children. **Peculiarity**, on the other hand, is far from neutral in suggesting an unpleasant *attribute* that is quite noticeable: a *peculiarity* in his shuffling walk; a *peculiarity* of mind that insisted on an exact order in doing even the smallest task; a *peculiarity* of the northern climate.

Feature and **mark**, like *peculiarity*, refer to something quite noticeable, but *feature* most readily suggests something positive, while *mark* may suggest either positive or negative aspects. *Feature* most specifically refers to physical appearance: an aquiline nose that was her most attractive *feature*. In more general uses, it may refer to an unusual or outstanding aspect of something: the siesta that is a distinguishing *feature* of life in Mexico. In the entertainment or advertising worlds, *feature* is used to refer to a special or added attraction: the *feature* of the evening's entertainment; the new automobile's compactness as an added *feature*. *Mark* is stronger than *feature* in suggesting something that sets its possessor apart: generosity as the *mark* of a civilized person. But it has negative uses that compare with *peculiarity*: the sadism that is the disfiguring *mark* of all oppressive regimes. In this use, *mark* differs from *peculiarity* in suggesting an intrinsic rather than accidental or external departure from the norm.

Trait and **quality** refer to more abstract *attributes* than *peculiarity, feature,* or *mark. Trait,* most specifically, is used to describe abiding behavior patterns, rather than single or momentary actions: a *trait* of suspiciousness that underlay all his relationships with people; *traits* of fortitude and industry that spelled survival for the settlers of a new world. *Quality* is more general than any of the other nouns here; it may suggest a passing aspect or an abiding one; it may suggest positive or negative *attributes*. It may imply measurable, concrete aspects, but is often used, contrarily, to suggest a vague or subtle gathering of impressions: a *quality* of despair in her drawn face; a strange *quality* of light in the room; *qualities* of exuberance and spontaneity that made the people easy to live with. See TEMPERAMENT.

charming

bewitching
captivating
enchanting
entrancing
fascinating
winning

These adjectives are superlatives used mainly to describe the pleasing manner of an attractive person, usually a woman. **Charming** emphasizes gracious behavior or elegance of manner, especially in social situations: Her *charming* considerateness made everyone feel at ease. It applies readily to feminine accomplishments or apparel: a *charming* table setting; a *charming* gown. Used of men, it suggests sophistication and suavity: the *charming* man with the slight French accent. Originally, it suggested being put under a magic charm; the force of this original meaning is still felt, perhaps, when *charming* refers to a beautiful scene or landscape: the *charming* mountain views we glimpsed through the windows of our train.

Bewitching, **enchanting**, and **entrancing** also once suggested being put under a magic spell. Now, used to describe an attractive woman, they do not suggest social grace so much as qualities of freshness, strangeness, or exotic allure, all considerably less innocuous than anything implied by *charming*. One might call the woman next door *charming*, for all her simplicity, but one would think twice about calling her *bewitching*—unless one lived in a rather unusual neighborhood. *Bewitching* most strongly suggests this exotic quality; *enchanting*, through overuse, is more innocuous than its two companions—shading off toward *charming*. *Entrancing* still has some of its freshness left, suggesting an ability to command an onlooker's stunned, almost hypnotized attention: stupidly staring back at every *entrancing* smile she gave him. The same scale of forces for these three prevails when they are used to describe scenery. None of them would be a likely description for a man.

Captivating and **winning** suggest a different and fainter submerged metaphor—of military conquest. They might both be most precisely used to imply an initial resistance on the part of the onlooker. *Winning*, however, suggests warm-hearted sunniness of disposition, whereas *captivating* carries an overtone of sexual allure and vivacity. *Winning* may also pertain to a single act, while *captivating* applies more easily to an entire manner of behavior: her *winning* appeal to him for help; his fading resistance to the *captivating* figure she made, standing alone and silent on the moonlit piazza. Both adjectives may describe men, in which case an attempted conquest of a woman is implied, *winning* referring to an ingratiating pleasantness of manner and *captivating* to a rakish insouciance. [She quickly forgot his *winning* courtesy and consideration when she saw the *captivating* smile of the man who rode by in the white convertible.] *Winning* would have little use in describing scenery, but *captivating* might suggest a collection of fanciful qualities that sweeps one away in spite of one's distrust for the strange or unusual: one of thousands who surrendered wholeheartedly to the *captivating* uniqueness of Venice.

Fascinating has perhaps suffered less from overuse as a superlative than these other adjectives. Although more general in application, it still can suggest, like *entrancing*, a prospect that is almost hypnotic in its inviting quality. It applies to men as well as to women, to any attractive scene or view, or to any idea or thing that is extremely interesting. In all cases it is like *captivating* and *winning* in suggesting the ability to overcome resistance, however strong: Against his will, he found himself caught up again and again in the life of this most *fascinating* of peoples. See BEAUTIFUL, LIVELY, PLEASING.

Antonyms: *dull*, REPULSIVE, *tedious*, UGLY.

chatter

babble
gibber
jabber
prate
prattle
yak

These verbs all refer to confused, rapid, incoherent, or worthless talk. **Chatter** is the most general; it may refer to quick rambling talk that is light, idle, or inconsequential, or it may refer to a din of voices all speaking at once: the woman who pretended to listen silently as her husband *chattered* on and on; people *chattering* in the backyard like a flock of magpies. *Chatter* is perhaps most appropriate to describe a high-pitched voice. **Babble** suggests the almost idiotically meandering talk of a person or group of persons: the drunkard who *babbled* out his life history to everyone in the crowded bar; the U. S. Senators in the cloakroom who *babbled* in one continuous uproar.

Jabber is a jocose, slangy way of referring to rapid interchanges of a conversation one doesn't understand or considers trivial: two merchants *jabbering* away in their bargaining for the sheer delight of hearing their own voices. The suggestion is even stronger in *jabber* of a frenetic pace without letup. **Gibber** is more strongly pejorative than *jabber* when applied to people. It suggests that the sounds produced are meaningless: dancers who *gibbered* in grunts and groans that seemed to keep time with the music. *Gibber* may be purely descriptive when applied to animals: monkeys *gibbering* back and forth in the branches overhead. **Prattle** shares with *jabber* and *gibber* suggestions of unintelligible sounds, but if confined to children or sounds in nature, the result is not pejorative: a baby *prattling* contentedly after nursing; a lazy waterfall that *prattled* to itself all day. If used of adult speech, of course, *prattle* suggests stupidity or childishness: the homeless man who *prattled* to himself on the park bench.

In **prate**, the suggestion of frenetically paced group speech present in *chatter* and *babble* is absent, as well as the unintelligibility present in those verbs grouped with *babble*. *Prate,* on the contrary, most readily suggests a tedious monologue full of the speaker's self-importance: a teacher who *prates* on disconnectedly but relentlessly about everything that comes into his head. **Yak** is a slang term for the action of conversing that is neither necessarily hectic nor unintelligible; it suggests, instead, a contented, relaxed flow of talk that is idle or trivial: His favorite pastime at college was *yakking* with friends at all-night bull sessions. *Yak* can also carry a pejorative implication, in which case constant, frenetic, and noisy talk may be indicated: She was nearly driven mad by the way her husband *yakked* at her without letup. See CONVERSATION, CRY, RAILLERY, TALKATIVE.

cheer

encourage
exhilarate
gladden
warm

These verbs refer to the raising of someone's morale or to the creating of a positive or lively frame of mind. **Cheer** suggests, most concretely, that some occurrence has given a boost to an otherwise despondent outlook: We were *cheered* that the sun had finally come out and would at least dry our damp clothing; *cheered* by news that one helicopter had sighted a feeble fire farther up the mountain slope. **Encourage**, like *cheer*, may refer to a raising of morale; as such it implies a resulting frame of mind that is less hopeful than with *cheer: encouraged* to look back on the considerable distance they had come, but still uneasy about the distance they had yet to travel. In another context, *encourage* may suggest the awakening of interest in someone else through sympathetic concern:

All the students had been *encouraged* by their teacher to take their writing seriously.

Gladden may suggest the same situation as *cheer*, but like *encourage* it can function in its own context, without reference to the raising of a flagging morale: *gladdened* by their success at building a fire big enough to be seen a good distance off; *gladdened* by the news that he had become the grandfather of twins. *Gladden* can sometimes, however, sound faintly outdated or a shade too formal when compared with *cheer* and especially with *encourage*. **Warm** may refer to a revival of morale or to a simple intensity of emotion deeper than that implied by *cheer* or *gladden: warmed* by the ease with which they had cleaned up what had seemed the hopeless mess before them; *warmed* to know that their savings would go toward seeing their grandchildren through college.

Exhilarate is unique among these verbs in suggesting a situation in which one is filled with a bracing exuberance and zest: He felt listless until the sea breeze *exhilarated* him and steadied his nerves. See ENCOURAGE, JOYOUS, LIVELY, MERRIMENT.

Antonyms: *chill, depress,* DISCOURAGE, *dispirit,* RIDICULE, *sadden.*

cheerful

blithe
cheery
happy
sunny
winsome

These adjectives refer to positive frames of mind or to a brightly optimistic disposition. **Cheerful** suggests an extroverted and open manner that is warm, pleasant, and contented: She smiled back at the *cheerful* faces of her students; the *cheerful* vacationers at the resort. **Cheery**, by contrast, can suggest a *cheerful* manner that is forced or intrusive in its attempts to make others feel better: the *cheery* nurses in the hospital who proved to be such a nuisance. *Cheery* can sometimes be less unpleasant in tone: giving me a *cheery* wink as I passed by.

Happy suggests an inward state of contentment that does not necessarily show itself in any outward bustle such as *cheerful* or *cheery* may indicate: so *happy* at the news that tears gathered in his eyes and ran down his cheeks. **Sunny** refers particularly to an untroubled disposition that is warm and friendly: a *sunny* laughter that rang out from the kitchen; the *sunny* expressions of children at a circus.

Both **blithe** and **winsome** suggest a lack of seriousness in manner. *Blithe* particularly indicates an almost reckless insouciance or indomitable lightheadedness: a *blithe* way of stuffing unpaid bills in a drawer, as though doing so would take care of them; a *blithe* willingness to try anything on impulse. *Winsome* contrasts with *blithe* by suggesting an almost staid sweetness or delicacy of manner, warm but subdued; it is most often applied to women: a *winsome* smile that in the next minute turned into an embarrassed blush. See BLITHE, JOYOUS, LIVELY, OPTIMISTIC.

Antonyms: *downcast*, GLOOMY, MISERABLE, SAD, *woebegone*.

choose
cull
elect
pick
select

The verbs **choose**, **pick**, and **select** mean take one or more from a number of things available—usually as a matter of preference. They may be used as exact synonyms: a family buying a lawn mower *chooses* (or *picks* or *selects*) the one best suited to the family's needs. However, these verbs have separate shades of meaning that may make one or another of them most appropriate in a particular context. In *choose*, for example, the emphasis is on the act of will exercised in making the decision and, sometimes, on the finality of the decision. When we say that young people *choose* careers, we imply that they are making voluntary decisions and that they intend to pursue those careers for the rest of their working lives. To *select* is to *choose* from several things (we *choose*, never *select*, one of two alternatives), and it suggests discrimination and a careful weighing of the reasons for the choice: At the beginning of the trial, a great deal of time was spent *selecting* the jurors. *Pick* is less precise in meaning than the other two verbs and can be used to cover situations in which neither decision making nor discrimination is required: A shopper in a supermarket, confronted by twenty cans of tomatoes of identical size and quality, will often *pick* the nearest one.

Elect usually connotes choosing from a limited number of alternatives. In its usual sense, it means *choose* a person for office by a majority or plurality of votes. [The high-school class *elected* him treasurer; The American people *elect* a president every four years.]

Cull means *pick* the good from the bad or, conversely, the bad from the good: A chef who is about to cook dried beans usually *culls* them first to remove dis-

colored beans. See DECIDE, DISCRIMINATE.
Antonyms: FORSWEAR, REJECT.

circumlocution
euphemism
euphuism
indirectness
periphrasis

These nouns indicate a roundabout way of expressing ideas or of referring to something. **Circumlocution**, derived from Latin roots that mean speaking around, is quite formal. **Periphrasis**, derived from comparable Greek roots, is even more formal and more technical in tone. Both pertain to the substitution of lengthy phraseology for more simple expressions: the *circumlocutions* of a candidate trying to win friends on both sides of every issue; judicial rulings that are clogged with *periphrasis*, peppered with whereases, and understandable by no one. *Circumlocution*, being slightly more common, has gathered more connotations; it can suggest avoidance of direct statement out of squeamishness, insincerity, self-interest, or a misplaced desire for elegance: the emphasis of diplomatic protocol on its own strange set of polite *circumlocutions*. *Periphrasis*, by contrast, is more restricted to a grammatical context and is perhaps more neutral in simply indicating the choice of a longer rather than a shorter expression of comparable function. "In order to" is sometimes a needless *periphrasis* for "to."

Indirectness is a much less formal, much more general, and much clearer synonym for the previous pair of nouns. It refers to the avoidance of simple or forceful expressions for whatever reason: an *indirectness* of style that stems from his reliance on the passive voice and his constant reference to himself as "one." By contrast, **euphuism** is highly specific. It comes from the name of a literary character, *Euphues*, the subject of two Elizabethan works of fiction by John Lyly. It refers to a ridiculous straining after an elegant prose style by clothing a paucity of thought in orotund parallelisms, flowery similes, and other verbal frills.

Euphemism, sometimes confused with *euphuism*, comes from Greek roots meaning speak well. It refers to a specific tendency in speech or writing that involves substituting a mild, inexact, or technical-sounding term for a more forceful, clear, or blunt term when the latter is thought capable of giving offense. *Euphemisms* are commonly substituted for words pertaining to parts of the body, death, sex, and bodily functions. "Limb" was a Victorian *euphemism* for "leg." Some use the *euphemism* "pass away" instead of saying "die." "The departed" is often used as a *euphemism* for "the dead." See TALKATIVE, VERBOSE.

Antonyms: *brevity, conciseness, condensation, directness, succinctness, terseness.*

circumscribe

    bound
    contain
    encircle
    enclose
    encompass
    envelop
    surround

These verbs refer to something that lies on all or many sides of something else. **Circumscribe** is the most formal and the most precise in reference, specifically indicating the drawing of a line around a plane figure so as to touch as many points of the figure as possible: a square *circumscribed* by a circle. Used to describe geographical situations, it need not adhere to this strict geometrical definition, but it still suggests something hedged in on all sides: a small country completely *circumscribed* by mountains. In other uses, the verb emphasizes the restriction of something within set limits: severely *circumscribing* the freedom to dissent in time of war. **Encompass** means to take in or embrace. Like *circumscribe,* it may refer to a line drawn around a figure, but it more particularly indicates something set within a circle. It may suggest, furthermore, a setting of limits but more often implies a measuring of natural capacities: a view that *encompassed* all of the campus; a mind that could *encompass* only a few obvious truths; an erudition that *encompassed* amazing expanses of abstruse knowledge.

Bound almost exclusively pertains to the setting of limits found in *circumscribe.* It may not, however, necessarily suggest a total hedging in on all sides by the same medium: a city accessible to motorists from the north, although *bounded* on the south and east by jungle, and on the west by desert. **Surround**, by contrast, suggests something hedged in on all sides by the same thing, and thus it might be thought a less formal substitute for *circumscribe. Surround,* however, often emphasizes an undesirable, hostile, or dangerous *circumscribing*: a cabin *surrounded* by the wilderness; decimated troops *surrounded* by enemy forces; watching the wolves *surround* the injured elk. *Surround* can, of course, be used without negative implications: *surrounded* by the smiling faces of his friends. **Encircle** is closest to *surround* in its generality, but it suggests a

tighter cluster about a central object and most often indicates a deliberate grouping for a definite reason: Oppressed serfs throughout the *surrounding* countryside joined together to *encircle* the castle.

While the previous verbs suggest, in simplest terms, a two-dimensional *encircling,* the remaining verbs all may indicate a three-dimensional gathering of one thing about another. **Envelop** refers most strictly to such a situation. It suggests the total *surrounding* of something, especially by folds or layers, so as to cover up or obscure the thing within: a porcelain vase *enveloped* in cotton; an airplane *enveloped* in fog; He *enveloped* the injured woman in the folds of his cloak. In more metaphorical uses, it may refer to a pervasive atmosphere or a totally preoccupied state of mind: *enveloped* by a sense of warm, sleepy contentment. It may also have overtones of protectiveness or secrecy: the overarching love with which she *enveloped* her son; an episode *enveloped* in mystery. **Enclose** is similar to *envelop* except that the latter often suggests an amorphous material in which something else may become lost or blurred, whereas *enclose* may suggest a hollowed solid or anything especially designed to fit around something else: a clock *enclosed* by a glass bell. *Enclose* suggests specifically a difficulty of access and often carries overtones of imprisonment or protectiveness: radioactive substances *enclosed* in heavy lead containers; a couple *enclosed* in a world of drab routine; a sleeping child *enclosed* in its mother's arms. **Contain** may refer to the mere presence of one thing inside another: plants that *contain* potassium; the safe that *contained* the jewels. But it may more specifically suggest the resistance of the thing *contained:* measures that might *contain* the vandalism of the students. It has also become a recent fad word in the terminology of power politics: the deployment of missile bases to *contain* the aggressor. See BOUNDARY, CONFINE.

cite

    adduce
    quote
    refer

These verbs are concerned with the presentation of supporting evidence in discussion, analysis, or argument. **Cite** is a highly specific verb, precisely directed to this concept. To *cite* an example is to bring it forward as proof or illustration of a point. *Cite* almost always suggests a backing up of assertions by authoritative investigation or knowledge, rather than a mere hazarding of guesses. In particular, *cite* often implies a collection or repository of sources or examples that any other investigator could easily go to for corroboration:

The bibliography *cited* more than a hundred works the author had consulted. *Cite* may also suggest that a complete and detailed presentation of an argument is being given: to *cite* the reasons behind the United Nations' delay in responding to the Iraqi attack on Kuwait.

Of all these verbs, **refer** is the least definite in suggesting how much or how little corroborating evidence will be presented. A treatise might merely *refer* to well-known facts in passing, on the assumption that they will be familiar to everyone. On the other hand, especially in verbal discussions, *refer* may imply the looking up of authoritative information about the point in question: to *refer* to the dictionary; turning to the Bible in order to *refer* to the exact wording of a disputed quotation.

Adduce means bring forward for proof or consideration, and may refer to an example, argument, or item of evidence. It suggests a succinct listing of the details that support a case, although each detail might be sketched rather than developed in full: *adducing* reasons why the United States should have entered World War II in 1939. One might *refer* to definitive proof that the world is round, but one would have to be more specific in order to *adduce* the reasons why this is known to be true. In other instances, *adduce* may be closely synonymous with the other verbs in this set, but it is much more formal and may seem unduly erudite or stuffy in tone.

Quote refers to an exact, word-for-word citation of one's sources. If one *cites* another person's arguments, one may be paraphrasing them. But if one claims to be *quoting* those arguments, then one is responsible for reproducing them exactly as they appear in the source. [The President had his aides pass out typescripts of his speech, since he was all too familiar with the inability of journalists to *quote* his remarks accurately.] See QUOTATION.

claim

perquisite
right
title

These nouns are concerned with establishing ownership or possession of land, money, or other valuables. A **claim** may be an actual document that permits one to possess land formerly in the public domain—or it may be the land itself: a *claim* of only a few acres that seemed worthless until gold was discovered nearby. In a more general sense, a *claim* may be an assertion of legal or moral entitlement to something that is held, withheld, or owed to someone by another:

the drama coach who made a *claim* on the estate of the deceased actress; the protectorate's *claim* to full independence; an injured workman's *claim* to compensation. **Title**, like *claim*, may also refer to an actual document that gives one possession of land or real estate. But unlike a *claim* that one may earn or come to possess by following a certain set of procedures, a *title* cannot usually be had except by purchase or inheritance. [The prospector staked, then filed, his *claim*; Her uncle's will gave her *title* to the condominium.]

A **perquisite**, more often called a fringe benefit, is something that accrues to one as an added advantage of one's usual job or position: *perquisites* that included unlimited free travel. It may suggest a monetary consideration in the form of a tip or bonus; and it may be specified in writing, as in a union contract, or may be an unwritten understanding between employer and employee.

A **right** is the most general of these terms and might substitute for any of them. In its narrowest sense, it may imply a legal proof of ownership, or a contractual agreement that has been put into writing. In its larger sense, it may refer to those things to which someone feels entitled without actually possessing them; such a *right* may be a moral, ethical, emotional, or tactical one: a *right* to ten percent of all proceeds from the book's sales; a child's *right* to love and understanding; the inalienable *rights* of life, liberty, and the pursuit of happiness. See RIGHT.

clarify

elucidate
explain
explicate
interpret

These verbs refer to attempts at removing confusion or making something understandable. **Clarify** usually pertains to words or actions that are introduced to make clear an earlier event, situation, statement, or state of affairs: a position paper released to *clarify* her voting record on past legislation; contradictory answers he made no attempt to *clarify*; adding details to the sketch that would *clarify* the spatial relationships; a plot structure that needed *clarifying*. **Elucidate** is a more formal substitute for *clarify*. While the root of *clarify* refers literally to clearness, the root of *elucidate* refers to light. To *elucidate* something, therefore, is to throw light on it. The verb's use reflects this in indicating any enlightening process that puts an end to confusion: searching for the clues that would *elucidate* the mystery; psychological theories intended to *elucidate* human behavior. Thus, *elucidate* in its very formality has a wider range of application than *clarify*. **Explicate** is more restricted and specific in use than the foregoing. It refers to a point-by-point discussion of a complex matter, especially as in the paraphrase and analysis of a literary text: asking each student to *explicate* one difficult poem; popular books that attempt to *explicate* difficult scientific theories.

Explain and **interpret** are far less formal than the previous verbs and have wider ranges of use. A person may *explain* a thing by describing its form or structure, tracing its origins and development, showing its operation or use, or citing its validity and the relations of its parts. Hence, an expert might *elucidate* one detail of a complex matter without *explaining* the whole. In its most informal sense, *explain* suggests a verbal attempt to justify actions or to make them understood: trying to *explain* why they missed the party. When *explain* is closer in meaning to *elucidate,* it may suggest a total falling into place of a causal sequence: experiments designed to *explain* the mechanics of heredity; the discovery of several notes that *explained* his homicidal outburst. *Interpret* is like *explicate* in suggesting a point-by-point treatment of an earlier situation, pronouncement, or event so that it can be understood; it is like *elucidate* in implying the use of knowledge or insight to cast light on some baffling problem or puzzle, though it differs in stressing personal judgment or understanding: to *interpret* a symbolic dream; to *interpret* an obscure piece of writing. In a limited sense, *interpret* may refer to oral translation from one language to another: A skilled linguist was needed to *interpret* the statements of the visiting head of state. Less specifically, *interpret* may imply any sort of after-the-fact analysis, in which case it may point to a less exhaustive or technical approach than *explicate*: a highly trained journalist who *interpreted* economic trends for the layman. See EXPLANATION, INFORM.

Antonyms: *becloud, bedim, befog, complicate,* CONFUSE, *obfuscate, obscure.*

class

caste
estate
order

These nouns, as here considered, refer to groupings in, or divisions of, a stratified society. **Class** is the most general. It refers primarily to a social division of society, as the middle *class*, but a *class* may also be an economic division, as the working *class;* a functional division, as the managerial *class;* or a division embracing persons with other common characteristics, as the educated *class. Classes* are based on such things as lineage, income, and occupation. A **caste**, by contrast, is a strictly hereditary division of society—especially one of the four Hindu social *classes* in India. The highest of these is the Brahman, or priestly, *caste*. A member of the lowest *caste* was formerly called an untouchable, his touch having been counted as pollution by Hindus of higher station. A person is able to move from one *class* to another, but where a rigid *caste* system is in effect, he cannot escape from his *caste*.

An **estate** is a *class* of people with a distinct political or social status, having in common special duties, privileges, powers, or limitations with respect to government. An *estate* was originally one of the three *classes* of feudal society in Europe—the *Estates* of the Realm being the clergy, the nobility, and the common people. The political power of the press later caused the journalistic fraternity to be dubbed the fourth *estate*. In a general sense, *estate,* like *class,* may be used to indicate rank, position, or social standing: a lady of high *estate. Class* is also applied to things or services as a measure of quality: first-*class* as opposed to tourist-*class* accommodations.

In one sense, **order** is close to *class* in indicating a stratum of society or a cohesive social or professional group: the scorn of the aristocracy for the lower *orders.* Specifically, *order* often refers to the rank or position of an ordained Christian clergyman—a bishop being in the highest *order* of the ministry, a priest in the second, and a deacon in the third. In traditional angelology, *order* designates one of the nine grades or choirs of angels, which are, in ascending rank, angels, archangels, principalities, powers, virtues, dominations or dominions, thrones, cherubim, and seraphim. *Order* may also refer to an honorary society to which members are named by a sovereign as a mark of the highest distinction: The *Order* of the Garter is the highest *order* of knighthood in Great Britain. See CLUB, POSITION (rank).

clean

fresh
immaculate
spotless
stainless

These adjectives refer to anything that is unsoiled by use or neglect or that is untainted by dirt or grime. **Clean** emphasizes freedom from dirt, grime, or stain. A thing may be *clean* because it is new, unused, or unmarked: a *clean* sheet of paper. More often, *clean* suggests that something has been freed of soil or the marks of use in order to be used again: *clean* dishes; *clean* clothing. Less concretely, *clean* can refer to an absence of fault or failing that combines in some uses with its reference to the absence of marks, implying a place where faults might otherwise be marked down in a list: a *clean* slate; a *clean* record. *Clean*'s implications of purity further extend to the moral sense, referring to that which is innocent, especially of sexual impropriety: a *clean* mind; *clean* jokes. *Clean*, however, can refer simply to what is well intended and harmless: good *clean* fun.

Fresh is often used in apposition with *clean* to emphasize newness or lack of use as well as purity: *fresh, clean* snow; a *fresh, clean* shirt. It may also suggest something revivifying in its purity: *fresh* air. Used in reference to failings, it suggests not an absence of faults but the putting aside of past mistakes: a *fresh* start; *fresh* approaches. **Spotless** refers to an actual absence of marks or blemishes. It is, however, more emphatic than *clean* and carries implications of neatness and tidiness as well: a *spotless* room. Otherwise, *spotless* may simply be a hyperbolic substitute for *clean*, though it may differ in describing something never sullied: a *spotless* employment record.

Stainless may be used in a way closely resembling *spotless*. Much more often, however, it indicates something that cannot be stained, especially something designed with this quality in mind: *stainless* steel dinnerware. In this sense, something that is *stainless* need not necessarily be *clean*. **Immaculate**, the most formal of these adjectives, can function like *spotless* as a hyperbole for *clean* in all situations: an *immaculate* suit. On this level, it reflects its Latin root, which means literally without spot. But *immaculate* also has a wider range of application to moral propriety and is particularly relevant in a religious context, meaning sinless: hermits who strove to lead *immaculate* lives. The doctrine of the *Immaculate* Conception holds that the Virgin Mary was conceived untainted by original sin. See INNOCENT, PERFECT, SANITARY.

Antonyms: *adulterated, contaminated,* DIRTY, *grimy, impure, marked, polluted, stained, sullied, tainted.*

clear

definite
distinct
unmistakable

These adjectives refer to something that stands out in vivid or sharp relief from its surroundings. **Clear** is the most general and informal. It suggests something that is not the least bit confused, vague, or fuzzy and therefore is easy to understand or perceive: *clear* directions on how to reach the resort; the *clear* lettering of the handmade poster. Where *clear* may emphasize lack of confusion or ambiguity, **distinct** is restricted to sharpness of impression or lack of blur: instructions that were *clear* enough if only he had spoken in a more *distinct* voice. *Distinct* can also suggest well-defined outlines: the right focus for getting a *distinct* image. Or it can suggest something that stands out noticeably: the *distinct* note of annoyance in her voice.

Definite relates to the lack of ambiguity implied by *clear* and to the sharpness of outline or impression implied by *distinct:* setting up *definite* rules of procedure; a *definite* litmus reaction that proved the presence of acidity. **Unmistakable** intensifies the implication of *distinct* and suggests a noticeable forcefulness not to be overlooked; *unmistakable* emphasizes the presence of evidence that removes all possibility for doubt: an *unmistakable* nod of her head; the *unmistakable* wail of a siren. See DEFINITE, SPECIFIC, SURE.

Antonyms: *blurred, confused,* DOUBTFUL, FOGGY, *fuzzy, muddled,* OBSCURE, *unclear, unintelligible,* VAGUE.

clergyman

cleric
divine
ecclesiastic
prelate
religious
theologian

These nouns refer to those members of a religion who are set apart from its ordinary followers either by the responsibilities of leadership or by other duties. **Clergyman**, now sometimes called *clergyperson*, is the generic term for all persons set apart in this way; it applies equally well to leaders of Catholic, Protestant, and Jewish faiths: cardinals, bishops, and other *clergymen* who met at the Second Vatican Ecumenical Council in Rome; a conference of Lutheran, Presbyterian, and Methodist *clergymen;* a study group composed of Jewish seminarians and *clergymen.* Just as clergy contrasts with laity, so *clergyman* contrasts with layman to distinguish authorized leaders from ordinary members: a closer relationship between *clergymen* and laymen. In Christian faiths, *clergyman* more specifically indicates someone set apart by ordination, someone who is regularly authorized to preach the gospel and administer sacraments; in addition, it can include in Catholic, Orthodox, and Anglican usage anyone who lives in holy orders: priests, monks, and other *clergymen*. At its most general, *clergyman* may be applied to the leaders of other religions at least when no more appropriate term from that religion suggests itself: Buddhist *clergymen*.

Cleric may refer, like *clergyman,* to any member of the clergy, but its use is restricted to the more ritualized or hierarchic faiths. Most specifically it refers to someone distinguished by a tonsure, although it now can suggest any *clergyman* whose ordination is symbolized by clothing markedly different from that of a layman: a procession of *clerics* in their colorful regalia. Unlike *clergyman, cleric* may sometimes give a contemptuous tone when used in criticism, not so much of a church itself, but of church leaders regarded as corrupt: *clerics* who flout their duties and ignore the needs of the faithful.

Theologian represents a much more specific concept, referring to anyone who formulates or clarifies the doctrines and thinking of a religion; *theologian* may occasionally be applied to members of other than the Western religions: the Hindu *theologian* Shankara. In any case, it suggests a learned, philosophical, or well-reasoned approach. Theoretically, *theologian* can apply to anyone accomplished in such technical discussion, male or female, *clergyman* or layman. In practice, a *theologian* has most often been a *clergyman* of the religion his thinking deals with: the Jewish *theologian* Maimonides who influenced the thought of St. Thomas Aquinas. While *theologian* suggests an official or orthodox approach, this is not always necessarily implied in practice: the *theologian* Arius whose doctrines were declared heretical in the fourth century A.D.; *theologians* of decades past who formulated the controversial "God-is-dead" theory. While **divine** may refer in a general way to a *clergyman*, particularly one highly placed, *divine* at its most specific refers to a *theologian* whose doctrines are accepted and honored by his religion: church *divines* of the early centuries whose main task was to combat such heresies as Arianism and Manicheanism.

Ecclesiastic refers to any *clergyman* in a church with an emphasis on a clergy arranged in a ranked and structured hierarchy, thus applying particularly to Catholic, Orthodox, and such Protestant churches as the Anglican: an *ecclesiastic* in the Church of England. **Prelate** more specifically refers to an *ecclesiastic* of superior rank and authority, as a bishop or cardinal, or to a dignitary of a particular church. *Prelate*, even more than *cleric*, can be given a negative ring by someone critical of the clergy: *prelates* who grow fat and rich while ordinary people starve.

While **religious** is restricted in reference to someone living in holy orders, usually in the context of the more formalized faiths, *religious* is unique here in that it applies equally well both to a man or woman in such orders: a young woman who wished to become a *religious* and retire to the sheltered life of the convent. [Not always mandatory for parish priests, celibacy nevertheless was always in force for the *religious,* both monks and nuns.] See MINISTER.

climactic. Do not confuse the adjective *climactic* (of a climax) with the adjective *climatic* (pertaining to weather conditions).

clique

circle
coterie
group
set

These nouns refer to a small cluster of friends that excludes outsiders and confers status on those who belong. Of these, **clique** is the most pejorative in tone and points to the smallest number of members. It also most strongly suggests both secrecy and snobbishness; in its quasi-official rigidity, in fact, it may all but resemble a social club: a clearly defined *clique* of teenagers who set style and fashion for their high school; a *clique* of conservative officers within the War Ministry. No person would describe his closest friends and himself as a *clique*—except to disparage them and himself. **Circle**, by contrast, carries no pejorative judgment and could be used descriptively either by an outsider or by a member of a social cluster: a *circle* of Impressionist painters in the 1890's; my *circle* of friends. *Circle* implies less intimacy than *clique*, but does suggest mutuality of interests, frequency of gathering, and, possibly, decorous civility carried out more formally than *clique*: Gloria Steinem and her *circle* of influential feminists.

Coterie, although more formal than either, more closely resembles *clique* than *circle*. It is not necessarily as pejorative as *clique*, however, and points to a larger cluster of friends with perhaps wider interests, less exclusive status, and the possibility of greater social fluidity. While every member of a *clique* or *circle*, for example, would be well acquainted with every other member, the members of a *coterie* might be on a more personal or familiar basis. Also, a *clique* or *circle* might point more strictly to sociability as a motivating factor, while *coterie* may more often suggest some uniting ideal or purpose beyond mere camaraderie: the *coterie* of Fabian socialists whose ideals were ultimately embodied in the British Labour Party.

Group and **set** are much less restricted in meaning than these other nouns. *Group,* when referring to social clusters, may range in suggestiveness from the intense intimacy of *clique* to a much vaguer casualness that includes all the friends and acquaintances one happens to have: my *group* at college; a *group* of young parents who met in the park over their baby carriages. *Set* indicates a much larger *group* of members than any of these other nouns; while it may be used pejoratively to point to snobbishness, like *clique,* it may be used more neutrally to indicate a particular social *group* that can be classified as to status and similar interests. Where *clique* all but suggests a club, *set* all but implies a class or caste of people. Most important, members of a *set* need not even know each other: modish dress that obviously indicated they were members of the fast-living jet *set. Set,* used of a smaller *group,* is even more emphatic about status, although this need not approach the snobbishness implicit in *clique:* falling in with a *set* of young women executives who spend their weekends in the Hamptons. See CLUB.

club

association
federation
fraternity
league
lodge
order
union

These nouns all apply to organized groups of people or things. A **club** suggests intimacy and informality as well as good fellowship. *Clubs* may be designed for a variety of purposes, but social *clubs* are usually of an exclusive nature; membership depends upon the personal judgment, feelings, or prejudices of the established members rather than upon any objective qualification. Political *clubs* are less exclusive, but payment of dues and attendance of periodic meetings of a more or less social nature characterize all *clubs.* The word *club* has lately become popular in commercial enterprises because of its pleasant connotations of comfort, relaxation, and fellowship; thus, we find it used in book *club,* which is simply an **association** of potential book buyers for the purpose of obtaining books at somewhat reduced prices. *Association,* then, applies to more formal and businesslike relationships that may obtain between organizations as well as individuals: the American Automobile *Association;* the American *Association* of University Professors; an *association* of law schools.

Federation applies especially to a cooperative organization of states or semi-independent groups for a specific, mutual purpose, as to conduct foreign affairs, or, as was the case of the American *Federation* of Labor, to strengthen the bargaining position of each of its member **unions**. The most common sense of *union* refers to the labor *union,* an organization of workers that represents the collective interest of its members in dealing with employers. In another sense *union* is close to **league**. A *union* or *league* is a combining of forces for some common end: the American Civil Liberties *Union;* the *League* of Nations. But *union* sometimes signifies a closer and more enduring relationship than *league:* The United States is often called the *Union.*

Fraternity may refer to a fraternal society such as the Freemasons or to a Greek-letter *fraternity* of college students. The latter are usually social and are run much like *clubs,* but some *fraternities* are devoted to service, and others, like Phi Beta Kappa, have an intellectual basis for membership. A **lodge** is a local branch of a secret or fraternal society. **Order** denotes a society with common aims and obligations, as a fraternal *order* or a religious *order:* The *Order* of the Odd Fellows; the Masonic *order;* the Franciscan *order.* A religious *order* is an organization of monks, nuns, or priests who have taken vows pledging themselves to live under a certain discipline or to perform certain social or religious duties. See CLIQUE.

clumsy

awkward
bungling
gawky
inept
lumbering
ungainly

These adjectives refer to actions lacking in skill or grace or to the faulty results of such actions. **Clumsy** indicates halting or imprecise movement, a propensity for making mistakes, or results that reflect these things: a *clumsy* walk; her *clumsy* attempt to match the colors of the original; a *clumsy* sweep of his hand that sent the vase toppling; the *clumsy* dialogue of the play. While the defects suggested by *clumsy* result from lack of muscular coordination, skill, talent, or training, **awkward** suggests similar but less serious defects that stem from misproportion or more especially from an unnerved state of mind: an *awkward* build; an *awkward* grammatical construction; a mutual suspicion that made for *awkward* silences in their talk; shyness that left him flustered and *awkward.* [One student's work is sensitive but still *awkward;* the others are without exception hopelessly *clumsy.*]

Bungling specifically stresses a propensity for making mistakes, and to an even greater degree than is true for *clumsy.* It also focuses on the inexpert handling of delicate matters rather than a *clumsy* physical carriage: his *bungling* mismanagement of the whole affair. Similarly, **inept** refers less to physical movement than to an abject and total failure to accomplish a desired result: a completely *inept* attempt at humor; an *inept* movie.

Ungainly specifically suggests a lack of grace that may or may not result, like *awkward,* from some innate misproportion: an *ungainly* attempt to retrieve the fallen napkin; an *ungainly* body incapable of agile movement. **Gawky** is much more emphatic about the physical basis for *awkward* or *ungainly* action; it may specifically suggest long, thin, or attenuated limbs: the usual *gawky* adolescent. **Lumbering**, by contrast, suggests ungraceful physical misproportion that stems from an overly heavy or outsized build: the big brute who *lumbered* after me down the stairs; the slow pace of the *lumbering* play. See GAUCHE.

Antonyms: *adroit, clever, dexterous, graceful, handy, skillful, sure.*

clutter
chaos
confusion
disarray
disorder

All these nouns mean a lack of order and arrangement. **Clutter** implies that objects are jumbled together in heaps, while **disorder** means they are not in their normal places. *Clutter* emphasizes the miscellaneous or various nature of the mess, whereas *disorder* points to the lack of proper arrangement of the individual objects, and thus usually refers to spatial relationships within an area. [Finding a particular book amid the *clutter* of papers and books on his desk was indeed a challenge; to discover a rare clock in the *clutter* of a used furniture shop; Burglars left the apartment in a state of *disorder*—the contents of every bureau and desk drawer scattered about the floors.] *Disorder* may of course refer to any lack of order: riots and civil *disorder.* **Disarray** refers specifically to the lack of orderly arrangement, and may apply to people, especially if usually in a disciplined arrangement, as well as to things. [The troops retreated in *disarray;* The office, usually so neat, was in complete *disarray* after we moved.] *Disarray* may also be used of one's clothing or person. [Her hair was in *disarray;* Jarred and shaken from his fall, he began to adjust his clothing, which was in a state of *disarray.*] *Disarray* is a rather formal or literary word and would be out of place in any informal context; thus, it is seldom used in speech.

Confusion, as here considered, suggests that things are so disordered that it is difficult to identify the individual objects in the general *clutter:* Burglars left things scattered in such *confusion* that it was days before we could determine what had been stolen. **Chaos** implies both extreme *disorder* and nearly total *confusion:* After the bombing attack, the city was in *chaos.* See JUMBLE.

Antonyms: METHOD, *neatness, order,* SEQUENCE.

coincide
agree
correspond
jibe
tally

These verbs all refer to close similarity in relationship between separate things. **Coincide**, **correspond**, and **tally** are related in their application to two or more things that conform to one another or share certain characteristics. *Coincide* means to conform exactly—to have identical elements. [The birthdays of twins usually *coincide;* It is fortunate when young persons' career goals and the wishes of their parents *coincide.*] To *correspond* is to have comparable elements. A national dish may *correspond* to one in the cuisine of another culture; evidence given in court should *correspond* with the facts in the case. *Tally* means to *correspond* in the sense of being consistent with. [The calculations of two scientists working on the same problem *tallied* exactly; Saying that the earth is flat does not *tally* with scientific observations.] **Jibe** is a colloquial term that, like *tally,* emphasizes the accordance or consistency of facts, elements, relations, etc.,: His version of the accident does not *jibe* with that of the other witnesses. *Jibe* thus points to fitting into an overall consistent pattern rather than a point-by-point correspondence between two separate things.

Agree is the most general verb in this list, and in this context stresses the sharing of like characteristics, attitudes, or elements. It can be used in place of each of the other verbs in this list in many constructions. [His version of the accident should *agree (jibe, correspond)* with that of the other witnesses; plans *agree* (or *coincide*); figures *agree* (or *tally*).] *Agree* can indicate any degree of likeness, from a slight similarity to virtual identity. See ADAPT.

Antonyms: CONTRADICT, DISAGREE.

cold

chilled
chilly
cool
frigid
frosty
gelid
icy

These adjectives refer to a relatively low temperature or to an unexcited, disconcerted, or unfriendly attitude. In reference to temperature, **cold** may refer to something desirably low-key: a *cold* drink on a hot day. Aside from this situation, however, *cold* more often connotes an unpleasantly low temperature: *cold* weather; a *cold* wind; numbed through in the *cold* rooms. **Frigid** and **frosty** are intensifications of *cold*, specifically referring to temperatures below freezing. *Frigid* factually stresses something that has been frozen solid or a temperature enabling this: *frigid* cuts of meat in the freezer; a week of *frigid* weather. *Frosty* may suggest a slightly warmer temperature, one at which frost first begins to form or breath vapor can be seen: windows turning *frosty* overnight; *frosty* winter gales. Like *frigid*, **gelid** and **icy** imply a temperature *cold* enough to result in the production of ice: a *gelid* mass of hailstones; a clear but *icy* day. *Icy* may also be merely a hyperbole for *cold: icy* waters; *icy* stares.

In reference to temperature, **cool** often suggests something pleasant or mildly low-key: a heat wave followed by *cool* weather; a winter that was *cool* but not *cold;* moving from direct sun into the *cool* shade. **Chilled** refers to someone who has become *cold* or something that has been caused to turn *cool: chilled* to the bone; *chilled* wine. **Chilly**, by contrast, refers more often to air or weather midway between *cool* and *cold:* a *chilly* autumn wind; a *chilly* house. *Chilly,* in fact, may suggest an erratic coming and going of *cold* winds: *chilly* gusts.

When these adjectives refer to emotional states, their interrelations differ. *Cold* may refer to an unresponsive attitude or, more drastically, to hostility: a book she remained *cold* to from beginning to end; giving him a *cold* look. In their greater intensity, *frosty* and *icy* usually stress the hostility implicit in *cold:*

replying to him with *frosty* disdain; moving with an *icy* anger. *Frigid,* however, is now so often used specifically of sexual unresponsiveness in women that it may sound odd or comic in any other emotional context: psychotherapy for women said to be *frigid.*

Cool suggests reserve based on shyness, lack of enthusiasm, or disapproval: a *cool* response to all his ideas; curt answers filled with a *cool* contempt. It may also suggest an ability to remain objective or impartial or to avoid anger or panic: sorting out the arguments with a *cool* objectivity; keeping a *cool* head during the crisis. *Chilly* suggests manners that are standoffish or openly hostile: bidding a *chilly* good-night to the guests who had overstayed. *Chilled,* by contrast, pertains mostly to a discouraged or horrified reaction to something else: *chilled* to see our store of ammunition dwindle; *chilled* to see a trail of blood leading into the bathroom.

Gelid has a rather literary tone and connotes the kind of *cold* numbness produced by unfriendliness, hostility, fear, or horror: nervous laughter that turned into *gelid* silence when she recognized his murderous intent. See ALOOF, DISTANT, IMPERTURBABLE.

Antonyms: *balmy*, HOT, PASSIONATE, WARM.

color

dye
paint
stain
tinge
tint

All these verbs mean impart color to something. **Color** is the most general of these and stipulates neither the extent of the process nor the materials used nor the object *colored.*

Dye means permanently change the color of something, as fabric or hair, by impregnating it with a *coloring* agent: to *dye* a white dress red by soaking it for several hours in a *dyeing* solution.

Stain means either *color* an object chemically, as to *stain* wood, or impart to an object a color foreign to it through use, negligence, or the like, as to *stain* one's clothing with spilled soup.

Paint is apply color to an object or a surface for the purpose of decorating it, as to *paint* a chair or a wall. The substance used in *painting* is usually a durable one that preserves as well as decorates.

Tint and **tinge** mean *color* something slightly. To *tint* is to impart a light or pastel color for decorative purposes; to *tinge* is to modify the basic color of something slightly or superficially, as to *tinge* ivory yellow by frequent handling. See DISCOLOR.

Antonyms: *bleach.*

comfort

ease
leisure
relaxation
relief
repose
rest

These nouns refer to a feeling or situation of pleasurable serenity. **Comfort** suggests the possession of complete peace of mind and physical contentment, either through the satisfaction of all needs and desires or through the elimination of anything unpleasant or disturbing: airlines that are expected to vie with each other over details of passenger *comfort;* prescribing a pill that would allow him to sleep in *comfort;* beachgoers seeking *comfort* from the heat wave. **Relief** is specifically restricted to this last possibility of *comfort,* stressing the removal of unpleasant or painful stimuli. Even here, *relief* is more restricted to expressing the mere absence of negative elements, whereas *comfort* might suggest replacing them with something positive: a medication for *relief* of sunburn; finding *relief* from her doubts but little *comfort* in the new doctrine.

Ease and **relaxation** refer exclusively to positive states and so relate to a side of *comfort* in contrast to simple *relief. Ease* has the widest range of any of these nouns, referring to things that make for contentment, like *comfort,* but going beyond it to suggest utter naturalness, lack of tension, or profound mental and physical peacefulness: taking our *ease* in the cool of the garden; the *ease* with which she made the arrangements; a smile that put us immediately at *ease;* never having felt so full of *ease* in his life. *Relaxation* is much more limited in reference than *ease;* it refers particularly to a state of freedom from or dwindling away of tension: a secluded corner where she could read with complete *relaxation;* a *relaxation* of hostilities; arm muscles paired in a continual opposition of tension and *relaxation. Relaxation* also has a special informal use to pertain to recreation: asking him what he did for *relaxation.* **Leisure** is the most restricted of these in relating exclusively to this last use of *relaxation. Leisure* refers most specifically to one's free time after work, regardless of how the time is spent: having the *leisure* to pursue a new hobby; executives who carry office tensions to the *leisure* of the golf course.

Rest and **repose** are an intensification of possibilities for *ease,* suggesting extreme peacefulness and quiescence approaching sleep. *Rest,* in fact, may be used synonymously with sleep, or as a group word to include both waking and sleeping *relaxation:* recommending plenty of *rest* for the patient following the operation. As this example shows, *rest* may be used like *relief* to suggest a restorative process. *Repose* is the most formal of these nouns and gives a lyrical tone. It suggests an utter stillness or lack of movement, implying a complete cessation of both desire and tension. Where *relaxation* can suggest a noisy letting off of steam, *repose* always suggests a profound quiet, as of contemplation: a *repose* so deep he didn't hear the conductor asking for his ticket; the town's old-world sense of decorum and *repose.* See RETIRE.

Antonyms: *agitation, nervousness, restlessness, unrest.*

command

direction
directive
injunction
instruction
order

These nouns pertain either to an authoritative statement that someone is to do something or to the giving of knowledgeable advice or guidance. **Command** and **order** are the least formal of these nouns referring to the stated demand of a superior. Of these, *command* is the more formal and more general; it may pertain to an overall plan that is to be executed, whereas *order* might pertain more to a limited action or to a detailed part of such a plan: They received headquarters' *command* to attack at dawn, along with the special *orders* each unit was to follow. In addition, *command* is more forceful, peremptory, and less impersonal: Your wish is my *command;* a standing *order* to remain in uniform during off-duty hours. But *command* can refer to a position of control: the general's ten-year *command* of the infantry division.

Directive and **injunction** are considerably more formal than the foregoing and are much more limited and specific in their application. *Injunction* now pertains mostly to a legal context, where it indicates a court *order* that is backed by the threat of punishment for disobedience. An *injunction* often takes the form of a *command* to refrain from a specified action: an *injunction* that prevented the union from following through on its strike threat. *Directive* refers to *orders,* often detailed at length, that those in *command* send down through channels to gain the compliance of all affected personnel. Where the previous nouns can suggest either oral or written statements, *directive* most often suggests written guidelines for action. *Directive* can seem to apply euphemistically to advice that carries no explicit threat of punishment for disobedience, but the rulings of a *directive* are usually mandatory and beyond appeal: a *directive* issued to all executives concerning a step-up in production during the next quarter; a battalion's *directive* on changes in the dress uniform; the dean's *directive* on admissions procedure.

Direction and **instruction** both have applications referring to *orders* that may not be contravened; in this sense both are extremely formal. *Direction* would suggest a less detailed oral or written statement than *directive;* it is also less forceful and more euphemistic in tone: a *direction* on hiring practices that was sent down to the personnel department. Often it can apply to informative but mandatory guidelines: the company's *directions* concerning the issuance of new stock certificates. In the context of *orders, instruction* stresses that a desired action cannot be done without including the necessary information as part of the *command:* junior officers awaiting the *instructions* of the company commander; the judge's *instructions* to the jurors; She left detailed *instructions* to her administrative assistant about preparations for the annual meeting. When the giving of information is not suggested by *instruction,* it can be even more euphemistic than *direction:* the manager's *instruction* to curb personal telephone calls.

The last pair of nouns pertain more often and less formally to the giving of knowledgeable advice or guidance. In the plural, both can indicate a programmatic or diagrammatic plan for a relatively complicated action that one wishes or chooses to perform. *Directions* would be more appropriate for a one-time action, *instructions* for an action one may wish to learn by heart or perform more than once: printed *directions* for assembling the components of the sound system; *instructions* for using the microwave oven. *Direction* can apply, of course, to information about reaching a place: She asked for *directions* to the railway station. *Instruction* most commonly relates to an entirely separate context pertaining to teaching and learning. See DEMAND, LAW, REQUEST, TEACH.

Antonyms: CONSENT.

communicable
catching
contagious
infectious

These adjectives are used to describe diseases.

Communicable and **contagious** are synonymous in designating disease that is conveyed by direct contact with an affected person or animal, or by contact with a secretion or discharge or by some article touched by the person or animal. Measles can be called either a *communicable* or a *contagious* disease. *Communicable* is a broader term than *contagious* in that it is also applied to diseases transmitted by some intermediary agent, such as an insect. Malaria and yellow fever are examples of such *communicable* diseases. **Infectious** refers to a disease caused by the invasion into the body and the resulting growth and action of pathogenic microorganisms, especially bacteria and protozoa. Botulism and wound infections are *infectious* diseases. **Catching** is an informal adjective used in place of all three of the others but more often as a substitute for *communicable* and *contagious* than for *infectious.*

Antonyms: *noncommunicable.*

compact
compressed
concise
condensed
constricted
dense
miniaturized
solid

These adjectives refer to confinement or weightiness in a relatively small space. **Compact** in its most general use suggests a physique that is small but firm and shapely. In a more specific and technical sense, *compact* suggests that the essentials of something useful have been reduced to a smaller scale for convenience: a *compact* automobile; *compact* luggage for air travel. An intensification of this trend toward utilitarian smallness is designated by the fairly recent term **miniaturized**, which refers to the making of smaller and smaller electronic equipment through the use of semiconductor devices; this makes inclusion of more equipment feasible in situations where bulk and weight are critical, as in space travel: the *miniaturized* computer; the *miniaturized* radio.

Solid and **dense** emphasize weightiness, but *solid* does not necessarily suggest reduction to a small space, only the rigidity or firmness of a material. In reference to a physique, it suggests one without fat or flabbiness: *solid* muscle. *Dense* suggests the crowding of a heavy substance into a confined space; it may, unlike *solid*, refer to gases or liquids as well as solids: *dense* fog; a *dense* forest.

Concise, **condensed**, and **compressed** suggest

progressively greater confinement in space; one use of this progression is to suggest brevity in writing or the absence of wordiness. *Concise* suggests the use of exactly as many words as are required to express something and no more; it would apply more usually to technical, factual work, but may apply to imaginative prose: a *concise* report; the *concise* sentences of Hemingway. *Condensed* suggests the boiling down of a longer piece of writing to its rudiments: a *condensed* book. *Compressed* suggests extreme conciseness, but not necessarily that something longer has been shortened: a *compressed* statement that will explain the already *condensed* report. *Condensed* and *compressed* also have specific uses in the physical sciences. *Condensed* refers to the heating of a liquid so that water is driven off and a *denser* or semi*solid* substance remains: *condensed* milk. *Compressed* in this context refers to the putting of a gas under pressure to make it occupy less space: *compressed* air.

Constricted suggests extreme confinement in general, with an added note of uncomfortable limitation: *constricted* movement in the crowded subway car. See MINUTE, SHORTEN, SMALL, TERSE.

Antonyms: *extended, loose,* VERBOSE.

compare

approach
approximate
correspond
parallel
resemble
savor of
smack of

These verbs refer to things that are roughly similar but not exactly alike. **Compare** suggests that one thing is like another in some significant way, however unlike in others: a war that *compares* to the Korean conflict in its evident stalemate of constructive alternatives. In the imperative, *compare* may also be an invitation to regard two things side by side in order to note their differences as well as their similarities: *Compare* these examples of Rembrandt's early and late styles. **Resemble** is not readily used in the imperative, but otherwise it is closely related to *compare*. Its stress, however, is on a closer likeness, indicating that one thing *compares* in a number of ways to something else. Also, *resemble* carries a stronger visual suggestion than *compare:* children who *resemble* their mother; a child who *resembled* someone I used to know; an argument that *resembles* an earlier but now discredited theory.

In many uses, **correspond** is a more formal word

for ideas suggested by *resemble:* an activist movement that *corresponds* to similar movements in the 1930's. *Correspond* has its own area of meaning, however, in suggesting things that are alike in that they match or complement each other: an availability of funds that seldom *corresponds* to the needs of researchers at work in the field. **Parallel** can also be used as a more formal substitute for *resemble,* but most often it suggests the separateness of two similar things: projects in the North that would *parallel* those underway in the deep South; proposals that not only *paralleled* but actually preceded Darwin's.

With **approximate**, the emphasis is on the roughness of the likeness: a bill that only *approximated* the demands of the lobbyists. This verb may also suggest that one thing falls short of matching another in obvious ways: designs that desperately attempted to *approximate* the latest Paris fashions. **Approach** is like *approximate* in suggesting that one thing cannot measure up to something with which it is *compared;* the special emphasis here, however, is on quantity or volume: inflation levels that only *approached* historical highs. Often, *approach* emphasizes a lower level: a book that *approaches* his others in quality.

Savor of suggests that one thing only vaguely *compares* to another in some almost elusive way. Thus, the amount of similarity suggested is even less than for *approximate* and *approach:* a novel that *savors of* a feeble attempt to mimic James Joyce; a northern port that nevertheless somehow *savored of* the Mediterranean in its whitewashed houses and tiled roofs. While *savor of* can suggest equally well an advantageous or unfortunate likeness, the more pungent and colloquial **smack of** almost exclusively suggests an undesirable similarity: an offer that *smacks of* bribery. *Savor of* and *smack of* tend to relate a single example to a larger category of things it *resembles,* however distantly. See COUNTERPART, DUPLICATE, SIMILAR.

Antonyms: *contrast, oppose.*

compel

coerce
constrain
force
necessitate
oblige

These verbs all denote the urging or driving of a person to do something or the obtaining of the performance of some action, all by use of irresistible physical or moral force. **Compel** may have as its agent a person, an impersonal entity, a law, an action, or a set of conditions, and its object may be a person or an action. A parent may *compel* a child to do his lessons by threatening to suspend his allowance; the government does not *compel* young men and women to perform military service; the law *compels* us to report all our income on pain of penalty; an attack *compels* one to defend oneself; a recession may *compel* an employer to lay off many employees; the government may take steps to *compel* compliance with the law.

Force suggests an actual physical process, the use of power, energy, or strength, to accomplish something or to subdue resistance: to *force* a confession out of someone; to *force* the enemy back; to *force* a lock; to *force* someone to change an opinion; to *force* a smile. **Coerce** can imply the actual use of *force* but very often suggests its potential in an attempt to secure surrender of will: A child may be *coerced* into obedience by physical punishment or by the threat of it.

Constrain has connotations of repression, restriction, confinement, or limitation. It means *compel,* but often suggests that the action being prompted or urged is in a negative direction or at least away from that which one may consider positive or pleasant: a man who was *constrained* by his weak heart to give up all forms of strenuous exercise.

Necessitate and **oblige**, as here considered, mean make an action necessary by the imposition of conditions that demand a response. There is often a suggestion of urgency about these verbs. [Reduction of income *necessitates* curtailment of spending; Courtesy *obliges* us to respond to an invitation.] See IMPEL, INDUCE, PROPEL.

compete
    contend
    oppose
    rival
    vie

These verbs refer to two or more people or factions struggling against each other to attain an objective. **Compete** is the most general of these, applying to the widest range of situations: pianists *competing* in the contest; baseball teams *competing* for the league championship; candidates *competing* for the office; armies *competing* for victory in the battle; businesses *competing* for the biggest slice of the market. As can be seen, the objective implied by *compete* can be, most concretely, a prize or award that is won by a single confrontation or, more abstractly, a share in something that accrues to one side for its continuing effort:

television programs *competing* throughout the season for the largest share of the audience.

Contend and **vie** suggest more strictly the moment of direct confrontation and thus are narrowed to one possibility for *compete. Contend,* however, adds a note of actual hostility or serious disagreement, where *compete* may suggest none; furthermore, *contend* often suggests a dispute carried on verbally, as in a debate: speakers who fell to *contending* about the least important points in the proposal. Even when the verbal implication is not present, the animus often remains: forces *contending* bitterly to win the uncommitted delegates. The implications of *vie* stress a series of countering maneuvers in an ongoing struggle: neighbors continually *vying* with each other as to who could display the greater number of status symbols. *Vie* is, however, more like *compete* than *contend* in lacking overtones of hostility.

Oppose may often, by implication, restrict the competing sides to two: extroversion as *opposed* to introversion; primary elections in which many *compete* for the right to *oppose* the other party's choice in the main election. This narrowing of sides to two is not always present in *oppose:* a debate in which many factions *opposed* each other. In any case, *oppose* does stress the choosing of clearly defined sides and suggests a greater rigidity of position than any of these verbs. It may suggest hostility, like *contend,* or at least a serious discrepancy of views not easily compromised: attitudes toward drug addiction that were sharply *opposed.* **Rival** can be used specifically to suggest a struggle of two or more sides to outdo each other: candidates who *rival* each other in popularity; dresses that *rival* each other in vulgarity. Even more specifically, *rival* may suggest that one performance nearly matches another: domestic wines that *rival* the best French imports; a role in which she *rivals* the best acting she has previously shown us. These special applications of *rival* in this context make it the most restricted in meaning of verbs grouped here. See ARGUE, CONTROVERSY, FIGHT, OPPONENT.

Antonyms: COINCIDE, *collaborate, cooperate.*

competent
    able
    capable
    efficient
    fit
    good
    qualified

These adjectives are applied to persons who exhibit more than average acquired or native skill in the performance of some act or operation. **Competent** attributes to the subject the ability to carry out the requirements of a specific task. By implication, the completed task is one that can be rated objectively as being either satisfactory or unsatisfactory: No *competent* tax accountant could possibly have made such egregious errors in making out your return. Thus, while *competent* can suggest expertise in a complicated field, adequacy rather than excellence may be indicated by it. A performing artist, for example, might be insulted if described as *competent: competent* musicianship but bereft of inspiration and nuance.

Able and **capable** at their most neutral may indicate the practicable or possible: an infant barely *able* to walk. *Capable* is stronger here in indicating potential, possibly unsuspected, whether for good or ill: a husband *capable* of more tenderness than his wife had ever allowed him to express; totalitarian governments *capable* of the most unspeakable enormities. Where the two adjectives approach *competent* in referring to above-average skill, *able* suggests versatility and resourcefulness, and *capable* a practical, problem-solving approach: an *able* architect; a *capable* programmer. *Capable* stresses trained proficiency for a specific task, whereas *able* suggests a wider perspective or potential: *capable* lawyers, well-schooled in corporation law; *able* children, eager for knowledge, though thwarted by a lack of training in the fundamentals of reading. Also, *capable* can be applied to things as well as animals: an electronic computer *capable* of storing millions of bits of information; a shipyard *capable* of producing two fully seaworthy ships a month. *Able,* on the other hand, applies only to creatures *capable* of performing an action.

Qualified stresses the possession of required skills and is generally applied to professions or trades for which a minimum of schooling or training is required. A *qualified* teacher has completed prescribed academic training but is not necessarily *competent.*

Efficient adds to *competent* the idea of a skill in making the most of the time and material available. A mechanic who is *competent* and *efficient* will perform a repair job more quickly and cheaply than a mechanic who is merely *competent.*

Fit and **good** are general adjectives often used in place of the others in this list. *Fit* is usually used predicatively: the manager is not *fit* for her position (meaning not *qualified,* not *competent,* not *efficient*). The specific meaning of *good,* when used in this sense, is indicated by the context. A *good* teacher is both *qualified* and *competent;* a *good* manager is both *competent* and *efficient.* See ADEQUATE, EXCELLENT, GENIUS, SKILL.

Antonyms: DEFICIENT, *incompetent, inefficient, unfit.*

complain
beef
bellyache
bewail
bitch
gripe
grouse
grumble
whine

These verbs refer to the act of finding fault with one's circumstances. **Complain** is the most general and also the most neutral of these, suggesting either justified or unjustified dissatisfaction with one's situation: They *complained* about the terrible brutality with which they were treated; *complaining* about imaginary slights from the neighbors. **Bewail** was once similar to *complain* in its neutrality, but its archaic flavor now makes it suitable only for the unsympathetic satire of *complaining* that is motivated by self-pity: like a tedious Puccini heroine *bewailing* her sad fate. **Grumble** suggests a habitual ill-humor that does not quite expect to be taken seriously: husbands who *grumble* every summer as they dutifully load the car for the family vacation; prisoners *grumbling* over the poor quality of institutional food. **Whine** implies a high-pitched, self-pitying tone, often used for a continually *complaining* woman or for a petulant child; its use suggests complete lack of sympathy for the subject: The patient *whined* on and on about how unfairly her psychotherapist had treated her. When applied to a man, it suggests weak or cowardly behavior: He *whined* about his bad luck while others put out the fire.

The rest of these verbs range from the extremely informal to slang. They also range, in the order of their discussion, toward less and less sympathy for the subject. **Gripe** can be used for any fruitless expression of dissatisfaction, but is especially pertinent to military life: The officers were told to beware of soldiers who have nothing to *gripe* about. This context has emphasized *gripe* as a normal everyday *complaining* about trivial things; it would not be used for outraged indignation or even serious dissatisfaction. **Grouse** implies a greater animus than *gripe* and may suggest a more pointed lashing out in accusation or insult: *grousing* about the food only when the cook could overhear them. **Beef** works as an intensification of *gripe* but does not necessarily suggest the bitterness of *grouse;* it can suggest an unjustified *complaining:* They *beefed* about mistreatment only to get front-page treatment in the newspapers. **Bellyache** suggests *complaining* that is interminable, tiresome, and completely without justification: continually *bellyaching* no matter how his roommates tried to shut him up. The slang word **bitch** is extremely general in its reference to *complaining*; it can range in application from the fruitless dissatisfaction indicated by *gripe* to the bitterness of *grouse*: He *bitched* about the weather, the food, and anything else that crossed his mind; They *bitched* about the favoritism the teacher showed to the daughter of the superintendent. See DEPLORE, DISAPPROVAL, UPSET.

Antonyms: *applaud, approve,* PRAISE.

complement. Do not confuse the noun *complement* (that which completes) with the noun *compliment* (an expression of praise).

compliant

agreeable
broad-minded
complaisant
obliging
suggestible
willing

These adjectives refer to a pleasant or tolerant manner, open to other people's demands or desires. **Compliant** suggests a passive nature readily molded to conform to the wishes of others, one easily persuaded with little effort: meekly *compliant* to even his harshest expectations. **Suggestible** is a less formal term for the same idea, but it has an additional implication indicating a naive or unguarded sensibility that can be influenced even by subtle or indirect methods: They disapproved of giving such violence-ridden fare to *suggestible* children.

Willing stresses a more conscious decision to do something and does not, unlike *compliant* or *suggestible,* suggest an innately weak or conforming nature: informing his father that he would be *willing* to run the errand for him; *willing,* eager students. On the other hand, **obliging** refers not to a conscious choice but to a nature that is cheerfully ready to assist or that will permit someone else to satisfy a wish: an *obliging* ticket agent; teenagers who mistakenly feel they must be *obliging* on dates or become unpopular. **Agreeable** stresses the cheerful side of *obliging:* an *agreeable* personality. It may also suggest anything that is simply pleasurable: an *agreeable* climate. But *agreeable,* in another use, can suggest an even more *willing*

and open attitude than *obliging:* finding that he was *agreeable* to anything she suggested.

Complaisant in one of its uses is simply a more formal term for *agreeable,* but with a greater stress on the conforming character suggested by *compliant:* his *complaisant* eagerness to please. *Complaisant* has a special use, however, to suggest a cheerful or hypocritical indifference to strict moral standards, either in others or oneself: parents who are permissive and *complaisant* about their children's behavior; a *complaisant* lover. **Broad-minded** is in some ways a more informal substitute for *complaisant* in this context; it suggests a lax regard for moral standards, although it does not necessarily imply a cheerful attitude. In other contexts *broad-minded* might suggest an admirable ability to see all sides of a question. Here, by contrast, it suggests, almost euphemistically, an ability to accept the misbehavior of others without protest: parties that put a strain on the most *broad-minded* of her older friends. See ADAPTABLE, LENIENT, MALLEABLE.

Antonyms: *narrow-minded,* STUBBORN, UNWILLING, WILLFUL.

compliment. Do not confuse the noun *compliment* (an expression of praise) with the noun *complement* (that which completes).

component

constituent
element
ingredient

These nouns all refer to parts of a whole. **Component** refers to a part that functions in association with other parts but that can easily be detached from them; this is in contrast to an organic whole in which the parts are fused or have lost their individual identity within the larger entity. In choosing audio equipment, for example, one can buy separate *components,* such as speakers, turntable, and amplifier, and wire them together oneself. Or one can buy a prepackaged console, designed as a single unit. The noun can suggest a more intimate relationship, as in chemistry, where it refers to a substance that in varying degrees is present in a mixture without being chemically integrated into it; in this case, a change in appearance or apparent loss of identity may be indicated: Salt is a *component* of seawater. **Ingredient** is a more general term, referring equally well to the unaltered substances mixed together in an amorphous mass and to the fused or transformed parts of an entity or organic whole: Turmeric is an *ingredient* of curry powder; a novel that has all the *ingredients* of an excellent mystery story.

Element and **constituent** both refer more strictly to essential, necessary, or intrinsic parts of a whole. *Element* comes from a Latin root meaning first principle; this is reflected in its use to indicate the rudiments of a subject: the *elements* of good writing. As in this example, the stress of *element* is often on simple or basic parts of a more complex whole. In chemistry, the noun refers to those basic substances, such as oxygen, mercury, and copper, that are irreducible by ordinary chemical means and that are the building blocks of all matter. *Constituent* refers more generally to a part that is necessary to the functioning of a whole. Such a part often loses its individual identity completely in contributing to the new entity; conversely, withdrawing it from the whole would drastically change the larger entity: The *element* hydrogen is a *constituent* of water. See ADDITION, PART.

Antonyms: *entity*, WHOLE.

compulsory

binding
de rigueur
imperative
mandatory
obligatory

These adjectives describe actions that are judged to be inescapably necessary. **Compulsory** suggests that someone in authority has imposed a course of action that may not be departed from: *compulsory* attendance of classes. It may further suggest that the *compulsory* ruling will be enforced by coercion if necessary, and that violators will be punished: *compulsory* blacklisting. **Mandatory** is like *compulsory* in suggesting an imposed rule: *mandatory* silence in the library. In contrast, it is milder than *compulsory* in that it stops short of suggesting coercion and punishment as methods of enforcing the ruling.

Binding also describes a ruling handed down by an authority, but it may specifically suggest a one-time decision concerning a specific dispute between two parties who agree beforehand to abide by the results: *binding* arbitration. It may also suggest that earlier, more tentative rulings have been appealed to an ultimate authority. [The teacher's *compulsory* ruling against wearing heavy gold jewelry to class was appealed to the principal, whose decision would be *binding*.]

Obligatory is like *binding* in its legal sense. In a more general use, however, it suggests something expected or made necessary by morality or conscience, rather than by a higher authority as in the previous adjectives: the *obligatory* chaperone at school dances. As such, its force is more what should be done than what is or must be done: notions of *obligatory* timidity she rejected. **Imperative** refers to a necessity dictated by circumstances rather than by an authority or a code of morality: It is *imperative* that we get food and water before sundown. If used to refer to imposed rule, it is more like *mandatory* than *compulsory*.

The phrase **de rigueur** is close to *obligatory*, but milder in referring to those acts or observances considered necessary according to etiquette or required by good form; it usually appears only as a predicate adjective: an unwritten rule that made formal dress *de rigueur* for attending most evening receptions. See INEVITABLE, SURE.

Antonyms: LENIENT, *optional*, *unnecessary*.

conceited

boastful
egotistical
proud
vain
vainglorious

These adjectives refer to a person who is afflicted with unwarranted self-admiration or a sense of superiority. **Conceited** pertains to an excessive affection for oneself that may be revealed by an uncritical smugness and aloofness from others: *conceited* children who walk home from school with their noses in the air. More specifically, *conceited* may point to a person who becomes swell-headed because of a particular accomplishment or occurrence, often a trivial one: She became unbearably *conceited* after the football captain asked her out on a date. **Vain** suggests a person who is extremely concerned about his personal appearance or the impression he makes on others. A *conceited* person might feel that his superiority is self-evident, whereas a *vain* person would more likely strive constantly to impress others or improve his appearance: The typical dandy of old was so *vain* about his appearance that he spent much time primping before a mirror.

Egotistical need not suggest an outward show, like *vain*, so much as an extreme self-preoccupation and lack of interest in the feelings or affairs of others. On the other hand, where *conceited* usually suggests that someone is self-admiring for clearly defined reasons, however specious, *egotistical* may suggest a more unconscious, narcissistic habit of mind: an *egotistical* snob who thought the world began and ended at Princeton. Sometimes, however, *egotistical* can point to the habit of calling attention to oneself and one's accomplishments while ignoring the interests of others: the *egotistical* artist who monopolized the conversation with talk of his work in progress.

Boastful and **vainglorious** concentrate on this last possibility of *egotistical,* both referring to self-praise and attention-seeking in public. *Boastful* emphasizes unsubtle and even boorish public displays of self-approval: After a few drinks, he usually became *boastful* about his pathetic sexual exploits. *Vainglorious* focuses more exclusively on hollow show, not necessarily verbal at all. The attempt may be more subtle than *boastful* self-praise, but conspicuous displays of status symbols are often involved: *vainglorious* young bankers calling attention to their elegance of dress.

Proud can indicate legitimate satisfaction at accomplishing a goal or honor: *proud* of his high score on the examination. It can also apply to things invested with real dignity: a *proud* history; *proud* mountains silhouetted in the sunset. When *proud* takes on a disapproving tone, it suggests a stiff-necked and unrealistic lack of humility: too *proud* to admit he had been grossly in error. See BOAST, CONFIDENCE, EGOISM, OVERBEARING.

Antonyms: *deferent, humble,* MODEST, TIMID.

conclusive
decisive
definitive
determining

These adjectives are concerned with those moments in a sequence of events that are crucial to bringing about a given result. **Conclusive** suggests a final act that settles questions at issue in a previous course of action: the unleashing of atomic bombs on Japan as the *conclusive* actions of World War II. *Conclusive* may be used in another sense to refer, not to the events themselves, but to a later analysis of them. In this sense, *conclusive* refers to an incontrovertible interpretation of these events as a whole: *conclusive* proof that Richard II was not the villain Shakespeare made him out to be. A **decisive** event differs from a *conclusive* event in that it need not necessarily be the last one in a given sequence. Indeed, it may be a situation present almost at the outset, with the whole following course of action merely corroborating it. [The South's lack of industrial development

was *decisive* to its defeat, long before a single shot was fired in the terrible Civil War.]

Determining, like *decisive,* may refer to something that comes early or late in a course of action. *Decisive* may be more suitable in describing a single overt act of choice, while *determining* might better describe underlying factors that are inherent in a situation and prejudice the outcome. [No matter how many *decisive* victories Justinian won, the split of East and West into two disparate cultures was the *determining* factor in his ultimate failure to reunite the Roman Empire.]

Definitive, when referring to an act, combines the meanings of both *conclusive* and *decisive.* It applies when a sequence of events has been in doubt until the very last act, which irrevocably settles things: Elizabeth's *definitive* victory over the Armada settled the question of British naval superiority for centuries. When *definitive* refers to a later analysis of events, it takes in all that is implied by *conclusive* in this sense, but adds to it implications of authoritative accuracy and incontestable interpretation not to be surpassed. In this sense, *definitive,* unlike *conclusive,* need not suggest the settling of controversy or the proposing of any thesis whatsoever; it simply suggests finality of examination and analysis: the *definitive* history of the Boer War; the *definitive* biography of Byron that strips away all myth and conjecture to show us the man as he actually was. See FINAL, OUTSTANDING, SIGNIFICANT.

Antonyms: *inconclusive, indeterminate,* PROVISIONAL, *tentative.*

condescend
deign
patronize
stoop
tolerate
unbend

These verbs refer to the treating of another person as one's inferior. **Condescend** suggests particularly the awareness of a social or class distinction, false or real, that one person bridges in dealing or speaking to someone beneath him or her. The person who *condescends,* however, calls attention to the difference and does not wish it forgotten. Once, *condescend* was simply descriptive: Her Highness *condescends* to recognize the foreign ambassador. Nowadays, in our egalitarian world, *condescend* has an almost exclusively negative implication: tourists who *condescend* to local people. **Deign** emphasizes choice; it implies that one could well have chosen an opposite, perhaps more appropriate, course. It is not necessarily restricted solely to dealing with one's inferiors: He didn't *deign* to reply to his colleague's accusation. The extreme formality of *deign* limits its use today, except for satirical effect: a salesperson who actually *deigned* to wait on me.

Stoop was earlier like *condescend* in emphasizing social station and like *deign* in suggesting choice, but it now has uses relating mostly to a discreditable moral act: cabinet officers who *stoop* to exchanging political favors. *Condescend* might suggest a generally grand, arch, or pompous behavior; *stoop* suggests single questionable acts. **Unbend** is more like *condescend* on this score, but its overtone, in contrast, is one of approval for a stuffy person who learns to relax or act less officiously. [Why does she have to *condescend* to me all the time? Can't she *unbend* a little and treat me like anyone else?]

Patronize, even more than *condescend*, suggests haughtiness of bearing and an overtone of looking down on someone: a teacher who *patronized* students by oversimplifying everything he taught. **Tolerate**, in this context, has gone through several shifts in usage. It has meant and can still mean simply accept: society hosts who will *tolerate* eccentric guests so long as they are artists. *Tolerate* at one point took on a note of reconciliation: learning to *tolerate* minority groups. Now this last use is avoided as too closely resembling *patronize* or *condescend*: Native Americans who wish to be accepted, not merely *tolerated*. See OVERBEARING.

Antonyms: *accept, respect,* REVERE.

confidence

aplomb
poise
savoir-faire
self-assurance
self-confidence
self-possession
smugness

These nouns refer to a psychological trait that involves a conviction of one's own worth or an unselfconscious certainty of succeeding at whatever is attempted, unhampered by doubt, hesitation, or fear. **Confidence** stresses a general optimism that all is or will be well: able to face the future with *confidence*. *Confidence* may also suggest fearless trust, whether well- or ill-advised: talking to the unfortunate people in the shelter with effortless *confidence*. **Self-confi-dence** restricts these possibilities to a general optimism concerning one's own capacities and accomplishment, suggesting a complete absence of timidity and, less positively, an aggressive bearing: social clubs set up to promote *self-confidence* in teenagers; a garish costume that matched the *self-confidence* with which she plowed her way through the startled members of the receiving line.

Aplomb and **self-possession** stress the ability to keep oneself under firm control. *Self-possession* suggests the restraining of conflicting impulses or the brushing aside of distractions, accompanied by a cool unemotional approach even in trying situations: calmly working his way through the customs inspection with unflustered *self-possession*. *Aplomb*, by contrast, emphasizes a total lack of self-doubt and may suggest a carefree or uncritical exuberance: Although she had never debated before, she faced her opponent with *aplomb*.

Poise stresses steadiness and balance and, somewhat like *self-possession*, suggests a calm sureness of manner able to cope courteously with any contingency: a shy and awkward adolescent who had turned overnight into a young woman amply endowed with grace and *poise*. With its emphasis on a mastery of social properties, **savoir-faire** relates closely to *poise* in stressing an intuitive ability to do the right thing socially and to get on well with other people whatever the situation: a *savoir-faire* that never deserted him whether he found himself among first-nighters at the opera or among bohemians in a Greenwich Village coffeehouse.

Self-assurance and **smugness** stress an extreme conviction of one's own worth, ability, or superiority. *Self-assurance* can be used either positively or negatively, but *smugness* is exclusively disapproving: an astonishing *self-assurance* in whizzing through an exam she had spent only a few hours preparing for; insisting with unblushing *self-assurance* that even the stupidest foreigner would understand his English if only he spoke loudly and clearly enough. *Smugness* suggests an uncritical vanity or pride in one's own privileged position and a failure to see things from other people's point of view. This puts it in strong contrast to *savoir-faire*, which stresses a sensing of what people will find pleasant and apt: the *smugness* with which she chose to stay at American hotels throughout Europe in order to avoid unscrupulous foreigners. See EGOISM, JAUNTY, OVERBEARING, ZEST.

Antonyms: ANXIETY, *diffidence,* DOUBT, *hesitation, shyness, timidity.*

confuse

bewilder
confound
dumbfound
nonplus

These verbs refer to a disordered emotional response to complex or puzzling experiences or events. **Confuse** is the most general of these and suggests the mildest disorientation: detailed directions that only served to *confuse* me further; *confused* by his sudden swings between exuberance and depression. The verb may also suggest only a temporary lack of equilibrium or resilience. **Bewilder** deepens the suggestions of *confuse* and adds a note of harried emotional discomfort: completely *bewildered* by the crossfire of conflicting commands by his parents. *Bewilder* suggests a disorientation that is longer lasting than *confuse* and that may paralyze one's ability to choose or act coherently: She was so *bewildered* by his accusations that she sat down and cried. **Confound** suggests a complete and possibly intentional undoing of someone by contravening that person at every point or by exposing the person to unfriendly scrutiny or ridicule: an appeal for help that was utterly *confounded* by red tape and bureaucratic double-talk.

Dumbfound and **nonplus** are closely related, both suggesting a momentary astonishment at some sudden occurrence or sharp retort. *Dumbfound* implies an acute emotional shock that leaves one speechless; *nonplus* suggests a more intellectual surprise at some irrational incongruence, leaving one unable to think clearly for a moment: The boy was *dumbfounded* at his mother's insistence that he explain where every penny of his allowance had gone; *nonplussed* by the strange costumes they saw everywhere in the bohemian section of the city. See DOUBT.

Antonyms: *CLARIFY, ENCOURAGE, hearten, reassure.*

congenital. Do not confuse the adjective *congenital* (existing since birth) with the adjective *genetic* (produced by genes).

consent

acquiesce
agree
assent
concur
subscribe

These verbs refer to a positive response or to a congruence between or among things. **Consent** is restricted to the giving of permission or the accepting of a proposal or request. [The sergeant *consented* to the private's request for an emergency leave; She *consented* to his proposal of marriage.] *Consent* always implies the power not to *consent:* The king gave willing *consent* to his son's marriage to a princess, and reluctant *consent* to his daughter's marriage to a commoner. Where *consent* often implies the permission of a superior, **assent** can indicate the approval of an equal. *Assent,* furthermore, is most often limited to an affirmative response to a statement or opinion: She *assented* to the doctor's assertion that her son was ill, but would not *consent* to having him hospitalized. **Acquiesce** suggests either lukewarm or minimal compliance or a compliance compelled by outside force or circumstances: With a shrug, the boy *acquiesced* in his mother's proposal that they go to the baseball game together; a spontaneous uprising that forced the government to *acquiesce* to the demands of its citizens. In the latter case, *acquiesce* does not suggest the uncompromised freedom to choose that is inherent in the previous verbs.

Agree is much wider in its application than the previous verbs. It can apply, like *consent,* to a positive response: After hearing his prepared statement, many on the committee *agreed* with his stand. But *agree* can also indicate congruence of opinion that does not involve statement and response, or even previous negotiation or discussion: I met the new manager today and found that we *agree* on basic policies. In its widest use, *agree* can indicate things that are alike: Both husband and wife were surprised to find that the balances in their checkbooks *agreed* to the penny. **Concur** is restricted to statements, findings, or opinions, but otherwise can indicate, like *agree,* positions that are found to be alike: The two scientists, working separately and unknown to each other, had reached conclusions that *concurred.* More often, however, *concur* refers to a common position reached by serious deliberation or negotiation: Each member of the committee finally *concurred* as to what position they should take in the controversy. *Concur* can also indicate *agreeing* to a position already taken by another or others: One Supreme Court justice wrote a separate but *concurring* opinion.

Subscribe indicates wholehearted approval for an already formulated position. The word's root suggests the signing of one's name beneath a statement. While *subscribe* may sometimes suggest this situation, more often it indicates only a comparable willingness to support and defend a position: a public-opinion poll showing that the voters *subscribed* to administration policy.

Sometimes the notion of a public avowal is completely absent: They *subscribed* in secret to discriminatory hiring practices. See APPROVAL, COINCIDE, ENDORSE, SUBMIT.

Antonyms: *CONTRADICT, DEMUR, DISAGREE.*

conserve

hoard
maintain
preserve
save
store

These verbs concern attempts to keep something intact or to possess it in greater quantities. **Conserve** pertains to the wise use of a valued item one already has, with the suggestion that it will be difficult to replace once it has been used up: leaflets requesting citizens to *conserve* water during the drought; efforts to *conserve* forest land from the incursions of timber speculators. **Preserve**, on the other hand, emphasizes keeping something valuable exactly as it is, without change and, in some cases, even without using it at all. It suggests greater urgency and, in contrast to *conserve,* may suggest that the item in question is literally impossible to replace once it is gone: proposals to *preserve* the house as it was when Poe lived in it; He was in favor of *preserving* the Bill of Rights without stricture or modification.

Maintain and **save** relate somewhat in the manner of *conserve* and *preserve. Maintain,* like *conserve,* emphasizes careful use and replenishment of a quantity, but suggests that a steady routine of work will be enough to keep the item in its present state. *Maintain* also does not necessarily suggest something of great value; it can pertain to anything one wishes to keep in good working condition: We can *maintain* essential services by insuring a steady flow of revenue; *maintaining* a house in good shape by an almost predictable annual outlay of time, effort, and money. *Save,* on the other hand, is somewhat more like *preserve,* suggesting greater urgency and the irreplaceability of what might otherwise be lost. If anything, it is more urgent (and certainly more informal) than *preserve,* especially in its sense of rescue: action that narrowly *saved* the country from defeat. In an informal context, however, it can function exactly like the more formal *conserve: saving* water during the crisis. Where it is distinct from all the verbs so far discussed is in suggesting the accumulating of a quantity. Both *conserve* and *preserve* concentrate on what one already has; *maintain* emphasizes the taking in and giving out to keep an unchanging balance. *Save,* however, can suggest the adding of new quantities to what already exists: She was *saving* money for a college education; As he grew older he took to *saving* bits of string he found in the street.

Store and **hoard** relate to this last meaning of *save. Store* suggests the piling up of goods that may be bulkier than those suggested by *save,* but as with *save,* the *stored* item may be valuable or worthless, may be *stored* for future use—or for no purpose whatsoever: reservoirs with which to *store* water against periods of inadequate rainfall; *storing* her books with friends until she returned from Europe; He *stored* every flotsam relic of his life without ever looking at it again. *Hoard* gives an unpleasant picture of someone *saving* or *storing* valuables out of fear, greed, or mental derangement: Everyone *hoarded* food during the famine; *hoarding* his money while living like a beggar. See POSSESS, RECOVER, REPAIR.

Antonyms: *disperse, dissipate, scatter, spend, squander, waste.*

consider

count
deem
reckon
regard

These verbs refer to a belief that something is as represented. **Consider** can indicate a belief reached after thoughtful deliberation or intimate experience. [All the critics *considered* the book a masterpiece; Most of the experts *considered* the Iraqi army to be a formidable opponent.] A favorable verdict is not always necessary: Scientists of that day *considered* his experiments to be without merit. **Regard** comes from a French word meaning look at. Compared with *consider, regard* often reflects its derivation by suggesting a more external assessment or, sometimes, a visual one: He *regarded* his daughter as a beauty, though others found her plain. Again, a positive judgment is not inevitable, despite the related use of *regard* referring to approval: They *regarded* him as a harmless fool.

Count and **reckon** can refer literally to numbering or to figuring sums; in the present context, they seldom carry this sense over, though they do refer to the forming of a judgment. Here, *count* is most often restricted to stock phrases: *counting* himself lucky; *counting* the day well spent. *Reckon* suggests the weighing of evidence on all sides: He was *reckoned* by everyone an honest man. But *reckon* has lost ground to its informal or dialectal use, meaning suppose or guess: I *reckon* it's time to go.

Deem is now somewhat formal and occurs perhaps more often in legal contexts than in other contexts. It refers more to opinion than belief, but to opinion arrived at after deliberation; if the opinion is that of a judge, it may well be as firm or binding as the belief implied by *consider* and *regard:* The judge *deemed* it inadvisable to hear the appeal. *Deem* almost always carries with it a note of authority: She was *deemed* a traitor by her own party. See STUDY, THINK.

considerate

attentive
diplomatic
helpful
tactful
thoughtful

These adjectives describe persons or actions that show a kind or courteous concern for other people. **Considerate** and **thoughtful** emphasize the unselfish spirit behind the act, the generous thought that prompts the deed. A *considerate* person is mindful of other people's feelings, aware of their circumstances, and responsive to their needs. He considers consequences before he acts, feeling that he should spare others needless annoyance, difficulty, or distress. A *thoughtful* person is *considerate,* but in a more positive way, having an active regard for others that leads him or her to anticipate their needs. He thinks of benefits he might bestow and then he acts, hoping to help others or to please them: *thoughtful* friends who offer to buy groceries for a shut-in; *considerate* neighbors who try not to disturb a convalescent with their noise. Both *considerate* and *thoughtful* are often followed by *of* plus an object. [She is *considerate of* older people; It was *thoughtful of* you to remember my birthday.] *Thoughtful* is also used for its connotations to describe a welcome remembrance: a *thoughtful* gift.

Attentive emphasizes continuing acts of courtesy, indicating an apparent thoughtfulness or devotion that may or may not be real. An *attentive* escort of an earlier time opened doors for his date, offered her his arm, and helped her with her coat. But he might have been either gentleman or gigolo, either genuinely *thoughtful* and *considerate* or eager to seem so for selfish reasons. [She was *attentive* to her sick sister, whom she loved; He became very *attentive* to his aunt when he learned the old lady was rich.]

Helpful is a matter-of-fact, workaday adjective, stressing a practical motive or result. A person or thing can be *helpful* by meeting a specific need—providing useful service or assistance: a *helpful* salesclerk; a *helpful* hint. [He is *attentive* in public but not *helpful*

around the house.] *Helpful* may at times imply little more than a willingness to assist, so it is sometimes used to claim or give credit for good intentions. [I wasn't meddling; I was only trying to be *helpful.*]

Tactful and **diplomatic** emphasize method, an ability to handle sensitive people and situations gracefully, without causing hurt or angry feelings. A *tactful* person is *considerate* of others and is careful not to embarrass, upset, or offend them. Such a person senses instinctively what to say and what to leave unsaid, often practicing restraint or taking a roundabout approach in order to be kind: a *tactful* suggestion that another hair style might be even more becoming; She knew it was a sore subject and, being *tactful,* did not bring it up. *Diplomatic* is a more formal term than *tactful* and suggests a deliberate rather than an intuitive courtesy. It presupposes the special tact required of a diplomat—skill in handling delicate or explosive situations, in mediating disputes, and in resolving differences through conciliation and compromise: a situation that requires *diplomatic* handling, not angry ultimatums; He was *diplomatic* in dealing with customer complaints. See BENEVOLENCE, GENEROUS, HUMANE, KIND.

Antonyms: *GAUCHE, HEEDLESS, inattentive, negligent.*

console

cheer up
comfort
condole
solace
sympathize

These verbs refer to the assuaging of unhappiness or grief. **Console** suggests the effort of one person to mitigate the serious grief felt by another: on hand to *console* him throughout his mourning. *Console* may specifically suggest the attempt to make up for a loss by offering something in its place: They tried to *console* her for losing the prize by taking her out to dinner. This making up for a loss may occur within the loser's mind: She *consoled* to think that she at least had an understanding husband to turn to. **Condole**, by contrast, is a great deal more formal than *console,* almost to the point of sounding fusty and pompous; it does, however, give the specific meaning of actively grieving along with someone else: parents who *condoled* with each other over the loss of their child. *Condole* has now been adopted for standard or formal expressions of regret: His fellow workers sent him a note *condoling* with him in his grief. This accounts for the tendency of *condole* to sound officious and insincere.

Comfort and **cheer up** are less formal than *condole* and even than *console;* they also can apply to less serious unhappinesses. Of the two, *comfort* has the wider range of use; it suggests a tactful and understanding ministering to someone who is unhappy: She *comforted* the grieving child with a tight embrace. This verb can also refer to thoughts within the mourner's mind that mitigate grief: *comforted* to know that everything had been carried out exactly as his friend would have wished. *Cheer up* is decidedly limited to active attempts to ease someone's mind over a less extreme unhappiness: She knew that if he failed to get the job she would have to exert every wile she possessed in order to *cheer* him *up;* a bubbling manner that *cheered up* the despondent men in the ward.

Solace is almost as formal as *condole* and might sound precious as a substitute for the more direct *comfort; solace* can suggest a tender intensity of feeling: Whitman's attempts to *solace* the wounded and dying during the Civil War. **Sympathize** in this context suggests an understanding and attentive manner to the needs of the grief-stricken. *Sympathize* implies a more passive role than these other verbs: *sympathizing* silently with the patient's rambling accounts of his many ills; all those who *sympathized* with us in our bereavement. See CHEER, ENCOURAGE.

Antonyms: *aggravate*, GRIEVE, HURT, *sadden*, UPSET.

conspiracy

cabal
junta

These nouns refer to a group of people who have joined forces for some secret purpose that is looked upon as evil and often has to do with the displacement or discrediting of an established authority or government. **Conspiracy** is the most general term; it can apply to any combination of persons united for the accomplishment of an unlawful or reprehensible end: a *conspiracy* of gangsters forcing restaurateurs to pay protection under the threat of personal harm; a *conspiracy* of financiers who were trying to wrest control of a large company from its owners; the *conspiracy* that assassinated Caesar. **Cabal** suggests a small, well-organized group of highly placed people intent on a clearly defined goal; this usually involves an attempt to bring about a power shift in some governmental structure or to overthrow someone in a position of great authority: a *cabal* of cabinet ministers seeking to overthrow the president and turn the republic into a dictatorship. **Junta** is the most specific of these nouns in that it almost always denotes a group of people united for political intrigue: a shaky regime ripe for

seizure by a military *junta. Junta* also may carry the implication of a temporary government during a crisis or of an emergency governing structure set up after a revolution: broadcasts by the *junta* promising free elections once the dissidents had been purged. See INTRIGUE.

consult

confer
negotiate
parley

These verbs refer to discussions held to clarify a question or reach an agreement. **Consult** emphasizes clarification as the motive, without necessarily suggesting ultimate agreement: The President *consulted* with his Cabinet on a variety of questions. Often *consult* may suggest the seeking out of an authority: *Consult* your dictionary when unsure of your spelling. Similarly, *consult* can suggest the applying of an inferior to a superior: The cashier said he would have to *consult* with the department manager about the matter. Sometimes, *consult* points to a secret or private discussion: Have you thought of *consulting* a psychiatrist? **Confer** also emphasizes clarification more than agreement, but here the notion of inferior and superior is less often present. What is stressed is the exchanging of views: union meetings at which members could *confer* with each other about work problems. *Confer* may suggest intimate and informal but not necessarily secret discussion: The coach sat up front in order to *confer* with the trainer.

Negotiate and **parley** are restricted to situations in which the main motive is the attempt to reach agreement between opposing sides or positions. Both suggest formal meetings. *Parley* comes from a French word meaning speak and applies to actual enemies attempting to resolve differences through words rather than force: Representatives of the French and English kings *parleyed* on the battlefield. *Parley* calls to mind the vanished world of warring European kingdoms and is less often used for comparable contemporary situations. The preferred verb now is *negotiate;* it applies to any formal meeting of opposing sides to settle their differences through compromise rather than through force or some other form of direct action or confrontation. [Labor and management finally *negotiated* a settlement after two weeks of bargaining, thus averting a strike; The Secretary General urged both sides to *negotiate* a settlement to the bloody war.] See ADVICE, ARGUE, CONVERSATION, INFORM.

contemptible

despicable

detestable
execrable

These adjectives refer to people, acts, or things that are unworthy, immoral, or intensely disapproved of because of bad behavior, bad execution, or bad taste. **Contemptible** indicates that something merits disapproval because it patently falls short of even minimal standards of worth or adequacy. The standard implied here is usually one pertaining to morals or conduct: the candidate's *contemptible* appeal to greed and prejudice; his *contemptible* rudeness to the guest of honor. But it can extend to any evaluating process: The concerto was a *contemptible* piece of trash. **Execrable** can apply through a comparably wide range, but in actual use it applies more often to bad taste or conduct than to immoral acts: dressed in *execrable* taste; an *execrable* lack of concern for the feelings of others. Because of this distinction, *contemptible* is the stronger word, even though it suggests something worthy of scorn, whereas *execrable* suggests something worthy of hearty condemnation.

Despicable and **detestable** are both stronger than the preceding pair, pointing to something worthy of hatred or intense revulsion. *Despicable* can sometimes apply to work or conduct that one finds utterly worthless: a *despicable* portrait; a *despicable* bore. But these uses shade off, with weakened force, into hyperbole. At its most intense, *despicable* suggests a fiercely negative judgment of immoral character or action: Few criminals, even the most vicious, are so *despicable* as the gangsters who traffic in narcotics and prostitution; a *despicable* dictator who sentenced thousands to prison and death. While *despicable* can be used less forcefully to register a personal opinion, *detestable* is more readily used in this way, since it can suggest an extreme aversion rather than moral outrage: He found early Italian opera utterly *detestable*. Even when the reference is to morals, this note of personal distaste may be present: We were amazed that no one else seemed to notice the *detestable* cruelty with which she treated her children. See DEPRAVED, REPREHENSIBLE, REPULSIVE.

Antonyms: *admirable,* EXCELLENT, MORAL.

contemptuous

audacious
disdainful
insolent
scornful
supercilious

Contemptuous, the strongest adjective in this list, means viewing something or someone as mean, vile, or worthless, and actively showing or expressing that view. Attributively, *contemptuous* is applied to a person's words or actions; predicatively, it may be used to describe the person. A man may utter a *contemptuous* remark; he may also be *contemptuous* of his associates.

Scornful and **disdainful** agree in their application to persons feeling or expressing contempt based on pride or a sense of superiority. The expression of contempt is often limited to the dismissal of the object as unworthy of attention. Like *contemptuous*, these adjectives are used attributively with expressions of contempt, and predicatively with the person expressing it: a *scornful* glance; a *disdainful* rejection; The nobles were *disdainful* of the peasants, *scornful* of their enemies. *Scornful* differs from *disdainful* in indicating greater emotional hostility to whatever is being condemned; *disdainful,* in comparison, may more readily suggest archness or haughtiness based on a sense of social superiority: a *scornful* attack by his enraged opponent; dismissing her young assistant with a *disdainful* nod. *Scornful* and *contemptuous* are closer in tone, but *contemptuous* suggests negative evaluation that may be expressed in ironic ways. *Scornful* points more to reaction than evaluation and might apply to more direct expression: a *contemptuous* look that suggested how worthless he found her proposal to be; a *scornful* outburst.

Insolent intensifies aspects implicit in *disdainful,* suggesting an arrogant or impudent pride that is expressed in rude behavior: the prima donna's *insolent* remarks about the conductor's ineptness. Where someone might be justified in feeling *contemptuous* or *scornful* of something—or even *disdainful*—*insolent* always indicates a peremptory or overweening grandiosity. **Audacious** applies to reckless behavior that is conspicuous and outrageous: His *audacious* manners are an effrontery to good taste.

Supercilious indicates a haughty or affected manner that is so excessive or unfounded as to become pompous or ridiculous: *supercilious* flattery; a plain-spoken man who was *contemptuous* of anyone displaying *supercilious* airs and grand gestures. *Supercilious* comes from the Latin for eyebrow; raised eyebrows are often characteristic of a *supercilious* expression. See CONCEITED, HOSTILE, OVERBEARING.

Antonyms: *considerable, humble,* POLITE, *respectful, reverent.*

contented

content
gratified

contented (continued)

pleased
satisfied

These adjectives refer to the appeasement of need or desire. **Contented** refers to the fulfilling of requirements to the point of satiation: *contented* cows; She pampered him so that he would feel thoroughly *contented.* By contrast, **content** almost exclusively appears as a predicate adjective and suggests, not the complete filling of needs or desire, but the willingness to accept a modest or reasonable amount: peasants who were thought to be *content* with their humble station in life; The reporter appeared *content* with the brief interview he was granted.

Satisfied is closer to *contented* than to *content* in suggesting complete appeasement of need or desire: gorging himself until he felt almost uncomfortably *satisfied. Satisfied* contrasts with *contented* in that the latter may more often refer to a state of mind akin to complacency, whereas *satisfied* more often suggests the filling of a particular need: dull, *contented* faces; *satisfied* with his score on the exam.

Gratified suggests unambiguous joy in the fulfilling of a need or desire; in this it is more intense than either *satisfied* or *contented:* a longing for excitement that was only fully *gratified* when he moved to the big city. *Gratified* can also function in a wider range than the other adjectives, suggesting happiness at a well-executed task, role, or duty: *gratified* at the way her students took up the challenges she laid down. **Pleased** is less intense than *gratified* and is the vaguest of these adjectives; it may suggest less demanding needs or desires to begin with: *pleased* with the refreshing simplicity of the light snack. It would seldom suggest, in fact, that a question of satiation exists, and may have more to do with the expression of mild approval: She was *pleased* at the courteous way in which he addressed her. See CHEERFUL, COMFORT, JOYOUS.

Antonyms: *discontent, frustrated, malcontent,* MISERABLE.

continuous. Do not confuse the adjective *continuous* (continuing without a break) with the adjective *continual* (continuing without stopping or with only brief breaks).

contradict

contravene
controvert

deny
disprove
gainsay
oppose
refute

These verbs refer to the rejection of a previous statement by argument or evidence. **Contradict** may indicate no more than disagreement with a statement: He flatly *contradicted* her assertion that he was too lazy to mow the lawn. In this case, no attempt at proof may be involved. *Contradict* also applies to an obvious discrepancy between statements or things where no proof is necessary: parents who *contradict* each other when giving orders to their children. [The findings of the two studies *contradict* each other; His voting record *contradicts* his claim to be a liberal.] In its widest application, **deny** can point to something refused or withheld: *denying* his request for a weekend pass; Substandard schools *deny* children the chance to learn. In the context of disputes, *deny* often suggests the specific situation of giving a negative answer to a charge or accusation: The treasurer hotly *denied* any misappropriation of funds.

Gainsay is more formal and is now rarely used in speech; it does suggest that someone gives vocal dissent to an opinion or accusation, perhaps arbitrarily, tersely, or abruptly, without supporting arguments: her habit of *gainsaying* anything he suggested. *Gainsay* most often appears now with a negative: arguments for an appeal that not even the most cautious judge could *gainsay;* new evidence that simply could not be *gainsaid.* Here, something is presented as so convincing or conclusive that an arbitrary rejection is not possible. **Oppose** is far less formal in tone than *gainsay* and applies widely beyond the context of dispute or argument. It can suggest unreasoning enmity to a position, with no attempt to argue or present evidence: They still *opposed* the new theory despite all the corroborating facts mustered in its defense. *Oppose* can also suggest reasoned disagreement: the superior skill that Lincoln revealed in *opposing* Douglas's arguments.

Contravene can function like *contradict* when it points to a discrepancy between statements or things, especially where one entity conflicts with another: No law can stand that *contravenes* the Bill of Rights. In terms of argument, *contravene* may point to an attempt to overthrow a whole trend of thought by making telling points: a speech in which he marshaled every available argument that might help him *contravene* the objections to the bill's passage.

The previous verbs are mainly concerned with situations in which one statement is at odds with another.

The remaining verbs all can indicate the situation in which a statement or position is demolished by facts or evidence. **Disprove** is the most forceful of these, indicating that a statement, proposition, theory, or even something accepted as a fact has been demonstrated as untrue by countering evidence: explorers who *disproved* the notion that the world was flat; He *denied* her assertion, but couldn't *disprove* it. When two scientific theories *contradict* each other, for example, further investigation will sooner or later *disprove* one or the other or both, whether in whole or in part. **Controvert**, a more formal term, points to someone who *opposes* a given view and wishes to *disprove* it by offering evidence: His opponents searched the data given in his report, hoping to find inconsistencies by which they could *controvert* his findings. When contrasted with *contravene,* the emphasis of *controvert* falls more heavily on proof: However much they *contravened* her conclusions, they could not *controvert* them. **Refute** can suggest the successful demolishing of an argument by reasoning alone, but it applies even more forcefully when supporting evidence is suggested: They *refuted* his claim of innocence with eyewitness testimony. See COMPETE.

Antonyms: *affirm, agree, corroborate, maintain,* UPHOLD.

contradictory

    conflicting
    contrary
    opposed
    opposite

These adjectives describe statements, opinions, concepts, methods, or emotions that are incompatible. The term **contradictory** refers to things that mutually exclude each other, so that both cannot exist in the same object at the same time, for example, life and death. In formal logic, two statements are *contradictory* if they cannot both be true and cannot both be false. In other words, the statements are so related that if one is true the other must be false, as *I am an American* and *I am not an American.* **Contrary** statements, on the other hand, cannot both be true, but they can both be false, as *I am an Italian* and *I am a Frenchman.* The falsity of either *contrary* statement proves nothing about the other, but the truth of one establishes the falsity of the other. In a general sense, *contrary* points to a basic difference in essence or disagreement in purpose or aim: a *contrary* viewpoint. Things are *contrary* when the highest degree of both cannot exist in the same object at the same time, but where a middle term is possible, partaking of the qualities of both. Thus, wisdom and folly are *contrary,* for the perfection of either excludes any trace of the other; yet most human acts and statements partake of both.

Loosely, *contradictory* may mean no more than differing significantly: *contradictory* versions of an accident. In this sense, *contradictory* and **conflicting** are often interchangeable. *Conflicting* means clashing and stresses discord, implying mutual antagonism, as of interests, feelings, or ideas: *conflicting* opinions of the intent of the Bill of Rights; The prospect of a return to his home town filled him with *conflicting* emotions.

Opposite comes close to *contradictory* in referring to things that are diametrically different in tendency, character, or point of view: *opposite* opinions; the *opposite* sex. But *opposite* is more likely to be applied to a difference in direction, position, or condition than to mutually exclusive statements. [The condition *opposite* to cold is heat; The direction *opposite* to north is south; Black and white are often said to be *opposite.*] Where *opposite* refers to position, tendency, or the like, **opposed** is chiefly used of feeling and intent. People who live on *opposite* sides of a fence may or may not be *opposed.* *Contrary* and *opposed* are often used interchangeably to mean differing from in any way: to do something that is *contrary* (or *opposed*) to another person's wishes. In other uses, *contrary* suggests active opposition, and *opposed* implies passive contrariness. A person holding a *contrary* point of view may propose that a different line of action be taken. But a person may be *opposed* to a line of action without proposing any alternative. Both *contradictory* and *contrary* may be used to describe persons who perversely beg to differ at every possible opportunity. See CONTROVERSY, DISPARATE, OPPOSED.

Antonyms: *accordant, acquiescent, agreeing, compatible, concordant, consenting, consistent, consonant, corresponding, harmonious.*

control

    administer
    direct
    govern
    manage
    regulate
    rule
    supervise

The verb **control** means exercise a restraining or dominating influence over a person or thing. **Regulate** means order or *control* by rule, method, or established mode. A major stockholder may *control* a large block of shares in a company. The police may attempt to *control* an unruly mob. The Securities and Exchange Commission *regulates* stock-exchange activity. A government may *regulate* its balance-of-trade payments by *controlling* exports.

Direct stresses guidance and refers to the exercise of leadership: to *direct* a play. *Direct* may refer specifically to the control or conduct of affairs: to *direct* a large corporation. In this sense, it is close to **manage**, which emphasizes operational control: to *manage* a hotel; to *manage* a campaign. Of the two verbs, however, *direct* implies a stronger, overall control, while *manage* often refers to the actual running or handling of specific affairs and may imply delegated authority. The President *directs* the nation's foreign policy. A person may be hired to *manage* a business for the owner.

The verb **administer** implies official management and direction of affairs: a well-*administered* state government. It indicates the performing of executive functions and may be used of government or institutional officials. The chief of a government agency *administers* the funds allotted to the agency. The chancellor or president of a university may *administer* the school's financial affairs. In a strictly legal sense, *administer* means act as an executor or trustee in settling or *managing* an estate: to *administer* the estate of a deceased or incompetent person. To **supervise** an operation or an employee is to be in charge of assigning, *directing,* and inspecting the work done. Like *direct, supervise* involves oversight and guidance, but it indicates a more personal control than *administer,* and, like *manage,* may imply the exercise either of personal or of delegated authority: to act as a group leader and *supervise* a dozen workers. A school superintendent may *supervise* the work done by the custodial staff. An office manager may *supervise* the work of several departments.

To **govern** is to *control* by authority, arbitrarily or constitutionally. *Govern* implies the exercise of knowledge and judgment as well as power, and usually involves systematic administration. To **rule** is more autocratic than to *govern,* implying the exercise of absolute or dictatorial power and the imposition of arbitrary commands. In a democracy, an administration *governs* with the consent of the majority. A dictator, by contrast, may *rule* (or *govern*) with an iron hand. In a less specific sense, *govern* often refers to the exerting of any *controlling* influence: What motives *governed* her actions? *Govern* may also mean keep in check, and in this sense it may serve as a more formal synonym for *control:* unable to *govern* (or *con-*

trol) his temper. See COMMAND, GUIDE, POSSESS, SUBDUE.

controversy

argument
bickering
conflict
contention
debate
discord
dispute
dissension
friction
quarrel
strife
wrangle

The nouns **controversy**, **discord**, and **dissension** mean a prolonged disagreement expressed in terms ranging from reasonable to belligerent. *Controversy* is generally applied to disagreements between groups, such as nations, political parties, or religious sects. Internationally, one speaks of the *controversy* over disarmament; politically, of the *controversy* over federal versus state power; and religiously, of the *controversy* over priestly celibacy. *Discord* is *controversy* carried to unpleasant lengths and implies an unlikelihood of easy resolution. *Discord* between branches of a family often lasts for generations. *Dissension* is factional *discord* and is often expressed in voluble protests or accusations: *Dissension* within the board of directors forced a change in management.

Argument, **debate**, and **dispute** mean verbal expressions of disagreement. An *argument* is usually between individuals and suggests a combined appeal to reason and to emotions. It may or may not result in a resolution of the disagreement. [An *argument* between parents regarding the rearing of their children may persist for years; The umpire always wins any *argument* about a close play in baseball.] A *debate* is an *argument* between selected individuals or groups, and is carefully controlled and monitored; it is normally limited to an appeal to reason and is usually an attempt to arrive at the truth rather than to overpower by tricks of oratory: A Congressional *debate* on a piece of proposed legislation is designed to bring out all relevant facts to enable members of Congress to vote on the merits of the bill. A *dispute* is an *argument* carried on over a long period of time and is often marked by heated clashes: The *dispute* over an international boundary produced a long exchange of strong allegations couched in diplomatic language.

Contention, **friction**, **conflict**, and **strife** mean disagreement carried so far as to be marked by ill will and sometimes by hostile actions. *Contention* is usually limited to verbal *discord* carried to extreme lengths and implies vying for a contested goal. *Contention* between rival camps at a political convention is often acrimonious. *Friction* implies a continuing disagreement between individuals or groups and is characterized by frequent clashes. *Friction* between labor and management can result in mutual recriminations, strikes, and lockouts. *Conflict* implies a disagreement so violent that resolution by action other than verbal must be resorted to: The *conflict* between Guelphs and Ghibellines in medieval Italy passed from *controversy* over papal authority to petty wars between city-states. *Strife* implies a *conflict* so basic and contestants so implacable that it is characterized by continuous hostility and an uncompromising attitude: The meanest tactics are often resorted to in the *strife* between contending political factions.

Bickering, **quarrel**, and **wrangle** mean *argument* about petty matters, usually carried on in a petulant manner. These nouns may be applied to individuals or groups, and carry a suggestion of opprobrium. *Bickering* suggests a prolonged exchange of ill-tempered remarks: Constant *bickering* seemed essential to their friendship. *Quarrel* is more general in application; it is usually highly personal and can range from a mild verbal *dispute* to a violent *argument:* a *quarrel* between neighbors about noisy children; violent *quarrels* in which she hurled pots and pans at him and he knocked her about like a rag doll. A *wrangle* is an angry or noisy *quarrel;* the suggestion of petulant intransigence is especially strong, and *wrangle* often implies an unwillingness to listen to reason or to be understanding of the other person's point of view: an embarrassing *wrangle* over who should pay the bill. See DISAGREE.

Antonyms: *agreement, coincidence, consensus, unanimity.*

conversation

chat
colloquy
dialogue
discussion
talk
tête-à-tête

These nouns refer to formal or informal vocal exchanges. **Conversation** and **discussion** are the most general, the former applying mainly to an informal social situation, the latter applying often but not exclusively to a formal or official situation. *Conversation,* of course, can and does take place at extremely formal gatherings, but in this case it points to incidental exchanges that are not usually the main point of such occasions. Much more often the tone of *conversation* suggests a relaxed, informal atmosphere, either festive or intimate: a party at which *conversation* flowed easily; a long *conversation* between the two of them over many cups of coffee. Any situation, however, in which two or more people speak to each other at some length can constitute a *conversation:* He warned the boy against getting into *conversations* with other passengers on the train. When *discussion* indicates formal or arranged situations, it still suggests a rambling or free-wheeling meeting in which people express their views or sentiments to each other: asking the committee to hold open *discussions* on the proposed housing project. *Discussion* can point specifically to a period that follows some sort of one-sided presentation, one during which audience reaction is heard: a *discussion* that was to take place after the play; the general *discussion* following her address. When *discussion* suggests an even more informal situation, it still differs from *conversation* in indicating a purposeful approach that limits itself to a given theme, possibly to arrive at conclusions or determine a course of action: family *discussions* in which each member can openly present grievances; an innocuous *conversation* that turned into a heated *discussion* of police brutality.

Dialogue and **colloquy** are more formal than the previous nouns, particularly the latter. *Dialogue* can refer to speeches in a play or to essays in play form. In the context of *conversation,* it suggests a two-person exchange, yet this distinction is commonly ignored. *Dialogue* has recently come to mean arranged *discussions* among people of dissimilar views: a new *dialogue* among the Protestant denominations and the Catholic church; a year-round *dialogue* between labor and management. *Colloquy* is an extremely formal substitute for *discussion* and is typically used of formal situations: an extended *colloquy* between the judge and the defense attorney. It may refer to a high-level arranged conference: a continuing *colloquy* on disarmament at the ambassadorial level. It might also be used humorously to suggest guarded verbal exchanges: my tense *colloquy* with the customs inspector.

Talk is both relatively informal and very general. It can serve as an informal substitute for *conversation,* with greater emphasis on intimacy, sincerity, and frankness: looking forward to having a good long *talk* with all his old friends; feeling relieved after their heart-to-heart *talk*. It can also refer to the substance of *conversations* or *discussions:* soirées where the people were interesting and the *talk* scintillating. *Talk* can also refer informally to a one-sided presentation, as a speech or a lecture: a *talk* on ways to reduce poverty. Sometimes, *talk* is a more general substitute for gossip: indiscreet behavior that caused *talk* among campaign workers.

Chat and **tête-à-tête** are emphatic about the informality and intimacy of the conversation they point to. But *chat,* the most informal of all these nouns, can refer to two or more people and most strongly suggests light, pleasant, and rambling *talk* in which personal matters, if touched on, are pursued without great intensity: an hour's *chat* about the doings of their mutual friends; a *chat* between mother and daughter about the mother's dating problems. By contrast, *tête-à-tête* specifically indicates a talk between two people (literally, head-to-head), in which the emphasis is on sincerity and frankness of a confidential, romantic, or even conspiratorial sort: seen having a *tête-à-tête* with her husband's employer; a courtship that consisted of long *tête-à-têtes* in dimly lit restaurants; a *tête-à-tête* between representatives of the two deadlocked candidates. See ARGUE, CHATTER, PATTER, SPEECH.

copy

> duplicate
> facsimile
> model
> replica
> reproduction

These nouns refer to an exact or approximate rendering of an original. **Copy** is the most general of these, applying both to exact and inexact renderings: a carbon *copy* of the letter; a Roman *copy* of the original Greek statue; manufacturers who mass-produce *copies* of Paris fashions; a poorly executed counterfeit *copy*. **Duplicate** and **replica**, by contrast, specifically stress the exactness of the *copy*. *Duplicate* may suggest an exact and valid replacement: applying for a *duplicate* of his marriage license. It may even refer more particularly to one of two identical things: sorting through her stamp collection for *duplicates;* a frieze that is the *duplicate* of one on the front of the building. In less precise usage, *duplicate* may shade off in reference to things that merely resemble each other, or to an accurate *copy:* an obelisk that is the *duplicate* of several in Egypt; a *duplicate* of the receipt. *Replica* refers most precisely to a *copy* made by the creator of the original: Rodin's habit of making a number of *replicas* each time he cast a statue. As in this example,

any sense of original and *copy* is obliterated. More loosely, however, *replica* is simply a more formal substitute for *copy;* it may even be popularly understood to mean a rough approximation: a *replica* of what an Elizabethan theater must have looked like.

Though more formal, **facsimile** is almost as general as *copy,* since the degree of exactness is not specified. Often *facsimile* is used to indicate only a schematic approximation of an original: a contest anyone can enter by sending in a box top or a reasonable *facsimile* thereof. Even in other uses, *facsimile* always suggests easily noticeable differences between the original and the *copy*. **Reproduction** is also vague about the degree of accuracy implied. Sometimes the stress is on a close resemblance to the original: a remarkably skillful *reproduction* of the original painting. Often, however, *reproduction* may be used to suggest a simplified or less expensive version of a prototype: applauding hand-sewn showpieces that will deluge the country as machine-stitched *reproductions*. **Model** is unique among these terms in specifically indicating an approximate rendering; it suggests a schematic approximation, often of reduced scale, which may precede construction of the original: a desk-top *model* of the second-generation supersonic transport plane; a working *model* of the new turbine. *Model,* in any case, seldom suggests the kind of *copy* that could be mistaken for the original; a functional or illustrative mock-up is more often indicated: using a *model* of the space station to show the maneuvering involved in docking. See COUNTERPART, DUPLICATE, SAMPLE.

Antonyms: *PROTOTYPE.*

corpse

> body
> cadaver
> remains
> stiff

These nouns refer to a dead person or animal. **Corpse** is the most general term here, applying to any physical specimen that is not alive. It is neutral in tone and is equally suitable in common, medical, or criminological parlance: identifying a *corpse* in the morgue; the *corpse* being wheeled into the autopsy room. **Body** is substituted for *corpse* in common speech when the latter is felt to be brutally blunt. Because *body* is both simple and factual, however, it does not give a euphemistic tone. One would certainly speak to someone bereaved about the *body,* not about the *corpse*. Where considerations for the feelings of others is not an issue, *corpse* is more exact, since *body* can, of course, refer to the living as well as the dead. In this neutral context, on the other hand, *body* might still be more appropriate than *corpse* for the recently dead.

Cadaver, most specifically, refers to a *corpse* used for medical education or research, excluding those examined in an autopsy merely to determine the cause of death. *Cadaver* may be used of nonhuman animals slated for medical dissection as well as of human *bodies*. Outside this medical context, *cadaver* would have overtones of grisliness or gallows humor.

Remains, in one context, is a euphemism used by undertakers who evidently consider *body* too indelicate to mention: The *remains* are to be moved tomorrow. This use intends, perhaps, to distinguish between the surviving soul or spirit and the physical part it leaves behind. *Remains* is more accurately descriptive of a *corpse* that has been partially destroyed—as in an explosion or other catastrophe. This possibility makes its use as a euphemism for *body* somewhat risky, and would strike some ears as vulgar and tasteless.

Stiff is a slang word for *corpse,* and has a bizarrely humorous quality owing to its association with gangland movies. Today it sounds a little dated. [Hey, Charlie, where'll we put the *stiff*?] One can imagine anyone using the term, however, who becomes so familiar with handling *corpses* that he or she begins to regard them utterly dispassionately as objects.

council. Do not confuse the noun *council* (an elected assembly) with the noun *counsel* (attorney).

counterpart

complement
correlate
opposite number
parallel

These nouns refer to something that resembles, completes, or corresponds to another thing. **Counterpart**, the most general, can function in all these ways, though it specifically suggests a close relationship between the two things considered. In reference to resemblance, it suggests a precise or near likeness: the very *counterpart* of his father. In reference to completion, it suggests two things that form an entity: finding that he had the first volume of the work but lacked its *counterpart*. In reference to correspondence, *counterpart* particularly suggests one of a matching pair of things that are alike but opposite: a coffee table that separated one piece of the sectional sofa from its *counterpart*. In this last sense **opposite**

number is sometimes used, but unlike *counterpart* it need indicate no likeness in appearance, only in function. An *opposite number* is a person or thing that corresponds to another in terms of relation of each to the sets of which they are part. In some instances *opposite numbers* may be physically opposed, as linemen in a football game; in others they may simply play similar roles, as third basemen of two opposing teams. Two account executives of different advertising agencies competing for the same account may be called *opposite numbers* or *counterparts*. It is to be noted that when the opposition becomes more a matter of role than of physical position, *counterpart* comes into play as a synonym for *opposite number*. But *counterpart* is in any event more elevated in tone.

Correlate indicates a much closer relationship than *counterpart*, but need not imply likeness at all. It indicates instead interdependence or reciprocity, with or without the suggestion that one of two things is a cause of the other: the anomie that is an inevitable *correlate* of homelessness. *Correlate* can, however, suggest one of two similar things, each existing in mutually exclusive areas; in this case any notion of causality is distinctly absent: tales of the Samurai that have their *correlate* in European Arthurian legends. **Parallel** is related to this last sense of *correlate*, but, in this case, a slighter resemblance may be suggested; again, no causality is implied. [The current abortion controversy has a *parallel* in the dispute over usury in medieval times.] *Parallel* can point to a more essential likeness, correspondence, or match, but the word's clear reference to the geometric situation of lines that run equidistant to each other gives strong implications of kinship but not of close contact or causality. *Parallel*, however, is the one term here that readily suggests similarity between several things, rather than just two: a plot line that has innumerable *parallels* in best-selling detective novels.

Of all the nouns treated here, **complement** puts the least stress on likeness and similarity; in fact, none at all need be suggested by *complement*. Instead, *complement* points to one of two things that together make up a whole. These two things, furthermore, need not be equal halves or mirror images as is the case with *counterpart*: a woman in whom intelligence and femininity were not antagonists but *complements*; a year-end bonus that was a small but by no means negligible *complement* to her annual earnings. *Complement* should not, of course, be confused with compliment, which refers to praise or flattery given by one person to another. See COPY, DUPLICATE, SIMILAR.

Antonyms: *antithesis, contradiction, contrast, opposite.*

countless

immeasurable
incalculable
innumerable

These adjectives refer to quantities or sizes that are great, infinite, or difficult to determine. **Countless** refers to large amounts that are difficult or impossible to total either because of their vastness or because their full extent is not known or unknowable: *countless* grains of sand scattered by the wind. Though the visible stars in the sky are often hyperbolically referred to as *countless*, they have in fact been counted, as well as those studied by other means. In the strictest sense, only those that may exist beyond any observation are *countless*, though these may be few or great or even infinite in number. Similarly, *countless* may refer to large quantities that cannot now be totaled: the *countless* numbers who died of malaria before the discovery of quinine. While *countless* may sometimes refer to instances in time, and **innumerable** may refer to quantities in space, the latter is particularly used for occurrences that cannot be totaled because of frequency or lack of record: *innumerable* instances in the past when a new idea was found dangerous to the established order. *Innumerable* is frequently used merely as a hyperbole for many: *innumerable* occasions on which he had stayed out all night carousing.

Immeasurable refers more strictly to spatial size or to dimensions that are either infinite or completely impossible to determine. Thus, unlike *countless* and *innumerable*, *immeasurable* is less likely to be used hyperbolically, whether to refer to greatness or difficulty of reckoning: distances that in an infinite universe would be literally *immeasurable; immeasurable* amounts of natural resources that were lost forever through misuse. **Incalculable** most strictly resembles the first pair of adjectives in referring to large amounts difficult to total. *Incalculable* may also be used like *immeasurable* for large volumes, but in this case the size may be hard to determine because of its uncertain dimensions: a deep trough on the sea floor, one of *incalculable* size. More commonly, however, *incalculable* refers particularly to the effects something has, when these are difficult or impossible to determine or can never be known: the *incalculable* effects of Luther's break with Rome, effects that still have not run their course; the *incalculable* benefits that ripple outward from even the most trivial act of kindness; aware that they were taking an *incalculable* risk. See INFINITE, MASSIVE.

Antonyms: *calculable, limitary, measurable, numbered.*

courage

backbone
fortitude
grit
guts
nerve
pluck
resolution

These nouns refer to a bold and determined attitude that is undaunted by difficulties and fearless in the face of danger. **Courage** is the most general, embracing all the rest. It indicates a dauntless spirit and the ability to act bravely under stress or to endure in times of adversity: the *courage* of the freedom fighters; the rocklike *courage* of a mother who lost three sons in the war. A person may show *courage* in response to circumstances, doing what is necessary despite the personal risk involved. But *courage* may also imply a firmness that arises from a strong belief in the moral rightness of a position or course of action: They have the *courage* of their convictions.

Fortitude is the most formal of these nouns, indicating firmness or strength of mind. It emphasizes the facing of obstacles with brave and unwavering resourcefulness: an ordeal that required every ounce of *fortitude* she possessed; the *fortitude* of a Daniel in the lion's den. **Resolution** is far less inclusive than *fortitude*. It implies a determination to be firm in conviction, faithful in allegiance, unswerving in course, or unwavering in devotion to a task. *Resolution* does not necessarily suggest fearlessness but emphasizes the firm pushing aside of any mental reservations or qualms about attaining an objective: the *resolution* with which the firefighter ran into the burning house despite the terror that must have possessed her.

Nerve may be compared to *fortitude* and **pluck** to *resolution*, although *nerve* and *pluck* are considerably more informal than the previous pair. *Nerve* is particularly emphatic in stressing the unflustered, cool, and steady daring with which someone takes calculated risks to win an objective: the *nerve* with which she drew herself hand over hand along the last section of the broken rope bridge. Sometimes, even more informally, *nerve* suggests brashness or rudeness in a social situation. [He had a lot of *nerve* to ask her for an invitation; You've got some *nerve* coming in here without knocking.] *Pluck*, like *resolution*, need not suggest the fearlessness of *fortitude* and *nerve*, but it does suggest a jaunty willingness to try anything, whether out of high spirits, conviction, or the zealous eagerness of the good sport: Any lowering of morale could endanger the *pluck* of our fighting forces; a stripling who showed more *pluck* on the march than many a seasoned scout.

The remaining nouns are more informal still, with less clearly defined spheres of separate meanings, all being colorful substitutes for *courage*. **Backbone** may suggest strength of character or stubborn determination, while **grit** may refer to a resolute spirit or a tenacious enduring power: having the *backbone* to endure ridicule for her unpopular views; showing his *grit* by taking every indignity the cruel teacher foisted upon him. **Guts**, a slang word, may imply a brash, hearty boldness or a presumptuous audacity: having the *guts* to ask for another assignment after failing so miserably in his previous assignments. But *guts* more often indicates an admirable display of *courage* when it really counts, and is in this sense synonymous with the cliché *intestinal fortitude:* the cop who showed real *guts* in a running gunfight with bank robbers; It took *guts* to stand up against the mob. See BRAVE, EFFRONTERY, OPPORTUNISTIC.

Antonyms: *cowardice, cowardliness, pusillanimity, timidity, timorousness.*

covenant
agreement
compact
concordat
contract

These nouns denote promises or understandings made between two or more parties as to a course of action.

Covenant carries strong overtones of obligation and responsibility. A *covenant* is often a solemn pledge made by members of a religious or other dedicated group to maintain and promote a body of doctrine or a set of principles: the *Covenant* of the Liberty of Worship drawn up in Scotland in 1557; the *Covenant* of the League of Nations.

Agreement is the most general and most positive term, suggesting that a settlement has already been reached. *Agreements* range in importance from those made informally between persons to those drawn up between countries or states. [By tacit *agreement,* Clark's friends all avoided any mention of his mentally ill wife; During the course of history, many *agreements* have been made between France and England.]

A **contract** is a formal *agreement* almost always in written form and enforceable by law. *Contracts* may be drawn up for the performance of work at a fixed rate and within a given period: a *contract* to deliver military supplies to the government; a *contract* signed by a teacher for the coming academic year. Or it may

be a binding, legalized *agreement* between persons: a marriage *contract.*

Compact carries the idea of a solemn *agreement* between persons or between political groups or states. A *compact* may or may not be in written form, but the chief guarantee of its being carried out is that each party is under strong pressures of obligation and mutual trust. [The two brothers made a *compact* that the family business would always be handed down to their descendants; Faust made a *compact* with Satan; The seven nations made a *compact* to regulate tariffs.]

Concordat is confined to formal *agreements* between the papacy and a national government to terminate or avert dissension between the Roman Catholic Church and civil power. See TREATY.

cowardly
craven
pusillanimous

These adjectives mean lacking courage to a degree that arouses disapproval and disgust. **Cowardly** is the most common of the three and is applied opprobriously to persons unwilling or unable to prevent their fear or timidity from influencing their actions unduly; it can also refer to the actions themselves: In frontier days, shooting a man in the back was considered *cowardly;* too *cowardly* to stand up and fight.

Craven and **pusillanimous** are formal words encountered mainly in writing and oratory. *Craven* is applied to persons or actions that are outrageously or abjectly *cowardly,* and that flagrantly violate the prevailing cultural standards of courage: The *craven* captive groveled at our feet, begging for mercy. *Pusillanimous* differs from the other terms in pointing more strongly to temperamental timidity than to fear as the basis of the resulting action or inaction. *Pusillanimous* represents a contemptible moral squeamishness rather than a physical cowardliness, although it is quite possible for the same person to be both *pusillanimous* and *cowardly.* What chiefly distinguishes the *pusillanimous* person, however, is an unwillingness to press for his or her rights: His *pusillanimous* reaction was to sigh and say, "Well, it really won't do to raise a fuss." See AFRAID, TIMID.

Antonyms: *BOLD, BRAVE.*

crack
breach
chink
cleft

crack *(continued)*

crevice
fissure

These nouns refer to a small gap or opening in a surface. **Crack** suggests an opening longer than wide, and may refer to a normal opening or to one formed by force, violence, or some malfunction: the *crack* under the door; faint *cracks* running through the base of the pillar; putting his eye to a *crack* in the partition. While *crack* may or may not suggest an opening through which light or air might pass, **chink** invariably suggests such an opening: the unfilled *chinks* between the logs forming the cabin wall; a *chink* in the dike through which water had begun to seep.

Breach suggests a gap in something that might impair its functioning and is made usually by wear or some sundering force: a *breach* cut by the enemy through our front lines, leaving headquarters vulnerable to attack. It may, however, refer as well to any natural gap of any size or shape in the distribution of items forming a group: a *breach* in the row of trees that widened out finally into a path. **Cleft**, by contrast, most commonly suggests a natural indentation in something: a *cleft* in his chin; in the *cleft* of a tree. It may also suggest something formed by wear or force: a bird perching where the lightning had made a *cleft* in the rock. In no case does *cleft* suggest an opening clear through to the other side of something, as is true of *chink.*

Crevice and **fissure** both usually refer to long *cracks* formed by natural forces at work in a terrain. *Crevice* most commonly suggests a *crack* in an incline or hillside: a mountaineer moving surefootedly from *crevice* to *crevice* in the mountain face. *Fissure*, by contrast, suggests a long slitlike opening in a more level surface: *fissures* in the ground formed by the earthquake; stretches of snow that tremored and broke open in *fissures* at every step they took. *Crevice* can also be applied outside this context: *crevices* between the bricks deep enough for the burglar to gain a toehold in the wall; using plaster of Paris to fill the *crevices* in the flaking paint and Spackle to seal up the smaller *cracks.* See HOLE.

create

compose
design
invent
make
produce

These verbs all concern the act of bringing something into being that did not exist before. **Create** may suggest conscious intention, aesthetic discrimination, power, control, or all of these. It is most appropriate for situations in which the raw materials and the finished product are very different from each other: a Supreme Being who *creates* the universe out of darkness and chaos; the novelist who *creates* a unique view of life by using everyday language; diplomats attempting to *create* world order out of the discords of warring nations. *Create* is also frequently used as a status word for far less significant pursuits: the fashion designer *creating* a new line of spring dresses.

Design and **compose** are like *create* in referring to aesthetic acts, but are more specific in their application. Someone who *designs* dresses, cars, or stage sets may simply execute the plans for these products, leaving their actual construction to lesser artisans. Thus, *design* emphasizes conception rather than building. Also, it suggests a less profound change from raw material to finished product than *create:* We can *design* schemes to prevent urban sprawl, but we can hardly *create* utopias from scratch at this late date. *Compose*, most specifically, refers to musical composition: to *compose* a symphony or a popular song. In this sense, it is more like *create* than *design.* In its passive use, however, the aesthetic implications disappear, and *compose* refers to the possibly arbitrary constituents of a group or object: a city *composed* of many ethnic strains.

Make, the most general of these verbs, is pivotal in that it may apply to aesthetic or scientific acts on the one hand, or on the other to production of any kind: artists who *make* sculptures; biologists who *make* new species through hybridization; nations that *make* hydrogen bombs; factories that *make* detergents. Because of the wide range of possibility of *make,* a more specific word is sometimes preferable.

Invent in a scientific or technological context is parallel to *design* in its aesthetic context. The person who *invents* a product plans and tests a new concept, though he or she may leave its production to others. Just as *create* has more status than *design* in the arts, so discover, as the highest goal of the sciences, has more scientific status than *invent:* Franklin discovered electricity, but Edison *invented* the light bulb.

Produce refers mostly to the turning out of work: the last years of his life in which Shakespeare *produced* no new plays. In another sense, however, the work implied by *produce* may be done by people who had no part in *creating, designing,* or *inventing* the product: theatrical technicians who *produce* what the playwright *creates;* seamstresses who *produce* the gowns fashion experts *design;* factories that *produce* the light bulbs based on the one Edison *invented.* See BUILD, CHANGE, DEVISE, FIND, MAKE, MOLD.

Antonyms: BREAK, DESTROY, KILL, *obliterate.*

creative
imaginative
ingenious
inventive
original
resourceful

These adjectives apply to the active, exploratory mind and to its products, describing creators or creations that employ ordinary materials in extraordinary ways. **Creative** suggests the entire process whereby things that did not exist before are conceived, given form, and brought to being. **Original** is more limited in scope and more specific, pointing to the creator not as maker but as source. The *original* mind, slipping free of the conventional and the commonplace, comes up with things no one else has thought of—the new idea, the different approach: an *original* insight; a highly *original* poet. The *creative* mind goes further, combining the fruits of experience and imagination in an *original* way to recreate reality in a new form: the *creative* process; a mind in *creative* ferment.

Where *creative* and *original* describe the mind, *creative* and **imaginative** have to do with the imagination. Great literary works are produced by the *creative* imagination, but the creators of such works and the works themselves are called *imaginative,* not *creative: imaginative* writers; *imaginative* literature. *Creative,* when applied to people and what they do, makes an elementary distinction. The *creative* people in an advertising agency are artists and writers, as distinguished from bookkeepers and sales personnel. *Creative* writing is the writing of fiction or poetry, as distinguished from the writing of fact or opinion. But *creative* is also used pretentiously in advertising lingo to mean novel, new, or different: *creative* hair styling.

Imaginative and **inventive** are alike in indicating an active fancy, a nimble exercise of mind, and both apply to works that are strikingly *original.* But where the *imaginative* person may visualize things very different from reality, the *inventive* person figures out how to put things together in a new way so that they will work. Inventiveness is a practical kind of creativity. It calls into play analytical qualities of mind, often in the service of a common-sense idea of what is needed.

The **resourceful** mind solves its problems despite limitations, finding whatever means are available and adapting them to its ends. Where an *inventive* mind poses its own problems, a *resourceful* mind copes with externally imposed problems. [The *resourceful* Scarlett O'Hara made a ball gown from her draperies.] An *imaginative* child may express himself or herself by drawing. An *inventive* child may do wonders with an Erector Set. A *resourceful* child may drape an old sheet over a card table to make a playhouse. Imposed limitations are not always implied by *resourceful,* however. Faced with the same abundance of toys, one child still might become easily bored; a *resourceful* child, by contrast, might soon begin to develop new games, using untried combinations of these elements.

The **ingenious** person is both *inventive* and *resourceful,* but above all brilliantly clever. *Ingenious* may, in fact, sometimes suggest a superficial cleverness indulged in for its own sake, without a cause. But *ingenious* is more often complimentary, an expression of admiring surprise at an ability to solve a problem neatly in a highly *original* way. Applied to products themselves, *ingenious* may indicate something unusually complex or intricate: an *ingenious* water clock. It can also suggest something deliberately devised to trick or mislead: an *ingenious* way of coping with absentees; an *ingenious* method for cheating on exams. See ARTISTIC, IMAGINATION.

Antonyms: BANAL, *dull, helpless, mindless, myopic, witless.*

credulous. Do not confuse the adjective *credulous* (too ready to believe) with the adjective *credible* (believable).

creed
doctrine
dogma
tenet

These nouns refer to the articles of faith on which a group of adherents are agreed. **Creed** most specifically refers to a concise statement of the essential points to which all believers must subscribe: the Athanasian *creed.* **Doctrine** suggests a particular stand that may be briefly summarized but that usually can involve complex or extensive theological discussion for full treatment: the easily affirmed *doctrine* of the Trinity to which so many church fathers devoted at least a volume of explanation. *Doctrine* may also refer to any item that makes up a *creed:* the *doctrine* of the Resurrection. By extension, *doctrine* can also sometimes refer, in other fields, to views generally subscribed to: the Keynesian economic *doctrine* of stimulating growth through an unbalanced budget.

Dogma refers to an authoritative stand or a bundle of such stands that all believers must accept as correct. A *dogma,* however, need not be of such first-rank importance as to be part of a religion's *creed;* it best suggests, in fact, an accretion of moral standards that have become institutionalized by time into an inflexible set of rules for the living of life: the shattering of worn-out *dogma* during the Reformation and Counter Reformation. By extension, *dogma* refers to any set of unquestioned assertions or attitudes in any field: Maoist *dogma* that branded the Soviet Union as a betrayer of the revolution. **Tenet** refers to an attitude, principle, or precept that may or may not be part of a body of *dogma* or *doctrine.* In any case, *tenet* suggests something more provisional in nature than these other nouns and thus more susceptible to change: holding to the *tenet* that the best military officers are those who come up through the ranks. See IDEA, OPINION, RELIGION.

crime

felony
misdemeanor
offense
treason
violation

These nouns pertain to the breaking of a law. **Crime** refers specifically to serious misconduct, **violation** specifically to lesser breaches of regulation; **offense** generically includes both kinds of lawbreaking: slums rife with theft, murder, and other *crimes;* a traffic *violation;* a scofflaw who repeats the minor *offense* of illegal parking and, by ignoring the tickets, becomes guilty of a major *offense;* a light sentence because it was a first *offense. Crime* may be used as an abstract noun to suggest all illegal activity: a mogul of organized *crime.* It may be used hyperbolically to mean any misjudgment: It's a *crime* to waste your money on such a movie. It may also imply a breach of moral standards: a *crime* against nature; a *crime* against humanity. Outside the legal context, *violation* may suggest a breaking of faith or the rape or desecration of something held sacred: the *violation* of a confidence; a *violation* of the test-ban treaty; soldiers responsible for the widespread *violation* of the captured city's women; the *violation* of holy relics. *Offense,* outside the legal context, may suggest extremely bad taste or injury to someone's sensibility: a film so ribald as to give *offense.*

Crime is commonly subdivided into two categories—

misdemeanors, the less serious, and **felonies,** the more serious *offenses.* The line between *misdemeanor* and *felony* is arbitrarily set by tradition or law. Thefts up to a certain amount of money, for example, are *misdemeanors;* over that amount, they become *felonies.* Severity of sentence may also be a determining factor. **Treason** is distinct in kind rather than degree from *misdemeanor* and *felony;* it involves a deliberate betrayal of one's country to an enemy, whether in peace or war. Of these three nouns, only *treason* is occasionally used in other than its legal sense. In this case it refers to some monstrous desecration or ethical violation: Nazi doctors whose experiments constituted moral *treason* against our most deeply ingrained human instincts. During periods of heated political controversy, *treason* is often used loosely to describe any act deemed unpatriotic or damaging to the national interest: In my book, burning our flag is an act of *treason.* See mischievous, sin.

Antonyms: *benefaction, good deed, service.*

crucial

acute
critical
pressing
urgent

These adjectives refer to the growing lack or need of something vital or to the turning point in an emergency or crisis. **Crucial** is the most general of these in that it can refer to either of these situations equally well: a *crucial* battle that would determine the outcome of the whole war. By contrast, **acute** usually refers to a lack or need that has intensified to crisis proportions: an *acute* water shortage; an *acute* lack of public housing. Less frequently, *acute* refers to other emergencies: the *acute* problem of air pollution in cities. In medical terminology, *acute* means grave or severe: an *acute* attack of bronchitis.

Critical is similar to *crucial* in that it refers either to an extreme lack or to a turning point: a *critical* absence of safety features in the new models; a *critical* showdown vote on the proposed legislation. *Critical* differs from *crucial* in often suggesting a more exact measurement of the lack, especially when even a slight decline could have far-reaching consequences: Another minute's lack of oxygen could be *critical.* The greater seriousness of *critical* as compared to *crucial* is also present when the reference is to a turning point. Where *crucial* may emphasize the absolute necessity that something happen in order to achieve a satisfactory result, *critical* more often suggests a balance between positive and negative outcomes that is beyond our power to influence: a decision that was to prove *crucial* to the great victory won that day; helpless to combat the *critical* weakening of the body's defenses. *Critical* can also be used to imply that something is scarce but vital: a list of *critical* materials.

Pressing and **urgent** are milder than *acute, critical,* and *crucial. Pressing* is especially so, since it can refer to a serious lack that is chronic rather than *acute:* a *pressing* need for changes that are not likely to be accomplished soon. *Urgent* suggests a closer approach to crisis, but the lack it points to might be one among many, without necessarily being the decisive one: faced with so many *urgent* needs that they had to decide which of them were the *critical* ones and which could wait a little longer. Both *pressing* and *urgent,* moreover, can refer to an emergency without necessarily referring to its turning point: a *pressing* matter; an *urgent* conference between heads of state. Both adjectives can refer to appeals rather than to the lack itself: a *pressing* request for funds; an *urgent* appeal for help. In all the various possibilities, however, *urgent* maintains its greater intensity when compared to *pressing.*

cruel

    bestial
    brutal
    nasty
    sadistic

These adjectives pertain to harsh or harmful acts that inflict pain on others or to inhumane temperaments and attitudes that are lacking in sensitivity or compassion. **Cruel** can apply to both the act and the attitude: the *cruel* way she mistreated the helpless child; *cruel* and vicious prison guards. While *cruel* can suggest gratuitous or unmotivated infliction of pain, *cruel* is also used to describe situations in which punishment may be deserved or thought desirable, but is meted out unjustly or excessively: a constitutional ban on *cruel* and unusual punishment; a *cruel* and repressive regime. But *cruel* can also apply to anything that causes pain or harm, even where any intent to hurt or punish is absent: the *cruel* sea; the *cruel,* inexorable forces of nature. By contrast, **sadistic** always implies a deliberate wish to cause pain and even more specifically focuses on inflicting pain for its own sake rather than out of necessity or as punishment. *Sadistic* suggests a warped mind that gets pleasure from seeing or causing other living things to suffer: the disturbed child who tore butterflies apart with *sadistic* gusto; a *sadistic* man who got sexual release only from flogging his partner.

Brutal and **bestial** both compare *cruel* behavior to that of animals. *Brutal* emphasizes a lack of sensitivity or compassion and can suggest a gross and unintelligent person given to the use of excessive and indiscriminate force in attaining an objective: Many a movie executive reached the top by trampling on others in the most *brutal* way. By contrast, it is possible to be both clever and *cruel;* also, the *sadistic* mentality may contrive intricate ways of inflicting pain. *Brutal* alone stresses sheer, savage force. Because of this, *brutal,* like *cruel,* can be used to refer to nonhuman actions, especially those that are harsh or energetic: The ship was beleaguered by the *brutal* pounding of the violent storm. *Bestial* is applied exclusively to humans; it does not point solely to forcefulness as does *brutal* nor necessarily to the inflicting of pain like *cruel* and *sadistic.* It indicates, instead, any sort of behavior that is thought unworthy of a human being because of its depravity, degeneracy, or viciousness: the *bestial* society that countenanced the enormities of Auschwitz and Treblinka. In a related use, *bestial* can apply to unrestrained or unnatural appetite of any sort: the *bestial* lust he felt for his own daughter. As Mark Twain pointed out, it may well be inaccurate to call *cruel* behavior *bestial,* since most animals inflict pain only out of such necessities as hunger and self-defense, whereas people have often been known to do so gratuitously.

Nasty is the mildest of these adjectives; at its most informal it can describe anything that is severe, serious, or harmful: a *nasty* cut. Used of behavior, it points to extreme unkindness or callousness and not necessarily to inflicting physical pain at all: She told them she wouldn't put up with their *nasty* remarks any longer. In describing personality, it can point to an extremely disagreeable temperament or to a habitual mistreatment of others: He woke up in a *nasty* frame of mind; a *nasty* person who treated other people like dirt. See DEPRAVED, HOSTILE.

Antonyms: *gentle,* HUMANE, *kind, merciful.*

cry

    bellow
    outcry
    roar
    scream
    shout
    shriek
    yell

These nouns all refer to a voice raised in excitement or urgency. Although each suggests most readily a particular emotion, all have been used interchangeably to pertain to any expression of intense feeling: joy, anger, pain, grief, despair, amazement, resentment, and many others. All of them, furthermore, pertain to one person's tone of voice, but are commonly used for groups of people when one wishes to suggest that the group responds almost unanimously to some event with a single reaction.

Cry, **shout**, and **yell** are the most general, emphasizing mainly the loudness of a voice or voices: a *cry* of delight; a tortured *cry;* a *shout* of approval that rang through the hall; a *yell* for help. *Cry* particularly suggests a surprised or involuntary response. In an informal context, however, *cry* is especially associated with emotions that result in tears: the woman who sat down and had a good *cry.* This informal use is sometimes present as an overtone in other uses of *cry:* watching her leave and *crying* for her to come back. *Yell* is especially relevant to a situation in which someone is calling for help: hoping their *yells* would carry far enough to be heard. *Yell* also has a particular use for *cries* of enthusiasm at sports events, either spontaneous or planned: cheerleaders who led the spectators in a school *yell; yells* of "Murder him" that were heard throughout the rink. *Shout* can relate to the situation of seeking help, but it also pertains particularly to the emotion of anger: an apoplectic *shout* from her husband that rang through the café.

Bellow and **roar** relate to this aspect of *shout* in being most appropriate for angry *cries. Bellow* suggests deepness of voice as well as loudness and thus implies a man's voice or that of a group dominated by men; it is also used for enraged animals, such as an angered bull: the platoon sergeant's *bellow* of disgust; a furious *bellow* from the wounded bull. *Roar* also suggests anger when it refers to a single person, but it is especially appropriate for describing the reaction of a crowd. In the latter case, the emotion need not be that of unanimous anger, but of a mingling of diverse emotions: the *roar* of praise and disapproval that swelled through the arena. *Roar* can, of course, also refer to any loud mingling of noises, neither human nor animal: the *roar* of the printing presses.

Shriek and **scream** refer most appropriately to *cries* of pain, terror, or surprise: the *shriek* of a woman trapped under piles of debris. In sharp contrast to *bellow, shriek* suggests high-pitched sound, discordant, grating, or whining: The woman's *shriek* of terror carried farther than the man's enraged *bellow.* Because of this implication, *shriek* is sometimes used of birds: the *shriek* of gulls above the harbor. It can also be used for any grating sound: the *shriek* of chalk against the blackboard. Like *shriek, scream* often implies a high-pitched, piercing sound: the *scream* of a siren. But it emphasizes loudness more than pitch, and more often than *shriek* may apply to hysterical or panicky shouts of men as well as women: Clutching his crushed foot, he let out a *scream* of pain. Both *shriek* and *scream* may be used hyperbolically in situations suggesting intense surprise: When she opened the present she gave a little *shriek* of joy; a *scream* of delight. And both are commonly used to describe the *shouts* of children.

Outcry relates to *shriek* as it pertains to *cries* of pain. But its most specific use is for an outburst of indignation, usually from a group of people: neighbors who watched the murder but made no *outcry.* The sense of protest is present also in metaphorical uses: newspaper editorials that cause a public *outcry* against such indifference. See CHATTER, SAY, SQUEAL.

curse
anathema
execration
imprecation
malediction

These nouns refer to the denunciation of something or the calling down of evil on someone. **Curse** is the only relatively informal noun here and the one most widely used in a variety of ways, and as a verb as well as a noun. Most informally, it can refer to any blasphemous oath or example of profanity but, more pertinent here, it suggests the denunciation of someone in whatever terms: *cursing* him for being unfaithful. Behind this use lies the more specific situation of appealing to a supernatural power to punish a wrongdoer or enemy: King Lear's calling upon the gods to *curse* his ungrateful daughters. *Curse* can also pertain to any condition seen as a handicap or misfortune: the *curse* of being a woman in a man's world. Behind this use lies the more specific situation of seeing the occurrence of some affliction as a punishment sent by fate: arguing that his misfortunes were a *curse* for his inconstancy.

Execration and **imprecation** are more formal substitutes for *curse* in the sense of denouncing or calling down harm upon someone. Of the two, *execration* is the more intense, suggesting greater violence and loathing: his *execration* of his son's misbehavior before the whole family. *Execration* can also refer to the denunciations themselves: the columnist's predictable *execrations* of the party in power. *Imprecation* derives from a Latin word meaning pray, and this was reflected in a now obsolete use of *imprecation* for any sort of praying. More recently, *imprecation* points exclusively to the expressing of wishes or hopes that someone will meet with misfortune. This may be expressed or merely thought, but *imprecation* suggests a private, even guarded expression to oneself of ill wishes, rather than the face-to-face denunciation of the person involved, as suggested by *execration:* muttering *imprecations* to himself against his former employer; voodoo *imprecations* conducted in secret and employing wax dolls through which pins are stuck.

Malediction and **anathema** are the most formal of these words. Where *execration* can refer to a face-to-face attack and *imprecation* to a completely solitary expression of ill will, both nouns refer most often to public denunciation expressed to arouse general disapproval. *Malediction* compares with its antonym, benediction, and may similarly suggest a formalized, ritual, or clerical denunciation: priestly *maledictions* against heresy within the church; a full-page ad taken by zealots to present their *malediction* against the administration's liberal policy. Its public nature can be seen in that *malediction* is sometimes used as a synonym for slander: spreading unfounded *maledictions* that amounted to character assassination of his former colleague. *Anathema* at its most specific refers to a formal ecclesiastical ban or *curse,* in which a person is excommunicated or a book or idea is condemned: pronouncing an *anathema* against the teachings of evolutionists. More generally, *anathema* can refer to anything disliked or detested by anyone: explaining that his former friend was now *anathema* to him.

Antonyms: *benediction, blessing.*

cursory

careless
hasty
scant
slapdash
superficial

These adjectives refer to giving less than full attention or effort to a demanding task. **Cursory**, the most formal of these, is also both the most specific and most inclusive, referring to a deliberately rushed or shallow treatment: rejecting the manuscript after a *cursory* glance at it; only a *cursory* attempt to help her client. The other adjectives here all emphasize one aspect of *cursory*. **Careless** suggests that the poor performance results from sloppiness and inattention to details: so *careless* as to render her best efforts *cursory*. **Hasty**, by contrast, emphasizes a refusal or inability to spend the time necessary for a more adequate performance: after a *hasty* thumbing through the pamphlet of instructions; a *hasty* consideration of the merits of the case. **Slapdash** approaches *cursory* in inclusiveness, since it combines the implications of both *careless* and *hasty*, suggesting a sloppy, rushed performance: trying to work from a *slapdash* sketch instead of a painstakingly executed blueprint.

Superficial limits *cursory* to a refusal or inability to look into the deeper meanings or complexities of something: a *superficial* analysis of the poem; *superficial* competence that could hardly withstand serious challenge. *Superficial* is in sharp contrast to *careless* and *hasty*, since one might give adequate care and time to an effort and still come up with a *superficial* result. Most often, in fact, *superficial* suggests an inability to do better and thus, unlike the other adjectives here, does not imply a deliberate refusal to meet the demands of something. **Scant**, in this context, refers specifically to brevity of effort: paying *scant* attention to class assignments. *Scant* differs from *hasty*, however, in emphasizing a short amount of time rather than work done too rapidly. One might have a great deal of time and still do *hasty* work; conversely, one might work methodically in the *scant* time allotted a task. Only in *cursory* are both the tendencies necessarily combined. See NEGLECT.

Antonyms: CAREFUL, *minute, painstaking, profound, searching, thorough.*

cut

gash
incision
slash
slit

All these nouns mean openings or separations of parts by edged or pointed instruments. A **cut** may be of any size and may be produced by any kind of instrument, whether intended for cutting or not. A bulldozer may produce a *cut* in a mound; the edge of a piece of paper may produce a *cut* on the finger. An **incision** is a *cut* made for the purpose of gaining entry. *Incision* is mostly used in surgery: an abdominal *incision* to expose an inflamed appendix. A **gash** is a long and broad *cut*, usually accidentally produced: Flying windshield glass produced a *gash* on the face of a witness to the accident. A **slash** is a long, often deep *cut*, usually administered with intent to injure with a sharp instrument such as a sword or a knife, and is produced by a long, swinging motion. A **slit** is a long, thin *cut* or *incision.* Some surgical *incisions* are mere *slits;* A letter opener is designed to produce a *slit* in an envelope.

Gash often suggests a jagged, ugly wound, whereas

slash stresses the length and depth of the wound, which may have been cleanly made; *slit* describes a more precisely made and usually narrower *cut*. [The *gash* on her leg from the barbed wire took thirteen stitches to close; The *slash* from the saber extended from his shoulder to his forearm; The *slit* in the patient's throat enabled the surgeon to insert a tube to assist her breathing.] See HARM, WOUND.

daily

daily
diurnal
everyday
quotidian

These adjectives refer to things that are commonplace or that occur every twenty-four hours or during daylight. **Daily** and **everyday** are the most informal of these. *Daily* refers most specifically to something that appears once every twenty-four hours: a *daily* newspaper; subject to tantrums that were almost a *daily* occurrence. It may also refer to things that inevitably occur each day, regardless of the number of times: Give us this day our *daily* bread. It may even suggest things accounted for by the day or things that differ from one day to the next: a *daily* record of expenditures; restaurants that have changing *daily* menus. *Everyday*, by contrast, refers almost exclusively to anything usual or ordinary, whether or not it can be said to occur once every twenty-four hours: the *everyday* life of the town. More specifically it refers to things appropriate for ordinary, humble occasions rather than for special events: their *everyday* clothes. It can even suggest that something is plain or drab: my *everyday* routine.

Quotidian and **diurnal** are much more formal. *Quotidian* is the more inclusive of the two in referring to aspects both of *daily* and *everyday*. It can indicate something that occurs *daily*: a *quotidian* fever. *Diurnal* suggests something that goes through its cycle of changes once every twenty-four hours: the *diurnal* motion of the stars. See TEMPORARY, USUAL.

Antonyms: *nightly, nocturnal,* UNPARALLELED, UNUSUAL.

danger

danger
hazard
jeopardy
menace
peril
risk
threat

These nouns refer to the possibility of harm or destruction. **Danger**, the most general of these, can refer to any situation that confronts one with an undesirable or injurious eventuality: He had stayed up so late that he was in *danger* of oversleeping and being late for work; discussions to reduce the *danger* of a military confrontation between the two nations. *Danger* is a familiar warning on road signs: *Danger—Curves Ahead.* As in the last example, *danger* often suggests a difficulty that can still be avoided through forethought. By contrast, **peril** exclusively points only to grave dangers and may sometimes suggest a worsening situation that can no longer be averted by the use of forethought alone: Many species are already in *peril* of extinction because of our destruction of their natural habitats. More broadly, *peril* can suggest the unpredictable *danger* that must be faced in pursuing a course of action: the great *perils* that the early arctic explorers confronted.

Risk is related to this last use of *peril*, but is more general and can indicate less extreme or imminent *danger*. At its most specific, it indicates the chance of misfortune that accompanies an act undertaken in hope of gain or benefit: a business insured against the *risk* of fire. Here, the negative possibilities can to some extent be foreseen and weighed against the possibility of success: a calculated *risk*. **Hazard** can function as a more formal substitute for *risk*, though it may suggest that greater *danger* attends the action. In this, it combines the gravity of *danger* suggested by *peril* with the weighing or taking of chances suggested by *risk:* the *hazards* of mountain climbing. *Hazard* can also function as a hyperbole for the predictable liabilities in any situation: He braced himself for the *hazards* of an encounter with the Internal Revenue Service agent. It is also commonly used to refer to taking an unwise *risk:* Storing newspapers in an attic presents a fire *hazard*. **Jeopardy** can substitute for *risk* at an even greater level of formality than *hazard*. It now mainly appears in the phrase *in jeopardy:* Such a gamble against long odds would put their venture *in jeopardy. Jeopardy* frequently appears in a legal context, where it indicates the *risk* of being convicted and sentenced; the phrase *double jeopardy* refers to the situation, barred by the Constitution, of standing trial twice for the same crime.

Threat and **menace** can both refer not to *danger* inevitably accompanying an act but to a malevolent or coercive *danger* independent or external to oneself: an escaped psychopath who was seen as a *menace* to the community. *Menace* suggests the possibility of violence or destruction and points to a graver *danger* than any of these nouns except *peril.* *Menace* can also refer more emphatically than *hazard* to something that represents an unwise *risk:* a rickety stairway that was a *menace* to life and limb. *Threat* is milder than *menace* and more general. Most concretely, it can indicate an expressed intention to harm: a *threat* against the attorney's life; a *threat* to expose him unless he continued to work for the gang. More generally, *threat* can indicate a situation or act that puts something in *danger:* provocations that were a *threat* to peace. See FEAR, PRECARIOUS.

Antonyms: *defense,* PROTECTION, *safeguard, safety, security.*

daring
adventurous
venturesome
venturous

These adjectives describe a fearless willingness to take risks. **Daring** stresses bold, decisive, forceful, or startling acts that set the performer apart and that may be viewed with awe or fear: a *daring* trapeze artist. Usually, *daring* implies admirable fortitude, cool-headed proficiency in the face of danger, or an unusual or original approach: a *daring* foray into enemy territory; a *daring* proposal to provide universal health insurance. Often, *daring* is favorable and implies the successful execution of an action: a *daring* novel brilliantly executed. Sometimes *daring* is used as a euphemism for risqué or salacious: *daring* photos of nude models. **Adventurous** indicates a habit of mind that is interested in exploring the new or untried, but *adventurous* gives fewer implications about the manner of execution. In this it is more general, being as applicable to a more relaxed or casual approach as to the decisive forcefulness indicated by *daring:* an *adventurous* mind that could painstakingly digest vast areas of new knowledge. Also, *daring* more often implies a single or specific goal, whereas *adventurous* can point to a general curiosity or zest for exploration: a *daring* maneuver; *adventurous* students off on a lark and ready to try anything.

Venturesome also concentrates more on single or specific goals, but is otherwise less rich than *daring* in its implication. It can suggest a canny—even prudent—weighing of odds before action, however unconventional the action itself may be: a *venturesome* gamble with penny stocks that paid off largely because of the speculator's shrewdness. **Venturous** is now less common in use, pointing to the taking of risks, but with no necessary implications of shrewdness or decisiveness: a *venturous* fellow who had at least learned to withstand setbacks. See BOLD, BRAVE, OPPORTUNISTIC, RECKLESS.

Antonyms: CAUTIOUS, COWARDLY, TIMID.

dead
deceased
defunct
departed
extinct
lifeless

These adjectives refer to something that is no longer in existence. **Dead** refers most concretely to any once-living thing that has died: his *dead* father; a *dead* rabbit; a *dead* tree. It can even refer to anything that no longer functions: a *dead* battery. By contrast, **deceased** and **departed** are exclusively restricted in reference to *dead* people. *Deceased* is a legal term that seems euphemistic in any other context, although it sometimes appears in ordinary use. *Departed,* by contrast, would strike many as a euphemism for *dead;* it is meant to be delicate by suggesting that the *dead* person has gone to a better world. Compared to *departed, dead* is simple, dignified, and universally unoffending.

Defunct and **extinct** contrast with the foregoing by not referring to the death of a living individual at all (except for comic effect). Although *defunct* could with all seriousness once be used of a *dead* person, it now applies mainly to the lapsing or closing down of nonliving things: a *defunct* literary magazine; an anthropomorphic attitude that is now *defunct* in the biological sciences; a *defunct* enterprise. *Extinct* refers to the lapsing of a whole species or line of individuals: when the brontosaurus became *extinct;* a family name that became *extinct* when the only heir died without issue.

Lifeless has a wide range of uses from the literal to the lyrical: *lifeless* inorganic compounds; dawn lighting the *lifeless* streets of the city. When used of someone *dead,* the implication may be of a recent death: staring down at her *lifeless* face on the pillow. See CORPSE, DIE.

Antonyms: *existent,* LIVING.

deception
chicanery
deceit

equivocation
fraud
trickery

These nouns pertain to the use of misrepresentation to win the trust or approval of others. **Deception** has the widest range of uses; at its mildest, *deception* can suggest a necessary or inconsequential misrepresentation: She referred to the pills as candy, a foolish *deception* intended to make it easier to administer them to the child. At its most disapproving, *deception* can point to selfish dishonesty: a candidate who practiced all kinds of *deception* on the voters to win their confidence. **Deceit**, which is wholly negative in tone, is considerably harsher than *deception* in its disapproval. It can suggest a habitual liar or schemer or refer to an involved plan to take advantage of someone else: the flagrant *deceit* by which he kept his wife from understanding his business affairs. Where *deceit* often stresses the dishonesty of one person to another, **fraud** more often points to a complex, more impersonal system for cheating all comers or the public at large. It often suggests official dishonesty or financial malfeasance: a land-development *fraud* that bankrupted dozens of retired persons. Sometimes, *fraud* is used hyperbolically for anything one finds utterly worthless: That movie was a total *fraud*.

Equivocation is most closely related to the mildest sense of *deception*, but can be even less severe, since it need indicate no intent to deceive. Instead, it points to an evasive or pussyfooting approach: Her *equivocations* sometimes seemed to be nothing more than a reluctance to give a straight yes-or-no answer. In some cases, *equivocation* is used as a mere euphemism for a lie: She denied having lied to me, although she admitted she had been guilty of an *equivocation* or two. **Trickery** points less to verbal misrepresentation alone than to the deliberate giving of false appearances. It is milder in its disapproval than *deceit* and *fraud*, although it can apply to either personal or public behavior. *Trickery* is a harsher term than *deception*, however, in suggesting the selfish seeking of gain, often by means of an illicit scheme: the *trickery* they practiced on their friends in order to appear more prominent than they were; He gained control of the corporation by *trickery* in manipulating the proxy votes entrusted to him. While **chicanery** suggests less serious offenses than do *trickery* or *fraud*, it adds a note of disgust for trivial or shoddy methods or goals: Press agents who will stoop to any kind of *chicanery* to gain publicity for their clients. See GUILE, TRICK.

Antonyms: *candor, frankness, honesty, sincerity, veracity*.

decide

determine
resolve
settle

These verbs pertain to the reaching of conclusions. **Decide** stresses the making of a choice regardless of how it is arrived at: jurors who have already *decided* what to think before hearing all the evidence; an investigative committee that took months to sift testimony and *decide* whether new legislation should be drafted. Sometimes a conclusive factor may be the subject: Above all, it was her earnestness that *decided* me. Using a passive construction is often thought to make the conclusion seem more objective, impassive, and official: It was *decided* at our meeting to adopt the honor system for the next semester.

Settle is considerably more forceful than *decide*, pointing exclusively to the reaching of a definite or final choice after a period of indecision or dispute: a new hearing to *settle* the question forever; She had considered a number of jobs before *settling* on a career in advertising. With *for*, *settle* can indicate a reluctant or compromise choice: They had wanted to spend a week in Rome but *settled for* a few days. A related context for **determine** pertains to investigation or discovery; here, in reference to choice, *determine* still implies thoughtful or searching consideration: She never asked for help in *determining* where to hang pictures. The force of *determine* changes considerably when it is used as a past participle to express a decisive choice, purpose, or conviction: He was *determined* to win the game. **Resolve** is closely related in meaning to this one sense of *determine*, referring to an even greater conviction or purpose with which something is *decided*. [He *resolved* to clear his father's name; I was *resolved* to become a ballet dancer.] *Resolve* can also refer to the *settling* of a question by a group, most often after debate: The student group *resolved* that draft deferments should be rescinded. More generally, *resolve* can refer, like one use of *decide*, to something that is conclusive: means to *resolve* the open questions surrounding the assassination. See CONSIDER, FIND, JUDGE.

Antonyms: *fluctuate,* HESITATE.

declare

advertise
announce
broadcast
enunciate
proclaim
publish

declare *(continued)*

These verbs refer to the releasing of information or rulings in official or public ways. More informally, **declare** can relate simply to forceful or direct assertion: She *declared* that she didn't want to see him again. This possible implication of forcefulness may or may not be present when *declare* applies to official rulings. [The judges *declared* the contest a tie; The military police *declared* the tavern off-limits.] In any case, *declare* here emphasizes an authoritative utterance.

Announce pertains almost exclusively to public or official statements, but these can be declared in any medium and they may be informative as well as authoritative decisions. [I called a press conference to *announce* my candidacy; They *announced* to the assembled guests that they were engaged to be married; The officials *announced* new rules to cover the championship bout.] On an informal level, **proclaim** can indicate the *declaring* of a considered and definite decision or judgment: She *proclaimed* the dress much too daring for her. Pertaining to official utterance, *proclaim* stresses extreme formality: the ceremony at which he would officially be *proclaimed* archbishop. It can also indicate resolute conviction: We *proclaim* these truths to be self-evident. **Enunciate** carries over its reference to clear speech when it applies to official statements, since here it stresses the careful but authoritative spelling out of detailed rules or doctrine: the pope who first *enunciated* the doctrine of the Assumption of the Virgin.

The remaining terms all now pertain primarily to the dissemination of information through various communication media. **Publish** pertains to books, magazines, newspapers, and other print media. **Broadcast** once referred merely to making something known far and wide, but more often now pertains to anything programmed on radio or television or announced over a public-address system. **Advertise** now indicates a paid presentation to win popularity for a product or candidate. Unlike *publish* and *broadcast,* however, *advertise* can suggest every conceivable medium in which paid messages can appear. A company may *advertise* its products by means of newspapers, magazines, television, billboards, even skywriting. See ASSERT, SLOGAN.

Antonyms: *censor, conceal, withhold.*

decrease

abate
decline
drop
dwindle
fall
sink
subside

These verbs refer to a lessening in numbers, intensity, or volume. **Decrease** and **dwindle** can both be applied widely but are particularly pertinent to a reduction in numbers. Of the two, *decrease* is the more general and has fewer connotations. [In winter, the number of arrests generally *decreases;* The number of nations supporting us *decreased* as the war dragged on.] Where *decrease* can apply as well to a reduction in undesirable things, *dwindle* usually suggests a loss of something valuable; it often gives a lyrical or elegiac tone and can suggest a wasting process. [Wildlife sanctuaries have *dwindled* alarmingly in the last decade; His health *dwindled* day by day.]

Abate and **subside** both point to a slow reduction in intensity: The ferocity of the enemy's counterattack *abated* after the second day. *Subside* can suggest in particular a return to calm or repose after agitation: a violent struggle after which he *subsided* into feverish sleep. Like one possibility for *dwindle,* both these verbs are often applied to a slow loss of strength or health.

Decline and **sink** are particularly relevant to a reduction in volume. *Decline* is more neutral and factual, whereas *sink* can give a lyrical or elegiac tone. While both can apply to illness, both also can refer factually to the gradual reduction in the measurable level of something: The volume of stocks traded *declined* as prices continued to *sink* throughout the day. Both refer metaphorically to downward movement, but *sink* is more graphic here and can suggest a quicker or more drastic shift: public acclaim that *declined* slightly at first and then *sank* rapidly when a vicious review was published. *Sink* is relatively informal when compared with the previous verbs.

Drop and **fall** both concentrate on a sudden shift downward or a reduction in numbers, intensity, or volume. Both, like *sink,* are relatively informal. A possible distinction between the two exists in that *drop* might more naturally describe a desired reduction and *fall* an unfortunate one. [The incidence of malaria *dropped* dramatically following completion of the swamp elimination program; The national dialogue *fell* to a new low, with name-calling and denunciation replacing rational discourse.] When *fall* is used with *off,* it applies more generally to any *decline,* slow or rapid, good or bad: Unemployment continued to *fall off* in the third quarter. See REDUCE, WANE, WEAKEN.

Antonyms: ENLARGE, ESCALATE, *grow, strengthen, wax.*

decry. Do not confuse the verb *decry* (disparage) with the verb *descry* (catch sight of).

dedicate
consecrate
devote
hallow

These verbs refer to a resolute commitment or a bestowing of honor, credit, reverence, or respect. **Dedicate** can pertain to a formal or public act in which something is metaphorically assigned to the honor or credit of someone who is not its immediate creator: I *dedicated* the book to my grandchild; a holiday *dedicated* to the memory of those who died in the nation's battles. Parallel to this, one may *dedicate* oneself to a particular goal; in this case, *dedicate* stresses resolution and conviction: He *dedicated* his life to the abolition of slavery. **Devote** relates almost exclusively to this last sense of *dedicate*, but it puts less stress on an idealistic commitment and more on something pursued out of warmth, affection, or personal inclination: a man *devoted* to his family; a loner *devoted* to a life of pleasure-seeking. Even where *devote* approaches *dedicate* in use, a more intimate or personal note is felt: From that moment on, she *devoted* herself to a simple life in service of others.

Consecrate and **hallow**, both relatively formal, are specifically religious in tone; at their most restricted, they suggest a ritual in which something is set aside for a sacred purpose: *consecrated* ground; *hallowed* be Thy name. Both apply outside the religious context to any extreme or solemn commitment, although *consecrate* here possibly applies more widely: a truly great President who *consecrated* himself to seeking and upholding the public good; a day set aside to *hallow* the founding of the country. See AWARD, ENTRUST, RESPECT.

Antonyms: *desecrate, dishonor, profane.*

deficient
inadequate
poor
unsatisfactory

These adjectives refer to what is substandard or low in quality. **Deficient** is by far the most specific and exact in meaning. It points to a lack of something required to accomplish a goal or purpose: a check returned because of *deficient* funds; Rickets can result from a diet *deficient* in vitamin D. Usually, *deficient* does not suggest a lack that is a matter of degree but one, whether small or large, that fails to meet a minimum level of need below which something cannot function at all. Applied to aspects of character, *deficient* suggests a flaw or failing, whether correctable or not, that makes someone unable to perform some activity: an armchair theorist *deficient* in practical experience.

Poor, the least specific and most wide-ranging of all these adjectives, applies in this context to a matter of degree rather than to a cutoff point at which something ceases to function: *poor* eating habits that, miraculously, did not result in a vitamin deficiency; anemia that resulted from a diet *poor* in iron. **Inadequate** relates more closely to *deficient* in indicating failure to meet minimal standards. *Deficient*, however, often points to a minimum that can be objectively measured, whereas *inadequate* can point to a more subjective evaluation: *deficient* by two votes of passing the proposed legislation; a pianist whose technique seemed *inadequate* to the demands of the pieces she had chosen to play. But *inadequate* can indicate lacks that are a matter of fact rather than of taste: a water supply *inadequate* to the needs of the city. By contrast, **unsatisfactory** stresses the first sense of *inadequate*, pointing more to subjective evaluation than to measurable lack: The teacher informed the boy that he was making *unsatisfactory* progress in his studies. It can also indicate a matter of degree, like *poor*: many brilliant scenes in a play that on the whole was *unsatisfactory*. As in the last example, *unsatisfactory* at its most literal can refer to a failure to give satisfaction or pleasure. See SCANTY, WEAK.

Antonyms: *ADEQUATE, good.*

definite
categorical
explicit
express
specific
unconditional
unequivocal
unqualified

These adjectives may all describe statements that are flat, clear-cut, and direct. **Definite** and **unequivocal** both refer to expressions unclouded by ambiguity. *Definite* is unique in suggesting decisiveness of choice; a *definite* answer would be one that is conclusive and perhaps binding. *Unequivocal*, in contrast, is more concerned with truthfulness and with expressions free of misleading possibilities. A *definite* agreement made in bad faith would not be *unequivocal*.

Categorical, **unqualified**, and **unconditional** refer to expressions reduced to the simplest statement possible, without reservations of any kind. *Categorical* suggests that possibilities for reply have been sorted out into a very few categories in advance: a *categorical* yes-or-no answer; a *categorical* denial of the charges. *Unqualified* is similar to but more sweeping than *categorical* in suggesting that the statement will hold true regardless of any limitations or restrictions that might be brought to bear. If a critic gives *unqualified* approval to a play, it means he or she found every aspect of it worthwhile—the acting, staging, sets, costumes, and dialogue—whether or not these things are mentioned item by item in a review. Because of this suggestion that details need not be given, *unqualified* sometimes suggests a rashness of judgment: *Unqualified* views are unwarranted in such a complex situation. *Unconditional* is more apposite to agreements or the making of bargains. It suggests that one's stand is not dependent upon provisos: *unconditional* surrender; an *unconditional* guarantee.

Explicit, **specific**, and **express** emphasize that the statement is spelled out, in all its details if necessary. This emphasis contrasts sharply with *unqualified,* and with the necessary brevity implied in *categorical.* In suggesting a stated rather than assumed situation, these adjectives are more like *definite. Definite,* however, is more concerned with clarity than with detail. One might infer that which is *definite,* but *explicit* implies an actual putting into words. [It was *definite* that he was to be a passenger on the boat, though he would not be *explicit* about his destination.] *Explicit* often tends to suggest the stating of choice among alternatives, while *specific* may simply emphasize accurate description without evaluation. *Specific,* more than *explicit,* also suggests full treatment in giving particulars: a *specific* block-by-block report on the city's housing needs. *Express* is slightly more formal than *explicit* or *specific* and means expressing in plain words what might already be implied. [An *express* agreement among honest men and women is seldom necessary.] See ABSOLUTE, CANDID, CLEAR, OVERT.

Antonyms: *ambiguous,* IMPLICIT, OBSCURE, *tentative,* VAGUE.

definitive. Do not confuse the adjective *definitive* (conclusive) with the adjective *definite* (clear and unmistakable).

delusion
fantasy
hallucination
illusion
mirage

These nouns refer to mental experiences that appear realistic or believable but, despite their vividness, have no objective reality. **Delusion** refers to the most extreme and inclusive form of this mental phenomenon, since it may combine vivid sensory imagery with complex notions or conceits; in a psychotic person, these *delusions* are mistaken for reality and are not voluntarily called up: a *delusion* that he heard voices urging him to kill; a *delusion* that he was Abraham Lincoln; the final stages of alcoholism in which *delusions* are commonplace. The phrase *delusions of grandeur* is a clinical term that is often used commonly for anyone with inflated self-regard.

Fantasy and **illusion** are considerably less extreme than *delusion,* referring to mental activity that everyone, not just a psychotic person, has commonly experienced. *Fantasy* applies mostly to an imaginary scene, such as that in a daydream, whether called up voluntarily or not, which is acted out mentally with vivid sensory imagery, but is not, except in the mentally ill, mistaken for reality. *Fantasy* may emphasize a general tendency of imagination toward the fanciful, whimsical, surreal, or grotesque: a *fantasy* in which she watched her parents mourning over her coffin; a delightful element of *fantasy* that makes some authors' ghost stories chilling and convincing. *Illusion* can refer to an ideational cluster of notions that everyone experiences, voluntarily or not, but which do not correspond to any objective view of things: under the *illusion* that he could accomplish the entire job without help. Two related, but milder, uses of *illusion* exist; one refers to the bundle of ideals or necessary lies some people maintain to buoy up their egos: an *illusion* that the society in which he lived was very near perfect; an *illusion* that he was well liked by his fellow workers. Another use of *illusion* refers to confused optical phenomena that trick the eye into seeing a situation as other than it is: Heavy fog had created an optical *illusion* that made the opposite shore appear much closer than it was. **Mirage** is specifically restricted to this last sense of *illusion:* a *mirage* that made the highway ahead seem to be flooded with water. When a person is under extreme stress, however, an inward mental disturbance may cooperate with deceptive optical clues to create something more similar to a *delusion:* Gasping through lips cracked by the desert sun, he claimed he saw a silver palace just over the next dune, unaware that the vision was nothing but a *mirage.*

Hallucination is mainly restricted to vivid sensory experience, like *fantasy,* but in its intensity a *hallucination* approaches the believability of a *delusion.* This experience would tend to occur involuntarily to any person under certain extreme circumstances, as during a long-term fever, after heavy dosages of painkillers or other drugs, during delirium tremens, or in connection with certain physical illnesses, such as brain tumors. In this sense, a *hallucination* might be most typically fleeting, like a waking dream. In other uses, however, *hallucination* may point to nervous malfunction expressive of a deep-seated mental imbalance, in which case it indicates one possible constituent of a psychotic *delusion.* See IMAGINATION, MISLEADING.

Antonyms: *actuality, fact, reality, truth, verity.*

demand

ask
claim
exact
order
request
require

These verbs all refer to rather forceful communications between a speaker and another person. **Demand** most commonly suggests a speaker in authority who bluntly insists upon being obeyed and does not intend to be contradicted: *demanding* your compliance with all our regulations. Its forcefulness may be weakened in some uses to a less blunt insistence: a book that *demands* your full attention; to be surrendered when the bearer *demands* payment. **Request** is considerably weaker than any sense of *demand;* it suggests a courteous statement of desire: *requesting* the bandleader to play her favorite tune. *Request* has a special relevance here, however, in that it is more and more used as a euphemism for *demand* in order to disguise the latter's harshness: The vice president firmly *requested* the manager's resignation. **Require** may suggest a stated set of rules listing necessary conduct: employers who *require* perfect punctuality and flawless performance. *Require* is like *demand* in suggesting authority and insistence, but unlike the latter in that it stresses need and may suggest an impartial code drawn up in advance. [No rational person would *require* the constant reassurances she *demanded.*]

Ask is like *request* in depending on context for whatever overtone of harshness or force it may suggest: *asking* timidly if he might see the menu again; political systems that *ask* for the complete surrender of all individuality. By contrast, **order** is like *demand* in its peremptoriness, suggesting power and authority on the part of the person who directs someone to do something. It is further removed than *demand,* however, from any suggestion of anger; like *require,* it may be quite impersonal, especially in a military context. [I'm not *asking* you to fire your weapons, I'm *ordering* you.]

Claim and **exact** involve a slightly different situation than these other verbs. *Claim* suggests that a right is being asserted: *claiming* this land in the name of the monarch; unions that *claimed* a right to share in the company's profits. *Exact* is stronger than *claim* in suggesting someone with enough authority to back up a *claim,* possibly with force, if necessary: a dictator who *exacts* grotesque extremes of obedience from underlings. In this, it is similar to but stronger than some uses of *require.* In other uses, *exact* shades off, like *require,* into impersonality, with less suggestion of force: states that *exact* tolls on newly built highways. See CLAIM (n.), PLEAD, REQUEST (v.), REQUEST (n.).

Antonyms: *FORGO, RELINQUISH.*

demur

balk
boggle
recoil
scruple
shirk
shrink
shy

These verbs refer to the act of hanging back from full participation or full assent. **Demur** suggests mild dissent or personal objection, possibly in reply to a direct request: gently *demurring* to her notion of leaving the party early. It may also imply hesitation prompted by doubt or indecision: Though urged to stay to dinner, she still politely *demurred. Demur,* in comparison with the other verbs in this set, might now seem too stiffly formal. **Scruple,** closely related to *demur* and only a little less formal, points specifically to hesitation or objection on moral or ethical grounds. [A single woman of that era often *scrupled* about being left alone with a gentleman; He did not *scruple* to tell lies when lying served his interests.] The verb *scruple* might now apply especially to overly fussy or niggling ethical distinctions. The note of propriety present in *scruple* is absent from **shy.** *Shy* emphasizes instead a looking aside or holding back out of fear, doubt, or caution. It thus suggests a more intense negation than *demur* or *scruple,* pointing to a reaction based less on reflection than on instinct. [The horse *shied* at the first hiss of the snake; The girl *shied* away from looking the strange man in the eye.]

Recoil and **shrink** relate more closely to *shy* than to *demur* or *scruple*. *Recoil* suggests a sudden springing back out of surprise, distaste, or fear. *Shrink* does not carry the implication of suddenness but emphasizes an indecisive cringing from something ominous, frightening, or even disgusting. [She *shrank* from entering the grimy tavern with him and once inside, she *recoiled* at every depraved face that met her gaze.] *Shrink* may also suggest excessive timidity: a *shrinking* violet.

Balk suggests a holding back that is more determined than *shrink*, but not necessarily sudden, as with *recoil* and *shy*. The determination implied by *balk*, in fact, extends to stubbornness: workers who *balked* at working under such poor factory conditions. *Balk* also has a special overtone implying that the subject has gone along with a situation as long as possible, but now stops short, calling a halt out of weariness or anger. [They *balked* at taking another step until their guide agreed to name a fee for his services; The donkey *balked* at climbing the next hill until it had food and water.] **Boggle**, by contrast, suggests a refusal at the outset, triggered by disbelief, shock, or amazement. In one sense, it is an intensification of *recoil*: senators who *boggled* at the President's astonishing proposal.

Shirk has a special sense that separates it sharply from these other verbs. Here, the holding back is an expression of laziness or unwillingness to cooperate: teachers who *shirk* their responsibilities to their students. See DISAGREE, HESITATE.

Antonyms: *accede, accept,* CONSENT.

denomination

church
cult
religion
sect

These nouns designate bodies of believers united in a common faith and form of worship. By derivation, **denomination** is precisely directed to this concept. It comes from the Latin word for name and applies to a religious group adhering to a particular creed under a distinctive name. In its broadest sense, *denomination* may refer to any such group: State aid to *denominations* is forbidden by the Constitution. The adjectival form, *denominational*, is often used in this sense as a synonym for parochial: *denominational* schools. But in a restricted sense, the noun *denomi-*

nation is commonly reserved for specific Protestant communions: Representatives of several Protestant *denominations* were present—Baptists, Methodists, Presbyterians. **Church** is interchangeable with *denomination* in this sense. The Methodist *denomination*, for example, is more often referred to as the Methodist *Church*. But *church* has a much wider range of application than *denomination*. In its broadest sense, it may refer to ecclesiastical organization and authority, as distinguished from secular authority: the separation of *church* and state. In the context of Christianity, it may designate all, or a major part, of Christendom. [All Christians are members of the universal *Church*; The Pope is the head of the Roman Catholic *Church*; The Archbishop of Canterbury is the highest prelate of the *Church* of England.] In its most strictly limited sense, it may refer to an individual congregation or to the building in which that congregation worships. [Which *church* do you belong to?; My *church* (or the First Presbyterian *Church*) is on 10th Street.] Also, where *church* stresses the union of believers in one body, *denomination* emphasizes separateness. Hence, in an ecumenical age of interdenominational activity, *denomination* is less often used in its religious context than formerly.

Religion is a general noun embracing all systems of religious belief. It can be used to refer to the major faiths or to their larger subdivisions: the Christian *religion*; the *religion* of the Mormons; the Jewish *religion*; the *religion* of the Essenes; Islam is the *religion* of Muslims. Like *denomination*, *religion* may sometimes emphasize differences in belief, and in this sense it is often used with reference to Catholicism, Protestantism, and Judaism: to marry outside one's *religion*.

Sect may designate a smaller group within a *denomination*, especially one that differs from the larger body in a particular matter of faith or worship. *Sect* is also used derogatorily of a relatively small, unorthodox *denomination*, to stress its separateness or peculiarity: *sects* that spring up and bank on emotional appeal. *Sect* acquired this derogatory connotation as a result of the many historical instances when *sects* were formed by groups that had split from their parent *religion* because of doctrinal discontent: the *sects* of the Gnostics.

The term **cult** is often applied to the forms or followers of a religious system that is looked on with suspicion or disfavor: The *cult* of Dionysus inspired orgiastic revelry during the celebrations of the Eleusinian mysteries. It also denotes a kind of worship or veneration that is not theistic in principle and is sometimes faddish in practice: the *cult* of nature; youthful worship that found momentary expression in the *cult* of James Dean. See FACTION, RELIGION.

deplore

bemoan
bewail
lament
mourn

These verbs refer either to sincere or censorious disapproval or to an aggrieved or regretful feeling of loss. **Deplore** often suggests a feeling of righteous indignation. It refers to thoroughgoing disapproval of what is perceived by some as an affront to decency, taste, propriety, or morality: to *deplore* a leader's vacillating policies; *deploring* the book's bad writing; *deploring* the lack of support for science; *deploring* the frankness of language in today's movies.

Bemoan and **bewail** are often used in tandem to suggest a *deploring* attitude that is overly solemn, hypocritical, or censorious: *bemoaning* and *bewailing* their capture as though they were innocent victims. Both verbs once were used with serious intent, but now they are mostly restricted to pejorative or satirical uses. While both indicate a verbal display of sorrow or grief, *bemoan* might suggest a greater incoherence, one more nearly reduced to wordless sounds; *bewail*, by contrast, might suggest a self-indulgent rush of sanctimonious or hypocritical rhetoric. Often no distinction can be seen between the two in actual usage: *bemoaning* the effort he had to make to support his family; loudly *bewailing* her husband's mistreatment of her to the neighbors.

Lament can also be used pejoratively or satirically, like *bemoan* and *bewail*; it more specifically suggests in this case a hypocritical or self-pitying expression of bereavement or loss: *lamenting* the passing of the good old days. *Lament* still has legitimate serious uses, however, to indicate sincere grief or remorse: *lamenting* the fact that it was her own lack of concern that had driven the boy from the house that night. **Mourn** has pejorative possibilities, but it is much more commonly used to refer to serious expressions of deep loss: the entire nation unashamedly *mourning* the loss of the great leader. See COMPLAIN, GRIEVE.

Antonyms: *applaud, approve, cheer, commend, PRAISE.*

depraved

corrupt
degenerate
evil
heinous
infamous
nefarious
vicious
vile
villainous
wicked

These adjectives describe persons, qualities, or actions that are morally base, malicious, or malevolent. **Depraved** is perhaps the most sinister. It points to utter perversion, meaning, by derivation, completely bad or totally immoral. In its most common use, it suggests a compulsive or willful turning away from the good, indicating a warped character or a twisted mind: a *depraved* sadist; *depraved* tastes. Where *depraved* tends to be absolute, **degenerate** is relative, implying a descent from a higher state or better condition. It may indicate moral, physical, or mental deterioration from a standard or norm: the *degenerate* heir to a fortune; the decline of a *degenerate* empire; a *degenerate* drug abuser. Since *degenerate* focuses on the results of degradation, however, it is commonly applied to persons or things that may never have been normal to start with: sexually *degenerate* persons; *degenerate* habits. **Corrupt** is clearer than *degenerate* in its implication of a lapse from a better condition, even when the resulting adulteration has totally vitiated any positive values that may originally have been present. But where *degenerate* is applied to low specimens of humanity, *corrupt* is often used of persons in high positions whose moral decay may not be apparent on the surface: a *corrupt* government, shot through with graft, vice, and venality; a *corrupt* official who was always receptive to a bribe.

Wicked and **evil** are both general words with wide application. *Evil* means morally bad: *evil* practices; *evil* companions. In an abstract sense, it is the polar opposite of good and can suggest utter and insidious malevolence: the eternal struggle between good and *evil* in the moral universe. Hence, *evil* can be a much stronger word than *wicked*, which implies sinfulness and may sound old-fashioned: a *wicked* and unrepentant old reprobate. *Wicked* is now often used in a humorous, tongue-in-cheek, or even admiring way: a tennis player with a *wicked* backhand.

Vile suggests something noxious or loathsome in its depravity, something utterly despicable or repulsive. A *corrupt* official might present a pleasant or attractive appearance, but *vile* indicates disgusting qualities that are readily apparent: a *vile* mass of putrescence. *Vile* may, however, be used in a looser sense as a colorful intensive of awful or terrible. [What *vile* weather! She's in a *vile* mood. Don't use such *vile* language.] **Villainous** suggests egregious wickedness and can be applied disapprovingly to anyone thought guilty of *evil* behavior: a *villainous* traitor. Even more than *wicked*, however, *villainous* now imparts an old-fashioned, melodramatic flavor to a denunciation: The *villainous* scoundrel absconded with the woman's life's savings; a *villainous* deed.

Unlike the other adjectives in this set, **infamous** refers to notoriety and ill fame, indicating a *vile* reputation. It points to *evil* that has gained wide publicity or that deserves universal condemnation, and it may apply to a person, action, or place: the *infamous* commandant of Auschwitz; the *infamous* Nazi concentration camps; his *infamous* act of treason. **Nefarious** is the most formal in the group and the least often encountered. It may suggest a glaring disregard for law or accepted morality, or a shocking disrespect for things that are worthy of reverence. It often has implications of premeditated group activity that is clandestine and underhand: the *nefarious* drug cartel; a *nefarious* scheme. **Vicious** calls to mind a mean, snarling animal baring its fangs and preparing to attack. It is used to describe persons, things, or ways of acting that are cruel or brutal, whether or not an *evil* act is intended: a *vicious* dog; a *vicious* gunman. *Vicious* may also mean spiteful or malicious, as in a *vicious* lie; *evil* or *depraved*, as in *vicious* associates; or morally injurious, as in *vicious* habits. **Heinous** comes from an Old French verb meaning hate. It is applied to something so atrocious as to inspire hatred, horror, or outrage: the serial killer's *heinous* crimes. *Heinous*, however, is distinctly high-flown or old-fashioned in flavor. See POLLUTE, PROFLIGATE.

Antonyms: *CHASTE, HONEST, INNOCENT, MORAL, PIOUS.*

deprecate. Do not confuse the verb *deprecate* (feel and express disapproval) with the verb *depreciate* (belittle, disparage).

descent

ancestry
lineage
pedigree

These nouns may designate collectively those from whom one is descended, or may indicate characteristics inherited from them. **Descent** is the most general. It is frequently used to refer to the nationality, race, or ethnic characteristics of one's immediate fore-

bears: persons of Swedish *descent*. **Ancestry** refers most strictly to all of one's progenitors on both sides: They could trace their *ancestry* all the way back to William the Conqueror. It may also, like *descent*, mean ancestral derivation, of whatever kind: a youth of royal *ancestry;* a mongrel of dubious *ancestry*. Unlike *descent*, however, *ancestry* sometimes points specifically to noble or distinguished forebears: She thought she was better than other people because of her *ancestry*. **Lineage** emphasizes a direct line of *descent* from a particular ancestor. It may embrace in one family, for purposes of genealogy, all the descendants of such a progenitor: St. Joseph is believed to have been of the house and *lineage* of David. *Lineage*, however, excludes all other branchings of the family tree. Many people are of the *lineage* of William the Conqueror, but the rest of their *ancestry* varies so greatly that their being of William's *lineage* has relatively little significance in accounting for their individual characteristics.

Pedigree stresses notable *ancestry* that is documented in detail and that usually includes many outstanding forebears. It may also refer to a list or table of *descent,* often a genealogical register of an animal. [A *pedigreed* pet is one of pure breed; Many dog owners are prouder of their pets' *pedigrees* than they are of their own.] See ANCESTOR, KIN.

desecration

debasement
defilement
profanation
sacrilege
violation

These nouns refer to irreverent or improper acts. **Desecration** is the opposite of consecration. It indicates the dishonoring of something sacred by wrongful use or irreverent treatment, and it commonly implies a conscious or intentional act. Specifically, *desecration* often points to the deliberate degrading, damaging, or destroying of a religious building or place: The stabling of horses in a church would be a *desecration;* the *desecration* of synagogues and cemeteries by ruffians. Outside a religious context, *desecration* may suggest the contemptuous abuse of anything that is held dear or regarded as sacred: a *desecration* of the American flag. **Profanation** is milder than *desecration* and less commonly used. It may or may not involve physical abuse of a sacred place, but focuses on a lack of proper respect or a callous or shocking act of irreverence: the *profanation* of a shrine by thoughtless sightseers; a cult that considered it a *profanation* to visit its temple without first undergoing a full day of fasting. Literally, *profanation* suggests a reduction of something sacred to the level of the secular, but it has few general uses outside the religious context. **Sacrilege** comes from a Latin word meaning temple robber. In a theological sense, it may imply improper use of a sacrament, as by one unfit to give or receive it. In a broader sense, it often points to an irreligious or taboo act that profanes the sacred character of a person, place, or thing in a shocking way: The primitive tribe considered it a *sacrilege* to utter the sacred name. *Sacrilege* is even less concrete than *profanation*, though, since the irreverence involved can consist of a thought as well as an act and need not occur within religious surroundings: It was deemed a *sacrilege* to question the witch doctor's teachings even for a moment.

Defilement suggests the dirtying or *profanation* of something that should be cherished or kept pure. In a religious sense, it may indicate the act of rendering something ceremonially (though not literally) unclean: the *defilement* of the temple by the presence in it of infidels. In a broader sense, it may indicate either a physical or spiritual sullying: the *defilement* of justice by prejudiced and corrupt officials. **Debasement** is less often used in a religious sense and does not suggest befouling or pollution. Instead, it focuses on a lowering in character, quality, or worth: determined to tolerate no *debasement*, however slight, of the club's standards. Applied to persons, *debasement* may indicate a public humiliation, as through verbal attack: The accusations he shouted at her during the banquet made his *debasement* of her complete.

Like *desecration* and *profanation*, **violation** may apply to the irreverent treatment of a sacred thing or holy place: the *violation* of the shrine by souvenir hunters; the vandals' *violation* of the sanctuary. But *violation* more often carries legal rather than religious connotations, suggesting the breaking of a law or a failure to abide by the terms of a binding contract: a *violation* of the tenure clause. Outside this specific context, it can be used of a sexual attack: medical tests to determine whether there had been a sexual *violation* of the woman. In its most general sense, it can refer to any outrage of decency: a *violation* of our sense of fair play. See CRIME, DISGRACE, POLLUTE, WORLDLY.

Antonyms: *consecration, purification, sanctification.*

descry. Do not confuse the verb *descry* (catch sight of) with the verb *decry* (disparage).

despair
desperation
despondency
discouragement
hopelessness

These nouns refer to a defeated, pessimistic attitude. **Despair** is the most general and informal of these. It implies loss or abandonment of hope and may suggest a permanent state of mind or a momentary one brought about by some calamity: lives doomed to want and uncreative *despair;* their silent *despair* at having lost the child. It may also refer specifically to pessimism about the future, whether momentary or permanent: a growing *despair* of ever getting a worthwhile job. **Hopelessness** relates exclusively to this last possibility of *despair*, implying a pessimism more deep-seated and long lasting: the utter *hopelessness* with which she regarded her narrow range of choices. *Hopelessness* may also suggest that someone's present position is extremely imperiled, with or without that person's realizing it: They were not yet aware of the *hopelessness* of their situation, given the lack of fresh water on the lifeboat.

Discouragement is much milder than the other nouns of this group. It restricts itself to one possibility of *despair* in that it pertains almost exclusively to a feeling of letdown at some misfortune or rebuff: the understandable *discouragement* with which he took the rejection of his application. *Discouragement* most often suggests a response to the thwarting or frustration of an ongoing process or effort; it can be momentary (as above), gradual, or total: growing *discouragement* to see everyone in the office promoted except him; a general *discouragement* with her life that she couldn't even explain or analyze. **Despondency** also pertains to a thwarted or frustrated feeling of letdown, but it is more intense than *discouragement* in suggesting more strictly a sense of total defeat that is expressed in lethargy, introversion, and apathy: days of *despondency* in which he hardly bothered to get out of bed; a long period of *despondency* before the first suicide attempt. *Despondency* relates tangentially to *hopelessness* in that such thoroughgoing defeat as it suggests usually implies as well a feeling that the future will not improve one's situation.

Desperation is unique among these nouns in suggesting such an intensity of *despair* that one may easily be goaded into wild, blind, or reckless action as a last resort. Thus, *desperation* contrasts with *despondency* and its implications of lethargy: fighting back at his tormentors with the *desperation* of a cornered rat; willing to risk anything in her *desperation*. See MISERABLE, MISERY, SAD.

111

Antonyms: CONFIDENCE, *encouragement*, EXPECTATION, *hope, hopefulness, optimism.*

despise

abhor
disdain
loathe
scorn

These verbs refer to a strong contempt or revulsion toward something. **Despise** indicates intense aversion or moral disapproval: I *despise* commercial television; those of us who *despise* bigotry. **Loathe** focuses mainly on aversion or dislike: Her husband *loathed* vegetarian meals. **Abhor**, by contrast, is stronger in suggesting outright hatred and hence extends to moral opprobrium better than *loathe*, which has been weakened by its extensive use for simple distaste: *abhorring* smug, priggish suburbanites and their moral hypocrisy.

Disdain suggests a feeling of superiority toward something or someone else; consequently, it can suggest an unwarranted self-righteousness in addition to its reference to distaste: an airy *disdain* for all those with less education. **Scorn** is a much stronger substitute for *disdain*, suggesting a haughty rejection or denunciation: *scorning* her ideas as though nothing could have been more repugnant. See CONTEMPTUOUS, ENMITY, REPULSIVE.

Antonyms: *admire, adore, appreciate, like,* LOVE, RESPECT.

despotic

autocratic
dictatorial
tyrannical
tyrannous

These adjectives suggest repressive rule by a single person or group. **Despotic** is the clearest of these adjectives in its disapproving indication of repressiveness and unrestrained power. This once was not always true, as the phrase benevolent despotism indicates. Now it more uniformly suggests a harsh and cruel wielding of power: *despotic* parents; a *despotic* executive. **Dictatorial** refers more neutrally to unrestrained power, usually in the hands of one person, and can apply whether this power is used fairly or harshly: a *dictatorial* regime that took over from the corrupt democracy that preceded it. *Dictatorial* does, of course, often carry the same disapproval as *despotic* and can imply the same harshness of rule: the reign of terror during Stalin's *dictatorial* leadership of the Soviet Union.

Tyrannical can suggest the arbitrary and abusive exercise of power concentrated in the hands of one person; it is now used less frequently to refer to government than to any mishandling of authority: a *tyrannical* office manager; a *tyrannical* union leader. **Tyrannous** is less commonly used than *tyrannical*, except for rhetorical flourish; it might refer to a whole situation, rather than to a person: *tyrannous* laws.

Autocratic is the most neutral of these adjectives, indicating one-person rule and referring descriptively to such a person's absolute power rather than to how it is exercised: an *autocratic* father. Context can give *autocratic* a disapproving flavor: an arrogant and *autocratic* foreign secretary. See AUTHORITARIAN, CRUEL, OVERBEARING.

Antonyms: COMPLIANT, *conciliatory, democratic,* LAWFUL, *representative.*

destroy

annihilate
demolish
eradicate
exterminate
extinguish
extirpate
raze
ruin
uproot
wreck

These verbs refer to the complete and usually forcible breaking up or damaging of something so that it is no longer recognizable or effective. **Destroy** is a general word with few overtones beyond its emphasis on force and thoroughness: the tornado that *destroyed* dozens of mobile homes in the town. **Ruin** is even more general, pointing only to the thoroughness of the damage; force, however, may not be involved and a single destructive act may not be at issue: manuscripts *ruined* by long exposure in the cold, damp cellar. **Wreck** suggests a battering action that breaks something up into an unusable mass or heap of fragments: companies that specialize in *wrecking* buildings. These three verbs particularly have a wide range of use beyond actual physical destruction. Here, *destroy* may suggest malevolent action that makes something impossible: escalation of hostilities that *destroyed* all hopes for a negotiated peace. *Ruin* points to anything that spoils or mars something good or desirable: a thunderstorm that *ruined* our picnic. *Wreck* suggests the breaking down of some cohesive unity: the constant squabbling that finally *wrecked* their marriage.

Demolish and **raze** are generally applied to big or substantial things, such as buildings or other edifices. A building is *demolished* if smashed to pieces, and *razed* if leveled to the ground. *Demolish,* unlike *raze,* is often used figuratively of the reduction of any complex whole to ruins: to *demolish* a social theory with a few incisive comments. *Raze* is used almost invariably of buildings or their remains: to *raze* the upright timbers left in the aftermath of the fire.

Annihilate is the most extreme verb in this list and literally means reduce to nothingness. As more commonly used, however, it denotes a severe degree of damage to a thing or person. An army may *annihilate* an enemy force by so damaging it as to render it incapable of further offensive or defensive action, but without literally removing all traces of its existence. A debater may be said to *annihilate* an opponent if he defeats him decisively.

Eradicate and **uproot** are etymological equivalents, but differ in their applications. To *eradicate* weeds is not only to *destroy* their visible parts but to pull them out by the roots and thus prevent their reappearance. *Eradicate* can also mean eliminate completely: The new vaccine *eradicated* all traces of the disease within three months. *Uproot* means pull up by the roots and is used figuratively as well as literally: trees *uprooted* by the hurricane; a family *uprooted* by the decision to build a highway through its property.

Exterminate, **extinguish**, and **extirpate** often mean destroy purposefully. *Exterminate* means wipe out or kill in great numbers: to *exterminate* insects by spraying with DDT. *Extinguish* means put out, as a fire; it is also used metaphorically as a synonym for die, implying a comparison between life and a spark or flame: The patient's life was finally *extinguished* by the onset of pneumonia. *Extirpate* refers to the rooting out or utter destruction of something: to *extirpate* a disease by destroying the organisms that cause it; to *extirpate* heresy within the church. See BREAK, HARM, REMOVE, VANQUISH.

Antonyms: BUILD, CREATE, DEVISE, *establish*, REPAIR.

devise

conceive
contrive
formulate
invent

These verbs are concerned with the development of plans for solving a problem. **Devise** and **contrive** both stress the actual working out of the plan, detail by detail. *Devise* is neutral in tone, making no comment on the value of the plan or its objective; it also emphasizes the tentative nature of the proceedings, suggesting that many possibilities are entertained, used, rejected, or revised: *devising* proposals to deal with air pollution; *devising* tactics that could win the battle. *Contrive* is similar in most respects to *devise* except for its tone, which may now suggest a conspiratorial or illicit plotting toward unworthy ends: *contriving* a foolproof scheme for robbing the bank. In a different but also negative sense, *contrive* may suggest unrealistic planning, needless complication, or artificial devices that avoid the problem rather than solve it: a law so *contrived* that the average person could not possibly understand or obey it.

Conceive refers to a point in the planning process that must precede *devising* or *contriving*. *Conceive* suggests the first ideas that form in a person's mind when faced with a problem, but before these ideas have necessarily been tested by the process implied in *devise*. He *conceived* of a hundred answers to his dilemma, but none helped him *devise* an escape from it. **Formulate**, by contrast, refers to an act that follows *devising*, in which the rough plan is spelled out, formalized, or put into words. Each step of the planning process may be evaluated separately. [The proposed law, while brilliantly *conceived,* has been poorly *devised* to do the job at hand; even worse, it is so vaguely *formulated* that it invites misinterpretation.]

Invent is much larger in scope than the other verbs here. It includes the entire planning process— *conceiving, devising,* and *formulating*. Also, its product is more often an actual object than simply a set of procedural techniques: *inventing* new synthetic fibers; *inventing* new techniques for coping with juvenile delinquency. See CREATE, INTEND, SUPPOSE.

die

bite the dust
depart
die with one's boots on
expire
go to meet one's Maker
kick the bucket
pass away
pass on
pass over
perish

Die is the simplest verb in this group, the most straightforward and direct way of saying stop living, that is, experience the permanent cessation of all vital functions. It is used figuratively in reference to any-thing that ceases to exist. [The smile *died* on his lips; The flames in the fireplace *died* slowly, keeping the room warm for an hour more.] To **die with one's boots on** originally designated the end of a person who *died* violently, especially in battle and in the kind of battle dress that included boots. Today, a person who *dies with his boots on* is one who *dies* while engaged in some activity, as his work, profession, etc., rather than during a period of prolonged illness or retirement. **Expire** means breathe out air from the lungs. This sense is extended somewhat euphemisti-cally to a breathing out of one's last breath and so is synonymous with *die:* The old man *expired* only after he'd made a final confession and received extreme unction. It is also used figuratively of things that cease to exist by reaching a natural limit: My lease will *expire* on September 30th of this year. To **perish** is to *die* untimely or in a violent way: Hundreds of settlers *per-ished* that year because of drought and famine. *Perish* is a rather literary word and is often used to denote complete destruction and decay: a civilization that *per-ished* of greed and decadence. **Depart** is a euphemism suggestive of the soul's leaving this plane of existence at the time of death and going on to another life elsewhere. **Pass away**, **pass on**, and **pass over** all are like *depart* in their implication of moving to an afterlife, while **go to meet one's Maker** is even more explicit in its designation of the terminal point of the soul's journey. **Bite the dust** and **kick the bucket** are both slang expressions for *die*. The former once pertained especially to death on the battlefield, where one literally *bit the dust* in a fall from a horse when wounded. Today, it applies not only to actual death but to the figurative death that is caused by failure or ruin: Another small business *bit the dust* this week. *Kick the bucket* is thought to be derived from the last act of a person who hangs him-self by fixing around his neck a noose that is attached to the ceiling and then kicking away an upturned bucket on which he or she has been standing. See CORPSE, DEAD, FATAL, KILL.

Antonyms: *PERSIST, survive*.

diligent
assiduous
industrious
persevering
sedulous

These adjectives describe the continual painstaking exertion of intense care and effort. **Diligent** suggests the accomplishment of work that is done well and that demands the worker's alertness and dedication to the task: her *diligent* efforts to clear her father's name. There is also an implication of wary watchfulness and the making of extremely fine distinctions: inspectors *diligent* enough to catch the slightest lowering of stan-dards.

Sedulous is considerably more formal than *dili-gent* but also stresses attentiveness, with a special over-tone of unwearying application to an exhausting task: a teacher who proceeded so rapidly that only the most *sedulous* student could follow her. **Assiduous** is only slightly less formal than *sedulous;* it emphasizes the ability to do a great deal of hard work. There is less implication that the work is done well, as in *diligent*, or that it is extremely taxing, as in *sedulous*. It does sug-gest dogged determination and an energetic approach: an *assiduous* struggle against the untamed land that every year brought forth larger and larger crops. [A poorly edited book requires the reader's *sedulous* attention to make up for the lack of *diligent* copy edit-ing and *assiduous* proofreading.]

Persevering has an area of meaning that sets it more clearly apart from the foregoing adjectives; it refers to an unremitting effort that is not weakened by momentary failures: to watch the *persevering* spider attempt to build its web time and time again. *Persevering* clearly indicates nothing about the quality or quantity of the work done, only about the unflag-ging nature of the effort: *persevering* in the keyboard-ing despite her exhaustion and her loss of accuracy and speed. **Industrious** also makes no comment upon the quality of the work accomplished, but it does stress constancy or speed of execution. It also suggests a cheerful or good-humored bustle: *industrious* bureaucrats who turn out mountains of reports in a day. See BUSY, CAREFUL.

Antonyms: *FLIPPANT, HEEDLESS, impatient, JAUNTY, lazy, negligent, procrastinating, SLOW*.

disagree
bicker
cavil
differ
dissent
object
quibble

These verbs refer to an expressed lack of concur-rence between the ideas of two or more people. **Disagree** may refer to any verbalized discord, whether trivial or fundamental, whether arising out of a dispute over facts or simply out of a contest of wills: *disagreeing* over which road to take; *disagreeing* as to when Shakespeare was born; those who *disagree* merely for the sake of controversy. **Differ** is milder than *disagree;* it might sound excessively formal to some ears, except in the phrase "I beg to *differ* with you." As a substitution for *disagree,* it can even sound euphemistic: urging them not to *differ* over so slight a matter. It has a real use, however, when one wishes to suggest lack of agreement that does not arise from hostility: *differing* on the causes of poverty but agreeing on steps to eradicate it. *Differ* can also suggest mere factual discrepancy from which no conclusions have yet been drawn: the detective who asked us to explain why our versions of the accident *differed.*

Object and **dissent** are more intense than either *disagree* or *differ* and suggest a more thoroughgoing dispute. *Object* most appropriately pertains to a single point of disagreement: *objecting* vehemently to his last inference. *Dissent,* on the other hand, would suggest the complete rejection of someone else's case, both formulated in detail. [Radicals do not merely *object* to a few scattered instances of injustice; they *dissent* from an entire way of living.]

Cavil and **quibble** pertain to the raising of petty objections to a line of thought. *Cavil* is the harsher of the two, with its implications of ill-tempered hostility: frowning negotiators who *caviled* at every new proposal merely in order to prolong the deadlock. *Quibble* may suggest the bad humor of *cavil* or it may refer only to a supersolemn, overrefined attention to detail that is sophistical in its nitpicking: scholastics *quibbling* over the number of angels that could dance on the head of a pin. *Quibble,* when it suggests contention, still stresses an almost legalistic pettiness: *quibbling* for hours about which candidate had the stronger platform. **Bicker** is an intensification of this sense of *quibble,* suggesting more hostility between the arguers, but with no lessening of the triviality inherent in the argument. Name-calling and groundless assertions, however, may be included as techniques of dispute: *bickering* about who should get up and turn out the lights. See CONTRADICT, DEMUR.

Antonyms: *CONSENT.*

disapproval
animadversion
aspersion
blame
criticism
reprehension

These nouns refer to negative judgments or attitudes toward something. **Disapproval** is the most general of these; it may refer to a fixed, irrational dislike of a person or to a specific instance of reasoned, analytic rejection of an idea or a way of behaving: meeting their efforts at friendliness with ever harsher signs of icy *disapproval;* attempting to demonstrate her *disapproval* of such a solution to their problems. **Criticism** is more exclusively restricted to this last possibility of *disapproval,* usually suggesting an expressed rejection of a specific thing because of its failure to meet certain standards: her constant *criticism* of his way of dressing; fierce *criticism* of every weakness in the debater's argument. *Criticism,* as commonly understood, most often suggests *disapproval,* although in more formal use it can suggest neutral analysis or even approving evaluation: the first work of *criticism* daring to claim greatness for so young an author. **Blame** does not suggest a measuring of something against standards; it stresses, on the contrary, an attempt to determine who is at fault for some failure or catastrophe that has already occurred. Thus, *blame* most specifically suggests the assigning of guilt or responsibility: fixing *blame* on the police for their handling of the investigation; taking the *blame* for the failure of their marriage.

The remaining nouns are considerably more formal than the foregoing and also suggest a much greater severity of *disapproval.* **Animadversion** is censure of a high, authoritative, and somewhat formal kind. It may suggest a single point in a more extensive *criticism,* especially one motivated by hostility: his expected *animadversion* upon the book's risqué language; a discussion that was nothing but a string of bilious *animadversions.* **Aspersion** suggests an even greater fierceness of attack than *animadversion;* its special emphasis is on ill-founded or reckless accusation of a defamatory nature, with the implication that such *criticism* is rendered in a sneering or self-righteous manner: unfounded *aspersion* of the petitioner's good faith; taunting her by casting *aspersions* on her truthfulness. **Reprehension**, unlike *animadversion* or *aspersion,* does not imply prejudiced or unjustified *criticism* but rather indicates a stern rebuke, reproof, censure, or reprimand directed against something blameworthy. *Reprehension* is supposed to be calm and just, motivated by good intentions; it is therefore a serious matter, even when mild, and is capable of great force, as expressed in the phrase *severe reprehension.* [He spoke out in *reprehension* of bossism; bigotry deserving of *reprehension.* See DISCIPLINE, MALIGN, REBUKE, REPREHENSIBLE.

Antonyms: APPROVAL, *credit, endorsement, praise.*

disassemble. Do not confuse the verb *disassemble* (take apart) with the verb *dissemble* (pretend).

discipline

> castigate
> chasten
> chastise
> correct
> punish

These verbs refer to acts taken by persons in authority to restrain or rectify the behavior of someone in their charge. **Discipline** in this context suggests remedial measures, harsh or mild, that are taken to effect an improvement in conduct; they are usually imposed in the form of precise regulations to govern misbehavior: strictly *disciplining* the class for every departure from the rules; *disciplining* his child unmercifully even for minor mistakes. **Correct** and **punish**, in their greater informality, can make *discipline* sound almost euphemistic by comparison. *Correct* refers specifically to the pointing out of error; this, of course, can be done as a help, but in this context it suggests some sort of imposed remedial measure: *correcting* children's tardiness by making them stay after school. Both *discipline* and *correct* seem to imply that an obedience to imposed rules will improve behavior. *Punish* is considerably more honest in its frankness, at least, by referring directly to the imposing of a penalty for undesirable performance: *punishing* her daughter by denying her a week's allowance; arguing that prisons should rehabilitate rather than *punish* lawbreakers.

Chasten is extremely formal but may range in suggestion from actual physical mistreatment to the imposing of any pain or affliction that leaves someone humble or tractable: the *chastening* of her careless ways by his withdrawn and bitter mood. It might particularly suggest the administering of harsh verbal reproaches: choosing a formal meeting of the board to *chasten* the office manager for her ill-advised policies. **Chastise** would now strike most ears as an outdated euphemism for physically *punishing* an inferior: a stout stick on the desk with which to *chastise* unruly students.

Castigate suggests, as does one aspect of *chasten,* a caustically severe verbal reprimand: *castigating* the speechwriters for their slovenly editing; The inspector was *castigated* for failure to check the electrical wiring thoroughly. See REBUKE.

Antonyms: *applaud,* ENCOURAGE, PRAISE, *reward.*

discolor

> stain
> tarnish

The verbs **discolor**, **stain**, and **tarnish** all mean change the color of something for the worse. *Discolor* shares with *stain* the specific meaning of changing something to a different color, *stain* emphasizing that this change is caused by foreign matter. Thus, after a fight, one's clothes are likely to be *discolored,* especially if they are *stained* with sweat, dirt, and blood.

Discolor shares with *tarnish* the specific meaning of depriving of color, or of dulling. *Discolor* is used in this sense when fading, streaking, or the like is referred to: curtains *discolored* by the action of sunlight. *Tarnish* is used to refer to the dulling of luster by action of air, dirt, water, or the like: silverware *tarnished* by the action of sulfur compounds in the atmosphere and in such foods as eggs. See DISFIGURE.

Antonyms: COLOR.

discourage

> deter
> dissuade
> divert

These verbs all refer to an intent to alter the actions or plans of another person by means of some kind of persuasion. **Discourage** suggests an attempt to prevent or repress an action by dulling a person's enthusiasm for it or by weakening his or her sense of purpose: The dean *discouraged* the student from enrolling for an extra course, because the student was already overworked. *Discourage* often presents a proposed action in an unfavorable light: I *discouraged* him from taking a position with that unknown and possibly unreliable insurance company. *Discourage* may also refer to actual, physical obstacles that make an action difficult if not impossible: Low hedges around lawns *discourage* visitors from walking on the grass.

Deter is stronger than *discourage.* To *deter* is to prevent from acting or proceeding by the consideration of danger, difficulty, or uncertainty that might countervail the motive for action. [Few penologists believe that the death penalty *deters* others from committing murder; Fear of the snarling watchdog *deterred* the salesperson from entering the house.]

When you **dissuade** someone from doing something, you try gently to bring that person around to your point of view by giving tactful advice or perhaps even by appealing to his or her better nature. *Discourage* and *deter* often involve stronger means of persuasion, even to the extent of browbeating, while *dissuade* refers to a milder method that is not always as successful. [When she became furious with her boss, I *dissuaded* her from rushing in to submit her resignation; Overweight people may be *dissuaded* from eating too much by friendly reminders that they will feel and look better when they begin losing weight.]

To **divert** is to turn another person's mind from one concern or occupation to another. *Divert* does not involve as much actual persuading as it does distracting the attention and offering an acceptable substitute. If you wish to *divert* a small child from littering the living room with toys, you may suggest that it would be fun if the child would help you by unpacking groceries in the kitchen instead. See QUELL, SUBDUE.

Antonyms: *ENCOURAGE, persuade.*

discriminate

differentiate
discern
distinguish

These verbs refer to an ability for making fine distinctions, or to the possession of qualities that set the subject apart from others of its kind. **Discriminate** pertains mostly to perceiving and evaluating differences among similar things: *discriminating* the real antique from the imitation; the connoisseur who can *discriminate* among several equally fine wines. **Discern** relates closely to *discriminate* but is somewhat more general in stressing an intense or accurate perception without necessarily implying that it is a sorting out of closely related items: *discerning* clearly the faint trail of clues that led to the identity of the murderer.

Distinguish, by contrast, can refer either to an ability of the perceiver or to the differences actually perceived. In the former case, it suggests the making of even finer distinctions than *discriminate* and making the distinctions among things even more closely resembling each other. *Distinguish*, consequently, stresses the skill needed for the detection of differences and, unlike *discriminate*, does not emphasize aesthetic evaluation as a part of the process. [She was unable to *distinguish* the gray shadow she made from all the other shadows in the garden; Anyone can learn to *distinguish* a Goya from a Velásquez, but only a real student of the period can *discriminate* between their styles.] *Distinguish*, however, when it refers to charac-

teristics of a thing perceived, is quite the opposite; in this case, it suggests drastically different and often superior qualities: amazing agility that *distinguishes* them from most other dancers.

Differentiate, in referring to qualities in something perceived, contrasts sharply with *distinguish*, suggesting slighter differences and differences seldom the result of excellence. [The yellows used to paint the sun were only faintly *differentiated* from the other yellows used throughout the whole sky; it took a sharp eye to *distinguish* one shade from the other.] *Differentiate* in the sense of making distinctions is most appropriate to a technical context: the entomologist who had *differentiated* sixty separate insect species. See FIND, PERCEIVE.

Antonyms: *blur,* CONFUSE, JUMBLE.

disfigure

blemish
deface
deform
mar

These verbs agree in meaning inflict injury or damage that spoils the appearance of a person or thing. **Disfigure** and **mar**, as here considered, imply comparatively permanent injury or damage; a person's face may be *disfigured* by scars, or the surface of a desk may be *marred* by deep scratches. The two verbs differ in that *disfigure* suggests a change in outlines or lineaments, whereas *mar* may suggest random nicks and scratches that do not substantially change appearance but may hamper effectiveness or functioning. [The church was *disfigured* by the half-built steeple; The phonograph record was so *marred* that it was almost impossible to listen to.]

Deface and **blemish** are often used interchangeably with *disfigure* and *mar*, but often imply less permanent damage or injury; a wall may be *defaced* by pencil markings, or a person's face may be *blemished* by pimples. *Deface* nearly always suggests flaws introduced into something originally not *disfigured;* deliberate malice is often suggested as the motive: campaign posters *defaced* by graffiti. Something, however, may be *blemished* by inherent defects: a program *blemished* from the outset by a lack of funds.

Deform implies a lasting change for the worse or deviation from the normal in the structure or form of something: a baby *deformed* by congenital abnormalities; *deformed* by a serious accident. See FLAW, HARM, STIGMA.

Antonyms: *adorn, beautify,* CONSERVE, *restore.*

disgrace

abase
debase
degrade
demean
humble
humiliate

These verbs indicate the act of stripping someone of pride, self-respect, rank, or reputation. **Disgrace** points to lowering someone in the estimation of other people: a scandal that *disgraced* the entire community. **Degrade** suggests indulging in disgusting or immoral habits or actions that destroy a person's character or publicly *disgraces* him or her: a fine mind *degraded* and dulled by drug use; accusations intended to *degrade* him and destroy his reputation. **Humiliate** can refer to any inner feeling or outward act that robs someone of self-respect: a husband who enjoyed *humiliating* his wife in public; She felt thoroughly *humiliated* by her lack of insight.

Debase suggests an action that reduces the intrinsic value of something: currency *debased* by inflationary measures; political discussion *debased* by an atmosphere of hysteria. As can be seen, *debase* may be more factual or descriptive than *degrade,* which suggests a more thorough but more subjective or moral sort of depredation.

The remaining verbs all concentrate on what one does to oneself. **Abase** can suggest sycophantic groveling or merely a ceremonial show of respect: *abasing* himself before the hardened criminals with whom he was confined; The vassal *abased* himself before the throne of his liege at the beginning of every audience. **Demean** suggests any lowering of oneself by unworthy motives or behavior: *demeaning* himself in his eagerness to meet the famous author. This verb can refer to a hostile act toward someone else: attempting to *demean* the witness by asking extraneous questions about her personal life. **Humble** can refer to an awesome experience: feeling small and *humble* as he stood gazing up at the Sistine murals. When not reflexive, *humble* functions as a milder substitute for *humiliate:* trying to *humble* her husband by making him account for every penny he spent. See IGNOBLE, REDUCE, SHAMEFUL.

Antonyms: *compliment, exalt, praise, raise,* RESPECT.

disinterested

dispassionate
fair
impartial
neutral
objective
unbiased
unprejudiced

These adjectives describe a willingness to listen to all sides of a case without prejudging it. **Disinterested** does not imply a lack of interest, as is sometimes mistakenly thought, but a receptive interest that does not take sides in a dispute, at least until the truth can be discovered: *disinterested* judges and jurors on whom our judicial system depends. To be *disinterested,* in fact, requires attentiveness to detail and an evenness of temper without implying coldness or lack of feeling. **Fair** is much more informal than *disinterested* and would be more appropriate to describe a decision or a person who makes a decision once a verdict has been rendered: I could tell by the *disinterested* attitude of the judge that he would give a *fair* verdict. Also, where *disinterested* stresses keeping an open mind, *fair* suggests the taking of a stand based on ethical considerations: striving to remain *disinterested* until she could arrive at a *fair* solution to the problem.

Impartial and **unbiased** are more closely related to *disinterested* than to *fair* in emphasizing open-mindedness. *Impartial* suggests literally taking no one's part; it implies, perhaps, a greater impersonality than *disinterested:* a judge free of all political pressures and thus aloof enough to remain *impartial.* While closely related, *unbiased* suggests someone who is inherently free of any predispositions toward conflicting sides or parties. A person who has such predispositions might still, by putting them aside, succeed in being *impartial,* but being *unbiased* suggests he or she has no predipositions to start with: a thorough familiarity with minorities that left him completely *unbiased* for or against them. In reference to reporting, *impartial* might suggest uninvolvement, while *unbiased* would suggest a *fair* treatment of all sides, even though a definite point of view emerges: I don't ask newspapers to be *impartial,* but I do expect them to be *unbiased* at least to the extent of distinguishing between fact and opinion.

Dispassionate and **unprejudiced** both emphasize the control of emotions rather than of thoughts. *Dispassionate* suggests someone unswayed by extraneous appeals designed to excite sympathy or indignation: remaining *dispassionate* amid wild accusations of nepotism and favoritism. It is even more strikingly different from *disinterested,* however, in being applicable not only to an *impartial* judge, but to an involved contender who remains low-keyed, even-tempered, and factual in argument: countering the hysteria of her opponent with a *dispassionate* presentation of the evidence. *Unprejudiced*, in this emotional context, relates most closely to *unbiased*, but *unprejudiced* seems more fundamental and thoroughgoing, more inclusive in stressing the absence of any irrational, deeply ingrained emotional blind spot. *Unprejudiced*, furthermore, might suggest an inward state, while *unbiased* would suggest the result or proof of this state in action. One could learn to behave in an *unbiased* way even though not wholly *unprejudiced:* a new law that requires *unbiased* hiring practices, whether the owners of a business are *unprejudiced* or not.

Neutral and **objective** both suggest an even greater distance than any of the foregoing adjectives. *Neutral* emphasizes the taking of no sides even to the point of rendering no final judgment whatsoever: jury trials in which the judge may remain *neutral* to the very end; *neutral* countries that refuse to be drawn into the dispute. *Objective* suggests an interest only in cold fact as distinct from belief, opinion, or attitude; unlike *disinterested*, it may also suggest lack of feeling: the *objective* attitude of scientists that would be fatal if extended to the sphere of human responsibilities. Some writers would argue that *objective* is necessarily a relative rather than an absolute quality. No one can argue that he or she is wholly *objective* about anything. Most of these adjectives, furthermore, are approving in tone—but only within the context of weighing and judging. They could all describe a moral weakness in other situations. [Who but a depraved person could remain unmoved and *objective* at the thought of a nuclear war?] See ALOOF, UNINTERESTED, UNINVOLVED.

Antonyms: *BIASED, prejudiced, unfair.*

dislike

  antipathy
  aversion
  distaste

These nouns are alike in pointing to a negative emotional response to someone or something. **Dislike**, the most general of these, has a wide variety of applications and can be substituted in most contexts for any of the other nouns here considered. It can be applied both to people and things: a *dislike* of crowds; His *dislike* for his work was overcome by his enjoyment of his salary.

Distaste implies a mild *dislike*, usually stemming from temperamental or constitutional inclination. It suggests, not always accurately, that one's taste or aesthetic sensibility has been offended by exposure to

something: a *distaste* for controversy; a *distaste* for sneakers Apart from intentionally jocular or comical contexts, *distaste* almost always describes things rather than people. It is commonly used with *for.*

Aversion is *dislike* that impels one to take steps to avoid the thing that offends; like *distaste*, it usually applies to things or animals rather than people. In formal contexts it more often suggests strong *dislike* amounting to a virtually uncontrollable desire to avoid: an *aversion* to snakes; an *aversion* to bloodshed. In less formal contexts, however, it often applies to mildly irritating things: an *aversion* to white wines. *Aversion* is commonly used with *to.*

Antipathy, whose etymological meaning is feel against, refers to an instinctive *dislike*. An *antipathy* is not so much irrational as nonrational—it is simply not thought out, only felt, and may incidentally be supportable on rational or ethical grounds: an *antipathy* to autocratic rule; an *antipathy* to politicians. See ENMITY, REPULSIVE.

Antonyms: *like, LOVE, penchant, predilection.*

dismal

  cheerless
  depressing
  dour
  forbidding
  grim

These adjectives describe appearances or prospects that are cold, unfriendly, or unpromising. **Dismal** suggests woebegone low spirits: the *dismal* sobbing of hungry children. Or it may suggest a course of action that portends unfavorable consequences: a chance for survival that was at best *dismal*. It can also suggest extremely uncomfortable or unpleasant surroundings: a room so *dismal* as to make her faintly sick to her stomach. **Grim** can be used in the same way as *dismal*. Once it might have added a note of horror to each of the situations discussed above, but it has been used hyperbolically so often that it may have lost much of its force. Its full seriousness can sometimes be recaptured: the *grim* efficiency of the firing squad; the *grim* leer of the psychopath. In more informal uses it has less force than *dismal*: the *grim* look the woman gave her friend; an exam that was really *grim*.

Depressing, which refers to a lowering of the spirits, has also been overused—so much so that it can apply very inexactly to any unwelcome situation: a *depressing* incident on my way to work; *depressing* weather; a *depressing* television program; her *depressing* gaiety.

Cheerless and **dour** are milder than *dismal* but still refer to unpleasant appearances. *Cheerless* most readily suggests a prospect that promises to be drab and unrelieved: a *cheerless* apartment that could be brightened considerably with a little effort. *Dour* most appropriately suggests ill humor: a *dour* glance that fully expressed his long-suffering pessimism. In describing a person, *cheerless* might suggest someone overly solemn: unable to tolerate the *cheerless* way she lived her life. *Dour* has a suggestion of sternness and, unlike *cheerless*, is seldom applied to anything but people or human qualities: A *dour* look was all the answer I got on how he liked the new boss; a *cheerless* day, overcast and drizzling.

Forbidding suggests an ominous appearance that promises to be unfriendly or threatening on closer acquaintance: the dank walls and barred windows of the *forbidding* castle. See BLEAK, GLOOMY.

Antonyms: *bright, cheerful, gay,* JOYOUS, OPTIMISTIC, *promising, uplifting.*

disparate

discordant
incompatible
incongruous

These adjectives are used to describe people or things that are dissimilar, or do not agree or go together. **Disparate** means unlike or unequal, as in kind, quality, character, or amount. It usually refers to differences that are so extreme as to make the compared people or things totally distinct: such *disparate* art forms as sculpture and the oratorio; The two facets of his personality were *disparate* enough to recall Dr. Jekyll and Mr. Hyde.

Discordant suggests the unpleasant effect that is the result of an association of two or more musical sounds that are not in harmony or concord: a modern orchestral work that was so advanced in melodic structure as to seem not merely dissonant but *discordant*. In general application *discordant* can refer to anything not in agreement with any other thing, but most often it is reserved for situations that imply the presence of opposition or conflict: Her ideas about the projected expenditures were so *discordant* with those of the other committee members that the meeting ended in a stalemate. When people are described as *discordant* it is because they exist in a disagreeable, quarrelsome atmosphere: a *discordant* family whose children left home as soon as possible to get away from their parents' bickering. Such people may be called **incompatible**—that is, unable to exist or get along with each

other in a pleasant or friendly way. In one way *incompatible* is milder than *discordant;* it does not necessarily imply the open clash or opposition that *discordant* does. It would be possible, for example, for two people to work together in a small office without open disagreement and yet be called *incompatible* because one is so much more talkative than the other that he disturbs the quiet person's working habits. In another way, however, *incompatible* is stronger than *discordant* since the incompatibility of two persons or things often implies the impossibility of their coexistence. Two *discordant* people might stay on in a place of employment, or as part of a family unit, continually fighting but nonetheless existing together. But *incompatible* strongly suggests the inability to remain together. Thus, *incompatible* is often used to describe couples whose marriage has gone on the rocks or whose contemplated marriage is thought of as unworkable. When *incompatible* is used in reference to things rather than people, there is the same suggestion of an incapability of mutual existence because of a basic difference in nature: the idea that matter and spirit are *incompatible;* the use of *incompatible* colors in a painting.

Incongruous designates that which is not in agreement or is not suitable, reasonable, or harmonious: his *incongruous* behavior at his father's funeral; the *incongruous* proportions of the building. It also suggests a lack of conformity, a being at odds with some accepted standard: a plan *incongruous* with reason. *Incongruous* sometimes has a connotation of the ludicrous or the absurd in the lack of agreement, harmony, conformity, etc., that it describes: Bea Lillie's *incongruous* combination of a formal gown and roller skates. See ABSURD, HETEROGENEOUS.

Antonyms: *consistent, consonant, harmonious, identical,* SIMILAR.

dissemble. Do not confuse the verb *dissemble* (conceal, pretend) with the verb *disassemble* (take apart).

distant

faraway
inaccessible
remote

These adjectives describe places considerably removed in space or time. **Distant** suggests that space is a barrier to easy contact: a country *distant* from our own. **Remote** takes up the suggestion of mere space as a barrier, but adds to it overtones implying isolation that results from being out of the way or off the beaten track: the *remote* interior that is harder to reach than many more *distant* places. **Inaccessible** almost exclusively emphasizes barriers other than space: a shortcut through the mountain that is, however, *inaccessible* in winter. **Faraway** suggests a *distant* place that might also be exotic or picturesque: *faraway* islands where people live simply and appear to bask all day in the sun.

Distant and *remote* also can refer to separation by time: ruins that were palaces in the *distant* past; a vanished culture *remote* from ours. In these uses, *remote* is an intensification of the lack of contact suggested by *distant*. In reference to future possibilities, *distant* suggests time as the barrier, *remote* other added difficulties that make for an unlikely prospect. [Complete disarmament is a *distant* possibility; The chances for negotiation are *remote*.]

In reference to attitudes, *distant* suggests a wandering mind: a *distant* look in his eye. *Faraway* suggests absorption in possibly pleasant fantasies of another kind of life: a *faraway* hint of wanderlust in his expression. *Remote*, however, stresses coldness of manner: a person who held herself rigid and *remote* in a chill silence. See ALOOF, DISINTERESTED.

Antonyms: *accessible, close, near, nearby, proximal, proximate.*

distrustful

    chary
    cynical
    disillusioned
    jaundiced
    mistrustful

These adjectives describe degrees of caution, doubt, or fear leading to a lack of faith in something or an embittered outlook. **Distrustful** refers to seemingly well-grounded suspicions of undependability or disloyalty that make one unwilling to give credence to something: inaccuracies in the report that made her *distrustful* of its conclusions; *distrustful* of adults who always spoke of how much harder they had worked when they were young. **Mistrustful** suggests a much less clear-cut suspicion, one that might amount to no more than a growing uncertainty mingled with an indefinable uneasiness and possibly even fear: increasingly *mistrustful* of her companion as he led the party deeper into the forest. *Distrustful* may suggest detached or informed judgment that guards one against taking a false step; *mistrustful* may suggest an anxious vulnerability that might already be exposed to or involved in danger because of a previous misstep.

Chary is more closely aligned with *mistrustful* in indicating a cautious, fussy, or grudging attitude, whether it is the result of natural timidity or painful experience. *Chary* suggests the same uneasiness or fear as *mistrustful*, but implies a hanging back from rather than involvement in a situation: *chary* of strangers; *chary* of eating undercooked food even after the epidemic was over. **Disillusioned** specifically suggests a posture of detachment or bitterness born of experience that has subverted one's hopes or ideals. [Had she been more *distrustful* of his extravagant promises, she wouldn't be so *disillusioned* now; He travels with people who try to appear *disillusioned* and blasé.]

Cynical indicates a *disillusioned* attitude that has hardened into extreme bitterness, although this may be leavened with resignation: She was *cynical* about my vow to quit drinking. *Cynical* can also point to a readiness to be *distrustful* on the basis of little or no evidence: *cynical* about any account of the altruism and idealism of young people.

Jaundiced is a more informal and colorful substitute for *cynical*, suggesting a hard-bitten skeptic who prefers to look at something or at everything from a negative point of view: He had a *jaundiced* attitude toward all proposals for slum clearance that differed in the slightest from his own; a person who was content to look at life with a *jaundiced* eye. See ANXIETY, CAUTIOUS, DOUBT, SKEPTIC, TIMID.

Antonyms: *confident,* SURE, *trusting.*

diversify

    variegate
    vary

These verbs mean give unlike characteristics or appearances to the members of a group of things. To **diversify** one's reading is to read about a number of different subjects; to *diversify* one's investments is to buy equities in a variety of industries.

To **vary** is to make different the successive elements of a series of related things. To *vary* one's diet is to eat different kinds of food at successive meals; to *vary* one's work routine is to break up one's day into segments devoted to various aspects of one's job rather than to concentrate on one aspect of it over a long period of time.

To **variegate** is to impart variety to a group of similar things by giving them different colors, shapes, sizes, and the like. Easter eggs are *variegated* by coloring, bouquets by arrangement, books by jacket design or choice of type. See DIVIDE, MIXTURE, RANDOM.

Antonyms: *solidify, unify.*

divide

allocate
allot
apportion
assign
distribute
prorate
ration

This group of verbs is concerned with the parceling out of a quantity, such as money or goods, among the members of a group. **Divide** is the most general of these and says the least about what means are used in the process. When two people or groups are to share in the quantity, *divide* carries implications of an equal division: Even though I put up more capital than you, let's *divide* the profits between us. This is not invariably true, however, and when more than two shares are involved, the implication of equality disappears completely: Thieves and pirates, according to legend, often *divide* their spoils unfairly.

Assign, **allot**, and **allocate** also carry no implication of a fair or equal division, but all three verbs suggest that someone in authority has determined how the quantity is to be divided. Of these, *assign* is the least and *allocate* the most formal. *Assign* carries the strongest implication of arbitrariness on the part of the one who *assigns*. The quantity being parceled out, furthermore, is more often tasks or roles than goods or money: How many chapters did the professor *assign?* *Allot* implies the matching of items on one list with those on another: I've *allotted* thirty dollars a month for carfare and ninety dollars a month for lunches. *Allocate,* as well as being the most formal of these three, is the most specific. It is most often used of a governing body's action in setting aside a fixed sum of money for a government program. Outside this governmental context, *allocate* would seem forced and stiff. [The legislature *allocated* $3 billion for highway improvement.]

Distribute is most used for the dispersing of a quantity in space or among the scattered members of a group. [The paperback edition of a book is usually more widely *distributed* than the hardcover version; This year, the corporation decided not to *distribute* dividends to its shareholders.]

The three remaining terms all imply a process of division that is equal, fair, or judicious—based on some fixed plan or equitable rule. **Ration** is specifically used for a method of sharing or *distributing* some scarce commodity when demand exceeds supply. It usually but not necessarily suggests a method of distribution based on need. [In wartime, meat and gasoline were *rationed.*] **Prorate** refers to the sorting out of a quantity into different sizes, based on some prescribed variable: Since you worked twice as long as I on the project, we should *prorate* two-thirds of the fee to you. To **apportion** is to determine the composition of a smaller group in proportion to a larger group. It most strongly suggests a just and fair parceling out, based on some objective standard: The Supreme Court ruled unconstitutional those state legislatures *apportioned* on any other basis than population. See DIVERSIFY, SEVER.

Antonyms: *commingle,* CONNECT, *fuse, unify.*

docile

amenable
submissive
tame
tractable

These adjectives describe a willingness to be managed, led, taught, or trained. **Docile** stresses a complete lack of unruliness that makes for easy handling; it comes from a Latin root meaning teachable and often appears in the context of education: *docile* pupils. **Amenable**, by contrast, suggests most strongly a goodwilled openness to suggestions or recommendations, but it does not imply the built-in acquiescent temperament of *docile:* Teenagers may not be the most *docile* creatures imaginable, but they are more *amenable* to sympathetic guidance than many parents believe.

Tractable suggests manageability to an even greater degree than *docile*. It comes from a Latin verb meaning handle; this is reflected in its use applying to the willingness of people to be led: a *tractable* audience that was willing to listen as long as the speaker had voice to exhort them with. *Tractable* can give a tone that is not flattering to the people it describes, since it can seem to discuss human beings as though they were a material or inanimate substance to be manipulated, a substance having no will of its own.

Tame and **submissive** point to the greatest amount of servility suggested by any of these adjectives. With *tame,* the servility may be innate or ingrained, as with domesticated animals: a *tame* horse. A *tame* animal may, however, be far from *docile* in temperament. *Submissive* at its mildest can indicate nothing more than meek humility before one's superiors, but in any case it suggests an extremely responsive attitude toward the needs, desires, or whims of another, sometimes to the point of humiliating abjectness: the ideally *submissive* wife of the Victorian era. See ADAPTABLE, COMPLIANT, MALLEABLE, OBEDIENT. **Antonyms:** *aggressive, inflexible,* STUBBORN, UNRULY, WILD, WILLFUL.

doctor

> chiropractor
> medic
> osteopath
> physician
> surgeon

These nouns all denote persons engaged in treating sick or injured people. **Doctor**, **physician**, and **surgeon** are all licensed practitioners of medicine and have one or more degrees from an accredited medical school. *Doctor* is the most general term, and it may also apply to specialists in related branches of medicine, such as psychiatrists, dentists, and veterinarians. A *physician* is a *doctor* who is engaged in general practice or in one of its many specialties, while a *surgeon* is primarily concerned with diseased conditions or injuries that require operative procedures. However, since in recent years medical knowledge has become such a vast field, more and more *doctors* are taking postgraduate training and are restricting their practice to pediatrics, gynecology, obstetrics, urology, and other specialties. As a result, many of these specialists are not only *physicians* but are often qualified *surgeons*. *Doctor* is the correct title for all of them and is a reference to their having earned the appropriate *doctor's* degree, as M.D. (*doctor* of medicine), D.D.S. (*doctor* of dental surgery), D.V.M. (*doctor* of veterinary medicine). Psychiatrists have earned an M.D. before taking their psychiatric training, whereas psychologists have not. Psychologists, however, like those pursuing any discipline in the arts and sciences, may earn a Ph.D. (*doctor* of philosophy), but this does not permit them to practice medicine.

An **osteopath** is a practitioner of a school of healing known as osteopathy, which stresses the importance of the musculoskeletal system and its proper functioning as a basis for health. An *osteopath* is a *doctor* by virtue of having earned a D.O. (*doctor* of osteopathy) and is now widely permitted by law to practice medicine, prescribe drugs, and undertake surgery when qualified. Often, the preferred method of osteopathic treatment is manipulation of the mus-

cles and bones, especially the backbone. A **chiropractor** puts a similar emphasis on the spinal area as basic to health and treats patients by manual adjustment and manipulation of this and related areas. Unlike the *osteopath*, however, the *chiropractor* does not practice internal medicine or surgery and is not trained to do so. Thus, although a chiropractor may have earned a D.C. (*doctor* of chiropractic) degree, his right to be addressed as *doctor* is disputed by some.

In its narrowest sense, **medic** refers to an enlisted man in the armed forces who is trained to assist *doctors* with medical duties in service hospitals or to work with the sick or wounded in combat areas. At its most informal, *medic* can be used in a more general or imprecise way to refer to any *physician, surgeon,* or hospital intern. See DRUG, HEALTHY, SICKNESS.

doubt

> dubiety
> skepticism
> suspicion
> uncertainty

These nouns refer to a lack of conviction that results in a reluctance to believe something or an inability to decide. **Doubt** is the most general of these and has the widest application. It can indicate dissent from a proposition because of evidence to the contrary, though this evidence may fall short of being conclusive: *There were growing doubts about the victory statement, based on scattered reports coming in from remote districts.* More often, *doubt* indicates a lack of full assent to a proposition that evidence alone can neither confirm nor deny: *He expressed considerable doubt that people are innately good.* In this sense, a lack of faith or trust may be indicated: *doubt about the existence of God; the first doubts concerning her husband's affection.* The phrase *in doubt* refers to something still unsettled or in question: *The result of the election remained in doubt until the next morning.* Used alone, *doubt* can also reflect this lack of decisiveness: *Tormented by doubt, he stood at the intersection of the two paths, not knowing which to take.*

Dubiety can function as a considerably more formal substitute for *doubt. Dubiety* may impart the notion of actively calling something into question rather than simply being passively unsure: *a touch of dubiety in his voice as he asked her to repeat her outrageous accusation.* On the other hand, *dubiety* can suggest a wavering between conclusions.

This last possibility for *dubiety* makes it a more formal substitute for **uncertainty**, which stresses wavering indecision for whatever reason, particularly as it relates to choice or outcome: She expressed *uncertainty* about whether she should marry. **Suspicion** more often concentrates on a single possibility, rather than on alternatives, and indicates a questioning *uncertainty* that something is what it purports to be: the first *suspicions* that their partnership would fail.

Skepticism is considerably more decisive in tone than the other nouns here, pointing to an unwavering posture of *doubt* until faced with undeniable proof: He greeted the child's protestations of innocence with amused *skepticism*. Often, *skepticism* suggests a rationalistic or scientific attitude—or an irreverent attitude toward the claims of religion or the occult: the necessary *skepticism* of science toward new scientific theories; Talking to the medium had only increased his *skepticism* about spiritualism. See UNBELIEF.

Antonyms: *assurance, certainty, confidence, conviction.*

doubtful

　　ambiguous
　　dubious
　　equivocal
　　problematic
　　questionable
　　uncertain

These adjectives relate to suspicion, indecision, or a lack of clarity. **Doubtful** can function in all three areas. [She was *doubtful* of his good intentions; still *doubtful* about which plane to take; The outcome of his appeal is still *doubtful*.] *Doubtful* can also be used as an indefinite way to impugn the worth or value of something: a youth of *doubtful* habits; a book of *doubtful* merit. **Dubious** is closely related to this last use of *doubtful*, but it carries a greater air of veiled insinuation and, relating to morals, may have more sinister overtones: a *dubious* person. The phrase a *doubtful* person, by contrast, would pertain to someone who did not know what to do. Similarly, an outcome that was *doubtful* would be one not yet decided; a *dubious* outcome would be an undesirable one. Referring to hesitation, *dubious* may suggest less basis on which to choose, but this may be accompanied by a sense of greater suspicion, wariness, or even danger: She was beginning to be *dubious* about the man's claim to be a licensed contractor. **Questionable** can be used euphemistically in reference to immorality: a house in which *questionable* activities were conducted. In other uses, it points to something genuinely open to doubt, analysis, or criticism: a *questionable* foreign policy.

Uncertain can refer, most simply, to an inability to choose: *uncertain* about which dress to wear. *Uncertain* also applies to a lack of clarity or evidence or to an unforeseeable outcome: an *uncertain* legend on the rusted sign; an *uncertain* dating of the new fossil discoveries; these *uncertain* times, in which there is little to be hoped for and much to be feared. **Problematic** emphasizes one aspect of *uncertain*, referring to something that cannot be definitely established by the available evidence: The ultimate origins of the Aztec and Mayan cultures are likely to remain *problematic*. *Problematic* can also pertain to results that are endangered or unclear because of an attendant pattern of complex causality: The need to secure multilateral approval on each item of a nuclear-control pact made disarmament *problematic*.

Both **ambiguous** and **equivocal** concentrate on a lack of clarity. *Ambiguous* can refer to either an intentional or unintentional failure to be precise or definite. [He kept making *ambiguous* remarks instead of straightforward yes-or-no replies; In explaining her stand, she only made everything more *ambiguous* than it had been to begin with.] *Equivocal* stresses an intentional wish to remain unclear; it can, in fact, suggest deliberate deception or the saying of one thing while meaning another. [She kept putting him off halfheartedly with *equivocal* replies to his request for promotion.] At its strongest, *equivocal* suggests something that might be thought of as morally compromising: They advised their son against putting himself in *equivocal* situations when he went out with new friends. But *equivocal* can also apply to what is merely *uncertain*, unprovable, or of *doubtful* validity, even when *dubious* motives are absent: statistical factors that make even the most scrupulous opinion pollsters *equivocal* in their findings. See CONFUSE, UNWISE, VAGUE.

Antonyms: CLEAR, *confident, decided,* DEFINITE, SURE.

dress

　　apparel
　　attire
　　clothes
　　clothing
　　costume
　　garb
　　garment

These nouns all refer to coverings worn on the body. **Dress** is the outer covering for both men and women, especially when suitable for a formal occasion: evening *dress;* court *dress. Dress* may be used specifically to mean the skirt and waist, usually in one piece, worn by women and girls.

Clothes and **clothing** are more general terms. *Clothing* denotes the entire covering taken as a whole. [In winter children need warm *clothing;* Aborigines in hot climates tend to wear little or no *clothing.*] *Clothing* need not be limited to the persons wearing it but may suggest the manufacturer or dealer: a factory that makes children's *clothing;* a secondhand *clothing* store; a sale of winter *clothing.* *Clothes* and **garments**, on the other hand, suggest that coverings worn on the body are made up of separate parts. When one speaks admiringly of a woman as having beautiful *clothes,* one means that everything she wears—coats, dresses, suits, shoes, hats, etc.—is in excellent taste and of high quality and is also very becoming to the wearer. *Clothes* may also be designed especially for various activities or for persons in a certain condition or time of life: sports *clothes;* school *clothes;* maternity *clothes;* baby *clothes.* A *garment* is an article of *clothing,* especially of outer *clothing,* but it may also be a piece of underclothing with a distinct function: a foundation *garment.* *Garment* may also apply as an attributive to *clothing* in general, and especially to its manufacture: the *garment* industry.

A **costume** is the characteristic *clothing* worn by the people of a given region, time, or group: the national *costume* of Bavaria; Elizabethan *costume;* cowboy *costume.* In this sense, *dress* is sometimes used interchangeably with *costume:* T. E. Lawrence often wore Arab *dress* in the desert. In its second sense, *costume* can also refer to the *clothing* worn by an actor during the playing of a role or by a person posing as an imaginary character in any situation. [As Hamlet, Booth wore a *costume* of black velvet and a long gold chain around his neck; My cousin went to the party in a pirate *costume.*] **Garb**, a rather literary word, is used chiefly with reference to the *clothing* characteristic of a profession or rank: the *garb* of a priest; kingly *garb.*

Apparel and **attire** are chiefly used of complete and elegant outer *clothing,* although *dress* has largely supplanted them in this sense. *Apparel* (often rendered as *wearing apparel*) is a somewhat formal word for both *clothing* and *clothes.* It carries more of the suggestion of a collection of separate *garments* in which a person is clad than does *attire.* *Attire* often stresses the impression that one's *clothes* may make upon others: the rich *attire* of a Renaissance pope; the strange *attire* of the eccentric old woman. See STYLISH, VOGUE.

drug
biological
medicament
medication
medicinal
medicine
narcotic
pharmaceutical
remedy
specific

These nouns relate to substances, natural or synthetic, that are intended to aid in the diagnosis, prevention, treatment, or cure of physical and mental disorders.

Drug is the most general, being applicable to any substance serving those purposes. [The doctor prescribed a new *drug* for her patient; Many *drugs* have been used in the treatment of malaria.] The plural form carries an added suggestion of improper or excessive use: an addiction to *drugs.* **Medicine** and **remedy** are close synonyms for *drug,* but both may be extended to other agencies or procedures supposedly conducive to health. [Sunshine and rest are good *medicine* for convalescents; The best *remedy* for overweight is careful dieting.] **Medicament** is a learned variant of *medicine,* seldom used nowadays. **Medicinal**, known chiefly as an adjective, is preferred by commercial enterprises concerned with the manufacture and marketing of *drugs:* the export of *medicinals* to South America.

Biological, generally used in the plural, denotes a class of *drugs* prepared from living animal sources and usually administered under medical supervision; serums, vaccines, and hormone products are *biologicals.* **Pharmaceutical** is a semiofficial term referring to all medical preparations made by *drug* firms, especially those meeting high standards of quality and obtainable from pharmacists only on prescription: cosmetics, *drugs,* and *pharmaceuticals* sold here.

Narcotic, in its medical sense, is a *drug* that has a limited, often variable capacity to relieve pain or induce sleep; morphine, codeine, and certain other opium derivatives are *narcotics.* It is this power, together with a strong habit-forming tendency, that has led to their widespread abuse and given both *drug* and *narcotic* a bad name: the traffic in *narcotics; narcotic* addiction. **Specific**, as the word implies, refers to any *drug* or *medicinal* that is adapted for the treatment, alleviation, or cure of some clearly identified abnormal condition. [Digitalis is a *specific* for many kinds of heart disease; The best *specific* for the control of diabetes mellitus is considered to be insulin.]

Medication has become popular as a generic term for anything that is given or administered to a patient undergoing therapy. This eliminates the possible unpleasantness of *drug* when it might be mistaken as applying to *narcotic* addiction rather than to prescribed treatment: nurses responsible for giving patients the *medications* specified by their doctors; a new *medication* to combat *drug* addiction. It can apply widely from the simplest *remedies,* such as aspirin, to the most complex. Also, it refers less harshly to the tranquilizers and other *drugs* used to control the symptoms of mental disorder, where a cure may not yet be known: hospital bed space freed by handling many of the mentally ill as outpatients who can be maintained by a program of regular *medication.* See DOCTOR, HEALTHY, SICKNESS.

dry

crisp
dehumidified
dehydrated
desiccated
dried
parched

These adjectives refer to things lacking in moisture. **Dry** is the most general, being equally suitable for describing solids, atmospheres, or climates: He wiped each dish until it was completely *dry; dry,* hot air in the sauna; New Mexico's *dry* climate. The remaining adjectives all stress that something containing moisture has been rendered *dry.* **Dried** is commonly used to describe foods from which moisture has been partially or totally removed as a way of preserving them: *dried* beef; *dried* peas; *dried* apricots. In some cases, preparation involves restoring water to the product, as with peas; in other cases, the food is used as it is. **Dehydrated** is a more formal and technical term for the same idea, although in this sense it more often applies to foods that have not only been *dried,* but powdered as well: *dehydrated* milk; *dehydrated* eggs. In other senses, *dehydrated* can indicate an unwanted loss of moisture: a fever that had caused the child to become dangerously *dehydrated.* **Parched** is a much less formal term that concentrates exclusively on this last possibility of *dehydrated,* referring to an undesirable or uncomfortable lack of or need for water: the *parched,* drought-stricken countryside; He had gulped down the last of the water in his canteen, but still felt *parched* with thirst.

Crisp applies almost exclusively to brittle or shriveled solids, particularly those in thin sheets or layers. Also, *crisp* suggests that this *dry,* brittle state has been arrived at by heating or cooking: *crisp* potato chips; the steaks they had burned to a *crisp.* This is not always true, however: *crisp* autumn leaves. **Dehumidified** is comparable to *dehydrated* in formality and would seem identical in meaning, but whereas *dehydrated* applies to solids, *dehumidified* most often applies exclusively to atmosphere: the amount of *dehumidified* air an air conditioner can put out. **Desiccated** can function as a much more formal substitute for *dried: desiccated* yeast. Here, it compares to *dehydrated* in suggesting a powdered substance. Much more often, however, *desiccated* is used in metaphorical ways, suggesting something wasted, old, dried-up, lifeless, or dull: the *desiccated* old fuddy-duddy. *Dry* and *crisp* also have metaphorical uses. *Crisp* can suggest a brusque, sharp, or efficient manner: She rejected his suggestion with a *crisp* remark; the *crisp* smile of the school clerk. *Dry* has an extremely wide range of metaphorical uses. It can indicate anything droll, boring, or lacking in humor: a *dry* remark, given with a deadpan expression; a *dry* book. *Dry* can also refer to an alcoholic drink that is free of sweetness: a *dry* martini. See HOT, STERILE.

Antonyms: *damp, deliquescent, moist, soggy, wet.*

duplicate

congruent
exact
identical
true

These adjectives refer to copies that are replicas of one another or reproductions of an original. **Duplicate** designates a copy that is just like another or others. It may indicate two corresponding copies, one of which is a second or extra copy: *duplicate* receipts, the original retained by the bank, the carbon returned to the depositor. Or it may apply to multiple copies that look exactly alike: a dozen *duplicate* prints of a photograph. A *duplicate* copy may be made with or from an original, as by use of carbon paper or a copying machine; or it may be made from a pattern, as a stencil, negative, or engraved metal plate: *duplicate* copies of a letter; *duplicate* copies of a book. At one extreme, *duplicate* designates a replica that is virtually indistinguishable from the original: a *duplicate* key. At the other extreme, it may indicate simply an accurate copy made at the same time or in the same form as the first: a *duplicate* copy of a tax report, kept for the taxpayer's personal records.

Like a *duplicate* copy, an **exact** copy or **true** copy is made from an original. But *exact* and *true* stress strict substantive accuracy and may or may not indicate correspondence in form. *Exact* implies a precise reproduction of all details in a standard or model. [Writing painstakingly in longhand, the student made an *exact* copy of the printed poem; By means of the photocopying process, one can easily make an *exact* reproduction of the printed page.] *True* indicates absolute accuracy in reproduction, conformity to fact, and consequent validity. It stresses content rather than form. [The college registrar certified the transcript as a *true* copy of the student's record; The Director of Vital Statistics certified that the birth registration card was a *true* copy of facts recorded on the birth record.]

Identical is applied to copies that are just like one another or that seem to be exactly alike. It is the strongest of these adjectives and implies correspondence in every detail. [As far as the eye could tell, the reproduction was *identical* with the designer's original.] Where a *duplicate* copy is clearly secondary, though it may be *exact*, *identical* implies equality, indicating mutual likeness: two women wearing *identical* dresses; *identical* prints made from a woodblock; Our suits are *identical*. In plane geometry, **congruent** refers to figures that are *identical* in shape and size, filling exactly the same space. Triangles are *congruent* if every point of one can be brought into correspondence with every point of the other in space, so that the flat figures would coincide exactly if they were superimposed. See ACCURATE, COPY.

Antonyms: *contrasted, different, dissimilar, faulty.*

eager

avid
desirous
enthusiastic
intent
keen

These adjectives describe a state of extreme readiness and interest in some prospective action or subject, suggesting a willingness to become involved in it. **Eager** may suggest a general thirst for experience of all kinds or an intense interest of a more specific nature: young, *eager* students ready to take on the world; *eager* for their first look at the Grand Canal. While *eager* most often suggests a period before involvement is possible, it may also describe the intensity of involvement itself: an *eager* lover. **Intent** relates to this last possibility of *eager,* suggesting an undivided concentration on the activity itself: *intent* on the book he was reading. It may also suggest a purposeful and determined search for something: *intent* on finding the cafés she had read about in books about Paris.

Avid and **desirous** pertain mostly to the period before involvement. While both may refer to an intense longing or craving, *desirous* might now seem old-fashioned or archaic to many: *desirous* of her hand in marriage. *Avid* still retains its forcefulness as an intensification of *eager,* suggesting a craving on the point of desperation: *avid* for news of the city; the *avid* reader of Westerns. Like *eager,* it may also describe actual involvement, but again with greater intensity: He dispatched the meal with a series of *avid* gulps.

Keen and **enthusiastic** both may suggest an extreme liking for or approval of something. *Keen* best describes *eager* involvement: children who watched the clowns with *keen* delight. Much more informally, *keen* indicates a special liking or appetite for something: *keen* on hiking. *Enthusiastic* is unique among these adjectives in applying mostly to participation rather than expectation, or to a favorable verdict on something already experienced or proposed. For example, a person can be *eager* for a vacation and *enthusiastic* about the plans he has made, but he cannot be *enthusiastic* about the vacation itself until it is underway or past. Thus, the adjective pertains to activity undertaken with gusto, verve, and exuberance, or to an extremely favorable judgment that contains few reservations: an *enthusiastic* group of mountain climbers; *enthusiastic* reviews of her first book. See PASSIONATE, PREOCCUPIED.

Antonyms: *deadbeat,* IMPASSIVE, *indifferent, listless, uninterested,* UNINVOLVED.

---

eager. Do not confuse the adjective *eager* (enthusiastic) with the adjective *anxious* (troubled).

---

eat

consume
devour
dine
gobble
gorge
sup
wolf

These verbs refer to the partaking of food. **Eat** is the most general, applying equally well to persons or animals: the woman *eating* a hot dog; horses *eating* oats. Only context can give further details: slowly *eating* a breakfast of hot chocolate and croissants; *eating* his sushi with great satisfaction. **Dine** and **sup** are relatively formal; both specifically refer to *eating* done by people. *Dine* can point to the day's main meal: She *ate* a light lunch so that she would be able to *dine* that night without a guilty conscience. Or *dine* can refer to any formal or special meal: She invited her entire staff to *dine* with her next week. *Sup* now sounds archaic and pretentious, though once it could refer to an evening or late evening meal: They had a nightcap and *supped* on leftovers once the guests were gone.

Unlike the preceding pair, **consume** can refer to people or animals, but its point in either case is the thoroughness of the *eating,* suggesting the utter and avid taking in of a food: a pack of lions able to *consume* the carcass of an impala in a single night; The hungry boy *consumed* every last scrap on his plate. Thus, *consume* can apply to any process that involves total destruction and in which one thing can be seen as feeding off another: the raging fever that was *consuming* her body. **Gorge** compares to *consume* but stresses *eating* or even overeating to the point of satiety or possibly discomfort, suggesting the gluttonous and indiscriminate stuffing down of food: the sleepy hounds lying about *gorged* with food; the fat man who *gorged* himself constantly with rich desserts.

Gobble emphasizes rapid *eating* rather than the thoroughness indicated by *consume* or the excessiveness possible for *gorge:* chickens that *gobbled* down the scattered breadcrumbs in a twinkling; I warned the girl that she'd get sick if she *gobbled* her food that way. **Wolf** also emphasizes quickness, but it indicates as well a ravenous ferocity or desperation. Since its obvious metaphor pertaining to one animal might make *wolf* tautological in that instance and inappropriate in others, the main point of the verb is to describe human *eating* in terms of a wolf's swift and rapacious feeding: *wolfing* down one canape after another as though he were starving; a movie that depicted Henry VIII *wolfing* down an incredible array of viands.

Devour can apply equally well to animals or people, though it is more general in its implications than the preceding, suggesting either the total consumption of something or the rapidity with which it is eaten: kittens that *devoured* the whole plate of catfood before the dozing mother cat could stir; hungry soldiers who *devoured* the tasteless creamed beef ladled out to them by the mess sergeant. Like *consume, devour* can have metaphorical uses, referring in this case to eager or enthusiastic taking in or, possibly, to the predatory destruction of something. [She *devoured* her French lessons so that she would be proficient by the time of her first trip abroad; All their assets were *devoured* by predatory loan sharks.] See ABSORB.

eccentricity
idiosyncrasy
oddity
quirk

These nouns all denote an aspect or peculiarity of a person's character or manner. **Eccentricity** is used to identify a characteristic, action, practice, or habit that differs in some way from what is usual or expected; it suggests a strangeness or irregularity that may be harmless but is an ingrained part of the personality. [Smoking cigars was the beautiful woman's only *eccentricity;* One of his *eccentricities* was a stubborn reluctance to entrust his savings to a bank.] By contrast, **quirk** is the most general of this group and suggests little as to the nature or the trait involved; *quirks* can be pleasant or unpleasant, amusing or irritating: Knuckle-cracking is an annoying *quirk. Quirk* originally referred to a kind of verbal trick or conceit. Bright retorts, plays on words, and subtle evasions all

were described as *quirks.* Although the term can be and still is used in this way, it more often now designates a distinctive trait of behavior rather than of speech. In any case, *quirk* can suggest a slight slip, flaw, or distortion: a keen mind, but one full of *quirks.* **Idiosyncrasies** are like *eccentricities* in that they are strange in nature, but *idiosyncracy* implies less a divergence from the general than an emphasis on the individual. *Eccentricities* are often an indication of mental aberration, *idiosyncrasies* the evidence of a strongly independent personality: His refusal to wear a tie at any time is one of my uncle's most admirable *idiosyncrasies.* **Oddity** is interchangeable with *eccentricity* because of its suggestion of the aberrant and peculiar. However, *oddity* is more often used to designate an odd or unique person or thing rather than a quality or trait. [What a collection of *oddities* he invited to his party! A bargain is an *oddity* in that store; all its merchandise is overpriced.] See CHARACTERISTIC, FLAW, TEMPERAMENT.

Antonyms: *commonness, conventionality, normality, ordinariness, typicality.*

ecology. Do not confuse the noun *ecology* (study of an environment and things living in it) with the noun *environment* (surroundings).

economic. Do not confuse the adjective *economic* (pertaining to economics) with the adjective *economical* (thrifty).

edge
border
brim
brink
margin
rim
verge

These nouns refer to the bounding line or outline of something. **Edge** refers to the thin line along one side of a thing: the south *edge* of the terrace. Or it may refer to the line between two sides or planes: the *edge* of an ax. In either case, *edge* refers to a line that does not circumscribe a figure but may form part of its perimeter. As such, it can refer to any sort of boundary: the ragged *edge* of the forest. Unqualified, however, *edge* often suggests a straight or sharp line: She tested the *edge* of the knife with her thumb. Metaphorically, *edge* may indicate the sharp line between two contrasting qualities or states or, particularly, the line delimiting an undesirable state: nations drifting closer to the *edge* of disaster.

Brink also indicates a line that is not circumscribing, but the stress of *brink* is on an abrupt division between high and low ground: the *brink* of the cliff; the *brink* of a valley. **Verge** once could refer literally either to a dividing or circumscribing line in as general a way as *edge,* but in the United States now is almost completely limited to metaphorical uses. Here, it suggests the imminence or nearness of an abrupt shift to some other condition, good or bad: on the *verge* of succeeding at last; on the *verge* of a breakdown. *Brink* functions similarly in a metaphorical way, except that it applies almost exclusively to the imminence of something undesirable: on the *brink* of war. It may also suggest speed, inevitability, and possible destruction as in falling off a cliff: In international affairs, *brink*manship was the tactic of risking nuclear confrontation in the hope that one could stop in time to avoid plummeting over the *brink*.

All the remaining nouns can refer to a circumscribing outline. **Border** and **margin**, furthermore, most often refer to plane figures. *Border* can indicate the area of such a figure that is nearest to its outside *edges:* They walked about the *border* of the park. *Border* can also refer to a circumscribing boundary that contrasts distinctly with what it encloses and thus sets off or frames the contained area: a black *border* around the portrait of the dead president; a modest *border* of lawn around the house. In this sense, *border* may imply an added, decorative *edge:* the lace *border* of her handkerchief. *Border* can, however, refer like *edge* to a dividing line, as in its common use for the boundary between two countries: the *border* between Canada and the United States. *Margin* emphasizes exclusively one aspect of *border,* pointing to the outer area circumscribing something, an area often distinct in appearance from what it encloses. Unlike *border,* however, *margin* more frequently refers to the emptiness, blankness, or lack of decoration that sets off and surrounds something: Typescript looks best when at least an inch of *margin* is left on all four sides of the page. To this implication of space left unused can be added the notion of its being saved for an emergency: *margin* for error.

Rim and **brim** also refer to a circumscribing outline, in this case that of a circle. *Rim* refers most specifically to the open lip of a cylindrical or rounded shape: She tested the *rim* of the glass to see if it was nicked; on the *rim* of the volcano. *Brim* can refer to the same open lip, but is most often associated with a situation in which a container is completely filled: a

teacup filled to the *brim*. This use extends to shapes that are not rounded: boxcars filled to the *brim* with grain. But *brim* has at least one use where it functions more like *border* or *margin:* the *brim* of a hat. See BOUNDARY, CIRCUMSCRIBE, PERIMETER.

Antonyms: CENTER, interior.

effect

cause
produce
realize

These verbs pertain to the accomplishing of results. **Effect** can refer to the successful accomplishment of an intended action: The pilot *effected* a takeoff despite the icy conditions. As in this example, the point of this use is often the overcoming of difficulty or a previous uncertainty as to outcome. *Effect* can also indicate putting into practice a previously formulated goal: We *effected* the plan with a minimum of fuss. No sense of difficulty or uncertainty need be implied here. When *effect* applies, however, to the formulating of a plan, goal, or solution, rather than to putting one into action, it takes on a different set of overtones: a board of mediators to *effect* a compromise in the newspaper strike. While initial resistance is implied, the goal reached is not necessarily known at the outset but is arrived at through experiment, innovation, and improvisation. Also, *effect* sometimes suggests a rough-and-ready or expedient result, if not a jerry-built one: ready to *effect* a solution to the problem by any means.

By contrast, the desired objective implied by **realize** is always seen in advance, at least in the sense pertinent here: to *realize* a longstanding dream. The stress of the verb, in fact, is on making actual or real something that has previously existed only as a plan or desire. **Produce** can also emphasize visible or actual results, but it can apply to intentional or unintentional as well as to both good or bad results: a plan that *produced* concrete improvements in its first year of operation; amendments that *produced* fiery outbursts on the floor of the Senate. At its most literal, *produce* can apply to the bearing of fruit or the creation of something: countries that *produced* bumper crops while famine raged; factories that *produce* armaments. At its most neutral, *produce* merely assigns actions or results to the factors or agents that brought them about: Penicillin can *produce* an extreme allergic reaction in some people.

Cause is most closely related to this last sense of *produce,* stressing the relationship between a result and the factors responsible for it. [A stroke can *cause* permanent paralysis; Continual conflict among city-

131

states *caused* the eventual decline of Greek civilization.] On this neutral level, *cause* points to the dispassionate or scientific tracing of a train of causality, often from the philosophical viewpoint of determinism. More informally, *cause* can apply to the laying of blame: parents who *cause* their children to grow up warped and apathetic. But a stress on inadvertence rather than on blame can be the point of *caused* in this use: He had unwittingly *caused* the accident by misreading a road sign. See CREATE, DECIDE, PERFORM, REACH.

Antonyms: DESTROY, *deter*, HINDER, PREVENT, STOP.

effort

exertion
pains
struggle
trouble

These nouns pertain to physical or mental application that is devoted to achieving a result. At its mildest, **effort** can be used in reference to measuring the amount of application a given task requires. [How much *effort* will it take to get the requisitions out on time? It takes little *effort* to keep your shoes shined.] With a slight increase in force, it can stress a more than ordinary attentiveness or thoughtfulness: students who make an *effort* to correct spelling errors; She decided to make a special *effort* to please him. When *effort* points specifically to a great outlay of energy, a challenging, difficult, or unpleasant task is implied: a real *effort* to win the race; a crisis that will require all our will and *effort* to survive; What an *effort* it took to endure the blabbering old busybody.

Exertion more readily suggests a considerable or exhausting outlay of *effort:* He stood gasping with *exertion* after reaching the summit of the hill; the mental *exertion* it took to make the accounts balance. Unqualified, *exertion* is more likely to apply to physical *effort,* but not always: Students on probation are expected to show greater *exertion* in their studies. **Pains** and **trouble** would also seem to stress expenditure of *effort* in the face of difficulty or resistance, but both nouns are used instead to indicate thoughtfulness or carefulness without necessarily suggesting great *exertion*. [She took *pains* to put her guests at ease; He'd be a good worker if he'd only take the *trouble* to get to work on time.] *Trouble* in particular can be used ironically to suggest a small *effort*, whereas *pains* can as easily be used for exacting *effort:* taking great *pains* with every detail of the program.

Struggle is the one noun here that almost exclusively points to extreme *efforts,* those called up not only by the difficulty of the task or the external resistance to its achievement but also by the determination, will, or zeal of the person involved: his heroic *struggle* to overcome all obstacles in a situation where it would have been a *struggle* merely to stay alive. When qualified, however, *struggle* need not always be so positive or approving: a feeble *struggle* to extricate herself; a hopeless *struggle* to escape just punishment. See LABOR.

Antonyms: *ease, facility, rest,* SLOTH.

effrontery

churlishness
impertinence
impudence

These nouns refer to aggressive rudeness born of vulgarity or egotism. **Effrontery** indicates an insult to good manners by someone who is pushy or conceited: the *effrontery* of the reporter to ask the boy's mother how she felt when she first got word of the accident; the *effrontery* to ask the distinguished guests whether they had read his book. As in these examples, *effrontery* often suggests offensive behavior that comes as a shock or surprise, but this is not always the case: I knew what he wanted and was only waiting to see if he would have the *effrontery* to put it into words. **Impertinence** is a shade milder than *effrontery,* suggesting an offense to good manners that results from action that is out of place or from an uncalled-for remark: his *impertinence* in coming to the party uninvited; her *impertinence* in asking about details of our private life. As in the last example, *impertinence* can sometimes point to a prying person who meddles in the affairs of others. In this case the stress is on aggressiveness rather than on arrogance. At its mildest *impertinence* can point to a mere lack of relevance: It is an *impertinence* in scholarly work to insist on assigning blame rather than analyzing actual conditions in an objective way. Usually, however, *impertinence* suggests impropriety or poor breeding.

Churlishness emphasizes this last possibility of *impertinence*, concentrating on grossly ill-mannered behavior that is the result of a crude, coarse, or vulgar background. This use reflects the derivation of *churliness* from a root referring to a lowborn person or one of the lowest rank. In addition, *churlishness* is the most extreme and disapproving of these nouns, implying an accompanying manner that is surly, contentious, hostile, and drastically inconsiderate: His constant quarrels with neighbors and chronic mistreatment of his children attested amply to his inescapable *churlishness*. Ill breeding may sometimes be absent as an implication: the brazen *churlishness* of the manager of the complaint department. **Impudence** relates more closely to *effrontery*, pointing to aggressive behavior that is not restrained by considerations of taste or courtesy. The noun's special stress, however, is on a contemptuous or obnoxious arrogance: the *impudence* to suggest that an Ivy League background made him better qualified for the job than applicants from the state university. As can be seen, *impudence* and *churlishness* contrast strongly in that *churlishness* can indicate a low or coarse background, whereas *impudence* can indicate a supposedly superior background. *Impudence* contrasts with *effrontery* and *impertinence* in that the latter nouns often point to specific acts; furthermore, these acts could conceivably be inadvertent. *Impudence*, however, points to an insufferable manner that is reflected in deliberate insolence: an *impertinence* that resulted mostly from sheer ignorance rather than from outright *impudence*. See BRASHNESS, CONTEMPTUOUS, OVERBEARING, RUDE.

Antonyms: *civility, courtesy, kindness, meekness, politeness, timidity.*

egoism

   conceit
   egotism
   narcissism
   self-importance
   selfishness
   solipsism
   vanity

These nouns refer to a preoccupation and concern only for oneself. **Egoism** and **egotism** are a related pair with a fine distinction in meaning. *Egotism* is disapproving in tone, suggesting someone with an inflated or unrealistic view of his or her own worth because of extreme self-preoccupation: the typical *egotism* of those who think the world owes them a living. *Egoism*, on the other hand, is a more ambiguous term. It might apply to persons who do not necessarily consider themselves superior but who nevertheless remain preoccupied exclusively with themselves: the *egoism* of the young executive seeking advancement. *Egoism* has been given a new slant of meaning, furthermore, by psychological theorists of the last half-century. Theories that stress the importance of a strong ego (or so-called positive self-concept) as a key to mental stability have made it possible for *egoism* to suggest healthy self-interest coupled with a solid sense of identity: the *egoism* normal to a small infant; activities that will develop a healthy *egoism* in adolescents.

Conceit and **vanity** stress the sense of inflated worth that is involved in *egotism*. *Conceit* suggests a general state of being puffed up about one's own imagined superiority to others, so extreme as to rule out self-assessment or self-criticism: a fathomless *conceit* that prevents him from working hard enough to perfect his real but unformed talents. *Vanity* suggests self-pride that is based not so much on a feeling of superiority to others as on an unrealistic admiration and love for self: the actress who requires constant obeisance and flattery to satisfy her *vanity*. *Conceit* no longer sounds as informal as it once may have, but *vanity* is still the slightly more formal of the two nouns. **Self-importance** is closely related to *conceit* and *vanity* but is more neutral and descriptive: diplomats who bustled about in a display of *self-importance*. Sometimes, *self-importance* can suggest considerations of status or involvement in serious or worthwhile affairs rather than a strictly personal *conceit*. [Some people spend hours before a mirror feeding their *vanity*, but is that any worse than your tedious concern with office protocol simply as a way of insuring your own *self-importance*?]

Narcissism and **solipsism** may once have been technical terms drawn respectively from psychology and philosophy, but they have now gained a wider currency, even in normal conversation, for the cluster of meanings discussed here. *Narcissism* in a psychological sense refers to extreme withdrawal into self-preoccupation and self-love. It has come to be used more loosely to substitute for *egotism*: the star system in the theater that is responsible for a most pernicious form of *narcissism*. *Solipsism* in a philosophical context refers to a disbelief in the existence of anything beyond the self; it now extends pejoratively to anyone completely wrapped up in a private world: the *solipsism* of many obscure writers who do not even attempt to communicate with their audiences.

Selfishness need not suggest an inflated sense of worth at all or even extreme self-preoccupation. Its main connotation is that of grasping greediness without concern for others: the *selfishness* of those lobbyists who press for legislation beneficial to special interests but harmful to the general public. Under certain circumstances, however, it need not be wholly pejorative; in this it may approach some uses of *egoism*: the natural *selfishness* of the three-year-old. See BOAST, BRASHNESS, CONFIDENCE, OVERBEARING.

Antonyms: *altruism, humility, meekness, modesty, shyness.*

elegant

- deluxe
- elaborate
- grandiose
- luxurious
- ornate
- sumptuous

These adjectives describe what is highly fashionable or formal in style as well as costly, detailed, or lavish. **Elegant** is the most general but least concrete of these, being an approving adjective that refers to what is striking for its taste and value: a set of books with *elegant* bindings. It may suggest rarity as well as refinement, but may or may not suggest a piling up of great or costly masses of detail: the heavy gold scrolls of the *elegant* picture frame; a room *elegant* in its bareness, being sparsely furnished with a few excellent examples of modern furniture.

Elaborate and **ornate** both specifically indicate great detailing, but neither necessarily carries the approving tone of *elegant*. *Elaborate* indicates a full-scale working out of something with painstaking care and thought: an *elaborate* epic poem with an amazing number of themes and intricate strands of imagery; *elaborate* charity balls that bored her silly; an *elaborate* hoax. *Elaborate* can also apply to argument or reasoning that is methodical, lengthy, and abstruse: an *elaborate* hypothesis. *Ornate* is more restricted to decoration, suggesting a denseness that is not so much orderly as sensual: *ornate* verbal imagery. *Ornate* stresses the finished effect more than the care or work that went into it. Sometimes, richness or costliness of the result is implied: an *ornate* piece of jewelry studded with several types of precious stones.

Luxurious and **sumptuous** specifically stress the sparing of no expense to create something fashionably lavish. These adjectives may or may not point to the tastefulness suggested by *elegant* or the amassing of detail emphasized by the previous pair, but they do indicate a showiness of general effect. *Luxurious* often suggests, as well, a setting arranged for comfort and convenience: the *luxurious* hotel; a *luxurious* stretch limo complete with television, telephone, and bar. *Luxurious* need not be approving; a *luxurious* airport that was in the most garish and banal taste possible. Often, however, *luxurious* is applied approvingly to things in nature, eliminating any notion of costliness but emphasizing denseness, beauty, or richness, as of visual effect: the *luxurious* plumage of the peacock; a *luxurious* forest floor of interlaced pine needles. *Sumptuous* is more likely to be restricted to things made by people; its root refers to expenditure, and this emphasis on costliness is frequently present: a *sumptuous* Gobelin tapestry; The *sumptuous* new opera house proved an aesthetic disaster. Used more loosely, *sumptuous* may indicate something well turned out, tasteful, or lavish, without necessarily implying expenditure: the only woman on the beach with a really *sumptuous* figure.

Deluxe comes from the French phrase that means *of luxury*. Thus, it might function identically to *luxurious*. *Deluxe*, however, very often refers to special accommodations: a *deluxe* compartment on the Orient Express; a *deluxe* hotel suite. In these and other cases, it can refer to added benefits, comforts, or values costing more than the ordinary versions: a *deluxe* leather-bound edition of the encyclopedia. Since the adjective has become chiefly a merchandising term, it is often used to be deliberately deceptive: proof that the canned olives labeled *deluxe* were not significantly different in quality from the regular grade.

Grandiose is the one adjective here that specifically and exclusively stresses a pretentious, inflated, or pompous striving for the *elegant* or *sumptuous*: a *grandiose* speech filled with empty rhetoric. In this sense, it has a more general range of applications than other adjectives here: a *grandiose* symphony that ran on for more than two hours; the *grandiose* delusions of some schizophrenics. See EXCELLENT, EXQUISITE.

Antonyms: *inexpensive,* MEDIOCRE, *plain, simple, unadorned,* USUAL, VULGAR.

embarrassment

- chagrin
- discomposure
- humiliation
- mortification
- shame

These nouns refer to a disconcerted state of mind brought on by the broaching or exposing of an impropriety or by some blow to the ego. At its mildest, **embarrassment** may refer merely to social uneasiness: her *embarrassment* at having to introduce her new friend. Or it may refer to a cringing from indelicacy: his *embarrassment* at overhearing the private conversation of his students. More to the point, however, it refers strongly to alarm at any public exposure of one's ineptness or impropriety: his *embarrassment* at not remembering the name of the distinguished guest; the *embarrassment* of being discovered by her parents in the arms of the stranger. **Discomposure** is more formal and is restricted to the milder sense of *embarrassment,* usually suggesting a social uneasiness for any reason whatever: greeting unexpected guests without being able to conceal his *discomposure.* **Chagrin** concentrates specifically on *embarrassment* because of a blow to the ego: She looked down with *chagrin* at her stained dress.

The remaining nouns all point to more severe states of *embarrassment* than the foregoing nouns. **Shame** suggests a guilty disgust for one's own actions: looking back with *shame* on the night's escapades; boiling with *shame* at having failed the examination. **Humiliation** suggests a public loss of self-respect or the respect of others; this can result through a person's own failure or through someone else's malicious attempt to discredit him: the *humiliation* of having to ask the dean for reinstatement; those who regard receiving welfare checks as a *humiliation;* false accusations that resulted in public *humiliation.* **Mortification** derives from a verb meaning kill and reflects this root in referring hyperbolically to someone almost destroyed by *shame* or *embarrassment:* her *mortification* at learning she had given all her money to confidence men. It is the most intense of all these nouns, except that frequent hyperbolical use has weakened its force considerably. See ANXIETY, TIMID, UNSETTLE, UPSET.

Antonyms: *BRASHNESS, composure, CONFIDENCE, contentment, exaltation, temerity.*

emotion

affect
desire
feeling
passion
sentiment

These nouns refer to subjective or affective states of mind rather than to objective or rational attitudes. **Emotion** is the most general and neutral, including all states of mind from the slightest shift in mood to the most intense or violent seizures: a wistful *emotion* that briefly clouded her eyes; a struggle within him of *emotions* so intense he could hardly speak. **Feeling** is similar to but more informal than *emotion.* It too can refer both to weak or intense states: a *feeling* of disgust at his shortcomings; Violent *feelings* broke out into ungovernable expression. *Feeling,* however, has a specific use to refer to a state of intense receptivity or expressivity: jurors who listened to the account with evident *feeling;* trying to play the piano piece with more *feeling.* While *emotion* might occasionally be used in this way, it sounds less natural in such a context than *feeling.*

Passion may once have been used in a fairly neutral way to describe strong *emotions* of all varieties; now, however, it is more strictly limited to sexual *feeling* or obsessive *emotions:* a *passion* for his wife undimmed by the years; an absolute *passion* for seeking out untraveled byways. In the sense of obsessive preoccupation, *passion* has so frequently been used hyperbolically that its force has been somewhat dulled and made trivial: a *passion* for garlic pickles. In its sense of sexual *feeling,* it can seem antiquated or euphemistic: an unholy *passion* for the fair sex. **Desire** is now the preferred word for suggesting sexual *feeling,* but it can also refer to any *feeling* of wanting or needing something: a *desire* for the opposite sex that is first expressed by playing practical jokes; a strong *desire* to see his native country once more before he died. In contexts where *passion* escapes the charge of fustiness, it would suggest a greater potential for action than *desire.* [He was aware of the *desire* that had led him to call on her again, but he was surprised at the overwhelming *passion* he felt at seeing her face smiling up at his.]

Sentiment may suggest a fixed attitude that is an abiding part of one's personality and that can be called up afresh as *feeling* by some external catalyst: politicians appealing to *sentiments* as safe as love of God, home, and mother. In a more general use, it can, like *feeling,* suggest any of a variety of strong *emotions.* It also has a special use, referring to the expression of an emotional stand: She spoke of her antiwar *sentiments* with great eloquence. **Affect** is the most formal and technical of all these nouns; it is used in psychiatric parlance to refer to an emotional state in its discernible psychological rather than physiological aspect. [The excessive *affect* with which she reacted to several of the inkblots was also reflected in changes in pulse and respiration; He was still in a state of shock and thus able to speak of his recent ordeal without *affect;* the typical catatonic's total loss of *affect*.] See ATTRACTION, IMAGINATION, PASSIONATE, PREOCCUPIED.

Antonyms: *indifference, insensibility, rationality, reason.*

encourage

embolden
foster
hearten
inspire
promote
support

encourage *(continued)*

These verbs all refer to the giving of help, hope, or succor. **Encourage** is the most general term and means give hope, confidence, or spirit, or give active help: to *encourage* a young writer with praise; to *encourage* new industry by granting tax abatements; a teacher who *encourages* students to form their own opinions.

To **embolden** is to give someone confidence to undertake something. Success with a short story may *embolden* (or *encourage*) someone to try writing a novel. To **hearten** is to renew someone's spirit, especially to the point of giving him or her fresh courage to pursue a course of action: a victory that *heartened* the weary army; a visiting dignitary *heartened* by the unexpectedly warm reception she was accorded. To **inspire**, literally to breathe in, is to infuse with confidence or resolution, or to fire with enthusiasm, as though a new and vibrant spirit were breathed into one's being: The example set by their valiant commander *inspired* the troops to take the hill in the face of heavy enemy fire.

To **foster** is, literally, to nurture, and by extension has come to mean *encourage* by extending aid: to *foster* (or *encourage*) growth in the economy by lowering taxes. But even in extended senses, *foster* often retains the idea of gradual cultivation: Rigid parental control *fosters* rebellion in children. In this sense *foster* is often used in contexts suggesting an unwise or at least controversial kind of help and is sometimes akin to cherish, at other times to instigate: to *foster* the illusion that peace can be preserved by preparing for war; overzealous arguments that tended to *foster* dissent and division.

Support, more than any of the other verbs, implies that without the assistance offered the thing helped might founder and fail. It depends on the help given to survive or grow: to *support* a dying industry by granting it government subsidies. In another sense *support* means back up or endorse: a lawyer's opinion that *supported* a litigant's claim. Or *support* may mean do what one can to help: to *support* the war effort by buying bonds.

To **promote** is to *encourage* the growth or success of something: tariff revision that served to *promote* world trade; a good example serving to *promote* good manners in the young. *Promote* implies an aggressive and deliberate kind of assistance, often with a specific aim in mind: to *promote* one's own welfare at the expense of others. See ENDORSE, IMPLANT, INCITE, STIMULATE.

Antonyms: *abash,* DISCOURAGE, *dishearten,* HINDER, *THWART.*

encroach
infringe
intrude
invade
trespass
violate

These verbs refer to an unwelcome advance, usually upon someone else's territory or privacy. **Encroach** emphasizes the slowness or subtlety of an advance that may at first have proceeded without a countering complaint, only to be recognized finally as a threat: powers of the executive branch that have gradually *encroached* on the rights of the other branches; a mother-in-law whose attentions are not meant to *encroach* on the privacy of the newly married couple; urban sprawl that *encroaches* on unspoiled countryside.

Intrude is more often limited to overstepping of personal privacy than to territorial expansion. It suggests a situation in which a person or group has deliberately withdrawn in order to escape interruption— but without success: parents who *intrude* on the secrecies of childhood. Unlike *encroach,* however, *intrude* may more often be unintentional or sudden: embarrassed at finding that they had *intruded* on the children's party. It can sometimes be used more generally, but the note of a personal situation is still retained: newspapers that attempt to *intrude* on the decision-making process.

Invade and **violate** are much harsher terms; they would never suggest unintentional acts, like *intrude,* nor gradual acts, like *encroach.* They may, in fact, suggest savagery and violence. *Invade* most readily brings to mind a military attack by one nation on another: the day Iraq *invaded* Kuwait. In other uses this context of military conquest is usually present as a negative connotation: forests *invaded* by timber speculators. *Violate* has both a sexual and a legal context: women *violated* by Serbian soldiers; a court ruling that basic constitutional rights had been *violated.* In more general uses, it can express outrage at unethical tactics: discrimination that *violates* the ideals most citizens hold sacred.

Infringe and **trespass** are mainly restricted to a legal context and are consequently less intensely negative in tone than *invade* or *violate. Infringe* most appropriately refers to the *violation* of a principle or a legal right, while *trespass* most appropriately refers to the illegal use of or *encroachment* on the property of someone else: laws that *infringe* on free speech; *infringing* on a copyright; hunters who *trespass* on a farmer's land. *Infringe,* thus, compares with *intrude,* but does not have the personal tone of *intrude*. *Trespass*, similarly, compares with *invade*, but need not imply a concerted attack. Both *infringe* and *trespass*, of course, have wider applications, although they carry connotations from these most specific uses. See INSERT, MEDDLESOME.

Antonyms: *desist, observe, respect, withdraw.*

endemic. Do not confuse the adjective *endemic* (commonly found in a particular district) with the adjective or noun *epidemic* (outbreak of a disease). See also PANDEMIC.

endorse
accredit
approve
confirm
O.K.
ratify
sanction

These verbs are alike in suggesting favorable judgment or support given someone or something. **Endorse** literally means write on the back of: to *endorse* a check. In its figurative sense, *endorse* means give approval and support to. [Local officials have *endorsed* changes intended to modernize the building code; a TV commercial in which a well-known actor *endorses* a brand of breakfast cereal; to *endorse* a political candidate.]

To **accredit** is to furnish someone with credentials or to invest with authority. *Accredit* suggests either formal acceptance of or the meeting of official standards: to *accredit* an ambassador; a school *accredited* by a professional association.

Approve is the most general term in this group of verbs and may indicate anything from mild acquiescence to enthusiastic support; moreover, it may refer to official endorsement or to a wholly personal reaction: to *approve* a subordinate's expense account; to *approve* one's daughter's choice of career. [The Congress *approved* unanimously the new stamp in honor of the poet; He had no choice but to *approve* the application for membership.]

Confirm, **sanction**, and **ratify** share with *endorse* the meaning of making legal or effective by *approving*. To *sanction*, the strongest of these terms, is to *approve* authoritatively or to make valid. Like *endorse*, it couples support with approval: a church that refused to *sanction* ordination of women; Public opinion *sanctioned* a more liberal view of abortion rights. *Ratify*

always suggests formal approval in an official and authoritative setting. [The Senate *ratified* the fair trade agreement; The Constitution was *ratified* by the original states.] *Confirm* is not as strong as either *ratify* or *sanction*, though it is sometimes used interchangeably with *ratify*. To *confirm* is to make valid or binding by approval or acceptance: The Senate did not *confirm* the President's nominee for the Supreme Court; a government arbitrator who *confirmed* an agreement reached between the union and management.

O.K. is an informal term that often implies a written expression of approval, as a signature or initials: The editor *O.K.'d* the manuscript for publication; a bank official who *O.K.'d* a shipment of gold bars. See ACKNOWLEDGE, CONSENT, ENCOURAGE.

Antonyms: *censure, condemn, disapprove, discredit,* REJECT, *reprehend,* VOID.

enlarge
amplify
augment
expand
increase
magnify

These verbs are comparable when they mean make something larger or greater. **Enlarge** points to size or dimension: to *enlarge* a photograph; to *enlarge* a house by adding a new wing; to *enlarge* a staff by hiring three new people. **Increase** may point to quantity or intensity as well as size: to *increase* one's stock of food before a hurricane. [Melting snow *increases* the flow of water in many streams during spring thaws; The safety of automobiles was *increased* by the addition of seat belts and air bags.] In other senses, *increase* may mean grow in number: May your tribe *increase*. Or to step up or accelerate: to *increase* the rate of productivity.

Expand may mean *increase* in range, scope, or volume as well as in size: to *expand* the economy by stepping up government spending. *Expand* conveys the idea of a general *enlarging* in all dimensions rather than one, and suggests an unfolding or opening out: to *expand* one's operation to include all aspects of the clothing business. *Expand* also can refer to the filling in or development of details: to *expand* a speech; to *expand* an equation. **Amplify** can also refer to the filling in of details, but stresses the addition of material for the sake of completeness, as by illustration. [The President was asked to *amplify* his statement that our goal was nothing less than total victory; to *amplify* a comment by providing reporters with background information.] As the contexts of these illustrations indicate, *amplify* is most often used of formal situations. In its more basic sense, *amplify* is nowadays used almost exclusively to refer to the increase in the strength of sound or of the electromagnetic waves that produce it: to *amplify* sound with the use of microphones.

Augment means add to and is in some contexts interchangeable with *increase* or *enlarge:* to *augment* (or *increase* or *enlarge*) a sales force. *Augment,* however, emphasizes the action of addition more than the increase in size and often suggests that the addition is a temporary expedient rather than a permanent or structural increase: to *augment* an infantry regiment with an artillery battalion. *Augment* may refer to intensity as well as amount: to *augment* an electrical signal by *increasing* the power, thus *amplifying* the sound.

Magnify means make something larger or greater either in fact or in appearance: A microscope *magnifies* objects by making them appear larger even though it does not *increase* their actual sizes. Sometimes *magnify* implies exaggeration, that is, it makes something appear to be larger or more important than it really is: to *magnify* a relatively trivial loss. See ESCALATE, EXTEND, SWELL.

Antonyms: *condense, contract, decrease, narrow,* REDUCE, SHORTEN.

enmity

animosity
animus
antagonism
hatred
hostility
rancor

These nouns are alike in denoting feelings of ill will or active dislike. **Enmity** is the quality or feeling that characterizes an enemy; it may be personal or impersonal, overt or hidden, but it is usually the result of a longstanding argument or of a prolonged series of conflicts, and hence is profoundly felt and not easily eradicated: The *enmity* between the two groups threatens to break into open war at any time. **Hostility** embraces the actions by which *enmity* is displayed; it is often used in the plural: The *hostilities* were marked by brief periods of savage fighting. *Hostility* also refers to the state of being hostile, that is, of feeling unfriendly or ill-disposed toward, often to the point of menace: The *hostility* between the two groups of demonstrators was marked by occasional scuffles; the *hostility* with which mothers in the park regarded the drug pushers.

Hatred is an intense dislike coupled with a strong desire to harm the object of one's feeling. *Hatred* is deep-seated and malicious and may be the end result of *enmity* or of prolonged *hostility:* the *hatred* felt for the Croats by some Serbians; Discrimination and persecution have created an atmosphere of *hatred* between the races in some parts of our country. *Hatred,* however, can also be applied to things and conditions, and may depend on instinct or temperamental aversion: a cat's *hatred* of water.

Antagonism emphasizes mutuality of ill will between persons or groups, and often implies temperamental incompatibility. Unlike *hostility, antagonism* seldom implies that harmful actions will result: Actors sometimes resent what they see as excessive guidance from their directors, and a feeling of *antagonism* may spring up between them. **Animus** implies a feeling of ill will or antipathy so deep-rooted and intertwined with character and background that a coherent explanation of its cause is seldom possible: to harbor an *animus* against intellectual women; an *animus* against government employees.

Animosity and **rancor** are stronger than *enmity,* but often less enduring; *animosity* suggests vindictive anger, and *rancor,* bitter resentment. [He nourished a feeling of *animosity* for his penny-pinching boss; a woman who felt *rancor* at being passed over for promotion by her company commander.] *Rancor* is intensely bitter *enmity* or *hatred,* often coupled with malice or even malevolence: *Rancor* over his party's humiliating defeat at the polls led him to organize a military coup with the aim of completely destroying the party in power. See DESPISE, DISLIKE.

Antonyms: *amity, camaraderie, fellowship, friendship, harmony, sympathy.*

---

enormity. Do not confuse the noun *enormity* (great wickedness) with the adjective *enormous* (immense) or the noun *immensity.*

enrage

anger
incense
infuriate

These verbs all mean arouse extreme displeasure, and usually antagonism, in a person or animal. **Enrage** means throw into a rage—in other words, put someone in such a state of frustration, anger, or annoyance that he is beside himself and may react compulsively or violently. *Enrage* always implies strong provocation: to *enrage* a wounded bull by taunting the beast with a cape; He was *enraged* by the policeman's rough treatment of the demonstrators.

Anger, a more general term, may apply to mild as well as severe displeasure: What *angered* her most was the lack of writing paper in the hotel room. *Anger* is often used as a participle to describe one's disposition: a diplomat not easily *angered* or flustered; He was always capable of being *angered* by trifles.

Incense literally means set on fire, and thus emphasizes the volatility and heat of anger. It need not, however, imply a long-standing or profound feeling, only one of great intensity: The mayor, *incensed* over the filthy condition of the hallways of the slum building he was inspecting, ordered an immediate investigation. *Incense* often implies sharp indignation resulting from a slight or incivility: She was *incensed* by the reluctance of the headwaiter to seat her because she was unescorted.

Infuriate is the strongest term of this group, implying a reaction so intense that one virtually loses control of one's actions. That which *infuriates* is felt to be unbearably offensive. [While the display of luxury by the French aristocracy of the eighteenth century *incensed* the poor of Paris, Marie Antoinette's purported suggestion that they eat cake if they lacked bread positively *infuriated* them.] *Infuriate* is often used hyperbolically in less formal contexts to indicate any degree of anger: She was *infuriated* by her friend's remark about her new dress. See ANGER, BOTHER, FRANTIC, OUTRAGE, UPSET.

Antonyms: *mollify, pacify, placate, quiet, soothe, tranquilize.*

entertain

amuse
divert
interest

These verbs concern activity that draws attention and makes time pass agreeably. To **entertain**, either oneself or others, is to provide some occupation that will afford pleasure or relieve monotony or boredom. *Entertainment* may be simple and personal at one extreme, or formal and public at the other, ranging from brief distraction and private hospitality to large parties and theatrical performances: children *entertaining* themselves with building blocks; to *entertain* out-of-town guests; a comedian and dancers *entertaining* soldiers overseas. *Entertaining* someone implies the putting forth of active effort: Let me *entertain* you; an *entertaining* show. **Amuse**, by contrast, focuses on

response: an *amusing* book; The Queen is not *amused*. To *amuse* people is to affect them in such a way that they are put or kept in a pleasant mood. In a nonspecific sense, *amuse* can suggest any form of distraction that contents the mind: Try to keep the child *amused*. Specifically, *amusement* emphasizes light *entertainment*, pointing to something that brings a smile or laugh or that is thought of as fun. A person may be *amused* by a clever thought, a bizarre sight, a game, a story, an evening's *entertainment*. But a performance of a Greek tragedy, which can *entertain* an audience by holding their attention and affording them aesthetic satisfaction, would not be said to *amuse*.

Divert is close to *amuse* but stresses that the *amusement* is not constant but is a temporary form of escapism. To *divert* is to draw the mind away from serious thoughts or pursuits, distracting the attention from work, worry, pain, or commonplace concerns and focusing it on pleasure: a *diverting* comedy. [An evening out may *divert* an over-worked couple; The students set aside one night a week for *diversion*.]

Interest is the most general of these verbs. To *interest* someone is to excite or hold his curiosity or attention, for whatever reason. [A psychopath *interests* a psychologist; The student found the lecture *interesting*.] But the specific sense in which *interest* compares with the other verbs in this set involves an awakening of attention by some *entertaining* expedient: The showing of slides *interested* the dozing student, and she sat up and took notice. See HOBBY.

Antonyms: *annoy, bore, tire.*

entire

complete
full
intact
total
whole

These adjectives describe things of which no part is missing, damaged, omitted, empty, or imperfect. **Entire** may apply both in concrete and in abstract senses, referring to a physical, numerical, temporal, or qualitative entity. [The *entire* continent seemed to be covered with snow; The *entire* cast was present for dress rehearsal; The *entire* day was ruined; His concern as a doctor was for the *entire* person, not just for the body.] **Whole** is more informal and more general than *entire* but is very close to it in meaning and may be substituted for it in the examples above. Both adjectives apply to that which is unbroken or undivided, but sometimes one or the other is used exclusively in a certain context. [When the Venus de Milo was *entire* (or *whole*), there were arms on the statue; A *whole* number is distinguished from a fraction.] *Whole* differs from *entire* in suggesting a moral or physical perfection that can be lost and recovered, as by the regaining of health: Your faith has made you *whole*. Here, *entire* is closer to **intact**, which refers to something that has remained in its original condition. [The second generation kept the family fortune *entire;* The heiress kept her father's art collection *intact.*] A thing is said to be *intact* if it has successfully resisted attempts made on its integrity, or if it has been subjected to destructive influences or forces and has come through unscathed. [She escaped from his clutches with virtue *intact;* Few buildings in the bombed city remained *intact;* Though subjected to brainwashing, the prisoner of war emerged with integrity *intact.*]

Complete focuses on the presence of all needed or normal parts, while **total** implies a measurable aggregate. Both may describe a collective entity: a *complete* set of dishes; the *complete* works of Shakespeare; his *total* earnings for 1993. *Total,* however, involves a precise determination of the size of an existent *whole*, and whether a *total* amount or number is added to or subtracted from, it still remains a sum *total* as long as it is inclusive and accurate. *Complete,* by contrast, means finished or perfected, implying the meeting of a standard or fulfillment of a goal. [The *total* number of jurors selected so far is nine, so the jury is not yet *complete.*] In an abstract sense the two adjectives are much more closely synonymous, describing that which covers everything without exception or reservation: *total* (or *complete*) destruction; a *total* (or *complete*) commitment. Both are also sometimes interchangeable with *entire:* He has *entire* (or *total* or *complete*) control of the business.

Full stresses content. In its most concrete sense, it implies that a receptacle contains as much as it can hold: to drink a *full* (or a *whole*) cup of coffee; a container *full* of water. Like *complete*, it may stress the presence of all belonging parts: a *full* dozen. It may also describe something that is maximum in size, extent, degree, or the like: a *full* moon as opposed to a crescent; a *full* load; *full* speed ahead. *Full* is close to *whole, entire,* and *complete* in implying that a thing is not deficient or that nothing is being omitted or withheld. To take a *full* course of treatment is to take a *complete* course or a *whole* course. But the other adjectives are stronger and more forceful in referring to something that is absolute and unlimited. [You have my *entire* confidence; I have *complete* (or *total* or *full*) confidence in you.]

All of the adjectives in this set, with the sole exception of *intact,* may be used as intensives: You've missed the *whole* point; It took us an *entire* week; a *full* four years; *complete* contempt; *total* abstinence. See FINISH, TOTAL.

Antonyms: *broken, damaged, destroyed, divided, empty, imperfect, incomplete, limited, partial.*

entrust

commit
confide
consign
delegate

These verbs involve the transfer of responsibility to someone else. **Entrust** stresses safety and reliance. A person may be *entrusted* with authority or with a specific task: to *entrust* an agent with power of attorney. A thing *entrusted* may be a specialized task or an object that needs protection: *entrusting* all her jewelry to the hotel safe; *entrusting* the canvassing of voters to a public-relations firm. **Confide** gives intenser overtones of safety, caution, or discretion: *confiding* enforcement of the new legislation to the federal courts. In this sense, it is more formal than *entrust* and has been overshadowed by other meanings of *confide* not directly related here.

Commit and **consign** are less personal than *entrust* and are more formal in this context. At its most general, *commit* means place a person or thing in someone else's charge: *committing* the child to a nurse's care. Specifically, it may involve the placing of a person in protective custody: to *commit* someone to a mental hospital. *Commit* often carries an undertone of giving something up for better or worse to forces beyond one's control: *committing* their chances for survival to the prospect of being sighted by a passing ship or plane. *Consign* suggests great impersonality and has a legalistic or commercial flavor: *consigning* the shipment to another railroad. In other cases, *consign* may suggest criticism for a lack of concern that allows power to fall into the wrong hands: *consigning* our most basic rights to the hazards of a kangaroo court. Both *commit* and *consign* may also sometimes focus on getting rid of a thing forever: to *commit* a paper to the flames; a critic airily *consigning* an author to oblivion.

Delegate is the most neutral verb of this group, implying neither the security and confidence of some, nor the impersonality of others. Its tone is one of description without evaluation. It suggests a bureaucratic context in which a leading executive is responsible for work that others will execute: the fatal flaw of being unable to *delegate* authority; *delegating* all but the most serious matters to a crack team of assistants. See APPOINT, REPRESENTATIVE, TRUST.

envious. Do not confuse the adjective *envious* (full of envy) with the adjective *jealous* (feeling resentment toward a rival).

environment. Do not confuse the noun *environment* (surroundings) with the noun *ecology* (study of an environment and things living in it).

epidemic. Do not confuse the noun *epidemic* (outbreak of a disease) with the adjective *endemic* (commonly found in a particular district) or with the adjective *pandemic* (occurring over a very wide area) or with the noun *pandemic* (a disease occurring over such an area).

equable. Do not confuse the adjective *equable* (even, unvarying) with the adjective *equitable* (fair, just).

equitable. Do not confuse the adjective *equitable* (fair, just) with the adjective *equable* (even, unvarying).

erase

cancel
delete
efface
eradicate
expunge
obliterate

These verbs refer to the removal of markings from a surface, possibly so that they can be replaced by other markings. **Erase** is the least formal and most general of these, referring to removal of symbols by any wiping or rubbing action: asking each boy to *erase* his own work from the blackboard; *erasing* the penciled guidelines after the lettering had been inked in. **Eradicate** is the most formal of these verbs. Aside from its etymological reference to rooting out, it applies here to the *erasing* of ink markings by a specially prepared chemical: revisions made in washable ink so that the editor could *eradicate* them if necessary.

Cancel and **delete** are less clear than the foregoing about the means used to cause the removal of markings. *Cancel* once pointed specifically to the crossing out of something: *canceling* every entry that was out of date. By extension, it may mean rescind or terminate: *Cancel* my subscription. *Cancel* also refers to overmarkings on postage stamps or to action that reduces the effectiveness of something: erratic behavior that *canceled* out the good impression previously made. *Delete* still chiefly refers to the editing of a text by removing unwanted expressions; this may be done by crossing out, *erasing, eradicating,* or covering the thing to be *deleted:* using red ink to *delete* objectionable phrases from the manuscript. **Efface** is also vague about the means of removal, but it may often suggest that markings have become partially or wholly indistinct, not by design but by time and attrition: weathering that had *effaced* the tombstone inscription; ideas whose vividness has been *effaced* by use. **Expunge** and **obliterate** refer to forceful and total removal, whether by design or not. *Expunge* compares to the less formal *delete,* but may suggest the total removal of a larger body of material by whatever means: *expunging* from the diaries all reference to people still living, and *deleting* a few remarks about figures out of the recent past. In any case, *expunge* suggests an uncompromising removal and the total disappearance of such material. *Obliterate* suggests even more force than *expunge,* even to the possible extent of damaging the surface or material on which the markings appear. Otherwise, *obliterate* compares to *efface* in sometimes suggesting indistinctness that results not by design but from the action of natural forces: fire damage that *obliterated* many passages in the manuscript; erosion that had nearly *obliterated* all trace of the earliest Minoan settlements. See DESTROY, VOID.

Antonyms: *impress, imprint,* INSERT.

erotic

amorous
arousing
concupiscent
desirous
passionate
sensual
sexy

These adjectives describe a state of being filled with sexual feelings, or things designed to call up such feelings. **Erotic,** stemming from a root meaning love, nonetheless stresses a specifically sexual love. *Erotic* can refer either to such feelings or to things eliciting these feelings: aware of his own *erotic* impulses; an *erotic* movie. **Sensual** can also refer to either situation, but it refers to sexual desire only by implication. Theoretically, *sensual* should indicate someone given to a life of the senses or something appealing to the senses, but it has been used suggestively, perhaps euphemistically, so often that sexual desire is inevitably a part of its reference, although not so strongly insisted upon as in the case of *erotic: a sensual* appetite for exotic women; *sensual* music to which veiled women danced.

Concupiscent is a learned synonym for lustful, coming from Latin roots meaning desire intensely. It focuses on fleshly desire that seeks its own gratification, as contrasted with unselfish love, and it carries the implication of original sin: a *concupiscent* husband, unfaithful to his wife; the *concupiscent* elements in human character.

Desirous, **amorous**, and **passionate** refer exclusively to someone filled with *erotic* feeling. *Desirous* may suggest a vague longing or lack, without an object in view, or it may suggest a specific sexual wish for a particular object: *desirous* of a kind of woman he had never met; He became more and more *desirous*, and she seemed more and more desirable the more she rebuffed his advances. In the latter case, *desirous* suggests a distinction between sexual eagerness and love. *Amorous* is consequently warmer in feeling, since it can suggest an affectionate desire for lovemaking or sex play: a wife turning away from her *amorous* husband. *Passionate* is more intense than either *desirous* or *amorous,* but it may or may not be divorced in its intensity from notions of affectionate love: a nymphomaniac making *passionate* advances to a strange man; proposals of marriage that grew more and more *passionate*.

Sexy is the most informal of all these adjectives. It may be applied to any person or thing that seems to project, radiate, or intensify sex appeal: a very *sexy* man; a *sexy* walk; a *sexy,* form-fitting sweater. Used of books, plays, movies, and the like, *sexy* points to a titillating preoccupation with sex: a *sexy* novel. **Arousing** refers solely to those things that call up sexual desire: a coy manner deliberately designed to be *arousing*. See EAGER, EMOTION, HOT, PASSIONATE, STIMULATE.

Antonyms: *sexless.*

escalate

increase
intensify
step up

These verbs refer to the heightening of something in scale, as pressure, tension, pay, or military activity. **Escalate** can imply either a gradual process or a series of sudden or surprise spurts. It is most often used for rising prices and pay rates or for military activity: factors causing the cost of living to *escalate* during the third quarter; a contract clause that would *escalate* their weekly pay to keep pace with rising prices; They *escalated* the war by mining enemy harbors. As in the second example, *escalate* can suggest two scales rising reciprocally, or one of these rising in response to or anticipation of the other: any aggressive act that would *escalate* the war to a new level of intensity on both sides. The verb's faddish appeal can be seen in the way it replaces simpler words in a wide range of contexts: We *escalated* our efforts to get the cabin built before summer.

Step up, by contrast, might more logically suggest a series of spurts with level intervals between them: businesses that must *step up* production during periods of seasonal demand. This notion is by no means held to, however, and *step up* can be used for any single or even gradual act of heightening: immigration quotas that were *stepped up* by the new law; directors who inevitably *step up* their pressure on the actors as opening night approaches.

Increase is a much more general verb than *escalate* or *step up* and can often replace either to advantage, with a possible gain in simplicity and clarity. While *increase* can apply to any buildup, its particular point is sometimes to indicate a gain in amount. [The number of people browsing in bookstores *increases* sharply during lunch hour.] **Intensify** is of comparable generality, but it is often directed toward a heightening of pressure, tension, or insistence: floods that *intensified* the force with which the river battered against the levees; the introduction of a plot device to *intensify* the movie's suspense; arrogant behavior that only caused the union leaders to *intensify* their demands. See ENLARGE, EXTEND, SWELL.

Antonyms: *DECREASE, LESSEN, REDUCE, WEAKEN.*

escape

abscond
flee
fly
retreat
run away

These verbs refer to a withdrawal from danger or from an unpleasant situation. **Escape** is the most general of these, applying to any sort of withdrawal. The verb, however, does carry connotations of urgency, though not necessarily of haste. [He lay perfectly still and played dead to *escape* capture by the enemy; She rushed down the stairs to *escape* her enraged pursuer.] **Run away**, unlike *escape,* specifically indicates swift movement and is most often restricted to actual physical action; on the other hand, it need not imply urgency: children who *run away* from home for no observable reason; burglars who will *run away* if caught in the act. Sometimes, the phrase is used without the physical implication: candidates who try to *run away* from controversial issues.

Retreat may suggest both urgency and haste but, unlike the previous verbs, need not necessarily suggest either. It is common in a military context, but is used widely outside this specific area: orders to *retreat* only in a desperate situation and then in an orderly, planned way. [They *retreated* in frantic, disorganized haste; the decision to *retreat* before any threat of confrontation arose; He *retreated* slowly and quietly to his room without being seen.] **Abscond** also pertains to a specific context but unlike *retreat* is almost exclusively restricted to it. It refers to embezzlement or theft in which property is illegally seized and carried off: the club's last treasurer, who had *absconded* with the funds. It is sometimes used jocosely for less serious situations: warning her not to *abscond* with the book he lent her.

Flee and **fly** both refer to a hasty escape and usually imply urgency as well: those who *fled* the burning hotel; Trojans who are always depicted as *flying* from the courageous Greeks. The only effective difference between these verbs now is that *fly* is much more formal than *flee* and, in fact, would sound archaic to most ears. Furthermore, the other and more common meaning of *fly,* pertaining to travel through the air, can make its use in this sense seem confusing, even comical: a child who *flew* from his kidnappers; refugees who *have flown* from persecution in other lands. *Fled* would seem preferable in both these circumstances. See AVOID, LEAVE (depart), RUN.

Antonyms: *confront, face, give up,* REMAIN, SUBMIT, *surrender.*

everlasting

endless
eternal
interminable
never-ending
timeless
unending

These adjectives all refer to that which has no beginning or no end, or exists outside or beyond time. **Everlasting** stresses something that endures through time, particularly something that once created will never cease to exist. **Eternal** contrasts with this by admitting the implication that the thing described has always existed in the past as well and thus has neither beginning nor end. [In Christian theology, the soul of each newborn infant is a fresh creation that is immortal and consequently *everlasting;* In Hinduism, the soul has no beginning and need never end and is consequently *eternal.*] *Everlasting* can also function as a negative hyperbole for a continual or constant annoyance or even for something that seems to take forever and has worn out one's patience or tolerance: her *everlasting* boasting; this *everlasting* war. When negative, *eternal* is used more loosely, less specifically, and with less force: his *eternal* lack of funds.

Timeless may refer more informally than *eternal* to something without beginning or end: the *timeless* laws of the universe. Even when used less literally, the adjective is mainly positive in its effect, referring in this case to something that does not go out of date but seems to be always fresh or relevant: the *timeless* poetry of Shakespeare. *Timeless* can also refer to something outside time or to a situation in which time seems to have stopped: It is possible to conceive of a *timeless* universe, but not one without space; the *timeless* moment of satori, or enlightenment. **Unending** refers more informally and exclusively than *everlasting* to something that has no end: the *unending* torment of souls condemned to hell; the philosophical view of the universe as being in an *unending* state of flux. Used less exactly, *unending* can be either an approving or disapproving hyperbole. In approval, it often suggests what is boundless as well as lasting: She gave her son *unending* love. In disapproval, a failure to get to the point may be implied: *unending* negotiations while the fighting continued.

Never-ending can point, perhaps more emphatically than *unending,* to what endures forever: the *never-ending* omniscience of God. As a loose hyperbole, *never-ending* can be positive, with a tone approaching that of *timeless* in this use, but with an additional suggestion of recurrent or continually renewed freshness: fairy tales that have been a *never-ending* delight for many generations of children. Used negatively, *never-ending* may have greater force, suggesting a tiresome refusal to come to a halt: a *never-ending* bore.

Endless is the most informal of these adjectives, has the widest range of uses, and is most open to the demands of context. It can refer to something without an end in time: the *endless* convolutions of matter and energy. But since it can also suggest something that continues without end through space, it can be ambiguous: a theory holding that the universe is *endless*. As a hyperbole, it can be approving, with implications like those for *unending: endless* admiration; a lovely afternoon that seemed *endless*. More often, it is loosely used as a harsh negative: *endless* delays during voter registration. **Interminable** is the one adjective here that is almost exclusively limited in use as a negative hyperbole for something that is long-lasting. It is more formal than *endless* but is less ambiguous than the latter in referring solely to time. It is also the most harshly disapproving: *interminable* filibusters that disrupt the orderly functioning of the legislature. See IMMORTAL, INFINITE, MONOTONOUS, PERMANENT, PERSISTENT.

Antonyms: *finite*, TEMPORARY.

examine

    audit
    inspect
    investigate
    scan
    scrutinize

All these verbs mean look something over or inquire into it, usually for a definite purpose. **Examine** is the general word; it can refer to a cursory look or a thorough study of all details. **Investigate**, **scrutinize**, and **inspect** mean *examine* thoroughly, but their connotations vary. To *investigate* is to make a methodical, searching inquiry into a complex situation in an effort to uncover the facts. *Scrutinize* suggests *examining* critically and with painstaking attention to detail: a printer *scrutinizing* a photographic transparency for specks of dust or other imperfections. *Inspect* usually implies that the object of one's attention is being critically compared to a standard of excellence, quality, or the like, with a view toward noting discrepancies or deficiencies in the former: fire officials *inspecting* an abandoned warehouse for potential fire hazards; a sergeant *inspecting* all the rifles of the squad. One may *examine, scrutinize,* or *inspect* a person, an inanimate object, or a situation; *investigate* is usually applied to situations or events, except in the case of formal inquiries into the lives or actions of a person suspected of a crime or applying for a job of a sensitive nature: to *investigate* the background of a potential member of the Secret Service. [The detective *investigating* the murder *examined* the body, *inspected* the scene of the crime, and *scrutinized* the weapon for clues.]

To **audit** is to *examine* accounts or records. Thus, to justify an increase in advertising rates, a magazine publisher may have an outside firm *audit* the circulation figures.

Scan is a verb that is undergoing a complete reversal of meaning. Its former meaning—*examine* closely and analytically—is still valid but is now applied chiefly to analysis of poetic meter: to *scan* Vergil. More frequently now, *scan* means glance quickly at something to get the gist of it: to *scan* a newspaper by glancing at the headlines. See HUNT, STUDY.

excellent

    choice
    first-class
    first-rate
    prime
    select

These adjectives refer to something rated as being among the best of its kind. **Excellent** points literally to something that excels other things. As such, it is often used to designate the highest class in a grading, rating, or ranking system: an eating guide that rated many restaurants as good or very good, but only a few as *excellent*. Often, however, as with most superlatives, *excellent* is not thought to be high enough in its praise and it takes second place to some other word: a debating team disappointed at getting an *Excellent* instead of a Superior rating.

Neither **first-class** nor **first-rate** admits of this sort of devaluation; one thing cannot be more *first-rate* than another. Both indicate the highest category in a ranking system. *First-class* can suggest a military or paramilitary system: a *first-class* scout; a *first-class* marksman. Even outside this context the adjective would suggest a set of clear categories into which things can be placed by objective evaluation: designating as *first-class* those cities with populations over 1,000,000; *first-class* mail; a *first-class* permit. As can be seen, any notion of excellence may well be absent from this adjective's meaning. Used more loosely and subjectively, *first-class* can describe anything one likes or approves of: a *first-class* fellow; a *first-class* movie. *First-rate* may sometimes suggest careful evaluation based more on imponderables than on objective categorization: feeling in *first-rate* health; a *first-rate* analysis of current political tendencies. But while inherent worth is usually indicated by the *first-rate*, it can sometimes point to something consequential rather than *excellent*: a *first-rate* world power. *First-*

EXILE

rate is even more open than *first-class* to uses indicating mere subjective approval: a *first-rate* friend; a *first-rate* party. Both adjectives can also indicate something that is thought to be supremely bad; *first-class* may lend itself more readily to this use, but in any case, it can give a more informal tone and may have comic force: a *first-class* heel; a *first-class* bore; a *first-rate* disaster.

Most specifically, **prime** indicates, under the grading system of the U.S. Department of Agriculture, the highest grade of beef or lamb; **choice** indicates a grade between *prime* and good. In other contexts, *prime* can refer to something of first significance, urgency, or value: television programs that appear in *prime* time; the *prime* need being to get the combatants to the conference table. *Prime* can also refer to anything that is excellent, best, most typical, or at its peak: *prime* theatrical fare; a *prime* example; athletes in *prime* condition. More neutrally, it can suggest the main part of something or what comes first: our *prime* reason for deciding to approve the bill; her *prime* concern being the safety of her children. *Choice*, by contrast, refers to something that fulfills high and discriminating standards. Oddly enough, *choice* often seems the stronger of the two adjectives in other contexts than the grading of meat. By implication, what is *prime* may be overlooked or easily available, whereas *choice* suggests the successful discrimination of what is both rare and *excellent:* their *choicest* wine from a vast stock that contained no bottle of less than *prime* quality.

Select can refer to lumber that is relatively free of blemish or knots. More generally, *select* compares with *choice* by stressing discrimination, but differs in often referring to a sampling of *excellent* things that cannot be presented in full: *select* highlights from ten Broadway musicals; only *select* programs appearing in the television listing. A weakening of the force of *select* may result by analogy with *selected*, which may indicate arbitrary compression or subjective sampling. See ELEGANT, EXQUISITE.

Antonyms: *bad, faulty, imperfect,* MEDIOCRE, *poor, second-class.*

excuse
alibi
apologia
apology

These nouns are comparable when they refer to causes, circumstances, or motivations that are put forth in order to defend, explain, or extenuate an action, viewpoint, or the like. An **excuse** is an implicit admission of wrong, but it is offered as a full or partial justification of one's actions. By contrast, an **apology**, in current usage, is an open admission that one has done wrong and is sorry for it. Whereas an *excuse* is a means of avoiding or mitigating the responsibility for one's actions, an *apology* is the contrite recognition of that responsibility. [His *excuse* for being late was that his train was delayed; He could only offer a frank *apology* for having forgotten about our dinner engagement.]

Apology and **apologia** both originally implied the intent of clearly setting forth the grounds for some action, conviction, or the like that others consider wrong or improper. *Apology* is now seldom used in this sense, *apologia* being preferred. [The convicted assassin stoutly defended his actions and wrote a lengthy *apologia* in explanation of the part he played in the plot.]

Alibi, in common usage, implies that an *excuse* is plausible rather than true. In legal use, however, *alibi* means a plea by an accused person that he or she was elsewhere when the crime was committed. Even in other contexts, *alibi* does not invariably suggest dubiety. [His *alibi* depended upon the eyewitness testimony of a taxicab driver; a desperate, last-minute *alibi* intended to save her from the wrath of her father.] See EXPLANATION, REASONING.

exile
banish
deport
expatriate
relegate
rusticate
sequester

These verbs refer to the sending away or placing apart of a person, group of people, or thing. In some periods of history, a government could **exile** a citizen, that is, force the citizen to leave the homeland. Although few if any modern nations now have such a punishment, *exile* has remained in the language as a metaphorical reference to any imposed or voluntary separation from one's home: Jazz Age writers who *exiled* themselves to Paris to learn the craft of writing; parents who *exile* their children to kindergartens simply to be rid of them for a few hours each day. **Banish** has a history similar to that of *exile*, but its present uses permit a wider range of application, suggesting any forcible removal: The judge ordered the hecklers *banished* from the courtroom; television commercials

145

promising that their product can *banish* washday drudgery, *banish* bad complexions, or *banish* acid indigestion in a twinkling. **Rusticate** means send or *banish* to the country and, in Great Britain, means punish university students by suspending them and sending them away temporarily.

Relegate, in reference to people, suggests disposing of them without much concern for their welfare: *relegating* minority groups to second-class citizenship; *relegating* freshman senators to a role of watchful silence. In reference to other matters, *relegate* suggests their assignment to an unimportant place: *relegating* his fears to a corner of her mind reserved for the trivial and forgettable.

Deport and **expatriate** both have current technical uses like those *exile* and *banish* once had. *Deport* refers to the official sending away of someone who is not a citizen: *deporting* the gangster who had entered the country illegally. *Expatriate* refers to the stripping of citizenship from someone, either by his own choice or by the nation's choice: a malcontent who *expatriated* himself to a country more to his liking; a law to *expatriate* those who serve in a foreign army.

Sequester means place apart or separate. It differs from the other verbs here considered in emphasizing separation rather than the action of sending away: to *sequester* a construction area in which blasting is necessary. In a related sense, *sequester* applies to people and is often used reflexively with the meaning of making private or secret or of being secluded. [She lived a *sequestered* life in a mountain village; He *sequestered* himself for the summer in a secluded cottage to write his novel.] The emphasis is still on placing apart, but additional stress is given to the motive—that of secrecy or seclusion. See IMPEL, PRIVACY, REMOVE.

Antonyms: *GREET.*

exonerate
absolve
acquit
exculpate
vindicate

These verbs all mean clear of guilt or wrongdoing. **Exonerate** means free from accusation or blame, and stresses freedom from future suspicion: The hearings before the subcommittee *exonerated* him of complicity in the swindle. To **absolve** is to set free from obligation or penalty attaching to an act: The aircraft company was *absolved* from liability following the investigation of the disaster. To **acquit** is to set free from

accusation, usually for lack of evidence, and often of a specific charge: to be *acquitted* of perjury in the first degree. [The motorist was *acquitted* of reckless driving; he was thereupon *absolved* from any claim for damages arising out of the collision.]

Vindicate means clear completely through the examination of evidence. [The accused accountant *vindicated* herself by producing all recent bank statements of the company; The testimony of witnesses *vindicated* the prisoner.] It may also refer to judgment that has been borne out by subsequent events: The justice's minority dissent was finally *vindicated* in later years, when the majority endorsed his arguments and reversed its former decision. **Exculpate** means free from blame or prove innocent of guilt or fault. Unlike *exonerate*, it does not necessarily imply that a formal charge was made nor that the blameworthy act was illegal or illicit. It may apply to any culpable action: Investigation *exculpated* the driver from suspicion of having caused the accident. See INNOCENT, PARDON.

Antonyms: *ACCUSE, inculpate.*

expectation
anticipation
expectancy
hope
outlook
prospect

These nouns all point to the future and the likelihood of certain events or conditions taking place. **Expectation** and **expectancy** are close synonyms meaning the waiting for something to happen, or the probability with which the awaited can be presumed to happen. [There had been no *expectation* of war among the general public when the Japanese attacked Pearl Harbor; Those who drop out of school may have to lower their *expectations* of success.] *Expectancy* is used to describe a state of tense *expectation:* There was an air of *expectancy* as the President was ushered to the podium to make his announcement. It is also commonly encountered in the phrase *life expectancy.*

Anticipation, in this context, is a strong *expectation* based on foreknowledge. [The *anticipation* of cold weather leads the householder to lay in fuel in the fall; building up the armed forces in *anticipation* of war]

Hope, as here considered, is *expectation* based on desire, with or without any likelihood that the hoped for will happen or materialize. [Parents have high *hopes* for their children; A man saves money in the *hope* that inflation will not wipe it out.]

Outlook and **prospect** refer to future probabilities based on present indications or analyses. [The employment *outlook* for the next year is based in part on contracts signed two years ago; The *outlook* for the weekend is good, with warm, sunny weather expected to hold up through Monday.] Whereas *outlook* may describe grim *expectations, prospect* is more often applied to *expectations* of success, profit, or comfort: The *outlook* was bleak; the *prospect* of taking off his shoes and settling down into an easy chair with a good book; good *prospects* for complete recovery from her illness. The association with pleasant *expectations*, however, is not invariable: The *prospect* of a bloody war was alarmingly increased. See FOREKNOWLEDGE, PREMONITION.

expedient. Do not confuse the adjective *expedient* (suitable for a particular purpose) or the noun *expedient* (a means to an end) with the adjective *expeditious* (done speedily and efficiently).

expeditious. Do not confuse the adjective *expeditious* (done speedily and efficiently) with the adjective *expedient* (suitable for a particular purpose).

explanation
annotation
commentary
definition
description
exegesis
explication
exposition
interpretation

The nouns in this list all mean an undertaking to make the meaning of something clear to oneself or to someone else. **Explanation** is the broadest and is applied to ideas, utterances, actions, or operations. It is often used in place of many of the other nouns in the list.

A **definition** is, etymologically, a setting of limits or boundaries. In this context it is used to give the precise meaning of a word or phrase, or to delimit a problem or an undertaking. In a debate, one is often required to give a *definition* (or *explanation*) of technical terms to be used.

A **description** is a detailed account of the important aspects of something. A *description* may have as its object merely the pleasure of the listener or reader: a *description* of a sunset. As here considered, however,

a *description* has a didactic purpose. Thus, to give a *description* of the parts of an intricate machine is to give an *explanation* of how it works.

An **exposition** is a long, detailed, often scholarly setting forth of all the salient points of an argument, proposal, theory, or the like: a theoretical physicist who published an *exposition* of her ideas in a scientific monograph. **Annotation** and **commentary** are *expositions* in the fields of law and theology, respectively, although both are also used in more general contexts as well. *Annotation* can apply to a single critical or explanatory note, whereas *commentary* applies to a series or body of notes or remarks.

Interpretation, in this context, is the application of imagination or insight to the *explanation* of a difficult passage in literature, a baffling problem, an action difficult to account for, a dream, or the like: a grave *interpretation* of the curt diplomatic message; a disputed *interpretation* of an obscure passage from Eliot's *The Wasteland*. Two other nouns, **exegesis** and **explication**, both formal, are synonymous with *interpretation*. *Exegesis* is applied primarily to Biblical interpretation, *explication* to explanation of difficult literary texts: concentrating on *exegesis* of the Apocrypha; *explications* once based exclusively on Marxist doctrine. See CLARIFY, NARRATIVE.

exquisite
fine
graceful
polished
raffiné
refined
soigné

These adjectives describe that which reflects rare beauty or delicacy in taste, fashion, or manners. **Exquisite** is extremely vague as a superlative used in any of these situations; to these notions it adds overtones of what is consummate in its execution, admirable in effect, and gives evidence of extreme sensitivity, discrimination, and fastidiousness: *exquisite* miniatures showing the greatest delicacy in their use of color; a ballet dancer of *exquisite* skill; an *exquisite* sunset, breathtaking in its beauty. *Exquisite* can also refer to that which is keen or acute: suffering the most *exquisite* torment.

Polished is metaphorical as it applies here, suggesting a correctness in manners and an elegance of grooming that has been carefully learned or inculcated: the *polished* society of years gone by. It can also refer to technical facility: a *polished* performance of the *exquisite* sonata. **Refined** extends the implications of *polished* to a larger range of uses. It can refer beyond manners to aesthetic excellence or taste in the widest sense, often suggesting the arduous process of separating what is valuable from what is dross: *refined* manners; a *refined* style, free of flaw or eccentricity; observing that art was nothing more than life *refined*. Often, however, *refined* can refer to that which has become too rigidly correct, mannered, lifeless, or genteel: a *refined* and bloodless prose style; *refined* taste that found the complexities of Greek drama too rich for its palate.

Soigné and **raffiné**, borrowed from the French, share an emphasis on good grooming. *Soigné* stresses elegance and modishness as well: the latest *soigné* fashions for women. *Raffiné* can indicate more general qualities of *refined* delicacy, subtlety, or cleverness: the *raffiné* wits of the mauve decade. *Raffiné* can point disapprovingly to something that is foppish, superelegant, or overrefined: new styles in men's clothing that give more than a hint of becoming dandified or *raffiné*.

Graceful most vividly suggests physical bearing or movement that is lithe, agile, and lyrical: a *graceful* walk. It can also indicate delicately smooth execution in the arts: a *graceful* modeling of the female body. It can point as well to manners that show poise, calmness, and correctness: her *graceful* way of making introductions. **Fine**, in this context, can refer to minute, delicate, or perfectly executed ornamentation or detailing: the *fine* carving of the filigree scroll framing the bas-relief. It can also suggest something *refined* or of high merit: *fine* manners; the *fine* arts. Less strictly, it can be a vague superlative for anything one regards favorably: a *fine* film; a *fine* painter; a *fine* friend. See ELEGANT, EXCELLENT, ORDERLY, URBANE.

Antonyms: CLUMSY, *coarse, common,* GAUCHE, *ROUGH, untutored,* VULGAR.

extend

    draw out
    elongate
    lengthen
    prolong
    protract
    stretch
    widen

These verbs agree in meaning increase in one or more dimension. **Extend**, as here considered, means increase a thing's length, breadth, or duration. An army may *extend* its supply lines; a bird *extends* its wings when soaring; and a tedious preacher may *extend* a sermon beyond the congregation's span of attention.

Lengthen and **draw out** mean *extend* a thing in length or in duration, but not in breadth. *Draw out* sometimes even implies a loss of breadth accompanying the increase in length; metal wires become both longer and thinner when they are *drawn out*. **Elongate** is used only to mean *lengthen* spatially, not in time, and like *draw out*, sometimes implies *extend* in length at the expense of breadth, but in any case suggests disproportionately great length: one of the sculptor Giacometti's mournful *elongated* figures.

Prolong and **protract** now usually refer to *extended* time, although *prolong* may also refer to space. *Prolong* implies an extension beyond natural or normal limits: to *prolong* the meeting until a quorum could be rounded up; to *prolong* a war by inept diplomacy and miscalculation of the enemy's aims. *Protract* means *draw out* or *extend* greatly in time; it is often used adjectivally: *protracted* negotiations covering four months of serious discussions.

Stretch, as here considered, means *extend* a thing in length, breadth, or in both dimensions: to *stretch* a rubber band; to *stretch* canvas; to *stretch* a sweater by pinning it while wet. *Stretch* is now also used as an adjective applied to articles of clothing made of synthetic fibers that can be *stretched* to fit a variety of sizes: *stretch* socks. **Widen** means increase only the breadth of a thing: to *widen* a highway by adding two lanes. *Widen*, like *extend*, may be used figuratively to apply to any broadening: to *widen* (or *extend*) one's interests to include the study of nature. See ENLARGE, ESCALATE, PERSIST.

Antonyms: *contract, cut short, narrow,* SHORTEN, *shrink, terminate, truncate.*

extenuate

    gloss over
    palliate
    whitewash

These verbs all mean make seem less wrong, evil, blameworthy, etc. **Extenuate** suggests the effort to lessen the blame incurred by an offense, while **palliate** implies concealment, as of the incriminating facts or the gravity of their consequences: to *extenuate* past neglect by present concern; to *palliate* the errors in a book. [Starvation may serve to *extenuate* an instance of theft; A doting parent may seek to *palliate* the excesses of an errant child.]

Gloss over stresses the disguising or misrepresentation of incriminating facts: to *gloss over* a mediocre academic record. To **whitewash** is to represent by completely false information or a dishonest judgment:

The accused man went free, *whitewashed* by a partisan board of investigators. See LESSEN, MISLEADING.

Antonyms: *enhance, exaggerate, heighten, intensify.*

extraneous

extrinsic
immaterial
inessential
irrelevant
superfluous

These adjectives describe whatever is not an inherent part of a given consideration or entity. **Extraneous** stresses something that is not necessary or has no bearing, but it is otherwise very general in its implications. It does suggest a difference in kind: sorting out hard facts from *extraneous* interpretations. The unnecessary element referred to may, if not excluded, be either harmless or deleterious: *extraneous* substances that make the sunburn preparation smell pleasant but have no healing effect; *extraneous* minerals in the water supply that made it unsafe to drink. **Superfluous** is different in its effect, often pointing to simple excess, not a difference in kind: wiping away the *superfluous* oil with a clean rag. Even where *superfluous* shows a less clear-cut contrast with *extraneous*, it still points to what is useless or redundant: a room cluttered with *superfluous* furniture.

By contrast, **extrinsic** functions as an intensification of *extraneous*, emphasizing that something is by its nature completely unlike a given entity or completely outside the scope of some concern: pointing out that oxygen consumption might well be *extrinsic* to the life cycle as it may have developed in other parts of the universe; literary standards that are *extrinsic* to any understanding of popular media. **Inessential** is more like *extraneous* in referring to what may be present and tolerated but is in any case not needed and may therefore be excluded by choice or necessity: an editor who helped the novelist cut those scenes of the book that were *inessential* to the main theme; ordering the people in the lifeboat to throw overboard everything that was *inessential* to their survival.

Immaterial refers not to what is unnecessary, in excess, or unlike something else, but to what has no effect or makes no difference: She told him it was *immaterial* to her whether he stayed or left. In the context of reasoning, *immaterial* may point to what contributes nothing to an objective proof and thus is unimportant: the judge's ruling that the political beliefs of the accused were *immaterial* to the question of guilt. **Irrelevant** also indicates what is unimportant or inapplicable, in this case because it lacks direct bearing on the concern at hand: proof that the mother's dreams were *irrelevant* to the development of the fetus. Most specifically, *irrelevant* suggests a lack of logical relationship, as in a non sequitur: injecting *irrelevant* details about the woman's life into our consideration of her candidacy. See MARGINAL, TRIVIAL.

Antonyms: *essential, intrinsic, material, relevant,* SIGNIFICANT.

faction

bloc
sect
splinter group
wing

These nouns refer to a loose grouping of like-minded people within a larger aggregate. **Faction** suggests a relatively small grouping that coheres because of attitudes or objectives that are different from those of others in the larger whole. A *faction*, by implication, is more concerned with winning acceptance for its views than for the welfare or effectiveness of the parent group; rather than compromise these views a *faction* might leave the parent body and form a rival group. Thus, *faction* may have pejorative connotations ranging from stubbornness, disharmony, to outright disloyalty: He begged them to set party unity above the bickering of *factions*. A **splinter group** is an even more cohesive and well-defined unit that has already broken away or is just about to break away from the larger parent group, usually because of doctrinal disagreement; it may be of doubtful stability or endurance: *splinter groups* that vote with their party in national elections but against it in local elections; a movement that was destroyed by its tendency to break into *splinter groups*. **Sect** is used primarily of religious groups that adhere to their own special doctrines and either remain loosely associated with a larger group or break away from it completely: the formation of a number of Protestant *sects*. *Sect* may also be used for any identifiable groupings within a dogmatic aggregate: Reactionary *sects* at work within dogmatic political parties.

Bloc and **wing** refer to far larger groupings than the previous nouns. Both also refer to much looser allegiances. *Wing*, however, need not suggest actual membership in some organized parent group so much as a definable position within a spectrum of possibility: a rare agreement between the left and right *wings* of the country's political sentiment; disclosures that should be satisfying to gadflies of the right *wing*. More strictly, *wing* can apply within an organized group, but still with the notion of an extreme position on that group's scale of values: cooperation between the left *wing* of the Conservative Party and the right *wing* of the Labour Party. One could not, obviously, refer to middle-ground sentiment by using *wing*. *Bloc* is not restricted, like *wing*, to suggesting polarization along a scale of values. It refers to a practical alliance of strength and consequently need not stress ideological intransigence: a power *bloc* made up of several political shadings. *Bloc* suggests a joining of forces fostered by threatened security, rivalry, and the will to survive: African delegates that vote as a *bloc* in the UN Assembly. It is sometimes like *wing*, however, in suggesting no parent group that overarches rival *blocs:* the neutralist *bloc* of nations; the rival power *blocs* of East and West. See ADDITION, COMPONENT, DENOMINATION, PART.

faint

black out
collapse
pass out
swoon

These verbs mean enter a state of unconsciousness, impairment of awareness, or extreme weakness. To **faint** is to lose consciousness suddenly because of a temporary deficiency of the blood supply to the brain. *Fainting* (for which the medical term is syncope) may be caused by emotional shock, pain, overexertion, or exposure to high temperatures. **Swoon**, once a synonym for *faint,* is now almost obsolete. *Swoon* appears widely in literature of the past, especially in the 19th century, where it often evokes the stock image of the delicate, vaporish lady of the Victorian period who habitually *faints* when under stress or in the grip of strong feelings: She *swooned* under the rain of his kisses; to *swoon* at the sight of blood.

Black out is used of airplane pilots experiencing partial or complete loss of vision and sometimes of consciousness, caused by rapid changes in velocity during flight. By extension, *black out* has come to mean experience any temporary memory lapse, usually without *fainting,* especially as a result of emotional tension or the consumption of large amounts of alcohol. [The accused claimed he had *blacked out* and did not remember strangling the victim; Jonathan was able to recall little of what happened at the party because he *blacked out* early in the evening.]

Pass out is an informal term for *faint:* to *pass out* from the heat; to *pass out* from fright. Unlike *faint, pass out* carries a suggestion of humor with little or no medical connotation, especially in its most popular use to describe falling into the stuporous sleep that overtakes some people after they have had too much to drink: a derelict who had *passed out* in a doorway; She was able to drink glass after glass of wine all evening without *passing out*.

Collapse is a much stronger term than the other verbs and may indicate grave illness. To *collapse* may also involve *fainting* but, from its literal meaning of giving way or caving in, *collapse* emphasizes a complete and sudden loss of vital strength or health, which may be either brief or prolonged: those who *collapse* into bed after an exhausting day; He *collapsed* from overwork; to *collapse* from nervous strain; to *collapse* with a heart attack. See SICKNESS, WEAKEN.

Antonyms: *come to, rally, revive.*

famous

celebrated
noted
notorious
renowned

These adjectives describe people or things that are widely known. **Famous** is the most general of these, the least formal, and the weakest in connotations. It refers to anything that has gained the attention of many people for whatever reason: a *famous* movie star; a country *famous* for its good cooking. While *famous* does carry a positive connotation, it may suggest popularity or general recognition rather than discriminating approval or inherent excellence: a meeting between the *famous* popularizer and the relatively unknown originator of the theory.

Celebrated and **renowned** are intensifications of *famous,* both adding the note of wide approval for accomplishment. *Renowned* is the more formal of the two and might seem too precious in some uses; its emphasis is also on the wideness of the acclaim rather than on discrimination. It is most useful now, perhaps, for places or things rather than for people: a world-*renowned* castle on the Rhine. It may also suggest something that has become legendary or is no longer available for an objective evaluation and must be approached through admiring but second-hand reports: the *renowned* band of Spartans who held Thermopylae. *Celebrated* refers, more objectively, to someone or something that has been given acclaim or honored with awards or prizes: a *celebrated* Nobel Prize economist. It can sometimes function like *famous* to indicate a more popular or less critical approval: the most *celebrated* of the *famous* movie stars. Sometimes, *celebrated* can be a less formal substitute for *renowned:* a love affair *celebrated* in song and story.

Noted is unique among these adjectives in suggesting that an accomplishment is singled out for notice because of its excellence. It is often used to describe a more intellectual kind of effort, indicating an authority or expert or their theories: a *noted* authority on beekeeping; a *noted* critic of feminist fiction. Because of this use, *noted* points to a much more limited general recognition than these other adjectives; a *noted* expert, while honored by others in his field, might not be known widely to the general public at all. **Notorious**, in sharp contrast to all these adjectives, indicates someone or something that has become *famous* because of its undesirable or offensive behavior: the *notorious* immorality of Hollywood in its heyday; a *notorious* gangster. See GREAT, OUTSTANDING, SIGNIFICANT.

Antonyms: *fugitive, inglorious,* OBSCURE, *unknown.*

farming

agriculture
agrology
agronomy
gardening
husbandry
tillage

These nouns refer to the cultivation of plants or the raising of animals, either as produce or for food. **Farming** is the most informal and can apply to the entire range of possibilities here or to a specialization: Wheat is the main product of *farming* in the Great Plains; chicken *farming*; cattle *farming*. **Agriculture** is more formal but just as all-embracing; it is widely used on all levels of speech. *Agricultural* is the preferred term when used of educational institutions that teach *farming* as a science: courses in *agriculture* at a state college.

All the remaining nouns emphasize particular aspects of *farming*. **Husbandry** now appears most often in the formal phrase *animal husbandry*, referring to the care and raising of all kinds of animals as an occupation. The phrase *good husbandry* indicates efficient and prudent management of the affairs of *farming*—or other concerns. [He had shown *good husbandry* in ordering seed when the prices were at their lowest; Young married couples often learn *good husbandry* of their income only after bitter experience.]

Tillage refers strictly to the planting, cultivating, and harvesting of crops, but is now less often used than *farming* for this activity. **Agrology** refers formally and specifically to the study of soil makeup and chemistry, often taught as a course in *agriculture*.

Agronomy, also extremely formal, is more general; it includes *agrology* in its wider concern with the best possible conditions for maximum land use and crop output: the *agrology* of alkaline soils; sensible techniques of *agronomy*, based on crop rotation and organic fertilizers.

Gardening, like *tillage*, is restricted to the raising of plants. In contrast with *tillage*, *gardening* is relatively informal and refers to the small-scale cultivation of fruits and vegetables for personal use or to the cultivation of trees and shrubs as a source of pleasure or beauty: Many families do some *gardening* in their backyards as a way of economizing on food bills during summer and fall; horticultural hints for *gardening* enthusiasts; interested in the profession of landscape *gardening*.

farthest

extreme
furthest
outermost
ultimate
utmost
uttermost

These words, both as nouns and modifiers, refer to the greatest distance, the most inclusive boundary of something, the point of its greatest extension, or to anything at its most ample or serious. **Farthest** and **furthest** are the superlative forms of farther and further. *Farthest* applies strictly to the greatest distance, whereas *furthest* cannot only apply identically, with no distinction in shading and meaning, but also to many other situations here, both literal and figurative, particularly where the notions of movement or progress are present. [Which of these cities are *farthest* (or *furthest*) from us? This line marks the *farthest* (or *furthest*) advance of the glacier; behavior reflecting the *furthest* departure from the norm.] **Outermost** is like *farthest* in referring strictly to distance, but it is even more specific in suggesting the outside of a plane or solid figure: the *outermost* layer of skin; the *outermost* provinces of the Roman Empire; the *outermost* planet.

Extreme and **ultimate** are considerably more general than the other words here; each, however, has an occasionally used area of specific reference. *Extreme* can apply like *farthest* and *outermost*: the *extreme* edge of the desert. When it refers more generally to great amounts, degrees, or intensities, it often suggests an unwise, excessive, or grave departure from the norm: the *extreme* left wing of the party; He always went to *extremes* with his drinking; an *extreme* illness. But *extreme* can be compared and, hence, may not be

as forceful as *furthest:* the more *extreme* of the two positions; Which of these *extreme* factions went *furthest* in its demands? *Ultimate* can refer to something that is last in space or either first or last in time: the *ultimate* island in the archipelago; the modern word's *ultimate* form in Indo-European; The mystery isn't unraveled until the *ultimate* chapter of the book. More commonly, *ultimate* refers to a final outcome: the *ultimate* results of our foreign policy. At its most general, *ultimate* functions more vaguely to indicate the most *extreme* or perfect form of something: the *ultimate* catastrophe; a hotel that provides the *ultimate* in luxury.

Utmost and the far less common **uttermost** are the most formal of these words and can refer generally to anything at its greatest, most *extreme*, or best. *Utmost* can apply like the last use of *ultimate:* the *utmost* in craftsmanship. An added suggestion here, as in its other uses, may be one of the *extreme* effort required to reach some goal: We will do our *utmost* to finish our work on time. *Uttermost* can seem like an intensification of *utmost* in some uses: a crisis that will demand our *uttermost* in time and patience. Often, *uttermost* suggests something severe or final: the martyr's *uttermost* sacrifice of his life; his *uttermost* agony. At its most specific and unlike *utmost, uttermost* can also apply more neutrally to distance: the *uttermost* tip of South America. See BOUNDARY, HIGHEST, SUMMIT.
Antonyms: *closest, initial, inmost, least, mildest, nearest.*

fat

adipose
buxom
chubby
corpulent
obese
plump
portly
stout

These adjectives describe a physique that is fleshy or overweight. **Fat** is the most informal and also the most concrete and direct: a man who was unbelievably *fat*. It does, however, recognize degrees of this condition: a boy who already looked slightly *fat*. By contrast, both **corpulent** and **obese** refer to excessive states of overweight; they are also much more formal than *fat*. *Obese* is the clinical term used to describe this condition when it is considered medically rather than aesthetically and with particular reference to its endangering of health; consequently, an unequivocally extreme case is indicated: the incidence of heart failure in *obese* persons. *Corpulent* refers literally to fleshiness of physique and thus may suggest bulk or overall heaviness rather than a medically *obese* condition; it would thus not require so extreme a case to become applicable: a smiling, *corpulent* Buddha.

Portly and **stout** are both genteel euphemisms for *fat,* especially used to describe elderly people. *Portly* suggests dignity of bearing in a figure of great girth; *stout* suggests, somewhat like *corpulent,* a general heaviness of physique: the *portly* matrons who served tea after the recital; the *stout* innkeeper with the cherubic face.

Plump and **buxom** indicate the slightest degree of overweight suggested by any of these adjectives; both can be approving rather than disapproving. *Plump* suggests a soft ripeness of figure that is thought attractive: Rubens's *plump* female figures that would today be considered *fat;* a *plump* baby. *Plump* can, of course, be used euphemistically: the *plump,* potbellied scoutmaster and his scrawny charges. *Buxom* is restricted to describing a *plump* or well-developed woman, especially one radiating sturdy good health: *buxom* pioneer women. Both this use of the adjective and its use as a euphemism for *fat* have recently given way to its specific use for a sensual and, particularly, a bosomy figure: especially *buxom* homecoming queens.

Chubby suggests a squareness of figure, filled out with fleshiness, that might be thought earthy or robust: the *chubby* little girl; the *chubby* man's twinkling eyes. *Chubby* sometimes has an aura of well-intended humor. **Adipose** is most strictly a biological term for fatty tissue itself; when used as a substitute for *fat, adipose* has comic effect, sometimes less well-intentioned than *chubby: adipose* ladies and gentlemen who rush to health spas. See HEALTHY, HUSKY, LARGE, MASSIVE.

Antonyms: *emaciated,* THIN.

fatal
deadly
lethal
mortal

The adjective **fatal** is used to describe anything capable of causing or actually has caused death; it carries a strong suggestion of the inevitability of fate: an illness that might not be serious for a young person, but will almost certainly prove *fatal* to old people. **Deadly** is interchangeable with *fatal* in this sense: Leukemia was formerly an inevitably *deadly* disease. *Deadly,* however, in a way that *fatal* cannot, can refer to a person who desires or seeks to cause the death of another person: The murdered man had many *deadly*

enemies. **Mortal**, like *deadly,* can be applied both to things or people that cause, are capable of causing, or seek to cause someone's death. In its reference to things, *mortal* differs from *fatal* and *deadly* only in the fact that it is usually found in contexts that detail a death that has already occurred. [He was struck down by a *mortal* blow to the head; Because of an ancient family feud, the two cousins had been *mortal* enemies from childhood.] **Lethal** refers to something that, because of some intrinsic quality in its makeup, is certain to cause death, and may indeed be present for the express purpose of causing death: Cyanide is a *lethal* poison.

With the exception of *lethal,* all these adjectives can be used to describe something that causes great fear or discomfort or that brings about disaster or ruin, but does not lead to physical death: a *fatal* mistake; a *deadly* insult; in *mortal* terror. See DEAD, DIE.

Antonyms: *enlivening, invigorating, life-giving.*

faultfinding
captious
carping
caviling
censorious
hypercritical
nitpicking
pedantic

These adjectives describe an attitude or act of disapproval that consists in attacking weaknesses, imagined or real, in someone else or in that person's behavior or achievements. **Faultfinding** is the most neutral of these adjectives in that it can conceivably apply to a helpful or friendly ferreting out of actual weaknesses: giving her penultimate draft to a friend who could be counted on to be openly *faultfinding.* More often, it is true, *faultfinding* suggests an eagerness to seek out weakness for its own sake, but even here the adjective is less severe in tone than the following adjectives: certain that the inspecting officer would prove to be tediously *faultfinding.*

Hypercritical suggests a harsher attitude than that suggested by *faultfinding,* pointing to someone overly eager to disparage, possibly out of a reluctance to recognize or honor good qualities in others: views so *hypercritical* that her companion wondered what on earth could possibly meet with her approval. In further contrast to *faultfinding,* a *hypercritical* person need not necessarily dwell on weaknesses in something at all; he or she may simply reject it wholesale as obviously inferior. **Censorious** is similar to *hypercritical* in allowing the possibility of a blanket rejection. It is even harsher in tone, however, suggesting an attitude that is exclusively negative in its judgments. Someone who is *hypercritical* might be expected to spell out views in some detail and to have, at least, some standards for measurement; someone *censorious*, however, might merely express a negative evaluation without explanation or without having such standards. The adjective, furthermore, has overtones of prissy or priggish ill will: easy for the contemplative man to be *censorious* of every attempt at acting out an ideal.

Captious suggests a further extreme than the foregoing adjectives, but not so much toward a greater severity of judgment as toward a truly irresponsible or whimsical refusal to be pleased by the most meticulous effort. *Captious* may suggest *faultfinding* that deliberately wishes to confuse rather than enlighten, especially when this results in fruitless argument: an interviewer who made *captious* remarks in order to get newsworthy responses from subjects.

Carping and **caviling** are better used to describe single acts of *faultfinding* rather than a *hypercritical* or *censorious* attitude. Both may suggest a zealous glee in scornfully condemning something on the basis of picayune considerations or niggling faults; some difference between them can be seen, however, by noting that *caviling* derives from words meaning jest, mock, or raillery, and *carping* from words meaning dispute or boast. *Carping* best suggests a pedantic railing at or making a mockery of something for small failures; *caviling* more often suggests strident or grating verbal attacks in which reasonable or generally acceptable propositions are imputed because of trivial lapses: a *carping* reviewer who thought a few split infinitives more important than the range and sweep of the work; the prosecution's *caviling* rebuttal that seemed to find proof of guilt in the defendant's nervous manner.

Nitpicking is a colorful adjective and noun that stresses an excessive concern with small or trivial faults or with making distinctions so fine as to be pointless; this concern may be either well-intentioned, though misguided, or deliberately hostile: diplomats busy at their *nitpicking* work while the world was going up in flames; an opponent who could find nothing wrong with my program and so had to content himself with *nitpicking*. **Pedantic** is an adjective that is less directly related to the notion of disapproval. It emphasizes, instead, someone intent on needless displays of learning or petty points of scholarship: a *pedantic* dissertation, full of musty footnotes and gobbledegook. In the context of disapproval, it is a more formal alternative for *nitpicking*: *pedantic* objections to practical

proposals. See DISAGREE, DISAPPROVAL.

Antonyms: *approving, commendatory, complimentary, encouraging, flattering, laudatory.*

favorable

auspicious
fortunate
good
happy
lucky
propitious
providential

These adjectives describe the gaining of benefit or advantage or the promise of such an outcome. **Favorable** can refer to a present situation that exposes one to positive possibilities: *favorable* influences absent from most slum schools. More simply, *favorable* may refer to approval: *favorable* reviews of the play. Most pertinent here, it pertains to signs that suggest an advantageous result: *favorable* indications that the stock market would recover rapidly.

Auspicious and **propitious** are restricted to this last possibility of *favorable*. Both suggest the foretelling of a beneficial outcome from preceding omens. Of the two, *auspicious* may better suggest an abundance of beneficial indications or conditions; *propitious*, the absence of negative or deleterious ones: *auspicious* signs that victory would be theirs by nightfall; *propitious* weather that promised a happy voyage. In another context, *auspicious* may be used to indicate a clairvoyant looking into the future: She tended to see *auspicious* rather than ominous portents in her customers' tea leaves. *Propitious,* by contrast, is more commonly used to indicate the promise or gaining of more practical advantages: a business contract that seemed *propitious* to both parties.

Strictly speaking, **providential** is a heightening of the supernatural possibility inherent in *auspicious*, suggesting divine intervention to bring about a *favorable* outcome: They saw the breaking of the storm as a *providential* blessing of their mission. Often, however, the force of *providential* is weakened to indicate anything that seems remarkably opportune: a *providential* escape from the avalanche. **Lucky** is a more informal synonym for this last meaning of *providential*, carrying no implication in current use of any divine or supernatural intervention. *Lucky* refers instead to a chance occurrence that proves beneficial: the *lucky* accident by which they met. In a less precise use, it can also refer to any positive circumstance, with less emphasis on chance: *lucky* to be living in a democratic country.

Good is the least formal and in its generality the least precise of these adjectives in referring to a positive circumstance: *good* results on the test. It can also refer to signs that augur a beneficial outcome: a *good* prognosis. **Fortunate** may once have implied a *favorable* augury; more often now, it indicates present success or *good* circumstances: contributions to those less *fortunate* than oneself. This implication even overshadows a use that relates to *lucky* in stressing more formally benefits that result from chance: a *fortunate* throw of the dice. One use of **happy** relates it to *fortunate* and *lucky*, suggesting advantages that result not from chance but from a discriminating choice of means that later events corroborate: Hiring her proved to be a *happy* decision. Sometimes, however, *happy* suggests fortuitous benefit, in which case the emphasis is on the beneficial outcome rather than, as with *lucky*, on the overcoming of odds: a *happy* accident. See BENEFICIAL, CHANCE, OPPORTUNE.

Antonyms: *adverse, bad, doomed, ill-fated, inauspicious, unfavorable, unlucky, untoward.*

fawn
butter up
compliment
flatter
toady
truckle

These verbs refer to seeking approval from others by praising them or behaving obsequiously or servilely toward them. **Fawn** can literally indicate the affectionate action of a dog toward its master, exhibited by licking him and sprawling before him, by tail-wagging, and by other forms of adoring behavior. Servile behavior of a comparable sort is suggested when a person acts in this way, although here *fawn* becomes contemptuous, whether the obsequious display is sincere or is undertaken cynically for self-advancement. [Only an uxorious husband could *fawn* on a woman the way he does; She *fawned* over her famous guests, but sneered at them when they were gone.]

Truckle and **toady** are both harsher in their contempt than *fawn*, although both are less vivid and specific about the behavior they indicate. *Truckle* indicates any sort of servility, whether exhibited because of necessity, cowardice, or self-interested obsequiousness: slaves who had to *truckle* to their harsh masters or be killed for insolence; He *truckled* to the repressive mores of his day for fear of being ostracized; peo-ple who bow and scrape and *truckle* to get ahead. As in the last example, *truckle* can imply a stooped, humbled carriage. *Toady* gives no visual suggestions whatsoever about manner or bearing, but it does suggest an attempt to curry favor with one's superiors by ingratiating actions: those who are willing to *toady* their way to success; an actress who needed an entourage of lickspittles and lackeys to *toady* to her.

The remaining verbs all emphasize praise as the means of gaining approval. Of all these verbs, **compliment** alone can be used approvingly. It can even indicate genuine admiration expressed for no ulterior motive: a teacher who was as ready to *compliment* deserving effort as she was to criticize slipshod work. But *compliment* often applies to praise given insincerely as an empty formality or as a self-interested gesture; in this case, the tone of disapproval is much milder than that of any other verb here. [He *complimented* her on her new dress without even looking at it; She refused to *compliment* the fatuous critic merely to win his approval.] **Flatter** concentrates exclusively on the paying of insincere compliments for whatever reason: She thought it could cause no harm to *flatter* her escort a bit, at least on his taste in wines; movie producers who expect to be *flattered* by the ambitious underlings who surround them. Sometimes *flatter* can indicate a surprising but genuine interest that is taken by the recipient as a not wholly deserved honor: She *flattered* us by coming early and staying late; *flattered* by the obvious sincerity of his concern.

Butter up is an informal phrase that suggests not only the obsequious behavior of *fawn, toady,* and *truckle* but also the insincere praise indicated by *flatter*. *Butter up* adds to these implications a completely cynical attitude behind the ingratiating acts and words and even a disrespectful or contemptuous attitude toward the person being courted: dropouts who claim to detest their middle-class parents but know how to *butter* them *up* when the need for help arises. See OBSEQUIOUS, PRAISE.

Antonyms: *carp, condemn, criticize, dominate, insult, tyrannize.*

ferment. Do not confuse the verb *ferment* (undergo fermentation) with the verb *foment* (arouse discontent, trouble, etc.).

fictional. Do not confuse the adjective *fictional* (of novels and short stories) with the adjective *fictitious* (not real).

fictitious. Do not confuse the adjective *fictitious* (not real) with the adjective *fictional* (of novels and short stories).

fight

> action
> battle
> bout
> clash
> engagement
> fray
> skirmish

These nouns refer to competition or conflict between hostile forces. **Fight** is the most general of these, ranging from suggesting any struggle toward a goal by one or more people to suggesting physical combat between numbers of people: a *fight* for life against great odds; a desperate *fight* to win the tournament at all costs; a *fight* that broke out between two pushers and soon spread to the whole neighborhood. **Bout** often suggests any sort of competition specifically between two people: a name-calling *bout* between the two legislators; a drinking *bout;* the *bout* for the heavyweight championship. *Bout* can, however, suggest the struggle of one person against some adversity: a *bout* with tuberculosis. And it can be used for larger groups, even including a military conflict, in which case it is mostly used for color: a shooting *bout* between the decimated guerrillas and the well-supplied government force.

Clash clearly refers to a two-sided conflict between comparable forces: a *clash* of wills between student and teacher. When physical combat is referred to, a hasty or unexpected *fight* may be suggested: a *clash* that ended before the artillery could zero in on vulnerable enemy targets. **Fray** suggests a free-for-all or melee that involves a number of people: a *fray* that broke out in the ghetto. It may also refer to the very heart of a military conflict: paramedics brave enough to work their way into the thick of the *fray*.

Battle refers most strongly to one specific *fight* that may be part of a larger or continuing war: a *battle* that produced the heaviest casualties of the war. The noun may refer more abstractly to some total war effort: our unceasing *battle* to drive the aggressor from our shores. *Battle* may also metaphorically describe *fights* or *bouts* outside the military context: a *battle* against drug abuse.

The remaining nouns are all more formal than the foregoing and all apply more exclusively to military combat. **Skirmish** suggests a quickly organized or localized thrust against an enemy force or a trivial, perhaps accidental, *clash* between combatants: night patrols sent out to engage the enemy in a series of small *skirmishes;* lines held without incident except for a few *skirmishes.* **Action** and **engagement** are both rather formal and colorless words to denote a *battle*. *Action* may suggest a full-scale struggle or a sporadic flickering of hostilities: a mopping-up *action* that proved decisive; enemy *action* that continued throughout the night. *Action* may also be used euphemistically to describe an actual war, usually for political convenience: a police *action* that really consisted of armed intervention in the deepening civil war. *Engagement* refers to a single *battle* in a war, suggesting that opposing armies in search of each other have met and are contending for victory: reporting an *engagement* of sizable forces east of the line of attack. See AGGRESSION, ATTACK.

Antonyms: *détente, pacification, reconciliation.*

filter

> exude
> percolate
> seep

These verbs all refer to the action a liquid or gas undergoes in passing through another substance or medium. To **filter** means to pass (a liquid, air, etc.) through a porous substance such as paper or cloth, in order to extract impurities or essences. Papers folded into the shape of cones and inserted in the mouths of test tubes or coffeemakers are familiar uses of *filters*. Photographically, certain kinds of light or certain colors are *filtered* by means of specially colored and constructed glass or plastic lens coverings.

Percolate means pass or cause to pass through fine openings or interstices. In coffeemakers, as the hot water passes through a container of finely ground coffee, the water extracts the essence of coffee and carries it along. *Percolate* emphasizes the process of passing through or permeating a substance; *filter* points to a particular means by which this process can take place. [Rainwater *percolates* through soil to form an underground reservoir; To get red, *filter* out the greens and blues; The spilled ink *filtered* through the blotter.]

Exude and **seep** mean ooze or trickle out through pores or small openings. *Seep* suggests a gradual and often accidental or unwanted movement of a substance into or out of something. [Gas *seeped* into the room; Air *seeped* from the balloon; Blood *seeped* from his wound into his bandages.] *Exude* is often used of natural or planned phenomena: to *exude* sweat; Gum *exuded* from the tree. It is also used figuratively with the sense of a powerful diffusion of any quality: to *exude* charm. See LEAK.

find

ascertain
detect
determine
discover
learn
locate
unearth

These verbs share the implication that something already in existence is being newly brought to light. **Find** and **discover** can both be used for an accidental or gratuitous gaining of knowledge; of the two, *find* is the less formal. [Explorers in Australia *discovered* flora and fauna *found* nowhere else in the world.] Both can be used, of course, to describe an intentional effort; *find* in this case may imply either a search for something new or the discovering of something lost but previously possessed. [He finally *found* the missing keys in a jacket he had put in storage for the summer; We know there must be a law that governs the odd gravitational behavior of certain stars, but it may take us decades to *find* it.] *Discover,* when it implies an intentional search, always suggests the acquiring of something that already exists but is new to the discoverer: Mendel raised crop after crop of snapdragons to *discover* the laws governing heredity. It should be noted that this sense of *discover* contrasts sharply with invent, with which *discover* is often confused. [Scientists may *discover* physical phenomena, but inventors find practical applications for exploiting the phenomena.]

Learn, **unearth**, and **detect** are equally able to suggest either intentional or accidental discovery, although they tend more strongly toward intentional discovery. Of the three, *learn* is the most general and informal, *detect* the most specific and formal. *Learn* in one sense can imply a minimum of effort in gaining unsought knowledge: It was only today I happened to *learn* the name of a song I'd been whistling for years. But the weight of usage here is on conscious, painstaking effort toward a predetermined goal: A pianist *learns* the secret of a major work only by practicing it intensively over a long period of time. *Unearth,* when referring to accidental discovery, implies the rediscovery of something lost or obscured by the passage of time: In her researches she was startled to *unearth* the manuscript of an unpublished major work by Boswell.

Again, the suggestion of deliberate search is more frequently present, in which case digging deep into a subject is suggested: The district attorney swore he would *unearth* the real facts in the case if he had to grill everyone who had ever known the dead man. *Detect* is more rarely applicable to accidental discovery: To her surprise, she *detected* a bright red glow emanating from a crater in the moon. It most often suggests deliberate, deductive investigation and the making of extremely precise observations: Her pulse was so weak and erratic that the doctor could barely *detect* it. In one use, *detect* has a sharply negative sense that contrasts with a positive use of *discover:* It may take time for the public to *discover* your real worth as a writer, but fortunately the vapidity of Smith's work has been quickly *detected.*

Determine, **ascertain**, and **locate** are almost exclusively suggestive of deliberate search and discovery. *Determine,* in fact, is charged with the suggestion of painstaking conscious effort, especially to resolve a controversy. [From the facts presented, the coroner's jury was able to *determine* conclusively that the death was not a suicide; You may not leave until you *determine* the acidity or alkalinity of the chemical placed before you.] *Ascertain* implies that the searcher began with an awareness of his lack of knowledge on a given matter and worked to correct it; in this it is similar to but much more formal than *determine*—even to the point of pomposity, except in very technical, legal, or scientific writing. [We shall one day be able to *ascertain* the exact nature of these subatomic particles; With careful research, it is possible to *ascertain* the often unspoken assumptions held by people of a particular historical era.] *Locate* is more specialized in meaning than either *determine* or *ascertain,* usually implying the fixing of an occurrence or thing in space. [All efforts have failed to *locate* the birthplace of Columbus; From her directions, it shouldn't be difficult to *locate* the beach house, even though you've never been in the area before.] See CREATE, DEVICE.

Antonyms: FORGET, MISLAY, *miss.*

finish

close
complete
conclude
end
finalize
terminate

These verbs are alike in meaning reach the end of a task or activity. **Finish** and **complete** mean bring to an anticipated end by doing all things necessary or appropriate to achieving that end. Although the two verbs may be used as exact synonyms, *complete* suggests the fulfillment of an assigned task and is therefore not always an appropriate substitute for *finish*. An author may *complete* or *finish* a novel; a reader might *finish* it, but one would not say that the reader *completed* it unless it was read as a school assignment.

Close and **conclude** emphasize the final stages that *complete* an action. [The district attorney usually *closes* his cases with a plea for conviction; The hymn sung by the congregation *concluded* the religious ceremony.]

End and **terminate** are more general in meaning. An action may be *ended* or *terminated* before it is *completed*. In addition, both *end* and *terminate* carry more of a sense of finality by suggesting a definite cutoff point. [Heckling from the audience *ended* the speech before the speaker had *concluded* his remarks; The truce *terminated* hostilities; If Congress refuses to appropriate funds, the foreign aid program will have to be *terminated*.]

Finalize has achieved currency, mainly in bureaucratic use, with the meaning of bring to a conclusion something that has been worked on for a long time or that has been held in abeyance: to *finalize* a budget estimate.

Antonyms: *BEGIN, initiate, open.*

fire

blaze
conflagration
flame

These nouns refer to the burning of something. **Fire** is the most general of these, referring both to slow or rapid burning, whether of small or great size: a wisp of tissue paper that caught *fire*, burned an instant, and then went out; a forest *fire* that covered hundreds of acres at the peak of its intensity. **Flame** may refer to one isolated small *fire*: reading his watch by the *flame* of a match. It may refer instead to each momentary fork or tongue of a larger *fire*: watching the largest log on the *fire* finally burst into *flame*. In this case, *flame* is often used in the plural to express the multitude of such elements making up a *fire*, or to indicate their diversity of placement: staring for hours into the flickering *flames*; The firefighter pointed to new *flames* licking through the roof and the second-story windows of the building.

Both **blaze** and **conflagration** stress intensity and rapidity of burning, with *blaze* functioning as an inten-

sification of *fire*, and *conflagration* as an intensification of *blaze*. In addition, *blaze* can give connotations of a controlled, cheerful warmth, while *conflagration* is more closely restricted to a widespread destructive or accidental burning: a comforting *blaze* roaring in the fireplace; a *conflagration* that destroyed much of Los Angeles. *Blaze* can also be used in ways that approach the suggestions of *conflagration*: a *blaze* that took the lives of six inhabitants and one firefighter. See CATASTROPHE.

flagrant

glaring
gross
rank

These adjectives refer to extreme, obvious, or outrageous failures or offenses. At its mildest, **flagrant** may be used to indicate what is deplorably obvious: *flagrant* indifference to the suffering of the poor. More commonly, however, *flagrant* is more emphatic in suggesting the public flaunting of blatant incompetence or impropriety: the editor's *flagrant* disregard of even the most common errors; the *flagrant* cynicism of politicians who work hand in glove with racketeers and gangsters. **Glaring** is even more emphatic about the obviousness of the failing, but is otherwise milder than *flagrant* in that it more often points to error, however inexcusable, than to unethical or immoral conduct: a play damaged by *glaring* faults. *Glaring* might also suggest an annoyed rather than disgusted reaction: exasperated by his *glaring* bad manners. Occasionally, *glaring* has the force of *flagrant;* even here, however, the misconduct that stands out is stressed: the *glaring* betrayal of a public trust.

With **gross** and **rank**, the emphasis shifts from the obviousness of faults to their extreme or offensive nature. *Gross* is often used simply to mean extreme: *gross* unfairness. More precisely, it suggests coarse or callous insensitivity to correct or decent standards of behavior: *gross* mistreatment of an innocent child. Another reference of *gross*—to heaviness—is often implicated in this context, suggesting an almost irreparable failing of great weight: an administration crippled by its own *gross* incompetence. *Gross* failings, however, need not be obvious: *gross* errors in the report that went completely unnoticed. *Rank* stresses disgusting offensiveness and tends to indicate moral corruption rather than simple error: the *rank* indecencies that occurred at the party. While the adjective, unlike *flagrant*, does not necessarily suggest a public display, it does suggest corruption that would be obvious to anyone exposed to it: a book that brought the rank improprieties of the former administration to public attention. As with *gross*, other meanings of *rank* affect its shadings here, especially its references to things malodorous or overgrown: a *rank* system of pay-offs that should have reeked of foul play to any impartial investigator; a tangled bureaucracy filled with *rank* inefficiency. See CLEAR, DEFINITE.

Antonyms: IMPLICIT, *mild, slight, venial.*

flaunt. Do not confuse the verb *flaunt* (display ostentatiously) with the verb *flout* (disobey openly).

flaw

    blemish
    defect
    failing
    fault
    foible
    imperfection
    shortcoming

These nouns indicate a lack in something that prevents it from being complete, wholly effective, or desirable. **Flaw** is the most general, suggesting the existence or presence of something that spoils an otherwise sound entity: a *flaw* in her ingenious plan; an admirable character cursed by the tragic *flaw* of pride. While *flaw* suggests something that detracts from completeness, effectiveness, or perfection, **fault** points to something that impairs excellence. A *flaw* can refer to something missing: The *flaw* in the weapon was its inability to detect targets rapidly. *Fault* usually refers to something present and to something inherent in the nature of a thing rather than external to it; *flaw* can refer to the superficial as well as to the profound. [The excessive length of her gown was surely a *flaw* in her costume; a central *flaw* in his argument that invalidated his entire position; a *flaw* (or *fault*) in the marble near the base of the statue; Snobbishness was his principal *fault*.] In connection with character, *flaw* is somewhat more elegant and dramatic than the more prosaic *fault*.

While *flaw* may or may not indicate something easily removed or overcome, **defect** often suggests a *flaw* so serious as to completely prevent functioning: a *defect* in the fuel lines that prevented the third stage from firing. Since *defect* is now often used of machines, its application to human personality sometimes indicates a judgmental or simplistic view of human nature, suggesting easily traceable explanations

for malfunction: probing for the *defect* that had made him resort to violence. In other contexts *defect* may refer to an error or the lack of something needed for completion. [A *defect* in judgment led to the accident; The *defect* in the microphone caused a crackling sound.]

Blemish refers especially to marks or qualities that disfigure or make imperfect. *Blemish* applies particularly to *defects* of the skin: a facial *blemish*. It may also be used figuratively: the first *blemish* on an otherwise spotless record.

Imperfection is closer to *flaw* than to *defect* in that it stresses malfunction less than incompleteness or lack of order: a slight *imperfection* in an otherwise beautiful design. Whereas a *flaw* may be self-evident, *imperfection* points more often to a lack that may be a matter of opinion. Like *defect*, *imperfection* also implies a criterion or an established canon by which to judge something: stylistic advances in her art that were regarded as *imperfections* by most of her contemporaries. And as *defect* relates to function, *imperfection* relates to form, drawing *defect* toward a scientific context, *imperfection* toward an artistic context. With *imperfection*, however, the judgment remains relative since no completely perfect thing exists.

Failing, **shortcoming**, and **foible** are the mildest of these nouns, suggesting a specific lapse in an otherwise sound entity. All three most commonly relate to personality, describing a characteristic way of behaving that is not desirable but does not vitiate goodness or overall effectiveness. *Foible* is perhaps the mildest of the three nouns, suggesting a slight but ingrained eccentricity that may easily be recognized by others and allowed for without causing great difficulties. A *foible*, in fact, may be almost harmless and even endearing: a love that was strengthened rather than weakened by their acceptance of each other's *foibles*. *Failing* may suggest a more severe *shortcoming* that has more serious consequences: a lack of compassion that can be an insurmountable *failing* in a husband or wife. Sometimes, the special point of *failing* is to indicate well-intentioned effort that does not succeed: the lack of convincing evidence that is the book's main *failing*. *Shortcoming*, like *failing*, may refer to failures or deficiencies in things as well as people, and in this sense compares with one sense of *flaw*: The chief *shortcoming* (or *flaw*) of the design was its relative unreliability. When applied to personality or character, it is milder than either *flaw* or *fault*, and is close to *failing* in meaning. [We all have our *shortcomings*—that man dotes on his wife, this one flirts with other women, a third flies into jealous rages at the slightest provocation.] See CHARACTERISTIC, DISFIGURE, ECCEN-TRICITY, LACK, MISTAKE, SIN, STIGMA.

Antonyms: MERIT, *perfection.*

fleet

armada
convoy
navy

These nouns all refer to organized groups of vessels. **Fleet** may refer to the entire number of ships of a government, including merchant vessels, whereas **navy** refers either to the warships of a country or to its entire military sea force, including personnel, shipyards, and equipment. *Navy* always implies a military purpose, whereas *fleet* need not. *Fleet* is used, however, to mean all the ships under one command in a particular area, and the command may be a military one. [The U.S. Sixth *Fleet* was assigned to the war in Southeast Asia; a Russian fishing *fleet* of trawlers.] *Fleet* is also commonly used to refer to a group of vessels or vehicles organized or viewed as a unit, or belonging to one company: a *fleet* of taxicabs. [A *fleet* of buses brought the Boston hockey fans to New York; Our *fleet* of tugboats was idled by the strike.]

Armada, the Spanish word for armed, means a *fleet* of warships. In this country *armada* is commonly associated with the disastrous experience of the Spanish *Armada*, which sailed against England in 1588, was defeated, and was virtually destroyed by storms.

A **convoy** usually refers either to the protecting escort accompanying ships at sea, as in dangerous areas during wartime, or to the ships being escorted. The noun need not, however, be restricted to ships; trains or trucks may also be considered *convoys*. *Convoy* is also applied to a group of military vehicles, such as trucks, personnel carriers, tanks, mounted guns, etc., traveling together in an organized way for protection or efficient movement, or to avoid impeding other traffic.

flimsy

frail
tenuous
unsubstantial

These adjectives refer to anything slight, weak, thin, or sheer and thus either lacking in permanence or vulnerable to damage or criticism. **Flimsy** is the most general in embodying all these meanings, particularly emphasizing a lack of density that makes for limpness rather than rigidity: *flimsy* cloth that clung to

her body; a *flimsy* stalk that caused the flower to droop in its vase. Less concretely used, *flimsy* may refer to inferior materials, worthlessness, implausibility, or low standards: *flimsy* books that come apart in one's hands; the *flimsy* reporting of tabloid newspapers; a *flimsy* excuse; a *flimsy*, meretricious movie. **Frail**, by contrast, concentrates more on slenderness, weakness, or enfeeblement; furthermore, it need not suggest limpness: the *frail* filaments used in light bulbs; the *frail* teacup of bone china; a disease that left him *frail* from loss of weight. *Flimsy* also suggests possible damage through tearing, *frail* through breaking or shattering. Used even more metaphorically, *frail* does not function with the same intensity of disapproval felt in *flimsy,* although it can give a negative tone: a grasp of orchestration too *frail* to give her symphonic ideas convincing weight. More often, however, *frail* can render a sharply contrasted connotation of pity: *frail* hopes long ago shattered by the brutal facts of city life.

Tenuous, like *frail*, can also emphasize thinness, although in this case weakness is not necessarily involved: a heavy free-floating sculpture hung from *tenuous* wires that made it seem light and airy. The particular relevance of *tenuous*, however, is to haziness: a *tenuous* fog that threatened to thicken by morning. Related to this possibility is its more metaphorical suggestion of vagueness or confusion: ideas too *tenuous* to test in a realistic research project. **Unsubstantial** is the most formal of these adjectives and emphasizes a lack of density, firmness, permanence, or stability: building houses out of paper and other *unsubstantial* materials. Less specifically, it points to something that is without basis in fact, cannot pass inspection, or that partakes of fancy or fantasy: *unsubstantial* theories; *unsubstantial* grounds for an appeal of the case; *unsubstantial* dreams of escaping her dreary existence. See TRANSLUCENT, TRANSPARENT, WEAK.

Antonyms: *firm, rugged, solid, sturdy, substantial, tough.*

flinch

cower
cringe
grovel
wince

These verbs refer to someone who shrinks from a person or action because of alarm, cowardice, or servility. **Flinch** indicates an involuntary and startled drawing back in the course of performing an action. [*Flinching* from the anticipated report of the rifle is the most common cause of poor marksmanship; He *flinched* as the doctor inserted the needle in his arm.] At its most concrete, as in these examples, the verb suggests a convulsed recoil or muscular spasm. It can function more abstractly to refer to any psychological reluctance or avoidance: She *flinched* from thinking about the husband and children she had left behind. While *flinch* most often suggests alarm or fear as the cause of the recoil, **wince** points to pain or discomfort as the motivating factor. The recoiling action, furthermore, may be slighter, briefer, or less noticeable than the action indicated by *flinch:* He gingerly touched his bruised shin and *winced* at the pain. *Wince* can function less literally for any pained response: She *winced* and blinked under his withering attack. In this context, *flinch* better suggests initial aversion or reluctance, while *wince* is better suited to describing a discomfited response.

Cringe is more general than the preceding pair and can function in the place of either, referring to any recoil caused either by fear or pain. The action may not be as intense or sudden as those of *flinch* and *wince,* but it may last longer: left standing by the rail to *cringe* under a steady onslaught of sea spray. Also, spasmodic movement is not suggested here so much as a crouched or stooped posture. This is especially true when *cringe* refers to servile, cowardly, or obsequious behavior: slaves who refused to *cringe* before the wrath of their master; a candidate who *cringed* from direct confrontation with his opponent; disgusted by the way she *cringed* and fawned before her dissertation adviser in rapt self-abasement.

Cower and **grovel** both relate more closely to *cringe* than to the first pair of verbs, emphasizing stooped or sprawled postures adopted out of fear, servility, or obsequiousness. *Cower,* however, can also indicate a fearful and trembling recoil or drawing back from danger, pain, or extreme discomfort: He *cowered* in panic as the horses stampeded toward him; oarsmen who *cowered* and groaned at each fall of the lash. In reference to obsequiousness, *cower* is now more specific, vivid, and disapproving than *cringe,* indicating someone who seeks approval by an extreme display of deferential humility: the sanctimonious remorse with which he *cowered* before the judge in hope of winning a lighter sentence. *Grovel* is the most extreme of all the verbs in any of the situations possible for this group; it specifically points to a sprawled or supine position, suggesting abject and incapacitating fear, loathsome servility, or self-abasing adoration: choked with sobs and *groveling* on the floor in terror as the two attack dogs fought; those who hope to influence policy by *groveling* before the policy makers and flattering their sense of self-importance; He worshiped his wife so that no amount of *groveling* seemed adequate to express his utter surrender to her. See ANXIETY, DEMUR, FAWN.

Antonyms: *brazen out, carry off, confront, face.*

flippant

casual
flip
fresh
nonchalant
sassy
smart
wise

These adjectives are all used to describe particular kinds of attitudes, speech, and behavior. **Flippant**, **flip**, **sassy**, and **fresh** are always unfavorable in connotation. They all imply impertinence or lack of respect; *flippant* and the colloquial *flip* also indicate an inappropriate levity in the face of something serious. The four can describe attitudes and actions, but very often relate to speech or writing. *Sassy* is distinctly dialectal in flavor. [She's a *sassy* little girl, disrespectful to her elders and peevish with her peers; His *flip* remark at the time of the accident was typical of his rudeness and bad taste; It is a *flippant* editorial, not at all in keeping with the importance of its theme; He was *fresh* when he was a child, and his manners have not improved with age.]

Unlike the foregoing adjectives, **casual** and **nonchalant** can be neutral or even complimentary in tone. Both indicate a lack of concern, interest, or excitement: a *casual* air; a *nonchalant* approach to business problems. *Nonchalant,* however, may suggest an attempt to be disciplined or detached: All during the meeting, Jessup maintained a *nonchalant* manner, even when the shouting was at its height.

Smart and the slang term **wise** are close in meaning to *sassy, flip, flippant,* and *fresh.* However, since other senses of *smart* and *wise* relate to the possession of intelligence or wisdom, there is sometimes present a suggestion of those qualities even when *smart* and *wise* are used in criticism or disparagement. The intelligence and wisdom hinted at are perverted by arrogance or a nasty wit, but they can make the distinction between someone being *smart* or *wise* instead of *sassy* or *fresh.* [She was a good editor, but she kept making *smart* remarks to the managing editor, and he finally had to fire her; The sergeant was court-martialed for being *wise* to his commanding officer.] When *smart* or *wise* is used in reference to a child, it describes someone who is unpleasantly assertive or forward. [The little boy was so *smart* to his mother that she sent him to bed without supper; A couple of *wise* kids broke the window of the new post office.] See CONTEMPTUOUS, SARCASTIC, UNINVOLVED.

Antonyms: POLITE, *serious, solemn.*

flood

deluge
engulf
inundate
overwhelm
swamp
whelm

These verbs mean cover with water or other liquid, as by a downpour, wave, or overflow. **Flood** is the most general. It indicates the submergence of something that is not normally under water: A leak in the plumbing *flooded* the basement. The noun *flood*, in its commonest meaning, refers to an overflowing of dry land by water, as when heavy, concentrated rainfall fills a stream beyond capacity. Hence, the verb *flood* means fill, overflow, drench, or submerge with water. [During spring rains the river *floods*; The river *flooded* extensive areas of the countryside; A calamitous storm tide *flooded* the coast; The hurricane *flooded* the beach cottage and did considerable water damage.] Figuratively, *flood* may refer to anything that seems to move in a full stream: Sunlight *flooded* the room. Or it may mean supply with an excess or abundance of anything: to *flood* an engine with gasoline; They *flooded* him with advice.

Flood comes from an Old English word. Its collateral adjective, *diluvial,* and its closest synonym, **deluge**, derive from the Latin word for *flood. Deluge* may designate a worldwide *flood* or one covering a considerable part of the earth's surface. Specifically, it applies to the rain of forty days and forty nights in the time of Noah—a cataclysm called either the *Deluge* or the *Flood.* In general use, however, where *flood* focuses on the rising flow of water in a swollen stream, *deluge* stresses the idea of an unremitting downpour. In a literal sense, the verb *deluge* may imply a drenching with torrents of water: Heavy monsoon rain *deluged* southern India, *flooding* the rivers. But the verb is most often used in a figurative sense, indicating any kind of profuse downpour or incessant stream: a candidate *deluged* with telegrams from supporters; an author *deluged* with offers of honorary degrees.

The verb **inundate** is synonymous with *flood* but is far more literary. *Inundate* goes back in derivation to the Latin word for wave. It is close to *deluge* in force and meaning, but it differs in its emphasis on a wave-like overflow. To *inundate* is to overrun with water and cover completely. [If the dikes of the Netherlands give way, the sea will *inundate* the lowlands; A submarine earthquake caused a tidal wave that *inundated* the peninsula.] In a figurative sense, *inundate* points to an overflowing abundance: a bookstore *inundated* with orders for a best seller; a mailbox *inundated* with junk mail; a congressman *inundated* by requests from constituents. *Inundate* may also mean overpower like an onrushing wave: The work piled up and threatened to *inundate* him.

Swamp is close to *inundate* but is much more informal. Literally, it means drench or submerge: The rampaging river *swamped* scores of villages during the *flood.* To *swamp* a boat is to sink it by filling it with water: The canoe was nearly *swamped* by the waves. In a colloquial sense, *swamp* means overburden with an unmanageable number or amount of anything: an Ivy League college *swamped* with applications; I'm *swamped* with work. *Swamp* may also suggest utter defeat or a thoroughgoing rout: The home team *swamped* the opposition.

Where *inundate* implies standing water covering a surface, **overwhelm** may suggest liquid going over and under, around and through. *Overwhelm* comes from a Middle English word meaning turn upside down. It calls to mind the overpowering force of a mighty wave that rolls over and buries everything in its path: Streams of lava *overwhelmed* the village at the foot of the volcano; a lost continent *overwhelmed* by the sea. *Overwhelm* is now more commonly used in figurative senses, often referring to abstractions: *overwhelmed* by grief; His foolhardy accusations opened the floodgates of suspicion, and unreason *overwhelmed* the land. **Whelm** is very close to *overwhelm* but sometimes conveys a greater sense of foreboding. It suggests a being enveloped on all sides by water or by something that covers and suffocates like water: A dust storm *whelmed* the wagon train; a town *whelmed* by an earthquake. *Whelm* is used with telling force by Gerard Manley Hopkins in *Spelt from Sibyl's Leaves:* "Our evening is over us; our night/*whelms, whelms,* and will end us." **Engulf** means swallow up, as in an abyss or bottomless gulf. It suggests a being utterly *overwhelmed* by waters—enveloped and buried beyond any hope of escape: The legendary island of Atlantis was *engulfed* by the sea and disappeared without a trace. See MARSH, VANQUISH.

flourish

flower
luxuriate
prosper
thrive

Flourish is comparable with the other listed verbs in the sense of increasing toward or being in a very desirable condition or a condition of maximum development. Thus, a farm is said to *flourish* when it is well tended and producing large crops, and a school of painters is said to have *flourished* at the time when most of its best paintings were produced. **Flower** means be in the best condition or period of development: The poet's talent *flowered* in his early twenties.

Luxuriate means grow or increase so abundantly as to reach or border upon excess: Dandelions *luxuriate* on untended lawns.

Prosper is applied to persons or enterprises that do well or succeed financially. A man may *prosper* through effort and good fortune, or his farm may *prosper* through good management and an absence of drought.

Thrive is generally applied to living things that enjoy physical growth or well-being. [Tropical plants *thrive* in a greenhouse; Most children *thrive* in summer camps.] *Thrive* is occasionally applied to nonliving things that by extension are considered living: a *thriving* community. See MATURE (v.).

Antonyms: *decline, die,* WANE.

flout. Do not confuse the verb *flout* (disobey openly) with the verb *flaunt* (display ostentatiously).

flow

gush
pour
run
spout
spurt
squirt
stream

These verbs refer to the movement of fluids or a mass of particles. **Flow** indicates continuous and free movement, and often suggests slow, steady, and untroubled passage: the broad river that *flowed* through my hometown; the prevailing air current that *flows* from west to east in the Northern Hemisphere; Salt once damp may refuse to *flow*. *Flow* can have a lyrical tone: We watched the river as it *flowed* on

under the bridge. By contrast, **run** is more matter-of-fact, although it is usually restricted to the movement of liquids. In this context, it is very general, suggesting any amount, channeled or unchanneled, moving in any direction: water *running* down the windshield; In which direction does the river *run?* In reference to streams or rivers, *run* may suggest movement faster than suggested by *flow*.

Pour most often suggests sharp downward movement: Soot *poured* out over the city; water *pouring* over the dam. **Stream** can also apply to a movement both of fluids and of particles, but is otherwise like *run* in suggesting any amount moving in any direction. However, it usually suggests more rapid or more forceful movement: tears *streaming* down the child's face; smoke *streaming* from the chimney. As in the last example, movement in a narrow band or through a small aperture is often implied: water *streaming* through the irrigation ditches; cars *streaming* past the scene of the accident.

Gush suggests surging, turbulent, or sudden movement, whether in a general upwelling or a rapid jet: blood *gushing* from his head; water *gushing* in a fine spray from the fountains. **Spout** more strictly refers to a continuous or intermittent jet: water *spouting* from the leaky pipe; Once wounded, the whale began to *spout* blood.

Spurt can suggest small or intermittent jets: He squeezed the plunger of the hypodermic until the needle *spurted* out a few drops. **Squirt**, when distinct from *spurt,* may suggest a wider or more diffuse spray: water *squirting* from the fire hose. More commonly, *squirt* is transitive: He *squirted* water at me. See FLOOD, LEAK, STREAM.

Antonyms: *congeal, freeze, stagnate.*

foggy

cloudy
murky
opaque
turbid

All these adjectives apply to what is obscure and confused or shows a lack of clarity. Even when used in an abstract way, the closely related **foggy** and **cloudy** can sometimes allude to distinctions between a fog and a cloud. The former is low-lying, enveloping, diffuse, and indefinite in configuration; the latter, partly because it is usually seen from a distance, is typically thought of as being a denser, more remote, and more clearly defined mass that may affect but does not impinge upon the viewer. Similarly, *foggy* can refer to

164

an enveloping obscurity or confusion in a thinker's mind: *foggy* generalizations without any substantiation in fact. By contrast *cloudy* can suggest remoteness, lack of relevance, or uncertainty that is external to the thinker or speaker: The prospect for passage of the bill was somewhat *cloudy*, in view of its evident unconstitutionality. As in this example, *cloudy* often refers to a future outcome, and *foggy* is more apt for present confusion: *cloudy* eventualities; I haven't the *foggiest* notion of what you're talking about. Both, of course, can serve as literal description: a *foggy* day; a *cloudy* day. *Cloudy* can also be used to describe milky or unclear liquids: *cloudy* tap water that clears after a few minutes.

Turbid literally means muddy or unsettled and applies particularly to suspensions of foreign particles within a liquid, such as particles of dirt in water. Whereas *cloudy* in this sense emphasizes a misty appearance, *turbid* stresses the presence of foreign material that pollutes, muddies, or unsettles the basic medium. *Turbid*, however, is probably more commonly used in figurative than literal senses. It may mean thick and dense, like heavy smoke or fog: a *turbid* smoke screen of deceitful hints and outright lies. It may mean confused or impure, suggesting a chaotic intermixture of incompatible elements: The stream-of-consciousness technique in fiction has been likened to a *turbid* confluence of fact, passion, and ratiocination.

Murky and **opaque** suggest lack of light. *Murky* can mean oppressively dark or, by extension, unclear and confused, as if seen through a mist. *Opaque*, which in its basic sense means impervious to light, suggests denseness and relative impenetrability: *opaque* writing, filled with erudite but inept allusions; a *murky* exegesis of an arcane work, full of dark, involuted clues to which only the dead author had the key. See OBSCURE, TRANSLUCENT, VAGUE.

Antonyms: *bright*, CLEAR, *sunny*, TRANSPARENT.

fold

crease
line
pleat
wrinkle

These words function as both nouns and verbs and apply to marks, grooves, ridges, or furrows made in a smooth surface. To **fold** something is to bend it over upon itself so that one part covers another: to *fold* a blanket; to *fold* a newspaper; to *fold* up a road map; Do not *fold*, spindle, or mutilate. Used intransitively, the verb *fold* means close together with the parts touching or facing: A fan *folds*. The noun *fold* may designate a *folded* or *folding* part, piece, or layer: the *folds* of the bellows of an accordion. The eyelid is a movable *fold* of skin that smooths out when lowered over the eye. A double chin is a fatty *fold* of flesh under the chin. *Fold* may also apply to a mark made by *folding* or the hollow between two *folded* parts: to tear paper evenly along a *fold*; She enveloped the child in the voluminous *folds* of her cloak.

A **line** is a long, straight, slender mark, as one crossing the brow: the *lines* in her pale, drawn face; a forehead *lined* by care. The *lines* in the palm of the hand indicate the flexional *folds* of the skin that make firm grasping possible. Palmists claim that the so-called life *line*, head *line*, and heart *line* are indicative of a person's fortune. A **crease** is a mark, ridge, or furrow made by *folding*. Like a *line*, a *crease* may indicate the place where something *folds*, but a *crease* is usually considered to be heavier than a *line* though shallower than a *fold*. Hence, when the hand is slowly closed, the *lines* in the palm first deepen into *creases*, then thicken into *folds*. *Crease* is also used of heavy *lines* about the mouth or eyes or on the forehead: A sullen scowl *creased* his brow. And it may indicate a line of soreness or tension that results from bending or twisting: The lumpy mattress put a painful *crease* in his back.

A **wrinkle** is a small *line*, *crease*, or *fold* in a smooth surface, as a furrow made in the forehead by raising the eyebrows. To *wrinkle* is to contract into alternate ridges and furrows: He *wrinkled* his brow in concentration. Permanent *wrinkles* in the skin may result from age, anxiety, or excessive exposure to the elements: a *wrinkled* old man. Applied to fabric, *wrinkle* indicates a temporary mark made by crushing or rumpling. The verbs *wrinkle* and *crease* are synonymous in this sense: Linen *wrinkles* (or *creases*) easily. The noun *crease*, however, may indicate a deliberate or permanent *line*, as one of the two sharp edges pressed into men's trouser legs. A **pleat** is a *fold* of cloth doubled on itself and pressed or sewn in place: a kick *pleat*; *pleated* draperies; a *pleated* skirt. *Pleat* may also indicate the way a thing is *creased* and *folded*: an accordion *pleat*. See CRACK.

Antonyms: *smooth*, *straighten*, *unfold*.

folk

nation
people
race
tribe

folk (continued)

These nouns refer to ethnic groups or subcultures that can be identified by specific acts or shared traits, whether physical or cultural. **Folk** is the vaguest and applies better to periods of history before the Industrial Revolution. It refers to the common people or peasants of those eras and is based on a class rather than an ethnic distinction. It would, in any case, be rarely used except as a combining form, referring to the products of this class of people: *folk music, folk culture, folk tales*. It has a modern informal use to refer to one's nearest relatives or to the community in which one may have grown up: the *folks* back home; I write regularly to my *folks*.

Nation can refer to any government, ancient or modern, but in this context it refers more particularly to nomadic groups that maintain a common culture, despite their being widely scattered: the American Indian *nations* of the far West; the gypsy *nation;* the Jewish *nation* that somehow survived despite its scattering during the Diaspora. **People** is a less confusing term to describe a group, whether scattered or not, of common ethnic and cultural background: a *people* as conscious of individual liberty as the Greeks; the *peoples* of the earth, each with a distinctive contribution to make toward defining mankind. **Tribe** is more specific than *people* or *nation* in referring exclusively to a closely knit primitive culture group: the *tribes* of Africa and the Pacific.

Race refers to those large divisions of humans into physical types that are determined solely by some combination of skin color, facial characteristics, and other imponderables. Physical anthropologists have concluded that all such attempts to define clear-cut *races* are inexact, subjective, and unscientific: the Caucasian or white *race*. See KIN, MANKIND.

foment. Do not confuse the verb *foment* (arouse discontent, trouble, etc.) with the verb *ferment* (undergo fermentation).

foreigner
    alien
    immigrant
    newcomer
    outsider
    stranger

These nouns pertain to someone who does not belong, either at all or as yet, to the group in which he finds himself. **Foreigner** specifically indicates that someone is a native or citizen of a nation other than the one he is now living in or visiting. *Foreigner* can theoretically be used in neutral description, but in the past it was so often used to express suspicion or disapproval that it is difficult to avoid this tone completely even in the most innocent use: the *foreigners* who moved in across the street from us. A *foreigner* who intends to remain permanently in his new country can be more neutrally referred to as an **immigrant**. Although this noun could also once be used pejoratively, its use as a precise legal term has kept it more viable and neutral than *foreigner*: an *immigrant's* visa. Until an *immigrant* becomes a citizen of the new country, providing that is his intention, he is known legally as an **alien**, that is, someone who resides in a country but is not a member of it: All *aliens* must register annually with the immigration bureau. Once a citizen, such a person is no longer an *alien*, but he might still be regarded as an *immigrant* by others so long as his speech, clothes, or living habits reflect his country of origin and depart from the national norm. The xenophobic or unfriendly onlooker could, in fact, call such a naturalized citizen a *foreigner* to express intolerance for any departure from the norm.

The remaining nouns are all more general and wider ranging in their implications. **Stranger** can indicate anyone who is not known to someone else or who is not familiar with or accepted as part of some group: She hurried past the beckoning *stranger;* great excitement when *strangers* came to a frontier town. **Newcomer** can refer more informally to an *immigrant,* but applies more widely to a person only recently accepted into a group, yet still largely unfamiliar with it: a *newcomer* to New York. *Newcomer* can also suggest an initiate to any area of experience: a *newcomer* to poetry. Where *newcomer* suggests recent membership, **outsider** stresses alienation from or rejection by a group: backhills people who were wary of *outsiders;* a boy who didn't have many friends in his class and preferred to remain an *outsider;* Both labor and management refused to call in an *outsider* to mediate the dispute. See BEGINNER, EXILE.
Antonyms: *citizen, inhabitant, native.*

foreknowledge
    farsightedness
    foresight
    forethought
    prescience

All these nouns deal with a shrewd, prophetic, or mystical ability to anticipate, predict, or see into the future. **Foreknowledge** can refer to a supernatural faculty: Augustine's treatment of God's *foreknowledge* and man's free will; a medium who claimed to have *foreknowledge* of future events. **Prescience**, the most formal of these nouns, can also point to such a faculty, although it is less often attributed to people than to the Deity: God's *prescience* is only one aspect of His general omniscience. Both nouns, however, can apply without any suggestion of the mystical or supernatural. In this case, *foreknowledge* would refer to having information concerning something that has not yet occurred: rapidly developing the same *foreknowledge* of weather conditions that we have long had of lunar and solar eclipses; She denied that she had any *foreknowledge* of the plot her husband hatched. *Prescience* indicates not the simple ability to anticipate but an acute and intelligent ability to see what lies in store in the future: their *prescience* concerning the problems that would await them in the New World; his *prescience* in seeing the dangers of overpopulation.

Foresight is an alternative for the last meaning of *prescience*. But more simply it can also indicate an ability to think ahead, prepare for eventualities, and take precautions against any undesirable possibility: She had the *foresight* to lock all the windows and doors before leaving on her vacation; the *foresight* to plan for the inevitable replacement of the automobile she drove. **Farsightedness** can refer both to an intelligent envisioning of the future, like *prescience*, or a practical tendency to plan ahead, like *foresight*. It adds to either situation, however, the specific ability to extend one's thinking and awareness to the distant rather than the near future: the *farsightedness* of those who framed our Constitution in allowing for the changing circumstances and needs of future generations. **Forethought** is close to *foresight* in meaning, but where *foresight* might be most aptly applied to envisioning circumstances that are independent of oneself, *forethought* suggests the careful planning out of something more completely within one's control: He could have avoided the accident by using *forethought;* writers who have the *forethought* to plan the general outlines of their work well in advance of the actual writing. See EXPECTATION, PREDICT, PREMONITION.

Antonyms: *heedlessness, hindsight, ignorance.*

forget

neglect
omit
overlook

These verbs refer to oversights or failures to remember or act. **Forget** suggests a failure to keep something in mind, either because of its unimportance or complexity, or because of an unintentional lapse: She *forgot* all about the gossip as soon as she reported it; *forgetting* the way to the station; *forgetting* to water the plants.

Overlook and **omit** are both more specific than *forget* in suggesting almost exclusively failures to act. The failure may be slight and excusable and may be either intentional or deliberate. *Overlook* concentrates on a failure to notice or check something: He *overlooked* the fact that the back door was not locked; politicians who deliberately *overlook* pressing needs of the city. The verb might also refer to a conscious decision to excuse someone's failing: He agreed to *overlook* her breach of confidence. *Omit* suggests a failure to act in a certain approved way. Extenuating circumstances may be implied for the reason of the failure, but conscious intention may also be a motivation: in my haste *omitting* to tell her where I was going; *omitting* to tell the doctor the whole story behind the child's injury. In a related sense the verb can refer to the deletion of something, usually because it might be thought disadvantageous or unpleasant: They *omitted* from the report any mention of the program's difficulties. Except in this sense of deletion, *omit* is the one verb here that might no longer sound fresh or natural in ordinary speech.

Neglect may suggest an inadvertent failure to act, but more often its connotation is one of deliberate inattention: His administrative assistant had *neglected* to double-check the correspondence file. [*Forgetting* one or two small details is one thing, but *neglecting* the major responsibilities of your job is something else again.] See CURSORY, NEGLECT.

Antonyms: *FIND, REMEMBER.*

forgo

give up
sacrifice
waive

These verbs indicate the surrendering of what one has had or is entitled to have. **Forgo** contrasts with **give up** in its greater formality, but otherwise these two terms are alike in being very general. When *forgo* applies to abstaining from or relinquishing pleasure or benefit, it usually implies a free choice based on principle: asked to *forgo* meat during Lent; actors who voluntarily *forgo* pay for a benefit performance. But *forgo* may also refer to any missed opportunity, regardless of reason: a youngster forced to *forgo* a chance for college because of lack of funds; an old refugee who had long ago *forgone* any hope of seeing his homeland again. *Give up* could be substituted in most of these instances, but whereas *forgo* usually implies relinquishing something in advance, *give up* often implies surrendering something that is already in one's possession: He *gave up* his seat to a handicapped person; farmers who *gave up* their land to the government only after a struggle. As in the last example, *give up* is more apt than *forgo* for a reluctant yielding, or one based on necessity or defeat. Intransitively, the term can mean surrender: enemy soldiers who had *given up*; I *give up!*

Waive stresses the voluntary yielding possible for *forgo*, but it is focused exclusively on yielding in advance a right to which one is technically entitled. [The defense *waived* cross-examination of the witness; Both sides agreed to *waive* the arbitration clause in the contract.] Sometimes, the implication of voluntary choice masks what is in fact mandatory: a law that required state employees to *waive* immunity in grand jury investigations or lose their jobs. **Sacrifice** can indicate both the involuntary and voluntary relinquishing of something, but its special point is the hardship entailed in doing so. If a voluntary surrender is indicated, *sacrifice* implies nobility or generosity in the actor; if an involuntary act is indicated, *sacrifice* stresses difficulty or even suffering: soldiers willing to *sacrifice* their lives for their country; those who *sacrifice* part of their income to help the disadvantaged; parents who must scrimp and *sacrifice* to send their children to college; prison conditions under which inmates are forced to *sacrifice* the last vestiges of their humanity. In some uses, neither generosity nor difficulty may be present: blithely *sacrificing* the lives of others to his own self-interest. See ABSTAIN, FORSWEAR, RELINQUISH, TEMPERANCE.

Antonyms: DEMAND, *keep, preserve.*

form

configuration
contour
figure
gestalt
outline
shape
structure

These nouns can refer to the entire pattern or ordering of something, its makeup or constitution, or its enclosing surfaces. **Form** is the most general, applying in all these ways: the sonnet *form;* Ice is water in solid *form;* rectangular in *form.* At one extreme, it can merely indicate external appearance: a *form*-fitting dress. At the other, it can contrast with *content* all the related patterns and techniques that make an organic unity of something: The author's keen sense of *form* sustained her through a project that could easily have gone awry.

Shape more readily suggests a three-dimensional bulk, but it is not restricted to this reference: the gnarled *shapes* of Monterey cypresses. *Shape* can also apply to the enclosing surfaces of both a plane or solid object: an elliptical *shape;* a dress designed to show off her lovely *shape.* When *form* and *shape* are contrasted, *form* usually suggests a prescribed or typical pattern, whereas *shape* suggests the individual relationships that a specific thing exhibits: the startling variety of *shapes* with which the sculptor had fleshed out the human and animal *forms* she had chosen as her subjects.

When **outline** and **contour** are contrasted, *outline* may apply to the bounding edges of a plane figure, whereas *contour* pertains exclusively to the enclosing surface of a solid figure: a star-shaped *outline;* the graceful *contours* of a pear. *Outline,* however, can refer more generally to the containing perimeter of any *shape,* plane or solid; in the latter case, it suggests one of a solid's possible silhouettes: the jutting *outline* of his chin in profile.

Figure refers in plane geometry to any *form* enclosed by three or more lines: A trapezoid is a *figure* bounded by four lines. In other uses, *figure* may suggest something reduced to its diagrammatic essentials, or to the characteristic *form* or set of *outlines* by which something is recognizable: eyes peeled for the familiar *figure* of an apple tree that marked the direct path to the farmhouse. At the same time, however, *figure* can refer to the details that fill out and give body to a *form:* a slow movement memorable for a complex pizzicato *figure* that recurs in the violins. Like *shape, figure* can refer to the human body, but with a greater emphasis on the total impression made by the relationship of part to part: a trim, clean-cut *figure;* He cut an imposing *figure* in his new tuxedo. **Configuration**, like *contour*, can refer to the *outlines* of a solid *shape,* but whereas *contour* can sometimes suggest gentle or smooth undulations, *configuration* can apply to any sort of *shape;* it is particularly relevant to landscape: a house designed by the architect to exploit and fit into the dramatic *configuration* of the cliff. In more general uses, *configuration* suggests the exact disposition of all the observable details within a *form,* as well as its external *outlines:* the lacework *configurations* of a snowflake; a *configuration* of jagged *shapes* within the symmetrical *form* of each inkblot.

Structure concentrates on the disposition of details suggested by one use of *configuration*. But *structure* may refer in addition to an underlying *form* that is not necessarily observable by a glance at the *outlines* of something: excessive fat disguising what was actually a perfectly formed bone *structure*. Also, *structure* emphasizes the organic relatedness of a whole, seen from the perspective of function: the complicated *structure* of the executive branch of the government; the *structure* of the diesel engine. **Gestalt** is the most inclusive of these nouns in pointing to the totality of details that go to make up a moment of experience, referring to all the factors that impinge on a single psychological state. *Gestalt* is drawn from *gestalt* psychology, which theorizes that the unity of such a totality is greater than the sum of its parts. *Gestalt* has since been applied more generally to anything that can be said to have organic *structure*: Each of the scenes in the novel contributed to a *gestalt* of guilt and redemption. See BOUNDARY, CIRCUMSCRIBE, PHYSICAL, PROTOTYPE, SIZE.

Antonyms: *content, formlessness, shapelessness.*

formal

> affected
> ceremonial
> ceremonious
> pompous
> proper
> punctilious
> ritual

These adjectives describe elaborate or precise modes of behavior. The crucial discrimination to be made among them concerns the positive or negative overtones they carry. The positive overtone suggests admiration for the skillful carrying out of a beautiful but complicated pattern; the negative overtone suggests abhorrence for an inflexible lack of spontaneity, sincerity, or naturalness. The choice of adjective may tell more about the speaker than about the behavior described.

Formal and **proper** are often neutral terms of description pertaining to correctness of behavior. *Proper* is almost exclusively restricted to this sense: the *proper* way of addressing a bishop. *Proper* may also indicate what is appropriate or customary in a specific situation: the *proper* clothing for mountain climbing. *Formal*, on the other hand, can only refer to highly stylized situations: a *formal* dinner. *Formal* dress, for example, would not be *proper* at a rock concert, whereas jeans and a T-shirt would be *proper* in this

instance, though *formal* in none. Both *proper* and *formal* can sometimes suggest the negative side to all these adjectives. [She would be more fun if she weren't so *proper;* They felt a lack of warmth in the overly *formal* congratulations he gave them.]

Ritual, **ceremonial**, and **ceremonious** are allied to *formal* in describing acts or manners that are stylized according to set rules. They describe behavior that is *proper* only in the most formalized ceremonies. *Ritual* is neutral or approving when it describes an act that is a part of such a ceremony, especially a religious one: the *ritual* procession of cardinals. It is more ambiguous when describing a *formal* gesture not part of such an occasion: He lit the candles with a *ritual* flourish. It can even suggest perfunctory, indifferent behavior: a *ritual* kiss on both cheeks. *Ceremonious* is most often used to describe people or their stylized behavior, while *ceremonial* is often restricted to those acts or artifacts that are part of an actual ceremony: The Japanese are never more *ceremonious* than when they enact together the *ceremonial* patterns of the bonodori dances. *Ceremonious*, in being more general, can refer to any ritualizing of behavior. If the behavior is *proper* to the occasion, *ceremonious* remains neutral; if not, it can suggest officiousness or artificiality: Her *ceremonious* attentions to the guests made relaxed conversation difficult.

Affected, **pompous**, and **punctilious** deal almost exclusively in the negative side to these adjectives. Only *punctilious* may suggest a positive value in fastidious concern for detail: the *punctilious* attention to protocol seen among diplomats. Where *punctilious* emphasizes the precise or overprecise carrying out of a code of behavior, *affected* is more likely to refer to an inappropriate pseudo-elegance of manner, especially of speech or gesture: his *affected* English accent; her *affected* bargain-basement idea of elegance. *Affected* behavior in a man suggests artiness or effeminacy; *affected* behavior in a woman suggests an inability to distinguish between a bad or cheap imitation and the real elegance she can only affect. *Pompous* refers mostly to inflated manners of a stuffy or officious kind, and tends to be used mostly in describing men. It would be used when super-solemn rather than effeminate behavior is indicated: the droning of the *pompous* judge. Thus, what one observer might call *affected*, *pompous*, or *punctilious*, another might call *formal*, *ceremonious*, or *ritual*. The observer's choice depends on what he or she considers *proper* or appropriate to a situation. See ARTISTIC, CONCEITED, ELEGANT.

Antonyms: *haphazard, improvisatory, informal, natural,* SPONTANEOUS.

forswear

abjure
disavow
disclaim
disown
recant
retract
take back

These verbs apply when a person rejects something, gives up past behavior, or withdraws from a previously stated stand or belief. **Forswear** indicates renunciation of past behavior; once, it referred to taking an oath to this effect, but now it can suggest an emphatic willingness to give up something completely. Most often, the verb suggests an open admission of guilt or fault arising out of such behavior: a country that *forswore* future military aggression after suffering a decisive defeat; no use asking alcoholics to make high-minded oaths *forswearing* drinking. Where *forswear* can suggest moral resolve or penitence, **abjure** is more forceful in sometimes implying an angry rejection; it also referred once to renunciation under oath, but less often applies in this way now: a union official who *abjured* mediation as a solution to the dispute, especially considering the unwillingness of management to negotiate; bitter disappointments that made her *abjure* marriage.

Disavow and **disclaim** are now most commonly used to deny complicity or responsibility; thus, both contrast with *forswear*, which often implies an admission of guilt. *Disavow* once could involve a formal oath; now it more often points to a refusal to acknowledge something as valid or an insistence that no connection exists between one's own stand and that of another. [The candidate *disavowed* completely the statement that had been attributed to him by newspaper reporters; The board *disavowed* the action of the executive and denied that his promises were binding on the company.] *Disclaim* can also function as a denial of responsibility, but its special point is the giving up of a right that might be offered in one's own behalf. [He *disclaimed* all complicity in the assassination plot; The company *disclaimed* any interest in the disputed land, even though the oldest deeds carried its name.]

Disown at its most general can suggest any sort of abandonment: The bureau *disowned* the project after the poor showing it made during its first year in operation. *Disown* is often used in a special way, however, referring to the total rejection of a disliked person, often a near relative: a father who *disowned* his son and wrote him out of his will.

The remaining verbs all deal with a retreat from previously stated positions. **Take back** is the most informal, applying to an apologetic withdrawal of anything one has previously said. [His friend kept him pinned to the floor until he *took back* the insult; She immediately *took back* her accusation once she saw how wrong she had been.] **Retract** can apply to the same situation, often indicating a formal, official, or public statement. [She threatened to sue unless her opponent *retracted* the libelous allegation; The defendant *retracted* his confession, claiming it had been coerced.] **Recant** once indicated the solemn *retracting* of a heresy by a former adherent: Witches were required to *recant* publicly or be hanged. It still applies to the repudiation of doctrine or ideology and is more forceful than *retract* in suggesting a total *disavowing* or abject capitulation, including an admission of past guilt and an implied promise to *forswear* the error in the future: those who *recanted* Communism after Stalin and Hitler signed their nonaggression pact. See ABSTAIN, FORGO, RELINQUISH.

Antonyms: ACKNOWLEDGE, ASSERT, *claim, uphold.*

fortuitous. Do not confuse the adjective *fortuitous* (happening by chance) with the adjective *fortunate* (brought by good fortune).

fortunate. Do not confuse the adjective *fortunate* (brought by good fortune) with the adjective *fortuitous* (happening by chance).

fragile

brittle
frail
frangible
friable

These adjectives describe things easily broken. **Fragile**, beyond this general meaning, may suggest weakness or delicacy as well: a *fragile* teacup; the shipping of *fragile* materials; her *fragile* health; a *fragile* embroidery of flower motifs. **Frail** carries its own implication of slenderness or enfeeblement, as well as of breakability or weakness: a *frail* scaffold; *frail* columns bearing the architrave; made *frail* by continuing bouts of malaria. The noun *frail* was an offensive slang term for a young woman, suggesting membership in the weaker sex.

Brittle, like *fragile*, need not suggest slightness or slenderness, and it is also less apt than either of the previous adjectives to indicate weakness or delicacy of construction. It refers to any hard material that tends to shatter easily under a direct impact: Glass is *brittle;* choosing building stones less *brittle* than marble or granite. More metaphorically, it contrasts sharply with the softness that may be implied by *frail,* suggesting instead a hard, brusque manner or appearance: giving him a *brittle,* contemptuous reply.

The remaining adjectives are considerably more formal than the foregoing and also more specific in meaning. **Frangible** may be used only to indicate breakability, but more relevantly here, is often applied to materials designed to be broken: a *frangible* capsule of ammonia that is broken and held under the fainting person's nose. **Friable** is even more restricted in meaning, referring exclusively to materials that can be crumbled easily: sandstone slabs that are not *brittle* but tend to be *friable.* Occasionally, *friable* can refer to anything vulnerable to being worn down: topsoil made less *friable* by the planting of trees. See BREAK (v.), FLIMSY, WEAK.

Antonyms: *elastic, flexible,* MALLEABLE, *strong,* SUPPLE, *tough.*

fragment

remnant
scrap
shred

These nouns refer to a small part or piece separated from a larger whole. **Fragment** stresses breakage. In a literal sense, a *fragment* is a broken piece or shard: Archeologists discovered *fragments* of a marble column; a prehistoric man expertly reconstructed from bone *fragments.* Where *fragment* is typically, though not always, used of a brittle substance, the other nouns in this set may all apply to bits and pieces of cloth or food. In a specific sense, a **remnant** is a piece of cloth left over, as from a bolt, after the final measured cutting: to buy carpet *remnants* on sale. In a general sense, it may refer to any remaining part or portion: the *remnants* of the unfinished meal. A **scrap** is a small, odd piece that has been cut, broken, or torn from a larger piece: a *scrap* of silk. *Scrap* may refer to paper as well as to cloth or food, and while *remnants* may be saved for future use, *scraps* are often discarded. Like *scrap,* **shred** may apply to a variety of substances. A *shred* is a long and narrow piece of strip, as one torn, cut, or shaved off lengthwise: *shreds* of carrot in a salad; *shreds* of crepe paper. Used of fabric, the plural *shreds* suggests a reduction to rags and tatters: In the fight, his suit was torn to *shreds. Shred*

may also refer to a stringlike piece of something, as food: *shredded* wheat.

All these nouns have extended, metaphorical uses. *Fragment* may designate any part incomplete in itself, existing, considered, perceived, or treated apart from a larger, inclusive context. *Fragments* may be the only extant work of an ancient poet. On the other hand, a *fragment* of a novel may be a piece of writing going up to the point where the writer broke off, leaving the conceptual whole uncompleted. *Fragment* may also refer to an isolated bit or part of anything abstract or immaterial. [Even the greatest scholar knows only a *fragment* of all there is to know; She overheard *fragments* of the conversation.] In a broad sense, *remnant* may mean a remaining trace or vestige of anything: *remnants* of early Indian settlements; a penniless aristocrat jealously guarding the *remnants* of past family glory. It may also refer to a small remaining number of people: the tattered *remnants* of the defeated regiment. *Scrap* and *shred* may apply to any particle or to the smallest amount: our last *shred* of hope; not a *shred* of evidence or *scrap* of proof. See PART.

Antonyms: *totality, whole.*

frantic

delirious
frenetic
frenzied
furious
hectic

These adjectives describe extreme states of confused and disordered action. **Frantic** is the most general in that it does not of itself suggest the reason for the extreme state: *frantic* with fear; a *frantic* dash for the departing train. *Frantic* does suggest desperation and ineffective haste; it also may stress action taken under extreme pressure: the *frantic* pace of the big cities. **Hectic** is specific in exclusively stressing this last sense of *frantic.* The note of desperation is not necessarily present, however, and the adjective may simply refer hyperbolically to a rush of events: the *hectic* days after the first discovery of gold; *hectic* traffic during rush hours. **Frenetic** also relates to this sense of *frantic,* but it may suggest suspense and excitement rather than the desperation of *frantic* or the busy swiftness of *hectic:* the *frenetic* final minute of the tied basketball game; a *frenetic* race against the printer's deadline.

Both *hectic* and *frenetic* have roots or older uses that refer to a feverish physical illness. Only **delirious,** however, would now be pertinent in this context, since it can literally suggest the confused mental state resulting from a fever. In other uses, it escapes the specific situation of physical illness, referring instead to wild excitement, but it still suggests hyperbolically a confused, helpless, or disordered mental state: the grandstand crowd that was flushed with victory and *delirious* with joy; the *delirious* new dances that emphasize self-isolation and dehumanizing incoherence. *Frantic,* used in a favorable sense, compares with *delirious* here. As a term of approbation, it may stress a wild aliveness or a joyfully giddy whirl: a *frantic* party; The music was *frantic.*

Frenzied intensifies the note of desperation in *frantic;* it suggests a person completely out of control, one who is goaded or driven by external or internal pressures to act in a completely disorganized way: the charging bull, *frenzied* by repeated wounding; the rioters shouting *frenzied* accusations. **Furious**, by contrast, suggests a fierceness of behavior stemming mainly from anger. This adjective is not nearly as intense as the others. A person might be *furious,* but not give the slightest sign of his emotional state; or he might give vent to his *furious* anger but still remain in control of himself: her cold but *furious* summation to the jury. The adjective may also merely suggest haste, like *frantic* or *hectic:* fast and *furious;* the *furious* rapids above the waterfall. See ANGER, FRENZY, PSYCHOTIC.

Antonyms: *IMPERTURBABLE, SLOW, TRANQUIL, unhurried.*

frenzy

delirium
hysteria
mania

These nouns refer to extreme states of mental agitation, craving, disorder, or abnormality. **Frenzy** is the most general of these in stressing extreme agitation of any sort for whatever reason: in a *frenzy* to meet the weekly deadline. Usually, this noun suggests an acting out of the mental state in rapid but possibly disordered movements: the *frenzy* with which they struggled to put out the fire raging through the building. It also suggests a spurt or seizure of emotion that goads one into action, rather than a steady or constant state: the *frenzy* of activity during harvest time. When *frenzy* refers to emotional imbalance rather than hyperbolically indicating frantic effort, the emotions suggested include hate, anger, terror, or other negative responses to externals: driven by a cold *frenzy* to kill her attacker. **Mania** in one of its particulars contrasts

strongly with this suggestion of negative response in *frenzy,* since it can refer to an extreme liking or craving for something: a *mania* for collecting rare books. Furthermore, a *mania* may be present over a long period of time without necessarily being acted out: never having indulged a secret *mania* for camping outdoors. In a psychiatric context, *mania* is used more strictly to refer to a mental disorder in which one is pervaded with a sense of well-being but acts in excessive and deranged ways: the *mania* that alternates with melancholy in the typical manic-depressive.

Where *frenzy* may suggest angry outbursts and *mania* a continual craving, **hysteria** suggests emotional seizures of grief or fear as expressed by uncontrolled sobbing: the *hysteria* of many aboard the burning plane. Uncontrolled laughter is also a possible result of *hysteria,* although such laughter would hardly stem from even an illusory happiness. Psychiatrically, *hysteria* refers to an abnormal condition that results from nervous malfunction or sexual repression and is characterized by violent emotional paroxysms and disturbances in sensory and motor functions: the crippled woman whose classic case of *hysteria* set Freud to devising his psychoanalytic theories.

Delirium indicates a deranged state that may be the by-product of fever, epilepsy, or alcoholism, or the primary effect of narcotic or psychedelic drugs. This noun may suggest agitation like that of *frenzy,* but it does not necessarily suggest any physical activity whatsoever; it does indicate a rambling or hallucinating mind: a *delirium* in which the woman thought she had stepped out of her body and looked back on it. More loosely, *delirium* can refer to any feverish state or nightmare-ridden sleep: a *delirium* of troubled dreams from which he awoke in a cold sweat. Hyperbolically, *delirium* is sometimes used to indicate uncontrollable excitement, wild emotion, or frenzied rapture: a *delirium* of joy. See DELUSION, FRANTIC, PSYCHOTIC.

friend

acquaintance
buddy
companion
comrade
confidant
crony
intimate

These nouns all refer to a close or informal relationship with another person, distinguished on one hand from formal business relationships and on the other from closer love or family relationships. One's **friend** in Shakespearean England meant one's mistress. Now it has lost this sexual meaning completely and means a person one is fond of and chooses to associate with. A business associate, one's spouse, or a member of one's family all may or may not be one's *friend,* while a *friend* may or may not be a person one would wish to work with or live with. An **acquaintance** is a person one has met and sees occasionally with cordiality but without intimacy: *acquaintances* who were destined never to become *friends.* **Companion** is ambiguous. It may suggest the closeness of *friend:* my constant *companion.* Or it may suggest the casual association of *acquaintance:* my *companions* on the cruise ship. In the case of *acquaintance* or *companion,* the noun stresses the physical presence of the person referred to; in the case of *companion,* however, the relationship might be controlled strictly by chance or necessity, without even the implied cordiality of *acquaintance. Companion* has recently come into use as a euphemism for lover and may suggest a heterosexual or homosexual lover: his long-time *companion.*

The rest of these nouns relate to the closeness of *friend,* each with a unique overtone that implies its own particular kind of closeness. **Intimate** suggests inseparable and affectionate friendship; it is less frequently used in this sense now, however, because the sexual reference of *intimate* in another context obtrudes here, where no note of sexuality was originally intended. **Comrade** has also suffered because of the obtrusion of another meaning of the noun. Originally used for a man's male *friend,* with jolliness and heartiness as overtones, it lost out to its specific use as a form of address among members of the Communist Party: Prince Hal's bawdy *comrades;* his *comrades* on the revolutionary council that governed the country.

Crony is now a more widely used informal noun for a close *friend* than either *intimate* or *comrade,* but it has a strong colloquial tang and implies the gossipy closeness of a clique: his *cronies* at the club. Its common form, old *crony,* suggests a relationship of long standing based on reminiscence: old *cronies* who on Saturday nights relive their experiences of the Vietnam War. Many slang words exist to describe close *friends;* the most common at present may be **buddy,** partially replacing such choices as mate, chum, and pal: my *buddy* at college. The frequency with which words for a male *friend* rise into and fall from favor may suggest an embarrassment over the affectionate side of friendship and a continuing search for a referent whose neutral and casual tone will be considered uncompromising in its manliness.

Confidant compares with *crony* in suggesting an exchange of gossip as the staple of a friendship. Where *crony* more commonly refers to a man's male friend, however, *confidant* refers more often to a woman's female *companion* and may thus be spelled *confidante.* A further implication suggests that the talk exchanged between *confidants* is not so much reminiscence as personal secrets. [Over the years, her hairdresser became her most trusted *confidant.*] See ACCOMPLICE, ASSISTANT, ASSOCIATE.

Antonyms: *antagonist,* OPPONENT.

frighten
scare
startle
terrify

These verbs mean fill with fear or apprehension. **Frighten** has the widest range of use. It often indicates a fear of physical harm, but it may also apply to fears rooted in emotion or arising from imagination. In an immediate sense, a person is *frightened* by a cause of fear addressed directly and suddenly to the senses and may react physically in a number of negative ways—shivering, shuddering, freezing, fainting, screaming, running, hiding, even having a heart attack. At one extreme, being *frightened* may involve only a brief pang or flutter of fear: *frightened* by a strange noise in the middle of the night. At the other extreme, it may imply dread or terror that paralyzes thought, motion, or response, leaving one in a state of shock: a pedestrian crossing absentmindedly against a traffic light, *frightened* into immobility by an onrushing car. *Frighten* is also used to indicate a fearful, apprehensive state of mind: The prospect of being deserted by her parents deeply *frightened* the child.

Scare is close to *frighten* in that it can imply either sudden, unnerving fear or a fearful, uneasy state. Even more strongly than *frighten,* it stresses a reflex physical reaction, whether literal or figurative: *scared* stiff. But *scare* is a more informal than *frighten* and may suggest a milder or more superficial form of fear. Unlike *frighten,* it is a child's word, and it emphasizes the immediacy of fear, whatever the cause. [He is *scared* of the dark; Our approach *scared* the rabbit and he ran.] *Scare* is also often used to suggest the deliberate stimulation of fear, as in games, teasing, initiation, practical jokes, or other forms of amusement, whether harmless or dangerous: a *scary* movie; to *scare* children with a ghost story. [I *scared* you, didn't I? The stunt pilot *scared* his passenger half to death with his daredevil feats.]

Startle stresses the element of suddenness, usually involving an involuntary reaction to an unexpected stimulus. A *startled* person may gasp, jump, draw back, or make a quick, jerky movement and then freeze. [You *startled* me—I didn't see you come in; *startled* by a rabbit running across his path.] In another sense, *startle* may indicate an inner, intellectual surprise at something unexpected: *startled* by their daughter's revelation but trying hard not to show it.

Terrify is the strongest of these verbs, suggesting extreme, overwhelming fear that is close to panic: The violence of the storm *terrified* the sailors. *Terrify* may be an intensification of *frighten* in the sense of fear that paralyzes all the faculties, physical and mental: too *terrified* to speak. But it may also suggest frenzied activity aimed at escaping a threatening situation: *terrified* people trying to get out of the burning World Trade Center. In a looser sense, *terrify* is sometimes used hyperbolically to imply intimidation or nervous agitation: *terrified* by the exam; *terrified* that he would be late. See AFRAID, INTIMIDATE.

Antonyms: *calm, comfort, quiet, soothe, tranquilize.*

frisk

    caper
    frolic
    gambol

These verbs all refer to movement that is high-spirited, zestful, and exuberant. **Frisk** suggests quick, playful, eager movements: dogs *frisking* in the park; letting the children *frisk* and scramble all day on the beach. The emphasis of **frolic** is close to that of *frisk,* but it stresses even more a playful, joyous activity: a playground where children skip rope, skate, and generally *frolic* without a worry in the world. *Frolic,* furthermore, can apply to a whole series of actions marked by joy, whereas *frisk* tends to suggest specific individual movements.

Caper and **gambol** are like *frisk* in indicating certain kinds of movement. *Caper* is the most specific, suggesting a dancelike way of jumping or leaping with a lively, bounding motion: teenagers *capering* around their beach fire far into the night; a nanny goat and her *capering* kids. *Gambol* suggests an impulsive series of skipping, bounding, or jerking movements that may seem unsteady, uneven, or erratic: lambs *gamboling* in the meadow after their sedate mother ewe. See PLAYFUL.

Antonyms: *mope, sulk.*

frown

    grimace
    pout
    scowl

These words, both nouns and verbs, are comparable in their denotation of the deliberate or involuntary distortion of a person's facial expression because of displeasure, annoyance, pain, or the like. **Frown** is the most familiar. As visually perceived, a *frown* involves a knitting, contracting, or wrinkling of the brows. As an expression, a *frown* can be a conscious or unconscious indication of displeasure. [The instructor *frowned* with annoyance when a student fell asleep during her lecture.] Mostly, though, a facial *frown* is involuntary. It can be a simple reaction to strong light: Many people who forgo sunglasses develop deep creases in their foreheads from *frowning.* A *frown* can also be the result of deep concentration or thought. [The novel was amusing, but it required such close attention that I often found myself *frowning* when I should have laughed.] In a figurative sense, however, *frowning* registers disapproval or distaste: to *frown* upon overindulgence in food or drink.

The word with the most extensive application is **grimace**. A *grimace* is a distortion of the features, either habitual or momentary, that is caused by some feeling or impulse. It is usually ugly and uncontrollable, as when it is caused by pain or annoyance. [The agonizing pain of arthritis left his face with a constant *grimace*; A *grimace* appeared on the storekeeper's face every time a child approached the shelf of fragile merchandise.] But a *grimace* can be a deliberate attempt to provoke laughter, as when someone makes a face: When the comedian's lines fell flat, she resorted to *grimacing* to get laughter from her audience.

Although **pout** can refer to a general sullenness of behavior, it more often is like *frown* in its designation of a particular facial expression. The verb *pout* means push out the lips, as in displeasure or ill humor. It is sometimes used in describing adults, but *pout* usually suggests the behavior of a child. [The little girl *pouted* all afternoon because her mother had refused to buy her a new bike.] A **scowl** is a lowering of the brows, much like a *frown.* It can indicate the same kind of displeasure or annoyance that a *frown* does. But the emotions that generate a *scowl* are usually stronger than those that produce a *frown.* There is a strong suggestion of anger, a threatening quality, and certainly an air of sullenness in a *scowl.* [His *scowl* hinted at the menace that lay behind his carefully modulated voice and calm demeanor.] See FOLD.

Antonyms: SMILE.

full-fledged
finished
perfected
seasoned

These adjectives are comparable when applied to something that has reached maturity or completion. **Full-fledged** is the most colorful. Its literal reference is to a bird whose wing feathers are fully grown, enabling it to fly. The noun *fledgling* is applied to a young bird that has just grown enough feathers for flight; by extension, it designates a person who is inexperienced or immature. But *full-fledged* stresses accomplishment, implying that a training or developing period is past and that full, independent status has been attained: a *full-fledged* teacher as opposed to a teacher trainee; a *full-fledged* doctor as opposed to an intern; *Full-fledged* pilots have finished flight training and won their wings.

Seasoned goes beyond *full-fledged,* suggesting not only qualification but maturity or experience. Applied to timber, *seasoned* indicates a drying or hardening process whereby the wood is made more suitable for use. Used of persons, it implies the development of expert skills and professional reliability through long practice: a *seasoned* ball club; a *seasoned* trouper, able to go on with the show despite laryngitis; a drill sergeant who turns raw recruits into *seasoned* soldiers. A *seasoned* politician is one who has become astute and adroit in practical politics through having weathered many campaigns.

Finished stresses polish and resulting elegance. *Finished* furniture has a stained and polished surface. An artist with a *finished* technique has polished her style to an ultimate degree. A *finished* musician, as contrasted with a merely competent one, has refined her skills and achieved excellence. **Perfected** is close to *finished* but is more emphatic in stressing consummate mastery or faultless excellence: A *perfected* technique is one mark of a virtuoso. See ATTAINMENT, EXQUISITE, FINISH, MATURE (adj.), PERFECT, REACH.

Antonyms: *apprentice, callow, fledgling, immature, inexperienced, raw, undeveloped, unfledged, unseasoned.*

fulsome. Do not use the adjective *fulsome* (excessive, disgusting) to mean *full, copious,* or *plentiful.*

further
advance
contribute
implement

These verbs refer to acts that give impetus to something already under way. **Further** is the most neutral of these in indicating any sort of action or effect, intentional or not, whether stemming from the primary agent involved or from an outside person, force, or factor: needing a rich patron to *further* his career; a pleasant voice that, without her realizing it, *furthered* the good impression she made on other people. *Further* can as easily be applied to undesirable developments: crisis conditions that *furthered* the spreading of hysterical rumors. **Advance** has more force than *further* and thus is useful for stressing intentional and decisive effort to *further* something desirable: selfless patriots who *advance* the cause of freedom. Despite these positive overtones, *advance* can be used, with the same increase in force, for undesirable developments: malnutrition that quickly *advanced* the progress of the disease Here, in fact, *advance* suggests the speeding up of a harmful process. *Advance* does not carry this added weight in some of its milder uses, where it simply indicates a moving forward, putting forward, or giving beforehand: armies *advancing* through the city; *advancing* his suggestion timidly; *advancing* part of next week's pay.

Contribute contrasts sharply with the foregoing by suggesting secondary factors that give helpful but not crucial assistance to something solidly under way. *Further* and *advance* can conceivably suggest aid without which no more forward movement would result. This is far less true of *contribute:* recalling the lucky accidents that had *contributed* to her hard-earned success. The secondary factors suggested by *contribute,* however, may derive from intentional or fortuitous acts or from established characteristics of the subject involved, as well as from external causes: political weaknesses that *contributed* to the economy's rapid decline. **Implement** is a fad word in governmental or sociological parlance for the act of making more effective those arrangements that exist in theory, though not always in fact: taking steps to *implement* the long-standing ban against press censorship. Sometimes, *implement* seems to suggest the putting into effect of newly established programs, or the enforcement of decisions that have been newly arrived at: *implementing* the new gay rights laws. See ENCOURAGE, GO.

Antonyms: *DELAY, HINDER, prevent, sidetrack.*

gather

assemble
collect
congregate
convene
mass
muster

These verbs all mean come or bring together into an organized body or group. In transitive uses, **gather** emphasizes bringing widely scattered things to one place, and **collect** suggests discriminating selection: to *gather* wildflowers; to *collect* art. When used of people or animals, *gather* and, less frequently, *collect* suggest some degree of necessity or compulsion: to *gather* refugees into one place. In intransitive uses *gather* and *collect* are often used interchangeably. [Autograph seekers *gathered* (or *collected*) around the movie star wherever she went; After the stirring sermon, parishioners *collected* (or *gathered*) around the new minister to offer congratulations.] But *gather* suggests a group formed by a more random process than *collect*. *Collect* usually emphasizes a gradual process of accumulation, often one by one, whereas *gather* may be used to describe the spontaneous forming of a group. [A few homeless beggars *collected* around the blaze for warmth; A crowd immediately *gathered* around the stricken man.]

Assemble refers to people or organizations and suggests their coming together for some joint purpose, though not necessarily a prearranged one: to *assemble* a convention to nominate a candidate; Congress *assembled* for a summer session to catch up on lagging legislation. **Congregate** suggests a more spontaneous or haphazard coming together. [People *congregated* on balconies to catch a glimpse of the new mayor; Students *congregated* under the dean's window to protest increased fees.]

To **convene** is to come together or meet in a body. It is a formal word and applies particularly to the *assembling* of a formally organized body of people. A scientific congress *convened* to discuss the effects of ozone depletion on human health.

Mass means *assemble* in great numbers: troops *massed* for an attack; Britons *massing* in the streets on Coronation Day. **Muster** is generally restricted to military use and is applied to parts or units of a force that come or are brought together. [Recruits *muster* for a roll call; a fighting force that *mustered* for a final attack] *Muster*, like *gather*, *collect*, and *assemble*, can be used of qualities or data as well as of things. [He could not *muster* the strength to raise his head from the pillow; to *muster* facts; to *gather* impressions on a trip to Europe; to *collect* anecdotes in preparation for a speech; to *assemble* data for a legal presentation.] See ACCUMULATE, SUMMON.

Antonyms: *disband*, SCATTER, *separate*.

gauche

boorish
maladroit
tactless
uncouth
unpolished

These adjectives describe a graceless mode of social behavior. **Gauche** refers to a person or actions that do not conform to the standards of a particular social group; such a person may be considered unsophisticated, vulgar, or ill-bred: American mannerisms that are thought *gauche* in England. The term may be used as a subjective evaluation of behavior that is innocent or harmless but also intentional. In the case of **maladroit**, the questionable behavior is inadvertent but results in injured feelings or resentment because it is ill-timed or in poor taste: wanting to bite his own tongue for having made such a *maladroit* remark. Also, *gauche* might more commonly describe the picture someone presents socially, whereas *maladroit* more often refers to a slip or breach of taste.

Tactless is closer to *maladroit* than to *gauche*, but it may refer not only to a momentary slip but to an ingrained habit of being thoughtless or inconsiderate of the feelings of others: a *tactless* reference to my recent divorce; a thoroughly *tactless* person who never knew when to keep still. **Unpolished** concentrates on *gauche* behavior that results specifically from a lack of good breeding or sophistication; furthermore, *unpolished* is not necessarily negative in its evaluation: a man whose shoes and manners were both noticeably *unpolished*; an *unpolished* simplicity of speech that was refreshing after the affectations of her city friends. **Uncouth** stresses a total lack of social experience and sophistication, but with no mitigating possibilities for a positive evaluation. It also implies harsh, offensive, or rude behavior: The *uncouth* manners of the waiter distressed all of us. *Uncouth* has an old-fashioned ring to it nowadays and is often used with an undertone of irony at the expense of the excessively sensitive or snobbish: She regarded all men as vaguely *uncouth*. **Boorish** is the harshest of all these adjectives in its disapproval. It makes no attempt to explain away disgusting or vile behavior in terms of inexperience; it simply condemns. The adjective suggests manners that are fawning, sycophantic, surly, or indelicate: a *boorish* lout who accosted her and insisted upon seeing her home. See CLUMSY, VULGAR.

Antonyms: *adroit*, CONSIDERATE, POLITE, URBANE.

gaudy

flashy
garish
meretricious
tawdry

These adjectives refer to tasteless displays of overdone finery or decoration, or to brazen, flaunting behavior. Of these adjectives, **gaudy** is the least negative in tone, but still points to excessive use of decoration or to any sort of vividness that approaches vulgarity: *gaudy* make-up; the *gaudy* neon signs of the Ginza. *Gaudy* may not imply disapproval at all in some circumstances, suggesting a wild or irresistible abandonment to spectacular designs: the *gaudy* lights of the carnival; the *gaudy* peacock. **Flashy** is an informal substitute for *gaudy*, referring to anything deliberately chosen out of exuberantly vulgar ostentation: *flashy* costume jewelry; a taste for *flashy* clothes that caused snickers among most of the women in the office. This adjective can also function without implying disapproval: a *flashy* sports car that was the envy of the neighbors; *flashy* beachwear designed for uninhibited summer fun.

With **garish**, the emphasis is wholly on extremely distasteful ostentation and more especially on a chaotic aesthetic effect resulting from the disharmony of elements in a design: green eye shadow that would have been thought *garish* in a bordello; the *garish* combination of striped pants, plaid jacket, and a clashing print shirt. *Garish* can also refer to loud, coarse manners: other patrons who left because of our *garish* behavior.

Meretricious and **tawdry** both emphasize decoration that is made of cheap or worthless materials. With *meretricious*, which derives from a Latin word for prostitute, the stress is on overuse, especially of phony or trashy gimmicks: *meretricious* gewgaws that made the living room look like a junk shop. The adjective has a special use to refer to aesthetic dishonesty or propaganda appeals: novels that make *meretricious* use

of sex to boost sales; *meretricious* campaign promises. *Tawdry* most simply may suggest cheapness combined with showiness in taste: a *tawdry* plastic tablecloth; a *tawdry* flowered sofa already beginning to fall apart. Used less concretely, *tawdry* may suggest unsavoriness or such an extreme abasement of taste as to be degraded and degrading: *tawdry* taverns where soldiers on leave could find women on the loose; *tawdry* magazines that peddle filth, scandal, and sleazy amusement to eager audiences. See SHOWY.

Antonyms: MODEST, *plain, quiet, simple, tasteful.*

gem

ice
jewel
jewelry
rock
stones

The noun **gem** denotes a cut and polished piece of mineral substance, either precious or semiprecious in quality. These mineral pieces are called **stones**, a term used especially by jewelers and one that can be applied to the mineral pieces in either their original or cut and polished form. Diamonds, emeralds, and rubies are precious *stones;* jade, amethyst, and garnet are semiprecious. **Jewel** can be used interchangeably with *gem*, although it more often designates a precious than a semiprecious *stone. Jewels* are cut and polished and usually set into a brooch, necklace, or other article of personal adornment. The article itself can be referred to as a *jewel,* but is probably more often described as **jewelry**. *Jewelry* embraces not only *gems* and *jewels* that have been set but also those articles of small worth known as costume *jewelry:* rings, pins, etc., manufactured with inexpensive metals, plastic, or imitation *stones*.

Gem and *jewel* are both used figuratively and informally to describe a person or thing that is valuable or highly thought of. A *gem* is something that has intrinsic worth, a *jewel* something one prizes for personal as well as objective reasons. [That Daumier is a *gem* of a lithograph; It's a *jewel* of a restaurant; the beef dishes are divine.] People characterized as *jewels* usually have done something to warrant the appellation. [My *jewel* of a nursemaid cares for our children as if they were her own.] People who are *gems* may be *jewels* as well, but they might be so named simply because of some prominent trait in their nature, even an eccentric one: Miss Skinner is a *gem*, the prototype of the devoted teacher.

Ice and **rock** are slang terms. *Ice* means diamonds,

but is used loosely to mean valuable *jewelry* of any kind. A *rock* is a precious *stone*, especially a large diamond.

general

accepted
common
popular
public
universal

These adjectives all imply wide appeal, use, influence, and the like. **General** means current among the majority of the persons, things, or class specified: the *general* opinion. A *general* favorite is widely liked. **Common** applies to many or a large part; a *common* belief is one widely shared. **Universal** applies to all members or to the whole of a class of things; a *universal* truth holds in all instances. [It may be said that good health is a *general* condition, that occasional sickness is *common,* and that death is *universal.*]

Accepted means commonly recognized, believed, or approved: Wearing a jacket and tie to a good restaurant was once an *accepted* convention. While *accepted* emphasizes willing compliance and approval, **popular**, as here considered, points to its etymological meaning, of the people, that is, the common people, and thus emphasizes source rather than extent of recognition: a *popular* myth that the bite of the tarantula causes madness; Watching TV is a *popular* pastime.

Public pertains to people at large or to the community. In its suggestion of an organized or quasi-organized body of people, *public* differs from the other adjectives here considered. [*Public*-opinion polls indicate a *general* feeling among the people that *accepted* standards of behavior are being deliberately flouted by students and others.] See PREVALENT, SINCERE, USUAL.

Antonyms: QUEER, SPECIFIC, *uncommon,* UNPARALLELED.

generous

bountiful
lavish
liberal
magnanimous

These adjectives refer either to considerate, tolerant persons who readily give of themselves or their money or to large helpings or sizable offerings. **Generous**, the most general, suggests kind concern and willingness to help others in tangible ways: a teacher *generous* with the time he devotes to after-class conferences; the *generous* habit of sharing her available money with less fortunate friends. It can also suggest tolerance rather than narrow faultfinding: *generous* in his estimates of the plays he reviews. When used of a helping of food or an offer of any kind, it suggests an amount greater than the receiver might have expected: a *generous* slice of beef; a *generous* offer to take a smaller down payment than usual. *Generous* is sometimes used ironically to suggest its opposite: *generous* with her criticism, frugal with her praise.

More formal than *generous,* **magnanimous** is more likely to refer to well-intentioned kindness than to monetary generosity. In this sense it may suggest courteous consideration given equally to everyone as a matter of principle, whereas *generous* is more likely to suggest a spontaneous impulse to help a particular person not so much out of principle as out of fondness: so *magnanimous* that she tended to forget that not everyone in the group shared her unselfish motives for belonging. *Magnanimous,* in fact, can sometimes suggest an unconscious condescension or paternalism toward inferiors: giving *magnanimous* praise for his hopeless efforts to balance their checking account. *Magnanimous* would not be used to describe a *generous* serving, but when used of an offer, it suggests restrained formality, possibly involving better terms than the receiver deserves: a *magnanimous* offer to buy the painting despite its unreliable provenance.

Bountiful is still more formal than *magnanimous* and in the sense of *generous* is now mostly reserved for references to the Deity: *Bountiful* Lord. It occurs in a satiric phrase referring to charity that is condescending, self-righteous, and smug: playing the lady *bountiful*. In more common uses, it suggests productivity and is often used for rhetorical effect: a *bountiful* harvest; the *bountiful* land.

Liberal and **lavish** most often refer to large servings or offers or to sizable expenditures of money: a sundae with a *liberal* sprinkling of nuts; a *liberal* trade-in offer on old cars; a *liberal* spender. *Lavish* goes beyond *liberal* in suggesting an excessive or unduly large amount or degree. In some senses it can suggest an excessive generosity adopted pretentiously for show: *lavish* displays of affection. In the stricter sense of *generous*, *liberal* can be used of a person, but here it suggests a permissive, easygoing nature: a doctor who was *liberal* about interpreting hospital visitation rules when doing so might raise a patient's morale. Sometimes *liberal* can even suggest carelessness or moral flabbiness: a *liberal* disregard for fine ethical distinctions. See BENEVOLENCE, PREVALENT.

Antonyms: *chary,* GREEDY, *niggardly, parsimonious, selfish, sparing, tight.*

genetic. Do not confuse the adjective *genetic* (produced by genes) with the adjective *congenital* (existing since birth).

genius

aptitude
bent
faculty
gift
instinct
knack
talent

These nouns all refer to innate or superior ability. **Genius**, the strongest, is conceived as a mental power far beyond explanation in terms of heritage or education and manifests itself by exceptional originality and extraordinary intelligence, surpassing that of most intellectually superior people: the *genius* of Leonardo da Vinci, whose notebooks, written in the late 15th and early 16th centuries, include designs of flying machines, improvements in weaponry, and complicated labor-saving mechanical systems utilizing gears and pulleys, as well as detailed scientific observations in biology, geology, and other subjects. *Genius* may be applied particularly to a single area: the artistic *genius* of a Picasso, whose unique achievement merits his dominant place in the history of art.

An **aptitude** is a natural or acquired ability to learn and become proficient, while a **faculty** is a particular mental skill or power. While *aptitude* suggests quickness in learning, often in gaining mastery of an academic discipline or artistic skill, *faculty* is at once more modest and more general in application, suggesting only an inhering attribute or skill. [He lacks completely the *faculty* of self-criticism; an early *aptitude* for mathematics; The child demonstrated her *aptitude* for music by the ease with which she picked out melodies by ear.]

Talent is a particular and uncommon *aptitude* for some special work or activity; it is conceived of as an inborn resource that may or may not be developed. Whereas *genius* applies to general intellectual or artistic superiority, *talent* is a specific natural endowment or **gift**: a *talent* for designing clothes for young women; a remarkable *talent* for staging and directing plays. *Genius* may also be used in the sense of special *aptitude:* to have a *genius* for turning a small invest-ment into a successful business. *Gift* is akin to *genius* but on a lower plane: the *gift* of a poet's sensibility and verbal acumen. *Gift* emphasizes the inborn quality of a skill. Unlike *talent, gift* does not necessarily imply creative ability or originality: a *gift* of intensely appreciating music; the *gift* of enjoying life. *Gift* may apply to any striking or remarkable personal ability or power.

Whereas *faculty* is most often used positively when applied to an interpersonal quality, *talent,* and especially *genius,* being progressively more exaggerated and figurative in such contexts, are often used negatively and emphatically, sometimes with comical effect. [He has the *faculty* of saying the right thing at the right time; He has a *talent* for saying the wrong thing at the wrong time; He has a positive *genius* for putting his foot in his mouth.]

An **instinct**, as here considered, is a natural *aptitude,* in which sense it is really an extension of its basic psychobiological meaning referring to an animal's innate tendency or response to act in ways essential to its development or preservation. *Instinct* usually implies innate disposition rather than *talent.* [Good salespersons know by *instinct* the best approach to take with any customer; He has the *instincts* of an athlete: he really goes all out to win.] *Instinct* can, however, be used of qualities that are not inborn but have been so thoroughly acquired that they seem as if they were: an *instinct* for making money; to develop an *instinct* for staying out of trouble. In this sense *instinct* is close to **knack**, which refers to an ability to do something readily and well; *knack* applies more often to social than to intellectual situations: a *knack* for knowing when to leave a party; Some people have the *knack* of being able to keep silent without making others feel ill at ease.

Bent refers to personal inclination or penchant; it does not necessarily imply an accompanying *aptitude,* but since it is human nature to like doing what one does well, *aptitude* and *bent* are often present in the same person. [My daughter has a mechanical *bent*—she's always tearing motors apart and putting them back together again; Politicians seldom have any aesthetic *bent;* From his earliest years he had a literary *bent,* but never showed much *aptitude* for creative writing.] *Bent* often suggests devotion and industry: She demonstrated her *bent* for music by willingly practicing six hours a day. See ATTAINMENT, SKILL.

genuine

actual
authentic

real
true

These adjectives all refer to the idea that something is in fact what it is represented to be. In this sense **genuine** is the most general of this group of adjectives and applies to anything having the origin, authorship, or character claimed for it: a *genuine* example of cuneiform inscription; a *genuine* painting by Goya; a *genuine* bargain. **Authentic** is often interchangeable with *genuine:* an *authentic* (or *genuine*) antique. But *authentic* emphasizes formal proof or documentation that an article is what it is claimed to be, whereas *genuine* simply asserts that the article is not spurious, adulterated, or counterfeit. [The geologists declared the fragment to be an *authentic* specimen of a rare fossil; an *authentic* Utrillo, verified by prominent art connoisseurs; an *authentic* replica of the drawing; *genuine* silver, unmixed with other metals.]

Actual means existing in fact, not imaginary, and is synonymous with one sense of **real**: an *actual* (or *real*) event in history. *Actual,* however, need not refer to physically existent things, whereas *real* usually does in this sense: an *actual* change in the rules; She was seen as a *real* person, not someone invented in a dream. *Real* also means being in accordance with appearance or claim, not artificial or counterfeit, and is in this sense often synonymous with *genuine:* a *real* (or *genuine*) alibi; *real* (or *genuine*) money. The emphasis on appearance, however, sometimes distinguishes *real* from *genuine:* a *real* feast (that is, a meal having the aspect of a feast); a *real* lecher (that is, a person having the appearance or manner of a lecher). *Genuine,* if used in these examples, would convey a more conspicuous sense of personal style and a greater degree of informality.

True means being *real* or natural: a *true* specimen; *true* gold. In many contexts it is interchangeable with *real* and often with *genuine* as well: a *true* (or *real*) feast; a *true* (or *real* or *genuine*) solution to a problem. Note that *true* in some contexts, as in *a true alibi*, is ambiguous, in that it can mean either conforming to the facts of the matter (that is, with the truth) or being in accordance with the appearance of a *genuine* alibi (that is, not appearing spurious or contrived). Obviously, a *true* alibi in the latter sense may well in *actual* fact be false. See ACCURATE, TRUTHFUL.

Antonyms: ARTIFICIAL, *fake, forged, imaginary,* SPURIOUS.

get

acquire
gain

obtain
procure

These verbs refer to coming into possession of something. **Get** is the most general of these, with a wide range of uses including every situation discussed here; it can apply to forceful seizure as well as to passive reception: The FBI always *gets* its man; *getting* the joke long after everyone else in the room was in hysterics. The use of *get* in idiomatic phrases is, of course, manifold and since some of these idioms may be informal, writers may feel the need to replace it wherever possible with **obtain**. *Obtain* is certainly more formal, but as a mere substitute for *get* it often may sound pretentious: *getting* her to sign the paper; *obtaining* her signature on the paper; urging people over 40 to *get* a physical checkup at least once a year; recommending that mature persons *obtain* a physical examination annually if not more frequently. *Obtain* is more precisely used in formal contexts where the stress is on the seeking out of something; here, *get* might not indicate clearly enough this intended meaning: an unmanned spacecraft that could *obtain* soil samples from other planets and return to earth with them.

Gain goes beyond *obtain* to indicate greater effort in the seeking process; it can indicate forceful seizure, as in the military sense: *gaining* the victory after a bloody battle. *Gain* can also suggest an increase in something already possessed, or a piece-by-piece process of *obtaining* something: *gaining* additional honors with each new book she published; *gaining* ground on the speeding car. **Acquire** points to a piecemeal process of possession that is continuous and often slow: *acquiring* a controlling interest in the company over many years of stock purchases; assiduously *acquiring* a fine collection of Impressionist paintings. As in these cases, *acquire* is often used in a context of financial transactions. It can also suggest the effort or exposure required to gain less tangible things, as in the learning process: wishing to *acquire* a speaking knowledge of French; forced to pretend that he had *acquired* a taste for broccoli.

Procure implies maneuvering to possess something, suggesting involved, contrived, or even shady dealings. Thus, the tone of *procure* ranges from neutrality to disapproval: the complicated requisition forms used by the Quartermaster Corps to *procure* supplies; a system of *procuring* favors from politicians. Most specifically, the verb can pertain to the act of pimping or pandering, that is, *obtaining* women to gratify the lust of others: a man who *procured* prostitutes for sailors in waterfront bars. This meaning of *procure* is often present as an overtone in its other uses. See ACCUMULATE, REACH.

Antonyms: *give up, let go, lose,* RELINQUISH.

ghost

   apparition
   phantom
   shade
   specter
   spirit
   spook
   wraith

These nouns refer to supernatural manifestations or appearances. **Ghost** is the general word for the appearance of a dead person in the semblance of his living form: the *ghost* of Hamlet's father. *Ghost* once could refer more widely to the soul or any nonmaterial being, but this survives only in a few phrases: the Holy *Ghost;* give up the *ghost*. **Wraith** contrasts with *ghost* in specifically indicating the *ghost*like manifestation of a person still alive but about to die: The *wraith* of her husband, long missing in action, appeared to her in a dream. *Wraith* can, however, refer less precisely to other supernatural manifestations. Metaphorically, it can refer to someone who is thin or to anything faint: the *wraith* of a child who sat in the refugee hospital; a *wraith* of smoke lazing up from the chimney.

Shade now sounds either high-flown or affected, except in the humorous exclamation *shades of,* suggesting that one thing is unfortunately reminiscent of another: "*Shades of* Cézanne!" she said with a yawn, after looking over her friend's new painting. **Spook** indicates downright cynicism, skepticism, or amusement at the notion that *ghosts* exist: men and women so thwarted by life that they begin seeing *spooks* just for excitement.

Spirit is the most general of these nouns in the sense of indicating any sort of nonmaterial existent being; this may include the souls of living things, the *ghosts* of dead things, the essence of bodiless forms that have never been born and never died, and, in fact, the godhead itself: *spirits* of unborn children; the *spirits* assigned by Hinduism to snakes, frogs, and water buffaloes; the angelic *spirits;* the creator *Spirit* of the universe. It can also, in another sense, contrast all nonmaterial or mental life with that of matter or body: living the life of the *spirit;* afflicted both in body and *spirit*. It can also refer less metaphysically to the essence of anything: the materialistic *spirit* of the age. **Apparition** can refer to any supernatural manifestation; often it suggests a detailed or narrative vision

vouchsafed to someone: an *apparition* in which Joseph was warned to take his family and flee to Egypt. It can also refer to the form seen in a vision: an *apparition* that had wings, wore a halo, and streamed with divine light. The noun may suggest a sudden appearance: an *apparition* that stopped them in the midst of their flight. Often, *apparition* suggests something pleasant or beautiful, which explains its usual metaphorical point: She was an *apparition* of loveliness in her new gown.

Specter contrasts with *apparition* in suggesting any sort of terrifying supernatural manifestation: the gruesome demon or *specter* that tormented those in the castle. Metaphorically, *specter* can suggest any unpleasant threat or prospect: the *specters* of want, hunger, and disease that hang over the world as the century draws to a close. **Phantom** can apply to any manifestation, pleasant or not. Its point may often be to raise the question of whether the appearance is real or illusory: Hamlet was unable to decide whether the *phantom* was really the *ghost* of his father or merely a guise worn by the Devil to secure his damnation. Metaphorically, *phantom* can point to any illusion, misconception, or bugbear: amputees who experience what are known as *phantom* limb phenomena; enticing the masses with the *phantom* of a future Utopia; raising the *phantom* of worldwide subjugation whenever universal disarmament is suggested.

gibe. Do not confuse the verb *gibe* (jeer) with the verb *jibe* (agree or fit with).

give

   accord
   award
   confer
   grant

These verbs all mean hand over freely to another. To **give** is primarily to transfer to another's possession without compensation, but the verb also has many extended senses; a boxer *gives* a blow, a clock *gives* time, a delinquent child *gives* trouble. *Give* is the most general verb in this group and may be used interchangeably with any of the others in most contexts.

Award usually implies that the thing *given* is deserved, and the giver is in some sense a judge. Thus, prizes are *awarded* to those who win contests, and damages are *awarded* to those who win civil lawsuits. **Accord** implies that the thing *given* either is deserved or is proper or suitable to the receiver for some other reason. Thus, one may *accord* praise to those who do good deeds, but may also *accord* respect to one's superiors merely because of their status.

To **confer** is to *give* in approval or as a reward: to *confer* knighthood; to *confer* an honorary degree.

Grant implies that one gives something out of generosity, mercy, or a sense of justice, often in response to supplication. *Grant* points strongly to the giver's discretion to do as he or she pleases, and to the would-be receiver as depending utterly on that discretion: a captain who *granted* his crew a shore leave; to *grant* a favor to a friend; to *grant* female students the privilege of entertaining men in their dormitory during certain hours of the day. See AWARD, OFFER, RELINQUISH.

Antonyms: *take back, withdraw, withhold.*

gloomy

dark
dreary
gray
murky
somber

These adjectives describe dimly lit, unpleasant places or pessimistic frames of mind. **Gloomy** is the most general of these adjectives. In reference to places, it can suggest poor lighting: *gloomy* hallways through which I had to grope my way. But it now more often suggests drabness: three *gloomy*, narrow rooms without a stick of furniture anywhere. In reference to a mental state, *gloomy* suggests someone who sees the hopeless side of any problem: his *gloomy* comments on the troubles they would have in clearing customs. In this context, *gloomy* has an overtone of criticism that suggests unnecessary worry. **Dreary** most appropriately describes drab surroundings rather than states of mind: escaping from a *dreary*, small-town existence. Used more loosely, *dreary* is often meant to convey disapproval of a situation both tedious and sordid: the *dreary* machinations of corrupt politicians.

Somber and **murky** may both describe dimly lit surroundings: a clouded moon that made the path *somber* and forbidding; London streets made *murky* by fog. *Somber*, however, is the one adjective here that may have positive overtones in suggesting a restrained despair or a subdued, stark simplicity of effect: her *somber* acceptance of the bad news that stood in such sharp contrast to his hysterical cries of self-pity; the novel's *somber* purity that removed it so decidedly from the charge of fashionable nihilism. The special overtones of *murky* suggest something clouded in confusing obscurity: motives that must always remain *murky* no matter how we attempt to reconstruct the actions of the killer.

Dark and **gray** suggest a literal dimness or a gloomy outlook: the *dark* house; the *dark* cast of his mind; another *gray* morning of mist and rain. In referring to states of mind, however, *gray* has a special overtone of dull, unrelieved sameness: the *gray* monotony of the days behind her, the *gray* stretch of days that still lay before her. See BLEAK, DISMAL.

Antonyms: *BRIGHT, CHEERFUL.*

go

advance
move
proceed
progress
rise

These verbs are comparable when they mean exhibit motion or other activity in a forward or upward direction or toward some specific goal. **Go** and **move** are the most general and include among their implications the ideas of **advance** and **rise**. *Advance* is the most explicit in indicating a forward direction, and *rise* is the most explicit in indicating an upward direction. Thus, an infantry unit may be ordered to *go* or to *advance* to the top of the next hill. An army may get an order to *move* or *advance* at dawn. Prices may *advance* or *rise*; a stagnant economy may be made to *move* or *advance*. A stalled automobile may be made to *go* or *move*.

To **proceed** is to begin or continue to *go* or *advance* in an orderly fashion, especially when used in the imperative. [*Proceed* to the next order of business; *Proceed* to the next crossroad.]

Progress means *advance* or *move* toward a definite goal. [A schoolchild *progresses* toward graduation; The moon *progresses* through its successive phases.] See LEAVE (depart).

Antonyms: *STOP (cease).*

gobbledegook

claptrap
garbage
gibberish
nonsense
officialese

These nouns all denote writing or speech that suffers from overuse of obscure, ponderous, or meaningless words, or that is worthless and empty of significance.

Gobbledegook (or *gobbledygook*) is confused or even unintelligible speech or writing, especially when it is used to express a simple idea. "Do not become involved in a colloquy with the bench, but proceed without undue delay to discharge your obligation for violation of the city ordinance" is *gobbledegook* for "Don't argue with the judge—pay the fine."

Officialese is the *gobbledegook* found in legal, governmental, educational, or other formal speech or writing. "There should be implementation to meet the unmet needs of that segment of society that is socially and economically oppressed and to provide motivation for mobility away from self-demeaning indigence and morale-destroying dependence" is *officialese* for "Let's get people off the welfare rolls who are able to work." Both *gobbledegook* and *officialese* make communication difficult and dull without making it more accurate.

Gibberish emphasizes the unintelligibility of difficult or esoteric expression that may sometimes be *gobbledegook* or sometimes a terminology or a language with which one is unfamiliar. [Higher mathematics is *gibberish* to most people; The Ainus of Japan speak a *gibberish* unrelated to any other language; Those who follow the stock market reports communicate in a *gibberish* all their own.]

In the context of this discussion **nonsense** stresses language that is absurd or that lacks meaning and common sense. *Nonsense* may suggest incorrect or irrelevant remarks arising from stupidity or ignorance: His comments are always *nonsense*. Or it may suggest deliberate playfulness in the use of language: Many children's rhymes and play songs are charming *nonsense*.

Claptrap is a form of expression designed to attract and win popular approval by use of cheap sensationalism or artifice. It stresses worthlessness and showiness: a piece of *claptrap* passing for a serious study of modern life; an impassioned political speech full of *claptrap*.

Garbage, here a slang term, carries stronger opprobrium than either *nonsense* or *claptrap* in that it is written or spoken language that is not only without merit but often objectionable. [She talks a lot of sentimental *garbage* about her dog having a soul; Even the most intelligent children are apt to have seen a vast amount of *garbage* on television by the time they have grown up.] See SLANG.

goodness
integrity
morality
probity
purity
rectitude
righteousness
virtue

Goodness has the broadest meaning of the nouns in this list and, as here compared, stresses inherent qualities of moral excellence and an underlying compassion. *Goodness* is applied to the Deity, to saints, and to persons whose actions are characterized by a transcendent humanity or ethical commitment.

The other nouns in this list are examples of moral excellence that is acquired or striven for. Of these, **morality** is the broadest, in that it may mean moral excellence based on religious teaching or on adherence to a code of ethics. **Righteousness** is limited mostly to religious use and means either a strict fidelity to divine law or a code of conduct based on it. **Purity** in this sense is also limited in its use. It is usually found in such contexts as a life of *purity*, *purity* of motives, and the like and implies an absence of faults rather than a positive striving for moral excellence.

Virtue is a broad word meaning moral excellence based on a conscious effort to do the right thing. Found often in religious contexts, *virtue* is also applied in connection with worldly, day-to-day actions.

Integrity, **probity**, and **rectitude** all imply a strict adherence to a stern code of ethics. *Integrity* and *probity* are based on an undeviating honesty that imputes broad *virtue* to the subject. *Rectitude* is a strict adherence to rules of right, justice, and the like and carries a strong suggestion of self-discipline. See BENEVOLENCE, FAVORABLE, HONEST, MORAL.

Antonyms: *badness, depravity, evil, foulness, immorality,* WRONGDOING.

gourmet
gastronome
glutton
gourmand

These nouns refer to people who have an intense interest in food. **Gourmet** indicates someone who is a connoisseur of good cooking and is knowledgeable and discriminating about food preparation and service. *Gourmet* suggests a taste for elegance and a concern for all aspects of the ritual of dining, including the selection of foods and wines that are thought to harmonize with each other: as much a *gourmet* of Indian as of Mexican or Chinese cuisine; thinking to pass himself off as a *gourmet* by criticizing the modest rosé she had chosen to accompany their seafood dinner. **Gastronome** is a more formal substitute for *gourmet* but, if anything, suggests even more knowledge about everything pertaining to food: expatiating like a true *gastronome* on the effect to be obtained by spicing the filet with marjoram instead of thyme.

Gourmand suggests someone for whom the eating of food itself is the primary interest. Although the *gourmand* may appreciate good cooking, he or she judges this more by its taste than by the canon of rules and regulations the *gourmet* or *gastronome* may be privy to: wives who treat their husbands like *gourmets* only to find them responding like *gourmands;* A *gourmand* must have originated the notion that the proof of the pudding is in the eating. **Glutton** is in sharp contrast to all these nouns by suggesting a person totally indifferent to the fine points of cooking and perhaps even to the taste of food. The main emphasis is on insatiable appetite and the devouring of food in great quantities: food so tasteless and ill-prepared that it could appeal only to a starving man or a *glutton*. *Glutton* is often used with humorous intention to describe an insatiable craving for a particular food: hot spells that turn some of us into *gluttons* for ice cream and watermelon. See EAT.

graphic

pictorial
picturesque
vivid

These adjectives describe things that have visual impact or are dramatically appealing. **Graphic** may refer as neutral description to work that uses the elements and techniques of visual design: training in all phases of the *graphic* arts. It also extends metaphorically to anything having the clarity and power of written, printed, diagrammatic, or visualized illustration: a *graphic* lesson in the pitfalls of befriending strangers; photographs that not only illustrate the article but lend it *graphic* force; giving *graphic* examples of how the two theories conflict. **Vivid** is much more general and less specific than *graphic*. Most strictly it suggests forceful visual representation or the use of dramatic *graphic* elements, especially color: the *vivid* colors of the painting; a self-portrait that was a *vivid* study of the sag and breakdown of flesh in old age. *Vivid*, of course, is used widely outside the visual arts for anything that has a heightened or concentrated dramatic impact: a speech denouncing his opponent in *vivid* terms; her *vivid* portrayal of Lady Macbeth.

Pictorial is often restricted to the neutrally descriptive aspect of *graphic*, referring to elements of visual design or to the fact that something is represented visually or contains pictures: *pictorial* maga-

zines; a film director strong in handling the *pictorial* elements but weak in giving a story line any sense of momentum. It may also refer to something that evokes visual images: a fiction writer with a flair for *pictorial* description. **Picturesque** is more closely related to *vivid* in stressing things having a dramatic visual impact. The special tone of *picturesque* often suggests that a scene is thought striking because it is panoramic, quaint, strange, or unusual in some other way: Uccello's *picturesque* battle tableaux; the *picturesque* minarets of Istanbul; a *picturesque* ride on the Staten Island ferry. See PORTRAY.

grasp

clasp
clutch
grab
grip
seize
snatch

These verbs express the action of laying hold of things with the hands. To **grasp** is to take hold of firmly: He reached out, *grasped* my hand, and shook it vigorously. To **seize** is to take hold of suddenly, with force. [The hawk *seized* its prey with its talons; She *seized* the reins of the runaway horse.] Both *seize* and *grasp* are general in application and may be used figuratively as well as literally. [I don't *grasp* your meaning; The army *seized* power.] **Grab** is more informal, suggesting roughness in *seizing* or undue haste in getting hold of something. [He *grabbed* the child's arm and pulled her out of the path of the car; You may have a piece of candy, but don't *grab*.] In some contexts, both *grab* and *grasp* may imply greed. [She was greedy and *grasping;* When his uncle died, he *grabbed* everything he could get his hands on.] To **snatch** is to *grab* abruptly, with a sudden jerk, but where one may sometimes *grab* with the arms in order to hold, one *snatches* with the hands in order to take away. [Instead of *grabbing* my mother, the thief *snatched* her purse and ran.] When both *snatch* and *grab* mean take, *snatch* implies greater haste and violence, suggesting urgency or desperation: Ravenous, the man *snatched* the pizza out of my hands. *Snatch* may express the *seizing* of something one has no right to, but this is not always the case. Still, the haste of a person who *snatches* is often prompted by fear of consequences, whether acting from good motives or bad. [She *snatched* the matches away from the child; The fireman *snatched* up the baby and carried him out of the burning house.] Both *snatch* and *grab* are also used in a more informal sense, meaning get in what little time is available: to *grab* a bite to eat before the show; to *snatch* a few hours of sleep between performances.

Where *grasp* and *grab* mean take hold of, *grasp* and **grip** mean hold. A person *grasps* with a firm but moderate closure of the whole hand. He *grips* with the strongest muscular closure of the hand he can exert. To *grasp* is to hold firmly; to *grip* is to hold tight. [He *gripped* my hand until it hurt; He *gripped* the railing to pull himself up.] **Clasp** may mean *grasp* firmly in or with the hand: The children *clasped* hands and formed a circle. Or *clasp* may mean hold in the arms in an encircling embrace: The child *clasped* her doll protectively. A person *clasps* or **clutches** something to prevent its escape or removal, but as *grip* implies a stronger *grasping,* so *clutch* implies a stronger *clasping:* She *clutched* the doll tenaciously. *Clutch* may simply mean *grasp* and hold firmly: roots that *clutch.* Or both *clutch* and *grasp,* when followed by *at,* may mean try to get hold of. A drowning man *clutches* (or *grasps*) at straws. But *clutch* implies a greater eagerness or urgency than *grasp* and may suggest desperation. Whether holding tight or only trying for a firm hold, the person who *clutches* feels frighteningly insecure. [She *clutched* her purse tightly, fearing a thief might *snatch* it; He *clutched* at my arm as he fell.] See CAP-TURE, CARRY.

Antonyms: *abandon, loose, release, relinquish.*

grateful

appreciative
thankful

These adjectives all indicate warm feelings or expressions of gratitude. **Grateful** and **thankful** are close in meaning, but one distinction is commonly observed in that *grateful* is used to describe our feelings of gratitude to another person, and *thankful* refers to similar feelings toward divine providence, fate, or some less immediate agency. One is *grateful* for a gift or a kind word, but *thankful* for good health or fair weather. **Appreciative**, more than the other two adjectives, indicates a demonstration of the gratitude a person feels: an executive assistant so *appreciative* of the opportunity for advancement her employer had given her that she worked overtime even when not asked to do so. See APPROVAL, ENDORSE, PRAISE.

Antonyms: *indifferent, ungrateful.*

grave

cenotaph
crypt

mausoleum
sepulcher
tomb
vault

These nouns refer to burial places of the dead. **Grave** is the most general, referring to any place where a body or bodies are buried: the mass *grave* outside Auschwitz; the *graves* in the cemetery near Omaha Beach; pyramids that were the *graves* for kings. While *grave* can also commonly be thought of as the pit or opening in earth into which a body is placed, **tomb** usually suggests some sort of enclosure, whether above or below ground, constructed to house the dead; it also often implies the existence of some sort of monument that contains the dead person and commemorates the person's life.

While **sepulcher** can be simply a more formal term for *grave* or *tomb,* it may also suggest an above-ground house or room in which the coffins of the dead are kept; such a chamber might adjoin or be part of a church. In any case, *sepulcher* tends to suggest an architectural display greater than that suggested by *tomb.* Most specifically, *sepulcher* may refer to a resting place for holy relics, especially when this is near or part of a church altar. A **mausoleum** specifically stresses the splendor and lavishness of a structure designed to hold one or more coffins. It would be a more exact term than *sepulcher* for such a building.

Both **crypt** and **vault** refer to burial chambers either wholly or partly underground. *Vault* suggests that the roof of such a chamber is arched, but not necessarily. *Crypt* is commonly used specifically for a *vault* that lies under the main floor of a church. Both nouns suggest a place for more than one coffin, although *vault* can also refer to a metal or concrete casing in which a coffin is placed before being lowered into a *grave.*

Although not a *grave* in the literal sense of being a burial place, **cenotaph** refers to a type of empty *tomb* or *mausoleum* erected in commemoration of the dead but not containing the remains, which have been buried elsewhere or have never been found.

great

eminent
illustrious
notable
noteworthy
preeminent
reputable

These adjectives describe persons distinguished either by social standing or by accomplishment. **Great** is the most general and informal of these adjectives and has a wide range of uses outside this context. Here, it may refer to groups that possess wealth, influence, or position: the *great* families of Boston. Or it may refer to an accomplished person or the person's accomplishments: a *great* composer; Newton's *great* discovery. *Great* is more far-reaching in the latter sense, since it implies that an accomplishment has been critically evaluated or tested by time in light of its contribution to art, knowledge, or humanity. The social sense of *great,* by contrast, merely implies the winning of status in a constricted or transitory sphere.

Reputable, while much more formal, functions like *great* in both ways. In either case, however, it may point to mere acceptance or absence of fault rather than to the genuine brilliance of a person or the person's work in its own right: a *reputable* family of successful merchants; a *reputable* scholar, a bit on the dry side; a *reputable* but outdated work on the subject. *Reputable* implies approval by those in a position to know rather than far-reaching fame. This makes it the mildest of the adjectives here. **Illustrious**, the strongest term here, shows the sharpest possible contrast with *reputable,* since it always suggests fame or glory. *Illustrious,* furthermore, is mostly restricted to the accomplished or to their accomplishments and may not necessarily indicate a *reputable* person at all: *illustrious* deeds; an *illustrious* poet who scandalized the *reputable* upper classes of his day. When used in the context of social standing, *illustrious* usually applies to people who have added brilliant accomplishments to wealth, status, or rank: an *illustrious* family that gave England some of its finest generals, statesmen, and thinkers over several centuries.

Notable and **noteworthy** are somewhat stronger in tone than *reputable,* but both apply more exclusively to accomplished people or to their accomplishments. Both adjectives would seem to point to something that merits attention, but in practice *notable* indicates those people or things that are actually known, respected, or admired, whereas *noteworthy* indicates what is worthy of attention but may not yet have received it: several *notable* authors who are scheduled to publish books in the coming season; the only critic to characterize the book as a *noteworthy* attempt despite its failure. In short, *notable* often suggests successful achievement, *noteworthy* a promising effort.

Eminent is considerably stronger in emphasis than all the preceding terms but *illustrious.* Here, however, *eminent* functions equally well in the contexts both of social status and of accomplishment: families considered *eminent* enough to be listed in the Social Register; an *eminent* scientist. *Eminent* has a dignified tone, suggesting solid, well-respected values, and points to the most admired members of a given class. This makes *eminent* less pertinent to the arts than to the academic disciplines, the sciences, or the learned professions: an *illustrious* painter; an *eminent* critic; an *eminent* Supreme Court Justice. **Preeminent** is a superlative for *eminent,* indicating a person who is the most respected of an already admired group. It also tends to suggest a position of great power and authority: the *preeminent* molder of taste in her era. Neither of this pair is likely to be used in describing an accomplishment. Moreover, in emphasizing respectability *eminent* and *preeminent* do not approach *illustrious* in suggesting widespread renown. A person may be *eminent,* even *preeminent* in a field and still not be in any way *illustrious.* See FAMOUS, OUTSTANDING, SIGNIFICANT.

Antonyms: *obscure, unknown.*

greedy

acquisitive
avaricious
covetous
envious
gluttonous
miserly
rapacious
stingy

These adjectives describe various kinds of insatiable desire for food, money, power, or material possessions. **Greedy**, the most general, is less formal than some of the other terms in this group. Although *greedy* can refer to a desire for money, power, or property, it more commonly relates to an inordinate desire for food. [He stuffed one chocolate after another into his *greedy* mouth; *Greedy* for profits, speculators lay waste virgin forests throughout the West.] *Greedy* less readily suggests the use of unethical means in seeking satisfaction: A *greedy* child left undisciplined may grow up to be a selfish adult.

Avaricious is a more formal term than *greedy* and suggests an unbalanced, almost fanatic desire for money or possessions: The *avaricious* child abandoned his toys as soon as he got them, but still cried for more. The overtones possible in *avaricious* relate it to three much more informal adjectives: **gluttonous**, **stingy**, and **miserly**. *Gluttonous* puts the emphasis on consumption, most commonly of food. [His *gluttonous* appetite made short work of all the leftovers.] *Stingy* emphasizes a lack of generosity, especially the reluctance to spend money. [She was so *stingy* that she never tipped a delivery boy.] *Miserly* refers more to the hoarding of money or property than to either the *gluttonous* consumption or the *stingy* use of it. [Their *miserly* piling up of wealth had not made up for their inability to bear children.] *Avaricious* persons may be either *gluttonous* or *miserly,* depending on whether they consume or merely possess wealth. In either case, such persons may or may not be *stingy.* Of these four adjectives, however, *avaricious* perhaps carries the strongest suggestion of being willing to use unethical means to satisfy a given desire. [The *avaricious* lawyer had cheated his own parents out of the title to their land.]

Acquisitive is considerably more neutral in tone than any of the other adjectives. It suggests the actual process of coming into the possession of goods whether by fair means or foul. In being more externally descriptive, it puts the emphasis on the act rather than on the desire. A poor person may desire possessions, but not actually be *acquisitive* until, by some means, there is an opportunity to assemble them. [Thoreau argues that our *acquisitive* tendencies prevent us from living unburdened, joyous lives.] In contrast to the neutrality of *acquisitive,* **rapacious** is the most strongly negative of all these adjectives. It blurs together desire and act, with overtones of brutality and violence. It emphasizes the taking of things against the will of others, by force or unethical means. [He was so *rapacious* in his lust for money that he impoverished entire families.]

Envious and **covetous** are opposed to *avaricious* and especially to *acquisitive* in suggesting more the intense desire for something than the act of possessing it. The desired item, furthermore, must necessarily belong to someone else. *Envious* implies the greater passivity of the two, referring to a hostile or inverted admiration for the belongings of another. Sometimes it is the impossibility of possessing them that provides the key. [He would always be *envious* of his brother's extraordinary success.] *Covetous* is the more intense of the two and the less passive, shading off toward *avaricious* in its potential for being acted upon. [The ninth and tenth commandments are a sharp condemnation of the *covetous* person.] Both *envious* and *covetous* can apply to a wider range of desired goods or qualities than the other adjectives grouped here. See EAGER, OPPORTUNISTIC, YEARN.

Antonyms: GENEROUS.

greet
accost
address
hail
salute
welcome

These verbs all refer to the words or actions offered or exchanged in the first moments of a meeting. **Greet** can indicate any sign of recognition or acknowledgment; on first glance it might be thought to suggest a warm, friendly, or cheerful response: *greeting* the children with a whoop of delight. But this is far from invariable: *greeting* him with a stiff, strained silence. **Welcome** is more specific than *greet* in indicating that one person receives another into a given situation, either as a newcomer or as one returning to it. Here, *welcome* may more often suggest a warm, official, or formal reception: *welcoming* him back into the household with a passionate embrace; a committee of sophomores to *welcome* the arriving freshmen; a ceremony *welcoming* the visiting dignitary to the city. But again, *welcome* need not always carry this positive tone: *welcoming* him each night with sullen stares and a stream of faultfinding remarks.

Hail now has largely been reduced to the special situation of *welcoming* someone as a high honor: a ticker-tape parade to *hail* the visiting astronauts. It can refer, in fact, to any ovation, without any notion of *welcoming* whatsoever. A related use pertains to calling out in order to attract someone's attention: *hailing* a taxicab; *hailing* an old friend on the street. Like *hail,* **salute** can indicate any act of celebrating or honoring someone: a benefit performance to *salute* the Oscar winners. It now functions in terms of meeting only in the military context, where it refers to the obligatory hand gestures presented in passing between officers or between officers and enlisted personnel.

In the context of meetings, **address** may focus on the manner of *greeting* or the exact terms used: *addressing* him by his first name. It may also suggest approaching a stranger or speaking to bystanders in general or at random: *addressing* her question to one of the women in the crowd; *addressing* his plea for help to everyone in the restaurant. In a wider context, of course, *address* refers to formal speech or planned discourse: *addressing* the convention in a seconding speech. **Accost** more clearly restricts itself to the situation of approaching or *addressing* a stranger, often in an unfriendly or threatening way: *accosting* one of the villagers and asking for directions; the ruffian who *accosted* me and demanded my purse. The verb has been used euphemistically for a number of kinds of physical or sexual assault; hence, it can often suggest any sort of violent attack: *accosted* on a dark street and mugged. See MEET, MEETING.

gregarious
    affable
    amiable
    cordial
    friendly
    outgoing
    sociable
    social

These adjectives all describe inviting or complaisant attitudes toward other people and are alike in suggesting either an openness or willingness to make the acquaintance of others. In its broadest sense, **gregarious** is applied to animals as well as people. It involves a basic tendency to associate with one's fellows, implying a natural disposition for group living: Men and sheep are both *gregarious* animals. In another sense, *gregarious* applies to people who actively seek the society of others, preferring company to solitude, but even in this sense the implication is present of wanting to be with others of one's own kind: students who are so *gregarious* they are unable to spend an evening alone for the sake of their studies. The more dialectal or folksy term **sociable**, on the other hand, implies the seeking of a personal acquaintanceship, often in conformity with prevailing cultural mores: In some parts of the United States people consider it *sociable* to drop in on one's neighbors for an unannounced visit. **Social** is more formal than *sociable* and applies more often in this sense to an individual's temperament than to an event, often defining one aspect of a person: the *social* side of his character; They've become very *social* lately, giving at least one party a month. When applied to temperament, **outgoing** is akin to *social* but more often suggests a sociological context: an *outgoing* personality. *Outgoing* indicates a person who is not indrawn, inhibited, or shy, but on the contrary expresses himself openly and makes acquaintances easily. Because such traits are attractive to most Americans, *outgoing* is often linked with other favorable terms: a sweet, *outgoing* child; a pleasant, warm, *outgoing* teacher.

Where the foregoing adjectives focus on the active individual whose *social* antennae go out to other people, **affable** and **amiable** indicate receptivity or accessibility to the gestures of others. Etymologically, *affable* means capable of being spoken to, that is, easy to approach. It suggests a benign and courteous attitude rather than one actively seeking new friends: The easy *affable* manner of Robert Frost endeared him to the audiences to which he spoke his poems. *Amiable* has more of a note of kindliness and suggests an openness to friendship. Unlike *affable, amiable* may also refer to a disagreement or dispute that is free from antagonism or ill feeling: An *amiable* rivalry existed between the two old friends.

Friendly has a wide variety of applications. It may, like *amiable*, mean free from ill feeling: a *friendly* argument. It may mean acting as or typical of a friend: *friendly* advice; Inviting us to stay the night was a *friendly* and hospitable gesture. *Friendly* may suggest an openness to a personal relationship based on the individual natures or interests of the people concerned; in this sense it differs from the more impersonal *amiable* and *affable* and the less individually oriented *gregarious*. [She was *gregarious* but not *friendly*; she liked to be surrounded by crowds of admirers but assiduously avoided personal relationships with any of them; He was an *amiable* sort—never said a harsh word about anyone—but no one ever got very *friendly* with him; Einstein had an *affable* nature, quick to appreciate wit and with considerable personal charm, but he was nevertheless known intimately by very few and could not truly be called *friendly*.] But *friendly* is also used more broadly to refer to kindliness in people and to the absence of antagonism or menace in animals. [He was a *friendly* fellow, always ready to lend a helping hand when needed; The dog seemed *friendly* enough until I tried to pet it.]

Cordial means warm and hearty and suggests sincerity of feeling as well; it is nowadays used most often of formal situations rather than personal ones involving the private lives of individuals: A *cordial* welcome was accorded the visiting minister of state; a *cordial* greeting. Its formal context and tone should not be interpreted as somehow vitiating the sincerity of feeling *cordial* connotes; it simply suggests a formal but nonetheless genuine expression of feeling: a long and *cordial* relationship between the violinist and his protégé. See BLITHE, COMPLIANT, FRIEND.

Antonyms: ALOOF, *antisocial,* HOSTILE, *introverted, retiring, unapproachable, unsociable.*

grieve
    lament
    mourn
    sorrow

These verbs refer to the inward feeling or active expression of unhappiness at a bereavement, failure, or loss. **Grieve** has the widest range of expressiveness, concentrating on thought or feeling. It implies anguish that may or may not be openly expressed: giving no sign he had spent the morning *grieving* over his failure to get a promotion; surprised at how many attended the funeral to *grieve* over the death of their friend. **Mourn** is similar to *grieve* but is more formal. In its most solemn sense, it implies deep emotion felt over a period of time: privately *mourning* their mother's death. But *mourn* is often used for a public show of bereavement that may or may not be sincere but is often ceremonial or ritualized: to wear black as a symbol of *mourning*.

Lament comes from the Latin word for wailing or weeping. It suggests giving vocal or verbal expression to a sense of loss or bereavement: loudly *lamenting* the loss of his job; *lamenting* his wife's tragic death in uncontrolled seizures of weeping. The verb is sometimes used in a less serious sense to indicate someone who tediously verbalizes trivial disappointments: *lamenting* to all his friends about how unfairly the teacher had treated him. **Sorrow** may suggest milder feelings or a less tragic loss than the foregoing verbs; it combines sadness with regret, contrasting with *lament* by suggesting *grieving* that is inward or, at most, quietly expressed: *sorrowing* over all their missed chances to get to know each other better. In some contexts, *sorrow* as a verb may sound faintly outdated. *Grieve* contrasts with *sorrow* and *lament* in that it may apply to a forlorn animal as well as to a human being: a man *sorrowing* for weeks over the death of his dog; a dog *grieving* over the death of its master. See DEPLORE, MISERABLE, WEEP.

Antonyms: *exult, jubilate, rejoice.*

grind

    champ
    chew
    chomp
    gnash
    masticate

These verbs all refer to the action of working the jaws and rubbing the teeth together. **Grind** is the most general. It means pulverize, reduce to fine particles, as by crushing or friction: *Grinding* bones helps keep a dog's teeth clean. *Grind* also means rub together with a harsh or grating sound: The noise of his teeth *grinding* kept his wife awake all night. To *grind* one's teeth in this way as a result of rage, pain, or anguish is to **gnash**. *Gnash* more than *grind* sounds like the action it denotes, but it is often used idiomatically rather than in a literal sense: Their eviction was marked by much weeping and wailing and *gnashing* of teeth. *Gnash* also means bite by *grinding* the teeth: a hungry lion, *gnashing* its kill.

Chew and **masticate** are synonymous in designating a crushing or *grinding* with the teeth. The difference between the two verbs is that *masticate,* in addition to being more formal than *chew,* is only used in reference to food that is swallowed after the crushing or *grinding* action. One speaks, for example, of *chewing* tobacco or gum but never of *masticating* them.

Champ and its variant **chomp** mean crush and *chew* noisily. Like *gnash,* they summon up lifelike mental images. [The young ranch hand *chomped* his dinner with as much gusto as he displayed when roping a steer.] *Champ* and *chomp* are also used idiomatically to refer to a restless biting action, and by figurative extension, to restlessness or impatience shown in any way: a horse *champing* oats; a convalescent *champing* at the bit in her eagerness to return to work.

group

    band
    body
    company
    gang
    party
    troop
    troupe

These nouns refer to gatherings of people. **Group** is so general that it may be used for small or relatively large gatherings that have come about by accident or intention: the *group* of parents waiting for the plane's arrival; a study *group* formed to keep track of the opposition's proposals. While these examples suggest relatively small gatherings, *group* may be used, especially in statistical contexts, for a large number of people: the thousands of people still in the undecided *group*.

Body is nearly as general as *group,* but considerably more vague; it may refer to organized *groups:* a legislative *body;* a Protestant *body;* a *body* of foot soldiers. It may also suggest dedicated followers or a majority: a solid *body* of Agatha Christie fans; the *body* of citizens who favor fair play. Except in standard expressions, such as student *body,* it might be effectively avoided in favor of a more concrete term for *group.*

Troupe and **company** both can refer to a traveling group of performing artists. *Troupe* has mostly gone out of use, however, except for such specialized *groups* as ballet, mime, or circus performers: a dance *troupe* setting out on tour; the carnival *troupe* that straggled into town last week. *Company* is now the preferred word for plays or musicals on tour; it also suggests a legal or formal organization: the national touring *company* of the Broadway hit. *Company*, unlike *troupe*, can also refer to performing groups that do not necessarily tour: a summer stock *company*; a repertory *company*. *Company*, furthermore, has a wider range of uses for various kinds of organized *groups*, such as military units or private businesses. It can also suggest a less well-defined array of like-minded people: a *company* of homeless families.

Troop, like *company*, can refer to a military *body*, but while *company* refers to a specific unit with a definite structure, *troop* is now seldom used in this sense. In the plural, however, it refers to soldiers in general: dispatching additional *troops* to the front.

Band and **party** both may have military uses. In this context, *band* would suggest a small *group* of soldiers who have perhaps accidentally fallen together during battle: the ragged *band* of survivors. *Band*, whatever its context, suggests a close working cooperation among the members: a *band* of experts on slum clearance. It may also suggest a furtive *group*, working secretly or illegally: a guerrilla *band*; a *band* of gangsters. *Party*, in its military context, suggests a detachment deployed for a specific purpose: the landing *party*. This suggestion of subdividing a larger *body* may be present in other uses: the *group* of canvassers being divided into smaller *parties*. *Party* may also refer to one side in a struggle or contract: a battle in which both *parties* suffered heavy casualties; both *parties* to the arbitration; a system of government based on two political *parties*.

Gang is the only noun in this set with mainly negative connotations, suggesting a *group* whose purpose is the performance of illegal, violent, or hostile activities: a narcotics *gang*; a teenage *gang*. But it can refer informally to one's cronies: the old *gang* that used to have coffee together in the diner. It can also refer to a select *group* of laborers: the section *gang* on the railroad. See GATHER, MEETING.

gruesome

    ghastly
    grim
    grisly
    hideous
    lurid
    macabre

These adjectives describe what is repellently ugly or extremely distasteful. **Gruesome** may be used as a hyperbole for anything evoking such a response: a

woman of *gruesome* taste. More precisely, however, *gruesome* refers to spectacles of physical violence, or an unhealthy interest in such things: the *gruesome* atrocities committed by both sides in the tribal wars; *gruesome* murders that suggested a psychopathic killer; the *gruesome* delight with which some newspapers played up the tragedy. **Grisly** is very close to *gruesome*, but is more intense in suggesting destructive violence that springs from a brutally sadistic or abnormal mind. It would thus apply less to impersonal destruction on a mass scale, such as might occur in wartime: *grisly* indications that he had played cat and mouse with his victims before dispatching them; the *grisly* detachment with which unspeakable experiments were performed on human subjects; a *grisly* interest in descriptions of deviant sexual behavior. *Grisly* can have comic force in referring to excessively labored or vivid accounts of a clandestine nature: eager to give everyone the *grisly* details of her neighbor's divorce.

Hideous, **ghastly**, and **grim** are much less specific than the previous pair. Each is popularly used as a hyperbole. *Hideous*, however, often has reference to extreme deformation or ugliness, and *ghastly* to something frightening or filled with horror: a car accident that left *hideous* scars on his face; the *ghastly* realization that she had lost her way in the forest. *Ghastly* has a more specific reference, however, to a ghostlike or deathlike pallor, or one resulting from fear: a *ghastly* face that spoke of the harrowing experience she had suffered. *Grim* suggests something stern or forbidding, even to the point of being terrifying: the *grim* aftermath of a bloody Civil War battle.

Lurid, like *ghastly*, may suggest an extremely pale appearance: a face *lurid* with fear and shock. Paradoxically, *lurid* also suggests redness such as produced by a smoky fire: the *lurid* torches of the enraged townsmen gathering in the courtyard. More generally, *lurid* refers to anything *hideous* in its vividness: the *lurid* marks of the whip across his back. *Lurid* has special use to refer to *gruesome* or sensational verbal descriptions or pictorial treatment: *lurid* accounts of the carnage left by the two-day battle; *lurid* photographs of the airplane crash. **Macabre** refers specifically to horror-inspiring ideas or spectacles of any kind, without necessarily pointing to physical destruction of any sort: the *macabre* sexual exploits attributed to witches. *Macabre* is derived etymologically from the French *danse macabre*, dance of death, and suggests a *gruesome* and frequently bizarre interest in or connection with death: *macabre* tales of bloodsucking vampires, zombies, and other supernatural phenomena;

the routine but nonetheless *macabre* preparation of a condemned prisoner for electrocution. See BIZARRE, REPULSIVE.

Antonyms: CHARMING, *delightful*, PLEASING.

guide

conduct
direct
lead
navigate
pilot
steer

These verbs all refer to the action of showing the way to something or someone. **Guide** and **conduct** mean accompany in order to show the way to a destination. *Guide* usually indicates a close or personal relationship or a joint effort between the two parties, whereas *conduct* stresses the fact of escorting and the unequal relationship between the two parties; *conduct* may even imply helplessness or coercion. [The police officer *conducted* the suspect to the station house; The Coast Guard vessel *conducted* the damaged freighter to harbor for repairs.] *Guide* is much more general than *conduct* and may apply to any direction given one's behavior, manner of life, etc. [She was always *guided* by her principles of honesty and fair play; *Guided* by the knowledge that he had only a year to live, he sold his business and went to Provence.]

To **direct** is to indicate a course without actually *guiding:* to *direct* a stranger in town to the railroad station. To **lead** is to *guide* by going ahead of. An usher *leads* playgoers to their seats; officers *lead* their troops into combat.

Both **navigate** and **pilot** mean determine and *direct* the course of a ship or airplane. To **steer** is to *guide* in a desired direction by a rudder or other means. *Pilot* and *steer* are also often used rhetorically to indicate *guiding* through difficulties or intricacies of any kind: to *steer* the ship of state through troubled waters. See ACCOMPANY, CONTROL.

guile

craft
cunning
duplicity

These nouns refer to the clever or perceptive manipulation of facts, appearances, or people in order to attain a goal. **Guile** suggests a wily and shrewd person who uses subterfuge and stratagems to gain a desired end: Don't try to match your inexperience with the *guile* of an unscrupulous antique dealer. At its

mildest, *guile* can indicate approval, if not admiration, for a clever person who has learned that indirect means are the only effective ones to use in some complex situations: the old prospector's *guile* in eluding those who tried to trail him back to the spot where he had discovered gold. When **cunning** is used with approval, it puts a greater stress on intellectual prowess than on subtlety born of experience: The detective had used all the *cunning* at her command to discover the murderer's identity. When *cunning* is negative, it is a harsher word than *guile;* in this case its stress is on ferocity or single-minded obsessiveness. It is often used, literally or metaphorically, in reference to animals: sheer animal *cunning;* a person with the *cunning* of a wolf.

Duplicity is less ambiguous in its application; it is always negative and refers either to double-dealing or to outright lying, in which case it may have a euphemistic flavor: price fixers who practice *duplicity* to cheat the public; She admitted she had been guilty of *duplicity* in claiming another engagement that evening. **Craft** is most like *guile* in suggesting someone practiced in using indirect means to get his way. But *craft* is less often used than the first pair, except in phrases that link it with one or the other: a woman capable of incredible *craft* and *cunning;* The best poker players are those for whom *craft* and *guile* seem to be almost second nature. See DECEPTION, TRICK (n.), TRICK (v.).

Antonyms: *artlessness, candor, ingenuousness.*

gullible

credulous
naive
trusting

These adjectives describe a readiness to believe what one is told. **Gullible** emphasizes that a person can be easily tricked or cheated; **credulous** is less intense, suggesting a willingness to believe on slight evidence, without implying the presence of trickery in presenting the evidence. *Gullible* might suggest the greedy hope of getting something for nothing, so easily exploited by confidence men. *Credulous* might more appropriately suggest religious or superstitious persuasion that does not necessarily result in material gain for either the persuader or the persuaded. A *credulous* person, furthermore, might be brought to believe something without acting upon it to his own harm, whereas a *gullible* person's belief, by implication, causes him to act in a foolish way that injures himself or others. [Hamlet fears being *credulous* of the ghost's story—he must corroborate it; Shakespeare's audience saw Othello less as a jealous man than as a *gullible* one, easily duped by Iago's machinations.]

Trusting suggests the same willingness to believe as *gullible* or *credulous,* but ranges from neutrality of tone to one of approval: a *trusting* woman alone in the big city; a people so *trusting* in the guarantees of a future life as to be unshakably free of temptation. **Naive**, on the other hand, suggests an inexperienced optimism, an unawareness of the compromises life entails. A *naive* person is certainly *trusting;* he is also likely to be *credulous* and would furthermore be thought *gullible* by the sophisticate. *Naive,* however, suggests an untried or untested person rather than one necessarily *gullible.* Only when the *naive* person has actually made a fool of himself by permitting himself to be tricked does he actually become *gullible.* See NAIVE.

Antonyms: *critical, disbelieving, doubtful, dubious, questioning, skeptical.*

193

happen

befall
occur
take place
transpire

These verbs all mean come about or come to pass. **Happen** is a general term and is widely used to mean come to pass, especially by chance. [It *happened* to snow that day.] It also means chance upon or come or go by chance. [We *happened* to be in town on the night of the concert; We *happened* on their country house by pure luck; I *happened* into the bank at the very moment the robbery was taking place.] **Befall** is like *happen* in meaning come about, but while *happen* can be used in speaking about pleasant or unpleasant things, *befall* is almost always used in reference to something unpleasant. [Disaster *befell* them when they were caught in Germany at the beginning of World War II.] *Befall*, too, is considered literary in tone and much more than *happen* suggests that destiny or fate has played a part in the situation described. [Bad luck and ill health *befell* him throughout his life.]

Occur and **take place** are both equivalent to *happen* in the sense of come to pass, but while *occur* can refer to something accidental or something planned, *take place* most often suggests the presence of design. [The accident *occurred* despite all the precautions taken to prevent it; The hearing is scheduled to *take place* tomorrow morning at eleven.] **Transpire** is sometimes used as a synonym for *happen, occur,* or *take place* in the sense of come to pass: She told me what had *transpired* at the court hearing. Although widely used in this sense, *transpire* tends to sound stilted and affected. This usage is considered erroneous by many people.

happiness

beatitude
blessedness
bliss
felicity
gladness

These nouns refer to states of well-being or to the pleasurable satisfaction that accompanies such states. **Happiness** is the most general term and may imply any degree of well-being from that of mere contentment or absence of sorrow to the most intense joy and sense of fulfillment. **Felicity** is a more formal and less often used term for great and sustained *happiness:* All people by nature seek ease of mind, but few can hope for unending *felicity. Felicity* is most often used of a pertinent or effective manner or style: a *felicity* of poetic expression.

Gladness is overflowing *happiness* and suggests an emotional reaction to a pleasant event, rather than a sustained state of mind: Their *gladness* at seeing us again was most touching.

Bliss in its commonest meaning points to complete, ecstatic *happiness* or to great contentment: the *bliss* of a young couple in love; the *bliss* experienced by a cat stretching in the sun. In the religious sense, *bliss* is a state of absolute *felicity* brought about by the submergence of the self into a divine infinity, as in the state of nirvana in Buddhism.

Blessedness and **beatitude** usually refer to intense spiritual *bliss. Blessedness* implies a *happiness* so profound as to be attributed to a deity or to unusually favorable fortune. *Beatitude,* a more formal and literary word, is supreme *blessedness* that approaches the transcendent. Its most familiar use is its application to the eight declarations of *blessedness* (The *Beatitudes*) occurring in the Sermon on the Mount in the New Testament. See JOYOUS, PLEASURE.

Antonyms: *grief,* MISERY, *sadness, sorrow, unhappiness.*

hard

arduous
difficult
laborious
perplexing
troublesome
trying

These adjectives describe efforts not easily made or problems not easily solved. **Hard** is the most general and informal of these, with a wide range of possible use: *hard* labor; a *hard* assignment; a *hard* struggle. As with the rest of these adjectives, *hard* does not suggest impossibility of success so much as the extremes of effort that will be required to attain it. **Difficult** is slightly more formal and somewhat more restricted in range as compared to *hard.* Where *hard* might suggest that a burdensome exertion alone is required, *difficult* frequently stresses a more complex task that may demand control or skill: the *hard* work of unloading the crates; the *difficult* job of weighing and inspecting fruit. *Hard*, furthermore, might suggest a firm or unmerciful stand, whereas *difficult* again stresses complexity, often of a puzzling kind: a *hard* master; a *difficult* employer; taking a *hard* line on these *difficult* problems.

Laborious and **arduous** are both more formal than the preceding pair, but are otherwise more closely related to *hard* than to *difficult*. *Laborious* is more restricted than *hard* in applying almost exclusively to the use of effort or exertion in accomplishing a task, with few suggestions of the skill that might be required and no reference to the complexity of a problem: the *laborious* job of digging new foxholes overnight. *Arduous* is even more formal than *laborious* and less restricted in suggesting burdensome effort or almost unmerciful firmness of stand: our *arduous* struggle to lay the carpet before the guests arrived; *arduous* regulations that apply to all tank drivers.

Perplexing relates closely to *difficult*, but is more exclusively restricted to describing a task or requirement that is *difficult* to understand. Thus, while *laborious* stresses effort, often of a physical kind, *perplexing* most often suggests the intellectual demands made by a task, and it would not be appropriate in describing effort of any sort: the *perplexing* job of finding the ten-cent discrepancy in the day's accounts.

Troublesome and **trying** also pertain mostly to *difficult* tasks rather than to the effort required to solve them. *Troublesome* suggests confusion or disorder or even unpleasant resistance; this contrasts with the intellectual demands made by a *perplexing* task: the *troublesome* job of interviewing every one of the suspicious neighbors. *Trying*, by contrast, is much less specific concerning the kind of resistance it points to; it may suggest any kind of obstacle that taxes the worker's patience, skill, or mental equanimity: too *trying* to be a baby-sitter for such a spoiled child. *Trying* goes beyond *perplexing* and *troublesome* in being applicable to effort as well, in which case it suggests the sapping of energy or will: finding the struggle to sit up too *trying* in her weakened condition. See LABOR, OBSTACLE, PUZZLE, STRESS.

Antonyms: SIMPLE.

harm
damage
disable
hurt
incapacitate
injure

These verbs all mean affect a person or thing in such a way as to lessen health, strength, value, beauty, etc. **Harm** and **damage** are both wide in application. *Harm* refers to living things and, occasionally, to inanimate objects: afraid that in his rage he would *harm* the child; worried that her belongings might have been *harmed*. The point of *harm*, however, is that it can suggest any sort of negative outcome and thus is widely used in an abstract way, especially when an immoral or unethical impairment is at issue: those who unwittingly *harm* the cause of peace. *Damage* stresses impairment of value or function, and while it can be applied to living things, it is more commonly used to refer to inanimate objects. [Her heart was slightly *damaged* as a result of her long illness; The gale *damaged* several houses; The governor *damaged* her chances for reelection by running an inept campaign.]

Hurt, the most informal verb of the group, is mainly but not wholly restricted to living things and is general in applying to both a severe or minor impairment: a puppy that had been *hurt* by the tomcat; a few scratches, proving that children are bound to get *hurt* when they play; badly *hurt* in the car crash; a reputation *hurt* by an enemy's vicious lies. **Injure** is a slightly formal substitute for *hurt*. But while *hurt* concentrates more on the registering of a pain that need not override usefulness, *injure* often indicates at least a temporary loss of some function: continuing to type as fast as ever, though he had *hurt* his fingers while repairing his truck; a bird that hopped about helplessly as if one of its wings had been *injured*.

Disable and **incapacitate** both intensify suggestions of *injure* in pointing more definitely to a temporary or permanent loss of function. Of the two, *disable* is more likely to suggest a partial impairment, perhaps permanent, but one that need not affect usefulness: serving as president, though *disabled* by polio. *Incapacitate*, by contrast, is more formal and tends to suggest total loss of function or effectiveness: the tragedy of an active person who had been *incapacitated* by a stroke. Both *disable* and *incapacitate*, however, go beyond the previous pair in their application to inanimate things: its retrorockets *disabled* by a misfire during blastoff; snow-clogged roads that would *incapacitate* any car not equipped with tire chains. See HURT, WEAK.

Antonyms: REPAIR.

healthy
hale
hearty
robust

sound
strong
vigorous
well

These adjectives characterize a good or superlative physical or mental state. **Healthy** at its most neutral may refer to an absence of illness; at its most positive it refers to normal or excellent functioning: a recovery that left her perfectly *healthy* provided she doesn't overexert herself; *healthy* minds in *healthy* bodies. **Well** and *healthy* are the most common of these words, if not the most informal, but *well* is more nearly restricted to the neutral implications of *healthy* rather than its positive ones: asking her physician when she would be *well* again. **Sound** is much more positive in tone, although, like *well*, it can refer simply to an absence of illness or defect: an alertness and liveliness that marked the baby from the beginning as having an unusually *sound* constitution. **Strong** takes a different slant than *sound*, emphasizing power of physique or forcefulness of mind, although these qualities may be possessed by someone who is not *healthy* or *well*: a *strong* athlete laid low by AIDS; Ruskin's *strong* mind becoming increasingly shadowed by mental illness.

The remaining adjectives all stress exclusively the side of *healthy* that refers to excellent functioning. **Robust** adds to the emphasis of *strong* implications of positive health: *robust* warriors who were never sick a day in their lives; a *robust* personality able to triumph over every adversity. *Robust* also has overtones of full-bodied zestfulness, manly eagerness, and ampleness of appetite: the *robust* and sometimes ribald songs of sailors; a *robust* interest in the opposite sex. **Hearty** concentrates mostly on these last aspects of *robust*, indicating an active expression of high spirits and the satisfaction of desire: a *hearty* appetite; living to a *hearty* old age. Here, a sexual connotation possible for *robust* is more clearly present, although *hearty* is more often restricted to refer to men: the *hearty* camaraderie of most bachelor's dinners.

Vigorous refers to forcefulness, like *strong*, adding to this a note of positive well-being; rosy cheeks and sparkling eyes that spoke of *vigorous* good health; a closely reasoned theory that revealed a *vigorous* mind at work. The adjective, however, is completely lacking in those connotations of *robust* and *hearty* that refer to masculine appetite: the *vigorous* skill with which her poems are written. **Hale** would suggest excellent functioning, although strictly it pertains to absence of illness or defect. In any case, *hale* sounds archaic, and except in stock expressions is now seldom used: *hale* and *hearty*. See BENEFICIAL.

Antonyms: *ill, sick, sickly, unhealthy,* WEAK, *weakly.*

heavy
burdensome
crushing
onerous
oppressive

These adjectives describe weight or pressure so severe that it is difficult to bear. **Heavy** is the most informal and the least intense, indicating something of relative weightiness. [He wondered if the floor could support the *heavy* piano; She insisted that the package was far from *heavy*.] Metaphorically, the noun suggests something difficult or unpleasant: a *heavy* duty; He went to meet her with a *heavy* heart. *Heavy* need not, of course, suggest the idea of a carried weight at all. **Burdensome**, by contrast, refers specifically to something that is *heavy* and must be carried or supported; it is also more formal and more frequently used in an abstract way: a *burdensome* obligation; the *burdensome* post of chief administrator. The implication is that while the weight or task is difficult, it can with effort be supported.

Onerous is thus an intensification of *burdensome*, being at the same time still more formal than the previous words. It is almost exclusively used abstractly for describing such things as supremely trying tasks or duties: the *onerous* burden of correcting more than a hundred themes a week. *Onerous* gives an implication of an unfair or unjust assignment of duties: class assignments that in one case were reasonable, in another extremely *onerous*. **Oppressive** relates to this last possibility for *onerous*, suggesting harsh or cruel demands that can scarcely be borne: an *oppressive* taskmaster; *oppressive* registration requirements applied to deny the vote to minority groups. **Crushing** is the most intense of all these adjectives and may suggest literally as well as metaphorically a weight or force that cannot be borne at all: the *crushing* impact of the plummeting airplane that buckled the bridge; poverty so *crushing* as to immobilize entire segments of society. See MASSIVE, SIZE.

Antonyms: *easy, light, mild,* TRIVIAL.

heedless
careless
incautious
inconsiderate
insensitive
thoughtless

heedless *(continued)*

These adjectives describe a lack of awareness that produces slipshod, dangerous, or offensive results. **Heedless** most strongly indicates inattentiveness, with disapproving suggestions of self-preoccupation, stubbornness, or indifference to the feelings or safety of others. [*Heedless* of everything but the striking impression she was making; *heedless* of his parents' sound advice; He kept making caustic remarks, *heedless* of whom he might offend; They let out sail, *heedless* of the gathering storm clouds.] **Thoughtless** is less disapproving in tone, suggesting a lapse or failure, possibly unintentional, rather than the determined disregarding indicated by *heedless:* a *thoughtless* mistake; He apologized for having been so *thoughtless* of her feelings. Consequently, it can be used euphemistically for *heedless,* although it occasionally expresses disapproval in its own right: the typically *thoughtless* and irresponsible behavior of some young people.

Inconsiderate relates most closely to *heedless,* and **insensitive** to *thoughtless.* Both *inconsiderate* and *insensitive,* however, concentrate more on doing injury to the feelings of others. *Inconsiderate* expresses almost as much disapproval as *heedless* in pointing to conscious, if not deliberate, discourtesy toward others: his *inconsiderate* insistence on playing his radio while his roommates were trying to study. *Insensitive* may suggest that the discourtesy is unintentional in that it stems from a lack of understanding for other people's needs: *insensitive* to how much they disapproved of his dropping in on them unannounced. *Insensitive* also suggests a lack of awareness for finer shadings of meanings than any other adjective here: *insensitive* to the nuances of diplomatic protocol.

Careless is the most general of these adjectives and can substitute, with a loss of preciseness, for any of them, regardless of the area of meaning involved. Most commonly, however, it is closest to **incautious** in indicating a *heedless* attitude to standards of accuracy or safety; laziness, indifference, or preoccupation may be suggested as possible reasons for the inaccurate or dangerous act: too industrious to be *careless* about his housekeeping; a sense of false safety that made them *careless* about locking their door at night; so rushed that she grew *careless* in totaling the last column of figures. *Incautious* is most specifically restricted to a *heedless* attitude toward safety, with the suggestion that this results from a *thoughtless* or *insensitive* recklessness: *incautious* about letting our children play without supervision. See IMPETUOUS, OBLIVIOUS, RECKLESS, RUDE.

Antonyms: *careful,* CONSIDERATE, OBSERVANT.

heretic
dissenter
nonconformist
schismatic
sectarian

These nouns pertain to people who espouse views in opposition to the doctrines of a religion or ideology. **Heretic** refers to a believer who willfully espouses a tenet that his or her church has officially declared to be anathema. Taking a stand on an issue the church has not ruled on would not make a person a *heretic.* And while the church may punish a *heretic* by ejecting the person or, at one time, putting him or her to death, a *heretic's* aim need not be to separate from the church but possibly to stay within and reform it. A **schismatic**, by contrast, may or may not have serious doctrinal objections to church teachings, but such a person's avowed aim is to establish a separatist faction or competing religious body. A *schismatic,* furthermore, would most likely be one of a group or its leader, whereas a *heretic* can be a single individual with or without followers: The early Protestants expected to be condemned as *heretics,* but didn't foresee that this would inevitably result in their becoming *schismatics.*

Dissenter and **nonconformist** both originally pertained to people who in some way opposed the established Church of England. A *dissenter* was someone who rejected a particular doctrine without leaving the church, while a *nonconformist* was anyone who would not give to the established church the loyalty required by law. Roughly speaking, a *dissenter* criticized from within the Church of England, a *nonconformist* resisted from without. **Sectarian** once referred to a *schismatic* who founded or advocated the founding of a denomination independent of the original church. Later, it could simply indicate a member of any denomination or sect. More recently, *sectarian* has been avoided altogether because it can imply a superior-inferior relationship between the original church and the later formation.

Dissenter and *nonconformist* are widely used outside the context of religion. In this case, *dissenter* usually implies someone who is extremely critical of some established order and wishes to reform it: youthful *dissenters* who were organizing a protest march. *Nonconformist,* by contrast, more often refers to someone who is idiosyncratic in personal behavior and appearance in such a way as to exhibit a sharp departure from custom; *nonconformist,* thus, need not suggest advocacy of any formulated ideological stand whatsoever: They called themselves *nonconformists* but were little more than pleasure-seeking exhibitionists and had no political commitment of any kind. *Heretic* and *schismatic* can occasionally be used of people carrying on doctrinal disputes about an authoritarian ideology; in this case these adjectives often have a humorous or ironic note: the party members whom Stalin decided to condemn as *heretics;* the infighting common among Trotskyite *schismatics.* See DENOMINATION, FACTION, SKEPTIC.

Antonyms: *adherent, compatriot, conformist, follower,* SUPPORTER.

hesitate

> falter
> flounder
> pause
> vacillate
> waver

These verbs refer to indecisive actions. **Hesitate** suggests a momentary stopping of activity because of uncertainty, reluctance, or a conflict of emotions: She *hesitated* fearfully between accepting him and denying him; the timid assistant who *hesitates* to interrupt the boss when she is in conference. The act of *hesitating,* of course, may imply a completely mental weighing of alternatives, or an initial immobility before a decision has been made. This contrasts strongly with **pause,** which can only imply an interruption of activity already under way. *Pause* is also the most neutral of all these verbs in referring to a temporary halt. While all the other verbs suggest uneasiness, however faintly, *pause* may suggest a preconceived plan and indicate no irresoluteness whatsoever: They *paused* for six counts between each pirouette. The point of *pause* may be brevity: He *paused* before each painting only long enough to note the painter's name. Or its point may be to stress the mere fact of the halt, without ascribing motive: uncertain whether she *paused* at the door out of fear or fascination.

Falter has a much clearer emotional overtone than *hesitate* or *pause.* It suggests either intense doubt, helplessness, awkwardness, or incompetence: He *faltered* midway in the denunciation as he saw new reasons to detest his opponent; pedestrians *faltering* across the dangerously icy street; an actor so drunk that he *faltered* through most of his lines. *Falter,* like *pause,* may suggest an interruption, but it can also suggest an extremely slow or faulty performance, as in the last example above. In this sense, **flounder** is an intensification of *falter,* referring to a bungled action that continues erratically because of panic or disablement: obviously unprepared from the way she *floundered* through the recitation; the sudden cramp that caused the swimmer to *flounder* desperately in the deep water.

Waver and **vacillate,** by contrast, return to the milder uneasiness of *hesitate,* although both may suggest a poorly continued action rather than a temporary halt or initial moment of indecision. Both, in fact, suggest an action that goes back and forth between two alternatives. *Vacillate* would be more appropriate to describe mental activity that veers between extremes. Where *hesitate* in such a context might suggest a suspension of will, *vacillate* suggests wild swings of choice. [While the interviewer *hesitated,* he *vacillated* between taking back the offer and urging her to accept.] *Waver* would be more appropriate to describe a physical act that reveals uncertainty. In this context, it is close to *hesitate;* one who *hesitates* may not move at all, however, whereas *waver* suggests slight, indecisive gestures and uneasy movement. [She *hesitated* so long on the stair that at last he came *wavering* up to her.] *Waver,* when it refers to mental activity, suggests less violent swings than *vacillate,* and between less clearly defined positions: He stood *wavering* among a thousand dimly imagined possibilities. See DEMUR, INCONSTANT.

Antonyms: *ascertain,* CHOOSE, *continue,* DECIDE.

heterogeneous

> miscellaneous
> mixed
> motley

These adjectives are used to characterize a collection or group of things or people that are not all alike, or are used to describe a mass made up of different elements. **Heterogeneous** emphasizes most strongly the differences among individuals or elements closely connected but not necessarily unified. [New York City has a *heterogeneous* population; The former tenants had left behind a *heterogeneous* pile of rubbish; Porphyry is a *heterogeneous* rock.]

Miscellaneous emphasizes diversity arising from lack of any unifying principle in selections and suggests things that have been brought together casually or by chance. [A small boy's pockets are likely to contain a *miscellaneous* collection of objects; Successful politicians tend to be on a first-name basis with hundreds of *miscellaneous* people.]

Mixed, as considered here, is often used interchangeably with the other adjectives discussed. Specifically, it suggests dissimilarity among elements or individuals in a group or mass, but seldom a diversity as extreme or fortuitous as that suggested by *miscellaneous*. [When you buy a can of *mixed* nuts, you can expect to get peanuts, cashews, Brazil nuts, almonds, and filberts; A *mixed* social gathering is made up of people of both sexes and a variety of backgrounds.]

Motley means literally having a variety of colors, but in this context it describes persons or things that are strongly contrasted or even discordant. Unlike *heterogeneous, miscellaneous,* and *mixed, motley* has a derogatory connotation. [Accidents always draw a *motley* crowd of onlookers; Being self-educated, he has read indiscriminately and absorbed a *motley* set of conflicting facts and concepts.] See DISPARATE, JUMBLE.

Antonyms: *homogeneous, identical, pure, uniform.*

hew
chop
cut
hack

These verbs mean penetrate and divide something by means of an instrument with a sharp edge. **Hew** usually means make or shape by means of heavy blows of a tool such as an axe or by wielding a chisel or adz: to *hew* logs into short lengths; to *hew* stones into proper shapes for building a wall. *Hew* may also indicate a destructive act, although in this sense it sounds high-flown and literary: to *hew* down a mighty oak; to *hew* one's adversary to pieces.

Chop means divide into two or many pieces or make by a blow or a series of blows with a hatchet, cleaver, knife, etc.: to *chop* onions into small pieces; to *chop* open a coconut husk; to *chop* a hole in the ice.

Hack means *chop* at something or mangle or slash it away entirely by irregular and clumsy blows of a tool. [The firefighters had to *hack* down the door to rescue the children; The vandals had *hacked* all the office furniture with knives; The little girl *hacked* off her long hair.]

Cut has a much wider application than the other verbs and may be a loose synonym for any of them. Frequently, an adverb must be added to make the meaning of the action clear: to *cut* up meat for a stew; to *cut* off a hangnail; to *cut* down a dead bush. In many instances *cut* suggests care and forethought in what one is doing. [It takes years for a butcher's apprentice to learn to *cut* meat; The first step in making a dress is to *cut* out the pieces according to the pattern.]

high
elevated
lofty
tall
towering

These adjectives describe something of a relatively sizable vertical dimension or something found or placed at considerable altitude. **High** functions in both these ways: *high* buildings; a little cabin *high* up in the hills. **Tall**, by contrast, is restricted to the first situation: a *tall* woman; a child *tall* for her age. Because of this, *tall* is preferred over *high* in more formal contexts to indicate vertical height: *tall* buildings. But the informal use of *high* in this sense remains secure: climb the *highest* mountain. *High,* in general, does tend to suggest altitude, *tall* relative dimension. *High,* furthermore, is used metaphorically to refer to mobility or intensity: *high* moral purpose; *high* spirits. *Tall* has fewer metaphorical uses, one of them being in reference to masculinity: *tall* in the saddle.

Elevated, considerably more formal than the foregoing, is like *high* in referring both to vertical dimension and placement at an altitude: an apartment house *elevated* several dozen floors above its neighbors; an *elevated* railway. *Elevated* has a special use to indicate anything that has been raised above something else: an *elevated* walkway for pedestrians; the *elevated* tiers of a rice paddy that ran halfway up the mountain. Metaphorically, *elevated* emphasizes nobility, dignity, or profundity: an *elevated* discussion of final causes. But it can suggest pretentious pomposity or inflated self-esteem: considering herself too *elevated* to eat with the common horde in the cafeteria; *elevated* diction.

Towering, by contrast, is restricted like *tall* to refer to things of considerable height, although it is an intensification of *tall,* almost to the point of hyperbole: the *towering* giant of a basketball star who was walking toward us; the *towering* redwoods in Mill Valley; *towering* skyscrapers. Metaphorically, *towering* is vaguer than *high* or *elevated,* making a hyperbolic plea that something be regarded as tremendously important or valuable: our *towering* need for solutions to present problems; a *towering* figure in feminist literature.

Lofty, like *high,* may refer either to stature or placement at an altitude: the *lofty* oak; the *lofty* mountain pass. Both these concrete uses may seem less than natural now, however, having a ring that would sound too pretentious in many situations. *Lofty,* like *elevated,* once was used metaphorically to indicate nobility and profundity, but this use could also be thought dangerously affected: the *lofty* efforts of our Founding Fathers. *Lofty* does have a specific use to suggest a sense of superiority that causes someone to withdraw and act in a cold or remote manner; in this case the adjective is disapproving or pejorative in tone: the *lofty* arrogance of the white suburbs; a *lofty* indifference of some writers to the pressing problems of their times. See OUTSTANDING, POSITION, STEEP, SUMMIT.

Antonyms: *base, degraded, low, short.*

highest
  supreme
  topmost
  uppermost

These adjectives characterize things that in some way stand over or above their surroundings or above similar things, either in a literal or a figurative sense. **Highest** is the most general. It may mean located at the greatest elevation: the *highest* story of a building; the *highest* peak in the mountain range. *Highest* also refers to something of greatest importance: the *highest* court of the land; the *highest* good. In reference to degree, amount, or size, *highest* is frequently used. [We pay the *highest* prices for old gold; The tide is *highest* at eleven o'clock; Yuma, Arizona, is said to have the *highest* temperatures in the United States; We have the *highest* regard for her opinions.]

The other adjectives in this group emphasize one or more of the meanings of *highest*. **Supreme** is applied especially to persons or things that are not only *highest* in rank, quality, or importance, but are also considered unequaled: the *Supreme* Court; Zeus, the *supreme* deity of the ancient Greeks. [The *supreme* moment of a gambler's life comes when he breaks the bank at Monte Carlo.]

Topmost may refer to a person who has the *highest* position in a specific situation: the *topmost* executive of the company. But it is more likely to be applied to something located at the greatest elevation: the *topmost* shelf of a closet; the *topmost* branches of a fir tree.

Uppermost is often used interchangeably with *topmost,* but it tends to be used more often to describe people or things that have the *highest* and most important position or receive the greatest amount of attention: the *uppermost* faction in a political party; the thoughts *uppermost* in her mind. See FARTHEST, STEEP, SUMMIT.

Antonyms: *bottom, deepest, lowest, undermost.*

hinder
  encumber
  hamper
  impede
  obstruct

These verbs mean put difficulties or obstacles in the way or progress of. **Hinder** is the most general term and the least strong in meaning. Specifically, to *hinder* is to delay or slow down a person or thing, and it may imply either active interference or an accidental action or condition. [The child's hysterical crying *hindered* the doctor from completing the examination; Bad weather *hindered* the military operation; Overcrowded schoolrooms *hinder* the education of our children.]

Impede means delay by a deliberate act, and it retains much of its original meaning of fettering the feet. *Impede* suggests stronger obstacles than does *hinder* and implies a forcible slowing down that is frustrating and even painful. [The crowds at the scene of the accident *impeded* the arrival of the ambulance; Many persons are *impeded* in their careers by a lack of belief in themselves.]

Hamper means *impede* by placing restraints of any sort that make action burdensome and difficult. [*Hampered* by four small whining children, the young mother had difficulty in getting on the bus; Too strong a sense of duty *hampers* enjoyment of life.]

Encumber, like *hamper*, suggests a *hindering* of action or motion by outside forces. However, in the case of *encumber,* the *hindering* comes about by the placing of a burden rather than by that of a restraint. [The burro was so *encumbered* with produce for market that it could scarcely walk; Debts *encumbered* the young family while the children were small.]

Obstruct is the strongest verb of this group. It implies not only a delay in action or movement, but often a complete halt by the placing of large, immovable objects in one's path. [The excavation has *obstructed* all traffic in this street for the past week; The bully *obstructed* the path of the small boy on his way home.] See STOP (arrest), STOP (cease), THWART, UNWILLING, WITHSTAND.

Antonyms: ENCOURAGE, IMPEL, QUICKEN, *spur.*

hint
  implication
  innuendo
  insinuation
  intimation
  suggestion

These nouns refer to signs or evidence, indirectly given or covertly present, from which certain meanings may be inferred. **Hint** is the most informal of these nouns and most often refers to a sign intentionally given to alert someone else to something that might otherwise be overlooked: giving him a *hint* that she wouldn't mind being asked for a date. *Hint* may also refer to clues unintentionally given: inadvertent behavior that was a *hint* of some deeper emotional disturbance. At an even further remove, *hint* may suggest a sign inherent in any set of data: a campsite that gave *hints* of recent use; a *hint* of fall in the air.

Suggestion differs from *hint* in that it may refer to more directly presented statements; even here, however, the emphasis is on a tactful presentation that stops short of insistence or flat recommendation: her *suggestion* that we try thinning the paint with alcohol. Less commonly than with *hint*, a *suggestion* may refer to inadvertent clues or to signs inherent in data: a *suggestion* of nervousness in the way he kept running his hand through his hair; a program emphasizing *suggestions* for improving the lives of city dwellers.

Implication, like *hint*, may refer to an intentionally given sign, although greater indirection is stressed: He backed up her *suggestion* that the child get ready for bed with a broad *hint* about a bedtime snack and an unspoken *implication* that the child might be punished for not obeying at once. More often, however, *implication* is restricted to indicating indirect evidence of any sort from which meaning can be inferred: arguing that the development of an inconsiderate selfishness was one *implication* of the permissive rearing of children; an *implication* of disapproval that underlay the author's seemingly objective treatment of his major character.

Intimation is alone among these nouns in stressing the gaining of an insight into the future: an *intimation* from the first day that she would not enjoy her new job. Sometimes, *intimation* may suggest a vague feeling or suspicion arrived at without evidence of any kind, either by intuitive or supernatural processes: an *intimation* that she would one day agree to marry him; an *intimation* that the world would come to an end on Friday. *Intimation* may also refer to intuitions or suspicions that do not pertain to futurity: getting any number of *intimations* that his friend's childhood had been unusually bleak and forbidding.

Innuendo and **insinuation** are closely related; both are set apart from the other nouns by concentrating mainly on intentionally given signs that bristle with unpleasant or hostile meanings. *Innuendo* can be seen as a negative *implication; insinuation* as a negative *suggestion*: making a thinly veiled *innuendo* that reflected on the morality of his opponent; a barrage of slight but mounting *insinuations* that she should perhaps give up trying to be a playwright. *Innuendo*, in addition, implies an unsupported or unsupportable personal attack that is never spelled out; *insinuation* may imply a process of worming one's way into someone's favor by obsequious behavior in order to harm that person or someone else: Cassius's *innuendoes* to Brutus about Caesar's untrustworthiness; Iago's *insinuations* concerning Desdemona's virtue. See PREMONITION, SYMPTOM.

Antonyms: *affirmation, assertion, declaration.*

hire
draft
employ
engage
enlist
recruit

These verbs refer to taking on someone to fill a job. **Hire** is the most informal and, because of this, may apply most naturally to a wage-earning rather than a salaried worker: *hiring* three new busboys. *Hire*, however, is often used of more exalted positions: *hiring* a new managing editor. Sometimes, *hire* suggests taking on someone for a specific or one-time job: *hiring* a plumber to install the new dryer; *hired* to kill a rival gangster. **Employ** is a more formal substitute for *hire* and is sometimes used for positions of greater prestige: *employing* her as guidance counselor. In governmental and official terminology, *employ* universally replaces *hire*: urging businesses to *employ* the handicapped. *Employ* goes beyond *hire*, however, in referring not just to the initial taking on of someone but to a continuing status. Thus, *employ*, which is euphemistic for other senses of the verb *use* and often for the simple act of *hiring*, is free of such a tone in this case: an operation that *employed* a staff of two hundred people; asking when he was last *employed*.

Engage seems unnecessarily indirect when used as a substitute for *hire* or *employ* in their most common senses. The verb has pertinence, however, in referring to a specific or one-time contracting for someone's services, especially when these are of a professional nature: *engaging* a gardener to cut her lawn each week; *engaging* a lawyer to argue their case in court. *Engage*, like *employ*, may also refer to someone actually at work, especially in fields where work comes in spurts: *engaging* extra summer help; an actress who was not *engaged* for the coming season.

Draft, **enlist**, and **recruit** have special relevance to serving in the armed forces, but all of them are used widely outside this context. *Draft* always carries the implication of service that is compulsory or involuntary: *drafting* college students into the army at the completion of their studies; *drafting* several club members to hand out sample ballots during the voting. *Recruit* contrasts sharply with *draft* in indicating an appeal for volunteers to undertake a task or position, not necessarily for pay: special training programs that made it easy to *recruit* young men into the Air Force; *recruiting* neighbors to help search for the missing child. Used transitively, *enlist* is a more general substitute for *recruit;* it may suggest seeking financial or moral support as well as the actual acquiring of someone's services: *enlisting* college graduates for the long-term government project; *enlisting* your help in the coming election. Used intransitively, *enlist* indicates volunteering for an assignment: *enlisting* in the Navy rather than waiting to be *drafted.* A confusion sometimes results because new arrivals or trainees in the armed forces, whether *recruited* or *drafted,* are called *recruits;* similarly, all noncommissioned personnel are called *enlisted* men (or women), though not all may have volunteered their service. See LABOR, LEASE, PROFESSION.

Antonyms: *buy, discharge, fire, purchase, retire.*

historic. Do not confuse the adjective *historic* (momentous, important in history) with the adjective *historical* (dealing with history).

history
annals
chronicle

These nouns denote a systematic record of past events. A **history** is a narrative that recounts events with attention to their importance, their mutual relations, causes, and consequences; it is therefore highly selective: Herodotus's famous *history* of the Persian wars; to commission an author to write a *history* of a company. A **chronicle** is a record of events in order of time; **annals** are similar but are divided year by year. Neither *chronicles* nor *annals* attempt to interpret events. A historian, for instance, might scan the *annals* of a political party before writing a *history* of its creation and growth; a magazine article might include a *chronicle* of the major political events of the last fifty years. See NARRATIVE.

hobby
avocation

pastime
recreation
sport

These nouns refer to play, leisure-time activities, or side interests pursued for amusement or pleasure. **Hobby** indicates an activity that may involve development of intricate knowledge about a limited field. It particularly implies collecting or tinkering activities, often done by oneself at home and seldom involving physical exercise for its own sake: a lifelong *hobby* of stamp collecting.

Avocation is more formal than *hobby* and may suggest a more dedicated pursuit of something with cultural or social value: a doctor whose *avocation* was playing cello in an amateur string quartet. More generally, however, *avocation* can group together the whole range of activities considered here, since its only restriction is its emphasis on something that is secondary to a person's livelihood, career, or central concern. **Recreation** is comparable in its generality to *avocation.* While it does not emphasize the distinction between main and secondary interests, it does suggest pleasurable relaxation and low-key activity that would not be found in most vocations. The stress of *recreation* is on play or games. Thus, unlike *hobby,* it can more often suggest activity that is done in groups and that includes physical exercise: camps offering a variety of *recreations* that include folk dancing, handicrafts, swimming, and boating.

Pastime is closer to *hobby* than the previous pair, indicating anything done to occupy one's leisure; by implication, *pastime* suggests busywork of little intrinsic worth: insisting that his painting was merely a *pastime* that kept him from being bored. This deprecatory note can be even more pronounced: few *pastimes* more foolish than autograph collecting. **Sport** is the one noun here that points to a *recreation* or *pastime* that is primarily a matter of physical exercise, and suggests especially competitive group or individual activity: We enjoyed playing baseball, football, and other *sports.* Unlike all the other nouns here, *sport* can indicate an activity pursued as a moneymaking vocation: He had performed so brilliantly on his college's tennis team that he took up the *sport* as a professional player. See PLEASURE.

Antonyms: *business, calling,* LABOR, *livelihood,* PROFESSION.

hole
cavity
excavation

hole (continued)

hollow
pit

These nouns are compared as they denote an unfilled space within a solid body. **Hole** is the most general and the most ambiguous; a *hole* in a stocking goes through it, a *hole* in a piece of timber may or may not go through, a *hole* in the ground does not go through the earth, but may be narrow or wide, shallow or very deep. **Hollow** and **cavity** refer to an empty space within something otherwise solid or filled; of the two, *cavity* is somewhat more learned or formal except for its popular use to describe a *hole* in a tooth: the pleural *cavity* in which the lungs are situated; the abdominal *cavity*. *Hollow* is frequently used of any depression or concavity in a surface: the *hollows* of the sea. **Pit** primarily denotes certain large natural *cavities*, especially in the ground; it is also used figuratively to suggest an abysmal depth, and is sometimes used to mean hell. **Excavation** is a man-made *cavity* or *pit,* as for the foundations of a building. See PIERCE.

Antonyms: *bump, projection, protrusion.*

home

abode
domicile
habitation
household
hovel
residence

These nouns refer to places or buildings in which people live, or to the people themselves. **Home** is the most general term, but it often means more than simply an occupied house or other dwelling. Specifically, *home* refers to a place where one lives on a more or less permanent basis and with which one has strong personal ties of affection and loyalty. [In our *home,* Sunday dinner in the middle of the day has always been the custom; Loving parents try to provide secure *homes* for children; The young soldier kept dreaming of *home.*] *Home* may also refer to a region or country in which one was born, brought up, or now resides. [Latvia is the *home* of the Letts; Although I have lived in California for five years, my *home* is Columbus, Ohio.] By extension, the natural habitats of animals or the places in which they seek shelter for the raising of their young are often spoken of as *homes:* the wolf's *home* in the rocky cave; the whale's *home* in the depths of the sea.

Residence is a more formal word for *home* and has the suggestion of an imposing or pretentious dwelling:

the mayor's *residence;* the *residence* of the college president. *Residence* may be used to distinguish a person's place of business or professional activity from his or her *home:* The doctor has her office in the city, but her *residence* is in the suburbs. A residential neighborhood is one made up largely of *homes* or *residences* rather than of commercial buildings. *Residence* is sometimes applied to housing provided by an educational or other institution for its students or staff members: a nurses' *residence;* a *residence* for graduate students; the *residence* of the Dean of Women. In a legal sense, a person may be said to have *residence* in the state of Masachusetts (that is, is registered to vote there, owns property there, etc.) although he or she temporarily lives and works in another region or country.

Abode is a somewhat high-flown, literary term for *home* and has a wide application, for it does not in any way connote the actual character of a *home. Abode* can also refer to a place such as a hotel, camp, or cottage by the sea in which one stays only temporarily.

A **hovel** is a small, wretched *home* and suggests squalor and poverty. [Medieval serfs lived in *hovels* on their lord's estate; Over the years, through neglect, the Tudor cottage became nothing more than a *hovel.*]

Habitation is a generic term and is chiefly applied to the dwellings of people who have settled, permanent *homes,* in contradistinction to nomads or gypsies, who habitually shift their *abodes* to find food, pasturage, or work.

Except in a legal sense, **domicile** is rarely used. *Domicile* denotes a *home* or *residence* over which the owner has certain rights and responsibilities by law and in which he or she intends to reside indefinitely.

Household refers to a domestic establishment, that is, to the persons dwelling together under one roof as a social unit, and not to any actual structure. It may include not only the members of a family or other organized group, but servants as well. A *household* may also consist of a single person living alone. When the Internal Revenue Service speaks of a head of *household*, it is referring to the person in a family who pays the costs of maintaining the *home,* such as rent, mortgage payments, taxes, and utilities. See HOUSE, LODGINGS.

homonym

homographs
homophones

The noun **homonym** is used with a variety of meanings. It is commonly used to mean one of two or more words pronounced alike but having different spellings and meanings, such as *fair* and *fare.* In more precise contexts such words are called **homophones**, from the Greek *homos* same + *phōnē* sound. *Homonym* is also sometimes used to mean one of two or more words that are spelled alike but differ in origin and meaning and sometimes in pronunciation, such as *wind* (a breeze) and *wind* (to coil). Again, in more precise contexts such words are called **homographs**, from the Greek *homos* same + *graphein* to write. *Homonym,* in precise usage, means a word identical with another in spelling and pronunciation but differing from it in origin and meaning, such as *bear* (animal) and *bear* (carry).

Unfortunately or not, *homonym* is well established in each of these senses and is perhaps most commonly used synonymously with *homophone*—that is, to refer to one of two or more words that sound alike but otherwise differ, such as *read* and *reed* or *whole* and *hole*.

hope

anticipate
await
dream
expect
foresee
wish

These verbs pertain to the attitude of looking forward to something that is to occur in the future. **Hope** suggests looking forward exclusively to some positive or favorable outcome; it may be well-founded in probability or completely beyond the pale of the possible: *hoping* that extra effort on the theme would bring her a higher mark; still *hoping,* despite the driving rain, that it would be sunny when they reached the beach. **Wish** suggests something considerably less plausible or likely than *hope: wishing* he could suddenly become a millionaire. Where *hope* may be part of an ennobling or heroic attitude, *wish* gives a flavor of idle childishness that is unwilling to take a realistic stand: *wishing* for the good things of life rather than working for them full of confidence and *hope.* **Dream** suggests an even more tenuous basis for looking forward than *wish,* implying a complete, if momentary, retreat from reality: *dreaming* of the day when his wife would be fully recognized as a distinguished writer. Unlike *wish, dream* can be used in a way that parallels the noble sense of *hope:* A man ceases to be human when he ceases to *dream.* Furthermore, both *dream* and *wish* are not necessarily restricted, as with *hope,* to future possibilities: *wishing* she had been born a princess; *dreaming* of a happier life on some other planet.

Anticipate is closer to *hope* in being restricted to thoughts of the future: *anticipating* the imminence of Christmas and the presents they would at last be permitted to open. But while the verb is frequently connected to thoughts of a pleasant outcome, it can also be used for imagining an unpleasant one: *anticipating* the eventual defeat of all their troops. **Expect** suggests looking forward either to a positive or to a negative outcome, but the point of this verb is that it concerns itself with supposed certainties: *expecting* any minute to hear his wife climbing the stairs, home from work; fully *expecting* the inevitable rush of abuse that would follow the unpleasant revelation. **Await** stresses a certain passiveness of attitude while watching for something imminent to occur, whether positive or negative, whether *expected* or not: *awaiting* her decision without the slightest clue as to what it would be; *awaiting* his passionately *hoped*-for return; grimly *awaiting* the fall of the guillotine blade.

Foresee introduces another aspect of looking forward to the future; it suggests an attempt to infer or guess what the future might be, rather than imagining an outcome either in accord with what is *hoped* or opposed to it: *foreseeing* by every sign that it would rain before morning. See PREDICT, SUPPOSE.
Antonyms: *despair, despond.*

hostile

bellicose
belligerent
unfriendly

Hostile, the strongest adjective in this group, connotes an attitude of intense ill will and a course of action based on that attitude: *hostile* intentions of the enemy; the malicious barbs of a *hostile* critic.

Unfriendly, as here considered, **bellicose**, and **belligerent** imply an aggressive readiness to fight and an attitude that is usually careless of the object of its ill will. [A *bellicose* nation is a warlike nation that tends to resort to arms with little or no cause; a *belligerent* tavern brawler who picked a fight just for the sake of fighting; an *unfriendly* tribe that attacked all interlopers without regard for their intent.] See ENMITY, VINDICTIVE.
Antonyms: *cordial, friendly, tolerant, warm.*

hot

burning
feverish
scorching
sizzling
sultry

hot (continued)

> sweltering
> torrid

These adjectives characterize relatively high temperatures. **Hot** is the most general and the most relative, depending on context for preciseness: weather *hot* enough to begin melting the snowdrifts; *hot* water; Even the coolest star is unimaginably *hot* by human standards. **Burning**, **scorching**, and **sizzling** are more specific in referring to temperatures that resemble or are the result of fire. Of these, *burning* is the most general; it is often used hyperbolically for anything *hot* or metaphorically for anything high-key: a *burning* sirocco; *burning* issues. *Scorching* is particularly relevant to a *hot*, dry atmosphere, although the implication of dryness is not always present: the *scorching* heat of a sauna as compared to the mugginess of a steam bath; humid, *scorching* weather. Metaphorically, it suggests anger: *scorching* disdain. *Sizzling* often hyperbolically suggests a *burning* that gives off sparks or spatters or that can sear upon contact: a pan of *sizzling* fat; sunbathers lying on the *sizzling* sand; *sizzling* weather. Metaphorically, it suggests luridness or arousal: *sizzling* pictures of half-clothed women.

Sultry, **sweltering**, and **torrid** concentrate more exclusively on one implication of the previous group, the one pertaining to weather. *Sultry* suggests humid heat: apparently in for another *sultry* summer. *Sweltering* is an intensification of *sultry*, suggesting an oppressive heat associated with heavy sweating or fainting: the customary siesta, made necessary by the *sweltering* noonday heat. *Torrid* is more matter-of-fact than the preceding pair, referring more to climate than to weather: the *torrid* zone; the Congo's *torrid* season. Of this group, both *sultry* and *torrid* have metaphorical uses referring to emotional excitement. *Sultry* suggests passionate moodiness or intensity, *torrid* a more specifically sexual context: the *sultry* beauties in his harem; a *torrid* love affair.

Feverish refers most literally to a high body temperature: He felt faint and *feverish*. Metaphorically, it can refer to haste and confusion: *feverish* attempts to meet the deadline. See HUMID, PASSIONATE, WARM.

Antonyms: *cold*.

hotel

> hostel
> inn
> motel

These nouns refer to buildings or groups of buildings that are set up to provide living quarters for customers, especially on a temporary basis. **Hotel** usually refers to a single building, large or small, in which rooms or suites are rented out on a fixed basis: *hotels* jammed by people pouring into town for the convention. Although *hotel* most often suggests accommodations for travelers or transients, it may also apply to more permanent arrangements: She had lived in the resident *hotel* for a decade. **Hostel** represents an older borrowing from the same source word as *hotel* and once meant the same thing. Now it almost universally refers to one of a chain of lodging houses for young people on cycling or hiking tours: He planned his itinerary so that each night he could stay in a welcoming *hostel*.

Motel is a portmanteau word for motor *hotel*; it refers to a roadside building or, often, a group of buildings such as a cluster of cabins, where people traveling by car may obtain lodgings: an attempt to choose among several *motels* along the highway. **Inn** also refers to a roadside *hotel*, but suggests a much more rustic setting than *motel* and is a place where travelers may obtain either food or lodgings, or both. Since *inn* has an archaic and convivial quality, it is often used pretentiously to refer to any sort of restaurant: your country *inn* in the heart of the city. Sometimes it serves as a genteel substitute for *motel:* a motor *inn*. See HOUSE, LODGINGS.

hound

> pointer
> retriever
> setter
> terrier

These nouns all refer to dogs used in hunting or tracking a quarry. **Hound** is by far the most general of these. Used loosely, it can merely be a more formal substitute for dog itself, giving an archaic or pretentious tone; used specifically, it can refer to a grouping of specific breeds. Between these two extremes, *hound* would most often be understood as referring to dogs that track quarry by scent or sight: They brought out *hounds* to track down the escaped convict; the packs of *hounds* used in fox hunting. Metaphorically, *hound* can suggest someone fixated on the pursuit of something: an autograph *hound*.

The remaining nouns are restricted to describing ways that hunting or sporting dogs track or capture their quarry. More specifically, of course, each may indicate a precise breed of dog or groups of such breeds. **Pointer** refers to a dog that signals the presence of quarry, such as birds, by fixing its body with tail uplifted and nose directed toward the prey. The

setter acts similarly, but adopts a sitting position in indicating its prey. A **retriever** is any dog that brings back shot or killed animals to its master, whether over land or water. **Terrier** refers to a dog that digs up burrowing prey, such as gophers or moles. But *terrier* has become more and more attached to particular breeds valued as pets, without indicating this hunting activity at all. See ANIMAL.

house

> building
> dwelling
> housing
> premises
> roof
> shelter

These nouns refer to structures in which people live or work. **House** refers generally to any sort of structure meant for living in. Though it may classically call up an image of a free-standing, one-family structure of moderate size, it can apply to a spectrum of habitations, from those considerably more to those considerably less extensive than this midpoint: the baronet's fifty-room country *house;* They bought a one-story semidetached *house* in the new development; a rickety one-room *house* built of unchinked logs; rows of grimy tenement *houses.* In informal use, *house* frequently refers to the place where one lives, even though it is a room or apartment or some other division of a larger structure: She takes the elevator to the tenth floor to play in Janie's *house.*

Dwelling is a more formal substitute for *house* and has fewer connotations, referring solely to any structure (or less often, to part of one) where people live. Its formality, however, makes it sound odd in other contexts than sociological discussion or the parlance of the construction industry: a study that compared children who lived in two-family *dwellings* with those in apartment *houses;* contractors who can mass-produce middle-income *dwellings* on a vast scale. Even in these uses, *dwelling* may sound like an unnecessarily inflated evasion of *house. Dwelling* can also have an aura of faded lyricism or religiosity, in imitation of its valid use in the King James Bible: the simple *dwellings* of upright men.

Roof and **shelter** are more informal and more colorful substitutes for *house* than *dwelling,* both stressing the minimal factors of utility or protection given by any sort of structure. *Roof* is a synecdoche for the whole *house:* two families sharing the same *roof.* But it may suggest temporary accommodations rather than permanent living quarters: anxious to get a *roof* over

their heads by nightfall. *Shelter* is useful as a general word with which to group together all living structures, permanent or temporary: people's basic needs of food, clothing, and *shelter.* It may even refer to any sort of protective retreat: a tree that provided *shelter* from the rain; to take *shelter.* Used as a specific reference to a particular structure, it is likely to suggest something rude or improvised: They collected driftwood to build a beach *shelter.* **Housing** is a general word referring to the supplying of or demand for living space of any sort: open *housing;* legislation in the areas of *housing* and education.

Building refers concretely to an actual structure, but it is not restricted, like *house,* to those designed or used as living space: farm *buildings* that included the farmhouse, a barn, and a silo. **Premises** is a technical term in insurance, legal, or criminological parlance. It may refer to a tract of land with *buildings* on it; to a *house, building,* or part of a *house;* or to the space occupied by a business: a policy insuring the *premises* against fire; suspicious characters seen on the *premises.* Sometimes it is used outside these contexts with comic effect: He got his golf clubs from the closet in the hope of getting off the *premises* without being seen. See HOME, HOTEL, LODGINGS.

humane

> benign
> charitable
> compassionate
> human
> humanitarian
> philanthropic
> sympathetic

These adjectives are comparable in the broad sense of expressing an interest in or concern for the welfare and happiness of others. **Humane,** the most comprehensive of them, implies considerateness in our dealings not only with people but with all living creatures and in situations involving either: a *humane* judge; *humane* treatment of animals; a *humane* management policy. **Benign** carries the suggestion of a mild, sometimes faintly condescending gentleness and tolerance, with a secondary meaning of harmlessness: a *benign* attitude toward the follies of others; a *benign* tumor.

Etymologically, **sympathetic** and **compassionate** mean the same thing: feeling or suffering, usually with another person. But *sympathetic,* from the Greek, has a wider, frequently more generalized and impersonal range than the Latin *compassionate.* One can be *sympathetic* with a point of view, a philosophy, belief, or way of life, or feel sympathy for the hardships of a fictional character, but *compassionate* implies a stronger and more directly personal feeling for suffering and misfortune at the individual level: His early life had taught him to be *compassionate* toward lonely and misunderstood children.

Charitable, **humanitarian**, and **philanthropic** all suggest a sense of obligation to aspects of life that are, or are regarded as, worthy of generous understanding and practical help. A *charitable* person is disposed to show a kindly and merciful attitude toward people in distress and to help them when possible. A *humanitarian* will generalize his or her interest in mankind along philosophic and often vaguely sentimental lines that disregard the individual in favor of the mass. A *philanthropic* person may be *charitable* and *humanitarian,* but has both the capacity and desire to be useful by giving substantial sums of money to specific causes, institutions, foundations, colleges, etc.

In all these distinctions the adjective **human** is a rock-bottom term that can be used wherever people are thought of apart from animals and inanimate nature and are regarded as capable of concern for and communication with others: a drop of *human* kindness. *Human* and *humane* are, however, different in their implications. Whereas *humane* can suggest an attitude of impersonal high-mindedness, *human* can often gloss over weakness or failings as being all too common and, therefore, forgivable. [It is *human* to err; little foibles that made the great man more *human;* After all, it was only *human* to do everything she could to win the prize.] But *human* can also suggest a flexible and tolerant attitude toward the imperfections of others: if he'd only stop moralizing all the time and be a little *human.* See BENEVOLENCE, CONSIDERATE, GENEROUS, LENIENT.

Antonyms: CRUEL, *hardhearted, parsimonious, selfish, stingy, unkind.*

humid
   close
   oppressive
   sticky

These adjectives are comparable in that they all are used to describe a condition of the weather. **Humid**, which means containing water or vapor, is the most specific term in the group because it refers to the measurable physical phenomenon called relative humidity. Relative humidity is the ratio, expressed as a percentage, of the amount of water vapor actually in the air at a specific time to the total amount that could be pre-

sent at the same temperature. *Humid,* therefore, alone or with a qualifying adverb can designate any state of atmospheric dampness: It was not *humid* yesterday, but it is very *humid* today, and the weather bureau predicts it will be even more *humid* tomorrow.

The other adjectives in this group are less precise in meaning but more colorful in tone. **Close** can refer to the weather or to a place. When one thinks of a *close* day it is in terms of being choked or suffocated by weather that is heavy, hot, and still. A room described as *close* has probably not been ventilated for some time; its unmoving air has grown stale and thick so that it induces an uncomfortable feeling of confinement. **Oppressive** is the most general of these adjectives; it can apply to any kind of harsh weather that causes depression or discomfort. A *close* day with a thunderstorm lurking and no breeze stirring is certainly *oppressive.* But so, too, is a day on which the wind never stops blowing, whether it be hot or cold, rainy or dry. It is true that *oppressive* is mostly used in reference to hot, sultry weather, but any climatic condition that produces a state of oppression can be characterized as *oppressive*: The mild Christmas season was followed by two weeks of *oppressive* cold that kept even the hardiest souls indoors.

In this context, **sticky** refers to sweatiness caused by an *oppressive* and *humid* warmth that does not encourage evaporation; this may result from weather, an unventilated atmosphere, or human exertion. An implication pertaining to the adhesiveness between layers, as of cloth to sweaty skin, may also be present: a *sticky* day; an overcrowded room that soon became damp and *sticky;* She stripped off her *sticky* running pants. See HOT, WARM.

Antonyms: *arid,* DRY, *parched.*

humorous
   comic
   comical
   droll
   facetious
   funny
   jocose
   jocular
   waggish
   witty

These adjectives refer to what causes or is intended to cause amusement or laughter. **Humorous** is most often restricted to successful attempts to amuse or to people who succeed in such attempts: a *humorous* story; a *humorous* fellow, full of diverting remarks.

Less often, *humorous* can refer only to the attempt: His *humorous* essays are not half as amusing as Thurber's. *Humorous* seldom refers to what is unintentionally laughable. *Humorous*, like humor, often refers to a warmhearted, sympathetic, or good-natured treatment of small failings or ironies, those that prompt smiles rather than laughter or derision.

Comic and **comical** relate instead to comedy, which can include the *humorous* but is a more general category, including slapstick, parody, or even caustic satire. *Comic* is a neutral word by which to refer to this category: *comic* writers. *Comic*, in fact, is now often used as a noun to refer to any comedian: stand-up *comics*. *Comical*, by contrast, can refer to anything or anyone whose effect is amusing, laughable, or absurd, whether such an effect is intentional or not: a *comical* misunderstanding that delighted spectators but caused the embarrassed delegates to call for a recess; He cut a *comical* figure in his pretentious finery. These distinctions are not always observed in the use of the two words.

Funny is the most general and the most informal of these adjectives, but it is focused mainly on whatever results in laughter: a comedian whose jokes weren't really *funny;* a howlingly *funny* slip of the tongue. When something or someone is inadvertently *funny*, it may be because of oddness, unfamiliarity, abnormality, or inappropriateness: the *funny* old man with the *funny* walk. This shades off into a description of anything strange or suspicious: His wife gave him a *funny* look. On the other hand, *funny* can categorize an attempt, like *comic*: professional *funny* men; *funny* business that was tedious and overdone. **Facetious** once could be approving, but now is exclusively an unfavorable description of silly or ill-timed attempts at being *humorous*: a *facetious* ass who always forgot the punch lines to the jokes he told; *facetious* remarks that kept sidetracking serious discussion of the problem.

Jocose and **jocular** are the most formal adjectives here and closely related in meaning. Both come from Latin roots meaning jest or joke and both can apply to a person given to jesting or to the amusement caused by such remarks. *Jocose* can sometimes function as a milder substitute for *facetious*, pointing to feeble attempts at humor, especially when they are heavy-handed or pompous: *jocose* inanities that were seen as stuffy. *Jocular* may imply a constant resort to jokes or wisecracks in the hope of cheering up or amusing others: *jocular* comments on the bad food and worse weather. It may sometimes apply to the deliberate turning away of a serious question by a light answer:

the *jocular* anecdote with which he disposed of the young man's objection.

Droll compares with one aspect of *funny* in pointing to someone who is whimsical or odd: the *droll* old curmudgeon. It can also refer to a *comic* impulse that is clever, deadpan, or laconic: the *droll* understatement of the British. It can also refer to *comic* work in a mordant or sardonic vein: Balzac's *Droll Stories*. **Waggish** can also indicate humor that is clever, but it also suggests a playful irreverence in someone given to private jokes or sly rejoinders: *waggish* remarks about the poor lady's grotesque and *comical* evening gown. **Witty** is more inclusive than *droll* or *waggish* in pointing to a brilliant or surprising play of intelligence in the delivery of amusing and trenchant observations on human foibles or follies: Oscar Wilde's *witty* repartee; a *witty* parody of campaign speeches. *Witty* can apply as well to the light and good-natured, like *humorous*, as to the caustic and withering: *witty* conundrums about trivialities; *witty* aspersions that cast doubt on the sincerity and competence of the playwright. See ABSURD, JOKE, RIDICULE.

Antonyms: *dull*, GLOOMY, SEDATE.

hunt

comb
explore
ransack
scour
search
seek
sleuth
track

These verbs indicate any effort at finding, catching, following, or examining something. **Hunt** at its most specific can refer to the activity of pursuing and killing animals, whether for food, profit, or sport: tribes that *hunted* buffalo for food; on a safari to *hunt* game. More generally, *hunt* can indicate an uncertain groping for something needed: He *hunted* for the light switch along the wall of the dark room. It can also indicate an urgent following: She *hunted* everywhere in the neighborhood for the tardy child. And it can point to any act of looking for something lost or missing: *hunting* for the missing book.

Track and **sleuth** relate closely to the aspect of *hunt* pertaining to following a quarry. *Track* can indicate the ability to detect a trail of clues: skilled at *tracking* the spoor of a wounded animal. It can also apply more widely for *hunting* anything fugitive or difficult to find: determined to *track* down every suspicious item in the expense accounts. *Sleuth* compares such action to detective work and can apply as widely. But here the verb refers more often to the search for clues itself, particularly where the quarry is not yet known: They *sleuthed* out every angle, however slight, that could lead them to the killer; clinicians to *sleuth* down symptoms that might help diagnose the strange illness.

Search and **seek** are considerably more general than the previous pair. *Search* may indicate the act of looking for a lost object or for an object presumed to exist: navigators *searching* for a western route to the East Indies. The verb may also apply to mere activity without clearly stated goals: young people *searching* for a cause that would give meaning to their lives. *Hunt*, by comparison to *search*, might suggest a more informed, purposive, focused, or relentless activity: They blocked off the canyon and methodically *hunted* down the trapped criminals. *Seek* can give a more archaic flavor than *search*, except in set phrases: *seek and find*; *seek and destroy*; *seeking* out directions, a place, or a person. The verb can also indicate vague desires or high-minded aspirations: negotiators *seeking* the good of all people; peacemakers who have always *sought* for an end to war.

Explore is like the aspect of *search* pertaining to activity that does not or cannot have a precisely stated goal in advance. *Explore* is much more clear-cut about this, however, since it always implies an attempt to learn more about an unknown: missionaries who were the first to *explore* the upper Mississippi; the thrill of *exploring* the streets of a strange city; an operation to *explore* the tissue surrounding the growth for any signs of malignancy. The action indicated by *explore* can, of course, have a stated general goal, but some sense of newness or unfamiliarity is always present in the verb.

The remaining verbs all involve the notion of a thorough or meticulous search of an area for evidence or for something lost or presumed to exist. **Comb** indicates a methodical, careful, minute, and orderly covering of possibilities, often giving a tone of desperation and sometimes implying a group search: a *searching* party that *combed* the hills for the missing campers. **Scour** compares with *comb* in thoroughness, but may suggest greater effort or intensity: They *scoured* their apartments for the missing keys. Although these verbs can be used interchangeably, *comb* might be more appropriate for small areas, since *scour* here can confusingly suggest the literal action of abrasion. **Ransack** indicates a strikingly different action, comparable in thoroughness, but implying a hasty, careless, or disorderly search: They had broken in and *ransacked* the darkroom for the incriminating roll of film, leaving behind a total mess. *Ransack* most often suggests the search of an interior, such as a house or room, and can often point to a furtive or illegal action. See EXAMINE, FIND, FOLLOW.

hurt
afflict
aggrieve
distress
pain

These verbs are used in referring to acts or situations that cause someone to feel emotionally upset or mentally injured. **Hurt** is the most general and informal of these verbs; it suggests a small mental injury: accusations designed to *hurt* and frighten the witness. **Pain**, in this context, now tends to sound archaic: *pained* by constant references to her sins. Because *pain* may sound unnatural or forced, it can sometimes give an unsympathetic tone: easily *pained* by the smallest slight. **Distress** has an extremely formal sound in most of its uses as a verb and can give a prissy or euphemistic tone: the manager who claimed to be greatly *distressed* by his sales staff's long lunch hours. It may seem more natural in describing a subjective state of mind: *distressed* by vague longings and poorly defined fears. **Aggrieve** has become so fusty-sounding that its only possible use is in the passive voice, for distraught states of mind: a parent deeply *aggrieved* by his children's disobedience. **Afflict** suggests a condition that is extremely uncomfortable or upsetting and further hints that the condition is one of long duration: *afflicted* by tensions that drove him to suicide. See HARM, WRONG.

Antonyms: *benefit, comfort, console, soothe.*

husky
beefy
brawny
burly
hulking
stocky
strapping

These adjectives describe strong, heavy, powerfully built, or masculine physiques. **Husky** refers to masculine muscularity. It derives from husk, referring to the tough covering shell of a seed; also, its other uses pertaining to dryness, roughness, or hoarseness provide connotations here. While *husky* suggests largeness of frame, it is more emphatic about the strength or muscular density of physique, particularly of the torso, with suggestions of coarseness or toughness. Thus, it serves as an antonym to lithe or supple and implies instead a possibly slower but more powerful body: the lithe physique best for runners and tennis players as compared to the *husky* builds required for wrestling or shotput.

Brawny and **burly** both intensify the emphasis of *husky* on massive or dense muscular development, suggesting in these cases a grossness of build beyond that of any well-proportioned and cleanly defined athletic ideal. *Burly* may carry connotations over from another word, identical in form, that refers to the knots and burls of a tree, in this case suggesting a thick bunching of muscles that may verge on the grotesque; an overall thickness of frame, at any rate, is implied, with suggestions of coarse or crude power that are even stronger than those for *husky:* the *burly,* lumbering stevedore with the thick neck and barrel chest. *Brawny* is less extreme in its implications than *burly,* emphasizing instead the sheer power inherent in muscular development. Where *husky* may particularly point to a developed torso, *brawny* suggests general

muscular density, such as that acquired through hard physical labor: a *brawny* lumberjack.

Beefy points to muscular masses but, unlike the previous adjectives, need not indicate power or density. *Beefy* can in fact suggest a fleshy grossness that may be repellent or flabby: the nightclub's *beefy* bouncer. **Hulking** and **stocky** both suggest sheer size or largeness of frame rather than pointing primarily to muscular development. *Hulking* particularly indicates a tall or looming male build: a *hulking* football player. *Stocky,* by contrast, emphasizes largeness rather than tallness of frame: a *stocky* plumber almost as wide as he was tall. Even more than *husky, stocky* can be used euphemistically for a fat or heavy body: a reducing clinic for *stocky* executives. **Strapping** combines the suggestions of sheer size in the last pair with the stress on muscular development in the first group. *Strapping* is often used to indicate precocious growth and development in boys or young men: a *strapping,* towheaded farmboy. See MASCULINE, PHYSICAL.

Antonyms: *THIN.*

idea

concept
conception
impression
notion
thought

All these nouns denote something that exists in the mind during the processes of perceiving, thinking, or willing. **Idea** is the most general term, applicable to almost any part or aspect of mental activity. [The *idea* of death is frightening to some people; I had no *idea* of going to the party; She encouraged her employees to communicate their most promising *ideas*.] A **concept** is an *idea* of a category or kind that has been generalized from particular instances. Thus, the *concept* of horse arises from the many horses we see. *Concept* also refers to a widely held *idea* of what something is or should be: The *concept* of government of many small nations has been influenced by the democratic institutions of the United States. The meaning of **conception** is much like this second sense of *concept*, but differs in that the *idea* of what a thing is or should be is here held by an individual or small group and is often colored by imagination and feeling: The child's *conception* of the universe is formed by her limited experience and her fancies. A **thought** is an *idea* based on intellectual activity and is not directly attributable to a sense impression: He has many *thoughts* on the matter. A **notion** is a vague or capricious *idea*, often without any sound basis: to have a *notion* that the stock market will rise. An **impression** is an *idea* that arises from something external. It suggests either a half-formed mental picture or a superficial view or conclusion. [An infant may have the *impression* that its father is a giant; My *impression* is that he was lying.] See OPINION.

ignoble

base
beggarly
cheap
low
mean
shabby

These adjectives are alike in describing persons or actions regarded as being far below common worth or dignity. **Ignoble** and **mean** originally meant of low birth but they are seldom used today to refer to social status. *Ignoble* denotes a lack or loss of noble or praiseworthy qualities and frequently implies a failure to meet ordinarily accepted standards of worth or excellence: the *ignoble* betrayal of a trust. *Mean* suggests a contemptible smallness of mind, or a petty, ungenerous nature: to repeat *mean* gossip. **Beggarly**, **cheap**, and **shabby** are close to *mean* in connotation, each suggesting the same nasty, sordid vulgarity. While *ignoble* could possibly describe the act of a person from whom we might expect a better sort of conduct, *mean, beggarly, cheap,* and *shabby* describe persons or actions for which we feel only scorn and disdain: a miserly landlord's *beggarly* treatment of an indigent tenant; the *cheap* quarreling of two brothers whose father had died intestate; the *shabby* charges and countercharges of rival political bosses. **Base** and **low** are alike in being strong words used to condemn that which is openly evil, selfish, dishonorable, or otherwise unmoral. As with *mean, beggarly,* or *cheap,* the character or action described as *base* or *low* is worthy only of contempt: a soldier guilty of *base* cowardice; a petty crook who was *low* enough to swindle a sick widow out of her life's savings. See CONTEMPTIBLE, SHAMEFUL.
Antonyms: MORAL, *noble.*

imagination

fancy
fantasy
reverie

These nouns refer to the mind's power to call up images, to picture or conceive things that are not actually before the eye or within the experience. At one time, **imagination** and **fancy** could be used interchangeably, but now the two terms are sharply distinguished both in application and in scope. Used in the broad sense of a basic mental faculty, *imagination* encompasses *fancy; fancy* is a playful or whimsical sort of *imagination.* Used in a restricted sense, *imagination* contrasts with *fancy; imagination* applies to the higher, creative faculty, and *fancy* is limited to a capriciously inventive play of mind. More serious in purpose than the *fancy,* the higher *imagination* creates a new form of reality, bringing forth things unknown or new by recombining the products of experience. The *fancy* is freer and more frivolous, following its whims and ranging further from reality: unbridled *fancy;* a flight of *fancy*. Where the higher *imagination* creates vivid characters that are true to life, such as Hamlet, Falstaff, and King Lear, the *fancy* dreams up delightful, nonexistent beings, such as elves, fairies, and woodland sprites. *Imagination* and *fancy* are also used to contrast false or misleading impressions with truth or reality. [No one moved in the bushes; it was only your *imagination;* Was it fact or *fancy?*]

Fantasy is *imagination* divorced from reality. The creations of *fantasy* may be delightfully bizarre or may be weird and grotesque, as in the case of science-fiction stories depicting strange people from Mars. Engaged in *fantasy,* the *imagination* projects unreal images or imaginary scenes on the screen of the mind, creating a dream world. [An amusement park full of figures from fairy tales may be called *Fantasy*land; In his *fantasies,* the meek little man was a bold, brave hero.] *Fantasy* and **reverie** both involve a withdrawal from the real world during which the mind is focused on its own imaginings, but where in *fantasy* there is an element of escapism, in *reverie* the mind is not actively fleeing reality but is simply not conscious of the world without. A *fantasy* is a vivid daydream directed like a drama by the mind. *Reverie* is an undirected wandering of the mind—an abstracted, dreamlike state during which *fancies, fantasies,* memories, or other imaginings preoccupy the mind and free it from conscious control. See ARTISTIC, CREATIVE, DELUSION.

Antonyms: *actuality, fact, reality, truth.*

imitate

ape
copy
impersonate
mimic

These verbs refer to reproducing the style or characteristics of something taken as a model. **Imitate** is the most general and neutral of these, referring to any attempt to repeat convincingly or tellingly the recognizable features of the model; this may be done unconsciously because of a lack of originality, semiconsciously out of admiration, or consciously as satire: He hadn't realized how much he tended to *imitate* his father's way of talking; a writer who slavishly *imitated* the works of his favorite poet, Keats; a brilliant parody that *imitated* the acting of movie queens of the silent screen. *Imitate* may also point to a conscious attempt at a serious resemblance for other than satiric effect: novelists who strive to *imitate* the speech patterns of real people; the cliché about art *imitating* life. It may also suggest following some example-setting prece-

dent: hairdressers who *imitated* the new British hair styles.

Copy stresses a conscious or at least semiconscious process; this may be done merely to duplicate information: He *copied* the relevant data out of the encyclopedia. It may also, like *imitate*, suggest following an admired or fashionable model: They *copied* in dress and speech the oldest member of their gang. Often, however, the verb suggests unethical appropriation: He found himself *copying* his friend's answers during the grueling exam. In a related context, the verb can also refer to mere mechanical duplication: the office *copying* machine.

Impersonate concentrates exclusively on a specific aspect of *imitate;* it refers to the assuming of another person's mannerisms or appearance, either for the amusement of others or to perpetrate a fraud: a nightclub entertainer who could *impersonate* half a dozen movie stars with amazing verisimilitude; a crime to *impersonate* a police officer. **Mimic**, in turn, concentrates on one aspect of *impersonate*, the acting out of someone else's mannerisms for humorous or satiric effect: She savagely *mimicked* the nasal whine of their teacher; a number in which he *mimicked* the vocal styles of several well-known singers. Sometimes, *mimic* is used contemptuously for any *imitating* of a style or vogue: a rash of local singers struggling to *mimic* a group of rap artists.

Ape is related to this last possibility of *mimic*, but can refer either to a conscious, contemptuous caricature or to less conscious, but slavish adherence to faddish models: They howled with laughter at the way he *aped* their manager's voice; adults who desperately try to *ape* the dance crazes of the young. See CARICATURE, COPY, DUPLICATE.

Antonyms: CREATE, *originate.*

immerse

dip
douse
duck
dunk
plunge
submerge

These verbs refer to the forceful pushing of something into water or another liquid. **Immerse** and **submerge** are the most formal and the most general in range of meaning. *Immerse* indicates the lowering of something into water so that all of it is below the surface: denominations that believe a person must be completely *immersed* in order to be properly baptized;

He *immersed* the cabbage in boiling water. *Submerge* also refers to putting something completely under water, but in this case the verb often suggests an object's being lowered to a greater depth than necessarily suggested by *immerse:* They weighted the old boat with rocks to keep it *submerged* at the bottom of the lake. Furthermore, *submerge* now often suggests the self-propelled sinking of a submarine: able to fire Polaris missiles while *submerged.*

The remaining verbs are much more informal and refer specifically to distinct kinds of *immersing* or *submerging.* **Plunge** suggests rapid and forceful motion, but not necessarily to any great depth: *plunging* the bunch of celery in water several times and shaking it vigorously; *plunging* from the overhanging cliff in a beautiful dive. **Dunk** most concretely suggests a partial lowering of something into a liquid; unlike *plunge,* the motion may be slow and gentle: to *dunk* a doughnut in coffee. **Dip** may suggest any kind of partial lowering, but most often, perhaps, would suggest a cautious, tentative movement: She *dipped* her foot into the water to see how cold it was. *Dip* may also apply to a brief but complete lowering: Easter eggs made by *dipping* them in bowls of dissolved food coloring. **Duck** now suggests the prankish forcing of someone's head under water: The lifeguard warned the boys not to *duck* each other if they wished to keep their swimming privileges.

While **douse** can be used like *plunge,* it more often indicates an action in sharp contrast with actions indicated by other verbs in this group. The liquid in this case is poured or sprinkled over something to drench, soak, or cover it; the only movement involved may be the downpour of water itself. [We got thoroughly *doused* by the sudden thunderstorm; He *doused* the face of the unconscious man with a glass of cold water.] *Douse* can even refer to a thorough soaking, however applied: plum pudding *doused* in brandy. See PERMEATE.

immortal
deathless
imperishable
undying

These adjectives apply to what cannot or will never die. **Immortal** is the one most likely to be used in theological discussion concerning the soul or the Deity: man's *immortal* soul; the *immortal* gods of the Greek pantheon. *Immortal* is also used loosely for any human accomplishment that seems particularly durable: the *immortal* works of Voltaire. It may also apply to the creator: the *immortal* Shakespeare; the *immortal* Jane Austen. **Deathless** and **undying** are more lyrical in tone, but both can function in the same theological or hyperbolic ways as *immortal. Deathless* was popular in the Romantic Age to typify aspiration or achievement but may now sound rhetorical and high-flown; sometimes it refers pejoratively to such uses: an unpublished writer who wrote *deathless* prose. *Undying* is less open to the charge of pretentiousness, partly because it is an accepted hyperbole for lasting sentiments as well as achievements: *undying* love; From that moment on he felt *undying* hatred for his oppressors.

While **imperishable** can also be used in ways identical to *immortal,* with a possible gain in vividness, *imperishable* can also indicate anything not subject to change or decay. When applied to something long-lasting but not in any case subject to physical death, *imperishable* may be more precise than the previous adjectives: the *imperishable* Elgin marbles; the *imperishable* will of people to survive and excel; a universe in which only matter and energy can be said to be *imperishable.* See EVERLASTING, IMMUTABLE, INFINITE, PERMANENT.

Antonyms: *mortal, perishable,* TEMPORARY.

immutable
fixed
indestructible
unchangeable
unchanging
unfading
unvarying

These adjectives refer to what does not change or cannot be changed. **Immutable** is the most formal of these words and refers strictly to that which cannot be changed. It often applies approvingly to a truth or principle unaffected by fashion or the passage of time: the *immutable* Golden Rule; the *immutable* justice and mercy of God. In referring to things beyond the scale of human impermanence, *immutable* need not always be approving, though it may connote humility or awe in recognizing them: the *immutable* physical laws of the universe. **Unchangeable** is a more informal substitute for *immutable,* but it also applies more widely to anything not subject to alteration: *unchangeable* hereditary traits. Often, *unchangeable* can be used disapprovingly of things that are too inflexible or rigid to permit vigor or growth: an *unchangeable* social order that stifled individuality.

Fixed can indicate something that appears in an *immutable* order: early astronomers who distinguished between the wandering planets and the *fixed* stars. But *fixed* can apply within the human scale, whether positively or negatively, to anything set, predetermined, habitual, or rigid: A child's personality is said to be *fixed* in the first five years of life; a woman of *fixed* opinions; a *fixed* stare. **Indestructible**, at its most literal, refers neutrally to what can never cease to exist: earlier theories that matter was *indestructible*. As a hyperbole, *indestructible* can refer approvingly to anything that withstands decay or change: the *indestructible* pyramids; They fought on against overwhelming odds with an *indestructible* determination to win the war.

Unfading can occasionally refer to materials that are colorfast but, more commonly, it refers in a general way to anything that retains its vividness over a long period of time: the *unfading* memory of their first meeting. The remaining adjectives stress what does not change, for whatever reason, rather than something that cannot be changed. **Unchanging** can merely indicate what is lasting: *unchanging* love. But it can be more specific in a series or sequence in which each item resembles every other: *unchanging* summer days; the tenderness and simplicity with which they moved through the *unchanging* ritual of their days. The adjective can also be disapproving in this sense: an *unchanging* routine that made them want to scream with boredom. **Unvarying** points almost exclusively to identical items in a series. It can be neutral or approving: He pronounced each word with *unvarying* precision. But it is often negative, with even greater force than *unchanging:* the *unvarying* daily round of their humdrum lives. See EVERLASTING, IMMORTAL, INVARIABLE, PERMANENT.

Antonyms: *changing, fading,* INCONSTANT, TEMPORARY.

impact

brunt
concussion
force
jolt
shock

These nouns refer to the energy with which objects are propelled, bear down, or collide. **Impact** is specifically restricted to an emphasis on the moment or point of contact between objects, one or both of which have been in motion: the *impact* of the meteorite on the earth's surface; the *impact* of two speeding cars. In emphasizing the contact itself, *impact* remains relative about the amount of stress developed: the faint *impact* of rain on his forehead; the mile-wide crater that

would result from the *impact* and explosion of so large a bomb. *Impact* is often used metaphorically for any effect: the *impact* of a tax cut on the economy. Here, again, it remains relative about the amount of effect engendered. The more formal **concussion** is closely related to *impact* in stressing collision but is even more specific, referring to the considerable destructive energy released, usually with resulting damage of a temporary or permanent nature, as in its reference to brain damage from a blow: suffered a *concussion* in the auto accident that would leave him handicapped for life. Even outside this specific use, it suggests a violent *impact:* delicate instruments that could not survive the *concussion* of a hard landing on the moon.

Jolt and **shock** are more informal than the previous nouns. They are both more general than but otherwise closely related to *concussion* in stressing the giving off of considerable energy, as in a collision or blow. *Jolt* may suggest a sudden shaking motion imparted to one body by another that is in motion: thrown back in her seat with a *jolt* when the driver suddenly slammed on the brakes. It is widely used in a more general context for any surprising or stunning occurrence: scientific discoveries that come like *jolts* to awaken the intellectual world. *Shock* suggests an abrupt and heavy *impact* or onslaught: reeling back under the first *shock* of the attack. But the noun's other meanings are inevitably present as overtones here, implying a numbed unbelieving response or physical collapse from injury: the *shock* with which she took the tragic news; a blow that sent him into a state of *shock.*

Brunt suggests an energetic bearing down that may or may not be supportable; once this may have referred particularly to abruptness of contact, much like *impact:* wiring that could not bear the *brunt* of any heavy flow of voltage. Now it refers more often to a steady demand that taxes endurance: the *brunt* of so many debts and so little earning power. **Force** is the most general of these nouns and may refer to the degree of energy with which objects make contact or to the amount of propulsion with which things move: grenades with enough *force* to blow up an enemy bunker; applying enough *force* to dislodge the nameplate; gamma rays that strike the earth's atmosphere with considerable *force*. See BREAK (n.), BREAK (v.), IMPEL, PROPEL.

impassive

apathetic
indifferent
insensible

phlegmatic
stolid

These adjectives describe a lack of emotional responsiveness. **Impassive** can pertain to a total lack of sensation or feeling: the *impassive* eyes of the corpse. Used in a less extreme way, it can refer to someone who remains unmoved by an emotional appeal: The judge stared down, remote and *impassive*, while the defense lawyer pleaded for clemency. With greater suggestiveness, *impassive* can often indicate someone who maintains a calm or unmoved exterior to conceal an emotional response: Only the faintest flicker of distaste betrayed the otherwise *impassive* expression with which the prime minister greeted the visiting head of state.

Apathetic and **indifferent** contrast sharply with this last possibility for *impassive*, since both point to a failure to respond. In addition, *apathetic* often carries a tone of criticism for a deplorable or pitiable lack of awareness, compassion, or empathy: students critical of parents who had grown *apathetic* about glaring social evils. Sometimes, this note of criticism may be absent: slum children already sunk in *apathetic* despair. Where *apathetic* can suggest an extreme state of anomie or listlessness, *indifferent* usually indicates a milder state of boredom or uninvolvement. Also, where *apathetic* can sometimes suggest someone dulled by adversity, *indifferent* can point to self-contentment as the motivating factor: The French ruling class had long been *indifferent* to the miseries endured by the peasants. But *indifferent* is less often condemnatory than *apathetic;* it can be neutral or even positive: people wise enough to remain *indifferent* to the exhortations of demagogues—without ever growing *apathetic* to the threat they represented.

Insensible refers to a lack of sensation or awareness that stems either from a physiological numbness, from a steeled and determined stoicism, or from extreme preoccupation: fingers that had grown stiff and *insensible* with the cold; freedom fighters who learned to be *insensible* to hunger, thirst, and suffering; so engrossed that he had become *insensible* to the passage of time. Less approvingly, *insensible* can refer to a callous lack of consideration for others: *insensible* to the needs of his wife.

Phlegmatic and **stolid** most often refer to a cast of temperament that is unemotional. *Phlegmatic* suggests a habitually *apathetic* or wishy-washy personality, lacking in forcefulness or vividness: a *phlegmatic* dullard as interesting as stale beer. By contrast, *stolid* suggests someone wooden, stiff, and unbending: a coarse, *stolid* jailer who could watch executions with-

out flinching. Whereas *phlegmatic* can indicate someone weak, passive, and yielding, even to the point of suggesting physical debilitation, *stolid* suggests a sturdy or unyielding rigidity or strength that is capable of surviving challenge: *phlegmatic* intellectuals who were no match for the *stolid* mass of the dictator's adherents. See DISINTERESTED, LISTLESS, OBLIVIOUS, UNINVOLVED.

Antonyms: EAGER, HUMANE, *responsive*.

impel

drive
motivate
move
prod
prompt

These verbs refer to whatever causes or contributes to the starting or continuing of an action. **Impel** always suggests considerable force; sometimes, this can apply to the movement of physical objects: an upward rush of sparks, *impelled* by columns of heated air that rose from the burning buildings. More often, *impel* refers to people acting under strong outward constraint or inner necessity: refugees *impelled* to flee before the advancing armies; legislators *impelled* by popular opinion to campaign for the passage of a bill; *impelled* by his desire to see her once more. **Move** is much more general; it can refer to physical motion without reference to force: The earth *moves* around the sun. When applied to the behavior of people, it stresses one aspect of *impel*, namely a forceful inner conviction or depth of feeling: *moved* by her appeal to enter the fight in behalf of the condemned man. Just as often, *move* refers to any surge of emotion: *moved* to tears; a film he found very *moving*.

Like *impel*, **drive** can suggest considerable force in reference to physical objects: leaves *driven* by the wind. It contrasts with *impel* because of its greater informality. In reference to what causes people to act, it can suggest a more direct outward goading than *impel*, or a greater inner obsessiveness than *move*: Christ *driving* the money changers from the temple; *driving* off the flies with a flyswatter; a psychosis that *drove* him to act out his fantasies; *driven* to drink by a jealous husband. **Motivate** is mostly restricted to expressing what causes people to act. It can be used in neutral causal explanation: What *motivated* him to commit the murder? Or it can indicate a conscious attempt to inculcate a desire for something: students *motivated* to learn by the encouragement offered by one good teacher.

Where all the previous verbs are equally applicable to initial and continuing action, **prod** and **prompt** both emphasize setting something in motion. At its most literal, *prod* suggests the use of a tool: He *prodded* the anthill with a stick. When applied to human behavior, *prod* suggests a one-time impetus of any sort: a smell of smoke that *prodded* the sleeping parents into action; a book that *prodded* the nation into a belated concern for the impoverished. *Prompt* literally refers to giving a speaker a cue, as in the theater: He still had to be *prompted* after two weeks of rehearsing; a television *prompting* device for speakers delivering written speeches. In more general uses, *prompt* is like *prod* in suggesting some type of stimulus to action. But where *prod* often suggests a start or jolt that makes one newly aware of something, *prompt* is more like *motivate,* though less formal, in its emphasis on causation: a misstatement of fact that *prompted* her to disagree with the host for the first time that evening; What *prompted* him to behave so rudely to their guests? See COMPEL, INCITE, INDUCE, PROPEL, STIMULATE.

Antonyms: *inhibit,* PREVENT, QUELL, STOP *(arrest),* SUBDUE.

impenetrable
impassable
impermeable
impervious

These adjectives describe the resistance of a thing to incursions upon or into it. **Impenetrable** suggests a solid mass of resistance that cannot be pierced or breached: miners trapped in the tunnel by an *impenetrable* mass of debris; rush-hour traffic that is almost *impenetrable* to the forgotten pedestrian; an *impenetrable* phalanx of avid bargain-hunters clustered around the sale table. The suggestion of an unbroken mass need not always be present; in this case, *impenetrable* may suggest the considerable resistance presented to anyone attempting to move through the medium: an *impenetrable* thicket of brambles. It may even be applied to things that allow incursions but thwart their purpose: a jungle *impenetrable* to a generation of explorers, all of whom it swallowed up effortlessly. Used of people, their expressions, or personality, the adjective suggests inscrutability, lack of response, or hostility: She responded to the suggestion with an *impenetrable* blankness. **Impervious** suggests even greater resistance to incursions than *impenetrable.* The failure to pierce an *impenetrable* object might still leave marks or superficial signs of damage. By

contrast, *impervious* suggests something that is literally beyond showing any change whatsoever from attempts to breach or affect it: gems *impervious* to scratching; metals *impervious* to cold and heat. As can be seen, *impervious* does not necessarily imply warding off efforts at piercing something so much as surviving vicissitudes without change. This is even more true in the adjective's less concrete uses, suggesting inscrutability or hostility, not inner strength, stubbornness, or determination that cannot be swayed by externals: They led a life *impervious* to criticism; infuriatingly *impervious* to her every suggestion; *impervious* to the temptations offered him if only he would compromise his stand.

Impassable and **impermeable** are both more narrowly restricted to specific contexts of resistance than the foregoing. *Impassable* refers to any blockage that makes travel impossible: roads that became *impassable* during the rainy season; heavy snows and avalanches that left the mountain route *impassable.* *Impermeable* refers, even more specifically, to a membrane through which certain fluids cannot pass. The membrane itself, of course, is not the same sort of barrier to passage as those implied by these other adjectives, since it might well be easily ruptured; also, the membrane may be selective in the substances to which it prohibits passage: tissues *impermeable* to carbon dioxide but not to oxygen. See COMPACT, HINDER, OBSTACLE, STOP (arrest).

Antonyms: *accessible, open, permeable,* VULNERABLE.

imperturbable
calm
collected
composed
cool
dispassionate
sober

These adjectives all characterize the absence of visible tension or excitement in persons when such reactions might well be expected. **Imperturbable** carries the sense of self-control based on temperament or discipline; it is perhaps most often used of a diplomatic or stately detachment and suggests more of a constitutional inability than a conscious refusal to panic: The *imperturbable* Secretary of State responded without asperity to the pointed questioning of the congressional committee members. When applied to attitudes or conduct rather than people, *imperturbable* means unshakable and suggests a strong, almost irrational devotion to a particular point of view: an *imper-*

turbable optimism that was not to be dampened by misfortune, however great.

Cool and **dispassionate** suggest a deliberate stifling of emotions in the face of disturbing influences. Where *dispassionate* emphasizes detachment and disinterestedness, *cool* points to resistance to excitability: to keep *cool* under enemy fire; a *dispassionate* surgeon; a *dispassionate* appraisal of the state of our economy. *Cool* is now used as a noun in a slang sense with the meaning of wits or composure: He completely lost his *cool* when the cop grabbed his arm.

Calm and **collected** are often used together with *cool* to suggest the complete intactness of mental resources in the face of difficulty. *Calm* stresses a quiet approach to a problem, devoid of hysterical actions or utterances, and *collected* stresses the application of appropriate mental or physical effort to the solution of the problem: to remain *cool, calm,* and *collected* in the midst of a violent demonstration.

Composed and **sober** in this context suggest dignified demeanor and conduct in the midst of confusion. *Sober* suggests a reasoned, quiet, and sometimes cautious attitude; *composed* indicates an even-tempered, self-controlled attitude. [The speaker remained *composed* despite the audience's heckling; Her *sober* approach to the crisis averted a catastrophe.] See TRANQUIL.

Antonyms: *agitated,* FRANTIC, NERVOUS, *shaken, touchy, volatile.*

impetuous

headlong
impulsive
precipitate
sudden

These adjectives are applied to actions or persons characterized by a lack of forethought, warning, or preparation. **Impetuous** and **impulsive** differ from the others in applying both to people and actions. *Impetuous* suggests more decisive or vigorous action than *impulsive* and often implies an unfortunate outcome as a result. *Impulsive* means acting on impulse, and since impulses can be good as well as bad, *impulsiveness* is not necessarily deplorable; it may even be considered endearing or attractive. *Impetuosity,* on the other hand, implies a rather childish inability to be patient or thoughtful before taking action. [Hers was a generous, *impulsive* nature, capable of spontaneous affection and warmth; an *impetuous* decision he soon would regret; to stamp his foot in an *impetuous* rage.] *Impulsive* need not always imply recklessness, and in

some contexts may only imply spontaneity and the lack of premeditation: an *impulsive* urge to reopen the door and check to see whether all the windows were closed before she left the house.

Headlong suggests a reckless disregard of consequences along with *impetuous* haste. Unlike the other adjectives here considered, *headlong* is used as both an adjective and an adverb; it is somewhat more formal when used as an adjective: a *headlong* advance into enemy territory; people rushing *headlong* into the store at the start of the sale; to plunge *headlong* into a business without adequate financial backing. Where *headlong* points to a complete lack of deliberation, **precipitate** suggests that what deliberation did occur was grossly inadequate to prepare for the ensuing action; a *precipitate* action is therefore premature and rash. [The editorial called the union's rejection of the wage offer *precipitate* and unwarranted.] **Sudden**, as here considered, suggests an abrupt or unexpected action but does not necessarily imply haste; it does point to either a spontaneous, unpremeditated act or a perception for which one is not prepared. [The crowd made a *sudden* rush for the door when someone shouted, "Fire!"; His *sudden* departure from the published text of the speech caught us by surprise; The *sudden* stop of the bus threw several people to the floor.] See HEEDLESS, RECKLESS.

Antonyms: CAUTIOUS, IMPASSIVE, IMPERTURBABLE, *thoughtful.*

implant

imbue
inculcate
infuse
ingrain
inseminate
instill

These verbs indicate the sowing or embedding of something in a receiving medium. **Implant** has the widest range of application. It can refer to a fixing or rooting in the ground: *implanting* the seedlings in a diamond pattern; *implanting* the flagpole at the top of the hill. It can refer to the inserting in tissue of a graft or device: a cutting *implanted* under the bark of the tree; *implanting* a kidney of the donor in his critically ill twin brother; *implanting* a plastic valve in the patient's heart. More generally, however, *implant* refers to the fixing of an idea in the mind, usually in the context of the educating of a child or student by a parent or teacher: a sense of decency *implanted* in her by her upbringing. In this use, the internalizing of rudimentary principles or attitudes is usually suggested, but rote training is not necessarily the technique by which the *implanting* is done. In any case, a deeply rooted and unshakable transfer of attitude or knowledge is implied. Such a fixing of ideas in one's own mind is not usually suggested by *implant,* but an unconscious process may be indicated, or even the fixing of qualities by heredity rather than environment: an innate curiosity that seems to have been *implanted* in him from birth. *Implant* at its most general can suggest the informing or propagandizing of any audience, whether overtly or subliminally: assumptions about cooperation and competition that every culture *implants* in its members.

Inseminate can still reflect its derivation by referring literally to the sowing of seed in soil. Much more commonly, however, the verb refers to the introducing of semen into the vagina or to the *implanting* of ideas in the mind: studying the reproductive cycle from the *inseminating* of sperm to the birth of the child; means for artificially *inseminating* livestock; teachers who *inseminate* a respect for authority in their students.

Infuse in its original Latin form meant pour in. It now carries a suggestion of this etymology in its reference to the introduction of something, as a quality, feeling, or idea into a receiving medium. Such introduction, it is implied, lends the medium inspiration, animation, or new significance: to *infuse* life into a dull party. **Imbue** has much the same connotation as *infuse,* but whereas *infuse* may indicate a temporary or superficial influence, *imbue* more often points to a change that deeply affects the receiving medium. Another difference between the two verbs is that *imbue* takes for its object the thing affected rather than the thing introduced: to *imbue* a student with confidence.

Ingrain means impress firmly on the mind or character. *Ingrain,* which is used almost exclusively in the passive or past participle, is like *imbue* in denoting an affecting influence that works into the inmost texture of the receiving medium: a deep respect for the truth had been *ingrained* into the child.

The remaining pair are restricted solely to the context of learning. **Instill** suggests a slow, subtle, possibly gentle transfer of attitude more than facts, one that reflects its derivation from a word meaning to put in by drops. Most often *instill* suggests a conscious imparting to someone who is at most only partially aware of the process: striving to *instill* in her son a distrust of his father; understanding how carefully her psychiatrist worked to *instill* in her an attitude of perfect trust; seeing how blindly everything in his drab environment had worked to *instill* within him a rage against the established order; nations that, without even realizing it, *instill* in their citizens an unexamined fear of outsiders. *Instill,* furthermore, is the only one of these verbs that can possibly suggest development of an attitude within oneself: a biographer who has not *instilled* in herself a proper objectivity toward her subject.

Inculcate limits this range of possibilities in *instill* to one situation, that in which both teacher and student are well aware of the learning process under way. A further limiting exists in that *inculcate* refers specifically to an *ingraining* of facts, ideas, or attitudes by the technique of laborious repetition: a generation of students who had not been *inculcated* with the rules of grammar. [English spelling cannot be reasoned out; it must be *inculcated,* example by insufferable example.] *Inculcate* more recently has taken on a disapproving tone to refer to the deliberate *ingraining* of propaganda or falsehoods in unsuspecting subjects: *inculcating* the doctrines of race hatred in innocent children. See INSERT, TEACH.

implicit

covert
latent
potential
tacit
unspoken

These adjectives describe things left unexpressed, unrealized, or unacted upon, though their existence or influence can often be detected. **Implicit** refers to something that is not revealed in words or action but can be inferred from the evidence: an *implicit* cultural assumption that men are superior to women; riots that were the expression of the violence *implicit* in day-to-day ghetto life; a weakness *implicit* in his approach to Renaissance art. **Potential** is close to *implicit* but stresses the capability of something to become active: on the lookout for *potential* customers; the *potential* good within a person. **Latent**, by contrast, stresses something that is not conscious or acted out, with no implication that it need ever be made manifest: a *latent* homosexual; musical talent that remained *latent* through a lack of training. Occasionally, *latent* can suggest something once in evidence but now hidden through accident or design: childhood fears that have become *latent* and fossilized in adulthood.

Covert is restricted to this last sense of *latent,* referring to something that is deliberately hidden or accomplished in secret. Thus, *covert* may even suggest a furtive acting out of something, a possibility that is in sharp contrast to the meanings of the previous adjectives: *covert* assignations that brought them together often, though both remained tied to their respective spouses. The stealth implied in *covert* usually points to unsavory or unethical misconduct, although this is not always true: hermetic readings of Scripture that saw it as a system of *covert* symbols for Gnostic doctrines; auctions conducted by means of *covert* signals between bidders and auctioneer. **Tacit** may apply in the same general way as *implicit*, but it does have specific relevance to agreements or understandings arrived at without verbalizing some or all of the conditions involved: a *tacit* understanding in the group that the newcomer would be watched closely; housing contracts that left *tacit* the illegal exclusion of minority groups from the neighborhood. **Unspoken** is restricted to one aspect of *tacit*, referring more informally to things not mentioned or said aloud. Like *covert* and *tacit*, *unspoken* contrasts with *latent* in indicating things one is conscious of and acts upon, but without expressing them: eyes glinting with her evident but *unspoken* disapproval of him; sexual assumptions that were left *unspoken* out of a sense of delicacy. See INHERENT.

Antonyms: *actual*, DEFINITE, *exposed*, *overt*, *plain*.

imply. Do not confuse the verb *imply* (suggest, hint) with the verb *infer* (reach an opinion from facts or reasoning). The distinction between these two verbs carries over into the nouns *implication* and *inference*.

improve

    ameliorate
    better
    meliorate

These verbs mean bring something to a higher level of quality, efficiency, etc. **Improve** is the most general verb in this group; it can mean increase, enlarge, correct, or raise, as in the following examples: to *improve* one's vocabulary; to *improve* one's understanding of world affairs; to *improve* one's habits; to *improve* one's grades. *Improve* thus refers to any means of making something higher in quality or more desirable in nature.

Better, more colloquial in tone, is in some contexts interchangeable with *improve*: to *better* (or *improve*) one's grades. But as a rule it has more narrow implications, often suggesting only a modest increase or elevation in knowledge or appreciation. Although *better* can

also be used to describe such situations, in contexts implying a profound or important elevation of status or quality, *improve* is more likely to be used: Through keen management procedures and substantial investment, the company *improved* its market potential. *Better* is often used reflexively with the sense of *improving* socially or economically. [She took the new job to *better* herself; He joined the country club with the hope of *bettering* himself.] *Better* so used often has a vulgar tone. The greater scope and importance that attach to *improve* become evident if one contrasts *improve oneself* with *better oneself*: He went to night school to *improve himself*.

Ameliorate is usually applied to conditions rather than to specific things and suggests that the conditions are in need of correction: The city council considered legislation to *ameliorate* the unsanitary conditions in slum areas. **Meliorate** has the same meaning as *ameliorate*, but is nowadays less often used. Both verbs, but especially *meliorate*, are extremely formal or literary: missionaries whose aim was to *meliorate* the pathetic ignorance of indigenous peoples. See ENLARGE, REPAIR.

Antonyms: *deteriorate*, *impair*, POLLUTE, ROT, *worsen*.

incite

    arouse
    exhort
    foment
    instigate
    provoke
    rouse
    stir up

The verbs in this list all mean stimulate vigorously into being or action. **Incite** means spur to action and may be applied to measures leading to salutary as well as deplorable results, to minor as well as profound changes: to *incite* others to greater effort by setting an example with one's own conduct; to *incite* a riot by making inflammatory speeches. **Stir up** is more informal than *incite* and more often applies to less serious disturbances or to attitudes of mind: an unruly boy who kept *stirring up* trouble when the teacher's back was turned; to *stir up* indignation. When applied to mental attitudes, as in the latter example, *stir up* is close to **arouse**. *Arouse* points specifically to awakening or opening one's eyes to a situation or point of view, whereas the more emphatic **rouse** indicates a call to action or to vigorous opinion likely to lead to action. [His speech *roused* the audience to such a fury that the police were forced to escort him away hastily for his own safety; The exhibition of poor sportsmanship *aroused* disgust and humiliation in all who witnessed it.]

Instigate and **foment** usually suggest the setting in motion of events that in some way threaten or upset the status quo. These verbs will therefore convey a negative or unfavorable connotation to the extent that one deplores violent change. *Instigate* suggests an insidious design to bring about some drastic action: to *instigate* an assassination; to *instigate* a plot to seize control of a government. *Foment* suggests an attempt to keep people or conditions agitated in order to bring about radical change or to promote dissension and discord: to *foment* rebellion; to *foment* mutiny. Whereas *instigate* emphasizes the act of initiating the design, *foment* stresses keeping it alive. *Instigate,* in addition, has a wider range of use and can point to any design, even one of noble motive, whereas *foment* is used most often of underhanded designs aiming at radical change: to *instigate* a change in the selection of municipal judges so as to improve the administration of justice; to *foment* fear and discord.

Provoke as here considered can be used, like *instigate,* to point to a variety of results, but it does not necessarily or even commonly imply conscious design. It may on the contrary imply spontaneous reaction: The slur *provoked* a sharp retort. Like *arouse* and *stir up, provoke* may also be used of the stimulation of a particular mental attitude: The arbitrary police action *provoked* (or *aroused* or *stirred up*) a public outcry for an investigation. *Provoke* emphasizes more strongly than the other verbs of this group the act that *incites* and its result: The outbreak of war *provoked* a call for an emergency meeting of the UN Security Council.

Exhort means urge earnestly; it suggests an attempt to persuade someone of a course of action by emphatic and even passionate argument or by appealing to that person's sympathy or conscience: The senator *exhorted* his colleagues to vote against the motion to censure him for his excessive tax-supported junkets. *Exhort* often implies a degree of desperation and can be close in meaning to beg or plead with, but more formal in tone: *exhorting* other students not to expose her cheating. See INDUCE, STIMULATE.

Antonyms: *DISCOURAGE, HINDER, SUBDUE.*

include
comprise
contain
involve
These verbs refer to an entity that takes in two or more parts or elements. **Include**, the most general, can indicate clearly defined subdivisions within a whole: The health club *includes* a gym, swimming pool, and sauna. It can pertain equally well to contents that are more imponderable or less tangible: a discussion that *included* extended treatment of the Vietnam War and the Persian Gulf War. *Include* can be useful, since it need not suggest an exhaustive listing of parts or elements: Our ten-city tour *included* a visit to Stratford. Often, *include* points to an additional feature, secondary element, or side benefit: The second book was more useful because it *included* a chronological table of the events under discussion. **Comprise** is a considerably more formal substitute for *include,* except that it most often indicates a complete or exhaustive breakdown of an entity into its parts or elements: The anthology *comprises* samples from the work of ten authors.

Most concretely, **contain** can indicate discrete things held or enclosed by a larger object: The bowl *contained* a variety of fruit. *Contain* functions much like *include* in indicating the parts or elements making up a whole. *Contain,* however, can function only when some sense of enclosure within the whole exists. One would not, for example, speak of a tour *containing* visits to various cities. Otherwise, *contain* compares with *include* and contrasts with *comprise* in not being restricted to an exhaustive listing. [The dictionary *contained* biographical entries on Washington, Jefferson, and Lincoln; Does your school building *contain* an auditorium?] Where both *include* and *contain* can point to concrete or material entities and their parts, **involve** almost exclusively concentrates on less tangible things and their elements: an argument that *involved* a discussion of basic principles. In this it compares with *comprise.* By contrast, *involve* need not suggest an exhaustive listing: Aside from its most widely known features, his philosophical system also *involved* a belief in reincarnation. See CIRCUMSCRIBE, POSSESS.

Antonyms: *exclude, leave out, omit.*

inconstant
capricious
chameleonic
changeable
erratic
fickle
mercurial
protean
These adjectives characterize things that change

frequently or rapidly, and things or people of unstable or disloyal natures. **Inconstant** and **fickle** denote unfaithfulness, usually in love. While *inconstant* can apply to a single betrayal of love, *fickle* applies to the inclination to move from one infatuation to another: a fiancé who proved to be *inconstant;* women who are *fickle* and promiscuous. *Inconstant* can sometimes refer more widely to anything showing variability: desert oases whose wells give an *inconstant* supply of fresh water; a politician who had been *inconstant* in his devotion to the principles of the party. In wider uses, *fickle* still applies to the basic situation of loyalty: young idealists who often prove *fickle* in their choice of causes to support.

Changeable and **erratic** are much more general than the previous pair and are less disapproving in tone. *Changeable* can register the neutral fact that something is capable of change: the *changeable* patterns of watered silk. Indeed, this capacity can be desirable: a camera with *changeable* shutter speeds. More often, however, *changeable* carries a negative tone in reference to people who habitually and readily take up and discard attitudes or opinions: a *changeable* sort who favored the war one day and opposed it the next. *Erratic* points more to an uneven or arbitrary course: the *erratic* path of the rivulet; an *erratic* person whose actions were usually completely unpredictable.

Chameleonic is most comparable to *changeable,* **capricious** to *erratic,* but both adjectives are alike in being more vivid than the foregoing and in being more exclusively concentrated on human characteristics. *Chameleonic* suggests the chameleon's ability, as a defensive camouflage, of changing color so as to blend with its background. Sometimes, *chameleonic* applies to human versatility in a neutral or approving way: students who are *chameleonic* in the diversity of their extracurricular activities; *chameleonic* in the way she could make herself appear at home with all sorts of people. More often, however, *chameleonic* suggests an insincere person willing to play any role that might offer momentary advantage: a *chameleonic* candidate who took prolabor stands before union audiences and probusiness stands at chamber of commerce dinners. *Capricious,* which is exclusively negative in tone, need not suggest insincerity, like *chameleonic,* but it does stress an arbitrary and high-handed attitude in which unfair choices are made, not on the merits of a case, but on the basis of personal taste or whim: a drama critic who seemed *capricious* in the way he bestowed praise or blame; a woman who was haughty and *capricious* toward her staff.

Mercurial and **protean**, alone of these adjectives, may suggest rapidity as well as frequency of change. *Mercurial* is most comparable to *chameleonic,* but where a negative tone preponderates in the latter's use, *mercurial* is more dependent on context to establish approval or disapproval. In favorable reference, it suggests a highly charged and energetic mental dexterity that is flexible to the demands of specific situations and responsive to opportunities for exploiting such situations: a *mercurial* artist who completely transformed the artistic possibilities of every medium she worked in. In negative uses, *mercurial* suggests an excessively volatile quickness and impatience that results in poor control and botched efforts: too *mercurial* to sit down and do the painstaking work of revision that his brilliant first drafts sorely needed. *Protean* refers to the ability of the demigod Proteus to change shapes as a way of eluding capture; often, *protean* can function in both positive and negative ways. Most often, however, *protean* refers favorably to someone gifted with diverse abilities and skills, which are exhibited in a remarkable proliferation of accomplishments: Michelangelo's *protean* imagination. Sometimes, *protean* refers more neutrally to anything given to change: a period of crisis in which the same basic dilemma appeared again and again in *protean* forms. See ADAPTABLE, HESITATE, TEMPORARY.
Antonyms: EVERLASTING, *faithful,* IMMUTABLE, INVARIABLE, *loyal,* PERMANENT.

incredulous. Do not confuse the adjective *incredulous* (unbelieving) with the adjective *incredible* (unbelievable).

indecent
immodest
improper
indecorous
indelicate
unseemly

These adjectives mean not conforming to accepted standards of social behavior, good taste, or propriety. **Indecent** is the strongest of this group. Primarily, it connotes condemnation of obscenity or licentiousness: *indecent* remarks directed at passing girls; *indecent* pictures; an *indecent* proposal to engage in unusual sexual practices. In its second meaning, *indecent* suggests a lack of decorum and a disregard for the feelings of others. [After his wife died, he remarried with *indecent* haste; Their appetite for gossip is absolutely *indecent.*]

Immodest and **indelicate** are applied to that which shows little sense of what is fitting or acceptable in a society that sets a high price on propriety. In one sense, *immodest* is close in meaning to *indecent*, having long been applied, especially to women, to revealing clothing or unrestrained behavior toward the opposite sex. [Few people now find the bikini *immodest*; My mother thinks my sister is *immodest* because she pursues boys.] *Immodest* has a second meaning of aggressive and boastful: the *immodest* self-seeking of a social climber; to brag in an *immodest* way about one's abilities. *Indelicate* is not as strong a term as *immodest* and suggests more a lack of tact and thoughtfulness than unconventional behavior. [It is thought by many to be *indelicate* to reveal one's salary; Subjects fit for the locker room are often too *indelicate* to be discussed at the dinner table.]

Improper and **unseemly** are used of conduct or actions that violate standards of good taste and the fitness of things. [It is considered *improper* for lawyers to discuss their clients' affairs publicly; It would be regarded as *unseemly* and ridiculous for a well-known philosopher to endorse the qualities of a patent medicine.] *Improper* is used often as a euphemism for *indecent* in the sense of obscene: to make *improper* advances.

Indecorous is applied to conduct that does not conform to established conventions of formality and manners, conduct generally consisting of minor infractions for which any of the other adjectives in this group would be too strong. [Loud laughter during a wedding ceremony is *indecorous*; She always felt *indecorous* when she was obliged to straighten her stockings in public.] See DEPRAVED.

Antonyms: MODEST, MORAL.

induce

cajole
coax
persuade
urge
wheedle

These verbs mean make one's will or views prevail over those of another. **Induce** means get another to do something by appealing to reason: to *induce* a woman to stop drinking; to *induce* a young driver to obey the traffic laws.

Persuade is the most general verb and may be substituted for any of the others. However, in its most specific sense, it means attempt to produce a desired action by an appeal to the emotions or the will. [After mother had been ill for a week, we finally *persuaded* her to consult a doctor; A newspaper article about the plight of slum children in summer *persuaded* her to send a contribution to the Fresh Air Fund.]

In this context, **urge** is the strongest term and means *induce* or *persuade* insistently and vigorously, usually with the strong intention of accomplishing one's goal: to *urge* a student to work harder; to *urge* an overworked couple to take a vacation.

Coax, **cajole**, and **wheedle** all mean *persuade* by using gentleness, tact, even artfulness. *Coax* implies the use of kindness and patience: to *coax* a sick child to eat by making a game of feeding; to *coax* a blind person to learn to cross busy streets. In an earlier sense, *cajole* meant *coax* or *persuade* by false promises and excessive flattery, but it now suggests more the idea of being agreeable and winning in order to get a person to do something: My outgoing friends were able to *cajole* the shy newcomer into attending the party. *Wheedle* implies the use of blandishments and wiles to obtain what one wants: They always *wheedle* money out of their father by hugging him and telling him how generous he is. See IMPEL.

Antonyms: DISCOURAGE, HINDER, *repel*, SUBDUE.

inevitable

inescapable
necessary
unavoidable

These adjectives describe events or conditions that cannot be prevented from happening. **Inevitable**, the strongest term, describes something that is bound to happen or be met with in the very nature of things. [Pain is *inevitable* when one breaks a bone; When the Japanese attacked Pearl Harbor, a declaration of war was *inevitable*.]

Inescapable is often used interchangeably with *inevitable*, but *inescapable* suggests something that may not be completely unalterable under a different set of attitudes or circumstances. [Whereas death is *inevitable*, earning a living is *inescapable* unless one has private means or is forced to live at public expense; He felt that his business failure was *inescapable*.]

When used in this context, **necessary** has less impact than *inevitable* and *inescapable*. Something that is *necessary* must logically occur because of an existing set of factors. [Hunger and disease are *necessary* concomitants of war; Crowded streets and shops are a *necessary* part of city life.]

Unavoidable is applied to events and conditions that are not always *inevitable*, but in specific instances

are incapable of being shunned or evaded: Accidents on our highways may be *inevitable*, but yesterday's accident was *unavoidable* because of bad weather and heavy traffic. See COMPEL, CONCLUSIVE, INEXORABLE.
Antonyms: *avertible,* CHANCE, *optional, preventable.*

inexorable

merciless
pitiless
relentless
remorseless
ruthless
unrelenting

These adjectives describe persons or things that persist, but not because of a feeling of compassion. **Inexorable** is the most formal. It may be used of unyielding, unappeasable persons: an *inexorable* foe; his *inexorable* will. But it is more often applied to inhuman or objective forces that cannot be avoided, stopped, or changed: Oedipus could not escape his *inexorable* fate.

Remorseless, **relentless**, and **unrelenting** are closest in meaning to *inexorable.* All imply a powerful, driving force and unceasing progress toward a goal: driving herself at a *relentless* pace; to apply *relentless* pressure; an *unrelenting* fight against crime. But *remorseless* is the most chilling of the three, as it may indicate utter unresponsiveness to human values: the *remorseless* progress of a fatal disease; the *remorseless* ticking of a time bomb. *Relentless* is sometimes close to *remorseless* in this sense, but it is usually less severe and is not always damning. In general use, it may apply to anyone or anything that shows no mercy and cannot be stopped by entreaty or appeal: a *relentless* public prosecutor; the *relentless* passage of time. Specifically, *relentless* is sometimes used as an intensification of tireless. As such it can imply a refusal to yield under punishing pressure: She pressed on *relentlessly,* intent on meeting her deadline. Or it may focus on an implacable persistence in hounding another: the *relentless* Javert pursuing Jean Valjean in *Les Misérables. Unrelenting* may be less extreme in its implications, sometimes suggesting a proper rather than a cruel refusal to relent. An *unrelenting* person may not be impervious to entreaty, but he or she is able to resist, even in the face of temptation: The father handled his disobedient son with *unrelenting* firmness. *Unrelenting* may also suggest the unshakable resolve and fierce dedication of someone firmly committed to a cause and not to be turned aside by obstacles: an *unrelenting* crusader for equal rights.

The remaining adjectives imply unfeeling harshness or cruelty. **Merciless**, like *inexorable,* is often used of impersonal forces: subjected to a *merciless* bombardment of noise; the *merciless* glare of the noonday sun. When the agency of persons is involved, it usually focuses on their instruments or acts rather than on their feelings: the *merciless* eye of the camera; a *merciless* beating. [A *merciless* mob of reporters descended on the bereaved family.] **Pitiless**, by contrast, is more often used to describe human beings as such. It suggests a steel-hard quality: her *pitiless* eye; a *pitiless* tyrant. *Inexorable, relentless,* and *pitiless* may all imply a refusal or inability to make or allow the slightest concession: *inexorable* logic; *relentless* reason; the *pitiless* efficiency of a machine.

Ruthless conveys a greater degree of harshness than any of the other adjectives, for it focuses on a fierce refusal to give any quarter. It is applied to persons who are so unsparing as to be cruel, driving forward single-mindedly and sometimes savagely, with brutal disregard for those they attack or exploit: a *ruthless* slave driver; *ruthless* in their criticism; *ruthlessly* frank. Applied to personal expression or action, *ruthless* may mean harsh, brutal, unsparing, cold-blooded, or cutthroat: *ruthless* methods; *ruthless* competition in the final round of the tournament. See INEVITABLE.
Antonyms: *alterable, changeable, clement, humane, lenient, placable, yielding.*

infer. Do not confuse the verb *infer* (reach an opinion from facts or reasoning) with the verb *imply* (suggest, hint).

infinite

boundless
illimitable
limitless

These adjectives characterize great quantities or things extending without end in space, time, or number. **Infinite** is the most general. Spatially, it refers to something that has no boundary: the assumption that space is *infinite.* It may also be a less precise substitute for eternal: a kind of immortality that results if matter is finite and space *infinite.* It may also refer strictly to quantity, as in mathematics, in which case it refers to a quantity that always exceeds any other. Theologically, it refers to something absolute or perfect: God's *infinite* mercy. Often, however, *infinite* is used hyperbolically for any great amount, or simply as a superlative: an *infinite* bore.

The remaining adjectives are primarily restricted to *infinite* quantities or size, but all may refer to things whose boundaries have not yet been discovered or cannot be formulated. In addition to these possibilities, **boundless** can specifically point to something that is unconstricted or unconstrictable: her *boundless* optimism. *Boundless* often refers hyperbolically to any great amount: the *boundless* energies of our productive nation. **Limitless** suggests a situation in which no end is in sight or in which there is as much of something as can be used or desired: a *limitless* supply of drinking water; a grand jury's *limitless* freedom to move in any direction while preparing a presentment. **Illimitable** is more formal than the previous adjectives and suggests, in addition to its shared meanings, something to which no boundary can practically be set. [Every source of energy in the universe theoretically emits waves that travel an *illimitable* distance.] *Illimitable* may also suggest *infinite* extension in one dimension: defining a line as having *illimitable* length but no width. See COUNTLESS, EVERLASTING, IMMORTAL, PERMANENT.

Antonyms: *circumscribed, finite, limited, relative.*

influence
   affect
   impress
   sway

These verbs all mean have an effect on a person's behavior, thoughts, or feelings. **Influence** means bring about a change in another's actions or thoughts by persuasion, example, or action, often of an indirect sort: *influenced* by a high school biology teacher to study medicine; *influencing* workers to produce more goods by praising them and improving their working conditions.

In this context **affect** means have an effect on another's feelings. [He is always deeply *affected* by Handel's music; Fear *affects* some people by making them powerless to act.] *Influence* and *affect* may both be used of things that tend to respond to outside stimuli or actions. *Influence* in this sense is usually used of intangible forces, and *affect* of physical forces: to *influence* public opinion through the press; to *affect* the size of a crop by using fertilizer. *Affect* may sometimes imply an undesirable result: Unusual exertion may *affect* the heart.

Impress means *affect* deeply and lastingly: *impressed* by the woman's prodigious talent; *impressed* by his stay in Venice.

Sway means change another's opinions or feelings

successfully in an intended way. It is a stronger verb than either *influence* or *affect*, implying the use of control or irresistible persuasion and often combined with the weakness of the one *swayed:* to *sway* a dissatisfied minority group by impassioned political speeches full of promises; a man so *swayed* by public adulation that he snubs his old friends. See ENCOURAGE, INDUCE, MALLEABLE.

Antonyms: *DISCOURAGE, HINDER, SUBDUE.*

inform
   acquaint
   advise
   apprise
   enlighten
   notify

These verbs mean call someone's attention to something or cause the person to receive knowledge of it. **Inform**, the most general term, loosely covers the meanings of the other verbs in this group. *Inform* usually points to the imparting of facts or information. [She *informed* her staff that she would be going to Europe on business for a month; This article *informs* us that the physical endurance of American children is inferior to that of most European children.]

Advise, **notify**, and **apprise** carry the connotation of more or less formal actions. *Advise,* in this context, is used in the sense of giving someone facts that involve his or her own interests: A lawyer should always *advise* clients of all their legal rights. *Notify* is the most commonly used term of these three, and it carries a note of urgency, demanding action or an early reply. [The girl's parents were promptly *notified* of her expulsion; He was *notified* by the board to report in three days with all his financial records.] *Apprise* is the most formal of these verbs and can sound dated or unnecessarily fancy. It may suggest supplying an interested person with facts in accordance with regulation or agreement: Suspects must be *apprised* of their constitutional rights before being questioned.

Acquaint and **enlighten** both mean impart knowledge of a wider scope than that suggested by the other verbs. *Acquaint* means make someone familiar with facts or a situation of some complexity: to *acquaint* oneself with the details of a new job; to *acquaint* the police with the mysterious lights that appear nightly in the abandoned house. *Enlighten,* as its root suggests, means bring information to light, usually about a particular point or situation. It carries more of an element of dispelling ignorance than does *acquaint.* [The mother *enlightened* her daughter concerning the true financial situation of the family; Careful daily reading of the newspaper will *enlighten* the reader as to what is happening at the United Nations.] See CLARIFY, CONSULT.

Antonyms: *misinform.*

informer

blabbermouth
fink
ratfink
squealer
stool pigeon
talebearer
tattler
tattletale

These nouns refer to people who divulge facts to which they are privy. When put next to the informal or slangy nouns given here, **informer** seems formal and dignified; it is also more general than the others. It often suggests divulging secrets or information concerning illegal or scandalous behavior: becoming an *informer* on the crime syndicate; encouraging children to act as *informers* against their parents. The disclosure itself may be covert or open and may be given out of vengeance, self-interest, or financial reward. The *informer* may decide to disclose information acquired in good faith, but also may have been intent at the outset on gaining and then betraying someone's confidence: an *informer* planted by the FBI to get evidence on a terrorist ring; publicly turning *informer* at the hearing to clear herself of a charge of complicity. The disapproving tone *informer* can give is milder than that of any other noun here. It can even have a neutral or approving tone: a conspirator who turned *informer* to help save his innocent children from persecution.

Blabbermouth, by contrast, seldom suggests covert disclosure done in reprisal or self-interest. Instead, the term indicates general loose-tongued behavior in someone willing to talk to anyone about anything, even when revealing his own secrets: a *blabbermouth* who betrays her friends daily without even being conscious of it.

Tattler, **talebearer**, and **tattletale** all can be used to describe someone who divulges information about someone else. Each of these nouns, however, has a special area of relevance. *Tattler* in particular relates to the collecting and spreading of trivial gossip of a faintly scandalous nature: *tattlers* who make their living by revealing titillating information about celebrities. It may also suggest the situation in which a child betrays playmates to a teacher, parent, or other outsider. *Tattletale* is perhaps more clearly related and restricted to such a context: The *tattletale* revealed to the teacher the name of the child who had taken the book. *Talebearer* suggests specifically a two-faced go-between who for reasons of his own pretends to inform each side exclusively about the other: labor mediators who lose their effectiveness as soon as either side suspects them of being *talebearers.*

Fink once was restricted to a labor context as an extremely pejorative way to refer to a turncoat who willingly informed on fellow workers. It and **ratfink**, a fad word, refer to anyone who is unsavory, contemptible, ridiculous, or inconsequential: the *fink* who stole my pencil; He acts tough, but in my book he's just a spineless *fink;* My landlord is a real *ratfink.*

Squealer and **stool pigeon** are slang words and the most pejorative in this group. Both may suggest a context of the criminal underworld but are widely used outside it. *Squealer* may refer to someone who divulges facts about his or her confederates for whatever reason: swearing he'd never be a *squealer* no matter how long the police grilled him. *Stool pigeon,* by contrast, refers specifically to a covert *informer* who inhabits the underworld or is planted there by the police; in either case, an *informer* furtively continues to convey information to the police as long as he or she remains undiscovered: convinced that one of their fellow prisoners had turned *stool pigeon* and had disclosed their plans for the jailbreak.

ingenuous. Do not confuse the adjective *ingenuous* (unsophisticated) with the adjective *ingenious* (clever at inventing).

inherent

essential
innate
intrinsic

These adjectives characterize things that are fundamental or necessary aspects of some larger pattern. **Inherent** refers to a principle that underlies or is implicit in a manifest pattern: an *inherent* tendency to get flustered in tense situations; the respect for human possibility *inherent* in all the literature of the Renaissance. When *inherent* emphasizes the implicit nature of a principle, it suggests something that may not be evident but can be inferred from the situation: a cool politeness that attempted to mask her *inherent* disrespect for most people. **Innate** suggests something deeply imprinted within a pattern and that may not be patently obvious, although it has its effect and, by implication, cannot easily be eradicated: gathering evidence to determine whether instincts are *innate* or learned responses; tendencies *innate* in all governmental impulses toward collectivism.

Essential does not necessarily suggest an underlying principle; something may be a quite evident and recent addition and still be *essential* if it is vital to the existence of the pattern to which it belongs: *essential* revisions in the proposed bill that would make it acceptable to the majority. Frequently, of course, *essential* does refer to fundamentals; even in this case, however, these fundamentals may be readily apparent rather than hidden or tacit: the *essential* documents on which our democracy rests. **Intrinsic** almost exclusively applies to fundamentals that underlie a larger design. *Intrinsic* suggests the irreducible minimum on which the design depends for its effectiveness; it also sometimes suggests that later or less *essential* excrescences may have coalesced about this minimum without necessarily impairing the functioning of the whole: the *intrinsic* decency of the man, regardless of every failure to live up to his own promise; *intrinsic* weaknesses of design that make some automobiles deathtraps, weaknesses not likely to be overcome by adding a few safety features. See INNATE.

Antonyms: EXTRANEOUS.

inheritance

bequest
birthright
heritage
legacy
patrimony

These nouns indicate property willed to someone, or anything handed down from the past. **Inheritance** is the most general of these. At its strictest, it refers to both the real estate and personal property (including sums of money) left to someone in a will. This is usually acquired upon the death of the person who made the will, although sometimes it may be reserved until the one receiving it reaches a certain age or meets certain conditions. Occasionally, *inheritance* may be used to indicate realty alone, especially an estate or family home. In a more general sense, *inheritance* refers to anything handed down by one's predecessors, from hereditary traits to cultural traditions: the *inheritance* of a recessive gene from his mother's side of the family; the precious *inheritance* of freedom guaranteed us by the Bill of Rights. **Bequest**, by contrast, functions solely in terms of willed personal property, often a sum of money, that comes to one by formal declaration

upon the death of the donor: stipulating that a number of small *bequests* were to go to close friends.

At their strictest, **legacy** and **heritage** contrast, since *legacy* refers like *bequest* to a willed gift of money or personal property, while *heritage* refers, more like *inheritance,* to real property that goes by right to an heir. More significantly, however, both nouns are similar in referring generally to anything that has come down from the past. In this use, *legacy* is likely to refer to abstract things such as qualities, attitudes, principles, or rights: the *legacy* of race hatred left us by the institution of slavery; a new openness about sexual matters, the *legacy* of Freud, Ellis, and others. *Heritage* has a particular pertinence to enduring concrete things such as monuments, buildings, or natural resources: our squandered *heritage* of untainted streams and virgin forest land; the cathedrals that are part of England's invaluable *heritage.*

In their strict senses, **patrimony** refers to an estate, usually real, inherited from one's father, while **birthright** can refer to property, real or personal, to which someone, especially a firstborn son, is entitled by birth: Esau's selling of his *birthright* for a mess of pottage. Much more commonly, however, both *patrimony* and *birthright* are used in more general senses. Here, *patrimony* can refer to anything derived from one's father or ancestors; thus, it is a restriction of the general sense of *legacy,* referring to family or ancestral traditions: taking up the Barrymore *patrimony* of theatrical accomplishment. Sometimes, however, *patrimony* is used even more generally, like *inheritance:* the rival *patrimonies,* still viable, of Athenian democracy and Spartan authoritarianism. In this context, *birthright* is used like *legacy,* though it is more emphatically reserved for qualities, attitudes, principles, and especially rights to which every human being is thought to be entitled: our inalienable *birthright* of free speech; a UN declaration naming specific freedoms as every person's *birthright.* See BEQUEST.

innate

congenital
hereditary
inborn
inbred

These adjectives characterize traits that are deeply ingrained as part of a functioning pattern. **Innate**, the most general of these, is the least specific in suggesting how or at what point a trait becomes of such intrinsic importance: an *innate* weakness of all battery-powered cars; an *innate* eagerness to learn that was challenging and exciting; questioning whether learned responses ever do become *innate*. **Inborn** and **inbred** are the most informal adjectives in this group; in effect, they split *innate* into separate halves. *Inborn* indicates those traits acquired before birth, *inbred* those traits acquired later through training: *inborn* musical ability; her *inbred* respect for other people's wishes. The split is not as neat as it appears, however, since *inborn* is not always clear about environmental influences during gestation, and *inbred* is not clear about the distinction between the contingent effects of environment during infancy and later training.

Congenital presents a conflicting set of meanings that render it vague and open to misinterpretation. In its most specific sense, it refers to traits acquired during gestation and not through heredity or later training: the tragic proof that thalidomide causes *congenital* deformities. In a completely contrary meaning, however, *congenital* refers to traits acquired at any time from birth onwards: a *congenital* liar. In this instance, it would seem clearer to use *habitual* or some other word. In still another instance, however, *congenital* can refer in a vague and general way to traits deeply imprinted, without specifying when the imprinting occurred; this would make it a more formal synonym for *innate*. *Congenital* is sometimes used in this context with humorous intent: the farmer's *congenital* distrust of city slickers.

In its biological sense, **hereditary** is distinguished from *congenital* in its reference to characteristics, as the color of the hair and eyes, that are transmitted or transmissible directly from an animal or plant to its offspring. In an equally specific legal sense, *hereditary* applies to that which passes, is capable of passing, or of necessity must pass by inheritance from an ancestor to an heir: a *hereditary* estate. In a more general way this adjective is used to refer to anything a person possesses that had to do with or was in some way a characteristic of one or more of his or her ancestors: the difficulty of dealing with a *hereditary* enemy toward whom one feels no personal animosity. See INHERENT.

Antonyms: *acquired.*

inner

interior
internal
inward

These adjectives refer to what lies below the surface, in the central or inside portion of something, or within its boundaries. **Inner** is the most general of these and has the widest range of meaning. It can have geographical pertinence: the *inner* regions of the

island. It can refer to a side that faces in: the *inner* edge of the terrace. It can also indicate the enclosed portion of something: an *inner* room of the tavern. In addition to these physical denotations, *inner* may suggest covert or unconscious mental activity: signs of an *inner* turbulence of emotion; an *inner* ripeness for change.

Interior also suggests the geographical context: the *interior* counties of the state. It has a special relevance for something hidden or obscure, suggesting enclosure: an *interior* courtyard in the Florentine style. And it refers, most strictly, to thought processes carried on without being spoken aloud: *interior* monologue.

The emphasis of **internal** is on something completely surrounded and covered from view: the *internal* organs of the body; suspecting *internal* injuries. It can also refer to mental activity, relating less to *interior* in this context than to *inner*, although its point is often a distinction between feeling emotions and expressing them: an *internal* uneasiness that became apparent when she began her nervous pacing.

Inward often refers to spiritual states: an *inward* rectitude of being. Sometimes, its emphasis is on invisible as opposed to visible states: outward behavior testifying to their *inward* state of grace. On a more mundane level, *inward* may indicate movement toward *interior* regions: their *inward* journey up the river, tracing its course upstream through the jungle. See CENTER.

Antonyms: *exterior, external, outer.*

innocent

blameless
guiltless
irreproachable
sinless
untainted
virginal

These adjectives characterize things that are perfect, free of fault or failing, or morally uncorrupted. **Innocent** pertains to freedom from immoral behavior: *innocent* children. This quality, however, may stem from self-restraint, inexperience, or lack of opportunity: chaperons who made certain that the picnic remained at a level of *innocent* fun. The adjective is often used more simply to denote lack of guilt for a wrongful act: pleading *innocent* to the charge of disorderly conduct.

Virginal relates to the aspect of *innocent* pertaining to freedom from immoral behavior; *virginal* is much more restricted than *innocent,* however, in specifically referring to chastity or to sexual immaturity, especially in women: his *virginal* bride. It may have a disapproving tone when this lack might be thought no longer appropriate or inherently admirable: a *virginal* woman. Sometimes, the adjective suggests the sweetness of youth: the *virginal* faces of young girls. **Sinless** is wider in range than *virginal,* but more restricted than *innocent* in pertaining exclusively to freedom from all sorts of behavior thought to be immoral: impossible to live a completely *sinless* life. *Sinless* implies a supporting theological view, since what is praised as *sinless* by one religion might seem pointless or irrelevant to another: ascetics who strove toward a *sinless* life by abjuring the eating of meat.

Guiltless functions more like *innocent.* It can refer to freedom from immorality, though without the emphasis on youth of *innocent* or *virginal:* a politician *guiltless* of the more obvious kinds of cynical dealings. *Guiltless* may also refer emphatically to blamelessness concerning a specific act: *guiltless* of the heinous crime. *Guiltless,* however, never substitutes for *innocent* in legal parlance. In the context of morality, **untainted** is used more abstractly than the previous adjectives, referring to something that has never been sullied by any sort of harmful influence; in tone it seems more passive than *innocent:* an attitude *untainted* by selfish thoughts; a life *untainted* by scandal. *Untainted* has its own concrete relevance to anything pure: water *untainted* by lead.

Irreproachable functions less on a theological or moral level than on the level of conduct, indicating a general propriety of behavior: an *irreproachable* teacher where her students' interests are concerned; a formal dinner *irreproachable* in every respect. **Blameless** operates, like *irreproachable,* in the sphere of ethics or conduct: *blameless* manners; a *blameless* life; finding him *blameless* in the accident. *Blameless,* however, is more restricted to a simple lack of fault, whereas *irreproachable* may suggest positive attainment of excellence: *blameless* but dull acting; *irreproachable* taste astonishing for its flair. See GOODNESS, MORAL, NAIVE, PERFECT.

Antonyms: *blameworthy, culpable,* DEPRAVED, DIRTY, *guilty, immoral, impure,* INDECENT, LEWD, *unchaste.*

inquiry

examination
inquest
inquisition
probe
study

These nouns all mean a seeking for information or truth. **Inquiry** is the most general term and is loosely applicable to all the others. An *inquiry* may range in importance from any request for information about ordinary matters to an investigation of an official nature: to make *inquiries* at the police station concerning road conditions; an *inquiry* made by the Board of Health about an outbreak of measles; an *inquiry* into alleged municipal corruption.

Examination is also a general term, but an *examination* is generally stricter or more formal than an *inquiry,* involving careful scrutiny or inspection: an *examination* of all the points in a formal argument; an *examination* of their motives for leaving the country. In law, an *examination* is an *inquiry* made by direct questioning or by the taking of testimony: The suspect underwent *examination* by the grand jury.

An **inquest** is an *inquiry* or *examination,* but its meaning is now almost entirely restricted to that of a judicial or legal investigation. In its best-known sense, an *inquest* is an investigation by a coroner (often aided by a coroner's jury) of the causes of a death when there is sufficient evidence to suspect that it occurred for other than natural reasons.

Inquisition and **probe** are both searching, official investigations of an individual or of a group, made in order to dig out facts proving the existence of illegal acts or of heterodoxy. *Probe* is an Americanism when used in this sense and denotes an investigation that goes deeply below the surface in a manner evocative of a surgeon's instrument exploring a gunshot wound. *Inquisition* is chiefly thought of in its historical meaning, that of the *examination* and punishment of heretics, as practiced by the ecclesiastical courts of Europe during the late Middle Ages and the Reformation. The term also is applied to the body of church officials engaged in this activity. In its more general sense, *inquisition* implies persecution by means of relentless investigation, and harassment by persistent and prolonged interrogation. As a proper legal procedure in modern times, *inquisition* has been largely supplanted by *examination* and *probe.* A *probe* is a thorough investigation by a legislative body or by a committee set up within such a body into alleged large-scale misconduct or illegal practices. A *probe* is usually made into activities considered hurtful to the government and its economy or to the rights of its citizens: a *probe* into a tax evasion on the part of a large corporation; a *probe* into the misuse of welfare funds.

A **study** is an *inquiry* made by gathering information in some detail in order to arrive at certain conclusions or to obtain a body of specialized knowledge: a *study* of the habits of the mountain gorilla; a *study* of the plant life of the Sargasso Sea. *Studies* are also conducted to gain an understanding of the causes of an undesirable social condition so that improvements may be made: a *study* of traffic patterns in a large city; a *study* of the incidence of recidivism among released convicts. See EXAMINE, PIERCE.

insert
interject
interpolate
interpose
introduce

These verbs may all express the act of breaking in on a flow of words in order to make an addition, alteration, or comment. To **insert** a letter, word, or group of words is simply to put it in, often where it has a perfect right to be. Specifically, *insert* suggests that a space must be made in written or printed matter so that the addition may be fitted in: to *insert* an ad in a newspaper; A caret [^] marks the spot where an omitted word or letter is to be *inserted* in a line. To **interpolate** a word, passage, or comment is to *insert* it where it does not belong—among words written or spoken by and attributed to another. *Interpolations* such as editorial comments, explanations, and helpful emendations are permissible if enclosed in square brackets, as in: "'I think [Parks Commissioner William] Sanders is doing a great job,' the mayor told reporters." *Interpolations* that are not permissible are additions made by other hands that are passed off as part of the author's original, for such *interpolated* matter corrupts the original text. To **introduce** something into a speech or piece of writing is to bring it in not only as an added part or insertion, but as a new part, a change from what is already there. [She was told that her paper would be more effective if she *introduced* further examples to illustrate her points; After Shakespeare's death, lesser playwrights *introduced* changes into his plays, *interpolating* spurious passages, stage directions, spectacle, and music.]

Both **interject** and the more formal **interpose** may mean *introduce* abruptly. These verbs, however, are specifically used of spoken comments that break in suddenly upon an otherwise even flow of speech. What is *interjected* is simply thrown in unexpectedly and forcefully, as an exclamation arising from a natural reaction. [When that politician's name was mentioned, the doctor *interjected* an oath into the conversation.] What is *interposed* is put in as a deliberate interrup-

tion, such as a protest or digression, and is meant to halt the speech or argument going on. [A student interrupted the lecturer, ostensibly to ask a question, but actually to *interpose* her own opinion; When, in the course of his summation to the jury, the prosecuting attorney began to repeat hearsay, the defense attorney jumped to her feet and *interposed* an objection.] See ADD, MEDIATE, REVISE.

Antonyms: *abstract, detach,* ERASE, *excerpt, extract,* REMOVE, *withdraw.*

insolvent
bankrupt
broke
impecunious

These adjectives characterize those who do not have enough money to meet their needs or pay their debts. **Insolvent** refers to a debtor whose liabilities outweigh his or her assets and who therefore cannot meet the claims of creditors. Both an individual and a business enterprise may be *insolvent*. [People thought her well-to-do, but she died *insolvent,* her estate being insufficient to liquidate her debts; Since the business was *insolvent,* it qualified as a tax loss.] In law, **bankrupt** refers specifically to a person or business that has been judicially declared *insolvent*. When, through the operation of a *bankruptcy* law, the actual *insolvency* of a debtor has been legally determined, his or her assets are taken into judicial possession for equitable distribution among creditors. The debtor is then granted by judicial decree a full discharge from legal liability for the indebtedness. For this reason, persons deeply and hopelessly in debt may choose to or have to declare themselves *bankrupt.* [Her business failed and she went *bankrupt;* the business went into *bankruptcy.*] Loosely, any person who is unable to pay his or her debts or who is devoid of resources may be called *bankrupt. Bankrupt* may also refer to utter ruin of any kind. In a figurative sense, it may mean destitute of some abstract quality, or hopelessly lacking, as in spiritual resources: a morally *bankrupt* society; a person *bankrupt* in spirit.

The remaining adjectives focus on a lack of money rather than on indebtedness, implying empty pockets rather than red ink. **Broke** is the everyday word. It is sometimes used informally as a substitute for *insolvent* or *bankrupt:* The business kept losing money and finally went *broke.* But *broke* is much broader in application than the previous pair of adjectives. People who cannot pay their bills may claim, or be said, to be *broke,* but they may also be *broke* without being in debt. Further, *broke* often applies to a temporary condition: a speculator often *broke* but never poor; flat *broke* the day before payday. **Impecunious** comes from Latin roots and literally means without money. It may refer to someone who never has much money or is frequently *broke*: an *impecunious* artist living in a garret. But *impecunious* is a rather high-flown, pretentious word and is often used in a self-conscious way to give a humorous, lightly mocking effect. [Sorry I can't go with you, but I'm rather *impecunious* at the moment.] See POOR, WEALTH.

Antonyms: *affluent, flush, loaded, prosperous, rich, solvent, wealthy, well-to-do.*

intend

    aim
    contemplate
    mean
    plan
    propose

These verbs mean have in mind the doing of some act or the attainment of some goal. **Intend** has the widest range of implication. It may involve no more than vague thoughts or halfhearted resolves. [I *intend* to clean out the attic sooner or later; The road to hell is paved with good *intentions.*] Or it may imply a firm decision taken with regard to an immediate or ultimate goal. [I *intend* to see to it that my son is not late again; They *intend* to work hard and save to put their children through college.]

Mean is synonymous with *intend* in both its strong and its weak sense, implying either a truly firm resolve or a merely professed purpose. [I *mean* to go, and nothing is going to stop me; I've been *meaning* to write you for weeks.] But *mean* is a less formal word than *intend,* well suited to everyday speech and writing, and it is more often used than *intend* to express a dubious, weak, or unrealized resolve. [I *meant* to visit her, but I never got around to it.] *Mean* is also used to claim or give credit for good *intentions* when an action has backfired. [I'm sure he *meant* well; I *meant* no harm—I only *meant* to help.] **Aim**, like *mean,* is informal in tone. It points, though, to an actual goal, purpose, or *intention,* as distinguished from an avowed one that is open to doubt. [What do you *aim* to do? I *aim* to succeed.] Further, *aim* may imply not only *intent* but also effort, though without the suggestion of failure often conveyed by *mean.* [I *aim* to please.]

Propose in one sense is closely synonymous with *intend:* He *proposes* to go on to medical school after college. But *propose* generally goes beyond *intend* and

aim in implying that an *intention* or design has been clearly formulated in the mind, and often announced to others. [What do you *propose* to do? I *propose* to rally the forces and attack at dawn; The chairman of the Bridge and Tunnel Authority *proposes* to build a new bridge across the narrows.] **Plan**, like *intend,* may sometimes imply only a vague goal or indefinite resolution that is not being presently acted upon: He *plans* to go to Europe someday. But *plan* may be, and often is, more definite than *intend,* implying the taking of active steps toward the realization of an *intention.* Such *planning* involves a consideration of the ways and means of achieving a goal and the making of arrangements in advance. [I *plan* to leave on August 4 and have made airline reservations for that date.] In an intransitive sense, *plan* and *propose* may be closely synonymous. [He is always *planning* but seldom carries through with his schemes; People never do all that they *propose.*] *Propose,* of course, may also mean make an offer of marriage.

To **contemplate** is to consider or anticipate, to turn over in the mind. *Contemplate* implies a greater immediacy than *intend, mean,* or *aim* but much less definiteness than *propose* or *plan.* [She *intends* to get married in the years after she is firmly established in her career; He is *contemplating* marriage but has not yet *proposed;* She is *contemplating* a trip to Europe, but she hasn't *planned* it yet.] See DECIDE, HOPE, MEAN, OFFER, PLAN, PURPOSE, TRY.

intimidate

    browbeat
    bulldoze
    bully
    cow
    daunt
    dismay
    overawe
    terrorize

These verbs mean make submissive, compliant, or subdued by inspiring fear. **Intimidate** is the most general, precisely directed to this concept. To *intimidate* someone is to manipulate him by using his own fear or weakness against him as a psychological weapon. The person who sets out to *intimidate* another aims to fill the chosen victim with a dread of unpleasant consequences to come if he or she does not comply. [The employer tried to *intimidate* her employees by threatening to move her business to Mexico if they formed a union; The parents were *intimidated* into paying the ransom by the kidnapper's threatening notes; Seeing the pistol was sufficient to *intimidate* the cab driver.] *Intimidation* may involve the use of violence or coercion to influence the conduct of another or to compel his consent, but when actual force is used, it constitutes a threat of future force that would be more deadly: The gang *intimidated* the witness by having him worked over in a dark alley. People may also be *intimidated* through their own shyness, cowardice, sense of inadequacy, or fear of embarrassment: so *intimidated* by the speaker's reputation that they were afraid to ask questions; *intimidated* by the surly waiter's sneer into leaving a larger tip than they had intended.

Cow and **overawe** point both to the cause and the effect of *intimidation*. *Cow* in this sense comes from an Old Norse word meaning tyrannize. To *cow* someone is to reduce that person to a weak, submissive state, breaking his spirit or overcoming his resistance by the use or threat of superior force: a tyrant of a father who *cowed* his children's spirits; cringing slaves, *cowed* by the overseer's whip; suddenly *cowed* by the sight of a policeman. *Overawe* does not imply the kind of fear and trembling suggested by *cow*. Instead, it focuses on reverential fear—respect that subdues or restrains one. [The peasants were *overawed* by the vastness of the cathedral; The explorer *overawed* the local population with his fine clothes and elaborate equipment.]

Daunt and **dismay** deal specifically with the kind of effect caused by *intimidation*. To *daunt* is to dishearten, frighten, or otherwise discourage someone from going on; it implies a loss of the will to keep trying. [*Daunted* by pioneer life, she decided to return to Boston; No number of failures and disappointments could *daunt* the researcher in her quest for a cure.] *Dismay* suggests a sinking feeling in the pit of the stomach. It points to a sense of hopeless discouragement in the face of obstacles or paralyzing fear in the face of a threat. [Their refusal to compromise *dismayed* me and left me confused; a young contender *dismayed* by the size and aggressiveness of the champion.]

The remaining verbs all focus on the act of *intimidating*. **Terrorize** and **bully** imply the deliberate incitement of fear as a method of *intimidation*. *Terrorize* is the more formal verb and presupposes a much greater degree of violence. It has political associations, often applying to unlawful acts of violence committed in an attempt to overthrow a government: Rebels *terrorized* the countryside, staging midnight raids, planting antipersonnel mines in every road, and appropriating food from the people. *Bully* is much more informal. As a noun, *bully* denotes a swaggering, aggressive person who is usually cowardly and who

intimidates weaker people. Children use *bully* for a larger or stronger child who picks on smaller or weaker ones. Hence, to *bully* is to push others around in this way, whether through brute force or through verbal taunts or threats: They had waited for hours, but he *bullied* them into letting him break in line in front of them. **Bulldoze** falls between *bully* and *terrorize* in force. This slang verb points to *intimidation* through the use of violence or coercion or through the threat of reprisals. Now, however, it may imply force of will or exercise of abstract power rather than physical force. [They tried to *bulldoze* her, but she stuck to her guns; The president *bulldozed* the businessmen into rescinding a price increase; one holdout trying to *bulldoze* the other jurors into changing their minds.] **Browbeat** implies mental harassment rather than a physical attack. To *browbeat* someone is to *intimidate* or *cow* him, or to try to do so, by means of a stern, overbearing, condemnatory manner. *Browbeat* may imply haughty, contemptuous, or rude treatment, or a bombardment of some kind that goes on without letup. [He was a meek little man, the perfect victim, *browbeaten* by his boss at the office and by his wife at home; The lawyer started *browbeating* the witness, trying to upset her and discredit her testimony.] See BELEAGUER, BRAVE, COMPEL, FEAR, FRIGHTEN.

Antonyms: *blandish,* ENCOURAGE, *enhearten,* INDUCE.

intrigue

conspiracy
machination
plot
scheme

These nouns refer to secret plans contrived to attain some possibly improper or illegal goal. **Intrigue** stresses behind-the-scenes manipulations, but it may or may not imply impropriety or illegality: a court rife with *intrigue* against the royal family; adept at the *intrigue* necessary to carry on a clandestine love affair; small-town *intrigue* that amounted to nothing more than trivial gossip. *Intrigue* may be a generic term for the sum total of secret maneuvering in a given social context. **Machination** more often refers, less inclusively, to a secret or semi-secret stratagem, a devious action, or an underhand maneuver that is part of a larger plan. It usually appears in the plural and suggests disapprovingly some impropriety of motive: *machinations* to make it appear that the innocent girl had committed the murder.

Plot suggests a specific, inclusive plan worked out in detail by a person or group, most often to gain some improper or illegal goal: the *plot* to assassinate Caesar; a *plot* to rig the jury. *Intrigue* or *machinations* may be resorted to as elements in furthering a *plot* or in its final carrying out. Both most often suggest subservience to the kind of master plan indicated by *plot*: certain that a *plot* of some sort was under way from the amount of *intrigue* they caught wind of.

A *plot* may sometimes be petty in scope, but **conspiracy** is applied chiefly to serious crimes, and there is something sinister about *conspiracy*. Specifically, in this sense a *conspiracy* is a *plot* involving two or more persons who plan together to commit an evil or unlawful act. [The investigative commission found no evidence of a *conspiracy* to assassinate the President; They uncovered a price-fixing *conspiracy* and indicted several industry officials.]

Scheme is much more general than the others in this group. Nothing at all improper or illegal may be referred to; the noun, in fact, might point exclusively to the devising rather than to the furthering or carrying out of a plan: suddenly coming up with a *scheme* that would solve their money problems. But *scheme*, unlike plan, often carries an unfavorable connotation, implying something underhanded and self-serving: the *scheming* Iago, devising a way to bring about Othello's downfall. See ACCOMPLICE, CONSPIRACY, PLAN.

invariable

constant
unchanging
uniform

These adjectives characterize things that are not marked by change or variation. Something is **invariable** if it recurs always in the same manner or at regular intervals. The succession of neap tide and spring tide is *invariable*. Something is **constant** if it remains the same or changes at a regular rate over a long period of time. The birth rate in some countries is *constant*, and in other countries the rate of population increase is *constant*. In mathematics and science, a *constant* is a number or quantity that does not change throughout a given discussion or operation. An absolute *constant* is fixed and cannot be changed. An arbitrary *constant* can be assigned any set value. In a more general sense, *invariable* and *constant* may mean continual or habitual. [She *invariably* forgets her keys; He is *constantly* changing his mind.] And while *invariable* more often applies to routine, both adjectives may be used to characterize abstract qualities that are enduring or reliable: an *invariable* stop at the newsstand; *constant* affection; *invariable* amiability.

Something is **unchanging** in this sense if its attributes remain the same for a long period of time. Weather and climate may be said to be *unchanging* in certain areas of the world. The biological processes of life may be called *unchanging*.

In one sense, **uniform** is close to *constant*, describing something that does not undergo changes in form or character, quantity or degree: a thermostat to maintain a *uniform* temperature. In another sense, *uniform* may suggest a bringing of separate things into a state of conformity, either basically or in some salient aspect: the need for *uniform* traffic regulations throughout the nation. [The hedges were clipped to a *uniform* height; All twenty volumes of the encyclopedia were of *uniform* thickness.] See IMMUTABLE, PERMANENT, PERSISTENT.

Antonyms: INCONSTANT, *variable*.

jaunty

chipper
debonair
insouciant

These adjectives are used to describe a brisk, unworried, self-assured person or the way in which such a person acts. **Jaunty**, which at its most positive refers to a lively, dashing urbanity, sometimes suggests a studied nonchalance—an attempt, often contrived or even forced, to appear suave or sophisticated that results in a kind of aggressive good humor: struggling hopelessly to look *jaunty* and interesting in his jogging clothes; the *jaunty* way he approached to ask her for a dance. **Chipper** refers more to a sprightly self-satisfaction that exudes good humor and health; however, *chipper* would refer to the good health of maturity rather than to the appearance of youth: Aging roués who still manage to look spruce and *chipper* are the despair of the moralist.

Debonair is more like *jaunty* in suggesting a reckless ease of manner that is filled with carefree good spirits: the typically *debonair* French lover. The noun has taken on an overtone that implies worldly sophistication as well: the eager and callow youth who for all his posturing is still naive, still far from being *debonair*. **Insouciant** translates literally from the French to mean worry-free; it also suggests gaiety of manner and sophistication: the *insouciant* Ivy Leaguers who travel from one party to another without a thought for tomorrow. See BLITHE, LIVELY, URBANE.

Antonyms: *SEDATE.*

jealous. Do not confuse the adjective *jealous* (feeling resentment toward a rival) with the adjective *envious* (full of envy).

jibe. Do not confuse the verb *jibe* (agree or fit with) with the verb *gibe* (jeer).

joke

gag
jest
pleasantry
quip
wisecrack
witticism

These nouns all denote something said or done to excite laughter. **Joke** is a general term, but specifically it refers to a brief narrative or anecdote with a funny ending. A practical *joke* is an act designed to surprise or embarrass another. **Jest**, which now sounds somewhat old-fashioned except in the phrase *in jest,* usually refers to a spoken remark, but may also be a playful act.

Whereas *joke* and *jest* emphasize humor, **witticism** points to a more intellectual exercise—that of wit—depending a good deal more on originality or irony of thought. **Quip** and **pleasantry** are comments intended to amuse, the former often imparting a sting and the latter scrupulously avoiding any painful effect. Both *witticism* and *pleasantry* stress nicety of phrasing rather than brilliance in idea.

Gag and **wisecrack** are the informal equivalents of *joke* and *witticism,* respectively. Like *quip,* but even more strongly, *wisecrack* implies a mocking or satirical motive. *Gag* often refers to a theatrical *joke,* as one prepared in advance of a performance. One speaks of the *witticisms* of statesmen, the *wisecracks* of political commentators, and the *gags* of nightclub comedians. See CARICATURE, RIDICULE.

journey

excursion
jaunt
junket
pilgrimage
tour
trip
voyage

These nouns refer to travel. While **journey** is the most general of these, it is now usually used of travel by land and often suggests the covering of considerable time or distance, with no necessary implication of a return: their transcontinental *journey* in covered wagons. **Voyage**, by contrast, is now usually used of travel by water: a long ocean *voyage* to South Africa.

Where both *journey* and *voyage* are relatively formal, **trip** is the more informal substitute for either. In this case, however, the covering of a shorter time or distance is suggested, and an eventual return to the starting point is often implied: He went on a *trip* to the nearest seaside resort during his vacation. In psychedelic slang, *trip* indicates an extended meditative or introspective sequence, whether drug-induced or not: He turned on and was soon off on a long *trip;* good and bad *trips;* strobes and screen projections guaranteed to send you on a *trip.*

Tour indicates a *trip* in which many places are visited, often by a circuitous route: a *tour* of Italy that included stops at Milan, Venice, Florence, and Rome. In a related use, the inspection of a much smaller area may be indicated: a *tour* of the castle. **Excursion** serves as a more formal substitute for *trip* or *tour;* it emphasizes a temporary departure from a given place and specifies a return to it. It can point to a sea or land *tour* or to a short outing: an *excursion* that would take us to several Aegean islands and return us to Athens after two weeks; an *excursion* to the beach, complete with picnic hampers and thermoses of cold drinks.

Pilgrimage indicates a *journey* taken to a place that has religious or emotional significance: the annual *pilgrimage* to Mecca; a *pilgrimage* to John F. Kennedy's grave. **Jaunt** and **junket**, by contrast, both suggest *excursions* for recreation or pleasure. *Jaunt* suggests a short *trip* or outing: a weekend *jaunt* to Fire Island. *Junket* is more specific in pointing to the *trip* of a public official whose expenses are paid, usually from public funds. While such *trips* may be authorized and connected with an official purpose, describing them as *junkets* often casts suspicion on this legitimate explanation and implies that the *trips* are nothing more than pleasure-seeking *jaunts:* a *junket* of Congressmen to the pleasure capitals of Europe.

joyous

ecstatic
elated
euphoric
happy
high
turned-on

These adjectives describe exhilarated or joyful states of mind. **Joyous** suggests a strong feeling of contentment or high spirits, often because of the expectation or realization of some good: *joyous* celebrations in anticipation of the end of war. *Joyous* is sometimes applied to people as a synonym for joyful, but is also used of something that promotes joy or is in itself an expression of joy: the *joyous* song of the hermit thrush.

Happy is the most general adjective of this group, but it is also the weakest, since it does not ordinarily imply the excitement and strong feeling indicated by *joyous* and by some of the other adjectives. In social exchanges *happy* is used in mild expressions of enjoyment or willingness. [I shall be *happy* to help you find a new job; We are *happy* to see you.] In its wider sense *happy* suggests contentment and fulfillment of one's aspirations and desires: to be *happy* in one's work; to have a *happy* marriage.

Ecstatic and **elated** both emphasize greater joy and delight than does *happy.* From its earlier meaning of being in a trancelike state of religious fervor, *ecstatic* suggests such an overpowering joy or mental exaltation: a young boy *ecstatic* in his first love; a traveler *ecstatic* over the art treasures of Florence. *Elated,* less forceful than *ecstatic,* points to the great pleasure and self-satisfaction that arise from success or good fortune: a novelist *elated* over the favorable reviews of her book; a young father *elated* over the birth of twins.

A person who is **euphoric** may outwardly resemble in behavior one who is *ecstatic* or *elated;* however, upon closer observation, it will be seen that the vigor and buoyancy are exaggerated and out of proportion to the stimulus. Although experienced at one time or another by many people, *euphoria* is commonly thought of as occurring during the course of certain mental disturbances or after the ingestion of alcoholic beverages or of certain drugs.

High and **turned-on** are terms used to describe more or less artificially induced exhilaration or *euphoria. High* is used most commonly and colloquially of a person who is animated and talkative after drinking an alcoholic beverage. [He usually gets quite *high* on just two drinks.] *High* is also applied to one who has taken a narcotic drug and is experiencing the resultant *euphoria* or contented lethargy. *Turned-on,* a slang term that originated among psychedelic drug users, is more frequently found as a verb, *turn on,* than as an adjective. In its narrowest sense, to *turn on* means either to begin feeling the effect of a marijuana cigarette or, transitively, in the sense of to introduce a neophyte to the practice. [Every Saturday night they and their friends *turn on;* Last week her college roommate *turned* her *on.*] It may also mean take or be under the influence of any narcotic or psychedelic drug: They *turned on* with LSD. By extension, *turn on* may also mean excite or attract strongly. [Bach's music always *turns* me *on;* Women with soulful brown eyes always seem to *turn* him *on.*] See BLITHE, CHEERFUL, LIVELY.

Antonyms: GLOOMY, *low*, MISERABLE, *morose*, SAD, *solemn*.

judge

    arbiter
    arbitrator
    referee
    umpire

These nouns all denote a person who makes decisions in situations in which there are conflicting views. **Judge** is the most general term. In its strictest sense, a *judge* is a government official who presides in a court of law and administers justice by hearing and deciding cases. By extension, *judge* is applied to a person who has the requisite knowledge, experience, and impartiality to make decisions or pass upon the merits of something. [Your doctor is the best *judge* of what will cure your illness; The *judges* at the fair awarded her a blue ribbon for her sow.]

Arbitrator and **arbiter** are sometimes used synonymously to denote a person or one of several persons chosen by disputing parties to settle their differences. However, in this sense, *arbitrator* is the preferred term. [In the labor dispute, three *arbitrators* were chosen by management and three by the workers.] *Arbiter,* a somewhat literary word, is more often applied to one who without official authorization or position has the prestige to make decisions or to set standards that others willingly follow. [Lord Chesterfield was the *arbiter* of elegant manners and good taste in his day; Dress designers are the *arbiters* of women's fashions.]

Referee and **umpire** may both mean *arbitrator,* but the two terms are more likely to be used in special contexts. Many sports are presided over by official *judges* who are appointed to enforce the rules of the game or contest and to settle disputed points. In baseball, tennis, and cricket, such an official is called an *umpire;* in boxing, ice hockey, and basketball, *referee* is the correct term. The rules of American football call for the presence of both an *umpire* and a *referee.* Outside the world of sports, *umpire* and *referee* have further meanings. *Referee* is applied technically to a lawyer to whom a pending legal case is referred, by means of a court order, for additional investigation and report. Although an *arbitrator,* a legal *referee* is usually appointed without the consent of the parties involved. In an important or complicated controversy, an *umpire* may be appointed to make a final decision in a case in which there is disagreement or a stalemate between the *arbitrators.* See LAWYER.

jumble

    conglomeration
    farrago
    hodgepodge
    medley
    mélange
    mess
    mishmash
    muddle
    olio
    olla podrida
    potpourri

These nouns are alike in referring to a disordered condition or to a confused or heterogeneous mixture of elements. **Jumble** and **muddle** both suggest conditions of extreme disorderliness resulting in confusion. *Jumble* suggests physical disorderliness, a lack of neatness, and brings to mind objects strewn about carelessly: The room was a *jumble* of books, papers, and soda cans. *Muddle* suggests the lack of clear or coherent organization and commonly refers to mental or intellectual disorder—confused thinking. [The club records were in a complete *muddle*—no one even knew how much money was in the treasury; Income tax returns always put me in a *muddle;* in a drunken *muddle* of misdirected antagonism.]

Conglomeration and **mélange** refer to heterogeneous collections of things. Both often carry critical overtones, suggesting that the collection is random or inapposite: a curious *conglomeration* of witticisms, quotations, word games, and other linguistic legerdemain, entertaining enough but lacking overall organization. *Mélange* more vigorously suggests inaptness or incongruity and is sometimes used derisively or contemptuously: a *mélange* of baby boomers, middle-class matrons, and Beltway pundits. **Medley** and **farrago** both refer to confused mixtures or masses of elements. *Medley* emphasizes the variegated, heterogeneous nature of the elements that compose it, whereas *farrago* emphasizes the irrational or confused juxtaposition of elements. A *medley* is necessarily various, but not necessarily composed of inharmonious or clashing elements: a *medley* of flavors. *Farrago* strikes a balance somewhere between *conglomeration* and **mess**: a *farrago* of outmoded ideas and half-understood theories.

Mess is the most general noun of this set as well as one of the strongest. In the sense here considered, it means a hopeless *jumble* of elements resulting in a state of confusion, or the confused state itself. It may refer either to physical disorder (After the ticker tape parade ended, the street was a *mess*), sloppiness or slovenliness (The manuscript was a *mess*, full of inkblots, scribbles, and deletions), or to any thoroughly disorganized condition (He's made a *mess* of his life).

Hodgepodge, **potpourri**, and **olla podrida** all refer in one sense to stews having a variety of ingredients. All also commonly refer to any miscellaneous collection of elements. *Hodgepodge* and the stronger term **mishmash** emphasize disorganization; they are the figurative analogues to an actual *jumble* of objects. [The comedy was a *hodgepodge* of sentimental cliché, coy sexuality, and jingoistic claptrap.] *Hodgepodge* bespeaks a lack of intelligent guidance or rational coherence. *Mishmash,* the most directly contemptuous noun of this group, is often used to suggest a badly mismanaged or botched undertaking, resulting in confusion and chaos: His heralded new political program turned out to be nothing more than the usual *mishmash* of stale slogans, unrealistic promises, and insincere flattery. *Potpourri,* as here considered, points to the lack of uniformity or similarity of elements and may imply a lack of discrimination or restraint as well: The movie was a *potpourri* of slapstick, melodrama, and bowdlerized history, in spite of which it still managed to include some genuinely funny moments. *Olla podrida,* borrowed from the Spanish, and **olio**, derived from *olla,* suggest a miscellaneous collection or *medley* of elements: an *olio* (or *olla podrida*) of political sentiment, ranging from the radical to the reactionary. See DISPARATE, HETEROGENEOUS.

jurisdiction
authority
dominion
power
sovereignty
sway

These nouns refer to the ability or right to rule. **Jurisdiction** is the most formal of these nouns and the most restricted in application. It indicates a legally predetermined division of a larger whole, a division within which someone or something has the right to rule or decide: A surrogate court has sole *jurisdiction* over the execution of wills; an election in which workers were to select the union that would have *jurisdiction* to represent them; the three-nation commission that was given *jurisdiction* over the internationalized city. **Sovereignty** approaches *jurisdiction* in formality, but it stresses absolute or autonomous rule over something considered as a whole. In this case, the official right to rule is not stressed so much as the fact of actual ruling, however this has come about: British mercantile interests that acquired *sovereignty* over the scattering of emirates adjacent to the port; nations traditionally suspicious of surrendering the slightest token of *sovereignty* to any supranational governing body; American revolutionists who rejected England's claim of *sovereignty* over the colonies.

Dominion is less clear-cut in its implications. It can refer, on one hand, to assigned partial rule, like *jurisdiction:* a constitutional provision that gave the states *dominion* over intrastate commerce. On the other hand, like *sovereignty,* it can refer to absolute control, although here it often refers strictly to the control of a superior over an inferior: the inescapable *dominion* of the rich and educated over the poor and unschooled. As an actual title for a territory, *dominion* can suggest a colony that has gained internal self-rule but whose external affairs still come under the *sovereignty* of the colonizer: a colony that advanced to the status of a *dominion* and finally to that of a republic. **Sway** can now sound old-fashioned; traditionally, it has referred to a sphere in which something has absolute control: the succession of European nations that held *sway* over various portions of Africa; Aristotle still holds *sway* over the thinking of some philosophers. As in the last example, *sway* is in danger of being taken in the sense of mere influence rather than absolute control; this possibility occurs because of an unrelated, verbal meaning of *sway:* a demagogue able to *sway* mass audiences to his point of view.

Authority and **power** are less formal than the other nouns here and more general in application. *Power* refers to any exercise of control over something, often with a stress on forcefulness or strength: The monarchy won universal recognition of its *sovereignty* only after the period of its greatest *power* had begun to fade. Often, this noun refers simply to the ability to choose, understand, or control: Only humans are thought to have the *power* to reason. A related use reveals the noun at its most general in referring to any sort of mental or physical strength or force: a work of great emotional *power;* brute *power* used to put down the revolt. *Authority* can indicate an officially determined right to rule: a committee given *authority* to rule on the credentials of disputed delegations. But *authority* can also refer to anyone exercising power, whether assigned to do so or not: a *power* gap in the new republic that remained until several tribal leaders assumed *authority* and formed a caretaker government. This noun can also indicate the taking on or delegating of responsibility: You have my *authority* to proceed with the investigation. As an abstraction, *authority* can indicate all sources of *power* taken as a whole: a child who always rebelled against *authority*. In related uses, it can refer to the expert or the definitive: an *authority* on antique glass; an actor who executed the role with consummate *authority*. See LAW.

K

keen

acute
astute
penetrating
perspicacious
sharp
shrewd

These adjectives characterize unusual mental agility or perceptiveness. **Keen** suggests both attributes, adding to them a vigorous and forceful ability to grapple with complex or obscure problems: a *keen* mind for fine distinctions. Sometimes, *keen* may suggest an ability to observe details and see them as part of a larger pattern: a *keen* understanding of the problems facing the civil rights movement. **Acute** suggests a finely honed sensitivity or receptivity to nuances that might escape others; it might also imply a high-keyed state of nervous attention that is not sustainable for long: an *acute* awareness of the slightest ambiguity in each statement made by her opponent; an *acute* alertness, heightened by the unusual silence of the jungle night.

Penetrating relates more to the vigorous agility suggested by *keen* than the high-keyed attunement implicit in *acute*. It stresses, however, the ability to see the root causes underlying details, where a *keen* mind might clearly see only the surface details. *Penetrating* may also suggest a brusque eagerness to get to basic principles, regardless of possible injury to the feelings of others: a *penetrating* analysis of the play's weakness that was unsparing in the harshness of its criticism. **Shrewd**, by contrast, suggests practical wisdom that does not necessarily look deeply into things at all but is wily and conscious of its own self-interest: a *shrewd* notion of how far he could go in criticizing the existing regime. Occasionally, *shrewd* can be used without this overtone of self-interest, but it still suggests cleverness rather than the impatient intensity of *penetrating*: a *shrewd* estimate of the materials the job would consume.

Astute suggests a thorough and profound understanding that stems from a scholarly or experienced mind in full command of a field: an *astute* assessment of the strengths and weaknesses of the plans for reorganizing the department; an *astute* evaluation of the gaps in our knowledge of how life evolved. **Sharp**, by contrast, suggests a mind that is generally capable but not necessarily well grounded in a given field. Its informality suggests the practical cleverness inherent in *shrewd*, but without that adjective's suggestion of self-interest: a *sharp* mind for figures; a *sharp* awareness of social niceties.

Perspicacious is the most formal of these adjectives; it stresses intensity of perception, without being rich in other connotations: a *perspicacious* remark that illuminated the problem for all of them. See ACUMEN, WISDOM.

Antonyms: BLAND, *languid*, SLOW, STUPID.

kernel

crux
gist
nub
nucleus
substance

The familiar phrase *the heart of the matter* comes close to summing up the meaning of these nouns. **Kernel**, originating in an Old English word for corn seed, soon broadened to include any seed or cereal grain within its protective coating, then the edible inner part of a nut, and finally its metaphorical sense as the central part of anything: The *kernel* of the problem lies in the interpretation of the evidence.

Gist derives ultimately from a Latin word meaning lie or rest. Its original meaning as a place of rest came to be extended to the ground or foundation on which something lay or by which it could be supported: the *gist* of an argument; the *gist* of the prosecution's case. The closely related noun **substance** (from the Latin for stand under or beneath) includes among its numerous meanings the same idea of the essential or central part of anything, of that without which it would lack stability and value. [Faith is the *substance* of things not seen; There is much *substance* in the critic's views on modern art.]

Crux, with its reference to the symbolism of the Cross, implies something pivotal, vital, and sometimes, as *crux* suggests, crucial: The closing of the Gulf of Aqaba proved to be the *crux* of the situation. **Nub** is an Americanism meaning much the same as *gist*, with an informal carry-over to the idea of a point or moral: the *nub* of the story; A student cannot go far wrong by giving the *nub* of the main idea in an opening paragraph.

Nucleus, though it comes from the Latin word for

nut, has not, like the related term *kernel,* acquired currency in a figurative sense. It has been and still is largely restricted to technical and scientific fields, where it denotes a central part or point around which other things are gathered, as in a cell, an atom, certain complex chemical compounds, and the like. Because the ideas of movement, change, and growth have become so closely associated with it, *nucleus* serves best only where such ideas are implied in the thought expressed: The *nucleus* of Plato's philosophy lay in his doctrine of the archetype. See BASIS, CENTER.

Antonyms: *periphery.*

kill

assassinate
butcher
dispatch
execute
massacre
murder
slaughter
slay

These verbs refer to the taking of lives. **Kill** is the most general, applying to any kind of death-dealing activity: a frost that *killed* all our fruit trees; an insecticide to *kill* roaches; two women *killed* in a car accident; a madman who threatened to *kill* me; soldiers *killed* in action. The generality of *kill* enables its use in situations where cause is assigned for other kinds of death: children *killed* by neglect; the rising number of people *killed* by heart disease. *Kill* can even apply where no life is actually lost: a veto that *killed* the bill; their decision to *kill* the news story after it had appeared in the early edition. **Murder** refers less ambiguously to the crime in which one person intentionally *kills* another: He admitted that he had accidentally *killed* his wife, but denied he had *murdered* her. Sometimes, *murder* can refer to a brutal *killing,* as in war: naked aggression in which one nation set out to *murder* the citizens of an adjoining state. Hyperbolically, it can point to the mishandling of anything: expressionless actors who *murder* their lines.

Assassinate is a form of *murder* in which someone *kills* a public figure, usually a political leader, for whatever reason: a continuing debate over the possibility that there was a conspiracy to *assassinate* President Kennedy. **Execute** can refer to capital punishment, which a state may exact in reprisal for certain crimes: *executed* for treason; The woman who *murdered* her husband was *executed* in a gas chamber. Sometimes, the verb can refer to an on-the-spot *killing* of enemies

or prisoners by an opponent, as in a war, occupation, or insurrection; here, the notion of legal sanction may be absent: the millions *executed* by the Nazis; a brigand who ordered his captives *executed* by firing squad. **Dispatch** can function like *execute* in reference to official or formalized *killing,* although it is not restricted to this sense. In any case, *dispatch* stresses efficiency and swiftness: The emperor ordered his rival *executed* by slow torture, rather than allowing him to be mercifully *dispatched* on the battlefield; the Reign of Terror during which hundreds were daily *dispatched* by the guillotine. The verb can also indicate the *coup de grâce* itself: a pistol with which to *dispatch* those not *killed* by the firing squad's volley.

Butcher and **slaughter** can both refer to the *killing* of animals for food. *Slaughter* is the preferred term in the meat-packing industry, possibly because *butcher* has implications of brutality or because *butcher* can also apply to the cutting or carving of meat at any point after the actual *killing.* Also, *butcher* sometimes indicates a small-scale operation, whereas *slaughter* can better suggest mass *killing:* a shed in which the farmer *butchered* pigs to feed his family; legislation recommending humane standards for *slaughtering* cattle in packing plants. Both *butcher* and *slaughter* take on extremely disapproving overtones when applied to the *killing* of people. *Butcher* here suggests bungling inexpertness or sadistic brutality: a rapist who *butchered* his victims with a razor; dictators who *butcher* those foolish enough to dissent. *Slaughter* suggests the *killing* of great numbers of people: Teutonic hordes who advanced across Europe, sacking and *slaughtering.*

Massacre usually applies solely to the brutal *killing* of large numbers of people. In this, it is close to one aspect of *slaughter,* but it is more specific in suggesting the wholesale and often total destruction of a group of relatively defenseless people, as in war, persecution, or revenge: the Incas who were *massacred* by the Spaniards; Herod ordered all infants in the land to be *massacred.* **Slay** can now sound outdated as a close synonym for *murder* or *slaughter* except in Biblical reference. [David *slew* Goliath; Charioteers were sent to *slay* the escaping Hebrews.] The past participle, *slain,* is now more frequently used than other forms of the verb: a battle in which twenty were *slain.* See DESTROY, DIE, ERASE.

kin

family
kindred

kinfolk
kinfolks
kinsfolk
kinsmen
relations
relatives

These nouns refer to people connected by blood or marriage. **Kin** is the general term for such people in the U.S. South. **Relatives** is the comparable term in the North. **Relations** can substitute interchangeably with *relatives,* except that it may also be the word of choice to indicate humorous or serious disparagement of the people to whom one is related. Also, *kin* is more likely to concentrate on blood relationship, whereas the other two are wider in scope by including in-laws as well. *Kin* is always construed as plural.

Family is a more restricted term, referring only to one's closest blood *relatives,* usually to those people living together in one household: a *family* composed of mother, father, one grandfather, and three children. *Family* can apply more widely to people past and present who bear the same *family* name: a distinguished Spanish *family* over three generations. **Kinsmen** often points to this same idea: He brilliantly upheld the honor of a long line of *kinsmen*. Unlike *kin, kinsman* has a singular form: a *kinsman* (or *kinswoman*) of mine. **Kindred** can refer to *relatives,* to lineage, or to a looser fraternal or tribal group: a clan in which the *kindred* are loyal to the same totem.

Kinfolk, kinfolks, and **kinsfolk,** like *kin,* appear preponderantly in the U.S. South and have no singular forms. All these nouns suggest a good many *relatives* who keep in touch or who act together, as in a clan. By contrast, one might have relatively few known *kin* and not be socially close to them at all. See DESCENT, FOLK.

Antonyms: *FOREIGNER.*

kind

category
sort
type

These nouns refer to groupings of similar things. **Kind** can indicate a grouping that has indisputable objective reality: a poker hand that contained four of a *kind*. More informally, it can also indicate a subjective notion on the part of a speaker that two or more things are alike in some way: I don't like people of that *kind;* the *kind* of room I can feel at home in. Often, however, *kind* can be used when no very serious reference to a larger grouping is actually intended: She was a friendly *kind* of person. **Sort** is even more informal

than *kind*. Occasionally, it can refer to clearly defined groupings that are objectively valid: a list of the *sorts* of trees that are hardy enough to grow in cities, despite the hazard of air pollution. But even more often than *kind, sort* suggests a subjective evaluation. Furthermore, it more often indicates a negative judgment: the wrong *sort* of person for her son to be associating with.

Type is only slightly more formal than the foregoing, but it points more clearly to objectively definable groupings: the four basic blood *types; types* of world literature. But it can be used in the same indefinite way as *kind* and *sort,* although it may carry over a note of greater conviction: What an ugly *type* of building. A special use of *type* refers to an individual or example as though it were the quintessence of a whole group: He was a Madison Avenue *type;* a Hollywood *type*. Some careful writers avoid this informal usage—or any use of the preceding nouns that may suggest the existence of hard-and-fast classifications where this is not the case **Category**, the most formal, applies exclusively to definable groupings, whether these reveal themselves in a material being analyzed or whether they are arbitrarily developed for the sake of order or convenience: self-evident *categories* based on the results of a single chemical test; She made *categories* of the things she wanted to take with her, things she wanted put into storage, and things to be discarded. See CLASS, PROTOTYPE.

kindle

fire
ignite
inflame
light

These verbs relate to ways in which something can be set on fire or made to burn, literally or figuratively. **Kindle** suggests the need for some preparatory effort or action before combustible material will burn. [He *kindled* a fire by setting a match to a few twigs; A smoldering cigarette can *kindle* a devastating forest fire.] In reference to people, *kindle* indicates the act of arousing, stimulating, or exciting. [The boy's interest in science was *kindled* by his visit to the laboratory where his mother worked; The speaker's eloquence *kindled* a lively enthusiasm in the audience.]

In the sense of burning or applying great heat, **fire** has numerous applications, both technical and figurative. One can *fire* a furnace, *fire* a gun, *fire* the pottery in a kiln, *fire* a hayrick. Metaphorically, it can have much the same meaning as *kindle,* but with the suggestion of a sudden burst. [Her imagination was *fired* by what she had read; The coach *fired* the team with the determination to win the pennant.] This compares with an analogous, chiefly literary use of **inflame** to mean excite to violent emotion or activity: The crowd was *inflamed* by the brutality of the police. In medical usage, however, *inflame* denotes a condition of actual heat, swelling, and soreness in some part of the body: an *inflamed* ulcer, complicated by infection.

Ignite is almost entirely restricted to the technical sense of a rapid and sometimes violent burning of something that has been exposed to a critical temperature by one means or another. [An electric spark *ignites* the gasoline in an automobile engine; A time fuse *ignited* the high explosives; Spontaneous combustion *ignited* the heap of oil rags.]

Light has a double reference, both to heat and to illumination. One can speak of *lighting* a fire or a furnace and *lighting* a lamp, with the knowledge that one result more or less accompanies the other, as when an electric current *ignites* the filament in an evacuated glass bulb, making it glow brightly. See BRIGHT, BURN, FIRE.

Antonyms: *darken, extinguish, quench, smother, stifle.*

knife

> dagger
> dirk
> misericord
> poniard
> shiv
> stiletto

These nouns all denote sharpened or pointed instruments commonly set in handles. **Knife** is the general term for any instrument used for cutting, piercing, or spreading, with one or more sharpened edges and sometimes with pointed blades. A *knife,* though it may be used as a weapon, is no more essentially a weapon than is a paperweight or a pair of shears, which can also be formidable weapons. For a *knife* used as a weapon, criminals have long had a word, variously spelled but now generally rendered **shiv**. In modern criminal slang it may refer to a switchblade *knife,* but the connection is not invariable. Should switchblade *knives* be replaced by other, perhaps more ingeniously concealed *knives, shiv* may well make the transition as effortlessly as it has many times in the past.

A **dagger**, unlike a *knife,* is made to be used as a weapon. *Daggers* are any sharp, pointed and edged weapons for stabbing. The printing mark (†) expresses fairly well the common shape of *daggers.* All the other terms here considered are specific kinds of *daggers.*

A **dirk** is a Highland Scottish *dagger,* rather long, with a straight blade. A **poniard** is a small *dagger,* especially one with a triangular or four-sided blade. A **stiletto** is a small *dagger* with a narrow blade that is comparatively thick in cross section. **Misericord** (or *misericorde*) denotes a *dagger* used in the Middle Ages to give the *coup de grâce,* or mercy stroke, to fallen knights. See CUT.

knit

> crochet
> darn
> tat
> weave

These verbs mean form a fabric from threads or other strands by various methods. **Knit**, **crochet**, and **tat** all imply the drawing of a single strand of yarn, cotton, silk, etc., into series of interlocking loops. *Knitting* involves the use of two large, slightly pointed needles (or a *knitting* machine) on which a series of interlacing loops are made into successive rows, the resulting fabric being transferred from one needle to the other at the beginning of each new row of stitches. *Crocheting* is a type of *knitting,* but it is done with a single needle having a hook at one end. Unlike the stitches of *knitting,* those of *crocheting* are not necessarily made in successive rows. Both *knit* and *crochet* nearly always imply direct construction of a garment or other article: to *knit* a sweater; to *crochet* a bedspread. *Tat* implies the making of an edging, as for a handkerchief, by means of a small hand shuttle that knots and loops a single thread into a lacelike strip that resembles *crochet* work.

Weave differs completely in principle from *knit, crochet,* and *tat.* In *weaving* fabrics, threads are entwined into a texture by interlacing on a loom two sets of strands, the warp and the weft (sometimes called woof) that are at right angles to one another. The warp threads, which run the long way of the fabric, are strung tightly on the loom; the weft threads are then passed back and forth, and over and under the warp by means of a shuttle. *Weave* is also used to describe the interlacing of straw and other pliable materials in making baskets, hats, etc.

To **darn** is to repair a hole in a garment or other cloth article by filling it in with yarn or thread, preferably by means of strands that are stitched across the hole and then filled in by transverse threads in the manner of *weaving.* See MAKE.

label

categorize
pigeonhole
tag

These verbs have to do with indicating the nature, function, purpose, disposition, etc., of anything that requires special identification, usually in the form of written or printed instructions. **Label**, at its most limited, can indicate the affixing of a slip that contains a printed, written, or visual legend. In this context, **tag** indicates one form of *labeling* in which such a legend is tied or strung to something by means of cord or wire: government regulations for *labeling* canned goods; certain packages that must be *tagged* as well as *labeled*. *Tag* may also better suggest a symbolic identification rather than a detailing of information: *tagging* diseased sheep with red markers and healthy ones with green markers. Used more generally, *label* has the wider range of application for any act of identifying something: a professor who was *labeled* by students a tiresome bore. As in this example, *label* can be humorous or sarcastic, but often it points disapprovingly to unfair identifications: those who *label* as dangerously liberal anyone interested in social welfare. With fewer general applications, *tag* can suggest a looser identification: He was *tagged* by some as a miser and by others as a prudent man. Or *tag* may be merely a more vivid or colorful substitute for *label:* a professor who was *tagged* a mean old woman.

Categorize is the most formal and neutral verb here; it applies to the classification of something within a larger system or division: an explanation of how books are *categorized* in the Library of Congress classification. Because of its earlier and still active use in philosophy and logic, *categorize* can indicate an arrangement that is both imperative and final, but just as often it can point to any arbitrary arrangement adopted for convenience in handling masses of data or detail. **Pigeonhole** suggests the same idea, but is often used, like one sense of *label,* to indicate disapproval for an attempt to fit something, in all its complexity, into simple and preconceived stereotypes: They were more concerned to *pigeonhole* the patient as a manic-depressive, schizophrenic, or what-have-you than to treat her illness. *Pigeonhole* may also apply to the filing away of something to be dealt with later or forgotten: He *pigeonholed* all suggestions for changing the work schedules. See KIND, ORGANIZE.

labor

drudgery
grind
toil
travail
work

These nouns refer to the effort required to accomplish a task, whether physical or mental. **Labor** most immediately suggests physical effort: the *labor* it would take to improvise a rope bridge across the chasm. From this sense, *labor* has become an abstraction for such effort: estimating that two-thirds of the repair bill went for *labor.* It also refers to a work force: a meeting between *labor* and management. An older sense of *labor* refers to childbirth: attended by a nurse during *labor.* When referring to mental effort, it suggests unusual difficulty: weeks of *labor* needed to balance the accounts; all the *labor* she put into documenting her claim. **Work** can apply to any situation in which either a short-term or recurring task is performed: It took hard *work* to get the car out of the rutted street; depressions that throw millions out of *work.* In a related use, *work* can apply to the result of someone's *labors:* her life*work;* a book that was the *work* of a distinguished group of scholars. It can also apply to something, as machinery, designed for a special function; this usually requires the plural: gas*works;* clock*works.*

Toil emphasizes the difficulty of the *work* it pertains to, but it is less often used now except for a high-toned effect, possibly specious: the *toil* of our forefathers to build a stronger nation; mothers who *toil* to better their children and are seldom rewarded. **Travail** emphasizes actual suffering, mainly because of its reference, like *labor,* to the pains of childbirth. *Travail* is, however, distinctly precious even in reference to childbirth, where the greater simplicity of *labor* gives both strength and dignity. In some contexts, particularly metaphorical, *travail* may nonetheless be useful: still unenlightened about the futility of war after centuries of *travail.*

Drudgery emphasizes *work* that is uninspiring, unpleasant, or arduous; it may suggest menial physical *work,* but can apply to any dull and unrewarding task. Unlike some other terms here, *drudgery* need not suggest hard or exhausting *labor* so much as unrelieved monotony: machines that take the *drudgery* out of factory *labor;* the unrelenting *drudgery* of exam week.

Grind is in some ways an intensification of *drudgery,* but it particularly emphasizes work done under pressure in a dehumanizing way, whether physical or mental; it suggests the unrelenting quality of such *labor* done over a long period of time: the twelve-hour *grind* of coal miners at the turn of the century; the daily *grind* of the office worker. See EFFORT, PROFESSION.

Antonyms: *idleness, leisure,* PLEASURE, *relaxation.*

laborer

jobholder
proletarian
wage earner
worker
workingman
workman

These nouns refer to people who earn their living by physical effort or by the practice of relatively simple skills. **Laborer** and **worker** have the least emotional tinge of any sort. *Laborer* specifically emphasizes physical effort, while *worker* is more general in applying to a wider range of tasks and reaching higher up the ladder of skills. [Automation hits hardest at the completely unskilled *laborer,* next at the blue-collar *worker,* and last at the white-collar *worker.*] By contrast with *worker,* however, **workingman** and **workman**, as well as *workingwoman* and *workwoman,* have a narrower or more specific range of application, *workingman* and *workingwoman* particularly being applicable at most to semiskilled labor: a full dinner pail for the average *workingman.* *Workman* and *workwoman* can suggest the possession of skills approaching those of the craftsperson: *workmen* who restore and refinish parquet floors.

Jobholder and **wage earner** are both ways of stressing the money a *laborer* or *worker* earns and the fact that both, at the moment of description, are actually holding a job or earning wages. Of the two, *jobholder* can apply more generally, since it stresses being in a position of employment more than the position itself, which could range from unskilled to skilled work. *Wage earner* distinguishes between someone who gets a paycheck and someone who is self-employed.

Proletarian originally denoted a member of the lowest class of ancient Rome. The term received a new lease on life from its use by modern political and economic theorists, particularly Karl Marx, to designate that class of a state or of the world which, lacking personal means of production, is forced to sell its labor for wages in order to live. See ARTISAN.

lack

absence
dearth
shortage

These nouns all denote a deficiency or nonexistence of something specified or implied. **Lack** is a general term meaning a total or partial insufficiency. [It was a *lack* of cash that prevented me from joining you at lunch today; A *lack* of beds in the cabin meant that three of us had to sleep on the floor all weekend.] Although *lack* can express a totality of deficiency, a qualifying adjective is often used with it to avoid any possibility of confusion: The young man displayed a complete *lack* of courtesy and tact in dealing with his employer. No confusion about total *lack* is possible when **absence** is used alone. *Absence* is the opposite of presence; it means nonexistence: The *absence* of a chairperson turned the meeting into a near riot. The difference between *lack* and *absence* is apparent when we contrast "a *lack* of sugar in her diet" with "an *absence* of sugar in her diet." The former suggests there is not enough sugar in the diet; the latter implies there is no sugar at all in the diet. *Absence,* of course, can also signify the state of being away. In the example cited, "the *absence* of a chairperson" denotes the nonexistence of a chairperson. If the phrase were "in the *absence* of the chairperson," it would be obvious that a chairperson existed but was not present at the time under discussion.

Shortage is synonymous with *lack* in designating a partial insufficiency, but more than *lack* it suggests an insufficiency of some established, required, or accustomed amount: There was a *shortage* of dairy products in the supermarket last week because of a delivery strike. *Shortage* also means the amount by which something is deficient: The *shortage* totaled $5000.

Dearth in a sense no longer used meant dearness or costliness. It later came to refer to the kind of *lack* or scarcity that makes something costly, especially food in time of famine. An extension of this sense gives *dearth* the meaning of a *lack* or scarcity of anything: a *dearth* of content in an essay; a *dearth* of oranges because of extended drought; a *dearth* of parental affection and discipline. See SCANTY.

Antonyms: *abundancy, adequacy, ampleness, copiousness, sufficiency.*

lame

crippled
halt
hamstrung
hobbled

These adjectives describe a partial or complete disablement, particularly of the legs or feet. **Lame** can refer to such impairment in a person or animal. It perhaps most often suggests a gradually worsening disablement or stiffening as from old age or arthritis. In many cases, walking might still be possible, though difficult: the *lame* woman who used a cane to get around; an old horse that had gone *lame* and had to be destroyed. *Lame* can also refer to other impairments, especially those involving muscular soreness or inflammation: a *lame* back that made sitting up straight excruciating. More generally, it can indicate something poor or awkward: a *lame* excuse.

Crippled can often suggest an accidental impairment: left permanently *crippled* by the collision. Also, it can suggest total loss of movement: telling the *crippled* child she would never regain the use of either leg. While *crippled* is thus more forceful than *lame,* it can be used as well for less devastating impairments: one hand *crippled* by rheumatism: a *crippled* woman who can walk only with the help of leg braces. **Halt** is now archaic sounding when used of a person who is *lame* or walks with a limp, except in stock phrases: a beggar who was *halt* and blind.

Hamstrung pertains most directly to cattle or other animals when the Achilles tendons of their hind legs have been purposely cut to make them incapable of walking or escaping: *hamstrung* bulls that were left behind to be picked up as stragglers. *Hamstrung* can also refer to the same condition in people, usually as the result of an accident: a torn ligament that left the track star *hamstrung.* More commonly, *hamstrung* refers to any frustrating setback: office procedures *hamstrung* by bureaucratic inaction. *Crippled* can also be used in a comparable way: a poverty program *crippled* by cutbacks in appropriations. **Hobbled** can indicate a less drastic way of impeding the movement of cattle or horses, by tying their legs so as to allow walking but not running or galloping: horses *hobbled* while grazing within the camp. Metaphorically, *hobbled* also suggests reduced activity caused by some frustrating factor: a bill *hobbled* in committee by obstructionist amendments. See HURT, POWERLESS, WEAK.

lanky

angular
gangling
rangy
rawboned
spindling
spindly

These adjectives apply to leanness that is emphasized by height, length of limb, or awkwardness of bearing. A *lanky* person is tall, thin, and long-limbed, being typically loose-jointed: a tall, *lanky* fellow; a *lanky* basketball player. **Gangling** is closely synonymous with *lanky* but implies greater awkwardness, as from disproportionate growth of the limbs during adolescence: a *gangling,* ungainly youth, all arms and legs. [He hurried toward me with long, *gangling* strides.] **Rangy** carries no hint of gracelessness but stresses physique. It was originally applied to animals having lengthy bodies and long limbs and therefore were well adapted for roving: *rangy* cattle. Now it is also used of slim and long-legged human beings: a *rangy* cowboy; *rangy* runners on our track team.

Angular presupposes prominent bones and suggests sharp edges: *angular* features; an *angular* adolescent. Along with bony leanness, it often indicates unprepossessing stiffness—whether evinced in awkward, jerky movements or in an unbending manner. Hence, when *angular* is applied to tall, thin females, it signals the absence of roundness, softness, pliancy, or grace: an *angular* headmistress with a cold eye and forbidding aspect. **Rawboned** is usually used of men and emphasizes a big, bony, often awkward frame. A *rawboned* person has a prominent bone structure and little flesh, but may be sturdily made though spare and *angular.* *Rawboned* carries the suggestion of crudity in build, of sharp or knobby bones jutting out: a ruddy, *rawboned* recruit.

The last two adjectives focus on abnormal leanness rather than a naturally *lanky* or bony build. **Spindling** describes a form so long and thin that it seems markedly out of proportion: The old man looked like an apparition—a tall, *spindling* wraith. **Spindly** adds to *spindling* the suggestion of physical weakness and frailty, describing a combination of height or length and matchstick thinness: a *spindly* invalid, pitifully wasted away; a child unable to stand on his *spindly* little legs. *Spindly* may also be used of a fragile, limblike appendage of a machine: the *spindly* aluminum legs of the spacecraft. See BONY, CLUMSY, THIN.

Antonyms: *FAT, HUSKY.*

large

big
giant
gigantic
king-size
mammoth
outsize

These adjectives describe things of more than normal size or of unusual mass. **Large** and **big** are both general and vague; both are acceptable in contexts ranging from the most informal to the most formal, although *large* would tend to be substituted for *big* in extremely formal contexts. *Big* suggests something of more than normal size, but it is particularly relevant to material or bodily mass, whereas *large* might suggest even greater departure from a norm. In this case, the implications of the adjective are less limited to the physical: a *big* stone; a *big* bully; a *large* house; trying on a *larger* size shoe; the *large* issues confronting us.

Outsize (or *outsized*) specifically suggests something too *large* to conform to the norm or be accommodated by an already established measure. While the adjective thus suggests an object of abnormal or excessive size, unusual mass is not necessarily implied: *outsize* typing paper that wouldn't fit the binder in which she kept her reports; extra-*large* beds for *outsize* people. **King-size** is a merchandising term that refers to a product that is longer or *larger* than the standard or usual size: *king-size* cigarettes; *king-size* beds.

Gigantic and **mammoth** are now mostly used as hyperboles, suggesting anything of extreme proportions. *Gigantic* derives from a Latin word for giant; *mammoth,* of course, can refer to the prehistoric elephantlike animal. *Mammoth* in the present context still may more readily suggest something physically *big,* whereas *gigantic* is more often used now for metaphorical instances: a *mammoth* skyscraper; a *gigantic* threat to our security. But this is by no means invariable: a *mammoth* weekend party; a *gigantic* brute of a man.

Giant differs from *gigantic* in often suggesting a physical change of scale or in referring to something reproduced in *outsized* dimensions: a science-fiction story about *giant* cockroaches. As a hyperbole, it can be used indiscriminately: a *giant* protest rally. In this example, reference to a *large* rally is no doubt intended, rather than to a rally of disgruntled giants. See MASSIVE, SIZE, TREMENDOUS.

Antonyms: *MINUTE, SMALL.*

laudable. Do not confuse the adjective *laudable* (praiseworthy) with the adjective *laudatory* (praising).

law

    canon
    code
    commandment
    constitution
    ordinance

regulation
statute

These nouns all denote rules of conduct or procedure that are imposed by some authority. **Law** is the broadest and most general term in this group. It designates a rule of conduct recognized by custom or decreed by formal enactment and considered by a community, nation, or other authoritatively constituted group as binding upon its members. *Law* also refers to a body of such rules.

A **constitution** is a collection of *laws* that establish the basic principles governing the actions of a government, corporation, or other body of persons organized for some purpose. The document that records such *laws* is also referred to as a *constitution.* **Code** also denotes a collection of *laws,* but these pertain to some specific subject or activity: a building *code;* the penal *code;* a *code* of ethics for lawmaking bodies.

A **statute** is a written *law* enacted by a legislative body and duly sanctioned and authenticated by constitutional rule. An act of Congress or Parliament would be considered a *statute.* In the United States, a *statute* enacted by a municipal body is called an **ordinance**; such *laws* cover local problems pertaining to traffic, zoning, sanitation, and the like.

Regulation is a general and less formal noun than the others in this group. It can designate any rule or principle, whether or not it has the effective force of enacted *law,* that is used to direct, manage, or control some system or organization.

A **canon** was originally a church *law;* it has since been extended to mean any principle regarded as established by common practice or by eminent authority: the *canons* of good taste. It has other, more specialized uses outside the legal context. **Commandment** is found almost exclusively in religious contexts because of its allusion to the ten injunctions given by God to Moses on Mount Sinai. See JURISDICTION.

lawful

    constitutional
    legal
    legitimate
    licit

These adjectives characterize ways of indicating what is permitted, allowable, countenanced, or sanctioned by custom or by some recognized authority.

Lawful implies conformity with laws, statutes, canons, precepts, principles, rules, etc., intended to regulate the conduct of those coming within their particular field of action. Thus, one speaks of *lawful* debts, a *lawful* claim, a *lawful* marriage, or of conducting a *lawful* business or making a *lawful* decision. **Legal** has nearly the same meaning, but is restricted chiefly to statute laws as they apply at certain times and places or under prescribed conditions. [Divorce is *lawful* but subject to various *legal* requirements before taking final effect; The *legal* speed limit within the town is 15 miles per hour.]

Constitutional refers to the fundamental laws and principles that have been adopted formally to govern the operations of a state acting as a unit toward those subject to its control and in its dealings with other states. [She stood on her *constitutional* rights; A *constitutional* amendment forbids slavery in the United States.] Strict usage distinguishes *constitutional* from all the other terms because of its direct reference to a document, instrument, or body of rules acknowledged as paramount in determining what is *lawful* or *legal:* The Supreme Court dismissed the appeal on *constitutional* grounds.

Legitimate originally meant whatever was declared to be *lawful:* a *legitimate* child; a *legitimate* heir to the throne; the *legitimate* owner of the land. It is now very generally applied to anything that is recognized by custom or in popular usage as conforming to established rules or standards, being regular, orderly, or acceptable in form, style, etc.: *legitimate* theater; a *legitimate* conclusion; *legitimate* procedures. **Licit** is the adjective form in English of the Latin verb *licet,* it is permitted. It is seldom used nowadays, and then in the sense of something strictly *lawful:* a *licit* marriage; *licit* traffic in drugs or liquor. From the same root we get *license, licentiate,* and *licentious,* as well as the far better known and more widely used negative form *illicit.* See PERMIT, RIGHTFUL.

Antonyms: *illegal, unconstitutional, unlawful.*

lawlessness

    anarchy
    disorder
    disturbance
    riot

All these nouns signify an absence, disruption, or breakdown of law and order. **Lawlessness** implies either that no law exists or that the law is not being enforced or obeyed: the *lawlessness* of a frontier town without a sheriff; the *lawlessness* of a band of outlaws. In a broad sense, this adjective may indicate disregard of any or all restrictive regulations: the *lawlessness* of children who are allowed to run wild. *Lawlessness* may also apply to actions that are not controlled or authorized by law or in accord with it: the *lawlessness* of his behavior; the *lawlessness* of a lynching. **Anarchy** comes from Greek roots that literally mean without a leader. At its most extreme, it implies the lawless confusion and chaos that result when no authority is exercised by anyone, either within or outside the law, and when no general rules of order are in effect: a newly independent colony plunged into *anarchy* by warring factions and a lack of central leadership; total *anarchy* after a world war, the only rules being every man for himself and survival of the fittest. In a general sense *anarchy* indicates the absence of government. Specifically, it may designate a community founded on the utopian principle that social order may exist without government, society being regulated by voluntary agreement and marked by absolute individual freedom. In a disapproving sense, *anarchy* can also imply utter license—freedom unchecked by self-regulation and unrestrained by submission to authority: the *anarchy* of rebellious youth, seeking liberty without responsibility.

Lawlessness and *anarchy* have to do with prevailing conditions. The remaining nouns, by contrast, apply to temporary breaches of the peace or to single incidents or outbreaks of unruly conduct. **Disturbance** is the mildest of these. A *disturbance* may be no more than a slight commotion or an annoying racket, and it can be caused by a single person or by any number of people: a drunk creating a *disturbance* in a bar; people throwing an all-night party who were charged with *disturbance* of the peace. **Disorder** is the most general of all these nouns, but here it applies specifically to a *disturbance* of proper civic order: a person charged with *disorderly* (an adjective) conduct. As a noun in this sense, however, *disorder* generally implies that a number of people are involved and that there is considerably more confusion and commotion than in a *disturbance:* an outbreak of *disorder* in the gallery of the legislative chamber before the demonstrators were ejected. **Riot** indicates the largest and most violent outbreak of the three. In law, a *riot* is a tumultuous *disturbance* of the public peace by three or more assembled persons who, in the execution of some private aim, act lawfully or unlawfully in a manner calculated to terrorize the people. As the word is commonly understood, a *riot* involves mob action, frenzy, and often violence: a race *riot;* a period of *riots* in Los Angeles marked by widespread vandalism, looting, and attacks on motorists. A *riot* often involves mass *lawlessness* but is usually not leaderless: a demagogue who deliberately inflamed the crowd to such a degree that they started a *riot.* See TURBULENT, UNRULY, UPRISING.

Antonyms: *discipline, law, lawfulness, legality, order, peace.*

lawyer

advocate
attorney
barrister
counsel
counselor
solicitor

These nouns all designate persons who have had legal training and are qualified to practice law. **Lawyer** is the general term for anyone versed in the law and duly admitted to the bar. *Lawyers* conduct lawsuits, advise clients of their legal rights and obligations, and may act on behalf of clients or plead their cases in court.

Attorney, often used as a synonym for *lawyer,* in its strictest sense denotes an agent (not necessarily a *lawyer*) empowered to act in a legal capacity for another person: While she was living in Europe, her brother had power of *attorney* over her property. When used interchangeably with *lawyer,* the correct term is *attorney-at-law.*

Counselor, as one who gives advice, is the common term of address of a judge to a trial *lawyer* during court proceedings. Some *lawyers* refer to themselves professionally as *counselors-at-law* if the greatest part of their work is given over to court cases. **Counsel**, as well as *counselor,* is a term of address used by a judge. But *counsel* may consist of one *lawyer* only or of a legal staff working as a unit to advise a client or to conduct a case in court: After consulting with *counsel,* the defendant pled innocent.

In Britain, a *lawyer* qualified to conduct court cases is called a **barrister**, while a **solicitor** may give legal advice and may prepare court cases, but usually may not conduct them.

Advocate is used of a trial *lawyer* in Scotland. This term is rare in the United States except in *judge advocate* and other military usages. See RECOMMEND.

league

alliance
coalition
confederacy
confederation
federation
union

These nouns refer to a group of nations, states, or other parties that have entered into association for a common purpose. **League** is the most general, embracing everything from private or semipublic organizations to regional, national, or international associations. It suggests, however, a specific, clearly defined area of common interest: The *League* of Women Voters provides civic information on issues, candidates, and voting procedures; During the Middle Ages, free towns in northern Germany and neighboring countries banded together in the Hanseatic *League* to advance and protect their commerce; The *League* of Nations, established in 1920, had as its primary purpose the preservation of world peace.

Alliance stresses common interest and the pooling of resources. It may be applied to families, referring to connection through marriage, but it is more often used of formal agreements between nations. In this latter sense, *alliance* implies that the nations involved surrender little or no sovereignty in banding together and that they are free to withdraw at any time. In a defensive *alliance,* all participating nations might agree to fight an aggressor if that aggressor attacked any one of them. The North Atlantic Treaty Organization (NATO) is a military and naval *alliance* of nations, organized under the North Atlantic Treaty of 1949. Presumably, a nation would remain in an *alliance* only so long as its leaders desired.

A **coalition** is a temporary association of rival groups, such as political parties or factions. In many countries *coalition* governments may be formed when one political party fails to win a majority of the votes cast in an election. Some members of both parties in Congress may form a *coalition* to defeat, or to secure passage of, a particular bill.

Both **confederacy** and **confederation** refer to a formal association of states under a central government, but both imply a jealous guarding of the sovereignty or prerogatives of the separate states. The central government may be largely confined to the direction of foreign affairs. In 1781, the American colonies adopted the Articles of *Confederation,* which bound them together in a *league* of common defense until 1789, when the ratified Constitution established a stronger federal government. Under the original *confederation,* each state retained its sovereignty, and the federal government was subordinate to the states, its powers being severely limited and restricted. Later, in 1861, the constitution of the Southern *Confederacy* was adopted; it was similar to the U.S. Constitution but differed in its emphasis on states' rights.

A **federation** is a *league* formed by independent states, clubs, or organizations that delegate part of their sovereignty to a central authority: the National

Federation of Music Clubs; the American *Federation* of Labor. In political terms, a *federation* is a single government formed from separate states or from separate local governments. Although the states retain jurisdiction over their own internal affairs, the central government has stronger powers than one established under a *confederacy* or *confederation* and is able to deal authoritatively both with the state governments and with the citizens of the states.

The United States is a *federation,* and a closely knit *federation* is a **union**. *Union,* like *alliance,* applies to the joining together of two persons in wedlock rather than to the consequent connection of their families. In its political sense, *union* designates a fusion of separate states in which the states have surrendered so much of their sovereignty that they are essentially one political entity: the former *Union* of Soviet Socialist Republics. See ACCOMPLICE, ASSOCIATE, CLUB.

Antonyms: *disunion, division, isolation, secession, separation.*

leak

   drip
   ooze
   trickle

These words, both verbs and nouns, apply to fluid that flows slowly or drops little by little. **Leak** stresses the idea of accident. It refers to the unintended entry or escape of a fluid that is meant to be excluded or contained. [The roof *leaks;* Milk is *leaking* out of the carton; The faucet is *leaking.*] The noun *leak* may designate a chance opening, as a hole, crack, crevice, or faulty closure, through which fluid may pass. [The boat has sprung a *leak;* They plugged the *leak* in the dam.] In other respects, *leak* is the least specific of these words. It may apply to air or other gas, light, electric current, etc.: a *leaking* faucet; a punctured tire *leaking* air. And unlike the other words, it may involve a fast, heavy, or steady flow as well as a slow, slight, or intermittent one: A *leak* in the plumbing flooded the basement.

Drip means fall in drops or let liquid fall in drops: rain *dripping* from the eaves; *dripping* trees; fat that *drips* from roasting meat; children *dripping* ice cream on the floor. Something that *drips* may be *leaking* or overflowing: a *dripping* spigot; a comb *dripping* with honey. A paper bag may *drip* when a container in the bag is *leaking. Drip* may also designate the sound of liquid falling drop by drop: the maddening *drip* of a *leaking* faucet. Where *drip* implies a broken, staccato movement, **trickle** is used of liquid that runs gently.

It indicates a slow fall or slight flow of liquid, either drop by drop or in a fine, thin stream: a *trickling* spout; a rivulet *trickling* over rocks; perspiration slowly *trickling* down his back. Fluid may *drip* or *trickle* either from a *leak* that was unforeseen or from an opening designed for the discharge of liquid. And *trickle* often suggests either that a flow has not been fully started or that it is petering out: Only a *trickle* of water came out of the garden hose.

Ooze indicates a slow leakage or a sluggish flow, as of a liquid squeezing out in droplets through small openings: sap *oozing* from a sugar maple; gravy *oozing* from a potpie; a wounded body *oozing* blood; Sweat *oozed* from his forehead and *trickled* down his cheeks. In an extended sense, *ooze* may be applied to any similar seepage: Vapors seemed to *ooze* out of the swamp. And it sometimes refers to the unctuous flow or easy movement of a substance that is thick and slippery: the *ooze* of oil; the *ooze* of mud between the toes.

In a figurative sense, *leak* refers to an unofficial or unauthorized divulging of information. [There was a *leak* in the security system; The news *leaked* out; An unnamed official *leaked* the story to the press.] *Trickle* may indicate movement in a very small stream, one thing or one person at a time: only a *trickle* of information; a *trickle* of visitors; workers *trickling* out of a building shortly before 5:00 P.M. The *trickle*-down theory presumes that benefits bestowed on those at the top of the economic ladder will gradually make their way down to those at the bottom. *Trickle* may also apply to an uncertain, rippling sound suggestive of *trickling* water: a *trickle* of applause. *Ooze* sometimes indicates the slow, silent escape of some vital quality: His courage *oozed* away. It may also imply the exuding of something as if through the pores: a politician *oozing* confidence and affability. *Drip* suggests being saturated or laden with something that seems to spill over in liquidlike drops: a voice *dripping* with venom; a dowager *dripping* with diamonds. See FILTER, FLOOD, FLOW.

learning

   erudition
   knowledge
   pedantry
   scholarship

These nouns refer to the mastery of facts and concepts in a given field. **Learning**, the least formal, suggests a background of orderly, prescribed instruction and study rather than a spontaneous or self-taught mastery of material: book *learning;* the *learning* required to understand the obscure allusions of some poets. A related use of the noun refers to the process of acquiring mastery: patterns of *learning* in young children. Sometimes, it refers to the sum total of all understanding and wisdom: libraries where accumulates all the *learning* of the ages.

Knowledge is more commonly used in this comprehensive way, referring to all that can be or is known: struggles to increase our *knowledge* of the universe. *Knowledge* is more than a store of facts in the mind; it also includes the contribution of the mind in understanding data, perceiving relations, elaborating concepts, formulating principles, and making evaluations. As applied to a person, *knowledge* need not refer to information acquired through a formal education, as *learning* does; rather, *knowledge* points to an acquaintance with facts or an understanding of actions and concepts: a poor *knowledge* of English grammar. [She had a better *knowledge* of human nature than the psychiatrist, for all his *learning*.] *Knowledge,* thus, need not suggest an academic background at all, but can result from observation and experience. This contrasts most sharply with **scholarship**, which emphasizes exclusively that aspect of *learning* pertaining to academic accomplishment. At one level, *scholarship* may suggest excellent work done in school: students receiving special awards for *scholarship*. At another level, it refers to care, precision, and accuracy in searching out information and presenting facts, implying a mastery of techniques necessary for advanced research in specialized fields: the definitive book on the Civil War, marked by its authoritative data and flawless *scholarship*.

Erudition refers to the personal mastery of a wide range of specialized *knowledge* in such a way as to combine both *learning* and *scholarship*. [He was not merely knowledgable, but exhibited extraordinary *erudition* on any topic that came up; the dazzling display of *erudition* required for the Ph.D. oral examination.] *Erudition* suggests a detailed grasp of the most abstruse or arcane points of *knowledge*. In this it compares with **pedantry**, which is a pejorative word for the same grasp of detail, however obscure. The negative force of *pedantry*, of course, suggests that such details are dogmatically exploited for their own sake as a pharisaical display, without regard for their relevance to important concerns or problems: the *pedantry* of scholastics busy refining Ptolemy while Copernicus and Brahe were altering the whole map of the heavens. See FAULTFINDING, STUDENT, TEACH.

Antonyms: *ignorance*.

lease

　　charter
　　hire
　　let
　　rent

These verbs mean get or grant the temporary use or possession of something, as a car, building, etc., in return for a certain payment. To do one of these things under the provisions of a governing contract is to **lease**. [I'm going to *lease* my apartment to a friend while I'm abroad next year; The land the oil speculator *leased* produced a gusher that made her wealthy.] **Hire** is most commonly used in reference to paying a set sum or certain wages for a person's labor or services: a *hired* hand on a farm. [We *hired* a driver to take us on a tour of the city.] Less commonly, *hire* indicates the granting of personal service or temporary use: to *hire* oneself out as a mathematics tutor during a vacation; to *hire* out beach umbrellas to bathers. It is also employed when one wishes to designate paying for the temporary, exclusive use of another's vehicle, premises, or the like. [I *hired* a cab to take me home from the party; The political club *hired* a hall to kick off its annual membership drive.] **Charter** is synonymous with *hire* in reference to vehicles, especially large public vehicles, as buses, airplanes, and trains: The graduating class *chartered* a bus for its trip to Mexico. *Charter,* however, also designates a specialized kind of *hiring* done in connection with a contract called a *charter party,* an agreement under which the whole or part of a vessel is *leased* for the conveyance of goods.

Rent is usually applied to the paying of an agreed amount of compensation for the use of real or personal property during a specified time. [Her family *rented* a house at the shore for the summer; Costumes for the play were *rented* from a theatrical supply house in New York.] *Rent* also means grant someone the temporary possession and use of land, premises, or property, and in this sense it is synonymous with *hire* and with **let**: rooms for *rent;* rooms to *let;* tuxedos for *hire*. [My aunt *rents* the top floor of her house to an old friend; Part of the estate was *let* out to tenant farmers.] See HIRE.

leave

　　depart
　　go
　　retire
　　withdraw

These verbs refer to the act of moving away from a previous position. **Leave**, in its generality, may stress the position being given up: *leaving* the office; *leaving* home; *leaving* the party early. It may also suggest, however, casting off something in the course of a movement: *leaving* behind a trail of banana peels. Or it may suggest passing by something one has not been in actual contact with at all: *leaving* one island after another in their wake. **Go** is even more general than *leave* and carries fewer connotations. In isolation, it stresses the act of moving away or passing along without reference to what one *leaves* behind: *going* forward through all sorts of terrain. *Go* may also imply movement away from a place, position, or starting point, especially when it is used as a command or signal, as in a race: Ready, set, *go!* In contrast to *leave*, however, *go* sometimes stresses the destination of a movement rather than its point of origin: just *going* to the grocery store for some bread.

Depart, like *leave*, emphasizes the starting point of a movement, though the destination is more often named; it is also more formal than *leave* and may suggest a planned *leaving* rather than *leaving* on the spur of the moment: *departing* for Europe next Wednesday; trains that *depart* (or *leave*) every hour on the hour. **Retire** stresses movement from a relatively public place to a more private one: *retiring* into the study, where they could talk freely. In a special sense, it means *go* to bed: The housekeeper said my father had *retired* for the evening. Its formality would make *retire* sound odd or antiquated in everyday conversation, except when it is used specifically to refer to the termination of one's active service or career: an aging opera singer who *retired* from the stage to teach voice. **Withdraw**, if used in a sense similar to the general meaning of *retire*, would sound even more antiquated, but it has a viable use when it suggests retracing one's steps away from a recent advance: the battalion that *withdrew* from positions seized the night before; *withdrawing* from her exposed vantage point at the uncurtained window. See DIE, GO, PRIVACY, QUIT, RELINQUISH, RETIRE.

Antonyms: *approach,* REMAIN.

leave

    abandon
    desert
    forsake

These verbs all mean quit a person, place, pursuit, party, or principle. **Leave**, the most general, is relatively free of the connotations that cling to the others. It is often used noncommittally to indicate a physical departure: He *left* his hometown and moved to the big city. *Leave* in itself gives no hint as to the motives behind or consequences of a departure. One person may *leave* a country to evade prosecution for a crime, while another may *leave* it merely to seek a milder climate. *Leave* may also refer in a more abstract sense to the termination of a connection or association: She *left* Berkeley but continued to live near the campus.

In other uses, *leave* may be closely synonymous with the other verbs in this group, though all the others are more emotionally freighted. **Abandon** denotes a complete giving up, especially of what one has previously been interested in or responsible for. It points to total relinquishment or withdrawal, sometimes under pressure of circumstances or in breach of duty. A person may rightly or wrongly *abandon* an attempt or an idealistic dream after encountering difficulties. A scientist may *abandon* an unpromising project to engage in more useful and rewarding research. A captain may give orders to *abandon* ship when the ship is sinking. A military commander may justifiably *abandon* an exposed position, but to *abandon* his troops or his post would be reprehensible. **Desert** adds to *abandon* the idea that a legal or moral obligation or trust is being violated. It means *abandon* a post, duty, relationship, or loyalty in violation of one's faith, oath, responsibility, or orders: a recruit who *deserted* the platoon under fire; a turncoat who *deserted* the party.

Leave, abandon, and *desert* are all applied to marital or family relationships but often differ in their implications. A man who *leaves* his wife may do so openly and may still contribute to her support. A mother who *abandons* her child utterly relinquishes personal responsibility, consigning the fate of the child to chance or to other people. A man who *deserts* his wife and children willfully *abandons* them, without legal justification, with the intent to renounce entirely all legal and moral obligation.

In a specific, intransitive sense, *desert* means *leave* military service without permission and with the intention of not returning. *Leave,* by contrast, may indicate no more than a temporary departure, while *abandon* may point to a position that has been *left*. [The sentry *left* her post for a few minutes; The soldier *abandoned* his post and *deserted*.] The past participles *abandoned* and *deserted* both emphasize the result of a departure, pointing to the condition of the place *left* empty or the plight of the person *left* alone: the helpless, forlorn figure of an *abandoned* child; an outpost *abandoned* to the elements; an *abandoned* building falling into ruin, *left* desolate by all its former occupants; a couple afraid to walk down a *deserted* street at night.

Forsake implies breaking off a close personal attachment and may refer to a spiritual as well as to a physical *desertion*. It often involves the letting down of a loved one or dependent and may point to a lack of positive action as well as to a negative *abandonment*. [He pleaded with his wife not to *forsake* her family; to *forsake* one's friends by failing to go to their aid when they are in trouble.] *Forsake* may also mean give up something that once was cherished or that formerly was freely indulged in or enjoyed. [Arthur Rimbaud *forsook* poetry at the age of nineteen; Doubts led the nun to *forsake* her faith and *leave* the church; In the ceremony, the groom promised to *forsake* all others and cleave only to his wife.] See FORSWEAR, QUIT, RELINQUISH.

Antonyms: *keep, persevere in, stay at, stay in, stay with, stick to, stick with.*

leftist
left-winger
liberal
progressive
radical

These nouns refer to those who favor changes, more or less drastic, in the political or economic system of a country. **Leftist** and **left-winger** arose as terms because in many European countries, conservatives are seated to the presiding officer's right, and their opponents are seated to the left. Most typically, a *leftist* might be someone who favors governmental solutions to social problems, favors the working class or the disadvantaged, and opposes unregulated business or the established powers of wealth and privilege. These views may extend to a belief in public ownership of the means of production or even to the belief in the necessity of a revolution to achieve social justice, as in some forms of socialism. The emotional tone of *leftist* would clearly depend on the persuasion of the speaker. It was more clearly taken as a pejorative in the recent past than at present. In a negative context, the noun may be used to imply that all *leftists* are revolutionists or extremists, which has given rise to such countering phrases as *democratic leftist*. At present, *leftist* appears with greater frequency in neutral description, even by those describing themselves. *Left-winger,* by contrast, was and still is largely pejorative and would be avoided except by those who condemn such stands.

Liberal, according to its etymology, pertains to someone devoted to freedom. In actual use, as opposed to conservative, it refers to someone who welcomes constructive change as a way of solving problems. Used as a political label in the recent past, *lib-eral* indicated someone to the left of a moderate and as such it could be used to express distrust or suspicion, if not the disapproval often implied by *leftist*. More recently, however, *liberal* has become almost synonymous with moderate to indicate someone who favors the present tendency to solve social problems through government action, provided no drastic alteration in the social structure is contemplated. Despite this shift in emphasis and because both major U.S. parties are middle-of-the-road, relatively few political candidates refer to themselves as *liberals*. Side by side with an approving use, a new pejorative use of *liberal* has emerged to criticize those who are seen as not going far enough toward solving fundamental problems. This use, of course, is favored by *leftists:* His political opponent accused him of being the typical *liberal* who paid lip service to integrated education and open housing, but did nothing about them. In Britain, *liberal* appears in the name of the party midway between right and left: the Conservative Party, the *Liberal* Party, and the Labour Party. Outside the political sphere, *liberal* can still refer in a wholly approving way to someone who favors tolerance, permissiveness, and constructive change, as in education and theology: a *liberal* who favored the new curriculum; those cardinals at the Ecumenical Council who became known as *liberals*.

Progressive has at least twice appeared as part of a U.S. third party to the left of Democratic Party *liberals*. The term would usually imply a stance more activist than that of a *liberal* but one more moderate than that of a *leftist*. On the other hand, *progressive* can sometimes be used to indicate a militance of the left: the *Progressive* Labor Party. Used more generally outside politics, *progressive* can suggest someone who is forward-looking and dynamic: a *progressive* businessman who had contributed to many community and civic programs. **Radical** is the one noun here that indicates an extremist stand, yet need not apply solely to extreme *leftists*: *radicals* of both the right and left. Often, however, particularly in historical discussion of the first half of the 20th century, *radical* can without qualification indicate a *leftist* who, unlike a *liberal* or *progressive*, wished to see drastic alterations in society, often by means of revolution: a freewheeling debate among Trotskyists, Wobblies, and other *radicals*. In other areas, *radical* indicates someone in favor of thoroughgoing changes in a system: *radicals* who propose that colleges abandon the grading system, the giving of degrees, and the assigning of required courses.

Antonyms: *RIGHTIST.*

leftover

- balance
- remainder
- residue
- rest
- surplus

These nouns refer to what exists as a superfluous quantity once the needed or used portion of something has been subtracted. **Leftover** is relatively informal in pointing to any such entity, concrete or abstract. Often, it suggests a survival from an earlier period: an idea that was a *leftover* from the McCarthy era. It particularly pertains to food not eaten at a given meal, suggesting something saved to be eaten later or prepared in a different way; in this use, it is often plural: observing that they'd probably be eating *leftovers* from the Thanksgiving dinner for weeks. **Residue** is much more formal and points more exclusively to actual material *leftovers,* but with the suggestion that these are wasted or unusable portions: scraping the *residue* of food from the plates before rinsing them. Most specifically, *residue* refers to dregs or to insoluble matter left behind by the filtration or evaporation of a liquid: hard water that leaves a chalky *residue* behind when it is boiled away. **Surplus** indicates something in excess of need, but in contrast with *residue,* this amount might be usable and possibly beneficial: agreeing to share in common any *surplus* of funds after all expenses were paid in full. *Surplus* is used particularly to indicate stored farm produce or excess military supplies: grain elevators for storing the season's wheat *surplus;* labeling the older model binoculars as *surplus.*

The remaining nouns are much more general, having fewer connotations about the nature of the *leftover.* **Remainder** and **balance** can both point to the amount left after subtracting one sum from another; the former often appears in the context of arithmetic, the latter in accounting. Both can be used more generally, however, to suggest a partial quantity viewed in separation from the whole for any reason: grating half the carrots and dicing the *remainder;* They discarded the obviously outdated books before deciding what to do with the *balance.* The only distinction here is that *balance* has a more formal tone and can sometimes sound out of place beyond its natural context of accounting.

Rest is the most general and informal of all these nouns; it can refer to anything that remains outside some designated amount. [He asked John to come with him and told the *rest* of the boys to stay where they were; I wondered how I'd live through the *rest* of the week; Only one of her reasons really mattered, but the *rest* were wide of the mark.] See MARGINAL.

lenient

- indulgent
- lax
- merciful
- permissive
- tolerant

These adjectives describe a flexible or complaisant attitude that shuns applying rules too strictly or that is more generous than standards of discipline or conduct might allow if interpreted literally. **Lenient** indicates a generous or indifferent lowering of standards, especially in the context of discipline meted out by a superior. It is the most neutral of these adjectives in its implications, although it can easily take on a tone of either mild approval or mild disapproval: a prep school that was more *lenient* than most toward minor infractions of the rules; arguing that regimentation militates against learning, while *lenient* approval assists it; He lacked a sense of responsibility because of his *lenient* upbringing.

Merciful and **lax** are distinct from all these other adjectives in adding to the general meaning an extreme emotional tone. They contrast sharply with each other as well, *merciful* regarding the *lenient* attitude from a strongly favorable viewpoint, *lax* from nearly as strong a negative viewpoint. *Merciful* furthermore suggests compassion, *lax* laziness, indifference, or slipshod incompetence. [He implored the judge to be *merciful;* The book's worth was invalidated by its *lax* standards of accuracy; When the spirit and letter of the law appear to be in conflict, a judge is *merciful,* not *lax,* in upholding the spirit.]

Indulgent is seldom neutral. It can carry a mild positive charge, suggesting generosity, in a context pertaining to affectionate relationships; sometimes in such a context, however, and in most other uses, it is more strongly negative, suggesting undiscriminating or irresponsible complaisance: a jolly, *indulgent* uncle; too *indulgent* of her children's every caprice or tantrum; a magazine *indulgent* of the unexamined prejudices and meretricious tastes of its readers. **Tolerant** is far less emotionally charged, approaching neutral description in most uses. In addition to indicating a flexible attitude toward rules or standards, it can suggest approval for an open-minded reluctance to make hasty judgments or disapproval for condescending rather than equal treatment: She informed her students that she could be *tolerant* of those who fell asleep in class provided they didn't snore; *tolerant* of the attitudes and beliefs of others; *tolerant* of but not enthusiastic about the latest fads.

Permissive is a much more formal adjective than the others, referring descriptively to an educational approach that permits a child's interest and capacities to determine course content and rate of progress: the *permissive* theories of progressive education. Less specifically, *permissive* may refer to an extremely *lenient* way of child rearing. [The children of *permissive* parents often give their own children an authoritarian upbringing, and vice versa.] Partisans of a *permissive* approach, in either context, might use the term in neutral description, but critics of this approach may well use *permissive* as a pejorative label: *permissive* theories that resulted, at best, in well-adjusted ignoramuses. Outside the contexts of education and psychology, *permissive* is widely used as a synonym for *tolerant*, but goes beyond the latter in suggesting not only open-minded detachment but a passive acceptance of involvement as well. See COMPLIANT.

Antonyms: *exacting, rigid, severe, stern, strict.*

lessen

    allay
    alleviate
    assuage
    lighten
    mitigate
    soften
    temper

These verbs all indicate the act of reducing the intensity or severity of something. **Lessen** is the most informal of these and the most general, applying both to a decrease in intensity and severity. It often suggests the subtracting of a part from a whole, as in its legal use: an appeal to *lessen* the sentence of the condemned man. But *lessen* can apply neutrally to any reduction in degree or quantity: The flight to suburbia *lessened* the number of middle-class families living in the city itself.

Lighten is metaphorically graphic in referring to a decrease in the weight of something; **soften** is comparably graphic in referring to a decrease in the harshness, roughness, or force of something. Both are often more favorable in their implications than *lessen*. *Lighten* would apply most naturally where an existing burden is partially lifted, *soften* most naturally where the full impact of something is prevented from being felt: technology that served to *lighten* the work load of factory employees; an attempt to *soften* the blow by telling her the good news first. In this context, **tem-**

per refers to making something more moderate, that is, more temperate: a sea breeze that *tempered* the noonday heat. But another use of *temper* gives a diametrically opposed meaning, referring to the act of hardening or toughening something: young bodies *tempered* by rigorous exercise. Thus, unless the context is clear, the use of *temper* can result in confusion.

The remaining verbs all emphasize a reduction in severity; they are also alike in pointing to the reduction or removal of something negative or undesirable, rather than the mere subtraction of one amount from another. **Allay** and **assuage** can both refer to the calming or satisfying of desire or appetite, but whereas *allay* can often suggest a partial lulling or pacifying, *assuage* might better indicate something approaching satiation: an attempt to *allay* their hunger by nibbling on roots and berries; a huge dinner that *assuaged* his ravenous appetite. In other uses, furthermore, where *assuage* remains more strictly tied to the notion of a need that requires satisfaction, *allay* can function more widely for any appeasing action: reassuring words that *assuaged* her fear; a codeine tablet to *allay* the pain. In the former example, *allay* would suggest less conclusive relief, whereas in the latter *assuage* would seem out of place.

Alleviate is closest to *allay* but is even more emphatic about partial relief; it is also restricted to situations in which something is made easier to bear. Thus, it is a more specific and more formal intensification of *lighten*: early attempts to *alleviate* conditions in mental hospitals that preceded this century's thoroughgoing reform of mental care; drugs to *alleviate* the pain of terminal patients. **Mitigate**, which comes from a Latin word meaning soften, can refer more formally to the partial lessening of need, pain, or hardship: programs to *mitigate* the disruptive effects of slum living; rehabilitative therapy to *mitigate* the aftereffects of strokes and heart attacks; the judge's decision to *mitigate* the sentence in light of the convicted person's previous record. See DECREASE, REDUCE, WANE, WEAKEN.

Antonyms: ENLARGE, ESCALATE, EXTEND, *heighten, toughen.*

lie

    falsehood
    fib
    prevarication
    rationalization
    untruth

These nouns refer to statements or formulations

that are misleading or contrary to fact. **Lie** is the most general of these, but it is restricted to a conscious and deliberate intention to distort the truth. [She told a *lie* about how much she had stolen; It was a *lie* that no nuclear arms shipments were being sent to the Persian Gulf.] In heated debate, *lie* is often applied more loosely to inadvertent misstatements or statements thought to be hypocritical: It's simply a *lie* that my opponent will carry out all these campaign promises without raising taxes. Sometimes, *lie* can apply to masking an unpleasant situation with a pleasant exterior: She was unwilling to live a *lie* for the sake of her husband's political future. In the idiom *give the lie to,* a conclusive disproof of an assertion or theory is indicated: evidence that *gave the lie to* their claim of having remained neutral during the crisis.

By contrast, **rationalization** is very specific, indicating a thought process by which one attempts to justify one's actions, either to oneself or to others, by consciously or unconsciously distorting the truth. Although psychologists may view all formulated explanations as *rationalizations,* the noun has become a fad word for ingenious but specious reasoning that puts one's own behavior in the most favorable light possible: The psychiatrist works to get behind the web of *rationalizations* to the real conflicts and anxieties they conceal; his *rationalization* that being late for work was a forgivable foible, considering how indispensable he was to the office; assassins whose *rationalization* was that they were only obeying orders.

The remaining nouns can all be used as euphemisms for *lie.* **Fib**, the most informal, is exclusively used in this way, suggesting a trivial, harmless, or forgivable *lie:* She turned him down with a *fib* about meeting her mother for dinner. *Fib* may now sound a bit dated. **Prevarication**, the most formal of the nouns here, would be taken by many as an overly fancy euphemism for *lie;* as such, it might be useful as humor or irony: comforted that the commandment prohibiting *lies* said nothing about *prevarication. Prevarication* can have a special area of meaning that refers not to bald misstatements of fact but to the deceptive statement of half-truths, but this distinction would be lost on many people.

Falsehood and **untruth**, as euphemisms, are less formal circumlocutions than *prevarication. Falsehood,* however, has a legitimate reference to any incorrectness, whether intentional or not: The *falsehood* of this prevalent notion is now inescapable. *Untruth* can sometimes refer to fictions that were never intended to mislead or be taken as fact: Novelists devise *untruths* that sometimes have a greater validity than

the statistical truths of the social sciences. See DECEPTION, GUILE, MISLEADING, TRICK (n.), TRICK (v.).
Antonyms: *honesty, truth, veracity.*

listing

catalogue
inventory
list
register
roll
roster

The nouns **listing** and **list** refer to any itemized series of names, words, etc., especially when recorded in a set order: a *list* of Representatives from the state arranged by county; a *listing* of drugs authorized for sale by the Food and Drug Administration. *Listing* is also used to mean an entry in a *list:* Please check your *listing* in the new telephone book and notify us of any mistakes.

Register and **roll** apply to *lists* of names. A *register* is a formal or official written record of names or transactions: a *register* of births or deaths. *Registers* are typically designed to preserve important information for future reference. A *roll,* on the other hand, is often a temporary *listing* of names, as of students in a class or soldiers in a military unit: The teacher called the *roll* every morning to see who was absent. Any *list* of names may be called a **roster**, but *roster* usually refers to a *list* of names of people enrolled for a particular kind of duty. In the U.S. Army and in other service organizations, duty *rosters* are maintained to ensure that special duties, such as guard duty and KP, are fairly assigned.

Inventory and **catalogue** refer to special kinds of *listings.* An *inventory* is a *list* of articles with the description and quantity of each. *Inventories* are periodically taken in warehouses, factories, and retail stores to record the numbers and kinds of articles in stock. A *catalogue* (or *catalog,* the standard spelling in most libraries) is a *list* or enumeration of names or objects, usually in alphabetical order and often with some accompanying description. A card *catalog* in a library lists the title and author of the book, periodical, etc., and other useful information, such as the number of pages, the copyright date, where and by whom the work was published, an identifying number, and sometimes an indication of the subject or contents. The *catalogue* of a mail-order house lists the articles offered for sale, with accompanying descriptions and prices. Figuratively, any methodical *listing* can be called a *catalogue:* She gave me a long *catalogue* of woes: his car broke down, he had a fight with his boss, he caught a cold, and so on. See ACCUMULATION, QUANTITY.

listless

lackadaisical
languid
languorous
lethargic

All these adjectives pertain to a lack of spirit or energy. **Listless** is the least formal and the most wide-ranging in application. At its most specific, *listless* can indicate slow or sluggish movement, at its most general a lack of the vibrance associated with good health or high spirits: He responded to my question with a *listless* shrug of his shoulders; the *listless* faces of children born into poverty. Most often, *listless* suggests a general apathy that may well be the result of disease or physical or mental fatigue.

Languid can also indicate a lack of interest or animation that may stem from poor health or fatigue, but it can also (and perhaps more often) indicate an avoidance of physical exertion as a matter of choice or temperament rather than of necessity: drooped in her *languid* pose on a bench while her friends walked from painting to painting in the exhibit. It can also suggest the affecting of a slow or lazy manner: the *languid* drawl with which he spoke. In a way that *listless* cannot, *languid* can indicate anything lacking in force: a *languid* wind that offered no relief from the heat. **Languorous** and *languid* both derive ultimately from the same French root, meaning languish. *Languorous* gives a distinct and specific meaning, however, that points to the affecting of an effete or indolent dreaminess: an era of crisis in which many retired to *languorous* meditation and disengagement.

Lethargic concentrates on the aspect of *listless* that pertains to sluggish movement, but it is slightly more formal than *listless* and is considerably more critical or disapproving in tone. *Lethargic* may, in fact, suggest laziness as the cause of this behavior: too *lethargic* to get his homework done on time. **Lackadaisical** concentrates on a different aspect of *listless*, the one referring to a lack of vibrance, spirit, or energy: reacting to the impassioned speech with a *lackadaisical* yawn; entrenched bureaucrats *lackadaisical* about proposals to improve the system. *Lackadaisical* can also refer to whatever is idle, indifferent, or empty of value: a *lackadaisical* attitude toward standards of accurate and objective scholarship. See IMPASSIVE, SLOTH, TIRED, UNINVOLVED, WEAKEN.

Antonyms: *energetic,* LIVELY, *spirited.*

lively

animated
brisk
buoyant
spirited
sprightly
vivacious

These adjectives all describe people, things, or actions that are full of or display great vigor and energy. **Lively**, the most general, suggests energy of motion and great activity: a *lively* kitten; a party that turned out to be a very *lively* occasion; a gathering in which there was much *lively* conversation.

Animated, close in meaning to *lively,* is normally limited in application to people or to behavior: an *animated* argument between two motorists; to become *animated* and talkative after dinner.

Buoyant, **spirited**, **sprightly**, and **vivacious** all suggest a manner of speaking or acting marked by energy and good humor. *Buoyant,* which carries the suggestion of its literal meaning of floating, describes an irrepressible or resilient energy in manner or outlook: *buoyant* laughter; *buoyant* confidence in the future. *Spirited* suggests a high degree of vitality, sometimes mixed with daring. [Young stallions are *spirited* animals; She made a *spirited* denial of having any knowledge of the crime.] *Sprightly* and *vivacious* add to the idea of energy the element of quick-wittedness and brightness: *sprightly* jokes; a *sprightly* old lady; a *vivacious* telling of a story; *vivacious* young women.

Brisk may be applied to actions that exhibit an abundance of energy: He passed us at a *brisk* walk. *Brisk* may also describe a sharp, businesslike manner that may approach curtness but also implies a controlled vitality: She always spoke to her subordinates in a *brisk* tone. See BUSY.

Antonyms: LISTLESS.

living

alive
animate
live

These adjectives all mean having life or manifesting signs of life. **Living**, **alive**, and **live** may be applied interchangeably to functioning organisms in contrast to those that are dead. *Living* may also refer only to the condition of not being dead. [She is England's greatest *living* novelist; My grandfather, at 93, is the oldest *living* stonemason.] By extension, *living* may also describe things that are full of energy and significance or are actually operative: the *living* faith of Buddhists; *living* languages. *Alive* applies to all degrees of life, from that which is barely evident to that which implies the utmost vitality and power. [The mortally wounded woman was unconscious but still *alive* when found; He is so *alive* that his presence in a room is electrifying.] *Live,* which is usually placed before the noun modified, may describe the condition of appearing in the flesh rather than being depicted in photographs, paintings, etc., or being preserved physically after death. [I was fully grown before I saw a *live* gypsy; Having seen the stuffed gorillas at the museum, the boy was delighted to observe his first *live* gorilla at the zoo.] In television and radio, a *live* audience or *live* actors are actually present at the time of transmission rather than appearing in a taped performance. When applied to certain things, *live* carries over the idea of vital functioning. [A *live* wire is one charged with electricity; We broiled the steak over *live* coals; Peace talks no longer were a *live* issue.]

Animate carries fewer connotations than do *living, alive,* and *live,* and is usually limited in application to *living* organisms as opposed to dead ones, or to inanimate objects, which do not possess life.

Antonyms: *DEAD.*

load

burden
cargo
freight

These nouns refer to something carried or transported. **Load,** the most general, may be used with any kind of carrier: a man with a *load* on his back; taking a *load* of soiled clothes to the laundromat; a wagon bringing in a *load* of hay; a flatcar with a *load* of cement blocks. *Load* also refers to the quantity carried or conveyed, as measured by the capacity of the vehicle or bearer: a car*load* of frozen foods; a truck*load* of newsprint. Sometimes *load* means anything that is unusually heavy or is borne with difficulty, either in a literal or figurative sense: the plum tree sagging under its *load* of ripe fruit; struggling under the *load* of monthly car payments.

Freight and **cargo** are both applied to goods or merchandise carried in large quantities over long distances. Trains, trucks, wagons, and the like are usually said to carry *freight. Cargo* is largely restricted to commodities carried by ships, and, in more recent times, by aircraft.

Burden now has limited use when applied to anything physical. [Donkeys and camels are still widely used in some parts of the world as beasts of *burden;* The carrying capacity of a ship and the weight of the *cargo* are both called the *burden.*] *Burden* has greater currency in meaning something borne with difficulty or something that weighs down, especially in a mental or emotional sense: too great a *burden* of responsibility and worry; a horse quivering under the *burden* of its three-hundred-pound rider.

loath. Do not confuse the adjective *loath* (unwilling) with the verb *loathe* (despise).

lodgings

accommodations
apartment
flat
quarters
suite

These nouns denote living space comprising a room or set of rooms that may occupy part of a building or exist as a unit within some larger unit. **Lodgings** and **accommodations** are equally vague in referring to any sort of living arrangements, usually temporary. *Lodgings,* especially in the United States, can sound old-fashioned; *accommodations,* while less informal in tone, is more current: troubadours who wandered through medieval France seeking *lodgings* for the night; asking her how she liked her *accommodations* at the hotel. The latter can also refer to a temporary, improvised setup, including the paraphernalia required to house a guest: setting up overnight *accommodations* for two more visitors by calling into service the living room sofa and a folding cot.

Apartment and **flat** are much more specific than the preceding, referring to sets of rooms usually rented and occupied for a longer term. As neutral description, *apartment* is the preferred term in U.S. speech, *flat* in British speech. In U.S. usage, however, *flat* often refers to an *apartment* without conveniences: a cold-water *flat.*

Suite is a widely applied term for any well-appointed set of rooms. It can refer to luxury *accommodations* in a hotel: the bridal *suite.* It can refer to a large or lavish *apartment:* the penthouse *suite.* It can also refer to a set of office rooms intended for conducting business: an executive *suite.* **Quarters** has almost as wide a range of usage; it can refer to specified buildings within a complex of other buildings (or to a part of a building or *apartment*) where certain kinds of people live: the nurses' *quarters;* servants' *quarters;* the former slave *quarters.* It has a particular relevance in military parlance, referring to the place where a specified group lives: officers' *quarters;* confined to *quarters.* See HOME, HOTEL, HOUSE.

loneliness
  alienation
  desolation
  disaffection
  estrangement

These nouns all relate to a lack or loss of friendship, love, or interrelatedness. **Loneliness** is the least formal and the most restricted in its application. It refers to a lack of companionship and usually implies an attendant feeling of unhappiness or unfulfillment: the stark *loneliness* of retired persons who live in rooming houses. *Loneliness* may refer to a feeling rather than an actual condition of isolation: Her *loneliness* was never more acute than when she sat in a crowded theater. Occasionally, *loneliness* can refer to a welcome state of seclusion or solitude: enjoying the *loneliness* of their life on the tiny island. It can also refer to the physical isolation of anything, whether regarded as pleasant, factually neutral, or unpleasant: the *loneliness* of a single tree silhouetted against a prairie landscape; the *loneliness* of their mountain cabin.

One use of **desolation** can serve as an intensification of *loneliness* in referring to someone utterly alone or inconsolably forsaken: the *desolation* of a homeless person. Often the noun can indicate an actual state of ruin or barrenness: the *desolation* left behind by the tornado; the *desolation* of Arizona's desert country. It can also refer to intense sorrow suffered because of a serious loss: the *desolation* she felt on hearing the news of her brother's death.

Disaffection is relatively formal; unlike the former pair, it most often suggests that an earlier fondness for someone has turned to indifference or mild distaste: She had regarded her husband over the years with a growing *disaffection.* Neither a complete separation from someone nor a transmutation of fondness into hatred need be suggested by *disaffection.* Often, however, it has a stronger charge when it indicates someone deliberately at work to cause a more drastic change in feeling or allegiance, as in intrigues of love or politics: a cruel person who actively promoted *disaffection* between the two friends; professional agitators who worked zealously to stir up *disaffection* and rebellion among the workers. **Estrangement** applies more exclusively to a voluntary *disaffection* that results in complete separation and, sometimes, a strong feeling of dislike or hatred that replaces an earlier fondness or love: It was impossible to keep their *estrangement*

secret, since they were living apart and had drawn up separation papers. Sometimes, the emphasis is on a process of cooling affection, without suggesting a complete break; here, it is close to *disaffection* but suggests a growing remoteness and lack of communication that may be involuntary: so busy with their careers that neither noticed the wedge of *estrangement* that was gradually being driven between them.

Alienation applies more widely than any of the other nouns. It can be used in a way resembling the last sense of *estrangement,* but with a clearer implication that no separation need take place: pressure that resulted in a feeling of *alienation* toward each other. The phrase *alienation of affection,* like *disaffection,* implies a deliberate attempt to bring about a reversal of feelings toward someone, but this use of *alienation* is now relatively uncommon. At its most general, *alienation* can apply to any feeling of unrelatedness, especially a hopeless feeling of distance from society's structure and concerns: minority groups that must also cope with their own feelings of *alienation* from a society that rejects them. This use of *alienation* derives ultimately from Marxism, in which it is a technical term for the separation of laborers from the fruits of their labor: Unlike the highly skilled worker who took pride in his work, the assembly-line worker may feel isolated and indifferent because of the *alienation* inherent in mass production. See LONELY, MODEST, PRIVACY, UNINVOLVED.

Antonyms: ALLEGIANCE, *camaraderie, companionship, fellowship, mutuality, reconciliation.*

lonely
  forlorn
  lonesome
  solitary

These adjectives characterize people or places that are set apart. **Lonely** is a broad term describing a state of mind induced by lack of companionship or the kind of sympathy companionship can provide. A *lonely* feeling can range from the mild sadness engendered by a casual instance of solitude to the great unhappiness and depression one might feel after a long period of separation from other people: a *lonely* young sailor feeling sorry for himself because his date had stood him up; a *lonely* woman whose eccentric ways had robbed her of the opportunity for anything but the most impersonal kind of social contact. *Lonely* can also be used to describe an unfrequented or deserted place: a *lonely* stretch of beach where it was possible to bathe in the nude. In reference to places, **lone-**

some intensifies the meaning of *lonely* to suggest a place not merely deserted but with an air of melancholy about it: *a house they had always considered overcrowded but now was* lonesome *and cavernous without children.* In its description of people, *lonesome* is again a stronger word than *lonely* but slightly less formal in tone. It often suggests the dejection felt when one is faced with the absence of someone to whom one has been very close: *a merchandising executive who never got over being* lonesome *when she had to leave her family for business travel;* lonesome *for a pet dog he'd raised from a pup and now was dead.*

Forlorn is more specific than either of the two preceding adjectives in its suggestion that the person described as such is alone because he or she has been deserted or abandoned: *wretched and* forlorn *in the sinister atmosphere of the deserted bus terminal, despairing of the arrival of a friend already three hours late.* A place referred to as *forlorn* may seem also to have been deserted and have the air of loneliness that characterizes remote or abandoned dwellings and locales: *a once-fashionable resort and now a* forlorn *ghost town.*

Solitary can mean *lonely* and can describe a person or place: *the* solitary *feeling one sometimes experiences in the middle of a crowded room; the* solitary *desert.* But *solitary,* in a way that none of the other adjectives in this group can, may suggest an aloneness that has been chosen rather than imposed. Thus, a person who is *solitary* by nature may prefer contemplation to companionship, and a *solitary* traveler may prefer traveling alone to being with a large group on an organized tour. See ALOOF, LEAVE (abandon), PRIVACY.

Antonyms: *accompanied, attended, escorted, protected.*

look

gaze
glance
glare
peer
stare

These verbs mean turn the eyes toward something either in an effort to see it or to convey a specific meaning or emotion. **Look** is the most general and may mean direct the eyes: *to* look *out the window; to* look *at pictures in a magazine.* One may also *look* in such a way as to communicate a particular feeling: *to* look *wistfully at a handsome new car; to* look *daggers at an uninvited guest.*

Gaze means *look* long and steadily, often with the implication of wonder, admiration, fascination, etc.: *to* gaze *at a beautiful view; to* gaze *into the eyes of a loved one.*

Glance refers to the act of *looking* briefly at something when one is preoccupied or in a hurry. [*On the bus I always have time to* glance *at the headlines in my newspaper.*]

Peer suggests a *looking* with a narrowing of the eyes and often a movement of the head, usually forward. To *peer* may mean to *look* inquiringly or searchingly or may indicate difficulty in seeing clearly. [*He* peered *surreptitiously into his wallet to see if he had enough money to pay the check; Nearsighted people often* peer *at you when they are not wearing their glasses.*]

Stare means *gaze* intently, especially with wide-open eyes, as in amazement, admiration, or fear: *to* stare *at a drunkard reeling down the street; to* stare *in terror into the muzzle of a loaded gun.* Stare may also connote insolence, or at least rudeness, on the part of the viewer, and may or may not be intentional. [*Children should be taught not to* stare *at handicapped people; The boys habitually gather in front of the drugstore to* stare *at girls.*]

Glare means *stare* fiercely or threateningly and always emphasizes hostility or fear: *a trapped fox,* glaring *at its captors; to* glare *at one's opponent in an argument.* See SEE, VISION.

loot

booty
haul
spoils
swag

These nouns refer to money, land, or goods seized by war, violence, or fraud. **Loot** in its oldest sense referred to goods seized specifically in war, especially goods of great value. More recently, it would better suggest money or goods acquired by theft: *jewel thieves dividing their* loot. Most recently, it has come to be used specifically for goods seized by rioters, roving singly or in bands: *estimates of the* loot *taken in three days of rioting.* In this sense, it distinguishes goods seized in this manner from ordinary stolen goods. In slang use, *loot* can refer simply to money, regardless of how acquired: *How much* loot *do you have on you?* By contrast, **swag** and **haul** are slang words for goods acquired by theft, although *haul* can also apply to the profits from any venture, legal or illegal: *counting up his* haul *from the lemonade concession.*

Spoils, like *loot,* once referred to goods seized in war, although it could refer as well to land so acquired. Occasionally it is used in the singular. Its most common meaning now, however, is money or advantages acquired through corrupt political practices: Largely honorary but highly paid appointive offices are among the *spoils* most reluctantly surrendered by machine politicians. Unlike *spoils* and *loot,* **booty** has not acquired latter-day uses and still refers specifically only to goods seized in war; in international law, it denotes goods seized on land rather than at sea. It is sometimes used figuratively for any acquisition, especially one taken by violence or robbery. See PLUNDER.

loud

> blatant
> boisterous
> clamorous
> noisy
> obstreperous
> vociferous

These adjectives describe sounds of high intensity or volume, or statements or ways of behaving that are excessive or strident. **Loud** is the most general of these, referring most concretely to sounds that are of high volume and carry considerable distances: playing his transistor radio so *loud* that neighbors could not sleep; foghorns *loud* enough to be heard nearly a mile inland; *loud* voices resounding down the hallway. *Loud* may also refer to offensive behavior or appearance: a *loud* sport shirt; people with garish tastes and *loud* manners. **Noisy** and *loud,* the most informal of these adjectives, differ in that *loud* refers to specific sources of high-volume sound, whereas *noisy* refers to a general density of sound emanating from many sources: a *loud* burglar alarm ringing in the deserted street; a maddeningly *noisy* neighborhood. *Noisy,* however, need not refer to sounds of high volume: the *noisy* chirring of crickets, low but incessant. While *noisy* has fewer applications to behavior, it may suggest relentlessness or impatience: using a *loud* speaking voice to reach a *noisy* audience; hating *noisy* arguments in which everybody shouted and used offensive language.

The remaining adjectives relate to specific but separate aspects of *loud* or *noisy.* **Blatant** refers most concretely to a raised, insistent voice, but it gives a disapproving tone: the *blatant* hucksters of the hard-sell television commercial. More and more often now, *blatant* is used for any distasteful appeal or obvious and vulgar disregard for the sensibilities: *blatant* lies; *blatant* bad manners that matched his disheveled appearance. **Obstreperous** is in every way an intensification

of *blatant:* the unruly screaming and shouting of her *obstreperous* children. It is also used to refer to distasteful manners, with a stress on deliberate rudeness, or to behavior that is out of control: *obstreperous* insults; *obstreperous* guests who ruined the party.

Boisterous emphasizes, without the disapproval inherent in the previous pair of adjectives, high spirits that result in *loud* or *noisy* behavior: *boisterous* group singing in the ski lodge. **Clamorous** specifically pertains to insistent or repeated entreaties, suggesting outcries at danger or a panicked disorder: the *clamorous* cries of miners in the blocked tunnel. In this sense, *clamorous* may sound somewhat outdated, but it is still used for any general din of *noisy* voices or general outcry: a quarter of the old town thick with the *clamorous* appeals of hawkers and vendors; theater lobbies filled with a *clamorous* hubbub during intermission. **Vociferous** refers to an insistent, urgent, or strident manner of speaking, sometimes suggesting anger or the determination to drive home a point: *vociferous* arguments between liberals and conservatives; a *vociferous* outcry for a recount of the vote. See NOISE, UNRULY.

Antonyms: *disciplined, peaceful, retiring,* SILENT, *soft, subdued,* TACITURN, TRANQUIL.

luminous

> gleaming
> glistening
> lambent
> lucent
> lucid
> lustrous
> refulgent

These adjectives refer to a soft radiance, mostly of reflected light. **Luminous** may describe a source of light, in which case it is very general, indicating the light's brightness or clarity: *luminous* stars. Yet, it can also specifically suggest a soft or barely perceivable radiance or one enclosed within or seen through something else: dim moonlight on *luminous* pine needles; the *luminous* dial of the wrist watch. **Lucent** and **lucid** share in these last meanings of *luminous,* suggesting particularly refracted or suffused light: the *lucent* pool of water; a *lucid,* cloudless day. Both, but especially *lucid,* suggest clarity as a carry-over from what is now their main use, to refer to transparency. **Lambent** also suggests a radiance of refracted light: the *lambent* fog surrounding the street lamps. It has a lyrical quality that suggests gentleness or beauty, but can seem overelegant in some contexts. **Refulgent** is even more in danger of this possibility, to the point of seeming precious. It specifically indicates a reflected brightness: the *refulgent* clouds above the setting sun.

Gleaming may indicate a source of light, in which case it merely suggests brightness: *gleaming* sunlight. In this use, it seems more natural and less formal than *luminous*. More specifically, *gleaming* may suggest the brightness of reflected light: the new skyscraper's *gleaming* walls of glass. Its overtones in this case are of spotlessness. *Gleaming* may also suggest dimness: the night's darkness punctuated by faintly *gleaming* birches. **Glistening** is almost exclusively restricted to reflected light. Except for this, it compares to *gleaming*, but suggests in addition to dimness an undulating reflection or a moist surface: *glistening* rain-drenched leaves. **Lustrous** suggests a more mellow reflected light than either *gleaming* or *glistening*, applying specifically to the soft shine of any smooth material: the *lustrous* gold of the wedding ring. See BRIGHT, SPARKLING.

Antonyms: *dull, dusky,* GLOOMY, *obscure.*

lurk

    creep
    skulk
    slink
    sneak
    steal
    prowl

These verbs all mean move furtively or stealthily, and all express an evident desire to stay hidden or unnoticed. **Lurk** can mean lie hidden or exist unnoticed or unsuspected: a snake *lurking* in the grass; What evil *lurks* in the hearts of men? But its most pertinent sense here is move secretly or furtively, always with the implication of menace: assassins *lurking* in the crowd. The implied danger is often vague and ill-defined, which increases the suggestion of menace: shadowy figures *lurking* in dark alleys.

Slink, creep, and **steal** all mean move quietly or furtively, but whereas *slink* and *creep* often suggest fear as a motive for remaining hidden, *steal* may suggest other motives. *Slink* often points to a sly, guilty, or abject attitude and suggests a cowering posture and fairly rapid gait: The beggar, refused a handout, *slunk* away into the shadows. *Creep*, in its basic sense, means move with the body close to or touching the ground: Marines *creeping* along through the underbrush. As here considered, *creep* often suggests timidity or fear as a cause of slow, very deliberate movement, regardless of posture: We *crept* up the staircase, our hearts pounding. But it can also mean any slow movement: The train *crept* along. *Steal* emphasizes the secrecy of a mission: He *stole* over to his friend's locker and dropped a frog in his shoe. Both *steal* and *creep* can be used figuratively. [A note of pathos *crept* into her voice; For the first time in his life, a feeling of pity *stole* into his heart.]

Skulk, more than *slink*, suggests guilt or shame as a motive for passing unnoticed: For months after being released from prison, he *skulked* around the house, ashamed to show his face during the day. But it may also suggest sober caution, even menace: to *skulk* past a gang of toughs; a waterfront street with clusters of figures *skulking* in front of every bar. Unlike *slink* or *creep*, *skulk* does not suggest any particular gait; it may imply the hunched-over posture of one wishing to remain undetected, but no mental picture is invariably associated with it. **Sneak** gives no clue at all either to posture or gait, thus emphasizing motive—the wish to remain unnoticed—to the exclusion of manner. *Sneak* can apply to trivial or innocent events as well as serious ones: to *sneak* into a ballpark; to *sneak* away from a party; to *sneak* into the kitchen for a snack. It suggests mischief or cowardliness more often than menace, and unlike *lurk* seldom or never suggests the threat of criminal acts.

Prowl means roam about stealthily in search of prey or plunder: lions *prowling* for gazelles. When applied to people, *prowl* can suggest danger or may emphasize only the predatory instinct: would-be muggers *prowling* for victims; young men *prowling* the streets (or *on the prowl*) for girls. In the U.S. a police patrol car may be called a *prowl car* because unless responding to a call it typically moves slowly and in an apparently random manner, as an animal might while searching for prey. Thus *prowl*, alone of these verbs, may suggest a benevolent motive for stealth. See HUNT, STEALTHY.

luxurious. Do not confuse the adjective *luxurious* (supplied with luxuries) with the adjective *luxuriant* (growing profusely).

machine

- apparatus
- appliance
- contrivance
- device
- engine
- mechanism

The noun **machine**, as here considered, is an assemblage of parts, movable and fixed, so constructed as to perform work when energy is applied to it. A *machine* may vary in size from, for example, a hand-operated numbering *machine* to a giant drop forge. Generally, a *machine* is thought of as more or less permanent and is expected to perform its work repeatedly or continuously over a long period of time.

Contrivance and **device** often mean a simple *machine,* sometimes improvised or makeshift, devised to perform a task once or for a short period of time. A belt that is attached to the rim of a drive wheel of an automobile to power a circular saw is a *contrivance* or *device.*

A **mechanism** may be a simple *machine* or one of the moving systems in a *machine.* Linotype *machines* included a *mechanism* for spacing words evenly.

An **apparatus** is a complicated *mechanism* consisting of several separate but connected parts, usually constructed for a special purpose and not mass-produced. A chemist's system of tubes and flasks is an *apparatus* constructed for a specific experiment or process.

An **appliance**, in current usage, is a household *machine* such as a washing *machine,* a vacuum cleaner, or an electric mixer.

An **engine**, properly speaking, is not a *machine* in the sense of something that performs a specific task; rather, it is a *machine* that converts energy, as heat, electricity, waterpower, etc., into mechanical power: the steam *engine;* the diesel *engine.*

malign

- asperse
- defame
- libel
- slander
- vilify

These verbs mean say or write something, often misleading or false, that is damaging to a person or a group of people. **Malign** is the broadest verb in the group in that the feelings motivating a person who *maligns* another can range from the simple ill will that may prompt a gossip to the bitter hatred or malicious ignorance that results in pernicious persecution: an author much *maligned* because of his romantic indiscretions; a reform candidate so *maligned* by crooked political bosses that she withdrew from a mayoralty race.

Asperse and **vilify** imply false accusations made in order to ruin someone's reputation. *Asperse,* literally meaning bespatter, often implies indirect or vague assertions made to reduce good repute. *Vilify* usually implies strong and direct abuse, such as name-calling. One may *asperse* a writer's integrity by suggesting indirectly that he has written lies, or *vilify* him directly by calling him a liar. *Asperse,* however, is extremely formal, and more commonly appears in the form of the plural noun *aspersions:* She accused the reviewer of casting *aspersions* on her work.

Defame can specifically indicate an attempt to destroy someone's good name. Like *vilify,* it suggests use of direct and harsh accusations, but *defame* is less commonly used in this way than *vilify.* Recently, it has acquired a meaning that refers to unfounded, broad denunciations of ethnic or religious groups: the myth of ritual murder that was repeatedly used to *defame* Jewish populations in many European countries.

In popular usage, **libel** and **slander** are applied to false accusations by any means. At their most restricted, however, they are legal terms that are periodically redefined by the courts. *Libel* invariably refers to written charges and *slander* to spoken charges. *Slander,* however, is now seldom the basis for court action. Where *libel* is concerned, proving malicious intent is paramount, but it has not always been necessary to prove that the charges themselves are false. Also, standards may be less stringent when someone is criticizing, even unfairly, the public acts of people in public life. See ACCUSE, BELITTLE, LIE.

Antonyms: *PRAISE.*

malleable

- ductile
- plastic
- pliable
- pliant

These adjectives characterize things that can be molded or bent. **Malleable** and **ductile** refer most specifically to the working of metals. *Malleable* indicates a metal, such as gold, that can be beaten easily into thin sheets or other forms. *Ductile* refers specifically to the ease with which a metal such as copper can be drawn out into a continuous wire. Sometimes, it can also refer to the readiness with which fluids will follow a given course. In this sense, water is more *ductile* than mercury. When these two adjectives are used to describe responsive minds, *malleable* suggests an innocent or unformed character that is easily impressed and can be decisively altered by the conscious attempts of another person or by propaganda: the age at which a normally *malleable* student is most open to influence, whether for good or ill. *Ductile* appears less commonly in this context; when it does, it suggests the capability of being subtly led toward a goal not always stated: a demagogue flattering his all too *ductile* audience.

Pliable and **pliant** are closely related. Used of physical objects, *pliant* often suggests something that resumes its shape after being bent: a *pliant* reed. *Pliable* is often used for something that will remain in any shape given to it: *pliable* putty; a *pliant* whip. When applied to character, consequently, *pliable* should suggest a greater openness to impression than *pliant:* half-truths purveyed to *pliable* minds; a readiness to learn that was *pliant* but not incredulous. Notwithstanding, *pliable* and *pliant* are frequently used with no discernible difference in meanings.

Plastic most often refers to any substance that can be molded and then hardened or set: *plastic* buttons; a *plastic* construction helmet. But *plastic* can refer to any synthesized substance, however treated, that is initially a liquid or gel: *plastic* shower curtains. Because of its overriding use in these cases, other uses of this adjective may be losing ground. *Plastic* can refer to an impressionable mind when it is still moldable, unformed, or not yet fixed: the first years of life, when the psyche is at its most *plastic*. It can also refer to the creative impulse in general or to sculptural or three-dimensional qualities: the poet's *plastic* ability to find new forms for new subject matter; a building considered strictly as a set of *plastic* values; the unique *plastic* designs of the choreographer's ensemble work. See ADAPTABLE, COMPLIANT, SUPPLE.

Antonyms: *inflexible, intractable, recalcitrant, refractory, rigid,* STUBBORN, *unyielding.*

mankind

Homo sapiens
humanity
humankind

man
men

These nouns refer to people taken as a group. **Mankind** points collectively to all people, past, present, or future, as an entity about which statements can be made. *Mankind* can sometimes tend to sound high-flown or flowery, suggesting a context of formal rhetoric or solemn oratory. It can also function as a personification that implies a unity of thought, action, and sensibility that can be generalized from the contradictory and diverse actuality. Hence, *mankind* may be used as a quasi-poetic or persuasive term rather than as a rendering of defensible or exact observation: arguing that *mankind* has always struggled forward no matter what the obstacles; basing his politics on his view of *mankind* as insatiably greedy and intent on self-aggrandizement. *Mankind* can, of course, appear more neutrally without these liabilities: the cultures of *mankind;* a multivolumed work attempting to take in the entire history of *mankind.* However, *mankind* has lost value as a term because of its inherent exclusion of *women.* (See also the discussion below of *humankind.*)

Humanity can have the same high-toned flavor as *mankind: humanity* in its age-old struggle for survival. By implication, however, *humanity* points more exclusively to favorable qualities, such as compassion, understanding, and the ennobling emotions: instincts of love and self-sacrifice that have always pervaded *humanity* in times of crisis. *Humanity,* in fact, can refer collectively to this bundle of ennobling or civilizing virtues, whether it is seen in a single person or in all people: a man of unmistakable sympathy and *humanity;* UNESCO's attempt to show the common *humanity* expressed in all the cultures of the earth. **Homo sapiens** is a scientific term for *mankind* as the only surviving species of the genus Homo; the term would appear in biological or anthropological discussion, particularly in making distinctions between this species and other animals: the relation of *Homo sapiens* to the other primates. *Homo sapiens* would sound affected in a more general context. **Man** can be used as a less formal or technical term in scientific discussion: studying the evolution of *man. Man* can also be used like the first two nouns, however, as a personification that includes all people of all times: *man's* incessant temptation to solve problems by using the fists instead of the brain. Because it infers exclusion of *women,* the noun *man,* like *mankind,* has lost currency as a term encompassing all people.

Humankind, the most formal of these nouns, can sound even more high-flown than *mankind* and *humanity.* Unlike *humanity,* however, it need not suggest only ennobling traits: the puerile attempts of *humankind* to understand the cosmos. Where *mankind* might be used to treat people collectively in narrative generalization, emphasizing a past-to-present progression, *humankind* lends itself especially to aphoristic statements about abiding traits, often stated in the historical present. [*Humankind* listens to the wisdom of its prophets once a week, to the bulletins of its warlords once an hour.] It must be pointed out that *humankind* is now preferred by many as a replacement for *man* and for *mankind*.

Men is like *humankind* in tending to suggest a present-tense statement about the enduring qualities of people, good or bad: pointing out that *men* are the only animals that kill for pleasure. Unlike *man*, *men* would seldom be used in scientific discussion. Both, of course, have traditionally included women in the implied grouping, but *men* is more ambiguous about this, since it can be used as well to mean all human males. *Men* is useful in historical discussion since it avoids the suggestion of personified unity implicit in *mankind*, applying where *mankind* cannot to point out diversity or conflict among people: the first attempts of *men* to settle disputes through reason rather than violence. See FOLK, KIN.

mannerism

affectation
air
airs
exhibitionism
pose
preciosity

These nouns pertain to the use of attention-getting devices or to the adoption of insincere, artificial, forced, or pretentious behavior. **Mannerism** and **affectation** disapprovingly indicate an instance of such behavior, but *mannerism* is milder, suggesting a noticeable but minor oddity of gesture or speech that may be either deliberate or habitual: adopting a few British speech *mannerisms* because she thought they conferred distinction; He waved his hands about as he talked—a nervous *mannerism* he had unconsciously picked up from his parents. Sometimes, *mannerism* can apply to any obtrusive stylistic device: self-conscious *mannerisms* that mar her prose style. *Affectation* concentrates more exclusively on the deliberate adoption of anything that is ornate or pretentious: speech studded with faded poeticisms and other *affectations*; He thought it was an *affectation* nowadays

to include finger bowls in the table settings. *Affectation* can also serve as an abstract collective for pretentiousness in general: Sincerity and simplicity are the archenemies of *affectation*.

Air and **pose** can both indicate a contrived appearance or manner adopted to create an effect or to impress others: She walked with an *air* of disdain past the members of the incoming class; his *pose* of being one of the world's foremost authorities on contemporary art. *Air* might well suggest a momentary attempt to create a certain mood; as such, it is less disapproving than *pose*, which suggests greater contrivance and willingness to deceive. *Pose*, in fact, can extend to roles assumed by swindlers or extortionists: his *pose* of being a blind man, adopted to win the sympathy of his victims. Both nouns, but particularly *air*, can also refer not to deliberate role-playing but to the mood or impression someone conveys: She faced us with an *air* of utter bewilderment; inadvertently discovered him pleading with his wife in a *pose* of genuine contrition.

Airs refers exclusively to grandiose *affectations* that do not correspond to one's real situation; its use is mostly restricted to a few stock phrases: giving oneself *airs*; putting on *airs*. **Preciosity** refers to a striving after a rarefied refinement that might appeal to an arty or genteel coterie: stilted speech and an overall *preciosity* of manner. Often, *preciosity* refers to artistic style or aesthetic taste: a *preciosity* that made him prefer the Pre-Raphaelite painters to Turner. By contrast, **exhibitionism** refers to any sort of attention-getting device. By implication such behavior may well constitute the opposite of refinement by being loud, garish, crude, or obstreperous: weightlifters strutting and flexing their biceps in unrestrained *exhibitionism*; the unruly *exhibitionism* of some habitués of the discothèque. In a psychiatric context, the noun can refer to a serious disorder in which a person has a compulsion to expose his genitals to a passing stranger or bystander. See CHARACTERISTIC, ECCENTRICITY, TEMPERAMENT.

marginal

inconsequential
minor
negligible
nugatory
peripheral
piddling

These adjectives characterize anything that has little bearing on a given question or that is slight in amount or importance. **Marginal** and **peripheral** both point to a small degree of value, usefulness, or importance: a *marginal* increase in pay. Of the two, only *marginal* can suggest something that an opposing force has almost but not quite canceled out: a *marginal* profit once costs had been accounted for; *marginal* culture traits left by an incomplete assimilation into the cultural majority. *Peripheral* is more restricted to something that has slight importance; at its most specific it can point to something that may be important in itself but is not relevant to a given situation: The Civil War was of *peripheral* concern to that period of California history. Both adjectives, of course, can indicate something that is distant from a center or lies at the edge of some entity: a book filled with *marginal* notations; *peripheral* vision.

Negligible adds to the general possibilities of the previous pair an implication of a slight amount, suggesting something so small that it can be safely ignored: arguing that even a *negligible* rise in atmospheric radioactivity is undesirable; a *negligible* variation that could not affect the outcome of the experiment. **Piddling** is a much more informal substitute for *negligible,* concentrating more exclusively on amount or value, particularly monetary: a *piddling* allowance. But it can also refer more vaguely as invective to characterize weak arguments or anything thought to be trivial: a *piddling* explanation; a *piddling* second lieutenant.

Both **inconsequential** and **minor** concentrate mainly on a lack of importance. *Inconsequential,* like *negligible,* can indicate a lack of relevance: an *inconsequential* objection to our plan. But it can function explicitly as indicating a lack of power or social status: an *inconsequential* person. *Minor* may function similarly to other adjectives here, but unlike them it can point to something of considerably greater importance, though such a thing would still remain clearly subsidiary, secondary, or subordinate to a main point or concern: any combination of *minor* failings that could yet add up to disaster; separating those important Elizabethan poets, major and *minor,* from those of *marginal* or *negligible* interest, while ignoring completely the totally *inconsequential.*

All the preceding adjectives emphasize a relative slightness of quantity or importance. **Nugatory** is the one adjective here that emphatically stresses an absolute and unqualified lack, in this case of worth or meaning: stylistic experiments that were *nugatory* both in sense and influence. See DEFICIENT, EXTRANEOUS, SCANTY, TRIVIAL.

Antonyms: *central,* SIGNIFICANT.

marsh
bayou
bog
everglade
fen
morass
paddy
quagmire
swamp

These nouns refer to stretches of land in which soil and water, often stagnant, are intermingled with no clear demarcations, a situation that results in unstable footing or presents resistance to navigation. **Marsh** indicates a shallow, stagnant expanse of standing water enclosed by wet and treacherous soil: a trail that swooped in a wide circle to avoid the *marsh.* **Swamp** suggests a large *marsh* that has some patches mainly of wet soil and others mainly of muddy water: They poled through the *swamp* in a flat-bottomed boat, but had to get out and drag the boat whenever it got mired. Both *marsh* and *swamp* may suggest the presence of vegetation such as grass or even trees; *swamp,* particularly, might suggest an almost impassable overgrowth.

At its most literal, **fen** can specifically suggest a *swamp* overgrown with vegetation and filled with fetid water. **Morass** more often indicates low-lying, soft, wet ground in which one can easily become mired. Both *fen* and *morass,* however, are now more often used metaphorically, *fen* for an evil or unsavory situation, *morass* for entangling complications into which it is easy to be drawn but from which it is difficult to escape, once involved: a city that was a *fen* of vice and corruption; a *morass* of work that threatened to overwhelm them.

The remaining nouns all suggest a *marsh* or *swamp* that has a specific locale and a particular set of topographic features. **Everglade** points to a low-lying subtropical swamp covered with tall grass: the Florida *Everglades.* **Bayou** indicates a marshy inlet or outlet of a lake or river; its root is a Louisiana French word borrowed from the Choctaw Indian word for a small stream: the *bayous* of the Mississippi delta. **Paddy** comes from the Malay, referring to flooded lowlands in the Orient where rice is grown: peasants working in the terraced rice *paddies.* **Bog** is drawn from an Irish word for soft, referring to wet, spongy soil that is overgrown with grass: peat *bogs* from which the Irish harvested a fuel for heating and cooking. *Bog* is the only one of these localized words that can apply more widely. In this case, it refers to soft, wet soil that provides only treacherous footing and from which it is difficult to extricate oneself; the metaphorical implications here are more clearly seen when *bog* is used as a verb: *bogged* down in another useless man-to-man chat with his father.

Quagmire, a close synonym of *bog* in its literal sense is especially used in the sense of a position or situation from which extrication is difficult: refusing to fall into the *quagmire* of military operations in the ethnically diverse Balkans. See PLAIN (n.).

massive

    enormous
    hefty
    huge
    immense
    ponderous
    vast

These adjectives characterize things of overwhelming size, scale, or weight. Most concretely, **massive** indicates a large mass, bulk, or weight: a *massive* boulder. Weight or bulk need not be implied, however, when *massive* points instead to something imposing or impressive in scale, scope, degree, or intensity: a *massive* painting; a decision that was to have *massive* consequences throughout the succeeding century. In a medical sense, *massive* points to something extending over or affecting a large area: *massive* swelling.

Ponderous and **hefty** are more restricted than *massive* in that both echo the stress on weight but put less emphasis on size. Relatively formal, *ponderous* points to heaviness that may be unwieldy or unbearable: pyramids made of *ponderous* stones said to have been inched into place. More often this adjective is used abstractly of something overserious or solemn to the point of dullness: a *ponderous* lecture on the immorality of our society. *Ponderous* can also suggest a heavy physical movement that is slow, tortuous, or lumbering: shuffling forward with a *ponderous* gait. Relatively informal, *hefty* can refer more readily to physical heaviness, as of a physique: a *hefty* weightlifter. Its unique area of relevance is to something that is heavy but meant to be picked up and carried: breathing heavily as she lifted the *hefty* briefcase.

Huge and **enormous** contrast with the previous adjectives in stressing size more than heaviness. In this sense, both can serve as superlatives for large, with *enormous* being the more formal of the two. In itself,

huge may suggest a looming tallness or largeness of frame: the *huge* football player; the *huge* balloon they inflated for the Thanksgiving parade. *Enormous* suggests extension in space on a scale that goes beyond the implications of *huge*: a *huge* man dwarfed by an *enormous* room. Both adjectives can be used metaphorically for something serious, critical, or urgent: the *huge* problems that must be faced in checking the population explosion; *enormous* questions remaining to be answered.

Immense is like the previous pair in stressing size more than weight. Where *immense* refers to material masses, it suggests something of dramatically or surprisingly large scale: an *immense* statue, fifty times life size. But, like *enormous*, *immense* frequently stresses extension in space, rather than mass: early explorers who got lost in the *immense*, uncharted Atlantic. Often, *immense* relates to totally nonmaterial or spiritual entities, with the implication of proportions so great as to swallow up things of normal scale: the *immense* void between the Milky Way and its nearest galactic neighbor. **Vast** concentrates exclusively on extension in space, with a complete absence of implications pertaining to weight or even to measurable or definable size: the *vast* emptiness of the unending desert. In comparison with *immense*, which can suggest three-dimensional largeness, *vast* more readily suggests two-dimensional extension: the *immense* volume enclosed by the cathedral's domed nave; the *vast* lawns surrounding the castle. See HEAVY, HUSKY, LARGE, SIZE, TREMENDOUS.

Antonyms: *MINUTE, SMALL, THIN.*

mature

    age
    develop
    mellow
    ripen

These verbs refer to the process of growing up or growing old. **Mature** is the most formal of these; in its most restricted sense, it indicates the natural attainment by a living thing of its adult or fullest form. [Caterpillars eventually *mature* into butterflies; Boys *mature* more slowly than girls, both physically and psychologically.] Outside this strict but neutral reference, *mature* can register approval for the gaining of wisdom, experience, or sophistication, particularly when this process is not necessarily inevitable: childhood hardships that *matured* him early.

Age, unlike *mature*, need not refer to fruition or tempering; instead, it more often refers to the changes that result from the passage of time: a study of how body tissue *ages*. *Age*, in fact, can often refer to negative or destructive changes that occur as a living thing grows old: lines and wrinkles that revealed how much he had *aged* since I had seen him last. *Mature* is sometimes euphemistically substituted for *age* in this sense, as though the former's positive reference to fruition might soften the latter's presumed harshness in suggesting declining vigor: She had *matured* into a lovely grandmother. *Age*, however, can apply to processed products with favorable force: whiskey that has been properly *aged*. Here, it suggests valuable or desirable qualities that only time can impart. When applied to inanimate objects in general, *age* applies less positively to the attrition resulting from time's passage: unpainted houses that had *aged* because of decades of exposure to the elements.

Develop is more like the first sense of *mature* in pointing to positive change in which an existing or rudimentary form is improved, evolved, or perfected. In referring to normal biological growth and change, *develop* can apply more generally than *mature*, since it can be used to refer to a part as well as a whole organism, and can indicate less ambiguously transitions other than the one culminating in adulthood. [When the breasts begin to *develop*, girls are well on their way to *maturing* into young women; The fetus *develops* lungs relatively late in the gestation period.] When *develop* does not refer to predictable biological change, it is more general in application, most often referring either to the improvement or detailed elaboration of something: She joined a gym to *develop* her body; a committee set up to *develop* a program for dealing effectively with air pollution.

Mellow concentrates on aspects of *mature* and *age* that pertain to the tempering imparted by time or experience. It specifically suggests a reduction in harshness or the moderating of an extreme position: As they *mature*, many men and women *mellow* into a more tolerant attitude toward life and society. In this sense, *mellow* is more positive than *mature* and *age*, since it gives overtones of glowing warmth, mildness, and amiability. **Ripen** is a less formal and more vivid term for *mature*, with the same reference to the attainment by something of its final or most *developed* form. At its most literal, *ripen* applies to fruit, describing the process that brings it to full flavor: McIntosh apples green a week ago have already *ripened*. Metaphorically, *ripen* often refers to the filling out or enlarging of a spatial form: the girl's *ripening* body. Used in a more general way in reference to people, *ripen* often suggests not the attainment of adulthood but a *mellowing* process in later life; here,

like one sense of *mature*, it often points to a gain in wisdom, but is in less danger of being seen as euphemistic: Rembrandt slowly *ripened* into a command of the insights typical of his last great phase. Sometimes, *ripen* refers more simply to any sort of increase or growth: The reader's interest is sure to *ripen* as he or she gets deeper into this new suspense novel. See FINISH, FULL-FLEDGED, OLD, PERFECT, REACH.

Antonyms: *regress*.

mature

adult
experienced
full-blown
full-grown
grown-up
of age

These adjectives characterize someone who is no longer a child or something that has attained its final stage. In a biological context, both **mature** and **adult** can refer descriptively to any living thing that has completed the cycle of growth and development normal to the first stages of its existence: Peach trees are considered *mature* when they begin bearing fruit; spots that have disappeared from the coats of *mature* deer; the *adult* fruit fly. *Adult* may sometimes suggest sharp and definable differences between young and *mature* individuals, whereas *mature* can suggest that such classification is less clear-cut or is a matter of degree: the average height of the fully *mature* Sequoia. In the context of neutral classification, *adult* is more often used as a noun than as an adjective when the reference is to people. By contrast, *mature* can suggest an old person, rather than one who has just attained adulthood, although in this case *mature* is often a euphemism: a dialogue between *adults* and youths; a dress shop for *mature* women. Both adjectives also refer to psychological stability in adults; here, they are used interchangeably as approving fad words for sane, rational, or considerate behavior: a person who had never learned to relate to others in an *adult* way; Both husband and wife must be tolerant and *mature* if their marriage is to retain its vitality.

Experienced indicates someone whose familiarity with something is based on considerable actual practice. By implication, this past immersion in a subject has resulted in superior understanding: an *experienced* proofreader; an *experienced* lover; an *experienced* leader. Sometimes, no gain in wisdom need be suggested by *experienced* so much as a piling up of involvements: She was *experienced* and worldly-wise, but had learned little from her many adventures. Also, *experienced* need not be restricted to adults: already an *experienced* actress at the age of ten. By contrast, **full-blown** can apply to anything that has reached its highest point of development, which may well be the point immediately preceding decay or senescence. Its literal reference is to a flower in fullest bloom, but *full-blown* applies widely beyond this situation: the film star's *full-blown* figure; the unearthing of a *full-blown* plot to overthrow the government. Sometimes, *full-blown* can have a critical tone for something excessive or overemphatic: a *full-blown* bore.

The adjective **grown-up** can be used as an informal alternative for *mature* or *adult* in reference to rational or sensible behavior: She told her son he would be given *grown-up* privileges as soon as he stopped acting like a child. Like *adult, grownup* (n.) often appears as a noun, particularly when used by youngsters: children who distrusted all *grownups*. **Full-grown** emphasizes that something has reached its normal size: a *full-grown* grasshopper; a hulking, *full-grown* adolescent. This attainment of full size may or may not correspond with the transition point at which the individual can be considered *adult*. By contrast, the phrase **of age** refers specifically to the transition point, often arbitrarily set by law, after which a person is considered to be *adult:* a young man can be drafted at nineteen, but may not legally come *of age,* at least in terms of voting, until he is eighteen. Anthropologically, the phrase *of age* can indicate the point at which a society accepts a young person as a *full-grown* adult. See FULL-FLEDGED, OLD, SUMMIT, URBANE.

Antonyms: *childish.*

mean

connote
denote
imply
indicate
signify
suggest
symbolize

These verbs refer to the agreed-upon ideas or things that words or signs stand for. **Mean** is the least formal and the most general in embracing every kind of import a sign may have, whether explicit or implicit. [A red traffic light *means* stop, and a green light *means* go; What do these symptoms *mean?* You will have to state exactly what these terms *mean;* Do his frequent outbursts *mean* he is capable of violence?] **Suggest**, by contrast, concentrates specifically on covert or implicit qualities or associations in signs or language: She claims to mean one thing, but her choice of words *suggests* quite another.

Indicate stresses a rough approximation of literal meaning, whereas **imply** stresses the unstated associative or peripheral overtones present in a sign or word: a flashing beacon to *indicate* that a stretch of road is undergoing repairs; a choice of imagery that *implied* a fear or contempt of women, whether unintentional or conscious. *Imply,* when compared with *suggest,* stresses subtlety or complexity of association; *suggest* stresses tentative alternatives in meaning or a permissible variety of interpretations: Mystery plots may *imply* that anyone may be guilty of the crime in order to *suggest* a bewildering array of false leads to the unwary reader.

Denote refers specifically to what a term literally *means,* while **connote** refers to the possible associations *implied* or *suggested* by a term. [Scientists are interested in stripping language down to what it can exactly *denote,* while psychologists, poets, and literary critics are interested in all the hidden or penumbral associations words *connote;* Bright *denotes* intense light, but in certain contexts it can also *connote* purity or beauty or other intangible qualities.] *Connote* is closer in meaning to *imply* than *suggest,* but it is more formal and technical than either and is best reserved for linguistic or epistemological discussion.

Signify and **symbolize** stand in roughly the same relation as *denote* and *connote,* with *signify* suggesting a simple, literal meaning and *symbolize* suggesting a cluster of abstract concepts that are invested in a word, gesture, or object. [The legend of a map tells what each sign and abbreviation *signifies;* The cross to the Christian and the mandala to the Buddhist *symbolize* a body of doctrines and beliefs that might require volumes to spell out.] *Symbolize* is different from *imply, suggest,* and *connote* in stressing a deliberate compression of complex ideas into a concrete token that stands for them. *Signify,* like *mean,* can be used in a more general way to emphasize any aspect of conveyed understandings; sometimes, *signify* is used especially to refer to the deepest import of an expression rather than to its more obvious or superficial aspects: analysis that gives not only the who, what, when, and where of the news, but also what these bare bones *signify.* See HINT, MEANING, SYMBOL.

meaning

implication
import

meaning (continued)

sense
significance
signification

These nouns refer to the ideas conveyed by words, phrases, symbols, actions, or events. **Meaning** has the widest range of use, embracing everything from specific, concrete denotation to a general suggestiveness. The *meaning* of a word, sign, or symbol is the idea it expresses, the object it designates, or the concept it conveys. Words may have both literal and figurative *meanings*, both of which can be expressed in definitions, but the *meaning* of a word in any given instance often depends upon the context in which the word is used. In less restricted usage, *meaning* may apply to anything expressed as a message or intent, whether verbally or in some other fashion: to look for an artist's *meaning* in her work. *Meaning* may also apply to motivation, purpose, consequence, or even justification. [We debated the *meaning* of his strange behavior; What is the *meaning* of this intrusion?; the real *meaning* of the statement.] Finally, in its most abstract, connotative use, *meaning* indicates expressiveness, pointing to the presence of insights or intimations without specifying what they are. [His speech struck us as being full of *meaning*, in contrast to the hollow declamations of the others.]

Signification relates to specific *meaning*. It points to an official or agreed-upon *meaning*, one recognized and understood by all who are acquainted with a given word, term, or symbol: the *significations* of standard abbreviations such as lb. and oz.; the *signification* of heraldic devices on a coat of arms; the legal *signification* of the word incompetent. **Sense** compares with *meaning* in a broad as well as a narrow application. It often points to different kinds of use or interpretation, implying that a word has two or more *meanings* or ranges of *meaning*, or that a text has two or more levels of *meaning*: a punster playing on widely different *senses* of the same word; the symbolic *sense* of *Moby Dick.* Unlike *signification*, which is confined to a fixed *meaning*, *sense* may indicate a connotation or understanding: He is a liberal in the best *sense* of the word. It may also refer to an overall *meaning* or impression: to get the *sense* of an article written in a foreign language even though some of the words may be unfamiliar. Something that makes *sense* conveys a clear, understandable, or logical *meaning*.

Import is less clear-cut than *signification*, indicating an intended *meaning* that may need interpretation. More than *meaning*, it indicates the grasping of an idea, pointing to someone's understanding of what has been suggested or expressed. [He stated the *meaning* of the passage in a paraphrase; Commentators explained the *import* of the dictator's speech; She correctly guessed the *import* of her friend's long silence.]

Implication applies to *meaning* that may have been hinted at but has not been actually stated or expressed in so many words. It emphasizes suggestiveness, referring almost exclusively to debatable possibilities of interpretation inherent in a statement, act, or situation. *Implication* is thus not nearly as certain as *import*, contrasting even more strongly with the precision and definiteness of *signification*. Nevertheless, the *implications* of a thing, read rightly, may be far more important to a proper understanding of it than its literal or surface *meaning*. [He was pleasant and polite, but the sinister *implications* of his remarks were not lost on his audience; She misinterpreted the *implications* of his letter and thus misunderstood his intentions.]

Significance is akin to *meaning* in its wider *sense*. It mingles *meaning* and importance, referring to the underlying ideas or *implications* that give a special relevance to words, deeds, symbols, or events. [Her remarks were fraught with *significance*, but few gathered their full *import*.] *Significance* may also be used in a specific *sense*, suggesting a need to determine which of several possibilities is most relevant. [The *meaning* of their statement rejecting negotiations was never in doubt; Its *import* of cooler relations between the two countries is also plain; What *significance*, if any, do you place on his mildness of tone?] See HINT, MEAN, SYMBOL.

means

agency
instrumentality
medium

These nouns refer to anything serving or used to accomplish a purpose. **Means** is the most general. In a concrete sense, it points to a device or contrivance used to carry out an action or perform an operation. [A hammer is a *means* of driving a nail; A cab was his customary *means* of getting to the theater.] In a broader, abstract sense, it refers to method, system, or technique: the *means* by which a politician may extend power. [The harnessing of falling water provides a *means* of generating electricity; Statistical analysis is a *means* of arriving at a fairly reliable forecast.] Ways and *means* are methods of accomplishing an end, and this phrase is sometimes specifically directed to governmental finance and fund-raising: the House Ways and *Means* Committee. *Means* may also be applied to persons and things considered in terms of their past, present, or potential usefulness. [She is our *means* of achieving victory; art for art's sake as opposed to art as a *means* of spreading propaganda.]

Agency suggests causation and implies active intervention. Unlike *means,* it would not be used of a passive tool employed by others in their action. Instead, it indicates a force, operation, or process that on its own produces a certain effect. [Carbon dioxide is converted into oxygen through the *agency* of plants; Corruption in government was exposed through the *agency* of the press.] Applied to persons, *agency* often indicates a deliberate working or acting on behalf of others: The dispute was resolved through the *agency* of mediators. An advertising *agency,* employment *agency,* or travel *agency* is a business that serves clients, acting in their interests and helping them attain their goals.

Instrumentality is much more formal than the foregoing but close to *means* in scope. It focuses on the instrument acting or being used to accomplish a purpose. [Through the *instrumentality* of the Travelers' Aid Society, the lost boy was found and returned to his parents.]

The noun **medium** has the greatest number of specific senses that relate to the overall concept of *means*—all stressing the intermediate position of the *means.* Unlike *agency, medium* may refer to an intervening substance through which a force may act or in which an effect may be produced. [Copper is a good *medium* for conduction of heat and electricity; Air is a *medium* of sound.] *Medium* may also designate a *means,* technique, or vehicle of expression, or the material used for such expression. [For her, poetry was a congenial *medium;* a sculptor whose favorite *medium* is stone.] In a spiritualistic sense, *medium* denotes a sensitive person, often a woman, who goes into a trance so that spirits may supposedly speak through her, using her as a mouthpiece for communication with the living. Other senses of *medium* refer to a more active intermediary. Here, most commonly, *medium* is applied to modern channels of communication, often appearing in its plural form *media.* Radio, television, newspapers, and magazines are known as mass *media.* Television is an advertising, entertainment, and news *medium.* A modern communications *medium* itself—the *means,* techniques, and effects of transmission—may seem to some to be more interesting and influential than the material or message the *medium* conveys. In this case, it is no longer a *medium* in the strict sense of the word, but an end in itself. See METHOD, PERFORMER, REPRESENTATIVE, WEALTH.

meddlesome

interfering
intrusive
nosy
obtrusive
officious
prying
snoopy

These adjectives describe someone who, without invitation, involves himself or herself in the affairs of others, or who hampers them with unwelcome attentions. **Meddlesome** can suggest either of these situations; if the former, unwarranted curiosity is implied; if the latter, a self-important insistence on giving advice is masked as helpfulness: not able to tell her what had happened until their *meddlesome* neighbor left; forcing upon them in the most *meddlesome* way advice about their trip. **Interfering** makes no reference to curiosity, but otherwise is close to *meddlesome,* except that it is more neutral and may suggest a less disagreeable or self-righteous approach. [A well-intentioned but *interfering* friend is no better than a *meddlesome* father-in-law.]

Prying, **snoopy**, and **nosy** stress offensive curiosity to the exclusion of other meanings. The extremely informal *snoopy* and *nosy* can suggest an avidity for spying on others, gathering gossip, or soliciting personal information by posing leading questions. *Snoopy* may suggest a sneaky or stealthy approach in acquiring information: a *snoopy* landlord looking through his tenants' closets while they are out; a *snoopy* child, always eavesdropping. *Nosy* may indicate more forthright methods, suggesting the act of sticking one's nose into someone else's business: *nosy* neighborhood gossips. The more formal *prying,* however, goes further than either of these to suggest an absolute violation of privacy by any means whatever: *prying* questions.

Officious is now generally taken to refer to someone who, unasked, bustles about making arrangements, volunteering advice, offering unwanted services, or giving orders as though he or she were discharging official duties. This meaning gives *officious* a degree of specificity not present in any of its synonyms: an *officious* assistant, so bossy that no one could abide him.

Intrusive may suggest a pushing of oneself where one is not wanted, or may point to undue curiosity: an *intrusive* guest, arriving uninvited and destroying their privacy. [She had always lived with us but was never *intrusive* in any way; Unknowingly *intrusive,* he had a knack for asking embarrassing personal questions.]

Obtrusive is applied to a person who disrupts other

people's affairs, either by calling attention to himself or herself or by making self-aggrandizing suggestions or *officious* offers. Where *intrusive* emphasizes a breach of privacy or other interruptive influence, *obtrusive* implies a loud, brusque, or unduly obvious way of butting in: maintaining a silent watchfulness that dampened the discussion with its *intrusive* disapproval; a member who disrupted the meeting constantly with *obtrusive* remarks. See EFFRONTERY, ENCROACH, OVERHEAR.

Antonyms: *incurious, inobtrusive, unobtrusive, unofficious.*

mediate
    intercede
    interpose
    intervene

These verbs refer to attempts to come between, reconcile, or compromise opposing extremes. **Mediate**, the most general of these, carries the greatest number of overtones. It refers to any attempt to bring extremes together or to function as a form of communication between them: *mediating* between labor and management in the dispute. In this example, the implication is that the intermediary can advise or show good will but not demand or order a settlement of differences. *Mediate* can also be applied to the divisive disagreement itself or to its resolution: to *mediate* a dispute by seeking a middle ground on which the disputants can agree; to *mediate* a compromise. In another use, *mediate* may indicate the occupying of a midway position between extremes: stable countries that have a sizable middle class to *mediate* between the extremes of wealth and poverty. The verb may also be used to define the action of linking or communicating: a church that *mediates* between God and believers.

Intercede stresses a coming forward to stop a dispute in progress from continuing or getting worse, although it does not necessarily suggest that such action will solve the dispute: asking the executive branch to *intercede* in the legislative struggle and prevent gridlock. *Intercede* is often used to suggest that a third party is being drawn into an argument in order to plead for one side or the other: asking us to *intercede* in her behalf.

Interpose contrasts with *mediate* in suggesting a blockage of communication between hostile forces. It resembles *intercede* in that no solution need be applied, but the suggestion of stalemate is stronger: an international police force that could be *interposed* along the borders between two hostile nations. Again, like *intercede, interpose* may indicate entrance into a dispute on behalf of one side, although in this case the action is limited, by implication, to defense: enabling the courts to *interpose* themselves between an unjust law and the rights of any person threatened by that law.

Intervene contrasts with these other verbs by suggesting from the outset a more self-interested attitude in disrupting a dispute, usually to favor one side or another. *Intervene* would not be likely to refer to a mere stoppage, but does often suggest an intensification of hostilities: a nation refusing to *intervene* in Serbia, though its sympathies lay with the Croatians. As in the last example, *intervene* can often suggest an unwanted meddling in other people's business, and thus can impart a pejorative tone. See INSERT, JUDGE.

mediocre
    commonplace
    fair
    ordinary
    passable
    second-rate
    so-so
    tolerable

These adjectives all characterize something less than good and express in varying degrees a sense of disappointment or dissatisfaction. **Mediocre**, the most general, suggests disappointment at the undistinguished quality of a thing. Calling a performance of a play *mediocre* means that the performance was neither very good nor very bad and suggests that one had expected it to be better. *Mediocre,* then, like the rest of these adjectives, is a relative term and, like most of the others, may be preceded by a qualifying adverb to emphasize its disparaging implications. [Considering his reputation as a gourmet, the dinner he served was surely *mediocre.*]

Ordinary and **commonplace** are probably closest to *mediocre* in meaning, but *ordinary* is broader in application and usually expresses a somewhat less severe judgment. [How was the book? Nothing very exciting, just *ordinary.*] *Ordinary* can also mean uneventful, in which case it connotes no disparagement at all: an *ordinary* summer day, with a cloudless sky and the hum of insects in the air. *Commonplace* stresses the disparity between one's expectation of originality or uniqueness and the disappointingly *ordinary* or vulgar reality. It often expresses the haughtiness or arrogance of one who has high standards or a keenly critical attitude. [It was a *commonplace* observation—anyone might have made it.]

Fair and **so-so** are close synonyms. Both occur more often in speech than in writing and are thus somewhat more informal in tone than *mediocre* and *ordinary*. Depending on the context (or tone of voice with which they are uttered), *fair* and *so-so* can range from cautious approval to moderate disgust. They are often deliberately used in a noncommittal way, as to conceal bad news or a low opinion, often out of politeness or from the wish to keep one's own affairs private. [How do you feel now? *So-so;* How did you like the book? *Fair.*] *Fair* is also used as a rank in a grading scale: excellent, good, *fair,* poor.

Passable and **tolerable** are examples of damning with faint praise. *Passable* suggests bare adequacy, expressing the attitude indicated by a shrug of the shoulders and "Well, things could be worse." If something is *passable*, one makes do with it out of necessity rather than choice. [She didn't really like the hat, but it was *passable* and couldn't be exchanged; The movie was *passable*—there were one or two good scenes, but the acting was bad and the plot fell apart near the end.] *Tolerable* has a wider range of meaning than *passable*. While it may mean barely adequate, it does not always emphasize *barely,* as *passable* does, but may in fact emphasize *adequate.* [It was a *tolerable* salary, one you could live on if you knew how to keep a budget.] When used to characterize someone's health, *tolerable* is informal and has a provincial or dialectal flavor.

Second-rate, when opposed to first-rate, is the most obviously derogatory of the adjectives in this group, but when it is used in a scale of values that includes even lower categories, it joins *passable* in being a backhanded compliment. [He's a *second-rate* writer, not fit to stand in the shadow of Hemingway or Faulkner; It's a good *second-rate* school, strong in some departments and weak in others, but certainly better than a great many other schools in this area.] See USUAL.

Antonyms: *distinctive,* EXCELLENT, *fine, good, original,* OUTSTANDING, *superior,* UNPARALLELED.

meet

    contact
    encounter
    get in touch with
    see

These verbs express the action of coming together with another or others. **Meet**, the most general, has the widest range of application. It may simply mean come upon: He *met* her there by chance. Or it may indicate a previous appointment: He promised to *meet* her at noon. In another sense, it may mean go to or be at the place of a traveler's arrival: They *met* her at the station, so she didn't have to hire a cab. In some contexts, *meet* refers to a formal introduction or to the making of a new acquaintance. [Have you *met* my mother? They *met* an interesting couple at the beach.] Or it may indicate an assembling, as for a conference. [What time does the committee *meet?*] In a restricted, literal sense, *meet* may stress a face-to-face approach. [She pulled out to pass and *met* a car head-on; While going to St. Ives, he *met* a man with seven wives.]

Of the remaining verbs, **encounter** is the closest synonym for *meet*, but it implies a casual or unexpected *meeting*. [He *encountered* many interesting people on his travels, whom he mentioned in his memoirs; They came sneaking around the corner and *encountered* a truant officer.] *Encounter* may also mean *meet* in conflict or face in battle. [They *encountered* one another on the dueling grounds; We *encountered* the enemy in small border clashes.]

The phrase **get in touch with**, conversational in tone, implies the establishing or renewing of communication. [When you are in London, I hope you *get in touch with* my son and daughter-in-law.] **Contact**, used as a verb meaning *get in touch with* is regarded by some as informal, but seems to be gaining acceptance in the written language. *Get in touch with* and *contact* are both useful when the means of communication is not indicated. [I haven't been able to *get in touch with* her, though I've tried writing, phoning, and going to her office; We'll *contact* you later; I will have to *contact* my lawyer before I can give you a definite answer.]

See in one sense is close to *encounter*, referring to a chance *meeting*. [I *saw* your sister downtown the other day.] In a special sense, it refers to the granting of an appointment, interview, or date, or to the reception of guests. [The doctor will *see* you now; He asked whether he might *see* her again; My mother is not *seeing* anyone today.] See MEETING.

Antonyms: *AVOID.*

meeting

    assemblage
    assembly
    conclave
    conference
    congregation

meeting *(continued)*

    congress
    convention
    convocation
    council
    coven
    gathering

These nouns denote the coming together of a number of people. **Meeting**, **gathering**, **conference**, and **assembly** are the most general and informal. As given here, these four nouns form a gradual progression toward greater specificity and formality. *Meeting* can apply to every situation in which two or more people come together by accident or design for an encounter, whether brief or prolonged. It can range in application from trivial or everyday situations to the most portentous or official occasions: the weekly Cub Scout *meeting*; a summit *meeting* of the heads of state. *Gathering* differs from *meeting* in its specific reference to a group of more than two people. It is like *meeting* in other respects, including its wideness of application: a chance *gathering* of people in a coffeehouse; the annual *gathering* of the clan. *Conference* has more formality than either of the foregoing. But, like *meeting*, it can imply a group of two or more people: a *conference* with my thesis adviser; the scheduled disarmament *conference* at Geneva. *Assembly* implies a *gathering* of many people and tends to suggest a planned rather than an unplanned *meeting*: the school's weekly *assembly*. It is also sometimes used to designate the lower house in as state legislature. [The governor was holding a *meeting* with her Senate leader to cut short the subcommittee's protracted *conference* on a bill the *Assembly* had already passed; The *gathering* of news reporters in the corridors was tense and restless.]

Assemblage, used as an exact synonym for *assembly*, would sound archaic. Even more important, it is often used currently in a pejorative sense: an *assemblage* of hypocrites and incompetents. A **coven** is an *assembly* of witches, especially a group of thirteen. When *coven* is used for a meeting of ordinary people, the tone is pejorative: a *coven* of sorority sisters intent on overthrowing their president.

The remaining nouns of this group are similar in being more specific than the previous ones and much more formal as well. **Conclave**, **congregation**, and **convocation** refer primarily to religious *assemblies,* though they can extend to other kinds of *meetings* as well. *Conclave,* most specifically, refers to the *gathering* of cardinals to elect a pope. Overtones of this use remain in more general applications, including solemnity, secrecy, and high purpose: political candidates elected by direct primaries or by party *conclaves. Congregation* is even more restricted in use, referring to the adherents of a religion who attend the same local church: the pastor's *congregation.* In a narrow sense, *congregation* can designate those actually present at a given service, and in a broad sense, it can embrace all of a church's parishioners. *Convocation* implies a *meeting* called by a higher authority: a *convocation* of the Episcopal clergy summoned by their bishop. *Convocation* is also used by university groups with no implication of being called together from above.

Congress, **convention**, and **council** often refer to governmental or political bodies. On an international scale, a *council* may include delegates from many nations. In ecclesiastical terms, *council* may refer specifically to a clerical parliament called to decide matters of church doctrine and discipline: the *Council* of Trent; the Second Vatican Ecumenical *Council.* An international *council,* however, is more often a secular agency or body: the Economic and Social *Council* of the United Nations; the UN Security *Council.* On a national or local level, *council* usually indicates either an appointed advisory committee or an elected administrative or legislative unit: the President's *Council* on the Fine Arts; the city *council.* In either case, it implies a small, select group, whereas *congress* and *convention* suggest larger *assemblies* or *gatherings.* A *council's meetings* may be closed to the public, like those of a *conclave* and unlike those of a *congress* or *convention.* Purely private organizations may also use *council* in their titles: the Duluth *Council* on Equal Housing. In all but the ecclesiastical use, a *council* consists of its members whether they are gathered in a *meeting* or not.

Congress is narrower in application than *council,* being most commonly used in a governmental sense, particularly of an elected legislative body: the United States *Congress.* Another meaning survives, however, in the names of some private associations: the *Congress* of Racial Equality; the *Congress* of Industrial Organizations. *Congress* may also refer to a formal *meeting* of the representatives of sovereign nations, having as its purpose the settlement of certain questions: the *Congress* of Vienna. *Convention,* in its political sense, refers to a scheduled meeting of delegates to pass resolutions and elect leaders (or nominate candidates): the quadrennial Democratic and Republican *conventions. Convention* is also often used to refer to a state or national *meeting* of members from various local branches of a private organization, as a professional association, social club, or fraternal order.

Business is conducted in this kind of *convention,* but many of these *gatherings* are looked on chiefly as social occasions: the Shriners' *convention* in Chicago. Where the term *convention* is typically used of national *meetings,* international *meetings,* as of scientists, are more often referred to as *congresses:* an international *congress* of geophysicists. See CONSULT, GATHER, GROUP, SUMMON.

melody

air
aria
lied
song
theme
tune

These nouns refer to a recognizable succession of pitches in the same voice, whether played or sung. **Melody** may refer to the pleasing or aesthetically satisfying quality of such an entity: a composer noted for exquisite *melodies.* Or it can refer neutrally to the leading voice in a musical composition: harmonizing the *melody* for a four-part choral arrangement. As a generic word, *melody* can refer to one of the three basic ingredients of music, the one pertaining to the linear sequence of intervals: *melody,* harmony, and rhythm.

Theme refers to a melody or recognizable sequence that is treated in a musical composition by such means as statement, development, and recapitulation. In this case, the sequence may occur or recur in any voice or even be spread out among two or more voices: a *theme* first stated in the cellos and then referred to in fragmentary form by other sections of the orchestra.

Song in its neutral senses usually refers to a *melody* rendered by the human voice: a *song* for soprano or tenor; a popular *song* recorded by the leading vocalist; folk *songs* performed by three singers to guitar accompaniment. *Song* can refer more widely to any rendering of *melody:* bird *songs;* whistling a *song.* In its most general sense, *song* may suggest approval for any sort of lyrical intensity, as of poetry: a poetic tradition rich in *song.*

Tune is more informal than *song* and suggests a *melody* that is simple, direct, and catchy: infectious folk *tunes. Tune* may refer to the music, as distinct from the words, of a *song:* uninspiring words set to a lovely *tune.* Often, *tune* suggests *songs* of less than the highest aesthetic rank: show *tunes;* the grating *tunes* of singing commercials.

Aria, derived from the Italian word for *song,* refers to any of the set pieces in traditional operas and oratorios. It contrasts the formal organization and lyrical intensity of such a piece, usually a solo, with the looser, more low-key passages of recitative that surround it. *Aria* more generally can function like *song* to refer to any instance of lyrical intensity, but particularly one in which a single person is given the floor to express himself, often in an ornate manner: one long *aria* about how cruelly he had mistreated her.

Air is the exact English counterpart for *aria,* but it is rarely used now except in reference to early English music, often indicating the self-contained simplicity of a folk *song* rather than the ornate flourishes of a formal piece composed as part of such longer compositions as an opera: Scottish *airs* and ballads.

Lied is the comparable German word for *song,* used in English to refer to the art-song form developed by such composers as Schubert and Wolf: the Schubert *lied* about a beggar. More often it is used in the plural, referring generically in this case to the German art-song literature or to art *songs* in general: an evening of *lieder.*

melt

dissolve
liquefy
thaw

These verbs refer to the process by which a solid is transformed into a fluid. **Melt** is the most general of these, referring to such a transformation of any solid: ice cubes that had *melted;* listing the temperatures at which various metals *melt.* Used metaphorically, *melt* indicates any emotional yielding, usually one in which rigidity or indifference gives way to responsiveness or affectionate concern: a tale designed to *melt* the hardest heart; feeling her resistance to his ideas *melting* away. **Thaw** is a specific instance of *melt,* stressing the application of heat as the cause of the *melting* process, and referring mainly to the transformation of ice or snow into water: signs that the snowdrifts had begun to *thaw;* wondering when the stream would *thaw.* But *thaw* has a special use in referring to frozen solids that remain more or less hard even after being subjected to warming: not certain whether the frozen vegetables should be plunged into boiling water or be allowed to *thaw* out first at room temperature. *Thaw* can also refer to any warming process: sitting by the fire to *thaw* out his cold feet. Metaphorically, *thaw* suggests a more gradual yielding to emotional warmth than *melt:* Their ceremonious reserve soon began to *thaw.*

Dissolve may function like *melt:* cakes of ice slowly *dissolving* into puddles. More strictly, however,

dissolve refers to the process by which a solid passes into solution in a solvent: *dissolving* the tablet in a glass of water; a cleaning agent that *dissolves* grease stains. By extension, *dissolve* is used of any supposed disappearance or eating away of solids: snowbanks that seemed to *dissolve* overnight; erosion that had *dissolved* acres of topsoil. Metaphorically, the verb can suggest a collapse after having yielded to a strong emotion: *dissolving* into laughter at his discomfiture; *dissolving* into tears at the news. **Liquefy**, the most formal of these verbs, gives a technical or scientific tone. Its usefulness lies in referring generically to any conversion into a liquid state, whether by heat or pressure, and applies to the conversion of both solids and gases: temperatures too low for mercury to *liquefy;* using high pressures to *liquefy* nitrogen. *Liquefy* is not commonly used to apply metaphorically to emotional states. See WARM.
Antonyms: *crystallize, freeze, harden, jell, solidify.*

merit

excellence
value
virtue
worth

These nouns are related in meaning in that in this context they denote desirable and praiseworthy qualities or traits. **Merit** refers to attributes that are commendable, though not necessarily superior, and may be predicated to that which has more favorable than unfavorable qualities: His first novel, though sketchy and immature, nevertheless has *merit*. When *merit* is qualified by a negative word, it tends to emphasize a preponderance of unfavorable characteristics rather than the presence of only a few. [As a work of serious scholarship in the field of history, the work has little *merit;* His singing is practically without *merit*.]

Excellence denotes qualities that are superior to an unusual degree, and it is much stronger and more positive in concept than *merit*. However, since *excellence* does not indicate perfection, it is often modified by an intensifying adjective. [The particular *excellence* of Thai cooking lies in its skillful blending of spices; We were impressed by the technical *excellence* of his draftsmanship.]

According to the meanings limited to these nouns as a group, **value** and **worth** have the sense of intrinsic *excellence*. *Value* points to characteristics regarded highly for their usefulness: the *value* of a sensible diet in maintaining good health; the *value* to a medical student of thorough undergraduate training in the biolog-

ical and physical sciences. *Worth,* on the other hand, applies to things esteemed more for their own sake than for their utility: the great *worth* of a close friendship; the *worth* of being able to take pleasure in small things.

Virtue, which in this sense has nothing to do with morality, is applied to qualities that give a person or thing its *value* or *worth*. [The only *virtue* of air travel is speed; Although this house lacks the *virtue* of architectural beauty, it is comfortable to live in.] See PERFECT.
Antonyms: *fault,* FLAW, *unworthiness, weakness, worthlessness.*

method

fashion
manner
mode
procedure
routine
system
way

These nouns refer to a set or habitual technique for doing a task. **Method** suggests a fairly elaborate group of techniques and stresses efficiency or accuracy as its goal. **Way**, by contrast, is much more general, since it can refer either to a single technique or to a complex operation; it is also more informal and carries no suggestions about the technique or operation itself, positive or negative. [The *way* most students study is appalling; they lack any sense of *method*.] *Way* does have a special use that refers to someone's characteristic approach to a problem: Don't mind him; it's just his *way*. It may even suggest a lifestyle: John's *way* of doing things; a paranoid's *way* of taking criticism; the democratic *way* of settling arguments.

Procedure, **routine**, and **system** relate to the elaborate efficiency implied by *method* rather than to the characteristic style that may be suggested by *way*. All three, however, stress an even greater elaborateness than *method*. *Procedure,* the most formal of these nouns, suggests an orderly set of *methods* established by a person or organization for coping with details: a *procedure* for withholding income tax; a *procedure* for moving a bill through Congress. *Routine* stresses unvarying, unimaginative, or rote *procedure*: The day's dreary *routine* never changed. *System* may refer to a bundle of *procedures* established by a person or organization, written or unwritten; it emphasizes the meticulous working out of every detail: the *system* for selecting Rhodes scholars. Unlike *procedure*, it can be used pejoratively, in which case it refers to a conservative, entrenched establishment: every genius who ever had to fight the *system*. It can refer neutrally, however, to any functioning entity: the body's circulatory *system*. It can also apply to any elaborate scheme, whether functional or not: a *system* for beating the slot machines at Las Vegas.

Manner, **fashion**, and **mode** refer more to a characteristic style than to an elaborate *method, procedure*, or *system*. All three may be used as less informal substitutes for *way*, with *mode* approaching excessive formality. Each, however, has its own nuances. *Manner* may suggest the good or bad carrying out of a *method* or the characteristic conduct of someone: results that depend as much on the *manner* of executing the plans as on the plans themselves; a querulous *manner* of speaking. *Fashion* may also stress execution, but is strongly influenced by its other meanings pertaining to styles of living: a new *fashion* of wearing her hair. *Mode* suggests the choice of one category out of many: street gangs as a *mode* of venting frustration and hostility. It is especially used in discussions of art: a *mode* of writing in which normal syntax is suppressed to give the effect of chaotic thought processes. See ACCURATE, COMPETENT.

migrate

emigrate
immigrate
move
travel

These verbs refer to the movement of people or animals from one place to another. **Migrate** suggests movement of a large group: the Teutonic tribes that *migrated* to Britain; mallards that *migrate* south in winter. **Emigrate** and **immigrate** refer to permanent movements, mainly of people, whether singly or in groups. *Emigrate* involves movement from a place; *immigrate*, movement to a place. [Irish families *emigrating* from their homeland during the potato famine were among many who *immigrated* to America in the nineteenth century.]

Move has a special sense of leaving one house or apartment for another: people *moving* from the city to the suburbs. Outside of this specific use, it is the most general verb here, suggesting any change of locale under any circumstances: *moving* rapidly through the crowd in search of the lost child. **Travel** has a special sense of taking a relatively brief trip to a place where one does not live, without intending to remain there: *traveling* to Europe on a tramp steamer; *traveling* from one port to another in search of excitement. In more general senses, it emphasizes the act of getting

somewhere: *traveling* to work by bus or subway. See JOURNEY, LEAVE.
Antonyms: REMAIN.

mind

brains
head
intellect
intelligence
reason
wits

These nouns pertain to the mental capacities or qualities of people. **Mind** is the most general and most neutral. It may refer exclusively to mental facility, requiring qualification to indicate how strong or weak it is: challenges that stimulate students with good *minds;* a *mind* unable to grasp modern scientific theories. *Mind* can also refer to a bundle of mostly conscious attitudes (including the will), or to the entire psyche, conscious or unconscious: those who have set their *minds* against intolerance; a *mind* afflicted by irrational impulses. The remaining terms are all more nearly restricted to mental ability or rational faculties.

Intellect and **intelligence** refer more exactly and more formally than *mind* to mental ability. *Intellect,* the more restricted of the two, refers mostly to reasoning ability. It can be used informally to describe mental alertness or accomplishment: a professor with an extraordinary *intellect*. Used more formally in description, it requires qualification to indicate degree: a mentally ill person with a weak *intellect;* the highly developed *intellect* characteristic of her family. Of the two nouns, *intelligence* is the more common, although it refers to a range of mental faculties wider than that suggested by *intellect*. Mental alertness, problem-solving ability, and keen perception of relationships are all implicit in *intelligence* when used without qualification: delighted to be working with students of *intelligence*. *Intelligence* can also suggest, with qualification, the degree to which these traits are possessed singly or in combination: weak in mechanical skills but otherwise showing strong *intelligence;* tests to determine the verbal *intelligence* of children.

Brains, **head**, and **wits** are all informal terms for aspects of *intelligence. Head*, the most restricted, usually pertains to a single faculty, often of a practical nature: a good *head* for figures; keeping a cool *head* throughout the crisis. *Brains* suggests a wider scope, like *intelligence*, but often refers to mental ability that has practical results: It takes more than *brains* to land a job these days. *Wits* refers specifically to alertness or sensitivity rather than to a general mental facility: warning her to keep her *wits* about her. Like *mind*, it can also refer to the conscious or rational *intelligence:* scared out of their *wits.*

Reason refers solely to the objective, rational part of the *mind;* it is one aspect of *intelligence.* In use, it is referred to as though it were a technique, rather than a faculty: using *reason* to trace the murderer from the few clues available. *Reason* may also, like one use of *wits,* refer in a commonsense way to normal sanity: lost his *reason.* As an abstract noun, it can indicate a rational, unemotional, open-minded approach: the hope that *reason* will overcome prejudice. See ACUMEN, KEEN.

minister. Do not confuse the verb *minister* (attend to people's needs) with the verb *administer* (manage the business affairs of).

minister
brother
father
monk
pastor
preacher
priest
reverend

These nouns refer to a religion's clergy—that is, those who lead a congregation in worship or belong to teaching or monastic orders. **Minister** refers exclusively to a member of a Protestant clergy authorized to administer sacraments and conduct religious services. Even more restricted in scope, **pastor** in this context refers to those *ministers* who have churches or congregations under their official charge. Someone with such a charge may, consequently, be called either a *minister* or *pastor,* although of the two, only *pastor* is used as a title: *Pastor* Jones. By contrast, a *minister* without a charge would not properly be called a *pastor* or be so addressed or titled. *Pastor* has a further use in that it can refer to a member of a Catholic as well as a Protestant clergy who is officially in charge of a congregation or parish.

Preacher and **reverend** also apply to the clergy of some Protestant faiths. *Preacher* is more informal than the previous nouns and, if officially sanctioned as a designation, might suggest denominations that eschew formality or ritual, or emphasize revivalism: farmers who rode into town to hear the new *preacher; Preacher* Smith. In other denominations, *preacher* might be used in informal speech to refer to the pas-

tor, particularly in the role of addressing a congregation in sermons; in this case, *preacher* may have a whimsical or affectionate tone—or it may be used contemptuously, depending on context: a sedate congregation clearly displeased by this fire-and-brimstone *preacher. Reverend* is an informal noun derived from its more formal adjectival use in reference to members of a Protestant or Catholic clergy. As an adjective it may properly appear as part of a title or courtesy phrase: the *Reverend* Dr. Jones. It may also appear in other set phrases before a name, such as the Right *Reverend* or the Most *Reverend.* It is often thought inappropriate or incorrect when any such title is shortened to the one word alone: *Reverend* Jones. Similarly, *reverend* as a noun may be informally substituted for *minister* or *pastor,* but many reject this usage.

In Catholic and Eastern Orthodox churches, **priest** designates a member of the clergy authorized to administer the sacraments; a *priest* in charge of a parish may be referred to as a *pastor,* but in any case may be addressed as **father**: *Father* Brown. [Good morning, *Father.*] *Father* is never used with an article, however, except to refer to the early founders of the church or, collectively, to its leaders: the church *fathers* who fought heresies on the one hand and persecution on the other; a meeting of the *fathers* of the church.

In these same faiths, **monk** refers to a man in holy orders, particularly monastic ones; such a man may or may not be a *priest* as well. If so, he would be referred to as *father;* if not, he would be referred to as **brother**. Unlike *father, brother* may well be used with an article: the poet who became a *brother* in a Trappist monastery. *Monk* and *priest* both may refer to comparable roles in other religions of the world, past or present: a Buddhist *monk;* a Druid *priest;* a Tibetan *priest.* See CLERGYMAN.

minute
infinitesimal
Lilliputian
microscopic
miniature
minuscule

These adjectives describe exceedingly small sizes or amounts. **Minute** describes something so small as to be seen with difficulty; it can, however, refer both to size and amount: a jade carving that teems with *minute* representations of plants and animals; a *minute* trace of poison discovered during the autopsy. It may emphasize that something is small to the point of having no significance or value; it may also indicate something so small as to require careful scrutiny if it is to be understood: a *minute* amount of radioactivity that can hurt no one; a *minute* crack in the wall that led to the amazing discovery. *Minute* in a related use may refer to the intensive scrutiny itself: a *minute* examination of the murder weapon.

Minuscule is derived from a word referring to an early script that used lower-case letters. While *minuscule* can still refer literally to such a script, more generally it indicates something extremely small, and as such is an intensification of the adjective *minute*. *Minuscule* can also refer both to sizes and amounts: a *minuscule* chess set with peg pieces, designed for travelers; a *minuscule* slackening of prices after active trading. When *minuscule* indicates amount, however, it is more likely than *minute* to suggest something unimportant or even petty: a *minute* inspection that turned up only *minuscule* defects in their procedure.

Infinitesimal more commonly applies to amounts so small as to be incalculable and insignificant for all practical purposes; more strictly, it reflects its relation to the adjective *infinite* by referring to something that is infinitely small. *Infinitesimal* is often used not so much literally as in exaggeration: making much of an *infinitesimal* error.

Microscopic, **miniature**, and **Lilliputian**, by contrast, refer most often to size. *Microscopic* literally refers to something too small to be seen without the aid of a microscope: the abundance of *microscopic* diatoms that flourish in the sea. *Miniature,* on the other hand, refers to something that is small but by no means invisible or even difficult to see with the naked eye. *Miniature* suggests most strongly the scaling down of something to small size, as a model. It relates, by derivation, to small-sized paintings and can still apply in this way. For other things, *miniature* may carry a note of amazement or wonder at the effective job of reducing the proportions of something; it can also suggest an effect of cuteness: a *miniature* dollhouse; a *miniature* castle used by children in fighting imaginary battles. *Lilliputian*, from Swift's tiny people in *Gulliver's Travels*, may be used to describe anything extremely small, petty, or trivial: problems *Lilliputian* compared with those facing all the homeless. See COMPACT, SMALL.

Antonyms: *LARGE, MASSIVE, TREMENDOUS.*

mischievous
bad
delinquent

disobedient
naughty

These adjectives characterize the behavior of people who defy convention or authority, as well as the people themselves, especially children. **Mischievous** is found in connection with the playful, teasing, but nonetheless irritating behavior that is part of every child's makeup at one time or another. It suggests that the harm done or trouble caused is neither lasting nor severe: The *mischievous* boy went through the house turning all the furniture around. When used to characterize an adult, however, *mischievous* suggests a manner or action that is more troublesome than playful, more harmful than teasing: a *mischievous* couple who broke up their neighbors' marriage by spreading rumors about the wife.

Naughty is commonly used by adults when speaking of a child's misbehavior, and sometimes humorously when speaking of the sexual attraction or peccadilloes of another adult. [You were a *naughty* boy, Johnny, breaking your sister's doll; an actress who built her reputation on being *naughty* but nice.] Although the application of *naughty* to children is usually confined to instances of trivial breaches of conduct, it is sometimes used to refer to more reprehensible action and in such cases can be considered a euphemism for certain senses of **bad**. *Bad* is a broad term that can at times be interchangeable with the most innocent connotations of *mischievous*. [What a *bad* little girl you are, smearing jelly all over mummy's new dress.] But it may also describe a child (and, of course, an adolescent or adult) who is willful, intractable, immoral, or evil.

Delinquent as an adjective means neglectful in duty or obligation: a *delinquent* father who spent more time playing poker with his friends than playing with his children. This meaning is not often found in reference to children or young people, possibly because of the common use of *delinquent* in the expression *juvenile delinquent*, which is taken to mean a young person guilty of antisocial or criminal behavior. It is unfortunate that this expression, which is specific in tone and pejorative in connotation, is applied loosely to young people who are indeed not juvenile delinquents but merely *mischievous, bad,* or **disobedient**.

Disobedient is another broad word. It refers simply to a failure or a refusal to obey, but its connotations when used to describe a child are different from those applying to an adult. Very young children who are characterized as *disobedient* might instead be called *mischievous* or *naughty;* they are rarely guilty of serious misbehavior, and their failure or refusal to obey is more an act of will than of reason. Older children, adolescents, and adults who are *disobedient* may be guilty of a major oversight or transgression: a *disobedient* student who was forced to leave school; a habitually *disobedient* soldier who was finally court-martialed after striking an officer. See BEHAVIOR, BOTHER, UNRULY.

Antonyms: *OBEDIENT.*

miserable

dismal
sorry
unhappy
wretched

These adjectives may be applied to the personal experience of physical and mental pain or depression or to the things that cause the pain or depression. They are also used to describe things that are below average in character, condition, or performance. When a physical, mental, or environmental state causes great suffering or unhappiness, it can be characterized as **miserable**. [I've been struggling along all day with a *miserable* headache; It is sometimes difficult to acknowledge that another person's lot may be more *miserable* than one's own.] The adjective also suggests something worthless or of inferior quality: to waste an evening at a *miserable* play. **Dismal** describes something or someone that lacks cheer or joy, and also characterizes the gloomy, depressed feelings that such a thing can provoke: a *dismal* day, hot and humid with threatening clouds hanging in the sky; feeling *dismal* after reading of the latest war scare. In referring to something that is below average, *dismal* hints at calamity or disaster: a new business enterprise that turned out to be a *dismal* failure. **Sorry** and **unhappy** describe unpleasant mental states. *Sorry* connotes the kind of sadness, major or minor, that is produced by loss, injury, misfortune, or the like. It may be aroused by one's own troubles or those of a friend, and it is often combined with a feeling of regret. [I'm *sorry* to see my vacation end—it's been a pleasant holiday.] *Unhappy* can be weaker than *sorry* if it merely indicates the absence of happiness: *unhappy* about having to go to a dull party. But *unhappy* can characterize a more lasting state of discontent: a profoundly *unhappy* man lacking friends and interests other than his work. When used critically, *sorry* often gives an indication of pity, ridicule, or concern. [What a *sorry* spectacle he made of himself when he got drunk; The world is in a *sorry* state.] *Unhappy* is less general and not as strong as *sorry* when it is used in criticism to mean unfortunate,

unlucky, not tactful, or inappropriate: an *unhappy* choice of words.

Wretched is stronger in tone than either *sorry* or *unhappy* in its indication of a severely distressed mental state but is interchangeable with *miserable* in reference to physical discomfort: the *wretched* civil rights worker whose wife was killed by bigots; She was feeling *wretched* as a result of a recurrent back problem. When used to describe quality, ability, or performance, *wretched* is strong again in meaning unsatisfactory or worthless: The opera performance was spoiled because the prima donna was in such *wretched* voice. See PATHETIC, SAD.

Antonyms: *CHEERFUL, CONTENTED, JOYOUS.*

misery

agony
anguish
discomfort
distress
passion
torment
torture

These nouns all denote suffering of body or mind. The suffering may be the result of some injurious external interference, as a wound, bruise, harsh word, etc., It may arise from an abnormality in bodily or mental functions, as disease, envy, or discontent. It may be occasioned by the lack of something one needs, as food or love.

Misery refers to a chronic or prolonged suffering, whether physical, mental, or emotional. There is a suggestion of hopelessness about this noun: the *misery* of the arthritic. **Distress** is too strong a term for little hurts, too feeble for the most intense suffering. It more often than not is applied to mental states, referring to any deep anxiety or the external circumstances that may produce it. Very commonly it applies to some prolonged trouble, as does *misery,* but *distress* more than *misery* implies at least a possibility of relief: the *distress* of an underprivileged child. **Discomfort** is the mildest of the nouns in this group, denoting little more than the absence of well-being and ease: the *discomfort* of a hot, humid day.

Agony, **anguish**, **torment**, and **torture** all refer to intense suffering of body or mind. *Agony* and *torture* are perhaps most closely associated with physical pain. *Agony* represents suffering, the endurance of which calls forth every human resource. Its severity is so great that *agony* is often used to denote the struggle and pain that may precede death: In his final *agony* he called for the religious comfort he had rejected for years. *Torture* puts great stress upon the agent that causes or inflicts it: Madmen who indulge in the *torture* of their victims before killing them; the recurrent *torture* of migraine. *Torment* and *anguish* suggest mental suffering. *Torment* hints at repeated or continuous instances of attack: the *torment* of an alcoholic husband. *Anguish* points to the extremity of grief that so terrifies the spirit as to be insupportable: the *anguish* they knew when their children burned to death, *anguish* so great that it turned into madness.

Passion, in the sense being compared here, is now limited to the New Testament account of the *anguish* and *agony* of Jesus Christ that culminated in the crucifixion. See HARM, HURT, PAIN.

Antonyms: *HAPPINESS, PLEASURE.*

mislay

lose
misplace
miss

These verbs refer to accidental losses. **Mislay** suggests the absentminded or disorganized act of putting something down where it doesn't belong, without remembering later exactly where it is: afraid he had *mislaid* the car keys; searching frantically for the *mislaid* deed to the house. The suggestion is that an item that has been *mislaid* is of relatively small size and somewhat difficult to keep track of. **Misplace** would not be so restricted: *misplaced* a boxcar of grain in one of the company's railroad yards. *Misplace*, furthermore, can suggest bad planning: finding that the table had been *misplaced* and was too near the open fire. The verb can also suggest an action that is intentional or unwise: deliberately *misplacing* the book on a shelf where no one could find it: *misplaced* admiration for another woman's husband.

Lose is the most general of these verbs, suggesting an accidental failure to keep hold of something one possesses: *losing* the change through a hole in his pocket. Whereas *mislay* and *misplace* suggest that the desired item may eventually be found, *lose* may suggest a permanent lack: He hadn't *lost* the letter; he had simply *misplaced* it. *Lose* in its generality has a much wider range of use than the other verbs: *losing* his way; *losing* the lucrative account to her competitor; trying to *lose* the man in the crowd.

Miss is much more specific in this context. It points to the moment when one becomes conscious of having *lost* something: first *missing* his wallet when he offered to pay for dinner. See FORGET.

Antonyms: *FIND.*

misleading

deceitful
deceiving
deceptive
delusive
dissembling

These adjectives characterize the giving or receiving of mistaken impressions. Although **misleading** is restricted to something apt to give a false impression, it is still the most general of these adjectives in that it can apply to great or small potential misapprehensions, whether fostered intentionally, unintentionally, or without any intent whatever: a *misleading* advertisement that deliberately left out the drug's side effects; peace offers that were *misleading* because of inexpert translators; clouds with a *misleading* appearance of calm.

Deceiving and **deceptive** would both seem stronger than *misleading* because an actual lie is implied rather than a misapprehension. Nevertheless, like *misleading*, *deceptive* also restricts itself to the possibility, somewhat greater in this case, of a mistaken impression, whether intentional or not. *Deceiving*, however, suggests both a deliberate and successful lie: vertical stripes that give a *deceptive* impression of greater height; patients who are assured by an intern's *deceiving* air of knowing what she is doing.

Dissembling refers to a deliberate pretense, whether believed or not, and **deceitful**, the strongest of all these adjectives, refers to a constantly *dissembling* manner and an ingrained habit of telling lies. **Delusive** functions like *deceptive* except that it suggests mistaken impressions so great as to constitute a complete derangement of mind or a flagrant departure from fact. Because delusions can be the result of mental imbalance, *delusive* often seems to suggest a self-imposed belief that corresponds to one's own wishes or needs. [With a *dissembling* diffidence, the *deceitful* Iago presents *misleading* facts, gives them a *deceptive* turn, and, with a *deceiving* concern for his victim, constructs a *delusive* theory of Desdemona's unfaithfulness.] See DECEPTION, GUILE, LIE, TRICK.

Antonyms: *HONEST.*

mistake

blooper
blunder

mistake *(continued)*

    boner
    contretemps
    error
    faux pas
    goof
    slip
    solecism

These nouns denote something done, said, or believed incorrectly or improperly. **Mistake** and **error** are the most common and general of this group. In many contexts they are interchangeable, but *error* often implies deviation from a standard or model, whereas *mistake* is preferred in the common situations of everyday life. [It was a *mistake* to suppose that George could ever get here on time; an *error* in logic or in arithmetic; a typographical *error*.] *Error* is also used in a theological sense to mean sin, since sin is perceived as deviation from the moral standards or theological truths established by religion.

A **blunder** is a blatant *error,* usually one involving behavior or judgment, and implying an ignorant or uninformed assessment of a situation. [Offering to negotiate with the enemy at that time was an inexcusable *blunder.*] **Slip** and **faux pas** (literally, false step) are minor *mistakes. Slip* emphasizes the accidental rather than ignorant character of a *mistake* and is often used to mean the careless divulging of secret or private information: a *slip* of the tongue. A *faux pas* is an embarrassing breach of etiquette. [He forgot she had remarried and introduced her with her first husband's name—a *faux pas* that made everybody momentarily uncomfortable.]

A **solecism** denotes any error, but especially a breach of good manners, grammar, or usage: Smoking in a restaurant is more than a *solecism* today; It is difficult to believe she could be guilty of the *solecism* "between you and I."

Blooper, **boner**, and **goof** all have a somewhat humorous tone and a distinctively American flavor. Americans apparently feel that if a *mistake* is outrageous enough it is funny, and this feeling is reflected in the variety of nouns available to describe such *mistakes. Blooper*, an informal term, is usually applied to particularly infelicitous mix-ups of speech, such as "rit of fellus jage" for "fit of jealous rage." A *boner* is any egregious and mindless *mistake.* The slang noun *goof* denotes an indefensible *error* honestly admitted, which contains in its admission a covert plea that the *goof* be regarded with indulgent forgiveness. [We really were guilty of a *goof* this time, weren't we?]

A **contretemps**, literally "counter to or against the time," that is, at the wrong time, refers to an embarrassing or awkward occurrence. The young woman who puts off an admirer by saying she is quite ill and then sees him that very night at a party learns the meaning of *contretemps* in a way she is not likely to forget. See FLAW, FORGET.

mixture

    alloy
    amalgam
    blend
    combination
    composite
    compound

Mixture and **combination** are the broadest of these nouns, all of which suggest the bringing together of diverse elements into a new whole. While *mixture* may apply to any materials joined in any way, it is perhaps most appropriate for the adding together of amorphous quantities in which there is no surrendering of individual particles to a new identity: a dry *mixture* of sand and gravel; a *mixture* of choice tobaccos; a *mixture* of peanuts and cashews. Metaphorically, it may suggest fortuitous collocations, as in a *mixture* of luck and perseverance, or it may suggest a mingling of opposites, as in a *mixture* of good and bad. *Combination* suggests a closer union of mingled elements, though not necessarily their fusion: a *combination* of tested ingredients. Metaphorically, it can imply a conscious selection of elements for effect: a striking color *combination* of blues and grays. It can also imply an eclectic distillation: a *combination* of prevailing dramatic styles; new *combinations* of proven therapeutic techniques.

Composite is more formal still than *combination,* but tends to imply that the materials have been patched or pieced together from disparate sources; in motion pictures, for example, a *composite* is a camera shot that consists of several superimposed images. The noun can, however, suggest a more complete fusion of elements: GI Joe was a *composite* of all the soldiers Ernie Pyle came to know as a war correspondent.

Blend suggests more fusion still and, generally, a loss of individual identity for the elements in a *mixture*: a *blend* of whiskeys. *Blend* suggests that skill, control, and conscious intention governed the making of the new whole. While many kinds of material can be used in a *blend,* the word suggests most specifically a *mixture* of fluids or gases.

Alloy and **amalgam** in their most specific senses refer to new metals made by fusing two or more metals in order to obtain valuable properties of each in the new combination. *Alloy* is the generic term for any such *blend*, while *amalgam* is a specific term referring to an alloy of mercury with another metal. Metaphorically, *amalgam* is loosely used to mean *combination*, but it most often suggests a confused *combination:* The child's account of what happened was an *amalgam* of fact and fancy. Metaphorically, *alloy* is often used to suggest the *mixture* of a fine quality with a baser one that reduces its purity: an *alloy* of love and possessiveness.

Compound, in its scientific sense, indicates the closest unity of any of these nouns; it refers to a chemical formed from two or more elements. Water, for example, is a *compound* of hydrogen and oxygen. In metaphorical uses, *compound* is less exact, meaning any *mixture* of things in fairly close relation to each other: a *compound* of wit and intelligence. See COMPONENT, DIVERSIFY.

modern

contemporary
current
present-day
recent
timely

These adjectives describe what is new or what exists now. **Modern** suggests a historical division of time including the present and what has gone immediately before it; this can be a comparatively long or short period. [The discovery of America in 1492 demarcates medieval from *modern* history; Several *modern* schools of painting were unheard of in the 1920's.] *Modern* may also distinguish something in vogue from something old-fashioned, or a present period from an older one: *modern* furniture that looked strange against the Renaissance flavor of the room's architectural details. Like *modern*, **contemporary** may be used to refer to a historical division that includes the present, but it usually suggests a much narrower slice of time than *modern:* the trends in *modern* times that have culminated in certain *contemporary* attitudes. On the other hand, *contemporary* can suggest the mere fact of present existence, while *modern* can suggest something new or vital in spirit: a *contemporary* but hardly *modern* thinker. **Present-day** suggests an even narrower slice of time than *contemporary* but is most often used simply as classification rather than to suggest a positive or negative judgment about value: arguing that *present-day* taste was evenly split between *modern* and traditional styles.

Recent and **current** stress what exists now; *recent* emphasizes factual classification of the immediately preceding past, a slice of time narrower than *contemporary* but more extended than *present-day*. *Current*, by contrast, emphasizes only those *recent* things still viable at this moment. [Of these three *recent* magazines only one is still *current*.]

Timely, like *current*, refers to things of the moment, but differs from *current* in its ability to refer to things of another time that have again become fashionable or pertinent: Machiavelli's advice on the uses of power is still *timely* in the struggle for corporate leadership.

Antonyms: ANCIENT, OLD-FASHIONED, *outdated*.

modest

humble
lowly
meek
retiring
shy
unassuming
unpretentious

These adjectives suggest an absence of assertiveness, a lack of vanity or presumption, or something moderate or small in scale. **Modest** is the only one that works equally well in any of these three areas of meaning: too *modest* for the aggressiveness demanded of him; touchingly *modest* about her tremendous success; a *modest* bank account.

Meek, **retiring**, and **shy** function only in the sense of unwillingness to call attention to oneself. Whereas *modest* here suggests an inbred wish to avoid indecorousness or boastfulness, *shy* suggests bashfulness based not on decorum but on timidity or a lack of social experience, or both. *Retiring* intensifies this sense of *shy*, suggesting the habit of avoiding any scrutiny altogether, though not necessarily out of fear. A *shy* person, for example, may go to parties but be afraid of taking part in them; a *retiring* person would avoid parties completely for unstated private reasons. *Meek* suggests a tractable mildness or submissiveness, but not necessarily an avoidance of confrontation as in these other adjectives: One boy was too *shy* to speak, but the others supplied us with *meek* answers to all our questions.

Unassuming and **unpretentious** are close synonyms to *modest* when it suggests a lack of vanity. *Modest* here refers to an understated acceptance of good fortune or recognition, or to behavior that at least acts out such an acceptance. *Unassuming* emphasizes one aspect of this, suggesting that one does not wish or demand that other people treat one in any special way. *Unpretentious* suggests having no illusions about one's relative importance or refusing to inflate one's worth out of proportion to the facts. [She was *modest* about winning the prize, *unassuming* in giving credit to those who had helped her, and *unpretentious* about the new importance it gave her.]

Humble and **lowly** relate to the meaning of *modest* that refers to something on a reduced scale. Whereas *modest* emphasizes moderate, *humble* and *lowly* suggest small. [*Humble* expectations are best, since even *modest* expectations are all too often disappointed.] *Lowly,* of course, suggests an even smaller scale than *humble* and is mostly used now in jocose clichés. [Let us consider the *lowly* househusband.] Unlike *lowly, humble* can also suggest a lack of vanity: a great man who is also *humble*. But in either sense it has more and more acquired a patronizing tone when used of other people and an air of sanctimonious piety when used of oneself: the *humble* poor; *humble* citizens like ourselves. In the last example, calling attention so blatantly to one's supposed lack of vanity is neither *unassuming, modest,* nor *unpretentious.* See DOCILE, SUBMIT, TIMID.

Antonyms: CONCEITED, OVERBEARING, *pretentious,* SHOWY.

mold

fashion
forge
form
model
shape

These verbs refer to a creative act that works some raw material into a state of beauty or usefulness. **Mold** suggests the working of some ductile or malleable material into the desired product: *molding* the clay into figurines; molten alloys that are *molded* into coins at the mint. *Mold* in more figurative uses retains the suggestion of a tractable material: inescapably *molding* the minds of their students for better or worse. **Form** and **shape** are considerably more general than *mold*. They include the act of compression implicit in *mold* but may suggest many other ways of working, especially with a less tractable raw material. *Form* carries the suggestion of giving outline to something previously less well-defined; it may also suggest putting the finishing touch on a product: *forming* a strong political platform from the many proposals that were submitted, amended, and finally approved. *Shape* suggests the bringing about of a more far-reaching change than is suggested by *form;* it may also suggest an impersonal cause-and-effect relationship: *shaping* an intricate

mosaic from bits of glass that lay about in seemingly confused and unrelated piles; policies that will *shape* our course for years to come.

Forge most strictly suggests heated metals that are worked with anvil and hammer: *forging* pieces for a wrought-iron balustrade. In figurative uses it suggests a great expenditure of labor to work out a solution against considerable resistance: negotiators who *forged* the final draft of the agreement. **Fashion** suggests none of the extremes of effort implicit in *forge;* it is very close to the literal denotation of *form* and *shape,* and is used figuratively in much the way that *mold* is, referring to the influence of instruction or conditioning on a person: *fashioning* a talented amateur into a brilliant actor. *Fashion* may sometimes suggest an improvised solution: *fashioning* from her hairpin a crude device with which to open the lock.

Model relates to *mold* in the specific sense of working a malleable raw material: children who *modeled* clay for an hour each morning. *Model* is more frequently used, however, in the sense of displaying an example of someone's work, especially in relation to designers of women's clothes: choosing mannequins to *model* an entirely new line of resort fashions. Another viable use of *model* refers to construction carried out along the lines of an earlier example: new countries that *model* their constitutions on ours; *modeling* her detective story on all the clichéd situations used in earlier bestsellers. See CREATE, MANUFACTURE.

mole

birthmark
freckle
melanism
nevus

These nouns denote pigmented or reddish marks or nodules on the skin that may be permanent and either are present at birth or develop later in life. **Mole** refers to a type of permanent spot that may vary in color from yellowish brown to dark brown. *Moles* are usually congenital in origin and may be large or small, flat or protuberant, with some having sprouting hairs. Occasionally, they may be removed either for cosmetic reasons or as a precautionary measure if they grow larger or undergo any change in appearance. At various times in history, a *mole* on the face of a woman, especially on the cheekbone, has been highly prized and referred to as a beauty mark or beauty spot because it serves to set off the whiteness of the skin.

A **birthmark** is often a *mole,* but *birthmarks* may also take other forms, most commonly that of elevated pink or bright red growths (in medicine called hemangiomas), sometimes covering large areas of the skin. Popularly called strawberry marks or port wine stains, such *birthmarks* are composed of clusters of small surface blood vessels and capillaries. No effective treatment is known for this type of blemish. **Nevus** is the technical term for both *mole* and *birthmark*.

Freckle applies to one of a large colony of small, flat, brown or tan spots on the skin, which are not congenital. They tend to appear on the fair, rosy complexion of people with sandy or red hair, multiply when the skin is exposed to the sun, and often fade or disappear entirely during the cooler seasons. Unlike *moles* or *birthmarks,* freckles are rarely considered blemishes, as they are very common and often are considered attractive.

Melanism is a fairly rare condition of the skin or deeper tissues in which there are abnormal deposits or patches of dark pigment, or melanin. *Melanism,* while sometimes present at birth, may arise from a disorder of pigment metabolism or as a result of constant handling of certain toxic substances, such as tar or pitch.

mongrel
    cur
    hound
    mutt

These nouns are comparable in that they all are used to designate a kind of dog, and in a pejorative way, a kind of person. A **mongrel** is any animal or plant of mixed breed, but especially a dog. Since there is a strong suggestion of illegitimacy about a *mongrel,* such a dog is often looked down upon by dog fanciers. It may, indeed, be this somewhat contemptuous feeling for *mongrel* dogs that has given the pejorative connotation to *mongrel* when it denotes a person who is not of a single race, whose parents are of different national or social backgrounds, or whose tendencies, political opinions, religious convictions, etc., are undefined or uncertain. [Ever since the governor took office, his only consistency has been his inconsistency; the man has proved himself to be a political *mongrel.*] **Cur** in its denotation of a dog is synonymous with *mongrel.* But whereas a *mongrel,* in spite of its ancestry, can be looked on as a worthwhile pet, a *cur* is despised by the dog lover as an inferior, ugly, or unfriendly beast. The same feeling reserved for *cur* greets the mean, malicious, cowardly, or otherwise objectionable person who is described by the same name: a man with pretensions to honor and bravery who proves himself a *cur* in the face of the slightest danger. **Mutt**, when it designates a dog, is synonymous with *mongrel* and *cur,* but even more than is true with *mongrel, mutt* frequently refers to a loved pet rather than to one that is thought to be worthless. A person who is a *mutt,* however, is stupid or doltish. Although such a person is not held in high esteem, he is usually not treated with the contempt or disdain accorded one called *mongrel* or *cur.*

Hound, like the other nouns in this group, is general in its designation of a dog of any breed or background. It can, however, be specific in a way the other nouns cannot, when it refers to any of several particular breeds of hunting dog. When *hound* denotes a person, it may characterize someone who is detestable in the way that a *mongrel* or *cur* is. But it may also refer, in an informal way, to a person who is fond almost to the point of addiction of a certain pastime, activity, food, etc.: a bridge *hound*; a pizza *hound*. See ANIMAL.

monotonous
    boring
    dull
    tedious
    tiresome

These adjectives are all used to describe someone or something that induces a state of dissatisfaction or weariness. **Monotonous** originally meant unvaried in inflection, cadence, pitch, or tone: It is incredible that a singer of her reputation has such a *monotonous* voice. This meaning was later extended to refer to anything so lacking in variety as to cause fatigue or annoyance: The views from my train window grew *monotonous* after less than an hour, and I found myself dozing off. **Dull** has many meanings, but in the sense being compared here, it is used to characterize a person or thing that is uninteresting, as from a lack of variety, spirit, attraction, delight, etc.: a *dull* performer; a *dull* book; a *dull* meal. That which is **boring** may be *dull* or *monotonous:* a *boring* movie unrelieved by dramatic conflict, wit, or even a decent bit of acting. *Boring,* however, more than the other adjectives in this group, can refer to the discontent and indifference known as ennui. This feeling may be a reaction to some person or thing, but it may also be the result of spiritual torpor and a general dissatisfaction with life. **Tedious** is like the preceding adjectives in meaning but goes beyond them in its suggestion that monotony or inactivity causes a repression of energy and an attendant physical discomfort: The month I spent confined to a hospital bed was so *tedious* I couldn't wait to get back to work. *Tedious* also refers to the kind of boredom one feels as a result of wordiness in speech or writing:

The lecture was so *tedious* that people began to leave the auditorium before the speaker was half done. **Tiresome**, like *tedious,* implies fatigue: a *tiresome* day filled with exhausting household chores. *Tiresome* also has connotations of annoyance that are stronger than those in the four other terms: a very beautiful woman, but *tiresome* because of her bad temper. See LISTLESS, NUMB, SLOTH, STUPID.

Antonyms: *diversified, exciting, interesting, stimulating, varied.*

moral
    decent
    ethical
    good
    honorable
    righteous
    self-righteous
    upright
    virtuous

All these adjectives characterize acts that are in accord with a code of right and wrong. **Moral** and **ethical**, once indistinguishable from each other, have recently taken on fine distinctions in meaning. *Moral* is now more often used in a quasi-religious sense, *ethical* in a quasi-legal sense: the *moral* rectitude of a saint; a law outlining *ethical* practices for legislators. *Moral* might be thought to include this narrower sense of *ethical,* making the one term generic, the other specific, but *moral* has more and more come to mean personal conduct as set by an external code or standard, especially when such conduct does not affect numbers of people: a *moral* standard that specified moderation in food and drink and an avoidance of worldly pleasures. *Ethical,* by contrast, is more and more taken to describe just and fair dealings with other people, not by the application of an external standard but by a pragmatic consideration of all aspects of a situation in light of experience. To put it most extremely, *moral* can often be taken to mean private, codified, rigid, and a priori; *ethical* to mean public, improvisatory, flexible, and a posteriori: agreeing, despite differing *moral* values, on *ethical* ways to work together. The split between the two adjectives, however, is by no means as sharp as this attempt to contrast them might suggest; they do overlap and can still be used interchangeably.

Upright and **decent** are more informal than *moral* and *ethical,* but they shade away from each other in much the same way as the first pair. *Upright* may suggest an inner *moral* strength, *decent* an outgoing *ethical* concern for others. While *decent,* in fact, has no pejorative uses, *upright* can sometimes suggest excessive rigidity: stiff-necked, *upright* Puritans.

Virtuous and **honorable** are slightly more formal than *moral* and *ethical,* but the same contrast in shadings can be felt. Here, *virtuous* suggests a private life free of blemish, whereas *honorable* suggests *decent* and *ethical* dealings with others: a *virtuous* man; women who are both competitive and *honorable.*

Righteous strongly suggests someone who lives almost faultlessly in accordance with strict *moral* standards. This adjective now is used somewhat less than previously except in such expressions as *righteous* indignation, which is indignation aroused by injustice or a lack of fair play. Otherwise, *righteous* tends to suggest priggishness, narrow-mindedness, and intolerance: an unambitious but gentle woman who had the misfortune of being married to a *righteous* man. The more common **self-righteous** is always pejorative and stresses pharisaism and an exaggerated sense of one's moral superiority compared with others. **Good** is a vague, general synonym for any of these adjectives and cannot be restricted to specific shades of meaning. See GOODNESS, HONEST, TRUST.

Antonyms: *dishonorable,* UNETHICAL.

moron
    dope
    dullard
    dummy
    idiot
    imbecile
    numbskull
    simpleton

All these nouns can be used as invective against someone considered stupid or foolish. **Moron**, **imbecile**, and **idiot** formerly functioned neutrally as classifications for degrees of mental deficiency, *moron* denoting a mild deficiency, *imbecile* a moderate level of deficiency, and *idiot* a degree of severe deficiency. Nowadays, the phrase mentally retarded child (or person) preceded by a qualifier such as mildly or severely is the preferred term, both in popular and technical writing, for any of these levels.

Dullard and **simpleton** lack the precise denotations of the previous group, but they do refer to a slow-witted rather than to a foolish person. *Dullard* is the more formal of the two and suggests a mild degree of mental deficiency that renders one passive, unresponsive, or imperceptive: appalled to find that her class appeared filled with *dullards* and borderline students on probation. *Simpleton* suggests greater deficiency; it has a faintly archaic flavor that sometimes brings to mind a touching innocence or sweetness of disposition: the class *simpleton* we all loved for his good nature despite his inability to learn.

The remaining nouns all are informal. **Dummy** suggests someone prone to foolish mistakes: *such a dummy that he kept setting himself on fire by smoking in bed.* Except for a much greater informality, **dope** is like *dullard;* but as used, it suggests ill-advised or foolish behavior rather than mental deficiency: *a dope to try swimming against such an undertow.* **Numbskull** must once have seemed a vivid coinage, but now, through overuse, has faded somewhat as a term for a hopelessly stupid person: *numbskulls who drop out of school.* See BLOCKHEAD PSYCHOTIC, STUPID.

Antonyms: *genius, intellectual, sage, savant.*

motive
incentive
inducement
reason
spur

These nouns all denote stimuli that prompt one to action. **Motive** connotes some impulse within a person—such as love, hate, revenge, or ambition—that impels the person to act with a strong sense of purpose: *The police believed the suspect's motive was jealousy; Her real motive for joining the club was not to make new friends, but to meet potential clients.*

Reason is the most general of these nouns, but in a specific sense *reason* implies a logical justification either to oneself or to others for an action by citing facts and circumstances. [*Her reason for entering the hospital was to undergo surgery; A severe handicap was the reason for his shyness.*] *Reason* may sometimes hint at a contrived excuse: *Although he had overslept, the reason he gave for his lateness was that he had been caught in a traffic jam.*

Incentive and **spur** are *reasons* for undertaking action with extra zeal. *Incentive* nearly always implies a reward for such effort *prizes offered as an incentive to the sales staff.* *Spur,* more strongly than *incentive,* suggests something external to oneself that causes a sudden increase in the rate of activity, as did the original meaning of *spur* in horsemanship: *Finding the cause of a disease often will provide a spur for research leading to a cure.*

Inducement denotes an attractive *reason* for choosing one thing rather than another: *The promise of a yearly bonus may be an inducement to an executive who is considering a job offer.* See STIMULATE.

mountain
cliff
hillock
hill
mesa
plateau
precipice
promontory
range

These nouns refer to projections of earth or stone that are elevated above the surrounding landscape. **Mountain** refers to a high-rising rocky projection that is typically steep and has a narrow summit. When *mountains* occur grouped together, they are collectively called a **range**: *the range of mountains running from Alaska to the southern tip of South America.* A **plateau** is a mountain that has a wide flat top, as though the peak had been sliced off or the *mountain* truncated at some midway point. *Plateau* may also refer to a much more extensive reach of highly elevated level ground that may not seem at all like a *mountain* to someone positioned on it anywhere but at its periphery: *people living on the great Arkansas plateau.* **Mesa**, a word borrowed from Spanish and used in the southwestern part of the United States, refers to a type of small, treeless *plateau.* It is a high, broad, and flat tableland with rocky slopes descending to the surrounding plain.

Hill indicates a projection of earth that is more low-lying than a *mountain;* such a shape may be of considerable size: *the Black Hills.* Or it may point to a slight rise of ground: *the hill at one end of the field.* **Hillock** specifically points to such a small *hill,* typically suggesting a brief grassy rise of indefinite or ragged shape: *leaving undisturbed occasional wooded hillocks on either side of the turnpike.*

The remaining nouns suggest abrupt or jutting outcroppings of rocky forms that may or may not be part of a *mountain.* **Cliff** indicates a high vertical shape that drops away suddenly to a lower level; it is particularly used to refer to the edges or side of a *mountain, plateau,* or *mesa: a widening highway cut into the cliff.* *Cliff* may, however, indicate a sharp break between two level stretches: *sauntering out to stand on the cliff overlooking the ocean.* **Precipice** is less general in referring almost solely to a sharply jutting vertical rise or overhang of rock or stone: *the precipice made by the steep side of the mountain.* **Promontory** specifically indicates a high point of land such as a *hill* or *cliff* that extends into the sea: *the lighthouse set on a promontory that dominated the surrounding landscape.*

Mountain and *hill* both have a wide range of metaphorical uses referring to great amounts, weights, or sizes: a *mountain* of work; this *mountain* of a man; a *hill* of papers on her desk. Used metaphorically, *precipice* usually suggests danger, as from falling: moving closer to the *precipice* of all-out war. See SUMMIT.
Antonyms: *PLAIN.*

move

relocate
shift
transfer

These verbs refer to the transportaton of something from one place to another. **Move** is the most general and informal. It can suggest the covering of slight or great distances: *moving* the desk a few inches to get better light; having the piano *moved* upstairs. As can be seen, *move* can imply great or little effort. It can also refer to the altering of position, as a part of the body, or simply an agitated back-and-forth motion: *moving* her hand to rest on his shoulder; *moving* about in her seat to get more comfortable; branches *moving* faintly in the breeze. Clearly, *move* has little connotation in itself and can often be replaced with a more vivid verb. *Move* does have exclusive relevance, however, for a person's changing of residence, including the transportation of belongings to the new address: *moving* from Baltimore to San Francisco; *moving* from a ground-floor apartment to one on the third floor.

Shift may specifically suggest a slight move: *shifting* the refrigerator so he could clean behind it; *shifting* her legs so latecomers could get past her to their seats. *Shift* can also stress an abrupt or considerable change in duties, or a reorganization that results in a physical *move: shifted* from his position as sales manager to one of the vice-presidencies; *shifting* the state capital from an out-of-the-way town to a more centrally located city.

Relocate is like *move* in referring to a change of location or residence. The change may be forced on one, as by a natural disaster or the condemning of one's dwelling: a tenement family that refused to be *relocated. Relocating*, however, may be done voluntarily in connection with one's business or job: If a better job were offered you in Cleveland, would you *relocate?* **Transfer** is a more formal substitute for *move*, but it is useful to indicate a change of occupation or station within the same large grouping; in this it is like one sense of *shift: transferred* from field work to administrative duties. *Transfer* in itself suggests neither promotion nor demotion but merely change of

function. The verb is also relevant for *shifting* that involves no actual movement: *transferring* his phone call to the personnel department; *transferring* the money from her checking account to her savings bank. See CARRY, GO, LEAVE, MIGRATE.
Antonyms: *REMAIN, rest,* STOP.

mutual

common
interchangeable
joint
reciprocal
shared

These adjectives characterize something that is possessed or can be used by two or more people or in two or more situations. **Mutual** and **reciprocal** are close in meaning, suggesting most simply some interaction between two parties, in which the same thing is given and taken on both sides: their *mutual* respect; a *reciprocal* lowering of tariffs between the two countries. *Reciprocal* is the more common term in official or technical contexts. Strictly speaking, neither would be used for groups of three or more. *Mutual,* however, is commonly used for any similarity of interests, views, feelings, even when the relationships are not *reciprocal:* a *mutual* interest in hiking that drew the two boys together; a *mutual* excitement felt by the whole audience; *mutual* funds.

Common escapes the objections that may be leveled at *mutual,* referring widely to something possessed by two or more people: speaking a *common* language; a *common* interest in silent movies. Because *common* can also mean ordinary, however, or even cheap or debased, the ambiguity of the adjective sometimes rules out its use, a fact that may justify substitution of *mutual.* A *mutual* friend would unmistakably be one that two or more people were friendly with, but a *common* friend might be a vulgar or coarse friend.

Joint exclusively emphasizes the actual possession of something by no more and no less than two people: a *joint* bank account. Since *joint* suggests a unity, as of two halves within a whole, it would not point to mere similarity of interests: a *joint* business venture in which both persons or organizations risk an equal amount of capital. **Interchangeable** involves a different concept altogether, applying to parts or elements that can be moved from one setting to another without loss of function or can be used one in place of the other: standardized shaving heads that are *interchangeable* from one model of electric razor to another. [Wapiti and elk are *interchangeable* words for a large North American deer.]

Shared gives a tone of even greater emotional warmth than is true for *mutual;* it also can indicate something actually divided up and used by two or more people: our *shared* lunch of bread and cheese. More generally, it can replace both *common* and *mutual* in many contexts, often with a gain in clarity or sense of intimacy: our *shared* language; pointing out that *shared* interests often lead to marriage.

Antonyms: *individual, inseparable, particular, separate, unshared.*

mystical
mysterious
occult

These adjectives describe matters beyond the ordinary range of knowledge, perception, or understanding, with the added suggestion of things kept secret or hidden from all but a favored few. **Mystical** emphasizes the idea of a direct, intuitive, deeply personal revelation, especially one of a spiritual or religious nature: the *mystical* visions of Saint Theresa; John Donne's *mystical* poems; a *mystical* belief in life after death.

An occurrence or phenomenon is **mysterious** if it contains elements that arouse one's wonder, stimulate one's curiosity, and baffle one's efforts to explain it: the *mysterious* universe; a *mysterious* ailment; the *mysterious* properties of a new drug. Here, the possibility of a rational explanation remains, the obscurity being the result of inadequate rather than unobtainable knowledge.

Occult means hidden or concealed and has come to be applied chiefly to magical arts and practices, as astrology, alchemy, or divination. Those who were versed in such secret matters were said to have *occult* powers, not to be freely divulged to others and exerted only under special conditions, usually determined by the practitioners. Thus, while one may speak of an experience as *mysterious* where the causes are unknown but ascertainable, as *mystical* when it is unique, spontaneous, and usually incommunicable, *occult* implies some agency unknown in human experience without whose deliberate intervention something would not have occurred. See BIZARRE, OBSCURE, SUPERNATURAL.

Antonyms: *PLAIN.*

naive

- artless
- guileless
- ingenuous
- provincial
- rude
- unaffected
- unsophisticated

Like the rest of these adjectives, **naive** suggests either a lack of urbanity or a candid simplicity. It also suggests a trusting innocence that has not yet been tested; *naive* ideals may be appealingly or exasperatingly out of touch with hard facts, but a *naive* person is limited in experience, not necessarily stupid. **Unsophisticated** is more specific than *naive* in suggesting a lack of worldliness, whether one is experienced or inexperienced; *unsophisticated* may be used as praise or as criticism, depending on the user's attitude toward urbanity: a plain, *unsophisticated* man who can say a lot in a few words; so *unsophisticated* they didn't know what a black-tie dinner was. Unlike *naive*, *unsophisticated* does not necessarily imply a willingness to trust: carnival barkers who misjudged as *naive* their *unsophisticated* but hard-headed audience. **Provincial** suggests lack of exposure to experience, like *naive*, but implies most specifically a life remote from any metropolis or one sheltered from fashionable taste and ideas: *provincial* rednecks who guffawed at the sight of male ballet dancers wearing tights. *Provincial*, in emphasizing remoteness of place, need not suggest innocence: Emily Dickinson and the Brontës were *provincial* but hardly *naive*. **Rude** suggests an extremely unformed taste or character, possibly as a result of a *provincial* life, but it comes near suggesting uncivilized and illiterate, except in rare instances of positive use: a *rude* but honest and stalwart people.

The remaining adjectives deal with the manner in which *rude*, *provincial*, *naive*, or *unsophisticated* people may behave. **Ingenuous** is closest to *naive* in suggesting someone who is overly confiding, unsubtle, or unwary. Unlike *naive*, however, this need not result from a lack of experience. It may be used in a positive sense: the sweetly *ingenuous* child. It may also be used critically: so *ingenuous* as to give away your secrets to anyone at the slightest prompting.

Unaffected refers to unpretentious manners or spontaneous informality. While it is exclusively positive in tone, what one person might consider *rude* behavior, another might think *unaffected*. Also, *unaffected* manners might be considered the mark of urbanity, whereas *provincial*, *naive*, or *unsophisticated* people, by putting on airs unnatural to them, might exemplify the opposite of *unaffected* conduct. **Guileless**, like *unaffected*, is wholly favorable in tone, but it refers less to the contrast between informality and formality than to a simple lack of deceitfulness; a person with pretentious manners might still be *guileless*. Nor does *guileless* necessarily suggest trusting unwariness like *naive*, or eagerness to share confidences like *ingenuous*. Aside from its stress on honesty, *guileless* thus says less about a person than the other adjectives. Similarly, an urbane person and a *provincial* or *unsophisticated* person might or might not be *guileless*, but their ways of showing this quality or lack of it would differ markedly.

Artless, very like *unaffected*, once unambiguously referred to a winningly open and spontaneous manner. This meaning may still be intended, with its implied distrust of all art and formality as mere contrivance, but it may now also be used to mean ungraceful or awkward: a radiantly *artless* smile; the *artless* hostess who stumbled over every introduction. Unless context makes clear which meaning is intended, *artless* should be avoided. See GULLIBLE, SINCERE.

Antonyms: FORMAL, *pretentious, sophisticated*.

name

- call
- christen
- designate
- dub

These verbs mean entitle a person or thing for purposes of identification or designation to a particular function, office, or honor. **Name**, the most general, means fix the thought or idea of someone or something in word form so that the person or thing may afterward be specifically known or recalled to mind. [The province was *named* Alberta; They *named* their child Janet.] *Name* also means mention or refer to by *name* in speech or writing. [The teacher asked her pupils whether any of them could *name* all the Presidents of the United States in five minutes.] *Name* also means identify or accuse by *name* or by *naming*. [Can you *name* that flower? He was *named* as a murder suspect in this morning's paper.] *Name* finally means select or nominate for or appoint to some purpose or position. [July 1st has been *named* the date for the annual office picnic; My father was recently *named* to the City Council.] **Call** means *name:* to *call* the baby Michael. It can mean address or speak of by a specific *name.* [Don't be formal, *call* me Joe.] *Call* is also used when a descriptive word is mentioned to characterize someone. [Don't you *call* me a liar; William I of England was *called* the Conqueror.]

Designate means *name* or entitle by some distinctive word, symbol, expression, etc.: The points of interest on the map are *designated* by letters of the alphabet. *Designate,* like *name,* also means select or appoint, as by authority, for some specific purpose, duty, etc., [Four officers were *designated* to receive the Bronze Star; The president of the club *designated* those members she wanted to serve on committees for the charity ball.] The comparable sense of *name* differs only slightly in that it is used more often than *designate* when emphasis is placed on announcement rather than selection.

Christen is the most specialized of the verbs in this group, since it refers to the formal Christian rite of baptism. In its original meaning, *christen* was synonymous with baptize, but it has come more and more to suggest the *naming* of a person at baptism rather than the entire ceremony: The infant was *christened* Erica. By extension, *christen* is used when inanimate objects are *named,* particularly in ceremonies analogous to baptism: to *christen* a ship.

Dub is the most informal verb in the group even though it refers in its original meaning to the formal act of conferring knighthood by tapping on the shoulder with a sword. Today, *dub* means nickname or give dignity or character to someone by means of some title or descriptive expression. [My friend Charles was *dubbed* Shorty when he was a child and he has never outgrown the nickname; It is unfair to *dub* someone a coward merely because he refuses to fight.] See APPOINT, CHOOSE, LABEL.

narrative

anecdote
legend
myth
saga
story
tale
yarn

All these nouns refer to the verbal account of an occurrence, whether real or imaginary. **Narrative**, the most formal and general of these, can serve to categorize whatever has as its impulse the recounting of events rather than the lyrical expression of feeling or the evocation of mood, character, or place: forms of *narrative* in Victorian prose. More specifically, it can refer to a recitation or recounting of actual events: a day-by-day *narrative* recounting her experiences during the AIDS epidemic. Sometimes, it is used humorously for a long-winded recital of grievances or past miseries: a rambling *narrative* of the ways her three husbands had mistreated her. Often, particularly as a generic term, it appears as an adjective: *narrative* poetry; *narrative* skill in prose fiction.

Story can function as an informal substitute for *narrative* in many instances: the *story* of her narrow escape from the concentration camp. Often, *story* indicates an account of fictional occurrences, clearly understood as such, told for the entertainment of a hearer or reader: He improvised a bedtime *story* for his daughter. In reference to written fiction, *story* serves as a literary category, indicating a compact prose form, the short *story,* or refers to the *narrative* element in any writing: reviewers who feel impelled to retell a novel's *story* before appraising it. Because of the reference of *story* to fictional accounts, it can be used for any explanation: a *story* she invented to explain why she was late; the suspect's *story.*

Tale can relate to this last use of *story,* applying to any exaggerated version of events, whether told to deceive or amuse: a tall *tale* about his life as a Broadway actor. *Tale* can also categorize one kind of literary *narrative*—a recital by a storyteller, in poetry or prose, of actual, fictional, legendary, or allegorical events: The Canterbury *Tales.* **Yarn** is the most informal of these nouns and usually indicates a colorful *story* or tall *tale,* whether composed of embroidered truth or outright fiction; *yarn* implies that the *story* or *tale* is told orally or imitates such a telling: Mark Twain's *yarn* about the Jumping Frog of Calaveras County. **Anecdote** can refer to any compact *narrative,* spoken or written, true or fictional. *Anecdote* suggests greater brevity than would be the case for either a *story* or *tale,* but it is otherwise general in its application: an *anecdote* about something that happened to her daughter at college; a lecture constantly interrupted by pointless *anecdotes* and other digressions.

Myth indicates a *narrative,* in whatever form, that recounts the doings of gods, heroes, and humans before the dawn of history. The *myths* of a given culture were usually taken seriously as explanations of the supernatural origin of the society, although later writers and artists may elaborate upon these *myths* or create new ones without ever giving them credence: Greek *myths;* Scandinavian *myths;* Balinese *myths.* A legend may include elements of *myth*, but is a more extended recounting in some set form of fabulous happenings, whether these are given credence by author and audience or are accepted as fictions. Often, *legends* may derive from a period later than the creation of *myth* and may have an underpinning of historical truth: *legends* that grew up around the exploits of Richard the Lion-Hearted. Sometimes, *legend* can refer to present-day *stories* that have evolved to explain local events or customs: a persistent *legend* that the house on the hill was once the site of a murder. Saga refers to an extended *narrative* that mixes *myth* and *legend* to recount the epic *story* of demigods or heroes: the Volsunga *Saga*. Less specifically, *saga* can refer to any epic chronicle, even of historical events: a *saga* of the Civil War. Used even more loosely, *saga* can refer to any long-winded oral *narrative* about past experiences. See ALLEGORY, HISTORY, NEWS, NOVEL, TELL.

native

aboriginal
autochthonous
endemic
indigenous

These adjectives designate persons or things that belong to the place in which they are found or in which they originated. That which is born or produced in a specific region or country is **native** to it: a *native* Californian; architecture *native* to New England; birds *native* to South America. *Native* may also be used of things that have been naturalized in a place for some time; thus, one may speak of the coffee plant as being *native* to Brazil, although it was introduced into that country from Africa several hundred years ago.

Indigenous is more restricted in meaning than *native* in that it excludes the possibility of introduction from elsewhere, as of a species of animal or plant, or a race of people. [The platypus is *indigenous* to Australia; Eskimos are *indigenous* to the Arctic regions.] *Indigenous* may also be applied to things that originate in a specified place. [Cliff dwellings are *indigenous* to the southwestern United States; The Irish have a rich *indigenous* folklore.]

Aboriginal is used chiefly of primitive peoples (aborigines) having no known or recorded ancestors and inhabiting a region at its earliest known historical time: The Ainus are the *aboriginal* people of Japan. Less frequently, *aboriginal* is applied to *native* or *indigenous* plants and animals.

Endemic is used of plants or diseases that are *native* to, and usually restricted to, a specific region or part of the world because they are peculiarly adapted to flourish there. [The maguey plant is *endemic* in Mexico; Cholera is *endemic* in the Orient.]

Autochthonous, which originally meant "sprung from the earth itself," is a less common synonym of *native*, *aboriginal*, and *indigenous*. It is now most often used in geology of rocks and minerals produced in the places where they are found rather than brought in by some external agency, such as a glacier. See ARISE, BEGIN, PROTOTYPE.

Antonyms: *alien, foreign, immigrant.*

neglect

dereliction
negligence
thoughtlessness

These nouns pertain to failure to give proper attention and care where it is due, and they are all condemnatory. **Neglect** and **negligence** are sometimes not clearly discriminated in meaning, but *neglect* refers to the act and *negligence* to the quality or trait of character of a person careless and irresponsible in actions and attitudes. Of the two, *neglect* is the stronger word. *Neglect* of one's appearance suggests slovenliness, while *negligence* as to one's appearance indicates only a lack of concern for style or smartness. A child may suffer from parental *neglect*, but it is *negligence* on the part of the parents if the child is improperly cared for. In law, *negligence* is a violation of the obligation to take care and caution in what one does, especially when it involves the rights and safety of other people. A driver who knowingly operates a car with faulty brakes, thereby causing an accident involving another car, is guilty of gross *negligence*.

Dereliction carries a sense of greater culpability than *neglect* or *negligence*, because *dereliction* is a deliberate and reprehensible *neglect* of a responsibility, rather than merely a careless one. A surgeon who performs an operation while intoxicated is guilty of *dereliction* of duty toward the patient.

Thoughtlessness strongly implies oversight rather than willful *neglect*. People who are usually careful to think before they act or speak may occasionally be guilty of *thoughtlessness*. Others, through lack of imagination or understanding of the needs and feelings of other people, are to be blamed for *thoughtlessness* when they habitually cause irritation or displeasure without appearing to realize it. See CURSORY, FORGET, HEEDLESS.

Antonyms: *attention, attentiveness, care, concern, consideration, thoughtfulness.*

neighboring

abutting
adjacent
adjoining
contiguous
juxtaposed
tangent

These adjectives characterize things nearby or things that touch each other. **Neighboring** is the most informal of these and suggests only that things are close to each other but not necessarily touching: a shopping center that drew its customers from the *neighboring* communities; no one in the *neighboring* apartments was awakened by the sounds. In geometry, a line that is **tangent** to a circle touches that circle at one and only one point; this meaning is often apparent even in more ordinary uses: a road that does not go through the city but runs *tangent* to it.

Adjoining indicates a closer relationship than the previous adjectives, suggesting a side-by-side placement having a common boundary: asking the hotel for *adjoining* rooms with a connecting door between them; French doors that opened on the *adjoining* patio. **Abutting** indicates an even closer relationship than *adjoining*, stressing an actual touching of elements, although not necessarily a side-by-side placement. The special implication here is of things driven together by force to gain strength or structural soundness: the roofbeam and its *abutting* crossbeams; a network of *abutting* boardwalks. When these implications are not present, *abutting* functions much as *adjoining*, except that it does not necessarily suggest a side-by-side relation: a number of chapels *abutting* the apse of the cathedral. **Contiguous** is more formal than *adjoining* and *abutting* and much less specific about the actual placement of elements to which it refers. Thus, any kind of contact whatsoever can be indicated: gardens *contiguous* to each other; a hallway *contiguous* to all the rooms of the railroad flat.

Adjacent can suggest a relationship like that indicated by *neighboring*: an explosion that brought people pouring out of the *adjacent* houses. It can also indicate the sharing of a common boundary in a side-by-side arrangement, as in the geometry term: *adjacent* angles; *adjacent* plots of land. But *adjacent* has a special use to indicate things of the same kind that do not touch but are not blocked from each other by things like them: *adjacent* islands; *adjacent* farmhouses. **Juxtaposed** also has a use distinct from those of other adjectives here. While *juxtaposed* can function like *neighboring* or *adjoining*, it most specifically suggests incongruous elements brought into close contact.

Juxtaposed often carries connotations of conflict, abruptness of placement, or surprise at contrasts: a city in which modern structures and some two centuries old are strikingly *juxtaposed;* opposing forces that found themselves *juxtaposed* the next morning on either side of the river. See BOUNDARY, EDGE.

Antonyms: *dispersed, far-flung, scattered, separated, unattached, unconnected.*

nervous

edgy
excitable
fidgety
flighty
jittery
jumpy
on edge
restless
uptight

All these adjectives suggest a state of tension, anxiety, or worry. **Nervous** and **restless** are probably the most general, but whereas *nervous* refers to an inward condition, *restless* suggests an outward manifestation of anxiety. A person can be inwardly *nervous* and outwardly calm, but if *restless*, the person shows it, as by shifting from one foot to the other, repeatedly getting up and sitting down, or pacing the room. *Restless* may also be used figuratively, suggesting the free inquiring attitude of the scientist or the adventurer: a *restless* mind, never satisfied with easy generalizations; Her *restless* spirit urged her on to ever greater feats. In this sense, however, *restless* often has a somewhat strained rhetorical ring. *Restless* describes a temporary condition called into play by a particular situation. A person may be *nervous* by disposition and not because of any particularly anxious situation: My father always has been a *nervous* person.

Edgy and **jumpy** both indicate an extremely *nervous* state and are somewhat more informal than either *nervous* or *restless*. An *edgy* person is irritable and combative, ready to take offense at slight provocation, whereas a *jumpy* person is extremely *nervous*, seemingly ready to jump. In this sense *jumpy* is synonymous with **on edge**, although one is usually kept *on edge* waiting for important news, whereas a *jumpy* person compulsively anticipates being shocked or surprised. [The day I start catching a cold I feel *edgy*, ready to snap at everyone; We were kept *on edge* for days, waiting to find out whether our son had passed his examinations; The war veteran still became *jumpy* whenever he heard a car backfire.]

Fidgety, more than the other adjectives discussed so far, suggests *nervous* body movements, especially small aimless gestures with the hands. It thus refers to an outward sign of inward nervousness or apprehension: The *fidgety* professor played with his eyeglasses as he lectured. *Fidgety* usually applies to people who habitually fidget—fussy people, worriers.

Jittery is also marked by body movements, but it often suggests fright as well as nervousness. A *jittery* condition may be caused by a menacing or dangerous situation: The thieves became *jittery* when they heard the news bulletin describing them accurately. Animals may also be *jittery*: The horses became *jittery* upon hearing thunder.

Excitable and **flighty** are alike in suggesting enduring temperamental qualities of human beings. *Flighty* implies an inability to keep one's attention fixed in a levelheaded manner on any one particular subject. A *flighty* person skips from subject to subject in a *nervous*, virtually random manner that suggests the flitting of a butterfly. It often indicates a shallow mind easily distracted by inconsequential events: The couple's conversation was so *flighty* that there was no way to discover what they were really talking about. An *excitable* person is one who is easily aroused to a high pitch of enthusiasm or emotion. *Excitable* may be applied to persons of either sex, but is usually confined to the young or inexperienced. [He was of an *excitable* nature; at the slightest hint of criticism he would stamp out the door in a rage.]

Uptight is a slang word for *nervous*. In its earlier use among jazz musicians, it referred to a feeling of being so sure of oneself that one could play without sheet music. Through misunderstanding, *uptight* now applies generally to someone who is tense, anxious, or disturbed, either because of a specific problem or a *nervous* disposition: ghetto youngsters who are *uptight* about police brutality; adolescents critical of the *uptight* world of their middle-class parents. See AFRAID, ANXIETY, FLINCH.

Antonyms: IMPERTURBABLE, *self-controlled, self-possessed, steady,* TRANQUIL.

neutralize
counteract
counterbalance
offset

These verbs denote a matching of one extreme with another so that a stable or static situation results. **Neutralize** suggests that this stability is achieved by adding a substance that will cause a change in structure: an alkali that will *neutralize* the excessive acidity of the soil; an antidote to *neutralize* the poison. *Neutralize* often suggests that some danger or threat is rendered harmless: government programs to *neutralize* the effects of poverty. It can also refer, however, to the frustrating of some positive tendency: the doubt and suspicions that surrounded her intentions and *neutralized* all her efforts to make peace.

Counteract is more forceful than *neutralize* because it suggests an act that not only restores things as they were, but may carry the action past that point into the opposite direction: They worked vigorously to *counteract* the community's apathy; pills to *counteract* her anemia by building up her red blood cells. **Counterbalance**, however, suggests an equalizing of one weight by another: *counterbalancing* the demands of labor and management with a concern for the nation's welfare.

Offset suggests most specifically the replacing of something lost by a new thing equivalent to it: trying to *offset* gambling losses by speculation in stocks; The low selling price more than *offset* the disadvantages of the house they bought. See BENEFICIAL, PERMANENT.

news
data
facts
information
intelligence

These nouns denote various types of acquired or derived knowledge. **News** is knowledge of recent events or developments of interest to the public at large, especially as reported in a newspaper or in a radio or television broadcast. *News* may also be the report or broadcast itself. [The *news* from Italy is that spring floods have severely damaged the crops; After dinner we listened to the *news.*] *News* may also concern something one did not previously know, or recent doings of which one hasn't heard. [What you have just told us about plastics made from soybeans is *news* to me; Please write and give me all the *news* about your family.]

Information is the most general term and is applied to any knowledge acquired from observation, from reading or study, or from talking with others. Although such knowledge is often accepted as valid, it may not necessarily be true or accurate. [The old man gathers *information* about his neighbors by spying on them through the window curtains; A hysterical person at the scene of an accident is a poor source of *information* about what actually happened.] *Information* is also timely or specific knowledge about an event or subject of interest. [Hundreds of sources supply *information* about the space program; Before leading the platoon into combat, the lieutenant called headquarters for *information* on the enemy's position.]

Facts are pieces of *information* that are known by observation or proof to be true or real. [Research scientists must work with *facts;* A witness in a murder trial is assumed to know the *facts* in the case.]

Data (the plural of *datum,* a Latin form) is a formal noun for facts or figures that have been gathered systematically and from which conclusions may be drawn: *Data* are usually amassed for scientific and statistical purposes, and the *information* obtained is often fed into a computer for rapid processing. The singular form *datum* is sometimes used by scientists and engineers to mean a single item of information, but it is common to see *data* used as a singular form to mean information or a body of facts: Little *data* is available on the frequency of repair of that car.

Intelligence is now a high-flown and literary term for *information* or *news* that is communicated by or received from another person: Last week we received *intelligence* of the reporter's whereabouts from the consul in Madrid. In a restricted sense, *intelligence* is the collecting of secret *information* about an enemy, as by political police, a government agency, or military authorities: an officer assigned to *intelligence.* The term applies also to the *information* or *facts* so collected as well as to the staff of persons occupied with this process: one of our functions is evaluation of *intelligence* gathered by electronic eavesdropping; Army *intelligence.* See TELL.

Antonyms: *conjecture,* OPINION.

noise

blare
clamor
clatter
din
hubbub
racket
sound
uproar

The nouns **noise** and **sound** are both general terms that designate sensations excited in the ear. *Sound,* the more general, embraces sensations of all qualities, whether loud or soft, pleasant or unpleasant, significant or insignificant: the soft, sibilant *sound* of two young students whispering in class; the horrifying *sound* of a scream in the night; the different *sounds* that two conductors get out of the same orchestra. *Noise,* though more specific than *sound,* is general in its application to all loud, confused, or irritating *sounds. Noise* may consist of high-intensity *sound* from a single source, *sound* that is loud, harsh, sharp, shrill, strident, or grating: the *noise* of a buzz saw; the *noise* of a vacuum cleaner. Or it may be a confused commingling of clashing *sounds:* the *noise* of a construction project, with its hammering and drilling, the whine of machinery, the shouts of the laborers. In one sense, *noise* is part of the unnoticed natural background of existence: office *noises.* In another sense, *noise* may designate distracting *sounds* that annoy because of special sensitivity or circumstances. [The *noise* of children eating popcorn spoiled the movie's most dramatic scene; Please stop rocking your chair—you're making too much *noise.*] *Noise* may also be applied to neutral *sounds* that are merely perceived and noted: the soothing *noise* of water falling; She continually makes groaning *noises* in her sleep.

Din denotes loud *noise* that goes on without letup, often with maddening or deafening effect. It implies an inescapable onslaught of *sound,* sometimes involving an assault on the eardrums: the thunderous *din* of a gong; the earsplitting *din* of a factory. **Blare** is a loud, brassy *sound* of constant, unremitting intensity. It impinges on privacy and preoccupies the consciousness: the *blare* of a loud radio; the *blare* of a car horn that will not shut off. **Clatter** indicates a rattling *sound* or a rapid succession of short, sharp *noises:* the *clatter* of a wagon on cobblestones; the *clatter* of a typewriter.

Hubbub designates a general, confused *noise,* as of many voices heard simultaneously: the *hubbub* in the courtroom before the judge calls for order; the *hubbub* of the stock exchange. *Hubbub* may also refer to any *noise* arising from hustle and bustle: He tried to make himself heard above the *hubbub* of a busy intersection. **Clamor** implies a loud outcry kept up by insistent voices. It is often expressive of a vehement public protest or demand: the furious *clamor* of the hungry mob; the *clamor* of the press for reform; the public *clamor* for repeal of the law. But *clamor* may also apply to any noisy commotion or confusion of *sounds:* the *clamor* of children scuffling in the schoolyard; the *clamor* of noisy bluejays and chirping chickadees. **Uproar** refers to an unrestrained outpouring of *sound,* as in outraged shouting, clamorous protest, or boisterous laughter. It implies the spread of turbulence, agitation, or excitement through a crowd, with a consequent eruption of *noise* and disorder. [The judge's motion to dismiss the charges threw the courtroom into an *uproar;* The class fell into *uproarious* laughter over the professor's Freudian slip.] **Racket** implies *clatter, clamor,* or commotion—a loud, percussive *sound* or a confused combination of *noises* that can rapidly get on one's nerves: the *racket* of hammering; The boys are making such a *racket* that I can't hear myself think. See LOUD, MONOTONOUS.

Antonyms: *calm, hush, quiet, silence, tranquillity.*

noisome. Do not confuse the adjective *noisome* with the noun *noise. Noisome* means harmful, noxious, evil smelling, offensive.

novel

    fiction
    romance
    story

These nouns denote extended works of imaginative prose. **Novel**, the most specific and exact of these terms, refers to any work that normally has a plot, characters, action, and dialogue but that does not refer to real people or events: bestselling *novels;* those who consider *Don Quixote* the first full-length *novel.* By contrast, **fiction** is more general, since it is the group term for all forms of imaginative prose, including the short story, the novella, and the *novel.* Since the *novel* is in one sense the most important form of *fiction,* however, the group term is often used with a special pertinence to this one form: a poor season for *fiction* thus far, in that no new major *novel* has yet appeared.

Romance is more difficult to pin down to an exact meaning. A related word in German is equivalent to our word *novel,* reflecting the development of the *novel* out of accounts of fabulous or legendary materials in the Middle Ages. In literary discussions, *romance* is often restricted to works showing this emphasis on the fabulous or legendary, or it may be used more broadly to apply to *novels* with a strong mythic or allegorical bent: Malory's gathering together and rewriting of the Arthurian *romances;* Hawthorne's *novels* seen as being essentially *romances.* Contrary to a misconception, *romance* would never in literate use refer merely to *fiction* that concerns itself with love affairs.

While **story** most commonly is an abbreviated way of referring to an established form, the short *story,* it is sometimes used loosely and informally for any work of *fiction* with narrative thrust: novelists who concentrate on telling *stories* filled with physical violence. *Story* is

also sometimes applied to the plot element of any *fiction:* a paragraph giving the *story* of the *novel.* See NARRATIVE, POETRY.

Antonyms: *nonfiction.*

numb

    anesthetized
    deadened
    insensible
    paralyzed
    stupefied

These adjectives describe a loss of sensation, ability to move, or mental responsiveness. **Numb**, the most informal, is primarily related to loss of sensation brought about by any means whatever: hands that were *numb* with cold; her tongue still *numb* from the novocaine; a leg *numb* from his having sat so long in one position. More metaphorically, *numb* suggests loss of emotional affect or mental alertness: tragic news that left him *numb;* looking at the questionnaire with *numb* bewilderment. **Anesthetized** is the most formal and most specific of these terms, referring to loss of sensation, if not of movement or consciousness as well it specifically suggests a medical use of drugs intended to make someone incapable of feeling pain: taking a pulse count of the *anesthetized* patient; the *anesthetized* side of her mouth. Used metaphorically, it functions much like *numb,* but with greater intensity: wondering if his dull, *anesthetized* manner was the result of an unhappy love affair.

Deadened may indicate, more informally, an *anesthetized* condition: drilling the *deadened* tooth. In other uses it is more like *numb,* but may suggest a partial or complete loss of sensation or movement: hearing that had been *deadened* slightly by the blast; nerve damage that had permanently *deadened* both legs. In terms of mental responsiveness, *deadened* suggests an acutely apathetic and depressed state of discouragement or hopelessness: minds *deadened* by conformity; *deadened* expectations. **Paralyzed** takes up one aspect of *deadened* exclusively, referring to a loss of ability to move: learning to walk with a brace on the *paralyzed* leg. Used of emotions or mental states, it suggests the absence of will or the inability to function: *paralyzed* with fear. It can even be used jocosely for total unconsciousness: drinking until they were *paralyzed.*

Insensible, at its most formal and precise, refers exclusively to loss of sensation: a local anesthetic used to render the area *insensible* to pain. More loosely, it can suggest resistance to rigorous sensation: Eskimos amazingly *insensible* to cold. In another context, it refers to unawareness, rather than to loss of sensation: talking on, *insensible* to her forbidding frown. It may also refer to complete unconsciousness: falling *insensible* to the floor. It has little application to mental states. This contrasts sharply with **stupefied**, which is almost exclusively restricted to describing states of shock or incoherence: *stupefied* with disbelief; giving the alarm clock a *stupefied* scowl. It contrasts with *numb* and *anesthetized* in this context by stressing surprise or mental befuddlement rather than a draining away of feeling. It contrasts with *deadened* by stressing confusion of mind rather than dullness. And it contrasts with *paralyzed* by suggesting a partial, though bleared, consciousness rather than a nonfunctioning one. See IMPASSIVE, LISTLESS, SLOTH.

Antonyms: *AWARE, LIVELY.*

nurse

> care for
> mind
> minister
> tend

These verbs share the meaning of looking after or taking care of someone or something. **Nurse** is specifically applied to looking after the sick, injured, or infirm: Her husband patiently *nursed* her back to health after the heart attack. In this sense it implies intimate care and close, devoted supervision, although it may also refer to a more formal and professional relationship, as that between a trained nurse and a patient. **Tend** may imply devoted concern, but it is a concern based more upon a sense of duty, charity, or religious conviction than upon a personal feeling for the individual being helped. [It is the duty of physicians to *tend* the sick; The medic selflessly *tended* (or, more informally, *tended to*) the wounded soldiers before dressing his own wound.] *Tend* may also apply to things, thus emphasizing its essentially impersonal connotation: to *tend* machinery; to *tend* a furnace.

Minister is close in meaning to *tend* and *nurse*, but today it may sound somewhat rhetorical or stuffy when applied exclusively to the care of the sick. *Minister* is more often applied nowadays to general wants, especially to spiritual succor, and even in such contexts is more formal than *tend* or *nurse*. [An elected representative must *minister* to the needs and aspirations of the community, city, and state; As doctors *minister* to the body, so do members of the clergy *minister* to the spirit or soul.]

Care for is the most general term of this group. In the sense here considered, it can mean looking after all the needs of a child, *tending* an invalid, *nursing* a convalescent back to health, or *ministering* to the unwell: The foster mother *cared for* those boys as faithfully as if they had been her own sons.

In the sense being compared here, **mind** means look after, watch over, or take care of. It most often suggests a temporary charge rather than a permanent devotion: to *mind* someone's children; to *mind* sheep; to *mind* a store while the owner is at lunch. See PAMPER, PROTECT.

Antonyms: *SLIGHT.*

obedient

dutiful
good
well-behaved

These adjectives are alike in meaning morally or intellectually disposed to respect authority or custom and to follow the dictates thereof. **Obedient** stresses an acknowledgment of the authority vested in some person, organization, etc., The common usage of *obedient* in reference to children suggests the nature of the compliance implicit in the word: a soldier who refused to be blindly *obedient* to the commands of an ignorant superior. Alone among the adjectives considered here, *obedient* has an extended application to physical objects that respond to or act in accordance with some superior force or natural law: a ship *obedient* to the wheel. **Dutiful**, even more than *obedient*, suggests the influence of outside conditions, such as customs or ethical demands. *Dutiful* men and women have a strong sense of respect or obligation: a *dutiful* child; a *dutiful* parent

While *obedient* and *dutiful* connote a manner of acting dependent upon external circumstances, **good** refers to behavior that is the result of inner demands. Thus, *good* children are docile by nature; they are easy to manage or teach because of their own inclinations. A *good* worker, in the context of this comparison, is one who follows instructions because of a personal desire to please and do what is expected.

Someone who is **well behaved** may be that way because of training or because of his or her makeup. Yet, the suggestion of outside influence is strong; *well behaved* is used to characterize the kind of conduct that has standards established by the society in which a person lives: The young teacher was pleased to have a class that appeared more than usually *well behaved*. See ADAPTABLE, COMPLIANT, DOCILE, MALLEABLE.

Antonyms: *MISCHIEVOUS, STUBBORN.*

obligation

duty
function
office
responsibility

These nouns are comparable in denoting that which one is bound to fulfill or perform. **Obligation** refers generally to anything one is compelled to do, or to forbear from doing, by law, contract, promise, morality, or the like. It often implies immediate pressure to carry out or to refrain from a particular action: a legal *obligation* to serve the nation. **Duty** is often used interchangeably with *obligation,* but it more often refers to that which springs from an interior moral or ethical impulse rather than from external demands: He volunteered for the dangerous mission out of a sense of *duty. Duty* is applied to a particular task and frequently has a more general reference than *obligation:* to put *duty* before pleasure. **Function** refers to activity demanded by one's position, profession, or the like. It focuses on objective purpose, as discharged in the performance of particular *duties:* She managed to perform the *functions* of a teacher but without any inspiration at all. **Office**, as here considered, refers to the services, *functions,* or *duties* connected with a position of trust. [He swore to faithfully discharge the *office* of vice president; reconciled through the good *offices* of their attorney.] **Responsibility** refers to any *obligation, duty, function,* or *office,* for the fulfillment of which one may be called upon to answer to a particular person, the public in general, or a Divine Being: It is the *responsibility* of the President of the United States to defend and uphold the Constitution. See COMPEL, RESPONSIBLE, STINT.

Antonyms: *RIGHT.*

oblivious

absentminded
abstracted
inattentive

These adjectives describe a mind that is lost in thought, lacks alertness or awareness, or is given over to some matter other than the one at hand. **Oblivious** stresses lack of awareness, either because of deep thought or poor concentration: so fascinated with solving the problem that he was *oblivious* to the odd looks his fellow passengers were giving him; wandering thoughts that made him *oblivious* to the question the teacher had just asked. **Inattentive** stresses exclusively this last possibility of *oblivious,* indicating an inability to keep the mind focused on the subject before it: *inattentive* to the demonstration the diving instructor was making. This inability can be the result of restlessness, distraction, weak intellectual powers, or even a willful indifference to detail: children who grow *inattentive* during long class periods; a bored programmer, *inattentive* while making corrections.

Abstracted stresses a mind far removed from mundane considerations before it, especially because of obsessive or intrusive thoughts and feelings: so *abstracted* by the beauty of the sunset that they quite forgot how soon night would fall; the *abstracted* smile the widow gave other mourners at the funeral. **Absentminded** may function exactly like *abstracted* at a more informal level. More importantly, however, it is unique among these adjectives in pointing to a fixed or ingrained tendency to lose one's bearings because of intrusive concerns: the typical *absentminded* professor, rapt in solving an equation while crossing the campus; An *absentminded* movement of his hand caused the goblet to tip over. See FORGET, PREOCCUPIED.

Antonyms: AWARE, OBSERVANT.

obnoxious

hateful
odious
offensive

The adjectives listed here describe a person or thing that arouses dislike, distaste, hostility, or opposition. **Obnoxious** is used to refer to that which is extremely disagreeable or even disgusting to one's personal feelings, ideas, or tastes. Very often the reasons for viewing something as *obnoxious* are subjective, but they are nonetheless strong enough to make one try to avoid the *obnoxious* person or thing. [I can't stand him—he's a thoroughly *obnoxious* young man who thinks he knows it all.]

Hateful and **odious** describe that which excites intense dislike or aversion, the former usually suggesting an attendant feeling of enmity, the latter associated with contempt or repugnance. Although these adjectives are sometimes used interchangeably, *hateful* implies an angry mental response to something that outrages or arouses violent antipathy: the *hateful* animosity of bigots. *Odious* often suggests something so disgusting that it evokes a physical as well as a moral or intellectual response: getting sick to one's stomach upon reading of the *odious* atrocities committed in some countries of Central America.

Offensive is the mildest term in this list. It has wide application and can be used to characterize anyone or anything that is unpleasant or disagreeable: the *offensive* sight of garbage in an apartment hallway; a series of *offensive* remarks that finally led to a bitter argument. See CONTEMPTIBLE, DEPRAVED, REPREHENSIBLE, REPULSIVE.

Antonyms: HUMANE, *lovable*, PLEASING.

obscure

abstruse
arcane
cryptic
recondite

These adjectives characterize things kept secret or hidden, or things difficult to perceive or understand. **Obscure**, the most general and least formal, is now most often used to indicate things indistinct or difficult to grasp, although it still may reflect its derivation from a root meaning dark. [The letters of the sign were made *obscure* by rain; *obscure,* involuted reasoning that thoroughly confuses students; a path that grew more and more *obscure* as the light faded.] When the reference is to understanding, *obscure* may imply disapproval because something is not clear: misled by the deliberately *obscure* language of the contract. *Obscure* may, however, refer with greater neutrality to something that is not clear, without necessarily implying any intent to confuse: allusions that were apparent in Shakespeare's own time but have long since become *obscure.*

Cryptic and **arcane** specifically stress things that are hidden or that have been deliberately made remote from easy understanding. *Arcane* can refer to something kept secret as a mystery: *arcane* religious symbols only the high priest could interpret. More generally, it may refer to a purposely pedantic reliance on *obscure* references in order to show off one's learning; in this sense, like *obscure*, *arcane* can carry a disapproving tone: *arcane* footnotes that not even a specialist in the field could be expected to understand. *Cryptic* may refer to the occult, but more generally it indicates something enigmatic or puzzling, often something deliberately made to seem meaningless, except to the initiate: *cryptic* signs and handclasps that were part of the lodge's ritual. *Cryptic* may also refer to something too brief to be understood: a *cryptic,* one-word clue.

Abstruse and **recondite** may refer to things secret, hidden, or difficult to grasp, but their special area of usage here is in referring to scholarly complexity. *Abstruse* suggests a formal or learned style filled with difficulties that tax the mind: *abstruse* legal documents that supported his claim to the office. *Recondite* is even more emphatic about the difficulty or complexity of a study or approach: needing fewer *recondite* books on the subject and more that might help ordinary people understand the new discoveries. Hence, by extension, *recondite* can refer to knowledge remote from the mainstream and accessible only to a few authorities: the *recondite* teachings of a

minor medieval philosopher. See MYSTICAL, VAGUE.
Antonyms: CLEAR, *explicit,* PLAIN, *transparent.*

obsequious
    abject
    menial
    servile
    slavish
    subservient
    sycophantic

These adjectives apply to persons guilty of, or to behavior characterized by, excessive deference, flattery, imitation, or obedience. **Obsequious** shares with **abject** an awareness of low station or a feeling of low self-esteem that reveals itself in fawning behavior. *Obsequious* strongly suggests an attitude consciously assumed in order to placate a superior in hopes of getting what one wants, or to escape unpleasant consequences: serfs who bowed with *obsequious* politeness to members of the gentry; a failing student who was maddeningly *obsequious* to her teacher. *Abject* conveys the sense of being cast down in spirits or a loss of self-respect that results in a humiliated cringing or a pitiable fawning on others: to make an *abject* apology even though one is not at fault; a beggar so *abject* that he plucks at the sleeves of passersby. In a related sense, *abject* designates something unusually degraded or wretched: the *abject* poverty of millions of people in Africa.

Sycophantic is sometimes used interchangeably with *obsequious,* but is more strongly pejorative. *Sycophantic* suggests a parasitical and self-seeking relationship to someone in a superior position, rather than an attitude of sincere respect: a dictator's *sycophantic* yes men; the *sycophantic* fans who surround a movie star.

Menial, **servile**, and **slavish** are applied to extremely *abject* persons or behavior. In former times, when class distinctions were more pronounced and rigid, these adjectives were applied as a matter of course to those at the bottom of the scale: a *menial* servant; a *servile* jester; a *slavish* retainer. Nowadays, these terms are more likely to be applied to actions or attitudes: his *menial* unobtrusiveness; *servile* obedience; *slavish* attention to the needs of others.

Subservient is a somewhat weaker synonym for the other terms in suggesting truckling or servility. It is more often used to refer to a person who properly serves as a subordinate or, more commonly, to a thing that has been used to promote some end or purpose. See FAWN, FLINCH.

Antonyms: *contumelious, impudent,* OVERBEARING.

observant
    alert
    attentive
    aware
    discerning
    perceptive

These adjectives characterize someone with a sharp eye for detail or a keen ability to discern the real meaning of a situation. **Observant** suggests someone who notices details another person might miss: Only the most *observant* spectator would have known which player had the ball. **Discerning** and **perceptive** include this emphasis of *observant*, but add to it an ability to evaluate or understand the observed details. *Discerning* stresses the ability to tell apart two or more similar things—or to evaluate slight differences by means of one's inherent good taste: the *discerning* reader who shuns bad imitations of last year's bestsellers. *Perceptive* stresses the ability to understand or make understandable the details one has observed: a *perceptive* comment on programs needed to combat illegal drug use.

Attentive resembles *observant* more than *discerning* and *perceptive;* it stresses the ability to concentrate on a matter without distraction or wavering of any kind: students who suddenly become *attentive* in the week before exams; congressmen who are *attentive* to the wishes of their constituents. **Aware** and **alert** also resemble *observant,* but they are more general than the other adjectives here. In a different context, *aware* can point merely to being conscious; here, however, it suggests acute responsiveness to other people or to one's surroundings: discussing how they could become more *aware* of each other's problems. *Alert* is similar to, but an intensification of, *aware;* it suggests a sharp, highly receptive state of mind that is on the lookout for some event to occur, especially a dangerous or threatening event: so *alert* that not a single error in the report slipped past her; *alert* for any sign of change in the critically ill patient. See DISCRIMINATE, KEEN, VISION, WISDOM.

Antonyms: OBLIVIOUS, PREOCCUPIED, *unaware, unmindful.*

obsessed
    addicted
    addictive

obsessed *(continued)*

compulsive
disciplined
obsessive

In the general sense of being independent of or contrary to a person's conscious will, these adjectives have both a popular and a technical use.

To be **obsessed** is to be excessively troubled, disturbed, worried, or preoccupied by virtually anything at any time, anywhere, for whatever reason or cause. [He was *obsessed* by fear of contracting AIDS; The thought of losing the large order *obsessed* the sales manager.] **Obsessive** implies a similar mental state but carries the idea of some deep character defect or personality maladjustment requiring careful, often extended psychiatric attention. Thus, one may be temporarily *obsessed* by unpaid bills or a forgotten address, but have a persistent *obsessive* fear of debt or of losing one's memory.

Compulsive suggests an insistent, unwanted, and repetitive emotion, attitude, or activity that has little relation to normal standards of behavior and whose omission leads to acute mental distress: a *compulsive* need to wash one's hands or rearrange furniture; *compulsive* eating; a *compulsive* striving for perfection. In this sense it is usually linked with *obsessive* as a psychiatric term for a large number of mental disorders: an *obsessive-compulsive* neurosis.

Disciplined is comparable to the other adjectives in this group chiefly as it implies submission to controls imposed either by some outside authority or by oneself. The submission may be involuntary or enforced: *disciplined* prisoners of war. It may also be consciously accepted as a means to some personal end: a *disciplined* course of action; *disciplined* behavior toward one's superiors.

Addicted and **addictive** both suggest a strong attachment to or dependence upon something. *Addicted* may often mean little more than a persistent devotion to some form of socially acceptable activity or pursuit: *addicted* to the theater, to sports, to reading or travel. Usually, however, *addicted* suggests an emotional or physical dependence incompatible with normal behavior: *addicted* to drugs or alcohol. Such dependence is emphasized by *addictive,* which has come to mean habit-forming in a bad or unhealthful sense: *addictive* drugs; *addictive* narcotics.

Antonyms: *instinctive, natural,* SPONTANEOUS.

obstacle

bar
barricade
barrier
difficulty
hurdle
impediment
snag

These nouns denote anything that checks or halts progress, either in a literal or a figurative sense. **Obstacle**, **barrier**, and **hurdle** present the most trouble in overcoming. An *obstacle* is something one must either remove or go around before being able to proceed. [A huge tree blown down by the storm was an *obstacle* to traffic; Poor grades may be an *obstacle* to playing varsity sports.] A *barrier* is an *obstacle* or obstruction that temporarily impedes progress, but is not necessarily impassable. [Writers never tire of depicting the *barriers* that arise between parents and growing children; The thick walls and moats of castles were built as *barriers* against attackers.] A *hurdle* is a *barrier* that one must surmount in order to continue. *Hurdle* usually suggests challenge and a good probability of success: Inventors face many *hurdles* before their brain-children reach the market as salable products.

A **bar** may be either a physical *obstacle* or a condition that prevents entry or passage: the *bars* of the lion cage; race, color, and creed as *bars* to membership. A **barricade** is always a physical *obstacle* and is usually conceived of as being a hastily erected *barrier* against advancing soldiers, rioters, or large crowds: Man the *barricades!*

Impediment suggests something that, so to speak, entangles the feet and interferes seriously with freedom of action or movement. There is a tendency to view an *impediment* as more or less permanent. [His severe speech *impediment* made it nearly impossible for him to be understood; Legal insanity is an *impediment* to making contracts.]

Snag is literally part of a dead tree that, lodged under the surface of a body of water, may damage boats. Figuratively, *snag* points to a hidden *obstacle* one comes upon without warning and which is annoying or troublesome but rarely serious: Their plans for going into business sound ideal, but there is sure to be a *snag* somewhere.

Difficulty is the most general of the nouns in this group and may be applied loosely to any troublesome state of affairs: to have *difficulty* in learning higher mathematics; the *difficulty* of driving a car through deep mud; to have financial *difficulties*. See EFFORT, THWART.

Antonyms: *help.*

occasional

infrequent
rare
scattered
sporadic
uncommon

These adjectives characterize things or actions that do not occur often. **Occasional** means happening now and then at irregular intervals, and it carries the idea that recurrence can be expected: to make *occasional* trips to a museum; to attend an *occasional* cocktail party. **Infrequent** means occurring at greater intervals, and it neither suggests nor precludes recurrence: Total solar eclipses are *infrequent*.

Rare and **uncommon** go a step further than *occasional* and *infrequent* in that they are applied to that which is met with so seldom as to approach the unique. [It is *rare* to find wisdom in the young; Snow in Florida is an *uncommon* sight; The prothonotary warbler is a *rare* bird in this state; That was an *uncommon* act of charity.] *Rare* has the added sense of precious: a *rare* medieval manuscript; a *rare* sapphire.

Scattered and **sporadic** both mean occurring in space or time in an irregular or random pattern. *Scattered* emphasizes things that are part of a group but have large, unequal spaces between them: *scattered* homesteads on the Nebraska plains; *scattered* showers; *scattered* applause from a bored audience. On the other hand, *sporadic* describes things that occur here and there with little or no continuity: *sporadic* outbreaks of smallpox; *sporadic* sniper fire from rooftops.

Antonyms: *frequent*, INVARIABLE, *often*, USUAL.

odious. Do not confuse the adjective *odious* (detestable, hateful) with the adjective *odorous* (smelly).

odorous. Do not confuse the adjective *odorous* (smelly) with the adjective *odious* (detestable, hateful).

offer

bid
present
proffer
propose
tender
volunteer

All these verbs involve making services available or giving suggestions. **Offer** is the most general; each of the other, more specialized verbs isolates one facet of its total possibilities. *Offer* and **volunteer** may both refer to a generous extending of aid, services, or a desired item. This generosity may or may not follow a specific request from someone who is, in any case, free to reject or accept the gift: *offering* to do the dishes; freely *volunteering* information to the timid tourist. When a request precedes the act of *offering* or *volunteering*, the implied situation is usually that of someone asking one or more members of a group to perform a task. Those who *volunteer* agree by free choice rather than by submission to selection or command: only two trainees naive enough to *volunteer* for extra duty.

Offer and **bid** share the context of a competitive attempt to close a contract. Here, the very opposite of a generous and spontaneous giving is indicated: *offering* the dealer five dollars less than the asking price on the radio; *bidding* low deliberately in the hope that no one would bid more. Usually, the act of *bidding* follows a request or invitation, but the *bid* would be accepted only if its terms were the most advantageous of those received. The one who *offers* or *bids*, however, is committed to the stated terms if acceptance follows.

Offer, **propose**, and **present** all share the context of putting forward ideas or suggestions in argument or discussion. *Propose* can also be used in a contractual situation, as in *proposing* marriage, in which case no previous request is implied and no following acceptance or rejection is certain. But the one who *proposes* something is bound to follow through if accepted. In the context of argument or discussion, however, *propose* and *offer* indicate a much more tentative situation, implying that a course of action has been suggested or a new idea brought forward not so much to be accepted or rejected as to be explored and possibly shaped by further discussion: *offering* a new slant on the problem; *proposing* several possibilities for coping with the crisis; *presenting* the pertinent facts without comment. In any case, *propose* implies at least temporary advocacy of an idea, whereas *present* suggests a much greater tentativeness still; indeed, a debater may *present* an argument for the express purpose of refuting it.

Present also has applications comparable to *offer* that range outside the context of discussion. Both suggest humility in certain courteous phrases: *offer* my condolences; *present* my apologies. Both may indicate bringing something forward for display or appreciation: the same producer who *offered* you last year's greatest hit; *presenting* six new productions in the fall season. *Present* and *offer* here suggest generosity, but if the public must pay admission to see what is displayed, these verbs can become unpleasantly self-congratulatory and euphemistic.

Proffer and **tender**, now going out of fashion, were once used to suggest something *proposed* or *offered* in a deferential way. They still are used in some extremely formal phrases: *proffer* my regrets; *tender* my resignation. Their use in other situations might now seem affected or coy. See TELL.

Antonyms: *FORSWEAR, REJECT, withhold.*

officious. Do not confuse the adjective *officious* (asserting one's authority) with the adjective *official* (pertaining to a position of authority).

old
aged
elderly
matriarchal
patriarchal
senile
superannuated
venerable

These adjectives describe persons who have passed youth and middle age. **Old**, the most general, has the widest range of application. It may indicate strictly chronological age, referring to the latter part of life: *old* age; an *old* man. But it may also focus on the negative qualities associated with *old* age, as loss of health, strength, or motivating force: He was *old* at forty, but she still has her youthful spirit at seventy-five. **Aged** often indicates a longer life span than *old,* applying to persons of very advanced years; it is more formal than *old* as well as more limited in application. Specifically, it often points to changes wrought by aging, suggesting physical decline, though not necessarily implying disability: an *aged* man advancing slowly, with the aid of a cane; an *aged* crone. In a social context, the designation home for the *aged* has largely replaced the plain (or blunt) term *old* folks' home; the former may be preferred because it more easily suggests debilitation that might demand institutional care. **Elderly** is more favorable than either of the foregoing. It is a polite term, often connoting the dignity rather than the weight of years: their *elderly* parents. An *elderly* person has passed middle age but is generally regarded as younger than an *old* person, both in age and in vigor: a resort hotel catering to *elderly* couples; an *elderly* gentleman with a twinkle in his eye.

Superannuated and **senile** stress the negative aspects of aging. *Superannuated* emphasizes the idea of being considered too *old* to continue in one's job. In a specific sense, a *superannuated* person is one who has been retired because he or she has passed an arbitrary age limit, such as sixty-five: a *superannuated* pensioner. In an extended sense, *superannuated* means too *old* to be useful or efficient and has a disparaging tone: *superannuated* election workers, half-blind and hard of hearing but given jobs at the polls by party officials. *Senile* implies a much more marked incapacity or decline. A person may be *aged* or *superannuated* without being *senile*. *Senile*, from the Latin word for *old*, points to mental or physical infirmity accompanying extreme *old* age. *Senile* atrophy, for example, involves a wasting away of tissue and a consequent emaciation of the body. Most specifically, however, in general use, *senile* stresses the enfeebling effects of age on the mind. [She has grown *senile*—her memory is going and she is in her dotage; He is as *old* as she, but his mind is as keen and clear as ever.]

Venerable, **matriarchal**, and **patriarchal** stress the positive aspects of aging. *Venerable* emphasizes the reverence, respect, and deference owed to one's elders. It focuses on the dignity of advanced age, implying that the person held in reverence is worthy of veneration, as because of wisdom, position, or achievement: a *venerable* father; a *venerable* sage. *Venerable* can also suggest a distinguished appearance: *venerable* white hair. *Patriarchal* and *matriarchal*, respectively, mean like a patriarch or matriarch—the leader of a family or progenitor of a community or group. Both are close synonyms of *venerable* but carry overtones of power and authority, such as might be exercised by an ecclesiastical leader. [The head of the firm was a *matriarchal* old woman who struck awe in her underlings; an actor with a hoary beard and *patriarchal* bearing, often cast in Biblical epics; a *patriarchal* tribal chief.] See MATURE (v.), MATURE (adj.), REVERE, WEAK.

Antonyms: *adolescent, boyish, girlish, juvenescent, young, youthful.*

old-fashioned
antediluvian
antiquated
archaic

obsolescent
obsolete
out-of-date
passé

These adjectives characterize anything time has passed by because of its age, inefficiency, or displacement by something superior, or because of changing tastes. **Old-fashioned** suggests that something has gone out of use because of an arbitrary change of custom: *old-fashioned* platform shoes for women. *Old-fashioned* can also suggest a change in technology rather than in taste: *old-fashioned* 78 rpm phonograph records. It does not necessarily imply that the outmoded or superseded thing in question no longer exists physically: the *old-fashioned* wedding dress she had treasured for twenty years. Sometimes, *old-fashioned* can nostalgically describe something valued for its quaintness, its formality, or its wholesome simplicity: the high prices still paid for *old-fashioned* Tiffany lampshades; an *old-fashioned* wedding with all the trimmings; plain, *old-fashioned* home cooking.

Out-of-date and **passé** share with *old-fashioned* an emphasis on an arbitrary change of taste and style. *Out-of-date* is descriptive and neutral and may refer to a lack of factual validity as well as to a change of taste; *passé* carries a tinge of contempt for something no longer in vogue: statistics that rapidly become *out-of-date;* full of *passé* notions about which hair styles are chic and sophisticated.

Antediluvian, literally before the Flood, is a hyperbole for ideas more neutrally expressed by **antiquated** and **archaic**. *Antiquated* suggests the continued existence of something very old and now functioning badly, if not already superseded by a more efficient or useful arrangement: an *antiquated,* treadle-operated sewing machine. *Archaic* may also suggest something old but still surviving; in this sense, it implies a given period in the past and can be used solely to classify rather than to evaluate: the *archaic* dress of the Amish; a statue carved in the *archaic* manner. In other senses, *archaic* refers to something extremely old and not now in general use; in this case it can be a more formal or technical substitute for *old-fashioned:* many *archaic* declensions that were abandoned during the development of the language. The hyperbolic *antediluvian* is mostly used humorously for any of these meanings of *antiquated* or *archaic,* with the added suggestion, when it pertains to ideas, of an extremely conservative or reactionary temper: an economic policy as *antediluvian* as a troglodyte.

Obsolete and **obsolescent** refer to different moments in the same process. *Obsolete* indicates what has already passed totally from use or adherence or what has been completely superseded; *obsolescent* points to what is now passing away: The death penalty for theft in Western society has long been *obsolete,* but for graver crimes it is only now becoming *obsolescent. Obsolescent,* as well, has a special reference to arbitrary modifications of a product that are deliberately introduced not to increase its usefulness but to make earlier models seem *passé:* Automobiles were formerly designed to become *obsolescent* in a single year.

Obsolete, obsolescent, and *archaic* are all applied to words that are now seldom or never used. An *obsolete* word is no longer used either in speech or writing, usually because it has been supplanted by a different word: Oscitate, meaning yawn, is now *obsolete.* An *obsolescent* word, though still in use, is becoming *obsolete.* Much modern slang rapidly becomes *obsolescent. Archaic* words were current at some time in the past, and appear in literature and in the Bible. Unlike *obsolete* words they are still used, either for effect, because they have an unmistakable flavor of their period or milieu, or else by persons whose vocabularies were formed in a distinctively earlier era. "Methinks" and "I trow" are *archaic.* See ANCIENT, UNUSUAL.

Antonyms: *à la mode, avant-garde,* MODERN, STYLISH.

opening

aperture
gap
interstice
orifice

These nouns all denote an empty space or a hole in something. **Opening**, the most general, refers to any vacant or unobstructed space, as a hole or passage. It can be substituted for each of the other nouns here considered in many contexts: an *opening* cut in a fence for pedestrians to be able to watch the construction going on in an excavation; an *opening* in the ground serving as a sump. An *opening* in a forest is a tract where few or no trees grow. Thus, an *opening* may be either natural or contrived. **Gap** usually applies to a wide crack and suggests a deviation from the normal or regular conformation: a *gap* between two teeth; a *gap* in the wall of the shack. *Gap* is also used abstractly, indicating a break in continuity: a *gap* in one's memory.

Aperture is more formal than *opening* and applies to any *opening* or cleft in a surface, regardless of the nature of the cause: windows regarded as *apertures* in walls; *apertures* in the foliage. The *aperture* of a camera is an *opening,* often adjustable in diameter, through which light enters the lens. **Orifice**, from the Latin word for mouth, refers to an *aperture* or *opening* into a cavity or enclosed place and therefore suggests a point of access or entry: the *orifice* of a chimney; the *orifice* of a test tube; Smoke belched from the *orifice* of the volcano. *Orifice* is much used in medical contexts in reference to *openings* into body cavities. The pulmonary *orifice,* for example, is the *opening* of the pulmonary artery into the heart. **Interstice** is a formal word suitable only in contexts where preciseness of description is necessary. It refers to one of a series of narrow spaces or *openings* between adjoining things or parts. [The *interstices* of a sweater knitted with thick wool are comparatively large; If the *interstices* in a fisherman's net are too large, too many fish will escape through the meshes.] See CRACK, CUT, HOLE, LEAK.

opinion

belief
conviction
estimate
impression
sentiment
view

These nouns designate thoughts or feelings about a subject. **Opinion** ranges from purely personal prejudice to relatively authoritative judgment. At both extremes, however, it implies a prior formulation of ideas or conclusions regarding a matter in dispute or under consideration. At its most individual, it involves evaluation, indicating an expression of personal thought, feeling, preference, or taste. [What is your *opinion* of the latest fashions?] In a more conclusive sense, it may represent an expert judgment in a matter of objective fact or truth. [In the *opinion* of my doctor, I should be well enough to travel by next week.] In all cases, however, *opinion* is carefully distinguished from fact. An *opinion* may be held with confidence, but it still falls short of positive knowledge and is open to challenge. [She sought the *opinion* of several experts, but even they disagreed.] In a broader frame of reference, *opinion* may indicate prevailing ideas many people hold in common: public *opinion*. At its most definite, it designates the formal announcement of the conclusions of a court: the majority *opinion* of the Supreme Court, citing precedents and constitutional principles in support of the decision.

Sentiment and **view** relate to personal *opinion* and frequently appear in the plural. *Sentiment* stresses feeling rather than reason, often indicating an idealistic approach or emotional stand rather than

a pragmatic one. It is now encountered only in certain contexts. [His Fourth of July speech was full of patriotic *sentiments;* the *sentiment* expressed on a greeting card; A competent lawyer will try to assess the *sentiments* of a jury before launching a defense; I agree with you—those are my *sentiments* exactly.] *View* stresses the personal element, emphasizing an individual attitude, approach, or point of focus. [In my *view*, the scheme seems unworkable; a newsletter monitoring congressional *views* on abortion; a novelist's *view* of society.]

Impression and **estimate** stress the element of uncertainty in venturing an *opinion*. An *impression* arises from external factors, whether it leaves its mark on the senses or the mind. It may indicate the first reaction of the mind, before the due consideration that warrants an *opinion,* and may imply a superficial *view* or conclusion: the danger of judging on the basis of first *impressions*. In other cases, *impression* may emphasize vagueness of recollection, or caution and uncertainty in stating a *view*. [My *impression* is that she was lying, but I couldn't swear to it; He had the *impression* they had met before.] Unlike an *impression*, an *estimate* does not reflect an uncertain memory or mind; instead, it involves a personal appraisal or a value judgment. An *estimate* is based on the pertinent facts available at the time, the implication being that other, unknown factors might enter in at a later stage. [The final bill was considerably higher than the contractor's *estimate*.] An *estimate* also involves a consideration of the different aspects of a thing, or a weighing of pros and cons, with the attendant possibility of error in judgment. [After reviewing her first batch of work, what is your *estimate* of her ability?; a critical *estimate* of Henry James.]

Belief and **conviction** are examples of positive *opinion*. A *belief* is something accepted by the mind as being true without certain proof. It may either originate in the mind or be instilled in the mind by others: a child's *belief* that monsters lurk in the dark; a boy's *belief* in Santa Claus. *Belief* has a wide range of application, embracing ideas, theories, philosophies, religious creeds or tenets, and superstitions: a *belief* that men are basically good; the Christian *belief* that Jesus was the son of God; the *belief* that Friday the 13th is unlucky. *Belief* itself may range from simple, unquestioning acceptance to deep emotional involvement: *belief* in a news report; *belief* in a friend's innocence. Sometimes, however, it may convey a lingering uncertainty. [It's my *belief* that she'll succeed, but only time will tell.] A *conviction* is a strong *belief* arising from a deep-seated feeling of certainty. *Conviction* often implies the overcoming of previous doubt or skepticism. [The voyage of Columbus to America was based on a *conviction* that the world was round; to have the courage of one's *convictions*.] See BELIEVABLE, EMOTION, IDEA, SUPPOSE.

opponent

adversary
antagonist
competitor
enemy
foe
rival

These nouns all designate a person or thing that opposes or is hostile to another person or thing. **Opponent**, the most general term in the group, designates a person engaged in some kind of disagreement, competition, opposition, or conflict. Because of the wide range of uses for *opponent*, it cannot be said by definition that an *opponent* is hostile or not hostile; only the context in question can determine this qualification. [The two women had become fast friends when they were *opponents* in a chess tournament; *Opponents* of the proposed legislation defeated it in a bitter fight on the Senate floor.] **Antagonist**, unlike *opponent*, can refer to an impersonal agent: Science and superstition are eternal *antagonists*. When applied to a person, however, *antagonist* suggests more hostility or sharper opposition than *opponent* does: His political *antagonist* was determined to use every possible means to defeat the governor's bid for reelection. **Adversary**, like *opponent* and *antagonist*, is a general word with a wide range of application. [The district attorney has a kind of intuition that makes her a formidable courtroom *adversary*; Army and Notre Dame always are worthy *adversaries* on the gridiron.] But *adversary* usually suggests a person or side that not only opposes another in fact, but does so with hostility or malignity: The two countries were ancient *adversaries* and had gone to war against each other many times.

Rival and **competitor** both denote a person who seeks the same object or end for which another is striving, but whereas a *competitor* may be impersonal and contend without hostility, a *rival* is usually motivated by feelings that can make him or her inimical or malicious. [The small store owner often welcomes a nearby *competitor* to stimulate business; The two men were not only *rivals* for the same job but also for the same woman, a situation that caused extreme ill will between them.]

An **enemy** is most often a person who is moved by feelings of animosity to an attempt to harm or destroy: Because of the family feud, the two cousins were *enemies* from birth. *Enemy* can, however, suggest opposition without hostility, or merely a feeling of dislike. [Smog is the *enemy* of healthy lungs; She seems to have more *enemies* than friends.] In military language, all who fight on the opposite side are referred to as *enemies*, or, collectively, as the *enemy*. No personal animosity is implicit when *enemy* is used in such contexts; individual ill feeling may or may not exist. **Foe** is much like *enemy* in definition, but it is more literary in tone. It suggests a hostile spirit and purpose in all contexts except the most impersonal. [The U.S. and Germany were bitter *foes* in two world wars; Ignorance is the *foe* of progress.] See COMPETE, ENMITY, OPPOSED.

Antonyms: *ASSOCIATE, FRIEND.*

opportune

advantageous
convenient
expedient
politic

These adjectives characterize easy, timely, fortunate, or practical actions that promote self-interest and the hope of gain or advancement. **Opportune** has the widest range of application. It may suggest chance action that gives unexpectedly good results: an *opportune* change of plans that placed them far from where the disaster occurred; an accidental encounter that proved *opportune*. More commonly, however, it suggests a conscious choice with an eye to suitability or timing: an *opportune* moment to bid for the vice-presidency. Often, *opportune* suggests action taken to ingratiate or advance oneself; a note of insincerity may sometimes be present: making *opportune* remarks he knew would flatter his superior.

Advantageous lays stress on favorable results; these may be arrived at by chance or design, but the adjective in any case often suggests a self-interested rather than altruistic attitude: happening on the most *advantageous* spot for viewing the sunset; seeking out the most *advantageous* positions from which to attack the enemy; driving the most *advantageous* bargain possible; lobbying for legislation *advantageous* to his backers. **Convenient** suggests considerations of ease and comfort: an apartment *convenient* to subway lines. *Convenient* is often used, however, to suggest that these considerations have outweighed such ethical concerns as truth or fairness: telling *convenient* lies, careless of whom she hurt; *convenient* excuses; *conve-*

nient compromises that would offend no one but accomplish nothing.

Expedient and **politic** refer much more strongly to self-interest. Most neutrally, *expedient* can indicate an improvised or temporary solution taken out of necessity: an *expedient* repair job that would at least get them to the next town. The conflict between self-interest and ethics is amply apparent in most other uses, however: appealing to the city's ethnic minorities as an *expedient* political gesture; twisting the facts outrageously whenever he thought it *expedient*. *Politic* is milder than *expedient*, suggesting actions governed more by immediate practical considerations than by any larger view: those who think it *politic* never to disagree with their employers. *Politic* certainly suggests insincerity and the currying of favor, if not the disregard of ethics possible for *expedient*: another excruciating attempt to be *politic* about his son-in-law's views on current events. See BENEFICIAL, CHANCE, FAVORABLE, OPPORTUNISTIC.

Antonyms: *disadvantageous, idealistic, inconvenient, inexpedient, inopportune, unseasonable, untimely.*

opportunistic
ambitious
aspiring
pushy

These adjectives are comparable in that they all refer to people who desire or are actively striving toward the attainment of some goal. **Opportunistic** describes a person who takes advantage of every opportunity that contributes to achievement of his or her ends, and who is relatively uninfluenced by moral principles or sentiment: an *opportunistic* young man who rose quickly from office boy to office manager by callously using everyone who could further his career. **Ambitious**, like *opportunistic*, is applied to someone who utilizes opportunities but, unlike *opportunistic*, need not always have pejorative connotations. *Ambitious* people may or may not be principled. What they must always be is eager and active in the pursuit of the wealth, power, honors, or whatever else they have chosen as a goal: a talented singer who was not *ambitious* enough to make the grade on Broadway. Someone who is *opportunistic* or *ambitious* might at times be described by the more informal and almost always derogatory term **pushy**. In its application to different people *pushy* may suggest offensiveness, bossiness, or crudeness: a *pushy* social climber; a *pushy* advertising trainee. **Aspiring** is a milder and more neutral adjective than the others in this group. It does not necessarily have the suggestions of drive and energy implicit in *opportunistic* and *ambitious*, and it is certainly devoid of the pejorative connotations in *pushy*. *Aspiring* persons seek something above themselves, as excellence for its own sake, and *aspiring* usually implies lofty ideals: an *aspiring* politician who refused to compromise principles in return for favors from party regulars. See BOLD, OPPORTUNE, RECKLESS.

Antonyms: *indolent, lazy,* TIMID, UNINVOLVED.

opposed
adverse
antagonistic
averse
inimical

These adjectives characterize unfavorable, harmful, or hostile forces, conditions, or opinions. **Opposed**, the most general, is usually applied to persons. It refers to mental resistance or a contrary view, whether or not action is taken against anything. [All *opposed* to the motion made their views known before a vote was taken; One delegation *opposed* to the amendment decided to abstain from the vote so as not to block passage of the main bill.] **Antagonistic**, when applied to persons, indicates a much deeper rancor than *opposed*. It suggests ill feeling, whether smoldering or out in the open: *antagonistic* rivals as contrasted with friendly opponents; a delinquent boy, highly *antagonistic* towards persons in authority. In a less personal sense, *antagonistic* may stress incompatibility of aims: Capitalism and socialism are *antagonistic* economic systems. Used of forces, it may indicate a counteracting or neutralizing effect: *antagonistic* muscular reactions.

Adverse is applied to inanimate forces or conditions that are unpropitious or detrimental, working against the interests of a person or thing: *adverse* winds; *adverse* circumstances; an *adverse* ruling in the lawsuit, denying his claim to compensation. *Adverse* may even point to what is ultimately disastrous or calamitous: *adverse* fortune or fate. **Averse** and **inimical** when used of personal attitudes imply opposition, unfriendliness, or hostility. [She was *averse* to giving an inch in the discussion; We were not *averse* to increasing aid to Third World countries; His attitude is *inimical* to our project; a former colony, now *inimical* to the parent country.] Used of forces and conditions, *inimical* implies a basic conflict of interest or an inherent incompatibility, as between nature and purpose: *inimical* and irreconcilable interests; a climate *inimical* to the development of an agricultural economy. See HOSTILE, OPPONENT.

Antonyms: *compatible, complementary,* FAVORABLE, *friendly, well-disposed.*

optimistic

confident
hopeful
sanguine

These adjectives characterize positive frames of mind. An **optimistic** person is one who cheerfully expects things to work out satisfactorily in the future. This attitude may be grounded in fact or may merely represent a determined attempt to look on the bright side of things regardless of the evidence: unofficial polls that made her *optimistic* about the outcome of the election; still *optimistic* after more than a week adrift that they would be sighted. The *optimistic* attitude may, in fact, be grounded in a fear of facing actualities or in blind faith.

Sanguine emphasizes almost exclusively a habitual frame of mind that anticipates good fortune. It can sometimes suggest an unfounded *optimistic* view that flies in the face of fact: so *sanguine* about the future he didn't bother to work toward realizing his goal. *Sanguine* is more formal than *optimistic.*

Hopeful is not as strong as the previous adjectives; a *hopeful* person may desire a specific outcome without being certain it will come about: still *hopeful,* long after her *optimistic* mood had left her, that a miracle would occur. **Confident,** by contrast, stresses conviction and certainty about the future. *Confident,* furthermore, may imply a conviction based on a knowledge of the facts: first-quarter sales figures that made them *confident* their business would succeed. *Confident* may also suggest self-assurance: someone who walked with a *confident* bearing. See CHEERFUL, CONFIDENCE, FAVORABLE, HAPPINESS, JOYOUS.

Antonyms: *cynical, defeatist, pessimistic.*

orderly

natty
neat
tidy
trig
trim

These adjectives refer to good grooming or to systematic arrangements. **Orderly** is the most general and least formal. In terms of something well cared for, it refers more to places or things than to personal appearance: an *orderly* array of reference books; an *orderly* studio. *Orderly* suggests a considerable mass of details that without deliberate efforts at arrangement can easily become disarrayed. Clarity may be the motivating factor behind such an effort: an *orderly* presentation of the points to be discussed. But the adjective can indicate superficial rather than meaningful arrangement: an *orderly* but not very searching mind. **Tidy** need not imply the arrangement of as many details as *orderly,* but it does suggest greater adherence to the arrangement chosen, even to the point of possible severity or rigidity: a pleasant, *orderly* playroom where the children were building a model airplane; a room so *tidy* it seemed doubtful that anyone actually lived in it. Sometimes, the adjective can suggest a happy, feminine touch, but conversely it can sometimes point to primness instead: a *tidy* bedroom with pink curtains and a simple dressing table; a father who kept scolding his children about keeping their rooms *tidy.*

Neat is the least formal of these adjectives and applies much like *tidy,* but without the latter's possibly unfavorable implications. Unlike the previous pair, however, *neat* applies as well to personal appearance as to places and things. In any case it suggests careful, uncluttered arrangements or simple, fastidious grooming: a *neat* kitchen; wearing a *neat,* newly pressed skirt; He was always *neat* in everything he did. But, *neat,* like the preceding adjectives, need not imply cleanliness, as can be seen from the phrase *neat* and clean. Something may be carefully arranged and yet not clean, although the two often go hand in hand: The room was as *neat* as she had left it, although dust had settled over everything; a room that had been left *neat* and sparkling by my roommate. **Trim** contrasts with *orderly* by emphasizing a sparseness rather than a quantity of detail; it also points to simplicity, compactness, and precision: the *trim* lines of her well-tailored jacket; the man's *trim* haircut; a row of *trim* cottages. In reference to physique, *trim* suggests an appealing slimness: the woman's *trim* figure; a swimmer's *trim* body.

Both **trig** and **natty** apply mainly to personal appearance, particularly to clothing. Both may be more relevant to men than to women. *Natty* is often used humorously to indicate something extremely stylish, even something overelegant: a tuxedo with *natty* silk lapels; the boy's *natty* Edwardian clothes. *Trig* can apply as well to good grooming in general: a *trig* Marine; a *trig* secretary in her stylish suit. *Trig,* in fact, can apply to something stiff and formal to the point of severity: the *trig* world of Wall Street with its colorless uniformity. See CLEAN, EXQUISITE, STYLISH.

Antonyms: *chaotic, disorderly, messy, untidy.*

ordinance. Do not confuse the noun *ordinance* (rule, decree) with the noun *ordnance* (weapons, military supplies).

ordnance. Do not confuse the noun *ordnance* (weapons, military supplies) with the noun *ordinance* (rule, decree).

organize
arrange
classify
marshal
order
sort

These verbs refer to imposing a shape upon a mass of details in accordance with some plan or system. **Organize** indicates the most thoroughgoing shaping of materials of any of these verbs, since it can point to the achieving of either sequential or spatial form, or both. [She *organized* the speech so that her most telling points came last; The architect *organized* multi-leveled shopping arcades around a central plaza.] In any case, while *organize* can imply the shifting about of items, it more often goes beyond this to suggest an altering of each and the fusing or fitting of part to part to form a new unity. A common use applies to the shaping of work systems: a business *organized* into two separate but interlocking corporations; an administrator good at *organizing* new government programs from scratch; a union drive to *organize* white-collar workers.

Arrange most often indicates the shifting about of items according to a plan, but without necessarily altering the items themselves: the job of *arranging* his vast library by subject and author. While *arrange* stresses sequence, a more complex spatial arrangement may be indicated: the painter's genius at *arranging* the graphic elements of a work within an overall design. A greater reshaping of details is also suggested when *arrange* refers to the creation of music to accompany a melody or singer: the composer who *arranged* her songs for voice and orchestra. **Order**, like *organize*, can point to a thoroughgoing shaping and reshaping of elements, but in this context is more formal and can be confused with its more common use referring to the requisition of something: catalogs for *ordering* spare parts. Nevertheless, *order* can function, especially in an aesthetic context, to refer to one aspect of the creative process: his ability to *order* the most disparate facets of contemporary life into a harmonious whole.

Classify refers to a categorizing process that at its most mechanical stands in sharp contrast to the creative acts that *organize* and *order* suggest. *Classify*, however, can sometimes refer to the creating of the categories themselves: the obsolete binomial system for *classifying* animal and plant life. At its mildest, *classify* can indicate the identifying of examples according to existing types, possibly with no actual *arranging* or re*arranging* whatsoever: a walk on which they noted and *classified* every tree they came across. **Sort** suggests the selection of items according to type; this process is closely related to the categorizing process indicated by *classify*. Often, *classify* indicates a previous evaluative judgment, and *sort* indicates the disposing of items according to this evaluation: He *sorted* out the books he had earlier *classified* as worth saving. **Marshal**, the most specific of these verbs, serves as an intensification of *arrange*. In this case, items are brought together and *ordered* for greatest efficiency or for the most forceful effect possible: She *marshaled* instance after instance of job discrimination in her statement before the appeals court. At its most literal, *marshal* refers to the maneuvering of troops to greatest military advantage: an order to *marshal* troops on both sides of the mountain pass. See CHOOSE, CREATE, FORM, HARMONIOUS, LABEL.

Antonyms: *bungle, dishevel, disorganize, muddle.*

origin
basis
cause
root
source

These nouns refer to the antecedent, beginning, initiator, or motivating principle of something. **Origin** suggests a beginning of something in time or place, or something out of which another thing arises: the *origin* of the contract theory of government in the Middle Ages; the *origin* of the Mississippi; the birth trauma as the *origin* of fear and anxiety.

Cause exclusively involves time, but the span of time need not be as long as that implied by *origin*: Friction was the *cause* of the fire. *Cause* also refers specifically to the notion of one thing arising out of another, rather than merely to the notion of beginning.

Basis may refer to a causal relation in time but more generally it suggests a principle that underlies some actuality: respect for law as the *basis* for a peaceful society.

Root and **source** involve metaphorical comparisons to a tree or a river. *Root* is most like *basis*, and source most like *origin:* poor schooling that is at the *root* of the unemployment problem; Greek civilization as the *source* of our democratic ideals. See ARISE, BASIS, BEGINNING, KERNEL.

Antonyms: RESULT.

ornament

adorn
beautify
bedeck
deck
decorate
embellish
garnish
trim

These verbs refer to lavish, detailed, or colorful additions to something that make it seem attractive, pleasant, or festive. **Ornament** indicates the addition of detail that makes something more picturesque: the iron deer that *ornamented* the lawn. *Ornament* is also common as a noun, referring in this case to possibly gaudier details: *ornaments* for our Christmas tree. **Decorate** is more widely used than *ornament*, applying especially to places or things: They *decorated* the bandstand with red, white, and blue bunting. Where *ornament* can sometimes suggest the addition of one or few details, *decorate* often suggests a more thoroughgoing approach that affects the whole area in question: a wall *decorated* in stripes of blue and green enamel. **Trim** is less formal than the previous pair. In the context of Christmas tree decorations, it can refer to everything added to the tree: the *ornaments*, lights, and tinsel used to *trim* the tree. In other situations, it can often refer to color or design applied to *decorate* the edges or accent points of something: a white house *trimmed* with green.

Embellish indicates the adding of flourishes or accent points, like *trim*, rather than the treatment of an extensive area, like *decorate*. The special implication of *embellish*, however, is that such flourishes are the expressions of the decorator's zest or are taken gratefully by others as making a material livelier or more interesting. Also, the flourish may be part of the material itself rather than an extraneous addition to it. [The oil portrait was *embellished* with crosshatching of vibrant color; a speech *embellished* with amusing anecdotes.] Sometimes, *embellish* can refer to the elaboration rather than to the decoration of something: the wealth of detail with which she *embellished* a simple plot line. *Embellish* can also suggest partial falsification or outright dishonesty: *embellishing* his dull life with

fictitious adventures; He didn't lie so much as *embellish* the truth a little. Both *ornament* and *embellish* can also refer to musical flourishes (such as grace notes or trills, also collectively called *ornaments*, ornamentation, or *embellishments*): Baroque composers often expected performers to *ornament* the melodic line during performances. **Garnish** is similar to *embellish* in indicating the inclusion of accent points to make something more lively or appealing and is now most often applied to foods: an omelette *garnished* with parsley.

Adorn and **beautify** often apply to substantial external changes made to give something a more pleasing appearance. *Adorn* can also apply to the adding of accents, but more often it suggests the clothing or dressing up of something in attractive materials: women *adorned* in jewels and furs. *Beautify* can sometimes refer specifically to the applying of makeup, but it can also apply generally to any attempt to make something more attractive: mascara to *beautify* the eyes; a program to *beautify* the nation's highways. *Beautify* can also indicate *decorating* something in a heavy-handed way: motels *beautified* with chrome and neon.

Deck and **bedeck** can also sound old-fashioned in reference to the adding of festive *trimming* or layers to something, though they survive in songs and poems: *Deck* the halls with boughs of holly; a garden *bedecked* with rosemary. Both can be effective as irony: a yokel whose hair was *bedecked* with hay; a dude *decked* out in his best togs. See ELEGANT, GAUDY.

Antonyms: DISFIGURE, *mar*.

orotund. Do not confuse the adjective *orotund* (imposing, dignified, pompous, with full voice) with the adjective *rotund* (plump, rounded).

outrage

aggravate
bug
exasperate

These verbs refer to being annoyed, disturbed, or incensed by or at something. **Outrage** points to the most intense or extreme response indicated by any of these verbs, but it may suggest the least direct emotional involvement in that one may be an onlooker rather than a participant or victim: *outraged* by the international outcry against our proposal. Thus, *outrage* can suggest attitudes of moral disapproval, prudery, or haughty indignation at some displeasing display. Even where a more personal involvement is suggested in emotions approaching anger, *outrage* applies to one's response to the actions of others, though seldom to what is done to oneself: *outraged* by his daughter's extravagance. Occasionally, the verb can suggest a more direct involvement; even here, it suggests response to behavior or attitude rather than to physical or violent conflict: *outraged* by his repeated insults.

The formal **exasperate** and the informal **bug** both introduce the personal element often lacking in *outrage*. *Exasperate* may suggest a final and complete breaking down of patience after repeated annoyance: so *exasperated* by his snoring that she slept on the sofa. This notion of a buildup, however, need not be present: *exasperated* by the innuendo implicit in the reporter's question. In any case, *exasperate* emphasizes an angry though possibly momentary loss of calm or control: *exasperated* to the point of incoherence. *Bug* may refer as an informal word to any displeased response to something annoying, whether the annoyance is intended or not: *bugged* by the sloppiness of the new paint job; *bugged* by his snide remarks about the way I dressed. *Bug* may suggest a process of growing annoyance, some single instance of anger, or even a continuing philosophical attitude of disapproval: *bugged* by my heavy drinking; a TV commercial that really *bugged* me; those who are *bugged* by middle-class materialism. Also, *bug* can be used for a deliberate attempt to annoy someone else: trying to *bug* him about his refusal to share housekeeping. *Bug* differs in one respect from *exasperate* in that loss of control may or may not be implied by the word; it can apply equally well either to a reaction that never rises above passive disgruntlement or to an *exasperated* or *outraged* response.

Aggravate focuses more directly on a slow process of growing annoyance, but without suggesting that emotions have reached their boiling point. In this use it is an informal adaptation of the verb, taken over from its reference to the worsening of an already bad situation: at first *aggravated* and finally maddened by the continual crying of the sleepless infant. Often, however, *aggravate* is used more loosely: so *aggravated* (more appropriately, hurt or annoyed or *exasperated*) by the reprimand that he wouldn't speak to me for days after. See BOTHER, ENRAGE, UPSET.

Antonyms: *favor, please,* SATISFY, *soothe.*

outrageous
atrocious
monstrous
scandalous
shocking
unspeakable

These adjectives characterize behavior that is intolerable or immoral, or taste that is extremely vulgar. **Outrageous** can function in any of these ways. When its reference is to morality, it suggests irredeemable depravity: an *outrageous* distortion of truth. In reference to impropriety, it suggests extreme disapproval for conscious audacity: *outrageous* manners for which he didn't even bother to apologize. In reference to taste, it tends to be merely a vague hyperbole: her *outrageous* notion of how to select a wardrobe. **Shocking** may apply either to an act of extreme immorality or to an unexpected or astonishing breach of manners: a *shocking* disregard for human life; his *shocking* rudeness to the elderly man. Where *outrageous* suggests an indignant response, *shocking* suggests a startled one. *Outrageous*, consequently, implies the stronger reaction of the two. Both may be used in a positive way: Tuscany's *outrageous* loveliness; the woman's *shocking* beauty.

Scandalous and **unspeakable** are more closely restricted to manners alone. *Scandalous* suggests a furor-creating breach of conduct; *unspeakable* suggests a violation of decency beyond the power of words to describe: their *scandalous* quarrels in full view of the neighbors; an *unspeakable* oaf. In a more prudish age, both adjectives could actually refer euphemistically to anything thought indelicate: *unspeakable* frankness; the play's *scandalous* suggestiveness. *Unspeakable*, however, has maintained a wider range of viable uses than *scandalous: unspeakable* cruelty; *unspeakable* taste.

Atrocious, like *outrageous*, can still refer to extremely immoral acts: such *atrocious* customs as slavery and flogging. **Monstrous**, similarly, can still describe something extremely immoral, abnormal, or deformed: the *monstrous* policy of genocide. But *atrocious* and *monstrous* have so often been used hyperbolically for anything bad or unpleasant that their original senses have been diluted: *atrocious* weather; *monstrous* luck. As hyperboles, both are commonly used to describe extremely bad manners or vulgar taste: *atrocious* rudeness; a *monstrous* style of painting. See DEPRAVED, GAUCHE, GAUDY, REPREHENSIBLE, VULGAR.

Antonyms: *appropriate, commendable, decorous, discreet,* HUMANE, POLITE, *tasteful.*

outspoken
forthright

open
plain-spoken
straightforward

These adjectives refer to statements that are simple, direct, or forceful, or to a guileless or tactless manner. While **outspoken** applies approvingly to vigorous statements of one's position or sentiments, it can also suggest a brusque manner or an indifference to the feelings of others. In any case, it is the strongest adjective here, carrying overtones of fearlessness and aggressiveness, as well: an *outspoken* critic of the automobile industry's reluctance to provide dramatically increased gasoline mileage; an *outspoken* fool who blustered and stormed but never got his facts right. Used in a more general way, *outspoken* can indicate, with greater neutrality, a willingness to take a stand or express oneself: She urged the girl to be *outspoken* about her needs and desires.

Where *outspoken* often implies criticism of others, **open** often suggests someone's willingness to speak frankly with another person: successful marriages in which both partners are *open* with each other. *Open* can also refer more specifically to an unthinking or fearless lack of secrecy, particularly in its adverbial form: They carried on their affair quite *openly*, without shame or guilt. *Open* can also apply to whatever is widely known, or to public statements deliberately made for the record: an *open* secret; an *open* scandal; an *open* avowal of her intention to compete for the research grant. By extension, *open* can indicate whatever is tantamount to a direct or public acknowledgment: He gave me a smile that was an *open* admission of his contempt for our immediate superior.

Straightforward most often applies to a character trait; it indicates a lack of deviousness in the way someone deals with other people. While it suggests unflinching directness in making requests of others, it need not suggest either a lack of consideration, as is possible for *outspoken*, or a willingness to be exposed and vulnerable, like *open*: a courteous but *straightforward* request to hear our reasons for disagreeing with them; a *straightforward* refusal to give me the facts about his past. **Forthright** is more closely related to *open* in suggesting either a readiness to respond to the requests of others or a sincere statement that does not hedge or involve evasion: a *forthright* person, always willing to give her opinion for whatever it might be worth; a *forthright* expression of his dissatisfaction with the work done on the community project.

Plain-spoken is like *straightforward* in indicating directness, but adds to this implications of simple and unambiguous utterance: She replied to their complex arguments with a *plain-spoken* refusal to cooperate. *Plain-spoken* can also function more emphatically to indicate a terse or blunt statement that flatfootedly rejects circumlocutions and euphemisms: He argued that it was merely being honest and *plain-spoken* to speak about starvation where these sharecroppers were concerned, and not about food shortages, hunger, or malnutrition. See BRUSQUE, CANDID, SINCERE, TRUTHFUL.

Antonyms: *CAUTIOUS, insincere, MISLEADING, subtle, TACITURN.*

outstanding
distinguished
dominant
foremost
paramount
predominant
preponderant
prevailing
prominent

These adjectives characterize something of unusual distinction or relevance by reason of its excellence or motivating force. **Outstanding** is the most general and least formal of these adjectives; most appropriately, it suggests excellence: an *outstanding* scientist of the past century. It may, however, suggest a feature that is sharply distinct from its surroundings: the *outstanding* impression of squalor that the town left us with. *Outstanding* may also refer to the most important of a number of causative factors: frustration as the *outstanding* cause of the prison riots. **Foremost** is considerably more formal than *outstanding*, but is otherwise similar in its uses. It more strongly suggests that the excellence, distinction, or power being referred to is the most important of many contenders for first place: the *foremost* interpreter of Bach; the *foremost* port of the region; the *foremost* reason for the legislators' change of attitude. When referring to a person's excellence, *foremost* may suggest formal or official recognition and approval more than actual superiority: Kozeluch was the *foremost* composer of his day despite Mozart's *outstanding* creative triumphs.

Distinguished stresses almost exclusively this last connotation of *foremost*, emphasizing merit that has been publicly recognized or honored: *distinguished* composers who, unlike their obscure colleagues, do not have to struggle to get a hearing for their music. **Prominent** does not always carry the suggestions of excellence conveyed by *foremost* or *distinguished*. It may point to status gained on other grounds entirely,

315

or merely suggest familiarity to a wide audience: socially *prominent* families; a novel that became *prominent* because of its sensationalism.

Dominant dwells mostly on causative force or a position of power: From her *dominant* position as chief executive officer, she saw fit to overrule the suggestions made by the *foremost* authorities; the corporation, consequently, failed to make an *outstanding* contribution to the nation's economy. **Paramount** strictly suggests a singular superiority rather than a most important excellence out of many—or even out of a few: lack of civilian morale as the *paramount* cause of our defeat. In many contexts, however, *paramount* might be thought excessively formal. **Predominant** and **preponderant**, on the other hand, imply a narrower advantage over the nearest contenders. *Predominant* suggests a recent ascendancy or points to a factor that is closely related to other factors almost as important; the era when religious tolerance became *predominant;* an electorate for whom the issues are the *predominant* consideration out of many extraneous factors vying for their attention. *Predominant* is less often used to refer to people; in comparison with the power and control suggested by *dominant,* it suggests less clearly defined or less decisive factors: the *predominant* apathy of the people that enabled the radical party to gain its *dominant* position. *Preponderant* may function similarly to *predominant,* but it may specifically suggest quantity rather than ascendancy. [All kinds of trees flourish in the region, but the *preponderant* species is the maple; Caution was *foremost* in the minds of a *preponderant* number of voters.]

Prevailing is closely related to *predominant* and *preponderant,* but it suggests an ascendancy that, while usual, is by no means uninterrupted or continuous: *prevailing* westerly winds. It may also suggest a consensus that is decisive but far from unanimous: the *prevailing* bipartisan foreign policy. See CONCLUSIVE, FAMOUS, GREAT, SIGNIFICANT.

Antonyms: *MEDIOCRE, USUAL.*

overbearing
arrogant
domineering
haughty
imperious

These adjectives describe the character or actions of persons who are possessed of an exaggerated pride or who, often because of such pride, behave in an overly determined, commanding, or even tyrannical way. **Overbearing**, **domineering**, and **imperious** refer to the latter group, persons in whom we can recognize a strong desire to exercise authority or at least to force their wishes on others; all three suggest that the insistence on being dominant is based on a real or assumed superiority: an office manager who was *overbearing* in her relations with her staff; a young man who never attained any independence and initiative because he was always under the thumb of a *domineering* father; a multitude of *imperious* demands that were met with reluctance and ill will.

Arrogant means unduly proud of wealth, station, learning, achievements, etc., Because of an exaggerated sense of self, *arrogant* persons take upon themselves more power or authority than is rightly theirs: the generals' *arrogant* seizure of the powers of state at the end of the civil war. **Haughty** is much the same as *arrogant* in denotation, but there is in a *haughty* person more feeling of pride and less compulsion to dominate than in someone who is *arrogant. Haughty* persons thinks highly of themselves while holding others in contempt, and may be rude and boorish or at least icily reserved in treating those they look upon as their inferiors: a *haughty* socialite who refused to attend her daughter's wedding because she disapproved of the groom's parents. See CONCEITED, CONTEMPTUOUS, PEREMPTORY.

Antonyms: *deferential,* DOCILE, MODEST, OBSEQUIOUS.

overhear
bug
eavesdrop
monitor
snoop
tap
wiretap

These verbs all refer to the action of listening in on or prying into the private conversations or affairs of others. To **overhear** is to listen to something being said without the knowledge or intention of the speaker or speakers. *Overhearing* is the most innocent action in this group, because it is accidental in nature. The only time it suggests a lack of innocence is when we know the *overhearing* mentioned went on for so long that the accident turned into an intention. "I couldn't help but *overhear* what you said to so-and-so" is often a euphemistic way of saying "I happened upon your private conversation and stayed on to enjoy it." The word for which *overhear* would be the euphemism in this case is **eavesdrop**. To *eavesdrop* is to listen in secret to some kind of private exchange. Unlike *over-*

hearing, *eavesdropping* is never unintentional. Even if one were to blunder into a situation where one *overhears* something private, the *overhearing* does not turn into *eavesdropping* without thought and decision: I took a booth next to the one where Marge and Jim were dining and before long I was *eavesdropping* on their conversation.

To *eavesdrop* by means of an electronic receiver is to **monitor**. The receiver may be planted almost anywhere and is designed particularly to listen in on conversation with military, political, business, or criminal significance. *Monitor* is also the word used to designate the act of observing or surveilling accomplished by a person or by a camera: Police *monitored* the suspect's comings and goings with a TV camera planted in a building across the street from the suspect's home.

To **bug**, an informal term, is to put a hidden listening device in a room, telephone circuit, etc., The device, which is called a *bug,* an informal noun, can be so small that it might be concealed as part of a person's clothing or jewelry: He soon became expert at planting *bugs*; Our embassy was *bugged* so completely that we had to close it down.

To **tap** or **wiretap** is to cut into a telephone or telegraph circuit for the purpose of secretly intercepting conversations and messages. [All conversations having to do with the planned merger were *wiretapped* by a competitor; She hired a private detective to *tap* her husband's office phone.]

Snoop is a general term that might be used in place of any of the verbs in this group except the innocent *overhear*. While *snooping* has always designated a sneaky, unsavory way to pry, its conversion from a personal to an electronic technique has given *snoop* much more sinister connotations than it ever had before. See ENCROACH, MEDDLESOME.

overt

open
patent
public

These adjectives characterize things made amply evident by direct expression. **Overt** indicates attitudes, feelings, and behavior that are put into words or acted upon, rather than intimated or suppressed: an *overt* declaration of his intention to quit; an *overt* homosexual; rebellious feelings that had passed the talking stage and were about to become *overt*. **Patent** stresses that something is unmistakably obvious and clear: a grasp and discrimination that are *patent* on every page of the book. *Patent,* however, frequently carries a pejorative tone: a *patent* lie; *patent* irrespon-

sibility; the *patent* invitations of streetwalkers in Times Square.

Open characterizes things done in an honest or unashamed manner, indifferent to criticism or reproof: easy to be *open* if you have nothing to hide; arguing that the gun laws were *open* invitations to violence; an *open* declaration of their stand on the controversial proposal. While people may be *open* with friends about their beliefs, they may still not wish to make **public** either their affairs or attitudes. *Public,* thus, is an extreme case among these adjectives, suggesting a deliberate revealing of oneself to the populace at large: a *public* announcement that she would no longer be responsible for debts incurred by her husband; a *public* address on foreign policy; voracious audiences who turn the private lives of movie stars into *public* scandals. See CANDID, PLAIN (adj.), TRUTHFUL.

Antonyms: IMPLICIT, *private, secret,* STEALTHY.

OX

bull
bullock
calf
cow
heifer
steer

These nouns come into comparison in denoting domesticated cattle, whether raised for milk and meat or used as draft animals. **Ox** is a general term when it is used in zoology to refer to any bovine animal, whether wild or tame. Specifically, an *ox* is an adult castrated male animal, once widely used to pull carts and plows but now common only in agrarian economies. **Bullock** and **steer** are also adult castrated males, but *bullock* is more closely related in meaning to *ox* in that *bullock* also suggests a draft animal, while *steers* are raised for their beef and hides. When one refers to beef cattle in general, it is acceptable to refer to males, females, and young animals as *steers*.

A **bull** is an adult uncastrated male animal kept usually for breeding purposes only. In Spain and elsewhere, special strains of cattle are bred to provide *bulls* for the ring.

Cow and **heifer** denote female bovines. The *cow* is the mature female of any variety of cattle, but the noun calls to mind the familiar animal kept as a milk producer on dairy farms. *Heifer* is a young *cow,* especially one less than three years old that has not yet produced young or given milk.

Calf is the newborn or very young offspring of the cow, and the term applies to either sex. *Bull, cow,* and *calf* are also used to denote the male, female, and young of a number of unrelated animals, as elephants, whales, moose, walruses, and alligators.

With various implications, *ox, bull, cow, calf,* and sometimes *heifer* are applied figuratively to human beings. *Ox* suggests slowness, clumsiness, and slow-wittedness: dumb as an *ox;* big as an *ox. Bull* empha-sizes brutish masculine strength and virility: to roar like a *bull;* a wrestler with the strength of a *bull. Cow* may be applied objectionably to an obese and coarse woman, while *heifer* may suggest a plump country girl. The awkwardness and bumbling of a *calf* is evoked when the term, now literary and obsolescent, is used of a gawky, callow young man.

pain

- ache
- pang
- stitch
- throe
- twinge

These nouns denote sensations of discomfort or suffering. **Pain**, the most general term, can be used in place of any of the others in this group. *Pain* can be of long or short duration, in a local or a general site, and of mild or great intensity: anxious about an off-and-on *pain* in the abdomen. An **ache** is an often long-lasting *pain*, usually dull rather than sharp and associated with a particular organ or body part: a stomach*ache;* a tooth*ache.* A **pang** is a sudden, sharp but transient *pain* that is likely to recur: the *pangs* of hunger. A **twinge** is much like a *pang,* but milder in intensity and often one that causes a muscle to contract: a *twinge* of rheumatism. A **throe** (usually in its plural form) is a violent, often convulsive *pain,* such as that associated with a mortal wound, the effects of many poisons, or a violent physical process: the *throes* of childbirth. A sudden, sharp, piercing *pain,* often followed by a cramp, is called a **stitch**: a *stitch* in the side that made her wince.

All these nouns except *stitch* have figurative application to mental or spiritual suffering: the *pain* of separation; the *ache* of loneliness; a *pang* of remorse; the *throes* of indecision; a *twinge* of regret. See HARM, HURT, MISERY.

Antonyms: *health,* PLEASURE, *well-being.*

pale

- ashen
- cadaverous
- livid
- pallid
- wan

These adjectives describe things, particularly complexions, that are lacking in color. **Pale** is the most general and informal and is the only adjective here that can refer to a relative lightness of color, permanent or natural: *pale* Scandinavians and swarthy Italians; choosing the *palest* shade of blue for the bathroom. More often, however, *pale* suggests a temporary loss of color because of emotion or sickness: growing *pale* with fear; looking feeble and *pale* after the long illness. In these cases, it is the change in color that is emphasized. Yet, the change need not be negative: The eastern horizon was *pale* with the first hints of dawn. Because of the adjective's association with illness, it can refer more generally to an undesirable weakness or dullness: a *pale* performance in an otherwise strong cast. **Ashen** is a much more restricted intensification of *pale;* it refers mainly to an extreme but possibly temporary loss of facial color and usually points to an abnormal or undesirable state: a face *ashen* with shock; troops that looked haggard, even *ashen,* from the long march; the *ashen,* pinched features typical of undernourished Bosnian children. The adjective can also refer to the grayish dull appearance of something that has been vividly colored: storm clouds that turned the bright summer sky *ashen* and somber. **Cadaverous** is an even more restricted and more intense substitute for *ashen.* It refers almost exclusively to a facial or bodily state and indicates a more permanent unhealthy or deathly look. In addition to a *pale* appearance, *cadaverous* suggests a wasted or diseased gauntness as well: the *cadaverous* faces of some fashion models; the *cadaverous* survivors of concentration camps. Although *cadaverous* compares this kind of look to that of a corpse, *cadaverous* is used to describe a living person.

Pallid and **wan** are both more formal than the foregoing, and both can sound somewhat archaic or precious. *Pallid* particularly has been overused as a more genteel or supposedly more elegant substitute for *pale.* In reference to facial appearance, *pallid* concentrates on unhealthy states rather than those resulting from temporary emotional seizures: the sick child's *pallid* cheeks. It would sound incorrect or affected to use *pallid* to describe things that naturally lack color: *pallid* snow. *Pallid* is useful, however, as a disapproving word for anything dull, dreary, or unspirited: facing the crisis with inept formulas and a *pallid* lack of imagination. Here, the adjective's suggestion of preciosity is sometimes consciously brought to bear with critical intent: *pallid* Victorian poetry. *Wan* is more restricted to facial appearance and less open to criticism on the grounds of preciosity; it emphasizes a loss of vigor, temporary or permanent: the *wan* faces of miners who seldom saw the sun; *wan* and wasted by disease.

Livid has almost lost any usefulness it once may have had by the contradictory meanings it has gathered to itself. Coming from a Latin adjective meaning black and blue, *livid* can refer clinically to a bruised, discolored skin. Many people, however, would tend to misunderstand *livid* when used in this way. Parallel to this use, *livid* can refer to a face flushed or purplish from intense emotion, particularly rage: absolutely *livid* when she heard the news. The connection with rage has become so customary that no change in coloration whatever need be suggested by *livid*. In contrast to this and to the adjective's suggestion of a flushed or a bluish cast, *livid* can also indicate a colorless or *ashen* appearance: the *livid* lips of the corpse. While some purists insist that only this last suggestion is valid, such a use would be widely misunderstood. See BONY, GRUESOME.

Antonyms: *colorful, flushed, glowing, ruddy.*

pamper
baby
coddle
humor
indulge
mollycoddle
spoil

These verbs mean treat someone with special favor, care, protectiveness, or privilege. To **pamper** people is to cater to them, to furnish them with everything they need for ease or comfort: to *pamper* an invalid. *Pamper* may imply treatment so tender as to be weakening or debilitating: an aristocracy so *pampered* and overprotected that it could not cope with change. Whereas to *pamper* someone is to lap that person in luxury, to **indulge** someone is to let that person have what he or she wants. The noun *indulgence* involves making an exception, yielding to wishes or inclinations usually denied; it suggests a relaxing of normal or proper restraint and a permissive sanctioning of pleasure. A person may *indulge* himself or another person: *indulging* oneself in the luxury of sleeping late; a grandmother who *indulges* the children so much that she undermines parental discipline. Preferences, desires, and needs may also be *indulged*: indulging a taste for wine to the point of insobriety. One **humors** other people only. To *humor* people is to go along with them, complying with their moods, fancies, or capricious demands, no matter how silly. [She *humored* her husband by driving back to the house yet again to see whether the gas had been turned off; Though tired, he pretended he was Superman to *humor* the child.]

To **baby** someone is to treat that person like a helpless infant who can't assume responsibility. To **coddle** someone is to treat him or her with much more solicitude than warranted, going to great lengths to spare or protect that person. **Mollycoddle** means much the same as *coddle*, but is a stronger word and particularly suggestive of the overprotection by which some parents insulate their children from experience and hardship, perhaps preventing them from growing up. *Baby, coddle,* and *mollycoddle* are often used sarcastically or in exaggeration. [They *babied* you in high school, but you'll have to stand on your own two feet in college; You're in the Army now, so don't expect any *coddling* here; He claimed people on welfare were being *mollycoddled*.]

Alone among these verbs, **spoil** emphasizes effect, the damage to the disposition resulting from overindulgence. According to folk psychology, one *spoils* children by giving in to whims and whining, letting them have their own way, according privileges unearned and undeserved; as a result, the children may well come to demand special privileges as a matter of right, and may become self-centered, conceited, and selfish. [Stop acting like a *spoiled* child; His grandparents would *spoil* him if we let them.] Adults may be *spoiled* in a different way by growing used to unearned luxuries, so that they no longer can be content with what they had before. [Wintering in Palm Beach has *spoiled* me forever.] See CARESS, LENIENT, PLEASING, PROTECT.

Antonyms: *deny, discipline, neglect, withhold.*

pandemic. Do not confuse the adjective *pandemic* (of a disease, occurring over a very wide area) with the adjective *epidemic* (of a disease, spreading rapidly through a community). Do not confuse the noun *pandemic* (a pandemic disease) with the noun *epidemic* (an outbreak of an epidemic disease). See also ENDEMIC.

parasite
freeloader
hanger-on
leech
sponger

These nouns refer to someone who attaches himself or herself to someone else in order to gain a portion of the other person's money, goods, or advantages. **Parasite** and **leech** both call to mind biological organisms that attach themselves to a host as a source of nourishment, often harming the health of the host or causing death. *Parasite* is the generic term for all such forms of life; *leech* refers specifically to a bloodsucking worm that acts in this way. As might be suspected from this, *parasite* is the vaguer of the two when the reference is to people, and *leech* the more pejorative. *Parasite* can refer to the draining off of any sort of benefits from someone else: a gigolo who lived as a *parasite* off the generosity of rich women; a real *parasite* who habitually looked the other way when a waiter presented a bill. *Parasite* can suggest a spineless person who gains another's confidence by hypocrisy or subterfuge. *Leech* is much harsher in its disapproval and indicates both a more ravening and more tenacious approach: *leeches* who clung fast to generous friends while there was the slightest advantage to be gained; such a *leech* that his patron was driven into bankruptcy.

Freeloader and **sponger** are more informal than the previous pair and suggest a more hit-and-miss approach to gaining benefits from others. *Freeloader,* the more informal of these nouns, suggests someone who makes himself or herself easily available to partake of someone else's hospitality, with no thought of ever returning it. *Freeloader* is particularly suggestive of the hasty and voluminous dispatch of someone else's food and drink: *freeloaders* who invited themselves to dinner three or four times before we got wise to them; *freeloaders* at the party who found the host's cache of expensive Scotch and made short work of it. *Sponger* refers to a person with any sort of gain in mind and may be especially suggestive of a person who never returns borrowed items, or of a person in a public place who manages to get free drink or food: fearing that borrowing a cup of sugar would make her new neighbor think she was a *sponger; spongers* adept at getting tourists to buy them endless drinks. As can be seen, *sponger* need not imply a permanent relationship and is less severe in its criticism than *freeloader* and certainly than *parasite* or *leech.*

Hanger-on is the mildest of these nouns, suggesting someone who has formed a more lasting relationship with a host; rather than snatch at benefits, the *hanger-on* may simply wait timidly for benefits as they are offered: a *hanger-on* who seemed always present, as though in hope of receiving a scrap of affection; *hangers-on* who were content to flatter me in exchange for an invitation to my parties. See FAWN, OBSEQUIOUS.

Antonyms: *host.*

pardon
condone
excuse
forgive
overlook
remit

These verbs mean free a person from the consequences of guilt, or pass over a blameworthy action without censure or punishment. **Pardon** is a more formal term than **forgive** or **excuse** and in its strictest sense implies the authority to punish—and set free—officially: The governor *pardoned* three men and a woman who had been unjustly convicted. *Forgive* means *pardon* with compassion, usually on a directly personal level. [A wife may *forgive* an unfaithful husband; A saint always *forgives* his enemies.] *Excuse* means *forgive* a minor offense, breach of etiquette, etc.: We *excused* her brusqueness because we knew she was under severe strain. *Excuse* may also be used of larger offenses that are not criminal nor of a personal nature: The company *excused* the guard for falling asleep while on duty. *Pardon, forgive,* and *excuse* are all used in polite exchanges to convey regret for having caused inconvenience. In this usage, *pardon* and *forgive* tend to sound stilted and sententious and are used less often than *excuse:* to *excuse* oneself for jostling a fellow passenger on a bus.

Condone and **overlook** mean *pardon* or *forgive* tacitly by accepting without redress actions and situations that merit censure. *Condone,* more than *overlook,* suggests toleration of more serious offenses—offenses of a public nature, such as breaches of the law: Child labor is still *condoned* in some states by officials who consider themselves upright and conscientious. One also *condones* faults that are similar to one's own: A man who cheats on his income tax and on his expense account tends to *condone* these practices in his friends. *Overlook,* a weaker verb than *condone,* suggests indulgent disregard of minor lapses in behavior: to *overlook* a child's sloppy table manners; to *overlook* a bright student's occasional failure to complete an assignment on time.

Remit, once a close synonym of *pardon,* is the most formal of all these verbs and its use is limited to ecclesiastical and legal contexts: to *remit* sins; to *remit* a fine for disturbing the peace. See EXONERATE.

Antonyms: *condemn, convict, penalize, punish.*

part
passage
piece
portion
section
segment
subdivision

part (continued)

These nouns refer to something looked at as an entity in isolation from the whole of which it is a member. **Part** is the most general of these, referring to a quantity, sometimes amorphous or unspecified, of a particular whole: asking for a *part* of my sandwich; in one *part* of the book I'm reading. It can also refer to some independently structured member of a totality: the spare *parts* needed to repair the car.

Piece and **portion** relate exclusively to that aspect of *part* suggesting a quantity drawn from a whole. *Piece* is especially appropriate in reference to flat stretches of material, land, etc.: a *piece* of property; a *piece* of yard goods. *Piece* can also be used for other quantities: a *piece* of pie. *Portion* is most appropriate in reference to servings of food or to abstract qualities: a cafeteria that serves up lavish *portions;* a woman who is blessed with enviable *portions* of wisdom and tolerance. *Portion,* unlike *piece,* also has a specific use in reference to an amount of time: spending a *portion* of each summer at the beach. **Passage** is more informal than *portion* and is even more commonly used to refer to periods of time, especially to elapsed time: a *passage* of ten years during which I traveled little. It also has a special use in reference to *parts* of art works, such as literature and music: a *passage* from Gershwin that echoed in his mind whenever he thought of Paris; the *passage* in her book in which she comes out most strongly for freedom of the press.

The remaining nouns refer to clearly defined entities or groupings within a larger, structured unity. **Subdivision** is the most specific of these, suggesting a rigid logical organization of *part* to *part* within a complex framework, such as a bureaucracy, a schematic drawing of surveyed land, a legal document with numbered or lettered paragraphs, or any detailed outline or system of classification: such catalogued *subdivisions* of nonfiction as biography, history, and travel. **Segment** can refer to a specified *part* of a geometrical figure or to some natural *subdivision:* the *segments* of an orange. It can also be used as a more formal word for a *piece* of some linear quantity, such as thread or wire: laying a new *segment* of cable to connect the two stations. **Section** is the least specific of these three nouns; it is more closely restricted than *segment* to refer to a structured part of an organized entity, but suggests less complexity than *subdivision:* that *section* of the Justice Department dealing with civil rights infringements; a wealthy *section* of town. When *section* approaches *part* in generality, it suggests a definable slice of a whole, sometimes isolated for the convenience of close inspection: calling our attention to a *section* of the portrait in which a later overpainting was clearly noticeable; the *section* of her will in which she assigned her art collection. See ADDITION, COMPONENT, FRAGMENT.

Antonyms: *entirety, entity, gestalt, totality, unit, whole.*

passionate

ardent
burning
fervent
fervid
fiery
impassioned
vehement
zealous

These adjectives describe intense states of desire, dedication, or conviction. **Passionate** and **impassioned**, both drawn from a Latin word meaning suffer, are most commonly used for states of desire, with a strong overtone of sexuality. *Impassioned* is more inward and passive and less ambiguous than *passionate* when applied to people, suggesting a deep and abiding feeling. *Passionate* is less lofty in tone and suggests that the desire is more a matter of appetite. *Passionate* may even suggest a lack of discrimination: *Passionate* as he was, he had never truly loved any of his many mistresses. It may, of course, be used without suggesting such negative connotations: Lawrence preferred the *passionate* to the rational life. When applied to the effective expression of strong feeling, *impassioned* is the more usual choice: an *impassioned* speech.

Ardent, **fiery**, and **burning** describe intense feeling in terms of fire. Of these, only *ardent* is free of negative implications in describing both desire and dedication: an *ardent* lover; an *ardent* patriot. *Fiery* would not be useful to describe states of desire, except for poetic effect, in which case it might be seen as a cliché: *fiery* embraces. In describing dedication, it suggests angry rather than *impassioned* conviction, and even wildness or instability: *fiery* demagogue; *fiery* denunciation. *Burning,* for both desire and dedication, has become a cliché, avoided by thoughtful writers: *burning* passion; *burning* issues.

Fervent and **fervid** come from the same root, meaning boil. Their relationship is somewhat like that of *impassioned* and *passionate*. *Fervent,* like *impassioned,* implies being filled with abiding feeling; *fervid,* an intensification of *fervent,* suggests feverish intensity and a greater compulsion to act, with the same overtones possible as for *passionate*. Both *fervent* and especially *fervid,* however, have become somewhat stilted in tone.

Zealous and **vehement** are both more applicable to dedication than to desire. One might perhaps speak of a *zealous* lover, but hardly of a *vehement* one. *Zealous* refers most strictly to intense religious conviction, although it applies as well to unwavering adherence to any set of beliefs or attitudes: a *zealous* convert; a *zealous* football fan. *Zealous* suggests that one is prepared to act on one's beliefs without question. This gives a strong negative overtone of fanaticism: the *zealous* witch-burners of Salem. *Vehement*, even more strongly than *zealous*, implies belligerence and challenge, but unlike *zealous*, *vehement* is more often applied to things or attitudes than to people: a *vehement* reply; a *vehement* gesture; He was *vehement* about civil rights. See BURN, EAGER, EMOTION, EROTIC, HOT.

Antonyms: IMPASSIVE.

pathetic

moving
pitiable
pitiful
poignant
touching

These adjectives characterize the compassion, concern, or empathy that can or should be aroused by viewing the situation of another living thing. **Pathetic** pertains to compassionate concern or sorrow that is or should be inspired by those less fortunate than oneself. It stresses circumstances in which a sufferer is reduced to helplessness: the *pathetic* struggle of the fawn to free itself from the steel jaws of the trap; those *pathetic* cases in which children get little love from either parent; his *pathetic* cries for help. The adjective usually implies that an innocent victim has unjustly or unfairly been harmed through no fault of his or her own. **Pitiful** may be used exactly like *pathetic*, but *pitiful* has a wider range of uses beyond this context. It can, for example, be used even when the victims may have contributed to their own plights or are entirely responsible for their situations: the *pitiful* loneliness of the alcoholic. It may also be used of persons who may not see themselves as victimized in any way and who, in fact, may seem more fortunate than others: the Iraqi leader's *pitiful* outbreaks of incoherent rage against his most loyal advisers; strutting and boasting about her beauty in a most *pitiful* way.

Poignant and **touching** are closely related and both depart from the situation of victimization or misfortune to indicate anything that arouses tender compassion or empathy. *Touching* is the more informal of the two, suggesting a winning appeal or inevitably affecting scene: the mother cat's *touching* zeal for the welfare of its kittens; his *touching* request for one last chance to prove himself. *Touching* most commonly suggests an audience that is actually affected by a scene, whereas *pathetic* and *pitiful* may imply no audience at all or one that is hardhearted: a *pathetic* figure whom no passerby found the least bit *touching*. This same distinction holds for *poignant*, which emphasizes the arousal of a bittersweet responsiveness that combines pity and longing or other contradictory emotions. *Poignant* once emphasized the presence of any sort of keen feelings, but it now points more often to an ambivalence inherent in subtle or gentle shades of compassion, wistfulness, or nostalgia: Her *pitiful* face had not seemed *touching* to him at the time, but recalling it now filled him with a *poignant* sorrow and delight.

Moving functions more like *touching* and *poignant* than *pathetic* and *pitiful*, but it suggests the arousal of emotions stronger than those indicated by the other adjectives. *Moving* applies to compassion and empathy but also to a wide range of emotions beyond them: the anger aroused by his *moving* demand for an investigation of the tragic fire; a *moving* scene of reconciliation at the end of her short story. Except when applied to a work of art, *moving* often suggests an arousal to action: a *moving* appeal that the *pathetic* victims of the plot be compensated for the injustices they suffered. **Pitiable** is unique among these adjectives in stressing that someone is deserving of pity whether or not this condition is noticed by others—or even detectable by them: a *pitiable* emptiness that he kept hidden under an outwardly happy and successful life; poverty made all the more *pitiable* by the indifference of the town's most fortunate citizens. See MISERABLE, PATHETIC, SAD.

Antonyms: *farcical, ludicrous, ridiculous, unaffecting.*

patience

forbearance
long-suffering
masochism
resignation
stoicism
sufferance

These nouns refer to a voluntary self-control, restraint, or passivity that helps one endure waiting, provocation, injustice, suffering, or any of the other unpleasant vicissitudes of life. **Patience** is almost exclusively positive in tone. Most often it refers to a willingness to wait without becoming disgruntled or anxious: showing great *patience* while waiting to learn the outcome of the election. More generally, the noun can suggest a kindly tolerance for other people's shortcomings, including an ability to remain unperturbed when facing someone else's slowness or other quirks: the *patience* with which she went over the lesson until the slowest student in the class could understand it; responding with a kind of blank *patience* to her companion's tumultuous comings and goings. Where *patience* implies little difficulty in putting up with annoying situations, **forbearance** indicates a determined struggle against giving in to negative feelings. Thus, the stress of *forbearance* is on self-controlled abstinence from hasty or ill-tempered action, whatever the provocation: answering with such *forbearance* that only his flushed face showed how angry he really was. In this sense, *forbearance* is positive in tone, more strongly so than the blandness of *patience* and its implications of passivity. But *forbearance* can refer less positively to an attitude that is disposed to endure annoyance or actual harm: minority groups no longer willing to meet indignities with mealy-mouthed *forbearance*.

Sufferance and **long-suffering** both suggest the passive endurance of pain or wretchedness, and so emphasize passive submission. This attitude can as easily be presented as a positive virtue or as a failure of nerve. Of the two, *sufferance* suggests a more conscious choice in indicating the ability, possibly learned, to endure pain or evil that might destroy someone else: their *sufferance* of the scapegoat's role through centuries of maltreatment. More often, however, *sufferance* may suggest a generous tolerance for the foibles of others—or an immoral or permissive failure to take a stand in the face of evil: pragmatic in her good-humored *sufferance* of student pranks; the average citizen's apathetic *sufferance* of the regime's repressive laws. *Long-suffering* is more informal and less wide-ranging, referring to the *patience* with which injuries or misfortunes are endured, especially over a great period of time: facing his wife's invalidism with hard-bitten grimness and *long-suffering*. *Long-suffering* can also be negative when it suggests a person who glories in unhappiness instead of attempting to alter the situation: the tedious display of *long-suffering* with which she recounted every cruelty imposed by her husband.

Stoicism and **resignation** refer to a more profound and abiding general life-view than the previous nouns. *Stoicism* most specifically names the philosophy originated by Zeno, who advised us to be superior to all life's passions—joy, grief, pleasure, pain. In general use, *stoicism* is taken, however, to refer mainly to the ability to endure pain. Unlike *long-suffering*, even the popular sense of *stoicism* emphatically stresses the enduring of pain without complaint or comment of any sort and usually with complete equanimity: the *stoicism* of the few who can be tortured to death without once crying out for mercy. Only in ethical or philosophical discussion can *stoicism* take on a critical tone, suggesting a sterile attitude in which evil is accepted as inevitable rather than actively opposed: an invidious *stoicism* that allowed otherwise decent citizens to tolerate affronts to their self-respect. *Resignation* is much more likely than *stoicism* to be ambiguous in tone. In pointing to unresisting acquiescence and surrender to the inevitable, especially to misfortune, *resignation* can suggest a noble or dignified response to tragedy—or a craven acceptance of a degrading situation: the stark *resignation* with which she stood beside her husband's coffin; railing at the *resignation* with which most voters viewed the corrupt political machine that ran the city. *Resignation*, like *patience*, also can be less charged when force or compulsion is present: hopeless *resignation* to his fate after twenty years of incarceration.

Masochism is related to the other nouns here in that it refers to the enduring of pain, but it is in sharp contrast to them by indicating a neurotic willingness to suffer or even the conscious or unconscious seeking out of painful experiences: the *masochism* inherent in drug addiction. The noun is drawn from psychiatric terminology, where it is sometimes compounded with its opposite in the term *sadomasochism* because of the intimate connection between the neurotic pleasures of inflicting and suffering pain. But *masochism* is used widely outside the clinical context for any tendency toward assuming a martyr's role, enjoying one's own miseries, or exposing oneself to needless pain: Only a streak of *masochism* in her could have allowed her to stay married to such a brutal man. See ALOOF, HEEDLESS, MISERY, NUMB, PAIN, SLOTH.

Antonyms: ANGER, *impatience, militance, restiveness, sadism.*

patter

chitchat
palaver
small talk

These nouns refer to glib or trivial discussion or conversation. **Patter** and **palaver** are the most general. *Patter* emphasizes rapidity and insincerity of speech, whereas *palaver* stresses a lack of content or an intent to flatter or deceive. *Patter* can indicate mechanical recitation, reflecting its derivation from a reference to the hasty saying of the Paternoster; it can also refer to rehearsed comedy routines, or to bodies of dialect or jargon. Drawing from this range of use, *patter* in its conversational context adds to its emphasis on rapidity the connotations of rehearsed or at least predictable conversational patterns: the conventional *patter* exchanged at faculty parties; tedious *patter* about the weather and high cost of living. A note of condescension is usually present. *Palaver* is also condescending, suggesting exchanges devoid of substance. *Palaver* can refer to a public discussion or conference, reflecting its original reference to a parley between indigenous persons and an explorer or missionary, in which condescension is clear. More often, however, *palaver* can refer to an informal group discussion, possibly assembled in haste to decide on a course of action: the *palaver* of neighbors gathered in front of the house from which the strange sounds were coming. It can also refer to the disorganized uproar of voices from any group: a general *palaver* that did not die down until the conductor interrupted the concert. In either case, *palaver* has a distinctly informal tone.

Chitchat and **small talk** are both restricted to idle conversation. *Chitchat,* the most informal of all the nouns considered here, combines the predictability suggested by *patter* with the lack of substance indicated by *palaver.* In contrast to *patter,* however, *chitchat* may point to a slow pace and, unlike *palaver,* does not suggest group discussion so much as a random exchange of banalities or gossip: the kind of *chitchat* that was a sure sign the cocktail party was dying on its feet. The phrase *small talk* also refers to trivial talk but suggests as well that such conversation may be the result of choice or inhibition and may serve as an icebreaker or as prelude to more interesting matter: waiting for the *small talk* to give way to a real discussion of the issues confronting the group; planning bits of *small talk* with which to become part of interesting conversations she heard at the party. See CHATTER, CONVERSATION, JOKE, RAILLERY.

penniless

destitute
indigent
necessitous
needy
poverty-stricken

These adjectives describe people who are poor, who do not have enough money to maintain a decent standard of living, or who have lost their means of subsistence. **Penniless** usually refers to someone who has undergone a sudden, calamitous loss of money and property but may not be in real want. [At the time of the stock-market crash in 1929, many wealthy people found themselves *penniless;* John's father left his family *penniless.*] *Penniless* may also be applied to those who make no real attempt to be economically stable, or who are unequipped to do so: *penniless* panhandlers on every street corner; a *penniless* artist who devoted all her energies to her painting.

Poverty-stricken is the most comprehensive term and may be substituted for any of the other adjectives in this group. It is generally used, however, to describe people who lack the resources to make life even passably comfortable, either through economic stress or because, as in the case of members of some religious orders, they have chosen a way of life in which they must forgo many necessities and all luxuries. *Poverty-stricken* points to a condition that is more or less hopeless and permanent, or at least tends to go on for a long period: *poverty-stricken* tenant farmers who never realized any cash from their crops. *Poverty-stricken* is used also to describe conditions and situations that exhibit or even cause poverty: a *poverty-stricken* country with little industry; the *poverty-stricken* homes of Native Americans on some reservations.

Destitute emphasizes poverty of such severity that one is deprived of such necessities as food, clothing, and shelter: a *destitute* slum family evicted for not paying rent; *destitute,* lost children wandering about in a bombed-out city.

Indigent indicates a state of less dire want than do *poverty-stricken* and *destitute,* and it is sometimes used in opposition to affluent. *Indigent* is applied to those suffering from what used to be known as genteel poverty, in which circumstances are straitened but something of the former outward facade is preserved: The *indigent* old couple, who find it hard to make ends meet on a pension, manage to keep their home neat and tidy.

A **needy** person is one who is certainly *poverty-stricken* or even *destitute,* but *needy* implies an inability to maintain oneself without some help from public or private assistance: Christmas dinners provided for the homeless and *needy; needy* children who receive free health care at the clinic.

Necessitous is a close synonym of *poverty-stricken* and *needy,* but it now tends to sound literary and is infrequently used. See INSOLVENT, POOR.

325

Antonyms: *affluent, moneyed, opulent, rich, wealthy, well-heeled.*

people
   herd
   hoi polloi
   masses
   mob
   populace
   rabble

These nouns refer to the citizens of a country or a region when considered collectively. **People**, the most general, is usually neutral in implication; it can be used simply as the plural of person, as a reference to all the inhabitants of a given place, as a reference to public opinion, or as a way to distinguish between a group and its leaders: only two *people* in the entire restaurant; the *people* of Mexico; wondering what *people* would think; politicians who deliberately mislead the *people*. **Populace** is even more consistently neutral than *people* and is more restricted in meaning, referring almost exclusively to the inhabitants of a given place: Nearly the entire *populace* turned out to see her. It is often used in statistical accounts and has consequently gained a technical flavor. *Populace*, however, comes from an Italian pejorative and is sometimes used in this older way: too grand to be seen riding the subways with the *populace*.

All the rest of these nouns, with varying degrees of intensity, provide pejorative ways of referring to common people or the lower classes, attributing to them vulgarity, ignorance, or gullibility and implying in the user of these nouns a conscious or unconscious snobbery. **Masses** and the phrase **hoi polloi** are the least pejorative of these, for differing reasons. *Masses* specifically suggests the lower classes: hiding behind a tawdry sentimentality for the *masses*. Leftist political thinkers, however, have sometimes used *masses* in a positive or outraged sense that blunts the noun's pejorative force: the exploited *masses*. *Hoi polloi* refers more to the ordinary citizen than to class stratification. Careful writers remember that *hoi* is the Greek definite article: candidates seeking the vote of *hoi polloi*. An extraneous article is frequently added by less careful writers: swilling beer with the *hoi polloi*.

Mob in this context implies that the general public can be considered an ignorant unity joined together by fear and anger, one easily swayed by demagogic special pleading: wit and grace too refined to be appreciated by the *mob*. **Herd** is more negative than *mob* and stresses conformity, a gullible willingness to be led, or

frantic but meaningless activity: a conservative taste in clothing that set them apart from the *herd;* specious appeals for peace that won widespread support from the *herd;* the nine-to-five *herd* of commuters.

Rabble is the most pejorative of all these nouns; it suggests a disorganized, poverty-stricken group of ignorant people. When it is applied widely to groups of people, it expresses contempt for democratic ideals: explanations of tax reforms that were good enough for the *rabble*. For this reason, a demagogue is often called a *rabble*-rouser. See FOLK, KIN, MANKIND, POOR. **Antonyms:** *aristocracy, elite, nobility, royalty.*

perceive
   descry
   espy
   make out

These verbs all mean become aware of through one of the senses, or apprehend with the mind. **Perceive** is the most general term since it has application to all the senses: a master chef able to *perceive* the most subtle seasoning used in any dish; a conductor who could *perceive* even the slightest variation from true pitch in each instrument. *Perceive* is most often used in reference to the sense of sight: to *perceive* a car coming toward them. But *perceive* has definite implications of recognition that are not present in the verb *see*. [The object I saw far off was too shrouded in fog for me to be able to identify it, but as we drew closer, I *perceived* it to be an old windmill.] *Perceive* denotes mental as well as sensory observation when it is used to mean come to understand: to *perceive* the nuances in different philosophical propositions; to *perceive* the difficulties inherent in any business enterprise.

Descry and **espy** are sometimes used interchangeably because they both imply catching sight of something that is partly hidden, in the distance, or otherwise difficult to see. But there are differences between *descry* and *espy* that should make their usage more precise. *Descry* suggests careful observation of the distant or obscure, and there is more implication of effort and attention in *descry* than in *espy,* which hints at a chance, sudden, or unexpected discovery. [A sentinel on duty *descried* the approach of an enemy patrol; She turned around just in time to *espy* an old friend disappearing in the crowd.] *Descry* also refers to the kind of discovery that is the property of the mind and not the eyes. In this sense, *descry* means understand or come to realize by examination and investigation: to *descry* the true nature of a complicated crime; to *descry* the differences between two seemingly similar passages of music.

The phrase **make out** is less formal than the others in this group. It can mean see, but it is less simple than *see* because of its suggestion of difficulty or effort. [The room was so dark it was impossible to *make out* her expression.] It can also denote mental seeing as, for example, deciphering or understanding. [Can you *make out* the inscription on this old coin? It was difficult to *make out* what the lecturer meant.] See ACUMEN, LOOK, SEE, SENSATION, VISION.

Antonyms: *misapprehend, misconceive, miss, overlook.*

perfect
consummate
flawless
ideal

These adjectives characterize something that is the ultimate of its kind. **Perfect** suggests completeness and lack of blemish; it may refer to something imaginary or hyperbolically to something that exists: the *perfect* son; having spent a *perfect* evening. When referring to something that exists, it can also mean utterly typical: a *perfect* example of Romanesque architecture. It may refer to negative attributes as well as positive, in this case stressing total badness: a *perfect* fool; a *perfect* villain. **Flawless** relates closely to the aspect of *perfect* that emphasizes lack of blemish: a *flawless* apple. But *flawless,* unlike *perfect,* tends only to suggest an absence of negative qualities. Because of this, it is not used to indicate total badness, since it would make no sense to refer to a *flawless* fool. Furthermore, something can be *flawless* and yet far from *perfect:* a *flawless* but mediocre performance.

Consummate is closely related to *perfect* in its sense of ultimate completeness: a *consummate* pianist. Here it gives an overtone of slow maturation through disciplined effort. Like *flawless, consummate* does not usually refer to imagined excellence, largely because it stresses actually achieved qualities. Unlike *flawless,* however, it is often used to suggest total badness, like *perfect:* a *consummate* liar.

Ideal has the most strongly positive implications of any of these adjectives. It suggests the greatest excellence one can imagine: an *ideal* democracy that would require *ideal* citizens. If used to describe something that exists, the resulting hyperbole invites disbelief: the divorce that ended what everyone saw as an *ideal* marriage. As with *flawless,* it would make little sense to speak of *ideal* badness. While *ideal* can mean archetypal in the philosophy of Platonism, this specialized use does not intrude into other meanings. In general,

ideal is stronger than *perfect,* because something may be typical, complete, or without blemish, and still be far from *ideal.* Of course, in ordinary use, both are interchangeably used to mean anything pleasant: a *perfect* evening; an *ideal* vacation spot. See ENTIRE, FULL-FLEDGED.

Antonyms: DEFICIENT, *flawed, imperfect.*

perform
conduct
do
execute
fulfill

These verbs all mean carry out in action, as an assignment or a task. **Perform** is precisely directed to this concept, though **do** is the most general term. When the two verbs are synonymous, *perform* conveys a greater formality than *do,* or implies a greater degree of difficulty and intricacy: to *do* a trick; to *perform* a feat; to *do* odd jobs; to *perform* an operation; to *do* one's best; to *perform* a miracle. *Perform* also differs from *do* in stressing the idea of a ritual or a formal public presentation: to *perform* a marriage ceremony; to *perform* a symphony. It implies the rendering of a work or the carrying out of a rite that already exists, while *do* may suggest spontaneity and improvisation: to *perform* a play or a piece of music; to *do* impressions. In another comparison, to *do* a play is to undertake it and prepare it for presentation: The repertory company is *doing* Ibsen this season. To *perform* a play is to give it before an audience: They are *performing* Shakespeare in the park tonight.

Perform can also mean discharge an obligation, duty, or command: She wouldn't promise what she could not *perform.* In this sense, it is close to **fulfill,** which stresses accomplishment of something pledged, hoped for, or anticipated: to *fulfill* an obligation; to *fulfill* expectations; to *fulfill* a campaign promise. Of all these verbs, *fulfill* puts the greatest stress on completion or consummation, the realization of potential or capabilities. Hence it implies an ultimate performance: The prophecy was *fulfilled;* a novelist who failed to *fulfill* her early promise.

Conduct is close to *perform* but stresses direction, leadership, or supervision: to *conduct* an experiment; to *conduct* a survey. With reference to music, it is used of a single person and means direct the performance of a work: to *conduct* an opera. **Execute** is like *perform* in several senses. *Execute* can suggest intricacy, meaning *perform* something demanding expert skill or faultless technique: to *execute* a tricky maneuver; a ballerina *executing* a tour jeté; a skater *executing* a perfect double axle. Or it can point to accomplishment, meaning follow, carry out, or put into effect: to *execute* an order. It differs from *perform* in another sense, however, implying creation of a work according to a plan or design rather than the artistic rendering of a completed work: an artist skillfully *executing* a portrait; a seamstress *executing* a dress designer's design. See ARTISAN, PERFORMER, SATISFY.

performer
agent
doer
executive
factor

These nouns refer to a person who acts for himself or others. At its most general, **performer** may indicate the one who carries out an action: the *performer* of a contract. It may also indicate someone who can accomplish goals: children who are poor *performers* in school. In these senses, *performer* can also apply to inanimate objects: a report that named the cars that were the best *performers*. On a more specific and less formal level, *performer* is much more widely used to indicate any sort of entertainer: clowns, acrobats, and other circus *performers*. **Doer**, unlike *performer*, has no widely used specific sense and is even less frequently used in its corresponding general sense: separating people into the *doers* and the dreamers. In such uses, *doer* can sound like an offhand coinage.

Executive at its most formal can refer to someone who actually does a job, either for himself or herself, or for others; this is best illustrated by the compound nouns of certain titles. An *executive* director is one who actually directs the work of a group, although someone else may have the honorary title of director. In its most common use, *executive* indicates a person who belongs to the best-paid bracket of a business, the one concerned with making decisions: *executives* who rank high enough in the firm to have a private office with a window.

Agent and **factor** refer to a person who does something on the behalf of someone else. Businesspeople, authors, and actors all may hire *agents* to conduct their affairs. A *factor* is an *agent* in business affairs exclusively, one who for a commission will finance an undertaking or carry it out. See ARTIST, PERFORM.

perimeter
circumference
girth

periphery

These nouns refer to the outside boundary of a shape, taken as a whole. **Perimeter** can refer both to the bounding lines that enclose a plane figure and to the total length of this boundary: They posted No Trespass signs along the *perimeter* of the estate; the ins and outs of fjords that add hundreds of miles to the *perimeter* of the Norwegian coastline. The noun can also refer to the outer edges of something far less clearly defined: the shifting *perimeters* of each task force in the battle zone. **Periphery** relates most closely to this last sense of *perimeter*, referring more vaguely to the outer edges of something, especially as seen from within: a planet on the *periphery* of the solar system; less familiar with the paths that ran along the *periphery* of the camping areas. Sometimes, *periphery* is seen as applying mainly to solid objects, but this is not always true. It does have a more generalized use to suggest something that is far from the center of things and thus of little importance: an official position that was on the *periphery* of the administration's center of power.

Circumference refers to the *perimeter* of a circle, both to the line itself and to its total length. By extension, it can refer to the bounding line of any curved shape, plane or solid: a hundred seats along the outside *circumference* of the amphitheater; a barrel four feet at its widest *circumference*. **Girth** refers specifically to the circumference of a curved solid, particularly the waist or belly of a person or animal: the *girth* of a redwood at its base; a strap too short for the *girth* of the horse; a fat man of astonishing *girth*. See BOUNDARY, CIRCUMSCRIBE, EDGE.
Antonyms: *CENTER.*

period
age
cycle
eon
epoch
era
generation

These nouns can serve as arbitrary labels given to sequences of time. **Period** is the most general of these, and **eon** the least definite. *Period* can describe any passage of time, great or small: a rest *period* of five minutes; the stormy *period* of adolescence. In reference to history, *period* can loosely characterize a sequence of time as a convenient aid to discussion, without claiming that such a sequence is homogeneous or self-contained: the *period* of artistic ferment between the wars. By contrast, *eon* is used, often in the plural, to indicate an immeasurably long stretch of time. While otherwise vague in reference, *eon* explicitly rejects any notion of uniformity in the *period* alluded to: the *eons* before the appearance on the planet of human beings; the *eons* remaining before the sun's extinction. **Cycle** is much more clear-cut at its most restricted, referring to a single and complete instance in a recurring pattern of time. [A *cycle* of the sun takes a year, while one *cycle* of the moon, revealing all its phases, takes twenty-eight days; the life *cycle* of the hookworm.] Sometimes, *cycle* can refer to the recurring pattern itself: the business *cycle* and its alternation between bull and bear markets.

Epoch most strictly indicates an event of such significance that it can be said to usher in a new *period* in history: The bombing of Hiroshima marked an *epoch* in human history. More often now, *epoch* is used to refer indefinitely to a compact or self-contained *period* in human history, recognizable because of a consistency in its emphases or concerns: the *epoch* of Spanish conquests in the New World. **Era** refers exclusively to such a self-contained *period* of history, although the time span implied may be longer than that suggested by the extended use of *epoch:* Cubism, Abstractionism, and Pop Art have all been *epochs* in the modern *era.*

Generation refers to the *period* between the birth of parents and the birth of their offspring, sometimes calculated for human beings as twenty or twenty-five years; it may also refer to the offspring themselves: They were the first of their *generation* to attend college. More pertinent here, *generation* has become a fad word for typifying any *era*, often shorter than twenty years, in which young people coming of age seem involved in concerns or behavior more characteristic of them than of their parents: the Silent *Generation* of students in the Reagan *Era;* unconventional young people who considered themselves members of the Love *Generation.*

Age might often suggest a longer *period* than *epoch* or *era*, one that could be typified in terms of some dominant interest or person: the *Age* of Shakespeare; the Atomic *Age;* the *Age* of Jackson. Some writers feel that *age* is preferable to *era* in such designations, since the former is factual in tone, whereas *era* can possibly sound pretentious or inflated.

In geology, paleontology, and archeology, the terms *era, period, epoch,* and *age* have been assigned arbitrary definitions. In paleontology, the paleozoic *era* is divided into the *age* of invertebrates, the *age* of fishes, and the *age* of amphibians. In geology, the paleozoic

era is divided into *periods,* such as the Permian *Period,* which is further subdivided into *epochs,* such as the Thuringian *Epoch.* In archeology, the basic division is an *age,* determined by the predominant culture, as the Stone *Age,* the Bronze *Age,* and the Iron *Age.* The Stone *Age* is subdivided into *periods* or *eras,* as the neolithic and paleolithic *periods* or *eras.* See EVERLASTING, MODERN, OLD-FASHIONED.

permanent
abiding
durable
enduring
indelible
lasting
perennial
perpetual
stable

These adjectives characterize that which does not change, pass away, or fade. **Permanent** is a broad word meaning continuing in the same place or condition without change for an indefinitely long period of time: the *permanent* foundation of a building; the *permanent* effect of French on the English language; *permanent* damage to the spinal cord. **Lasting** is closely synonymous with *permanent*, but is used to refer to something that may end sooner or later: a *lasting* friendship; the *lasting* effects of having fought in Vietnam. **Enduring** is stronger than either *permanent* or *lasting*, as it implies great resistance to time and to change: the *enduring* grandeur of Bach chorales; the *enduring* influence of Christianity. **Perpetual** is perhaps the strongest adjective in the entire group and emphasizes the sense of continuing endlessly in time. It refers chiefly to an activity that is not susceptible to interruption: the *perpetual* flow of the river; *perpetual* motion. In everyday talk *perpetual* is used of things that are annoying or seem to continue for maddeningly long periods of time: a *perpetual* rain; their *perpetual* complaints. **Durable**, less closely related to the above adjectives, describes that which is able to continue for a long time in the same state and has the power to resist change, decay, and wear: *durable* woolen cloth; the *durable* granite of the cliff; the *durable* and indomitable spirit of the gold prospector.

Perennial differs from the other adjectives in that it originally stipulated a set period of time—a year. In one sense it has come to mean *lasting* for one year or recurring every year: *perennial* plants. Now, by extension, it means both *permanent* and *perpetual* in describing something that is unceasing and also impervious to change: the *perennial* rise and fall of the tides; the *perennial* ties between parents and children; poverty, the *perennial* problem in our cities.

Stable applies to that which has a firmness of character or position so as to resist change or displacement: a *stable* currency; a *stable* economy. *Stable*, alone in this group, is applied to human personality as marked by steadfastness of purpose, emotional balance, and the ability to handle stress: a nervous, excitable teacher not considered *stable* enough to continue in his job.

Indelible means permanent in the sense of not being easily erased or obliterated: *indelible* strawberry stains on a tablecloth; an old letter written in *indelible* ink; a scene of horror that left an *indelible* impression on his memory.

Abiding refers to that which has continued and will continue for a long time. It is applied mostly to feelings and abstract concepts: *abiding* love; *abiding* truth. Now found mostly in poetry and literature of the past, it is best replaced by *lasting* or *enduring*. See EVERLASTING, IMMORTAL, IMMUTABLE, MONOTONOUS, PERMANENT, PERSISTENT.

Antonyms: *brief, short-lived,* TEMPORARY.

permeate

imbue
impregnate
penetrate
pervade
saturate
supersaturate

These verbs express the action of passing into and spreading through every part of something, such as a liquid or a gas. **Permeate** focuses directly on this concept. It emphasizes both entry and diffusion, indicating infiltration through pores. It may be used in a physical sense: a waterproof fabric, treated with a substance that keeps water from *permeating* it; spring rains that *permeate* the earth. Or it may apply to a sense impression: Cooking odors *permeated* the air. It is especially expressive, however, in figurative contexts with reference to intangibles. [The atmosphere of Ireland *permeated* the pub; The spirit of the times *permeates* her novels; A sense of peace and contentment *permeated* the room.] **Penetrate** comes from a Latin verb meaning put within. More strongly than *permeate*, *penetrate* stresses the initial entry into something and usually implies the overcoming of resistance. [A powerful headlight beam was needed to *penetrate* the fog; Here no sound can

penetrate; Penetrating cold chilled him to the bone; tissues that allow certain liquids to *penetrate* while preventing passage of others.] *Penetrate* is also used of a figurative breakthrough and may sometimes refer to a deep or lasting effect made on the mind or emotions: a psychiatrist using hypnosis to *penetrate* a patient's amnesia; an attempt to *penetrate* the boy's protective hostility.

Pervade comes from Latin roots meaning go through and marks a shift in emphasis from entry to effect. Where *permeate* refers to an action like that of a gas that diffuses through all the pores or intermolecular spaces of a solid or another gas, *pervade* describes the action of a gas that fills all the open space of a chamber. Hence, a gas *pervades* a room by *permeating* the air in the room. In extended senses, *pervade* is more closely synonymous with *permeate;* it may be used of any quality, idea, force, influence, or sensation diffused throughout all of a thing. [The influence of the former headmaster still *pervades* the school; A strange stillness *pervaded* the garden, like the hush before a storm; In the eyes of the priest, God *pervaded* all of creation.] **Impregnate** goes beyond *permeate* and *pervade*. It stresses the new qualities or characteristics gained by a substance through which some other substance has been diffused: air *impregnated* with poisonous gases. It is also used figuratively: Every page of the work is *impregnated* with her prejudices.

Saturate comes from a Latin verb meaning fill up, and **supersaturate** is an intensification of *saturate*. In chemistry, a solution is said to be *saturated* when the solvent can hold no more of the solute under existing conditions of temperature and pressure: water *saturated* with salt. A *supersaturated* solution is one carried beyond the normal degree of *saturation*, made to hold more solute by a mechanical process of heating and cooling. A slight shock or the addition of one more bit of solute to such a solution can suddenly produce crystallization. When air becomes *saturated* with water vapor, having a relative humidity of 100%, the excess vapor begins to condense as dew; when *supersaturated*, the air contains an amount of moisture more than sufficient to *saturate* it, as in a fog. In general usage, *saturate* means fill anything to the utmost extent of its capacity for absorbing or retaining. Going well beyond *permeate*, it often suggests a thorough soaking or a being thoroughly soaked. [Moisture *permeated* the wall, leaving it damp; Rain *saturated* their clothes, leaving them sodden; A swamp is land so *saturated* with water as to be unfit for tillage.] *Saturate* is also used figuratively. [His mind was *saturated* with facts after hours of cramming for the exam; She *saturated* herself in the culture and customs of her adopted land.] *Supersaturate* also has extended uses, referring to more of anything than can be absorbed or accommodated: a *supersaturated* labor market, resulting in a high rate of unemployment.

Imbue comes from a Latin verb meaning wet, soak, or dye. In a physical sense, it suggests the imparting of a color that soaks in and *saturates* the whole: The dye *permeated* the cloth, *imbuing* it with a rich red color. In a figurative sense, *imbue* means fill or *impregnate,* as with emotions, ideals, or other intangible qualities. [She *imbued* her son with the principles for which she fought; fighting men *imbued* with patriotism; a strangely sinister place, *imbued* and *saturated* with an atmosphere of evil.] See IMPENETRABLE, IMPLANT, PIERCE.

permit
allow
authorize
let

These verbs refer to the act of not preventing. **Permit**, **allow**, and **let** are loosely related, *permit* being the strongest of the three. To *permit* is to grant leave to or empower by express consent. *Permit* suggests authority that could prevent something from occurring if it chose: The chairman recognized the delegate and *permitted* him to speak. *Allow,* used positively, means grant as a right or privilege: a youth *allowed* to stay out until midnight and *permitted* to use the family car on occasion. *Allow* and *permit* are often used interchangeably; *allow,* however, is a less formal term and often carries the idea of not attempting to hinder. *Permit,* by contrast, implies a greater or lesser degree of approval and may indicate official sanction. [The nurse *allowed* the visitors to remain beyond the hospital visiting hours, though such visits were not *permitted.*] *Let,* the least formal of these verbs, may sometimes suggest permission or consent, but may imply no more than a failure to prevent or restrain. [He asked the boss to *let* him leave an hour early; Don't interrupt them—*let* them speak their piece.] A person may *let* things happen passively, either through choice or through indifference, carelessness, error, or inattention. [He decided to *let* his hair grow; She decided to *let* her insurance policy lapse; They forgot to shut the windows and thereby *let* the rain in.] As opposed to *permit, let* may point up a lack of, or failure to exercise, preventive authority: a timid, unassertive man, always *letting* people take advantage of him.

Authorize is stronger and more formal than *permit* and is more limited in application. It implies positive approval of a proposed course of action by an authority empowered either to *permit* or to forbid it. [The State *authorized* construction of a new expressway; The firm *authorized* use of company cars by sales personnel after working hours.] *Authorize* may further imply the delegation of authority: a UN official *authorized* by the secretariat to initiate formal negotiations. See ENDORSE, LENIENT.

Antonyms: *enjoin, forbid, interdict, prevent, prohibit.*

perquisite. Do not confuse the noun *perquisite* (allowance, privilege, etc., given in addition to salary) with *prerequisite* (qualification required as a condition for admission, advancement, etc.).

persist
continue
endure
last
survive
weather

These verbs all refer to something that goes on existing. **Persist** at its mildest can indicate the lingering on of something beyond the point at which one would expect it to terminate: A dwindling hope of restoring the monarchy *persisted* for a century. At its most forceful, *persist* suggests a tenacious will to exist, as in a hardy or stubborn struggle against odds: a species that *persisted* despite the depredations of floods, glaciers, famine, and plague. Less favorably, *persist* can indicate an annoying or obstinate insistence that goes on without letup. [He *persisted* in quibbling about fine points in the contract long after everyone else was satisfied; Why do you still *persist* in bothering us with demands for money?]

Continue is much more general than *persist;* it is also less definite, since its neutrality is uncolored by implications of any sort. *Continue* refers to any ongoing process after its start and before its conclusion: an announcement that the bombings would *continue;* her hope that she would be able to *continue* in school; The riot *continued* to rage for a third day. Sometimes, *continue* can specifically point to a resumption after a halt: Please *continue* with what you were doing before I came in. **Last** refers specifically to something that *continues* to exist, particularly when this is not necessarily inevitable: the few masterpieces from each age that will *last* centuries. At its most literal, *last* can refer to remaining viable or alive, or it can be used in connection with measuring duration: perfume with a scent that *lasts* a long time; He *lasted* out the fever but succumbed to a minor infection; an avant-garde film that *lasts* eight hours.

Endure can be used as a more formal substitute for *last:* a body of poetry that will *endure.* The verb has richer associations when it is used transitively. As a transitive verb, it suggests the same dauntless struggle for existence against odds that *persist* can refer to, but without overtones of obstinacy, since *endure* is almost wholly favorable in tone: patriots willing to *endure* torture and even death to defend their country; the traditional siesta that helped us to *endure* the broiling summers of the tropics. Intransitively, **survive** indicates *continued* existence: Somehow, we *survive.* Often, *survive* implies the successful overcoming of an ordeal or threat to existence: Of those wounded in the battle, only three *survived.* Transitively, *survive* compares with *endure,* except that the latter suggests a strength and permanence that can overcome obstacles intact, whereas *survive* is open to the implication of greater frailty or subsequent impairment: Although many died or *survived* only as mental wrecks, a few of the hardiest explorers could *endure* every punishment the jungles offered.

Weather is restricted to a transitive sense that points to the *surviving* of crises or exposures to danger. *Weather* may apply to *lasting* out difficulty without change or impairment, but more often it suggests an altered state, though this may often be one of increased maturity or mellowness: She *weathered* every conflict in their marriage without the slightest difficulty; an increased sense of self-confidence among law students who *weather* the agonies of their freshman year; people who *weather* a first heart attack with only slight impairment. See MATURE (V.), REMAIN.

Antonyms: *collapse,* DIE, *fade, fail,* STOP (*cease*).

persistent
ceaseless
continual
continuous
incessant
unceasing
unremitting

These adjectives characterize that which continues or is repeated without letup. **Persistent** can indicate an unflagging series of efforts, favorably implying determination or unfavorably implying a meddlesome attitude: his *persistent* efforts to better himself from his first job as a lifeguard to his appointment as district attorney; annoyed by the stranger's *persistent* questions. *Persistent* is very general, however, since it can also apply to anything of long duration or to any series of repetitions: finally awakened by the *persistent* ringing of the alarm clock; the *persistent* brushing of oak leaves against our bedroom windows.

Continuous refers exclusively to something that is unbroken throughout its entire length, no matter how great and whether its extension is through time or space: a *continuous* expanse of wall without door or window; a *continuous* hum in one of the word processors. **Continual**, by contrast, pertains exclusively to something that, despite short or great intervals of rest, is repeated over a long period of time: the *continual* coming and going of trains in the depot; a *continual* pounding at his door; the *continual* bickering of their parents.

Unremitting is an intensification of *persistent* in both its positive and negative uses. When positive, *unremitting* can indicate earnest dedication, suggesting an undaunted or relentless series of efforts or attempts: Robert the Bruce watched as the spider tried again and again with *unremitting* patience to weave its web. When negative, *unremitting* suggests inflexibility or stubbornness; in this case, it can function more like *continuous* since it suggests an unalterable or unbroken extension of something through time: an *unremitting* hatred that had not diminished over the years.

The remaining adjectives all characterize something that continues without a break. While all three can be used in this way, **incessant** is often used now particularly for anything that occurs in quick repetitions over a long time span: the *incessant* crashing of waves against the rocks. *Incessant* can also apply forcefully to annoying or meddlesome repetitions: *incessant* phone calls from the bill collector; the *incessant* whining and complaining of the child. **Ceaseless** and **unceasing** are close in meaning, but *ceaseless* might be the word of choice for uninterrupted action, *unceasing* for unchanging attitudes: her *ceaseless* vigil by the sickbed; the loud and *ceaseless* playing of his radio; *unceasing* devotion. *Ceaseless,* thus, can be a more emphatic substitute for *continuous* in its temporal application, while *unceasing* can be a milder substitute for the favorable sense of *unremitting.* See EVERLASTING, INEXORABLE, INVARIABLE, MONOTONOUS, PERMANENT, STUBBORN.

Antonyms: OCCASIONAL, *periodic,* TEMPORARY.

perspicuous. Do not confuse the adjective *per-*

spicuous (easily understood) with the adjective *perspicacious* (having great insight).

physical

bodily
carnal
corporal
corporeal
fleshly
fleshy
material
mesomorphic

These adjectives refer to matter or the body as distinguished from the mind or spirit. **Physical** sums up the whole range of possibilities in these adjectives, some aspects of which each succeeding adjective concentrates on to the exclusion of others. It can refer to the matter and energy of the universe and the science that treats it: the *physical* sciences. Anything apparent to the senses can be described by *physical*: the *physical* remains of a vanished culture. It can also refer to the body: *physical* beauty; a *physical* defect. Or it can distinguish the body from the mind: tests to determine whether the heart pains were *physical* or psychological in origin. In dualistic philosophy, *physical* contrasts with spiritual: rejecting *physical* attachments for enduring spiritual values. Most concretely, if somewhat euphemistically, *physical* can refer to sexuality: *physical* love.

Corporeal more clearly contrasts with the spiritual or immaterial than *physical*: positing a spiritual basis underlying all *corporeal* things. It can also refer to anything organized into an entity: *corporeal* property. **Material** is a less scholarly sounding term than *corporeal* in its reference to matter or to *physical* objects: the *material* universe; their *material* possessions. *Material* is often used to distinguish object-oriented values from more idealistic ones: the *material* greed fostered by advertising. **Corporal** now refers exclusively to the body, intensifying the negative possibilities of *physical* in this sense by emphasizing most often what is applied to or inflicted on the body: *corporal* punishment. Beyond this stock phrase, *corporal* is less often used than the more direct **bodily**. The latter can be neutral in itself, or it can be opposed to the mental or spiritual: *bodily* sensations carried to the brain; those *bodily* appetites considered sinful. Related to the last possibility, *bodily* can refer specifically to sensual or sexual pleasures, possibly in a disapproving way, although this use may now sound old-fashioned: *bodily* desire.

Fleshly and **carnal** concentrate on this last implication of *bodily*, *fleshly* appearing in a religious context and *carnal* most often in legal terminology. *Fleshly*, however, can sound even more old-fashioned than *bodily*: *fleshly* dissipations. One use of *carnal* is so familiar as to have reduced its use in other ways, referring specifically to sexual intercourse in *carnal knowledge*. Where *carnal* once could refer simply to sensual or *bodily* appetite, it now might be misunderstood as explicitly indicating the sexual: a *carnal* licentiousness that characterized Venetian society. **Fleshy** is useful as a neutral designation for soft *bodily* tissue as opposed to bone and sinew: wounded in the *fleshy* part of the upper arm. This adjective can even refer to flabby muscle or fat tissues: his torso having grown noticeably *fleshy* over the years. Although much more formal and technical, **mesomorphic** relates to *fleshy* in referring to a body in which muscular tissue has been favored by development over nervous and digestive tissue: neurasthenic, pyknic, and *mesomorphic* body types. More loosely, as a fad word, *mesomorphic* can refer merely to a substantially developed muscularity: a gung-ho *mesomorphic* first sergeant.

Antonyms: *mental, spiritual.*

pierce

penetrate
prick
probe
stab

These verbs indicate the forcing of a sharp, pointed instrument into something by means of a driving or cutting action. **Pierce** may suggest merely the cutting of any opening into something, though more often it is used to indicate the cutting of a hole entirely through a thin layer to its other side: a screen *pierced* to let light through; *piercing* a balloon; a hat *pierced* by a hatpin; instruments used to *pierce* ears. By implication, the opening through the layer is made by a sharp, thin object such as a needle or lance. **Stab**, by contrast, suggests that something is merely cut into, not *pierced*. Furthermore, *stab* suggests the use of a bladed instrument such as a sword or knife rather than something needlelike, as with *pierce*: *stabbing* the man with a dagger. **Prick** is more nearly comparable to *pierce*, but specifically may suggest a light, glancing thrust of a needlelike instrument to make a small opening in or through a thin layer: *pricking* the blister with a heated needle; thorns that *pricked* her skin as she ran.

Penetrate is more formal and more general than

the foregoing. It may suggest the partial or complete passage made by any sort of instrument: measuring the depth to which the bullet had *penetrated* the flesh; a facade of marble *penetrated* by three rows of windows. *Penetrate* may also suggest the achieving of any sort of entrance into or through something, whether along an existing passageway, through a discontinuous mass, or through a permeable membrane. In these cases, the act may by implication be difficult but may be achieved without altering or actually *piercing* the medium itself: brave explorers who first *penetrated* the interior of Africa; light that *penetrated* the dusty windows; tissues that allow certain liquids to *penetrate* while preventing passage of others. **Probe** suggests a deliberate, cautious, or exploratory attempt to *penetrate* something; the passage may already exist or may be made by the act of *probing*: carefully *probing* the cavity with a toothpick; two men sent in to *probe* the tunnels for possible survivors; scalpels with which to *probe* the tumor for signs of malignancy. See CUT, HEW, PERMEATE.

pile

agglomeration
heap
mass

These nouns denote the result of processes through which things or particles are gathered together. **Pile** suggests that the things gathered were brought together, usually by a person, rather than accumulated by chance or natural processes. It further suggests that the accumulated things were placed in some sort of order, one on top of the others, for example, or in layers. Finally, the things in a *pile,* such as the blocks in a *pile* of building blocks, are usually all of the same kind and, more than likely, of about the same size and shape.

Heap implies a more casual gathering of things than *pile.* The things, which eventually take the form of a mound, are thrown together carelessly or haphazardly, and there is usually no evidence in a *heap* of selection or special arrangement: a *heap* of old clothes in the attic. **Agglomeration,** even more than *heap,* suggests a chance coming together of its parts, those parts being heterogeneous and not compacted, connected, or consistent: a room that was an *agglomeration* of so many different styles of decorating that it seemed more the work of an eccentric than of an eclectic.

A **mass** is an assemblage of things that together make up a single body. There is in *heap* an indication of adherence or coherence of the individual parts or objects and a suggestion that the final accumulated *mass* has no definite shape but is relatively large in size: a *mass* of clay; a *mass* of flowers. See ACCUMULATION.

plain

bush
desert
outback
pampas
prairie
range
savanna
steppe
tundra
veldt

These nouns refer to large areas of usually level country that may be farm or grazing land, or unsettled wilderness. **Plain** is the general noun here for such countryside, giving no information in itself as to fertility or other topographical facts: the great *plains;* the cities of the *plain.* **Steppe** suggests a specific geographical locale, that of Russia, but is otherwise general, like *plain,* with as little indication of fertility or infertility: Mongol tribes that fanned out across the *steppes.* While **desert** suggests no geographical placement, it does specifically point to barren and infertile regions lacking in rainfall and composed mainly of sandy soil or undulating sand dunes: the Sahara *desert;* an irrigation project intended to make the *desert* fruitful.

All the other nouns here point to a specific kind of countryside and suggest as well a specific geographical locale. **Prairie** suggests the fertile but largely unforested *plains* of the U.S. Midwest: the rich loam of Nebraska *prairies.* **Veldt** points to the fertile *plains* of South Africa; these are by and large grassy but unforested and filled with an array of wildlife. Unlike the *prairies* of North America, much of the *veldt* has not been converted into farmland and is still wild and pristine. **Bush,** less exclusively, suggests land that is wild, unsettled, and covered with scrub growth, as in East Africa: steps taken to encourage cattle-raising in the *bush. Bush* is also applied to the backcountry of certain other lands, especially Australia, designating an extensive, unsettled or sparsely populated region thought of as being uncivilized, rugged, or wild. The Canadian *bush* is unsettled northern forest land. **Outback** indicates the backcountry of Australia and New Zealand, referring particularly to the arid and unsettled northerly regions of Australia: the untapped resources of the Australian *outback.*

The **pampas** are the great treeless *plains* of South America, extending from the Atlantic to the Andes, south of the Amazon River. Like the East African *bush* country, the *pampas* are used mainly for cattle grazing, the land not being fertile enough to yield much in the way of cereal crops: gauchos who ride herd on the Argentine *pampas*. **Range** is the equivalent North American term for the same kind of countryside: cattle raised on the Wyoming *range*. This *range* country is bordered by more fertile *prairie* country on one side and mountainous countryside or *desert* on the other, intermingling features of both.

Savanna, used of country in the southeast part of the U.S., designates a tract of level, treeless land covered with low vegetation. More broadly, the term refers to a large area of tropical or subtropical grassland, as an African pasture or a South American campo, covered in part with trees and spiny shrubs, and found in regions undergoing alternate rainy and dry seasons. **Tundra**, by contrast, refers to a flat or rolling, treeless, often marshy *plain* of Arctic or near-Arctic regions, as of Siberia, the Scandinavian countries, and the northernmost parts of North America. The *tundras* have permanently frozen subsoil and are poor in vegetation, though they are covered with moss in summer and furnish forage for such animals as reindeer: Finns who raise reindeer on the *tundra* in northern Finland. See BACKCOUNTRY.

Antonyms: *MOUNTAIN.*

plain

apparent
conspicuous
evident
manifest
obvious

These adjectives all mean readily perceived. **Plain**, the most general, means clear and understandable and suggests strongly that there is little possibility of confusion or mistake in perceiving the object concerned. [The *plain* fact of the matter is that the man lied; His guilt is *plain*—the stolen money was found in his briefcase.]

Apparent and **evident** are close synonyms, both indicating the easily perceived or recognizable. Of the two, *apparent* is perhaps more commonly used when referring to something visible, although both adjectives are used to describe mental perceptions as well as sensory ones. [It was soon *apparent* that our horse was winning the race; From the quick success of the business, it was *evident* that she had invested wisely; He

spoke with *evident* sarcasm.] Because *apparent* can also mean seeming to be, as opposed to being in fact, its use may be ambiguous (especially before nouns), and *evident* may therefore be preferred in some contexts. For example, *apparent defeat* could mean that the defeat was more *evident* than real; *evident defeat*, on the other hand, states flatly that the defeat was *plain* and makes no suggestion of reality contradicting appearance.

Obvious, **manifest**, and **conspicuous** mean immediately *apparent*, unmistakably true; all imply that the issue is so unequivocal and *plain* that contradiction would be absurd. *Manifest* suggests that outward signs or actions may be taken as revealing inward character; it points to openness and explicitness as qualities that make something *plain: manifest* disapproval of another's actions, expressed in forthright language; The *manifest* bias of the judge, referring to the young defendant as a punk, disqualified him from presiding over the trial. *Conspicuous* implies that something stands out, unavoidably striking the eye or mind as different or irregular: a *conspicuous* defect in the fabric; a *conspicuous* typographical error, with one whole line of type printed upside down; a discrepancy in the company accounts so *conspicuous* that no auditor will fail to notice it. *Obvious* describes something too *conspicuous* to be concealed and too *apparent* to be disputed: an *obvious* gimmick to compensate for the playwright's flagging invention. *Obvious* is often used to point up the disparity between form and meaning in disingenuous gestures: an *obvious* pitch for maintaining the status quo concealed within a high-flown plea for law and order; Though couched in elegant diplomatic language, the note *obviously* threw cold water on any hopes we had for U.S. aid. See CLEAR, DEFINITE, FLAGRANT, OVERT.

Antonyms: *concealed, hidden, imperceptible, IMPLICIT, inconspicuous, secret.*

plan

blueprint
design
program
proposal
scheme

These nouns refer to sets of ideas developed to accomplish a desired result. **Plan** is both the most informal and the most general. It can refer at one extreme to a tentative, unverbalized cluster of notions, at the other to a detailed final draft stating the precise methods by which to proceed: a vague *plan* to go there sometime; final *plans* for a merger that filled six filing cabinets. **Scheme** is also informal, but is restricted in meaning either to a vague, unverbalized notion or to surreptitious or unsavory ideas. Unworkability may be implied in the former case, conspiratorial plotting in the latter: coming up with *scheme* after *scheme* for getting rich quick; a carefully planned *scheme* for blowing up the two buildings.

Design and **blueprint** both relate to the side of *plan* that suggests a detailed final draft. *Design* can suggest harmony and order as the salient feature of the *plan;* it can also suggest a symbolic rather than literal rendering of the work to be done: a building noteworthy for its simplicity of *design;* an architect who made the grand *design* had his staff fill in the details. *Blueprint,* by contrast, suggests minute attention to every detail: a complete *blueprint* for enforcing the new law.

Proposal can suggest tentativeness, like *plan,* but it strongly implies collaboration through discussion, or a hierarchic situation in which approval of a *plan* must first be obtained: a *proposal* for spending the afternoon in the park; a *proposal* approved by the Senate but defeated in the House. **Program** may suggest a detailed set of *proposals* but, alone of all these nouns, it most specifically suggests a *plan* that is actually being carried out: the tenth anniversary of the health *program.*

playful
frisky
frolicsome
sportive

These adjectives refer to an inclination to take part in pleasurable activity. **Playful** is the most general and the most neutral in indicating any mood of levity that does not directly contribute to the accomplishing of essential or practical tasks: distracted from her sewing by the *playful* kitten; husbands who expect to return at night to well-kept homes and to lively and *playful* wives, who themselves have careers. **Frolicsome** is an intensification of *playful* in that it suggests the positive presence of exuberant spirits that make one wish to undertake madcap or zany adventures on the spur of the moment: a group of *frolicsome* youngsters who decided to drive to the beach at four in the morning. The overtone of sexual adventurousness present in *playful* is intensified here: *frolicsome* couples at the picnic.

Frisky, like *frolicsome,* also pertains to high spirits, but stresses as well an extremely active physical energy that may be nervous, impatient, headlong, and irre-

pressible: three or four *frisky* colts cantering about the pasture; a first round of drinks that made him feel *frisky* and insouciant. *Frisky* is even more pertinent to sexual adventurousness than *frolicsome,* but may stress, more informally in this case, lusty impatience rather than good-humored desire: giving her boyfriend a swat whenever he became too *frisky.* **Sportive** may suggest an inclination to merrymaking in almost as neutral a way as *playful,* though it is considerably more formal than these other adjectives: coffeehouses that are gathering places for *sportive* teenagers. *Sportive* may also refer specifically to an interest in games or sports: taking down his golf clubs every spring when the weather makes him feel *sportive.* More often, *sportive* refers to a specifically sexual interest although it need not suggest either the levity inherent in *frolicsome* or the impatience possible for *frisky*: cocktail lounges where *sportive* career women can meet unattached males on the make. See LIVELY, MISCHIEVOUS.
Antonyms: *LISTLESS, SEDATE.*

plead
appeal
beg
petition
sue

These verbs refer to a humble, deferential, urgent, or formal request for help. **Plead** may suggest a dignified humility, but in any case it stresses urgency: *pleading* for another chance. Even in legal uses, where it is now formalistic for any request or for a stating of position, as in *pleading* guilty, its implications of urgency can still be felt: *pleading* for mercy. **Beg** is much more informal than *plead* and devoid of legal application. Furthermore, it may join to the urgency implicit in *plead* a note not so much of humility as of abjectness: *begging* with them at least to spare the life of the child. In less extreme uses a sense of debasement may still be present, suggesting an insistent, continual harrying of someone in a position to grant a favor: *begging* hopelessly for a second chance; *begging* to be allowed to go outside and play.

Appeal may not always suggest as great an urgency as *plead,* but it suggests an even greater dignity, implying a request based on reference to moral imperatives: *appealing* to the crowd's sense of fair play. Legally, it suggests a request in the name of justice that one's objection be sustained or that a decision against one be reversed: *appealing* to the judge for a ruling; *appealing* to a higher court. **Petition**, like *appeal,* suggests an address to authority. It is much more formal, however, except when it refers in a political context to the backing up of a request by the signed approval of others: *petitioning* to get a separate line on the ballot. There are some situations in which this implied gathering of signatures is not present, and *petition* refers to a routine way of making a request: *petitioning* her neighbors to support the fund drive.

Sue is seldom used intransitively in the legal sense and is extremely formal to the point of stuffiness in more ordinary contexts, except in some set phrases: *sue* for redress; *sue* for peace. See DEMAND, REQUEST.

Antonyms: *command,* DEMAND.

pleasing
agreeable
attractive
engaging
enjoyable
gratifying
nice
pleasant

These adjectives characterize anything found interesting and satisfying. They are, as a group, words that are associated with mild pleasures and comforts rather than with intense feelings or passionate commitments. **Pleasing** and **pleasant** are, with one exception, the mildest of these adjectives, referring to a positive response to a setting, person, idea, or thing. The response, however, is not so deep that one would be unable to turn away without regret. *Pleasant* suggests something naturally appealing because of its cheerful exterior or warm disposition. *Pleasing* may suggest, beyond this implication, a conscious attempt to please: a *pleasant* view of the harbor; a *pleasing* waiter. When *pleasing* does not refer to such a conscious attempt, it is nevertheless slightly stronger than *pleasant* in suggesting something more satisfying or better able to hold the attention; also, *pleasant* may refer more to mood, *pleasing* to comeliness: a *pleasant* smile; a *pleasing* figure. **Nice** is milder than either of the foregoing and can, of course, refer to any kind of positive response whatsoever. Having no connotations of its own, it is susceptible of any implications that context may give it.

Agreeable, where it goes beyond *pleasing,* suggests something especially in harmony with the wishes of the beholder: an *agreeable* afternoon spent chatting with friends; an *agreeable* city for an art lover to be stranded in. **Attractive** and **engaging** are stronger than either *agreeable* or *pleasing* in suggesting something that draws or holds one's attention. *Attractive* stresses comeliness that draws attention; *engaging* suggests liveliness or some other appeal that makes it difficult to turn away from: a woman who chose her clothes to set off her *attractive* figure; valued at parties because she was such an *engaging* conversationalist.

Enjoyable and **gratifying** stress actual satisfaction rather than the ability to draw or hold attention. *Enjoyable* is of a mildness comparable to that of *pleasing,* but *gratifying* suggests a greater intensity of pleasure than any other adjective here. [The musical comedy sounded *attractive* enough to make us risk a visit, but while some of the numbers were *enjoyable* and a few of them actually *engaging,* the evening was far from *gratifying.*] The special force of *gratifying* lies in its suggestion that something has answered a deeper expectation or need; in this sense *gratifying* is an intensification of *agreeable:* a truly *gratifying* friendship based on long, *agreeable* talks. See CHARMING.

Antonyms: BAD, *displeasing,* OBNOXIOUS, REPULSIVE, *unattractive,* UNGRATIFYING.

pleasure
delectation
delight
ecstasy
enjoyment
fun
glee
joy
rapture

These nouns all denote feelings of satisfaction or happiness. **Pleasure** is the most general term in the group. In its mildest sense, *pleasure* may be no more than an expression of politeness, or convey the absence of discomfort. [I have the *pleasure* of presenting our commencement speaker; The patient rallied and was able to take some *pleasure* in her surroundings.] *Pleasure* may arise from a stimulation of the mind or the senses: the *pleasure* they found in books; the *pleasure* of watching a spectacular sunset. In its strongest sense, *pleasure* emphasizes gratification of the senses, especially of sexual appetite, or it may refer to a round of futile and frivolous amusements that exclude meaningful activity. In this meaning *pleasure* may have a pejorative implication: the *pleasures* of the flesh; a rich young man who passed the time in relentless pursuit of *pleasure.*

Delight may be a strong feeling of *pleasure,* but it is likely to be sudden and transient: *delighted* cries of children on Christmas morning; to take *delight* in winning a chess match. *Delight* may also refer to that in which one takes quiet *pleasure* over a long span of time: the *delights* of a childhood spent on a farm.

Ecstasy and **rapture** denote intense or extreme exaltation, originally that accompanying religious or creative experience, but currently that of intense *pleasure* or *delight*. From earlier usage, *ecstasy* connotes a trancelike state wherein one stands beside oneself, conscious neither of surroundings nor of self, but only of what one contemplates or feels: the *ecstasy* of a saint during a mystical experience. *Ecstasy* still implies such intensity of feeling that other perceptions are clouded over: the *ecstasy* of first love. *Rapture*, in its original sense, connotes being seized or lifted up, as by divine power. It is now closely related in meaning to *ecstasy*. Both nouns are commonly used hyperbolically to describe almost any degree of *pleasure* or excitement: in a state of *ecstasy* at being accepted at the college of her choice; a child *ecstatic* over a new puppy.

Joy is sometimes used interchangeably with *pleasure, delight, ecstasy*, or *rapture*, but it implies greater intensity than does *pleasure*, longer duration than does *delight* and is seldom so intense an experience as *rapture* or *ecstasy*: the *joy* of watching the signs of spring returning after a hard winter; the *joys* of living in a warm family setting.

Enjoyment and **delectation** may be used as mild synonyms for *delight, joy*, or *pleasure*. However, both denote action accompanying these feelings rather than the feelings themselves. *Enjoyment* is the savoring of what is pleasing; *delectation* implies a giving over of oneself to something that amuses or diverts: the *enjoyment* of conversing with good friends; the *delectation* of the theater.

Fun denotes lighthearted playfulness or jesting. [He is full of *fun*; We enjoy insulting one another in *fun*.] *Fun* is also a general term that may apply to any diversion that affords *enjoyment*, or to the *enjoyment* itself. [Picnics are *fun*; We had *fun* riding our bicycles in the park today.] It may also be applied to an activity that engages one's interest or imagination, an activity that may prove to be more than a diversion and may involve hard work: the *fun* of learning to play the piano; a fortunate person who finds both *fun* and challenge in work; raising pedigreed dogs for *fun* rather than for profit.

Glee, once a common synonym for exuberant *joy* or for merriment, has in recent times taken on strong overtones of a malicious pleasure in another's discomfiture or bad luck: clapping their hands in *glee* at the defeat of their opponent; the ghoulish *glee* of an 18th-century crowd at a public execution. See CHEERFUL, CONTENTED, HAPPINESS.

Antonyms: AGONY, *displeasure*, MISERY, *sadness, sorrow, suffering, unhappiness.*

pledge
bail
bond
collateral
guarantee
security

These nouns refer to a promise backed up in some way and reinforced by the commitment of one's honor or material possessions. **Pledge** is the most general of these, applying in any case where someone solemnly promises to remain loyal to a principle or to undertake a given task: the *Pledge* of Allegiance to the Flag; a *pledge* of $10,000 to the Alumni Fund; a *pledge* to have the alterations completed by Friday. Only the person's honor backs up the promise in this case. **Guarantee** is like *pledge* in that it is a verbal offer, but it is often backed up by an agreement, legal or otherwise, to make good any loss from failure to perform as promised: a money-back *guarantee* to anyone dissatisfied with the company's product; a six-month *guarantee* on the television set for any repairs needed during that period.

Bail is a sum of money offered as a *pledge* by someone charged with a crime, assuring the court that he or she will appear for trial at a specified time. The alternative to posting *bail* is to remain in prison until trial; if the accused fails to appear, the amount *pledged* as *bail* is forfeited. **Bond** is comparable to *bail* in that a sum of money is posted, but differs in that the sum is set aside on behalf of someone not accused of crime but who, despite evidence to the contrary, might make off with money or valuables the person must deal with directly at work: supermarkets that place their cashiers under *bond*; bank tellers are generally under very high *bond*.

Collateral indicates the private possessions of value that one puts up when taking out a loan and which one forfeits if the loan is not repaid: She used stocks as *collateral* for the loan she was taking out. *Pledge* is sometimes substituted euphemistically for *collateral*: a small loan that stipulated the *pledge* of her best coat. **Security** can also be substituted for *collateral*, in which case it stresses the retaining of the valuables by the person making the loan. More often, *security* refers to a sum of money put up upon signing certain kinds of contracts, as when one leases a house or apartment; if the conditions of the contract are not met, the sum may be forfeited: one month's rent as *security*, in addition to paying for the first month in advance. See ASSURE.

plenitude. *Plenitude* (abundance) is spelled correctly. *Plentitude* is a common error.

plunder

loot
pillage
ravage
sack

These verbs all suggest the act of laying waste to something or stripping it of anything of value. **Plunder** most specifically suggests the roving of armed persons through recently conquered territory in search of money and goods: generals who allowed the city to be *plundered* while the inhabitants cowered behind locked doors. It can also be applied, however, to the seizing of anything by force or fraud: innocent victims *plundered* of their life savings by fake cancer cures. It can also suggest the devastation of something for financial gain: timber speculators who *plundered* irreplaceable forest lands. It is also used as a hyperbole for any act of depleting: guests *plundering* our liquor cabinet.

Pillage is less common and more formal than *plunder* and is restricted to the act of stripping conquered people or lands of money and goods during wartime: Visigoths who *pillaged* churches. In extended usage, *pillage* may refer to any unscrupulous swindle or self-serving theft: He *pillaged* other writers and appropriated entire passages.

Sack is more extreme than *pillage,* not only implying seizure of all valuables but usually suggesting wholesale destruction as well. A strong word, it is typically restricted to a context of war: the Greeks who *sacked* Troy; Union armies *sacking* mansion after mansion along the route of their march. **Ravage** means lay waste or wreak havoc, as by *pillaging* or burning. It has fewer implications of a search for valuables than *sack* and has many figurative uses suggesting devastation: samurai who *ravaged* towns and farms; the disease that *ravaged* his body; open-pit mining that *ravaged* the countryside.

Loot might once have been exactly synonymous with those meanings of *plunder* and *pillage* restricted to the context of war, but it now more commonly suggests seizing valuables by theft or riot, especially when these forays are disorganized or complete random: *looting* the museum of two valuable paintings and destroying five others; bands of rioters who broke store windows and *looted* the displays. See LOOT.

poetry

doggerel
jingle
poesy
rime
verse

These nouns refer to verbal compositions that have greater intensity than prose or normal speech, a quality achieved by heightened language, imagery, rhythms, or sound relationships. **Poetry** and **verse** are frequently used together for contrast, with *verse* indicating all such attempts at heightened effect, and *poetry* indicating successful attempts: winnowing out true *poetry* from the mass of *verse* written by the Victorians. This distinction has been losing ground recently. *Verse*, unqualified, can suggest light or trivial products that make no attempt at any heightening of intensity: greeting-card *verse*. *Poetry*, by contrast, is more and more used neutrally in a generic way, depending on qualifiers for any indication of success or failure: writing voluminous amounts of both good and bad *poetry* in his middle years. *Poetry* still retains a positive tone when used in a wider, less exact way: a view of life touched with *poetry*. Here, it points to an indefinable emotional intensity.

Doggerel refers specifically to bad *verse*, usually suggesting trivial, banal work full of clichés, inept images, and tedious rhythms: the *doggerel* scribbled on the walls of school rest rooms. As a pejorative hyperbole for any *poetry* one does not like, *doggerel* still need not impugn the writer's attempt at intensified utterance—only a total failure to achieve it: critics who agreed that the most honored poet of the preceding era had seldom written anything but *doggerel*. **Jingle**, by contrast, usually does not point to a serious attempt at intensity, but suggests instead an extreme simplicity of language coupled with singsong or monotonous rhythms. It may have a neutral or descriptive relevance: nursery *jingles*. More often, *jingle* suggests disapproval for tedious meter used to drive home an insipid or commercial message, often one set to music: advertising *jingles*. **Rime** once functioned much like *verse*, referring to work done in traditional form. At one point, in fact, it could be used as a generic term for all *poetry*: his essay on *rime*. *Rime* now sounds odd and archaic and would not be used except for satirical purposes: reciting his poem, "The *Rime* of the Elder Statesmen." **Poesy** could once be used in as general a way as *poetry*, but with a more lyrical and approving tone. Now, however, the only use of *poesy* is to express caustic disapproval of *verse* that is overelegant, precious, or genteel: his tattered sheaf of *poesy* about life's trials and tribulations. See NARRATIVE, SLOGAN.

Antonyms: *prose.*

poison

 bane
 toxin
 venom

These nouns refer to substances capable of impairing health, damaging tissues, or destroying life by their chemical action upon an organism or its parts. **Poison** is the most general of these words, being applicable to any such substance, natural or synthetic, that is deadly when swallowed, inhaled, or brought into contact with the skin. [Many useful drugs and medicines, when taken improperly or to excess, are *poisons*; Prussic acid and carbon monoxide gas are both lethal *poisons*.] **Toxin**, though closely related in meaning, has become a specialized term for *poisons* developed by metabolic processes in and by animal, vegetable, and bacterial organisms and capable of producing disease or serious harm. [Tetanus is caused by *toxins* formed in the body by invading bacteria; Curare, a powerful *poison* used to tip arrows, is a *toxin* extracted from a plant and is used in medicine as a muscle relaxant.]

Venom is now generally restricted to the toxic liquid secreted by various animals, especially snakes, scorpions, and some insects, and injected into victims as an offensive or defensive weapon. **Bane**, from an Old English word meaning killer, has become archaic in the sense of *poison*, but is still found in the popular names of certain plants such as hen*bane*, wolfs*bane*, and rats*bane*, containing substances once believed poisonous to these animals.

In figurative use, *poison*, *bane*, and *venom* denote that which corrupts, harms, or destroys: the *poison* of malicious rumors; an alcoholic who is the *bane* of his family's existence; the *venom* of the rejected woman's spite. See DRUG, FATAL.

polite

 civil
 courteous
 courtly
 mannerly
 well-behaved
 well-mannered

These adjectives characterize a manner of social intercourse that is designed to please, or at least not to give offense. **Polite** implies punctilious observance of the forms of speech and action customary among well-bred persons: It was not *polite* of him to reply to your question so hastily and with such an obvious lack of thought. **Civil** is weaker than *polite*, suggesting nothing more than an avoidance of rudeness: a clerk who was always *civil* but never really interested in helping customers. To be **courteous** is to be *polite* while having also a warm regard for the feelings and dignity of others: a police officer who managed to be *courteous* to an abusive person. **Courtly** means *polite* or *courteous* in a ceremonial way, as befits a royal court; it is applied to men and implies an old-fashioned or elegant observance of formal courtesies, especially toward women: a *courtly* gentleman; a *courtly* diplomat.

Mannerly and **well-mannered** are alike in suggesting the kind of politeness evidenced by strict adherence to a code of etiquette. Since there are no overtones to these adjectives, there is no indication whether someone called *mannerly* or *well-mannered* is actually *courteous* or merely careful about outward appearances. **Well-behaved** can mean *mannerly* or *well-mannered*, especially when it is used to describe a child well versed in social graces. *Well-behaved* is often used to refer to the discipline or control demonstrated by a person or, especially, by a group of persons in a difficult or trying situation: a crowd that was surprisingly quiet and *well behaved* considering how long they had to wait in the hot, stuffy room. See BEHAVIOR, CONSIDERATE, URBANE.

Antonyms: GAUCHE, *rude.*

pollute

 adulterate
 contaminate
 pervert
 vitiate

These verbs refer to tainting or dirtying something or otherwise impairing its integrity, purity, or effectiveness. **Pollute** now most commonly indicates a physical befouling that renders something noisome or noxious to health or life: [Some factories *pollute* our water supply by dumping untreated chemical wastes into streams and rivers; The fumes from furnaces and motor vehicles have *polluted* the air and shortened life expectancy.] Recent usage of *pollute* has focused so heavily on such instances that other uses are taken as metaphorical extensions of this meaning: political debate *polluted* by recriminations and unfounded allegations. Actually, an earlier use of *pollute* referred directly to any defiling of sanctity or of physical or moral purity: temples *polluted* by barbarian invaders.

Contaminate refers to the spreading of harmful or undesirable impurities through something previously free of taint. The resulting impurity may be negligible or, as is the case for *pollute*, thoroughgoing and widespread. In addition, where *pollute* often indicates readily apparent or grossly visible impurities, *contaminate* is often the word of choice where the change is slow, devious, unsuspected, or not noticeable by ordinary means: an order to burn all linens that may have come into contact with smallpox victims or have been otherwise *contaminated;* arguments that the atmosphere had not been seriously *contaminated* by radioactive fallout from the testing of hydrogen bombs. In other uses, *contaminate* is milder than *pollute* in that it can sometimes suggest a temporary tinge rather than an irrevocable stain.

Adulterate has special relevance to food products to which harmful, low-quality, or low-cost substances have been deliberately and deceptively added in order to defraud the buyer: hamburger *adulterated* with bread crumbs and food coloring; milk *adulterated* with water. Theoretically, *adulterate* can apply to other products debased by additives, even where there is no intent to defraud, but such uses are rare. In its widest applications, *adulterate* can apply to any mixture of good and bad where the bad seems deliberately included by the producer in the hope that it will go unnoticed: academic curricula *adulterated* with courses on everything from rap music to surfboard acrobatics.

The remaining verbs apply more generally than the foregoing and do not have specific applications to a concrete situation. **Pervert** indicates misdirecting something, leading it astray, or turning it in a wrong direction, as away from the good, pure, and moral, and toward what is considered depraved or evil: television personalities who *pervert* discussion programs into platforms for the airing of prejudices; a beautiful novel that was willfully *perverted* by Hollywood into a sex-and-sadism spectacular. As can be seen, *pervert* suggests a grotesque or hideous transformation; this makes it even more emphatic than *pollute* in comparable uses, although here complete alteration is indicated, rather than the inclusion of additives: an attempt to *pervert* the truth by appealing to dishonest, ignorant, and irresponsible bigotry. A specific sense of *pervert* once referred to something that caused sexual deviation, but this use is more and more avoided because of its judgmental tone.

Vitiate is the most general verb here, having no area of concrete reference. It applies widely to whatever can be seen as nullifying the value of something: an overweening arrogance that *vitiates* all his efforts to make friends. *Vitiate* sometimes is used only for impairment rather than complete destruction: an irresponsible act that to some extent *vitiates* our claim that we are seeking peaceful solutions to the crisis. More often, however, it suggests that one thing cancels out or invalidates another: pay raises *vitiated* by the rising cost of living. See DIRTY, DISCOLOR, HARM, HURT, SOIL, WASTE.

Antonyms: CLEAN, *purge, purify,* SANITIZE.

polygamy
bigamy
polyandry
polygyny
trigamy

These nouns refer to a married state in which someone has more than one spouse. **Polygamy** is a general term for any situation in which more than two people are knowingly joined in marriage. This can be a husband with more than one wife, a wife with more than one husband, or a group marriage in which two or more husbands are married to two or more wives: a text dealing with the practice of *polygamy* in primitive cultures. Outside an anthropological context, *polygamy* is often understood to refer directly to the situation of a husband with two or more wives, since this departure from monogamy has been more widely dealt with (and perhaps practiced) than other departures: the *polygamy* of the early Mormons. **Polygyny** would be the strict anthropological term for the situation in which two or more wives are married to one husband: linking the practice of *polygyny* with cultural assumptions about the innate inferiority of women; the disappearance of *polygyny* from Turkey following the emancipation of women.

By contrast, **polyandry** points specifically to the marrying of two or more husbands to one wife: matriarchal cultures that have *polyandry* as a concomitant. **Trigamy**, an infrequently encountered term, refers to the state of having three wives or three husbands at the same time, or to the state of having been married to three wives or three husbands at different times. **Bigamy** refers as a legal term in Western civilization to the crime of being married to more than one spouse at the same time; *bigamy* functions for either sex. At first it might seem that the term is a legal substitute for the word *polygamy*, but one can be guilty of *bigamy* without practicing *polygamy*, through discarding one spouse without a legal divorce and marrying another while claiming to be unmarried. *Bigamy* usually suggests a situation in which there is deception of at least one of the spouses, since few people in a monogamous society consent presumably to marrying someone already married. Even in instances where a deceiving bigamist sets up two households and alternates visits to both, a true situation of *polygamy* does not exist, since *polygamy* most often indicates spouses who knowingly share the same household and are married to the same person as well.

Antonyms: *monogamy, monogyny.*

poor

> disadvantaged
> hard up
> lower-class
> underprivileged
> unemployable

These adjectives describe people who are unable to obtain sufficient money or possessions to afford them a decent standard of living. **Poor**, the most general term, is applied to those who live in more or less constant poverty, or to anything characterized by or resulting from poverty: *poor* migrant workers; *poor* housing; a *poor* neighborhood. *Poor* is often a derogatory term pointing at the squalor, ignorance, and immorality believed by some to exist among those who do not have enough money.

Underprivileged and **disadvantaged** are euphemisms employed by social scientists, welfare workers, and journalists to describe the children of *poor* parents. *Underprivileged* is vaguely and categorically applied to those who, because of economic oppression and illiteracy, are deprived of many of the basic necessities that most people take for granted. *Disadvantaged* is more specific than *underprivileged* and stresses the need for granting full civil rights and effective schooling to the young who are the victims of poverty and racial discrimination. *Disadvantaged* also suggests the psychological damage that *poor* children may suffer.

Hard up is an informal phrase for *poor*. But to be *hard up* often implies only a temporary shortage of money rather than a state of continuing need: so *hard up* before payday that she had to go without lunch; farmers *hard up* because of a crop failure.

Lower-class is used to describe that group of people occupying the lowest social and economic position in any society that has a long-established caste system or observes class distinctions based on occupation, education, and income. People who are *lower-class*

tend more often than not to be *poor,* but the term is also used in a snobbish way to suggest lack of ambition, crude manners, and low educational attainments.

Unemployable refers to people who for various reasons are unable to work at any job or remunerative occupation. It is now used widely of young people, especially *poor* ones, who have been so handicapped in their early schooling that they cannot be trained for useful employment. In a wider sense, people who are *unemployable* may be those of advanced age or those who have physical and mental disabilities preventing them from working. See INSOLVENT, PENNILESS.

Antonyms: *privileged, upper-class,* WEALTHY, *well-to-do.*

portray

> delineate
> depict
> describe
> represent
> sketch

These verbs refer to the vivid presentation of material in some medium of communication. **Portray**, most specifically, suggests capturing a likeness, usually of a single person: a painting that *portrayed* the actress in her most successful role. It is frequently used, however, to refer to the detailed discussion of any subject, whether concrete or abstract: an article that attempted to *portray* the lives of three American families. Even in its most abstract uses, *portray* still suggests catching something in its most characteristic aspect. **Depict** is similar to *portray* but more general in suggesting the artistic recreation of any scene: *depicting* the landscape at the moment of its full autumnal ripeness. Where *portray* suggests catching the most revealing aspect of something, *depict* suggests a choice between equally valid possibilities: *depicting* the nineteenth century in light of the Industrial Revolution. *Depict* may also suggest a deliberate departure from reality: actually *depicting* me, without a shred of evidence, as a scheming charlatan.

Delineate, in the graphic arts, usually refers to a line drawing, but one that is subtle and careful about accuracy and detail. In other media it suggests the same fullness and vividness: *delineating* in a magazine article all the undercurrents of dissent that affected the election; the actor successfully *delineated* the complex character of Malcolm X.

Sketch is used in application to a quick, usually undetailed, rendering of a subject, but one that is nonetheless readily recognizable. While *sketch* may imply haste, it does not necessarily indicate carelessness or inaccuracy: quickly *sketching* a dress that was being modeled in a fashion show; *sketching* out the main points of the subject matter she would cover exhaustively later in the term.

Represent and **describe** depend less on the context of the visual arts for their implications. Of the two, only *represent* can be used in this context at all, in which case it is more like *depict* than *portray:* a woodcut *representing* the harbor as it appeared to the first settlers. In any context, *represent* can imply a symbolic or typical rather than a literal rendering: a classic statue that *represents* the human body as devoid of individuality; *representing* nuclear proliferation as the greatest threat to world peace. It can also suggest the arbitrary choosing of one thing to stand for something else, even when there is no resemblance between them: In describing the beleaguered country at dinner, he used water glasses to *represent* the various warring populations. *Describe,* most specifically, suggests the citing of details that will create a visual image in the mind of an audience; it thus suggests a context of discussion: a novelist who can vividly *describe* a landscape; a patient able to *describe* her symptoms accurately. Unlike *represent* and *depict, describe* necessarily suggests a literal, realistic rendering. See GRAPHIC.

position
rank
standing
status

These nouns refer to the relative degree of respect someone is given by society or attains through accomplishments. **Position** is the most general, indicating one's relative acceptance by society, recognized professional attainments, or place in any structured order: families of wealth and *position;* a scholar of unimpeachable *position* in the academic world; assuming the *position* of treasurer for the club. **Standing** is more vague than *position,* referring to one's place, high or low, in any graduated order: people without *standing* in their own communities; a member in good *standing.* In the latter example, the sense is restricted to minimal acceptance that puts one on an equal footing with others of a group.

Rank may function in the same three areas as *position,* but it tends to suggest a more definable placement, such as one indicated by a specific title given by a hierarchical order: the highest *rank* of the nobility; attaining the *rank* of associate professor that year.

Rank is particularly pertinent to military *positions:* the *rank* of captain. **Status** has become the most fashionable of these nouns to refer to all the indefinable qualities that constitute social or professional success: teachers of high *rank* but little *status* among their colleagues. Unqualified, it suggests social acceptance: the constant striving for *status* in the middle classes. In this use, *status* often has a negative tone and suggests the placing of undue emphasis on material values. See CLASS.

possess
have
hold
keep
own

These verbs refer to the relationship between people and their belongings, or to things and their attributes. **Possess** and **own** both stress belongings; *possess* is slightly more formal: people who *possess* large quantities of material goods; families who *own* at least two television sets. *Own,* however, suggests some legal act of acquisition, whereas *possess* may refer to goods that now belong to someone, however acquired: time payments that enable customers to *possess* goods before they can be said to *own* them fully. *Possess,* furthermore, is often used to relate something to its attributes, while *own* is unlikely to be used in this way: a face *possessing* great strength of character.

Have is the least specific of these verbs and is far less clear than the rest about the kind of relationship suggested. It may be used as an informal substitute for either *possess* or *own:* a way of smiling that *has* great charm; families that do not *have* at least one car.

Hold and **keep** add suggestions of retention or control to *possess* or *own. Hold* can mean guard something against seizure, even from someone who may rightfully *own* it: *holding* the land despite legal notices to surrender it. Compared to *have,* it stresses conviction: *have* an opinion; *hold* an opinion. *Hold* can also substitute for *own,* in which case it has a legal tone and may suggest resources not actually *used: holding* estates in Ireland they have never seen. It can be used in reference to something put in trust for someone else who actually *owns* it: *holding* the money for you until you come of age. *Keep* may suggest preventing someone else from *possessing* something: *keeping* aspirin away from children. It may also stress safety or emotional attachment: *keeping* bonds in a safe; wishing to *keep* the program as a souvenir. See CARRY, CONSERVE, CONTROL, INCLUDE.

Antonyms: *borrow, dispossess,* RELINQUISH.

postpone

adjourn
defer
delay
suspend

These verbs mean put off to a future time. **Postpone** usually suggests putting something aside until something else occurs, or is done, known, obtained, etc. [The conference will be *postponed* for two weeks; We are *postponing* our trip until the weather improves.] However, *postpone* is often used without this limitation and may imply the intention of putting off an activity until some undetermined future time: to *postpone* activation of the plan.

Adjourn means *postpone* until another day or place. It is customarily applied to a meeting of an organization or any formally constructed gathering, such as a legislative or deliberative body, that is brought to an end, especially with a view toward assembling again at a specified time or place. [The hearing will be *adjourned* until tomorrow morning at ten o'clock; Congress always *adjourns* in time for an approaching election.]

Delay means *postpone* to an indefinite future time, usually because of obstacles that impede progress. It has the strong implication of lateness or tardiness. Often such obstacles are unavoidable: Their arrival will be *delayed* by traffic. On the other hand, *delay* may suggest failure to do something at the expected or proper time either through carelessness or reluctance: to *delay* fixing the roof although it leaks badly; to *delay* having a tooth pulled.

The suggestion of arbitrary lateness and putting off that resides in *delay* is absent from **defer**. Etymologically, *defer* means to refrain from dealing with, and implies the intentional *delaying* of an action in a more emphatic way than does *postpone:* to *defer* payment of one's bills until the Christmas bonus is paid.

Suspend, in this sense, is to discontinue or to withhold temporarily but indefinitely, pending fulfillment of certain conditions. [Bus service will be *suspended* until the highway is repaired; A scientist *suspends* judgment until all the facts are in.]

Antonyms: *schedule.*

powerless

helpless
impotent
paralyzed

These adjectives characterize an inability to act in one's own behalf. **Powerless** indicates an inability to act because of outside resistance. **Helpless**, by contrast, suggests someone incapable of action because of personal inadequacy, without reference to externals. These distinctions are completely at variance with what both adjectives might seem to suggest (lack of power; lack of external help): a decision by her superiors that left her *powerless* to act; *helpless* as an infant that must be nursed and watched every second of the day. Both *powerless* and *helpless,* of course, can be used in a context more appropriate to the other; *helpless,* especially, can refer to someone literally without aid or assistance: a last survivor who was *helpless* to prevent enemy troops from capturing the bunker.

Paralyzed in this context compares an inability to act with muscular disablement; **impotent** here compares the same inability to sexual disablement. Both adjectives suggest a will or desire to act that some other impulse has contravened: a mind *paralyzed* by its own excessively fine distinctions; embarrassment that rendered her *impotent* to speak. Both adjectives can also refer to a will made *powerless* or a normal routine frustrated by external forces: a city *paralyzed* by a strike; red tape that left the chairman *impotent* to innovate or experiment. *Paralyzed* is the more intense of these two, suggesting a greater crisis and a greater difficulty of resolution. The sexual metaphor inherent in *impotent,* furthermore, is always in danger of surfacing and making the word sound unintentionally comic in this context. See WEAK.

Antonyms: HEALTHY, *potent, powerful.*

praise

acclaim
eulogize
extol
laud

These verbs all pertain to the act of commending someone or something. **Praise** is the most general of these and the least formal. It can refer to overall approval: He *praised* his friend as the finest person he had ever met. Or it can refer to a specific accomplishment: All the critics *praised* the new play for its originality and emotional impact. *Praise* can sometimes suggest the approval of a superior: a teacher who never forgot to *praise* the slow learner who struggled to master the day's lesson. When the situation is reversed, homage to the Deity is usually involved: They *praised* God for their safe deliverance from the perils of the winter. At its weakest, it can refer to the mere paying of compliments that may or may not be sincere: Confidence men usually *praise* the shrewdness of the gullible victims they are fleecing.

Laud indicates the highest of *praise* and may suggest recognition of a special or formal kind: a citation that *lauded* her for her twenty years of service. *Laud* can indicate excessive *praise* as well, or *praise* that is formalized, officious, or ceremonious: a set of annual awards broken down into so many categories that even bit players stood a chance of being *lauded*. By its very formality, **extol** also suggests formal *praise*. The derivation of *extol*, from a Latin root meaning raise up, is reflected in its suggestion of an intention to elevate or magnify the recipient: She was publicly *extolled* by the department head on the occasion of her promotion to full professor.

Eulogize often suggests formal *praise* given in a public speech, although *eulogize* can also apply to a written tribute. It can imply a public or official testimonial, particularly one delivered at a funeral: friends who came forward to *eulogize* the dead hero. **Acclaim** suggests applause or vocal approval, especially by a mass of well-wishers: The convention *acclaimed* the nominee with an unrestrained demonstration of support. Used more generally, *acclaim* can suggest widespread popularity or public backing: Newspapers *acclaimed* the court's decision; a singer *acclaimed* far and wide for her unique vocal style. See APPLAUSE, AWARD, RESPECT.

Antonyms: BELITTLE, *censure, condemn, discredit.*

precarious
insecure
unstable
unsteady

These adjectives characterize a stance or position that is endangered by lack of balance, poor footing, wavering strength, or changing conditions. **Precarious** is the most formal of these and most restricted to the situation of a dangerous imbalance for whatever reason: the ladder propped at a *precarious* angle against the wall; a *precarious* perch on the ledge. It can also refer to things that can put one in danger of falling: a *precarious* path that wound its way along the mountainside; sand dunes too *precarious* to build on. In less concrete situations, *precarious* stresses risk or danger more than the possibility of imbalance or falling: a *precarious* theory that could only lead to war. Unless the adjective's overtones are remembered, however, a mixed metaphor may result: his *precarious* resistance to change.

Insecure also indicates an untenable position, but it is wider in application and less open to mixed metaphor. It suggests exposure to threat or danger of any kind: rendering *insecure* the enemy's position in the valley by capturing the surrounding foothills. *Insecure* has also become a fad word for psychological states of uncertainty, doubt, or confusion: a boy made *insecure* by his parents' conflicting demands.

Unstable and **unsteady** also refer to untenable positions. *Unstable* emphasizes impermanence, suggesting a foundation capable of changing or shifting: a Venetian palazzo built on an *unstable* island that has been sinking for a century. It may also suggest infirm support of any kind: adding crosspieces to strengthen the *unstable* uprights of the bookcase. *Unstable*, in a wider context, can refer to a substance that tends to break down or change drastically: an electrically charged, *unstable* form of oxygen. It can also refer to an erratic or dangerous personality: an *unstable* eccentric who conceived great schemes that would never be executed; an *unstable* sociopath capable of committing murder without a qualm. The more informal *unsteady* concentrates on one aspect of *unstable*, indicating a lack of firm support: a short leg that made the table *unsteady*. It can, however, also point to any sort of wavering: *unsteady* flashes of light; capable only of divided and *unsteady* attention. See DANGER.

Antonyms: *firm, safe, stable, steady.*

predict
augur
divine
forecast
foreshadow
foretell
prognosticate
prophesy

These verbs refer to attempts to indicate the course the future will take. **Predict** is the most commonly used in the widest variety of situations; it can range in suggestion from hazarding a guess or wish to making an astute statistical estimate about the likely outcome of an event: *predicting* he would be miserable without her; *predicting* the results of the election with amazing accuracy. As in the last example, it is commonly used to refer to the activities of professional pollsters. Like *predict*, **forecast** can range in use from the general or vague to the specific, but in this case its most specific use—for *predicting* weather—has crowded out other uses of *forecast*: Tiros satellites that make it easier to *forecast* hurricanes.

Divine and **foreshadow** both concern suggesting

rather than *predicting* the future, especially through the giving or assessing of subtle hints or clues. *Divine* implies the action of someone capable of reading present evidence in all its ambiguity and seeing where it must lead: the first political commentator to *divine* in Iraq's threats the imminent upheaval of the Persian Gulf nations. *Divine* originally suggested powers of clairvoyance, but it is now seldom used in this sense. *Foreshadow,* unlike *divine,* does not necessarily imply a shrewd reading of clues; it can refer to anyone or anything that gives an indication of what is to come: Hitler's plan of action *foreshadowed* the actual course of events so unmistakably that anyone should have been able to *divine* it. *Foreshadow* is often used to refer to the hinting by a storyteller of what will happen eventually in a story: the novelist's skillful *foreshadowing* of her heroine's tragic decline.

Like *divine,* **augur**, **prophesy**, and even **foretell** once suggested a supernatural ability to read the future. Now these verbs have mainly lost this use, although they still suggest, unlike *predict* and *forecast,* a future that is already set and determined rather than one that can be rationally assumed from the evidence at hand. Of these three, *augur* is most like *divine* in implying a reading of subtle omens and clues as a way of prefiguring what is to come: *auguring* from a host of economic indicators that the decline would continue unabated. Like *foreshadow,* *augur* can also refer to the sign or clue itself: a trend that *augured* well for the company. *Prophesy* sounds more portentous than *augur,* suggesting authoritative wisdom and acumen: the only pundit to *prophesy* a rapprochement with China. Both *augur* and *prophesy* are sometimes used in place of *predict* and *forecast* to give a higher tone or to suggest unerring accuracy; many would find the uses questionable: polltakers *auguring* a record turnout. *Foretell* now has fewer residual implications of the supernatural than *augur* and *prophesy,* as well as being far less formal. It would, however, still sound odd as a substitute for *predict* or *forecast.* Like *foreshadow,* *foretell* can refer to the clue rather than to its practitioner: signs of a struggle that *foretold* a violent end for the missing couple. It is often used negatively in referring to the past: Who could have *foretold* that the outing would end in tragedy?

Prognosticate comes from a different context altogether from the verbs just discussed. It suggests a knowledgeable look at the symptoms of a disease in order to determine its likely outcome. This gives it a specific pertinence to medicine similar to *predict* for polltaking and *forecast* for meteorology. Used outside this area, *prognosticate* suggests inside knowledge or perspicuity, but is often used comically or pejoratively: *prognosticating* the effect a third pickle would have on his digestion. See

EXPECTATION, FOREKNOWLEDGE, HOPE, PREMONITION.

premonition

forerunner
harbinger
inkling
omen
portent
precursor
presentiment

These nouns refer to a sense, indication, or sign of something to come. Most, but not all of them, partake of the prophetic, and some directly involve superstition. A **premonition** is instinctive, based on an indefinable feeling rather than on actual information received. It may be good or bad, may come in sleep or wakefulness, and may be either borne out or proved false by later events. [A *premonition* that she would win led her to buy three raffle tickets; He had a *premonition* of his father's death.] Some *premonitions* are purely irrational or superstitious; others, possible instances of extrasensory perception. **Presentiment** is close to *premonition* in meaning but is more formal in tone. Etymologically, where *premonition* stresses the idea of an advance warning given to the mind, *presentiment* points to a sort of inner perception, usually an instinctive feeling of foreboding, a sense that misfortune or calamity is at hand: a terrifying, but unfounded *presentiment* that his life was in danger; a *presentiment* that the Pan Am plane would go down. Like a *premonition* or *presentiment,* an **inkling** is an intimation of something yet unknown. Getting an *inkling* of something, however, does not require prophetic powers or ESP. Instead, the ability to interpret natural signs, pick up hints, or guess on the basis of a paucity of information is involved. [A few veiled hints she dropped gave me my first *inkling* of her purpose.] Unlike the other nouns, it is often used negatively in disclaiming or denying knowledge of something. [I haven't an *inkling* of what they will do.]

Omen and **portent** designate outward and visible signs that are regarded as prophetic and are subject to interpretation. Both strongly imply a superstitious response. To those who believe, there are both good and evil *omens.* A stork nesting on the roof, for example, is considered a good *omen.* A black cat crossing one's path is thought to be an evil *omen.* Unlike an *omen,* which may be favorable, a *portent* more often, though not always, indicates impending evil. A *portent* may be a sign, an event, a wonder, a natural or unnatural phenomenon: a sailor's belief in luck and in supernatural *portents*. It may be something to marvel at, as a flaming comet, or it may be something heavy with foreboding, as a total eclipse. [Calpurnia's *premonition* of Caesar's death came in a prophetic dream; Casca saw a fiery tempest, a slave with a flaming, unburned hand, a lion in the Capitol, and other *portents*.] *Omen* and *portent,* modified by adjectives like black, bad, ill, or evil, may also mean ominous significance: a bird of evil *omen;* a cloud of black *portent.*

The remaining nouns refer to a messenger or herald who signals the approach of a coming person or thing. Formerly, a **harbinger** was a courier who rode in advance of a party to arrange for lodging. Now, though *harbinger* may mean anyone in the vanguard whose job is to prepare the way, it is more often used figuratively of a person or thing that heralds the approach of a change. [An autumn frost is a *harbinger* of winter; The robin is a *harbinger* of spring.] Unlike the other nouns in this set, **forerunner** and **precursor** may indicate hindsight rather than foresight, pointing to an advance sign that is seen as such only in terms of later events. Both nouns have the same etymological meaning, *precursor* meaning *forerunner* in Latin, but now differ somewhat in use. *Forerunner* more strongly retains the original sense of a person who goes ahead as a messenger to proclaim the coming of another. John the Baptist is known as the *Forerunner* since he heralded the coming of Christ. **Precursor** was also used of John the Baptist, but where *forerunner* stresses the announcement of the coming of a more important person, *precursor* implies a laying of the groundwork for a later, more significant accomplishment. Both *forerunner* and *precursor* may refer to a predecessor in a particular line of development, or an advance indication of something to come. [John Wyclif was one of the main *forerunners* of the Reformation and an important *precursor* of Martin Luther.] Used of signs or symptoms, both nouns may be unfavorable in tone. [Overweight and shortness of breath can be *precursors* of a heart attack; a border conflict that turned out to be the *precursor* of a world war; Widespread moral corruption and decadence are often the *forerunners* of national decline.] See ANXIETY, EXPECTATION, HINT, PREDICT, SYMPTOM.

preoccupied
absorbed
engrossed
involved

These adjectives describe persons whose complete attention is held or whose total concern is aroused by a particular subject. **Preoccupied** points to a mind taken up with a certain line of thought to the exclusion of other matters that may be competing for attention. It may suggest a dedicated and voluntary concern for something: *preoccupied* with details of the merger plan. More often, it suggests an excessive or involuntary brooding about something: so *preoccupied* with her career that she neglected her family; indications that thoughts of suicide had *preoccupied* the child for months. It may also suggest a mind lost in haphazard thought of any kind whatsoever and, consequently, inattentive to the matter at hand: a clerk who met my question with a vacant and *preoccupied* stare.

Involved pertains to commitment more than to concern, and it can be used for active behavior as well as for mental states: students *involved* in politics; readers who become deeply *involved* in suspense novels.

Absorbed and **engrossed** contrast with *preoccupied* in being almost wholly positive in connotation. Both refer primarily to a voluntary, almost eager, attentiveness to or interest in something. *Engrossed* suggests complete intellectual concentration: *engrossed* in studying the committee's report. *Absorbed* may suggest an emotional interest that is even more complete: utterly *absorbed* by the slow unfolding of the movie. *Absorbed*, furthermore, may suggest an intensity of interest in one's own activity: so *absorbed* in telling his story that he failed to notice the growing restlessness among the listeners. See BUSY, EAGER, OBLIVIOUS.

Antonyms: *distracted,* UNINVOLVED.

prerequisite. Do not confuse the noun *prerequisite* (qualification required as a condition of admission, advancement, etc.) with the noun *perquisite* (allowance, privilege, etc., given in addition to salary).

present
bonus
gift
grant
gratuity
lagniappe
largess
tip

These nouns denote something given freely to a person, group, or institution for use or pleasure. **Present** and **gift** are applied to anything, large or small, material or nonmaterial, that is given without expectation of return or compensation. *Present* and *gift* may be used interchangeably to denote things bestowed upon another: a birthday *present;* a Christmas *gift.* However, *present* is a less formal word than *gift* and is more likely to be applied to things of nominal cost, while *gift* may suggest something of considerable value. [Each child brought a *present* to the teacher; The foundation made a *gift* of a million dollars to the university.] An admirable quality or talent that seems to have been bestowed miraculously by nature is also called a *gift,* but never a *present:* the *gift* of prophecy; a *gift* for writing poetry.

Largess is a somewhat pompous word for a *gift* conferred ostentatiously, often among many recipients. *Largess* hints at condescension on the part of the giver and is often used ironically: a ne'er-do-well who was given a job through the *largess* of his congressman; the poor who live on the *largess* of public assistance.

A **grant** is a *gift* of money or its equivalent to a person or an institution to enable accomplishment of a specific end: a *grant* to a research chemist; a *grant* to a technical college to develop a humanities program. *Grants* commonly involve considerable sums and are often given by public authority: a *grant* of land to establish an agricultural college.

A **bonus** is something paid or given in addition to what is usual or stipulated. Employers may give their staffs cash *bonuses* at the end of the year, or they may reward valued employees with a *bonus* of an extra week of vacation. A *bonus* is also a *grant,* as of money or insurance, to citizens who have rendered military service.

Gratuity and **tip** both imply an unspecified sum of money given voluntarily in return for a service or the expectation of special attention. *Gratuity* is the more formal word and points to a more substantial *gift* than does *tip:* a *tip* to a waiter or porter; *gratuities* to servants in the household for many years. **Lagniappe**, used chiefly in Louisiana and southeast Texas, is especially a small gift given to a customer as a *bonus,* but more generally is a *gratuity* or *tip.* See BEQUEST.

prevalent
abundant
ample
common
copious
plentiful
prevailing
rife

widespread

These adjectives describe something present in great quantities or something frequently encountered. **Prevalent** may indicate a great incidence of something either in time or in place: ideas *prevalent* in the Renaissance; varieties of wildflowers *prevalent* in the Rockies. *Prevalent* most often suggests factual observation without any attempt to evaluate the thing observed. **Prevailing** goes beyond *prevalent* to suggest that the thing observed has existed and continues to exist in such quantity as to surpass any other kind of thing that might be compared to it. This may often be a matter of subjective evaluation: discussing what he regarded as the *prevailing* theme of the modern British novel. [While many forms of life are *prevalent* throughout the world, man and the insect are perhaps the two *prevailing* forms in nearly every habitat.]

Abundant, unlike *prevalent* and *prevailing,* is mostly restricted to observations about a particular place rather than a particular time: an *abundant* harvest; a cultural life more varied and *abundant* than in some larger cities. *Abundant* usually suggests a valued or desirable quantity, even though it may occasionally suggest frequency to the point of oversupply. **Common**, by contrast, shades off to suggest something that by its frequency becomes usual or ordinary: the *common* people; an experience *common* to every traveler. *Common,* furthermore, can apply to time as well as place, much like *prevalent:* a style of dress *common* in the 1980's. Neither *abundant* nor *common,* however, suggests the notion of dominance present in *prevailing.* [Although revolutionary ideas were *abundant* and poverty was *common,* the *prevailing* temper of the times was one of indifference.]

Rife and **widespread** both emphasize aspects of *prevalent. Rife* suggests the unchecked or unregulated spread of something: a time *rife* with conflicting theories of art; Bribery and corruption were *rife* in the local courts. As suggested by the last example, *rife* is frequently used to suggest a heavy incidence of something undesirable, thus making a sharp contrast with *abundant. Widespread* most specifically refers to place rather than time, suggesting something that is not so much *common* as occurring over a large area: the *widespread* misconception that Darwin had argued that we were descended from apes; paperback publishers who have had a *widespread* effect on the country's reading habits; tests to determine whether the cancer was *widespread.*

Plentiful, like *abundant,* relates to a desirable quantity or even a superfluity of something: a region in which work is never *plentiful;* an island where edible fruit is so *plentiful* that it is allowed to rot on the trees. **Copious** indicates an even greater quantity than *plentiful* and sometimes requires the interpolation of "supply of," "number of," etc., before the operative noun: The squirrel gathered a *copious* store of nuts. However, the interpolation is unnecessary when reference is made to a volume, outpouring, profusion, cascade, or flow: His writings were *copious; copious* tears. *Copious* can also serve as a more formal intensification of *abundant,* sometimes indicating a superfluity: a *copious* harvest; a scholarly treatise with *copious* footnotes. **Ample**, in contrast to *copious,* means both just enough and more than enough, and so tends to imply an amount between enough and *plentiful; ample* but not generous servings; an *ample* income; *ample* room for a family of five. When used of a person, *ample* can also refer, in a humorous way, to generous or excessive size: her *ample* bosom. See GENEROUS, OUTSTANDING.

Antonyms: *OCCASIONAL, SCANTY.*

prevent
    avert
    forestall
    obviate
    preclude
    stop

These verbs mean keep from happening or doing. **Prevent** is the comprehensive term for the group. Used of human agency, it implies precautionary or restraining measures taken to hinder, thwart, or block a thing. These measures may involve forcible restraint. [Armed guards *prevented* us from entering the palace; They tied him up to *prevent* his escape.] The measures may also be positive steps taken to ward off potential trouble: concessions and reforms made to *prevent* future riots; negotiations to *prevent* a stalemate; fabric waterproofed to *prevent* damage by rain; It is easier to *prevent* illness than to cure it. *Prevent* is also used of a nonhuman agency or chance cause that acts as a hindrance; in such cases, only the effect of the agent is stressed and no motive is attributed to it. [Rain *prevented* us from going (or *prevented* our going) on the hike; A sprained ankle *prevented* her participation in the championship game.] **Stop** in this sense is more informal than *prevent* and has greater immediacy. Where *prevent* often implies forethought and advance preparation to keep something from occurring, *stop* focuses on responsive action to the circumstance at hand. [Don't try to *stop* me from leaving.] Further, *stop* may refer to the halting or ending of an action already in progress. [*Stop* him from hitting me; to *stop*

an alarm from ringing; to *stop* a revolt by the use of armed force.] *Prevent*, which at first had only the anticipatory meaning, has also come to apply to the *stopping* of an action at any stage, with the implication that the ultimate consequences of the act have been avoided: The enemy passed the outworks and were barely *prevented* from capturing the fortress.

To **preclude** is to *prevent* by anticipation or to rule out by necessity. *Preclude* is used not of persons but of events, circumstances, decisions, or the like. It suggests a door shut in advance, as a consequence of a prior action, occurrence, choice, or commitment. [Walls and bars *precluded* the possibility of escape; Our decision to vacation in Europe *precludes* our going to California this year; Professional duties *precluded* her from accepting the invitation.] **Forestall** is like *preclude* in emphasizing anticipation, but it implies deliberate deterrence. Where *preclude* points to circumstances that make an occurrence impossible, *forestall* involves taking preventive countermeasures in time to turn something aside or temper its effect. [He *forestalled* criticism by coming forward to confess his faults; She *forestalled* my question by bringing up the subject herself; In 1933, Roosevelt closed the banks to *stop* gold shipments abroad and to *forestall* runs on the banks.]

Avert, more strongly and more specifically than *forestall,* implies warding off a threat or danger. It points to the taking of effective countermeasures just in time to keep something disastrous from happening. [He swerved sharply to the right and narrowly *averted* a collision; The mayor and other local leaders *averted* a riot by rushing to the scene of the disturbance.] **Obviate** is the most formal verb in this set. It means dispose of, referring to a risk, difficulty, objection, or the like that is met squarely and cleared out of the way. [A settlement out of court would *obviate* a long-drawn-out lawsuit; traveler's checks to *obviate* the risk of lost or stolen cash.] See AVOID, DISCOURAGE, HINDER, STOP (arrest), THWART.

Antonyms: *EFFECT, facilitate, PERMIT.*

principle
    assumption
    axiom
    theorem

These nouns are comparable in denoting statements of fact or generalities that are universally or widely considered to be true and fundamental. **Principle** has the greatest range of meaning of all the terms in this group, but in the context of this discrimination it refers to an elementary proposition held to be basic in any system or chain of reasoning, conduct, or procedure: a theological *principle;* the *principle* of self-government. In logic, an **assumption** specifically designates the minor or second premise in a syllogism. Less specifically, *assumption* refers to any assertion about reality that is unproved or debatable: the danger of basing scientific conclusions upon *assumption.* **Axiom** originally denoted a proposition, usually one agreed upon as the basis of an argument or demonstration, whose truth was so self-evident as to be indisputable: using the *axiom* that every effect must have a cause to prove the existence of God. In current usage, *axiom* often indicates any *principle* that people universally receive and act upon as if it were true, rather than something deemed necessarily true. A **theorem** is a proposition that is not self-evident but is susceptible of rational proof. Since *theorems* are deduced from *axioms, axioms* are often called first *principles,* and *theorems* are called secondary *principles.* See BASIS.

privacy
   isolation
   seclusion
   solitude
   withdrawal

These nouns refer to being alone with others or by oneself, without a chance of being seen, overheard, or interrupted. **Privacy** adds to this general meaning strongly positive overtones of freedom and intimacy, such as a person has at home, whether alone, with his family, or with chosen friends: eavesdropping devices that threaten people's *privacy*; a Supreme Court decision affirming a married couple's right to *privacy.* When used outside the context of the home, *privacy* suggests conditions approaching this state, often presented as a luxury or added feature: the *privacy* afforded by a box at the opera; a large ward of the hospital that afforded patients little *privacy;* asking where they could go to talk in *privacy.* In one sense, **seclusion** is an intensification of *privacy,* suggesting a situation offering even greater protection from interference than one's own home: preferring to work in the *seclusion* of a mountain retreat. Also, *seclusion* suggests surroundings that protect, separate, or shield one from any sort of notice, whereas *privacy* may give practical but not total protection: feeling free to talk in the *privacy* of their railway compartment, though their *seclusion* was rendered incomplete by an uncovered window that looked out onto the corridor. In a more specialized and not necessarily positive sense, *seclusion* suggests a deliberate hiding from the outside world, either to meet with, evade, or wait for someone: the grove of trees that gave *seclusion* to the lover's lane; seeking *seclusion* from their enemy in the hidden cave; waiting to ambush the officer from the *seclusion* of the dark alley.

Isolation can function like *seclusion,* but it can also stress the state of being cut off from the outside world, whether by compulsion, choice, or circumstance: keeping his captives in *isolation* by removing them to a deserted farmhouse. As can be seen, *isolation* may suggest the condition of being utterly and involuntarily alone or cut off from others. While *privacy* and *seclusion* can suggest freedom from interference or harm, only *isolation* can suggest inaccessibility to help or aid. Less strictly taken, *isolation* still refers more sternly to total exclusion of the external: hoping her friends would understand her insistence on complete *isolation* during the period of mourning; erratic ferry service that contributed to the island's sense of *isolation* from the mainland; the *isolation* of the ghetto from the rest of the city.

Solitude can be a more positive and high-toned substitute for *isolation,* but mostly in the latter's voluntary senses: longing for the off-season *solitude* of a seaside resort. In an extended sense, *solitude* can refer more generally to the stillness or peacefulness of a setting: the lofty *solitude* of the mountain peaks. **Withdrawal** places its emphasis on an act rather than a state, stressing voluntary removal of oneself from distraction or, less positively, rejection of the outside world: his *withdrawal* each night into the *privacy* of his home; their self-preoccupied *withdrawal* into their own affairs. The movement suggested by *withdrawal,* however, need not be from public view into *seclusion,* but from one place to anywhere else: a *withdrawal* from home life into the concerns of her hectic office life. In a psychological sense, *withdrawal* has become a fad word for any indication of introversion or introspection, even extending to catatonic or autistic states: the boy's *withdrawal* from the other students. See ESCAPE, LEAVE, LONELINESS, LONELY, MODEST.

Antonyms: *company, gregariousness, publicity.*

procrastinate
   dally
   dawdle
   dillydally
   lag
   loiter
   shilly-shally

stall

tarry

These verbs refer to the postponing of a duty or to the leisurely, aimless passing of time. **Procrastinate** and **stall** both emphasize the putting off of serious questions, but *stall* can suggest any sort of delay to gain time, whereas *procrastinate* suggests occupying oneself with other, often trivial, matters. *Stall,* furthermore, can indicate a brief pause, as before answering a question, while *procrastinate* indicates the protracted dragging out or delaying of something over a longer time. [His hemming and hawing was only a ruse to *stall* the reporters before answering their questions; When faced with a deadline on a term paper, he lolls about on his bed, daydreams, goes out to movies, or does anything he can think of to *procrastinate* a little longer.] *Stall* can, however, refer to a longer delay, in which case it suggests greater ill will than *procrastinate:* legislation *stalled* in subcommittee.

Dawdle may refer to a kind of *procrastinating* in which a given duty is pursued halfheartedly and phlegmatically rather than put off or put aside: He knew that if he *dawdled* over the dishes, his wife would take over in a fit of exasperation and do them herself. But *dawdle* may also refer to a leisurely passing of time, with no sense whatever of postponing a duty: In the hour between trains, he *dawdled* in a bookstore near the station. **Tarry**, which can sound quaint or affected, means hang behind or stray off course; a deliberate act of *procrastinating* may be implied: Don't *tarry* on your way home from school. Most frequently, *tarry* now more often applies to aimless or leisurely stops along a course: a couple who decided to *tarry* another week in the quaint village.

Loiter means stand about aimlessly or move from place to place in a slow, rambling way: *Loitering* forbidden; a tourist who *loitered* about the town square, browsing through the shops. The verb seldom suggests the delaying of a task, although legally it can refer to a misdemeanor and so can suggest an improper or sinister motive. **Lag** can suggest something that lacks impetus or falls behind a desirable rate of progress: when interest in school begins to *lag;* a theory that our social consciousness has *lagged* behind our technological accomplishments. *Lag* may be used in a more literal way, without the disapproval inherent in the previous examples: a fifteen-mile hike during which those with blistered feet soon *lagged* behind.

Shilly-shally suggests the evasive tactic of *stalling* for time or an attempt to avoid taking a stand: She was not one to *shilly-shally* when disagreeing with her colleagues. Most simply, *shilly-shally* can indicate any weak vacillating or *procrastinating* behavior: Officials *shilly-shallied* about technicalities while fires in the city raged out of control. **Dally** can indicate the leisurely passage of time where no postponing of duty is implied: a vacation in which they could *dally* as long as they wished in any place they liked. *Dally* can also add a special note of pleasurably relaxed and even amorous *dawdling*, influenced by a related use of *dally:* members of the government who themselves had *dallied* with young women. More disapprovingly and with no note of playfulness, *dally* can indicate an indecisive wasting of time: shoppers who *dally* over the prepackaged cuts of meat in supermarkets. **Dillydally**, an alternative form, more readily suggests *procrastinating:* He *dillydallied* over choosing a movie until it was too late to go to one. See HESITATE, POSTPONE.

Antonyms: *decide, persevere, push on,* QUICKEN.

profession

field

job

occupation

specialization

trade

vocation

work

These nouns refer to the long-term duties that people take on as a livelihood or main interest in life. **Profession** suggests a position that cannot be attained without a considerable amount of higher education, and that involves one creatively in mental rather than manual labor. *Profession* once referred mainly to the three learned *professions*—law, medicine, and theology—but it is now often used to confer status upon many other ways of earning a livelihood: the teaching *profession;* the acting *profession;* making friends mostly among other members of the plumbing *profession.* Even when *profession* is used more strictly, it need not suggest dedication on the part of a member. By contrast, one sense of **vocation** specifically stresses this dedication: finding early that he had a *vocation* for the ministry, though he ended up in the legal *profession* instead. Moreover, *vocation* stresses a long-term commitment to something that is not necessarily equated with the earning of a livelihood: choosing painting as a *vocation* and earning her keep by waiting on tables. Less specifically, *vocation* can be a neutral reference to one's form of employment; as such, it may or may not include the *professions,* but in any case it can sound euphemistic or high-toned when so used: calling together a representative sampling of people from all walks of life and from every *profession* and *vocation*. **Occupation** is restricted to this last neutral possibility for *vocation*, though *occupation* escapes the danger of sounding over-elegant or euphemistic: drawn from *occupations* as diverse as medicine and carpentry.

Trade, **work**, and **job** may suggest a range of *occupations* from skilled labor to the most menial of positions. Of the three, *trade* implies the dignity of learned skills in which inventiveness and manual labor are combined: programs designed to teach a *trade* to school dropouts; the building *trades*. *Work*, which is very general, can apply to any sort of effort: the *work* of raising a child. In a professional context, it suggests the set hours of full-time employment: getting to *work* on time. Less specifically, it can point to a *vocation* or *occupation* in general: asking her what sort of *work* she did. *Job* is commonly used to refer to any sort of gainful employment, whether permanent or temporary: hunting for a summer *job;* getting *jobs* for the unemployed. *Job* ranges in application from a single task or piece of *work* to a regular position of employment. It may suggest either skilled or unskilled labor, for its commonness gives it informal currency in any context: the *job* of turning out first-rate psychiatrists; an editorial *job* with a publishing house; to do a good *job* of mowing the lawn.

Field is an informal word, and **specialization** a formal word, for referring to smaller groupings within *occupations:* a medical student who intended to specialize in the *field* of obstetrics; a general knowledge of law but with a *specialization* in divorce cases. See ARTISAN, LABOR, LABORER, STINT.

professor

> don
> graduate assistant
> instructor
> lecturer

These nouns refer to academic positions or duties germane to higher education. **Professors** are the highest-ranking teachers in a college or university. Usually, *professors* have tenure by virtue of status, qualification, or seniority: advancing from assistant *professor* to associate *professor* and finally to full *professor* in the shortest possible time. **Instructor** indicates a college teacher without the title of *professor* and so has lower status, often without tenure: *professors* to teach the upperclassmen and *instructors* to teach freshmen.

A **graduate assistant** is a student working for an advanced degree, usually the doctorate, who is hired to teach one or more sections of a required course on the freshman and sophomore levels.

Lecturer often indicates a teacher who instructs by means of formal verbal discourse. In some American colleges and universities, *lecturer* denotes a temporary or part-time appointment at various salary levels but often without standard academic rank. At other colleges, particularly in Europe, *lecturer* may be a rank in itself, and often such a person may actually be a *professor*. *Lecturer* may also indicate a person invited to give a single talk or group of talks and thus is a teacher who remains outside the academic hierarchy entirely: a guest *lecturer* invited to give a term of lectures on modern art. Also, some large classes are taught by *lecturers* and then broken down into smaller discussion groups, taught by *instructors*. **Don** indicates a teacher in British and other colleges who is neither a *professor* nor a *lecturer,* but who instructs students individually, a technique that forms the basic method of the students' education. Such a faculty member may have or may attain both rank and tenure within such systems. See LEARNING, TEACH.

prohibit

> ban
> debar
> enjoin
> forbid
> interdict

These verbs are alike in referring to a declaration that something must not be done or to an action that prevents something from being done. To **prohibit** is to give some formal command against or, more specifically, to make some authoritative legal enactment against. There is in *prohibit* an implication of readiness to use such force as may be needed to give effect to the enactment: In our city, smoking in government offices is *prohibited* by law. **Forbid** is a less formal word than *prohibit* and suggests a personal relationship between the people involved in the *forbidding:* She *forbade* her son to leave the house unaccompanied.

The remaining verbs in this set are less general than *prohibit* or *forbid*. **Ban** and **interdict** suggest *prohibiting* by ecclesiastical or civil authority. *Interdict* is chiefly known for its ecclesiastical use: to *interdict* the administration of the sacraments to heretics. *Ban* frequently implies moral condemnation or disapproval: a textbook that had been *banned* in Texas. **Debar** means shut out or exclude, as from some place or condition. It hints strongly at the action of an irresistible authority or inner necessity: His plea of insanity was *debarred* by his own admissions. **Enjoin** has specific application to legal contexts. It means *prohibit* or command by judicial order or injunction: railroad workers who were *enjoined* from striking for ninety days. See COMMAND, STOP.

Antonyms: *ENDORSE, PERMIT.*

project

> activity
> enterprise
> operation
> program
> undertaking

These nouns refer to the execution of a systematic plan for realizing an explicit objective. **Project** and **program** might both seem to refer literally to a proposed plan rather than one being carried out, but in actual usage these nouns can apply to such a plan at any stage of its existence, from conception to completion. *Project* is the more general of the two and can apply equally well to the planned task of a single person or to such a task involving a number of people: a *project* to teach himself French on weekends; the government's highway construction *project*. *Project* is often used to refer to the result achieved by such work, long after its planning and completion: the six-block housing *project*. *Program* is more formal and more abstract than *project* and applies most often to group work. Where *project* might suggest a single self-contained objective, often requiring physical labor, *program* can suggest a more complex set of such *projects* or the application of largely mental or administrative effort: an antipoverty *program* that would develop a number of neighborhood *projects*.

Activity is the most general of these nouns. While it need not suggest a plan or objective, it is often used to refer to the work done on a *project* or carried out by a group. It stresses the actual carrying out of something that continues without any point of completion: kindergartens that emphasize unprogrammed playtime *activity;* college students who slight their studies for extracurricular *activities;* settlement houses offering such *activities* as literacy training, citizenship courses, and folk dancing.

Operation is close to *activity* in its generality, suggesting continuing motion without necessarily implying the possibility of completion: studying the *operation* of the federal courts. It has come to have a special use in reference to a complex *program* designed to achieve a defined goal; this use, bor-rowed from the military, follows the capitalized word with a colorful epithet: *Operation* Desert Storm; *Operation* Headstart.

Enterprise and **undertaking** are the most formal of these nouns. *Enterprise* may suggest improvisation toward a less clearly defined goal and may imply an element of risk; it may also suggest boldness and strenuous endeavor: a perilous *enterprise* that few thought had a chance of success. On the other hand, it may refer to any business *activity*. [Watchmaking and banking are the chief *enterprises* of the country.] *Undertaking* is more general than *enterprise*, but unlike *activity* it suggests both considerable forethought and the possibility of completion: agreeing to the *undertaking* only after exhaustive discussion of other possibilities. It can sometimes sound like an unnecessarily fancy substitute for one of its less formal synonyms. See BUILD, CREATE, LABOR, MAKE.

propel

> press
> push
> shove
> thrust
> urge

These verbs refer to the generation or application of force to move a thing onward or away. **Propel** is the most general, referring to the act of driving someone or something forward by whatever means: *propelled* through a revolving door. The verb is most often used, however, of a mechanical force or a separate source of power; an explosive that *propels* a projectile from a gun; a fuel that serves to *propel* a missile or a rocket; a boat *propelled* by steam or by an outboard motor.

Push generally implies physical contact between the mover and the moved. It specifically indicates force or pressure exerted on or against one side of an object to move it forward, in the opposite direction, or out of the way. The force employed may be slight or considerable: to *push* a baby carriage; to *push* a stalled car. Applied to persons, *push* often implies impatience and consequent rudeness: to *push* ahead of someone at a counter. *Push* has many other shades of meaning depending on context: to *push* a reluctant parachutist out of a plane; to *push* a person off a diving board. **Shove** is close to *push* but is generally a stronger word, implying a greater degree of forcible pressure or physical effort: to *shove* a boat away from shore with a pole. More often than *push*, *shove* indicates exertion, as in *pushing* a heavy object along a surface: to *shove* a boat into the surf. Used of persons, it may imply greater belligerence or determination than *push,* focusing on rough haste or blunt rudeness in *pushing* insistently: *shoving* everyone aside, elbowing and jostling his way to the front. *Push* and *shove* are often used in tandem: passengers *pushing* and *shoving* in the subway.

To **thrust** is to *push* suddenly and forcibly, as on impulse or because of some stimulus. [The child *thrust* out his hand, asking for candy; Shy and embarrassed, the boy *thrust* the corsage at his date; Othello, in a jealous rage, *thrust* Desdemona aside.] Unlike the other verbs here, *thrust* often implies a putting of one thing into another. It may mean put a person forcibly into some situation: to *thrust* a prisoner into a cell; to *thrust* an unwilling child onto the stage. Or it may refer to the act of *pushing* into something with a sharp or pointed instrument: to *thrust* a pin into one's skin; a matador who *thrusts* a sword into a bull. In an extended sense, *thrust* can mean have anything forced upon one against one's will: Unwanted publicity was *thrust* upon her.

Press and **urge**, in this context, point to an outward influence that *propels* one toward a goal. *Urge* may be used of physical force: to *urge* a horse on with a whip or with spurs. More often, however, *urge* indicates strong persuasion, the psychological exertion of a prompting or impelling influence: She *urged* us to accept her plan. *Press* refers almost entirely to psychological stress. It is stronger than *urge* in implying greater insistence and urgency, with overtones of demand: *pressing* them to meet the deadline; He *pressed* me for an answer; *pressing* hard for needed reforms. *Push* is used figuratively in a similar way, meaning *press* persistently or promote or advocate vigorously: to *push* for a change in the law; to *push* a new product. See IMPEL.

Antonyms: *DISCOURAGE, PULL, STOP.*

protect

defend
guard
harbor
safeguard
shelter
shield

These verbs mean preserve from harm, injury, or attack. **Protect** is the most general term. It suggests from its etymology the providing of a covering or other barrier to ward off harm: to *protect* against frostbite; to *protect* a country from surprise attack. **Guard** means *protect* with extreme care and watchfulness against actual or potential danger: to *guard* a prisoner; Secret Service personnel who *guard* the President; to *guard* against hurting someone's feelings.

Shield suggests even more strongly than *protect* that something is placed between that which is to be *protected* and the impending source of harm or injury: to *shield* one's face from blows with an upraised arm; *shielding* one's eyes from strong light; overly protective parents who *shield* their children from disappointment or failure.

Safeguard implies that danger is not yet present and may even be remote, but that planning against its eventuality is prudent. [Vaccination *safeguards* us from smallpox; Saving money regularly during your working years will help *safeguard* your old age.]

Defend emphasizes present danger and means *protect* by use of force or other measures. [The American colonists fought to *defend* their liberties; Every girl must learn to *defend* herself while playing with aggressive boys.] By extension, *defend* means uphold or vindicate actions, opinions, decisions, etc., against censure, punishment, or unfriendly criticism: to *defend* one's right to hold certain political views; to *defend* the reputation of a wrongly accused man; a lawyer *defending* her client in court. *Defend, guard,* and *shield* are not as complete in indicating success in warding off harm as is *protect*. One may *guard, shield,* or *defend* a person or thing in vain, but that which one *protects* tends to be secure and safe.

Shelter and **harbor** both mean *protect* by offering, or by being, a place of refuge or safety. *Shelter* is usually applied to providing cover from inclement weather, physical danger, or attack. [*Sheltered* from the cold in its cave, the bear slept until spring; They were *sheltered* from the rifle fire by a huge boulder.] *Shelter,* like *shield,* can also convey the idea of *protecting* in a manner that serves to inhibit or keep in a state of ignorance: The Victorians believed in *sheltering* girls and women from sexual knowledge. *Harbor* almost always has connotations that are unfavorable or that may even suggest illegality: Improperly supervised operating rooms may *harbor* germs; to *harbor* a fugitive from justice. In its figurative use, *harbor* points to a cherishing in the mind, often secretly, of thoughts, motivations, plans, etc., that are unacceptable or hostile: to *harbor* grudges; to *harbor* ruthless ambitions that may never be realized. See NURSE, PAMPER.

Antonyms: *ATTACK, PLUNDER.*

protection

asylum
cover

refuge
sanctuary
shelter

These nouns are alike in denoting a place where one is guarded or defended from attack or injury; they also are used to designate the condition of safety or security such a place provides. **Protection** is the most general and widely applied noun in this group. It can refer to anything that shields from harm or destruction. [A strong defense system offers *protection* from sudden attack by an enemy; A storm cellar is intended to provide *protection* from tornadoes.] **Shelter** usually connotes temporary *protection,* as from exposure to the elements: the awning under which we found *shelter* during the shower. **Refuge** suggests the safety one seeks when threatened or when one has escaped from danger or distress: a prisoner on the run who took *refuge* in an abandoned shack. Figuratively, *refuge* refers to any expedient used for safety or defense: His final *refuge* was a web of lies and deceit. **Cover** is *protection* that affords safety through concealment. It can be the natural *shelter* of shrubbery used by wild birds. It can be an object, a house, etc., that serves as a shield during an attack: Take *cover* in the barn as soon as you hear gunfire. It can be a military tactic used by troops, vessels, etc.: Most Allied landings in World War II would not have been possible without air *cover.*

Asylum and **sanctuary** are related in meaning. *Asylum* originally denoted the inviolable *refuge* from arrest or punishment offered by the temple in ancient times; *sanctuary* was the later Christian equivalent. Today, such immunity from arrest, punishment, or persecution is generally fixed by political boundaries. *Asylum* and *sanctuary* are most often applied, therefore, to the *protection* offered a political refugee by a foreign country or its diplomatic officials: A dictator deposed by a successful revolution may find *asylum* (or *sanctuary*) in another country. *Sanctuary,* by extension, has also come to refer to areas set apart for the *protection* and preservation of wildlife: a bird *sanctuary.* See ESCAPE, PROTECT.

Antonyms: AGGRESSION, DANGER, *distress, harm, hurt, injury.*

prototype
archetype
exemplar
ideal
original
pattern
urtext

These nouns refer to the representative, perfect, or earliest form of something. **Prototype** indicates the first example of a type from which other examples are developed or upon which they are modeled: the anthropoid *prototype* of modern human beings; The Homeric epics became the *prototypes* upon which Vergil, Milton, and others based their epic poems. *Prototype* can also indicate the first full-scale model of something: the *prototype* of a plan for urban housing projects, built to demonstrate its advantages. Less specifically, *prototype* can also indicate any sort of precursor of a later instance: Roger Bacon was the *prototype* of the modern scientist.

Pattern can apply to the plans for a product rather than to the *prototype* or the later creations made from its specifications. It often suggests blueprints or templates to be followed in constructing the product: new dress *patterns* on sale. More generally, *pattern* indicates the design or configuration that something actually takes: the *pattern* of imagery in *Hamlet* that pertains to bodily injury and disease; *patterns* of culture. But *pattern* can also refer to the perfect representative of a type, or to any example thought worthy of emulation: Castiglione was the very *pattern* of the Renaissance courtier.

Original is close to *prototype* in distinguishing the first or genuine product from copies or later versions: He prepared an *original* and two copies; a painting copied from an *original* in the Louvre; a close comparison of the two dresses, one a signed *original,* the other a mass-produced copy; a collation of all manuscript copies with the *original.* **Urtext,** the most restricted of these nouns, is from German and refers to the earliest version of a musical or literary work, whether written or printed and whether extant or not: an argument that presupposed a vanished *urtext* upon which the existing version is modeled.

Archetype can also refer to the earliest version of a literary work, referring strictly to a manuscript that no longer exists: whether it is possible to reconstruct the *archetype* from the many incomplete copies in existence. *Archetype* refers much more widely, however, to the abstract conception of a perfect type. In Platonism, *archetypes* are the general or pure forms of which existing things are imperfect copies: For Plato, all chairs, however various in design, can be said to reflect in their chairness the same *archetype,* just as there are *archetypes* for justice, goodness, and such institutions as a republic. Jung initiated a modern redefinition of *archetype* to refer to those forms and symbols in the unconscious of all people that theoretically reflect the history of the species: a myth that deals with *archetypes* of guilt, death, redemption, and rebirth. More loosely, *archetype* can refer to the quintessential elements something contains: recurrent *archetypes* of conflict and resolution that can be seen in the living patterns of every family unit. *Prototype* and *archetype* are sometimes loosely substituted for one another, but strictly speaking, *prototype* suggests an early, possibly unrefined version that later versions may reflect but depart from; *archetype*, by contrast, suggests a perfect and unchanging form, real or imaginary, that existing things can more or less approach but never equal.

Ideal is a much simpler word for some of the meanings indicated by *archetype*. However, it usually suggests an imagined perfection, formulated as a goal to strive for or as a measure against which to test something that exists: describing his *ideal* of what a city should be like and comparing this with the monstrosities produced in the trend to urbanization. As can be seen, *ideal* may indicate a personal rather than universal set of desirable qualities, whereas *archetype* refers to what is generally and invariably true of all examples, at least in essence. *Ideal* can also point hyperbolically to an instance seen as an embodiment of perfection: She is his *ideal* of everything that can properly be called womanly. **Exemplar** concentrates exclusively on this last possibility of *ideal*, pointing to an instance that seems the perfect realization of its type: the *exemplar* of the prima donna at her most grandiose and temperamental. See ARISE, FORM, KIND, NATIVE.

Antonyms: COPY, COUNTERPART, DUPLICATE.

proverb

adage
aphorism
apothegm
epigram
epigraph
epitaph
maxim
motto
saying

These nouns all denote forms of brief expressions of what are supposed to be accepted truths. A **proverb** is a homely illustration of a general truth and is couched in condensed and practical terms, as in "A fool and his money are soon parted." An **adage** is a time-honored and widely known *proverb*, such as "Actions speak louder than words."

A **maxim** is a practical rule of conduct or action, such as, "Neither a borrower nor a lender be." A **motto** differs from a *maxim* in that it states a guiding principle or belief rather than a precept. *Mottoes* are sometimes prefixed to literary works, but they commonly are chosen by a group, an institution, a nation, etc., as an expression of a purpose or ideal. ["Semper fidelis" is the *motto* of the Marine Corps; "In God we trust" is the *motto* of the United States.]

A **saying** is a figure of speech or a remark of any type that is current. *Sayings* are repeated often, sometimes to the point of losing their freshness. [As the *saying* goes, "He has bats in his belfry"; As I always say, "Live and let live."] *Saying* also has the general meaning of any noteworthy or pungent observation, especially one of a group culled from the writings and speeches of well-known figures. One speaks of the *sayings* of Marcus Aurelius or the *sayings* of Benjamin Franklin.

The remaining nouns all refer to expressions that are more consciously literary or clever than are *proverbs* and *adages;* furthermore, their authorship is more often known. An **epigram** is a brief, pointed remark in verse, prose, or conversation that expresses a witty or even satirical observation: "The only way to get rid of a temptation is to yield to it," wrote Oscar Wilde, a composer of brilliant *epigrams*. **Epigraph** is sometimes confused with *epigram*, but it refers strictly to a brief quotation, rich in implications, that introduces a piece of writing: Eliot used a quotation from Conrad as an *epigraph* to his poem "The Hollow Men." Less commonly now, *epigraph* can also refer to the inscription of a *motto* in some material such as stone or metal: the *epigraph* on the coin. **Epitaph**, often confused with *epigram* and *epigraph*, refers to a verse or prose inscription on a tombstone. Whether signed or anonymous, an *epitaph* may be composed for the occasion or consist of a quoted *adage* or *motto:* her hobby of collecting *epitaphs* found in old graveyards.

An **aphorism** is a thought-provoking remark that does not yield all its meaning so readily as an *epigram* and aims at profundity rather than wit. An *aphorism* may be embedded in a longer work, as the following observation from King Lear: "As flies to wanton boys are we to the gods; they kill us for their sport." In other cases, authors have deliberately written groups, sequences, or even books of *aphorisms*: the *aphorisms* of Kafka. An **apothegm** is a startling or paradoxical assertion, such as Swift's "There is nothing in this world constant but inconstancy." See TRUISM.

provisional

conditional
contingent

dependent

These adjectives characterize a tentative act, decision, or situation subject or subordinate to factors that are either in evidence or thought likely to come about. **Provisional** may refer merely to something adopted for the moment out of temporary necessity or until something better can be arranged: a *provisional* army. More pertinent here, *provisional* often suggests a situation that is allowed to exist provided certain results are forthcoming: given *provisional* status as a nonmatriculated student until his first-term grades become available. *Provisional* usually suggests that the crucial factors determining ultimate status lie in the future.

Dependent, by contrast, may indicate something subject to factors past, present, or future: rapid growth that was *dependent* upon the groundwork laid in the last century; a sense of well-being *dependent* mainly on overall physical health; accepting the new liberal policies, *dependent* only upon how they worked out in practice. *Dependent* also may suggest factors to be imposed or stipulated as part of an agreement or contract: an increased allowance that would be *dependent* on how it would be spent.

Conditional stresses almost exclusively this last sense possible for *dependent*, suggesting an agreement that will be honored by one side if the other side lives up to its terms: *conditional* approval of the book, provided certain passages are deleted. *Conditional*, less specifically, may mean tentative: could give only *conditional* praise to the content of the report before studying the transcript in detail. **Contingent** may refer at its least complex to something liable to happen: fearing that defeat was *contingent*. It may also indicate something unforeseen or occurring by chance or accident: *contingent* catastrophes. More pertinent here, *contingent* suggests a cause-and-effect relationship of any sort: a political victory wholly *contingent* upon the personal popularity of the winner. *Contingent* may also suggest something *dependent* upon an uncertain event or condition. [Historical processes are *contingent* upon so many imponderables as to make the approach of the scientific determinist untenable.] See FLIMSY, SUBORDINATE, TEMPORARY.

Antonyms: CONCLUSIVE, DEFINITE, *independent*, PERMANENT.

pseudonym
    alias
    nom de guerre
    nom de plume
    pen name

The noun **pseudonym** is a fictitious name used in place of one's actual, or legal, name. *Pseudonym* is the most general term in this group and includes all the others. It does not suggest a discreditable motive for concealing one's identity but may be adopted merely because it is more striking or easier to recall than one's actual name. **Pen name** and **nom de plume** (a term coined in England from French elements) both refer specifically to a fictitious name an author signs to a book, article, or other literary work. [Voltaire was the *pseudonym* (or *pen name*) of François Marie Arouet; Mark Twain was the *pseudonym* (or *nom de plume*) of Samuel Clemens.]

An **alias** is a name taken to conceal one's identity, often for suspect purposes. An *alias* is often assumed to avoid the consequences of a criminal record or to confuse law officers. On the other hand, a reformed criminal or a person who has been involved in a scandal may move to another area to make a fresh start and there take an *alias* to avoid publicity. In the legal sense, *alias* is not only an assumed name but may be another name by which a person is known to some people. Unlike the other nouns here, *alias* may be used adverbially: Jason Miller *alias* James Minton.

Nom de guerre (adopted from the French and meaning war name) is a *pseudonym* adopted by a person who must conceal his or her true identity in order to retain freedom of action. Consequently, many persons engaged in controversies or in political activities opposing a prevailing regime find it necessary to adopt *noms de guerre*. [Lenin was the *nom de guerre* of Vladimir Ulyanov; Currer Bell was the *nom de guerre* (and the *pen name*) of Charlotte Brontë because she found it easier to publish her works under a masculine name.

psychotic
    crazy
    demented
    deranged
    insane
    lunatic
    mad
    psychopathic

These adjectives characterize serious mental disturbances. **Psychotic**, the most precise of these, is used by psychiatrists to describe a person who exhibits a total break with or withdrawal from reality; it contrasts with *neurotic*, which describes someone with a distorted view of reality. A *psychotic* personality may be antisocial, violent, or merely passive: *psychotic* delusions; *psychotic* acts of cruelty; *psychotic* apathy.

Psychotic may also be used by sociologists to describe, less precisely, acts that are extreme departures from social norms: a *psychotic* split between duty and simple humanity that resulted in the establishment of concentration camps. *Psychotic* has also entered the popular consciousness, where it can be used imprecisely as a term of opprobrium: my *psychotic* brother-in-law.

Psychopathic is even more likely to be used in a popular context, although here it is more often a high-toned substitute for vicious or brutal: a *psychopathic* killer. In psychiatric use, however, *psychopathic* describes someone who has no sense of social responsibility but does not exhibit a break with reality. While this condition may result in violent or criminal acts, it may also result in extreme withdrawal or passivity.

Demented at its most precise indicates a person whose mentality has degenerated from a previous level that was more nearly normal: brain damage that left him *demented*. More often, however, *demented* is used loosely to characterize anyone who seems possessed by odd obsessions or eccentricities: his *demented* fear of strangers. **Insane**, a term no longer used by psychologists or psychiatrists, is still used in law to refer to someone so mentally disturbed as to be unable to distinguish right from wrong: a trial that hinged on whether the man on trial was *insane* at the time of the murder. In popular usage, it may also refer to things that appear foolish or ridiculous: an *insane* scheme for making a million in the stock market. *Insane* can even be used as a superlative for anything intense, exciting, or pleasurable: an absolutely *insane* party. **Deranged** is less likely to be used in either a psychological or legal context, but in a general way it has validity in formal usage to refer to mental or emotional drives or balances that have become disordered: *deranged* by fever; *deranged* from lack of food and water; She suffered a shock that left her *deranged*.

The remaining adjectives no longer have valid uses in either psychological or legal discussion, or even in general formal use. **Lunatic**, in fact, is now less often used on any level of speech because of its old-fashioned sound; its root refers to a belief that the moon could cause mental disturbance. It is still used sometimes comically or disapprovingly for odd or undesirable behavior: a *lunatic* notion that our citizens should be able to own weapons of mass destruction. It is also commonly found in the expression *lunatic* fringe, which denotes followers or devotees of a movement, idea, etc., who are extreme or fanatical in their enthusiasm. By contrast, **mad** and **crazy** are used widely to refer popularly to mental disturbance. *Mad*, the more formal of the two, may suggest profound mental disorder. Informally, *mad* can also refer to anything silly, flamboyant, pointless, unrealistic, or irrational: a *mad* feathered hat; a *mad* hope that help might still come; a *mad* desire to wreak vengeance on his imagined oppressor. Careful writers avoid *mad* when it means angry: remarks that made her *mad* at me. *Crazy* is the most informal of these and refers popularly to someone who is extremely neurotic or *psychotic*. *Crazy* also has a wide range of additional uses to refer to the eccentric, odd, troubled, or desiring: a *crazy* collection of furniture; a *crazy* dread of failing the exam. It can even express approval for something that goes to extremes: a *crazy* scheme for making extra money over spring break. See FRANTIC, FRENZY.

Antonyms: *SENSIBLE.*

pull

drag
haul
tug
yank

These verbs refer to the action of moving something toward one or in the same direction in which one is moving. **Pull**, the most general verb in the group, embraces all the other terms within its meaning: *pulling* the wagon behind him; *pulling* a straw from the broom; *pulling* the body out of the crevasse. While *pull* can suggest movement in any direction, **drag** usually refers to horizontal motion or motion up an incline; it suggests laborious effort over rough ground or against friction, resistance, or gravity: *dragging* his feet across the floor; *dragging* the dead pilot out of the airplane; *dragging* each stone for the wall up the hill. **Haul** is like *drag* in suggesting laborious effort and rough going, but it is like *pull* in suggesting movement in any direction: *hauling* the loaded basket up two stories by a long, sturdy rope; *hauling* the raft over the sandbar. It also has a special use in the transportation industry for moving heavy materials or equipment: flatboats that *haul* iron ore from Duluth to the steel factories.

Tug and **yank** both refer to intermittent or quick pulls on something: *tugging* at my sleeve to ask directions; *tugging* at her chains. *Yank* suggests abruptness and ill humor and, unlike *tug*, is more often used of a single motion than of a series of small, quick motions: *yanking* me off the platform; *yanking* the picture from the wall. See IMPEL.

Antonyms: *PROPEL.*

purpose

- aim
- end
- goal
- object
- objective

These nouns refer to the result toward which one chooses to direct an activity. **Purpose** may suggest either a resolute, deliberate movement toward a result or the desired result itself: filled with high *purpose;* explaining the *purpose* of the tedious exercises. The specific overtone of *purpose* in either use is that of meaningfulness: unable to comprehend a universe without *purpose;* a cruel act done on *purpose.* The other nouns in this group do not carry this implication and concentrate mostly on the desired result rather than on the manner of moving toward it. Of these, **goal** is closest to *purpose* in suggesting a selected result that can be won only with difficulty by dedicated effort: sticking stubbornly to their *goal* of prison reform. The emphasis on choice is more invariable here than with *purpose,* which might be supplied by someone else. A *goal* suggests a personal determination: a tutorial system whose *purpose* was to let all students realize their own educational *goals. Goal* is sometimes used in a vaguer way to mean the general trend or direction a person or group takes, without implying any final result: the *goals* of a free democracy; asking himself what his *goals* should be.

Aim is often used in this vague way, suggesting a general tendency: the *aims* of education; his *aim* in life. In the singular, it implies a more concrete choice than *goal,* one that can be given succinctly. When used of a desired result, *aim* is most appropriate for a small or short-term *goal* and is consequently less dramatic in tone than *goal* or *purpose:* going to Venice with the *aim* of seeing as many Tintorettos as possible. *Aim* also suggests less emotional involvement in the outcome than *purpose* and *goal,* and less determination that it will be achieved. **End** is more formal than the foregoing nouns and is most specifically appropriate to philosophical or ethical discussions: theorizing that the *end* of exogamy is species differentiation; the *ends* of a just society. Because *end* has other meanings that are more common, it is often restricted in this sense to uses in which it contrasts with the manner of achieving a given *goal:* arguing that the *end* justifies the means.

Object and **objective** would seem too close in meaning to differentiate, but each has a context in which it is the more appropriate term. *Object* and *objective* are more formal than the other nouns of this group and are often used for impersonal planning of an abstract or general nature: limited desegregation as an *object* of the court's decision; economic *objectives* of the administration. *Object* would be most appropriate for an *aim* or *goal* that can be stated in a few words; *objective* suggests a wider, more intangible set of *goals* that includes a good many imponderables. *Objective,* however, has a military use for a specific or limited *goal:* identifying Hill 104 as our company's *objective. Object,* by contrast, nearly always suggests specificity or singleness of *purpose:* the *object* of her search; the *object* of his fantasy life. See INTEND, PLAN, PROJECT.

puzzle

- conundrum
- enigma
- mystery
- problem
- riddle

These nouns apply to things that are hard to solve, answer, or understand. In a limited sense, all are questions, tasks, or entertainments that have set answers or solutions and are devised to challenge the wits. A **puzzle** is a game or contrivance that tests one's ingenuity or patience. To work a jigsaw *puzzle* or a crossword *puzzle,* one must fit together pieces or words in a certain way. A **problem** is an exercise in learning that tests the ability to apply theory, knowledge, and technique. To work a *problem* in mathematics, one must use given facts to find the missing ones: The *problem* asks students to find the average speed of a car on a trip when the distance traveled and the travel time are known. A **mystery** in this comparison is a story, novel, play, or movie that arouses curiosity or suspense: a murder *mystery.* To solve a *mystery,* one must follow clues and interpret evidence in order to find a plausible explanation for perplexing events. In actuality, a *mystery* story is plotted and solved by its author, who must keep the reader guessing until the end.

Enigma, **riddle**, and **conundrum** apply to questions or statements designed to perplex. An *enigma* is a deliberately obscure or ambiguous statement, a dark saying meant to hide as much as it reveals: The Delphic oracle spoke in *enigmas.* A *riddle* is a puzzling question stated as a problem to be solved by clever ingenuity. *Riddles* may be significant, requiring a grasp of metaphor or the ability to comprehend a paradox. The *riddle* of the Sphinx was an *enigma* that only Oedipus could interpret: "What goes on four legs in the morning, on two at noon, on three at night?" "Man—in infancy he crawls, in his prime he walks, in age he leans on a staff." On the other hand, a *riddle* may be merely clever, depending on a pun, as: "What is black and white and red (read) all over?" "A newspaper." A *conundrum* is a *riddle* that hinges on a pun and involves some fanciful point of likeness or difference between things, as: "What is the difference between a floorwalker and a sailor?" "One oversees sales and the other sails overseas." *Conundrum* is an adult word for a child's game— a kind of *riddle* at best ingenious, at worst inane.

In a broader sense, all these nouns may be applied to anything that baffles or perplexes. *Problem* is the most general. Any person or thing that causes difficulty may be called a *problem*. A *mystery* was originally something beyond human understanding: the *mystery* of creation; religious *mysteries*. But *mystery* is now freely applied to puzzling things that have not been explained or are not fully understood. [Her disappearance has remained a *mystery*; Why he went there is a *mystery* to me.] *Riddle* is close to *mystery* in this sense but stresses the idea of eventual solution: the unsolved *riddle* of the common cold. An *enigma* is a tantalizing *mystery*, something darkly veiled or utterly baffling: His biographer passed over the subject's wholesome public image to probe the *enigma* of his private life. Applied to human beings, *enigma* stresses internal contradictions, the presence of opposed traits that make a person hard to understand. *Puzzle* is close to *enigma* in this sense but is a less romantic and more pragmatic word, emphasizing the fitting together of pieces to find a solution: Though many tried to figure our leader out and to predict what she would do, she remained a *puzzle*. *Conundrum*, the most specific of these nouns, is the only one never applied to a person. When used in an extended sense, it means a *problem* that seems to defy solution but that invites conjecture. See CONFUSE, OBSCURE.

puzzle
baffle

mystify
perplex

These verbs mean confuse or present difficulty in understanding or solving something. **Puzzle** may suggest only a mild curiosity and therefore only a mild frustration at the inability to decipher the meaning of something: *puzzled* by his neighbor's stares. As in this example, the *puzzle* suggests that enough hints or clues have been picked up to indicate that something is not normal, without enabling one to determine what is wrong. On the other hand, *puzzle* can merely suggest the remarking of a situation that is unusual in some way: *puzzled* by the friendliness of the strange country's inhabitants.

Mystify suggests a greater loss of detachment than is true for *puzzle* and a greater frustration at not being able to get at the meaning of something. By implication, a person must have many more clues to be *mystified* than he or she needs to be *puzzled*; *puzzle* might also suggest an initial stage of investigation, *mystify* a later one: first *puzzled* and then thoroughly *mystified* as to why she never mentioned her husband in the hundreds of diary entries she made.

Where *mystify* most appropriately suggests astonishment in the face of an unyielding enigma, **perplex** stresses actual discomfort as the attendant emotion; it may also imply a more personal involvement with overtones of worry and uncertainty: *perplexed* by their refusal to tell her where they were vacationing. **Baffle**, the most intense of these verbs, combines the sense of astonishment implicit in *mystify* with the emotional discomfort implicit in *perplex*. It suggests someone rendered unable to act or offer hypotheses in the face of a strange or inexplicable experience: The odd noises and flashes of light in the empty house completely *baffled* me. See CONFUSE.

Antonyms: *CLARIFY, INFORM.*

Q

quantity

amount
number

These nouns refer to the total size, sum, or extent of something measurable. In general use, **quantity** suggests that something is considered in its totality, in terms of mass or bulk: a sufficient *quantity* of food to last a week. *Quantity* is the property of a thing that admits of exact measurement. In order to express a *quantity* in precise terms, however, it is necessary to divide it into units of some kind, measuring it in terms of magnitude, volume, size, sum, weight, or length. A *quantity* of water in a storage tank, for example, can be measured in gallons. **Amount** is often very close to *quantity* in meaning but may differ significantly in its use. It implies that the thing thought of in sum or in the aggregate can be broken down into units or parts that can be measured, counted, or otherwise specified: a large *quantity* of gravel; a limited *amount* of time; a large *amount* of money; a considerable *amount* of work. *Amount* rather than *quantity* is the word generally used of immeasurable or intangible things: They went to a considerable *amount* of trouble. It is *quantity,* however, and not *amount,* that is set over against quality, indicating the contrast between bulk or output and the immaterial value of excellence.

When used collectively, **number** points to a collection of individual things that can be counted, referring to things physically or symbolically separate, not merely separable into units. Where *amount* emphasizes the whole, *number* focuses on the parts: an *amount* of money; a *number* of coins. Where *quantity* stresses measurement in bulk, *number* stresses individual items: a *number* of peaches; the *quantity* of peaches contained in a bushel basket. *Number,* like *quantity,* may be either specific or vague. It may refer to an indefinite or unspecified *quantity.* [When he moved, a *number* of his books had to be left behind; A limited *number* of seats are still available.] Or it may refer to a specific sum or total count of units or individuals: The *number* of students absent is 6. When *number* is preceded by "the," it is used with a singular verb: The *number* of jobs is increasing. When preceded by "a," it is used with a plural verb: A *number* of graduates plan to apply. *Number,* when used with "a," and otherwise unqualified, can imply that the *amount* referred to is relatively large: A *number* of people have signed the petition. Both *number* and *quantity* when used in the plural can indicate a large *amount* or group or a sizable collection. [*Quantities* of surplus materials are available; *Numbers* of people complained when the proposed shutdown was announced.] See PART, TOTAL.

quash. Do not confuse the verb *quash* (annul, reject legally) with the verb *squash* (primary meaning: squeeze).

quell

calm
placate
subdue
suppress
tranquilize

These verbs all mean restore to a state of peace, quiet, or order. **Quell**, **suppress**, and **subdue** mean put an end to a disturbance, such as a riot or a revolt, by use of persuasion or force. Persuasion, force, or both may be used to *quell* an uprising, with the verb suggesting the taking of measures to discourage the participants in order to keep the situation from getting out of hand: The sergeants were able to *quell* the melee in the barracks by ordering all the soldiers to stand at attention. Used figuratively, *quell* may mean allay or quiet: to *quell* foolish fears; the mother's happiness in the event apparently *quelled* the pains attending childbirth. *Suppress* in this sense means *quell* by taking specific actions that not only will put down a disturbance completely but will frustrate any attempts to revive it or to start a similar one. *Suppress* suggests a complete crushing and overpowering, often swift and violent in nature: to *suppress* a mutiny by hanging the ringleaders. *Subdue* takes as its object the participants in a disturbance and implies that they not only are reduced to order but, by the imposition of controls (such as curfews or threats of reprisal), are also rendered more or less incapable of resisting further. In addition to the implication of conquering completely, *subdue* also carries the idea of taming or rendering mild and gentle, often after great difficulty: The great stallion was finally *subdued* and broken in as a riding horse.

Calm and **placate** are milder in meaning than the foregoing verbs and apply only to the quieting of violent movement or emotion. *Calm* is the more general term here and implies causing a state of quietude that may only be transient. [The nurses *calmed* the anxious patient with soothing words and small attentions;

While awaiting trial, the angry prisoner *calmed* down enough to cooperate with her lawyer in preparing her defense.] *Placate* always involves appeasement and means *calm* anger, resentment, hostility, etc., by making concessions or yielding to demands: Only by offering to do extra work at the end of the term could he *placate* the teacher who seemed determined to fail him.

Tranquilize is rarely used in the sense of *calm* or pacify and almost always refers to the effect produced by drugs designed to reduce anxiety and nervous tension. See DISCOURAGE, DOCILE, SUBJUGATE, VANQUISH.

question

grill
interrogate
quiz

These verbs refer to the asking or demanding of information. Of these, **question** is the most general in meaning and the most neutral in tone. At its most restricted, it may be used as a more formal substitute for ask, in the sense of making a single or specific query: *questioning* the woman at the information desk about how to exchange the merchandise he had bought. More pertinent here, however, is its use to suggest the asking of a series of questions to bring information to light: *questioning* the witnesses for details about the physical appearance of the killer. *Question* may also suggest an informal situation: *questioning* her about why she was so late in getting home from school. Often, however, *question* points to an official or formal situation: The suspect was brought to the station house to be *questioned* about his connections with the murdered man. **Interrogate** is a much more formal substitute for *question* and is mostly restricted to an official examination: warning them that the prosecutor would *interrogate* them about embarrassing matters.

Grill is much more informal and applies specifically to intensive *interrogating* in which someone is pressured to reveal information: a dozen known criminals who had been rounded up and *grilled* for hours about their activities on the night of the holdup. The pressure may be psychological, but can extend to physical torture: using torture in *grilling* the captured guerrilla. **Quiz** suggests the use of much less strenuous methods than *grill* and may apply to more ordinary situations; it does, however, suggest intensive *questioning: quizzing* her children about everything they did. Often, *quiz* suggests an educational context, referring in this case to short informal tests, oral or written, conducted to test their mastery of assigned work: *quizzing*

the students twice a week on their outside reading. See DEMAND, EXAMINE, INQUIRY, QUESTION (n.), REQUEST (v.).

quick

fast
precipitate
rapid
swift

These adjectives refer to rapidity of movement. While **quick** can apply widely, it often refers less to rate of motion than to the suddenness or brief duration of a one-time action: a *quick* leap; a *quick* response to my question; The hand is *quicker* than the eye. It can also apply to a readiness to act: *quick* to take offense. When *quick* indicates something of short duration, it often implies haste: He ate a *quick* breakfast and rushed off to work. While **fast** can also apply in a wide variety of ways, it is more apt than *quick* for referring to something in sustained motion, indicating here a high rate of speed or a capacity for such movement: a *fast* car; a *fast* getaway; You're speaking much too *fast* for me to follow you.

Rapid and **swift** are both more formal than the preceding pair and apply equally well to sudden or sustained movement: a *rapid* river; a *rapid* burst of gunfire; a *swift* change of mood; a *swift* runner. *Rapid* has a special connotation relating to beneficial or advantageous speed; by contrast, both *quick* and *fast* can apply as well to catastrophic haste: a *rapid* recovery from his illness; *rapid* progress in slum clearance. A special connotation of *swift* relates to speed that is smooth, undisturbing, uninterrupted, or seemingly effortless: a *swift* transition without hesitation or awkwardness; a communications network that was *swift* and silent in operation. Also, *swift* can give a lyrical overtone: the *swift* fading of autumn into winter.

Precipitate is the one adjective here that stresses sudden change or abrupt movement: too late to halt the *precipitate* decision to divorce; the *precipitate* fall of stock prices. See SPEED, SUPPLE.

Antonyms: LISTLESS, SLOW.

quicken

accelerate
expedite
hasten
hurry
rush
speed

These verbs mean move or cause to move faster.

Quicken suggests greater animation in the performance of an action, as well as a shorter time required for its completion; it is close in sense to **accelerate**, which denotes an increase in the rate of movement, growth, progress, etc., of a thing. [The dancers *quickened* their steps; Neglect *accelerates* tooth decay.] **Speed** differs from *quicken* and *accelerate* in that it always implies rapidity of movement: The auto *sped* along the road; to *speed* production by providing better working conditions. **Hasten** indicates urgency, or sometimes a sudden and premature result. [The storm's approach *hastened* our departure; As the time for the guests' arrival approached, he *hastened* his dinner preparations.] **Hurry** and **rush** are similar to *hasten,* but suggest in addition precipitate or confused motion. [The late arrivals were *hurried* to their seats; The stricken man was *rushed* to a hospital.] *Rush* suggests greater urgency than *hurry:* They suddenly *rushed* out of the room. **Expedite**, more especially a business term than any of the other verbs of this group, means process quickly, as by giving special attention to, in order to save time: The delivery of your new automobile will be *expedited. Expedite* thus has a distant and formal tone that distinguishes it from emotionally charged words like *rush* and *hurry.* See IMPETUOUS, SPEED.

Antonyms: *DELAY, HINDER, STOP.*

quit

    drop out
    leave
    resign

These verbs refer to the act of giving up or withdrawing from employment, school attendance, club membership, or other activities. **Quit** and **resign** emphasize the voluntary relinquishing of a position, membership, or office. *Resign* usually suggests the presentation of a formal letter declaring one's decision. *Quit*, a less formal word, is likely to be applied to employment for which wages, rather than a salary, are paid, or to a group activity that is not highly structured: to *quit* a factory job after a row with the foreman; to *quit* playing on the neighborhood baseball team. *Quit* strongly hints at making up one's mind without much forethought or planning for the future. In more general usage *quit* can refer to the cessation of any activity: to *quit* reading.

Leave is the most general verb of this group; it does not imply much beyond the fact of ceasing to be part of a specific group, even in the narrower sense here considered. A person who *leaves* a job may be planning to take a better one, may have been dismissed, or may have reached retirement age.

The phrase **drop out** means withdraw from participation or membership, usually following a period of loss of interest and of discouragement in the face of increasing competition. *Dropping out* is more negative and more passive than *leaving, resigning,* and *quitting. Dropping out* is most commonly applied to adolescents who *leave* school before earning a diploma and who thereafter may find it difficult to obtain employment. By extension, certain people, such as alcoholics, may be said to be *dropouts* (noun) from life itself. *Drop out* is sometimes used favorably to suggest the action of rejecting false social values: to *drop out* of the race for the almighty dollar. See LEAVE (abandon), LEAVE (depart), RELINQUISH.

Antonyms: *BEGIN, REMAIN.*

quotation

    blurb
    excerpt
    extract
    quote

These nouns refer to short supporting passages from a longer work or another person, or to brief evaluations cited in praise or blame. **Quotation** refers specifically to a passage from another source, clearly indicated as such. It suggests a word-for-word rendering of what the other person said or wrote: failing to make clear in the text what was summary and what was *quotation* of her opponent's argument. Brevity is usually but not always an implication of *quotation:* justifying his viewpoint by extensive *quotations* from available sources. While *quotation* can apply even to a few words, **extract** and **excerpt** suggest longer passages from another source. *Extract* usually refers to several lines of a paragraph, especially when these are set off from the text in which they are cited by the use of indentation or smaller type: concluding the review with a twenty-line *extract* from the title poem. *Excerpt* suggests a longer passage still and may be presented in and for itself, without comment: Two magazines published *excerpts* from the novel.

Blurb and **quote** are much more informal terms than the other nouns here considered. *Blurb* refers to commendatory words cited on the dust jacket of a book or in advertisements for a play or movie. A *blurb* may comprise or include *quotations* from critics, or be an entirely anonymous account designed to persuade potential customers to read or see the work. *Blurb* is also used pejoratively to denote the extravagant and insincere praise common in such writing: a *blurb* comparing the author favorably to Homer and Shakespeare. *Quote* is a shortened form of *quotation*, used in much the same way as the full word. Its natural context is the field of journalism, where it suggests a brief comment by someone, either with or without attribution: Reporters were calling the Pentagon for *quotes* on the Libyan attack. See COPY, DUPLICATE.

raid

foray
incursion
invasion

These nouns refer to a physical and hostile entering of someone else's territory. **Raid** suggests an organized but temporary encroachment: boys planning a *raid* on the neighbor's orchard; an unexpected *raid* on the jungle stronghold of the enemy. As in these examples, stealth and surprise may be suggested as planned elements of a *raid. Raid*, however, can be used humorously for less hostile acts: laying in a supply of cold cuts for the expected midnight *raid* on the refrigerator. **Foray** suggests a more scattered, less organized overrunning of territory than *raid;* it may be haphazard and impulsive as well and even briefer and more limited. A *foray's* sole motivation may be an intent to wreak gratuitous havoc or to plunder and pillage: students who went on *forays* into town; a *foray* behind enemy lines.

Incursion is the most formal of these nouns and is often used in a technical sense to indicate a violation of a nation's territory by another nation: arguing that the overflight could be considered an *incursion* on French airspace. In this sense it may suggest any encroachment: an *incursion* on First Amendment rights. *Incursion* can also be used less technically for any hostile entrance, usually sudden, into another's territory: an armed *incursion* into Cambodia. **Invasion** resembles *raid* in suggesting an organized violation of territory, but it specifically suggests a much more complicated and long-range operation that is usually carried out with the intention of effecting a seizure or change of a permanent sort: the Allied *invasion* of Normandy. Occasionally, *invasion* suggests a large-scale but unplanned *incursion:* the Danish *invasion* of Britain that occurred over several centuries and took the form of sporadic but repeated *raids* and *forays. Invasion* can also suggest any unwanted intrusion: an *invasion* of privacy. See AGGRESSION, ENCROACH, FIGHT.

raise

elevate
hoist
lift
uplift

These verbs all mean place in a higher position. **Raise** commonly implies a physical gesture or activity, although it is often applied in figurative senses to any improved condition or motive: to *raise* one's hand; to *raise* one's spirits with kind words. **Elevate**, when applied to a literal rise in position or altitude, sounds pretentious, *raise* being preferred in most such contexts. When applied figuratively to a rise in rank or distinction, however, *elevate* is commonly and easily used on a variety of levels: She was *elevated* from major to colonel; to *elevate* one's goals.

Lift suggests the use of physical effort in moving something to a higher position, and **hoist** often signifies *lifting* by mechanical means. When *hoist* is used in place of *lift*, it signifies a greater expenditure of effort, comparable to what would be required in *lifting* something by mechanical means: to *lift* a book off the table; to *hoist* the automobile aboard the ship; The firefighter *hoisted* the man to her shoulder before descending the ladder. **Uplift** may be used to mean *raise* aloft, but is more commonly used today to mean *elevate* morally or mentally: *uplifted* by their audience with the Pope. See ESCALATE, IMPROVE.

Antonyms: *depress,* DESCEND, *lower.*

random

casual
desultory
haphazard

These adjectives characterize an aimless, irregular, or erratic procedure. **Random** suggests something arrived at through accident or arbitrary choices; it implies lack of specific direction or intent: a *random* gathering of friends; They followed a *random* route through the forest; having *random* thoughts on ways to redecorate the apartment.

Casual points to something that happens without intention or plan and may give a sense of freedom and ease: a *casual* meeting on the street; a *casual* question; a *casual* stroll. On the other hand, it may also suggest indifference or unconcern: a *casual* handshake; showing by his *casual* manner that he was unaffected by the loss.

Desultory stresses a procedure marked by stops and starts but includes the lack of plan implied by *random* and the lack of formality implied by *casual:* a *desultory* talk of old friends interrupted by silences and lapses. Less favorably, *desultory* can suggest wandering attention, instability, or inconsistency: her *desultory* attempts to keep their correspondence active. **Haphazard** is even stronger in negative implications than *desultory;* it is used almost exclusively in a disapproving way for unsystematic work or behavior that is indifferent to accuracy and efficiency: *haphazard* and slapdash experiments on which no sound conclusions can be based. See CHANCE, CURSORY, OCCASIONAL.

Antonyms: *FORMAL, INVARIABLE, ORDERLY.*

ravage. Do not confuse the verb *ravage* (devastate) with the verb *ravish* (rape).

ravish. Do not confuse the verb *ravish* (rape) with the verb *ravage* (devastate).

reach

accomplish
achieve
attain
earn

These verbs refer to successfully executing a task or arriving at a goal. **Reach** stresses arrival, regardless of whether the goal has been chosen in advance or whether great or little effort has been expended: We *reached* an unfamiliar quarter of the city after an hour of aimless walking; those few who *reach* the finish line in the hazardous obstacle course. *Reach* can also indicate effort that expresses intention rather than successful completion: He *reached* for a book on the shelf above his head. **Earn** can point to the automatic accruing of money or benefits because of one's work or situation: How much do you *earn* a week? Some of my stocks *earn* handsome dividends. More pertinent here, *earn* can suggest a struggle to acquire a special position or distinction: She worked hard to *earn* her Phi Beta Kappa key. *Earn* can also indicate the awarding of an honor or benefit because of the excellence of some completed task: a novel that *earned* her a Pulitzer Prize. In this case, the honor need not be foreseen or worked toward as a goal.

Achieve and **attain** can both emphasize the *reaching* of an intended goal, usually through sustained effort. *Achieve* can indicate the working out of a set or standard procedure, whereas *attain* more often applies to a goal toward which someone has aspired without being sure of success: a series of experiments that *achieved* their purpose; They *attained* a decisive victory in the hard-fought battle. When these verbs apply to acquisition of a possibly unanticipated distinc-

tion, their implications are different. In this case, *achieve* may indicate a deserved success, won because of merit or effort, whereas *attain* is open to other implications: a searching book that *achieved* an awakening of the nation's conscience to the problem of AIDS; a trivial play that *attained* a successful run on Broadway.

Accomplish can stress completion of a set task: He *accomplished* the building of the bookcase, although the result was a rickety affair. More favorably, *accomplish* can function like *attain* to indicate something executed with distinction: the first to *accomplish* the difficult work of deciphering the Minoan script. While *accomplish* always indicates success, whether minimal or exceptional, it often concentrates on interpretive or technical skills rather than creative or original work: a pianist who was able to *accomplish* the difficult passage in the sonata with ease and brilliance. See GET, PERFORM.

Antonyms: *bungle, fail, fall short, miss.*

read

browse
devour
leaf
peruse
scan

These verbs refer to taking in and comprehending written or printed words. **Read,** the most general of these, yields no more connotations beyond the shared meaning for the whole group. It is, however, the one verb here that can apply to the act whether silently or done aloud: *reading* the letter over to herself; *reading* the tale aloud to his students. **Peruse,** by contrast, specifically means *read* carefully and with close attention, suggesting a demanding or complicated text that requires concentration and effort: *perusing* the contract in detail before agreeing to sign it. Sometimes, *peruse* is substituted for *read* without these implications attached, as if elegance could be achieved by using a long word where a short one will do: quickly *perusing* the road sign before applying the brakes.

Devour also can refer to thorough *reading,* but it points not to a studious approach but to a zealous or enthusiastic infatuation for certain authors or genres: *devouring* every book Hermann Hesse wrote; *devouring* at least two murder mysteries a week. Unlike *peruse, devour* can suggest rapid *reading* that may or may not be retentive, and sometimes it can point merely to a habitual or methodical total consumption of a periodical: the enforced silence in our house while father *devoured* the evening newspaper.

The remaining verbs point to hasty or cursory *reading*. **Browse** can indicate the act of strolling through a bookstore or library and sampling books or periodicals without *reading* any, possibly as a way of selecting something to buy and *read* more thoroughly: *browsing* through the biographies. This meaning of *browse* has been extended to other kinds of shopping: *browsing* in a toy shop to see whether he could find anything his son might like. *Browse* can also apply to the idle sampling of passages from a book or periodical: *browsing* through the magazine without finding anything he wanted to read.

Leaf suggests the quick turning of pages in search of a particular item, with *reading* restricted to glimpses at key words or passages until the desired entry is found: quickly *leafing* through the phone book to find the numbers of a few nearby restaurants. But *leaf* can also indicate an idle looking over of a magazine or newspaper, especially one heavily illustrated, as a way of passing time; here, *leaf* would suggest little serious purpose or little intention of *reading* much or for long: *leafing* through some old magazines until a barber was free. **Scan** indicates the act of glancing down the body of a text to take in rapidly the gist of the material. Thus, this action is more methodical than the actions indicated by *browse* and certainly of *leaf: scanning* the articles that might give the information he needed, then *browsing* about in a few related entries, and finally *leafing* past the sports and fashion sections to the television listings. See STUDY.

ready

> disposed
> prepared
> set
> willing

These adjectives suggest the accomplishment of whatever training or conditioning is necessary as a preface to action. **Ready** is the most general of these, suggesting anything from a momentary potential for a certain kind of behavior to a long period of discipline prior to an undertaking: *ready* to tell him exactly what she thinks of him; *ready* to perform her first heart operation. In the first kind of use, *ready* suggests a ripeness for action that may have been building for some time; in the second it suggests a delicate tuning process. *Ready* may also suggest something that is easily available: a *ready* answer to a complex question. **Prepared** stresses the aspect of *ready* that suggests the active, conscious deliberation and effort that pre-

cede action: a student thoroughly *prepared* for the final examination. A more general use of *prepared* stresses a psychic resilience by which one can face alternatives not necessarily known in advance: conscientious parents whose children are *prepared* for the disappointments as well as the joys of life; *prepared* for any eventuality. **Set** suggests plans that have become definite or preparations that are complete and final: all *set* for the big party; *ready, set,* go.

Disposed and **willing** emphasize a different aspect of the period just before action, stressing desire rather than training or even conditioning: He was *willing* to take on the immense job, though he was poorly *prepared* for it. While *willing* implies an agreeable or voluntary choice, *disposed* suggests an innate proclivity or a settled and favorable attitude toward the impending action: *Disposed* as they were to telling the truth, they were hardly *ready* to tell all they knew. In a use closer to *ready* or *prepared, disposed* suggests a last positioning previous to action: two battalions *disposed* for an attack on the air base. See EAGER, OBSERVANT, ORGANIZE, PLAN. **Antonyms:** *disorganized, inexperienced, unprepared,* UNWILLING.

reasoning

> deduction
> induction
> inference
> ratiocination

These nouns refer to exact, objective thought that deals with provable fact and abides by the rules of logic in tracing premises to conclusions. **Reasoning** is the most inclusive of the nouns here, indicating an attempt to draw conclusions by the use of valid methods of thought while remaining impartial and admitting for consideration only unbiased data. **Ratiocination** is a more formal noun for the same concept, but it may occasionally suggest a mind moving from one conclusion to another in a long, complex, even tortuous process: a cogent and convincing piece of *reasoning* demonstrating the common origin of all the races; a process of *ratiocination* that led her to unpleasant conclusions.

An **inference** is the movement from premises to conclusion, so *reasoning* may be said to be the attempt to make valid *inferences,* and *ratiocination* the puzzling out of a chain of *inferences.* If **deduction** is used in reaching an *inference, reasoning* proceeds from general premises regarded as proved or true and may reach a specific conclusion. [All men are mortal; I am a man; therefore, I am mortal.] **Induction** is the opposite process, in which *reasoning* collects all the particulars that relate to a problem and draws a general conclusion that explains their behavior. [Every man he knew of had died, sooner or later. Therefore, all men are mortal.] The laws of science, such as the law of gravity, are first *inductions* from particulars. Once these laws are considered valid, however, they become the basis for any number of *deductions*, provided that these are derived according to the rules of logic. See THINK.

rebuke
admonish
censure
reprimand
reproach
reprove

These verbs are comparable in meaning to express disapproval, either mildly or sharply, of some fault or misdeed. To **rebuke** is to criticize or call down with sharpness, often with abruptness, and usually in the midst of some action or course of action: to *rebuke* a worker whose clumsiness was responsible for the breakdown of operations in the department.

Admonish and **reprove** indicate mild forms of disapproval. *Admonish* may be used in giving warning or counsel where no wrong is implied and often refers to duty that might have been forgotten or might in the future be forgotten: to *admonish* a student about the lateness of his assignments. *Reprove* also suggests mild or even friendly criticism designed less to chasten than to help correct a fault or pattern of misbehavior: to *reprove* a child for telling fibs.

To **reproach** is to express the kind of disapproval that arises from a personal hurt, anger, or grief at someone's thoughtlessness or selfishness: *reproaching* her husband for having forgotten their wedding anniversary.

Censure and **reprimand** agree in indicating a formal and, usually, public or official disapproval. *Reprimand* suggests a direct confrontation between offender and critic; one may *censure* directly or indirectly: the judge who sharply *reprimanded* a witness for being evasive and uncooperative; to *censure* a senator for flagrantly violating ethical standards; a newspaper editorial that *censured* corruption in city government. See DISAPPROVAL, SCOLD.

Antonyms: *ENDORSE, PRAISE.*

reckless
daredevil
foolhardy

precipitate
rash

These adjectives characterize persons and actions that show a heedless defiance of danger and a seeming lack of regard for consequences. **Reckless** and **rash** are applied to persons acting or actions undertaken without regard for the risks involved in terms of the end sought. *Reckless* implies wild, irresponsible action or emotion, indicating at worst a dangerous lack of self-discipline or self-control, and implying at the least a devil-may-care attitude or a frightening absence of forethought. *Reckless* may indicate extreme carelessness or unconcern in respect to oneself or to others. What distinguishes a *reckless* act from a brave one is not always the action itself but rather the attitude motivating it and the circumstances behind it. A police car or fire truck may, with siren sounding, drive at great speed through the streets and through red traffic lights without being *reckless*. A joy rider doing the same thing would be guilty of careless and *reckless* driving. *Rash* is not as extreme as *reckless*. *Rash* points to overhasty action taken in the heat or emotion of the moment, without due caution or regard for consequences. [Quitting his job in anger was a *rash* action that he soon regretted; Don't do anything *rash*.] A *rash* or *reckless* accusation is one that disregards the possible consequences to both the accused and the accuser, himself, who might be sued for libel. **Precipitate** suggests an action undertaken without sufficient forethought: a *precipitate* leap from the cliff.

Foolhardy implies boldness exercised without consideration or judgment, pointing to action that is daringly *reckless* or downright foolish. A *foolhardy* person rushes into peril from lack of good sense or forethought. Swimming out beyond one's depth when tired or immediately after eating is a *foolhardy* action. **Daredevil** differs from the other adjectives here in indicating the deliberate taking of chances, with an implication of calculated risk. It points to some sort of public exhibition, often describing a professional who performs sensational feats to entertain onlookers: a *daredevil* racing driver; a *daredevil* stunt pilot. *Daredevil* further suggests a certain amount of flair and debonair defiance: a death-defying aerialist performing *daredevil* feats. See BRAVE, DARING, HEEDLESS, IMPETUOUS.

Antonyms: *calculating,* CAREFUL, CAUTIOUS, *chary.*

recommend
advise
advocate

counsel
prescribe
suggest

These verbs refer to spoken or written assistance given to someone who is trying to decide upon a course of action. **Recommend** indicates a positive declaration in favor of a particular alternative or set of possibilities: *recommending* a change of occupations that would give her life new meaning; *recommending* ten books as essential to any understanding of the question she had raised. *Recommend* can apply equally well to situations in which help has or has not been solicited: enthusiastically *recommending* a walk before breakfast to everyone they met; asking her to *recommend* a good tailor. **Advocate** is the most like *recommend* of the rest of these verbs in emphasizing a positive declaration by the person giving assistance; drawn from legal terminology, it is even stronger than *recommend* in suggesting an ardent espousal of a given course of action: *advocating* complete abstinence as the best way to combat alcoholism. In this context, *advocate* can imply tenacity or an unwelcome intrusion: *advocating* his theories on social adjustment to people far less disturbed than he. **Prescribe** compares with *advocate* and *recommend* in the sense that a positive statement is made, but it is more specific in relating mainly to a doctor-patient relationship in which the doctor *prescribes* remedies for an ailment. The patient has sought the doctor's assistance and is usually not compelled to abide by what is *recommended.* This gives it a less ardent, more matter-of-fact tone than *advocate,* but a more authoritative cast than *recommend: prescribing* a good dinner and an exciting movie as the best way to cure the blues.

Advise and **suggest** are much milder than the foregoing verbs. They do not necessarily indicate that any one alternative is *recommended* as a solution to the problem in question. *Advise* implies an extensive and detailed examination of a person's situation, with several possibilities for action opened up simply by getting another insight into any difficulties: *advising* me on what to expect from the various careers I was considering. When used as an exact substitute for *recommend,* it adds an implication of politeness or of reluctance to seem overbearing. [May I *advise* you not to lend him large sums of money? Would you *advise* me where I should vacation this summer?] *Suggest* implies a single, tentative proposal that is not insisted upon: In *advising* me, he *suggested* several possibilities for revision. In some cases, the tentativeness implied by *suggest* may result from a fear of being rejected: *suggest-*

ing timidly that dining out together would be enjoyable.

Counsel has come to have a specific reference to psychologists or guidance personnel: *counseling* them on the dangers of experimenting with drugs. In other uses, it still implies some quasi-official situation, with a stress on seriousness and formality: contending factions that *counseled* the president in secret. In ordinary uses *counsel* is more formal than *advise,* sometimes excessively so: *counseling* her daughter on how to behave after the prom. See ADVICE, INDUCE.

recover
reclaim
recoup
regain
restore
retrieve

These verbs refer to getting back something that has been lost. **Recover** is the most general; it can refer to finding a lost item by chance or accident as easily as by intention and effort: *recovering* the missing boot while searching the attic one day for something else; only *recovering* her position of eminence among scientists in the last days of her life. **Retrieve**, most concretely, suggests something that has not so much been lost as slipped beyond reach and requires some effort to *recover: retrieving* the floating paddle by reaching out over the stern.

Recoup is drawn from legal terminology to mean, in ordinary use, a *recovering* of something similar to or equivalent to a disastrous or negligent loss: *recouping* his losses at Atlantic City by embezzling company funds. Like *recover,* **regain** stresses getting back the very thing lost, but in contrast it tends to be restricted to a deliberate and laborious search or effort: *regaining* the hill lost the night before to the enemy; *regaining* her eyesight after several operations; *regaining* the heavyweight championship in last week's fight.

Reclaim and **restore** both suggest bringing something back to its original condition; *reclaim* is used largely of land or large areas, *restore* of buildings or art objects: *reclaiming* good farmland from the polluted swamps; *restoring* the house to the way it looked in 1820. *Reclaim* may also suggest an interval in which the right to a position or to a property has been transferred or disputed: *reclaiming* rights to the inheritance after a protracted legal battle. See CONSERVE, REPAIR, SAVE.

Antonyms: *MISLAY.*

reduce

abate
curtail
diminish
lower

These verbs mean make or become smaller or less, but they are not in all cases interchangeable. **Reduce** has the widest range of connotations and is also the most general. It means make less in size, amount, number, extent, or intensity: to *reduce* household expenses; to *reduce* a labor force during a slack season; to *reduce* speed on a highway undergoing repairs; to *reduce* the acreage of a farm by selling off a field. *Reduce* further means bring to an inferior rank, position, or financial condition: a couple *reduced* to renting out rooms to make ends meet; a sergeant *reduced* to private after a summary court-martial; an executive *reduced* to doing her own keyboarding because of the cutback. When applied to losing weight, especially when deliberate, *reduce* is popularly used intransitively: My mother and father are always trying fad diets in order to *reduce*.

Abate means *reduce*, as in strength or degree, usually from an excessive intensity or amount. In this sense, it is most frequently an intransitive verb. [The screams began to *abate* once the police arrived; After taking aspirin, she found her pain *abating*.] In a legal sense, *abate* is used transitively and means do away with completely or make null and void: to *abate* a nuisance; to *abate* a writ.

Curtail means *reduce* abruptly and radically, as by cutting off or cutting shorter than was originally intended. *Curtail* is used chiefly of nonmaterial things and conveys the idea of the unexpected: a vacation *curtailed* by a hurricane that damaged their cottage; to *curtail* a pointless argument by turning on one's heel and leaving the room; to *curtail* useless government spending.

Diminish is a more accurate term than *reduce* when one wishes to stress the idea of removing part of something so that there is a manifest and sometimes progressive lessening, but not to the point of total disappearance. *Diminish* may suggest either the loss of something valuable or a lessening of that which is undesirable. [As people approach old age, their energy may *diminish;* As her confidence increased, her anxieties about the new job *diminished*.]

Lower means make less, especially in value, degree, or level. It is not as emphatic or precise a verb as *reduce* in this sense, although fairly close in meaning: to *lower* prices on shopworn goods; to *reduce* payments on a mortgage. In extended senses, *lower* points to a lessening by undermining or weakening. [He could not bear to *lower* himself by asking relatives for help; Frequent colds *lower* resistance to more serious infections.] See DECREASE, LESSEN, WANE, WEAKEN.
Antonyms: *enhance,* ENLARGE, ESCALATE, EXTEND, *raise.*

---

refer. Do not confuse the verb *refer* (direct attention to by mentioning) with the verb *allude* (direct attention to without mentioning). The distinction between these two verbs carries over into the nouns *reference* and *allusion*.

---

reject

decline
refuse
repudiate
spurn

These verbs mean be unwilling to accept, receive, or take into account a person or thing. **Reject** means fail to accept or grant and carries overtones of casting aside as useless, valueless, or unsuitable. [The judge *rejected* my appeal for a new trial; The notion that the earth is flat was *rejected* centuries ago.]

Refuse and **decline** mean fail to comply with or to do something. *Refuse* is the stronger of the two and often stresses firmness, at times even rudeness: to *refuse* to obey an order. It also suggests the idea of withholding: to *refuse* money to a beggar; to *refuse* an offer of marriage. *Decline,* on the other hand, means *refuse* politely and is applicable to invitations to social events or to a courteous offer of help: to *decline* an invitation to a dinner party; a blind person who *declined* help when crossing a street. *Decline* may be used in place of *refuse* when an atmosphere of formality prevails: The witness *declined* to answer certain questions.

Repudiate and **spurn** emphasize more pointedly than the foregoing verbs a refusal to recognize or have anything to do with a person or thing. *Repudiate* (which once meant cast off a wife) points to a disowning or rejection of something once held more or less dear: to *repudiate* one's religious beliefs; an author who *repudiates* the revolutionary ideas expressed in her earlier work; to *repudiate* one's relatives because of their critical attitude. *Spurn,* derived from an Old English word meaning kick out, emphasizes even more strongly the idea of driving or pushing away roughly and contemptuously: *spurning* the attentions of a man she despised; *spurning* the suggestion that he get his hair cut and put on a clean shirt. See DISCARD, REMOVE.

Antonyms: *accept,* ACKNOWLEDGE, DEMAND.

religion
belief
creed
faith

These nouns refer to a more or less codified set of ideas concerning the cause, nature, and purpose of the universe. **Religion** is the most specific of these, suggesting an organized body of traditional doctrines that are reflected in a more or less complex set of institutions for fostering these doctrines: the Christian *religion;* the Buddhist *religion;* the Hindu *religion.* Within one of these large groupings, *religion* is sometimes used to refer to its denominations or sects, but this use is mostly eschewed in formal speech or writing: the Catholic *religion;* the Lutheran *religion.* **Faith** is often substituted for *religion* to put less emphasis on institutionalized tradition and more on devoted adherence: the Jewish *faith;* the Christian *faith.* Because of these implications, *faith* is more often used of a subdivision in one of the larger categories: the Catholic *faith;* the Eastern Orthodox *faith.*

Creed stresses an exactly delineated outline of dogma and doctrine and thus may refer to small or large divisions, even within a sect, where doctrinal differences are at issue: the several extant Mormon *creeds;* the Moravian *creed. Creed* may also be used for any codified statement of principles: a sportsman's *creed.* **Belief** is the vaguest of these nouns; it may refer to groupings large or small: a *belief* in the tenets of Islam; the *beliefs* of Taoism; the Quaker *belief.* Its stress is on wholehearted assent to details of doctrine. *Belief* is also commonly used to indicate assent to each item of doctrine: a *belief* in life after death; the Buddhist rejection of *belief* in a supreme being. It may also point away from any organized *religion* whatsoever to a purely personal conviction about final causes: her own highly idiosyncratic *belief* in an all-powerful but not always beneficent God; a *belief* in atheism. See CREED, DENOMINATION, SKEPTIC.

Antonyms: *atheism,* DESECRATION, *impiety, irreligion, unbelief.*

religious
devout
pious
reverent
sanctimonious

These adjectives are comparable in that they all are used to characterize the thoughts, feelings, and actions of people, insofar as they pertain to religion. **Religious** embraces all the other terms in the group. It can mean simply of or having to do with religion: *religious* literature; the *religious* life. It can describe anyone, from a person who observes nothing more than the minimum obligations of a faith to a person genuinely devoted to a way of life that reflects a deep love of God as well as adherence to the tenets of one of the systems set up to worship God: an opportunist who found it profitable to be *religious* on Sundays; a truly *religious* woman who has been able to make the Christian ideal viable in every aspect of her life.

Devout and **pious** are alike in suggesting a dedication to religion that is evidenced by the observance of established ceremonies and ritual. They differ, however, in that *devout* always implies that earnest *religious* feelings motivate the performance of *religious* obligations, whereas *pious* may indicate the hypocrisy of one whose *religious* behavior is merely outward show: a *devout* belief in the tenets of Orthodox Judaism; a *pious* fraud whose mind is more devoted to gossip than to gospel. **Sanctimonious**, which is never used now in its original meaning of holy or saintly, is stronger than *pious* in its reference to spurious sanctity: a *sanctimonious* old man whose condemnation of other people's actions was a mask for his own immorality.

Reverent, which means feeling or showing reverence or respect, is applied to the character or actions of persons who evince great sincerity of *religious* belief and observance, and is closer in meaning to *devout* than to *pious.* See REVERE, SACRED.

Antonyms: *atheistic, impious, irreligious, irreverent.*

relinquish
abdicate
cede
renounce
resign
surrender
yield

These verbs mean let go or give up. **Relinquish** is the most general and neutral term in the group. It can indicate no more than the release of one's grasp: She *relinquished* the oars. It can denote the letting go from one's direction or possession, usually voluntarily but sometimes reluctantly. [A good parent *relinquishes* control over grown children; A creditor may *relinquish* a claim in consideration of a concession.] **Surrender** means give up under compulsion to any person, passion, influence, or power: He *surrendered* his savings to his creditors. **Yield** is close to *surrender,* but implies milder compulsion and therefore some softness, concession, respect, or even affection on the part of the person who *yields:* She *yielded* the floor to her opponent. **Cede** means give up, usually by legal transfer or as the result of a treaty; it is most often used in reference to the concession of territory: France *ceded* Alsace-Lorraine to Germany in 1871.

Abdicate and **resign** refer to the formal giving up of some office or position along with its attendant rights, power, etc. *Abdicate* applies specifically to a monarch's relinquishment of a throne; *resign* is used to designate the action of a president or other elected or appointed official, or a person working in business: George III threatened to *abdicate* his throne; forced by ill health to *resign* her position as chief executive officer. **Renounce** means declare against or give up formally and definitively: to *renounce* the pomps and vanities of the world; to *renounce* one's citizenship. When used in place of *abdicate, renounce* suggests that the giving up is done for something considered to be more important: Edward VIII *renounced* his throne for the love of a woman. See ABSTAIN, FORGO, FORSWEAR.

Antonyms: *cherish, claim, maintain,* POSSESS.

remain

abide
linger
stay
tarry

These verbs all mean continue in one place. **Remain** and **stay** are often used interchangeably. *Remain*, in its narrower application, means continue in one place after the removal, departure, or destruction of other persons or things, whereas *stay* implies the temporary continuance in one place of a guest, resident, or the like. [Little more than the shell of the building *remained* after the explosion; We were invited to *stay* for supper.] If the fact that others have left is made explicit, either verb may be used: He *remained* (or *stayed*) in his seat after all the other students had gone home. But if the writer's intention is to contrast *staying* with leaving, *remain* has more impact. [All of them had left their seats and gone home hours ago; she *remained*.]

Abide, as here considered, means *stay* somewhere

a long time and often connotes residing. *Abide*, a formal verb, is often used in legal or other contexts requiring a term neutral in emotional connotation and precise in meaning: The child *abode* (or *abided*) with grandparents for three years before returning to his parents.

Linger implies reluctance to leave, usually because what one is doing is pleasant; to **tarry** is to stay beyond the proper time for leaving, and more strongly than *linger* implies excessive delay. *Tarry* is not commonly used today apart from consciously stylized, rhetorical, or old-fashioned contexts; it has a romantic ring that makes it inappropriate in prosaic contexts. [The candidate *lingered* behind her entourage to shake the hands of supporters; *Tarry* not with your loved ones, but join us in righteous battle.] See DELAY, RESIDE.

Antonyms: GO, LEAVE *(depart).*

remember

memorize
recall
recollect
remind
reminisce
retain
review

These verbs refer to the act of summoning up the past, to its spontaneous cropping up in the mind, or to the fixing of information in the memory for future reference. **Remember** can refer generally to any mental glance at the past, voluntary or involuntary: He caught himself *remembering* how his first wife would have cooked the same meal; struggling to *remember* where she had been at the time the murder took place. But *remember* often specifically suggests the staying power of a vivid past event or circumstance: I can still *remember* every detail of my college dormitory room. **Recall** is more formal than *remember* and more often indicates a voluntary summoning up of the past, whether silently for oneself or aloud for others. [He *recalled* his last evening with his fiancée whenever he felt depressed; In the closing speech to the jury, the prosecutor *recalled* the mass of incriminating evidence he had developed during the trial.] Unlike *remember,* however, *recall* can refer to something in the present that resembles and therefore calls up something in the past: a view that *recalled* to him the village he had stayed in before the war. **Remind** concentrates more exclusively on this last possibility for *recall:* a boy who *reminded* me of my brother. But *remind* can also suggest a conscious effort to insure that something will be *remembered* in the future: a note on her calendar to *remind* herself of their luncheon date; a monument to *remind* future generations of sacrifices made in their behalf.

When used interchangeably with *recall*, **recollect** can have a regional flavor: I don't rightly *recollect* when I saw him last. But *recollect* can apply without this flavor to the act of casting one's mind back over past events in a leisurely and ruminative manner, whether silently or aloud. *Recollect* can suggest the active process of piecing together dimly *remembered* details: He settled back with great relish and began to *recollect* battles in the war he had witnessed firsthand. **Reminisce** is restricted to this last use of *recollect*, adding a positive note of pleasant nostalgia; *reminisce* may also suggest a tendency to dwell on or brood over the past: daydreams during which she *reminisced* about the life she had before marriage; cronies who sit around *reminiscing* about the good old days.

Retain can point to the staying power of a memory that often comes to mind involuntarily or without effort: He *retained* an image of his father going off to hunt. In more neutral uses, *retain* can involve holding on to facts or details one is trying to learn: a test to measure how much of the argument they *retained* an hour after reading. **Memorize** is more specifically directed to this situation, indicating a conscious and laborious effort to commit something to memory in exact detail: actors who quickly *memorize* their lines; trying to *memorize* every line and angle of his face.

Review suggests an orderly summoning up of the past in summary form, applying particularly to past lessons or to facts one is trying to *memorize:* a final week to *review* the material before the exam; *reviewing* the schedule item by item before setting out. See HISTORY.

Antonyms: *FORGET, ignore, repress, suppress.*

remove

dismiss
eject
eliminate
evict
expel
oust

These verbs refer to getting rid of something or moving it to a new position. **Remove** is the most general of these and the most colorless. It ranges in tone from neutral or factual description to suggestions of

rejection, disapproval, or the use of force: *removing* the compact disc from its box; *removing* the sheets from the bed; *removing* a corrupt administrator from office; ordering the sergeant-at-arms to *remove* the angry man from the chamber.

Dismiss is less likely to suggest the use of force, but otherwise is richer in connotations than *remove.* It can suggest the routine release or sending away of a subordinate: *dismissing* the servant as soon as the guests arrived; *dismissing* the class promptly at three o'clock. It can suggest the routine or disapproving termination of employment: *dismissing* the consultant with thanks once the project is complete; *dismissing* her assistant for persistent lateness. More pertinently here, *dismiss* can suggest a swift, abrupt, or final rejection. [She *dismissed* him with a wave of her hand; We *dismissed* the idea of bicycling through the mountains.]

Eliminate at its mildest pertains to the routine or methodical disposal of something: organs that *eliminate* bodily wastes; *eliminating* from the list five books she had already read. *Eliminate* can also suggest determination, if not force: *eliminating* from the list of candidates members whose dues were in arrears. At its most extreme, *eliminate* can suggest ruthless or systematic destruction: a wave of killings as one gang set about *eliminating* the other; measures adopted to *eliminate* other ethnic groups.

The remaining verbs are all more specific in pointing to the use of considerable force to *remove* something, although none suggest destruction. **Oust** and **evict** emphasize the resistance given by the thing being *removed* from its previous position. *Oust* is restricted to those implications of the previous verbs pertaining to termination of employment or discharge from office: *ousted* from party leadership by unanimous vote; a revolution fomented to *oust* the dictator. *Evict* is even more specific in applying exclusively to *removing* tenants from occupancy; most often, it suggests the gaining of legal approval to carry out this act: The officers who *evicted* the family carried its belongings out to the curb.

Expel and **eject**, like *oust* and *evict*, may both suggest a forcible *removing* from office or occupancy, but they are more general than any of these verbs except *remove. Expel*, however, has its own area of special relevance in applying to the punitive *dismissing* of a student from school for objectionable behavior: students *expelled* for cheating. *Eject* is the most emphatic of this group in stressing the use of force; it pertains most appropriately to a physical or bodily removal: the spent cartridge *ejected* by the rifle; calling the police to *eject* demonstrators from the clinic. See DESTROY, EXILE, MOVE.

Antonyms: *POSSESS, retain.*

renewal

rebirth
recrudescence
rejuvenation
rejuvenescence
renaissance
renascence

Central to these nouns is the idea or fact of a return to some previous condition, usually but not always thought of as desirable. **Renewal** can apply to anything good, bad, or indifferent that returns, repeats, or begins again: a *renewal* of the argument or discussion; the *renewal* of a lease or mortgage; an unexpected *renewal* of health and spirits.

Rebirth, in the sense of being born again, has only a figurative use. Though one can speak of a *rebirth* as well as a *renewal* of confidence, a contractual relationship of limited duration, such as a contract, treaty, copyright, or patent, is subject only to *renewal*. The distinction brings out the idea of an innate, self-sustaining vitality in something that had been or long seemed to be dead: a *rebirth* of hope.

Rejuvenation and **rejuvenescence** mean a *renewal* of youth, with emphasis on recovery of lost or fading strength, vigor, alertness, or resilience of body and mind. [They looked back upon the trip abroad as having provided a veritable *rejuvenation;* Disappointment followed his hopes of *rejuvenescence* after the costly operation.]

Recrudescence, derived from a Latin word meaning become raw or bleed again, finds its primary use among physicians to describe a breaking out afresh, as of a disease, sore, or wound that had appeared to be healing. In this unfavorable sense of a relapse, it may properly be applied to the recurrence of anything considered evil or objectionable: the *recrudescence* of bigotry; a *recrudescence* of Nazism.

Renaissance and **renascence** are formal words for *rebirth* and are given special rank as descriptive terms in the history of human culture. *Renaissance,* the more common spelling, is a French form, while *renascence* comes from Latin roots meaning be born again. Either can be used for a widespread awakening of interest in some rediscovered aspect of life or learning, and both imply a sense of discovery and an attendant burst of accomplishment: a *renaissance* in Far Eastern studies; a literary *renascence*. The *Renaissance*

refers to the period of vigorous intellectual and artistic awakening in Western Europe extending from about the 14th century to the 16th. This period gave its name to *Renaissance* man, now also *Renaissance* woman, denoting a person of fresh life, vigor, and creativity, whose interests are universal and whose accomplishments go beyond a single field.

Antonyms: *aging, loss, subsiding, termination.*

repair

correct
fix
mend
rectify
remedy
renovate

These verbs refer to the changes made in something to restore it or to set it right. **Repair** emphasizes work done on an object that is broken, damaged, or not in proper working order: to *repair* a TV set; to *repair* shoes; the cost of having an old car *repaired*. By extension, it can refer to any effective restorative action: diplomats who work to *repair* a disruption in trade relations. **Fix** is an informal word for the same set of meanings as *repair:* the time it takes to *fix* a flat tire. But while *repair* usually suggests a broken object to begin with, *fix* can apply to anything that needs attention or has gone awry: *fixing* curtains for the bare windows; a friend who could *fix* things between the child and her angry parents. **Mend** suggests the *repairing* of something broken, torn, or worn threadbare: a torn page *mended* with tape; to *mend* old clothes. But it can go beyond this to suggest a knitting and healing of injured parts in living things: tying the bent branch in place until it could *mend;* splinting the leg until the broken bone began to *mend*. Thus, it may suggest a return to health and peace in wider contexts: eager to *mend* the rift between the two factions.

The remaining verbs apply less often to the concrete context of a broken object and are both more general and more vague in referring to steps taken to improve something imperfect or to improve a bad situation. **Correct** suggests the supplying of correct answers or the pointing out of errors: needing a special teacher to *correct* his halting mispronunciations; parents unwilling to *correct* and discipline their own children. A pedagogical atmosphere, in fact, is often suggested by *correct*. **Remedy** more obviously suggests a medical situation, but it appears in a wide range of contexts, implying an effort to find solutions to bothersome problems: steps to *remedy* poor living conditions so that children can grow up normally. *Remedy* may suggest alterations in a system rather than a complete reorganization: They hoped to *remedy* the company's lackluster performance by making a few personnel changes. *Remedy* often suggests a search for one of many possible solutions, unlike *correct,* which gives the impression that a simple, right-and-wrong dichotomy exists.

Rectify, by contrast, stresses a more thoroughgoing change in something; one *rectifies* something wrong by setting it right, insofar as amendment is possible: to *rectify* a factual error; finally *rectifying* a miscarriage of justice. It is the most formal of the verbs here and, in the sense discussed, the most abstract. **Renovate** applies strictly to the *repairing* and updating of an old or run-down building: a program to *renovate* slum housing. Sometimes, *renovate* can apply to the less desirable modernizing of a venerable or distinctive building merely because it is old or thought to need modernization: a committee set up to protest the proposal to *renovate* a row of 19th-century houses. See CONSERVE, RECOVER, REVISE, SAVE.

Antonyms: *BREAK, DESTROY, REPLACE, TEAR.*

replace
>   displace
>   supersede
>   supplant

These verbs refer to a situation in which the place of one thing is taken by another. **Replace**, the most informal and most neutral of these verbs, refers to any substitution for whatever reason: She *replaced* the amber beads with a string of pearls to see which she liked better. *Replace,* however, is especially used to indicate the substitution of something new or functioning for something old, worn-out, or lost: an offer to *replace* the missing volume of the encyclopedia; *replacing* the burned-out light bulb; He *replaced* the battered pillows with new ones.

Displace, by contrast, indicates the dislodging or forcible removal of one thing by another, without necessarily suggesting that the first had become unusable or ineffective: republics in which new regimes *displace* old ones with wearying predictability; the growing number of employees being *displaced* by computers. **Supplant** is even more restricted than *displace,* usually suggesting that the old thing is deliberately uprooted, rendered ineffective, or wiped out so that the new thing can take over; the process, furthermore, may be immediate or gradual: European settlers who *supplanted* the indigenous populations they encoun-

tered; new models and fashions that vie to *supplant* each other.

Supersede is the most formal of these verbs and indicates that a substitution occurs because the new thing is better, more modern, or more effective than the old: consumers who have been taught to believe that this year's models actually *supersede* those of the year before; informed economic planning intended to *supersede* random approaches. *Supersede* may sometimes suggest mere substitution because of greater authority: cease-fire orders that immediately *superseded* all previous orders to attack. See CHANGE, DESTROY.

Antonyms: *CONSERVE, keep, REPAIR, SAVE.*

reprehensible
>   blameworthy
>   culpable
>   deplorable
>   opprobrious
>   regrettable

These adjectives describe undesirable acts or circumstances that are worthy of criticism, sorrow, or pity. **Reprehensible** exclusively stresses disapproving criticism for egregiously bad behavior or character: the *reprehensible* diffidence of public officials in taking firm stands on the city's problems; a *reprehensible* criminal who robbed many people without the slightest twinge of guilt. **Opprobrious** is the strongest adjective in this group. It characterizes something that not only merits criticism but also deserves disdain or scorn. There is often an implication of general rather than merely personal censure involved in anything *opprobrious:* the *opprobrious* commercialization of Christmas.

While **culpable** refers to something deserving of censure, its main stress may be on an attempt to assign guilt or blame for an accident, misdeed, or failure: *culpable* negligence; He displayed *culpable* ignorance in handling what started out as a routine personnel problem. *Culpable* is milder than the foregoing adjectives in that it would not be used for outrageous or egregious violations of a legal or moral code. **Blameworthy**, like *culpable,* is concerned with assigning guilt for failure or misbehavior; its tone may be factual and neutral: an investigation to determine which of the officials involved in the scandal were the most *blameworthy.* More generally, however, *blameworthy* can express censure, although it seldom suggests the moral outrage of *opprobrious:* a *blameworthy* lack of concern for the impoverished.

Regrettable is the mildest adjective in this group.

It need not denote a critical attitude of censure at all, but rather a sympathetic understanding of someone's failings: a *regrettable* lack of decisiveness that marred the effectiveness of an otherwise brilliant person. It contrasts with the previous adjectives even more dramatically when it expresses pity for circumstances beyond human control: It is *regrettable* that such a talent died. Sometimes, *regrettable* is used in a polite or genteel way to express disapproval in terms of sympathetic disappointment: your *regrettable* absence from my dinner party. *Regrettable* can even be used more forcefully as an ironic understatement for a severely critical reaction: I find it *regrettable* that Smith chose to display her inadequacies to us so conclusively by taking on a demanding role.

In many ways, **deplorable** is an intensification of *regrettable.* On one hand, it can express consternation and distress over what may not be anyone's fault: the *deplorable* accident that crippled her for life. But when used critically, *deplorable* is harsher than *regrettable* and does not mask its criticism in irony or understatement: *deplorable* living conditions; a *deplorable* lack of compassion. Like *regrettable,* however, *deplorable* would not be used for outrageously hardened, cruel, or brutal behavior. See CONTEMPTIBLE, DISAPPROVAL, REPULSIVE.

Antonyms: *admirable, EXCELLENT, INNOCENT, praise-worthy.*

representative
  agent
  delegate
  deputy
  proxy
  substitute

These nouns are alike in denoting a person empowered to take the place or position of another. **Representative** in its wider application means a person or thing that stands for, acts for, or takes the place of another. In its narrower application *representative* means a person who acts for another or others in a special capacity. [*Representatives* in Congress act for their constituents in legislative matters; American ambassadors are *representatives* of the President of the United States.]

A **substitute** is a person or thing that can be used instead of another person or thing. [Honey can be used as a *substitute* for sugar in many recipes; Men drafted during the Civil War were allowed to hire *substitutes* to serve in their place.]

In general, **agent** means a person authorized to act

on behalf of another or on behalf of a corporate entity. [The business *agent* of a union acts on behalf of the union in financial matters; In a dictatorship, all government officials are personal *agents* of the dictator rather than *representatives* of the people.] In its more restricted sense, *agent* means one who acts on behalf of one of two parties. [A real estate *agent* acts on behalf of the landlord in transactions between landlord and tenant; A theatrical *agent* acts on behalf of the client.]

A **proxy** is one who acts as an *agent* for another at a ceremony or in an election. [Marriages by *proxy* were common during World War II: if the groom was overseas, another person would act as his *proxy* at the ceremony; Most stockholders vote for directors by *proxy;* that is, they authorize an *agent* to vote on their behalf.]

Delegate and **deputy** usually refer to *representatives* who are closely bound by instructions; the use of the title *representative* rather than *delegate* or *deputy* often implies a lack of such instructions, or less binding ones. Thus, Congressional *representatives,* once elected, are free to vote for or against legislation as they see fit, but *delegates* to a presidential convention may be required to vote for the winners in the primary elections. A *deputy* is usually a person who acts under powers granted by a superior. A sheriff's *deputy* may have the power to arrest only if empowered to do so by the sheriff. See ASSOCIATE.

repulsive
  abhorrent
  abominable
  disgusting
  loathsome
  repellent
  repugnant
  revolting

These adjectives all characterize what is extremely ugly, deformed, or shocking, or anything that deserves to be hated or causes aversion or nausea. **Repulsive** can refer to visual appearances that are hideous, or to behavior worthy of condemnation because of its crudity or immorality: a *repulsive* painting; such *repulsive* habits as belching and picking his nose. **Repellent** can refer literally to the warding off of something: an insect-*repellent* spray. Otherwise, it is an intensification of the possibilities for *repulsive:* the *repellent* cruelty with which he treated dogs. Both adjectives strongly imply a shocked or outraged reaction to the thing described, even suggesting a physical drawing away from the object or a desire to drive it away: No matter how she tried to conquer her distaste, she found the wounded soldier too *repulsive* to touch; using a cane to smash the *repellent* art object.

Abhorrent derives ultimately from a Latin expression that refers to a horrified bristling, shuddering, or shivering action. A comparable distaste, almost physical in its intensity, may well be indicated by *repellent,* although now it applies less to appearance than to something that affronts sensibilities or moral sense: the *abhorrent* policy of terrorism. In the context of moral indignation, *abhorrent* is the most forceful adjective here. **Loathsome** is closely related to such a use of *abhorrent,* but where *abhorrent* might apply best as a sweeping condemnation of group action or behavior, *loathsome* applies equally well to single acts or individuals: his *loathsome* mistreatment of his wife. In reference to group action, *loathsome* is less emphatic because it may more clearly imply an aversion or disapproval not necessarily shared by others: *loathsome* customs the newcomer found impossible to accept.

Disgusting and **revolting** are more like the first pair in suggesting a shocked or outraged reaction that can sometimes find physical expression. *Disgusting* can suggest an actual queasiness stimulated by something objectionable, whereas *revolting* can imply physical nausea or a psyche that reacts in rebellious upheaval to such a phenomenon: She found his cooking methods unsanitary and *disgusting;* impossible to be polite when confronted with his *revolting* impertinence. Both adjectives lose any suggestion of such intense reactions when applied more generally, especially when used as loose hyperboles for irritation or annoyance: *disgusting* incompetence; a *revolting* development.

Repugnant also emphasizes a reaction of distaste or aversion, but is more formal than the previous pair. Also, because *repugnant* is less often used in loose exaggeration, it is considerably more forceful in effect: *repugnant* conditions in uninspected food-processing plants; a *repugnant* indifference to human suffering. It is, however, less forceful than *abhorrent;* it would show a want of feeling to speak of *repugnant,* rather than *abhorrent,* crimes against humanity, since the latter not only expresses distaste but moral outrage as well.

Abominable is closer in tone to *abhorrent* and *loathsome* in stressing that something merits severe condemnation and hatred: *abominable* working conditions. *Abominable* has suffered from overuse and exaggeration to a greater degree than the other adjectives through its application to things that are only relatively

unpleasant: an *abominable* weekend of rain. Also, *abominable* has been popularized as part of the phrase *abominable snowman,* referring to a legendary or imaginary man-beast reputed to exist in the mountains of Tibet; widespread humorous references to and extensions of this phrase have nearly incapacitated *abominable* for any serious use. See CONTEMPTIBLE, DEPRAVED, OBNOXIOUS, REPREHENSIBLE.

Antonyms: *admirable, alluring, amiable,* CHARMING, *commendable,* EXCELLENT, PLEASING, *splendid.*

request
appeal
application
invitation
petition
requisition

These nouns refer to oral or written statements asking someone to grant a wish or satisfy a need. **Request** is the most general and informal. Unless contravened by context, it suggests courtesy and genuine desire, but no necessary certainty that what is asked will be granted: a *request* that he be released in time for Christmas; able to supply on *request* any book in print; a pianist who closed his programs by playing *requests;* a written *request* that she recommend him for the fellowship. An **appeal** would suggest an urgent *request* for aid: *appeals* for donations to help victims of the earthquake. It may also imply the dissatisfied seeking out of another opinion: an *appeal* to the rest of the group to settle their disagreement. In reference to written *requests, appeal* stresses a formal or urgent turning to a higher authority: an *appeal* to the Supreme Court for a reversal of the decision. *Appeal* may also be used to indicate the arousing of special motives in the person addressed, not necessarily by verbal means: an *appeal* to his sense of fair play; an *appeal* to readers' prurient interests.

Invitation cannot suggest a *request* for aid and is completely lacking in any sense of urgency. It suggests, rather, the making of a courteous offer to someone either of hospitality or some other kindness or benefit: an *invitation* to join her for coffee after the meeting; an *invitation* to attend their wedding; an *invitation* to deliver the principal address. *Invitation* has a less concrete use for an *appeal* to specific motives in the person or group singled out for attention: a look that was really an *invitation;* an unenforceable regulation that was an *invitation* to lawbreaking.

The remaining nouns are mostly restricted in meaning to written *requests*. **Requisition** is the most formal of these, indicating a detailed statement of the need for food, supplies, or shelter: putting in a *requisition* for a new personal computer. **Petition** is close to *appeal* in suggesting submittal of an urgent *request* to a higher authority. In a legal context, however, *petition* may imply the throwing of oneself on the mercy of the authority: a last *petition* to the governor for clemency. Outside the legal context, it suggests the gathering of many names in support of a candidate or in support of a policy: the deadline for filing nominating *petitions*; a drive to collect signatures on a *petition* to be sent to the president. In its older sense of *request, petition* is now seldom used and would tend to sound stuffy. **Application** suggests most strongly a routine written *request* for consideration: a three-page job *application;* turning in her *application* for a fellowship; making *application* to join the fraternity; an *application* to enter the contest. See DEMAND, SEEK.

request
apply
ask
invite
seek
solicit

These verbs concern the situation in which one person proposes a solution for a need or desire, leaving the person addressed free to decline or accept the proposal. **Request** implies the use of a courteous manner in expressing a need: *requesting* directions from a police officer; He *requested* help from the librarian in locating a book he wanted. *Request* is sometimes used as a euphemism: *requesting* his immediate resignation. **Ask** is more informal and more general than *request* and does not necessarily imply courtesy: curtly *asking* the surly waiter for another glass of water. Whereas both *request* and *ask* in themselves suggest some unfulfilled need or desire on the part of the speaker, **invite** often suggests that someone else is given permission to fulfill such a desire: a sign *inviting* passersby to enter and browse about the shop; *requesting* that she be permitted to attend the party, even though she had not been *invited*.

Seek contrasts with the foregoing verbs in suggesting any kind of action taken in gaining help or fulfilling a desire, without being restricted in possible meanings to the *requesting* of help in speech or writing: *seeking* approval in the faces of the audience as he spoke. Furthermore, while *request* often suggests a one-to-one relationship of an appealer and one appealed to, *seek* points to an effort to get an answer from a num-

ber of sources: *seeking* directions from everyone along the way who seemed the least bit friendly. *Seek* may also imply an insistent manner: *seeking* the necessary document through a bureaucratic maze.

Apply, as now used, mostly suggests a written statement addressed to an institution expressing a desire to be considered for a position: *applying* for a job, a scholarship, a sabbatical, a credit card. **Solicit** suggests a canvass of likely prospects in the attempt to gain some consideration, often of a business nature: carnival hawkers *soliciting* onlookers to buy tickets to the sideshow; prostitutes *soliciting* any man who came along. In more general uses, comparable to those of *request, solicit* now seems archaic, if not clouded over by unpleasant connotations from its more common use: a teacher *soliciting* the earnest attention of his students. See PLEAD.

resentment
huff
offense
pique
umbrage

These nouns are comparable in denoting a feeling of displeasure directed at the cause of some real or imagined wrong or injury. **Resentment** and **offense** refer to the strongest emotions characterized by this group. *Resentment* describes a sense of grievance that is internal and suggests a persistent or recurrent brooding rather than a sudden outburst of passionate anger. *Offense* designates a state of hurt feelings less extreme than *resentment* and lacking the strong sense of grievance implicit in that noun. There is also in *offense* no suggestion of an abiding emotion but rather one that is transitory because less serious. [She cherished a deep *resentment* toward her employer for having denied her a promotion; Reporters and photographers alike took *offense* at the way the star behaved during the interview.]

Pique, which comes from a French word meaning to prick or sting, denotes a sudden feeling of mingled pain and anger that is usually slight and transient. *Pique* often arises from wounded vanity or sensitiveness: leaving the party in a *pique* because of an imagined slight on the part of the hostess. **Umbrage** is a deeper and more persistent displeasure at being ignored or overshadowed or being subjected to any treatment one deems discourteous or disrespectful: to take *umbrage* at the criticism because he thought it unfair and belittling. **Huff** is much like *pique* in suggesting a petty, usually passing, sense of injury because of a blow to one's pride: in a *huff* because his boss had chewed him out in front of his secretary. See ANGER, BOTHER, ENRAGE, UNSETTLE.

Antonyms: *PATIENCE, PLEASURE.*

reside
dwell
inhabit
live
occupy
settle

These verbs all mean make one's home more or less permanently in one place. **Reside**, the most formal term in the group, is preferred to any of the others when a legal and permanent abode is being emphasized. [When the trooper stopped me for speeding, he asked me where I *resided;* A U.S. senator is expected to *reside* in the state he or she represents.] *Reside* may also suggest tenancy of an elegant or imposing home: The wealthy banker *resides* in a town house off Park Avenue. **Live**, though close in meaning to *reside,* is more general when applied to having any established or permanent home, whether one is referring to the actual abode or a city, country, etc., in which it is located: to *live* in New York City; to *live* in the big house on the corner; to *live* in Europe. *Live* may also mean maintain a domicile in a specific place, either temporarily or indefinitely: President Roosevelt *resided* in Hyde Park, but during his presidency he *lived* either in Washington or in Warm Springs, Georgia.

Dwell, in the sense of *reside* or *live,* is normally limited to poetical or literary usage, especially of the past: to *dwell* in marble halls. In an extended sense, however, it is commonly used of states of mind or of surroundings of a particularly limited nature. [Schizophrenics *dwell* in a web of fantasy and hallucination; The philosopher *dwells* in the realm of ideas; A physician *dwells* in the world of the sick.]

Inhabit carries less of the implication of having a fixed abode than do *reside* and *live.* When used in this sense, it tends to sound high-flown or archaic. Rather, it points to people or animals *living* in large areas or adapted to specific physical environments. [Before the arrival of the Europeans, Africa was *inhabited* by many tribal peoples; Fishes and certain mammals *inhabit* the ocean.] *Inhabit* may also lay stress on the using of a place as a home or shelter: an old tenement *inhabited* by families on welfare; burrows *inhabited* by wild rabbits.

Occupy is applicable both to places where people *live* and to premises given over to business enterprises,

and it carries the implication of taking over and holding possession. [The Lewis family *occupies* the house next door; The insurance company *occupies* a large building downtown.]

Settle differs from the foregoing verbs in that it refers to a town, country, region, etc., in which one has established a permanent home, not to the home itself. [They *settled* in San Francisco last year and like *living* there; The Amish *settled* parts of rural Pennsylvania and usually *live* on farms.]

resolution
decision
determination
resolve

All these nouns can refer to the taking of a stand or to the acting out of a purpose with unflagging fixity. In the first situation, **resolution** suggests the conscious or formal spelling out of a position: a New Year's *resolution;* a *resolution* adopted unanimously. When *resolution* refers to behavior, it still suggests a conscious choosing of goal and methods that infuse the action with vigor and, often, with ethical purpose: She administered the spanking with *resolution;* behaving with steadfast *resolution.* **Determination**, in reference to action, contrasts with *resolution* by suggesting an almost stubborn willpower more than a conscious spelling out of goals or principles: He drove in each nail with *determination. Determination,* furthermore, may suggest an undivided emotional and mental assent to the action one is performing, whereas *resolution* could suggest an intellectual choice that has actually overcome an emotional reluctance: attacking the tempting meal with lusty *determination;* They flinched at the icy water but strode into it with *resolution. Determination,* in the sense of taking a stand, suggests studious investigation: arbitrators who will hear both sides before making their *determination.*

Resolve, of course, is closely related to *resolution.* In the sense of choosing, however, it does not suggest the same spelled-out complexity or formality as *resolution,* pointing instead to a single instance in which a person takes a stand once and for all: a *resolve* to pass the test no matter how much study it took. In referring to action, *resolve* also relates more to single instances of vigorous application; here the note of difficult obstacles or inner reluctance is heightened, although the ethical suggestion may be absent. [With renewed *resolve,* she tried again to climb the sheer wall; Despite their repugnance, they flung themselves into the unpleasant task with great *resolve.*] **Decision** is the least forceful of any of these nouns in both possible situations. In reference to taking a stand, *decision* can apply to any situation, serious or trivial: Truman's *decision* to drop the bomb; a *decision* to stay home with a good book. More simply, *decision* can refer to a choice among alternatives: our *decision* to vote for a third-party candidate. In reference to action, *decision* suggests a lack of hesitation or hanging back rather than an approach based on ethical or willed conviction. It does impart a note of acting with dispatch and, perhaps, of using an ability to improvise as one goes along without stopping repeatedly for a new search after methods or motives: acting with *decision* while others still debated. See ALLEGIANCE, OPINION, SURE.

Antonyms: DOUBT, HESITATION, *irresolution, vacillation.*

respect

consideration
deference
esteem
honor
regard
reverence
veneration

These nouns refer to an admiring attitude or to courteous treatment. **Respect** and **honor** can imply both these possibilities. When describing an attitude, the nouns suggest an almost awed admiration for a person's views, accomplishments, or behavior, and the person so admired is often one's superior: feeling a deep *respect* for the old woman because she had met all the challenges of a very difficult life; astounded to learn that an employee who had been held in such high *honor* had been dismissed from the department because of his political views. *Respect,* in a way that *honor* does not, can refer to a feeling for one's equal: a real *respect* for her opponent's intelligence. When *respect* and *honor* refer to a manner of treatment, they suggest a courteous, sometimes humble approach: paying the founder every conceivable *respect;* doing *honor* to one's parents.

Regard is similar to *respect* or *honor* in that it can refer either to attitude or to treatment. The attitude suggested by *regard,* however, suggests approving friendliness more than humble admiration. It may sometimes suggest the attitude of a superior toward a favorite: happy to have won the employer's *regard.* In any case, *regard* is less austere than *respect* or *honor:* classmates who held her in evident *regard.* When *regard* applies to treatment, it contrasts with the two preceding nouns by referring to a thoughtful or atten-

tive concern rather than humble courtesy: giving the matter my special *regard;* treating the interviewer with uncommon *regard.*

Esteem suggests a favorable opinion of a person that is based on worth but is joined with a feeling of warm interest in and sometimes attraction toward the *esteemed* person: hurt by the growing indifference of a coworker whom he had held in high *esteem.*

Reverence and **veneration** are alike in suggesting a profound *honor* or *respect* for someone or something. *Reverence* implies that feelings of love are mingled with *honor* or *respect;* it can refer to an attitude or treatment, the object of which is looked on as exalted or inviolable: regarding her grandmother almost with *reverence;* to have *reverence* for the Constitution; treating a great work of art with the *reverence* it deserves. *Veneration* refers more to attitude than treatment and implies *respect* mixed with awe, as for that which we consider to be not only of great worth but almost hallowed: *veneration* for a dead hero; *veneration* for the cause of civil rights.

The remaining nouns relate almost exclusively to treatment. **Deference** is restricted to possibilities of *respect* in this use. It suggests an even greater formalized courtesy and need imply nothing about the true feelings of the person showing such *deference:* a briefing on what signs of *deference* the visiting head of state would expect. **Consideration**, by contrast, relates almost solely to possibilities of *regard* in this use. Here, even greater overtones of warmth are present, with thoughtfulness and concern more clearly motivated by sincere feeling: showing an unbiased *consideration* for both sides in the dispute. As with *respect* and *regard, deference* might be more appropriate for suggesting behavior toward a superior, *consideration* more appropriate for an inferior: parents who demand to be treated with *deference* by their children, yet give little *consideration* in return. See PRAISE, REVERE.

Antonyms: *contempt,* DISLIKE, *disrespect, repugnance.*

responsible

accountable
answerable
liable

These adjectives characterize the agreement by which one takes blame or credit for the results of an endeavor of which one has charge. **Responsible**, the most general of these adjectives, not only suggests such an agreement but applies beyond this to anyone mature or able enough to discharge difficult or exacting duties, to delegate authority wisely, and to perform capably despite unforeseen obstacles. More strictly, it suggests the relationship between the performer of duties and the taskmaster: *responsible* to the people alone for adequate performance of their duties. In a negative situation *responsible* may also refer exclusively to the assignment of blame: a jury trying to decide whom to hold *responsible* for the accident. Much more restricted in scope than *responsible*, **liable** refers exclusively to this last possibility of assigning blame; in a legal sense it can even refer, most strictly, to the payment of monetary damages in a mishap: laws that hold the driver *liable* for any injury to passengers.

Accountable, like *liable*, has a legal or technical sense, but in this case *accountable* refers to the situation of stewardship in which the steward must demonstrate the wise use of things put in his trust: an administrator who is directly *accountable* to the president for the funds allocated to her department. **Answerable** has a less technical ring to it than *accountable* and can apply as well to nonlegal situations: arguing that parents were to be held *answerable* for the widespread discontent of teenagers; evolutionary changes that are *answerable* to corresponding changes in the earth's environment at the time of a species' emergence. See OBLIGATION.

Antonyms: *irresponsible, unaccountable.*

result

consequence
denouement
effect
outcome

These nouns refer to events that are caused, determined, or set in action by, or that bring to completion, antecedent events of which they are the outgrowth. **Result**, the most general, indicates a causal link between the two events: unemployment that was the direct *result* of attempts to balance the federal budget. It may often suggest an earlier action that is taken to gain a particular goal: pacifying words that had their intended *result* of reducing tension. Sometimes, *result* may suggest earlier action taken experimentally to determine or measure what then will happen: evaluating the *results* of the double-blind cancer test. **Effect** emphasizes even more strictly than *result* the notion of causality and consequently gives a more objective, almost scientific tone. *Result*, furthermore, may suggest a unique or unpredictable one-time action, while *effect* emphasizes a principle that underlies a chain of events and continues to work in other instances: a

childhood familiarity with firearms that had a tragic *result;* the *effect* of radiation on the heredity of fruit flies.

Consequence may refer to simple causation in a neutral way: prosperity that was the *consequence* of expanded governmental spending. More often, however, *consequence* suggests a negative *result* or at least the negative concomitant of an otherwise desirable *effect:* arguing that the rise in lung cancers was a *consequence* of widespread smoking; willing to tolerate the degree of inflation that was the inevitable *consequence* of full employment.

Outcome and **denouement** relate to *result* in emphasizing more strongly a unique or one-time conclusion to a sequence of events. The informal *outcome* suggests finality or resolution: hearing of the fight he had been in, but not of its *outcome*. The notion of causality here is far less strong than in the previous nouns: a tragic *outcome* for the happy marriage. *Denouement* is the most formal of these nouns; at its most restricted, it refers to the final working out of plot in a fictional narrative, especially a play: a dramatic conflict that is resolved in the surprising, but completely believable *denouement*. This noun is often extended to other areas of use, where it functions as a more formal synonym for *outcome,* especially when events are dramatic, suspenseful, and unpredictable: a vote of censure that came as a *denouement* to the charges and countercharges aired during the congressional investigation; a Pyrrhic victory on the battlefield that had as its *denouement* an inconclusive statement issued by the peace conference. See FINISH, PURPOSE.

Antonyms: *ORIGIN.*

retire

fall asleep
go to sleep
grab some shuteye
hit the hay
hit the sack
sack out
turn in

These verbs all relate to entering into or being in the state called sleep. The most formal term in the group is **retire**. It can simply mean go to bed: We *retired* early that night because the day's activities had been so strenuous. It can also suggest a withdrawal to a private place where one can be alone, read, write, etc., before actually going to bed: We went to see Jim after dinner, but his father informed us that he had *retired* for the evening. **Fall asleep** and **go to sleep** are common idioms. The first stresses the natural, passive suspension of consciousness that occurs when one ceases being awake: I *fell asleep* as soon as my head hit the pillow. The second can mean the same thing: to *go to sleep* quickly. But it can also suggest the deliberate action involved in going to bed: Let's *go to sleep* now and clean up this mess in the morning.

Turn in is a colloquial equivalent for *go to sleep* in the sense that implies the action of going to bed: We *turned in* at ten and slept for twelve hours straight. It can also suggest the same kind of withdrawing that *retire* does: I *turned in* right after dinner to finish the detective story I'd started the night before.

Hit the hay and **hit the sack** are both slang expressions meaning go to bed. **Sack out** is also slang for go to bed, but it can mean *fall asleep* and even can suggest sleeping for a long time or at least for as long as one wishes: I can't wait to *sack out* tonight. Another slang expression for sleep is **grab some shuteye**. It can be used to refer to an ordinary night's rest or to even a longer than normal period. But it often indicates a short sleep or nap: I'm going to *grab some shuteye* before the party begins. See LEAVE.

revere

adore
idolize
reverence
venerate
worship

These verbs refer to the warm respect and honor with which one may regard an admirable person or institution. **Revere** is less formal but warmer in tone than **reverence**, which emphasizes solemnity. It is more appropriate for an institution or idea than a person, and is perhaps excessively formal in some cases: a virtuoso who still *reveres* his old teacher; the underprivileged who are asked to *reverence* the goals of a free society.

Worship and **venerate** both function directly in a religious context; in this case, *worship* might be reserved for expressing one's attitude to the divinity, while *venerate* could apply to an exemplary religious person, idea, or aspect: *worshiping* God and *venerating* the saints. More broadly, in other contexts, *venerate* is often used in conjunction with the notions of dignity and advanced age: *venerating* the old man for the wisdom and courage he had always shown. *Worship* can be used more generally: a father who *worships* his children. But sometimes it may suggest an excess and uncritical respect: people who *worshiped* the scoundrel as though he were a demigod.

Adore suggests the greatest tenderness and warmth of any of these verbs, and while it has a religious use, it functions in other contexts with fewer religious overtones than its synonyms: *adoring* the name of God; boys who *adore* their mothers. However, *adore* suggests the situation of love at a distance or the putting of someone on a pedestal more than it does a realistic, equal sharing of affection. **Idolize** is an extreme example of the overtones inherent in *adore*. While its pejorative possibilities should be clear in suggesting a slavish, servile, helpless love, *idolize* is often used without negative intent: a man who *idolizes* rather than loves; a writer who *idolized* the novels of Dostoevsky. See RESPECT.

Antonyms: *blaspheme, contemn,* DESPISE, REJECT, SCOFF, SLIGHT.

revise

amend
emend
rewrite

These verbs refer to changes in an existing statement, especially a written one, usually with a view to its improvement. **Revise** suggests large or small alterations, mostly in a piece of writing, in order to make it sounder or more in keeping with a given intention: *revising* the story to give it a tauter, more dramatic forward movement; ideologies that are constantly *revised* in the light of changing circumstances. **Rewrite**, by contrast, suggests a more thoroughgoing change and is more exclusively restricted in use to refer to manuscripts or documents. While it may be used in reference to a single sentence or to an entire book, major alterations in structure or theme rather than in style or expression are most often indicated: arguing that Jefferson had *rewritten* Paine's first attempt at a declaration of independence; the star who insisted that the part be completely *rewritten; rewriting* the conclusion of the novel in such a way as to change the theme and outcome of the whole book.

Amend indicates the change made in a document by adding new sections, particularly at the end: *amending* the Constitution so that it gave specific rules on presidential succession. While *amend* would thus seem to suggest less possibility for change than the previous verbs, a document can in theory be *amended* so that all its provisions are nullified and replaced by completely opposite or different provisions. **Emend**, by contrast, suggests a textual change, small in extent, that is accomplished in the body of the work itself, usually by someone other than the original author:

scholars who *emend* Shakespeare freely when they decide that the existing texts are garbled; lazy minds that wrench a great writer's words out of context and then further *emend* them to suit their own taste. See INSERT, REPAIR.

ridicule

derision
irony
mockery
sarcasm
satire

These nouns refer to the act of holding something up for disapproval or contempt. **Ridicule** suggests a conscious, usually verbal, attack on something to make it appear ludicrous: heaping *ridicule* on her desire to find a job. **Derision** suggests a fiercer attack, one designed not only to prove something ludicrous, but contemptible as well; *derision* is often used in the context of a public display of such contempt: heaping *derision* on the tax system; audiences who greeted her singing with catcalls and *derision*. **Mockery** may suggest a lighter, more subtle approach than *ridicule*, but it is characterized by the same motivating contempt as *derision*: stung by the note of *mockery* in his remarks. *Mockery*, however, is often used in a special way for an act that leaves a person open to intense disapproval: making a *mockery* of the democratic process.

The remaining three nouns relate more closely to techniques for making something seem ludicrous or contemptible. **Irony** is the technique of saying the opposite of what you mean: his deliberate *irony* in referring to the bejeweled visitors as generous and compassionate. **Satire** suggests a less subtle assault through such techniques as overstatement, *ridicule*, or laughter-provoking *derision*: unsettling many officials with his pointed *satire* on their bungling methods for coping with the crisis. *Satire* may also refer to any work using *ridicule*: Pope's *satire* on the bad writers of his day. **Sarcasm** is most often restricted to the making of brief, unpleasant remarks that are motivated by hostility and contempt: replying with *sarcasm* to anything she would suggest as a solution to their difficulties. See CARICATURE, HUMOROUS, JOKE.

Antonyms: *PRAISE.*

right

freedom
liberty
prerogative
privilege

These nouns refer to the fundamental claims a person can properly make or to a person's unfettered ability to choose. **Right** suggests a concrete claim established by legal, ethical, or religious sanctions: the *right* to own property; the *right* to equality before the law. Although someone claiming a *right* may argue that it is inherent, a person's *rights* are seen differently in various cultures: the *right* of a Muslim to have several wives; the *right* of a serf to remain immovably on his land. **Liberty** is a more abstract and general notion suggesting the opportunity to choose among alternatives. A document such as the Bill of Rights spells out those conditions a citizen may construe as *rights*: the *right* to life, *liberty*, and the pursuit of happiness. *Liberty* may sometimes, in fact, refer to an unwarranted breach of someone else's *right* to consideration or privacy: taking the *liberty* of phoning you directly; unbridled *liberty* without regard for the *rights* of others. Civil *rights* are now understood to refer to racial equality, while civil *liberties* are understood to refer to all the rights enumerated in the U.S. Constitution and its amendments.

Freedom is close to *liberty* in its abstract generality but stresses a total lack of constraint more than the opportunity for choice: clothes cut to allow *freedom* of movement; rulers who took it as their right to suppress *freedom of speech*.

Prerogative and **privilege** are much more specific in their meanings than the other nouns here. *Prerogative* refers to a *right* one has by virtue of age, sex, or position: a host's *prerogative* to turn away uninvited guests; the *prerogative* to change one's mind; an employee's *prerogative* to receive adequate severance pay. *Privilege* suggests advantages given as favors or added luxuries rather than as *rights*; a *privilege* may be given as a concession in exchange for something else. [Arriving early gave her the *privilege* of an unhurried dinner; College education is taken as a *right* rather than a *privilege*.] See BENEFIT, RIGHTFUL.

rightful

deserved
due
equitable
fair
just
merited

These adjectives characterize anything that is fitting, proper, or called for by legal or ethical standards. **Rightful** suggests that something is in accordance with some objective set of standards: a *rightful* heir to the property; the *rightful* place of women in society.

Rightful is often used when something thought true or fitting has been challenged: protesting that he was still their *rightful* monarch. **Just** also emphasizes an objective set of standards by which to judge whether something is fitting, but here the standards, by implication, are legal or moral ones: a *just* trial; arguing that a *just* society should forbid segregation of any kind.

Due emphasizes appropriateness or reasonableness: promising to answer in *due* course; a *due* punishment. In emphasizing moderation and practicality, *due* can sometimes seem a denial that objective standards exist and thus imply an arbitrary judgment: asserting that there was no conflict between the censorship law and a *due* regard for civil liberties. *Due* can also imply something that has accrued with time or has been left outstanding: juries that allow criminals to escape their *due* punishment.

Deserved and **merited** both emphasize the earning of something: a *deserved* honor; a *deserved* punishment; a *merited* award. As shown in these examples, *deserved* can be used both positively and negatively, whereas *merited* is more often used only for positive achievements. **Fair** is the mildest and most general of these adjectives; it is also the most subjective in suggesting an appeal to reasonableness and open-mindedness: a referee who was scrupulously *fair* in all decisions; claiming it wasn't *fair* that she had to do more work than her brother. **Equitable**, more formal than *fair*, suggests a solution that is just and reasonable to all parties concerned, but not necessarily wholly satisfactory to all. It is often used in contexts indicating an acceptable compromise rather than those susceptible of sharp distinctions between right and wrong: The wage agreement was *equitable* to both management and unions, although both had misgivings about certain aspects of the settlement. See LAWFUL, MORAL, RIGHT.

Antonyms: *evil, illicit, improper,* OUTRAGEOUS, *unlawful, wrongful.*

rightist

conservative
fascist
reactionary
right-winger
tory
traditionalist

These nouns refer to people who in valuing the past are opposed to change in the present. **Rightist** would seem to offer a neutral description of a person with such a belief, especially in the area of politics, but in actual U.S. use, *rightist* carries a tinge of disapproval. In other parts of the world, *rightist* might be avowedly descriptive, but in the U.S., where both parties are middle-of-the-road, few people would accuse a candidate of being a *rightist*. **Conservative** and **traditionalist** are much more neutral and can, in addition, be used for many other areas of activity beyond the political. Especially in Britain, where it is the name for a major political party, *conservative* carries the positive implication of wishing to conserve time-tested values handed down by wise leaders who struggled to realize them in the past. In political discussion in the United States, however, this implication may suggest instead a refusal to innovate and an extreme caution toward or dislike for any extension of governmental authority. In a wider context, *conservative* suggests a rejection of modern or contemporary styles or tastes: political liberals who are *conservatives* when it comes to taste in art and music. *Traditionalist* is more appropriate in this wider context than *conservative,* since it cannot be confused as a reference to politics; it suggests a person who judges things in the light of clearly defined standards evolved over a long period of time: *traditionalists* whose paintings show no influence of the avant-garde ferment.

The rest of these nouns refer more exclusively to political alignment. **Tory** has been used as a generic term for any *conservative,* especially one who is a proponent or beneficiary of privilege, status, or an entrenched establishment. This noun has faded from political use in the United States, but it is the popular name for the *Conservative* Party in Britain. **Right-winger** is a much more informal substitute for *rightist;* its very informality intensifies the disapproval felt in *rightist.* No *conservative* would call himself a *right-winger:* party hacks and *right-wingers* who surrounded recent presidents.

Reactionary and **fascist** are both extremely pejorative. *Reactionary* is the milder of the two, suggesting a person who wishes to wipe out the political innovations of a previous period by returning to an older, more rigid governmental scheme: *reactionaries* who oppose Social Security. *Fascist* as a descriptive term refers to a person who espouses a strong authoritarian government based on naked power rather than on the consent of the governed; *fascist* also frequently suggests theories that one racial or ethnic group is superior to others. In political invective, *fascist* is used loosely by liberals for anyone who disagrees with them: *fascist* hatemongers who voted against the bill. See OLD-FASHIONED.

Antonyms: LEFTIST, *Whig.*

rite

ceremony
liturgy
observance
ritual

These nouns refer to the prescribed way of conducting a formal event of significance. **Rite** now pertains mostly to a religious service, referring to the entire service as an entity: the Anglican *rite;* the *rites* of puberty in primitive societies. **Ritual** includes but goes beyond this meaning by referring to the formal manner of conducting a *rite:* Puritans who objected to the emphasis on *ritual. Ritual* has become popular to describe any action conducted with great formality, seriousness, or inflexibility: the opening-night *ritual* of waiting up for the drama critics' reviews; the mysterious *rituals* people undergo in health spas; his little *ritual* of expressing approval of everything she said. More and more, *ritual* in this context is open to a pejorative tone that disapproves of cut-and-dried ways of behaving.

Liturgy, like *rite,* pertains mostly to religious services, but it is even more restricted in use to refer solely to the body of text and actions used by a Christian denomination, especially one that emphasizes *ritual:* bishops called together to codify the *liturgy;* differences in *liturgy* among the Catholic, Episcopal, Eastern Orthodox, and Lutheran Churches.

Ceremony and **observance** are not confined to a religious context. Both can refer to any stylized commemorative event: discussing whether they would be married in a religious or civil *ceremony. Observance* can imply the formal use of *rituals,* like *ceremony,* but it is the most general of these nouns in suggesting any kind of commemoration whatever, formal or informal, festive or solemn, public or private: a gala *observance* of Independence Day; a quiet *observance* of their wedding anniversary. See RELIGION.

rob

embezzle
extort
milk

These verbs refer to the taking of something from someone without permission. **Rob** is the most general of these, referring to any such situation; it often suggests a one-time act involving a use of force, as in housebreaking, or the threat of force, as in an armed confrontation: the couple whose house was *robbed* when they were away; *robbed* in a holdup.

Extort and **embezzle** are more formal, and each has a particular area of relevance. *Extort* refers specifically to an official who compels someone to give the official something to which he or she is not entitled, possibly in exchange for an improper favor: fire inspectors who *extorted* bribes from landlords before declaring their buildings free of violations. Money need not always be involved: *extorted* party-line obedience from the officials by threatening to reveal their part in the kickback scandal. *Extort* thus has a connotation that suggests any sort of shady, underhanded, or unsavory dealings, not necessarily by an official: mothers who *extort* allegiance from their children by emotional blackmail. *Embezzle* applies much more strictly to a single situation, that of covertly taking money from an employer by doctoring the relevant financial records; usually, an accountant, treasurer, cashier, or someone else entrusted with other people's money is involved in this crime.

Milk can mean get money or other benefits from someone by means of threats, flattery, persuasion, or any sort of unethical means; it strongly suggests the tapping of a portion of some larger amount: gangsters who *milked* protection money from every merchant in Chicago. *Milk* can also refer to small amounts acquired with difficulty: *milking* his friends for free meals. Thus, at one extreme, *milk* can be a substitute for *extort,* where outright illegality is involved, and at the other indicate the act of freeloading, which may be annoying or unethical but certainly is not illegal.

robbery

burglary
holdup
larceny
mugging
stickup
theft

These nouns refer to the taking of someone else's possessions against the person's will. **Robbery** most often suggests a face-to-face confrontation between robber and victim in which the victim surrenders valuables because of threat or violence. **Mugging** is a *robbery* that occurs with an actual carrying out of violence, so that the victim is rendered helpless or unconscious and then divested of valuables. **Burglary**, by contrast, most often indicates robbing a house of its valuables, usually with the intention of avoiding a confrontation with the owners because they are asleep or absent. **Holdup** and the informal word **stickup** can substitute for *robbery* and can also refer to the robbing of premises, such as a train or bank, when groups of people must be confronted and cowed.

Theft and **larceny** are more general and abstract than these other nouns; *theft* can apply to any taking of property against the will of the owner, whether by stealth, confrontation, or fraud. *Larceny* is the legal term for *theft,* but includes even the attempt to take property, whether successful or not, provided the position of the property in question has been changed, however slightly. Each of the states fixes a specific value to measure the seriousness of a *larceny.* If the value of stolen goods is under this amount, the theft is called petty *larceny* and a light sentence would apply upon conviction; if over, grand *larceny* has been committed, carrying a heavier sentence.

rot

    decay
    decompose
    molder
    putrefy
    spoil

These verbs refer to the breakdown of dead organic tissues by natural bacterial processes. **Rot** is the least formal and most forceful of these verbs, suggesting an advanced point in the process of breakdown; the tissues at this point might or might not smell foul but they would in any case be almost unrecognizable, as compared to their former state: a fear of plague that had left dead bodies to *rot* in the streets; a snail that had completely *rotted* away inside its shell; leather bindings that had *rotted* in the damp basement; leaves left to *rot* in the compost heap. **Spoil**, by contrast, refers to an earlier point in the process of organic breakdown; it is especially applied to foods that have turned bad or begun to turn: milk that had *spoiled* in the refrigerator; drying strips of beef in the sun so that they would not *spoil.*

Decay is more matter-of-fact than *rot* and applies generally to the whole process of breakdown, but particularly to the end point of total destruction: a corpse that had already *decayed,* leaving only the skeleton intact; seaweed that lay *decaying* on the beach. **Decompose** is a more formal substitute for *decay,* but is almost clinical in its reference to a point between *spoil* and *rot* at which tissues may be distended and ruptured by a buildup of gases: formaldehyde to prevent the specimens from *decomposing;* treatment plants to *decompose* sewage more rapidly.

Putrefy refers to the same point in the process as *decompose,* stressing particularly the presence of foul or poisonous gases and noxious odors: salmon that had spawned and died and now lay *putrefying* in the shallow water; garbage that *putrefied* in heaps on the neglected beach. **Molder** might now be thought too precious or euphemistic a substitute for *decay.* It means *decay* gradually and turn into dust: their remains *moldering* in the tomb; old castles *moldering* on the Rhine. See CORPSE, DEAD, DIE.

Antonyms: *bloom,* FLOURISH, *grow.*

rotate

    gyrate
    revolve
    roll
    spin
    turn
    twirl
    whirl

These verbs all mean have or impart a circular motion. **Rotate**, **revolve**, and **roll** describe three different circular motions, though they are frequently used interchangeably. A body *rotates* around its own axis or center. A body *revolves* around a center outside itself: The earth *revolves* around the sun. A body *rolls* on a plane or other surface with which its circumference is in continuous contact: A wagon wheel *rolls* on the ground and *rotates* on its axle.

Gyrate is sometimes used loosely as a synonym for *revolve.* However, *gyrate* emphasizes spiral or helical movement about, or as if about, a central point or axis, while *revolve* indicates circular or elliptical movement: an eagle *gyrating* majestically up into the sky for a thousand feet; the violent, *gyrating* winds of a cyclone.

Turn is the most general verb of this group and may be used as a synonym for any of the others. It most commonly applies to rotary motion, however, and is thus most often used in place of *rotate:* The earth *turns* on its axis. *Turn,* less colorful and less precise denotatively than the other verbs, implies nothing about speed or the complexity or course of the circular movement in question.

Spin, **twirl**, and **whirl** all mean *turn* or cause to *turn* rapidly and continuously. *Whirl* usually implies greater speed than the other two verbs, while *twirl* often refers to a complicated series of movements of something manipulated by the hands or fingers. *Spin* emphasizes the continuity of the action, and usually the narrow compass of the circular motion; it may, however, apply to any action of *turning:* The earth *spins* on its axis. [The wind *whirled* the leaves around the yard; a drum majorette *twirling* her baton while strutting at the head of a parade; to *spin* a top.] *Spin* and *whirl* may also be used for any abrupt circular motion: The car *spun* (or *whirled*) around out of control. *Whirl,* more often than *spin,* has the connotation of lack of conscious control or design: The sensations *whirled* through his mind too rapidly for him to assimilate. See CIRCUMSCRIBE, GO, MOVE.

rotund. Do not confuse the adjective *rotund* (plump, rounded) with the adjective *orotund* (imposing, dignified, pompous, with full voice).

rough

    bumpy
    crenelated
    crooked
    jagged
    rugged
    serrated
    uneven

These adjectives describe things that are not smooth or straight. **Rough** and **uneven** are both general and vague in their implications. *Rough* can specifically indicate a coarse-grained surface: *rough* sandpaper. At its most specific, *uneven* suggests something, as a line, configuration, or surface, that has more noticeable ups and downs: an *uneven* margin; *uneven* landscape. *Rough,* however, may also indicate irregular or *uneven* ground that is impenetrable, steep, or difficult to traverse: *rough* terrain. Less concretely, *rough* can indicate anything unrefined, harsh, or difficult: a *rough* sketch; *rough* treatment; a *rough* job. *Uneven* in its other uses stays closer to its reference to something with irregular variations: *uneven* patches of shrubbery scattered across the meadow; an amusing but *uneven* play. It can also refer to something unsymmetrical, unmatched, or disarranged: a face with *uneven* features; The pictures on the walls were slightly *uneven* in placement.

Bumpy and **rugged** are much more specific in their reference to *rough* or *uneven* surfaces. *Rugged* applies mostly to landscape, stressing an extremely *uneven* topography or a resistance to smooth passage: *rugged* mountains; *rugged* waves; a *rugged* dirt road. *Rugged* carries implications of harshness or toughness, as can be seen in more general uses of the adjective: a *rugged,* masculine build. *Bumpy* can refer to small surfaces as well as to landscape. In both cases, *bumpy* may suggest a generally smooth stretch that nevertheless has small hollows and lumpy projections: After an hour of sanding, the boards were still quite *bumpy.* Often, *bumpy* refers to anything that results in travel that is full of jolts: a *bumpy* road enclosed by *rugged*

hills; Our jet traveled through air pockets that made the ride extremely *bumpy.*

Crooked refers specifically to undesirable departures, great or small, from the horizontal or vertical. [All the pictures on the wall were *crooked;* a *crooked* tower; The seams of his sweater are *crooked.*] In more general uses, *crooked* can refer to anything skewed: *crooked* shelves. Occasionally, *crooked* can be used with poetic force to describe something that is naturally *uneven* or *rugged:* a range of *crooked* mountains. **Jagged** can also be used in this way, particularly of steep or extremely *uneven* topography: the *jagged* lip of the crater. More specifically, *jagged* refers to small-scale shapes with sharp or needle-like edges such as those that result when something brittle is broken or shattered: the *jagged* edges of the broken bone; *jagged* pieces of glass. As in the last example, *jagged* can refer primarily to an *uneven* configuration rather than to *rough* surfaces.

Serrated and **crenelated** are the most technical and specific of these adjectives. *Serrated* refers to any saw-toothed configuration or edge: a *serrated* knife. *Crenelated* refers most specifically to the regular notched upper edge that is typical of battlements: *crenelated* castle walls. It can apply more widely to any edge with deep notches: leaves distinguished by their *crenelated* edges. See KEEN, MOUNTAIN, STEEP.

Antonyms: *even, fine, smooth, straight.*

run

    jog
    lope
    race
    sprint
    trot

These verbs refer to movement on foot that is faster than walking. **Run** is the most general. To *run* is to move by regular, bounding steps in such a way that both feet are off the ground during part of each step. *Running* (noun) is a rapid, continuous motion and usually implies haste. A person may *run* in pursuit, in order to escape, out of eagerness, for exercise, or toward a goal in competition: to *run* for the bus; to *run* away from an assailant; to *run* to meet a friend; to *run* in a race. To **race** is to *run* very fast, often at top speed. *Race* implies urgency in *running.* It may suggest the pressing need to reach a goal in time: They *raced* for cover when gunfire was heard. Or it may focus on a challenge, an attempt to outstrip competition in a contest of speed: I'll *race* you to the corner. Horses and dogs are *raced* as a form of sport. Athletes *race* in track meets, as in the 100-yard dash or the relay. To **sprint** is to *run* at top speed, typically for a short distance: to *sprint* 100 yards. As a noun, *sprint* may denote a short race *run* at full speed throughout. But *sprint* may also indicate a short burst of speed in the course of a longer race, especially in the home-stretch: She passed the lead runner on the outside and *sprinted* across the finish line.

Trot and **jog** emphasize the up-and-down motion of restrained *running*. To *trot* is to go at a brisk, bouncy gait midway between a walk and a run. When a horse or other quadruped *trots,* it moves one front leg and the opposite hind leg together, then shifts to the other diagonal pair: The dog *trotted* up, wagging its tail. A person who *trots* bobs up and down, body upright and knees lifted high, shifting his or her weight from leg to leg, but maintaining a quick, constant pace. [The child *trotted* obediently after her father; The candidate *trotted* around the park to show that he was in good condition.] To *jog* is to go at a steady, unhurried *trot*. Where *trot* may imply a need for moderate speed, *jog* suggests the slow, jolting pace of one who is in no rush. [The tireless old fellow *jogged* along, completing his first lap around the block; The batter *jogged* back to the dugout.]

Where *jog* and *trot* denote workaday, sometimes humorous, ways of running, **lope** stresses the freedom of a leisurely and swinging gait. A person or animal that *lopes* is free from strain or pressure and is able to maintain speed for a long time without tiring. Applied to quadrupeds, *lope* indicates an easy, bounding movement or relaxed *running:* the grace and ease of a fox *loping* along. A horse that *lopes* moves at a slow gallop or canter. Applied to persons, *lope* suggests a long, loose, swinging stride in walking: a lanky Texan *loping* along.

In a looser sense, *run* may simply mean hurry off: Oh dear, I'm late; I've got to *run*. *Race* may mean rush or dash: She *raced* to the phone. *Trot* suggests determination but may imply no more than a brisk, hurried walk: I'll *trot* up there on my lunch hour. In a figurative sense, *run* may mean be a candidate, and *race* (noun) may indicate any competitive contest: to *run* for office; to *run* in a congressional *race*. *Jog*, on the other hand, suggests an utter lack of competitiveness, an easygoing indifference: He *jogs* along doing odd jobs, seemingly unconcerned about his future. *Race* may also suggest the tendency or compulsion to speed toward a goal: Her thoughts *raced* ahead, anticipating the solution. Or it may emphasize the desperate need to utilize time to the utmost: The doctors *raced* with the clock to save the child's life. See SKIP, WALK.

sacred

> blessed
> consecrated
> divine
> hallowed
> holy

These adjectives describe things a particular religion holds to be dedicated to its god and worthy of adoration. **Sacred** suggests something associated with a divinity as being worthy of reverence: a temple *sacred* to Apollo; a mountain thought to be *sacred* by Shintoists. In another use, *sacred* can simply mark off from everyday life a sphere of things belonging to a religion: the strict separation of *sacred* and secular laws; *sacred* and profane love. **Consecrated** may suggest most specifically that human beings, by completing a prescribed ritual, have recommended something to their divinity as being of special worth: the bishop who *consecrates* (verb) a king. One would, thus, say that the king was *consecrated* to his God, but not necessarily that he was *sacred* to his God. Reinforcing this distinction, *consecrate* (verb) can also mean give over or dedicate to a deity or even to some other ideal: *consecrating* himself to the civil rights struggle. **Divine** is more like *sacred* but goes even further in suggesting something that is of a deity or issues from the deity: holding that the Pentateuch was *divine* in origin. Like *sacred, divine* also can distinguish the religious realm from more ordinary ones: St. Augustine's effort to mediate between the *divine* and mundane worlds.

The remaining terms, like *consecrated,* suggest something that has been made worthy of worship. Of these, however, only **blessed** (adjective) may suggest the official or ritual declaration such as *consecrated* may indicate. At its most specific, *blessed* is the title for a deceased person who has been beatified by the Roman Catholic Church in an appropriate ceremony. More generally, *blessed* indicates something worthy of reverent adoration or something given significance by the particular act of a clergyman: the *blessed* Bible; a crucifix that *has been blessed* (verb) by the Pope. **Hallowed** may suggest that something has been made an object of adoration or it may, less specifically, refer to something that is in actual fact revered: the *hallowed* saints; her wish to be buried in *hallowed* ground. **Holy** is the least specific of the adjectives in this group, suggesting anything dedicated to God or anything righteous or godly: the *holy* church; the *holy* days of Lent; a *holy* man from Calcutta. See REVERE.

Antonyms: *lay, temporal,* WORLDLY.

sad

> blue
> dejected
> depressed
> despondent
> disconsolate
> lugubrious
> melancholy

These adjectives all characterize unhappy or despairing states of mind and, in some cases, situations that cause or are evocative of such feelings. **Sad**, the mildest and most general term, is also the least explicit, giving no hint as to how downcast a person may be or for what reason. One may feel *sad* because of the passing of summer, or *sad* because a child leaves home to be married. A funeral may be a *sad* occasion, but so may the cutting of a virgin forest for timber. A monkey peering out of a cage may have the *sad* eyes of a lonely old man.

Dejected literally means cast down in spirits and suggests a temporary state of disappointment and discouragement brought on by some external event: *dejected* when she failed to win the prize; *dejected* because a friend failed to greet them on the street.

Depressed and **despondent** both apply to more prolonged states of sadness. *Depressed* describes an emotional state in which both physical and mental activity may be slowed down, sometimes to the point of apathy. The *depressed* person is flooded with feelings of hopelessness and low self-esteem, and tends to brood. To the casual observer, one who is *depressed* may appear to be so without apparent cause or, at most, for insufficient reasons. *Despondent* is sometimes used interchangeably with *depressed,* although the former often connotes great grief and a feeling of helplessness because of some catastrophe: *despondent* because they lost all their money in the stock market; *despondent* over the death of a child; a patient *despondent* because his condition does not improve.

Melancholy suggests a habitual pensiveness and sadness that may not necessarily be unpleasant. It stresses the presence of sorrow rather than of pain. [During the Romantic period it was fashionable in literature to have a *melancholy* outlook on the world and turn one's back on liveliness and joy.] In the past, *melancholy* has been applied to persons suffering from the marked lowness of spirits associated with mental illness. It is rarely so used today, *depressed* and *despondent* having supplanted it in this sense. *Melancholy* may also describe things and places that have an adverse effect on one's good spirits: the *melancholy* sound of the whippoorwill; the *melancholy* news of a friend's bad luck; the *melancholy* beach, deserted and strewn with dead seaweed and snow.

Disconsolate means refusing or unable to accept consolation or comfort, as after a loss or disappointment. *Disconsolate* is more literary than *despondent* and carries the suggestion of an outward expression of sorrow or pain rather than of listlessness: a *disconsolate* couple weeping before the smoking wreckage of their home.

Lugubrious, while actually meaning *sad* or *dejected,* is now applied almost exclusively to a person or thing that is so excessively mournful or solemn as to be ludicrous. [Our Sunday school teacher used to regale us with accounts of the *lugubrious* fates awaiting bad children; A bloodhound has long ears, pendent chops, and a *lugubrious* expression.]

Blue is a loose synonym for *sad, depressed,* or *despondent.* It does not suggest the extent or depth of such a feeling except in context, and it tends to sound informal. [She was *blue* because her best friend stayed away from her party; A retired person often becomes *blue* when no longer engaged in meaningful activity.] See DESPAIR, GLOOMY, MISERABLE, PATHETIC.

Antonyms: BLITHE, CHEERFUL, *excited, exhilarated, exuberant, gay, glad,* JOYOUS, *jubilant,* LIVELY.

salary

    compensation
    emolument
    fee
    honorarium
    pay
    stipend
    wage

These nouns refer to the money given for work. **Salary** and **wage** denote the set amount of money paid periodically to an employee. *Salary* usually pertains to money received by white-collar workers or by executives in managerial positions; it implies a sum figured by the week, month, or year and paid weekly or at longer intervals. *Wage* usually pertains to the earnings of skilled or blue-collar workers and on down the scale to manual and menial positions; it often implies an hourly rate paid weekly or biweekly: an executive *salary* starting at $40,000 a year; a minimum hourly

wage of $4.75; the low *wages* paid even for skilled labor.

Pay and **compensation** are the informal and formal terms, respectively, for *wages* or *salary* in general: the gulf between the scale of *pay* for clerical workers and that for teachers; amateur golf competitions that rule out contestants who have played the game for *compensation. Pay* is the preferred term in the military for the regular amount paid to personnel. In any case, *pay* most often suggests a permanent, recurring amount of money. *Compensation* in some cases might sound overly formal or roundabout, but it can pertain generally to a set amount that is paid once for a given service or for one performance.

Fee and **stipend** are specific forms of *compensation* in the last sense described above. A *fee* is usually charged by a professional person as a sum set in advance for performing a specific, one-time function: the doctor's *fee* for a general examination; asking the lawyer what the *fee* would be to take a case to court. A *stipend* is most often an allowance, also set in advance, but in this case applying mostly to students who are awarded such a grant of money in the form of a scholarship or fellowship in order to pursue their studies: a handsome *stipend* granted for advanced research. *Stipend* has been extended to any grant of money awarded for any reason: Two geneticists, a poet, and four sociologists were awarded *stipends* under the foundation's fellowship program.

Honorarium technically refers to the *compensation* given to a professional person for services rendered when law or custom forbids a set *fee:* an *honorarium* given a poet for a public reading of her work. Often, however, *honorarium* can become a mere euphemism for a *fee* so low that the honor of doing the work must make up for the inadequate *compensation:* literary magazines that give ten-dollar *honorariums* for critical articles from college teachers who must publish to further their careers. **Emolument** is the most formal of these nouns and would seem a needless circumlocution when it substitutes for the already formal *compensation. Emolument* has a unique area of relevance, however, when it suggests the money that becomes available to one upon being appointed to a particular office; often this may include, by implication, fringe benefits, an expense account, or other indirect monetary perquisites in addition to the stated *salary* or *fee:* the perfectly legal *emoluments* that sometimes go along with certain appointive offices.

sample

    case
    example

illustration
instance
specimen

These nouns refer to a specific thing or piece of data summoned up to represent or verify a general type or thesis. **Sample** usually indicates something that is physically present for inspection as a representative of some larger entity. [The interior decorator had brought along *samples* of the fabrics selected for the upholstery; The enclosed essay is a *sample* of my writing.] Most concretely, **illustration** may indicate graphic material that accompanies a written text to supplement it or help explain it: a book on architecture with beautiful *illustrations;* a geometry textbook with numerous *illustrations.* But *illustration* can refer to any citing of specific material to supplement, explain, or demonstrate a thesis or train of thought: He threw in two humorous anecdotes as *illustrations* of his main point. *Illustration* can also refer to something that is merely alluded to rather than actually presented: She cited the slaughtering of Incas in *illustration* of her argument that genocide was not uncommon.

Specimen stresses even more than *sample* the physical presence of a representative individual. *Specimen* is also clinical in tone, suggesting a laboratory or scientific context: microscopes set up with *specimens* of the four blood types; rock *specimens;* display cases with *specimens* of many insect species. As in the last case, *specimen* can often imply that something is dead or has been killed, but this is not always so: cages to separate the healthy *specimens* from those that had contracted the disease. Beyond the scientific context, *specimen* can apply to anything that seems representative of a type or larger whole: a perfect *specimen* of absurdist fiction; checking the endorsement against other *specimens* of her signature. When applied to a person, *specimen* suggests someone noticeably typical, eccentric, or physically impressive; in this use, an ironic tone may be present: a standard *specimen* of the middle-class liberal; odd *specimens* of underworld life; a real *specimen* of a man.

Example is the most general of these nouns. While it may indicate something physically present as a *specimen,* more often *example* suggests the citing of supplementary material, comparable to the similar use of *illustration.* But *example* often implies brief citations given for clarity rather than to corroborate a thesis: a list of *examples* showing faulty and correct constructions to illustrate each grammatical rule. The implication that an *example* is an aid to learning or study comes to the fore when the context is that of discipline: a punishment that was intended to make an *example* of him before the whole class.

Instance points to a concrete *example* or *illustration* of a general thesis, particularly one drawn from the past: asked to cite *instances* of oligarchic rule in European history. *Instance* can also refer to an isolated or minor occurrence in the present: scattered *instances* of rioting even after the major flareups were over. Sometimes, *instance* can refer to exceptions rather than typical *samples:* a few *instances* of disagreement at the otherwise harmonious meeting. Or *instance* can apply to details that are part of an occurrence, even when no general thesis is being proved or defended: noting *instances* of the crowd's behavior as the news came in. **Case** can function vaguely in place of other nouns here, but it may refer particularly to a greater body of material looked at in some detail: a presentation of *cases* in which open conflict existed. By contrast, *case* can refer to a whole argument rather than to its *examples:* the *case* for nuclear disarmament; the district attorney's *case* against the suspect. It can also refer to a specific medical or psychiatric *instance:* her analysis of some hundred cancer *cases. Case* often suggests a significant or unusual body of details isolated for intensive study because of their puzzling or controversial nature: the strange *case* of Mark Twain; an investigation of alleged *cases* of levitation by Hindu gurus. See COPY, COUNTERPART, DUPLICATE, PROTOTYPE.

sanitary

antiseptic
aseptic
hygienic
sterile

These adjectives characterize what is healthful, clean, germfree, or germ destroying. **Sanitary**, the most informal, pertains mostly to what preserves or is favorable to health, particularly by virtue of its cleanliness. But since it has a quasi-medical tone and suggests a degree of cleanliness beyond that of the word clean, it can also imply a germfree condition: A common drinking cup may be clean without being *sanitary.* **Hygienic** is much broader in scope than *sanitary;* used of things preserving or promoting health, *hygienic* can refer more readily than *sanitary* to other aspects of healthfulness than those pertaining to cleanliness or freedom from germs: stressing that moderate exercise is *hygienic.* But it can refer generally to freedom from germs where the additional implications of extreme cleanliness in *sanitary* would be inappropriate: It is not *hygienic* to have a well situated on lower ground than a cesspool.

The remaining adjectives relate exclusively to the absence or destruction of germs causing disease or infection. **Sterile** refers particularly to things made free of germs: *sterile* bandages; using only *sterile* instruments; precautions to make sure the wound remained *sterile*. **Aseptic** refers especially to the absence of germs from living tissue, or to the absence of putrefactive infection; in this, it is restricted to one aspect of *sterile*, with a gain in precision. This lack of infection, however, may be fortuitous rather than induced: a cut that had luckily remained *aseptic;* using *sterile* instruments so that the incision would be *aseptic*. **Antiseptic** can also refer to something kept *sterile* against germs or infection, including living tissue, though it applies to other things as well. In its particular area of relevance, however, it points to the counteracting of infections by the destruction of germs that may already be present: an *antiseptic* solution of sodium perborate. See CLEAN (adj.), HEALTHFUL, SANITIZE.

Antonyms: *noxious, polluted, soiled, unsanitary.*

sanitize

decontaminate
disinfect
fumigate
sterilize

These verbs mean clean something so as to free it of germs, pests, or other unhealthful encroachments. **Sanitize** indicates thorough cleaning, with the implication that anything unfavorable to health has been removed, especially anything that might spread infection or disease: a ruling that secondhand clothes must be *sanitized* before being resold; an ultraviolet unit for *sanitizing* toilet seats. **Sterilize** specifically suggests the destruction of bacteria or microorganisms that cause infection or disease: the high temperatures used to *sterilize* surgical instruments; *sterilizing* the wound by applying antiseptic. **Disinfect** is even more specific, because it implies the presence of an infection or of infection-causing germs: a liquid designed for *disinfecting* toilet bowls; an antibiotic that would act to *disinfect* the inflamed tissue.

Fumigate means subject to smoke or fumes in order to kill germs or insect pests: to *fumigate* a sickroom to prevent the spread of contagion; to *fumigate* an apartment by spraying it with insecticides. **Decontaminate** may sometimes apply in a general way. It has gained a specific meaning, however, that refers to the destroying or neutralizing of poisonous

chemicals or radioactivity that has pervaded an area: teams sent in to *decontaminate* all but the central area irradiated by the atomic explosion. See SANITARY.

Antonyms: *POLLUTE, SOIL.*

sarcastic

biting
caustic
cutting
mordant
sardonic

These adjectives characterize sharp, contemptuous behavior toward someone, especially verbal behavior. **Sarcastic**, which comes from a root meaning tear flesh or sneer, describes a person, statement, expression, attitude, or tone of voice that is heavily ironic to the point of being snide. A *sarcastic* comment is generally scornful or taunting in tone, often expressing the opposite of what it literally says. *Sarcastic*, in fact, often points to obnoxious arrogance, lacerating mockery, or wryly contemptuous teasing. **Mordant** is a less common term with the same meaning as *sarcastic: mordant* wit; a *mordant* speaker. By contrast, **sardonic**, from a root that refers to a poison causing fatal, laughterlike convulsions, emphasizes a less direct or aggressive approach in favor of a mocking or sneering attitude that may be witty, ironic, or laughter-provoking. Where *sarcastic* and *mordant* suggest an attempt to express and inspire contempt, *sardonic* stresses the intent to ridicule. Also, *sarcastic* suggests single, *ad hominem* utterances, whereas *sardonic* may suggest a more far-reaching attitude of somber cynicism that is not always directed at a person: his *sarcastic* remarks about the so-called speed and competence of the waiters; his *sardonic* view of the possibilities for social reform; She kept her audience in stitches with the *sardonic* quips she tossed off; meeting the students' *sarcastic* laughter with a chilling, *sardonic* smile.

Biting refers most specifically to remarks alone, but suggests incisive or telling utterances that may express animus but need not be personal in intent: a *biting* critique of bureaucratic inefficiency. **Cutting** is close to *biting*, but *cutting* specifically indicates a harsh, personal rejection: a *cutting* remark on his bad manners; turning away from them with a *cutting* disdain. **Caustic** comes from a Greek root meaning burn. It points to a critical attitude that is so sharp in its expression as to be searing, scathing, or corrosive: the *caustic* satires of an embittered author; a brilliant critic whose *caustic* wit made her many enemies. See CONTEMPTUOUS, RIDICULE, SCOFF, SOUR.

Antonyms: *complimentary,* FAVORABLE, *flattering.*

satisfy

answer
ease
fill
fulfill
meet
palliate

These verbs are concerned with an adequate response to a foregoing requirement, need, or expectation. **Satisfy** can be applied in all three cases, stressing in each the completeness with which something measures up to standards set in advance: *satisfying* all requirements for a degree; unable to *satisfy* a craving for pickles; a movie that could hardly *satisfy* the claims made for it. **Fulfill** functions in all three settings and may also suggest thoroughness of response; its special overtone, however, implies a more-than-mediocre performance or one that is profound or sets high standards: *fulfilling* the duties and obligations of the post with distinction; imaginative play projects that would *fulfill* the need for creative experimentation; high expectations that were ultimately *fulfilled.* In each of these cases, *satisfy* might suggest adequacy, but only *fulfill* would imply going beyond set boundaries.

Answer, fill, and **meet** are more like *satisfy* than *fulfill* in suggesting adequacy but no more. *Answer* suggests an exact matching of candidate and specifications: an executive who would *answer* these requirements. If the specifications are demanding, of course, *answering* them might be a measure of excellence more than a mere proof of adequacy: a director who interviewed hundreds of ingénues before finding one who *answered* to all demands of the role. *Fill* applies best to the situation of eradicating a lack and may leave open the question of performance: She was hired to *fill* a staff vacancy, but despite excellent recommendations, she didn't *satisfy* our expectations. *Meet,* more than any of the foregoing, may suggest a minimal measuring up to standards, or the difficulty of attaining them: They barely *met* the deadline; drinking just enough water to *meet* the minimum weight restriction for paratroopers. It may also stress reluctance or suggest an either-or condition: *meeting* his demands with an air of unwilling surrender; They refused to negotiate unless three conditions were *met.*

Ease and **palliate** apply only to the situation of responding to a lack, both stressing that it is partially *filled* but not wholly *satisfied:* Troops were flown in to *ease* the shortage of rescue workers. *Palliate* is even more negative than *ease,* suggesting the lack has been disguised or concealed but not altered in any basic way: laws that have *palliated* the disease of discrimination without curing it. See ADEQUATE, SURFEIT.
Antonyms: *miss, refuse, worsen.*

save

deliver
ransom
redeem
rescue

These verbs are comparable in meaning free a person or thing from some dangerous or unfavorable situation or condition. **Save** is a general verb with broad application. It can refer to the help offered when a person or thing has already been subjected to some kind of danger or threat of injury: plunging into the lake to *save* a drowning child. It can designate the protective measures taken to ward off an impending disaster: inoculating a community to *save* it from the threat of an influenza epidemic. In less serious situations, *save* can suggest the careful treatment employed to avoid fatigue, damage, etc.: Help *save* your eyesight by using good lighting. In all these senses, *save* goes beyond the immediate helpful action to suggest the preservation of the person or thing that is *saved* for further life or use. *Save* also has a theological reference to a freedom from spiritual death or the consequences of sin: a belief that his soul would be *saved* by devoting his life to good works.

The sense of **deliver** being compared here is rather formal in tone and is almost never used in reference to things. Like *save,* it means free or protect from some real or potential danger, harm, etc., The most dedicated work of his attorney *delivered* the condemned man from prison.

Ransom and **redeem** are alike in denoting the securing of the release of a person or thing from bondage, captivity, detention, pawn, etc., upon payment of a sum of money or some equivalent. *Ransom* has special relevance to the release arranged for a kidnapped person: willing to pay any price to *ransom* their infant child. *Redeem* commonly suggests the recovering of something through payment of a sum of money: to *redeem* mortgaged property; to *redeem* a pawned coat. In theological contexts, *redeem* has specific reference to Christ's salvation of mankind from the power of sin by his death on the Cross.

Rescue is interchangeable with the first meaning of *save* in its implication of aid to someone in imminent danger: brave firefighters *rescuing* people from a burning building. Less commonly, it refers to the protective measures used to *save* something that is being threatened by injury or destruction: steps taken to *rescue* the abandoned building from decay. See CONSERVE, RECOVER, REPAIR.

Antonyms: *DESTROY, HARM, lose, SENTENCE.*

savory

piquant
pungent
spicy
tangy

These adjectives all signify sharp in smell, taste, or flavor. **Savory**, **tangy**, and **piquant** mean pleasantly sharp in taste. *Savory* emphasizes most strongly the agreeable nature of the taste and in a related sense means appetizing, whether sharp in taste or not: to eat every *savory* morsel of a delectable stew. *Piquant* suggests tartness and emphasizes vividness of taste and strength of flavor. *Tangy* usually implies a touch or impression of tartness rather than a heavy or long-lasting dose: a *tangy* soft drink. It is mild in force and is more common in informal contexts than either *savory* or *piquant*. In extended senses *savory* can refer to anything eagerly received: a *savory* bit of gossip. *Piquant* suggests something that is lively and charming, and therefore of compelling interest: a *piquant* account of a contretemps with a butcher; Audrey Hepburn had a *piquant* quality that endeared her to all filmgoers.

Spicy means highly flavored and usually but not necessarily implies that the strong seasoning is pleasant: a *spicy* dish that included red pepper and horseradish; so *spicy* that we had to gulp water between bites. In its figurative sense *spicy* means somewhat improper or risqué and implies that certain details are used to pique interest as spices are used to enhance flavor: a *spicy* story of young lovers.

Anything acrid or prickly to the senses is said to be **pungent**. A *pungent* odor is strong, keen, and penetrating: the *pungent* aroma of smoking fish; The *pungent* odor of sulfur resembles that of rotten eggs. *Pungent* writing is colorful, sardonic, or sarcastic, and is characterized by a piercing or penetrating quality that is at once memorable and forceful. [The *pungent* style of H. L. Mencken left its mark on my writing; a *pungent* satire of middle-class life.] See SMELL, TASTY.

Antonyms: *BLAND, insipid, tasteless.*

scanty

exiguous
inadequate
insufficient
meager
scarce
skimpy
sparse

All these adjectives describe things that are limited in quantity or deficient in amount. What is **scanty** is barely adequate or not quite enough, whereas what is **meager** is not nearly enough. A *scanty* meal may be ordered by a dieter, whereas a *meager* meal suggests the pinch of poverty and may be poor in quality as well as small in amount. **Exiguous** is a more formal adjective than *scanty* or *meager* and carries the same meanings: an *exiguous* income. **Skimpy** is a more informal term than *meager*. Unlike *scanty*, *skimpy* indicates deliberate stinginess, often suggesting that more could or should be provided. *Skimpy*, thus, often implies disapproval or dissatisfaction, while *scanty* may suggest a more serious deficiency: a *skimpy* serving, considering that it was a $500-a-plate dinner; a *scanty* stock of emergency provisions. *Meager* is expressive of real want, implying that more is not only desirable but is badly needed: The social worker claimed it was impossible for his client to live on her *meager* pension.

Insufficient and **inadequate** are limited by definition to what is not enough to fill requirements or meet needs. These adjectives are less descriptive than *exiguous, scanty, skimpy,* and *meager*, but they are broader in application and better suited to formal contexts, being applied to abstractions as well as to material things: The urchin's *scanty* clothing was *insufficient* for the winter, affording him *inadequate* protection against the cold. Although *insufficient* and *inadequate* are often used interchangeably, *insufficient* is a purely quantitative term, being applied to what is not enough, whereas *inadequate* may be qualitative as well, being applied to what is not good enough. *Insufficient* evidence can only mean not enough evidence, but *inadequate* evidence can mean either that the evidence is *insufficient* or that it is of dubious quality.

Sparse and **scarce** also refer to what is not abundant, but they deal with occurrence and do not necessarily involve need. *Sparse* is opposed to dense or thick, describing what is widely scattered in isolated clumps: *sparse* vegetation; a *sparse* crowd scattered thinly through the auditorium. What is *scarce* is temporarily in short supply, hard to get at a given time or in a given place: During World War II, sugar was *scarce* and had to be rationed. See LACK.

Antonyms: *ADEQUATE, PREVALENT.*

scarify. The verb *scarify* (make slight cuts in skin or tissue) has nothing to do with *scare*.

scatter
broadcast
diffuse
disperse
disseminate

These verbs mean separate and distribute widely. **Scatter**, the most general verb of this group, simply indicates the act of driving away or throwing about in different directions. [The wind *scatters* seed everywhere; With one bound the cat *scattered* all the pigeons.] **Broadcast** and **disseminate** both suggest the *scattering* of seed, but *disseminate* is now used exclusively in figurative senses, whereas *broadcast* retains its literal meaning of sowing by *scattering*: to *broadcast* seed. In a related sense *broadcast* and *disseminate* both mean make public or publish: to *broadcast* gossip; to *disseminate* the Gospel. *Disseminate* is broader in scope than *broadcast* and implies a wider audience and usually a longer duration: a lifetime of *disseminating* knowledge and spiritual guidance to those in need of it. *Broadcast*, on the other hand, may indicate only a single occurrence of making something public; in the sense here considered, it has a formal tone and sounds more appropriate in old-fashioned contexts than in contemporary ones: It was indelicate of the man to *broadcast* the intelligence that his wife was cuckolding him. Today, of course, *broadcast* has become more widely used to refer to the transmission of sounds by radio or television: a radio station that *broadcasts* news every hour on the hour; to *broadcast* a baseball game. Although *broadcast* is used of television as well as radio, telecast, formed on analogy with *broadcast*, and the more common televise may in time replace it in such contexts.

Diffuse emphasizes the relationship between the area covered and the relative density of the material spread out over it: the greater the area, the lower the density of the material. [The cloud cover *diffused* the light of the sun; The *diffused* light of the candles on every table lent a pleasant, intimate air to the restaurant.] Whereas *diffused* often indicates a graduated lessening of intensity over a broad area, **disperse** suggests a wide and sometimes forcible *scattering* of elements or individual things: The police quickly *dispersed* the unruly crowd. *Disperse* is often used figuratively: to *disperse* doubts and fears and instill confidence. See DIVIDE, PERMEATE, SPREAD.

Antonyms: *GATHER, UNITE.*

scoff
gibe
jeer
sneer
taunt

These verbs mean show disapproval or scorn by making remarks intended to belittle or disparage. To a greater or lesser extent, all of them have a hostile intent. To **scoff** is to speak slightingly and with derision of something usually accorded honor, reverence, or respect by people in general: to *scoff* at someone's fervent patriotism; to *scoff* at advice given by one's elders; to *scoff* at the teachings of a church.

Sneer carries a much stronger feeling of cynicism, superciliousness, and the deliberate wish to wound. To *sneer* is to make a contemptuous contortion of the facial muscles while uttering brief, cutting remarks that are intended to cast an unfavorable light on whatever is being attacked: to *sneer* at an adolescent's attempts to be independent; to *sneer* at the furniture in someone's home.

Jeer means *scoff* in a rude and open way. It carries the suggestion of mocking laughter and even shouting or booing: During the French Revolution crowds *jeered* at prisoners on their way to the guillotine.

Gibe and **taunt** mean rail at someone with sarcastic and contemptuous remarks: During the radio interview, the nasty critic *gibed* at the young novelist for imitating Hemingway. *Gibe*, however, also retains some of the meaning residing in its French derivation—treat roughly in play—and *gibing* may also be good-natured bantering or twitting: The two old men who strolled daily in the park constantly *gibed* at one another about their political opinions. *Taunt* is stronger than *gibe*. It means insult and upbraid in a defiant way and also carries overtones of reproach: The pupils *taunted* the new boy because he did not know how to play softball. As in *gibe*, there may be an element of teasing in *taunt*, but such teasing is likely to be harsh and cruel. See DESPISE, LAUGH, RIDICULE, SARCASTIC.

Antonyms: *PRAISE.*

scold
berate
chide
upbraid

These verbs pertain to the criticizing of one person by another. **Scold** is the most general and least formal of these. Often it can suggest an instance of reproof for misbehavior that is meted out by a superior, such as a parent or teacher: She *scolded* the child for being late. In this situation, *scold* may imply a distinction between a verbal reproach and reprimands that involve some form of punishment. Because of this, *scold* can sometimes suggest ineffectual attempts at discipline: We *scolded* our children frequently, but made no attempt to correct their unruly behavior. *Scold* can even suggest continual nagging to no purpose, whether about serious faults or about trivialities; here, the relationship need not be between superior and inferior: a woman who constantly *scolded* her husband about his low pay.

Chide, more formal than *scold,* is more exclusively focused on reproofs for specific failings. It can, however, suggest a wider range of emotional contexts, ranging in reference from angry rebukes or taunts to charitable efforts to help someone surmount shortcomings: gently *chiding* students every time they misspelled a word; the fury with which she *chided* the legislators for their lack of compassion.

Upbraid stresses the lengthy expression of displeasure or criticism, often of a total performance rather than a single failing. This may take the form of a harangue, a tongue-lashing, or a pep talk exhorting someone to better behavior. [He *upbraided* them about the sloppy way they kept track of their charge accounts; The coach *upbraided* the team for bungling play after play.]

Berate can be used in a vague way for the administering of any sort of reproof, but more often it can suggest total rejection of something or someone as being valueless, a judgment that can be delivered with no view to improving future performance. In this case, *berate* can also suggest an attitude of scorn or contempt for the thing being criticized, which is more often a whole pattern or way of life than a single instance of misbehavior: a young man who *berated* his parents for their social values. [A teacher who *berates* and belittles students is only admitting an inability to teach them anything.] See DISAPPROVAL, FAULTFINDING, MALIGN, REBUKE.

Antonyms: *PRAISE.*

scoop

bail
dig
ladle
shovel
spoon

These verbs all describe the use of implements in moving something from one place to another. **Scoop**

suggests a twisting or probing motion, often involving a good deal of effort, used to press into a substance and lift part of it out: to *scoop* ice cream out of a container. In informal use *scoop* is also used to mean gather into a heap, especially hastily: He *scooped* up the coins, thrust them in his pocket, and ran away.

Dig, the most general verb of this group, can be applied to any vigorous act of pressure or penetration: He *dug* a finger into my ribs menacingly. In its primary sense, however, *dig* means break up, turn up, or remove earth, as with an implement, claws, or fingers. [Gophers keep *digging* up the soil; She *dug* at the ground with the heel of her shoe; The workmen *dug* up the street with pneumatic drills.] *Dig*, unlike *scoop*, suggests a straight thrust into a substance, and whereas *scoop* emphasizes the process of lifting out, *dig* usually emphasizes the going in. [The cook *scooped* out some sugar and sprinkled it over the cake; to *dig* up buried treasure.] Also, *scoop* suggests open or shallow indentations in a surface, whereas *dig* can apply to any sort of excavation: *digging* miles of underground tunnels.

Shovel suggests a laborious, regularly repeated *digging* motion with a long-handled implement. *Shoveling* is hard work and typically involves the movement of something that does not yield easily or is heavy, such as earth, rock, or snow. The tools used to *shovel* vary in size from children's toys to huge, power-driven devices used for moving mounds of earth and boulders; therefore, the word *shoveling* in isolation indicates little about the amount *shoveled*.

Spoon and **ladle** point to the transferral of liquids from one vessel to another, as from a pot to a bowl. *Spooning* suggests smaller portions than *ladling*, which can indicate gross, careless, or hasty disposal of a substance: to *spoon* out medicine carefully; *ladling* out soup to hungry people. **Bail**, unlike the other verbs here considered, indicates the emptying of a boat of water to keep it from becoming swamped: After each wave, all hands started *bailing* with anything that would hold water.

section

area
locale
neighborhood
quarter
region

These nouns refer to parts of geographical or demographical entities. **Section**, the most general, can pinpoint a part of a city or country or even some natural formation: the *section* of desert surrounding the oasis. In its demographic sense, it might suggest a homogeneous population: the Spanish-speaking *section* of Harlem. But when the geographic sense predominates, no such limitations are applicable: diverse ethnic groups in that *section* of the country. In surveying, *section* can specifically indicate a plot of land one mile square, comprising 640 acres. **Area** suggests a larger, possibly less clearly defined subdividing of some entity: an *area* of the country that breaks naturally into two *sections* of opposing political attitudes; *areas* of coastal waters infested by sharks; an *area* of the city where the poorest families live. *Area* can also refer to computed square units: suburbs taking up one-third of the state's total *area.*

Region indicates an even larger subdivision than *area;* it would not be used to refer to a *section* of a city, for example, but would most often suggest a considerable stretch of territory with some unifying principle that distinguishes it from the surrounding territory: the main dialect *regions* of the United States; Russia's arctic *region.*

The remaining nouns stress the pinpointing aspect of *section,* suggesting even more clear-cut or smaller subdivisions. **Quarter** refers specifically to a *section* of a city that has a noticeable homogeneity or its own identifying flavor: the French *quarter;* the bohemian *quarter.* **Neighborhood** can indicate most concretely a residential grouping in towns or cities: a friendly *neighborhood.* Its implication of communal peaceableness need not be present: a racially tense *neighborhood. Neighborhood* can also be used to indicate something that is merely nearby or adjacent: in a *neighborhood* with accessible public transportation.

Locale can refer to any pinpointed environment: a *locale* in which fresh water was plentiful. More concretely it can refer to the exact place of an occurrence or event: unable to fix the *locale* where the scuffle took place. It can refer as well to the scene or setting of a work of art: The *locale* of the play was an unnamed Ivy League college; paintings that had Paris as their *locale.* See SITE.

sedate

earnest
grave
serious
sober
solemn
staid

These adjectives characterize anything that lacks or eschews frivolity or merriment because of social restraint, unsparing dedication, or urgent conditions. The emphases of **sedate** and **staid** are on restraint in

manners or behavior. *Sedate* points to unruffled self-possession and implies a flawless exterior of correctness, politeness, and propriety: a *sedate* gathering of quiet but interesting people; *sedate* matrons who sit supreme and secure at the bridge table. *Sedate* can sometimes apply critically to people or manufactured things that are genteel or too refined: the *sedate* indifference of well-bred Victorians to the miseries of the lower classes. But when applied outside the context of human affairs, *sedate* can refer more generally to anything serene or tranquil: the *sedate* hush of Indian summer. *Staid* is now used most commonly in a way comparable to the negative possibility for *sedate,* referring to manners that are straitlaced, unbending, prim, and pompous: plays that shock the sensibilities of *staid* ladies who attend Broadway matinees.

Solemn once could refer almost exclusively to an extremely formal and awe-inspiring religious ritual: a *solemn* requiem mass. This was extended to other rituals or formalities expressing a total commitment: a *solemn* oath; a *solemn* dedication to the cause of freedom. Now the adjective can also refer to a person or manner unleavened by lightheartedness: the *solemn* faces of couples awaiting news of the air disaster. As a term of disapproval, it can point to someone needlessly gloomy or lacking in humor: *solemn* parents aghast at the most innocuous amusements of their children.

When applied to a lack of humor, **serious** is much more neutral in tone; depending upon context, it can be approving, disinterested, or disapproving: a play she spoke of as the only really *serious* attempt at contemporary drama currently to be seen on Broadway; promising to give the suggestion her *serious* consideration; He couldn't bear people who were so *serious* all the time. In a comparable context, **grave** emphasizes an extremely *serious* manner that is intense and unrelieved. It may suggest as well a concerned, anxious, or troubled state: She gave him a *grave* look that showed how alarmed she was; inspecting his son's report card with a *grave* frown. When both adjectives apply to a state of urgency or crisis, *serious* suggests an uncertain condition that could well result in danger or failure: *serious* condition following the heart attack. *Grave,* however, may well suggest a state too far gone to expect full recovery, although it can be applied for emphasis to less extreme conditions: a *grave* lack of food on the lifeboat; a *grave* problem facing the nation. Both *grave* and *serious* can also be used for anything thought extremely bad; in this case, *grave* is again an intensification of *serious:* a *serious* lack of concern for others; a *grave* defiance of the law.

Sober and **earnest** apply more strictly than the

foregoing adjectives to human behavior and attitudes alone. *Sober* can refer at its most restricted to someone who is free of the influence of alcohol or illegal drugs: a test to determine whether the driver was *sober*. Used more generally, *sober* can suggest a wide-eyed, clearheaded approach, particularly in response to a *serious* or *grave* situation: a *sober* look at the growing political danger. It can also indicate unwavering devotion to a task: a life spent in *sober* dedication to the advancement of medicine. *Earnest* stresses this last possibility for *sober* and adds implications of zeal, selflessness, and single-mindedness: the *earnest* pursuit of her studies; *earnest* retired persons who express their idealism by joining the Peace Corps. *Earnest* can also apply to a momentary involvement in which someone is engrossed or becomes impassioned: *earnest* attention from his originally restless audience; *earnest* requests for more information. Neither *sober* nor *earnest* is useful in expressing disapproval for someone who is habitually *solemn* or overly *serious*. See DEDICATE, EAGER, FORMAL.

Antonyms: *easygoing, flighty, frivolous,* JAUNTY, *light-hearted.*

see

inspect
look
notice
observe
regard
watch
witness

These verbs refer to the attentive viewing of something. **See** is the most general of these, with a wide range of uses outside this context. Here it suggests equally well an accidental or deliberate viewing of an occurrence: happening to *see* the suspect in an alley; eager to *see* the outcome of the game. Because *see* is so general, it carries few connotations beyond those that context may give it. **Watch** stresses attention or fascination. Whether the viewing begins by accident or design, *watch* suggests the complete engagement of interest, at least while the watching continues. By contrast, one may *see* something happen and turn away without interest: *watching* the spider attempt to spin its web for the third time. *Watch,* furthermore, is common as an imperative, whereas *see* is much less frequently so used: Just *watch* what happens when I press this button.

Look is like *see* in suggesting no particular connotations for the act of viewing something: *looking* lazily out over the city; *looking* frantically for some sign that would indicate where the path lay. *Look* is like *watch,* however, in being frequently used as an imperative: *Look* at the lizard on that rock. In this use, *look* suggests the effort needed to *see* something before it disappears, whereas *watch* in the imperative might suggest a necessary attendance on a whole process about to begin. **Witness**, like *see,* is less frequently used in the imperative, but is more emphatic than *see* about an attentive viewing of an entire experience: coming in time to *witness* the changing of the guard; *witnessing* the gun battle from a second-story window. *Witness* may suggest either a deliberate or an accidental viewing.

All the remaining verbs can be used in the imperative as well as the declarative, but in either case, their emphasis on attentiveness is apparent. **Notice** suggests the taking in, almost by chance, of a small detail that may yet be important to some larger pattern: *noticing* that he kept his fist clenched in his pocket as he talked. In the imperative, *notice* is a call to attend to some small detail that might otherwise be overlooked: *Notice* the small scratch on the handle of this pistol. **Regard** suggests viewing at a distance in a safe, prearranged position or with a definite emotional attitude: *regarding* with suspicion the movements of the man across the street. **Observe** is like *regard* in suggesting a process of viewing something from one or more vantage points, but it implies a detached, almost clinical frame of mind engrossed in a detailed examination: *observing* the customs of the tribe for two full years. Like *watch, observe* in the imperative suggests a process about to unfold. Only its slightly greater formality distinguishes *observe* from *watch* in this usage: *Observe* the expression on her face when she hears the verdict. Of this group of verbs, **inspect** puts the most emphasis by far on a thorough and detailed examination of something through direct handling or involvement with it: *inspecting* the child's body for any sign of the recurring rash; *Inspect* these photographs of the two murder weapons. See EXAMINE, FIND, PERCEIVE, STUDY.

Antonyms: *disregard, ignore, miss, neglect, overlook.*

send

deliver
dispatch
forward
ship
transmit

These verbs refer to the moving of objects or materials from one point to another. **Send** is the least formal and most general of these verbs, carrying no implications about what is *sent* or how: *sending* my answer by return mail; *sending* trunks ahead by boat. With *send*, however, the movement is viewed specifically from the point of origin rather than from its destination: wondering if she ever received the letter I *sent* a month ago.

Dispatch suggests urgency or speed: *dispatching* three fire engines to combat the blaze; *dispatching* a messenger who would arrive before sundown. *Dispatch* may also suggest a central agent who assigns vehicles to specific tasks: *dispatching* taxicabs by radio to all points in the city. With **deliver**, the movement of an object can be viewed exclusively in terms of the point of destination: Most manufactured goods were *delivered* to San Francisco by water or stagecoach. But in the context of retailing, *deliver* is often synonymous with *send*: trading only with stores that *deliver*; asking them to *deliver* the groceries in an hour.

Forward and **transmit** imply a movement that is less than direct. *Forward* suggests an intermediate or incorrect destination from which the object must then travel to its ultimate goal: a variety of Russian goods that are *forwarded* through Sweden; *forwarding* the letter to his new address. *Transmit* may suggest the *sending* of the contents or equivalent of a document or thing, rather than the original itself: *transmitting* the details of the conference to the president; *transmitting* the message by ship-to-shore telephone. **Ship** indicates the moving of produce or effects by sea, air, rail, or truck. It now usually suggests a commercial operation and, if effects are involved, transportation that is unaccompanied by the owner: left our furniture to be *shipped* after us once we were settled in new quarters; goods scheduled to be *shipped* by boxcar or trucks. See GO, MOVE.

Antonyms: *keep, receive, retain.*

sensation

feeling
percept
perception
sense

These nouns are comparable but not closely synonymous when used to refer to a response to a stimulus or to the ability to make such a response. In a technical sense, **sensation** is applicable to an impression originating either from within or from outside the body and conveyed to the nervous system by the organs of seeing, hearing, touching, tasting, or smelling. However, *sensation* does not necessarily imply an identification of the stimulus: to experience a *sensation* of warmth. In general usage, the meaning of *sensation* is extended to include not only sensing but also the attendant emotional and mental responses: to have a *sensation* that everyone is staring at you; a recollection that brought a *sensation* of sadness.

Sense, as here considered, may refer strictly to the physical agencies (taste, touch, sight, hearing, and smell) by or through which a person or animal receives impressions. In the plural it is applicable to the total awareness of the world around one: She came to her *senses* in a hospital bed. Whatever one experiences through the *senses* is a *sensation*.

Perception in this context involves interpretation of a stimulus and recognition of the object that produces a *sensation*. *Perception* is always based on experience and is the process by which people become acquainted with their environment. Whereas a *sensation* does not suggest the agency of the mind, *perception* implies that the stimulus creating a *sensation* has been registered, however unconsciously, on the brain.

Percept, closely related in meaning to *perception*, is a term in psychology and is applied to the immediate knowledge and recognition of an object gained by perceiving it. A dog will have the *sensation* of seeing or even of smelling a chair; it knows the chair is an obstacle to be walked around, but will gain no *percept* or *perception* of what a chair is.

Feeling, the most general noun in the group, is sometimes used loosely in place of *sense, sensation,* and *perception*. *Feeling* applies more precisely to the faculty by which one perceives *sensations* of pain, pressure, heat and cold, contact, etc. It may also refer to kinesthesia—the *perception* of muscular movement, tension, or tone derived from the functioning of nerves connected with muscle tissue, skin, joints, and tendons: After John's spinal injury, he had no *feeling* in his legs. See AWARE, EMOTION, OBSERVANT, PERCEIVE.

sensible

lucid
rational
reasonable
sane

These adjectives characterize an intelligent and objective approach to problems or behavior that is temperate, fair, and sound. **Sensible** puts less emphasis on intelligence than on common sense; it suggests an attitude that is prudent, calmly controlled, considerate, understanding, and aware of consequences by virtue of distilled experience: the few *sensible* children who refused to indulge in the foolish fads of the day; a *sensible* approach to a controversial subject; the plain, *sensible* people who are the backbone of the nation. **Reasonable** is similar to *sensible* in emphasizing the value of distilled experience, but its connotations are slightly different in suggesting an approach or situation that is fair, just, objective, or unemotional in its avoidance of extremes: a *reasonable* price; *reasonable* men and women who eschewed the witch-hunting hysteria that was convulsing Salem; asking her son to be *reasonable* about his demands for the family car. Oddly enough, **rational** rather than *reasonable* is the adjective here that is most emphatic about the value of reason as a guide; this contrasts with the stress on experience implied by the previous adjectives. Most specifically, it points to a problem-solving process of thinking that employs valid or logical methods in reaching conclusions: a *rational* way of going about the myriad tasks involved in city planning; a *rational* explanation for the enigmatic events surrounding the catastrophe. *Rational* may also indicate a coherent mind, one that is not mentally imbalanced or at the mercy of overpowering emotions: becoming more *rational* as the tranquilizer took effect; psychiatrists who debated whether the accused man was *rational* enough to stand trial.

Lucid and **sane** are both directed to this last meaning of *rational*. *Lucid* indicates a mind free of internal pressures or distortions: *lucid* intervals between bouts of catatonic depression. It can refer to a *rational* approach or train of thought that is particularly clear, understandable, or helpful in its simplicity: a *lucid* argument against the theories advanced in the article. *Sane* is commonly used in ordinary speech and in legal terminology to refer to someone who is not psychotic. *Sane* has no usefulness, however, to psychologists: declared to have been *sane* at the time of the murders; struggling to stay *sane* in a mad world. *Sane* also has a use akin to *reasonable* in referring to a fair, just, or *sensible* approach: *sane* legislation to deal with the problem; *sane* attitudes toward disciplining children. See ACUMEN, MIND, WORKABLE.

Antonyms: *confused, impractical, incoherent,* PSYCHOTIC, *unreasonable.*

sentence
condemn
convict
doom

These words have to do with judgment—the finding of guilt and the imposing of punishment. **Sentence** and **convict** are legal terms, and both may be nouns as well as verbs. To *sentence* offenders is to state the penalties they must pay for crimes or misdemeanors. To *convict* defendants is to find them guilty of the offenses with which they are charged. A person on trial who has been *convicted* by a jury is then *sentenced* by a judge: She was *convicted* of second-degree murder and *sentenced* to from twenty years to life in prison. The noun *sentence* denotes the penalty imposed on a defendant. A *sentence* may be pronounced (or a person may be *sentenced*) in cases where guilt is admitted by the accused, is determined by a judge, or is found by a jury: let off with a suspended *sentence* and a light fine; *sentenced* to ninety days; the death *sentence*. The noun *convict* is a term applied to a person serving a *sentence* in prison: an escaped *convict;* an ex-*convict*.

Condemn and **doom** imply severe or irrevocable judgments. Where *convict* and *sentence* are factual and neutral, *condemn* and *doom* can express emotional disapproval for excessive punishment or harsh treatment: an innocent man *condemned* to die; *doomed* by shreds of circumstantial evidence. The connotations of *condemn* and *doom* can be misused by defense lawyers or crime reporters to win sympathy or to bolster a sensational approach. *Condemn*, however, has a more neutral use to indicate something that does not measure up to official minimum standards of health and decency: a building *condemned* as a health hazard. Sometimes, the disapproval inherent in *condemn* in official use has advisory rather than legal force: The bar association *condemned* the lawyer's actions but did not disbar her. *Doom,* referring originally to Doomsday, the day of the last judgment, can still sometimes suggest supernatural powers believed to determine a person's fate: *doomed* to hell for his profligate life.

When *condemn* and *doom* apply more widely, *condemn* is still likely to carry implications of a conscious and overt judgment that is harsh, excessive, and cruel: Croats *condemned* to concentration camps. *Doom,* by contrast, stresses hopelessness and inevitability that may be the result of deplorable circumstances as well as human callousness: children *doomed* to ghetto life. See DISAPPROVAL, KILL.

Antonyms: EXONERATE, *free, liberate.*

sentimental
effusive
gushing
maudlin

mawkish
mushy
romantic
slushy

These adjectives characterize emotionalism that is excessive, unrealistic, false, or affected. **Sentimental** once could refer neutrally or approvingly to the capacity for feeling deeply about serious matters; it is occasionally still used approvingly, though even here it applies to more trivial emotions, particularly to nostalgia: She kept the ribbon from her corsage as a *sentimental* memento of her first formal dance. Otherwise, *sentimental* is widely understood as disapproving in tone, pertaining to an inappropriate willingness to be moved at the slightest prompting or by situations that do not warrant genuine feeling. *Sentimental* does not censure all feeling, only that which is trivial, forced, or excessive; no one would think it *sentimental* to weep at the death of a friend; many people, on the other hand, would think it *sentimental* to supply a funeral and tombstone for, say, a pet dog that had died. **Romantic** has gone through a similar shift, although the split in meaning still exists. It once referred to the expression of deep feeling, or the valuing of feeling above form. As such, it names an artistic era or indicates works of art from any era that display this legitimate emphasis. Those who prefer a different emphasis, however, can use *romantic* disapprovingly to point to chaotic or formless emotionality: *romantic* blithering about originality and artistic freedom. On a much less formal level, *romantic* can refer descriptively or approvingly to things pertaining to love between a man and woman: glances that hinted of her *romantic* interest.

Effusive and **gushing** both refer to copious displays of any sort of emotion. *Effusive* may be approving or neutral: *effusive* in their thanks for the host's hospitality. More often, it emphasizes excessive or insincere displays: finding his *effusive* flattery unbearable. With *gushing*, only disapproval is possible, pointing with more severity to extreme or silly displays: the *gushing* letters they wrote. **Mushy** at its most informal suggests contempt for *romantic* love: rejecting any interest in girls as being *mushy*. It can also suggest a rejection of trivial or *sentimental* attitudes toward such emotions: a *mushy* love story. **Slushy** is even more critical of such attitudes toward love than *mushy*. It suggests a rejection of love seen as occasions for self-pity, weeping, and a *sentimental* evasion of reality: *slushy* soap operas.

Maudlin and **mawkish** are considerably more formal than the previous pair and more specific in meaning. *Maudlin* derives ultimately from the second name of Mary Magdalene, who was often depicted with her eyes swollen from weeping; *maudlin* now suggests strong disapproval for excessive emotionalism, especially of a tearful sort: a *maudlin* tearjerker that enthralled its audience. *Mawkish* emphasizes the falsity of excessive emotions, their awkwardness and feebleness, or their offense against good taste. Unlike *maudlin*, *mawkish* applies to any sort of emotion and is even stronger in its pejorative overtones: *mawkish* appeals to the prejudices of his audiences. See BANAL.

Antonyms: *cynical*, IMPERTURBABLE, *objective*, *realistic*, *sardonic*, *unmoved*.

separate

detach
disconnect
disengage
dismember
disunite

These verbs refer to the breaking down of a grouping into smaller units. They are all alike in suggesting some division other than a splitting into equal parts. **Separate** is the most general in suggesting either a sorting out of items from an amorphous mixture or the taking apart of things intimately joined or fused: *separating* the scored examination papers into percentile groupings; *separating* the whites and yolks of three eggs. Used intransitively, *separate* may also stress volition: members of the tour who wished to *separate* from the main group.

Detach and **disconnect** are restricted mostly to the taking apart of solid objects that retain their individual identities after the separation: *detaching* the check from its stub; *disconnecting* the lamp from the wall socket. *Detach* specifically suggests the removing of a part from a larger whole, especially when the two are designed to come apart as an added convenience in their functioning: *detaching* the bayonet from his rifle so that he could use it as a machete; *detaching* one platoon as a backstop for the rest of the company. *Disconnect* does not suggest this part-from-whole relationship so much as it indicates the separation of linked objects or components: *disconnecting* the turntable in order to plug in the tape recorder. In more general uses, *detach* may suggest the removal of a small part from a larger mass: *detaching* the snail from the glass wall of the aquarium. *Disconnect* may suggest any loss of contact: complaining to the telephone operator that they had been *disconnected*.

Disengage may suggest withdrawal from contact,

especially from a close-fitting, interlocking, or inter-mingled union: *disengaging* the pieces of the puzzle; *disengaging* himself from the project. It may also suggest taking something out of operation: *disengaging* the safety catch.

Dismember and **disunite** stress a deleterious breaking apart. *Dismember* suggests removing a part from a whole, but contrasts strongly with *detach* in rejecting the implication of a designed or normal uncoupling: *dismembering* the butterfly by pulling off its wings. *Disunite* suggests most specifically the breaking up of an amorphous group so that it can no longer function as an entity, even though no visible rupture may have taken place: a political party so *disunited* that it was unable to agree on a platform. *Disunite,* alone of these verbs, would almost always suggest a breaking down into many smaller units: internal dissension designed only to *disunite* us and turn us into squabbling factions. See SEVER.

Antonyms: *combine, consolidate, engage.*

sequence
progression
series
succession

These nouns are alike in denoting a group of things that come or are brought together in some particular order or according to a plan. They are further alike in that the order they refer to is one in which the things grouped together follow each other. **Sequence** designates a following in space, time, or thought and suggests that the things brought together reflect some logical system: making sure the chassis parts were added in proper *sequence;* the *sequence* of arguments in a discourse. **Succession** emphasizes the following, one after the other, of similar objects or events, without interruption. Unlike *sequence, succession* can, but does not necessarily, imply a logical ordering: a *succession* of hereditary monarchs; a *succession* of catastrophes.

Progression fixes the attention chiefly upon the act, process, or state of moving forward and has particular reference to mathematics and music. A mathematical *progression* is a *sequence* of numbers or quantities, each derived from the preceding by a constant relationship. Musical *progression* can designate either a *succession* of tones, chords, etc., or the movement from one tone or chord to another.

A **series** is a number of things ordered or arranged according to a similarity of nature or on the basis of like relationships. Although it is therefore much like *sequence* or *succession, series* suggests the individuality

of the connected things rather than that they merely follow one another: a long *series* of successes in the theater. See ORGANIZE.

sever
cleave
split
sunder

These verbs refer to the breaking or cutting apart of something by force. **Sever** is a formal term for any such action, though it often specifically suggests the cutting of a part from a larger whole: an accident that *severed* his legs; being sure to *sever* auxiliary shoots from a plant so that they will not weaken the main stem. **Sunder** is an even more formal word for forceful separation, but it more often pertains to breaking something into two halves or equals. *Sunder* is now rarely used except in metaphoric senses: a civil war that *sundered* brother from brother.

Split may suggest any forceful cutting or tearing action: *splitting* rails with a sharp ax; *splitting* his pants when he bent over. In one of it senses, however, it relates closely to **cleave**, since both verbs can refer to a voluntary separation within an entity, usually into equal halves: the way cells *split* during mitosis; a club that *split* up after the group's graduation. Where *split* is informal, often extremely so, *cleave* is nearly as formal as *sever* and *sunder* and may, most specifically, suggest a biological context: when the egg begins to *cleave* after fertilization. *Cleave* can be confusing, however, since it can apply to clinging fast as well as to breaking apart. Outside the biological context, *cleave* is mostly used as a metaphor: the ship's prow, gaily *cleaving* the waves. More specifically, *cleave* can refer to the cutting action of an instrument, for example, a meat cleaver: carefully *cleaving* the steak into equal portions. See DIVIDE, HEW, PIERCE, SEPARATE.

Antonyms: *fuse.*

several
divers
diverse
few
sundry
various

These adjectives characterize small groups of more than two members. **Several** emphasizes the fact that more than two are involved; **few** adds to this minimal restriction an unspecified maximum restriction, emphasizing the smallness of such a group: *several* friends dropped in during the day, but only a *few* stayed for dinner. Both adjectives are useful precisely because they are vague, but neither has any connotative richness.

Diverse and **divers** are different in pointing to a larger, though still restricted group. Furthermore, each adds implications that make both more specific than *several* and *few*. When *divers* is substituted for *several*, it stresses the variety or disunity within the grouping: *divers* attitudes expressed by the panel members. *Divers* may have an archaic sound to it, but in any case it is more formal than *diverse*. *Diverse* is even stronger in its emphasis on dissimilarities among members of a group. In fact, *diverse* may suggest a deliberate selection to give a representative cross section of types that are varied or diversified in form or kind: an anthology representing the *diverse* kinds of poetry being written by contemporary poets.

Sundry, in contrast with *diverse*, emphasizes the randomness of differences among members of a group indefinite in size. *Sundry* carries a tone of casual but deliberate approximation: the *sundry* skills that go into making up a musical comedy. It can also suggest dissimilar things viewed in isolation rather than collected in a group: *sundry* times and places. **Various** is less formal than *sundry* but is more matter-of-fact about a wide representation of differing things, whether actually grouped together or looked at in isolation: *various* trees dotting the landscape; *various* sorts of people out for a walk. A common phrase couples this pair of adjectives, but with no gain in specificity or flavor: *various* and *sundry* Madison Avenue types.

Antonyms: *none, one.*

shackle

　chain
　fetter
　handcuff
　manacle
　tether

These verbs refer to being tied or bound up so that one cannot move freely. **Shackle** refers literally to the binding of ankles or wrists or both. The bands or straps used can be attached to another person or group so *shackled* or to a post or stationary object: *shackled* hand and foot to the prison wall. Figuratively, *shackle* suggests something that frustrates progress along a certain line: youthful minds already *shackled* by the prejudices of their parents; a government *shackled* by an inflexible foreign policy.

Manacle and **fetter** both deal with a separate and specific aspect of *shackle*. *Manacle* refers to the binding of hands or wrists, *fetter* to the binding of feet. As with *shackle*, the binding may be by a band or strap; both hands or feet may be *manacled* or *fettered* together, or one of each may be attached to one of another person's: raising her *manacled* hands in protest; one hand *manacled* to the policeman who arrested him; *fettered* so that he could barely walk about his cell; convicts *fettered* to each other by a heavy chain. In figurative uses, these distinctions are frequently forgotten, and both verbs are used interchangeably with *shackle*. On this level, however, *fetter* suggests less loss of freedom than *shackle,* and *manacle* an even greater loss: a slow-moving program that was *fettered* by congressional caution; an apathetic populace *manacled* by desperate need and squalor. In using any of these three verbs figuratively, the literal image remains strong, so ridiculous comparisons should be avoided. [The hand that rocked the cradle was *fettered* to the home; The current generation is *shackled* to its lust for speed and rapid changes of pace.]

Handcuff and **tether** are still more specifically restricted than the foregoing verbs. A *handcuff* (noun) is two circles of metal connected by a short chain. As with *manacle,* both wrists of a person may be *handcuffed* together, or one wrist may be *handcuffed* to another person's wrist or to a fixed object. *Tether* most specifically suggests an animal tied to a fixed stake by a cord or chain that is attached to its neck, giving the animal a limited circle in which to move or graze. Figuratively, *tether* implies setting a limited area within which freedom is permitted but beyond which it is impossible to go: *tethered* within a four-year program of required courses; a group *tethered* to tedious pieties that no longer mean anything.

Chain, while specifying the material with which the binding is done, is the most general verb here in that it can refer to any manner of binding whatever. Unlike the other verbs, it can also suggest a more complete loss of freedom: *chained* so that he could neither stand, sit, nor lie down at full length. Figuratively, it suggests an impediment to free movement that is difficult to overcome: *chained* to archaic notions of economics. See CONFINE, THWART.

Antonyms: *extricate, free, liberate, release, unchain.*

shake

　quake
　quiver
　shiver

shake *(continued)*

shudder
tremble

These verbs refer to agitated movements that are quick, slight, or intense and are often involuntary expressions of strain or discomfort. **Shake**, the most general, is unique in this group because it can designate something that is done to as well as by a person or object: *shaking* her fist in rage; branches *shaking* in the wind. **Quiver** is more specific in suggesting a rapid but almost imperceptible vibration: ropes that *quivered* tautly under his hands; a network of ripples that *quivered* momentarily across the surface of the pool; almost *quivering* with delight. **Quake** suggests a more violent upheaval: the ground *quaking* beneath them as the bombardment began; his heart *quaking* with panic.

The remaining verbs apply best to the involuntary *shaking* of a person or animal; when they are used of natural objects an anthropomorphic overtone persists. **Tremble** is like *quiver* in suggesting a quick but slight movement; to this are added implications of uneasy or nervous discomposure: hands that *trembled* with eagerness as he opened the letter; leaves *trembling* in the faint breeze.

Shiver is like *tremble* except for specifically suggesting coldness or fear as the cause of the slight, rapid movement: beginning to *shiver* as the intense cold pervaded the room; *shivering* inwardly at the thought of having to explain why they had stayed away so long. **Shudder** suggests a more intense *shaking* than either *tremble* or *shiver*, suggesting horror, revulsion, or extreme pleasure as possible causes for the involuntary movement: *shuddering* at the touch of her gnarled hand. Although *shudder* may be nearly as intense as *quake*, it may suggest movement less noticeable to an onlooker: *shuddering* breathlessly in the doorway until the pursuer had raced past. See TOTTER, VIBRATE.

sham

bogus
fake
mock
phony

These adjectives suggest imitations or substitutes that are poorly or unconvincingly executed. **Sham** specifically suggests the hypocritical acting out of roles or the display of pretended virtues so as to result in a deliberate or unconscious travesty of the real thing: *sham* piety that sorted ill with their actual behavior; a *sham* marriage entered into to qualify for citizenship. **Mock** is close to *sham* in suggesting an outrageously

bad or hypocritical pretense to virtue, especially when done with overblown grandiosity: windy oratory full of *mock* patriotism. *Mock*, however, has a growing use as a neutral term to describe something intended to deceive no one but having a usefulness of its own: *mock* turtle soup; a *mock* battle.

Fake suggests a copy or substitute that may but need not be intended to deceive: *fake* loyalty that won his employer's admiration; buying a *fake* fur to wear in cold weather. **Bogus** stresses the inherent worthlessness of the copy or imitation: *bogus* sentiment; *bogus* currency. **Phony**, aside from its simple pejorative use for a deliberate deception, stresses conscious hypocrisy that is never self-deceiving: a *phony* scholar who freely plagiarized the work of others. *Phony* is the most informal adjective of this group and perhaps most pejorative in its assault on priggishness and pretentiousness: a *phony* show-off. See ARTIFICIAL, SPURIOUS.
Antonyms: *GENUINE*.

shame

abash
discomfit
embarrass
faze
mortify
rattle

These verbs express various shades of meaning implicit in the general idea of feeling or of making others feel uncomfortable in situations or under circumstances that involve a loss of self-esteem. **Shame**, the strongest of them, implies a painful sense of guilt or of degradation arising from a consciousness of acting in an unworthy or dishonorable way. [She *shamed* him by her courage in the emergency; He was *shamed* by his failure to pass the test.] **Mortify** is somewhat milder, suggesting humiliation or chagrin resulting from an unpleasant experience: The teacher was *mortified* by her pupil's poor showing. (Note that in this sense it can sometimes be replaced by *ashamed: mortified* by or *ashamed* of one's behavior.) It may also signify punishment or decay: to *mortify* the flesh by fasting; the *mortification* of gangrenous tissue.

Embarrass means make self-conscious or uncomfortable: a woman *embarrassed* by her mother's intolerant outburst at the party. It may also denote the checking or hindering of thought, speech, or a course of action: an *embarrassing* setback to his plans; to *embarrass* an opponent by asking awkward questions. **Abash** means confuse or disconcert, as by arousing a sudden consciousness of inferiority. [The child was *abashed* by his mother's reproof; No amount of scorn or ridicule could *abash* him.]

Discomfit still carries its former military sense of defeating or routing an enemy: He took satisfaction from having *discomfited* his rival. More loosely, it can be used, instead of *embarrass* or *abash*, to suggest discomfort short of humiliation or defeat: *discomfited* because they had lost the directions. **Faze** carries the meaning of worry, vex, or disturb and is generally used in the negative sense: He was not *fazed* by the attacks made on his character. **Rattle** implies a state of emotional confusion or agitation: The speaker was *rattled* by the constant interruptions. See EMBARRASSMENT, UPSET.

Antonyms: ENCOURAGE, UPHOLD.

shameful

disgraceful
dishonorable
ignominious
scandalous

These adjectives all characterize conduct or a condition that violates standards of probity or morality. **Shameful** and **disgraceful** express strong disapproval and often shock at someone else's transgressions. Both adjectives are commonly used for emphasis to reveal profound indignation on the part of the speaker or writer. They are more meaningful in suggesting attitude than in objectively describing shocking situations: a *disgraceful* exhibition of poor sportsmanship; a *shameful* display of ingratitude. Strictly speaking, a *shameful* act would bring shame or obloquy upon the person performing the act, and a *disgraceful* act would bring disgrace. This distinction is not commonly observed, and all that can be said is that *disgraceful* usually indicates a greater degree of indignation than *shameful*. *Shameful* may also suggest a note of sadness rather than contempt, as at an unfortunate condition: It was *shameful* how flabby the former athlete had become. *Disgraceful* would be too strong in this context; it is limited more usually to acts felt to be outrageous: a *disgraceful* misuse of federal funds.

Dishonorable, though also revealing a highly critical attitude, has more objective relevance than either *shameful* or *disgraceful* and retains more of its original sense of imputing dishonor. It is a formal term of high seriousness and would not ever be applied to comparatively trivial circumstances involving manners or the like. *Dishonorable* applies to one's character and to one's good name. [It was *dishonorable* of him to take credit for having written a book he had not written; The soldier received a *dishonorable* discharge for desertion.]

Ignominious and **scandalous** are both closely related to *shameful*. *Ignominious* suggests behavior that subjects one to humiliation; *scandalous* suggests sensational actions that flagrantly violate accepted standards of morality and hence stimulate reactions of intense revulsion or contempt. [Her *scandalous* affairs shocked her friends; In the U.S., the fate of some public officials who are convicted of crime may be *ignominious*—once they leave prison, they find themselves forgotten.] *Ignominious* is now widely used to refer to anything that diminishes one's self-respect: She suffered through an *ignominious* silence when asked to explain her absence. See BAD, DISGRACE, EMBARRASSMENT, IGNOBLE, OUTRAGEOUS, REPREHENSIBLE.

Antonyms: *exemplary, glorious, honorable, proud, reputable, upright, upstanding.*

share

commune
join
partake
participate
relate

These verbs pertain to the coming together of two or more people to accomplish a common task or pleasure. **Share** is the most general of these and is relatively informal. It may suggest the mere dividing of a portion or activity: *sharing* the profits; *sharing* the cleanup job to make it go faster. Often, however, an added note of friendliness or warmth of feeling is present: *sharing* an intense, unspoken sympathy. **Join** is like *share* in its informality; it may also stress good fellowship, especially in the sense of banding together for a common activity: neighbors who *joined* together in rebuilding the stricken family's home; spontaneously *joining* in on the refrains of the song. This note of voluntary goodwill, however, may be totally absent: forcing them to *join* in digging the mass grave. *Join* often suggests the action of a person who becomes part of an existing group: *joining* the tour in Rome.

Participate, although considerably more formal, is like one aspect of *join* in suggesting a joining or taking part in group activity: a shy student who finally learned to *participate* in the group discussions. *Participate* implies a more active role than is necessarily the case with *share* or *join:* members who *join* the club and *share* in its ideals but still do not *participate* in the club's programs. **Partake** is closer in meaning to *share* than to *join* or *participate,* although it is more formal than any of these verbs. It might, in fact, seem excessively formal in some cases. It suggests most specifically the receiving or taking of portions, especially of food: picnickers who *partook* of a sumptuous though improvised feast. Sometimes the emphasis on food is felt so strongly that *partake* is used even for a person eating alone: *partaking* of her solitary meal.

Commune is more like another aspect of *share* in emphasizing an intense give-and-take of quiet but warm feeling: They *communed* with wordless, unhurried glances. Like *partake*, *commune* may be used of a lone person, in which case it might suggest an internal dialogue or a silent responsiveness to one's surroundings, especially a natural setting: a woman who sat *communing* with experiences long past; *communing* with nature. The last example is a stock phrase that illustrates a certain preciousness that may be present when *commune* appears in this context.

Relate in current usage has become a fad word referring to interpersonal relationships: an autistic child completely unable to *relate* to anyone; people who *relate* to others only superficially. See ASSOCIATE.

shore

bank
beach
coast
littoral
strand

These nouns refer to land lying along a body of water. **Shore**, the most general of these, refers to any sort of land that borders a large water mass, such as a lake or ocean: the *shores* of Lake Superior; the western *shore* of the Atlantic. As can be seen, *shore* most strictly regards this meeting of land and water from the view of the limit set on the water. **Coast** reverses the view, indicating the limits set on the land. Also, *coast* is most pertinent to a long stretch of land taken as a whole, making it most appropriate in reference to land masses along an ocean: the British *coast;* the states along the Pacific *coast*. One would speak of the *shore* of a small island, rather than of its *coast*.

In contrast to these nouns, **bank** applies specifically to any sort of land bordering a river: the *banks* of the Wabash. *Coast* would never be used in this sense and *shore* seldom, perhaps only when emphasizing a river's width: calling to them from the opposite *shore* of the river. *Bank,* however, has an additional specific reference to a steep slope or jut of land above the water's edge: diving from the *bank* into the swimming hole. In this sense, *bank* would suggest a moderate jut of earth beside a pond or river; if higher land or a stony outcropping beside a lake or tidal water is in question, the nouns bluff or cliff would be more appropriate in connotation. **Beach** contrasts sharply with *bank,* referring to a gradual slope, especially of sand, rather than to an earthy steepness. A *beach* may exist, however, either beside fresh or salt water, lake or ocean, and even along a river: a *beach* formed along the wide bend of a river; Greek islands with naturally sandy *beaches*. *Beach* may also specifically suggest a sandy *shore* that has been designed for public use: opening two new *beaches* in the last three years.

Strand and **littoral** both apply mainly to ocean *shores*, or at least to land along tidal water. *Strand* may now sound old-fashioned or stilted, but it does refer specifically to the area of land between high and low tide: When the tide was out, we walked along the *strand*. *Littoral* can refer to exactly the same area as *strand* but without risking a stilted tone: sea pools along the *littoral*, where many sea creatures live between high tides. It is extremely formal and technical in tone, however, and can also refer to both the strip of land and the shallow water that lie to either side of the water line: ecological studies of the Aleutian *littoral*.

shorten

abbreviate
abridge
curtail
cut
dock

These verbs are comparable in their denotation of reducing the length, extent, or duration of something. **Shorten** means make or seem to make short or shorter, and can refer either to dimension or duration: angry with the new fashion that forced her to *shorten* all her skirts; forced to *shorten* her lunch hour because of a heavy work schedule; hoping to *shorten* the waiting time in his office.

Curtail and **cut** imply *shortening* through removal of a part of the whole. *Curtail* suggests a lessening, as in quality or effectiveness, because of the removal of some important part: a department store whose business suffered when it *curtailed* deliveries to suburban customers. *Cut,* which suggests an editing process, may or may not remove something important: Some movies seen on TV suffer when they are *cut* badly to fit into a *shortened* time slot. **Dock** has the specific meaning of *cut* off the end of something: *dock* a dog's tail. It also is used specifically in the sense of reduce: wages *docked* for excessive lateness.

Abridge and **abbreviate** carry the idea of *shortening* so that what remains represents the whole adequately. *Abridge* suggests *cutting* away of nonessentials while retaining the core. *Abbreviate,* generally used in reference to words or phrases, implies *shortening* by compression or omission of parts, the remainder standing for the whole: to *abridge* a novel for inclusion in a magazine; the *abbreviated* name of an advertising agency. See COMPACT, DECREASE, LESSEN, REDUCE.

Antonyms: ENLARGE, EXTEND.

show
display
evince
exhibit
manifest

These verbs refer to the revealing, demonstrating, or clarifying of something. **Show** is the most informal and general of these, with a wide range of possible uses: *showing* his teeth when he smiled; *showing* off her diving ability. *Show* is particularly useful to indicate acts that communicate an attitude or result in a visible or unmistakable sign: *showing* enthusiasm for the sketches; a gift chosen to *show* how much she cared.

Evince and **manifest** are the most formal of these verbs and are both restricted in use to suggest the giving of a sign. *Evince* may point to a subtle or slight exposure or to something that shows itself in a rudimentary or initial state: first *evincing* a grudging interest in the work project and finally becoming absorbed in it; her cool manner *evincing* a restrained hostility toward their new friend; a flair for color and form that first *evinced* itself in grade school. *Manifest* indicates an unmistakable or much clearer revealing. Unlike *evince,* it would suggest something that requires no investigation but is plainly evident to anyone: a hunger that *manifested* itself in strange ways; a region *manifesting* a luxuriance of flora and fauna.

Display and **exhibit** both emphasize an exposure such as results from deliberately putting something on full view. *Display* may suggest a painfully obvious or flaunting exposure: *displaying* his drunkenness openly on the street; beach bums *displaying* their physiques. *Exhibit* may stress instead a more matter-of-fact tone, suggesting that something is almost clinically put on view for consideration or evaluation: *exhibiting* the murder weapon to the jury; a gallery *exhibiting* a new painter's work. Both, however, can function less specifically as more formal substitutes for *show: displaying,* by a sign, a readiness to depart with him; *exhibiting* slight nervousness as he read the poem. See HINT, MEAN, MEANING.

Antonyms: *cloak, conceal, disguise, hide, mask, suppress.*

showy
colorful
loud
ostentatious

These adjectives characterize persons or things that are conspicuous because of their vivid or garish physical makeup or because of some striking or vulgar manner of behavior. **Showy** is a neutral term and may be used in either a complimentary or critical way. It can refer to a great or brilliant display, and in this sense may characterize such things as beauty, ability, technique, performance, or achievement: a *showy* floral arrangement, done with originality; a pianist with a *showy* technique. In its pejorative sense *showy* suggests a cheap display and is used to describe persons or things that in some way are offensive to good taste: a *showy* team of ballroom dancers whose performance was more gymnastic than graceful; the *showy* furniture chosen by someone with little knowledge of interior decoration.

Colorful may suggest an abundance of color or colors, usually bright and vivid, and often contrasting: a *colorful* afghan so beautiful that I use it as a wall hanging. *Colorful* can also describe something picturesque and full of variety: a *colorful* novella about life in the Old West. Finally, it can characterize a person who draws attention by a striking, individualistic, or even eccentric manner: my *colorful,* crotchety grandfather; a *colorful* character actor whose off-stage life was as flamboyant as his acting.

Loud and **ostentatious** are more definitely pejorative in connotation than *showy* or *colorful. Loud,* in the sense being compared here, is synonymous with the critical meaning of *showy.* In reference to objects, it denotes flashiness and offensively bad taste: a *loud* jacket with clashing colors and a jarring pattern. When *loud* describes a person or behavior, it suggests crudity and vulgarity: a *loud,* coarse businessman whose back-slapping behavior failed to hide his ruthlessness. *Ostentatious* is not as pejorative as *loud,* but is nonetheless critical in its depiction of vain pretense or uncalled-for exhibition. It suggests the overly elaborate, flashy display that fails to impress because of its excess: an *ostentatious* copy of an English manor house that looked ridiculous in its Midwest setting. See ELEGANT, GAUDY, VULGAR.

Antonyms: *MODEST, plain, quiet, simple.*

sickness

ailment
complaint
disease
disorder
illness
infirmity
malady
malaise

These nouns all refer to poor health or to an episode of poor health. **Sickness** and **illness** are the most informal of these terms, and both refer to an episode of bad health, no matter what its duration. While the two nouns are used interchangeably, *sickness* might be the more usual and general choice, *illness* the slightly more formal one. Also, since *sickness* can sometimes refer specifically to nausea alone, *illness* is sometimes used to avoid this implication when it would be inappropriate: overcome with *sickness* shortly after eating the contaminated food; an *illness* that can result in blindness if left untreated. Furthermore, *sickness* can sometimes imply an episode that temporarily incapacitates one, whereas *illness* can imply a longer-lasting siege that is accompanied by impairment but not cessation of normal functioning: a *sickness* that kept him in bed for two weeks; an *illness* that caused her little difficulty in youth but began to take its toll as she reached middle age. *Sickness* can suggest external causation of the acute episode, while *illness* can suggest inherent weakness or malfunctioning as the source of chronic poor health. Also, *illness* is the word of choice for all mental disturbance, from mild neurosis through severe psychosis: the growing incidence of mental *illness*. When *sickness* is substituted for this neutral use of *illness,* an emotional coloration is added, implying greater seriousness or urgency or suggesting an attitude of condemnation: These odious crimes are enough of the killer's *sickness*. With a similar emphasis, *sickness* is often used in a more general way: a pervasive *sickness* in American society that predisposes us to violence.

Disease is often popularly thought to apply only to *sickness* that is infectious or communicable: *diseases* bred by poor sanitation. But *disease* can refer as widely as *sickness* or *illness* to any kind of bad health, with the advantage that its very generality yields no implications as to whether the sickness is acute or chronic, mild or harsh, or long or short in duration: a form of heart *disease* caused by a genetic defect; a case of Parkinson's *disease;* cancer and other *diseases* whose ultimate causes are still unknown; such mild viral *diseases* as the common cold. By contrast, **disorder** usually refers to a malfunction of mind or body that may be mild or serious, infectious or inherent, but is seen in some imbalance, as a metabolic or chemical defect, or in the improper working of some mechanism: hormonal *disorders* such as cretinism; a mental *disorder* typified by aural hallucinations. *Disorder* can be useful because it leaves open the question of cause and points strictly to symptoms indicating that something is awry.

Malady is a more formal synonym for *disease* that may seem outdated in descriptive use, although it has a note of alarm that makes it useful in metaphorical situations: the denial of female sexuality that is a *malady* endemic to Western civilization. **Malaise** refers to an indefinable sense of ill-being: a predictable *malaise* that is the first sign of the onset of the *disease*. It aptly describes a psychological state in which someone feels ill at ease or disquieted for whatever reason: an abiding *malaise* that jaundiced our view of world affairs.

Infirmity applies most concretely to a weakness of mind or body, but it may now sound too genteel as a substitute for *disease* or *disorder*. This is true as well in its extended uses: an *infirmity* that kept him in a wheelchair for years; needless cruelty that mocks at the *infirmities* of others; her tendency to exaggerate— the one *infirmity* in an otherwise admirable personality. **Ailment** can refer to a symptom or collection of symptoms that causes noticeable discomfort: What exactly is your *ailment?* *Ailment* too can sound outdated, although sometimes it can have an informal or regional thrust: Lumbago is the one *ailment* that keeps him on edge day in, day out. *Ailment* once focused more clearly on the enervation or depletion of one's sense of well-being. **Complaint** now functions as an informal substitute for symptom: Frequent faintness was a *complaint* he learned to live with. Sometimes, *complaint* can specifically indicate symptoms that are confided to one's doctor: cards on which she carefully noted every *complaint* of her patients. See COMMUNICABLE, FLAW, WEAKEN.

Antonyms: *health*.

significant

consequential
grave
important
momentous
serious
vital
weighty

These adjectives characterize factors that are outstanding or crucial, or that have considerable force or effect. **Significant** suggests something that is outstanding because it is especially meaningful or excellent; no urgency or forcefulness, however, is necessarily suggested by *significant*: a *significant* trend in opinion polls; a *significant* but often overlooked masterpiece of Hellenistic art. **Consequential** stresses that something is meaningful, cannot be overlooked, or has considerable impact on succeeding events, especially of a negative nature: a *consequential* contribution to the theory of cultural diffusion; a *consequential* decision to refuse the colonists representation in Parliament. In another context, *consequential* can often refer merely to the possessing of wealth or status: the town's two or three most *consequential* businesspeople.

Important, the most general of these adjectives, is also considerably less formal than the preceding adjectives. It may refer to something rife with meaning, but it can also suggest almost every sense that any other adjective here more specifically points to. In any case, *important* has been weakened by overuse, especially in the superlative, referring now to anything mildly interesting, noteworthy, or of value: one of the most *important* battles of the war; an *important* new talent; an *important* trend toward smaller families.

Momentous and **vital** both refer to things that are crucial or essential. *Momentous* stresses the great and immediate impact of an event, though it also points to *significant* ramifications or results, like *consequential*, but without any suggestion that these need be undesirable: a *momentous* turning point in evolution; the *momentous* decision to bomb Hiroshima. *Vital*, in contrast to *momentous*, can indicate an element that is organic and essential to the well-being or functioning of the whole: a *vital* organ of the body; raw materials *vital* to the economy. Deriving from the Latin word for life, *vital* often means crucial, or of life-and-death importance: a *vital* error; a *vital* question. It can also describe something dynamic, full of life and energy: a *vital* young executive; a *vital* work of art.

With **grave** and **serious**, the emphasis shifts to something urgent or crucial and to something that promises to have an extremely undesirable outcome. *Grave* is the more restricted of the two, specifically suggesting something that may well have a fatal conclusion: a *grave* illness; a pilot in *grave* danger. Occasionally, *grave* can refer more generally to something ponderous or solemn, with no suggestion of a negative outcome: addressing me in a *grave* manner; a *grave* treatise on the science of ethology. *Serious* is

considerably less formal and more general than the other adjectives here. Like *grave, serious* suggests the crucial, ponderous, or solemn, but with less emphasis on urgency and even less on negative eventualities. Like *important, serious* has been weakened by overuse, especially in the superlative: a *serious* flaw of character. Categorically, *serious* can distinguish the sober from the pleasant, light, or comic: a *serious* expression on her face; a *serious* discussion. In this use, it is a milder substitute for *grave;* here, neither *grave* nor *serious* necessarily suggests something unusually meaningful or effective.

Weighty refers to factors that are not easily disregarded: *weighty* considerations that militated against an attack. But it can also refer to a decisive preponderance or to presentations that are excessively lengthy, abstruse, or solemn: *weighty* data that disproved the argument for spontaneous generation; a *weighty* treatment of the origins of Roman fertility cults. See CONCLUSIVE, OUTSTANDING.
Antonyms: *insignificant*, MARGINAL, TRIVIAL, *unimportant.*

silent

noiseless
quiet
still

These adjectives are comparable when they are applied to persons or things that make no sound. **Silent** simply means refraining from speech or being without noise; it does not necessarily suggest serenity or motionlessness: His *silent* reproach was accompanied by vigorous gestures; a *silent* movie; a *silent* conversation between mutes who communicated by sign language. Because *silent* implies only the absence of sound, it can be more emphatic than any of the other adjectives: The crowd fell *silent* at the news that the president had died.

Quiet and **still**, although denoting silence, have different implications. *Quiet* implies freedom from activity; *still* suggests an unruffled or tranquil state, and often implies that the calm is an interlude between periods of noise or agitation. In most contexts, therefore, *silent, quiet,* and *still* are not interchangeable without changing the sense: a *quiet* street; a *quiet* neighborhood; a *still* forest. Note that there is a sense of permanence about *quiet* but none about *still*, which suggests the potentiality of the opposite of stillness: a *still* moment in the eye of the storm. On the other hand, when referring to the absence of speech, and especially if used predicatively, *silent, quiet,* and *still* may be interchangeable: a child who keeps *silent* (or *quiet* or *still*). Even here *still* is ambiguous, since it may also suggest the absence of fidgeting.

Noiseless is used in commerce, usually to refer to machines that are inherently noisy, such as air conditioners and the like, in order to persuade consumers to purchase a brand that is supposed to be *quieter* than others. Like most advertising claims, *noiseless* must be taken as a relative term, in this case meaning comparatively *quiet*. In more precise contexts *noiseless* means literally without any noise: the *noiseless* flight of an owl; the *noiseless* tread of a cat. In this sense it is synonymous with *silent*. See SPEECHLESS, TACITURN, TRANQUIL.

Antonyms: *LOUD, TALKATIVE.*

similar

easy
alike
comparable
parallel

These adjectives characterize persons or things that in some way or to some extent resemble each other. **Similar** and **alike** are close in that each means like one another in whole or part. [My shoes are *similar* to the ones you wore yesterday; The two office buildings are *alike* in size and shape.] The difference between *similar* and *alike* has to do with the extent of resemblance they indicate. Both adjectives can be used in reference to a slight degree of likeness. [I don't understand how you could have mistaken one car for the other since only their colors are *similar;* The cousins are *alike* in age, but otherwise as different as day and night.] But when identicality is to be indicated, the one adjective in this group conveying this meaning is *alike*. [All the houses in this block are *alike*.] It is interesting to note in this connection that by employing modifiers, *similar* and *alike* may be made to express more or less resemblance: somewhat *similar* in taste; not at all *alike* in price. Even with modifiers, however, identity can only be expressed by *alike,* since we can speak of two things being exactly *alike* but not exactly *similar*.

Things that are **comparable** are capable or worthy of being examined together with reference to their likeness or unlikeness, or in order to ascertain their relative excellence or defects. [The performance of this reasonably priced CD player is *comparable* in quality to that of more expensive units; The music of Irving Berlin, while outstanding in its way, is scarcely *comparable* to that of Beethoven.] **Parallel** is used when comparing things that show a great likeness,

whether real or apparent, or that have great similarity in their development, construction, history, operation, tendencies, etc. [The first hundred days of that administration were not at all *parallel* to those that came later; Can you point out any *parallel* passages in her first and second symphonies?] See COMPARE, COPY, COUNTERPART, DUPLICATE.

Antonyms: *CONTRADICTORY, contrasting, different, dissimilar, diverse.*

simple

easy
effortless
elementary
facile
simplified
simplistic

These adjectives all characterize things that are made, done, understood, etc., without undue difficulty, but they are not close synonyms. **Simple** and **easy** are the most general terms. In this context *simple* refers to something that is not complicated or intricate and is therefore capable of being quickly grasped by the mind. *Easy* points to that which requires little effort to do: a *simple* problem in long division; the *easy* job of preparing a meal from precooked frozen foods. In popular usage, *simple* and *easy* are often used interchangeably, and their connotations tend to become blurred: twelve *easy* lessons in Italian for the tourist; a task so *simple* that a child can perform it.

In its most precise sense, **elementary** is applied to rudiments or first principles, as of a branch of learning or of a skill, and is therefore concerned with basic or introductory material that may not necessarily be *easy* or *simple: elementary* electronics; *elementary* Greek. By extension, *elementary* is occasionally used as a synonym for *simple* in implying the absence of complexity, but here the meaning tends to merge with that of fundamental. [Her poems deal with the *elementary* themes of the changing of the seasons and the inexorability of nature; The television drama had the usual tiresome, *elementary* story line.]

Facile and **effortless** both apply to that which is achieved, performed, or activated with apparent *ease*. *Facile* was once a close synonym of *easy* but now carries somewhat derogatory overtones. It may describe that which is superficial in a bad sense or even spurious: the *facile* smile of hairdressers. *Facile* is also used of something that shows signs of having been done with too little expenditure of effort or with undue haste. It further suggests the careless or undisciplined use of skill or dexterity: a *facile* prose style of an author with little to say. *Facile,* in an extended sense, also points to glibness: the *facile* tongue of the born gossip. *Effortless,* while it can mean making no *effort* or being passive, is more often used to describe action or activities that appear *easy* to perform, but whose smoothness conceals a mastery achieved by long practice and control: the pianist's *effortless* playing of a difficult sonata; the trapeze artist's *effortless* somersaulting high in the air. *Effortless* may also refer to natural endowments impossible for others to emulate: the *effortless* flight of the eagle; the spectacular, but *effortless,* leaps of the impala.

Simplified means rendered less intricate or difficult and thus capable of being more easily understood, performed, or used. The term presupposes an original condition of complexity that has been reduced to bare essentials: *simplified* English spelling in which the words are written as they sound; the teaching of fractions *simplified* by cutting an apple into halves, thirds, and quarters; a *simplified* process for making steel. *Simplified* may also have a pejorative meaning when used to describe something that suffers from being made overly *simple* to the point of distortion or uselessness: the candidate's *simplified,* cliché-ridden suggestions for solving the complex problems of the poor. **Simplistic,** alone among these adjectives, means oversimplified: a *simplistic* view of the world, in which everyone or everything is either good or bad. See BASIC.

Antonyms: *complex, complicated,* HARD, *intricate.*

sin

> error
> fault
> indiscretion
> misdeed
> transgression
> wrong

These nouns refer to acts that violate religious, ethical, or moral standards. **Sin** has an exclusively religious connotation, referring to any act proscribed by religious doctrine: a sect that considers going to a movie a *sin.* It may also be used metaphorically for any act judged improper or outrageous: a *sin* to show up so late; a *sin* against humanity. **Transgression** is often used as a fancier word for *sin,* as though its weightier syllables more clearly indicated opprobrium. In other uses, it may suggest any violation of an agreed-upon set of rules: a clear *transgression* of the Geneva Convention.

Wrong and **misdeed** refer to evil or unjust actions; both may imply either a religious context or, more vaguely, a wider ethical context. *Wrong* suggests the giving of hurt or injury to someone: those who would unthinkingly do a *wrong* to their neighbors. The wrongful act implied by *misdeed* does not necessarily suggest hurt to others, but *misdeed* often seems euphemistic when used for *sin:* repenting her *misdeeds.*

Error and **fault** also sound euphemistic when substituted either for *sin* or *wrong.* Except in such clichés as "the *error* of my ways," *error* seems to suggest that a *sin* or *wrong* is an unintentional mistake rather than a deliberate choice. *Fault* suggests an imperfect result, a flaw, or a blemish; when used euphemistically for *sin,* it seems to excuse bad conduct by suggesting that perfection, however much desired, is impossible. **Indiscretion,** most strictly, refers to an unwise or improper action, but it has become a vogue word for such *sins* as adultery, as though to minimize the *wrong* committed by attributing it to a momentary lack of judgment: a woman guilty of an *indiscretion.* See CRIME, FLAW, MISTAKE, UNETHICAL.

Antonyms: *benefaction, good deed,* GOODNESS, *kindness.*

sincere

> genuine
> heartfelt
> honest
> open
> unfeigned
> wholehearted

These adjectives mean free from pretense, concealment, reservation, or falsehood. **Sincere** is the most general and the most positive in tone, suggesting a complete absence of hypocrisy and an exact identity between appearance and reality, with added implications of friendliness, interest, and kindness: a *sincere* expression of gratitude that went beyond mere formality. **Honest** and **genuine** stress truthfulness. *Honest* may be considerably more neutral than *sincere* and may describe an isolated instance of truth-telling as easily as it suggests an unvarying character trait: Even the least *sincere* person occasionally makes an *honest* statement. *Genuine* is closer to *sincere* than *honest* in its positive warmth of tone, emphasizing that a person or thing is really what it seems: She showed *genuine* regret. In another sense, someone may be *genuine* but neither *honest* nor *sincere:* a *genuine* confidence man.

Open and **unfeigned** suggest, negatively, a

refusal to play roles that might conceal one's true nature and, positively, a willingness to risk exposure and to tell all one knows. *Open* emphasizes telling the whole truth: begging her to be *open* with him, even if she did not like him. It suggests fearlessness of consequences and can veer over into suggesting an unnecessary or hurtful frankness: to show *open* hostility. *Unfeigned* does not necessarily suggest that the complete truth is told or expressed, but it does suggest a lack of posturing or archness: *unfeigned* delight in being with them, despite her suspicions about their intentions. Sometimes, *unfeigned* may suggest a sudden or unwilling revealing of one's true feelings: an irrepressible outburst of *unfeigned* disgust.

Heartfelt and **wholehearted** stress the aspect of *sincere* that pertains to warmth of concern and deepness of kind or friendly feelings. *Heartfelt* can indicate a rare inward intensity that is assented to completely: giving the widow his *heartfelt* sympathy. *Heartfelt*, however, is in danger of seeming too flowery in many instances. *Wholehearted* escapes this danger by suggesting thoroughgoing dedication without reservation, or an undivided response to experience: giving the proposal our *wholehearted* approval. It also suggests emotional exuberance or enthusiasm: *wholehearted* merrymaking.

Often, *sincere* is linked with another adjective here as a clarifying intensification, as though *sincere* were limited in its force. The phrase *sincere* and *genuine* seems to suggest that even sincerity by itself can be pretended; *sincere* and *honest* suggests that one can be *sincere* in one's intentions and yet be in error or fail to give the whole truth; *sincere* and *open* suggests that one can be concerned and *honest* and still be shy and reserved or hold back something important. Light is also cast on the felt limitations of *sincere* by another common type of doublet: *sincere* but *mistaken*; *sincere* but *misguided*; *sincere* but *ill-tempered*. These phrases imply that one may mean well yet fail to do the right thing, as because of a lack of knowledge, understanding, or control of one's emotions. See BRUSQUE, CANDID, GENUINE, OUTSPOKEN, OVERT, TRUTHFUL.

Antonyms: *affected, dishonest, dissembled, feigned, halfhearted, hypocritical, insincere, pretended, put-on, SPURIOUS.*

sing

chant
hum
intone

To **sing** is primarily to utter a succession of articulate musical sounds, especially with the human voice. In *singing*, the sound of the words differs from speech sound in that the vowels are lengthened and the pitches clearly defined. *Sing* has also come to mean produce any succession of musical sounds. One says that a bird *sings*, that a brook *sings*, or that a skilled performer can make her violin *sing*. By extension, a poem or a piece of imaginative prose may be said to *sing* when read aloud, because the cadences are pleasing to the ear.

To **hum** is to *sing* a tune, usually with the lips closed and without articulating the words. On the other hand, any monotonous, murmuring sound may be referred to as *humming*. [Bees *hum* as they fly from flower to flower; The flywheel in the powerhouse *hums* softly as it spins; The streets of the city *hum* with traffic.]

Chant and **intone** are closely related and mean *sing* in a solemn and somewhat uniform cadence a piece of repetitive music such as a plainsong, psalm, or canticle. *Intone*, however, suggests more gravity and less resemblance to music than does *chant*. [A priest *intones* the words of the Mass, but a choir *chants* the responses.] In its more extended meaning, to *chant* is to recite something repetitiously or monotonously in a singsong manner. [An auctioneer *chants* the amounts of money bid for items to be sold; Children *chant* rhymes as they jump rope.] See MELODY.

site

location
place
point
scene
setting
spot

These nouns all denote regions, localities, or particular portions of space. **Site** is almost always restricted to an area of ground, small or large. It may be one that has been set aside for a particular use or activity: a building *site;* a factory *site;* a recreation *site*. Or a *site* may be a circumscribed locale where some event has occurred: the *site* of the battle of Bull Run; the *site* of the beheading of Anne Boleyn.

A **location** is usually a *site* considered in relation to its surroundings or noteworthy for some specific feature. [The *location* of the house is near the highway; The prison guards could not discover the *location* of the escape tunnel; A post office should be built in a central *location*.]

Place is the most general term and may be substituted in an indefinite sense for all of the others. *Place* may mean a small, circumscribed area: to take one's *place* in line; hanging one's coat in the proper *place;* to find a parking *place*. Buildings, dwellings, cities, towns, or larger localities are all loosely called *places*. [The bank is her *place* of business; We are furnishing our *place* with antiques; He comes from a small *place* in Idaho; She sent postcards from faraway *places*.]

Setting and **scene** are both *places* or surroundings in which events (real or imaginary) occur or have occurred, and in this sense they may be used interchangeably. However, *setting*, rather than *scene*, is often limited in meaning to the *place* in which the incidents of a play or narrative are laid. [The *setting* of *Macbeth* is Scotland; India is the *scene* of many of Kipling's short stories.] *Scene* is more likely to be used of *places* in which actual events have occurred, but it suggests a less definite area than does *site*. [The meadow at Runnymede was the *scene* of the signing of the Magna Carta; A dark alley was the *scene* of the murder.] A *scene* may also be a wide or even panoramic landscape or view. [The wild mountain *scene* lay spread before us.] In a spatial sense, *setting* suggests a scenic environment or one with special characteristics: a cabin in a woodland *setting*.

A **spot** is a specific *place*, either indoors or outdoors, of limited extent: a night*spot;* a beautiful *spot* in which to have a picnic.

In the sense treated here, a **point** is a particular *place* without reference to the size or shape of the space occupied. It suggests a fixed *location* from which position and distance may be reckoned, as when one says he sails from *point* to *point* during a cruise. Otherwise, *point* is simply a *place* of definite, though unstated, size: to visit *points* of interest abroad. See SECTION.

size

area
bulk
expanse
extent
mass
scope
volume

These nouns refer to the measure of something large or small in quantity or degree, or in a plane or solid space. **Size** is the most general, being applicable in all these situations: a country of great *size;* a melon the *size* of my head; the *size* of the state's population; the *size* of the increase in the cost of living. By contrast, **area** and **expanse** are restricted most specifically to surface measurements. *Area* is most often used in neutral description or to focus attention on a partic-

ular region: pinpointing *areas* of discontent in Latin America; a small *area* of tenderness just behind my left ear. *Expanse* suggests a space larger than *area:* an *expanse* of timberlands; an inflamed *expanse* of skin across his chest. *Area* is also used to indicate a certain portion of an abstract whole: an often overlooked *area* of research.

Volume, **bulk**, and **mass** all specifically refer to three-dimensional spaces. *Volume* may be used in indicating the amount of cubic space something takes up or the quantity needed to fill a container: a room with a *volume* of a thousand cubic feet; estimating the *volume* of water needed to fill the pool. It is also used for amplitude of sound and arbitrarily for some other measurements: an increasing *volume* of trunk calls each day. By contrast, *bulk* does not suggest precision of measure, but does refer to a considerable *size* that may not be proportionate to its weight: cereal packages of deceptive *bulk*. *Bulk* has a special use for indicating a major portion: taking on the *bulk* of the work herself. In scientific usage, *mass* refers to a quantification of matter underlying gravity and weight. In ordinary use, *mass* emphasizes weight, density, or quantity, and may specifically suggest a large *bulk* of uneven outline: *masses* of debris left from the explosion. Less specifically, *mass* may suggest a great amount: a *mass* of student papers to correct and grade. *The masses* (plural) are the ordinary or common people: Our avowed intention is to improve the lot of *the masses*.

Extent and **scope** may be used to indicate linear or plane distances, like *area*, or more generally to indicate degree. In surface measurement, *extent* suggests an effort to determine the distance something reaches to, especially a linear distance that is subject to change: estimating the *extent* of river made brackish by saltwater from the ocean; reports on the *extent* of the captured territory. Used to indicate degree, *extent* is more flexible in application but less specific in meaning, only vaguely suggesting a metaphor of physical penetration: the *extent* to which they plumb the unyielding subject matter. Where *extent* implies a linear distance, *scope* implies a two-dimensional area that something has mastered or controls: bulletins on the *scope* of the flood's destructiveness. Much more commonly, *scope* is used figuratively to indicate degree of mastery or breadth of concern: a book of immense range and *scope;* the *extent* of his reach; the *scope* of her knowledge. See BOUNDARY, PART, SECTION, SITE.

skeptic

agnostic
atheist

skeptic *(continued)*

doubter
freethinker
unbeliever

These nouns designate people who question or reject accepted beliefs, particularly religious dogma. The relatively formal **skeptic** and the relatively informal **doubter** are alike in emphasizing someone who questions or is not sure of a given belief. *Doubter* most often refers to uncertainty about a belief already put forward; this may be a body of religious dogma or any isolated, nonreligious theory: evangelists who swept through the Midwest to convert *doubters*; a detailed investigation of the assassination, with conclusions that should convince the most conscientious *doubter*. *Skeptic* can function in both these ways, but its main emphasis is on the questioning of accepted beliefs, perhaps not so much from a position of open-minded uncertainty as from one of an a priori conviction about where the truth lies: a confirmed *skeptic* about the value of any of the great religions. Most specifically, *skeptic* can refer to a philosophical belief that no final truths can be known, whether in any area of knowledge whatever or in some particular area: a *skeptic* about the validity of psychoanalytic theory. Less precisely, *skeptic* may refer to a person with a disengaged attitude of moral cynicism toward the worth or value of life as a whole: a *skeptic* who watches with an indifferent eye the fads and inanities of the time.

Freethinker and **unbeliever** are more closely tied to a rejection of religious belief than the previous pair. *Freethinker* is an approving word, *unbeliever* a disapproving word, for a person who rejects the truth of a given religion or of all religions. *Unbeliever* might most often be used by a group of religious adherents to describe anyone not of their faith: a fanatical sect that regarded members of other religions as *unbelievers* doomed to suffer the torments of hell. More precisely, *unbeliever* would indicate someone who belongs to no organized religion, or someone without religious beliefs of any sort. This sets it apart from *doubter*, which might indicate someone who belongs to a religion but is wavering in his or her convictions: addressing the sermon to *doubters* rather than to outright *unbelievers*. *Freethinker* emphasizes someone who has asserted the right to think and decide for himself about religious dogma. *Freethinker* need not point to unbelief, but rather to a nonconforming, heterodox approach that picks and chooses from one or many religions those things, if any, that seem worthy of belief: a *freethinker* who subscribed to the Sermon on the Mount, the Upanishads, and the writings of Darwin, Freud, and Lao-tzu; a *freethinker* who objected to the attitude of most religions toward women.

Agnostic relates roughly to *skeptic* and *doubter*, while **atheist** is more comparable to *unbeliever*; both terms can be used in neutral description rather than in approval or disapproval. As widely used by the public press, political leaders, and some popular magazines, however, *atheist* is a contemptuous term: *atheistic communism*. *Agnostic* suggests someone who feels that no religious certainty is possible and that no proof or disproof of such a thing as the existence of God is valid: neither a believer nor *unbeliever*, but an *agnostic*. *Atheist* is the most specific of these nouns in being restricted to someone who does not believe in the existence of any sort of divinity: an *atheist* with a rigorous moral code based on the Ten Commandments. See DISTRUSTFUL, DOUBT, DOUBTFUL.

Antonyms: *believer, bigot, pietist, religious, zealot.*

skill

adroitness
artistry
deftness
finesse
flair
mastery

These nouns refer to ability that may be the result of training, talent, perceptivity, or a combination of some or all of these qualities. **Skill** is the least formal of these, the most general, and the most clear-cut in reference. It may refer, most simply, to relatively commonplace abilities gained largely through training: *skill* at keyboarding. But it may also refer to ability that training alone could not account for without considerable natural talent: the *skill* of the prima ballerina. Even in this situation, however, *skill* would suggest a necessary adjunct of artistic accomplishment rather than its lifeblood. With **artistry**, the situation is quite the reverse. Here all the imponderables of exquisite performance and accomplishment are indicated, and while training, talent, and taste play their part, they work in concert with other less common qualities: the *artistry* of a great violinist. Because of the strong praise conferred by *artistry*, it is often used hyperbolically of nonartistic acts to suggest how creatively even a seemingly mechanical task may be approached: the *artistry* with which she tossed the Caesar salad.

Deftness and **adroitness** are much nearer *skill* than *artistry* in their implications. *Deftness* may suggest simple manual dexterity when this natural ability has been highly trained: his *deftness* in handling the complex program. Less concretely, it can suggest a trained ability to handle any sort of difficult situation: the *deftness* of a good diplomat in avoiding embarrassing incidents. *Adroitness* also may pertain to *skill* at physical manipulation, but it is better able than *deftness* to suggest knowledgeable appropriateness of behavior in potentially charged situations: the *adroitness* of a conference leader in turning a discussion away from heated topics. It is more likely than *deftness* to refer to an artistic act at a higher level than technical *skill*: the *adroitness* with which the author managed the convoluted structure of her novel.

Just as *deftness* and *adroitness* are more closely related to *skill*, so **finesse** and **flair** are more closely related to *artistry*, though they suggest aspects of *artistry* rather than its equivalents. *Finesse* pertains to unusually excellent formal technique that joins to ordinary *skill* such imponderables as exuberance, taste, perceptivity, wit, or cleverness: the chess champion's *finesse* in defensive and offensive play. Someone crediting an artist with *finesse* rather than *artistry*, however, would be suggesting a lack of emotional depth or maturity: the flawless but shallow *finesse* of the young pianist. *Flair* is the one noun here that need not suggest thorough training; what it points to instead is a natural talent surprising in its forcefulness, whimsy, colorfulness, or vivacity: a *flair* for watercolors that is all the more impressive considering her lack of experience in the medium. In reference to admittedly trained people, however, *flair* can suggest work with zest or dramatic impact that goes beyond mere *adroitness* or *finesse*: writing with *flair* despite the rigid limitations of the heroic couplet. Less exaltedly, *flair* can refer to anything very striking about someone's personal taste: a way of dressing that showed a *flair* for exploiting bold patterns and colors within the bounds of good taste.

Mastery is ambivalent in that it can apply to simple training, like *skill*, or to the highest of attainments, like *artistry*: *mastery* of her complex task on the assembly line; magnificent murals that are the apex of Michelangelo's *mastery*. See ACUMEN, ATTAINMENT, GENIUS.

Antonyms: *clumsiness, incompetence, ineptitude.*

slang
argot
cant
jargon

These nouns refer to congeries of specialized and nonstandard words and expressions used by a subculture or subdivision within a larger group sharing a common language, especially when such expressions would be thought illiterate, odd, or unintelligible by many users of the language. **Slang** is the extremely informal language used by the members of an in-group in place of more usual expressions; *slang* may include abbreviated or made-up words, novel expressions, grammatical distortions, and other violations or departures from accepted usage. Sometimes, the expressions of an in-group that gain popularity or a wider understanding are still considered *slang* by some people so long as they remain distinct from standard or formal usage.

Argot refers to the *slang* of a very limited group that feels threatened by the hostility of society as a whole. *Argot* was once restricted to the *slang* of criminals or thieves, but it can now apply to any use of language by minority groups that is marked by protective euphemisms and codelike secretiveness: the popular adoption of the word *camp* from homosexual *argot*; comparing the *argots* of the carnival worker and the jazz musician; Mr. Charlie and ofay are slang terms for the white man in the *argot* of the African-American ghetto. **Cant** once was exactly synonymous with *argot* in referring to the private language of thieves, but now it generally refers especially to the inflated, ingrown, or pompous language of a respected profession, especially in the social sciences: a learned paper full of sociological *cant*.

In a technical sense, **jargon** refers to a simple crossbreeding of two languages to facilitate communication, such as pidgin English. More generally, *jargon* would be understood as referring to the extremely technical terms in use among specialists in any abstruse field: words like tweeter and woofer and other bits of *jargon* bandied about by audio enthusiasts. See GOBBLEDEGOOK.

slaughterhouse
abattoir
packing house
packing plant
shambles

These nouns denote buildings in which animals are slaughtered, butchered, and processed for market. **Slaughterhouse** may refer to a place where all these things occur in an organized way as a business endeavor, but it may also refer to a structure set aside for nothing but the killing of animals for whatever reason, though not necessarily for processing and marketing: *slaughterhouses* set up for the killing of cattle found to be diseased. The vividness of *slaughterhouse* may have been thought unpalatable; in any case, the colorless term **packing plant** is now the most common way to refer to the building or complex of buildings where the killing of animals and processing of meat are carried out as a commercial enterprise: the *packing plants* of the major meat packers. **Packing house** is sometimes used instead of *packing plant,* but it can be confusing in that it might imply a small-scale, one-building operation and might indicate a place where the processing, rather than the killing, is done: delivering sides of beef to the *packing house* for grading.

The term **abattoir** is usually confined to a place where animals are slaughtered for food and is not in wide use as a substitute for *packing plant,* except in English-speaking Canada. Because of its French root, *abattoir* might also suggest a European context, or it may be used as the basis of literary metaphors: the *abattoirs* of Belsen and Buchenwald. **Shambles,** referring exclusively to the place where animals are killed, is seldom used in this literal way in current speech; metaphorically, its reference to wholesale butchery of any kind is not even felt any longer as a reflection of the literal meaning: the smoking *shambles* of the battlefield. Killing of any sort, in fact, is not necessarily evoked by *shambles* so much as a complete disordering of things: electricians who made a *shambles* of the kitchen we had just cleaned. See CLUTTER, KILL.

slave

bondmaid
bondman
peon
serf
thrall
vassal

These nouns refer to someone deprived of liberty, serving involuntarily, or otherwise at the mercy of a master. **Slave** is the most common of these and the one with the widest range of uses. Specifically, *slave* refers to someone who is owned by another and has no civil rights, particularly someone who serves involuntarily or is given no pay for services performed. Most countries now prohibit the possession of *slaves,* a practice endemic throughout history, as in the case of conquerors who commonly made *slaves* of conquered peoples. Trade in *slaves* still persists, however, in some parts of Africa and the Near East. In a more general sense, *slave* is often used now in informal speech to refer to anyone victimized by someone or something: a paternalistic company that not only expected its employees to work like *slaves,* but to be grateful for the chance; a *slave* to her own narrow egotism.

Bondman and **bondmaid** are now archaic except in a historical context; they refer to a man or woman bound to serve without wages. Unlike *slave,* these nouns could suggest a contractual agreement that might last for a certain term only and in which a degree of freedom was permitted to the *bondman* or *bondmaid.* On the literal level, **thrall** and **vassal** are also archaic, but unlike the previous pair, both have surviving figurative uses. *Thrall* once indicated someone bound to personal service in a household; *vassal,* by contrast, indicated someone who was the master of his own affairs but pledged to serve his lord in war in exchange for protection within the lord's domain. Thus, in its literal historical meaning, *vassal* contrasts sharply with these other nouns, since it could apply to people of any intermediate rank between the *slave* and the absolute master: barons who rebelled against being kept as *vassals* to their king. When used figuratively, *thrall* can suggest someone intangibly bound to something, as a habit: a *thrall* to tobacco. Also, because of legends in which the use of black magic could make one an unwilling *thrall* to an evil person, *thrall* can suggest figurative enchantment, particularly a state of involuntary fascination: held in *thrall* by the exquisite music. *Vassal,* by comparison, is more often used to refer to any kind of forced allegiance or dependency: East European countries that are no longer *vassals* of Russia.

Serf, like *bondman,* is now mostly archaic except in historical reference. Under feudalism, a *serf* was bound to an estate and could not leave it; whoever owned the land was perforce the *serf*'s master. The *serf,* however, did have rights, unlike the *slave,* in that no one could drive him from the land nor deny his right to be there. *Serf* can be used loosely for anyone in servile subjection, but this use can sound imprecise or far-fetched. In Latin America, **peon** once referred most specifically to someone held in involuntary servitude until he or she had paid a debt. Since this arrangement often proved permanent in practice, *peon* now refers to anyone so ridden by poverty as to be virtually a *serf* or, loosely, to any poorly paid laborer. Used figuratively in English, *serf* refers informally but contemptuously to an underling or, in the plural, to the ordinary mass of people: a public statement full of platitudes, written strictly for consumption by the *peons.* See OBSEQUIOUS.

Antonyms: BOSS, *lord.*

slight

disregard
ignore
neglect
snub

These verbs indicate a failure to pay proper attention or respect to something. **Slight** makes the failure a matter of degree: it suggests that whatever attention or respect has been given is totally inadequate to the situation at hand: deliberately *slighting* the ambassador by placing her at the far end of the table; *slighting* his studies to concentrate solely on extracurricular activities. **Snub** is more restricted in emphasizing the aspect of *slight* that pertains exclusively to manners and propriety; in this case, however, the lack of respect is unsubtle and overt rather than implied. *Slight* also usually suggests a single, dramatic action rather than a gradual process of attrition: deliberately *snubbing* us by turning and walking away in the middle of a sentence. Whether or not a person has been *slighted* may be a matter of interpretation; there can be no doubt about someone's having been *snubbed*.

Neglect is mainly restricted to the aspect of *slight* that suggests an inequitable division of attention, except that in this case the amount of attention given is even less than is true for *slight*. *Neglect* may, however, suggest either an intentional or unintentional failure of attention, unlike *slight* and especially *snub*, where the failure is most clearly conscious and deliberate: a research project that caused him not so much to *slight* his students as to *neglect* them altogether in his usual absentminded way. *Neglect* in its very generality can also apply to situations where courtesy or propriety is the issue: a woman who never *neglects* the slightest expression of uneasiness shown by her guests.

Disregard and **ignore** are like *neglect* in applying to the more general context of failures in attention, but both verbs suggest a complete rather than a partial failure. In this case, *ignore* particularly stresses an intentional refusal to take account of a warning: *ignoring* the detour signs until he pulled up at a washed-out bridge. *Disregard* implies a denial of attention to something because of superior knowledge or more pressing considerations: asking the jurors to *disregard* his testimony as false and contradictory. While *ignore* suggests that something has been rejected without any conscious consideration, *disregard* can suggest a careful, wholly conscious evaluation that results in dismissal: eager to show that however she might *disregard* his advice, she would never *ignore* it. When these two verbs apply to manners, *ignore* compares with *snub* in stressing deliberate rudeness, but whereas *snub* refers to the commission of an offensive act, *ignore* refers to the omission of even minimal courtesies: *ignoring* the guest of honor all evening. In this context, *disregard* is unique among these verbs in having a use that suggests the act of deliberately overlooking someone else's discourtesy: *disregarding* the public outburst as inconsequential and unworthy of an answer. See CONTEMPTUOUS, DESPISE, FORGET, NEGLECT, SCOFF.

Antonyms: *attend, cherish, consider, heed, prize, tend, value.*

sloth

acedia
anomie
apathy
autism
catatonia
indolence
torpor

These nouns refer to extremely dull, unresponsive, or inactive states due to laziness, sluggish health, or mental depression. Classically one of the seven deadly sins, **sloth** stresses extreme inaction due to laziness, a state amenable to a simple effort of the will. *Sloth* is sharp in its disapproval and suggests the unpleasant concomitants of sloppiness, untidiness, or uncleanliness: filthy, disheveled rooms that gave eloquent testimony to his life of *sloth* and debauchery. Unlike *sloth*, **torpor** may be applied to animals, people, or in fact to anything lying quiescent. Also, *torpor* does not necessarily suggest a willed sinfulness and is consequently less disapproving. *Torpor* does point to a more lasting or deep-seated state close to that of sleep or hibernation and may suggest an unbroken outward uneventfulness: a *torpor* in which he stared out the window for days on end.

Acedia and **apathy** add to the connotations of the previous pair the suggestion of a state of mental unresponsiveness. *Acedia* (or *accidie*) sometimes replaces *sloth* in lists of the seven deadly sins, but it is now more widely thought of as referring to a state of mental depression, implying a despair so profound that no action or attitude is thought possible or desirable: bouts of frenzied activity alternating with months of hopelessness and *acedia*. *Apathy* is a much more informal substitute for this last use of *acedia*, suggesting emotionless unresponsiveness that may stem from discouragement or low morale: looking upon his parents' quarrels with growing pessimism and *apathy*. *Apathy* is often used sociologically to refer to a limp, passive attitude toward injustice among groups of people: slum children who face their constricted future with understandable *apathy;* the *apathy* of the German middle classes when faced with the rise of Hitler.

Anomie is specifically used in a sociological context to refer to a widespread social *apathy* that results in alienation, breakdowns in communication, hostility, and the weakening of norms of conduct. *Anomie* has become a fad word, used in less specialized contexts: the new delinquency among children of affluent parents, reflecting a widespread *anomie* among the wealthy. Sometimes *anomie* can suggest a breakdown of norms that sets the stage for chaotic or anarchic violence; in this sense, its suggestion of action puts it in sharp contrast with the other nouns here. By comparison, the more general **indolence** refers strictly to an aversion to exertion or work. While this could conceivably give *indolence* a sociological context, more often it is used as a more formal substitute for laziness, emphasizing a deliberately chosen state of inactivity: the pampered *indolence* of the jet set. But *indolence* need not always be disapproving: a glorious week of *indolence* at the beach.

Autism and **catatonia**, highly formal and technical terms from psychiatry, describe extremely withdrawn states of mental unresponsiveness. *Autism* at its most general can indicate a tendency toward daydreaming and introspection; at its most concrete it is used specifically to describe an extreme withdrawal in children that retards or destroys the development of such normal functions as speech: the years of intensive face-to-face effort involved in treating a single case of *autism.* *Catatonia* indicates a similar kind of extreme withdrawal in schizophrenic adults, in which the psychosis takes the form of apathy, complete passivity, and inability to initiate the simplest actions: patients who, afflicted with *catatonia,* sit in the same uncomfortable positions for hours rather than shifting to a more comfortable posture. See IMPASSIVE, LISTLESS, UNINVOLVED.

Antonyms: *activity, concern, diligence, industriousness, interest, involvement, liveliness.*

slow

deliberate
dilatory
gradual
laggard
leisurely
retarded
slack
sluggish

These adjectives are here compared as they apply to persons who do not accomplish things quickly or to actions that consume a great deal of time, often more than is considered necessary. **Slow**, the most general, means extending or occurring over a relatively long span of time. *Slow* may be positive in its application to persons: a *slow* but meticulous cabinetmaker; a person *slow* to anger. It may also suggest such undesirable traits as laziness or stupidity: *slow* in his work because he is always on the phone; a woman of such limited ability that she is *slow* to understand the simplest directions. Often, *slow* indicates no more than not fast in progress or prompt in action: proceeding down the street at a *slow* walk.

Gradual and **leisurely** are never applied to persons. *Gradual* stresses advancement by *slow* or even imperceptible steps or degrees, but it involves continuing progress: a *gradual* change for the better in one's health; to make *gradual* improvements in an old house. Anything *leisurely* is performed with no thought of a time limit and may be *slow* or simply unhurried and relaxed: a *leisurely* drive; a *leisurely* meal.

Deliberate in this context adds to *slow* the connotation of caution and care. A person who is *deliberate* acts after weighing all aspects of a situation; a methodical person tends to plan work in a *deliberate* manner.

Dilatory and **laggard** bring to *slow* the concept of delay. The *dilatory* person wastes time by being *slow* in doing what he or she could or should do promptly and procrastinates either through lack of self-discipline or an unwillingness to apply effort: a *dilatory* correspondent. *Laggard,* a stronger and more censorious word, implies lingering and falling behind in progress through laziness and a refusal to make an effort: *laggard* in paying debts; *laggard* in finding summer jobs, relying on their parents to support them.

Slack and **sluggish** both stress having little motion or alertness. To be *slack* is not only to be *slow,* but to be negligent in the performance of duties: police who are *slack* in enforcing traffic rules; a *slack* worker. Used of a period of time, it refers to a temporary lessening of activity in some endeavor: a *slack* season in the garment industry. *Sluggish* more than *slack* implies reluctance and sometimes an inability to move forward: a *sluggish* digestive system; a *sluggish* river. In a general sense *sluggish* is often applied to both physical and mental lethargy: to feel *sluggish* in hot, humid weather; a mind too *sluggish* to entertain new ideas.

At one time **retarded** meant *slow* or delayed, but it has almost completely lost its general meaning. It is now limited to describing persons who are *slow* or backward in mental development and in the ability to learn skills. See LISTLESS, SLOTH.

Antonyms: *agile, fast,* LIVELY, *quick, rapid, speedy.*

small

diminutive
little
petite
short
squat
tiny
wee

These adjectives describe people or things of relatively reduced dimensions. **Small** and **little** are the most general and informal. Both may be used loosely and interchangeably, but *little* without doubt suggests the more extreme departure from a norm: a *small* man; a *little* man. *Small* may suggest a slight reduction of proportions that is noticeable but not necessarily objectionable: a *small* house that would do perfectly for the two of them. *Little,* by contrast, suggests a reduction in scale that may be drastic: a *little* doll-house.

When *small* and *little* refer to the physical proportions of a person, they suggest an overall reduction of scale, with *little* the more extreme. By contrast, **short** is restricted to a reduction in the scale of normal physical height: the *shortest* boy in the class; a man who appeared to be *shorter* than he actually was when he stood beside his tall wife. In this sense *short* may also be applied to parts of a human or animal body: a dwarf with *short* arms and legs attached to a trunk of normal size; The zebra has a *short* neck compared with that of the giraffe. In reference to things, *short* is applied to that which has relatively *little* linear extension or vertical length: a *short,* dead-end street with only three houses; skirts so *short* that they resemble tunics. *Short* may also emphasize that something does not measure up to a standard or need in some way: a board that was too *short* to reach from one bank of the stream to the other; cheating by playing with a *short* deck of cards. **Squat** is an intensification of *short,* referring particularly to something that is of reduced vertical height but is not comparably reduced in its other dimensions, giving a low, wide silhouette: Romanesque churches that look *squat* beside their soaring Gothic counterparts; a heavy, *squat* man who waddled along.

Diminutive and **petite** are intensifications of the meanings implicit in *small.* Both are more formal and

are particularly used to refer to women's figures that are pleasingly trim and compact: a shortage of *petite* sizes in informal gowns; showing off the *diminutive* figure she had earned by dieting. While *petite* would seem affected when applied to things other than women's figures, *diminutive* can be used for anything of reduced overall proportions: *diminutive* apples.

Tiny and **wee** are intensifications of *little,* suggesting such a drastic reduction of scale as to put the thing described outside established norms. *Tiny* may suggest a miniature or model of something: *tiny* toy soldiers. In another use, *tiny* can more simply express surprise at something extremely *small,* even when it is of normal size: a *tiny* baby; a *tiny* insect that lit on the palm of my hand. *Wee* almost inevitably sounds precious or cute, except possibly in children's literature: a *wee* lamb; a *wee* elf. Used euphemistically by adults, it suggests a humorous intent: wondering if they might have a *wee* drink together before leaving for the party. See COMPACT, MINUTE.

Antonyms: HIGH, LARGE, MASSIVE, TREMENDOUS.

smell

aroma
bouquet
fragrance
odor
scent
stench
stink

These nouns denote that which is perceived through the nose by means of the olfactory sense. **Smell** is the most general word, including all the rest, and **odor** is its closest synonym. They are often used interchangeably, and both may be applied to pleasant, unpleasant, or neutral sensations. But *odor* is the more nearly neutral word, being freer of connotations than *smell* and better suited to scientific contexts. *Odor* tends to take its character from the words that qualify it: a pungent *odor;* a foul *odor. Smell* has a character of its own—a simple, hearty, forthright quality better suited to the kitchen than to the laboratory: cooking *smells. Odor* may sometimes signify a more delicately pleasing perception than *smell:* the clean *smell* of soap; the spicy *odor* of incense. And whereas a *smell* may sometimes be a blend of separate emanations, an *odor* is more commonly traceable to a single source: the *smell* of the sick room; the *odor* of formaldehyde.

An **aroma** is an *odor* both pleasing and distinctive, such as that given off by good food as it cooks or by good pipe tobacco as it burns. An *aroma* may be savory or smoky, or it may be delicate or spicy; but it is always stimulating to the senses: the *aroma* of fresh coffee. **Bouquet** is applied primarily to the delicate *aroma* that distinguishes a fine wine: She lifted the wine glass and sniffed the *bouquet* appreciatively.

A **scent** is any *odor,* natural or artificial, that is or may be faintly diffused through the air. A *scent* is always delicate and often pleasing: the *scent* of a sachet. **Fragrance** is a sweeter, fresher, more pervasive *scent:* the lingering *fragrance* of lilacs. *Scent* and *fragrance* are the words properly applied to dusting powder and perfume. *Smell* and *odor* seem inelegant in such contexts, except when *smell* is used with simple sincerity, as by a child: He liked the *smell* of his mother's perfume.

Applied to the natural emanations of human beings, *smell* and *odor* often signify something unpleasant or offensive, though the nouns are not limited in this way: the *smell* of sweat; body *odor.* *Fragrance* is used only of women and often occurs in popular writing, connoting a fresh, clean *smell:* the *fragrance* of her hair. *Scent* denotes the characteristic *odor* of an animal—a faint residual *odor* that lingers along the ground over which the animal passed. A natural human *odor* is referred to as a *scent* only when the person in question is being tracked down like an animal: Bloodhounds followed the *scent* of the escaped prisoner. *Scent* and *smell* may also denote the olfactory sense itself, but *scent* is usually reserved for animals, especially dogs, and suggests an unusually sharp sense of *smell:* the keen *scent* of the bloodhound.

Stink and **stench** are strong words and are applied to foul, offensive *odors, smells* that make persons hold their noses or that sicken them. Of the two, *stink* suggests a sharper sensation; *stench,* a more sickening one: the *stink* of sweaty feet; the *stench* of gangrene. Both *stink* and *stench* apply to what is rotting or decaying, but *stench* denotes the stronger and more overpowering *odor:* the *stench* of a vast open grave.

Bouquet and *stench,* being the most specific of these nouns, are seldom used figuratively. But *odor, stink,* and *smell* are often so used. [There was an *odor* of fear in the air; They made quite a *stink* about it; It had the *smell* of foul play.] See SAVORY.

smile

grin
simper
smirk

These nouns denote a facial expression in which the mouth is silently widened and its corners are upturned in order to convey such emotions as affection, amusement, confidence, irony, polite approval, or disdain. **Smile**, the most general, refers to any such expression regardless of the emotion being conveyed: giving the child a tender *smile;* swaggering down the street with a bright *smile;* unable to suppress a *smile* at his naiveté; the bitter *smile* she wore during her opponent's rebuttal. Because the expression itself suggests pleasure or approval more readily than other emotions, *smile* can even refer to the stereotyped mannerism put on automatically for other people in the absence of sincere emotion of any sort: the maddening and invariable *smile* most flight attendants wear when listening to requests or complaints.

The remaining nouns restrict themselves in reference to particular emotions or situations that motivate the *smile.* **Grin** indicates a greater widening of the mouth than *smile,* especially one that exposes the teeth, and suggests spontaneity, greater emotional intensity, and friendly warmth, pleasure, mirth, or high-spirited amusement: giving her his best all-American-boy *grin;* the *grin* with which she greeted her old schoolfriend. *Grin,* derived from a root referring to howling or groaning, is sometimes used for a less amicable or even ferocious baring of the teeth: the *grin* of a snarling wolf; the wounded soldier's *grin* of pain. In this use, *grin* may be a colorful substitute for grimace, which is more precise.

Simper and **smirk** are sometimes equated as indicating the same sort of silly or fatuous expression, but strikingly different connotations surround each noun. *Simper* suggests smugness and self-righteousness and may even imply primness: the Wife of Bath's complaisant *simper;* a mutual admiration society in which they could exchange *simpers* of superiority as they faced the uninitiated. *Smirk* may be used with precisely these same overtones. But where *simper* may suggest the reflection of an abiding inward sense of hypocritical superiority, *smirk* more often suggests a momentary outward expression of derision or hostility: a teacher who tricks students into giving incorrect answers and then greets them with a *smirk;* a man in handcuffs regarding his captors with a *smirk.*

Antonyms: *FROWN.*

soil

besmirch
dirty
smudge
sully

These verbs mean make or become unclean, impure, or stained with foreign matter. As implying the degree of uncleanness and its undesirability, **soil** is somewhat milder than **dirty** and refers largely to the inevitable staining with dust and grime, especially of wearing apparel and linens, that occurs from ordinary use: to *soil* a towel by not thoroughly washing one's *dirty* hands; a shirt collar *soiled* with sweat. In this context *dirty* is often substituted for *soil*, but *dirty* usually suggests creating an unclean condition that not only offends the aesthetic sense but may be injurious to health. Something that has been *dirtied* is often harder to clean than something that has been *soiled*: to *dirty* a neighborhood by throwing garbage on the sidewalks; to *dirty* upholstery by putting one's muddy shoes on it; to *dirty* a city's air with industrial fumes.

Smudge means *soil* literally by begriming, as with soot, or by smearing, as with ink or dirty fingers. It often implies a degree of uncleanness as mild as, or milder than, that implied by *soil*, and suggests not making something *dirty* as much as it does spotting or staining it: Try not to *smudge* the drawing.

Dirty and *soil* are sometimes used figuratively in the moral context of character assassination: to *soil* a spotless reputation; to *dirty* an honored name.

Besmirch and **sully**, now found largely in literature of the past, have virtually lost all their earlier meanings of *soiling*, *dirtying*, or *smudging* in a physical sense. Rather, *besmirch* is used to mean damage or dim the luster of, as one's honor or good repute: a reputation undeservedly *besmirched* by vicious gossip and slander. *Sully* is used in the same way, but carries a hint of greater injury and condemnation: his fame and standing as a diplomat *sullied* by the publicizing of his many sexual involvements. See DIRTY (adj.), DISCOLOR, POLLUTE.

Antonyms: *bleach,* CLEAN, *purify.*

solecism. Do not confuse the noun *solecism* (error in language usage, offense against good manners) with the noun *solipsism* (philosophical theory that the self is the only knowable thing).

solicitude
care
concern
worry

These nouns agree in denoting a troubled state of mind. **Solicitude**, the most formal term, often implies anxious attention or devotion to another's welfare: The *solicitude* shown him by his neighbors touched him deeply. *Solicitude* is especially used when the involve-ment of others is disinterested, stemming from feelings of charity or brotherhood rather than from intimacy or blood relationship: the *solicitude* of the mayor toward all residents.

Care arises from responsibility or affection for others, and may vary from mild **concern** to profound **worry**: *care* for one's children. *Concern* is the absence of indifference, and hence implies voluntary involvement: *concern* for the nation's welfare. *Worry* implies an oppressive and fretful anxiety, and is often needless or excessive: distraught with *worry* over his daughter's absence. *Worry* is the most personal and most intensely felt of these nouns, although it is sometimes used of impersonal situations to indicate irrational *concern*: burdened with all the *worries* of the world. *Care* implies an intimate and often deep attachment. *Concern* is more detached and may only indicate a formal response to an impersonal situation: The President expressed *concern* over the situation in the Balkans. See ANXIETY, WORRY.

Antonyms: *aloofness, indifference,* NEGLECT, *unmindfulness.*

Solipsism. Do not confuse the noun *solipsism* (philosophical theory that the self is the only knowable thing) with the noun *solecism* (error in language usage, offense against good manners).

solve
decipher
decode
unravel

These verbs denote working out or clarifying a puzzle or mystery. **Solve** means answer a question or work out a problem, often one deliberately set as an exercise: *solving* the ten equations assigned for tomorrow's math class. *Solve* can also refer to explaining any set of events by finding a workable way of dealing with them or by seeing the deeper meaning behind them: *solving* the problem of peace through world diplomacy; *solving* the dilemma of accounting for the national debt by viewing it in terms of the national accounts index. **Unravel** functions most nearly like this general sense of *solve*. The emphasis is on the untangling of a knotty problem, especially by means of research or analysis: an investigative body at work to *unravel* the motives of the assassin; an essay attempting to *unravel* the meaning of the poem.

Decipher and **decode** are alike in specifically referring to the act of making intelligible a message that has been systematically garbled to confuse an unwanted reader: *deciphering* enemy messages; *decoding* the message by feeding it through a computer programmed to turn it back into English. In this context, *decipher* refers to translating messages scrambled according to a key or prearranged scheme, whereas *decode* refers to translating agreed-upon symbols that may be arbitrary or random. Thus, *decoding* normally requires a code book in which the plain text and encoded equivalents are listed; *deciphering* only involves knowledge of the key or system, for example, 1 for A, 2 for B, etc. *Decipher* is more often used than *decode* in a metaphorical way, in which case it refers to explaining puzzling or enigmatic signs: finally *deciphering* the look he had given her. See CLARIFY.

Antonyms: *baffle,* CONFUSE, PUZZLE, *stump.*

sophistry

casuistry
hairsplitting
sophism

These nouns refer to oversubtle argumentative techniques that place more emphasis on form than content, often with the intent of misleading or deceiving an audience. **Sophistry** and **sophism** both derive from a Greek word for wisdom and relate to the Sophists, a pre-Socratic school of philosophers interested in the logical expression of philosophical truth. In Socrates' day, however, the name was taken over by paid philosophers who taught logical and rhetorical techniques and were concerned more with persuasive forms of discourse than with a search for truth. Thus, both nouns now indicate false argument intentionally used to deceive. While the difference between the two nouns is slight, *sophistry* might be most useful as a generic term, *sophism* as a reference to specific examples: campaign oratory filled with *sophistry;* a statement on taxation that was a *sophism* pure and simple.

Casuistry has a Christian theological rather than classical Greek background; it refers to the science or doctrine of ambiguous cases of conscience, involving questions of moral right and wrong. The reasoning involved in this sort of argument was often so subtle and complicated that *casuistry* has come to be used with the same pejorative tone that *sophistry* has acquired. It still applies, however, particularly to disputes about ethics or morals: a governor who has abandoned the *casuistry* surrounding arguments over capital punishment. **Hairsplitting** is more specific than *sophism, sophistry,* and *casuistry* in applying to any sort of argumentative discourse in which finicky atten- tion is given to fine points of method or substance in such a way as to lose sight of significant questions: descending to *hairsplitting* about side issues whenever her opponent discussed the main issue. See CONTROVERSY, DECEPTION.

soup

bouillon
broth
chowder
consommé
porridge
stew
stock

These nouns denote either liquid food or food having a liquid base. **Soup** is the most general and most inclusive. It is made by boiling meat, vegetables, or a combination of ingredients in water. *Soup* may be purely liquid—whether thick, or thin and clear—or it may consist of bits of solid food in liquid: tomato *soup;* chicken *soup;* vegetable *soup.*

Liquid that has had meat, fish, or vegetables boiled in it is called **stock** or **broth**. *Stock* stresses that the liquid is a by-product or an ingredient, not a food in itself: to strain beef *stock;* to skim off fat from chicken *stock*. *Stock* may be used as a base in making *soups*, sauces, or gravies. Beef *stock*, for example, is often an ingredient in canned vegetable *soup;* vegetable *stock* is often used as a liquid base for homemade *soups*. When *stock* is prepared as a separate liquid food— whether for use as a thin, strained *soup*, a packing fluid, or a fluid base—it is called *broth*. Beef *broth* may be made by boiling marrow bones, beef shin, vegetables, and seasonings together, then skimming and straining the *stock:* a *soup* of noodles and ground beef in beef *broth;* a can of boned turkey with *broth*. *Stock* used to make *broth* is sometimes clarified: a chicken *soup* recipe calling for two cans of clear chicken *broth*.

Bouillon is a clear *broth* made by boiling and simmering lean beef, chicken, or other meats, then straining and clarifying the *stock*. Such *stock* may be dehydrated and sold in the form of *bouillon* cubes that are reconstituted by being dissolved in hot water. **Consommé** is a clear, strong, concentrated *soup* of meat or meat *stock* (and sometimes vegetables) boiled, strained, and seasoned: beef *consommé;* chicken *consommé*. *Consommé* is richer and more nutritious than *bouillon* or *broth*. It may be served hot, as a clear liquid; or, if it contains gelatin, it may be refrigerated, jelled, and served cold.

Where *stock, broth, bouillon,* and *consommé* are purely liquid, the remaining dishes consist of food cooked in liquid. **Stew** is a preparation of meat or fish and various vegetables simmered together gently in water or milk. Beef *stew* may contain small chunks of beef and diced vegetables in beef *broth*. Oyster *stew* may contain oysters, oyster *broth*, butter, cream, and whole milk. **Chowder** is a thick *soup* often made with milk. It usually consists of clams, fish, or corn stewed with potatoes and onions, often bacon, and sometimes other vegetables: clam *chowder;* corn *chowder;* fish *chowder* made with halibut fillets and fish *broth*. **Porridge** is a soft food made by boiling oatmeal or other meal in water or milk until it thickens. *Porridge* may also denote a thick *broth* or *stew* of vegetables with or without meat.

sour

    acid
    acidulous
    acrid
    bitter
    caustic
    tart

These adjectives refer to sharp tastes or smells or to harsh dispositions and behavior stemming from them. When used of tastes, **sour** refers to the characteristic sharpness produced by acids. **Acid** itself refers more directly to such a taste. **Acidulous** indicates a taste that is partially *acid* or mildly *sour*. **Tart** refers to a sharp taste that is pleasantly *acid* or piquant in taste. **Acrid** pertains to any strong or sharp smell, but can also apply to sharp tastes produced either by acids or alkalis. **Bitter** is restricted to sharp tastes produced mainly by alkalis, but can also apply to strong unpleasant smells. If the *bitter* taste or smell is mild, it might be regarded as savory or pleasant; if quite strong, it might become wry or unpleasant, or be capable of lingering on, causing discomfort. **Caustic** suggests a sharp smell such as a strong alkali might give off; it can be used of tastes only as a hyperbole, since it also refers literally to alkalinity intense enough to eat away or corrode organic tissues.

These adjectives, on their most literal level, are fairly clear in their neutrally descriptive distinctions from one another. In describing harsh disposition or behavior, however, their shadings of meaning are somewhat blurred. *Sour* applies almost solely to mood or disposition, suggesting a pessimistic, disenchanted, or excessively solemn attitude: wearing a *sour* expression no pleasantry could soften; recalling her former idealism with a *sour* smile; having to confront his *sour* face. *Bitter* suggests an even fiercer gloominess that arises from a sense of having been unjustly treated or from a deep-seated anger that smolders without catching fire: a *bitter* man who saw nothing worthy of admiration no matter where he looked; *bitter* accusations concerning the division of the money. *Tart* applies more appropriately to particular instances of behavior and suggests impertinence or sassiness: giving a *tart* answer to the teacher's scolding. *Acid* and *acidulous* are difficult to distinguish except for the greater formality of the latter; *acidulous* might sometimes suggest an abiding mood, and *acid* an actual expression: an *acidulous* temper; an *acid* remark. In any case, *acid* seems considerably stronger in its suggestions of harsh or gratuitous hostility: *Bitter* at his own lack of success as a playwright, the critic was negative and *acid* in all his comments.

Acrid and *caustic* are the most intense of these adjectives in pointing to harsh dispositions or expressions. *Acrid* applies best to mood: an *acrid* curtness of manner. It can also apply, however, to expressions: an *acrid* scowl disfiguring her face. *Caustic* perhaps suggests an even fiercer hostility than *acrid*, since it carries over here its implication of corrosive power: often filled with a *caustic* rage; *caustic* aspersions on his friend's abilities; answers so *caustic* as to suggest a mental imbalance. See SARCASTIC, SAVORY, VINDICTIVE.

Antonyms: BLAND, *kind*, OPTIMISTIC, *sweet*.

sparkling

    flashing
    flickering
    glimmering
    glittering
    scintillating
    shimmering
    twinkling

These adjectives characterize wavering coruscations of light, whether reflected from a moving surface or emitted unsteadily by the source of light itself. **Sparkling** would seem to suggest the throwing off of sparks, but as now used it is almost exclusively restricted to uneven, bright flashes reflected from light-catching objects: *sparkling* diamonds. **Glittering** is close to *sparkling* in meaning; *sparkling* perhaps suggests more intense stabs of more fleeting light, while *glittering* might suggest a larger mass of reflecting material that can be seen over a longer time and that casts reflections less dependent on an exact perspective: a *sparkling* drop of dew; the *glittering*, rain-washed garden. In more general uses, *sparkling* suggests exuberance or animation, while *glittering* may have connotations of gaudiness, cheapness, or evil: her *sparkling* smile; *glittering* trinkets; *glittering* generalities; the *glittering* greed in his eyes.

Flashing, when used for sources of light, suggests most strongly a regular alternation of light and darkness: the *flashing* red of the traffic light. Used for reflected light, it does not suggest regularity so much as intensity; it may not even suggest wavering light at all: the *flashing*, sunlit windows. Like *sparkling*, *flashing* may suggest liveliness, but more often of an unpleasant nature: the *flashing* eyes of rage. Both **twinkling** and **scintillating** describe, most specifically, starlight that appears to waver because of the moving atmosphere through which we see it. *Twinkling* can seem coy outside its nursery-rhyme context, but may escape this in descriptive uses: the *twinkling* lights of the city far below. *Scintillating* has overtones of brilliance and has been overused in figurative contexts to suggest elegance and wit: *scintillating* conversation.

Flickering, **glimmering**, and **shimmering** all suggest a subdued or dim wavering of light. *Flickering* mostly relates to sources rather than reflections of light, but suggests a more sporadic or irregular wavering than the earlier adjectives: patches of clouds that let through only *flickering* sunlight. *Flickering* has been overused to describe firelight: *flickering* logs on the andirons. *Shimmering*, in contrast, stresses reflected light that undulates quickly in a soft or dazzling blur: *shimmering* water. *Glimmering* may apply either to sources or to reflections; more than either of its two companion terms, it stresses fitfulness and dimness, suggesting a source fainter than for *flickering* and undulations slower than for *shimmering*: the last coals of the *glimmering* fire; traces of moonlight in the *glimmering* darkness of the room. See BRIGHT, LUMINOUS.

Antonyms: *dull,* GLOOMY, LACKLUSTER.

specific

definite
explicit
express

These adjectives characterize a communication that is without ambiguity, vagueness, or evasion. With **specific**, the emphasis is on a lack of vagueness achieved by detailed rather than general treatment: *specific* instructions on how to cope with every conceivable problem. **Definite** refers either to clarity and distinctness or to expression that is conclusive or unconditional: a map that would give them a *definite* notion of their whereabouts; promising to have a *definite* yes-or-

no answer within a week. As in the last example, *definite* may indicate extreme brevity, whereas *specific* tends to suggest exhaustive treatment. Something that is *specific*, furthermore, may still be unclear or inconclusive, regardless of its concreteness and detail: a study that was *specific* in listing alternatives but not *definite* about which might give the best results.

Explicit stresses an exact spelling-out that leaves nothing to be guessed at or confused by. When descriptions or instructions are involved, one would normally have to be both *specific* and *definite* to be *explicit*; if a judgment is involved, one would have to be *definite*, but not necessarily *specific*: an *explicit* list of all campaign expenditures; a brief remark that made *explicit* her dislike of Picasso. *Explicit* may tend to relate to questions, *definite* to answers: an *explicit* request that he give a *definite* reply. **Express** is similar to, but an intensification of, *explicit*. It suggests emphatic directness that avoids the tacit or evasive: unwilling to disobey an *express* command. *Express* also is often related to the posing of questions or the stating of one's desires: her *express* wish that she be cremated. See ACCURATE, CLEAR, CONCLUSIVE.

Antonyms: *ambiguous, evasive,* OBSCURE, VAGUE.

spectator

fan
kibitzer
observer
onlooker
peeping Tom
voyeur
witness

These nouns denote someone watching an event. **Spectator** can indicate someone present at a sporting event or other happening; no direct participation is implied, but the term often suggests that a *spectator* has made the effort to attend or be a member of the audience: *spectators* at the tennis match; *spectators* lined up to watch the parade. Less often, *spectator* can suggest the opposite: millions of people who unexpectedly became *spectators* at the world's first televised homicide. **Onlooker**, by contrast, more often suggests an accidental or chance viewing of some event: *onlookers* who happened to be present when the bridge collapsed. *Onlooker* may also suggest someone who has deliberately withdrawn from events he or she might well have participated in: He chose to remain an *onlooker* during most of the family's quarrels.

Fan and **kibitzer** are more informal than *spectator* and *onlooker*, but both specifically suggest the interested and voluntary viewing of something. *Fan* relates to *spectator* in particularly emphasizing the ardent advocacy of a given artist, performer, or team: They performed in a hall that held thousands of screaming *fans;* booed by *fans* for the home team. *Fan* need not, however, imply a physical gathering at all: a *fan* of the prolific mystery writer; a market of *fans* for every new record they made. *Kibitzer* relates to *onlooker* in indicating someone on the sidelines of an event, but who in this case can't refrain from commenting on the action, or otherwise meddling in it, even to the point of being drawn into direct involvement: *kibitzers* at ringside who shouted advice to the champ; a personal argument that at first attracted *kibitzers* and finally turned into a general brawl.

Peeping Tom and **voyeur** denote *onlookers* who deliberately spy on others. *Peeping Tom,* the more informal of the two, may sometimes suggest a devious attempt to gain information, but more often it suggests a person who gets erotic pleasure from spying on unsuspecting people who are not fully dressed: a *peeping Tom* who kept watch on the apartment bedrooms across the street from him. *Voyeur* is the psychiatric term for such a person, although here the term includes, as well, any sort of erotic pleasure derived from looking rather than active involvement, even where stealth is not present: permissive parents whose open intimacies tend to make *voyeurs* of their children.

Observer is uniquely relevant to someone specifically assigned the role of watching rather than participating, particularly someone who remains impartial and has no authority to affect the outcome: UN *observers* deployed as a peacekeeping force in the truce zone. *Observer* can also indicate the role assumed by someone, such as a commentator or critic, who is a perceptive viewer of events and reports on them or analyzes them: a keen *observer* of the art scene. In this case, it is the *observer* who may have the audience, whereas the things he or she reports may not. **Witness** may suggest accidental viewing, like *onlooker: witnesses* to the accident. It may also suggest someone who deliberately experiences something in order to report it: a crusading *witness* to racial injustice. It may, in fact, refer to the report itself: bearing false *witness. Witness,* in the legal context, can refer either to *onlookers* or anyone else called to testify in court, or to people called on to observe and certify a transaction: *witnesses* who gave conflicting testimony; needing two *witnesses* to make the ceremony legal. See SEE, VISION.

Antonyms: *participant,* PERFORMER.

speech
address
discourse
harangue
homily
lecture
oration
sermon

These nouns apply to public speaking, denoting talks delivered before an audience. **Speech** is the most general and least formal word. A *speech* may be either extemporaneous or prepared; it may express feelings, ideas, or opinions; impart information; relate experiences; set forth a program; or outline a position: a campaign *speech;* a ghostwritten *speech;* an impromptu *speech;* an after-dinner *speech.* An **address** is a carefully prepared, formal *speech,* as one delivered by a distinguished speaker or made on a ceremonial occasion: an inaugural *address;* a valedictory *address.* Also, where *speech* emphasizes the act of talking, *address* stresses the fact that an audience is in attendance: a malcontent making *speeches* on street corners; the President's annual *address* to Congress.

An **oration** is an eloquent *address* meant to stir the emotions of a group or mass of people. It treats some important subject in a dignified style and manner, according to the rules of oratory, and is usually delivered on a special occasion, as at a celebration or a funeral: Mark Antony's *oration* over the body of Caesar; Lincoln's Gettysburg *Address* is an *oration.* Since true orators are rare, however, the term *oration* may also be applied to a pompous *speech* designed for showy, oratorical effect: an old-fashioned, small-town, Fourth-of-July *oration.* A **harangue** is a long, loud, vehement *speech* appealing to passions or prejudices. It may be an extemporaneous tirade and is often intended to inflame those to whom it is addressed and to spur them to action of some sort: the *harangues* of a demagogue. In a looser sense, *harangue* may apply to any long, bombastic *speech,* typically a tiresome one: endless *harangues.*

Where *oration* and *harangue* emphasize the character of an *address,* the remaining nouns stress content and purpose. A **discourse** is a fairly long, carefully prepared, well-organized *speech* on a definite subject: a *discourse* on Vergil; a collection of religious *discourses.* A **lecture** is a *discourse* on a given topic intended to inform and instruct a group of students or some similar audience: a *lecture* course in college, as distinguished from a seminar; a series of museum *lectures* on modern art. *Lecture* derives from a Latin verb meaning read. The most effective *lectures* are not read, but giving a *lecture* does imply extensive previous preparation, including the writing down of what is to be said.

Both **sermon** (the general word) and **homily** (the more erudite term) may mean an instructive religious *discourse* delivered by a clergyman to a congregation. Originally, a *homily* was a *discourse* or *lecture* explaining a Biblical text, while a *sermon* was an *address* from the pulpit dealing with dogma or ethics. Now the opposite distinction is sometimes made; a *sermon* takes its theme from Scripture while a *homily* gives ethical guidance. In the Middle Ages, *homilies* written by learned churchmen were often read in churches, being used as approved *sermons*. Hence, the branch of theological study that treats of the art of planning, writing, and delivering *sermons* is called homiletics.

In informal use, *lecture, sermon,* and *harangue* may all imply didactic moral instruction, referring to formal reproofs, stern rebukes, lengthy reprimands, or earnest exhortations to duty. [He gave the boy a *lecture* on lateness; She was subjected to a *harangue* on ingratitude; "All right, I'll do it," I said. "You don't have to preach me a *sermon* about it."] See CONVERSATION.

speechless

dumb
inarticulate
incoherent
mute

These adjectives all characterize an inability or unwillingness to speak or produce sound or be intelligible. **Speechless** often refers to a transitory inability to speak because of shock or powerful emotions: *speechless* at the news. But *speechless* sometimes can also indicate an impairment of speech functions: The brain damage resulted in an aphasia that rendered her permanently *speechless*. Much more commonly, however, **dumb** or **mute** refers to any such sort of permanent inability to speak. *Dumb* may refer to this inability when caused by some defect of the speech organs, whereas *mute* is often the word of choice when the inability results, instead, from never having heard speech sounds, as in deafness sustained since infancy: a child who was *dumb* because of deformed vocal cords; a technique for teaching *mute* children to speak despite their deafness. Sometimes, *mute* is substituted for *dumb*, regardless of cause, since *dumb* can also

apply informally as a pejorative word for mental dullness. This linking of two unrelated deprivations may once have been deliberate, but it is now felt to be both inaccurate and cruel. *Dumb* can also function like *speechless* to indicate a temporary loss of speech, though it can refer as well to an inability to make any sort of sound because of shock or emotion: *dumb* with fright. In this context, *mute* more often refers to a deliberate refusal to speak: She answered his question with *mute* contempt; a prisoner who stolidly remained *mute* under excruciating torture. When the reference is not to people, *dumb* refers to a possibly natural or normal incapacity for speech but not necessarily to an inability to produce sound: *dumb* animals. In a similar situation, *mute* may refer to complete soundlessness: the *mute* hush of the forest at dusk. The verb form of *mute* is of interest here, since it refers to altered or subdued sound: *muted* trumpets.

Inarticulate can be a vague and confusing word, since it can refer to what is soundless, *speechless,* unintelligible, confused, or halting. Only context can make clear which notion is intended: His mouth worked to form words, but he remained completely *inarticulate;* gasping in *inarticulate* fright; lines in the play that were lost because of *inarticulate* mumbling; an *inarticulate* presentation of her ideas; simple lessons that help stutterers become less *inarticulate*. **Incoherent** can sometimes be substituted for *speechless,* but most often it clearly implies confused statements or halting speech: an *incoherent* essay filled with circumlocution and digression; stammered accusations and *incoherent* outcries. See SILENT, TACITURN.

Antonyms: *articulate,* TALKATIVE, VERBOSE.

speed

alacrity
celerity
dispatch
haste
hurry
promptness
swiftness
velocity

These nouns refer to rapid motion or to the immediate execution of a task. **Speed, swiftness**, and **velocity** are the most general of these, with *speed* the least formal and *velocity* the most formal. *Speed* can be used of any rapid and continuing motion: The *speed* of the racehorses was amazing. It is especially appropriate in referring to vehicles, machines, or inanimate projectiles: *Speed* and more *speed* are what the racing enthusiast is after. It can, of course, refer to the rate of motion and not necessarily to fast motion at all: The tortoise crept along at an agonizingly slow *speed*. *Velocity* has only scientific or technical uses and would sound pretentious in other situations. It can refer to rapid, continuing motion, but is more often used for rate of motion. [The rocket attained an orbit of dizzying *velocity*; The *velocity* of sound falls far short of the *speed* of light.] *Swiftness* does not apply to rate of motion but is otherwise almost interchangeable with *speed*. It is slightly more formal, however, and would be used less for vehicles and machines than for living things. It may have a lyrical or poetic quality that is by no means trite or stilted. [The mallards streamed across the sky with a *swiftness* that dazzled onlookers; A ballet dancer must possess both strength and *swiftness*.] Unlike *speed*, *swiftness* often also refers to a brief interval: the *swiftness* with which she correctly answered my questions.

Haste and **hurry** both refer to a rushed manner of behavior. *Haste* is equally appropriate to formal and informal contexts and tends to imply the ineffective performance of a task, as in the motto *Haste* makes waste. When this overtone is absent, an extremely brief or partial action is still implied: Forgive the *haste* with which this note is written; I will soon send a long letter. *Hurry* is more informal than *haste*, but otherwise similar in its possible overtone of ineffectiveness: How can you avoid mistakes when you're in such a *hurry?*

Dispatch is much more formal than either *haste* or *hurry* and is opposed to them in implying rapid action that is both efficient and thorough. It also suggests the total completion of a task. [Where could he find an assistant who could work with such *dispatch?* The *dispatch* with which the children finished the leftovers astonished the adults at the table.] **Promptness**, while slightly less formal than *dispatch*, also suggests an efficient *swiftness*; it is restricted, however, to refer to punctuality or to the accomplishment of a task in a given time. [Haste cannot make up for your lack of *promptness*; Despite the interruption of communications, the correspondents turned in their reports with their customary *promptness*.] It can also refer to the briefness of an interval of time: The *promptness* of your reply delighted me.

Alacrity and **celerity** are the most formal of these nouns and apply more to readiness in a person's attitude than to *speed* of motion. *Alacrity* implies a cheerful willingness to act: The waiter's *alacrity* in greeting us and finding us a table surpassed the *speed* with which our food was served. *Celerity* may also be used in this way but, unlike *alacrity*, it can apply simply to the *speed* of a continuing motion: The ungainly look of an ostrich is belied by the *celerity* with which it can outdistance its more graceful enemies. Both nouns tend to sound pretentious or stilted. See QUICK, QUICKEN.

Antonyms: DELAY, *languor, slowness, sluggishness.*

spendthrift
improvident
prodigal
thriftless
wasteful

These adjectives refer to the extravagant or imprudent spending or use of one's resources. **Spendthrift** is the most informal of these terms and the most clear and specific. It points exclusively to the spending of one's money in ways that are excessive, unwise, or unnecessary: putting their children on strict allowances to cure them of being *spendthrift*. By itself, however, *spendthrift* carries no implications about the money available to such a spender or about the consequences of such spending: a legendary *spendthrift* millionaire; the penurious rich and the *spendthrift* poor. *Spendthrift* was once, perhaps, more disapproving than it necessarily is now: uncomplaining when hard up, but *spendthrift* with windfalls.

Of the remaining adjectives, **prodigal** is closest in meaning to *spendthrift*, though it refers beyond the spending of money to any lavish or foolish extravagance, often one of awesome proportions: a *prodigal* shopping spree; the *prodigal* extravaganzas Hollywood once turned out. *Prodigal* may be used without disapproval for extreme generosity: *prodigal* in the time she spent with interns who needed help. In any case, it emphasizes the amount of expenditure involved, whereas *spendthrift* can conceivably suggest the unconcerned spending of what one has, regardless of the amount. Sometimes, *prodigal* is understood as referring to someone who, after having wasted all of his substance, returns home in repentance, after the Biblical parable of the *prodigal* son.

Improvident, the most formal of these adjectives, indicates the unwise use of anything, with a specific emphasis on failing to foresee or provide for the future: the *improvident* grasshopper in the fable that, unlike the industrious ant, had failed to lay in supplies against the winter; *improvident* bon vivants who live with no thought for tomorrow. **Thriftless** relates to

427

improvident in pointing to someone unable to save money or live economically, but the emphasis on futurity is not necessarily present: the average bachelor's *thriftless* hit-or-miss budgeting of income. *Thriftless* is distinct from *spendthrift* in that no squandering need be implied; an impoverished family could not be *prodigal*, though it might or might not be *spendthrift* with what resources it had. It would most likely, however, be compelled to be thrifty.

Wasteful is the most general of these adjectives in applying widely beyond the context of spending money; it suggests an unwise or reckless misuse of resources that fails to get full benefit from them: *wasteful* to spend so much on a dress you'll wear only once; *wasteful* of the company's time, though miserly with my own; tragically *wasteful* of natural resources that can never be replaced. See GENEROUS, RECKLESS.

Antonyms: CAUTIOUS, *frugal, miserly, niggardly, thrifty.*

spontaneous

  extemporaneous
  impromptu
  improvised
  impulsive
  unplanned
  unpremeditated
  unrehearsed

These adjectives characterize actions taken on the spur of the moment or without forethought. **Spontaneous** includes both these ideas and may often include suggestions of naturalness, frankness, and good humor: the child's *spontaneous* answers to all our questions. Sometimes, *spontaneous* is deliberately contrasted with such adjectives as routinized or conformist: the *spontaneous* exuberance of teenagers when they feel free to be themselves. In another use, *spontaneous* is sometimes restricted in reference to voluntary rather than coerced action, or to action that comes about by general agreement arising out of immediate circumstances: a *spontaneous* decision to vote for the insurgent candidate despite the pleas of the incumbent; a *spontaneous* protest demonstration that began with a handful of disgruntled students. **Impulsive** is far less positive in its implications than *spontaneous*. It may, in fact, suggest someone governed by or at the mercy of his or her whims or moods without regard for others. *Impulsive*, consequently, lacks the overtone of good humor present in *spontaneous* and can apply to ugly or disruptive actions as well as to pleasant ones: an *impulsive* generosity that

alternates fitfully with equally *impulsive* temper tantrums. In some cases, *impulsive* can be used to describe actions occurring on the spur of the moment: supermarkets that display their wares to encourage customers to make *impulsive* purchases.

Unplanned is the most neutral of these adjectives in stressing only the lack of forethought and carrying no emotional overtones about the quality of the action: an *unplanned* stopover in San Francisco because of engine trouble; an *unplanned* interview that enabled the speakers to explore questions in depth. **Unpremeditated** is the most technical of these adjectives; in legal terminology, it refers to an *impulsive* crime committed without forethought and therefore *unplanned*. This would be less serious than the same crime devised in advance. Except in a legal context, it would sound stiff as a substitute for *unplanned* or *impulsive*, unless a comic touch were intended: a party that became an *unpremeditated* disaster.

The remaining adjectives pertain mostly to a context of public speaking or musical and theatrical performance. **Extemporaneous** refers specifically to a speech delivered with few or no notes, but especially without a written version of the speech to be given: ministers long accustomed to working all night on an *extemporaneous* Sunday sermon; the call-in program that by its very nature had to be *extemporaneous*. **Impromptu** pertains, most specifically, to a kind of musical performance in which the music played is invented as the performer goes along: an overblown piano fantasy that was surely *impromptu*. *Impromptu* is also often used of speeches delivered on short notice: *impromptu* speeches tacked onto each seconding motion. In this area, *impromptu* can be distinguished from *extemporaneous* in that the latter may be a matter of choice, even when the speech has been set long in advance, whereas *impromptu* suggests being called on to speak when one is not expecting it and is therefore of necessity unprepared. [The dean gave the same *extemporaneous* reprimand, word for word, to every student caught cheating; nor did he flicker an eyelid as he listened to the students' *impromptu* replies.]

Both **unrehearsed** and **improvised** can be used in either a musical or a theatrical context. *Unrehearsed*, here, may suggest that a set piece is to be performed, but that the players have not previously practiced it. In this context, *improvised* would suggest a basic structure within which the players have considerable opportunities for *spontaneous* invention. Although *improvised* is generally used in a neutrally descriptive way, *unrehearsed* can sometimes suggest a negative judgment: Jazz is necessarily *improvised,* but it is ridiculous to think of it as *unrehearsed.* In a more general context, *unrehearsed* approaches *spontaneous* in its implications, stressing a voluntary and *unplanned* telling or acting out: She asked bluntly if the witness's testimony was freely given and *unrehearsed. Improvised* can suggest a rough-and-ready substitute for something lacking or the making of decisions as one goes along: an *improvised* tent pole made from a stripped branch; an *improvised* tour, taking them from place to place as the spirit moved them. See VAGUE, WANDER.

Antonyms: *definite, forced,* FORMAL, *stylized.*

spread

circulate
distribute
propagate

These verbs refer to the gradual gaining of ground by something. **Spread** is the most informal and general of these, with particular usefulness in referring to the ground gained by a species, a disease, an idea, or a cultural mannerism: deciduous trees that slowly *spread* over most of the world; rats that *spread* bubonic plague throughout Europe; a rash *spreading* over most of my body; ideas that *spread* more rapidly in an age of instant communications; men's fashions that *spread* quickly from London to New York. **Propagate** also refers to something that gains ground or adherents. It suggests a conscious, laborious effort to stimulate the healthy growth of something: *propagating* a new species of grapefruit. It can also apply to an insidious or harmful *spreading* of information: *propagating* the myth of racial superiority for devious ends.

Distribute and **circulate** lack both the negative implications possible for *propagate.* They are both most often neutral in their concentration on techniques for the wide *spreading* of something through space. *Distribute* emphasizes easy access and is particularly relevant in reference to periodicals: noisy trucks that *distribute* newspapers throughout the city. The point of *distribute* may be making available something to everyone concerned, or parceling out a given quantity among a group: *distributing* a copy of the new insurance plan to everyone in the office. *Circulate* is less concrete in reference than *distribute;* it may also refer to *distributing* periodicals: a paper that is *circulated* to homeowners. More often, however, this word, as a verb, refers to actual movement through a mass: arterial blood that *circulates* oxygen throughout the body. *Circulate* may also point to a movement of ideas or mannerisms among a circle of people: conservative notions that *circulate* among the power elite. See ENLARGE, PERMEATE, ESCALATE, SCATTER.

Antonyms: ACCUMULATE, DESTROY, GATHER.

spur

goad
nag
needle
sting

These verbs refer to the act of inciting or taunting someone or something. **Spur** can refer literally to horseback riding, indicating the urging of a horse forward by jabbing it in the sides with one's heels or with devices worn on the heels for this purpose: He *spurred* his horse forward. In other uses, *spur* can similarly point to anything that jogs or jolts awareness or that stimulates interest: a speech designed to *spur* the nation on toward its goal of a just peace. Unlike other verbs here, *spur* can be used with no implication of a negative or punitive act, often pointing instead to a pleasant arousal of eagerness or desire that results in speeded-up action: a lively plot that will *spur* the most lethargic reader to forge ahead to the book's completion.

Goad referred originally to a spear or pike used to drive animals forward. Unlike *spur, goad* seldom leaves completely behind this notion of a harassing action that forces someone or something to move forward: editorials that attempted to *goad* the government on to fulfilling its promises. Sometimes, *goad* can indicate a penchant for troublemaking without implying any constructive effort at reform: She constantly *goaded* her son about what she saw as the failings of his wife. Or *goad* can indicate being bothered and distracted by the pressure of external forces: people *goaded* by the heat; *goaded* by the demands of her job into a nervous breakdown.

Sting particularly suggests chagrin because of some rebuff or because of the worrying action of one's conscience. [He was *stung* by your refusal to greet him on the street; Her act of duplicity *stung* every time she thought of it.] **Needle** can also refer to the workings of conscience: constantly *needled* by the growing conviction that they had failed their children. More often, however, *needle* refers to an insistent and possibly insidious wearing away by one person of another person's self-esteem or vanity, usually with little attempt at constructive criticism: a playwright who loved to *needle* middle-class audiences about their values. Occasionally, a serious impulse at reform can be indicated: *a gadfly who* needled *the administration about its failures in urban renewal until it was* goaded *into reexamining its housing program.*

Nag stresses the repetitious insistence with which someone carries on trivial criticisms of someone else. *Nag* typically is applied to the actions of a wife who berates her husband for failings, large or small, but it can apply more widely: *a* nagging *boss; leaders who know how to get results without constant* nagging. *Nag* can also apply to any moderate but annoying persistence: *a* nagging *back pain.* See BOTHER, FAULTFINDING, INCITE, STIMULATE.

Antonyms: *palliate,* QUELL, *quiet,* STOP, SUBDUE.

spurious

apocryphal
counterfeit
forged
shoddy

These adjectives characterize something false or worthless, particularly when it is passed off as being genuine or valuable. **Spurious**, the most general of these, derives ultimately from a Latin word for bastard. It is harshly condemnatory in tone, whether or not an attempt to deceive is implied. It rarely now refers to illegitimacy: *a* spurious *heir.* More often it refers to something that has been mistaken for the real item: spurious *paintings attributed to old masters.* Often, the adjective leaves no doubt that deception is involved: *a candidate who made* spurious *campaign promises in order to get elected.* But when *spurious* applies to reason or logic, a deliberate attempt to mislead need not be involved: *Invalid assumptions lead to* spurious *conclusions; an attempt to demonstrate that the thesis was* spurious *in every detail.*

Counterfeit and **forged** are exclusively focused on deliberate attempts to deceive or defraud. Most typically, *counterfeit* pertains to false money, *forged* to false signatures, as on a check: counterfeit *twenty-dollar bills; a* forged *endorsement on the traveler's check.* Both adjectives can also apply to anything that is made to pass for something authentic or valuable: *a* counterfeit *painting;* forged *papal decretals.* Usually, *forged* retains some implication of a false signature that seems to validate a product or document, but *counterfeit* applies more widely to anything insincere: *an attempt to deceive the public with their* counterfeit *optimism over the results of the government*

action; the counterfeit *concern he lavished on his wife in public.*

Shoddy can still occasionally refer to a fabric of reclaimed wool. By extension, it now refers universally to anything inferior in materials or construction: shoddy *housing developments sure to become the slums of the future.* Shoddy *can also point to any vulgar or pretentious imitation or anything cheap that purports to be of superior quality:* shoddy *nightclubs whose meretricious glitter is designed to trap tourists.* Sometimes, shoddy *stresses whatever is unsavory, worn-out, or of dubious reputation: the bum's* shoddy *clothes; the* shoddy *red-light district; a* shoddy *criminal lawyer.*

Apocryphal is the most restricted of these adjectives in that it always applies to accounts of the past whose truth or accuracy cannot be determined. In reference to disputed theological documents, the implication is that such works have been rejected from the accepted or official canon: the apocryphal *sayings of Jesus that are excluded from the New Testament.* Outside this context, *apocryphal* can refer less negatively to what is legendary or unprovable: *an* apocryphal *story about Lincoln as a young boy.* Here, it can refer to any body of myth and anecdote that grows up around an object of reverence or curiosity: apocryphal *feats attributed to Babe Ruth.* See ARTIFICIAL, DECEPTION, SHAM.

Antonyms: ACCURATE, GENUINE, SINCERE.

spy

agent
agent provocateur
counterspy
double agent
secret agent

These nouns all denote a person who secretly gathers information about persons or about countries other than his or her own, usually for destructive purposes. **Spy** is the most general term. In a narrow sense, a *spy* is one engaged in espionage—that is, a *spy* is sent into a belligerent country to obtain military or political secrets. If captured, especially in time of war, a *spy* is subject to execution. In a wider sense, *spy* is derogatory and is applied to anyone who uses underhand and furtive methods of observing the activities of others, usually for personal gain: *The president of the firm has* spies *in every department.*

Agent and **secret agent** are now preferred over *spy* when signifying a person employed by a government to engage in espionage. An *agent* or *secret agent* enters a foreign country under a disguise and usually resides there for a time. The intent is to learn the military secrets and other facts about that country which will be of use to the *agent's* own government. An *agent* may also be sent within the borders of a belligerent power to commit acts of sabotage that will weaken the defenses of the enemy. *Agent* or *secret agent* may also be applied to investigators within a government who probe into treasonable activities, counterfeiting, or other infringements of federal laws: an FBI *agent*.

A **counterspy** is an *agent* who spies on the *secret agents* of the enemy, often within the *secret agents'* country, in order to thwart their activities and destroy their efficiency.

The **double agent**, or double *spy,* is employed simultaneously by two opposing countries and engages in espionage against both of them while pretending to be working for only one. A *double agent* may actually be loyal to one country or may practice deception toward both sides. *Double agents* often make effective *counterspies.*

Agent provocateur is a French term designating a *spy* who is planted in a trade union, political party, or other organization in which there are conflicting loyalties. The method of the *agent provocateur* is to gain the trust of the members of the group and to stir them to actions or declarations that will incur punishment. *Agent provocateur* also carries a suggestion of opprobrium, since the *agent provocateur* may be acting against and betraying his or her own kind. See OVERHEAR, SPECTATOR, STEALTHY.

squash. Do not confuse the verb *squash* (primary meaning: squeeze) with the verb *quash* (annul, reject legally).

squeal
cheep
chirp
peep
screech
squawk
squeak

These words are imitative of the shrill cries made by certain birds, insects, or animals. All may be used as either nouns or verbs, and most apply to human sounds as well and have other, extended applications. A **squeal** is a shrill, high-pitched, somewhat prolonged nasal cry, the sort of sound that is made by a young pig. **Squeak** denotes a shorter, weaker cry—a very high-pitched, thin, sharp, penetrating sound, as the little piping noise made by a mouse. One may *squeal* out of surprise, excitement, fright, pain, anger, or protest: children *squealing* with delight; to *squeal* in terror at a horror movie. One may *squeak* because of a high-pitched voice or laryngitis: The boy's voice was changing and would go from a deep tone to a shrill *squeak* without warning.

Screech and **squawk** refer to shrill, harsh cries or to sounds that are strident or raucous. A *screech* is a long, harsh, piercing sound—a grating scream or shriek: a small owl that *screeches* weirdly instead of hooting. One may *screech* out of pain, terror, or anguish: a *screeching* woman trapped in a burning building. *Screech* is also disdainfully applied to a loud, high singing voice that sounds terribly forced and strained: That soprano isn't singing—she's *screeching!* A *squawk* is a shrill, harsh cry such as is made by a parrot or a frightened hen. *Squawk* is also applied to any sound reminiscent of such a cry: a *squawking* radio.

Chirp, **cheep**, and **peep** denote the high, thin, pointed sounds made by young birds. A *chirp* is a clear, bright sound—a short, sharp, high-pitched cry, as one made repeatedly by a bird or insect: *chirping* sparrows; the cricket's *chirp.* A person may make a somewhat similar sound (or chirrup) by drawing the breath through the closed lips, as in greeting an infant or urging on a horse. A *cheep* is a faint, shrill sound—a weak, feeble *chirp* or *squeak:* the *cheep* of a small bat. A *peep* is the kind of tiny cry made by a newly hatched chick: the *peep* of a frightened mouse. Applied to human utterance, *chirp* means talk or say in a quick, vivacious way, or cry out cheerfully with birdlike enthusiasm: "Good morning," *chirped* the children.

Applied to things, *squeak* designates a shrill, creaking sound indicative of stiffness or friction: the *squeak* of new shoes; a *squeaking* hinge. *Squeal* refers to a loud, drawn-out, nasal sound reminiscent of a hurt, protesting cry: *squealing* brakes. *Screech* implies a harsher, more earsplitting noise: The subway train *screeched* to a stop.

In idiomatic speech, to *squeak* by or *squeak* through is to make it by a hairsbreadth, to succeed by an extremely narrow margin: He managed to *squeak* through the course. In slang usage, to *squeal* is to turn informer, betraying one's confederates, as in crime: You'd better not *squeal* if you know what's good for you. To *squawk* is to complain or protest loudly in a harsh, shrill way: He really *squawked* when he found the hotel didn't have their reservations. A *peep* is the slightest sound one can make, especially a sign of dissatisfaction: I don't want to hear a *peep* out of you. See CHATTER, CRY.

stand

attitude
policy
position
posture

These nouns are comparable when they indicate a point of view or conviction about a practical matter, usually one expressed in words. **Stand** and **position** both refer to definite, expressed convictions about single issues that are the focal points of disagreement, debate, or controversy. *Stand* often implies an emotional commitment, although it does not exclude intellectual or rational grounds for one's feeling: to take a strong *stand* in favor of amending the abortion law. *Position* implies a more dispassionate and restrained attitude, often one decided upon after lengthy deliberation. [My *position* on civil rights is well known; He took the *position* that salvation depended upon good deeds as well as piety.]

Policy implies a definite structure of convictions based on an assessment of needs, interests, goals, or principles: The United States government follows a *policy* of promoting democracy in Central America. In less formal contexts *policy* may mean any general rule of conduct: It's bad *policy* to continue lending money to friends who make no effort to help themselves. **Posture** in recent years has come to mean *policy* in a formal sense: the defense *posture* of the U.S. But *posture* may indicate also the actual disposition of forces: a military *posture* that embraced the deployment of intercontinental ballistic missiles. In its several implications, *posture* may also include the sense of **attitude**. *Attitude*, a more general term than the others here considered, indicates a personal or institutional feeling, often unexpressed and vague in nature: the sympathetic *attitude* of the government in dealing with problems of the homeless. In this it is at the other pole from *policy*, which represents a clearly formulated and precise enunciation of one's view. *Posture* is therefore useful in suggesting a hardening of *attitude* without going so far as to imply a firm *policy:* the neutral *posture* of the U.S. in the Arab-Israeli confrontation; the belligerent *posture* of India toward Pakistan resulting from unresolved border disputes. See OPINION.

standard

criterion
gauge
measure
test
touchstone
yardstick

These nouns refer to sets of rules or principles by which to evaluate the quality of something. **Standard** implies an objective, impartial rule or set of rules spelled out in advance: the army's *standards* for physical fitness; research that does not meet our *standard* for accuracy.

Gauge and **measure** may both suggest an actual physical tool to determine the dimensions or attributes of a product: a *gauge* (also, in technical use, *gage*) for determining the thickness of wire; an anemometer or other *measure* of wind velocity. Rather than the yes-or-no evaluation suggested by *standard, gauge* and *measure* suggest an objective assessment of attributes. In more metaphorical uses, *measure* is the less formal of the two: agricultural production as a *gauge* of the economy's effectiveness; an honor system that will be a *measure* of our students' character.

Test emphasizes the act of evaluation. The previous nouns suggest that means exist for evaluation and for assessment, without necessarily implying that they will be used. *Test* strongly implies an actual application of these means: combat as a *test* of a soldier's bravery. [The *standards* applied so rigorously in our factory are nothing compared with the real *test* to which customers put our product in daily use.]

Criterion, the most formal of all these nouns, suggests the independent existence of *standards* that stress excellence. The implication is less strong than the discriminations suggested by *criterion. Criterion,* therefore, may suggest implicit taste as a more important part of a *test* than the mechanical application of an objective *measure* or *gauge:* candidates who feel that the sole *criterion* for office is the ability to win votes; a philosophy that requires each person to state the *criteria* behind every judgment that is made.

Touchstone and **yardstick** are metaphorical in suggesting something against which any attempt may be contrasted. *Yardstick,* the most informal of any of these nouns, implies a set of rules that are based on common sense, are easy to apply, and give a cut-and-dried answer: a low rate of unemployment as the least ambiguous *yardstick* of an economy. *Touchstone,* by contrast, suggests a set of imponderable values that cannot be spelled out so much as embodied in an earlier work against which the work in question is compared: Greek and Elizabethan tragedies that are the *touchstones* for all later theatrical effort. *Touchstone* suggests a rarefied level of aesthetic discrimination based on tradition and precedence; it may even suggest preciosity: new artists who shattered the *touchstones* of Victorian sensibility. See CONTROL.

stealthy

clandestine
furtive
sneaky
surreptitious
underhand

These adjectives characterize things done in concealment so as not to be noticed or found out. **Stealthy** comes from an Old English word meaning steal. It suggests the quiet of an animal moving on padded feet, slyly stealing up on its prey or warily making its way past its enemies. [The scout made a *stealthy* approach to the enemy position; The escaping prisoners moved with *stealthy* tread until they were out of earshot of the sleeping guards.] **Furtive** comes from the Latin word for thief. It suggests the quick, nervous movements of someone who feels guilty or fears capture: the *furtive* manner of an escaped convict; A *furtive* glance confirmed his fears—he was being followed. **Surreptitious** comes from Latin roots meaning snatch secretly. It describes something forbidden that is done or enjoyed on the sly, at an opportune moment when no one is looking: the *surreptitious* reading of a friend's private diary; a dieter's *surreptitious* snack.

Clandestine comes from a Latin word meaning in secret. It suggests the wariness of a person who hides what he is doing because of the social or political danger of discovery. What is done *clandestinely* either is illicit or is considered to be so, being kept under wraps because it is frowned on by society or forbidden by those in authority: a *clandestine* meeting of young lovers; the *clandestine* meeting of a local official and racketeers. Where a *surreptitious* act is done quickly, a *clandestine* activity may be carried on over a long period of time: a *clandestine* love affair; a *clandestine* publication of an underground organization.

Sneaky and **underhand** carry the suggestion of cheating, of unfair dealings and self-serving manipulations behind the scenes. Where the other adjectives emphasize the fear of detection, *underhand* suggests a sly and crafty secrecy practiced not for protection but for gain—a stooping to trickery, deceit, or fraud for one's own profit: to win an election by *underhand* means. *Sneaky* is more general and less formal than *underhand,* and emphasizes the deceitful nature of one's actions more than the selfishness of one's motives. It suggests a *clandestine* or roundabout man-

ner concealing an insidious calculation: There was something *sneaky* and sinister about him; her *sneaky* habit of filching coins from her mother's purse. See LURK.

Antonyms: *obvious, open,* OVERT.

steep

abrupt
precipitous
sheer

These adjectives characterize terrain that rises or drops away sharply or that approaches the vertical. **Steep**, while indicating a relatively sharp inclination or a considerable departure from the horizontal, is alone among these adjectives in indicating a gradual or steadily increasing slope, usually one that is difficult to negotiate. The relativity of *steep* can be seen in the fact that a grade too *steep* for a railroad locomotive might be considered a gentle rise for someone on foot; terrain too *steep* for a burro to climb might not be *steep* enough to interest mountain climbers. Another connotation, even more subtle and not always present is the special suitability of *steep* for a rise viewed from below.

By comparison, **abrupt**, while referring to a much sharper slope, often suggests an incline viewed from above. [We were winded by our long climb upward along the *steep* path; They were confronted by an *abrupt* chasm as they emerged from the forest.] This distinction, however, does not always hold. *Abrupt* suggests sudden discontinuities in a terrain rather than the gradual change implicit in *steep;* consequently, a sharp contrast with surrounding topography is a special point of *abrupt:* the *abrupt* and dramatic looming up of the giant sculpture out of nearly level countryside.

Like *abrupt,* the remaining adjectives pertain to a nearly vertical incline. **Precipitous** has special relevance to an incline viewed from above. *Precipitous,* by association with the adjective *precipitate,* also brings to mind suddenness or unexpectedness in referring to a nearly vertical incline that is clifflike. Thus, the unique point of *precipitous* may be its suggestion of an *abrupt* drop that is dangerous or perilous: a frail rope bridge over the *precipitous* chasm. It can be used, however, without this implication: looking up at the *precipitous* rise of skyscrapers along both sides of the street. **Sheer** is related to *steep* in suggesting an incline viewed from below, but it is more intense than *steep; sheer* often refers to a nearly vertical slope that may be impossible, not merely difficult, to negotiate: the *sheer* face of the high wall that stood between them and their freedom. *Sheer* also has a special implication that concerns the vertical face itself, suggesting one without break, foothold, or cranny: the *sheer* surface of the cliff where not even a blade of grass could take root. See CLIMB, DESCEND, HIGH.

Antonyms: *flat, gentle, gradual, level, low, plain.*

sterile
arid
barren
childless
infertile
unfruitful
unproductive

These adjectives refer to a lack of yield or value or to the inability to have children. **Sterile** functions in all these senses: *sterile* soil; a *sterile* discussion; determining whether it was the husband or wife who was *sterile.* **Barren** is the only other adjective here that applies to all three situations, but it is less technical sounding and more dramatic than *sterile:* the *barren* desert; a debate that was *barren* of results; a *barren* woman. In the last sense, *barren* has a Biblical ring and applies to women (or a union) rather than to men. Also, *barren* is less often used than *sterile,* since it may seem critical rather than factual. *Sterile* itself, however, can seem overly harsh to some; this may be one reason why **infertile** is often substituted for it, although *infertile* may refer to lack of success at having children for any reason, without necessarily implying that either the man or woman is biologically *sterile.* *Infertile* is also used in the agricultural sense, although its increasing use in reference to childbearing may have diminished its usefulness here: topsoil rendered *infertile* by excessive alkalinity. **Childless** is the only adjective here that refers exclusively to people whose sexual union does not result in offspring. It points, however, to the simple fact of this lack, whether it comes about involuntarily or by choice: a *childless* couple; deciding to remain *childless* for the first few years of marriage; the adoption of children by those who are *childless.*

The remaining adjectives have no reference to childbearing, but do refer to other senses grouped here. **Arid** most concretely suggests a lack of yield because of excessive dryness or heat: miles of *arid* sand dunes; an *arid* climate. In terms of values, *arid* suggests dullness or lack of results: an *arid* play; an administration *arid* of new ideas. **Unfruitful** and **unproductive** are closely allied and can apply to a lack of yield or of value. *Unfruitful* would seem most open to the former, *unproductive* to the latter: an *unfruitful* use of land; an *unfruitful* season; mediation that was *unproductive* of changes on either side. This neat pattern, however, is far from being the case in actual use: *unfruitful* summit conferences; *unproductive* stretches of swampland. In any case, *unfruitful* tends to sound more dramatic or colorful, and need not suggest something totally *barren* of yield or value: crop yields that doubled after *unfruitful* harvesting techniques were abandoned. *Unproductive* gives a more factual tone and tends to suggest a more nearly complete lack of any result whatever: detectives stymied by their *unproductive* search for clues. See DRY, STERILIZE.

Antonyms: *bearing, productive,* VIABLE, *yielding.*

sterilize
castrate
emasculate
geld
hysterectomize
neuter
spay
vasectomize

These verbs refer to the act of rendering a person or animal incapable of producing offspring. **Sterilize** is the most general of these, referring to people, animals, and even plants, and to any sort of action that makes reproduction impossible: a controversial proposal to *sterilize* mental defectives; *sterilizing* fruit flies by exposing them to radiation; hybrid corn that is detasseled to *sterilize* it against self-pollination. In reference to people, *sterilize* may refer to accidental or deliberate acts and to acts bringing about temporary or permanent infertility in either men or women. It may also refer to an occurrence that causes no apparent alteration of the body, as with exposure to radiation, or to an operation in which reproductive organs are altered or removed.

In practice, **neuter** is most often limited in reference to the deliberate removing of reproductive organs from either male or female animals: having both their male and female cats *neutered.* Fix and alter are common euphemisms for *neuter.* **Spay** functions like *neuter* but is applied exclusively to female animals: a *spayed* bitch. **Geld,** similarly, applies to the *neutering* of male animals: a *gelded* horse. Sometimes, however, *geld* can be applied to animals of both sexes, but this wider use is open to misunderstanding.

Castrate can apply both to men and male animals

in specifically indicating the removal of testicles, less often to women in indicating the removal of ovaries. In the case of animals, *castrate* is clearer and more forceful than either *neuter* or *geld: castrating* hogs to fatten them for market. Applied to men, *castrate* would now suggest only sadistic punishment or a surgical necessity, as to prevent the spread of a cancer, but this was not always so: harem guards who were *castrated* to insure the inviolability of the odalisques; choirboys *castrated* to preserve their soprano voices. *Castrate* now carries the meaning of render impotent, either literally or figuratively, by psychological means, especially by threatening a person's masculinity or femininity: women who *castrate* their husbands by continually humiliating them in public.

Emasculate may apply to male animals but is more commonly restricted to men. *Emasculate* differs from *castrate* in referring more to the damage than to the actual removal of reproductive organs: *emasculated* by flying shrapnel. *Emasculate*, however, is sometimes used euphemistically for *castrate*. Figuratively, *emasculate* refers, like *castrate,* to any act that reduces a man's sense of manliness. While less dramatic than *castrate* in this use, *emasculate* would seem to have greater metaphorical felicity, since no physical alteration is necessarily suggested by *emasculate. Emasculate* is also used as a generally applicable metaphor for weaken: amendments that *emasculated* the new law.

Vasectomize and **hysterectomize**, the former applying to men, the latter to women, are medical terms for surgical operations that *sterilize* the person operated on. These terms are more commonly used in their noun forms: vasectomy and hysterectomy. To *vasectomize* is to perform a duct-cutting operation that is chosen specifically to make a man infertile and is believed to have no effect on body chemistry. To *hysterectomize* is to remove the uterus and sometimes the ovaries and fallopian tubes to stop uncontrollable uterine hemorrhaging, to remove large fibroid tumors, or to eradicate a cancerous condition. The operation is never done simply to achieve infertility, as it is irreversible and, if both ovaries are removed, can have a deleterious effect on the body's chemical balance. See STERILE.

Antonyms: *fecundate, fecundify, fertilize, fructify, impregnate, inseminate.*

stick
adhere
cleave
cling
cohere

These verbs all mean become or remain closely and firmly attached. **Stick** and **adhere** express the idea of maintaining a close or permanent union by or as if by gluing or cementing together. *Stick* is less formal than *adhere* and conveys in addition the establishing of such an attachment: two young men who intend to *stick* together in college; to *stick* a label on a package. *Stick* may also imply perseverance, as in working at something or in keeping to an ideal, bargain, etc.: *sticking* doggedly at the physics homework until long after midnight; *sticking* to her principles of fair play; *sticking* to an agreement made in a moment of optimism. *Adhere,* which is always used intransitively, may sound formal and stiff when applied to things: a stamp *adhering* to a postcard.

Cohere, also an intransitive, refers to the *adhering* or *sticking* together of the particles of a substance, which then form a whole or mass that is resistant to separation: Plaster of Paris *coheres* only when water is added. Figurative usage may indicate the achievement of logical consistency: An argument *coheres* only if it validly bridges the premise and the conclusion.

Cling is used to indicate a close attachment caused by entwining, clutching, or hanging on, rather than by gluing or otherwise causing surfaces to *adhere:* ivy *clinging* to brick walls; a baby gorilla *clinging* to its mother. In the sense of holding on to attitudes, beliefs, or emotional states, *cling* used as a synonym for *adhere* often has derogatory connotations suggestive of the presence of anxiety or dependency: a widower *clinging* to his grown son; people who *cling* to their prejudices.

Cleave, in the sense of *adhere* or *stick,* is now largely a literary or Biblical term for being closely attached, as in a human relationship marked by fidelity: to *cleave* to one's spouse through sickness and misfortune. In a few contexts, *cleave* is still used to literally mean *adhere* or *stick* closely: In his terror his tongue seemed to *cleave* to the roof of his mouth. See TIE.

Antonyms: LEAVE *(abandon)*, SEPARATE, SEVER.

stigma
blot
brand
mark
stain
stigmata
taint

These nouns refer, by means of a metaphor of disfigurement, to the lasting harm or discredit that may attach to someone because of an impropriety or injustice. As treated here, they all imply a distinction between such a disfigurement and those flaws present as an innate part of one's character. A person may acquire a **stigma** because of some improper act of his own or, more arbitrarily, because of an unfortunate situation not of his own making: prevented from seeking office by the *stigma* of her perjury conviction; the glazed eyes and pinched minds of children who already show evidence of bearing the *stigma* of poverty. Sometimes, the special point of *stigma* is the disapproval of society rather than actual injury done to the person disapproved of: a culture that puts a *stigma* on anyone interested in the arts.

Stain, **blot**, and **taint** are almost exclusively restricted to the discredit someone has brought upon himself or herself; the discredit, furthermore, most often is the result of a breach of morals. Of the three, *stain* suggests the greatest or most serious breach: a *stain* on his reputation he could never eradicate. *Blot*, by contrast, can be used almost euphemistically to extenuate a breach as accidental or slight: a record, like anyone else's, that showed a *blot* or two here and there. Clashing with this implication, *blot* appears sometimes in orotund rhetoric to mean an especially heinous disfigurement: a political machine that is a *blot* on our city. In this sense, it is part of a common but shopworn expression: a *blot* on the escutcheon. *Taint* suggests a moral breach slighter than either *stain* or *blot*. Leaving aside the use in which *taint* refers to a slight but innate flaw, it still stresses a vague or subtle imprint and may suggest, in fact, a less permanent discrediting than any of these other nouns: surrounded by the *taint* of scandal that surely would fade with time. Even the underlying metaphor here is unique in suggesting a slight but permeating discoloration more than a single but plainly observable scar.

Mark is the least specific in this context and carries the fewest overtones. It has so many other uses that its sense of disfigurement would have to be made clear by context: a *mark* against him; accusations that left a *mark* on the entire family. **Stigmata** is the one noun here that does not imply shame or dishonor, referring instead to *marks* said to appear miraculously on the hands and feet of certain saints, *marks* that correspond to the wounds inflicted at the Crucifixion.

A **brand** was originally a *mark* burned on criminals or slaves to proclaim their status; it is now an easily identifiable design put on cattle with a hot iron to indicate ownership. Figuratively used, *brand* is a close synonym of *stigma*, but suggests even greater dishonor or notoriety, which like the burned-on *mark* is difficult or impossible to eradicate: a man bearing the *brand* of having informed against his comrades; the *brand* of illegitimacy once placed on innocent children. See BURN, DISFIGURE, ECCENTRICITY, FLAW.

stimulant. Do not confuse the noun *stimulant* (anything that quickens or promotes activity of some physiologic process) with the noun *stimulus* (incentive).

stimulate

enliven
excite
galvanize
titillate
whet

These verbs refer to that which arouses interest, motivates to action, or satisfies and invigorates. **Stimulate** is the most general of these, applying in all three situations: a remark that *stimulated* my curiosity; a crisis that finally *stimulated* Congress into voting new funds for the cities; a bull session that *stimulated* all those present. **Excite** can also apply to the arousal of interest, but in this sense it has a more formal tone than *stimulate:* a book that *excited* much comment. More often now, *excite* applies to anything that brings forth an intense emotional display: They feared the news would *excite* the patient too much; ethnic slurs that *excited* the crowd to a fury.

Enliven applies solely to what is both arousing and invigorating: an outspoken couple who could always be counted on to *enliven* a party; outdoor sculpture to *enliven* the dull facade of the skyscraper. **Galvanize**, by contrast, applies strictly to setting something decisively in motion, particularly after a period of vacillation or disorganization: fresh troops to *galvanize* our flagging offensive; a tragedy that *galvanized* the city government into action.

Titillate and **whet** also apply exclusively to one aspect of *stimulate,* indicating an initial arousal of interest or desire. Most concretely, *whet* applies to an appetite for food: hors d'oeuvres to *whet* the appetite. Similarly, when *whet* applies in other contexts, it usually suggests partaking of a small sample that leads to a desire for some larger portion: government action that only *whetted* the desires of African Americans for full equality; an opening chapter that *whets* the reader's interest. By contrast, *titillate* need not suggest actual sampling. While it can operate like *whet* in the context of food, it more often suggests a tempting action achieved through allusion, insinuation, or promises of what is to come. It implies raising eager expectations of whatever kind, whether or not these promises are later fulfilled. [The delicious appetizer *titillated* my palate; Rumors of secret information on the assassination *titillated* our curiosity; a jacket illustration designed to *titillate* readers of pornographic novels.] See INCITE, INDUCE, KINDLE, QUICKEN, SPUR.

Antonyms: *deaden, dull, enervate,* QUELL, SUBDUE.

stimulus. Do not confuse the noun *stimulus* (incentive) with the noun *stimulant* (anything that quickens or promotes activity of some physiologic process).

stint

assignment
chore
duty
hitch
job
task

These nouns refer to a limited, one-time, or nonrecurring piece of work. **Stint** and **hitch** are most clear about the limited or temporary nature of the work. *Stint* suggests the limited period of time in which something is done. [He never starred in a long-running play, though he did several short *stints* off-Broadway; wandering from one college to another, including *stints* at Harvard and Oxford.] Where *stint* suggests a relatively brief undertaking that is voluntary or agreed-upon, *hitch* suggests a limited commitment of longer duration that may not be a matter of choice; it frequently appears in a military context: doing a two-year *hitch* in Japan before returning home. In the military, *hitch* may refer to one's whole period of service, long or short: the new six-month *hitch* followed by annual summer training; NCO's who plan to do the whole twenty-year *hitch*. **Assignment** is both more formal and more general than the preceding and is applicable in a great many contexts. It indicates a limited commitment that is even more likely to be involuntary than is the case with *hitch*: chafing at the unpleasant *assignment* that had fallen to him. However, this need not always be so: volunteering to take on the two-week *assignment*. Furthermore, *assignment* can refer to a permanent, long-term role: her *assignment* to the appellate court, where she served for twenty years. Or it may specifically apply to a student's homework: a hard arithmetic *assignment*.

Chore and **task** both indicate a circumscribed or short-term undertaking, whether voluntary or not, and suggest an undertaking that will require a relative amount of effort. The two nouns contrast, however, in that the more general *task* is more nearly neutral in its connotations, whereas *chore* suggests something onerous, arduous, or even unpleasant, despite the short duration suggested: relishing every *task* that fell to her, no matter how pesky; complaining about how much he hated the *chore* of washing dishes after every meal. Also, *task* is less specific about duration and can suggest effort arising out of personal commitment or obligation: the *task* of political reform, to which she selflessly devoted her best efforts throughout a long life. *Chore* nearly always suggests grudging reluctance: when going to parties becomes a *chore* rather than a pleasure. Used in the plural, it applies to routine household or farm duties and has a homey ring: to do *chores*.

In the context of a specific, short-term effort, **job** and **duty** emphasize different aspects of *task*. *Job* is neutral and general, open to the qualification of context: looking forward to the *job* of building the garage on weekends; dreading the exasperating *job* of doing her income tax. *Duty*, by contrast, stresses either an involuntary or unpleasant *task* or one that calls up devoted commitment or dedication: my reluctant *duty* to set your punishment; students put on dormitory *duty*; the painful *duty* of sorting through his father's effects; glad to undertake the *duty* of caring for the child. See OBLIGATION, PROFESSION.

Antonyms: HOBBY.

stop

arrest
block
cease
check
discontinue
halt
prevent

These verbs refer to the act of bringing something to an end or a complete rest. **Stop** in its generality has few specific implications, being open to any coloration context gives it: to *stop* in mid-sentence; They *stopped* the bandit dead in his tracks.

Arrest, **check**, and **block** suggest a *stopping* of motion or activity by the application of a countering force: words that *arrested* his wild attack and left him speechless. All three verbs, however, can suggest an interruption or prevention of activity that might well begin again once the countering force is removed. [The child's development may have been *arrested* by an overly permissive regimen; therapy to *check* the course of the disease; *blocking* the enemy's access to the sea.] *Arrest* most specifically suggests the freezing of something just as it was at the time activity ended. *Check* suggests keeping something hemmed in so that it cannot continue. *Block* suggests the interposition of an obstacle that cannot be overcome.

Discontinue relates particularly to a manufactured item that is gradually phased out of production: a notice that they would *discontinue* several lines of spare parts listed in their catalog. It may also refer to the gradual abandonment of a habitual way of doing things: The practice of binding the feet of women was finally *discontinued.* In other uses, it may seem a long-winded way to say *stop.*

Cease most often suggests an abrupt *stopping:* The officer ordered me to *cease* my whistling. **Halt** also suggests suddenness, but it may suggest as well a *stopping* of motion brought about by authority or force: brusquely *halting* her at the gate with a demand to see her papers. **Prevent** can apply to anything that results in *stopping* or forestalling an action by whatever means. The action in this case may be blocked before it has been set in motion: a thorough grounding in fundamentals to *prevent* reading difficulties in later life; a program to *prevent* drug addiction rather than treat it once it has taken hold. *Prevent* can also apply to a countering force, but only the potential or psychological effectiveness of such a force may be indicated: maintaining troop readiness to *prevent* being overwhelmed by surprise attack; a puritanical streak that *prevented* her from surrendering to momentary pleasure. See CAPTURE, INHIBIT, PREVENT, QUELL, SUBDUE.

Antonyms: *ACTIVATE, BEGIN, continue, EFFECT, IMPEL, QUICKEN, SPUR.*

stop

cease
desist
halt
quit

These verbs refer to the act of coming to rest or of breaking off previous activity. **Stop** is the most general, least formal, and most commonly used, yielding the fewest specific suggestions about the way in which activity is concluded: a clock that *stopped* and started erratically; listening for a pulse to find out if the patient's heart had *stopped;* where the paved road

stops and a dirt trail takes over. **Cease** carries the specific implication of a total extinction: a newspaper that has *ceased* publication. It may sometimes suggest abruptness: As suddenly as it began, the rain *ceased.*

Halt is similar to *cease* but has specific reference to the abrupt, decisive termination of movement: *halting* only at the edge of the cliff; demonstrators who marched into the square, *halted* in its center, and then threw themselves down on the pavement. **Quit** may also indicate an arbitrary *halting,* but this is usually voluntary or agreed upon: They worked until 5:00 P.M. and then *quit.* Most often applying to work or effort, *quit* can sometimes suggest disgruntlement or defeat: an administrator who *quit* her job to protest government policy; Battered as we were, we refused to *quit.* It may also suggest cessation because of enfeeblement or lack of energy: The motor coughed and sputtered, turned over a few times, and then *quit* on us. **Desist** is the most formal verb here. It is applied to an active agency and implies forbearance. Specifically, it presupposes the existence of opposition or resistance to continuance, or the presence of obstacles that seem insurmountable: finally *desisting* in his fruitless efforts to find the missing heir. It is often coupled with *cease* in legal parlance: ordered to *cease* and *desist* from false advertising. See BREAK, DEMUR FINISH, HESITATE, STOP (arrest).

Antonyms: *begin, GO, PERSIST, start.*

stream

brook
creek
rill
river

These nouns are comparable in denoting a body of water flowing in a watercourse or channel. **Stream,** the most general, embraces all the others in its meaning. A **rill** is a tiny *stream,* the smallest of those under discussion. A **brook** is usually a primary *stream* emerging from a spring. A **creek** is a *stream* that is larger than a *brook* and usually flows through a valley. A **river** is a large *stream* of water that discharges into a larger body of water, such as the ocean, a lake, or another *river.* In popular usage, *brook, creek,* and *stream* are often used interchangeably.

Of these nouns, only two are used figuratively as well as literally. *Stream* and *river* both may refer to a continuous flow of anything, as well as to a flow of water. [A *stream* of people issued from the theater; The battlefield was covered with *rivers* of blood.] See FLOW, SHORE.

street

alley
avenue
boulevard
highway
road
superhighway
throughway
turnpike

These nouns refer to open ways for public passage, particularly for the movement of vehicles rather than of pedestrians. **Street** is a generic term for all such public ways within a town or city: the intersection of the two busiest *streets* in the neighborhood. **Avenue** can sometimes be used more formally as a generic term similar to *street,* but more often *avenue* serves as a complement to a specific sense of *street;* this sense refers to towns or cities laid out with *streets* running in one direction, crossed by *avenues* running in the other. In this case, *avenues* are often the wider or more important of the two intersecting systems. In other cases, however, *avenue* can refer to any sort of *street,* wide or narrow, and can form part of the name of the *street:* Garrison *Avenue.*

Alley and **boulevard** indicate sharply contrasting kinds of *streets. Alley* suggests a narrow, sometimes dead-ended, *street* behind or between buildings, that exists solely to permit access for deliveries, pickups, or the parking of vehicles: carrying out the garbage to the collection cans in the *alley.* While *alley* may be perfectly neutral in this sense, it often has connotations of an unsavory darkness, dankness, or uncleanness: parks, rather than *alleys,* for children to play in. Sometimes, *alley* can be used with an affected quaintness for any *street,* particularly a narrow one, even though it permits through traffic and is faced by buildings or houses: Minetta *Alley.* While *boulevard* can be applied to any city *street,* particularly a wide one, it has connotations in sharp contrast to *alley,* suggesting a residential *street* enhanced by greenery or an intervening strip containing grass and shrubbery: expensive houses facing on a landscaped *boulevard.*

The remaining nouns refer mostly to public ways outside towns and cities. **Road** here is as informal and general as *street,* with an even wider range of connotation. It can suggest anything from a dirt path for vehicles to the most modern and sophisticated **highway.** *Highway* now refers to any paved *road* constructed for motor traffic: federal funds for building *roads;* small towns whose main *streets* are wide places in the *road;* turning off from the main *highway* onto a winding gravel *road.* Unqualified, *highway* has few imponder-able connotations; *road* has many. It can refer to any course that leads to a certain destination: the *road* to nuclear disaster.

Throughway, **turnpike**, and **superhighway** refer exclusively to a specific kind of *highway.* A *turnpike* is any sort of *highway,* public or private, that cannot be used without payment of a toll: low on money and wishing to avoid the *turnpike. Turnpike* gives connotations of rapid travel, uninterrupted by stoplights or intersections, and a landscaped drive unmarred by billboards or other advertising. *Throughway* (often spelled thruway) and *superhighway* carry none of these pleasant connotations, referring specifically to express routes built to handle capacity traffic undistracted by stops or intersections. While a *throughway* and a *superhighway* may well be *turnpikes* and vice versa, *throughway* and *superhighway* better suggest a mazed labyrinth of traffic systems built with no eye for aesthetic appeal: a six-lane *throughway* (or *superhighway*) walled in from the countryside by gray concrete. See JOURNEY.

stress

pressure
strain
tension

These nouns are comparable in denoting the action or effect of a force upon a person or thing. **Stress** designates any force or combination of forces acting on a body or part of a body, as by pressing, pushing, pulling, stretching, compressing, or twisting, and by such action causing a change in the shape or size of the body acted upon. When used in reference to a person, *stress* indicates a condition of emotional or intellectual distress. There is a suggestion in *stress* of some external stimulus, such as injury or shock, that exerts a compelling or constraining influence to which the person involved cannot adequately adjust: a serious gastrointestinal disorder that resulted from the *stress* of anxiety and grief.

Strain, when used in relation to an object, denotes the change in shape or size of that object when it is acted upon by a *stress.* A suggestion of the natural resistance an object makes to the action of *stress* is carried over to the meaning of *strain* when it pertains to persons. Resistance implies effort, and a person undergoing *strain* is subject to the physical, mental, or emotional distress that severe effort entails: the constant *strain* of trying to make ends meet on a substandard wage; the *strain* of working while suffering from a painful back ailment.

In their application to things that are inanimate,

tension and **pressure** may be classified as types of *stresses*. *Tension* is an elongating *stress* caused by a force that pulls or stretches an object in one direction. *Pressure* is a kind of *stress* characteristically produced by fluids; its special property is that its force is the same in all directions. In designating the condition of a person, *tension* hints at a state of mental *strain* whose peculiarity is its manifestation in physical distress, as in headaches or taut muscles: a tranquilizer to reduce nervous *tension* after an unsuccessful job interview. *Tension* has also come popularly to denote any state of *strained* relations like that caused by conflict or hostility between persons or groups of persons: the dangerous *tension* existing between the two countries. *Pressure,* more than the other nouns in this group, specifically points to the things that produce a state of *strain* or *tension* rather than to the state itself. It can apply to anything from a minor and temporary difficulty to major, continuing misfortune: the *pressure* of an active social life; job *pressure;* the *pressures* of poverty. See ANXIETY, IMPACT, NERVOUS, PROPEL.

strong
hardy
muscular
powerful
stalwart
sturdy
tough

These adjectives characterize what is vigorous, well built, durable, or resistant to change or pressure. **Strong**, the most general, pertains to what has force or to what is rugged in construction or build: a *strong* headwind; a *strong* workbench; a *strong* body. It can also apply to what is vigorous, intense, vivid, or persuasive: a *strong* government; a *strong* tranquilizer; a painter who worked with *strong* colors; a *strong* argument. At its most general, *strong* is still relative, implying what is greater in degree than usual: a *strong* suspicion.

Powerful can function as an intensification of *strong:* a *powerful* argument. It can also indicate the ability to deliver great amounts of energy: a *powerful* turbine; a *powerful* bomb. It can particularly suggest the considerable ability to overcome resistance or opposition: a *powerful* fighter against oppression; a *powerful* army. Where *powerful* can be used to refer to someone who is physically *strong,* **muscular** is almost exclusively limited to this application, specifically suggesting a *strong,* well-built body: a *muscular* athlete. Of these three adjectives, however, only *pow-*

erful necessarily indicates an absolute capacity for applying considerable force: pioneer women who proved at least as *strong* as the men they accompanied across the prairies; *powerful* wrists that enabled him to flick a bat around as though it were a straw; a *muscular* weightlifter who couldn't fight his way out of a paper bag.

Sturdy and **hardy** both refer more strictly to what is durable or resistant to change or pressure. But *sturdy,* like one sense of *strong,* can refer as well to what is well built: a *sturdy* footbridge that could easily support the weight of a small truck. When applied to physique, *sturdy* suggests solidity without necessarily implying the development indicated by *muscular:* a *sturdy* boy. *Hardy* emphasizes the ability to withstand force or adversity. It is typically applied to strains of plants or animals: a *hardy* species of corn that is unaffected by drought conditions; sled dogs *hardy* enough to withstand arctic weather. In application to people, it can refer to someone able to survive difficulty or a difficult way of life: the *hardy* life of physical activity at summer camp.

Tough at its most restricted can indicate a surface or covering that is thick, dense, horny, or callous—a surface impervious to wear or damage: the *tough* hide of the alligator. More informally, *tough* can apply to physical strength or stamina, sometimes with an added implication of coarseness or brutality: *tough* recruits; the *tough* bouncers most nightclubs employ. Even more informally, *tough* can refer to what is difficult: a *tough* problem. **Stalwart** is the most formal of these adjectives; nowadays, it points more to qualities of courage and loyalty than to physical strength per se: *stalwart* braves willing to fight the settlers; a *stalwart* political supporter. See HEALTHY, HUSKY, MASSIVE.
Antonyms: *POWERLESS, WEAK.*

stubborn
adamant
headstrong
obdurate
obstinate
pertinacious
pigheaded

All of these adjectives suggest a tendency to persist in an opinion, belief, decision, or course of action, generally with more force than reason. People may be **stubborn** by disposition, showing this quality in most of their behavior and in most situations, but may be **obstinate** in a particular instance: Dick had always been a *stubborn* boy, but he was particularly *obstinate* in his dislike of homework. **Pigheaded** usually suggests *obstinate* stupidity: His *pigheaded* refusal to accept facts makes discussion impossible. **Adamant** implies a hard and unyielding attitude that may be the result of a strongly felt or carefully thought out conviction regarding some important matter: The ambassador was *adamant* in insisting that all prisoners be released from the detention center. A similar attitude, but carrying the idea of harshness and a lack of feeling, is implied by **obdurate**: The foreman was *obdurate* in holding to rigid production schedules. Both *adamant* and *obdurate*, however, can point approvingly to a principled refusal to compromise, unlike these other adjectives with their implications of arbitrary egocentricity.

Pertinacious, though not necessarily deprecatory, usually suggests a kind of perseverance in a course of action that can be annoying or seem unreasonable to others: The lawyer's *pertinacious* harping on the same point unnerved the witness. **Headstrong** indicates a strong-willed self-direction and an impatience with restraint. A *headstrong* person cannot be held back by advice or argument and may be reckless or hotheaded in his or her actions: a *headstrong*, impetuous youth, rushing into things without forethought; His *headstrong* attempt to seize control of the party was political suicide. See AUTHORITARIAN, OVERBEARING, PERSISTENT, UNRULY.

Antonyms: *ADAPTABLE, COMPLIANT, DOCILE, MALLEABLE.*

student

disciple
learner
protégé
pupil
scholar

These nouns refer to someone involved in studies, in attempting to gain a set of skills, or in devotion to a patron or master. **Student** is the most general noun here for such a person. At its most specific, it forms a complementary pair with **pupil**. *Pupil* now usually refers to a young person in grade school, while *student*, in this context, refers to one in high school or college: demonstrating that more kindergarten *pupils* end up as college *students* than do children who enter the first grade without previous educational experience. But whereas *pupil* itself has few uses outside this situation, *student* can displace *pupil* on the one hand and refer on the other to the most advanced or specialized expert or authority in some field: a musi-

cologist who was a keen *student* of Beethoven's later work .

Scholar can function as a more formal substitute for *student*, but it is unique in having two special areas of relevance. *Scholar* may be used at any level for a *student* who excels in studies: an unruly child who turned out to be a real *scholar*. More often, *scholar* refers specifically to an advanced specialist, without any suggestion that the person is still pursuing a course of formal education; in fact, it may suggest an extremely learned authority on a given subject: *scholars* who were able to test the theory by collating all existing copies of the folio text of the play. **Learner** is much more informal than *scholar* and emphasizes the other extreme—a beginner rather than an authority in some field of knowledge. Furthermore, *learner* applies less to youngsters than to adults who are purposely acquiring some new set of possibly simple skills. The situation pertains not so much to someone seeking formal education as to any sort of novice or beginner: insisting that she have a *learner's* permit before driving the family car.

Disciple and **protégé** both pertain exclusively to someone devoted to a master or patron. Most strictly, *disciple* suggests a religious situation: the *disciples* of Buddha who codified his writings; the twelve *disciples* of Christ. In general use, *disciple* refers to an ardent advocate of any prominent figure or theory: an early *disciple* of Freud, though never of Freudianism per se. *Disciple* often has a contemptuous ring, suggesting someone subordinate or unimportant in himself, possibly because of a slavish devotion to or imitation of another: teenagers who become *disciples* of the newest singing sensation; business executives who pick sycophants as *disciples*. *Protégé* indicates a situation in striking contrast to *disciple*. Here, a young or unknown person of talent is assisted or patronized by someone who is securely established, either as an artist or merely as a person of financial means: a wealthy benefactor who demanded nothing in return for the money she gave her *protégés;* a master sculptor who, seeing the boy's talent, took him on as a *protégé. Protégé*, like *disciple*, can have a contemptuous ring to it. In this case *protégé* may suggest even greater servility in the subordinate but adds to this a suggestion of overweening vanity in the superior or benefactor. See BEGINNER, LEARNING.

Antonyms: *master, patron,* PROFESSOR, *teacher.*

study

consider
contemplate

study (continued)

ponder
weigh

These verbs mean apply one's mind to a subject in order to learn about it, to resolve any questions it poses, or to reach a decision concerning it. **Study** implies a careful attempt to learn all the aspects of the subject or problem under scrutiny before making plans or taking definite action. [Meteorologists *study* information sent back to earth from weather satellites before making forecasts; A city council *studies* proposals submitted for urban renewal.]

Consider is more general than *study;* it can imply either momentary and casual attention given to something, or deep, prolonged concentration: *considering* whether to brave the snowstorm and drive to the movies or to stay at home; *considering* how much insurance they would need to guarantee the education of their children. *Consider* may also point to an objective judgment reached after careful *study:* We are *considering* your manuscript for publication, but feel it needs extensive abridgment.

Contemplate implies thinking about something, as for a long period of time, but usually simply for its own sake and with no definite, pragmatic end in view: We have long *contemplated* the possibility of living in Europe for a year. In its related meaning of looking at intensely, *contemplate* suggests leisurely and pleasurable reflection: He *contemplated* the Bayeux tapestry for an entire day.

Ponder and **weigh** both mean examine all sides of a question in one's own mind in order to make a careful evaluation. These verbs differ from *study* in that they emphasize the making of a choice between conflicting data, opposing claims, or the like, rather than the acquiring of knowledge by searching into a body of information. *Ponder* suggests that the matter is a serious one and deserves careful deliberation: Before casting a vote, a responsible citizen should *ponder* the records of all candidates. *Weigh* may also be applied to important considerations: The judge advised the jury to *weigh* the arguments and testimony presented by both sides. When the decision to be made is of minor significance, *weigh* is to be preferred to *ponder:* to *weigh* the advantages of going to the beach or to a ball game. See EXAMINE, READ, SEE, THINK.

Antonyms: *NEGLECT, scan, SLIGHT.*

stupid

asinine

dense
dull
dumb
obtuse
slow
thick
unintelligent

These adjectives characterize a lack of intellect, perceptivity, or wisdom. **Stupid** and **asinine** are the harshest of these and are more likely to be used to disapprove of rather than to describe someone. *Stupid* may suggest either a weak mentality or foolish behavior, whereas *asinine* is most often restricted to the latter: a *stupid* fellow; a *stupid* mistake; an *asinine* middle-aged man dressing like a teenager. Because of this limitation, *asinine* is even more disapproving than *stupid;* its reference is to a beast of burden, the ass, traditionally considered *stupid* and obstinate.

Dense and **thick** both concentrate on the aspect of *stupid* pertaining to a weak mentality, emphasizing an inability to understand simple facts or remember clear instructions. *Thick* may sound more formal, but it is also less harsh than *dense,* which suggests an impenetrable slowness of mind. Also, *thick* may apply to a single act, while *dense* more often refers to a rooted characteristic: a bit *thick* of him not to get the joke; so *dense* he had to be talked to like a child.

Dumb in this sense is restricted to an extremely informal level when applied to *stupid* people: a *dumb* bunny; a *dumb* cluck. Purists frown on it in this use, because it means mute in other situations: the offensive expression deaf and *dumb; dumb* animals. **Obtuse**, by contrast, is perhaps the most formal adjective here, referring to slow-wittedness, whether revealed by a particular act or by a person's whole character: a laughably *obtuse* misunderstanding of her request; an *asinine* television show specifically designed for the ignorant and *obtuse.* While *obtuse* may seem more objective at first glance, its formality adds a note of withering scorn not present in the previous adjectives.

Dull and **unintelligent** are both used more objectively to describe people or behavior revealing low mental ability. *Unintelligent* is almost completely devoid of emotional connotations: *unintelligent* answers to complex questions. Since mental ability is a matter of degree, however, *unintelligent* may mask subjective judgment except when used comparatively: gearing her lessons to the more *unintelligent* among her students. *Dull* can be used to express disapproval of the *stupid* and boring: a man too *dull* to be able to work a child's crossword puzzle; a *dull*-witted fool.

Dull is often used more objectively, however, to refer to less than average mentality and sometimes serves as a euphemism for the more straightforward *unintelligent:* a special class for *dull* learners. **Slow** is used as a synonym for *dull:* a class for *slow* students. See BLOCK-HEAD, MONOTONOUS, MORON.

Antonyms: BRIGHT, *clever*, CREATIVE, *intelligent*, KEEN, *smart.*

stylish

chic
dapper
fashionable
modish
smart
spruce

These adjectives characterize grooming and clothes that are fastidious, elegant, well designed, or in accordance with current taste. **Stylish** emphasizes something designed and executed so as to display a flair for what is in vogue. In this *stylish* is close to **fashionable**, but is less formal, suggesting a more dramatic appearance, based on more transitory standards. By contrast, *fashionable* emphasizes elegance, correctness, and possibly a simplicity of expensive taste that is not likely to become dated so quickly: Leather coats were *stylish* for a season, but cloth coats will always be *fashionable. Stylish* is also more open to being used as a contemptuous term: beehive hairdos and other *stylish* vulgarities. *Fashionable,* however, can also be applied to transitory or disapproved-of vogues: The sack, the shift, and the miniskirt all had their *fashionable,* brief moments of glory. *Fashionable,* furthermore, is more likely than *stylish* to be applied to men: the double-breasted suit that has again become *fashionable.* Used of men, *stylish* is likely to suggest a specialized subculture when it is not openly contemptuous: the *stylish,* bowler-hatted men of London's financial district; the dirty jeans and torn T-shirt thought *stylish* among young people.

Chic is in every way an intensification of *stylish,* except for its greater formality. Its French flavor points to that country as a source of high fashion for Western women, a fact emphasized by the adjective's restriction to female grooming. If anything, *chic* suggests an even greater concern for the last word in modernity, with emphasis on the exclusive and expensive: outraged to discover that her *chic* evening dress, a signed original, was being sold in department stores all over town.

Modish sometimes concentrates on the negative

aspects of *stylish,* suggesting a concern with vogue to the neglect of good taste, comfort, or decorum: women who looked like cadavers in their *modish* chalk-white makeup. By contrast, **smart** concentrates on a different aspect of *stylish,* referring to the dramatic impact of good design. *Smart,* however, puts less emphasis on vogue than any of the previous adjectives and suggests instead boldness of clean lines and simple cut, particularly those conceived of as being suitable for a specific occasion: her *smart* riding outfit. Where *chic* suggests the apex of femininity, there is something of the opposite in *smart,* although its forcefulness need not suggest mannishness. *Smart* does tend to emphasize overall appearance rather than any one aspect. *Smart,* of course, can also refer to comparable aspects of male grooming without suggesting effeminacy: his *smart* Ivy League suit. This paradox makes *smart* useful in joint descriptions: a *smart,* well-turned out couple.

Dapper and **spruce**, by contrast with the previous adjectives, are mainly reserved to describe aspects of male grooming. *Dapper* may indicate the last word in formality and correctness: looking *dapper* in a tuxedo. More often, however, *dapper* suggests overelegant and even prissy grooming: quipping that he reminded her of the *dapper* little gentleman on wedding cakes. *Spruce* suggests masculine neatness and cleanness, with an emphasis on simplicity and timeless correctness of costume rather than conformity to *fashionable* vogues: sailors looking *spruce* in their whites. Also, more than any other adjective here, *spruce* often bears directly on grooming to the exclusion of dress: coming back from the barber looking *spruce* and clean shaven. Occasionally, *spruce* can refer to a woman's costume; in this case, it emphasizes trimness and neatness: her *spruce* skiing outfit. See ARTISTIC, ELEGANT, EXQUISITE, MODERN, ORDERLY, VOGUE.

Antonyms: *dowdy*, OLD-FASHIONED, UGLY, *unkempt.*

subdue

check
constrain
curb
inhibit
repress
restrain
suppress

The pacification or putting down of unruly forces is suggested by all these verbs. **Subdue** is the mildest, suggesting a gentle but firm power exerted to moderate an impulse that might otherwise be dangerous: *subduing* an impulse to tell the boss what he thought of her. *Subdue* implies that the threatening force has been put down but not necessarily altered or diminished in any basic way. **Inhibit**, consequently, goes further than *subdue* in suggesting a fundamental altering of the rebellious impulse; this is achieved, by implication, through blocking its chances for growth or decreasing the area within which it can continue operating effectively. *Inhibit* often refers disapprovingly to the diminishing of natural or healthy instincts: tariffs that would *inhibit* free trade; overly restrictive or permissive parents who *inhibit* the normal development of their children.

A similar relationship holds between **check** and **curb**. Like *inhibit*, *check* suggests the prevention of further growth; *curb*, on the other hand, suggests the moderating force implicit in *subdue:* merely wishing to *curb* some thoughtless tendencies in her pupils, while *checking* altogether any tendency toward openly hostile acts. *Check* is stronger than *inhibit,* however, in sometimes implying the complete rooting out of an impulse. Similarly, *curb* is much stronger than *subdue* in suggesting the use of considerable force, when necessary, in order to counter any threatened unruliness. Because it suggests difficulty and struggle, in fact, *curb* has greater force than *check,* even though the latter points to the complete extirpation of an impulse: A few concessions wisely made would have completely *checked* the revolution; now, whole armies thrown into the breach may be insufficient to *curb* it.

Repress and **suppress**, besides sounding so similar, are often used almost as though they were different spellings of the same word. They are differently defined by psychologists, however, and even in ordinary use a contrast in meaning can be observed. In psychology, *repress* indicates a process of returning to the unconscious mind fears and impulses so that they cannot easily be called up again; this process occurs without the subject's knowledge. *Suppress*, in contrast, relates to an effort of will in putting away an unpleasant thought; this act may or may not be conscious, and the *suppressed* idea can more easily be recalled for consideration. The ordinary uses of these two verbs reflect a similar comparison; *repress* is felt as the stronger here, often implying a harsh or excessive stamping out of dissent or rebellion. Except for its greater force, it is thus similar to *check* and *inhibit.* *Suppress* suggests bringing something under control, like *subdue* and *curb,* although it suggests the use of greater force than either.

Constrain and **restrain** are a comparable pair, but they are more clearly distinguished in common use than *repress* and *suppress. Constrain* indicates forcing someone to do something against his or her will and carries an overtone of disapproval for such an act: *constraining* their daughter from dating. *Restrain* suggests a gentler, advisory moderation and may sometimes refer to a self-imposed discipline. As such, it can be used with a tone of approval: *restraining* himself from drinking to excess. See CONTROL, DISCIPLINE, STOP (arrest), SURMOUNT.

Antonyms: *INCITE, STIMULATE.*

suggestive
earthy
off-color
Rabelaisian
racy
raunchy
risqué
scatological

These adjectives characterize expression or behavior that is concerned with sexuality or bodily functions. **Suggestive**, the mildest of these terms, emphasizes not frankness on these matters so much as allusions or innuendoes considered to be in bad taste: *suggestive* commercials that are more titillating than the programs they are used to publicize. Even so distant an approach to frankness as *suggestive* can imply was once condemned; now, *suggestive* can be used in disapproval of any leering indirectness about sex, even where frankness itself might now be thought quite innocuous: a parental lecture on the facts of life that is bewildering and *suggestive* rather than dispassionate and informative.

Risqué suggests a closer approach to frankness on sexual matters in that boldness of allusion is stressed. Except for someone who is extremely straitlaced, *risqué* has fewer legitimate uses in today's relatively tolerant atmosphere, since many kinds of direct references to sex are not thought particularly bold: It was once thought *risqué* for a woman to dine alone with a man in his apartment; gentlemen who traded *risqué* jokes once the ladies had retired after dinner. **Off-color** has been similarly affected, although its vagueness still permits its application, particularly to jokes of any sort that hinge on sexual matters: an *off-color* joke currently making the rounds of the student dormitory. Dirty joke is a more common description of this kind of humor.

The remaining adjectives are not restricted to sexuality. Of these, **earthy** is the broadest in application. If once it was disapproving for something coarse or crude in reference to sexual and bodily functions, it now may be descriptively neutral or even approving: the *earthy* humor of Chaucer and Shakespeare. *Earthy* may even suggest a sentimental nostalgia for the supposedly simpler and more direct life of earlier times: the trend to urbanization that has robbed us of our *earthy* acceptance of the natural processes of birth, copulation, death, and decay. **Racy** can apply to accounts that are erotic, pornographic, or *earthy,* but in this case it suggests fast-paced action and a linguistic forcefulness gained through frank and direct expressions: a *racy* book about marital infidelity. When *racy* applies to actions, it can indicate *earthy* behavior marked by high-spirited energy and linguistic gusto: a person whose *racy,* pungent speech and erotic prowess might put Don Juan to shame.

Raunchy is an informal term with a variety of applications. It can refer to personal uncleanliness or to an *earthy* disregard of hygienic niceties: He felt *raunchy* after three days of hiking in the forest; a beer-guzzling, *raunchy* brute of a husband. It can also refer to an intense but unappeased building up of sexual appetite: *raunchy* submariners on leave.

Both **Rabelaisian** and **scatological** emphasize *earthy* expression or behavior. *Rabelaisian,* like *racy,* indicates high-spirited zest, but stresses a penchant for good-humored tomfoolery involving a preoccupation with sexual and excretory functions. The eponymous term *Rabelaisian* is derived from the French writer Rabelais, whose work reflected such concerns: the *Rabelaisian* wit of many contemporary Southern novelists; a *Rabelaisian* rascal who delighted in playing obscene practical jokes on his friends. *Scatological* is a term of neutral description for a fascination with excrement or with the excretory functions. It is useful in discriminating work with this emphasis from other possibly obscene material that is focused on sexual functions: the *scatological* emphasis in the works of Jonathan Swift; soldiers whose language is larded with obscene and *scatological* references. See EROTIC, INDECENT.

Antonyms: BLAND, *decorous, genteel,* INNOCENT, *prissy.*

summary
abridgment
abstract
digest
outline

précis
synopsis

These nouns refer to a short description of the main points of a longer work or presentation. **Summary,** the most general, refers to any attempt to condense into as few words as possible an extended train of thought: a day-to-day *summary* of the proceedings in the murder trial; closing each chapter with a *summary* of its main arguments. *Summary* implies a pithy paraphrase, with no attempt to catch the style of the original. Also, it refers almost exclusively to something that follows after and is based on the extended presentation, or even concludes it—as suggested by the common phrase in speechmaking: in *summary.* **Abstract** and **précis** both refer to *summaries* written most often by someone other than the original author; hence, they are seldom part of the original presentation, though they follow it and are based upon it. Like *summary,* they stress brevity and the schematic representation of essential points with no attempt to preserve flavor. *Abstract* most specifically refers to a scholarly or legal citation that gives the gist of what may be a complex argument or study: a quarterly containing *abstracts* of recent doctoral dissertations; an *abstract* of the proposed legislation. *Précis* may suggest a lengthier treatment than *abstract* and one adhering to the exact ordering of points in the original; also, it is not restricted to legal or scholarly fields, applying to any *summary* of thought or argument in an essay or other nonfiction prose: each sentence in the *précis* representing a paragraph in the essay; space that permitted *abstracts* but ruled out *précis* of research projects. *Précis* can even refer to a list-like presentation of entire fields of knowledge: a *précis* of Renaissance art history.

Outline and **synopsis** relate to *précis* in that they both retain the point-by-point ordering of the original; they are both most often a skeletal setting down of these points, but may be drawn up either by the author or someone else before, as well as after, the writing of the original. Within these possibilities, *outline* covers a wider range than *synopsis.* It often suggests a numbered and lettered list containing nothing more than key words or phrases, but may present an extended prose paraphrase: a *summary* of French history written in the form of an *outline;* drawing up an *outline* of the author's arguments. *Synopsis* usually refers to a plot summary of a piece of fiction. Ordinary prose sentences are most often used, rather than the numbered and lettered list suggested by *outline.* It may tell in capsule form events treated in a completed work or those planned for a projected work: submitting the first chapter of a novel and a *synopsis* of the unwritten remainder; writing *synopses* of novels submitted as candidates for film treatment. *Synopsis* may also refer to a paragraph that retells previous action and introduces an installment of a serialized work of fiction.

Abridgment and **digest** refer to more expanded treatment, suggesting condensation rather than a capsule paraphrase of the original. Consequently, what is presented after this shortening process may still be substantially in the original author's words and style. Of the two, *abridgment* suggests the least modification of the original; it may refer, in fact, merely to the excision of a small number of passages: an *abridgment* in which passages involving sexual frankness were omitted. *Abridgment* can, however, indicate a greater amount of change: several characters and the entire subplot that did not appear in the *abridgment;* a useful one-volume *abridgment* of Gibbon. *Digest* refers to a boiled-down recasting of the original to present its essentials in shorter space. Although the original author's style and flavor may be retained at times, other passages may be rewritten for the sake of clarity or brevity: a concise *digest* of the judge's long dissent. *Digest* may also refer to a collection of condensed pieces: a quarterly *digest* of articles pertaining to space research. In some scholarly or technical uses, *digest* may suggest nearly the sort of brevity implicit in *abstract:* a *digest* of all the articles presented at the medical convention. See SHORTEN, TERSE.

summit

> acme
> apex
> climax
> peak
> pinnacle
> zenith

These nouns refer to the highest point of something. **Summit** and **peak** both refer most concretely to mountains; *peak,* however, can indicate the whole mountain or its upper part, whereas *summit* is specifically restricted in reference to the topmost surface alone: climbing the *peak* to reach the *summit.* In metaphorical use, this distinction is lost. Both nouns refer to the position of greatest importance, intensity, or power. *Summit* is the more formal of the two and has come to refer specifically to high-level conferences, as between heads of state: the settling of nuclear policy at the *summit. Peak* suggests the point or moment at which something is most typical or at its

best: when the Roaring Twenties were at their *peak;* a book produced when she was at the *peak* of her powers. *Summit* is less often used in this metaphorical way.

Pinnacle can refer to a turret or more commonly to a *peak* or its *summit.* It may, however, sometimes suggest a leaner, taller silhouette than *peak.* Used metaphorically, it functions as a hyperbolic substitute for *peak,* often in stock combinations that approach the cliché: the *pinnacle* of success. **Acme** can theoretically refer to a *summit* but now is almost exclusively used in a metaphorical way to refer to some abstract quality at its quintessential; it also appears in stock combinations: the *acme* of perfection. **Apex** refers to the vertex of an angle but can also indicate the tip or top of something or something at its maximum or its turning point: a debate that reached its *apex* the next afternoon. All three of these nouns can become empty metaphors, especially when used indiscriminately because of their imagined status or elegance.

Neither **zenith** nor **climax** makes any literal reference to a mountain *peak* or *summit. Zenith* refers to the celestial point directly overhead. Metaphorically, it suggests anything at its highest development; as such, it is a useful intensification of *peak:* fearing that their candidate's popularity had reached its *peak* too early, before campaign intensity was at its *zenith.* Also, *zenith* is more often used to suggest something positive, whereas *peak* is not so restricted: Her mastery of painting technique was at its *zenith* when the taste of her times had reached a *peak* of vulgarity. Most concretely, *climax* refers to the turning point of a play or a kind of rhetorical buildup in an oration. Metaphorically, *climax* is especially pertinent to indicate the point of fullest development in something that grows or has cyclic stages: picking only flowers that were at their *climax.* See CONCLUSIVE, HIGHEST.

Antonyms: *base, bottom, foot, nadir.*

summon

> beckon
> call
> conjure
> invoke
> send for
> subpoena

These verbs refer to an appeal for help, a mustering of forces or resources, or a request for a group or a person to gather or draw near. The most general are the relatively formal **summon** and the informal phrase **send for.** Since neither verb indicates what means are used to make the request, both can be convenient when only the request itself is of importance or when a variety of means is used in a gathering process. [The dying man *sent for* his only son; The cabinet was *summoned* to an emergency meeting by presidential aides.] *Summon* often implies an official or formal request or demand that someone come or appear: The pope *summoned* all cardinals and bishops to the ecumenical council. *Summon* can also apply to a mustering up of forces or resources: an attempt to *summon* up her last reserves of strength. *Send for* often implies the delegation of a task: We stayed at home and *sent out for* food. The noun form of *summon* can also refer specifically to a notice to appear in court: served with a *summons*. **Subpoena**, both as verb and noun, is exclusively restricted to this sense: Both sides may *subpoena* witnesses to testify.

Call can specifically indicate a *summoning* of someone by means of the spoken word or a vocal exclamation: He *called* to her from the other side of the street; the wordless wail with which she *called* for help. In other uses, *call* can refer to paying a visit or the arrival of an escort: a friend who promised to *call* on us; the hour at which he would *call* for me. More pertinent here, *call* can indicate the expression of a recommendation or demand: a biting speech in which he *called* for a new approach to public housing. *Call* can indicate the act of telephoning: I'll *call* you tomorrow. *Call up* can refer to *summoning* spirits or recollections—or to making any imaginative notion real and vivid by describing it in detail: a face that *called up* in her mind the image of her dead son; He *called up* for his audience a vision of what our city centers might look like if city planners were ignored. *Call* has a wide range of uses, often involved literally or metaphorically in some reference to a *summoning* process.

Beckon specifically refers to any *summoning* done by a gesture of the hand: *beckoning* me to his side; She asked them to follow her and *beckoned* them forward. **Conjure**, like one use of *call,* can specifically indicate the *summoning* of spirits or recollections, but it more often refers, like the same use of *call,* to vivid descriptions of an imagined state: a house that *conjured* up her forgotten childhood; a speech in which he *conjured* up for his colleagues the specter of all-out war. **Invoke** can refer to a call for supernatural favor, particularly at the opening of a formal or official gathering: the minister who *invoked* God to guide the convention in its work. In wider uses, *invoke* can refer to any action in which something real or imaginary, tangible or intangible, is called into play: a plea for the pro-

posal in which he *invoked* the memory of the late president; They *invoked* the mounting evidence of discrepancies in the report as justification for a full investigation. See GATHER, NAME, PLEAD, REQUEST.

Antonyms: *dismiss, POSTPONE.*

superficial
flat
obvious
shallow

These adjectives characterize effort or understanding that is not searching or profound or that does not go deep. **Superficial** and **shallow** may both literally indicate a lack of depth: *superficial* wounds; *shallow* water. In this context, *superficial* suggests a cursory or hasty approach, an undue interest in trivialities, or a personality that by choice is not genuine or sincere: a *superficial* glance at the newspaper; a *superficial* life of self-indulgence; giving him a polite but *superficial* welcome. In contrast, *shallow* applies not to a refusal to go into something deeply, but an inability to feel, sympathize, or understand: those who rush into marriage with only the *shallowest* notions of what love and responsibility entail; a *shallow* indifference to the sufferings of others; a *shallow* anthropocentric view of the universe. *Shallow* might seem the more condemnatory of the two adjectives, except that *superficial,* in suggesting a better or more painstaking effort is possible, would seem to indicate less forgivable failings: a *superficial* approach to the problem that was the result of a lazy, rather than a *shallow* mind.

Obvious and **flat** more often refer to the poor results to be expected from *superficial* efforts or *shallow* approaches. *Obvious* is very general and has a wide range of uses. In this context, it may pertain to effort that attempts to go beyond the *superficial* but fails: an *obvious* treatment of problems better dealt with by other scientists; an *obvious* plot that vitiates the playwright's ability to create genuine conflicts. In this context, *flat* suggests an *obvious* result without any sign of ability or desire to accomplish more: the novel's *flat* characters. It can also suggest something that has lost any value it once had: a story that was widely admired in the 1890's but seems *flat* to us today. As can be seen, both *obvious* and *flat* are often used to criticize works of art, particularly of a narrative sort, with *obvious* applying to action or plot, *flat* to the creation of character: The author's *superficial* approach, his *obvious* story line, and his *flat* characters all betray a *shallow* mind. See BANAL, BLAND.

Antonyms: *deep, GENUINE, profound.*

supernatural

magical
miraculous
preternatural
superhuman

These adjectives characterize things and occurrences that are or seem to be breaks with the natural order, or unexplainable departures from ordinary reality. **Supernatural** would seem unambiguous in referring to anything that is literally beyond nature or cannot be explained by commonsense experience or the scientific method, especially to phenomena of a divine or heavenly character. However, some people would exclude the possibility of such phenomena. To them, *supernatural* might be used to express skepticism or disbelief: priestly hocus-pocus and *supernatural* rigmarole. Furthermore, *supernatural* has gathered suggestions that make it particularly relevant to the context of occultists and spiritualists. Since many believers would find such interests heterodox, this flavor of *supernatural* restricts its use in a more general religious sense.

Magical has far less complicated implications; now it refers strictly to acts or things believed to confer *supernatural* powers: a *magical* charm to drive out evil spirits. This meaning makes it useful to anthropologists in describing aspects of primitive cultures whose religion is animist. More loosely, *magical* may refer hyperbolically to anything charged with meaning and emotion or awe-inspiring: the *magical* moment when the entire earth became visible to the orbiting astronaut. **Miraculous** is, of course, used in a religious context to refer to *supernatural* acts of saints or deities: the *miraculous* ability to levitate attributed to some Tibetan lamas; the *miraculous* changing of water into wine during the marriage at Cana. On a less elevated plane, *miraculous* is often used to refer to a last-minute or unexpected stroke of good fortune: a *miraculous* escape from their pursuers.

Preternatural puts contention to rest by specifically indicating those things that seem beyond explanation in terms of ordinary reality, but that are the result of unusual or rare causes: a *preternatural* ability to do complicated sums in her head. [Science works with *preternatural* phenomena in hopes of including them eventually within the circle of what we consider natural and explainable.] **Superhuman** indicates powers beyond those possessed by people, but again overtones obtrude. One might speak of the *superhuman* force of a hurricane or the *superhuman* compassion of God, but such descriptions might seem obvious, therefore trivial or irreverent. More often *superhuman* is used as a hyperbole for human effort that seems extreme: his roommate's *superhuman* powers of concentration. See BIZARRE, MYSTICAL, UNUSUAL.

Antonyms: *earthly*, NORMAL, STANDARD, USUAL, WORLDLY.

supple

agile
limber
lithe
nimble
resilient
spry

These adjectives suggest a smooth working of parts, especially in reference to a well-conditioned physique. **Supple** suggests a body capable of effortless movement: Unlike swimming, weightlifting does not lead to a *supple* build. Used of physical objects, *supple* suggests that something can be bent without breaking or without becoming permanently distorted: *supple* branches trembling in the breeze. Used more abstractly, *supple* suggests something relaxed rather than taut or something smoothly articulated: the rhythmically insistent yet always *supple* music; a cool, *supple* mind able to make fine distinctions.

Of the remaining adjectives, **lithe** and **limber** are closest in meaning to *supple*. *Lithe*, in fact, is often used in tandem with *supple*: *lithe* and *supple* dancers. *Lithe* tends to suggest gracefulness and trimness of figure. *Limber* more specifically suggests a body brought into condition through training: Even naturally *lithe* and *supple* bodies need disciplined exercise to remain *limber*. While both *lithe* and *limber* are less often used of inanimate objects that can be bent, *lithe* is sometimes used, like *supple*, to describe character. Its special emphasis here is on an economic spareness: a *lithe*, understated style of writing.

Agile and **resilient** both stress quickness of response in addition to a smooth working of parts. *Resilient* specifically emphasizes a rapid rebounding into shape, *agile* the ability to move quickly yet gracefully: the *resilient* layer of pine needles under our feet; the *agile* leap of the doe. Both can also refer to qualities of mind. Here *agile* stresses the ability to think quickly without faltering: an *agile* aptness for finding the significant pattern in a mass of data. *Resilient* suggests an innovating mind that is not bound by deadening routine or habit: a *resilient* hopefulness in the face of seemingly insoluble dilemmas.

Like *agile*, **nimble** points to quickness, but here the gracefulness of movement is less emphasized than lightness and dexterity: the *nimble* fingers of a pianist. **Spry** emphasizes unexpected quickness and is often used to describe an old person still *agile* in movement: a *spry* old man who still plays tennis. See ADAPTABLE, MALLEABLE, QUICK, THIN.

Antonyms: CLUMSY, HEAVY, SLOW.

supporter

adherent
disciple
follower
partisan

Supporter is the general noun for one who allies himself or herself with a cause or shows allegiance to its leader. [James Madison was one of the early *supporters* of the Bill of Rights; A political candidate needs the help of *supporters* to win an election.]

Follower and **disciple** are related in emphasizing devotion to a leader rather than to a doctrine or cause. A *follower* plays a more passive role than a *supporter* or a *disciple*. A *disciple* is one who studies under a leader or influential teacher and puts the leader's teachings into practice, perhaps to the point of proselytizing for the leader: Christ had many *followers,* but it was his *disciples* who spread his doctrines.

Adherent places emphasis on support of the doctrines rather than of the leader. Thus, one would call Lenin an *adherent* of Marxism (not an *adherent* of Marx).

Partisan means a zealous *supporter* of a person or cause, right or wrong, sometimes to the point of wrongheadedness and obstinacy: The candidate is a strong *partisan* of the president and his domestic policy; a violent *partisan* of the conservative cause. Since World War II, *partisan* has taken on the additional meaning of a dedicated rebel who supports a cause by guerrilla tactics: In World War II, Italian *partisans* helped the Allies conquer northern Italy. See ASSISTANT, STUDENT.

Antonyms: *antagonist,* OPPONENT, TRAITOR.

suppose

assume
conjecture
guess
imagine
postulate
surmise

These verbs refer to the tentative adoption of an idea or interpretation in the face of incomplete evidence or uncertainty. **Suppose** and **guess** are the most informal and general of these. Both can be used, especially in speech, to present a proposal or opinion in a tentative way, making it come as a suggestion rather than as a directive. [We'd better get going, I *suppose;* It's getting late, I *guess.*] Both can also indicate any hazarding of opinion, however well- or ill-informed, but *guess* is more likely to suggest a completely arbitrary notion or a more thoroughgoing lack of information or authority. *Guess* can even suggest a bluff or a futile groping in the dark without hope of success: tests that enable students to *guess* at random when they have no idea of the correct answer. *Suppose,* by contrast, more often suggests a shrewd notion based on some evidence: able to *suppose* how upset you were just from the expression in your eyes. *Suppose* also can point to something adopted experimentally or to something entertained simply for the sake of argument: asking him to *suppose* what he would do if he were in such a situation. Although *suppose,* like *guess,* implies a lack of certainty, there must be some grounds, however scanty, for *supposing* something. [You're only *supposing* this on hearsay; you have no proof.]

Imagine exists in a wider context, indicating either a creative act or a deliberate entertaining of something totally contrary to known fact. In the present context, *imagine* relates more closely to *guess,* suggesting a paucity of evidence on which a supposition is based: *imagining* all the wild stories of the neighbors to be true. *Imagine* emphasizes the role of invention or fancy in influencing perception: He *imagined* he heard a scraping noise. Even so, *imagine* carries over from its other contexts vague connotations of sympathy, understanding, or reassurance, as in its common use as a stock phrase in speech. [You'll enjoy the movie, I *imagine.*] When related to the context of argument or reasoning that surrounds *suppose,* *imagine* indicates a more thoroughgoing fabrication: largely *imagining* the existence of such a prehistoric tribe, rather than demonstrating its existence.

Assume and **postulate** relate most closely to *suppose* in suggesting a context of argument or reasoning. *Assume* is the less formal of the two, emphasizing a conclusion based on little or no validating evidence; as such, it can suggest a general context pertaining to psychological rather than to logical mental operations: *assuming* that life owed us a living; She *assumed* he wouldn't want to see her again. In argument, *assume* is even clearer than *suppose* about agreeing to adopt a tentative stance in order to test a proposition: *assuming* the report to be valid just to see how its recommendations might affect our policies in the next decade. In the stricter context of logic and reasoning, both *postulate* and *assume* point to things that must be accepted as given prior to the reasoning process: *preferring an explanation that requires us to postulate (or assume) the fewest preconditions at the outset. Postulate* is exclusively restricted in reference to the setting up of a theory in order to test its merit, so it is more precise than either *assume* or *suppose:* scientists who are traditionally driven to *postulate* a series of explanations until they find one that will stick.

Conjecture and **surmise** are comparable to *postulate* in formality, but comparable to *suppose* and *guess* in generality. *Conjecture*, used as a noun as well as a verb, relates closely to *guess*, stressing incomplete or inadequate evidence serving as a basis for judgment. A shrewd *conjecture* may include elements of intuition, extrapolations based on experience, a good sense of probability, and plain luck. When used without qualification, *conjecture* often indicates mere guesswork, unsubstantiated by any evidence and hence without much credibility: *aimless conjectures about conspiracies organizing the assassination; He conjectured that the rescue party would arrive by first light. Surmise* relates to the aspect of *suppose* that indicates a shrewd notion based on evidence. It points to an ability to detect clues and draw valid conclusions from them; its connotations suggest detachment and an ability to reason dispassionately: *quickly surmising that he had called on them at an inopportune time. Surmise* conveys a greater degree of certainty, or at least better grounds for drawing a conclusion, than any of the other verbs here considered. See CONSIDER, DECIDE, REASONING.

Antonyms: *actualize, execute, finalize, know, prove, validate.*

sure

  certain
  definite
  doubtless
  positive

These adjectives all mean free of doubt or uncertainty. **Sure** and **certain** are used interchangeably in most contexts, but *certain* may emphasize the indisputable character of what is referred to. *Sure* is more indiscriminately used. [One thing was *certain:* Democrats will think twice before nominating a national candidate with only a local reputation; She was *sure* she could make the five o'clock train.] Both adjectives, but especially *sure*, may serve as polite substitutes for a hopeful but less-than-*certain* attitude. "I'm *sure* I'll be there on time" can mean "I think (or I hope) I'll be there on time."

Positive is somewhat more emphatic than *sure* or *certain* in stressing the absolute absence of doubt and the incontestable nature of one's conviction. [I was *positive* I had seen her face before; I could not possibly have been mistaken on that point.] **Definite**, influenced by its more basic meaning of precisely defined or limited (as in *definite* boundaries), is usually used in contexts that suggest a narrowing of choice or elimination of doubt, and often carries the meaning of no longer open to question, settled beyond doubt. [Her choice of a running mate is now *definite*.]

Doubtless is more often used as an adverb than as an adjective. Indeed, its use as an adjective today strikes most ears as rather formal or dated. [It was his *doubtless* conclusion that the verdict was justified by the evidence.] As an adverb, *doubtless* often functions as a polite substitute for "one supposes" or "one would like to believe," or in contexts that show equivocation or skepticism. [*Doubtless* he had not meant to offend me, but the tone of his remarks was certainly insulting; It was *doubtless* true that the deal was legal, but one wondered whether it was ethical.] See CLEAR, SPECIFIC.

Antonyms: DOUBTFUL, *improbable, unlikely, unsure, wavering.*

surfeit

  cloy
  dull
  glut
  pall
  sate
  satiate

These verbs mean diminish, satisfy completely, or take away an appetite for something, often because of overexposure to it. **Surfeit** suggests an oversupply of something that may be appealing in itself but that causes antipathy in quantity: *eating second and third helpings of the plum pudding until he was surfeited;* a *public surfeited* to the point of boredom by the violence displayed on the television screen. **Glut** restricts itself to one aspect of *surfeit*, concentrating on the notion of oversupply without necessarily suggesting any concomitant antipathy: *a society glutted, yet ever more avid for sexually provocative entertainment.*

Sate and **satiate** once suggested appeasement of hunger or appetite, but now they suggest overindulgence to the point of discomfort. Of the two, *satiate* is the milder and more abstract and is still sometimes used for simple appeasement: gulping water from the offered canteen until his thirst was *satiated*. *Sate* almost invariably suggests the discomfort of overindulgence, especially in specifically sensual pleasures; the resulting discomfort may be felt as an enfeeblement of the senses or a sybaritic exhaustion or ennui: collapsing into sleep at last, *sated* with drink and carousing.

Dull specifically emphasizes an overtone of *sate* pertaining to sensory enfeeblement through overexposure: senses *dulled* from days of partying; Don't *dull* your hunger by wolfing down chocolates. **Pall** suggests that an attractive or desired object has lost its appeal through overexposure: a face whose beauty *palled* on him the more he looked at it; an interest in theories of conspiracy that *palled* soon after the new movie was issued. **Cloy** suggests a sense of heavy oppression or suffocation caused by excessive gratification of an initially pleasing sensation, especially a sweet smell or fulsome manner: a strong scent of lilacs in the room that soon *cloyed*; a maternal love that *cloyed*. See EAT, GOURMET, SATISFY.

surprised

amazed
astonished
astounded
flabbergasted
stunned

These adjectives mean filled with wonder or incredulity because of a confrontation with something unexpected. To be **surprised** is to meet with something that momentarily, at least, sets one back and then may or may not afford pleasure: The child's *surprised* blue eyes upon opening my present were thanks enough; no longer *surprised* at the drunken behavior of her business associate. *Surprised* can also suggest a certain amount of moral condemnation, as when a person says, "I'm *surprised* at you!"

Astonished is stronger, indicating that a person has had more than an ordinary reaction to the unexpected: The *astonished* visitor spoke only of how the town had changed in ten years.

Amazed suggests great wonder or bewilderment in the face of something that seems impossible or highly improbable: a teacher *amazed* to find that three poor students had made marks of 100 on the test. **Astounded** and the informal **flabbergasted** express extreme difficulty of belief. A woman may be *astounded* to learn that her dearest friend has been spreading malicious gossip about her. Describing her reaction to another friend, she might say, "I am *flabbergasted!*"

Stunned indicates shock and even speechlessness: the *stunned* congregation listened as their pastor revealed his criminal past. See CONFUSE, PUZZLE, UPSET.

Antonyms: *IMPERTURBABLE.*

swarthy

dusky
tanned
tawny

These adjectives indicate a dark or brownish coloring of the skin. Both **swarthy** and **dusky** signify skin of a dark cast, but they differ radically in connotation. *Swarthy* may be used neutrally in description: a tall man with a *swarthy* complexion. But it has been used so often to describe fictional characters of a romantic and sometimes vaguely sinister aspect that these associations accompany *swarthy* more often than not: a *swarthy* Mediterranean in a Gothic novel. *Dusky* has exotic rather than suspicious connotations, a quality of mystery rather than menace. It seems somewhat lyrical or literary when applied to skin, suggesting a darkness of coloring that might have been dusted on like powder, a shadowy quality like an aura or an overlay: a *dusky* Moor; the *dusky* skin of the island girls.

Tawny and **tanned** suggest a warm coloring between dark and fair. *Tanned* describes skin darkened through exposure to the sun: a *tanned* complexion achieved in eight days at the beach. *Tawny* indicates a natural coloring that is yellowish, somewhat orange, or reddish brown. *Tawny* is seldom used of human beings except to describe the color of hair: a *tawny*-haired youth.

Antonyms: *fair, light, light-skinned,* PALE, *white, whitish.*

swell

bulge
dilate
distend
inflate

These verbs agree in meaning become or cause to become larger. **Swell,** the most general, means increase in bulk or dimension in any way, as by adding air or by absorbing moisture: a mosquito bite that *swelled* to the size of a quarter; a mountain brook rapidly *swelling* into a river. **Inflate**, on the other hand, specifically means expand by filling with gas or air: to *inflate* a balloon or a tire. Both *swell* and *inflate* are commonly used in extended senses; *swell* can apply to any large increase, *inflate* always, and *swell* sometimes, applying to disproportionately large or exaggerated increases: a tiny company that *swelled* into a giant corporation almost overnight; to *swell* the funds of the charitable organization to a new high; His sense of importance *inflated* rapidly. *Swell* in many contexts has a suggestion of morbidity or unnatural size, illustrated by its metaphorical use in the expression "a *swelled* head," meaning an *inflated* self-esteem.

Bulge implies *swell* outward, usually in one particular direction. [Sacks filled with fluid *bulge* at their weakest spots; The policeman's coat *bulged* where his service revolver was holstered on his chest.]

Distend means expand or stretch out because of pressure exerted from within. [When you take a deep breath and hold it, your lungs *distend;* A nursing mother's breasts *distend*.] Whereas *distend* implies an enlargement in all directions, **dilate** usually implies a two-dimensional enlargement, and is most often applied to the eyes: Eyes may *dilate* with surprise; Pupils *dilate* when one moves from a sunny to a darkened room. See ENLARGE, EXTEND.

Antonyms: DECREASE, *deflate, depress, extract*.

symbol

badge
device
emblem
hallmark
sign
token

These nouns refer to a tangible or visible indication of a detectable or agreed-upon meaning. **Symbol** is the most complex in its references, emphasizing in all its uses something deliberately made to embody or constructed to communicate a certain meaning. A *symbol* may be arbitrarily arrived at: the *symbols* of the alphabet; white as the *symbol* of purity. Or it may be developed by charged circumstances: abolitionists who saw in John Brown the *symbol* of their cause. In an aesthetic sense, *symbol* may refer to an element carefully chosen and deployed to have a desired effect: a series of unrelated misfortunes in the novel that became *symbols* for the protagonist's state of mind.

Sign is often used in place of *symbol* to refer to a simple, arbitrary representation of an agreed-upon meaning: the *sign* of the cross; waving the white flag as a *sign* that they want to surrender. Even on the simplest level, however, *symbol* and *sign* are often used in tandem to indicate different things; for example, letters and the words they make are referred to as *symbols*, punctuation marks as *signs*. The former yield meanings, the latter phrasings or intonations. On other levels as well, *sign* refers to an arbitrary indication from which simple, agreed-upon meanings or instructions can be deduced. Correspondingly, *symbol* refers to an indication that embodies a greater range of meanings. These must be deduced from the exact deployment of the *symbols* and cannot always be paraphrased without loss. The higher animals as well as human beings use *signs,* but only human beings create *symbols:* the typical shriek that monkeys make as a *sign* to warn others in the tribe of an imminent danger. [Documents such as the Bill of Rights endure as *symbols* for human aspirations that are not even necessarily enumerated in them.] More loosely, *sign* is widely used for any sort of telltale fact from which information can be deduced: looking for *signs* that the disease had run its course; a *sign* that inflation was on the way.

Emblem suggests a visual *symbol* that stands as the distinctive device of a group or nation: the eagle that is an *emblem* of the United States; the hammer-and-sickle *emblem* of the former Soviet Union. **Badge**, most strictly, is an *emblem* that designates membership or rank in a military or paramilitary unit or an honor given by it: the *badge* of the Second Division; a merit *badge;* the *badge* of Eagle Scout; opening her coat to show her police *badge*. Sometimes, *badge* can be used as a more colorful substitute for *emblem:* wearing the scarlet letter as the *badge* of her disgrace. **Hallmark** originally referred to a distinguishing mark stamped on sterling silver; now it may refer to an *emblem* chosen to represent a group or business: the drawing of a comet that appeared as a *hallmark* on the company's stationery. Even more generally, *hallmark* can refer to any unmistakable or outstanding feature by which something can be recognized: the wit that was the *hallmark* of her presidency; integrity, the *hallmark* of a gentleman.

Device, in this sense, refers to a symbolic figure or design, usually with a motto or legend, in a coat of arms borne upon a shield. It may also denote any *emblem* that has been adopted by a person or a family. By extension, the colophon of a publisher and an easily recognizable symbol used as a trademark are sometimes called *devices*.

Token most often refers to something offered as a

symbol or reminder of an attitude or understanding: giving him a kiss as a *token* of her love; keeping the medals as a *token* by which to remember her dead son. More recently, *token* may suggest a partial effort or a minimal compliance: asking for a deposit as a *token* of her intention to buy the book; businesses that hire one member of a minority as a *token* of their intention to integrate. See MEAN (V.), MEANING.

symptom
    clue
    indication
    prodrome
    syndrome

These nouns refer to evidence from which a whole situation, such as the presence of a disease, may be inferred. **Symptom** relates closely to a medical context, applying to any manifestations of unusual functioning that may or may not be relevant to a diagnosis: unexplained *symptoms* of dizziness and nausea. Similarly, each abnormal condition or disease gives off characteristic *symptoms*: required to name the telltale *symptoms* for hundreds of diseases. A **syndrome** is the set of *symptoms* that always occur together and are characteristic of a particular disease, whether physical or mental. A *syndrome*, however, is not the sum total of random *symptoms* detected in someone at a checkup, but only those that fit together into the typical picture of a specific disease or ailment: the *syndrome* for a type of hepatitis that includes yellowing of the skin, extreme fatigue, and certain digestive disorders; delusions, the hearing of voices, and a feeling of being persecuted that are inevitable parts of the paranoid's *syndrome*. *Syndrome* has become a fad word for any set of characteristics commonly found in association, usually used with a negative tone: immediately recognizing in him the political extremist *syndrome*. **Prodrome**, a medical term, unlike *syndrome*, does not refer to a collection of *symptoms* but to any single *symptom* that is premonitory of an approaching disease: the chronic anemia that may be a *prodrome* for leukemia.

While **indication** and **clue** may be used in a medical context, both are also used widely outside it. *Clue*, of course, relates more directly to the field of criminology than to medicine. As such, it refers to the evidence by which a crime may be solved or from which a whole situation may be inferred: gathering *clues* at the scene that could lead them to the killer. In a wider context, *clue* can refer to any telltale evidence whether given intentionally or inadvertently: seeking some *clue* as to how she felt about his novel; noticing several *clues* suggesting a community of interests. *Indication* is the most general of these nouns and can point to any piece of telltale evidence in any context: *indications* of the drug's effectiveness; *indications* that a quarrel had immediately preceded the murder; giving her *indications* that he enjoyed her company; some guidelines that are good *indications* of a country's economic health. See HINT, MEAN (V.), PREMONITION, TESTIMONY.

taciturn

close
reticent
secretive
uncommunicative

These adjectives are alike in meaning restrained in speaking to others or reserved in manner. **Taciturn** characterizes a disposition to speak little, and then grudgingly; it conveys the strong suggestion of a dryness of manner bordering on unsociability. ["Yes," was his *taciturn* response to the complex question posed; a cold, *taciturn* nature that seldom could be aroused to the point of uttering a complete sentence.] **Reticent** implies a reluctance to speak freely about particular matters, especially about one's private affairs, rather than a quality of temperament, as is the case with *taciturn*. [He became *reticent* when asked to divulge his income; *reticent* about discussing her life before marriage.] **Close**, like *taciturn*, indicates a habit of temperament rather than a particular instance. A man who is *close* says little of his own affairs, perhaps because he has something to hide. **Secretive** makes the explicit accusation of knowing concealment and is broader than the other adjectives here considered in not necessarily applying to what is unsaid; it may apply instead to the manner of what is said: something *secretive* about him, although he answers questions readily enough. *Secretive* implies suspicion or mistrust on the part of the observer: Why is she so *secretive* about her friends?

Uncommunicative, like *taciturn*, implies an unwillingness to speak even when speech is called for, but strongly points to unsociableness as the underlying motive for such reluctance: police occupied with interrogating an *uncommunicative* suspect; disturbed children who were sullen and *uncommunicative*. *Uncommunicative* may, however, also indicate a lack of verbal facility: school dropouts who are *uncommunicative* because they are unsure of themselves. See ALOOF, MODEST, SILENT, SPEECHLESS, TERSE, TIMID, UNWILLING.

Antonyms: *communicative*, TALKATIVE.

talisman

amulet
charm
fetish

These nouns denote something regarded as having magical powers. A **talisman** is a material object that is supposed to work wonders because it possesses and transmits certain qualities. It is believed to have a positive power in itself. A *talisman* may be carried on the person or, like Aladdin's lamp, be put to use as desired or needed. Aaron's rod in the Old Testament is a *talisman*, as are the magician's wand and the cap of invisibility in folklore. In a figurative sense, a *talisman* is something that produces or is capable of producing extraordinary effects: The young queen's dignity and beauty were *talismans* against unfavorable public opinion.

In common use, *talisman* and **amulet** are frequently confused. An *amulet* is a piece of stone, metal, bone, or wood inscribed with a magic incantation. It is almost always worn on the person and is supposed to protect the wearer from danger, disease, and witchcraft, or to ensure the wearer of success, as in love or war. Unlike a *talisman*, an *amulet* is supposed to confer passive protection and not produce active magic.

Charm is the most general of these nouns and includes anything that has occult powers. *Talismans* and *amulets* may both be referred to as *charms*. In modern times the small metal miniatures worn on chains or bracelets, and called *charms*, are no doubt a carryover from the old or primitive custom of wearing *amulets*. In the strictest sense, however, a *charm* is the uttering of words or rhymes supposed to produce magical results. By extension, *charm* is the power to allure or delight: the *charm* of a beautiful child; the *charm* of Mozart's music.

In animistic religions, a **fetish** is an object worshiped by primitive peoples because they believe it to be the dwelling of a friendly spirit. Among such objects used as *fetishes* are stones, teeth, carved bits of wood, and plants. Figuratively, a *fetish* is something to which one is excessively devoted: people who make a *fetish* of cleanliness. Psychiatrically, it can refer to any object or part of the body on which a deviant's eroticism is fixated: confessed to a *fetish* for women's gloves; a foot *fetish*. See SUPERNATURAL.

talkative

gabby
garrulous
glib
loquacious
voluble

These adjectives refer to the tendency or ability to

talk smoothly readily, tediously, continually, or at length. **Talkative** is relatively informal and, most often, neutral in tone. It describes people who are easily engaged in conversation or given to expressing themselves verbally with little prompting. Context can make the word negative: a *talkative* bore. But more commonly it is descriptively neutral or even approving. When the latter is true, *talkative* may suggest an outgoing person: good to be among people who were friendly and *talkative* after facing the hostile silence of the villagers. **Gabby**, the least formal of these adjectives, refers to a compulsive talker and as such is firmly negative in tone: a *gabby* clutch of graduate students exchanging the latest gossip. *Gabby* can be used without harsh intent, however, when it is meant humorously or in self-deprecation: missing the *gabby* bull sessions he'd enjoyed at college; apologizing for having been so *gabby*.

Voluble and **glib** pertain specifically to the ease with which someone is able to converse or speak. Of moderate formality, *voluble* once pointed to a pleasing facility in speech, gesture, manners, and writing, but now it pertains more strictly to free-and-easy verbal smoothness. *Voluble* may be approving in tone or indulgently critical: a beautifully modulated baritone voice that contributed to the impression he made of being a *voluble* speaker; a *voluble* neighbor, always eager to tell me the local gossip. *Glib,* by contrast, is more harshly and consistently negative in tone, referring to a smooth, slick, and possibly vulgar way of speaking, as one adopted to mask insincerity, superficiality, or dishonesty: the *glib* flattery doled out at literary cocktail parties; a student long on *glib* answers but short on thoughtfulness; a *glib* spokesperson for a government official.

Unlike the previous pair, **loquacious** and **garrulous** are less concerned with verbal smoothness than with talk that is incessant or lengthy. Of the two, *loquacious* is less clear-cut in tone. When positive, it serves as an intensification of the favorable implications of *talkative*, with a suggestion of the fluency implicit in *voluble:* an earnest and *loquacious* advocate of open housing. When negative in tone, it can suggest an overbearing insistence on holding forth without regard for one's listeners: *loquacious* guides who will not let you examine a masterpiece in silence; a *loquacious* public speaker who always spoke far beyond the time allotted. *Garrulous* is wholly negative in tone and as such is an intensification of the negative possibilities in *loquacious. Garrulous* suggests a nonstop talker who is rambling, wordy, possibly foolish, and usually tedious. It suggests someone who is unable to be concise or who insists on monopolizing conversations: a *garrulous* old man who kept interrupting their chat with boring accounts of his latest fishing trip. See CHATTER, PATTER, VERBOSE.

Antonyms: *SILENT, SPEECHLESS, TACITURN, TERSE.*

tasty
delicious
flavorful
palatable
toothsome

These adjectives characterize the pleasant sensations accompanying an agreeable taste or flavor. **Tasty** and **delicious** are more common in speech and less formal than the other adjectives here considered. *Tasty* merely refers to a fine flavor; *delicious* stresses more strongly the great pleasure that attends a fine food: a *tasty* dessert; a *delicious* imported pâté that was gobbled up by the guests. *Delicious*, moreover, is not necessarily restricted to pleasure induced by taste: a *delicious* silence in the park when cars are banned from the roads within it. Taste is, however, the most common association with *delicious*.

Palatable implies more modest or equivocal pleasure than any of the other adjectives of this group. *Palatable* is now most often used to mean acceptably good or agreeable, especially when the thing tasted has not been regarded as *tasty:* Missionaries found the indigenous food *palatable* if not always *delicious*. In its extended senses, *palatable* refers to some saving feature that makes acceptable an otherwise unattractive thing or condition: Being sent down to the minor leagues was made *palatable* to the ballplayer by a promise that he would get to play every day.

Flavorful literally means full of flavor but is more commonly used to mean having a strong and pleasant flavor: a *flavorful* brew of tea. **Toothsome** suggests a succulent or voluptuous quality attending a pleasant taste. In figurative uses, in which *toothsome* is perhaps more commonly used today, the quality of being appetizing or sensually attractive predominates: a *toothsome* bevy of beauties. It is often thus used, as in this example, with a humorous or sardonic tone. See SAVORY.

Antonyms: *BLAND, dull, flat, flavorless, foul, inedible, tasteless, unappetizing, unsavory.*

tax
assess

impose
levy

These verbs pertain to a government's exacting of money or other forms of support from its citizens or those dealing with them. **Tax** is the most general and least formal of these. It refers almost exclusively to the raising of money, although this may be done through a variety of means: the average citizen who ends up being *taxed* according to income, general purchases, real estate holdings, buying of imported goods—and even amusements and luxuries. One of the points of *tax* is its emphasis on the actual collection of money. This contrasts with **assess**, which points to a determining of the basis for *taxing* someone; the reference of *assess* now is usually to the *taxing* of real estate: *assessing* property at a higher valuation because of improvements made on it. In related uses, *assess* may also refer to determining the amount of a fine: damages *assessed* by the court at $10,000.

Impose may suggest the determining of fines, punishment, or taxes in individual cases: *imposing* stiff fines on scofflaws; *imposing* a light sentence on the first offender. More closely related to *tax*, however, is the reference of *impose* to a governmental decision, general in nature, to tap new sources of revenue or support: *imposing* additional taxes on business expansion; *imposing* military service on young men and women. When its emphasis is on determination rather than collection, *impose* is like *assess*, except for its indication of a general decision. A legislative body might *impose* terms concerning the amount and source of new revenue, after which each affected person might be *assessed* and then *taxed* accordingly. *Impose* in these senses has neutral force, but it can easily be given overtones of repressive or arbitrary willfulness: a staggering burden of taxation *imposed* on those who can least afford it; a policy of *imposing* unjust taxes on the colonies. **Levy** may sometimes be used to indicate determination, like *assess* or *impose*. But more appropriately, as its root suggests, it refers to the actual raising—that is, the collection or exaction of the amount *assessed* or the duty *imposed:* a stabilizing of prices when the new tax began to be *levied;* British officers who *levied* troops and quarters from the colonists. See COMPEL, DEMAND, OBLIGATION.

teach
educate
indoctrinate

instruct
school
tutor

These verbs refer to the process by which knowledge is imparted to students. **Teach** suggests a guided process of assigned work, discipline, directed study, and the presentation of examples. It may or may not suggest an academic context: *teaching* his daughter to change a tire; *teaching* pupils the letters of the alphabet. Intransitively, however, *teach* refers to *teaching* thought of as a profession: deciding he would *teach* after he graduated from college; *teaching* in the freshman English program. **Educate** is more formal and less specific than *teach;* it cannot substitute for *teach* in any of the examples above, referring in a more general way to a long-range, wide-scale academic process: *educating* the coming generation by means of new methods. Sometimes, *educate* suggests the accomplishing of greater results than *teach:* schools that *teach* but fail to *educate* their students.

School is used rarely as a substitute for *teach* and suggests an especially thorough process: *schooling* the class in the essentials of arithmetic; parents who had *schooled* their children in the social graces. Oddly enough, as in the last example, *school* need not suggest an academic context at all, though it does indicate a special effort or training, often to master complex rather than rudimentary matters: thinking to *school* himself in making the fine distinctions the new job would require; having *schooled* herself simply to ignore angry outbursts. **Instruct** is closer in function to *teach* than *educate* or *school*. It is more formal, however, and is mostly restricted to the specific situation of guided training or to the imparting of information or commands: one teacher to give the lecture classes, another to *instruct* the discussion groups; a manual *instructing* the buyer on the installation of an air conditioner; *instructing* the aide to come in an hour earlier on Monday.

Tutor refers to a special one-to-one relationship between teacher and student: English universities in which each student is *tutored* by a don. Often, *tutor* refers to remedial or special work done outside the classroom on a one-to-one basis: offering to *tutor* her in French in exchange for German lessons; hiring a graduate student to *tutor* him in his worst subjects. **Indoctrinate**, alone of these verbs, suggests the inculcation of propaganda or prejudices rather than unbiased knowledge: parents who *indoctrinate* their children with race hatred; schools that unwittingly *indoctrinate* their students with middle-class values. See IMPLANT, LEARNING, STUDENT, STUDY.

tear

rend
rip
rive

These verbs are comparable in that they all refer to a pulling apart of a material or an object, or to the separating of two objects that are firmly bound together. **Tear**, the most general verb in the group, has the widest application. It can denote the pulling apart of a seamless piece of material, as cloth or paper, suggesting in this case that the edges of the resultant pieces are rough or irregular: *tearing* an old sheet into cleaning rags. It can refer to the damaging action of such a pulling apart: cursing under his breath when a nail *tore* a hole in his trousers. It can be used in application to an injury or laceration: *tearing* her skin while picking roses. Figuratively, *tear* can mean disrupt or distress: a political party *torn* by dissension; a sight to *tear* one's heart.

Rip has special application to the division of a fabric by *tearing* along a line of least resistance or by cutting or breaking a row of stitches: *ripping* a dress apart along its seams. It can also designate any kind of *tearing* or cutting that is accomplished with harshness or violence: *ripping* open an old wound.

Rend and **rive** have even stronger overtones of violence than *rip* in their referral to a *tearing*, splitting, or pulling apart by force: buildings *rent* by an earthquake; a tree *riven* by lightning. Figuratively, *rend* and *rive* are like *tear* in their application to dissension or painful affliction: a nation *rent* by civil war; a heart *riven* by despair. Today, however, *rend* and *rive* tend to sound lofty and poetical. See CUT, SEVER.

Antonyms: *REPAIR.*

teem

abound
overflow
swarm

These verbs refer to great amounts or dense clusters. **Teem** and **swarm** both refer to the rapid, independent movement of particles in a small space or cluster. Of the two, *swarm* is more concrete and more limited in application outside this literal situation: bees that *swarm* around a hive; traffic that *swarmed* over the bridges leading to the city; enemy soldiers that *swarmed* toward us down the hill: a section of the city that *swarmed* with peddlers. *Teem* is even more emphatic about the frenetic nature of the activity referred to. While *teem* can have literal application, it is more often applied figuratively. Unlike *swarm*, which can often carry a negative tone, *teem* frequently suggests approval for anything that seems infused with vibrant life: Shakespeare's plays that *teemed* with insights; a novel *teeming* with memorable characters and incidents; a new generation *teeming* with exuberance and iconoclasm. When *teem* applies in a more nearly neutral way, it still can have a tone of panoramic lyricism: the *teeming* slums of the city.

Overflow can specifically refer to a fluid that overruns its container: flood waters that *overflowed* sandbag barriers. In figurative use, *overflow* suggests approval for qualities that someone or something possesses and gives off in copious amounts: a personality that *overflowed* with kindness and generosity. Less often, *overflow* can refer to any superfluity, as of emotion: pinched, bitter faces that *overflowed* with sullen distrust. **Abound** is the most general of these verbs and the vaguest in its implications; it suggests a generous portion, usually of favorable qualities: a country that *abounds* in architectural masterpieces; those of us who still *abound* in goodwill. Used negatively, *abound* can contribute an ironic forcefulness: an administration that *abounded* in broken promises. See FLOW, GENEROUS, PREVALENT.

Antonyms: *vacate*, WANE, WEAKEN.

tell

convey
impart
narrate
recite
recount
relate
report

These verbs are comparable in the general sense of communicating with others in speech or writing. **Tell**, the least formal of the group, is applicable in many contexts where other verbs would be more exact or pertinent, but it is the term of choice in the sense of making something known or of disclosing or revealing: He would not *tell* who was to blame.

Narrate and **relate** imply conscious and deliberate attention to the communication of a story, suggesting an orderly arrangement of details with a view to continuity, completeness, and artistic effect. [Defoe *narrated* the adventures of Robinson Crusoe on his desert island; Homer *related* the misfortunes of Odysseus after the Trojan War concluded.]

Recount carries the idea of a more careful enumeration of the particulars of whatever is being communicated: The witness *recounted* the events leading up to the crime. **Recite** may be used in the same sense but is more pertinent when it refers to something clearly remembered or repeated from memory: to *recite* the Gettysburg Address. **Report** implies giving an account of something with a more formal attention to details and to accuracy in the presentation of the relevant information: The committee *reported* its findings after a thorough investigation.

Convey has the primary meaning of carry or transport from one place to another; by extension, one can *convey* information or *convey* an impression or idea. **Impart** means disclose in the sense of sharing with another person: to *impart* one's suspicions about a crime. See CHATTER, CONVERSATION, SPEECH, UTTER.

temblor. The noun *temblor* (earthquake) has nothing to do with the verb *tremble* or the noun *trembler*.

temperament

character
disposition
nature
personality

These nouns refer to a person's mental makeup or emotional state. **Temperament** refers most commonly to a cast of mind that is revealed by the fixed or habitual ways a person responds to life. *Temperament* may suggest either an innate or a learned pattern, but it does point to something deeply ingrained or unconscious rather than something reflecting an arbitrary or conscious choice. Otherwise, *temperament* can indicate any sort of mental or emotional state: a frivolous *temperament;* a *temperament* marked by restless curiosity. *Temperament* can also typify a group of people: the no-nonsense British *temperament*. When unqualified, however, *temperament* indicates a tendency toward intense and moody rebelliousness; this is a more informal use of the word: a child marked by *temperament*.

Disposition can refer to an enduring frame of mind, whether innate or learned, but it points more strictly to emotional qualities that are only one part of the more formal *temperament:* a grouchy *disposition;* the sunniness of her usual *disposition*. *Disposition* contrasts most sharply with *temperament*, however, in that it can be used for transitory emotional states: coming to work in a foul *disposition*. **Nature**, in contrast to all these nouns, is the most emphatic about the innate and irrevocable aspect of the traits it points to. *Nature* can also point to the widest range of traits, including emotional, mental, and physical qualities: by *nature* a timid little man of mediocre intelligence;

those *natures* that are unhesitatingly compassionate. *Nature* is also the only one of these nouns that is commonly used when generalizing about traits inherent in humans as a whole: anthropologists who challenge our culture-bound notions about the *nature* of humanity.

Character and **personality** both point to bundles of mental and emotional traits, innate and learned, that distinguish one person from another. *Character* points to the fully developed lifestyle of an adult or group and often relates to moral fiber: drinking companions of questionable *character;* the stern but resourceful *character* of the Pilgrims. *Personality* pertains more to the entire indefinable emotional coloration that a specific person gives off: her winsome *personality;* a *personality* crippled by arrogance and impatience. Used without qualification, *character* suggests moral forcefulness, *personality* emotional appeal: He has *character* but no *personality*. In this use, both nouns can apply to anything thought to exhibit these qualities, especially when they are distinctive in their force or appeal: a face with *character;* paintings completely lacking in *character;* a striking city, full of *personality*. Used in this way, *personality* has become so popular that it is in danger of sounding trite through overuse. See CHARACTERISTIC, ECCENTRICITY, GENIUS.

temperance

abstinence
continence
self-denial
sobriety

These nouns refer to an avoidance of pleasurable excesses. **Temperance**, correctly used, refers to a wise moderation of indulgence in such pleasures, but as commonly used it suggests a complete rejection, especially of alcohol: a *temperance* that extended to declining drinks until sundown; the question of *temperance* that inflamed women against the evils of whiskey. **Self-denial** and **sobriety** are, of themselves, vague as to the extent to which avoidance may or should go. *Self-denial* is, of course, more general than *sobriety* but is firmer in tone than *temperance* in its most general sense, suggesting an attitude of refusing to give in to the demands of one's own body: a Spartan *self-denial* that made young men impervious to extremes of heat and cold, to hunger, and to the threat of death; a Victorian code of morals that stressed prudish *self-denial*. *Sobriety*, by contrast, usually applies in this context strictly to nonintoxication by alcohol. A person, of course, may be intoxicated one day and in a state of *sobriety* the next. More broadly, *sobriety* may suggest a soberness or solemnity of mien: the grim *sobriety* in the faces of the jury.

Abstinence and **continence** are much clearer than *self-denial* and *sobriety* as to the extent of denial involved; they emphasize a total avoidance of sensation. In this they are at odds with the more general implications of *temperance*. *Abstinence*, in context, may refer to an avoidance of alcohol or sexual satisfaction or the like: a complete *abstinence* from salty foods. *Continence* usually is taken to mean an avoidance of sexual intercourse in particular, but at its most general it can suggest a range of possibility similar to *self-denial:* maintaining a certain *continence* toward extracurricular activities, the better to concentrate on studies. See ABSTAIN, AVOID, FORSWEAR, REJECT.

Antonyms: *avidity, excess, hedonism, indulgence, intemperance.*

temporary

ephemeral
evanescent
fleeting
momentary
passing
transient
transitory

These adjectives characterize things that last or that remain on the scene for only a brief time. **Temporary** is the most general term, implying a measurable but limited duration. Unlike most of the other adjectives in this set, *temporary* indicates what is meant or known to last for a limited time only: a *temporary* job; a medicine that gives *temporary* relief. Further, *temporary* often suggests makeshift arrangements made for the time being under the pressure of circumstances: *temporary* shelter from the storm. It is also used to soften the impact of a harsh reality: a *temporary* setback, not a final defeat.

Momentary, used literally, means coming and going away suddenly, in a moment: a *momentary* misgiving. It is also used to indicate relative brevity of duration: a *momentary* delay. **Passing** emphasizes the fact that a thing does not continue to occupy the interest for long, but runs its course fairly quickly: a *passing* fad. **Fleeting** is an intensification of *passing* in a literal sense, referring to something that passes almost instantaneously: a dilettante too preoccupied with the *fleeting* moment to do any serious work; I caught just a *fleeting* glimpse of my new neighbor.

Transient stresses the *temporary* nature of a stay or the brevity of a thing's duration. Though in common use as a noun, *transient* has a formal or literary

tone when used as an adjective: a *transient* joy. **Transitory**, like *temporary*, points to impermanence. It designates something destined to pass away, either fairly soon or, at least, eventually: *transitory* pleasures as opposed to sources of enduring satisfaction; a *transitory* stage of development.

In a literal sense, **ephemeral** refers to that which lasts only a single day. It is stronger than *transitory* in indicating not only certain but speedy extinction. For this reason, that which is *ephemeral* is looked upon as slight and perishable. [Our lives are *transitory;* A flower's existence is *ephemeral*.] *Ephemeral* can also sometimes carry a suggestion of contempt: the *ephemeral* popularity of a handsome actor who never learned to act. In extension, *ephemeral* denotes that which changes aspect rapidly or continuously: an *ephemeral* inspiration. *Ephemeral* is a rather literary word. **Evanescent** is lyrical and evocative. It refers to that which vanishes almost as soon as it appears, implying that a thing is tenuous, delicate, or unsubstantial by its very nature: the *evanescent* radiance of the sunset; an *evanescent* glimpse of the truth. See INCONSTANT.

Antonyms: EVERLASTING, IMMORTAL, IMMUTABLE, INVARIABLE, PERMANENT, PERSISTENT.

tempt

allure
attract
beguile
entice
lure
seduce

These verbs refer to things that awaken one's desires or prompt one to act upon them, possibly against the will. **Tempt** stresses the awakening of desire despite an initial reluctance; this may result from something that is appealing by its nature or from a deliberate attempt at arousal: an apple pie fresh from the oven that *tempted* him to disregard his diet; a woman who used all her wiles to *tempt* him into following her. **Seduce** stresses someone prompted to action or permission against the will: *seduced* by the excitement of the city I had hated so at first. The sexual connotation possible for *tempt* is insistently present in *seduce:* boasting about how many women he had *seduced*. If this is not borne in mind, *seduce* can be misleading in other contexts: not the first man who had been *seduced* by money.

The sexual connotations of both **attract** and **allure** are less insistent and obtrusive than in *tempt* and *allure*. *Attract* may give an objective tone in pointing to the winning of notice for any reason: an eccentric costume that *attracted* disapproving comment; a bonfire that might *attract* rescuers. In the context of desire, *attract* suggests being drawn to something because of its intrinsic appeal. No reluctance need be implied on the part of the beholder, no design on the part of the beheld: a vivacity that *attracted* every eye in the room; *attracted* to the woman who stood alone nearby. *Allure* suggests greater intensity of appeal than *attract: allured* by the breathtaking view before them. *Allure* may also suggest a deliberate effort to *tempt* someone against his or her will, even to the point of using deception: barkers who *allure* passersby into the sideshows by promising spectacles never encountered, once inside.

Lure is closely related to *allure*, but concentrates mostly on deliberate or deceptive attempts to influence someone, often for fraudulent or destructive purposes: cheese with which to *lure* mice into the trap; *luring* him into an alley where her confederate could rob him. *Lure* can also be used more innocently in a hyperbolic way: wondering how she could *lure* him into extending an invitation for dinner. **Entice** also suggests a deliberate effort to *tempt* someone into action but is vaguer about intent and motivation: hoping to *entice* them into joining our discussion group; psychopaths who *entice* children to go off with them. *Entice* can also be used more simply of appeal: *enticed* by her lively interest in foreign movies. **Beguile** once referred more exclusively to deceptive attempts to lead astray for unworthy purposes: *beguiled* by a promise of quick profits. *Beguile* has lost much of this negative force in uses that compare with *attract:* hoping to *beguile* him with fascinating repartee; an exuberance and zaniness she found *beguiling*. See ATTRACTION, EAGER, EROTIC, PLEASING.

Antonyms: *chill, dampen,* DISCOURAGE, *dissuade, repel.*

terse

compendious
laconic
pithy
sententious
succinct

These adjectives stress brevity in speech or writing, the avoidance of wasted words. **Terse** goes back to a Latin verb meaning rub off or rub down. Thus, it suggests polished style as well as pointed phrasing, implying elegance as well as economy of expression: a *terse*, vigorous style. In present use, *terse* emphasizes

extreme compactness, concentrated force, and a strict sticking to the point: a *terse* note of dismissal with no explanation. **Laconic** literally means like a Spartan, with reference to the habitual *terseness* of Spartan speech. A *laconic* speaker is so sparing with words as to seem stingy or exceptionally self-controlled. [He was reserved and *laconic*, a close-mouthed man; Someone said it with *laconic* brevity: "It's the economy, stupid."] Both a *terse* and a *laconic* remark may be so brief as to seem curt. But where a *terse* remark is complete and its brevity may be due to pressure of circumstances, a *laconic* remark may be puzzling and may suggest deliberate taciturnity: a *terse* battlefield command; "Trust me" was his *laconic* reply. *Terse* and *laconic* imply a certain austerity of utterance, but **succinct** suggests a more reasonable rationing of words. *Succinct* comes from Latin roots meaning gird underneath. It implies compression, avoidance of elaboration, exclusion of extraneous detail. Hence, a *succinct* statement is brief, clear, and concise, being confined to main points or essential meaning: a *succinct* summary of a rambling treatise.

The remaining adjectives emphasize content. **Pithy** literally means full of pith, and pith is the essential part of anything—the tissue at the center of a stem, the marrow of a bone. Hence, a *pithy* remark is one full of meaning and substance; it is both brief and forceful, containing the gist of a matter in concentrated form: a *pithy* aphorism; the *pithy* couplets of Alexander Pope. **Compendious**, like *pithy*, stresses substance, but substance drawn from many sources and summarized. A *compendious* work is both brief and comprehensive, encompassing and condensing a great mass of material: a *compendious* account of the Civil War; It required a true scholar to digest so much material and organize it into so *compendious* an introduction. **Sententious** comes from a Latin word meaning opinion. It indicates the condensing of general truths or moral principles into *pithy* maxims or aphorisms: the *sententious* wisdom of the Book of Proverbs. By extension, *sententious* may connote a moralizing attitude or a pompous, all-knowing tone: a speaker too *sententious* not to be tiresome. See COMPACT, SHORTEN.

Antonyms: *lengthy,* TALKATIVE, *tedious,* VERBOSE.

testimony

affidavit
deposition
evidence

These nouns may all denote statements made to a court of law. **Testimony** is any declaration made by a

461

witness who is considered to know the facts of a case. Giving *testimony* involves taking an oath and making statements in open court or before an official body in answer to questions put by a qualified public official. *Testimony* in its wider meaning is affirmation or proof of something: The ruined buildings of the city bear *testimony* to the thoroughness of the bombardment.

Both **affidavit** and **deposition** are types of legal *testimony* put into writing. Although occasionally used interchangeably, *affidavit* and *deposition* differ in several ways. An *affidavit* is a sworn document made voluntarily without cross-examination. Also, an *affidavit* may be accepted as *testimony* by a court when the testifier is unable to appear in person. A *deposition,* on the other hand, is made orally under oath in response to formal questioning, and is then taken down in writing. Unlike an *affidavit,* a *deposition* is subject to cross-examination.

Evidence, the most general term, includes the *testimony* of witnesses, *affidavits, depositions,* and all the facts and physical objects connected with a legal proceeding. In everyday use, *evidence* is anything that tends to prove a thing true. [Scholars have been able to unearth *evidence* as to the true authorship of the book; Her red eyes and sad expression were *evidence* (and also *testimony* to the fact) that she had been crying.] See REASONING.

theatrical

camp
campy
dramatic
flamboyant
histrionic

These adjectives have either a direct reference to the theater or are used to describe persons and things that exhibit qualities associated with the theater. **Theatrical** is used to describe anything connected with the world of the theater: a *theatrical* festival; a *theatrical* booking agency. It also connotes artificiality and show: His long hair and old-fashioned attire gave him a *theatrical* air that was sometimes interesting but more often merely eccentric. Since **histrionic** pertains especially to actors or their performing techniques, it has the most limited application: Her *histrionic* abilities are more at home before the camera than on the stage. *Histrionic,* by extension, is used to suggest the showy or affectedly emotional qualities one thinks of in connection with actors and acting: His *histrionic* display at the funeral was in bad taste. **Flamboyant** originally meant extravagantly ornate or

elaborately styled: a house with *flamboyant* architectural detail; an essay complicated by *flamboyant* prose. In a generalization of meaning, *flamboyant* came to imply brilliance or boldness and finally to suggest the same kind of affectation and showiness that *histrionic* does: the *flamboyant* foliage of autumn; a *flamboyant* style of dress; a *flamboyant* display of temper.

In its implication of an affected or showy manner, **dramatic** is like *histrionic* and *flamboyant:* She set all tongues wagging with her *dramatic* entrance. More than the other adjectives here, *dramatic* has direct pertinence to the drama and to things that are suitable to or characterize acting: a *dramatic* performance of the highest caliber; The short story was *dramatic* without being in the least sentimental.

Camp and **campy** were once restricted in use as homosexual argot to describe the supposedly telltale mannerisms of this in-group; these terms suggested behavior that was *theatrical,* artificial, exaggerated, effeminate, or ostentatious. Recently, *camp* and *campy* have become fad words that need not refer to homosexuality at all, but can be applied to any manifestation of popular culture that is so phony, banal, or vulgar as to merit amazement or admiration: *campy* movies from the 1930's; a *camp* feather boa she evidently thought was the last word in chic. These adjectives can now also describe deliberate attempts to reproduce such meretricious qualities in serious art or literature. In fact, *camp* and *campy* are in danger of being used so vaguely and broadly as to vitiate their usefulness. See EMOTION, PASSIONATE.

Antonyms: *colorless, drab, dull, prosaic,* SEDATE.

thin

lean
scrawny
skinny
slender
slim
spare
svelte
willowy
wiry

These adjectives mean the opposite of fat or plump, describing persons whose weight is low in proportion to their height. **Thin** is the most general. It suggests a lack of girth and a narrowness of frame, and may apply either to natural low weight or underweight: a tall, *thin,* distinguished-looking man; *thin* and weak after a bout of illness. *Thin* in itself is descriptive of appearance, but is often qualified by adverbs that express the degree of thinness or the attitude concerning it: too *thin;* terribly *thin;* pitifully *thin.* Like *thin,* **lean** and **spare** may have either positive or negative connotations. Both stress the absence of fatty tissue: a *lean* and hungry look. At the same time, both imply an underlying muscular strength—a sinewy and sometimes vigorous self-discipline: a *lean,* lithe runner with great stamina; a soldier's *spare* build. But *lean* and *spare* may also be expressive of hardship and deprivation, suggesting the strength to endure hard times with a minimum of sustenance: an old farmer's *lean,* hard frame; the *spare* form of a pioneer woman. In extended senses *lean* may mean fraught with want or hardship, not prosperous or productive: *lean* years. *Spare* can mean not plentiful, meager: a *spare* meal of beans and tea.

Svelte implies trimness and elegance of figure, and is often used in a complimentary way rather than as pure description: She slimmed down tremendously and looked positively *svelte.* This use is suggested by the derivation of *svelte* from Latin roots meaning pluck out. **Willowy** suggests a *lean* build marked by suppleness and grace: a modern dancer bending her *willowy* frame. *Svelte* is feminine in connotation and is always applied to women; *willowy* is not invariably applied to either sex, but since gracefulness is more common among women, *willowy* is more often associated with women.

Slim and **slender** refer to relatively slight bodily weight, especially as it appears aesthetically to an observer. *Slim,* which may apply to either sex, implies a trim figure or physique. It is most often used in the context of someone's losing or maintaining weight: He kept *slim* by dieting and exercising diligently. *Slender,* as applied to girls or women, often connotes gracefulness, litheness, frailty, or fragility: a *slender* slip of a girl. *Slender* may also be used of men, in which case it retains a suggestion of slightness of physique that is not considered unattractive or effeminate; often *slender* is complimentary, but whereas *slim* suggests firmness and strength, *slender* indicates lightness: a tall, *slender* man with a sensitive face. *Slender* is often applied to parts of the body: a *slender* wrist; *slender* arms.

A person considered overly *thin* may be called **skinny.** *Skinny,* a child's word, is always blunt and sometimes humorous or touching: a *skinny* little man. *Skinny* stresses the idea that a person is underdeveloped—nothing but skin and bone: a *skinny,* knobby-kneed little girl; tall, *skinny* models. *Skinny* may also imply a lack of strength or vigor: a *skinny* weakling who joined a health club. **Scrawny** means small and stringy, *lean,* bony, and undernourished: *scrawny*

urchins scrambling for coins. *Scrawny* is often applied to animals as well as humans: a *scrawny* chicken, too tough to eat. **Wiry** is usually used of persons, meaning *thin* but tough and sinewy. It describes one who is quite *slim* but deceptively strong: a *wiry* little man, as pugnacious as a bantam rooster. See BONY, LANKY, SUPPLE.

Antonyms: *FAT.*

think

cogitate
deliberate
meditate
muse
ponder
reason
reflect
ruminate
speculate

These verbs all mean set the mind to work in order to seek a better understanding of something, solve a problem, or get at the truth. **Think,** the most general, can refer to any use of the intellect to arrive at ideas or conclusions. One can *think* profoundly or superficially, seriously or frivolously: to *think* about whether a person's fate is determined by free will or by the force of circumstances; She *thought* about entering medical school. **Cogitate** is a rather pompously formal word that means *think* seriously or continuously; it is often used jestingly: The infant spent hours *cogitating* on the depth of his navel. However, it is occasionally used soberly about a baffling problem: tax specialists *cogitating* about how to simplify instructions to the taxpayer.

Meditate, muse, reflect, and **ruminate** mean *think* in a contemplative or leisurely manner. *Meditate,* the most general of these verbs, implies a serious and extended period of concentration: The author *meditated* on the theme of her book before sketching out the plot and characterization. *Muse* suggests a dreamlike, aimless, or conjectural succession of thoughts. [She *mused* about whether her brother would notice her new ring; He *mused* over what he would do if he won a lottery.] *Reflect* means look back in a thoughtful way over what has happened: a woman *reflecting* on the changes that had occurred during her long life. But *reflect* may also be used of any intellectual review: to *reflect* on the causes of urban rioting. In its basic literal sense *ruminate* is applied to certain animals and means chew the cud (food previously swallowed and regurgitated). Analogously, *ruminate* as here considered means turn a thought over and over in the mind: *ruminating* on his failed presidency.

Deliberate and **ponder** emphasize the slow, careful process of weighing possibilities or alternatives; *deliberate* stresses the slowness, and *ponder* the weighing of possibilities. Whereas *deliberate* suggests a methodical, rational process of decision making, *ponder* points to the solemnness and difficulty of the problem, to which there may be no solution. [The jury *deliberated* for four hours before recessing for lunch; They *pondered* the problem of maintaining national security without compromising individual freedom.]

To **reason** is to make logical or empirical generalizations based on evidence: The district attorney *reasoned* that the suspect's attempt to flee suggested guilt. **Speculate**, on the other hand, means theorize or conjecture on the basis of little or no evidence: At present scientists can only *speculate* on the nature and extent of life outside our solar system. See CONSIDER, EXAMINE, IDEA, IMAGINATION, MIND, OPINION, STUDY, SUPPOSE.

throng
crowd
horde
host
mob
multitude

These nouns refer to large gatherings, especially of people. *Throng* and *host* are the most formal. *Throng* emphasizes a group whose members are pressed together in a crush: a *throng* of shoppers fighting to reach the display tables of the department store. *Throng* can also suggest a mass of tightly grouped people moving with difficulty in the same direction: a *throng* of worshipers who followed the religious procession down the narrow streets of the village. *Host,* by contrast, suggests an archaic or Biblical tone; here, the group may well be spread out in space. *Host* may also be descriptive of an army or armed group of people: the heavenly *host* of angels who appeared to the shepherds near Bethlehem; a *host* of people spread out on the hillside in all directions; a ragged *host* of militia, falling before the gunfire of well-hidden rebels. *Host* can also suggest any vast group of things: a *host* of reasons for disbanding the cavalry.

Crowd and **mob** suggest sizable collections of people, but both are more informal than the previous pair. Like *throng, crowd* can suggest congestion but is even more emphatic about disorder within the group: a confused *crowd* that gathered to watch the burning house. *Crowd,* however, is used informally to describe large audiences of any kind, even the most orderly: the large *crowd* that had turned out to hear the performance. *Mob,* by contrast, stresses disorder in a *crowd* possessed by unruly or angry emotions and implies the erupting of violence or a state of riot: a *crowd* that turned into a rampaging *mob* when it learned that the injured boy had died before reaching the hospital. As a mere hyperbole, *mob* can be used informally for any great number: *mobs* of friends who came to the celebration.

Multitude, while not sharing the old-fashioned sound of *host*, gives an elevated tone in referring to an extremely large number. When *multitude* applies to people, it specifically implies their being spread out through space: the *multitude* gathered in Red Square to support the Russian leader. Like *host, multitude* can also apply to any great amount: presenting a *multitude* of reasons for reopening the case. **Horde** refers specifically to a *crowd* or *mob* that is threatening, unkempt, or unpleasant in some way: a *horde* of hungry peasants who gathered before the palace. In this context, *horde* suggests disorganization, fierce emotion, and a motley or ragged array of people. *Horde* can also refer to a pack or swarm, as of animals or insects: a *horde* of mosquitoes that circled the outdoor light; a *horde* of rats. Most specifically, and with a less negative tone, *horde* can refer to a nomadic tribe or army: the *horde* of Berbers who camped for the night outside the desert town. See GROUP, MEETING, PEOPLE.

throw
bowl
cast
fling
heave
hurl
pitch
put
sling
toss

These verbs refer to sending a hand-released projectile through the air by a swing of the arm. **Throw** carries the fewest implications about the manner in which the act is done or its emotional context: taking careful aim before she *threw; throwing* handfuls of grass everywhere. **Hurl** suggests *throwing* something with considerable force or ferocity, **heave** the lifting and *throwing* of something quite heavy: *hurling* stones and curses at their helpless victim; seizing a boulder and *heaving* it into the path of advancing soldiers. **Cast**, **pitch**, and **toss**, by contrast, suggest less force and greater swiftness in *throwing* lighter objects:

pitching pennies into an upturned hat; *casting* his line downstream and reeling it in against the current; lazily *tossing* darts at a picture of her political opponent. *Cast* has fallen into disuse except in the context of fishing and in certain stock phrases such as *casting* a net, *casting* dice, *casting* bread upon the waters. *Pitch* is specifically used in baseball to describe the *throwing* of the ball by the pitcher to the batter. Even in other contexts, *pitch* suggests care and accuracy of aim. **Bowl**, as a term used in cricket, means *pitch* or *hurl* the ball to the batsman, usually on one bounce, with the arm held fully extended, not bent at the elbow; otherwise, the *pitch* would be ruled a *throw*, which is illegal. In the U.S. *bowl* most commonly refers to the game of tenpins or similar games in which the ball is *bowled* by rolling it over a level surface. *Bowl* as a general term is current in both varieties of English with this sense of rolling. To **put**, in the sense here considered, means to thrust or push forward with the arm, with the full force of one's body behind the motion. The term is now used mainly of the competitive sport of *putting* the shot (a metal ball), an event in many track and field meets: To *put* a 16-pound shot over 60 feet requires great strength, coordination, and concentration.

Toss is used almost exclusively of light objects and may suggest a haphazard movement or one in which the notion of aiming for a target is absent: *tossing* confetti pell-mell; *tossing* aside a lock of hair that had fallen over her eyes. **Fling**, unlike *toss,* does not necessarily suggest a light object, but it is otherwise similar in implying aimlessness or a forceful wildness of movement: *flinging* down the briefcase on the table and stomping off. **Sling** once referred to the sudden force reminiscent of something thrown by a sling: this is less and less present as an implication of the verb. *Sling* now mainly suggests inaccurate or violent movements, possibly angry ones, as in the stock phrase *slinging* mud at your opponents. See DISCARD, PROPEL, ROTATE.

thwart

balk
foil
frustrate
inhibit

These verbs refer to the applying of force in a hostile way so as to repel or subdue any opposing resistance. **Thwart** suggests the outwitting of an enemy or the undoing of enemy's plans: sending troops to *thwart* the rebellion. *Thwart* often implies the use of cleverness instead of violence to attain an enemy's defeat and suggests action taken before the enemy has had time to move: the scheming villain whose designs on the maiden were always *thwarted* before the final curtain. *Thwart* has recently appeared frequently in a psychological context, suggesting barriers that prevent full realization of one's natural endowments: a perceptive intelligence that was *thwarted* from attaining its full scope by bad training, poor schools, and lack of opportunity.

Foil relates to the aspect of *thwart* that emphasizes the undoing of an enemy's plan before damaging action has been accomplished: *foiling* the assassination plot at the last minute by cutting communications. In some modern contexts, *foil* may sound melodramatic and old-fashioned. **Balk** relates to the aspect of *thwart* that emphasizes the imposing of barriers, but *balk* does not necessarily suggest the interruption of an otherwise natural or inevitable process: every effort at creative teaching *balked* by excessive paperwork.

Frustrate in its most general context suggests the confounding of an enemy by tactics short of an open confrontation in direct battle: *frustrating* Hannibal's drive toward the sea by hemming in his troops and engaging them in inconclusive skirmishes. Like *thwart, frustrate* can suggest the undoing of an enemy's plans before they can be executed, although in this case the result is less conclusive than with *thwart,* since here it can imply merely forcing the enemy into inaction or into delaying plans: *frustrating* every effort the prisoner made at getting word to confederates. When the situation of enemies is not involved, *frustrate* may suggest any sort of insurmountable obstacle that reduces someone to galling inaction: talented playwrights *frustrated* by the commercialism of Broadway.

Inhibit, like one aspect of *frustrate,* suggests the forcing of something into inaction rather than a complete routing of it: *inhibiting* inflation by raising taxes. Both *frustrate* and *inhibit*, however, have gained currency in a psychological context for suggesting barriers that impede normal development or prevent realization of natural desires. *Frustrate* here suggests an insoluble conflict between two forces working upon or within a person: *frustrated* by desires he believed it would be reprehensible to satisfy. *Inhibit* here specifically suggests the weakening or damaging of normal impulses: rules so rigid as to *inhibit* calm development of self-assurance; learning to *inhibit* impulses that would result in harm to others. See CONFUSE, SUBDUE.

Antonyms: *PERMIT.*

timid

bashful
coy
diffident
fainthearted
shy
submissive
timorous

These adjectives characterize a lack of ease in the society of others, or fearfulness in facing new experiences. **Timid** is the most general adjective in the group. It points to a reluctance to assert oneself or to undertake anything new or unknown without exercising caution. [The little boy was *timid* about going to school on the bus; A *timid* driver hesitates to pass trucks and buses on the highway.] **Timorous** is much stronger than *timid,* although they are often used interchangeably. *Timorous* emphasizes a greater apprehension and anxiety surrounding any experience that demands daring, independence, and confidence: a *timorous* young man unable to live his own life. *Timorous* may also describe one who is easily startled and seems to live in a constant state of fearfulness: a *timorous* teacher who could not control children.

Shy, **bashful**, and **diffident** share the meaning of showing unobtrusiveness and embarrassment in the company of other people. *Shy* implies self-consciousness and a fear of pushing oneself forward. It may suggest a lack of social poise arising from inexperience: so *shy* that talking to new acquaintances made his voice tremble. *Shy* may also point to a naturally quiet and retiring nature, often not without charm: His low voice and *shy* smile soon made him a favorite among his colleagues. By extension, *shy* is used of people who because of the nature of their culture tend to live by themselves, or to animals that evade observation by humans. [The Pygmies of equatorial Africa are a *shy,* primitive group; The shrew, a common field rodent, is so *shy* that even farmers rarely see one.] *Bashful* is usually applied only to children who are *shy. Bashful* may have somewhat humorous overtones as it suggests the awkwardness of a youngster struck speechless before strangers or shrinking from notice. When used of adults, *bashful* tends to sound condescending: such a *bashful* man when he has to talk to women. *Diffident* stresses a want of confidence in one's abilities, point of view, or even general worth. Although *diffident* persons are *shy* with others, their main difficulty is a hesitancy in expressing themselves or in trying new things.

Fainthearted is a somewhat scornful term as it implies not only a bumbling lack of courage but also uncertainty as to how to go about getting what one wants. Formerly, *fainthearted* was used of a *timid* or *shy* lover held back from declaring himself for fear of being rejected. Nowadays, it may be applied to any timidity that appears to be slightly ludicrous: too *fainthearted* to ask for a raise in pay.

Coy originally meant *shy* and was used chiefly of women who were discouraging advances from men. It now carries overtones of a feigned and consequently coquettish shyness meant to kindle amatory interest: She was *coy* over the telephone when he asked for a date, although she had flirted outrageously with him the evening before. The extended meaning of *coy* refers to a playful or sly unwillingness to reveal information or to make a statement: When I told him I had heard rumors of his promotion, he acted *coy.*

Submissive, in this context, means so *timid* or *timorous* that yielding comes more easily than resisting: a client too *submissive* to question the increase in price. See AFRAID, COWARDLY, DOCILE.

Antonyms: *audacious,* BRAVE, *confident,* DARING, *poised.*

tip

cant
careen
heel
list
slant
slope
tilt

These verbs mean turn from a vertical or horizontal position. To **tip** or **tilt** something is to incline it at an angle, lowering or raising one side or end. *Tip* suggests a slight, momentary, or accidental movement away from a balanced position. It is often applied to something turned downward, thrown out of balance, or turned over. [He *tipped* the pitcher too far while pouring the milk; She suddenly stood up and *tipped* the boat; The vase *tipped* over.] *Tilt* suggests a more decided or more stable shift of balance—a marked, permanent, or deliberate positioning at an angle: When the restaurant was closed, the chairs were *tilted* forward against the tables.

Slant and **slope** may refer to stationary things, and both stress line rather than movement. *Slant* is the more general. It simply indicates an oblique placement or position. *Slope* involves a change of level or direction and is most often applied to the lay of land: a *slanted* line; a *sloping* lawn. A roof or hillside may either *slant* or *slope;* but *slope* suggests the gentler, more gradual downward inclination—except when qualified to the contrary: The ground *slopes* sharply here. *Slope* is limited in application, but *slant* may be used in a figurative sense, suggesting a bias toward a particular point of view: objecting that they *slant* the news.

To **cant** something is to set it at a *slant. Cant* is close to *tilt* but is more formal and may imply a greater degree of permanence. An engineer *cants* the drafting table by setting one side higher than the other. To *cant* a timber is to cut off a corner or an edge so as to form a slightly *slanted* end: to *cant* off the end of a plank. In nautical usage, a ship that *cants* swings around, taking a position oblique to some definite line or course. In another sense, to *cant* is to pitch toward one side, and to *cant* over is to turn over in this way: a schooner *canted* by the wind; The boat *canted* over.

Careen, **heel**, and **list** are all nautical terms applied to vessels that lean sharply to one side. A ship, especially one under sail, *careens,* or *heels* over, from being buffeted by wind or waves. A ship *lists* when its center of gravity is displaced, throwing it out of balance: The freighter *listed* 10° to starboard. *Careening* or *heeling* is always toward one side or the other, but *listing* may be forward or astern as well. *Careen* may also apply to a ship standing in port and turned over on one side: They *careened* the ship to clean the bottom. In general use, *careen* is applied to moving objects, as vehicles, and means lurch or twist from side to side as if out of control: The car *careened* down the embankment. See TOTTER.

tired

> exhausted
> fatigued
> weary
> worn-out

These adjectives all pertain to a lessening or depletion of strength, energy, or spirit. **Tired** is a general term and in itself indicates no specific degree of loss of vigor: *tired* from mowing the lawn; eyes *tired* from reading; *tired* after running the marathon. **Weary** is sometimes used interchangeably with *tired* to refer to a general lull in physical energy: *weary* from a long day's work. However, *weary* more strongly suggests discontent and vexation arising from having put up too long with something that is, or has become, disagreeable: *weary* of getting up over and over again to soothe a colicky baby; *weary* of arguing with the boss; *weary* of seeing the same inane television shows every night. *Tired* may also be used in this sense: sick and *tired* of the same deadly routine.

Fatigued implies a painful reduction of strength, as by nervous strain, illness, or overwork. It is more precise than *tired* or *weary*: After his harrowing experience of being trapped in the mine, he became easily *fatigued*. As a symptom of a low state of health, *fatigued* is preferred over the other adjectives: getting up in the morning as *fatigued* as she had been the night before. In the sense of bored or *weary, fatigued* may function in a more formal and literary way: Mozart's music gave him a sense of elation, but he felt *fatigued* by Brahms' brooding lyricism.

Exhausted implies the draining of strength and energy, which may be restored by long rest or may be irreversible: too *exhausted* to eat dinner; *exhausted* by the hustle and bustle of city life; on his ninetieth birthday, *exhausted* and dying of old age.

Worn-out carries over to this context some of its more usual meaning of having been used to the point where value or effectiveness has been lost. Here it is informal and may cover the range of meanings from *tired* to *exhausted,* but it suggests the complete depletion of energy implied in *exhausted: worn-out* from years of working the rocky, unproductive farm. Generally, *worn-out* is loosely applied to any state of lagging energy or patience: *worn-out* by thirty-six holes of golf; *worn-out* from hearing the constant quarreling next door. See BORED, LISTLESS.

Antonyms: *invigorated, refreshed, relaxed, rested, strengthened.*

topic

> burden
> matter
> subject
> subject matter
> theme

These nouns refer to the major intent of a given speech or piece of writing. **Topic** presents the greatest variety of possible meanings. It can refer to the intent of a complete piece or utterance or to the point of a single sentence or paragraph within such a piece: the *topic* of her commencement address; the *topic* of every paragraph being carefully introduced in the first sentence. In conversation, *topic* can refer to something of general interest to all, whether introduced deliberately or by chance: the *topic* of the week at every cocktail party I went to. In any case, *topic* always suggests the explicit intent toward which expression is directed.

A number of *topics,* however, may be organized into the larger concern of an overall **subject**. And whereas *topic* usually refers to what is explicit, stated, or intentional, *subject* may also refer either to what is implied by a speaker or writer or to what can be inferred by an audience: the *subject* on which she chose to speak; unconscious references to violence, which was a constant *subject* of his talk. **Theme** refers more often to the emotional attitudes that underlie a *subject* and that unify the *topics* selected to illustrate it: His *subject* was poverty, but the *theme* he held to was the futility of attempting to cure it overnight. *Theme,* like *subject,* may refer to something explicitly or implicitly present: Is she aware that all her dreams are expressions of the same *theme. Theme* can also refer to any tone or attitude that gives unity to some variety of examples collected to make a point. This may be true of any collection, written or otherwise: a group of essays whose *theme* was the will to endure; a show of paintings whose *theme* was the vulgarity of modern life.

Burden, by way of its reference to the refrain of a song, can indicate something frequently repeated or dwelt on as a prevailing *theme:* Mark Antony's mocking phrase, calling Brutus an honorable man, becomes the *burden* of his oration. By way of its reference to a heavy weight, *burden* is often taken in the context of discourse to suggest a consequential, weighty, or solemn *topic;* even in this case, however, repetition is implied: the needless loss of life that was the *burden* of several editorials. **Matter** and the more commonly used phrase **subject matter** are like *subject* in designating anything that is the object of a discussion, concern, feeling, etc.: doing research on the *subject matter* to be discussed in the next class. *Matter* and *subject matter* are often used to distinguish the actual content of a discourse or piece of writing from its verbal decoration and rhetorical flourishes: less manner and more *matter*. See BASIS, KERNEL.

total
aggregate
sum
totality
whole

The nouns **total**, **aggregate**, and **sum**, as here considered, mean a result, as a number or amount, arrived at by adding or putting together all parts or elements of a particular group or mass. They may or may not suggest that the result contains everything that should be in it. The membership of an organization may be a *total* of 150; attendance at a meeting of the organization may be a *total* of only 50. An *aggregate* of statistical samples does not cover the entire range of what is being examined; the *aggregate* of a person's characteristics is a composite picture of the person. The *sum* of two or more numbers is fixed and complete; the *sum* available for financing a project is merely what is on hand and not necessarily the *sum* needed.

Totality and **whole** indicate the same kind of result denoted by *total, aggregate,* and *sum,* but here the result contains all the parts or elements that should be in it. The *totality* of a nation's productive capacity includes the *sum, total,* or *aggregate* of all its natural resources, productive establishments, labor force, and technical competence. The *whole* of a nation's economy is the *sum* of the value and capability of all its component parts. See ACCUMULATE, ACCUMULATION, ENTIRE, QUANTITY.

Antonyms: COMPONENT, PART.

totter
lurch
reel
stagger
teeter
wobble

These verbs refer to unsteady movement resulting from insecure balance. **Totter** and **teeter** would seem interchangeably close in their referral to the in-place movement of an object that is in an unstable position: a platter that *teetered* on the edge of the table before crashing to the floor; watching nervously while the statue *tottered* on its pedestal. But *teeter* carries a suggestion of the height of an impending fall, while *totter* implies that when an object falls, it falls no farther than its base: *teetering* at the head of the stairs before tumbling down; a drunken man who *tottered* to the sidewalk. *Totter* can also refer to unsteady movement along a path, especially suggesting the instability resulting from old age or weakness: The old couple *tottered* along; After being injured, he *tottered* along uncertainly.

Lurch can suggest a sudden, violent movement through space, especially a shift in the rate or direction of movement already underway: knowing the airplane would *lurch* every time it hit a pocket of warm air. *Lurch* can also suggest the irregular movement or walk of a person who is drunk, disabled, or disoriented in some way: watching him *lurch* dizzily up the stairs. **Reel** can indicate an irregular motion, like *lurch,* or a recoil from an impact that causes one to sprawl out or fall back: The train *lurched* and sent me *reeling* across the aisle; I *reeled* under his blows. Like *totter,* **wobble** can suggest both the unsteady in-place motion of an object and an ungainly walk. Used of an object, however, *wobble* need not suggest the precarious placement implicit in both *totter* and *teeter;* it can refer, instead, to a slight back-and-forth rocking motion resulting from uneven support: a short leg that caused the table to *wobble. Wobble* can also suggest any irregularity of continuing motion: a turntable that *wobbled* badly at low speeds. Where *totter* suggests age as the possible cause of an unsteady walk, *wobble* tends to suggest fatness or a misproportioned squatness of build: a fat man who *wobbled* down the street. **Stagger**, like *reel* and *lurch,* can refer to an abnormal or grotesque walk, suggesting the unsteady gait and uncertain balance of someone who is drunk or semiconscious: sleepily *staggering* to the telephone; drunkards who *stagger* into a hospital asking for help. See PRECARIOUS, VIBRATE, WALK.

tradition

convention
custom
ethos
folkways
manner
manners
mores
practice

These nouns refer to established patterns or instances of behavior typical of a group, community, or culture. **Tradition** in its broadest sense refers to knowledge, doctrines, and patterns of behavior transmitted from generation to generation. More specifically, *tradition* means a particular observance so long continued that it almost has the force of law: the *tradition* calling for the Queen to declare Parliament in session. **Custom** refers to the habitual pattern of behavior of a community or people. A *custom,* while well established in usage, does not have the force of a *tradition; tradition* emphasizes more strongly historical significance: the *custom* of shaking hands; the *tradition* by which the bridegroom places the wedding band on the finger of his bride.

A **convention** is a rule or approved technique, and is applied to the arts as well as to conduct: the *convention* in the Elizabethan theater of employing boys to enact the roles of women; the old *convention* of wearing a jacket and tie to business; demonstrators flouting *convention* by carrying signs displaying obscene words. While *custom* suggests a longstanding cultural habit relatively independent of the influence of ephemeral fashions, a *convention* might be considered an expression of the **manners** of a people. In this sense, *manners* refer not to etiquette but to the modes of social

behavior prevailing in a group during a particular period. Observing *convention*, therefore, implies a measure of conformity, even if unconscious, whereas observing a *custom* implies only the enacting of a habit shared with a great many other people. *Manners* in the sense here considered is often applied to literary works; a novel of *manners* is a novel describing the social attitudes and behavior of a group of people—often a stratum of society—in a given place at a given time. **Manner**, on the other hand, refers to a typical or customary way of doing something, especially a characteristic style used in one of the arts: painted in the *manner* of Rubens. **Practice** refers to a usual way of acting, working, or behaving—in short, a *custom*—but, unlike *custom*, implies a voluntary choice: the whalers' *practice* of discarding the fins; the physicians' *practice* of charging patients fees according to their ability to pay. In a related sense, *practice* refers to individual habit: It was her *practice* to read several books a week for pleasure.

Ethos, **mores**, and **folkways** are terms most often encountered in sociological contexts. *Ethos* means the underlying and distinctive character or spirit of a people, group, or culture. The *ethos* of a group is seldom recognized by the members of that group, but it is nevertheless implicit in their *manners* and finds expression in their *folkways. Folkways* is not restricted to behavioral patterns but applies also to patterns of thought and emotional attitude. Thus, *folkways* is more closely allied to *tradition* than to *manners. Mores* refers to the established, traditional *customs* or *folkways* regarded by a social group as essential to its preservation and welfare: the Christian *mores* of marriage and family life; ascetic Puritan *mores. Mores* is often used, however, to refer to any prevalent moral attitudes or social *customs:* teenage *mores* placing a high value on going steady. See HISTORY, RITE, USUAL.

tranquil

calm
placid
quiet
serene
still
undisturbed
unruffled

These adjectives all indicate freedom from violent movement or emotion. **Tranquil** and **calm** both describe an absence of turmoil and agitation. However, *tranquil* implies an enduring condition, while *calm* points to a more transient one: a long, *tranquil* life; a *calm* interlude during a hurricane. In terms of personality, both adjectives retain much of this same distinction: a *tranquil* mind given to reflection; remaining *calm* and in command of herself during the crisis.

Quiet and **still**, as here considered, imply an absence of bustle and commotion as well as the secondary suggestion of consequent silence. *Quiet* is the more relative term and describes that which is peaceful and is characterized by little excitement, but which is not necessarily silent: a *quiet* village; a *quiet* evening spent at home; a *quiet* man who does his work unobtrusively but well. *Still* may verge on the absolute. On the one hand it emphasizes a contrast with motion: the *still*, humid air of an August night; the *still* face of the dead woman. It may also point to the overcoming of an inherent tendency toward movement: On Sundays the great turbines are *still;* The unhappy parishioners were *still* until the long sermon came to an end.

Serene suggests that which is elevated above earthly turmoil: a *serene* blue sky. In referring to persons, *serene* implies the presence of an almost otherworldly calm and peace of spirit that has been reached through self-fulfillment and a philosophical acceptance of what life brings, or through religious faith: a *serene* old age passed in puttering about in the garden; the *serene*, kindly face of the mother superior.

Placid, when used to describe persons, indicates an untroubled, even temperament little given to anger or other strong emotions. *Placid* may have an unfavorable connotation in suggesting an unimaginative, bovine dullness of personality: a large, *placid* girl who seemed to pass unmoved through the uncertainties of adolescence. In referring to things, *placid* points to that which is prevailingly *calm* and *tranquil:* a *placid* lake hidden among the hills.

Undisturbed and **unruffled**, being negatives, are usually applied to the absence of superficial agitation rather than to the lack of turmoil implied by the other adjectives in this group: Apparently *undisturbed* by the open hostility shown him, the *unruffled* senator completed his biting criticism before relinquishing the floor. See BLAND, IMPERTURBABLE, SILENT.

Antonyms: *agitated, disturbed, excited,* FRANTIC, NERVOUS, TURBULENT.

translucent

blurred
diaphanous
filmy
veiled

These adjectives characterize materials that obstruct total or perfect vision but through which light can penetrate. **Translucent** may refer either to something that permits an imperfect view or to something that merely allows the passage of light with little or no view possible: the *translucent* silver of the brook through which the pebbled bottom could be seen; partitions made of *translucent* panes of frosted glass to give the occupants of each cubicle complete privacy. **Blurred**, by contrast, usually indicates specifically a particular point between a near-perfect view and no view at all. This would be the point at which figures or images could be seen hazily or, possibly, distortedly through the refracting medium: wiping her hand across the *blurred* windshield. In metaphorical uses, *blurred* emphasizes distortion or lack of soundness: a *blurred* treatment of the issues under discussion.

The remaining adjectives all suggest vision that is *blurred* because of thin intervening layers or tissues, whether spread evenly or in distorting folds. **Diaphanous** indicates the least obstruction, suggesting an extremely thin or delicate gathering of folds: a formal gown with a *diaphanous* outer sheath of organdy; *diaphanous* wisps of clouds that did nothing to mask the sun's rays. **Filmy** suggests a greater obstruction of vision than *diaphanous,* but may apply either to an even layer or a gathering of folds: a *filmy* glaze of condensation on the cold crystal pitcher. When *filmy* characterizes cloth, it resembles *diaphanous* but is less formal: stitching together yards of *filmy* chiffon. With **veiled**, the emphasis is on a greater obstruction of vision than *diaphanous* or *filmy,* with particular reference to a cloth designed for partial concealment, as of the face: thick clouds that *veiled* the sun. In metaphorical uses, a deliberate partial disguise may be implied: a *veiled* hint. See BRIGHT, FOGGY, LUMINOUS, TRANSPARENT, VAGUE.

transparent

clear
crystalline
limpid
lucid
pellucid

These adjectives characterize materials that not only permit the passage of light but present no obstruction to vision. **Transparent** gives a tone of technical precision: a roll of *transparent* tape; frosted glass in the lower part of the window and *transparent* glass above. In metaphorical uses, the tone of *transparent* shifts drastically to emphasize what is obvious, especially when a poor attempt at deception is referred to: a *transparent* falsehood they didn't even bother to justify. **Clear**, in reference to unobstructed vision, emphasizes freedom from blur or blemish: letting the water run until it turned *clear; a clear* day. In this sense, it is often simply a more informal substitute for *transparent*. In metaphorical uses, however, *clear* is in sharp contrast to *transparent* and its suggestion of obvious deception; in this case, *clear* means lack of obscurity: *clear* and concise explanations.

Limpid, **pellucid**, and **crystalline** are more lyrical in tone than *clear* and *transparent*. *Limpid* suggests a view through a refracting medium, particularly water, that is unclouded and untroubled: the stillness of the *limpid* water on the inland side of the reef. In metaphorical uses, *limpid* suggests simplicity or serenity: the *limpid* loveliness of her smile. *Pellucid* is lyrical, sometimes to the point of preciosity, and its stress may be on the unblemished fragility of the refracting medium: a *pellucid* soap bubble. In metaphorical use, *pellucid* is in even more danger of preciosity, referring to a remarkably *clear*, sweet, or delicate quality: a choir boy's *pellucid* soprano. *Crystalline*, in this sense, conveys the sparkling *transparent* quality of quartz: the *crystalline* air of mountain regions; the *crystalline* lens of the eye. In an extended sense, *crystalline* may refer to that which is either literally or figuratively clear-cut and distinctly outlined: a leafless tree standing in *crystalline* sharpness against the sky; the *crystalline* clarity of her prose.

Lucid is seldom used nowadays to refer in a literal sense to something so *clear* or *transparent* as to permit unobstructed vision. *Lucid* once was widely employed in this way in literature. Its application now is principally to treatments that are understandable and unambiguous: a *lucid* explanation of black holes; a *lucid* prose style. *Lucid* may also refer to mental processes that are *clear* and rational, especially in persons who may experience periods of remission from a mental illness: From time to time he would be free of delusions and hallucinations and *lucid* for days. See FLIMSY, TRANSLUCENT.

Antonyms: *FOGGY, OBSCURE, VAGUE.*

treacherous

disloyal
false
hypocritical
specious
traitorous

treasonable
unfaithful

A betrayal of trust is implicit in all these adjectives. **Treacherous** implies strong moral condemnation. It refers to a tendency or a disposition to imperil or betray someone to whom one has shown apparent loyalty and goodwill: a *treacherous* coworker who secretly denounced me; a *treacherous* dog that bites its master. *Treacherous* may also mean dangerous or unreliable, especially when applied to things: roads that become *treacherous* during a rain; *treacherous* times in our history. **Disloyal** is the most general of these adjectives, suggesting either frank or covert hostility toward anything one has paid allegiance to: *disloyal* to the standards of the profession; situations in which political dissent is thought *disloyal*. **Unfaithful** narrows its implications to one possibility in *disloyal,* being used now mainly for personal situations. A man may be *disloyal* to his country, but *unfaithful* to his wife. One aspect of **false** relates to these adjectives, especially in the phrase *false* friend. Here, it suggests a total or irreparable breach, as in the case of a *treacherous* friend. A *disloyal* or *unfaithful* friend, unlike a *false* friend, could conceivably have erred and yet repent later.

Specious and **hypocritical** both suggest a misleading contrast between appearance and reality or between stated beliefs and actions. *Specious* once suggested no more than a pleasing appearance, but now it is taken most often to mean a deliberately dissembling manner or to suggest something that seems true but proves *false: specious* reasoning; *specious* declarations of friendship. *Hypocritical* suggests either a conscious or unconscious discrepancy between what one claims to be and what one does. In the context of betrayal, the stress would fall on conscious dishonesty: *hypocritically* promising to reduce taxes.

Treasonable is closely related to the aspect of *disloyal* that refers specifically to betrayal of cause or country. It is more likely to be applied to acts, however, than to people, and sometimes suggests behavior approaching or tantamount to treason rather than betrayal: insisting that the demonstration was not *treasonable,* either in effect or intent. **Traitorous**, the most formal of these adjectives, may now sound slightly old-fashioned. Like *treasonable,* it is also most often restricted to betrayal of one's country. In contrast, *traitorous* is most appropriately used to describe people, although it can be used of acts as well. In any case, it suggests deliberate betrayal rather than a close approach to it: a *traitorous* officer who relayed war secrets to the enemy. See CRIME.

Antonyms: *CANDID, HONEST, loyal, MORAL, SINCERE.*

treaty

coexistence
détente
entente
pact

These nouns denote types of agreements or political adjustments between nations. **Treaty** is the general term for a formal contract drawn up after diplomatic negotiations and in accordance with international law. *Treaties* may end wars, provide for the purchase of territory, or contain provisions to ensure peace. Many *treaties* are named for the places in which they are ratified: the *Treaty* of Westphalia; the *Treaty* of Versailles.

In recent times, **pact** has frequently been substituted for *treaty:* the Kellogg-Briand *Pact;* the Locarno *Pact.* In general, however, *pact* often suggests a less important and less binding agreement than does *treaty.* One would always refer to a decision to cease international hostilities as a *treaty,* but one to regulate trade between otherwise friendly countries is likely to be called a *pact.* In its wider meaning, *pact* is any covenant made between two or more persons or groups in which each agrees to carry out a certain action: a *pact* between rival companies to raise prices; a suicide *pact.*

Entente, a shortened form of *entente* cordiale, a French term meaning understanding, is an informal compact, rather than a *treaty,* between governments with reference to the conducting of foreign affairs or cooperation in the event of military aggression from without. An *entente* may or may not be set down in the form of a document; it may simply be a pledge made between heads of states.

Détente is a lessening in, or a suspension of, strained relations between governments, especially after a military crisis has been averted. A *détente* may be uneasy and temporary or may lead eventually to an *entente.*

Coexistence, a fairly new word in diplomacy, is the simultaneous existence, through a policy of mutual noninterference, of two or more nations differing widely in ideology. *Coexistence* differs from an *entente* in that it is a more or less neutral state of affairs, often implying mere forbearance for the sake of preventing war. *Coexistence* may come into being after a *détente;* on the other hand, it may be the forerunner of an *entente.* See COVENANT.

tremendous

colossal
herculean
prodigious
stupendous
thumping
titanic
whopping

These adjectives describe anything extremely great in size, scope, scale, intensity, or importance. **Tremendous** not only suggests something extraordinarily large or vast but something unusual, striking, or astonishing in magnitude: a *tremendous* skyscraper; issues of *tremendous* consequence. *Tremendous* is often used loosely as a hyperbole for anything interesting or pleasant: a *tremendous* party. **Prodigious** can refer to sheer size, but more particularly it suggests anything preternatural to the extent of being a prodigy or marvel; it also can be used vaguely in hyperbole: a basketball player of *prodigious* height; a *prodigious* blow to the economy. It may also refer to something achieved with effort, or to precocious development: a *prodigious* technological triumph; the girl's *prodigious* ability to work differential equations. **Stupendous** could once refer to any phenomenon that staggered the mind, but it has suffered more from overuse than the previous pair and now may seem mere overstatement: a *stupendous* success.

Colossal and **titanic** both derive from references to large bodies. *Colossal* comes from the Colossus of Rhodes, the huge statue that was one of the wonders of the ancient world. *Titanic* refers back to the Titans, a race of giants in Greek mythology. Some echo of these origins remains in that *colossal* may stress monumentality, while *titanic* may stress force and power: a *colossal* facade of marble blocking the sky; a *titanic* effort to arm the nation following the sneak attack. Both are overused as hyperboles. Like the previous pair, **herculean** has a classical origin, the hero Hercules. *Herculean* suffers less from loss of meaning through overuse and can still refer not only to a powerfully built man, but to selfless labor dedicated to accomplishing seemingly insuperable tasks; this shade of meaning is also a reference to the *prodigious* feats of Hercules: *herculean* athletes; the *herculean* job of fighting drug smugglers.

Thumping and **whopping** have a colorful, informal sound that saves them from the gray vagueness that some of these adjectives have acquired through overuse. *Thumping* hints at the physical sound a large or plump object might give off or, less concretely, suggests ripeness, health, or perfection: a *thumping* ten-pound baby. *Whopping* may deliberately suggest an awareness of overstatement in characterizing hyperboles or outright lies: a *whopping* excuse for being late. In a more general way, it can refer to anything that seems forceful or decisive: a *whopping* landslide election victory. See HUSKY, LARGE, MASSIVE, SIZE.

Antonyms: *MINUTE, SMALL, TRIVIAL.*

trick

artifice
blind
dodge
evasion
maneuver
ruse
stratagem
subterfuge
wile

All of these nouns involve an intention to deceive. **Trick** is the most general and may apply to any device used to fool someone, whether in earnest or in fun: a mean *trick* to obtain money; prankish schoolboys' *tricks.*

Artifice has a general meaning of artistic skill or even the created work itself. One of its meanings, however, relates it to this set of nouns, in denoting expedients used to gain an end. In this sense *artifice* means something contrived especially to win out in a situation. It has connotations of cleverness and may or may not suggest an unethical approach. [The labyrinth was an *artifice* created by Daedalus to imprison the Minotaur; Pretending to be a sightseer was a harmless *artifice* if it enabled him to speak to the attractive woman standing nearby.]

In **blind** and **subterfuge**, the element of an unethical deception or disguise is stronger. A *blind* usually involves role-playing, whereas a *subterfuge* can be a momentary deception that invites the onlooker to mistake a person's real intentions. [His job as a bartender was a *blind* for selling narcotics; Her sudden illness was a *subterfuge* to prevent her son from leaving home.]

Both **wile** and **ruse** imply cunning pretenses in order to persuade, but *ruse* may be more innocuous than *wile,* which suggests taking unfair advantage. [The *ruse* of having a later appointment enabled her to leave the meeting early; All his *wiles* could not persuade them to entrust him with the money.]

Dodge and **evasion** are much more harmless in tone, implying the avoidance of a confrontation rather than the active initiation of a false situation. [The actor changed the subject quickly, a *dodge* to avoid admitting his age; She had built her career on a succession of *evasions.*]

Stratagem and **maneuver** are drawn from mili-

tary parlance to describe carefully plotted offensive or defensive tactics. Both imply conscious, calculated planning. [His *stratagem* for winning approval was to agree with everything they said; Announcing her candidacy was only a *maneuver* to prevent me from gaining the nomination.] See DECEPTION, LIE, MISLEADING, TRICK (v.).

trick

deceive
delude
dupe
hoodwink
mislead

These verbs all mean use secret or underhanded devices to make someone believe something that is not true or to accept as real or worthwhile something that is false or valueless. **Trick** suggests the accomplishment of such a purpose by means of a plot, maneuver, artifice, wile, etc.: to *trick* a fugitive into believing he has eluded his pursuers. To **deceive** is to *trick* by the distortion of truth or reality: a bookkeeper who *deceived* employers by manipulating accounts.

To **delude** or **mislead** is to lead into error, as by a series of deceptive or alluring utterances or demonstrations. Both verbs suggest evasion or avoidance of the real facts of a matter rather than deliberate misrepresentation: propaganda designed to *delude* the public about the true extent of civilian casualties during the bombing; unethical teachers who *mislead* untalented, gullible students into thinking they can become successful musicians.

To **dupe** is to take advantage of a victim's naiveté or credulity in *deceiving* the victim about the reality, truth, or value of something: farmers being *duped* by shills at a fair. **Hoodwink** means befuddle the mind to the point at which truth and falseness are indistinguishable: an attorney who *hoodwinked* a jury by confusing the issues. See DECEPTION, MISLEADING, STEALTHY, TRICK (n.).

trite

cliché
hackneyed
shopworn
stale
stereotyped
stock
threadbare

These adjectives characterize expressions or ideas that have lost freshness and meaning through overuse and so insult good taste by their superficiality, obviousness, or banality. **Trite** and **cliché**, while negative in tone, do not carry the same degree of opprobrium suggested by the rest of these adjectives. *Trite* is milder but more general than *cliché*, referring to overused expressions, obvious ideas, or a style that relies on either or both of these: a *trite* simile comparing her teeth to pearls; a story beautifully written but concerned with the *trite* theme of adolescent loneliness; the standard Independence Day speech, *trite* in delivery and sentiment. *Cliché* (or *clichéd*) in contrast more often refers to expression alone: coinages such as "promotionwise" that can become *cliché* almost overnight. Occasionally, it goes beyond these restrictions: a few *cliché* characters that marred an otherwise good play. In any case, the fault of overuse indicated by *cliché* is more serious than that suggested by *trite*.

Hackneyed and **shopworn** are the most condemning of these adjectives. *Hackneyed* points to expression, style, and content that befit a hack writer, that is, someone hired to do routine and commercial, if not trashy, writing: the *hackneyed* jargon of soap opera magazines. Extreme cheapness or vulgarity of expression is often indicated by *hackneyed*, and possibly dullness and lack of serious intent. Expressions might become *trite* or *cliché* by striving pathetically for elegance or loftiness: no longer possible to speak of rosy-fingered dawns without being *cliché*. *Hackneyed*, however, suggests low, narrow meanness undiluted by striving of any kind. *Shopworn* carries less opprobrium than *hackneyed*, but it vividly characterizes anything whose appeal and interest have worn out through overuse: *shopworn* political talk about a candidate's image, ethnic appeal, and other claptrap.

Stale and **threadbare** emphasize that something, now overused, might once have been fresh or novel. Both, like *shopworn*, apply here metaphorically. *Stale* suggests comparison to perishable food, *threadbare* to the wearing out of cloth. *Stale* is unique in suggesting a process of dating that need not result through overuse: *stale* Victorianisms that are disappearing from the language. When overuse is suggested, the emphasis is on a lack of liveliness: a campaign speech that was a *stale* reiteration of respect for God, country, and motherhood. *Threadbare* points to overuse that results in an expression's ultimate meaninglessness: *Threadbare* metaphors like "kick over the traces" no longer have any meaning for most people. It should be pointed out in passing that, because of their metaphorical colorfulness, *shopworn, stale,* and *threadbare* are themselves in danger of becoming *trite* through overuse.

Stock and **stereotyped** suggest things mass-produced, struck from a mold, or deliberately made to resemble forerunners. *Stock* may suggest a situation in which originality is not expected or desired: *stock* formulas for constructing hit musicals. *Stereotyped* suggests oversimplification of complexities to the point of caricature, however recognizable: the *stereotyped* figure of the beautiful in automobile commercials. Both *stock* and *stereotyped*, however, can refer to an audience's expectation of being given the comforting or the usual, or even the desire to see something according to standard patterns: the *stock* response when the image of a baby is flashed on the TV screen; *stereotyped* attitudes toward minority groups that persist even in the face of evidence to the contrary. Of the two, *stereotyped* is more critical and severe in this situation. See BANAL, BLAND, OLD-FASHIONED, SUPERFICIAL, TRUISM.

Antonyms: CREATIVE.

trivial

measly
paltry
petty
picayune
puny
trifling

These adjectives all mean small or insignificant. **Trivial** is used to characterize that which is ordinary or commonplace and hence of no special value or import: to interject a *trivial* remark. Yet, *trivial* is not always opprobrious and may sometimes be used in reference to something unimportant because it is easy to deal with: to dispose of *trivial* business in the morning. That which is **trifling** is so *trivial* as to be unworthy of notice: a *trifling* distinction. *Trifling* is also applied to small amounts of money: The cost of the book is *trifling*.

Petty and **picayune** are alike in implying small-mindedness, but *petty* has overtones of meanness and spite while *picayune* has special relevance to a narrow or rigid point of view: a *petty* gossip who delighted in making trouble; a *picayune* politician who hadn't come up with a new idea in ten years. *Petty* can also be used to describe any small, minor, or subordinate person or thing: a *petty* irritation; a *petty* officer. *Picayune* is much like *trivial* when it refers to something small: Why should we quibble about such a *picayune* sum? And it can be like *petty* in expressing a carping meanness: It was *picayune* of him to criticize me before the other women.

Paltry and **measly** are derogatory and are applied to anything contemptibly small. *Paltry* suggests that the thing it describes should be larger or greater: a *paltry* contribution to the charity. *Measly* hints at scantiness and stinginess: a *measly* serving of stew for a hardworking man.

Puny specifically refers to a person whose body is feeble, underdeveloped, or weak: Poverty, with its attendant miseries, had turned a normal baby into a *puny,* neurotic child. By extension, *puny* can apply to anything insignificant or enfeebled: a *puny* attempt to solve a problem beyond his knowledge and experience. See EXTRANEOUS, MARGINAL, SCANTY.

Antonyms: *SIGNIFICANT.*

truism
    bromide
    platitude
    saw

These nouns denote sayings that express self-evident truths or oft-repeated assumptions. **Truism** is the most neutral of these: the *truism* about the fool and his money being soon parted. Often, however, *truism* refers to statements widely regarded as true or accepted as fact: setting out to disprove the *truism* that the world was flat. Since it is needless to point out what is obvious, *truism* can also carry a critical tone: lectures that were no more than a collection of *truisms.*

In the case of **platitude** and **saw**, the tone is decidedly critical. Unlike *truism,* the statements referred to by these nouns need not be self-evident or even true; they do suggest ideas that have been repeated so often as to be no longer vivid or meaningful. *Platitude* suggests an attempt at wisdom that expresses, instead, a commonplace sententiousness: weather that made a mockery of the *platitude* about March coming in like a lion; fathers who wish to be helpful concerning their sons' problems but can only spout embarrassed *platitudes* to them. *Saw* refers to any well-worn saying whose point may be wit rather than wisdom, but that has become pointless through repetition or misapplication: countering her *saw* about a penny earned by quoting the one about being penny-wise but pound-foolish.

Bromide is the most disparaging of all these nouns. It denotes a stereotyped, inane remark made as though it were an original idea or observation. *Bromides* are usually uttered by people who exhibit a lack of imagination and intellectual perception: the *bromide* that it's not what you learn in college that counts but the friends you make there. See BANAL, PROVERB, TRITE.

Antonyms: *witticism.*

trust
    confidence
    faith
    reliance

These nouns denote the feeling that a person or thing will not fail in loyalty, duty, or service. **Trust** and **faith** suggest the greatest degree of conviction in this context. *Trust* indicates a feeling of certainty that someone or something will not fail in any situation where protection, discretion, or fairness is essential: their *trust* in us to defend them if they are attacked; placing her *trust* in him to protect her secret; unwilling to put any *trust* in banks. *Trust* emphasizes this feeling of certainty whether it is justified or misguided: an investigation proving that their *trust* in him was warranted; misplaced *trust* in someone who proved to be a charlatan. *Faith* is an intensification of *trust,* suggesting an even deeper conviction of fidelity and integrity, often in spite of no evidence whatever or even in the face of contrary evidence: *faith* in her son's goodness despite innumerable examples of his inability to keep out of trouble; blind *faith* in his partner's loyalty; an unquestioning *faith* in the powers of psychiatry. *Faith* emphasizes such a deep-seated conviction that it is appropriate in a religious context to refer to belief that is based on steadfast loyalty rather than on demonstrable evidence: a pious *faith* that remained unshakable in the face of every misfortune.

Confidence and **reliance** more often suggest *trust* based on the proven reliability of someone or something. One can intuitively *trust* someone at first glance, rightly or wrongly, but *confidence* suggests a conviction born of time-tested familiarity; it also pertains specifically to a feeling that someone or something will not fail or behave differently than in the past: a record that merits the *confidence* of all voters; *confidence* in her ability to survive the crisis, based on her many narrow escapes in the past; a diabetic's *confidence* in the efficacy of insulin. *Confidence* sometimes is detached from any notion of evidence as a basis for *trust:* a buoyant *confidence* that everything would work out all right. *Reliance* is even more specific than *confidence,* pointing to an actual dependence on someone or something, whether out of choice or necessity: speeding along with complete *reliance* on the effectiveness of his brakes. Often it suggests the need for protection of the weak by the strong: the *reliance* of emerging countries on the foreign-aid programs of the world's affluent nations. Sometimes, *reliance* indicates something resorted to as a solution to a specific problem: the administration's *reliance* on increasing taxes to support education. See ALLEGIANCE, ENTRUST, MORAL.

Antonyms: ANXIETY, *distrust,* DOUBT, UNBELIEF.

trustworthy

dependable
reliable
trusty

These adjectives characterize personal qualities of people in whom one has great confidence. **Trustworthy** implies that one's confidence is complete and profound: a *trustworthy* friend. **Reliable** suggests competence and consistency: A *reliable* judge is one who has a record of sound opinions. *Reliable* persons can be counted on to do what they have promised to do or been told to do: a *reliable* babysitter. When applied to things, *reliable* means adequate, serviceable, or true; a reference book, for example, might be called *reliable* if its information is accurate. **Dependable** is akin to *reliable,* but a little more subjective; *reliable* is often used of relationships based on service between superiors and inferiors, whereas *dependable* more often suggests an attitude of personal allegiance rather than one of honesty or scrupulosity in performance of a duty. One goes to a *dependable* person confident of receiving loyalty, support, or aid: a *dependable* ally. When applied to things, *dependable* suggests stability and consistency of performance: a *dependable* headache remedy.

That which has been found *reliable* in the past is **trusty**, though it may not merit as much confidence as something *trustworthy:* a *trusty* prisoner; a *trusty* sword. See ALLEGIANCE, SURE, TRUST, TRUTHFUL.

Antonyms: HEEDLESS, INCONSTANT, *irresponsible,* negligent.

truthful

good
honest
reputable
veracious

These adjectives all refer to estimable qualities. **Truthful** and **veracious**, stemming respectively from the Old English and Latin words for true, are close synonyms that mean habitually telling or disposed to tell the truth. *Veracious* is considerably more formal and more limited in application; it is used principally of a person's habitual tendency rather than of particular instances of truth-telling: a *veracious* (or *truthful*) man; a *truthful* remark. **Honest** and **good** are rich in connotations; as here considered, *honest* means not given to lying, cheating, or stealing, and stresses the virtuous and worthy motivation and principles of a person to whom the adjective is applied. *Truthful* and *veracious,* by contrast, while usually complimentary, since truth is highly valued, do not necessarily suggest an accompanying nobility of character: a *truthful* but malicious retort; He was *veracious* but unkind. *Honest* in this sense implies holding nothing back; it suggests an extreme candidness, even at one's own expense: an *honest* admission of his failure. *Good* may suggest honorable motives and noble character even more strongly than *honest,* but unless placed in a limiting context suffers from vagueness. By itself *good* is little more than a reflection of the high opinion of the writer: a *good* reporter; a *good,* straight answer. **Reputable**, although it refers specifically to a *good* reputation, implies that the reputation is justified. *Reputable* may be used of a solid, respectable, dependable person highly regarded by the community, or it may be applied to a firm known for the consistently high quality of its goods or services: a *reputable* doctor; a *reputable* store. On the other hand, *reputable* may simply mean well known or greatly esteemed for one's achievements: a *reputable* physicist. See CANDID, DISINTERESTED, MORAL, SINCERE.

Antonyms: *bad, cheating, corrupt, lying,* TREACHEROUS, *underhanded, venal.*

tryst

assignation
date
rendezvous

These nouns refer to prearranged meetings of an intimate nature, often secret, illicit, or amorous in intent. **Tryst**, the most specific, points almost invariably to a secret meeting, often at night, in a hidden place. *Tryst* hints at furtiveness and so strongly suggests a meeting of lovers that it could sound odd when used of any other encounter: a midnight *tryst* in the garden. **Assignation** specifically indicates secrecy as well, but it also strongly suggests an illicit meeting. A *tryst* might occasionally be perfectly innocent, not causing surprise or alarm if known about by others. In contrast, *assignation* denotes a meeting with an amorous or sexual purpose: arranging an *assignation* with an actor while I was away.

Rendezvous emphasizes prearrangement, but it

may or may not be secret or unsavory in implication. Often, it can suggest a simple matter of synchronizing independent movement so as to coincide at a planned time and place. It appears in contexts of romantic love, conspiracy, and military tactics: a café where the lovers held their *rendezvous;* the bus depot in which the addict and his connection made their *rendezvous;* a *rendezvous* of the two patrols in Zone A at 0600 hours. **Date**, by contrast, is the most general and informal of these nouns and is not often likely to suggest either a secret or illicit meeting. Most commonly, it suggests an evening of shared entertainment of an unmarried couple: college students who confine their *dates* to weekends. *Date* can apply as well to any sort of pre-arranged meeting at any time for any purpose: a luncheon *date* with another lawyer in her office; a *date* with my son. See MEETING.

turbulent

blustering
riotous
stormy
tempestuous
tumultuous
violent
wild

These adjectives characterize extreme agitation, either of external physical forces or of internal emotional states. **Turbulent** suggests troubled, tumbling, erratic, chaotic, or confused activity or a whirl of uncontrolled emotion: *turbulent* anxieties that drove him to suicide; *turbulent* airflow around a badly streamlined airplane; a *turbulent* mob of jostling, jeering workers. As in the last example, the physical and emotional applications of *turbulent* may often coalesce.

Violent and **wild** are the most general of these adjectives. *Violent* stresses destructive or uncontrolled physical force: a *violent* hurricane. In reference to human action, it stresses extreme agitation and often harmful or vicious behavior: the *violent* manner in which he pounded the lectern with his fist; trying to keep the *turbulent* crowd from becoming *violent;* a *violent* person capable of commiting murder. *Wild* suggests an untamed state of nature: the Lewis and Clark expedition over *wild,* uncharted prairies and mountains. Used of a person, *wild* can suggest uncontrolled, uncivilized behavior: cursing and stomping about like a *wild* man. It can also suggest derangement

or immorality: a woman who went *wild* and stabbed three children; staggering from the lifeboat with *wild* eyes; a *wild* party.

Stormy and **tempestuous** can refer to *turbulent* weather, but also to human emotion. In either case, *tempestuous* suggests greater force or intensity: *stormy* weather that had run its course by morning; *tempestuous* winds and rain that hammered the island for three days. Used of emotions, *stormy* indicates great agitation, but there is no necessary implication of potential harm or of an unpleasant outcome: *stormy* lovers' quarrels that end in tearful reconciliation. In this context, *tempestuous* suggests forceful or disordered emotional intensity, but like *stormy,* no necessarily harmful or lasting result: a brief, but *tempestuous,* love affair. *Tempestuous* can suggest the running of a range of emotions at their highest pitch; consequently, it sometimes is used in describing art, particularly works from the romantic era: a *tempestuous* piano concerto. **Blustering** is related to *stormy* and *tempestuous* in that it can refer to weather, but by contrast it suggests erratic gusts of wind or rain. As applied to emotions, however, *blustering* has a drastically different set of connotations, usually suggesting hasty, rash, angry outbursts of uncontrolled speech or action: *blustering* about the office and breaking out in fits of *violent* fury that he directed at me.

Both **riotous** and **tumultuous** can apply to *turbulent* or *violent* groups of people. In this use, *tumultuous* is like *turbulent,* while *riotous* is even more forceful than *violent*. *Tumultuous* stresses noise, mass crowding, and erratic activity, but does not necessarily suggest potential danger or destructiveness; it can, in fact, indicate the opposite: *tumultuous* crowds that gathered to hail the returning troops; *tumultuous* applause for her performance. A *riotous* crowd, by contrast, is by implication one verging on angry mob action: an orderly meeting that became *riotous* as more and more people called for lynching the suspect on the spot. *Riotous* can refer to any sort of bewildering array or profusion: a field *riotous* with colorful flowers. It is, however, less likely than *tumultuous* to describe emotions. In this context, *tumultuous* suggests an extreme upheaval accompanied by surges of contradictory feelings during which the rational mind cannot sort out or control the developing confusion: a *tumultuous* state of combined anger and fear. See LAWLESSNESS, UNRULY.

Antonyms: *TRANQUIL.*

U

unbelief

disbelief
incredulity

These nouns are comparable in that they denote a chronic tendency or temporary disposition to withhold belief. **Unbelief** refers to the absence of positive belief, especially the lack of belief in God and any of the religious faiths based on belief in God. More than the other two nouns in this group, *unbelief* suggests a chronic mental quality rather than a particular instance of doubt: the impossibility of trying to harmonize the *unbelief* of an atheist and the conviction of a Catholic dogmatist. In theological usage, *unbelief* has condemnatory force, since it implies willful rejection of manifest truth.

Disbelief refers to a positive conviction that a particular act, statement, doctrine, etc., is untrue, even in the face of its asserted validity. It hints at a one-time or temporary rejection instead of a continuously doubting state of mind: so committed to his point of view that he dismissed with *disbelief* all evidence of his error; A look of *disbelief* replaced the smile on her face.

Incredulity is a disinclination to accept as true whatever has been suggested as such; it is based on skepticism and a disposition to criticize or object. *Incredulity* indicates a set frame of mind more than does *disbelief,* but less so than *unbelief:* extravagant claims for a product that were met with *incredulity* by knowledgeable buyers. See DOUBT, DOUBTFUL, SKEPTIC.

Antonyms: *credulity,* OPINION, RELIGION.

unethical

amoral
immoral
nonmoral
unmoral
unprincipled
unscrupulous

All these adjectives can apply to acts that go against the codes that society establishes to regulate social behavior. **Unethical** in its generality has the widest range of uses, applying particularly to any act that harms another person: *unethical* campaign practices, such as appeals to bigotry and character assassination. *Unethical* has a popular connotation, as well, that suggests a breach that is unfair but not so apparently harmful to someone: insisting that it was *unethical* to curry favor with an instructor. By contrast, **immoral,** at its most general, can point to much graver or more serious harm: believing that it was *immoral* to sanction violence in the Balkans. (Here, *unethical* would surely be a weak way of typifying the action under discussion.) In popular usage, *immoral* more concretely points to sexual misbehavior: parents so hopelessly old-fashioned and puritanical that they considered dancing an *immoral* activity. *Immoral,* of course, can be applied like *unethical* to anything one disapproves of.

Unscrupulous and **unprincipled** both apply to people willing to do anything for their own gain, regardless of whom they harm. *Unscrupulous* is the less condemning of the two, suggesting someone who would commit any venial breach of taste, conduct, or manners for self-aggrandizement, though perhaps stopping short of anything outright illegal or at least anything that would get the person into trouble: an *unscrupulous* office manager who would betray any confidence in his vain hope of ingratiating himself with the front office. *Unprincipled,* by contrast, suggests an even more rapacious attitude: an *unprincipled* pusher who made her living by ruining people's lives.

Amoral points to behavior that is at variance with society's codes of behavior because of ignorance, indifference, or a more or less principled rejection of these values: the *amoral* lives of new bohemians who see old values as institutionalized cruelty. **Unmoral** and **nonmoral** mean not within the realm of morality. [A baby is *unmoral;* Meteorology is a *nonmoral* study.] See DEPRAVED, SIN, WRONGDOING.

Antonyms: MORAL, *principled, scrupulous.*

unexceptionable. Do not confuse the adjective *unexceptionable* (with which no fault can be found) with the adjective *unexceptional* (quite ordinary).

uninterested. When your intention is to indicate *uncaring* or *not interested,* use *uninterested;* when your intention is to indicate *unbiased,* use *objective, unbiased,* or *disinterested.*

uninvolved

apathetic
bored
indifferent
unconcerned
unmoved

These adjectives suggest a lack of participation in an activity, or a lack of sympathy for it. **Uninvolved** is the most general as well as the most neutral in tone. It suggests an attitude of standing apart from an activity as well as from its benefits or consequences: preferring to remain *uninvolved* in the counterfeiting scheme; seeking jurors *uninvolved* in the problems of the neighborhood. One may have strong feelings about an activity but choose to be *uninvolved* because of fear or other pressures. **Unconcerned**, however, stresses lack of interest or sympathy: those citizens totally *unconcerned* by the international crisis. It may even suggest carefree abandon: blithely *unconcerned* about the piling up of their debts.

Indifferent and **unmoved** are intensifications of *unconcerned,* suggesting a complete lack of feeling. *Indifferent* might especially apply to an uncaring attitude about the outcome of something when faced with two or more choices: equally *indifferent* to every entrée on the menu. It can also suggest a lack of response to an emotional appeal: *indifferent* to the attorney's passionate summation. *Unmoved* is an intensification of this last sense of *indifferent,* referring particularly to a situation designed specifically to elicit a given reaction: a maudlin play that left me completely *unmoved. Unmoved* also suggests a refusal to perform a suggested action: an appeal that left the student body *unmoved.*

Apathetic and **bored**, even more than *unmoved,* suggest resistance to arousal. *Apathetic* suggests a general lethargy or dullness of feeling in a person or a group: citizens awakening from an *apathetic* acceptance of injustice and prejudice. *Bored* is more narrowly specific in meaning, suggesting an *unmoved* response to a particular event, but does not necessarily imply the inactivity of *apathetic: bored* and restless children; members of the audience so *bored* by the tedious play that many left after the first act. See ALOOF, DISINTERESTED.

Antonyms: *concerned, engaged, interested, moved.*

unite

blend
coalesce
combine
fuse
join
merge

These verbs all refer to the bringing or coming together of several different elements to form a whole. **Unite**, stemming from Latin *unus,* meaning one, emphasizes the completeness of the process and the singleness of the resulting entity: to *unite* forces to overcome their enemy; to *unite* two families in marriage. **Combine** means bring together into close union; it is more general in application than *unite* and does not emphasize so strongly the completeness of the process of coming together. For example, to *combine* military forces would not exclude the possibility of each force's retaining a separate command, but to *unite* forces would imply the formation of a single force under one command. *Combine* is used in a wide variety of contexts. [To succeed as an artist one must *combine* talent and discipline; To get gray, one *combines* black and white.] Thus, *combine* may suggest mixing or compounding, a connotation lacking in *unite.* **Blend**, even more strongly than *combine,* suggests a mingling of different elements; unlike *combine,* it specifically refers to the obscuring or harmonizing of various components: to *blend* modern and medieval architecture; to *blend* sugar and egg whites to make a meringue. **Merge**, like *blend,* suggests the loss of separate identity of ingredients, but it does not imply the physical act of mixing or mingling together different elements: The two railroad companies *merged* to cut costs.

Join, the broadest verb of this group, can mean become part of, bring together or connect, or put together in close contact: The path *joins* the road; to *join* two wires; to *join* hands. **Fuse** means *join* by or as if by melting together. Whereas *fused* wires, therefore, are connected by being melted together, *joined* wires might be attached with solder or be intertwined. *Fuse* in other contexts implies a solid, lasting connection: The feeling of persecution and a sense of defeat became *fused* in our minds. **Coalesce** suggests a gradual or natural growing or coming together, as the segments of a broken bone. [The operation set the bones in position to *coalesce;* The sections of a baby's skull are not fully *joined*, but *coalesce* after a few years.] In extended senses *coalesce* suggests two separate courses that gradually *merge* into one: The idea of nationalism and the traditional mistrust of foreigners *coalesced* to form a policy of isolation. See GATHER, MIXTURE.

Antonyms: *SCATTER.*

unparalleled

extraordinary
singular
special

These adjectives are used to describe someone or something that differs from the ordinary or the usual. That which is **unparalleled** is different in that it has no parallel or equal; it is unmatched. It suggests not so much a uniqueness of kind as an overwhelming superiority or quantity: her *unparalleled* achievements in astrophysics. That which is **special** has some distinguishing or individualizing characteristic: These machines are all identical in their surface design, but each one is *special* in its interior construction. Something *special* might be designed for or concerned with a specific purpose: The hospital has over fifty *special* diets for different kinds of illnesses. *Special* can mean peculiar or even unique: Each problem that crosses my desk is *special*. It is often used to refer to the exceptional in amount or degree: a *special* fondness for French cooking. *Special* is the most comprehensive term in this group; anything described by one of the other adjectives could certainly be called *special* as well. **Extraordinary** means greatly beyond the ordinary or usual. It is a neutral word that can function in either a complimentary or a critical description: *extraordinary* kindness; *extraordinary* wickedness. It can also, like *special,* be used to refer to something that is employed for a specific purpose: an envoy *extraordinary.* **Singular** has a wide range of meaning. In the most precise usage, it implies that whatever is being described is the only one of its type: a phenomenon *singular* in the history of this experiment. In an extension of this sense that is less limited in application, *singular* refers to the uncommon, the rare, or the *extraordinary:* a woman of *singular* charm. Finally, *singular* has to do with the kind of difference from the usual that is characterized as odd or eccentric: It is difficult to excuse his *singular* behavior at the engagement party. See BIZARRE, ECCENTRICITY.

Antonyms: *GENERAL, USUAL.*

unruly

intractable
recalcitrant
refractory
restive
uncontrollable
ungovernable

unmanageable
wayward

These adjectives apply to persons or things that rebel against restraint or defy control. **Unruly** stresses a boisterous quality—the tendency to burst free from restrictions or to get out of line. An *unruly* person or thing is disposed to resist discipline but can be brought under control: *unruly* boys creating a disturbance; to plaster down an *unruly* cowlick. **Wayward** goes beyond *unruly* in indicating willfulness and immorality. It suggests a straying from the straight and narrow, and sometimes connotes potential delinquency or sexual promiscuity: a home for *wayward* minors. Like *unruly, wayward* may be applied to a piece of hair that will not stay in place: a *wayward* curl.

Restive emphasizes impatience and irritation—a chafing under restraint and a struggle against coercion. A *restive* horse impatiently resists control or struggles to break free. A *restive* area is ready to rebel: a *restive* community, ripe for a riot. By extension, *restive* has come to mean restless or fidgety, discontented with the status quo: an inattentive, *restive* audience, impatiently waiting for the intermission.

Intractable, **refractory**, and **recalcitrant** are more formal adjectives that indicate an obstinate refusal to yield. An *intractable* person or animal stubbornly resists being led, guided, restrained, or influenced: The boy was shy and quiet, yet strong-willed, independent, and *intractable,* as stubborn as a mule. Applied to things, *intractable* means difficult to manipulate, treat, or work: The source material was *intractable,* and there was little the librettist could do with it. *Refractory* implies more activity of resistance, suggesting an active rather than a passive disobedience. *Refractory* persons are both obstinate and rebellious, determined to protest the dictates of authority: a *refractory* lad, doing just the opposite of what he is told. A *refractory* metal or ore is one that resists heat or ordinary methods of reduction. [Fire clay, a *refractory* material used to make crucibles and furnace linings, resists the highest temperatures of the blast furnace without melting.] *Recalcitrant* comes from Latin roots meaning to kick back. It is close in meaning to *refractory* but more extreme, implying uncompromising resistance or a disposition to be defiant: A *recalcitrant* student who not only refused to obey any rule but threatened a teacher with violence.

Unmanageable, **ungovernable**, and **uncontrollable** apply to things that are hard to handle or impossible to control. An *unmanageable* person or animal will not submit to guidance or direction. An *unmanageable* thing is incapable of being handled or dealt with successfully: a heavy but not *unmanageable* work load. That which is *ungovernable* cannot be regulated by rules or agreed-upon restraints; it defies any attempt to tame it or to bring it under orderly, rational control: an *ungovernable* land, beset with warring factions and internal strife. *Ungovernable* often suggests a loss or lack of self-control: an *ungovernable* temper. *Uncontrollable* is the most extreme of these adjectives. It applies to that which goes beyond the bounds of control, as by being involuntary, instinctive, irrepressible, or wild: *uncontrollable* muscle spasms; *uncontrollable* anger. See LOUD, MISCHIEVOUS, STUBBORN.

Antonyms: *ADAPTABLE, COMPLIANT, DOCILE.*

unsettle

   annoy
   irritate
   nettle
   put out
   rile

These verbs refer to an uneasy or exasperated response to external factors or causes. **Unsettle** is the least intense of these, suggesting someone who has been unnerved or vaguely disquieted by something; the cause may be a specific distraction or a more indefinable mood or atmosphere: *unsettled* by the wailing of an infant in the next apartment; *unsettled* by the institutionalized coldness of the office. Even in the active voice, *unsettle* does not suggest an intentional attempt to unnerve someone so much as a subjective or intuitive response to an existing state of affairs. One would not be likely to say: He deliberately *unsettled* me. But one could say: Oddly enough, his mere presence *unsettled* me. In contrast, **annoy** can indicate both an intentional disturbance and a disturbed response. [You appear intent on *annoying* her; I was *annoyed* by his incessant grumbling.] In any case, *annoy* indicates a greater degree of emotional upset than does *unsettle:* His whistling *unsettles* me a bit, but I can't say it *annoys* me all that much.

Irritate suggests a repeated, abrasive action that *annoys* by draining a person of patience or good humor; nothing is too trivial to *irritate,* if the observer is high-strung: Her habit of tapping her fingers on the chair while she read *irritated* him. **Nettle** suggests being temporarily aroused to anger or pique, often because of something considered damaging to one's self-respect: *nettled* by his willful disregard of her advice; *nettled* by the critic's casual rejection of my arguments. *Nettle,* as in these examples, often implies

a sense of indignation occasioned by a real or fancied slight.

Rile is in every way an intensification of *annoy,* but it is also more informal; it might, in fact, be considered dialect by some. Also, *rile* emphasizes response without suggesting an intended cause: *riled* by their unthinking rudeness; I didn't mean to get you all *riled* up over nothing. **Put out** is related more closely to *unsettle* than to *nettle* or *rile. Put out* points to the vague dissatisfaction of someone who has been displeased, inconvenienced, or disappointed. [He was *put out* by the way everyone at the party ignored him; She tried to get her work done but was terribly *put out* by the constant interruptions of the contractor; Only a sullen silence suggested how *put out* he was over not getting his promotion.] As in the last example, *put out* can imply a minimal, passive, or withdrawn response; this may also be true for *unsettled.* In contrast, *annoy* and *irritate* suggest a more agitated or noticeable response. In the active voice, *put out* refers more exclusively to inconvenience: I hope we haven't *put* you *out* by staying so late. See ENRAGE, BOTHER, INCITE, OUTRAGE, UPSET.

Antonyms: *calm, relax, relieve, soothe, tranquilize.*

unwilling

   averse
   disinclined
   hesitant
   loath
   reluctant

These adjectives indicate refusal to assent to something, or a cautious, grudging, or indecisive attitude toward it. **Unwilling** points to a flat rejection and is the most forcefully negative of these adjectives: *unwilling* to lend him the money and *unwilling* even to discuss it. *Unwilling* can also indicate someone involved in something contrary to his or her wishes: the ancient mariner's *unwilling* listener. **Loath** (or *loth,* as it is also spelled) can be taken as having negative force equal to or surpassing that of *unwilling;* this may stem from overtones supplied by the verb loathe: *loath* to do anything detrimental to her reputation. In common use, however, *loath* can suggest resistance to or distaste for something without implying the adamant refusal inherent in *unwilling: loath* to go to the opera, but doing so to please his family. This is especially true when one feels compelled to do something whether willingly or not: *loath* to acquit the defendant, though the lack of conclusive evidence left no other choice. To illustrate the contrast with *unwilling,* it can be said that many draftees are probably *loath* to enter military service, but pacifists are more likely to be *unwilling* to serve. On the other hand, one might not be *loath* to do something and yet remain *unwilling:* keenly interested in the assignment but *unwilling* to do it for so little money.

Averse suggests distaste that may be innate but in any case is so strong as to be unalterable. This deep-seated distaste, however, may or may not result in an *unwilling* response: so *averse* to crowds that he went to great lengths to avoid them; *averse* to the idea of taking a second job, but agreeing to it because of her desperate financial situation. **Reluctant** may sometimes suggest firm resistance to something: insisting he was and would remain *reluctant* to vote for any bill liberalizing the abortion law. More often *reluctant* indicates a grudging or provisional consent: finally giving *reluctant* permission to test the drug on human beings, but only under strict control. **Disinclined** is similar to *loath* and even more to *averse* in suggesting distaste for something. It suggests a weaker resistance than *loath* and *averse,* however, and may point to a cautious or prudent attitude that is habitual or is based on experience or evidence: *disinclined* to opt for total withdrawal of forces. *Disinclined* is alone in this set of adjectives in applying to opinions, views, or judgments as well as to consent or action: *disinclined* to believe the man's story; *disinclined* to take the reports of flying saucers seriously. Sometimes, *disinclined* is used as a circumlocution for a more direct term of disapproval. **Hesitant** suggests the least resistance of any of these adjectives. It can, in fact, refer merely to indecisiveness or immobilizing caution: faced with so many confusing choices that he was *hesitant* to commit to any. See OPPOSED, STUBBORN.

Antonyms: EAGER, FAVORABLE, *inclined,* READY, WILLFUL.

unwise
ill-advised
imprudent
injudicious

These adjectives are low-key, unemotional words used to call the wisdom of actions or decisions into question without giving offense. All are politely or mildly critical, emphasizing the absence of a positive attribute rather than the presence of a negative one. And all may be used either to express disapproval or to convey a word of warning. **Unwise** is the most general adjective here and may serve as a less precise substitute for the others. When used in expressing an opinion on something already done, it implies an alterna-

tive considered to be wiser: an *unwise* choice. When used as an advisory or precautionary term, it may sometimes imply considerable risk and possible danger: Making speculative investments without adequate savings is *unwise.* **Injudicious** is milder, suggesting not so much lack of judgment as failure to exercise the best possible judgment in a sensitive situation. Where *unwise* may refer to something foolish or risky, what is *injudicious* is ill-considered or indiscreet. [The official made hasty, *injudicious* remarks; His *injudicious* eagerness to buy the antique encouraged the dealer to raise its price.] *Unwise, injudicious,* and **imprudent** all point to a lack of foresight, a failure to think ahead and anticipate consequences. But *imprudent* emphasizes a lack of discretion, implying that greater precautions might be taken or that greater circumspection might be shown. [The doctor thought it *imprudent* for the patient to take a long trip; Many colleagues felt it was *imprudent* of him to encourage even his poorest students.]

Ill-advised is perhaps the least offensive of these inoffensive terms. Where *unwise* might imply a personal failure in judgment, *ill-advised* suggests that the person was acting on bad or inadequate advice: You were *ill-advised* to sell the stock, as it has good growth potential. *Ill-advised* may also be applied to an action or project: an *ill-advised* strike that forced the employer to go out of business. *Ill-advised* may also be used to warn someone against taking action without getting enough sound advice beforehand: It would be *ill-advised* to abandon the project before all the preliminary studies are complete. See ABSURD, HEEDLESS, RECKLESS, STUPID.

Antonyms: CAREFUL, CAUTIOUS, CONSIDERATE, *judicious, provident,* SENSIBLE.

uphold
back
champion
defend
maintain
support
sustain

These verbs are concerned with protection or assistance given in the face of difficulty or hostility. **Uphold** specifically suggests an active attempt to prevent something from giving way or from falling into danger or neglect: a performance that *upheld* the sport's tradition of fair play. **Back** can also apply to the protection of principles or ideas, but it is very often used in a more personal way, suggesting that one person stands behind or subscribes to the efforts of another who has exposed himself or herself to danger or disapproval. *Back* can therefore suggest a more passive role than *uphold*: careless of their own safety in *upholding* the cause because they believed others in the community would *back* them up. *Back* may also specifically suggest the choosing of sides in a contest: voters who had *backed* the dark horse.

Defend and **champion** suggest action in the face of hostility. *Defend* is smaller in scope than *champion*, stressing protection of a challenged right or position. The extent of the action taken, however, may be slight or great: *defending* her reputation with a well-placed word or two; *defending* his friends from injury by throwing himself on the live grenade. *Champion* specifically stresses a more active, offensive role and may suggest taking the place of someone less able to act. It may also suggest a single-handed offense, as opposed to most of these other verbs, which imply that many could conceivably cooperate in protection or assistance: the only newspaper that insistently *championed* the right of the convicted person to a new trial.

Support and **sustain** are like *back* in suggesting the assistance of something that is in an exposed or endangered position. *Back,* however, suggests more determination than either of these verbs in themselves. *Support* states the mere fact of aid or favor without any implication of resoluteness or permanent commitment: *supporting* her in the primary but not in the general election. Unlike *back* and *support, sustain* cannot apply to the choosing of sides in a contest. It can go beyond *support* in other situations to suggest a continuing loyalty: *sustaining* his support for the cause over more than a decade. In another use, *sustain* can suggest the granting of a point or the giving of peripheral aid without taking sides on larger issues: asking the judge to *sustain* her objection concerning the tactics of her opponent; friends who *sustained* his morale during exam week by popping in often with coffee and snacks.

Maintain may suggest resoluteness in the context of advocacy: *maintaining* that the confession had been coerced. In other situations, it may suggest continuing *support* that may, however, be minimal or less than adequate: The absent father *maintained* the payments over many years, but they were never enough to *sustain* the whole family. See ENCOURAGE.

Antonyms: *betray,* DESTROY, *drop.*

uprising
civil war
counterinsurgency
insurgency
insurrection
rebellion
revolt
revolution

These nouns all denote some kind of effort to defy or overthrow a government or other form of authority. **Uprising**, the broadest term, may be substituted in a general way for any of the other nouns. Specifically, it may refer to a minor or unsuccessful act of popular resistance: an abortive *uprising* of the slaves on a Georgia plantation. It can also apply to those localized signs of unrest and discontent that indicate the imminence of widespread conflict: the first *uprisings* in Germany and Austria, which led to the Peasants' War of 1524–1526. **Rebellion** is an armed resistance or *uprising* against a government, often on a large scale and frequently doomed to failure. If successful, however, a *rebellion* may become a **revolution**, which involves overthrow and replacement of a government or political system by the people governed. In a wider sense, *revolution* can denote any extensive or drastic change in economic institutions, in ideas, or in mores: the Industrial *Revolution*, which began in England in the mid-18th century; the *revolution* in manners and morals that followed World War I.

Insurrection points to an organized effort to seize power, especially political power, while **revolt** emphasizes protest against oppression or other intolerable conditions. Unlike *insurrection, revolt* has the extended meaning of any refusal to go on tolerating an allegiance or a powerful authority: a *revolt* within an established church.

Insurgency has almost the same meaning as *insurrection,* but it usually designates a better organized kind of *revolt,* and is often used today to refer to revolutionary activity that is aided by foreign powers. **Counterinsurgency**, a word most common in current news and propaganda media, is any measure designed to combat revolutionary activity or guerrilla warfare.

If an *uprising, insurrection,* or *insurgency* continues for a long time without being effectively countered, the country of its origin may be said to be in a state of **civil war**. *Civil war* denotes armed conflict openly carried on between parties or sections of the same country, whether or not both parties involved are legally recognized as belligerents. In the usual sense of the term, *civil war* involves factions (generally two), each trying to gain control of the existing government. In this way, a *civil war* differs from a *revolution* in that the emphasis is not on overthrowing a regime. The American *Civil War* differs from the above concept in that the South seceded and wished to become a separate nation. See CONSPIRACY, CRIME, INTRIGUE, LAWLESSNESS.

upset

    agitate
    demoralize
    disconcert
    disturb
    exacerbate

These verbs refer to acts that cause or result in emotional upheaval. **Upset** is the most general and the least formal, stressing a complete or sudden loss of mental equilibrium, although this may not be accompanied by an outward show: finally admitting she was deeply *upset;* ridicule deliberately designed to *upset* him. *Upset* usually suggests a temporary state of mind from which one can normally recover in time: It *upset* him all morning until his usual sense of calm returned. Although *upset* can imply a more permanent derangement, **disturb** is now more frequently used in this sense: juvenile delinquents who are emotionally *disturbed.* In this case, *disturb* suggests a mental disorder that may verge on psychosis. When *disturb* refers to a momentary upheaval, it suggests a milder anguish than *upset* and possibly one more gradual in onset. It might also imply a deepening uneasiness difficult to objectify: She was growing more and more *disturbed* that he had not phoned to explain the delay. **Agitate** is more like *upset* in suggesting a sudden upheaval, but it contrasts with *upset* in specifically suggesting an unavoidable outward show of one's turbulent state of mind: The news so *agitated* him that he babbled incoherently. The turbulence may also be the intensified expression of a chronic nervousness rather than the result of deep emotional shock.

    Demoralize and **disconcert** indicate a less intense upheaval than the foregoing verbs, suggesting that something has reduced one to a state of complete ineffectiveness. Of the two, *disconcert* more nearly resembles *upset* in implying a sudden onset accompanied by no necessary outward show, but resulting in momentary mental disarray. In contrast, *disconcert* most often suggests an upheaval that results from some specific confrontation: *disconcerted* by remarks made about his taste. Although *demoralize* may indicate the slightest emotional upheaval of all these verbs, it nonetheless suggests a gradual and long-term exhaustion or sapping of the will because of a hopelessly snarled situation or the unremitting pressure of hurtful hostility: bureaucratic inefficiency that had thoroughly *demoralized* the staff; *demoralized* and

embittered by the dean's continuing harassment.

    Exacerbate refers to the worsening of anger, irritability, pain, etc. In this context, *exacerbate* can function as an intensification of any of these other verbs: first *upsetting* her with the news that he was leaving her and then *exacerbating* the hurt by proceeding to call her vile names. *Exacerbate* may also mean exasperate or irritate, but this usage tends to sound informal. See COMPLAIN, CONFUSE, DISTRESS, EMBARRASSMENT, ENRAGE, FRENZY, OUTRAGE, PUZZLE, SHAME, SURPRISED, UNSETTLE.

Antonyms: *calm, relax, relieve, soothe.*

urbane

    cultivated
    genteel
    sophisticated
    suave

These adjectives all deal with qualities of mind or manner characteristic of well bred, worldly wise, or educated people. Virtually every one of the terms here discussed is sometimes used in a derogatory, disapproving, or humorously condescending way.

    Urbane means having a refined or polished manner, such as befits one who is well traveled, well bred, or long habituated to the society of **cultivated** people; an *urbane* conversation about continental cuisines. *Cultivated* indicates a sophistication acquired through formal education or purposeful experience: a *cultivated* appreciation of abstract art. *Cultivated* speech is educated speech, as distinguished from the speech of the ignorant, untutored, or illiterate. When applied to people, *cultivated* often stresses knowledge and the appreciation of the arts, whereas **sophisticated** can suggest superficiality, indicating overly polished manners and sometimes a skeptical or jaded attitude toward life: Too *sophisticated* for plain fare, she frowned as we placed the food before her. *Cultivated,* however, can also be used derogatorily to mean contrived or affected: a carefully *cultivated* British accent designed to impress friends.

    When *sophisticated* is positive in tone, it points to advanced perception and an appreciation of culture that comes with study or experience; in such contexts even the toughness or worldly-wise quality *sophisticated* connotes may be viewed with admiration: Although the play was considered strong stuff by provincial audiences, *sophisticated* New York playgoers found it weak tea. When applied to things, *sophisticated* often means using advanced and complicated technological techniques: a very *sophisticated* but useless missile defense system. In its association with scientific achievement, *sophisticated* acquires a wholly positive character; there are few things valued more highly than modern technology.

Genteel conveys derogatory or humorously condescending connotations in most current uses. *Genteel* formerly meant well bred or refined, but now usually means too consciously *cultivated.* To call people or their manners *genteel* implies anxiety about appearing *cultivated,* with the result that they appear pretentious or ridiculous: Her *genteel* manners made it impossible for her to grasp a coffee cup without elevating two fingers, even though the coffee frequently sloshed out onto the floor as a result. Buildings are sometimes described as being shabby *genteel,* indicating a ludicrous incongruity between the splendid original decor and its present poorly maintained condition or old-fashioned style. The personification suggests someone who has seen better days and is now trying with only moderate success to appear respectable.

Suave means smoothly pleasant or ingratiating; it may be purely descriptive and neutral in tone, and in this sense is close to *urbane* in meaning: a *suave* and masterfully executed bow. But it may be associated with a surface politeness, oily manner, and glibness in speech: At first she found him attractive and *suave,* but she soon recognized his basic vulgarity. See BLITHE, EXQUISITE, GREGARIOUS, POLITE.

Antonyms: *BRUSQUE, GAUCHE, NAIVE, VULGAR.*

usual
    accustomed
    common
    conventional
    customary
    habitual
    ordinary
    regular
    wonted

These adjectives are used to describe things that happen in the everyday course of events or are accepted by most people as normal and natural rather than as novel or strange. **Usual** is applied to whatever recurs frequently, steadily, or with relative constancy. Unlike some of the other adjectives here, *usual* may be applied to natural happenings as well as to occurrences based on the customs of a community or the habits of an individual. [Thunder is the *usual* sign of an approaching storm; Flowers are the *usual* gift for a shut-in; Chess is their *usual* pastime.]

Regular, **ordinary**, and **common**, in the sense of

usual, have equally wide applications. *Regular* emphasizes a conformity to the established or natural order of things. [Overtime is work in excess of the *regular* weekly schedule; Most of us thrive on *regular* meals and *regular* hours of rest.] *Ordinary,* implying such conformity less strongly, connotes an absence of exceptional or striking characteristics: My *ordinary* workday is nine hours. *Common* also emphasizes the unexceptional, but may in some usages suggest less frequency than does *usual:* the *common* household accident of slipping in the bathtub; the *usual* congratulations one extends to new parents.

Customary, **habitual**, **wonted**, **accustomed**, and **conventional** seldom refer to natural occurrences except metaphorically. In most cases they indicate what is *usual. Customary* is applied to something that characterizes a given community or person. [It is *customary* for Tibetans to put yak butter into their tea; It is *customary* for our family to sleep late on Sundays.] *Habitual* refers to acts or qualities in individuals that have been strengthened by constantly repeated actions: a *habitual* chain-smoker; a *habitual* gambler. *Wonted,* an adjective that now sounds bookish and quaint, emphasizes habituation but is applied both to personal habits and social customs when less stress is being laid on their fixity: returning home each evening at his *wonted* hour. *Accustomed* is often used in place of *customary* or in place of *wonted,* but it suggests fixed custom less strongly than does *customary* and is less stilted than *wonted.* It often implies simply getting used to something: *accustomed* to reading the paper at breakfast; her *accustomed* attitude of optimism. *Conventional* is the strongest of these adjectives in suggesting the following of established custom or usage, and it emphasizes the general agreement accorded to it: It is *conventional* for friends to shake hands when they meet on the street. See DAILY, GENERAL, MEDIOCRE, NORMAL, TRADITION.

Antonyms: *OCCASIONAL, SPECIFIC, UNPARALLELED.*

usurp
    appropriate
    arrogate
    confiscate
    preempt

These verbs all mean claim or take possession of something. To **usurp** is to seize and hold in possession something, such as a position or status, that belongs to another person and to which one has no legal right, and to exercise the authority and enjoy the privileges stemming from such a position. *Usurp* pertains especially to the forcible seizure of kingly power: an upstart pretender trying to *usurp* the throne.

Appropriate, as here considered, denotes the lawful or unlawful acquisition for one's own use of something originally belonging to another or to no one in particular. Thus, farmers may legitimately *appropriate* water for irrigation from streams running through their farms; if unscrupulous, they may also *appropriate* parts of a neighbor's land.

Arrogate means claim, demand, or take that which belongs to another. It differs from the other verbs in this group in its suggestion of the overbearing or haughty manner that accompanies *arrogating*: a department chairman who *arrogated* the right of deciding how each professor could spend allocated research funds.

Confiscate means *appropriate* by authority something that belongs to another, but not necessarily for one's own use: Customs officials have the right to *confiscate* goods being smuggled into their country.

Originally **preempt** referred to the securing of the right of purchase of public land. In general usage, *preempt* means establish a prior claim to something sought by others: arriving early at the theater so as to *preempt* an aisle seat. See GRASP.

Antonyms: *RELINQUISH.*

utter

express
pronounce
voice

These verbs all refer to the communication of facts, thoughts, feelings, etc., especially through speech. **Utter** can apply to the making of any audible vocal sound and is thus not confined to those disciplined sequences of sound called speech: to *utter* a cry of warning; to *utter* a scream of terror; to *utter* a loud oath. *Utter* often emphasizes the violence or suddenness of the sound produced, as in these examples. It may also apply to normal speech, but it is used only to describe or summarize discourse, not in direct or indirect quotations. [He *uttered* what we were all thinking; She *uttered* the opinion that not all people were equal in ability.] One would not say, however, "He *uttered*, 'I will go,'" nor "He *uttered* that he would go." *Utter* may be used, as exemplified by the sentences in brackets above, to contrast speech with silence and to suggest a bold speaking out. In this sense *utter* is close to **pronounce** in meaning, but *pronounce* is more solemn in tone and more suitable to formal proceedings than ordinary discourse: The judge *pronounced* her opinion with a grave and impressive air; to *pronounce* judgment; to *pronounce* him guilty. Influenced by its phonetic sense of articulating sounds in producing speech, *pronounce* may suggest an orotund or dramatic manner of delivery.

Voice, which is more informal than either *pronounce* or *utter*, means put into words, especially a feeling or opinion rather than facts or statements: to *voice* the suggestion that club members owing dues be suspended. *Voice* thus literally means give voice to something thought or felt, and is synonymous to one sense of **express**, a much broader term: to *voice* (or *express*) an unpopular opinion. *Express*, however, may refer to any means of exposing feelings, ideas, etc.: a musical theme that *expresses* melancholy; Picasso's *Guernica expresses* a profound horror of war; to *express* anger by frowning; The habitual dress and habits of some young people may be interpreted as *expressing* contempt for the values of older people. See ASSERT, DECLARE, VERBAL.

vague

dim
hazy
indefinite
indeterminate
indistinct
obscure

These adjectives all refer to that which is not clear to the senses or to the mind. To be **vague** is to fail, whether intentionally or accidentally, to state precisely what one means or to make oneself clearly understood. [He had *vague* memories of his childhood; The senator was *vague* about her plans, saying only that she would not refuse to run again if nominated.]

Indefinite means not precisely defined or limited; **indeterminate** means not definite in extent, amount, or nature: *indefinite* frontiers; an illness with *indeterminate* symptoms. In short, *indefinite* means *vague*, but with the emphasis on blurred outlines or a lack of focus; that which is *indeterminate* may be quite definite, such as specific symptoms accompanying an illness that nevertheless give no clear indication as to the nature of the underlying disease. An *indeterminate* number may be definite, but cannot be known: An *indeterminate* number of rioters dispersed before the police arrived.

Obscure, **indistinct**, **hazy**, and **dim** refer to various ways by which something is blurred or hidden. *Obscure*, the strongest adjective, may suggest a difficulty in perception caused by a murkiness of the atmosphere, or it may suggest a difficulty in understanding caused by the complex, abstruse, or ambiguous nature of the material presented. In either case the result gives only an *indistinct*, partial view of something still hidden from sight or sense: *obscure*, muffled sounds; an *obscure* outline; an *obscure* passage of the Bible. *Indistinct* emphasizes the faintness of the impression on the senses or mind as well as the blurred outlines of the whole; it is thus synonymous with one meaning of *vague*: *indistinct* (or *vague*) memories. *Hazy* and *dim* suggest different ways in which perception may be rendered *indistinct*. *Hazy* implies a glary atmosphere impenetrable to sight; *dim* points to darkness. Whereas *hazy* conveys a strong sense of confusion, uncertainty, and blurred impressions, *dim* stresses the difficulty of seeing or perceiving. [Though heavily sedated, she had a *dim* awareness of what was happening; Her husband had only the *haziest* of notions about what she did at the office.] See DOUBTFUL, FOGGY, MYSTICAL.

Antonyms: *CLEAR, DEFINITE, PLAIN, SENSIBLE.*

vanquish

conquer
overcome
overpower
overthrow
overwhelm
rout
surmount

These verbs all mean get the better of, especially by using physical force in battle. **Vanquish** means defeat utterly in battle, while **conquer** gives greater emphasis to gaining mastery or control over the defeated and their territory: to *vanquish* the enemy; The Romans *conquered* parts of Britain in the 1st century B.C. *Conquer* may apply to a geographical area or a political entity, whereas *vanquish* refers specifically to military forces. Both verbs may be used in extended or figurative senses: to *vanquish* fear; to *conquer* disease; to *conquer* one's shyness.

Overpower and **overwhelm** imply a disastrous defeat in which the defeated are rendered helpless by a sudden onset of superior power. *Overpower* stresses greater strength, as in numbers or weaponry; *overwhelm* implies complete and utter dominance, a one-sided victory that virtually constitutes a **rout**. *Rout*, strictly speaking, implies that the defeated are put to flight. [An army that has been *overpowered* or *overwhelmed* may either surrender or be *routed*.]

To **overthrow** is to defeat an opponent so thoroughly that the opponent is deprived of position or power: a government *overthrown* by an adverse vote; a champion prizefighter *overthrown* by a challenger.

Surmount literally means rise above and is now used chiefly to refer to getting the better of difficulties, obstacles, or the like: Peace negotiators must *surmount* mutual suspicion and resentment. **Overcome** suggests *overpowering*, as in *overcoming* one's enemies, but now is applied chiefly to getting the better of something nonmaterial: to *overcome* temptation; to *overcome* handicaps. See DEFEAT, DESTROY.

Antonyms: *capitulate, ESCAPE, lose, SUBMIT, succumb.*

venal. Do not confuse the adjective *venal* (able to be bribed; of conduct: influenced by bribery) with the adjective *venial* (of a sin: pardonable).

venture

bet
chance
dare
gamble
hazard
risk
stake
wager

Central to this group of verbs is the idea of confronting an uncertain or precarious situation with the intention or hope of obtaining a satisfactory outcome.

When the purpose is to show courteous disagreement or resolve, **venture** is preferred. [I *venture* to contradict you; She *ventured* to insist on major changes in procedure.] But if the emphasis is on challenge or defiance, the otherwise closely synonymous **dare** is more often used. [I *dare* you to do it; He wouldn't *dare* cancel the contract.]

Bet, **gamble**, and **wager** carry the suggestion of pitting one's wits, knowledge, and resources against a set of equally probable events, only one of which is or can be favorable: to *bet* on the races; to *gamble* away a fortune at roulette; to *wager* that the candidate would win the election. *Gamble,* though applicable in virtually every situation covered by the other terms, implies a more reckless commitment under less favorable circumstances: to *gamble* (not *bet* or *wager*) on the stock market. **Stake** also has the same general sense: to *stake* one's reputation on the outcome. More specifically, *stake* means give money or assistance in advance to further a venture, on condition of sharing in any gains. [I *staked* a large sum on my friend's new business.]

Chance means happen or come about accidentally: She *chanced* to find us at home; it may also refer to a more or less deliberate attempt to bring some desired but problematical event to pass: I'll *chance* it. In this latter sense *chance* is nearly interchangeable with **risk**, but *risk* contains an added suggestion of damage, loss, or injury that is not to be ignored: The general *risked* the entire campaign on the outcome of one battle. **Hazard** points up the same distinction: to *hazard* all their winnings on the next fall of the dice. But it may also substitute at a milder level for *venture*: to *hazard* a guess. See DANGER, DOUBTFUL.

verbal

oral
spoken
vocal

These adjectives relate to various forms of utterance. In strict usage, **verbal** refers to the actual words used and does not exclude the possibility of a written communication: a *verbal* dispute; *verbal* translations from the Greek; He gave his *verbal* consent to the proposals.

Oral and **spoken** mean uttered or communicated by mouth: an *oral* examination in defense of one's dissertation; the *oral* tradition of epic poetry; a *spoken* account of their adventures. The distinction between *oral, spoken,* and *verbal* is often blurred by a tendency to confuse a written (or printed) communication with one that is only *spoken. Verbal,* in short, can mean *oral* or *spoken,* but is less precise when so used: *verbal* testimony.

Vocal retains its original and primary meaning of voice, and means having or endowed with the power of utterance: *vocal* cords; *vocal* music; *vocal* creatures. As such *vocal* refers to anything from meaningful speech to a confused murmuring or shouting. [He was always *vocal* in his objections; The crowd was *vocal* in its welcome of the new leader.] See UTTER.

verbose

diffuse
pleonastic
prolix
redundant
repetitious
wordy

These adjectives refer to the use of more words than necessary to make a statement. **Verbose** is formal, **wordy** informal, but both are similar in pointing to an excess of words in speech or writing, without specifying further: a *verbose* chapter on foreign affairs; a *wordy* poem on a familiar subject. *Verbose* is more general than *wordy,* however, since in addition to describing a specific example of excessive verbiage, it is the more likely of the two to typify a writer or speaker, particularly a speaker, who habitually uses more words than necessary or is extremely garrulous: a *verbose* anecdotist who left audiences stony-eyed with boredom.

Redundant and **pleonastic** can pertain to a particular example or an entire statement, but rarely to a writer or speaker. In any case, they both refer to excessive verbiage that results from tautological or unnecessary expressions. *Redundant* is of moderate formality and is restricted almost completely to indicating an excess caused by tautology: *redundant* phrases like essential requisite or fundamental basis. It is also more likely to pinpoint specific examples than to typify an entire style. *Pleonastic*, by contrast, is the most formal of these adjectives; it can refer to specific *redundant* examples: a speech full of *pleonastic* phrases. But it is more general in pertaining as well to a speaking or writing style that is *wordy* or riddled with *redundant* expressions, especially when the style is complicated or pretentious: the *pleonastic* superelegance of the standard Victorian sermon.

Except for *wordy*, **repetitious** and **diffuse** are the least formal of these adjectives. Both specify a particular fault that results in a *wordy* or *verbose* style. *Repetitious* points to excess because of the needless restatement of already established points: *repetitious* commercials that relentlessly hammer home their slogans. *Repetitious* can also refer to the speaker or writer: a *repetitious* debater whose arguments approached the simplemindedness of propaganda. *Diffuse* suggests an excess of words that results when a discourse is spread out, rambling, or poorly ordered in its movement from statement to statement: an essay so *diffuse* that it becomes almost impossible to grasp its central idea.

Prolix approaches *pleonastic* in formality, but is somewhat different from the rest of these adjectives in indicating a discourse that is both unnecessarily long and tedious, with the suggestion that the overall approach is excessively intricate or complicated: a *prolix* contract unintelligible to anyone but a legal expert. *Prolix* can also refer to specific examples of involuted syntax. [A *prolix* sentence can result when too many phrases interrupt the normal flow from subject to verb.] See CHATTER, CIRCUMLOCUTION, MONOTONOUS, TALKATIVE.

Antonyms: *SILENT, SPEECHLESS, TACITURN, TERSE.*

vessel

boat
craft
ship

These nouns denote types of hollow structures capable of floating and of carrying considerable weight, which are used to move goods and people over water. **Vessel**, in accordance with its original meaning of a hollow receptacle, suggests a large structure, especially in terms of its function of carrying goods or people or of being engaged in a specific type of commercial enterprise: a merchant *vessel;* a passenger *vessel;* a whaling *vessel.*

Ship is applied to large seagoing *vessels* when the type of propulsion is being stressed: a steam*ship;* a

motor*ship;* a sailing *ship. Ship* also carries the implication of a *vessel* that has distinctive and even personal qualities for those who sail it. [The captain and the crew all went down with the *ship;* The Bounty was a notorious *ship;* it was a gallant *ship.*] In literature and in figurative uses, *ship* suggests poetic and emotional overtones that are not inherent in any of the other nouns here considered. ["I have seen old *ships* sail like swans asleep"; "Sail on, O *Ship* of State!"]

Boat and **craft** may both be used as general designations for all these structures. *Craft* is more generalized than *boat* in that it does not have any specific connotation as to size, use, or means of navigation. Although *craft* is somewhat indefinite in meaning, *craft* may be used in the singular: Our *craft* was moving at nine knots. More commonly, *craft* is a collective noun: hundreds of sailing *craft;* a lake full of small *craft;* a fleet of fishing *craft. Boat* is applied loosely to water*craft* of any size: to cross the river by ferry*boat;* to go to Europe by *boat;* to race a sail*boat.* In a narrow sense, *boat* is applied to any small, open *craft* propelled by oars, sails, or a portable engine: a row*boat;* a speed*boat;* a life*boat.* According to an old naval maxim, if a *vessel* can be hauled out of water it's a *boat;* otherwise, it's a *ship.*

These adjectives are comparable as they denote a capacity to produce or the power of producing, either in the biological or medical sense, or figuratively. The distinctions relate chiefly to the context in which they are used, although some hints are given by their etymology.

viable

fecund
fertile
fruitful
proliferous
prolific

Viable, from the French word *vie* (life), means capable of living and developing normally: a *viable* seed, egg, or newborn child. *Viable* has also been applied to anything thought of as being able to continue an independent existence, and in this sense has the meaning of workable or practicable: a *viable* plan or project; a *viable* arrangement.

Fertile goes back to the Latin *ferre*—bear, carry, bring—and means capable of producing or reproducing, whether in a material or figurative sense: a *fertile* woman; *fertile* soil; a *fertile* breed of cattle; a *fertile* imagination; *fertile* in ideas; a *fertile* resoucefulness in the face of difficulties. Note, however, that what is *viable* is not necessarily *fertile:* a seed or newborn child is *viable* but can become *fertile* only at a certain stage in its own development.

By extension, **fecund** suggests the actual productivity or yield of any *fertile* person or thing. [Queen Victoria was a very *fecund* woman; a *fecund* crop; *fecund* with ideas.] **Fruitful**, though often a close synonym of *fecund,* carries the idea of something that promotes further productivity along similar or related lines. [A properly fertilized soil is *fruitful* in crops; Newton's laws were *fruitful* for the future development of science; The lecture led to a *fruitful* discussion.]

Prolific is a contraction of a medieval Latin word with the literal meaning of make offspring or progeny. It is more widely used than *fecund* or *fruitful* to emphasize a rapid and abundant production of anything. [Rabbits are *prolific* animals; He comes of a *prolific* stock; Zola was a *prolific* writer of naturalistic novels.] **Proliferous**, coming from the same root as *fertile,* is generally restricted to biological and medical contexts: a *proliferous* growth of cells, buds, branches, or new tissue. See PREVALENT, WORKABLE.

Antonyms: *aborted, jejune,* STERILE, *stillborn, untenable.*

vibrate

  fluctuate
  oscillate
  sway
  swing
  undulate
  waver

These verbs refer to back-and-forth motion. **Vibrate**, the most general, suggests a rapid, continuing pulsation: feeling the train begin to *vibrate* with the steady roll of wheels along the track. **Oscillate**, a more formal term and often used in scientific contexts, applies to any regular shifting back and forth, as of a pendulum, or to any uncertain change of position: common stocks that *oscillate* in a cyclical way; attitudes that *oscillated* between extremes of despair and hope. Apart from technical contexts, and especially where uncertainty rather than regularity is intended, *oscillate* may sound stiff or ambiguous.

Swing, while much more informal, relates closely to *oscillate* in suggesting motion like that of a pendulum or of anything stationary at one end and free at the other: *swinging* apelike from vine to vine. Unlike *oscillate, swing* may suggest a curving movement, like that followed by a pendulum's weight: *swinging* the car around sharply to avoid being struck.

Undulate and **sway** are more specific than the foregoing verbs. *Undulate* suggests the slow, irregular alternation of swells and hollows in an elastic surface: smooth waves *undulating* across the bay. Unlike the other verbs treated here, *undulate* can also be applied to things completely at rest but composed of gentle swells and hollows: foothills that *undulate* gently along the highway. *Sway,* like *undulate,* may suggest the swelling and hollowing of a surface, but most specifically it suggests the slow back-and-forth movement of something standing upright: trees *swaying* in the first gusts of the storm. This contrasts with *swing,* which strongly suggests the movement of something attached at the top and free to move at the bottom, rather than vice versa.

Fluctuate and **waver** refer less to physical motion than to shifts in rate or changes of mind. *Fluctuate* suggests an irregular up-and-down motion or an uncertain or erratic course: stock prices that *fluctuate* for no apparent reason. *Waver* stresses indecisiveness or purposelessness: *wavering* between going to a movie and staying home. *Waver,* in referring to observable motion, suggests a faltering, unsteady course: the ragged caravan that *wavered* across the last mile of desert. See BOUNCE, ROTATE, SHAKE, TOTTER.

vindictive

  malevolent
  malicious
  mean
  rancorous
  resentful
  spiteful
  splenetic
  venomous

These adjectives characterize some of the least attractive aspects of human nature. **Vindictive** means spitefully vengeful, suggesting the harboring of grudges for imagined wrongs until the *vindictive* person, with satisfaction and perhaps even enjoyment, sees the object of his hatred suffer. **Spiteful** and **rancorous** emphasize the bitterness that attends feelings of malice and hate. *Rancorous* suggests a festering ill will, perhaps stemming from resentment over some real or fancied wrong. Unlike *vindictive* and *spiteful, rancorous* suggests a deep-rooted malice without implying a desire to hurt. **Resentful** is less intense than *spiteful,* since the *spiteful* person is actually prompted to vengeful acts, whereas the *resentful* person's indignant anger may be suppressed or inhibited. Indeed, resentment often arises from feelings of frustration akin to envy: The girl was *resentful* when the teacher selected another girl to be valedictorian; The *spiteful* boy deliberately broke the toy when he was told he couldn't keep it.]

Mean is applied to base or ungenerous feelings or actions. A *mean* person or attitude is small-minded, petty, and lacking in qualities of human consideration and fair play that we tend to regard as natural attributes of most people. [Their failure to invite the Harrises because they were poor was a *mean* act.] Related to this sense is the common informal use in the sense of vicious, ill-tempered, or dangerous: a *mean* gang, ready to mug and rob you if you're not careful.

Venomous and **splenetic** refer to feelings of malignant spite. *Venomous* retains some of its basic serpentine sense of able to give a poisonous sting, and thus stresses effect as well as motive. A *venomous* review of a book suggests sharp, biting, painfully acute criticism. It also suggests a personal and possibly *vindictive* motive, since the attack is too strenuous to issue from impartiality. *Splenetic* means fretfully *spiteful* or peevish. It relates to the traditional sense of spleen as the seat of various emotions, among them ill temper, melancholy, and spite. Thus, *splenetic* acts are moody and unpredictable, and stem from someone's nature or condition rather than from external causes. [The last words of the dying man were characteristically *splenetic:* "Hope to see you soon."]

Malicious and **malevolent** both imply the intent to do evil or to harm. *Malicious* is applied chiefly to actions and motives, *malevolent* to personal disposition. *Malevolent* has more sinister implications than *malicious,* implying a deep-seated antipathy that is manifested by wishing another ill: the *malevolent* nature of a miser; a cunning, *malevolent* smile; the *malicious* destruction of school property by vandals; a *malicious* lie. See ENMITY, RESENTMENT.

Antonyms: *benevolent, friendly,* GENEROUS, *genial, gracious,* HUMANE, *kind, well-meaning.*

vision

eyesight
perception
sight

These nouns refer to seeing, whether literal or metaphorical. **Vision**, at its most limited, can refer to the proper functioning of the eyes: 20-20 *vision;* cataracts that may blur *vision*. It can also indicate thoughtfulness, foresight, or sharpness of understanding: a woman of *vision*. **Sight** is a less formal term for *vision:* an injury that left her without *sight*. Both nouns

can also apply to something seen. *Vision,* here, would indicate something seen in a dream or hallucination, or something that may be illusory, imaginary, ideal, or supernatural: a *vision* that came to him in his sleep; a medium who summoned up a *vision* of his dead mother; her *vision* of a world free of war. *Sight,* here, may be a neutral reference to a look at something real: catching *sight* of the Statue of Liberty; the first *sight* he saw on debarking. More informally, it can indicate anything that looks odd or extraordinary: a badly overdressed woman who thought she looked a *vision* but was merely a *sight*.

Perception, like *vision,* can refer to seeing, but it is more general in referring as well to the action of any of the other senses: lacking *perception* of greens and reds; a sharp *perception* of mold and danger in the dark bedroom. *Perception* emphasizes not merely the registering of a phenomenon but the interpreting of it by the mind, often instantaneously: His trembling hands and blank stare confirmed her *perception* that the patient was extremely ill at ease. Carrying this tendency further, *perception,* like *vision,* can indicate any sharpness of understanding: a critic of keen *perception*.

Eyesight would seem to add nothing to the idea of *sight* itself, since no other organs than the eyes are able to see. Yet, *eyesight* is firmly established in usage: insured against the loss of *eyesight*. See LOOK, PERCEIVE, SEE, SENSATION.

vogue

fad
fashion
rage
trend

These nouns all refer to the prevailing acceptance or usage of things that are subject to change in form or style, as dress, décor, manners, etc. **Vogue** and **fashion** are sometimes used synonymously, but *vogue* is a more limited word than *fashion* in its stress on the amount of acceptance or usage of a way of dressing, decorating, etc., *Vogue* can designate a person or thing that enjoys temporary public approval: the comedian who became a *vogue* after one appearance on TV. It can refer to the approval itself: at a time when short hair and short skirts were both in *vogue*. It can also denote the period of the *vogue:* during the recent *vogue* of rap music. *Fashion,* more than *vogue,* is concerned with the clothing, furniture, behavior patterns, etc., in and of themselves. [Women's *fashions* of that era were unflattering and unfeminine; It has become the *fashion* for some members of royalty to appear as democratic as the average politician.] In reference to attire, *fashion* sometimes retains its original meaning of shape, mold, style, or make: I don't like the *fashion* of that coat. It also suggests the high social standing of people who are influential in establishing customs, making a style of dress popular, etc.: to be seen at the right places with people of *fashion*. A *fashion* that has a short but active life is a **fad**. It is the rapidity with which many people become interested and then lose interest in the *fashion* that distinguishes a *fad* from a *vogue:* The question in a clothing manufacturer's mind is whether short skirts will be a passing *fad* or a long-lived *fashion*. A **rage** is a *fad* that engenders great enthusiasm and, quite often, a lack of taste or judgment: a rock group that was a *rage* one week and a forgotten name the next. **Trend** literally means the general course, direction, or line of movement followed by a coastline, river, etc. By extension, *trend* refers to any general course, inclination, or tendency: to evaluate *trends* in modern education. More pertinent to this comparison is the meaning of a style or *vogue:* the *trend* toward bright colors and wild patterns in men's wear. See DRESS, STYLISH.

void

   abolish
   abrogate
   annul
   cancel
   invalidate
   negate
   nullify
   repeal
   rescind
   revoke

These verbs all mean put an end to something. **Void**, **abrogate**, and **cancel** are often used interchangeably with **invalidate** and with each other in specific contexts. To *invalidate* is to bring to an end the effectiveness of documents or claims. A faulty signature may *invalidate* a check. Evidence shown to be false may *invalidate* a claim in court. Negotiators may *void* disputed clauses in a contract, thereby *invalidating* its provisions. A government may *abrogate* a treaty, in effect *invalidating* it by declaring it no longer in force. A landlord may *cancel* a lease, thereby *invalidating* the tenant's claim to shelter and his own claim to payment.

   Abolish is applied to practices, conditions, or social institutions. [The Emancipation Proclamation *abolished* slavery; Most school systems long ago *abolished* corporal punishment.]

Nullify means prevent or end the effectiveness of some condition or activity. Often it means counterpose an action or a condition that renders an original action or condition futile or inoperative: Counterintelligence seeks to *nullify* the enemy's espionage efforts. **Negate**, as here considered, means prove an assertion false and thus render ineffective a claim based on it: The testimony of eyewitnesses *negated* the accused man's alibi. **Annul** either means end something existing or declare that it never really existed. A municipality may *annul* a charter and thus *abolish* its provisions. A court may *annul* a marriage, thus declaring that it never existed, rather than declaring a valid marriage at an end. To **repeal** and to **rescind** are to bring to an end the effect of a law or an order, respectively, and by depriving them or the authority behind them, *invalidate* them. The Twenty-first Amendment to the United States Constitution *repealed* the Eighteenth Amendment by declaring it no longer in effect. When issuing new regulations, a military headquarters may *rescind* earlier regulations governing the same subject.

   To **revoke** is to bring to an end something that has been authoritatively given, permitted, or granted. [Evidence of forgery *revoked* the Donation of Constantine, which purported to establish that the Emperor Constantine the Great gave the Western Roman Empire to the Papacy; King Louis XIV of France *revoked* the Edict of Nantes, in which King Henry IV had granted religious liberties to the French Huguenots; My license was *revoked* for driving while intoxicated.] See ERASE.

Antonyms: ENDORSE, *establish, legalize,* PERMIT, RECOVER, *reinstate, renew,* UPHOLD, *validate.*

vulgar

   coarse
   crude
   gross
   obscene

These adjectives are comparable in describing the character, speech, or actions of people who have in some way offended one's sensibilities or moral standards. **Vulgar** and **obscene** are similar in their suggestion of indelicacy or indecency. But *vulgar* points more to a lack of refinement or good taste, while *obscene* suggests a preoccupation with the pornographic: displaying shockingly *vulgar* table manners; a street person shouting *obscene* epithets.

   Literally, **coarse**, **crude**, and **gross** refer to physical properties and carry the idea of an absence of fineness or delicacy. *Coarse* suggests roughness: a *coarse* fabric. *Crude* points to rawness or a lack of preparation: *crude* oil. *Gross* is used in reference to excessive fat: *gross* features. In their figurative meanings, these three adjectives are applicable to persons and their behavior. *Coarse* and *crude* are like *vulgar* in indicating a lack of refinement, as in manners or language: *coarse* behavior that reflected complete absence of training in the rudiments of social conduct; a group of schoolboys making *crude* jokes about their teachers. *Gross*, the strongest in this respect, suggests a reversion to animal instincts: the *gross* behavior of an invading army. See INDECENT, SUGGESTIVE.

Antonyms: *EXQUISITE, POLITE.*

vulnerable

defenseless
exposed
untenable

These adjectives characterize something open to attack or left unprotected from possible harm. **Vulnerable**, the most wide-ranging of these, comes from a Latin verb meaning wound; reflecting its derivation, *vulnerable* can literally refer to the danger of physical wounding: the boxer's lowered guard left him *vulnerable* to a left jab. *Vulnerable* always stresses a lack of protection against physical or mental harm: an uncritical admiration of her teacher that left her *vulnerable* to exploitation. *Vulnerable* also is relevant in the context of argument, where it applies to an assertion that cannot be supported or corroborated or that is easily rebutted: a new policy statement *vulnerable* to attacks from left and right. In military strategy, *vulnerable* suggests a position that is liable to capture or encroachment by the enemy: attempts to lure the guerrillas into the open countryside, where they would be *vulnerable* to air attack; a *vulnerable* machine gun emplacement.

Defenseless refers strictly to an undesirable inability to ward off harm or danger. In this sense, it is more extreme than *vulnerable,* since it suggests an utter lack of protection or precaution, whereas *vulnerable* can suggest defenses inadequate to some danger or threat. [The most massive defense system would still leave the nation *vulnerable* to nuclear attack, though it might comfort average citizens to think they were not *defenseless.*] *Defenseless* also adds a note of complete helplessness: a *defenseless* child. **Exposed** emphasizes a lack of protection that might shield one from discomfort, harm, or danger: broken windows that left them *exposed* to the cold; a battle plan that left their left flank *exposed.* Sometimes, *exposed* can suggest an actual testing of something, whether or not the possibility of harm is involved: experiments in which rabbits were *exposed* to the drug. Sometimes, it is the risk rather than the harm that is emphasized: an attempt to track down everyone *exposed* to the bacillus; his odd ideas, which left him *exposed* to ridicule.

Untenable reflects its derivation from a French word in referring to what cannot be held, that is, defended or maintained. In the context of argument, *untenable* refers not only to a statement that may be refuted, as in the case of *vulnerable,* but to one that is inherently unsound. [Although the prosecution's case was *vulnerable,* the defense had chosen a line of reasoning that was inept and *untenable.*] In terms of military strategy or, by extension, any form of competition, *untenable* suggests a precarious position or deployment of forces that cannot resist attack: an *untenable* beachhead, *exposed* to attack on three sides. *Untenable* suggests a greater certainty of defeat than *vulnerable* and almost as much as *defenseless.* See POWERLESS, PROTECT, UPHOLD, WEAK.

Antonyms: *fortified, guarded,* IMPENETRABLE, *impregnable, invincible, protected, unassailable.*

walk

- amble
- saunter
- stride
- stroll
- strut
- swagger
- waddle

These verbs relate to ways people move on foot. All are of moderate informality. **Walk** is the most general and neutral of these, encompassing all manner of moving on foot short of running or leaping. **Stride** refers to a swift, purposeful way of *walking;* it suggests long steps and an energetic rhythm: *striding* through the depot well before the train would leave. **Amble**, **stroll**, and **saunter**, in sharp contrast with *stride,* suggest a slow, wandering movement without a clear-cut goal; each may furthermore suggest laziness, leisure, indecisiveness, or simply the enjoyment of *walking. Amble* emphasizes a leisurely but even movement, smooth and uninterrupted: *ambling* along without stopping at any of the displays. The smooth, swaying motion suggested derives from a horse's *amble,* in which two feet on one side are lifted together alternately with the two feet on the other side. *Stroll* emphasizes a slower movement, more wandering and aimless, with suggestions of many starts and pauses: *strolling* through the park with many a rest on benches they came across. *Saunter* suggests an even movement, like *amble,* but it indicates cheerfulness as well. One might *stroll* while attending to disagreeable thoughts, but one would hardly *saunter* in such a state of mind: whistling as he *sauntered* along the beach.

The rest of these verbs describe the manner of a person's walk rather than commenting on its larger intent. **Strut** and **swagger** intensify the cheerfulness of *saunter. Swagger* suggests showy overconfidence or egotism and functions mostly as a negative comment: *swaggering* before crowds of fans. *Strut* is even more disapproving in tone than *swagger,* suggesting an affected posture of bombastic self-importance: the candidate who *strutted* about the room like a latter-day Napoleon.

Waddle means *walk* with short steps, swaying from side to side like a duck. When applied to people, it suggests an awkward, laborious gait, such as that of a very fat person. See RUN, TOTTER.

wander

- meander
- ramble
- range
- roam
- rove
- stray

These verbs refer to motion or to travel that is slow, aimless, pointless, or without purpose or goal. **Wander** suggests a slow but possibly steady rate of movement. It usually indicates action that is idle or without purpose and is often applied to the movement of water, to travel, or to verbal discourse: a stream that *wandered* through the valley; nomadic tribes that *wander* through the desert from oasis to oasis; a disorganized speech that *wandered* from example to example without ever coming to the point. As can be seen, *wander* acquires a severely negative tone when applied to verbal discourse, emphasizing confusion or ineptitude.

In the same context, **meander** might suggest an amused rather than a disapproving tone: a backwoodsman whose anecdotes seemed to *meander* endlessly. More concretely, *meander* suggests the movement of water: brooks *meandering* through green meadows. *Meander* is less often used for travel, although here it can give a tone of amiable idleness: *meandering* around the theater district like a stage-struck child. When used in the context of travel, **ramble**, like *meander,* usually refers to a specific occasion rather than a habitual way of life. It can give a tone of pleasant relaxation, like *meander,* but is more concrete in suggesting a particular manner of walking, one in which a sauntering gait is linked with a start-and-stop unevenness of speed: We went *rambling* through the park every weekend; a couple who liked to *ramble* about the ancient ruins in search of a secluded picnic spot. When used of discourse, however, *ramble* takes on a negative tone like that of *wander,* referring specifically to any presentation in language that is lengthy, poorly organized, and full of digressions: yawning while his friend *rambled* on about one trivial grievance after another; an essay that *rambles* too much to have any persuasive force.

Unlike the previous verbs, **roam** and **range** may both suggest a more serious purpose behind the uneven or circuitous movement. [He *roamed* through six states in search of his lost brother; The student's report *ranged* through a dozen cultures that supported his thesis.] *Roam,* like *ramble,* can be used to indicate a pleasant stroll: *roaming* about the hills and enjoying the wildflowers. The implication of making a thorough search or having some other specific purpose in mind, however, is seldom completely absent: *roaming* about dusty museums in search of unauthenticated paintings. *Roam* is furthermore the only verb here that is specifically associated with the grazing or foraging activity of horses and other animals: letting her horse *roam* free so it could eat its fill of prairie grass. *Range* implies a thorough or systematic movement over a wide area: His search *ranged* over three continents and twice took him across the Pacific Ocean. More often it refers to a sorting through or presenting of diverse ideas. More formal than *roam, range* also suggests more certainty of purpose, a deliberately various course, and a wide grasp of far-flung materials: books *ranging* from popular fiction to learned treatises.

Rove and **stray** both most readily suggest negative aspects of idle movement. *Rove* can sometimes indicate, with an effect of cuteness, the pleasant overtones of *meander* or *ramble*. Often it suggests a greater intensity or a more clearly defined goal, but particularly a more fickle attitude toward the experience at hand. As such, *rove* often suggests a cynical inconstancy in love: always on the go, *roving* from one lover to another, never satisfied for long. *Stray,* by contrast, is the one verb here that specifically emphasizes someone who is lost or off-course; with this sense, *stray* can apply in any context, including those that circumscribe other verbs here: constantly *straying* from the main point of her talk; to *stray* from the prescribed route laid down by one's guide. Like *rove, stray* may refer to unfaithfulness in love; more generally, it refers to sinfulness of any sort: earnestly trying to win back a spouse who has *strayed;* inevitable that the party would *stray* from its original high principles. See CIRCUMLOCUTION, EXTEND, WALK.

Antonyms: REMAIN, *rest, settle.*

wane

ebb
fade
slacken

These verbs refer to a gradual decrease in quantity, size, rate, or intensity. **Wane** is used most concretely to describe the slow decrease in the bright portion of the moon after its full phase. It is widely used as well, however, for any process of attrition: watching the patient's stamina *wane* day by day; hoping the enemy's morale would *wane* as the siege continued. In such uses there is no implication of a cyclical recovery, as is true of the moon. **Fade** implies even more strongly an

irreversible process. Most concretely, it refers to a loss of intensity or distinctness in color or marking. The process suggested might be more drawn out than for *wane:* a memory that *faded* year by year. *Fade,* in fact, is often used to suggest attrition caused by the passage of time: a striking talent that the years had *faded.* **Ebb** refers to the running out of a tide; even in other uses, the reference is often to a diminished rate of flow: a pulse that *ebbed* and became almost indistinct. In general, *ebb* suggests a shorter period of time than *wane,* thus contrasting strongly with *fade.* On the other hand, both *ebb* and *fade* refer most often to a decline from a better to a worse state, whereas *wane* can be applied more widely: waiting for her anger to *wane* and her good humor to return. Inconsistently enough, however, *ebb* is sometimes used to suggest a slow recovery: feeling her strength *ebb* back.

Slacken is far less concrete than the previous verbs, referring neutrally to any slow decrease. *Slacken* suggests a decrease in rate, volume, or pressure: in the summer when the hectic pace *slackens* a bit. *Slacken,* unlike the foregoing verbs, may suggest a voluntary adjustment: *slackening* my stride so the child could catch up with me. See DECREASE, LESSEN, REDUCE, WEAKEN.

Antonyms: *brighten,* ENLARGE, *mount, multiply, rise, wax.*

want

beggary
destitution
indigence
pauperism
penury
poverty
privation

These nouns refer to a lack of what is desirable for or necessary to a decent standard of living. **Want** is the most general of these; as an abstract noun, it indicates an unwilling and harmful lack of the necessities of life: faces pinched by *want;* the people of the world who are seen as doomed to disease-ridden lives of *want. Want* can also be used apart from an economic context to refer to any sort of desire, whether momentary or abiding, whether deeply felt or trivial: returning to their homeland became for them a lifelong *want;* a man who caters to my every *want.* **Pauperism** and **beggary** concentrate on economic *want,* but both have become dated, since the forms of hardship they refer to are now less common. *Pauperism* refers to someone who, utterly without resources, has become a public charge; *beggary* refers to such a person who, while not a public charge, makes public appeals for money or handouts. Nowadays, the pauper would more likely be called a welfare client, the beggar a panhandler. Similarly, their condition would be referred to by one of the nouns discussed below. Either *pauperism* or *beggary*, however, may still be used for its strong connotation of helpless dependence on others: fearing that his ex-wives would reduce him to *pauperism* (or *beggary*).

Of the remaining nouns, **indigence** indicates the mildest degree of economic *want*, referring to the condition of someone who is poor and lacks ordinary comforts but is not desperate for the means to sustain life: a recession that reduced many families to a state of *indigence*. **Poverty** can indicate a more severe state of economic *want* than *indigence*: those living in *poverty* seldom have the means to acquire adequate food, clothing, or shelter. *Poverty* can, however, function as a generic term that includes all forms and degrees of economic *want*: the federal government's oft-announced war on *poverty*.

Penury indicates a state of *poverty* that cramps or hampers normal life; thus, it points specifically to a degree of *want* more severe than *indigence*. Even more severe is the state indicated by **privation**, in which the economic hardship has become painful or harmful: a life of ignominious *penury* wherein the loss of a few coins was tantamount to disaster; permanent damage to the body and brain because of malnutrition resulting from extended *privation* in childhood.

Destitution is the most severe of all these nouns in pointing to a state of *poverty* so harsh as to endanger life: the utter *destitution* of the peasants on the eve of the French Revolution. See INSOLVENT, PENNILESS, POOR.

Antonyms: *affluence, opulence, plenty, prosperity, solvency, wealth.*

want
covet
crave
desire
wish

These verbs refer to feelings of need for some sort of object or satisfaction. **Want**, the most general and informal, can range in intensity from expressing a weak preference or inclination to the most extreme states of need or passion: asking if he *wanted* more butter; not *wanting* to go to a movie; *wanting* the new sports car more than anything else in the world. *Want* can also express, more simply, a lack of the necessities of life, whether consciously expressed or not: peasants who *wanted* food, clothing, and decent homes.

Wish is also very general and wide-ranging in application. It can suggest mental fantasy, as in a daydream, and can express regret for past action or hopes about the future, whether realistic or not: *wishing* a Prince Charming would come along and rescue her from her drab existence; *wishing* he hadn't made a fool of himself the night before; *wishing* to do well on the exam tomorrow; *wishing* that one day she would be a millionaire. *Wish* can also be used as a slightly more formal equivalent of *want*: Do you *wish* another helping of meat?

Desire can also function as a more formal substitute for *want*: asking if he *desired* another drink; the many people who *desire* better education for their children. The special province of *desire*, however, is in referring to sexual or sensual appetite or need: a growing sexual hunger that more and more *desired* expression; *desiring* her intensely; *desiring* all sorts of sybaritic pleasures.

Crave relates most concretely to hunger: surprised to find himself *craving* a taste of Mexican food. *Crave* is widely used in other ways, however, to suggest either a mild hankering or a gnawing inclination: *craving* a change of pace in their humdrum life. It can even, by an analogy comparing hunger to sexual appetite, refer unambiguously to intense erotic need: *craving* another long kiss and close embrace. In this case, it stresses mere appetite, whereas *desire* might sometimes more inclusively suggest a tincture of love and affection as well. **Covet** most specifically refers to a longing to possess the material goods or anything that rightfully belongs to someone else: *coveting* her neighbor's land; *coveting* his friend's wife. As now used, *covet* may suggest a feeling as weak as that indicated by *wish* or as persistent as that suggested by *craving*. It may suggest harmless envy or a poisonous determination to possess: *coveting* the exuberance of the other people at the party; *coveting* the rare book that lay before her. See EAGER, EMOTION, EROTIC, GREEDY, HOPE, YEARN.

warm
lukewarm
muggy
stuffy
tepid

These adjectives suggest a temperature midway between cold and hot. **Warm**, the most general of these, can have positive, neutral, or negative force, depending on context: pointing out that the champagne was still *warm;* offering to reheat the *warm* coffee; a *warm,* cheery fire; an uncomfortably *warm* room. In reference to emotions, *warm* has an exclusively positive tone, indicating sincere interest or affection: our *warmest* regards.

Lukewarm and **tepid** at their most literal refer more neutrally to things that are not too hot. Of the two, *lukewarm* is less formal and more clear in its neutral emphasis on description: fabrics that must be washed in *lukewarm* water. *Tepid* more readily permits implications that something is too cool: water that had become too *tepid* for washing dishes. Both may refer to halfhearted or indifferent feelings. *Lukewarm* suggests interest that remains mild: *lukewarm* reviews of the play. *Tepid* is more emphatic in suggesting a lack of animation or enthusiasm: *tepid* evenings spent with dull people.

Muggy and **stuffy** both refer mainly to an unpleasantly warm atmosphere or weather. *Muggy* emphasizes warmth accompanied by oppressive humidity: staying *muggy* for days after the hot spell was over. *Stuffy* is restricted specifically to an *overwarm* and poorly ventilated area, usually indoors: becoming *stuffy* in the crowded lecture hall; the *stuffy,* airless bedroom. See HOT, HUMID, PASSIONATE.

Antonyms: *COLD.*

waste

    debris
    garbage
    junk
    pollutant
    refuse
    rubbish
    trash

These nouns refer to cast-off remains or leavings. **Waste** is the most general, referring to anything left over from some process, regardless of whether it can be used in some other process: bundling and selling the piles of newspapers as *waste;* more sophisticated sewage plants to process human *wastes.* **Refuse** suggests an accumulation of broken or unusable objects, especially bulky ones: a pool now filled with old tires, bottles, cans, and other *refuse.* **Rubbish** suggests a collection of items less bulky than *refuse* and may imply, as is not necessarily so with *refuse,* used-up remnants collected specifically for disposal: shoving sacks of *rubbish* down the incinerator. Sometimes *rubbish* is distinguished from *refuse* as being burnable, but this is not universally true. **Garbage** is the most

specific of these nouns, referring almost exclusively to uneaten or inedible remains from the kitchen that must be disposed of before they become a sanitary problem. By contrast, *rubbish* does not imply the same necessity for disposal, since it refers largely to undegradable materials.

Pollutants refers specifically to chemicals or industrial *wastes* that are emptied into waterways, sewers, or the air and result in environmental damage: *pollutants* from the exhausts of cars and buses; chemical *pollutants* from a single factory that kill thousands of fish annually. **Debris** refers to the random piling up or scattering of extremely bulky remnants or pieces of wreckage: a plane crash that scattered *debris* over several square miles; *debris* left behind after the construction job. *Debris,* like *refuse,* can be used for less sizable items, but in this case it still implies a random or bit-by-bit scattering: *debris* carelessly tossed into the ditches along our roads.

Junk and **trash** can both refer to worn-out or worthless castoffs. In an industrial context, *junk* can refer to old cars and other large machines collected for the reusable parts or metals in them. In a housekeeping context, *junk* can refer to smaller items of little or no value: broken teacups and other *junk.* *Trash* is close to *refuse* in its generality, but it suggests a collection of heterogeneous items of small size: After cleaning the attic, we swept up the *trash*, put it into the *garbage* pail, and hauled stacks of *junk* to the dump.

wave

    billow
    breaker
    chop
    comber
    ripple
    roller
    surge
    tsunami

These nouns denote upheaval of the ocean's surface. **Wave** is the general term, applying to any ridge or undulation moving on the surface of a liquid. A **ripple** is a very small *wave,* such as might be produced by a light breeze, or by an object dropping into still water. A **chop** is one of many small, irregular *waves* produced by opposing forces, as tide and wind. **Billow** is a poetic word for any *wave,* but especially for a *wave* of great height. A **roller** is one of the long, irregular *waves* that move swiftly outward from a storm center. High, curling *rollers,* such as those that produce whitecaps, are called **combers**. A *wave* that curls over into a mass of foam as it strikes the shore is a **breaker**.

Surge is the vaguest of these nouns; it is sometimes applied to a series of *breakers,* and sometimes to the rise and fall of the water's surface under any kind of *waves.* A **tsunami** is an extraordinarily large sea wave that is produced by an earthquake or by undersea volcanic eruption.

Wave, of course, has other uses that depend on particular aspects of its basic sense. The visual aspect is emphasized, somewhat poetically, in its application to any series of curves suggesting *waves* of the ocean: *waves* of grain. The turbulent power and regularity of *waves* are emphasized in the application of *wave* to a period of excitement or activity: A *wave* of enthusiasm swept the nation.

waylay
ambush
surprise

The verbs **waylay** and **ambush** mean attack suddenly from a place of hiding. *Waylay* is generally used when a person is set upon by robbers, assassins, etc., who have been lying in wait: armed thugs *waylaying* tourists who have lost their way. *Ambush* suggests that the object of attack is a military enemy: In guerrilla warfare, small contingents frequently *ambush* larger forces.

In the context of this discussion, the verb **surprise** means attack an enemy without warning, often but not necessarily from a place of hiding: Washington crossed the Delaware to *surprise* the British at Trenton. See ATTACK, CAPTURE, GRASP.

weak
debilitated
decrepit
feeble
frail
infirm

These adjectives refer to lack of strength or health or to an inability to bear strain or pressure. **Weak,** the most general of these, carries no implications as to how the lack of strength came about. It may be used in a purely physical sense: *weak* and dizzy after a fainting spell; born with *weak* eyesight; walls too *weak* to bear their own weight. Or it may refer to a lack of mental or moral strength, indicating instability of character or deficient willpower: a *weak* youth, easily led astray by bad associates. Sometimes, however, *weak* points to a lack of influence or authority: a government with a *weak* executive branch and strong legislature. Or, generally, it may refer to any lack of normal power, strength, or potency: a *weak* voice; *weak* coffee; a *weak* heart; a *weak* link in a chain.

Frail, when used of a person, stresses an extremely slender, delicate, or sickly physique: *frail* and undernourished children who stare out at us from the tenement. In other situations, *frail* suggests something easily broken or unable to resist an opposing force: *frail* columns long ago snapped in two; a *frail* theory that even the average student can refute. **Infirm** concentrates on a lack of soundness that is either inherent or results from aging, illness, or the like: an *infirm* constitution inherited from his father's family; a mind grown *infirm* with poverty, sickness, and old age. Used more abstractly, *infirm* suggests a thoroughgoing faultiness resulting from incorrect methods of working: *infirm* conclusions based on distortions of the evidence. It may also point to a lack of stability or firmness, meaning irresolute or insecure: *infirm* of purpose; an *infirm* prop.

Feeble suggests a lack of strength that results in a fitful but always subnormal performance marked by a pitiable lack of alertness or resilience: a hand so *feeble* it could scarcely lift the cup from its saucer; *feeble-minded.* When used of the human body, *feeble* generally suggests that a process of attrition has occurred. Used literally of things, *feeble* may mean faint or inadequate: a *feeble* light; a *feeble* cry; a *feeble* defense system. Used of abstract qualities or of ideas, *feeble* points to ineffectualness, pointlessness, or pitiable performance: a *feeble* effort at courtesy; a *feeble* joke; a *feeble* interpretation of the play.

Debilitated and **decrepit** specifically suggest the sapping of strength formerly present. *Debilitated* is more general in applying to any result of such a process: a body *debilitated* by disease; a house *debilitated* by long exposure to the elements. *Decrepit* specifically restricts itself to a loss of strength or usefulness because of advanced age: *decrepit* dodderers in the rest home; stairs so *decrepit* that they groaned under a child's weight. See BONY, FLIMSY, FRAGILE, POWERLESS, SICKNESS.

Antonyms: *energetic, hardy,* HEALTHY, HUSKY, *resolute, stout, strong, sturdy, tough.*

weaken
deplete
enervate
enfeeble
exhaust
sap
spend

Weaken, the most general verb of this group, refers to the lessening of strength or power of a person, organization, or force. [The majority party was *weakened* by the defection of several leading senators; He was so *weakened* by the disease that he could barely stand up.] **Enervate** and **sap** both mean lessen the vitality or strength of, and are applied only to people. *Sap* implies a gradual or insidious loss of strength; *enervate* focuses on a loss of vitality and a general lassitude, as after an illness, during a spell of hot weather, or because of a loss of moral fiber. [The emotional strain of attending to the dying man *sapped* all my strength; After her illness, she felt *enervated* and listless; The youth was *enervated* by dissipation.] **Enfeeble** is like *enervate* and *sap* in being used chiefly of human beings. It differs, though, in indicating an extreme *weakening,* as through long, debilitating illness or serious deprivation, and in suggesting a resultant helplessness: *enfeebled* by the spread of the cancer; prisoners of war *enfeebled* by undernourishment.

Exhaust means use up and empty utterly, while **deplete** means lower the resources of a thing. To *deplete* one's store of ammunition is to lower it to the point of danger; to *exhaust* it is to have none left. *Deplete* is often used of natural resources to express alarm at the wasteful use of unrecoverable materials: a bill that would prevent our preserve of virgin timberland from being further *depleted*. Where *deplete* refers to quantities, *exhaust* may also refer to qualities that cannot be measured. **Spend** is close to *exhaust,* but shares with *sap* the connotation of gradual exhaustion, a using up by degrees. [The candidate's energy was *spent* after two months of campaigning.] *Spend* and *exhaust* may apply to anything giving power. [The fuel was *spent* (or *exhausted*).] *Sap* and *enervate,* on the other hand, are always associated with life or with the life-giving spirit, and cannot be used of nonvital processes. [The fruitless battle to protect his reputation *sapped* his strength and *enervated* his spirit.] See DECREASE, HARM, LESSEN, LISTLESS, REDUCE, TIRED, WANE.

Antonyms: *energize, invigorate, replenish, revitalize, strengthen, vitalize.*

wealth
    assets
    chattels
    estate
    goods
    means
    property
    resources

These nouns refer to what one owns or has, as money, land, or other possessions of value. **Wealth,** considered in its concrete rather than its abstract sense, is a broad term meaning a store or accumulation of anything that people desire to possess. It is used especially of material things having economic utility or monetary value, and may be applied to individuals, groups, or inanimate entities: a man of *wealth;* a nation's *wealth.* In a broader sense, *wealth* may refer to the possession of nonmaterial things of value and may indicate a great abundance of anything: a *wealth* of experience; a *wealth* of learning.

The other nouns in this set are used to denote specific kinds of *wealth.* **Property** and **estate** generally refer to material possessions. *Property* is the broader term, referring to any object of value a person or group may lawfully acquire and own: private *property;* government *property. Property* may be either real or personal; that is, it may consist of *wealth* regarded as immovable or permanent, as land or buildings, or of *wealth* regarded as movable or temporary, as jewelry, books, furniture, and the like. *Estate* may refer to a usually extensive piece of landed *property* or to the residence built upon it: a country *estate.* In another sense, *estate* designates the entire *property* and possessions of a dead person or of a bankrupt: to settle creditors' claims against the *estate.* Certain intangible rights are also referred to as *property,* as copyrights, patents, and the like, and may be included in a deceased person's *estate.*

Assets is a legal and commercial term used to designate sources of *wealth* as opposed to liabilities. The *assets* of a person, partnership, or corporation are all of the real and personal *property* that could be converted into money if necessary for the payment of debts or legacies. In a literal sense, land, buildings, furniture, supplies, equipment, stocks, bonds, and savings are *assets.* By extension, useful characteristics and attributes are often referred to as *assets:* An outgoing personality is surely an *asset* in a sales career.

Means and **resources** are *wealth,* particularly material possessions, that can be readily used for general or specific purposes. A person of *means* is presumed to possess money or negotiable *assets* sufficient to procure satisfactions well beyond bare necessities. *Means* is sometimes qualified to indicate strictly limited funds: working men and women of slender *means.* Or it may simply refer to one's budget or to money available for spending: an expenditure beyond her *means;* to give children equal opportunity for education, regardless of their families' *means. Resources* implies the existence of a reserve supply of *wealth* or assets that can be drawn upon when needed. An individual's *resources* may include a bank account, business, and credit standing. A nation's natural *resources* include its raw materials, as water, oil, metals, and fertile soil, as well as its human *wealth*, as its scientists, artists, and trained workers. *Resources* can also refer to a person's skill and ingenuity in handling problems and dealing with situations: someone of many *resources*, invaluable in an emergency.

Goods is a limited term, referring to personal and movable *property*. It is usually reserved for merchandise or other salable wares. **Chattels** is broader than *goods* but is now generally limited to legal use. *Chattels* include *goods* and such other forms of *wealth* as promissory notes, mortgages, bonds, and the like. See CREATIVE, MEANS, POSSESS.

Antonyms: *debts, liabilities,* WANT.

wealthy

affluent
flush
loaded
opulent
prosperous
rich
successful

These adjectives all characterize people who possess a large share of money, real-estate holdings, and other things of value. **Wealthy** and **rich** are the most general of the terms that specifically apply to owning goods or having money. To call persons *wealthy* often suggests that they are established and prominent members of the community: one of our *wealthiest* citizens. *Rich* is blunter in tone and indicates only the possession of many goods or much money; it is therefore more forceful when the purpose is to emphasize the great extent of someone's wealth. [He was not merely *wealthy*—he was *rich;* By astute manipulation of her stocks she became a *rich* woman before she was forty.] *Wealthy* can be used flexibly to describe various levels of wealth: a moderately *wealthy* family. *Rich*, on the other hand, is an either-or word; one is either *rich* or not *rich;* although one can be very *rich*, seldom is one spoken of as being moderately *rich*. *Rich*, unlike *wealthy*, is widely used in extended senses to mean full, pregnant, or abundant: a *rich* find of rare minerals; a full, *rich* voice; an experience *rich* with meaning.

Affluent and **opulent** are formal words derived from the Latin words meaning, respectively, to flow, and power or wealth. *Affluent* thus suggests an abun-

dant flow of goods or riches, whereas *opulent* has a strong connotation of ostentation or showy display of wealth: an *affluent* community where every family owned at least three cars; an *opulent* tapestry woven with gold and silver threads. *Opulent* most often refers to the products of wealth, whereas *affluent* describes people or human societies that possess wealth.

The less formal **flush** and the slang **loaded** mean having plenty of money, especially money on hand at a particular time. [*Flush* with their race-track winnings, they went on a spending spree; We just got paid so we were all *loaded.*] *Loaded* may also mean simply *rich*, in the sense of having a lot of money. Both these adjectives differ from the others here considered in referring exclusively to money.

Prosperous and **successful**, while implying the acquisition of wealth, do not indicate simply the possession of money and goods. *Prosperous* means thriving or flourishing, and suggests a temporary or developing state of affairs: a *prosperous* farmer; a *prosperous* period of industrial growth; a *prosperous* business community. A *prosperous* person or group need not be *rich* nor even moderately *wealthy*, but merely one whose economic situation is relatively good or on the rise: The child felt *prosperous* when he found a dollar in the street. *Successful* moves one step further in broadening the context to include wealth as just one facet of meaning. As here considered, *successful* combines the sense of *prosperous* with the fulfillment of certain goals or ambitions, independent of wealth, and thus connotes a greater degree of stability or permanence than *prosperous; successful* bankers, for instance, are those who have achieved prominence in their field, whereas *prosperous* bankers are those who are doing well financially. Nevertheless, since success is often measured by one's wealth, the role of wealth in determining what *successful* means is not to be minimized; it is hard to conceive of a *rich* man or woman who will not be considered *successful* by most people, but it is not hard to imagine someone or something that is *successful* but not *rich:* a *successful* business in which the profit margin is small but reliable; A *successful* character actor for many years, he managed to live on his income by practicing frugality. See OUTSTANDING, PREVALENT.

Antonyms: *destitute,* INSOLVENT, *penurious,* POOR.

weep

blubber
cry
sob

weep *(continued)*

wail
whimper

These verbs all denote the inarticulate sounds and shedding of tears indicative of grief, pain, or other strong emotions. **Weep** and **cry** are close synonyms and are often used interchangeably. *Weep* is more often used in writing than in speech and gives greater emphasis to the shedding of tears than to the accompanying sounds. *Cry* usually gives primary emphasis to the sounds although, paradoxically, it may also describe the act of silently shedding tears. [She *wept* copiously over the death of her dog; She *cried* loudly in despair; The child *cried* himself to sleep.] *Cry* does not always indicate depth of feeling: The baby *cried* loudly after draining his bottle. Babies never *weep*. Both *weep* and *cry* can describe a variety of emotions: to *weep* with joy; to *cry* with fright; to *cry* from exhaustion.

Sob and **whimper** describe different varieties of *weeping*. To *sob* is to *weep* with audible convulsive catches of breath and the heaving of one's chest. *Sobbing* is usually accompanied by gasps and is akin to sighing. *Sob*, more than *weep* or *cry*, implies pathetic circumstances: The movie ends with the heroine *sobbing* desperately as her daughter dies in her arms. To *whimper* is to *cry* or whine with plaintive broken sounds; *whimper* introduces the suggestion of defenselessness or timidity and is most often associated with fright: a lost child *whimpering* for his mother. But *whimper* can also criticize ill-humored, unfounded, or self-pitying complaints: those who *whimper* about high taxes.

Blubber and **wail** stress the sounds accompanying *weeping*. *Blubber* means *weep* or *sob* noisily; *blubber* reflects an attitude of ridicule or contempt on the part of the person using the verb, and is thus more abusive than descriptive, although in some contexts it may be used humorously to emphasize the inappropriate loudness of the *weeping*. [I *blubber* like a baby at sentimental movies; A child your age shouldn't sit around *blubbering* over a lost toy.] *Wail* suggests a loud, unbroken, usually high-pitched *cry*. *Wailing* is traditionally associated with grief; a *wail* is a formal *cry* of mourning. Nowadays, however, *wail* is most often used to describe any sad or melancholy sound, whether in grief or not. Otherwise, it is used more informally, like *blubber*, as a term of contempt, implying a weak, self-pitying attitude: *wailing* as though he were dying every time he stubbed a toe.

All these verbs are also used to mean to say while *weeping, crying, sobbing*, etc. ["I don't have a home," she *wept*; He *blubbered* something about a package he'd lost.] See GRIEVE, SAD.

Antonyms: *rejoice*.

whim

caprice
crotchet
vagary
whimsy

The nouns **whim**, **caprice**, and **vagary** are all sudden and sometimes irrational notions, especially impulses to do something. A *whim* is a passing fancy or wish, often fantastic or odd. [On the first day of spring, the *whim* struck him to wear a carnation on his lapel; Queen Elizabeth I, although expert in statecraft, tended in private to indulge in foolish *whims*.] *Caprice*, stemming from the Latin word for goat, is a sudden change of mood, opinion, or purpose without apparent motivation. As implied by its etymology, *caprice* suggests an insistence upon having one's own way: a baby-sitter trying to control the *caprices* of a willful little girl; a patient whose various *caprices* against obeying the doctor's orders delayed his recovery. *Vagary* originally meant a journey or a rambling about and still suggests strongly unpredictable, erratic, or even irresponsible behavior: the *vagaries* of an employee who is usually late and always lazy. It is a stronger term than either *whim* or *caprice*. *Whim, vagary,* and *caprice* may also be used in figurative senses: to sail at the *whim* of tide and wind; the *caprices* of fortune; the *vagaries* of April weather.

A **crotchet** is a perverse idea or opinion about a particular subject and held obstinately despite its obvious untruth or contradiction to common opinion. [Mr. Midwick was well off, but his *crotchet* was that skimping on butter was a virtue.] *Crotchets* often concern minor points of doctrine or belief or merely trivial matters. [There is no *crotchet* so ridiculous nor any idea so silly that it cannot find wide acceptance.]

Whimsy, once considered a synonym of *whim*, now is applied almost exclusively to an odd, fanciful style of humor that delights and astonishes. *Whimsy* may appear in speech or actions, but it is more likely to occur in literature: the *whimsy* of Lewis Carroll; the whimsy of *The Wind in the Willows*. *Whimsy* may range from charming fancy to tongue-in-cheek drollery. See ECCENTRICITY, HOPE.

wild

feral
ferocious

fierce
savage

These adjectives describe actions, appearances, or living things that display brutality, violence, or lack of restraint. **Wild** is sometimes used loosely as a substitute for the other adjectives in this group: a *wild* tiger; *wild* eyes; a *wild* rage. Strictly speaking, that which is *wild* is simply unrestrained and often implies no anger or harshness: *wild* delight; *wild* terror; the *wild* west wind.

Feral, from its original application to an undomesticated or untamed animal, carries the suggestion when applied to people of the behavior of a beast of prey: the *feral* attack of an assassin in a dark alley; the *feral* appetites of those who enjoy watching public executions.

Fierce, in this sense, is applied mostly to people or animals who are frightening to others because of a forbidding aspect or the violence of their actions. [An angry gorilla has a *fierce* roar; My grandfather became *fierce* when he lost his temper; To be a good watchdog, a dog must be *fierce* toward strangers.]

Ferocious always denotes a tendency to violence or viciousness. It is more distinctly bloodthirsty than is *fierce*: the *ferocious* crocodile. Whereas *fierce* suggests vehemence and lack of control, *ferocious* implies an animalistic wildness that is extremely menacing: a *ferocious* man-eating tiger; a *fierce* dog. Fierce may also describe actions: a *fierce* battle in which both sides suffered heavy losses.

Savage emphasizes lack of training and a lack of those restraints practiced by civilized people in controlling their aggressive impulses: to make a *savage* attack against a political opponent; to be *savage* in one's revenge. More basically, it means not domesticated: *savage* animals.

Ferocious, fierce, and *savage* are all used in an exaggerated and sometimes playful sense to describe things that cause discomfort or excite anxiety: the *ferocious* heat of a July day; a *fierce* final examination; the *savage* crowding in a city slum. See CRUEL, UNRULY.
Antonyms: DOCILE, *domesticated, gentle, harmless,* TIMID.

willful

firm
hardheaded
hard-nosed
no-nonsense
strong-willed
tenacious
tough

These adjectives all describe more or less uncom-

promising or fixed states of mind. The differences between them reveal that obstinacy in itself can be adjudged either good or bad, depending on the motive behind it and the uses to which it is put.

Willful means bent on having one's own way, and therefore careless or indifferent of other people's feelings or wishes. It has critical if not damning implications, but is somewhat mitigated by its common association with children: The *willful* child insisted on wearing yellow socks with his blue trousers. When applied to adults, *willful* may be considered a sign of immaturity or unreasonable conceit: a *willful* decision, taken without regard to the welfare of the community. **Strong-willed**, on the other hand, is usually taken to be complimentary, especially if the person indicated is a man: a *strong-willed* leader of men. It is also used, however, to imply criticism less strong than *willful*, perhaps mixed with a certain degree of admiration. [Robert is very *strong-willed*; once he has made up his mind, he won't change it.]

Firm is decidedly favorable in tone. It means fixed and unshakable, and often implies deep commitment to a moral principle: a *firm* resolve to spend two hours each evening as a volunteer at the community center; a *firm* commitment to civil rights. *Firm* is also commonly used as a euphemism for obstinate, because it substitutes the motive of high moral dedication for willfulness or self-seeking; indeed, whether one calls people *firm* or stigmatizes them with a less attractive adjective depends upon whether one happens to share their convictions. Politicians are known for being *firm* (believers in democracy, supporters of the president, upholders of free enterprise, etc.). **Tenacious**, meaning tending to hold strongly, as opinions, rights, etc., is also much favored by men and women in the public eye: a *tenacious* defender of states' rights. *Tenacious* has the implication of hanging on, refusing to let go no matter what the odds against eventual victory. This can be interpreted as blind stubbornness or as fierce devotion to principle. Nevertheless, *tenacious* always conveys some respect; a *tenacious* adversary, for instance, may be disliked but certainly is not to be taken lightly.

Hardheaded, **hard-nosed**, **no-nonsense**, and **tough** all describe practical, businesslike, or ruthless attitudes All are on the whole favorable in tone, since all suggest that the people so characterized are doers, people who care primarily about results rather than about the means by which they are achieved. *Hardheaded* means having a shrewd and practical mind; *hardheaded* executives are not given to sentiment or to much thought about human feelings, although they are not necessarily unkind or inhuman. They simply regard such considerations as not worth thinking about. *Hard-nosed* was originally carnival slang and meant stubborn. In recent uses it appears to mean experienced, hard-bitten, unyielding, even ruthless in the pursuit of a practical objective: *a hard-nosed* approach to government spending; the stereotyped *hard-nosed* drill sergeant. *No-nonsense* means without time-consuming formalities or the rigmarole of polite intercourse and indicates a straight, blunt, even gruff approach, with the aim of getting things done quickly and efficiently even at the price of wounding someone's feelings or offending protocol. **Tough** in its primary sense means capable of sustaining great tension or strain without breaking. If one thinks of emotional rather than physical tension or strain, one has an excellent definition of its common colloquial use applied to people who are deemed shrewd and canny, not easily fooled or worn down by argument: a *tough* negotiator; a *tough* competitor. *Tough* and *no-nonsense* often appear together in informal or self-consciously modern writing: a *tough, no-nonsense* labor leader; A *tough, no-nonsense* take-charge administrator was needed to head the public housing program. See IMPERTURBABLE, OPPORTUNISTIC, STUBBORN.

Antonyms: *accommodating,* ADAPTABLE, COMPLIANT, DOCILE, *easygoing,* NAIVE, *tender,* TIMID, WEAK.

wind

    blizzard
    breeze
    cyclone
    gale
    hurricane
    squall
    storm
    tempest
    tornado
    twister
    typhoon
    whirlwind
    windstorm

The noun **wind** and its synonyms are terms for natural movements of air. **Windstorm** is a general term for movements of air that are so strong as to be a source of concern.

Breeze is a general term for a light *wind;* it is also, as are some of the other nouns treated here, defined precisely by the Beaufort meteorological scale, which is used by the U.S. Weather Bureau. The Beaufort scale defines a *breeze* as a *wind* having a velocity of between 4 and 31 miles an hour; *breezes* are further defined as light (4–7 miles per hour), gentle (8–12), moderate (13–18), fresh (19–24), and strong (25–31).

Gale is a general term for a very strong *wind* capable of doing considerable damage to property and usually regarded as hazardous for small craft at sea. The Beaufort scale defines a *gale* as a *wind* having a velocity of between 32 and 63 miles an hour; *gales* are further defined as moderate (32–38 miles per hour), fresh (39–46), strong (47–54), and whole (55–63).

Storm is a general term for any atmospheric disturbance, especially one marked by a great whirling motion of the air and accompanied by rain, snow, hail, etc. The Beaufort scale defines a *storm* as a *wind* having a velocity of between 64 and 75 miles an hour, thus placing it between a whole *gale* and a **hurricane**, which is defined as a *wind* having a velocity of over 75 miles an hour.

Whirlwind, **tornado**, **twister**, **cyclone**, and **typhoon**, as well as *hurricane*, denote winds that whirl helically around a central axis. Though *whirlwind* is the general name, it is chiefly used as a synonym for *tornado*, an extremely violent vortex of small diameter. A *tornado*, visible as a funnel-shaped cloud of dust that moves in a relatively narrow path, can be devastating in its destructiveness. In certain parts of the United States, a *tornado* is popularly called a *cyclone. Twister* is also a common popular name for a *tornado*, especially in the central plains. Technically, a *cyclone* is a vortex, usually hundreds of miles in diameter. In the northern hemisphere, the *wind* of a *cyclone* spirals counterclockwise around an area of low barometric pressure. A *cyclone* that originates over tropical seas deposits driving rain as it advances; such a *cyclone* originating in the West Indies is called a *hurricane*, and in the western Pacific, a *typhoon.*

A **squall** is a sudden and violent *wind* of short duration and is often accompanied by rain or snow. *Squall* is perhaps most commonly used to describe a *storm* at sea. A **blizzard** is a high, cold *wind* accompanied by blinding snow that accumulates to a considerable depth. **Tempest**, now a somewhat poetic term, can be applied to any *storm* of great violence, especially one involving both wind and rain, snow, or hail. See FLOOD.

wisdom

    discernment
    discrimination
    judgment
    sagacity
    sense

These nouns are comparable in denoting mental

qualities that have to do with the ability to understand situations, anticipate consequences, and make sound decisions. **Wisdom** is a broad term, embracing the meanings of all its synonyms in addition to outranking them all in suggesting a rare combination of discretion, maturity, keenness of intellect, broad experience, extensive learning, profound thought, and compassionate understanding. In its full application, *wisdom* implies the highest and noblest exercise of all the faculties of the moral nature as well as of the intellect: A truly great jurist bases decisions on *wisdom* gained from far more than study of the law.

Sense is also very general in meaning. It can refer to rational perception accompanied by feeling. Used this way it suggests an intense awareness and realization of the stimuli to which it is responding: a highly developed *sense* of right and wrong. *Sense* is also commonly applied to the ability to act effectively in a given situation, in this meaning being close to **sagacity**. Both terms suggest the kind of knowledge or know-how that is the result of broad experience and the thoughtful evaluation of such experience: a politician who showed good *sense* in avoiding mistakes made in a previous campaign; a *sagacity* that was reflected in all her business dealings. *Sagacity* can also suggest a searching profundity, like that of *wisdom:* the old man's *sagacity* about the dilemmas inevitable in a long life.

Discernment and **discrimination** are alike in denoting an analytic ability that enables one to see things clearly. *Discernment* is applied to the evaluation of character and is concerned with the kind of accuracy of observation that finds the real behind the apparent: By applying *discernment* in screening jury panels, lawyers can do much to secure impartiality for their clients. In another meaning, *discernment* can suggest the power to recognize quality or worth, as in a work of art: a music critic whose *discernment* of great talent has been proved time and time again. *Discrimination* is closely allied to the second meaning of *discernment,* denoting an ability to perceive subtle distinctions, even when they might be blurred to ordinary observation: chefs with such gustatory *discrimination* that they can recognize any seasoning, no matter how delicate, that has been used in preparing a dish.

Judgment is *sense* applied to making decisions, especially correct decisions, and thus *judgment* depends to some degree upon the exercise of *discernment* or *discrimination:* the fallibility seen in someone with a good heart but poor *judgment.* See ACUMEN, DISCRIMINATE, KEEN, OBSERVANT.

Antonyms: *folly, foolishness, imprudence, indiscretion, miscalculation, misjudgment, senselessness, silliness, stupidity.*

wistful

moody
nostalgic
pensive
plaintive

These adjectives characterize an introspective frame of mind that is sad, thoughtful, or intense. **Wistful** stresses sadness that is mild and bittersweet, often suggesting a light longing after something past or impossible: a *wistful* hour spent remembering her childhood dream of becoming a great writer; giving his father a *wistful* look. Sometimes, *wistful* suggests an aura of sadness that is not unpleasant and not attached to any specific aspiration: feeling tipsy and *wistful* as their last guests left the party. **Nostalgic** applies specifically to a longing for familiar or beloved circumstances that are now remote or irrecoverable. *Nostalgic* thoughts focus on actual events or people, whereas *wistful* thoughts may center on far-fetched hopes or past illusions. A *wistful* feeling may be casual or fleeting, but a *nostalgic* feeling is usually felt deeply and is often suggestive of a mood persisting for some time. [She opened the photograph album whenever she was in a *nostalgic* mood; *nostalgic* memories of boyhood street games whenever he passed through a lower-class neighborhood.] *Nostalgic,* which suggests both satisfaction and regret, usually implies a warmth and intensity of feeling lacking in *wistful.*

Plaintive may stress any sort of longing, sorrow, or wish expressed in words or song: a *plaintive* suggestion that they dine together some time; a *plaintive* melody. In current use, *plaintive* has drawn closer to *wistful* in not necessarily indicating utterance at all: looking after them with a *plaintive* smile. The emotion suggested in this use is a shade more intense than that of *wistful,* with a possible suggestion both of greater hopelessness and greater need or desire: the *plaintive* cry of a kitten separated from the rest of the litter.

Pensive, strictly speaking, can refer solely to a musing, reflective thoughtfulness: *pensive* chess players bent over the board. Very often, however, *pensive* is felt to imply a state of mind that is also tinged with sadness or resignation: feeling *pensive* and lonely as he watched the boat sailing out of sight. **Moody,** by contrast, can refer to a wide variety of emotions, including sadness, sullenness, or anger. Most typically, it might suggest any dark, depressed, and withdrawn state of mind, one considerably more intense than would be

true for other adjectives here: She would go about for days in a *moody* silence. *Moody* often implies a petulant or uncertain disposition: a *moody,* sulky child. See CONSIDERATE, IMAGINATION, SAD, SENTIMENTAL, THINK.
Antonyms: *airy,* FLIPPANT, HEEDLESS.

withstand

bear
cope
defy
endure
manage
put up with
resist

These verbs all mean tolerate, undergo, sustain, or oppose, as a trying or painful experience or the weight of superior authority. **Withstand** means hold out against someone or something and usually implies that the initiative for the action was taken by the opposing side: to *withstand* an enemy siege. It also suggests strong moral or physical qualities in the person or group doing the *withstanding:* to *withstand* forceful arguments because of firm conviction. *Withstand* may also be used in contests where the opposing force is a strong influence or attraction: Nobody can *withstand* her charms.

Put up with is used in reference to unpleasant or mildly harmful situations. [Our office manager won't *put up with* habitual irritability and complaints; If you can *put up with* a bit of cold air, I'd like to ventilate this room.] In some cases, **bear** is synonymous with *put up with.* [She can't *bear* her sister; For a long time, I couldn't *bear* living alone.] Usually, however, *bear* refers to a burden that weighs one down, as pain, sadness, or responsibility, and is suggestive of a test of one's physical or moral strength. [She *bore* the pain of childbirth without complaint; Of all the sorrows I have had to *bear,* none was so great as the loss of my father.] **Endure** is much like *bear* in pertaining to serious physical or mental hardship, but *endure* goes beyond *bear* in its suggestion of lasting strength in the face of a continual series or an unbroken period of trials. [The couple has *endured* so many emotional crises that everyone finds it amazing they are still together.]

One **manages** or **copes** in situations that require some searching for ways and means to overcome whatever problem or difficulty has been encountered. [The family *managed* by constant denial and rigid budgeting; My brother had to learn to *cope* with complicated social situations when he married a wealthy woman.]

Resist and **defy** imply more active opposition than the other verbs treated here. *Resist* means act counter to or fight against in order to stop, prevent, or defeat: to *resist* aggression by armed force; *resisting* the impulse to doze off by reminding himself of the penalty for falling asleep on guard duty. *Defy* implies even more open and bolder opposition and may convey a sense of daring or bravado if not outright belligerence: She *defied* the government's rule against meeting with foreign agents. *Defy* is usually used in connection with a superior authority: teenagers *defying* their parents by smoking openly. See COMPETE, CONTROL, FIGHT, PERSIST.
Antonyms: FORGO, RELINQUISH, *submit.*

workable

feasible
possible
practicable
practical

These adjectives refer to what is useful, sensible, suitable, or capable of being realized. In its most restricted application to an idea or proposal, **workable** indicates simply that something can be carried out in reality: a committee that presented several *workable* plans, though it didn't claim to know which would be most effective. *Workable* can, however, include in its meaning a proposal's likelihood of being effective: While both plans were perfectly sensible, only one seemed *workable* in terms of actually reducing delinquency. *Workable* can also apply to methods, plans, or systems already underway, in which case it refers strictly to proven ability to accomplish set goals effectively: many employee suggestions that proved *workable* once they were adopted. **Possible**, while general and wide-ranging in application, is restricted in this context to the most limited meaning of *workable,* suggesting something that can actually be carried out: the pair who first proved it was *possible* for people to fly. But *workable* can point merely to the chance that something may occur or to whatever is not ruled out as an eventuality by the nature of reality: vaguely *possible* that she could still win the election.

Feasible is more formal than the foregoing, but is otherwise like *workable* in pointing either to something's capability of being realized or to its success if carried out. It is distinct from *workable* in that *workable* views effective operation as if in a vacuum, whereas *feasible* may suggest a variety of impinging external factors that qualify performance; a design, for example, may prove *workable* under ideal conditions and yet not be *feasible* for ordinary use.

Practicable is the most restricted of these adjectives in meaning. It compares with *possible* in pointing solely to proposals that can be realized, but it is more limited in eliminating notions of mere occurrence or likelihood, concentrating instead on what can be produced, created, built, or put into effect. It compares naturally with and complements **practical**, which points mainly to something of proven effectiveness. Thus, *practicable* and *possible* relate like *workable* and *feasible*, but with a clearer set of distinctions in meaning. While there would be a *practical* use for a robot that could, for example, clean a house, the manufacture of such a device is not yet *practicable*. It is *practicable* to make compact disks three feet in diameter, but the ordinary user would not find them convenient or *practical*. See SENSIBLE.

Antonyms: DOUBTFUL, *impracticable, impractical, impossible, unlikely, unworkable.*

worldly
earthly
mundane
profane
secular

These adjectives characterize things of the world rather than of the spirit, or things pertaining to public, ordinary, or everyday life. **Worldly** indicates a liking for the goods and pleasures of the world; it often points with disapproval to such a liking when it is stronger than any interest in spiritual matters: a *worldly* prelate; a minister whose sermons attacked the godless and *worldly* members of the community. *Worldly* also suggests a sensualist who is cosmopolitan and sophisticated. Thus, a farmer with a zest for good food and drink would less likely be called *worldly* than a city dweller with the same appetites. In one sense, in fact, *worldly* can be neutral or even approving of such urbanity, suggesting someone who is well informed, discriminating in taste, and wise in the ways of the world: Benjamin Franklin's ambassadorship to France brought to Paris a clever and cultured man in the grand style, both *worldly* and *worldly*-wise.

Secular and **profane** are neither condemnatory nor approving but strictly neutral in classifying those things that pertain to a totally nonreligious sphere: a *secular* drama; *profane* art. *Secular* can also indicate something pertaining to the laity rather than the clergy: *secular* resistance to the orthodox church's attitude toward abortion. Most specifically, *secular* can refer to a member of the clergy who is not bound by monastic vows: a *secular* priest. **Mundane** refers to things belonging strictly to the ordinary world of everyday affairs, suggesting something practical, routine, or dull: idealistic students who criticize their affluent parents for having no concerns beyond the *mundane* worlds of the office and home. **Earthly** remains largely confined to religious use and is directly opposed to heavenly: this *earthly* paradise; *earthly* joys.

Antonyms: SACRED.

worry
brood
care
fret

These verbs are used in relation to interested, concerned, or troubled states of mind. **Worry** and **care** both express a wide range of emotional involvement. One may be said to *worry* when the feeling described is as mild as uneasiness: Don't *worry* if you're late for the meeting. On the other hand, *worry* is frequently used to convey a sense of deep anxiety: I'm *worried* sick about driving on icy roads. *Care*, in a way that *worry* cannot, denotes a purely objective interest: It is impossible that a man so involved with contemporary problems should *care* not at all about health care reform. *Care* can designate sorrow: to *care* about a friend's being out of work. Finally, *care* can indicate serious concern or anxiety: It was obvious from the press conference that the prime minister *cares* deeply about the recent worsening in relations between East and West.

Brood, like *care* and *worry*, denotes a concern about a person or thing, but more than the other two verbs, it implies a thoughtful and sometimes morbid dwelling on the object of concern, often to the point of moodiness or depression. [He *brooded* so long on his mother's illness that he sank into a state of melancholia; She *broods* continually about the abuse inflicted on her in childhood.] **Fret**, like *brood*, suggests a lingering state of mind, with the governing emotion being that of anxiety, grief, or unhappiness: Since her husband fell ill, she has done nothing but *fret*. Often in *fret* there is a suggestion of whining and complaining that is not present in *brood*: I pity his hypochondria, but I pity more the wife who has to put up with his continual *fretting*. See AFRAID, ANXIETY, BOTHER, SOLICITUDE.

wriggle
slither
squirm

wriggle *(continued)*

wiggle
writhe

These verbs refer to convulsed or contorted movements within a body. **Wriggle** can suggest a deliberate shaking or shuddering not intended to result in motion along a path: *wriggling* uncomfortably in his wet clothes; *wriggling* with delight as the waves broke over her. More often, *wriggle* does suggest forward movement achieved by a crawling or creeping action: *wriggling* into the tunnel with a flashlight in one hand; a caterpillar that *wriggled* down my back. **Slither** points exclusively to this sort of movement, but where *wriggle* may suggest jerking, awkward, or ungainly motion, *slither* implies a sinuous and graceful sliding of an elongated body, such as that of a snake: pythons *slithering* noiselessly over rock; a rope that *slithered* down the prison wall.

Squirm is nearly identical to *wriggle* in suggesting either in-place shaking or a forward crawl. In both cases, however, a greater amount of internal undulation is suggested by *squirm,* as well as more thrashing about: watching the stranded octopus *squirm* each time they stabbed at it; trying desperately to *squirm* free from the tangled bedclothes. In contrast to the foregoing verbs, both **writhe** and **wiggle** point primarily to in-place motion. *Writhe* would suggest a slower, less voluntary shuddering than *squirm* and even *wriggle;* it often describes the throes of someone in pain: bodies *writhing* in agony. But *writhe* can also suggest other kinds of contorted movement: *writhing* dancers. *Wiggle* suggests a side-to-side or back-and-forth motion: He can *wiggle* his ears; She seemed unaware of how much she *wiggled* as she walked. As in the last example, if forward movement is indicated, *wiggle* points to incidental motion rather than to motion that contributes directly to the gaining of ground. See ROTATE, SHAKE, VIBRATE.

wrong

abuse
maltreat
mistreat
oppress
persecute

These verbs all refer to unjust acts or to acts that harm other people. To **wrong** is to treat unjustly or harmfully without good cause: a woman who *wronged* her husband by mistakenly accusing him of infidelity; an innocent woman *wronged* by being sent to prison. **Abuse**, the most general verb in this group, covers all injurious use or treatment by word or act; it does not, however, always connote a deliberate act: an overweight man whose self-imposed diet *abused* his health; a police officer who *abused* her authority by searching a house without a warrant.

Both **maltreat** and **mistreat** usually imply base motivation for the actions concerned. *Maltreat,* however, suggests harsher or more consciously cruel treatment than *mistreat,* which can apply to acts whose chief effect is psychological rather than physical: accused of *maltreating* their dogs; an author who felt *mistreated* by her agent on grounds of neglect. *Mistreat* is thus more general than *maltreat* and need not imply physical abuse or even the desire to harm.

To **persecute** is to *maltreat* because of race, religion, or beliefs. **Oppress**, the strongest verb of this group, implies harsh and unjust use of force in keeping someone in subjugation. *Persecute* implies a deliberate, systematic, and often ruthless attempt to harm; *oppress* emphasizes action rather than motive and suggests the weighing down or crushing by the might of irresponsible authority. [The Puritans, *persecuted* for their religious beliefs, fled to America; The American colonists, feeling themselves *oppressed* by taxes and without due political representation, decided to revolt.] To *oppress* people is to deprive them of their liberty and often of their hope; to *persecute* them is to inflict suffering upon them. See DESTROY, HARM, UNSETTLE.

Antonyms: *favor, help,* NURSE, PROTECT, UPHOLD.

yearn

hanker
long
moon
pine

These verbs refer to a strong inclination toward something or an unfulfilled want that one may or may not take action to fill. **Yearn** points to an inclination continually present as a gnawing or unhappy feeling of lack for something, either for a clearly defined object or for something more abstract, less definite, or beyond one's reach: *yearning* for one look from her; *yearning* to have a real friend. *Yearn* must be used with care, since it can give a tone of sentimental overstatement: *yearning* for self-fulfillment, she knew not how. This tone can be deflated in brusque usages: *yearning* for a cold glass of beer. The likelihood of such a sentimental tone is even more heavily incurred by **pine**, which would now be thought old-fashioned in most situations. It can give an implication of long-term *yearning* so intense as to result in a wasting away of physical or mental health, as in folk ballads: missing her dead lover so much that she *pined* away and died. **Moon** satirizes such excessive grieving or *yearning:* all this adolescent *mooning* after a girl; girls *mooning* over the latest pop-cult heroes. The recent introduction of a slang meaning for *moon*—expose one's buttocks publicly as a gesture of defiance—has all but stripped the verb of the meanings here discussed.

Long is less open than *pine* or *yearn* to the charge of sounding high-toned, though such a tone is possible: humanity's age-old *longing* for freedom. More often, *long* points to a weaker, more enduring, or more hopeless want, if not to one totally impossible or contrary to fact: *longing* to be as handsome as the most popular boy in his class. It can apply informally to less extreme situations, however, pointing to any sort of emotional want: telling him how much she *longed* to lie in the sun for a solid week. **Hanker** specifically suggests sexual desire of a trivial, momentary, or frivolous nature: *hankering* after the woman sitting next to him on the long flight. *Hanker* can also suggest any mild desire, impulse, or inclination: *hankering* to see a good movie. See EAGER, EMOTION, EROTIC, GREEDY, HOPE, WANT.

yokel

hayseed
hick
rube
rustic

These nouns refer unflatteringly to rural, provincial, uncultured, or unsophisticated people. **Yokel** and **hayseed** are contemptuous terms for a person from a rural or farming background who is seen as uncultured or ignorant. The main difference here is that *hayseed* is more vivid and even more withering in its scorn: stuck in a resort filled with country *yokels;* a *hayseed* who seemed not to understand the simplest request for directions. Also, *yokel* can refer to any noncosmopolitan audience: taking a program of hackneyed piano pieces on tour, since they were sure to please the *yokels*. Both terms have the ring of a bygone era.

Hick can apply to someone in a provincial setting, including persons from towns or even cities considered to be removed from the center of things: attacking him for sneering at so-called *hicks* in Chicago and San Francisco who wanted to build their own cultural centers rather than depend on road companies from New York. Where *yokel* and *hayseed* usually place the provincial person in his hometown, *hick* can apply to someone who appears to be newly arrived in a cosmopolitan setting and is still unfamiliar with its ways: *hicks* who come to Greenwich Village to stare at the bizarre locals.

Rube, another old-fashioned abusive term for a person from a rural area, was originally carnival slang for any patron, viewing such a person contemptuously as being easily gulled, duped, or conned: the *rubes* who believed the heap of plastic bones was the skeleton of Goliath. **Rustic** is the most formal of these nouns—and the least uncomplimentary as well. It suggests a colorful, possibly even likable country eccentric who is set in his ways or appears to be quaint in his tastes: sketching the old *rustic* who sat whittling on the wharf. While all these nouns, by implication, indicate men, *hick, rube,* and possibly *rustic,* may refer to both men and women when pluralized: the dumb *hicks* in that town; an audience of *rubes* willing to believe anything; a quaint village peopled by genuine *rustics*. See BLOCKHEAD.

zero

aught
cipher
naught
null

These nouns come into comparison as verbal equivalents of 0, the symbol for nothing. The choice of which noun to use depends upon a context that may range from the archaic and informal to the mathematical and scientific.

Zero and **cipher** both come from the Arabic word *sifr,* meaning empty. In this sense *zero* has come to be the most commonly used to indicate the absence or negation of something. [Subtracting any number from itself gives *zero;* The results of all the tests were *zero.*] It is also regarded as the standard reference point in any scale of values, quantities, magnitudes, dimensions, etc. [The temperature was 10° below (or above) *zero;* The gambler bet on *zero* at roulette; Heavy fog reduced visibility to *zero.*] *Cipher,* though literally synonymous, cannot replace *zero* in any of the above examples. It is still thought of as representing any numeral from 0 to 9, a use carried over from the verb form meaning count or calculate. We can, of course, increase the value of any whole number by adding *ciphers* at the end of it, but the distinction is recognized by saying that the enlarged number, say 643,000, contains three *zeros,* not *ciphers.* However, the idea of nullity or nonentity is usually clear from the context, especially if we are using *cipher* in a figurative sense: Man is a mere *cipher* in the universe.

Naught (sometimes spelled *nought*), an Old English word for nothing, doubles for *cipher* in its literal sense. [This number has a lot of *naughts* in it.] But this use is rare and mostly colloquial, though less so than its clipped version **aught** (a *naught* taken as an *aught*). As an epithet for a person or thing devoid of merit or value, *naught* still has poetic force. [All his plans came to *naught;* There was *naught* to be done in the emergency but wait.]

Null is best known to us in the reduplicated legal phrase "*null* and void," meaning without force or effect, or invalid. But it also serves a useful purpose in indicating a negative result or outcome, especially in certain types of scientific work. [All the Geiger counter readings were *null;* The results of the first experiments to prove the value of the new drug were *null.*] See LACK.

zest

brio
dash
drive
energy
gusto
panache
pizazz
verve
zip

These nouns all denote states or attitudes of keen enjoyment, invigoration, or vitality. **Zest** expresses dynamic vigor along with uninhibited sensuous delight: The remarkable aspect of the life of Don Juan was not how many women he seduced but the *zest* with which he seduced them. In some contexts **gusto** and *zest* are interchangeable: He ate with *zest* (or *gusto*). But *gusto,* while intensely felt, is commonly associated with single events of short duration, whereas *zest* may signal a more profound or enduring characteristic. [After her illness she lost her *zest* for life; They traded insults with *gusto.*]

Energy emphasizes the vigor of physical action rather than a dynamic motivation. To eat with *energy,* for instance, suggests nothing more than the expenditure of a good deal of effort in hastily transferring food from plate to mouth, whereas eating with *zest* or with *gusto* expresses keen appreciation of the food. *Energy* is often used, however, as an enduring quality: A woman of considerable *energy,* she took a brisk stroll every morning right after breakfast.

Drive denotes *energy* stimulated by ambition: Fortunate is he who has lots of *drive* to get ahead in his work. This use of *drive* may have been influenced by the word's psychological meaning of a strong, motivating power or stimulus: the sex *drive.*

The U.S. Post Office rejuvenated **zip** by adopting the acronym *ZIP* code (Zone Improvement Plan) for its numerical system designed to speed the delivery of domestic mail. *Zip* means *energy,* get-up-and-go, vitality, zing: a song with plenty of *zip.* Apart from Post Office use, *zip*—like zing—has a dated quality. The verb *zip,* meaning go at great speed, does not share the archaic flavor of the noun; jets can still *zip* along. A fad word replacing *zip* in many contexts is **pizazz** (also spelled *pizzazz*), meaning drive, vitality, vigor, dash, and flair: a person full of *pizazz;* a car with *pizazz.* When applied to people, *pizazz* means something like charisma. [There is no doubt; Marilyn had plenty of *pizazz.*]

Brio, meaning spirit, suggests exuberant, often careless, vitality. [He spoke with tremendous *brio;* his speech, always loud no matter where he went, was punctuated with brilliant but unrepeatable oaths, and his gestures were appropriately flamboyant.] As a musical direction, the Italian *con brio* means with spirit, in a lively manner.

Dash and **verve** both emphasize a great and vigorous *energy*, but *dash* points more particularly to a brilliant or flamboyant style carried out with sophistication and speed, whereas *verve* stresses the enthusiasm and untiring nature of the effort. [Ethel Merman sang with *verve;* He toasted our health with exquisite courtesy and entertained us with considerable *dash.*]

Panache, derived from the Latin word for feather, literally means a plume or bunch of feathers, especially when worn as an ornament on a helmet. *Panache,* in its more common sense, is thus the equivalent of *dash,* even more strongly emphasizing the flourish of wit or brilliance of style with which something is done or said: the aristocratic jewel thief who pulls off his jobs with elegance and *panache.* *Dash* and *panache* both suggest an elegant independence of spirit amounting to an indifference to or contempt for popular manners or morals. See EAGER, LIVELY, PASSIONATE.

Antonyms: *blandness, dullness, exhaustion, hebetude, insipidity, lethargy, listlessness, weariness.*

Index

515

CHOOSE THE RIGHT WORD

cognizant AWARE 23

cohere STICK 435

COINCIDE 70

COLD (adj) 71

collapse FAINT (v) 151

colleague ASSOCIATE 18

collect ACCUMULATE 2

collect GATHER 177

collected IMPERTURBABLE 218

collection ACCUMULATION 3

colloquy CONVERSATION 89

colophon BRAND 46

COLOR (v) 71

colorful SHOWY 407

colossal TREMENDOUS 472

comb HUNT (v) 209

comber WAVE 500

combination MIXTURE 284

combine UNITE 480

comely BEAUTIFUL 29

COMFORT (n) 72

comfort CONSOLE 83

comic HUMOROUS 208

comical HUMOROUS 208

COMMAND (n) 72

commander BOSS 43

commandment LAW 248

commence BEGIN 29

commendation APPROVAL 13

commentary EXPLANATION 147

commit ENTRUST 140

common GENERAL 179

common MUTUAL 290

common PREVALENT 348

common USUAL 486

commonplace MEDIOCRE 274

commune SHARE (v) 405

COMMUNICABLE 73

COMPACT (adj) 73

compact COVENANT 93

companion FRIEND 172

company GROUP 190

comparable SIMILAR 410

COMPARE 74

compassionate HUMANE 207

COMPEL 74

compendious TERSE 461

compensation SALARY 390

COMPETE 75

COMPETENT 75

competitor OPPONENT 309

COMPLAIN 76

complaint SICKNESS 408

complaisant COMPLIANT 77

COMPLEMENT 77

complement COUNTERPART 91

complete ENTIRE (adj) 139

complete FINISH (v) 158

COMPLIANT 77

COMPLIMENT 77

compliment FAWN 156

COMPONENT (n) 77

compose CREATE 94

composed IMPERTURBABLE 218

composite MIXTURE 284

compound MIXTURE 284

compressed COMPACT 73

comprise INCLUDE 222

compulsive OBSESSED 303

COMPULSORY 78

comrade FRIEND 172

concede ACKNOWLEDGE 4

conceit EGOISM 133

CONCEITED 78

conceive DEVISE 113

concept IDEA 213

conception IDEA 213

concern SOLICITUDE 421

concise COMPACT 73

conclave MEETING 275

conclude FINISH 158

CONCLUSIVE 79

concordat COVENANT 93

concupiscent EROTIC 141

concur CONSENT 81

concussion IMPACT 216

condemn SENTENCE 400

condensed COMPACT 73

CONDESCEND 79

conditional PROVISIONAL 356

condole CONSOLE 83

condone PARDON 321

conduct BEHAVIOR 31

conduct GUIDE (v) 192

conduct PERFORM 327

confederacy LEAGUE 250

confederate ACCOMPLICE 2

confederation LEAGUE 250

confer CONSULT 84

confer GIVE 182

conference MEETING 275

confess ACKNOWLEDGE 4

confidant FRIEND 172

confide ENTRUST 140

CONFIDENCE 80

confidence TRUST 475

confident OPTIMISTIC 311

configuration FORM 168

confines BOUNDARY 45

confirm ENDORSE 137

confiscate USURP 486

conflagration FIRE 159

conflict CONTROVERSY 88

conflicting CONTRADICTORY 87

conform ADAPT 4

confound CONFUSE 81

CONFUSE 81

confusion CLUTTER 70

CONGENITAL 81

congenital INNATE 228

conglomeration ACCUMULATION 3

conglomeration JUMBLE 237

congregate GATHER 177

congregation MEETING 275

congress MEETING 275

congruent DUPLICATE 126

conjecture SUPPOSE 449

conjure SUMMON 446

connote MEAN 271

conquer VANQUISH 489

conscientious CAREFUL 54

conscious AWARE 23

consecrate DEDICATE 105

consecrated SACRED 389

CONSENT (v) 81

consequence RESULT 381

consequential SIGNIFICANT 408

conservative RIGHTIST (n) 384

CONSERVE (v) 82

CONSIDER 82

consider STUDY 441

CONSIDERATE 83

consideration RESPECT 380

consign ENTRUST 140

CONSOLE (v) 83

consommé SOUP 422

conspicuous PLAIN 335

CONSPIRACY 84

conspiracy INTRIGUE 233

conspirator ACCOMPLICE 2

constant INVARIABLE (adj) 234

constituent COMPONENT (n) 77

constitution LAW 248

constitutional LAWFUL 248

constrain COMPEL 74

constrain SUBDUE 443

constricted COMPACT 73

construct BUILD 51

CONSULT 84

consume EAT 129

consummate PERFECT (adj) 327

contact MEET (v) 275

contagious COMMUNICABLE 73

contain CIRCUMSCRIBE 64

contain INCLUDE 222

contaminate POLLUTE 340

contemplate INTEND 232

contemplate STUDY 441

contemporary MODERN 285

CONTEMPTIBLE 84

CONTEMPTUOUS 85

contend COMPETE 75

content CONTENTED 85

CONTENTED 85

contention CONTROVERSY 88

contiguous NEIGHBORING 296

continence TEMPERANCE 459

contingent CHANCE 59

contingent PROVISIONAL 356

continual PERSISTENT 332

continue PERSIST 331

CONTINUOUS 86

continuous PERSISTENT 332

contour FORM (n) 168

contract COVENANT 93

CONTRADICT 86

CONTRADICTORY 87

contrary CONTRADICTORY 87

contravene CONTRADICT 86

contretemps MISTAKE 283

contribute FURTHER 175

contributory AUXILIARY 21

contrivance MACHINE 265

contrive DEVISE 113

CONTROL (v) 87

CONTROVERSY 88

controvert CONTRADICT 86

conundrum PUZZLE 359

convene GATHER 177

convenient OPPORTUNE 309

convention MEETING 275

convention TRADITION 469

conventional USUAL 486

CONVERSATION 89

convert CHANGE (v) 59

convey CARRY 55

convey TELL 458

convict SENTENCE (n, v) 400

conviction OPINION 308

convincing BELIEVABLE 32

convivial BLITHE 39

convocation MEETING 275

convoy FLEET 161

cool COLD 71

cool IMPERTURBABLE 218

cope WITHSTAND 508

copious PREVALENT 348

COPY (n) 90

copy IMITATE 214

cordial GREGARIOUS 189

core CENTER 58

corporal PHYSICAL 333

corporeal PHYSICAL 333

CORPSE 90

corpulent FAT 153

contend COMPETE 75

correct ACCURATE 3

correct DISCIPLINE 116

correct REPAIR (v) 374

correlate COUNTERPART 91

correspond COINCIDE 70

correspond COMPARE 74

corrupt DEPRAVED 109

costume DRESS 124

coterie CLIQUE 68

COUNCIL 91

council MEETING 275

counsel LAWYER 250

counsel RECOMMEND 368

counselor LAWYER 250

count CONSIDER 82

counteract NEUTRALIZE 297

counterbalance NEUTRALIZE 297

counterfeit SPURIOUS 430

counterinsurgency UPRISING 484

COUNTERPART 91

counterspy SPY 430

COUNTLESS 92

COURAGE 92

courageous BRAVE 47

courteous POLITE 340

courtly POLITE 340

coven MEETING 275

COVENANT 93

cover PROTECTION 354

covert IMPLICIT 220

covet WANT 499

covetous GREEDY 187

cow INTIMIDATE 232

cow OX 317

COWARDLY 93

cower FLINCH 161

coworker ASSOCIATE 18

coy TIMID 466

CRACK (n) 93

crack BREAK (v) 48

craft GUILE 192

craft VESSEL 491

craftsman ARTISAN 15

craftsman ARTIST 16

crave WANT 499

craven COWARDLY 93

crazy PSYCHOTIC 357

crease FOLD (n, v) 165

CREATE 94

CREATIVE 95

creator ARTISAN 15

creator ARTIST 16

creature ANIMAL 10

credible BELIEVABLE 32

credit ATTRIBUTE (v) 20

CREDULOUS 95

credulous GULLIBLE 192

CREED 95

creed RELIGION 371

creek STREAM 438

creep LURK 263

crenelated ROUGH 387

crevice CRACK 93

CRIME 96

cringe FLINCH (v) 161

518

519

CHOOSE THE RIGHT WORD

CHOOSE THE RIGHT WORD

522

herculean TREMENDOUS 472
herd PEOPLE 326
hereditary INNATE 228
HERETIC 198
heritage INHERITANCE 228
hermaphroditic BISEXUAL 37
heroic BRAVE 47
hesitant UNWILLING 482
HESITATE 199
HETEROGENEOUS 199
HEW 200
hick YOKEL 511
hideous GRUESOME 191
HIGH (adj) 200
high JOYOUS 236
HIGHEST 201
highway STREET 439
hill MOUNTAIN 289
hillock MOUNTAIN 289
HINDER 201
HINT (n) 201
HIRE 202
hire LEASE 252
HISTORIC 203
HISTORY 203
histrionic THEATRICAL 462
hitch STINT 437
hit the hay RETIRE 381
hit the sack RETIRE 381
hoard ACCUMULATE 2
hoard CONSERVE 82
hoary ANCIENT 10
hobbled LAME 246
HOBBY 203
hodgepodge JUMBLE 237
hoi polloi PEOPLE 326
hoist RAISE (v) 365
hold POSSESS 343
hold-up ROBBERY 385
HOLE 203
hollow HOLE 203
holy SACRED 389
HOME 204
homily SPEECH 425
homographs HOMONYM 204
HOMONYM 204
homophones HOMONYM 204
Homo sapiens MANKIND 266
honest SINCERE 411
honest TRUTHFUL 476
honor AWARD (n) 22
honor RESPECT (n) 380
honorable MORAL 288
honorarium SALARY 390
hoodwink TRICK 473
HOPE (v) 205
hope EXPECTATION 146
hopeful OPTIMISTIC 311
hopelessness DESPAIR 111
horde THRONG (n) 464
host THRONG 464
hostel HOTEL 206

HOSTILE 205
hostility ENMITY 138
HOT 205
HOTEL 206
HOUND (n) 206
hound BELEAGUER 32
hound MONGREL 287
HOUSE (n) 207
household HOME 204
housing HOUSE 207
hovel HOME 204
hub CENTER 58
hubbub NOISE 298
huff RESENTMENT 378
hug CARESS (v) 54
huge MASSIVE 269
hulking HUSKY 210
hum SING 412
human HUMANE 207
HUMANE 207
humanitarian HUMANE 207
humanity MANKIND 266
humankind MANKIND 266
humble DISGRACE 118
humble MODEST 285
humiliate DISGRACE 118
humiliation EMBARRASS-MENT 134
humor PAMPER 320
HUMOROUS 208
HUNT (v) 209
hurdle OBSTACLE 304
hurl THROW 464
hurricane WIND 506
hurry QUICKEN 362
hurry SPEED 426
HURT (v) 210
hurt HARM (v) 196
husbandry FARMING 152
HUSKY 210
hygienic SANITARY 391
hypercritical FAULTFIND-ING 154
hypocritical TREACHER-OUS 471
hysterectomize STERILIZE 434
hysteria FRENZY 172

ice GEM 178
icy COLD 71
IDEA 213
ideal PERFECT 327
ideal PROTOTYPE 355
identical DUPLICATE 126
idiosyncrasy ECCENTRIC-ITY 130
idiot MORON 288
idolize REVERE 382
ignite KINDLE 243
IGNOBLE 213
ignominious SHAMEFUL 405
ignore SLIGHT 417
ill-advised UNWISE 483
illimitable INFINITE 225
illness SICKNESS 408

illusion DELUSION 106
illustration SAMPLE 390
illustrious GREAT 186
IMAGINATION 213
imaginative CREATIVE 95
imagine SUPPOSE 449
imbecile MORON 288
imbibe ABSORB 1
imbue IMPLANT 219
imbue PERMEATE 330
IMITATE 214
immaculate CLEAN 66
immaterial EXTRANEOUS 149
immeasurable COUNT-LESS 92
immemorial ANCIENT 10
immense MASSIVE 269
IMMERSE 214
immigrant FOREIGNER 166
immigrate MIGRATE 279
immodest INDECENT 223
immoral UNETHICAL 479
IMMORTAL 215
IMMUTABLE 215
IMPACT (n) 216
impart TELL 458
impartial DISINTERESTED 118
impassable IMPENETRA-BLE 218
impassioned PASSIONATE 322
IMPASSIVE 216
impeach ACCUSE 3
impecunious INSOLVENT 231
impede HINDER 201
impediment OBSTACLE 304
IMPEL 217
IMPENETRABLE 218
imperative COMPULSORY 78
imperfection FLAW 160
imperious OVERBEARING 316
imperishable IMMORTAL 215
impermeable IMPENE-TRABLE 218
impersonate IMITATE 214
impertinence EFFRON-TERY 132
IMPERTURBABLE 218
impervious IMPENETRA-BLE 218
IMPETUOUS 219
IMPLANT (v) 219
implement FURTHER 175
implication HINT 201
implication MEANING 271
IMPLICIT 220
IMPLY 221
imply MEAN 271
import MEANING 271
important SIGNIFICANT 408

impose TAX 456
impotent POWERLESS 344
imprecation CURSE 98
impregnate PERMEATE 330
impress INFLUENCE 226
impression IDEA 213
impression OPINION 308
impromptu SPONTA-NEOUS 428
improper INDECENT 223
IMPROVE 221
improvident SPEND-THRIFT 427
improvised SPONTANEOUS 428
imprudence EFFRONTERY 132
imprudent UNWISE 483
impulsive IMPETUOUS 219
impulsive SPONTANEOUS 428
impute ATTRIBUTE 20
inaccessible DISTANT 120
inadequate DEFICIENT 105
inadequate SCANTY 394
inane BANAL 26
inarticulate SPEECHLESS 426
inattentive OBLIVIOUS 301
inaugurate BEGIN 29
inborn INNATE 228
inbred INNATE 228
incalculable COUNTLESS 92
incandescent BRIGHT 49
incapacitate HARM 196
incautious HEEDLESS 197
incense ENRAGE 138
incentive MOTIVE 289
incessant PERSISTENT 332
inchoate BEGINNING 31
incidental CHANCE 59
incipient BEGINNING 31
incision CUT 99
INCITE 221
INCLUDE 222
incoherent SPEECHLESS 426
incompatible DISPARATE 120
incongruous DISPARATE 120
inconsequential MAR-GINAL 267
inconsiderate HEEDLESS 197
INCONSTANT 222
incorporate ABSORB 1
increase ENLARGE 137
increase ESCALATE 142
incredulity UNBELIEF 478
INCREDULOUS 223
incriminate ACCUSE 3
inculcate IMPLANT 219
incursion RAID 365
INDECENT 223
indecorous INDECENT 223

indefinite VAGUE 489
indelible PERMANENT 329
indelicate INDECENT 223
indestructible IMMUTABLE 215
indicate MEAN 271
indication SYMPTOM 453
indict ACCUSE 3
indifferent IMPASSIVE 216
indifferent UNINVOLVED 480
indigence WANT 498
indigenous NATIVE 295
indigent PENNILESS 325
indignation ANGER 10
indirectness CIRCUMLO-CUTION 63
indiscretion SIN 411
indistinct VAGUE 489
indoctrinate TEACH 457
indolence SLOTH 417
INDUCE 224
inducement MOTIVE 289
induction REASONING 367
indulge PAMPER 320
indulgent LENIENT 255
industrious DILIGENT 114
inebriate ALCOHOLIC (n) 7
inept CLUMSY 69
inescapable INEVITABLE 224
inessential EXTRANEOUS 148
INEVITABLE 224
INEXORABLE 225
infamous DEPRAVED 109
infectious COMMUNICA-BLE 73
INFER 225
inference REASONING 367
infertile STERILE 434
INFINITE 225
infinitesimal MINUTE 280
infirm WEAK 501
infirmity SICKNESS 408
inflame KINDLE 243
inflate SWELL 451
INFLUENCE (v) 226
INFORM 226
information NEWS 297
INFORMER 227
infrequent OCCASIONAL 305
infringe ENCROACH 136
infuriate ENRAGE 138
infuse IMPLANT 219
ingenious CREATIVE 95
ingenuous CANDID 53
ingenuous NAIVE 293
ingest ABSORB 1
ingrain IMPLANT 219
ingredient COMPONENT 77
inhabit RESIDE 379
INHERENT 227
INHERITANCE 228
inhibit SUBDUE 443
inhibit THWART 465

531